CASES AND MATERIALS

Law, Medicine, and Medical Technology

Lars Noah
Research Foundation Professor of Law
University of Florida

Barbara A. Noah
Research Associate, Health Law & Policy
Center for Governmental Responsibility
University of Florida

NEW YORK, NEW YORK
FOUNDATION PRESS
2002

COPYRIGHT © 2002 By FOUNDATION PRESS

          395 Hudson Street
          New York, NY 10014
          Phone Toll Free 1–877–888–1330
          Fax (212) 367–6799
          fdpress.com

ISBN 1–58778–169–7

TEXT IS PRINTED ON 10% POST
CONSUMER RECYCLED PAPER

Dedicated to the memory of Berndt G. Noah (1930–1993)

*

PREFACE

The most important discoveries of the next 50 years are likely to be the ones of which we cannot now even conceive.

–Sir John Maddox

In its broadest sense, the word "technology" refers to the application of knowledge.* In that respect, medicine has always centered on technology. With accelerating advances in biomedical knowledge, the number of therapeutic interventions continues to multiply. Instead of concerns about generating the information, the challenge has become how best to manage—in terms of both filtering and disseminating—the increasing quantity and complexity of clinically-relevant research findings. See Lars Noah, Medicine's Epistemology: Mapping the Haphazard Diffusion of Knowledge in the Biomedical Community, 44 Ariz. L. Rev. (forthcoming 2002); see also United States v. American College of Physicians, 475 U.S. 834, 850 (1986) (Burger, C.J., concurring) ("The enormous expansion of medical knowledge makes it difficult for a general practitioner—or even a specialist—to keep fully current with the latest developments . . . .").

In a narrower sense, the word "technology" refers to the objects produced by the application of scientific knowledge. Medicine involves the use of technology alongside the application of professional skill and judgment in the treatment of patients, and we may find ourselves in the midst of a radical transformation in the delivery of health care in this country. Of course, physicians have long made use of various instruments and medications, at first quite primitive but increasingly complex. See Audrey B. Davis, Medicine and Its Technology: An Introduction to the History of Medical Instrumentation (1981). Even so, the health care system has always emphasized the provision of professional services.

Dramatic changes in health care financing have shaken this tradition in recent years, but continuing technological advances also threaten to over-

---

* See XVII Oxford English Dictionary 705 (2d ed. 1989) ("A particular practical or industrial art."). For a recent discussion of the difficulties in defining medical technology, see Michael H. Shapiro, Is Bioethics Broke?: On the Idea of Ethics and Law "Catching Up" with Technology, 33 Ind. L. Rev. 17, 38-39 & n.43 (1999); see also Einer Elhauge, The Limited Regulatory Potential of Medical Technology Assessment, 82 Va. L. Rev. 1525, 1530 n.14 (1996) ("The technology assessment literature generally defines 'medical technology' as including not only machinery, devices, and drugs but also medical practices and procedures. This definition . . . somewhat confusingly seems to eliminate any distinction between technology and health care.").

take the classic service-oriented paradigm. As one physician observed in a recent book:

> Technology will confound almost any attempt to change the health care system or redirect its fundamental goals. Further, if there is one thing that can be singled out as the engine of the medical cost inflation now occurring everywhere in the world, it is the seemingly irresistible spread of technology into every level of medicine . . . . [L]ike the broom in The Sorcerer's Apprentice, technologies come to have a life of their own, not only because of their own properties but also because of certain universal human traits. Technologies come into being to serve the purposes of their users, but ultimately their users redefine their own goals in terms of the technology.

Eric J. Cassell, Doctoring: The Nature of Primary Care Medicine 62–63 (1997); see also Annetine Gelijns & Nathan Rosenberg, The Dynamics of Technological Change in Medicine, Health Aff., Summer 1994, at 29.

One can describe the magnitude of technological advances in health care in economic terms. For instance, in 1999 Americans spent in excess of $100 billion (approximately ten percent of health care expenditures) just on prescription drugs. See Susan Okie & Amy Goldstein, Drugs Driving Rising Health Costs, Wash. Post, Mar. 12, 2001, at A2. If one adds to that the cost of medical devices and equipment used in the provision of medical services, the centrality of technology in health care becomes even more apparent. The economic issues surrounding medical technologies also have political salience. See Robin Toner, Rising Drug Costs a Powerful Issue for National and State Politicians, N.Y. Times, Apr. 1, 2002, at A1. Who could have guessed that the price of prescription drugs would become one of the central issues in the latest Presidential election?

There is more to the subject, however, than expense. Technological advances challenge existing institutional relationships as well as mechanisms of supervision and control. In concluding his chapter on this technological imperative in medicine, Dr. Cassell noted a paradox: "Despite the enormous power of modern medical technology . . . , the power of the medical profession is at a low point. Doctors had greater public power in 1950, when technological power was modest." Id. at 79; see also George J. Annas, Some Choice: Law, Medicine, and the Market ch. 5 (1998) (offering a critical assessment of the enthusiasm for new medical technology). One theme running through these materials focuses on the interactions between health care providers and medical technologies, whether defined broadly as biomedical knowledge or more narrowly as the products utilized in the treatment of patients.

Of course, technological advances offer tremendous promise for promoting patient welfare. The story of past successes—ranging from the development of antibiotics, vaccines, chemotherapy agents, artificial joints, pacemakers, and magnetic resonance imaging (MRI) devices—is by now familiar. In the summer of 2001, the media tracked the progress of the first recipient of the AbioCor, a new generation of artificial hearts. A few months later, with the news that someone had mailed letters containing weapons-grade anthrax spores, public attention turned to antibiotics and vaccines as tools for responding to bioterrorism. In the near future, persons may have implanted microprocessors that can monitor numerous physiological parameters on a continuous real-time basis; expert systems might allow computers to download this information and provide a differential diagnosis; and gene therapies might allow for the delivery of precisely tailored biological treatments. See Bruce N. Kuhlik, The Regulation of Drugs and Biologics: Fifty Years into the Future, 55 Food & Drug L.J. 21, 22 (2000); Scott Hensley, New Race Heats Up to Turn Gene Information into Drug Discoveries, Wall St. J., June 26, 2000, at B1 (reporting that the completion of the Human Genome Project may lead to improved therapies). In 1999, recognizing these possibilities, more than 40 medical journals from around the world devoted one entire issue of their publications to the growing significance of medical technologies in health care. See David H. Mark & Richard M. Glass, Editorial, Impact of New Technologies in Medicine: A Global Theme Issue, 282 JAMA 1875 (1999); Caralee E. Caplan & John Hoey, Editorial, Impact of New Technologies in Medicine: Progress and Pitfalls, 160 Can. Med. Ass'n J. 66 (1999).

This is not a book designed for futurists, however, and we do not mean to suggest that the medical profession will be further marginalized, though the roles of health care providers no doubt will continue to evolve in the face of technological advances. Medical technology is already, and has been for some time, an essential aspect of modern medicine. Unfortunately, existing textbooks fail to give the subject adequate attention. For instance, one of the leading health law casebooks devotes essentially no attention to the regulation of drugs and medical devices by the Food and Drug Administration (FDA) or to the transmission of biomedical knowledge. See Barry R. Furrow et al., Health Law: Cases, Materials & Problems (4th ed. 2001). To be sure, issues concerning the control of medical technologies appear sporadically throughout this and similar texts, but the emphasis rests squarely on the service aspects of this industry: licensing chapters focus on state regulation of health care professionals rather than federal regulation of health care products; the tort law chapters focus on medical malpractice rather than products liability; the health care financing chapters focus on payment for services rather than medical equipment; and the materials about informed consent focus on the transmission of knowledge that occurs vertically (between physicians and patients) rather than horizontally (among clinical researchers and health care providers). In short, the subject of health law must concern itself with more than just efforts at supervising the provision of medical services.

Moreover, anyone with an interest in issues relating to the control of medical technologies will struggle to find any comprehensive treatment of these sorts of questions in other texts. For instance, one of the leading casebooks on products liability devotes all of 35 pages to a focused discussion of the special tort law principles governing prescription drugs and medical devices. See James A. Henderson, Jr. & Aaron D. Twerski, Products Liability: Problems & Process 433-68 (4th ed. 2000). Again, issues involving such products receive sporadic attention elsewhere in this and similar texts, but the subject deserves more thorough treatment than is possible in a general course on products liability. Similarly, administrative law texts often use the activities of the FDA to illustrate questions of agency procedure and judicial review. See, e.g., Jerry L. Mashaw et al., Administrative Law: The American Public Law System 128-34, 478-79 (4th ed. 1998) (describing the controversies involving FDA restrictions on saccharin and tobacco products). Even so, sustained attention to this powerful agency can only be found in a specialized but infrequently offered course. See Peter Barton Hutt & Richard A. Merrill, Food and Drug Law: Cases & Materials (2d ed. 1991).

This casebook attempts to blend the best of all of these fields by focusing on the regulation of medical technology. We intentionally use the word "regulation" broadly to encompass not just legislative and administrative agency controls on the creation and use of such technology but also less direct controls mediated through the systems of tort law, insurance, and intellectual property regimes, among others. Although organized thematically rather than sequentially in reference to a product's life-cycle, these materials consider the many ways in which society attempts to manage the production and application of medical technologies, tracing the research and development process from laboratory bench to ultimate use in the treatment of patients. Although students would benefit from some prior exposure to the numerous doctrinal subjects addressed—ranging across administrative law, constitutional law (esp. First Amendment issues), products liability and medical malpractice, insurance, patents and copyright, antitrust, and bioethics—not to mention the scientific issues that arise, we have tried to design the materials in a way that persons with widely different backgrounds will find equally accessible and hopefully valuable. We also hope that the Problems scattered throughout the book, including one lengthier exercise focused on questions of an attorney's professional responsibilities, will facilitate use in the classroom.

A note on editing: Deletions from materials are indicated by asterisk ellipses except when the omitted material consists only of citations or footnotes. Some citations within judicial opinions have been modified as appropriate to approximate the formatting guidelines of *The Bluebook: A Uniform System of Citation* (16th ed. 1996). All footnotes in judicial opinions or other sources are numbered according to the original (editors' notes use an asteriks footnote). We would like to thank our research assistant, Sonia Bretzmann, for double checking our work.

ACKNOWLEDGEMENTS

American Law Institute, Restatement of Torts, Second, Copyright © 1965, 1977 by The American Law Institute. Reprinted with permission of The American Law Institute.

American Law Institute, Restatement of Torts, Third: Products Liability, Copyright © 1998 by The American Law Institute. Reprinted with permission of The American Law Institute.

American Medical Association, Code of Medical Ethics, Opinion 8.135: Managed Care Cost Containment Involving Prescription Drugs. Source: Council on Ethical and Judicial Affairs, Code of Medical Ethics: Current Opinions. Copyright © 1996 by the American Medical Association. Reprinted with Permission of the American Medical Association.

Danzon, Patricia M. and Li-Wei Chao, Does Regulation Drive Out Competition in Pharmaceutical Markets?, 43 J.L. & Econ. 311 (2000). Copyright © 2000 by the University of Chicago. All rights reserved. Reprinted with permission of the University of Chicago and Patricia M. Danzon.

Goldberg, Steven, The Changing Face of Death: Computers, Consciousness, and Nancy Cruzan, 43 Stan. L. Rev. 659 (1991). Copyright © 1991 by the Board of Trustees of the Leland Stanford Junior University. Reprinted with permission of the Stanford Law Review.

Hall, Mark A., Rationing Health Care at the Bedside, 69 N.Y.U.L. Rev. 693 (1994). Copyright © 1994 by New York University Law Review. Reprinted with permission of New York University Law Review.

Heyman, Philip B. and Lance Liebman, The Social Responsibilities of Lawyers, 216–34 (1988). Copyright © 1988 by Foundation Press. Reprinted with permission of Foundation Press, publisher.

Hutt, Peter Barton, The Transformation of United States Food and Drug Law, Journal of the Association of Food & Drug Officials, Sept. 1996, at 1. Copyright © 1996 by the Association of Food and Drug Officials. Reprinted with permission of the Association of Food and Drug Officials.

Mahoney, Julia D., The Market for Human Tissue, 86 Va. L. Rev. 163 (2000). Copyright © 2000 by the Virginia Law Review Association. Reprinted with permission of the Virginia Law Review Association.

Makow, Lawrence S., Note, Medical Device Review at the Food and Drug Administration: Lessons from Magnetic Resonance Spectroscopy and Biliary Lithotripsy, 46 Stan. L. Rev. 709 (1994). Copyright © 1994 by the

the Seton Hall University School of Law. Reprinted with permission of the Seton Hall Law Review.

Saver, Richard S., Note, Reimbursing New Technologies: Why Are the Courts Judging Experimental Medicine?, 44 Stan. L. Rev. 1095 (1992). Copyright © 1992 by the Board of Trustees of the Leland Stanford Junior University. Reprinted with permission of the Stanford Law Review.

Shapiro, Michael H., Is Bioethics Broke?: On the Idea of Ethics and Law "Catching Up"with Technology, 33 Ind. L. Rev. 17 (1999). Copyright © 1999 by the Trustees of Indiana University. Reprinted with permission of the Indiana Law Review and Michael H. Shapiro.

Siegel, Laurel R., Comment, Re-Engineering the Laws of Organ Transplantation, 49 Emory L.J. 917 (2000). Copyright © 2000 by the Emory Law Journal. Reprinted with permission of the Emory Law Journal.

Sorum, Paul C., Limiting Cardiopulmonary Resuscitation, 57 Alb. L. Rev. 617 (1994). Copyright © 1994 by the Albany Law Review. Reprinted with permission of the Albany Law Review.

Wax, Amy L., Technology Assessment and the Doctor-Patient Relationship, 82 Va. L. Rev. 1641 (1996). Copyright © 1996 by the Virginia Law Review Association. Reprinted with permission of the Virginia Law Review Association.

The following cases have been reprinted with the permission of West Publishing Company:

Bernhardt v. Pfizer, Inc., 2000 WL 1738645 (S.D.N.Y. 2000).

Conant v. McCaffrey, 2000 WL 1281174 (N.D. Cal. 2000).

Lake v. FDA, 1989 WL 71554 (E.D. Pa. 1989).

Moran v. Pfizer, Inc., 2001 WL 315339 (S.D.N.Y. 2001).

Tivoli v. United States, 1996 WL 1056005 (S.D.N.Y. 1996).

Vess v. Ciba-Geigy Corp., 2001 WL 290333 (S.D. Cal. 2001).

*

SUMMARY OF CONTENTS

TABLE OF CONTENTS

TABLE OF CASES

Principal cases are in bold type. Non-principal cases are in roman type. References are to pages.

Law, Medicine, and Medical Technology

*

PART I

GOVERNMENT REGULATION

CHAPTER 1

FDA CONTROL: PRELIMINARIES

A. HISTORY AND OVERVIEW

Peter Barton Hutt, *The Transformation of United States Food and Drug Law*

J. ASS'N FOOD & DRUG OFFICIALS, Sept. 1996, at 1.

Government regulation of food and drugs extends back to earliest recorded history. Our modern era of food and drug regulation, however, began with the work of scientists and legislators in the 19th century in England and America. * * * [B]etween 1850 and 1900 virtually every state enacted some form of food and drug statute. Although resources were obviously limited and the science needed to police the food and drug industry was unsophisticated by current standards, our basic concepts of protecting the public health from adulterated and misbranded food and drugs find their origin in this formative era. * * *

When the United States Department of Agriculture (USDA) was created by Congress in 1862, * * * the Chemical Laboratory of the former Patent Office Agricultural Division was designated as the USDA Chemical Division. * * * During the first forty-five years of its existence—from 1862 to 1906—FDA [hereinafter defined broadly to include its predecessor agencies] had no statutes to enforce. * * * Reflecting this lack of statutory authority, FDA initially conducted its business in accordance with its formal title, the Division of Chemistry. It analyzed the food supply and provided advice to other parts of the Department on all aspects of agricultural chemistry but did not engage with the states in establishing national regulatory policy. * * *

[In 1897], the National Board of Trade (the predecessor to our current United States Chamber of Commerce) adopted a resolution establishing $1,000 in prize money for the best three drafts of a national food adulteration statute. The prize was won by George W. Wigner, a public analyst in England, who based his draft statute on the law that had recently been enacted in 1875 in England. Although the wording changed, all of the elements of food adulteration and misbranding included in Wigner's draft statute ultimately became part of the Federal Food and Drugs Act of 1906 and the Federal Food, Drug and Cosmetic Act of 1938 and still can be found in the law today. * * * At the time, however, there was a powerful obstacle in the way. A majority of Congress firmly believed that regulation of the manufacture and sale of food and drugs within the United States involved local matters that the Constitution left entirely to the states. Only the import and export of food and drugs was regarded as within the jurisdiction of the federal government. * * * State food and drug officials were early supporters of federal legislation. As a result of the increasingly national scope of our growing economy, they recognized the need for a federal leadership role to set national policy and standards that would be used throughout the country. * * *

Regulation of biological products represents the oldest form of government regulation of business in our country. * * * [I]n 1901 contaminated smallpox vaccine caused an outbreak of tetanus in Camden and a lot of tetanus-infected diphtheria antitoxin resulted in the death of several children in Saint Louis. * * * Congress promptly enacted the Biologics Act of 1902. The 1902 Act represented a remarkable turning point in the history of food and drug regulation, even though it was not appreciated at the time. For the first time in history, a statute required premarket approval by the government of a category of consumer products before any product within that category could lawfully be marketed. The 1902 Act required government approval of a product license application and an establishment license application for every biological drug intended for human use. Never before—and indeed, not for more than another fifty years—did Congress impose a similar regulatory requirement upon any other category of products. Equally remarkable, the 1902 Act explicitly authorized the Treasury Department to inspect any biologics establishment during all reasonable hours. This was the first federal law authorizing inspection of private manufacturing premises by the federal government. * * * It was to take seventy years before regulation of human biological products would be integrated into FDA regulatory responsibilities. * * *

The Federal Food, Drug and Cosmetic Act, which was enacted in 1938 to replace the 1906 Act, has now been in effect for fifty-eight years. Although its basic structure remains the same, and many of the original regulatory principles are unaltered, its substantive content is now unrecognizable. Its length has increased well over ten times as a result of dozens of extremely important substantive amendments. * * * The 1906 and 1938 Acts were extremely broad and general. They were drafted in the nature of a constitution, incorporating a broad mandate to protect the public against adulterated or misbranded products. The statutory requirements and prohibitions were written as general mandates, not operational rules. The details of implementation were left to FDA.

In more recent years, however, this has begun to change. * * * As a result of the numerous amendments to the 1938 Act during the past fifty-eight years, the statute today consists of very lengthy and complex provisions that have never been subjected to a comprehensive review and rationalization. Each amendment has been negotiated on an ad hoc basis, reflecting the prevailing balance of power in Congress and the Administration at the moment, without consideration of the need for consistency in language or policy throughout the entire statute. Different words are used to mean the same thing in different parts of the statute, different types of authority are granted with respect to similar matters, different enforcement powers are provided for comparable violations, and the relationship among all of the provisions in the statute is increasingly ambiguous. * * *

[T]he legislation that has often been most important in establishing national policy on food and drug regulation has been created in the aftermath of a major product disaster. As is often true under these conditions, the legislation has been shaped as much by public emotion as by rational policy design. There has often been insufficient congressional analysis and legislative history to guide FDA, the regulated industry and the courts in the intended meaning and application of the resulting statutory language.

The relation of any federal agency with Congress is always tenuous. Congress has two functions with respect to a regulatory program. First, it creates the agency and authorizes the program. Second, it conducts oversight to determine any weakness or limitations and to recommend changes in both legislative and administrative policy. During the first half of its existence, FDA was subjected to relatively little oversight from congressional committees. * * * Since 1960, there have been far more oversight hearings than legislative hearings regarding FDA. Virtually every aspect of the agency's work has been subjected to intense investigation.

For the first two decades of these oversight hearings, on all but one occasion the hearing was conducted to criticize FDA for failing to take adequate regulatory action against a product that the committee concluded was unlawful or for approval of a new product that the committee thought was unsafe or ineffective. On only one occasion was FDA criticized for not approving a new drug with sufficient speed. On literally hundreds of other occasions the agency was subjected to withering criticism for failing to protect against unsafe and ineffective products. This congressional criticism had a profound impact on FDA employees at all levels. Already risk averse by nature, they became even more conservative in implementing the FDA premarket approval authority. * * * After such a long time during which the congressional focus was on the failure of FDA adequately to protect the public against harm, FDA was ill-prepared to respond to charges that the agency was failing to promote the public health by fostering the prompt availability of new products. * * *

Over the past century, FDA and its counterpart state agencies have fared extraordinarily well in the courts. Often faced with complex scientific and technical issues, judges have been reluctant to overrule decisions made by FDA. * * * Not long after the 1906 Act became law, the Supreme Court unanimously upheld it as a valid exercise of the power of Congress to regulate interstate commerce. The Supreme Court has repeatedly upheld the power of FDA to protect the public from "lurking dangers caused by the introduction of harmful ingredients" and from "dangerous products," and has relied on "consumer protection, not dialectics" to interpret food and drug law in a way most likely to promote these objectives. * * * To be sure, neither FDA nor state agencies have an unblemished judicial record.

Occasionally on matters of substantive authority, but more frequently where the courts have perceived procedural irregularities, FDA has been overturned in the courts. Yet one has difficulty identifying a single court decision in the past century that struck a fundamental blow to the ability of FDA or the state agencies to protect the public health. * * *

For roughly the first half of its existence, until 1940, FDA remained a component of USDA. The agency was transferred from USDA to the Federal Security Agency in 1940 and to the Department of Health, Education and Welfare when it was formed in 1953, which later became the Department of Health and Human Services in 1979. From 1930 to the present, it has retained its present designation: the Food and Drug Administration. * * * FDA is our oldest federal regulatory agency, and for decades it was the only federal agency charged with jurisdiction over a broad range of consumer products. The Environmental Protection Agency, the Occupational Safety and Health Administration and the Consumer Product Safety Commission are all of relatively recent origin, created during 1970–1972. FDA thus towers over the field of regulation in the United States as our most venerable and respected regulatory institution. * * *

FDA regulates one-quarter of the United States economy. Yet FDA has never been a large government agency by federal standards and has commanded only a rather modest annual appropriation. [In 1995, the agency received almost $900 million in appropriations and employed more than 9500 individuals.] * * * [I]t is likely that user fees and other innovative sources of revenue for FDA will continue to be explored in the future. FDA has fared extraordinarily well in its appropriations during a period of severe restrictions on government funding, but this cannot last forever. In the coming years, FDA is likely to experience flat appropriations or a modest reduction. * * *

The history of progress in food and drug regulation over the past century is largely the history of the development of science, not the enactment of statutory provisions. The 1938 Act contains broad statutory mandates that are meaningless without the infusion of scientific knowledge that permits the development of specific operational rules. * * * Development of some of the most important principles of toxicology can be attributed to FDA scientists. * * * [T]hey gradually derived during the 1940s the now well-accepted rule of toxicology that a safe human dose may be determined by dividing the lowest no observed effect level (NOEL) in animals by a safety factor of 100. * * * [In addition, in the early 1970s, an FDA decision represented] the first use of quantitative risk assessment by any government agency. * * * FDA has long struggled with its identity as a "regulatory" or "law enforcement" agency on the one hand or as a "science" agency on the other hand. * * *

NOTES AND QUESTIONS

1. *Statutory evolution.* In 1997, Congress enacted the Food and Drug Administration Modernization Act (FDAMA), Pub. L. No. 105–115, 111

Stat. 2296, one of the most significant set of amendments to the 1938 law in decades, though, consistent with the recent pattern of legislative micromanagement, these latest amendments tinkered with rather than transformed the FDCA. See Richard A. Merrill, Modernizing the FDA: An Incremental Revolution, Health Aff., Mar.-Apr. 1999, at 96. Relevant provisions of the statute as amended over the years can be found in the Appendix, and they also are reproduced in appropriate parts of the text or in excerpted judicial opinions (though they may have been amended subsequent to the decision).*

2. *Agency lore.* Although of late it has not fared as well before Congress and the courts, and it recently has struggled with scandals and leadership problems, the FDA remains one of the most highly respected agencies in the federal government. See Stephen Barr, Users Mostly Rate Agencies Favorably, Wash. Post, Apr. 13, 2000, at A29 ("The FDA came out on top in the survey, with more than 80 percent of medical professionals, business regulatory officers, health and medicine advocates and the chronically ill responding with favorable impressions of the agency."). This translates into important clout for an agency that lacks the size and resources enjoyed by other regulatory bodies.

3. *Further commentary.* See Peter Barton Hutt & Richard A. Merrill, Food and Drug Law: Cases and Materials (2d ed. 1991); David F. Cavers, The Food, Drug, and Cosmetic Act of 1938: Its Legislative History and Its Substantive Provisions, 6 Law & Contemp. Probs. 2 (1939); Arthur H. Hayes, Food and Drug Regulation After 75 Years, 246 JAMA 1223 (1981); Symposium, The Protection of the Consumer of Food and Drugs, 1 Law & Contemp. Probs. 1 (1933); Developments in the Law–The Federal Food, Drug, and Cosmetic Act, 67 Harv. L. Rev. 632 (1954); see also Jonathan Liebenau, Medical Science and Medical Industry: The Formation of the American Pharmaceutical Industry (1987); Peter Barton Hutt, Food and Drug Law: Journal of an Academic Adventure, 46 J. Legal Educ. 1 (1996); Lars Noah, One Decade of Food and Drug Law Scholarship: A Selected Bibliography, 55 Food & Drug L.J. 641 (2000); FDA's Web Page <http://www.fda.gov>.

B. PRODUCT CATEGORIES AND INTENDED USE

The FDA regulates a wide range of consumer products, including food, food additives, dietary supplements, human and animal drugs, medical devices, and cosmetics. The lines of demarcation between these product categories are often unclear and sharply contested because the classifica-

---

* A note on numbering: The original sections of the Act were renumbered as codified in Title 21 of the United States Code, usually by adding a "3" at the beginning and dropping the middle "0" of the three digit section number (so FDCA § 301 becomes 21 U.S.C. § 331). Where there is no "0" in the middle (or at the end) of the original, the codified section numbers attach letters (so FDCA § 510 becomes 21 U.S.C. § 360, and FDCA § 511 becomes 21 U.S.C. § 360a).

tion will dictate whether the FDA has any jurisdiction and then what types of regulatory controls it might impose on the product. Cosmetics face the weakest controls (only after-the-fact policing for adulteration and misbranding) and new drugs face the most rigorous controls (including thorough premarket review in addition to after-the-fact policing), with dietary supplements, foods, color additives, food additives, and medical devices arrayed between these two extremes (and roughly in that order). Although this casebook focuses on human drugs and medical devices, the growing interest in unconventional therapies necessitates some discussion of dietary supplements, and the other product categories will be mentioned as necessary to illuminate definitional disputes.

1. DRUGS

United States v. An Article of Drug . . . Bacto–Unidisk

394 U.S. 784 (1969).

■ WARREN, CHIEF JUSTICE:

* * * Various antibiotics, known more commonly as "wonder drugs" under such familiar names as penicillin, aureomycin, terramycin, tetracycline, and streptomycin, have proved very useful since World War II in treating numerous infectious diseases. Produced biologically, however, these drugs tend to vary greatly in their quality and potency unless developed, and thereafter tested, under very carefully controlled conditions. Consequently, Congress enacted § 507 of the Food, Drug, and Cosmetic Act, directing the Secretary of Health, Education, and Welfare to promulgate regulations establishing such standards of identity, potency, quality, and purity as necessary to ensure the "safety" and "efficacy" of those antibiotics. At present, more than 30 antibiotic drugs are listed with accompanying regulations covering more than 700 pages in the Code of Federal Regulations.

With the proliferation of the various types of antibiotics, doctors found a need for a screening test to help choose which antibiotic to use in treating a particular infection. A diffusion test, using antibiotic sensitivity discs like the one in question here, soon became a widely employed screening method. In this test, a round paper disc, which has been impregnated with a specific antibiotic, is placed in contact with sample cultures, or isolates, of a patient's virus, grown in a special culture medium (agar) from a specimen of the patient's fluid (blood, spinal fluid, sputum, urine, etc.). In those places impregnated with an antibiotic to which the patient's infection is sensitive, no new isolate will grow, leaving a clear area (an "inhibition zone"); in those places impregnated with a drug to which the infection is resistant, the isolate will grow, leaving no clear area. The disc is used, in conjunction with a patient's specimen, in laboratory work exclusively, and never comes in contact with any part of the patient's body itself.

The discs had been in general use for some four years when, in 1960, the Secretary of Health, Education, and Welfare determined to regulate them pursuant to § 507. After notice and an opportunity for public partic-ipation, the Commissioner of Food and Drugs, under authority delegated by the Secretary, promulgated regulations requiring pre-clearance, batch-test-ing, and certification of antibiotic sensitivity discs. The Commissioner's action, the regulations noted, followed "numerous complaints by the medi-cal profession, hospitals, and laboratory technicians" and a resulting exten-sive survey of the use of the discs. That study found the discs unreliable in their statements of potency with resulting loss of safety and efficacy, and thus found it "vital for the protection of the public health" to adopt the regulations (25 Fed. Reg. 9370).

This case arose in May 1962 as an in rem seizure proceeding against an interstate shipment of a number of cases of sensitivity discs, manufactured by Difco Laboratories, Inc., under the trade name of "Bacto–Unidisk." In condemning the product pursuant to § 301 et seq. of the Food, Drug, and Cosmetic Act, the United States claimed, inter alia, that the product, as a "drug" within the meaning of the Act, had not been certified nor exempted from certification as required by § 507 and the regulations thereunder and was therefore misbranded under § 502. The seizure was proper only if the Secretary's regulations subjecting the discs to the pre-market clearance requirements were authorized by the Act. Since the scope of the Secretary's pre-market regulatory power over antibiotic drugs under § 507 depends ultimately on the Act's general definition of "drug" in § 201(g), the validity of the disc regulations allegedly violated turned on the coverage of the drug definition:

For the purposes of this chapter—

(g) (1) The term "drug" means (A) articles recognized in the official United States Pharmacopoeia, official Homeopathic Pharmacopoeia of the United States, or official National Formulary, or any supplement to any of them; and (B) articles intended for use in the diagnosis, cure, mitigation, treatment, or prevention of disease in man or other ani-mals; and (C) articles (other than food) intended to affect the structure or any function of the body of man or other animals; and (D) articles intended for use as a component of any article specified in clauses (A), (B), or (C) of this paragraph; but does not include devices or their components, parts, or accessories.

If, on the other hand, the product was a "device," only the misbranding, adulteration, and labeling provisions of §§ 501 and 502 applied, and the Secretary's disc certification regulations were invalidly promulgated. Al-though a "device" expressly cannot be a "drug" under the last phrase of the drug definition above,* a device is given almost a parallel definition in § 201(h):

The term "device" . . . means instruments, apparatus, and contri-vances, including their components, parts, and accessories, intended (1)

---

* In 1990, Congress amended the statute to, among other things, delete the exclusion of devices from the drug definition.

for use in the diagnosis, cure, mitigation, treatment, or prevention of disease in man or other animals; or (2) to affect the structure or any function of the body of man or other animals.

Finally, it was established at trial that of the various definitions given above, the operative ones in this case were § 201(g)(1)(B) of the drug provision and § 201(h)(1) of the parallel device definition; the essential question underlying the validity of the regulations, then, was whether the Bacto–Unidisks were "articles intended for use in the diagnosis, cure, mitigation, treatment, or prevention of disease in man or other animals." * * *

Although there was some testimony below debating the precise extent of the public health dangers posed by the sensitivity discs, the courts below declined to substitute their judgment for that of the Commissioner of Food and Drugs by determining whether his action was really necessary to protect the public health from a purely medical viewpoint. Rather, the courts below quite properly confined the inquiry to an examination of whether the disc regulations, even if medically unwise, were authorized by the Act, and more specifically, by the Act's definition of "drug." * * *

Respondent's primary contention here is that the sensitivity discs are not subject to any of the provisions of the Act because Congress did not intend it to cover articles used so indirectly in the "cure, mitigation, (and) treatment" of disease. Respondent uses the same two-step analysis relied on by the courts below: (1) Congress did not intend to write the drug definition more broadly than does the medical profession, and (2) the medical concept of drug is limited to articles that are administered to man either internally or externally. Alternatively, respondent argues, even if the Act's "intended for use" language does cover the discs, they must clearly be classified as devices. In view of the legislative history discussed below and the broad, remedial purpose of the Act itself, however, we hesitate to give the critical language such a narrow, restrictive reading in the absence of congressional direction to do so, and we therefore reject the contention that the discs do not properly fall within the purview of the Act. For the same basic reasons, we furthermore reject the argument that the discs, once found to come under the Act's coverage, must be classified specifically as devices and not drugs.

We need not stop to parse the language of the Act's definition of drug, for the district court found, and the parties do not disagree here, that a literal reading of the words "intended for use in the . . . cure, mitigation, (or) treatment" of disease "clearly has application" to the Bacto–Unidisk. Although respondent again urges that the disc itself does not "treat" a patient in the same way an antibiotic does in terms of personal application, the disc plays at least some role in the selection of the appropriate drug. Thus, the essential question for our determination is whether Congress intended the definition of drug to have the broad coverage the courts below and the parties agree its words allow. Viewing the structure, the legislative history, and the remedial nature of the Act, we think it plain that Congress intended to define "drug" far more broadly than does the medical profession. The reason for including a separate, almost parallel, definition of "devices" in the Act is, as the legislative history shows, relevant to congressional intent. It is therefore helpful to consider both the question of the Act's initial application and the question of the drug-device dichotomy at the same time. * * *

[T]he word "drug" is a term of art for the purposes of the Act, encompassing far more than the strict medical definition of that word. If Congress had intended to limit the statutory definition to the medical one, it could have so stated explicitly, or simply have made reference to the official United States Pharmacopoeia (or the National Formulary), as it did in the first of the three subsections of § 201(g)(1), and let the definition rest there. The historical expansion of the statute's definition, furthermore, clearly points out Congress' intention of going beyond the medical usage. * * *

The enactment of the 1938 Federal Food, Drug, and Cosmetic Act illustrates the expansion of the definition of drug. One of the changes contemplated in S. 2800, an early version of the Act, defined "drug" to include

> (1) all substances and preparations recognized in the United States Pharmacopoeia, Homeopathic Pharmacopoeia of the United States, or National Formulary or supplements thereto; and (2) all substances, preparations, and devices intended for use in the cure, mitigation, treatment, or prevention of disease in man or other animals; and (3) all substances and preparations, other than food, and all devices intended to affect the structure or any function of the body.

Senator Copeland of New York, who sponsored the Act, remarked about the inclusion of the word "devices" in his prepared statement introducing S. 2800 as follows:

> The present law defines drugs as substances or mixtures of substances intended to be used for the cure, mitigation, or prevention of disease. This narrow definition permits escape from legal control of all therapeutic or curative devices like electric belts, for example. It also permits the escape of preparations which are intended to alter the structure or some function of the body, as, for example, preparations intended to reduce excessive weight. There are many worthless and some dangerous devices and preparations falling within these classifications. S. 2800 contains ample authority to control them.

The definition was revised in S. 5, 74th Cong., 1st Sess. (1935), to include substances, preparations, and devices intended for diagnostic purposes, as well as for cure, mitigation, treatment, or prevention of disease. As the inclusion of the word "diagnosis" came before the Senate for consideration, a controversy developed on the floor, aimed more at the word "devices," which was not then before the Senate, than at the word "diagnosis." * * *

As a result of the criticism on the Senate floor, Senator Copeland proposed an amendment to add a definition of "device" to parallel that of drug, an amendment which was included when the bill was returned to the

Senate Committee on Commerce and later agreed to by the Senate without debate. The ultimate effect of the various amendments, of course, was still to include devices under the control of the Act for the first time, the goal Senator Copeland had originally set out to achieve. As Congressman Chapman of Kentucky explained to the House after the bill had passed the Senate, "For the first time it is proposed in a bill before Congress to control therapeutic devices.... There are hundreds of worthless contrivances being sold to and used by gullible people. Suffice it to say that a fake contraption for the cure of consumption is just as serious a menace to health as is a worthless drug sold for the same disease." 80 Cong. Rec. 10,236 (1936). * * * Thus, it is clear that two parallel definitions were provided for semantic reasons only; for the purposes of the Act, the two definitions had the same effect of subjecting both drugs and devices to the adulteration and misbranding provisions. No practical significance to the distinction between the two words arose until the pre-market clearance provisions, similar to the certification regulations for antibiotics enacted in 1945, were added after a drug tragedy in the fall of 1937.[17] The excepting clause of § 201(g)(1), stating clearly that a drug cannot be a device, was also added in 1938.

The historical expansion of the definition of drug, and the creation of a parallel concept of devices, clearly show, we think, that Congress fully intended that the Act's coverage be as broad as its literal language indicates—and, equally clearly, broader than any strict medical definition might otherwise allow. Strong indications from legislative history that Congress intended the broad coverage the district court thought "ridiculous" should satisfy us that the lower courts erred in refusing to apply the Act's language as written. But we are all the more convinced that we must give effect to congressional intent in view of the well-accepted principle that remedial legislation such as the Food, Drug, and Cosmetic Act is to be given a liberal construction consistent with the Act's overriding purpose to protect the public health * * * *

Respondent's alternative contention, that even if its product does fall within the purview of the Act, it is plainly a "device" and therefore by definition necessarily not a "drug," must also be rejected, we believe, in light of the foregoing analysis. At the outset, it must be conceded that the language of the statute is of little assistance in determining precisely what differentiates a "drug" from a "device": to the extent that both are intended for use in the treatment, mitigation and cure of disease, the former is an "article" and the latter includes "instruments," "apparatus," and "contrivances." Despite the obvious areas of overlap in definition, we are not entirely without guidance in determining the propriety of the Secretary's decision below, given the overall goals of the Act and its legislative history.

More specifically, as we have previously held in an analogous situation where the statute's language seemed insufficiently precise, the "natural

---

17. This was the "Elixir–Sulfanilamide" tragedy of September–October, 1937, where nearly 100 persons died as the result of consuming an untested drug.

way" to draw the line "is in light of the statutory purpose." Since the patient will tend to derive less benefit and perhaps some harm from a particular antibiotic if, though the drug itself was properly batch-tested, it was not the proper antibiotic to use, it was entirely reasonable for the Secretary to determine that the discs, like the antibiotics they serve, are drugs and similarly subject to pre-clearance certification under § 507. An opposite conclusion might undercut the value of testing the antibiotics themselves, for such testing would be a useless exercise if the wrong drug were ultimately administered, even partially as the result of an unreliable disc.

Furthermore, the legislative history, read in light of the statute's remedial purpose, directs us to read the classification "drug" broadly, and to confine the device exception as nearly as is possible to the types of items Congress suggested in the debates, such as electric belts, quack diagnostic scales, and therapeutic lamps, as well as bathroom weight scales, shoulder braces, air conditioning units, and crutches. In upholding the Secretary's determination here, without deciding the precise contours of the "device" classification, we need only point out that the exception was created primarily for the purpose of avoiding the semantic incongruity of classifying as drugs (1) certain quack contraptions and (2) basic aids used in the routine operation of a hospital—items characterized more by their purely mechanical nature than by the fact that they are composed of complex chemical compounds or biological substances. Finally, we are supported in the decision to uphold the FDA's determination that the sensitivity discs fall under the coverage of the Act and specifically under the drug provision thereof by the knowledge that the classification of these discs as drugs may not be as contrary to common medical usage as the district court and respondent would have us believe.[20]

In upholding the Secretary's construction of the Act, we are not unmindful of our warning that "[i]n our anxiety to effectuate the congressional purpose of protecting the public, we must take care not to extend the scope of the statute beyond the point where Congress indicated it would stop." 62 Cases of Jam v. United States, 340 U.S. 593, 600 (1951). Our holding here simply involves an obvious corollary to that principle, that we must take care not to narrow the coverage of a statute short of the point where Congress indicated it should extend.

United States v. Article of Drug ... Ova II

414 F.Supp. 660 (D.N.J.1975), aff'd mem., 535 F.2d 1248 (3d Cir.1976).

■ BIUNNO, DISTRICT JUDGE:

This case involves the question whether a kit of chemicals and equipment, marketed in interstate commerce by Faraday Laboratories, Inc.

---

20. See W. Dorland's Illustrated Medical Dictionary 449 (24th ed., 1965), where "drug" is defined as: "Any chemical compound or any non-infectious biological substance, not used for its mechanical properties, which may be administered to or used on or for patients, either human or animal, as an aid in the diagnosis, treatment or prevention of disease or other abnormal condition, for the relief of pain or suffering, or to control or improve any physiological or pathological condition."

under the name "Ova II," is a "drug" within the meaning of the Federal Food, Drug and Cosmetic Act. The kit is marketed with literature indicating its use for the purpose of performing, in the home, a "preliminary screening test" by which a human female, having some reason to suspect that she may be pregnant, may obtain an indication of probability that she is or is not pregnant. The United States (FDA) filed a complaint for forfeiture and condemnation of several thousand kits seized within the jurisdiction of the court, and Faraday, as claimant, resists that action. * * * Both sides agree that if it comes within any of the definitions of a "drug," it is also a "new drug" as defined by 21 U.S.C. § 321(p), and may not be marketed in interstate commerce without first filing a "new drug application" on the basis of which FDA determines that it is "safe and effective," 21 U.S.C. § 355. * * *

Turning to the Ova II kit, the facts are that it consists of two glass vials, and two bottles of solutions. Bottle A contains a solution of hydrochloric acid (HCl). Bottle B contains a solution of sodium hydroxide (NaOH). Use of the kit involves taking a quantity of fresh urine and reacting it with both solutions in the two vials, with differences between them in respect to the number of drops added and the time sequence of the addition. The presence or absence of distinct visual differences in the darkness of the two quantities of urine so treated forms the basis for the indication (distinct differences of color indicates absence of pregnancy, essentially similar color and saturation indicates pregnancy). This test is in glass, outside the body, using body fluids available by ordinary bodily processes (i.e., "in vitro" to use the technical term). The test does not involve the injection or ingestion of any material in the human body itself (i.e., "in vivo").

Items which are "drugs" as contemplated by the statute fall into two major functional categories. One such category is the "diagnostic" function. The other is the "treatment" function, in the broadest sense that embraces prevention and alleviation of pain or discomfort as well as "cure." Those items related to the treatment function are necessarily "in vivo." Something must be done, or applied to or placed within the body itself to provide treatment. At least in this country, treatment outside the body, as by inserting pins in a doll, is not considered to be treatment. Those items related to the diagnostic function may be either "in vivo" or "in vitro." The test of a urine sample for the presence of sugar is "in vitro," and is a means for diagnosing the disease of diabetes. The presence of certain enzymes in the blood, with the test performed "in vitro" may indicate heart disease in the form of a myocardial infarction. On the other hand, the Schick Test, which involves the intradermal injection of a dilute toxin, is an "in vivo" diagnostic procedure to determine susceptibility or immunity to diphtheria. Similarly, scratch tests which involve the tearing of the skin surface and the application of allergens are another example of "in vivo" diagnostic procedures for allergies and sensitivity to various substances. * * *

In the ordinary sense of the word "drugs," it would be rational to limit its meaning to items used or applied for diagnostic purposes to those employed "in vivo" and not for those employed "in vitro." There can be little question that for the entire array, this distinction will usually be valid. But an overlap between these two areas arises by reason of the decision in *United States v. An Article of Drug ... Bacto–Unidisk,* 394 U.S. 784 (1969). * * * Careful analysis of all the opinions in the case indicates that this conclusion reached to the outer boundaries of what might be found to be encompassed by the definition "drug." The fundamental rationale of the conclusion rests on the context within which the disc was used. The activating circumstances would necessarily involve the existence of a patient known to be ill, i.e., suffering from a disease, and that an infection was involved. Also involved is the circumstance that the identity of the infecting organism was not known. Without an item like the disc, a treating physician might be obliged to try one antibiotic after another, by way of "challenge and response" to find out what treatment would be effective. The disc, which applied a whole spectrum of antibiotics to a cultured specimen of the infected material offered a diagnostic tool for simultaneous testing of what would be effective.

On the face of the statutory language, the disc doubtless fell more clearly within the exception of a "device" carved out of the definition of a "drug." At best, the question was on the edges of the outer boundaries. The Supreme Court accepted a generous and broad construction, no doubt influenced by the life-and-death risks involved in achieving a correct diagnosis to identify the specific infection at the earliest possible moment, so that effective treatment might begin without avoidable delay. Considerations of like nature are non-existent here. The condition of pregnancy, as such, is a normal physiological function of all mammals and cannot be considered a disease of itself. Pregnancy is an execution of an inherent bodily function and implies no ailment, illness or disease. * * * A test for pregnancy, then, is not a test for the diagnosis of disease. It is no more than a test for news, which may be either good news or bad news depending on whether pregnancy is wanted or not. * * *

The key point is that no pregnancy test, including those recognized by FDA as not only "safe and effective" but also considered by it as the most "safe and effective" (a quality not required by the Act), is fully 100% reliable, and even if they were 100% reliable would disclose no more than that pregnancy exists or does not exist. No presently known pregnancy test is designed to or capable of differentiating between a pregnancy as such and an ailment or disease arising out of the pregnancy such as an abnormal pregnancy (i.e., tubal) or a pregnancy not indicated (i.e., in a female with hypertension or mental illness), or a disease (i.e., toxemia of pregnancy). These ailments or diseases have other symptoms, other conditions or history, and the like, that must be separately diagnosed. Neither Ova II nor any other pregnancy test attempts to do so. In the context of the issues here, the fact that there may be ailments or diseases related to pregnancy or associated with it is not an element that may be considered.

On the central question, then, the court is satisfied that there is no genuine issue on any material fact, and that Faraday is entitled to judgment as a matter of law. This determination rests on the view that the Ova II kit is not a "drug" within any rational sense that may be attributed to the term as defined. There is no dispute that FDA has the burden of persuasion. Taking each of the three definitions of a "drug," as set out in 21 U.S.C. § 321(g)(1), it is plain that the Ova II kit does not fall within any of them.

The first definition, i.e., recognition of an item in the U.S. Pharmacopeia, National Formulary, etc., cannot be taken literally. In the first place, none of these compendium publications is more than a privately sponsored set of standards of strength and purity, for medicinal use, which may properly carry labeling such as "U.S.P." or "N.F.," and the like. The overwhelming mass of items for which there are monographs are substances or chemicals whose use for medicinal purposes calls for a high degree of adherence to uniform standards of strength and purity. * * *

These compendiums and pharmacopeiae, being privately published, make changes from time to time. And thus the question arises whether they can have the force of law without running afoul of the principle that a legislative body may not lawfully delegate its functions to a private citizen or organization. Limited delegation of legislative functions to governmental agencies within the boundaries of an expressed norm, standard or guide is well recognized; but a delegation to private groups, and without such boundaries, is quite another matter. * * *

Since the Congress will not be presumed to have enacted an invalid statute, the first definition, i.e., recognition in the U.S.P. or other named compendium must be read [more narrowly] * * * * Under this interpretation, the Ova II kit is not a drug under 21 U.S.C. § 321(g)(1)(A), despite the fact that it contains sodium hydroxide and hydrochloric acid, since it is not labeled "U.S.P." etc., and is not marketed for medicinal use.

The second definition, namely articles related to the diagnosis of disease, etc., does not apply to the Ova II kit because its purpose is to indicate the existence or non-existence of pregnancy, which is not of itself a disease, and because no other pregnancy test attempts or purports to do anything more than Ova II does. The third definition, articles intended to affect the structure or any function of the body is obviously not applicable to any article which is used "in vitro," and in no way inserted in, injected in, ingested by or applied to the body. * * * In arriving at these conclusions and determinations, the court has not considered the implications of pending legislation, such as S.510, passed by the U.S. Senate on April 17, 1975 even though it would define a "device" as embracing in vitro reagents intended for use in the diagnosis of "conditions" (i.e., pregnancy), other than disease. * * * Summary judgment will be entered accordingly in favor of Faraday.

NOTES AND QUESTIONS

1. *Some other odd drugs.* In *Bacto-Unidisk*, the Court cited a lower court decision upholding the FDA's decision to classify a ligature product (using nylon suture material to tie off blood vessels during surgery) as drugs rather than devices. See AMP Inc. v. Gardner, 275 F.Supp. 410 (S.D.N.Y. 1967), aff'd, 389 F.2d 825 (2d Cir.1968); see also United States v. Loran Med. Sys., Inc., 25 F.Supp.2d 1082, 1086 (C.D.Cal.1997) (fetal cells injected to stimulate insulin production); Jay M. Zitter, Annotation, What Is "Drug" Within Meaning of § 201(g)(1) of Federal Food, Drug, and Cosmetic Act, 127 A.L.R. Fed. 141 (1995 & 2002 Supp.). For a contemporary version of antibiotic sensitivity discs, consider the following new technology currently under FDA review: a gene sequencing test for HIV designed to help physicians select from more than a dozen AIDS drugs those to which the patient's particular virus is least likely to develop resistance. See Andrew Pollack, When Gene Sequencing Becomes a Fact of Life, N.Y. Times, Jan. 17, 2001, at C1. Is this a drug? Could the FDA assert jurisdiction over a textbook on antibiotic therapies because it too is intended for use in the treatment of patients (and, if the information is incorrect, it would defeat the purpose of demanding pre-clearance of antibiotics)?

2. *U.S. Pharmacopeia and National Formulary.* In a lengthy appendix to the *Ova II* opinion elaborating on the nature of pharmacopeiae, the court noted that "their status generally is not unlike that of legal publications such as the Restatements and Model Codes adopted by the American Law Institute, or the Uniform Acts and Codes published by the Commissioner on Uniform Laws and approved by the House of Delegates of the American Bar Association." Even so, the concern that the first clause of the drug definition might represent an unconstitutional delegation of governmental authority to private parties has not troubled other courts that have faced this objection more directly. See White v. State Bd. of Pharmacy, 138 N.Y.S.2d 448, 452 (App.Div.1955); State v. Wakeen, 57 N.W.2d 364, 367–69 (Wis.1953); James O. Freedman, Delegation of Power and Institutional Competence, 43 U. Chi. L. Rev. 307, 333 (1976) ("In these cases, the private party's decision to include or exclude a particular drug is invariably made according to pre-existing professional standards in order to serve a particular professional need, rather than as a response to the legislation that gives such decisions a coincidental public effect."). Even so, the compendial recognition clauses in the drug and device definitions have fallen into disuse.

3. *Structure-or-function claims.* The courts have sustained FDA enforcement actions against products such as starch blockers (made from kidney beans) or guar gum when they are marketed as a weight loss aids that interfere with digestion because such claims reflect an intent to affect the structure or function of the body and trigger drug status. See American Health Prods. Co. v. Hayes, 744 F.2d 912, 913 (2d Cir.1984); Nutrilab, Inc. v. Schweiker, 713 F.2d 335, 338–39 (7th Cir.1983); United States v. Undetermined Quantities of "Cal–Ban 3000," 776 F.Supp. 249, 253–55 (E.D.N.C.1991); see also United States v. Undetermined Quantities of Bottles of an Article of Veterinary Drug, 22 F.3d 235, 239–40 (10th Cir.1994) (holding that a pet food additive containing subtherapeutic doses of an antibiotic and promoted as a way to reduce the odors resulting from intestinal bacteria qualified as a drug under both the "disease" and the "structure or function" clauses in the statutory definition); cf. E.R. Squibb & Sons, Inc. v. Bowen, 870 F.2d 678, 682–83 (D.C.Cir.1989) (noting that "the 'structure or ... function' definition, unlike the 'disease in man' definition, is relatively narrow, and was not intended to encompass all articles that might have some remote physical effect upon the body").

4. *Drugs vs. cosmetics.* Courts have sustained FDA enforcement actions against cosmetic products as unapproved new drugs when accompanied by claims that they affect the structure or function of the body. See United States v. An Article of Drug ... "Line Away," 415 F.2d 369, 372 (3d Cir.1969) (finding drug connotations in advertising claims for skin lotion containing bovine albumin); United States v. An Article ... Sudden Change, 409 F.2d 734, 739–42 (2d Cir.1969) (holding that a "face lift without surgery" claim for a lotion that had only a temporary physiological effect on the skin triggered drug status because some gullible consumers might take it literally); United States v. Kasz Enter., Inc., 855 F.Supp. 534, 539–40 (D.R.I.1994) (herbal shampoo marketed as promoting hair growth); cf. United States v. An Article of Drug ... "Helene Curtis Magic Secret," 331 F.Supp. 912, 917 (D.Md.1971) (holding that claims that a "pure protein" skin lotion could smooth facial wrinkles and cause an "astringent sensation" did not convert it into a drug); Jacqueline A. Greff, Regulation of Cosmetics That Are Also Drugs, 51 Food & Drug L.J. 243, 254–57, 262 (1996) (noting FDA efforts to regulate cosmetics as drugs based solely on the presence of an active ingredient such as fluoride in toothpaste). In the early 1990s, a company introduced a thigh cream product containing aminophylline for topical application (aminophylline is an ingested antiasthmatic prescription drug whose labeling warns of risks such as ventricular arryhthmias, convulsions, and death). See Pamela A. Simon et al., Skin Reactions to Topical Aminophylline, 273 JAMA 1737 (1995). Around the same time, several companies began marketing products containing alpha-hydroxy acids for reducing the appearance of wrinkles, and the FDA undertook investigations because of concerns that high concentrations could cause skin damage. See Laura A. Heymann, The Cosmetic/Drug Dilemma: FDA Regulation of Alpha–Hydroxy Acids, 52 Food & Drug L.J. 357 (1997); Paula Kurtzweil, Alpha Hydroxy Acids for Skin Care, FDA Consumer, Mar.-Apr. 1998. See generally Joseph A. Page & Kathleen A. Blackburn, Behind the Looking Glass: Administrative, Legislative and Private Approaches to Cosmetic Safety Substantiation, 24 UCLA L. Rev. 795 (1977).

5. *Intended use.* A product is regulated according to claims made for it rather than its composition. See S. Rep. No. 73–493, at 2–3 (1934) ("The use to which a product is put will determine the category into which it will fall.... The manufacturer of the article, through his representations in connection with its sale, can determine the use to which an article is to be put."). The mere presence of a chemically active substance would not satisfy this definition; the intended use of the substance must serve a diagnostic or therapeutic purpose or otherwise affect the structure or function of the body. Conversely, a chemically inert substance can qualify as a drug depending on the claims made for it. Thus, bottled water, which would normally be regulated by FDA as a food (and also by the EPA under a different statute) might be regulated (1) as a drug if labeled as a cure for cancer, (2) as a medical device (accessory) if labeled as a sterilizing agent for surgical instruments, or (3) as a cosmetic if labeled as a skin softener. See Bradley v. United States, 264 F. 79, 81–82 (5th Cir.1920) (holding that curative claims for mineral water made it a "drug"). More plausible classification problems arise with items like toothpastes (cosmetic or drug, depending, for instance, on whether anticavity claims are made, while denture cleansers are regarded as medical devices). The intended use of a product typically is determined by its labeling and any other promotional claims made by the seller. See, e.g., United States v. Article of Drug ... B–Complex Cholinos Capsules, 362 F.2d 923, 925–26 (3d Cir.1966) (radio broadcasts); Nature Food Centres, Inc. v. United States, 310 F.2d 67, 70 (1st Cir.1962) (public lectures); V.E. Irons, Inc. v. United States, 244 F.2d 34, 44 (1st Cir.1957) (oral representations made by authorized sales distributors); United States v. General Nutrition, Inc., 638 F.Supp. 556, 563–64 (W.D.N.Y.1986) (same); Hanson v. United States, 417 F.Supp. 30, 35 (D.Minn.), aff'd, 540 F.2d 947 (8th Cir.1976); see also 21 C.F.R. § 201.128 (defining "intended use"). More controversially, the FDA has suggested that "intended use" may include the seller's subjective intent even if never communicated to consumers, which would mean that promotional claims provide the best but not exclusive evidence of a product's intended use. See Richard M. Cooper, The WLF Case Thus Far, 55 Food & Drug L.J. 477, 485–86 (2000) (criticizing this interpretation); see also Meza v. Southern Cal. Physicians Ins. Exchange, 73 Cal.Rptr.2d 91, 94 (Ct.App.1998) (concluding that melaleuca oil used by a physician to treat warts qualified as a drug even though the seller made no therapeutic claims).

6. *Other puzzles.* The reference to "disease" in the definitions of drug and device may pose difficult questions of its own. See Lars Noah, Pigeonholing Illness: Medical Diagnosis as a Legal Construct, 50 Hastings L.J. 241 (1999) (excerpted in Chapter 11(C)(3)). The term connotes some sort of departure from normal physiological or psychological functioning. See Oxford Medical Companion 207 (1994) ("Any sickness, ailment, or departure from the generally accepted norm of good health. . . ."); Stedman's Medical Dictionary 492 (26th ed. 1995) ("An interruption, cessation, or disorder of body functions, systems, or organs."). Recall that, in *Ova II*, the court rejected the FDA's argument that pregnancy qualifies as a disease. Note also that Congress added the structure-or-function clause in 1938 so that the agency could regulate weight loss products. Nowadays, of course, many in the public health community characterize obesity as a disease—indeed, one of rather large proportions. In the course of regulating nailbiting and thumbsucking deterrents as non-prescription drug products, the FDA rejected an argument made by the sellers that these were simply bad habits rather than diseases. See 58 Fed. Reg. 46,749, 46,750 (1993). Finally, the agency recently proposed broadening a definition of the term "disease" in connection with its rules governing dietary supplement labeling, apparently in an attempt to narrow the range of structure-or-function claims that Congress had exempted from drug regulation. See 63 Fed. Reg. 23,624, 23,626 (1998).

Although the FDA backed off in the final rule, which meant that claims to treat various conditions experienced during pregnancy would be permissible, the agency decided to disavow one aspect of the rule after some expressed concerns about in utero exposure to dietary supplements. See Guy Gugliotta, FDA Cancels Labeling Rule: Firms Told Not to Market Dietary Products to Pregnant Women, Wash. Post, Feb. 10, 2000, at A2.

PROBLEM #1. *THE BATTLE AGAINST BAD BREATH*

Your client has developed a new mouthwash product. It contains an antibacterial agent, but the bacteriostatic action in the mouth is entirely superficial. One of your competitors claims in labeling that its mouthwash product "stops bad breath," which the FDA has accepted as a simple deodorancy claim—because it suggests that the product only masks odors—and, therefore, subject to regulation as a cosmetic. See 59 Fed. Reg. 6084, 6088 (1994). Another competitor claims in labeling that its mouthwash "kills the germs that cause bad breath," which the FDA historically had allowed as making an appropriately qualified antibacterial claim also subject only to cosmetic regulation. See William Gilbertson, FDA OTC Drug Standards Versus Cosmetic Standards, 21 Drug Info. J. 379, 382 (1987). Your client, anxious to attract customers of these other well-established products, has proposed a number of items for its labeling: (1) "contains a powerful new antimicrobial chemical;" (2) "kills germs," (3) "fights halitosis," and/or (4) "kills germs that cause the common cold." Could the FDA subject this product to regulation as a drug?

2. DIETARY SUPPLEMENTS

National Nutritional Foods Association v. Mathews

557 F.2d 325 (2d Cir.1977).

■ ANDERSON, CIRCUIT JUDGE:

Plaintiffs-appellants, producers and vendors of vitamin preparations, appeal the dismissal of their action seeking declaratory and injunctive relief against regulations promulgated by the Food and Drug Administration (FDA) * * * * Acting under the rule-making power vested in the Secretary of Health, Education and Welfare, § 701(a) of the Act, 21 U.S.C. § 371(a), and delegated to the Commissioner of Food and Drugs (Commissioner), 21 C.F.R. § 2.120(a)(1), the latter, on December 14, 1972, announced his proposal to adopt regulations restricting the sale of Vitamins A and D in dosages exceeding 10,000 IU and 400 IU, respectively, to prescription sales. 37 Fed. Reg. 26,618. Employing the notice-and-comment procedure of the Administrative Procedure Act, 5 U.S.C. § 553(c), the Commissioner solicited comments from interested persons concerning the proposed regulations. Over 2,500 written comments were received. On August 2, 1973, the Commissioner summarized the comments, answered the criticisms of the proposed regulations, and, upon determining that the regulations were in the public interest and should be adopted, ordered that they become effective on October 1, 1973. 38 Fed. Reg. 20,723.

During the period when the proposed Vitamins A and D regulations were under consideration by the FDA, formal administrative hearings were held on proposed labeling statements and standards of identity for "Food for Special Dietary Uses." These regulations, covering the vast array of vitamin and mineral preparations, were adopted as parts 80 and 125 of 21 C.F.R. on August 2, 1973, to become effective January 1, 1975. As part of the FDA's regulatory scheme for the sale of vitamin and mineral dietary supplements, the Commissioner promulgated new U.S. Recommended Daily Allowances for the vitamins and minerals considered essential to human nutrition and for which there was available scientific evidence to show the level of ingestion nutritionally necessary. The U.S. RDA upper limits for Vitamin A is 2,500 IU for children under four years of age, 5,000 IU for adults, and 8,000 IU for pregnant and lactating women. The upper limit for Vitamin D is 400 IU for all age groups. As part of the general Dietary Supplement regulations, the FDA determined that all preparations containing more than the upper limit of the U.S. RDA per serving for any vitamin or mineral on the list is a "drug," 21 C.F.R. § 125.1(h), thus subjecting such products to the rigorous provisions of subchapter V of the Act. When the Commissioner promulgated the specific Vitamins A and D regulations, therefore, the levels restricted to prescription sale under these regulations were already denominated "drugs" under the general Dietary Supplement regulations.

In *National Nutritional Foods Association v. FDA*, 504 F.2d 761 (2d Cir.1974), this court, on a petition to review the general dietary supplement regulations under § 701(f) of the Act, 21 U.S.C. § 371(f), determined that the evidence supporting 21 C.F.R. § 125.1(h), classifying as "drugs" all vitamin and mineral preparations containing dosages in excess of the U.S. RDA's upper limits, was insufficient to bring such preparations within the statutory definition of "drug" * * * *

When the Commissioner adopted the Vitamins A and D regulations, he concluded that the available evidence showed that the U.S. RDA upper limits were adequate for all known nutritional needs; and, in view of the fact that there was no evidence to establish a food value or nutritional use for Vitamins A and D at higher levels, the ingestion of these vitamins at the regulated levels is "appropriate only for therapeutic uses and thus are properly classed as drugs." 38 Fed. Reg. 2073 (1973). The Commissioner based the drug classification for all vitamin and mineral preparations in excess of the U.S. RDA contained in 21 C.F.R. § 125.1(h) solely upon lack of nutritional usefulness for most people. This court, however, held in the course of invalidating the general drug classification in § 125.1(h), that "demonstrated uselessness as a food for most people" is an insufficient basis upon which to establish a drug classification under § 201(g)(1)(B) of the Act. * * *

In proposing the Vitamin A and D regulations, however, the Commissioner indicated that an additional basis for the drug classification was the widespread promotion of the products for therapeutic uses. The Commissioner did not fully develop this rationale at the time of the promulgation of the regulations, and this court, therefore, was not in a position to evaluate whether the evidence of promotion for therapeutic uses was sufficient to render the drug classification not arbitrary or capricious and in accordance with the statutory definition of a drug. * * *

In determining whether an article is a "drug" because of an intended therapeutic use, the FDA is not bound by the manufacturer's subjective claims of intent but can find actual therapeutic intent on the basis of objective evidence. Such intent also may be derived or inferred from labeling, promotional material, advertising, and "any other relevant source." In remanding this case, this court expressly indicated that evidence that Vitamins A and D at the regulated levels were used "almost exclusively for therapeutic purposes" when coupled with lack of a recognized nutritional use, would be sufficient to show that high dosage Vitamins A and D products were intended for use in the treatment of disease.

In proposing the regulations, the Commissioner emphasized the potential for toxicity and the widespread promotion of the intake of high doses of Vitamins A and D to cure a variety of ills. To show objective therapeutic intent, the Commissioner's affidavit submitted on remand relied upon three factors: (1) widespread promotion to the public in the use of high potency Vitamins A and D preparations for the treatment of various ailments; (2) lack of recognized nutritional usefulness; and (3) potential for toxicity from the ingestion of large doses of these vitamins over extended periods of time.

Potential for toxicity was cited in the statements of proposal and adoption of the regulations as supporting the limitation of high-dosage Vitamins A and D preparations to prescription sale in the interest of public safety. In his affidavit, the Commissioner admitted that "[i]n promulgating these regulations, concern over the public harm that could be done by these high potency therapeutic preparations weighed more heavily upon my mind than any other single factor." The Commissioner also indicated that evidence of toxicity was further objective evidence of therapeutic intent because it was unreasonable to believe that one could intend that a toxic product be used as a food.

Plaintiffs assert that toxicity is irrelevant to the issue of therapeutic intent and, although the key element in determining that a drug should be limited to prescription use under § 503(b) of the Act, it has no bearing upon whether an article is a drug. The Government argues, on the other hand, that toxicity is relevant to therapeutic intent and that the Commissioner must make the decision of whether there should be a regulation which classifies an article as a food or as a drug, for the purposes of the Act. Although an article may be recognized as a food, this does not preclude it from being regulated as a drug. The determination that an article is properly regulated as a drug, however, is not left to the Commissioner's unbridled discretion to act to protect the public health but must be in accordance with the statutory definition. Toxicity is not included as an element in the statutory definition of a drug. It is relevant as a factor * * * * Such evidence, however, only presents a further indication that the excessive intake of Vitamins A and D may not be nutritionally useful and does not provide the objective evidence of therapeutic intent necessary to support these regulations.

There is no evidence in the administrative record that the manufacturers and vendors of Vitamins A and D preparations, at the regulated dosages, represent through labeling, promotional materials, or advertising that these products are effective in the cure or treatment of disease. They are sold as "dietary supplements." The district court dismissed the complaint on the ground that the record evidence of lack of nutritional usefulness, when coupled with the evidence of widespread promotion of high-dosage preparations of Vitamins A and D for therapeutic purposes, established that the drug classification was not arbitrary or capricious. The district court relied upon three sources for its determinations that there was widespread promotion of these products for therapeutic purposes: (1) the Commissioner's experience; (2) the medical and popular literature in the record advocating the therapeutic use of these vitamins; and (3) the large number of comments to the proposed regulations which indicated a desire to continue using Vitamins A and D for therapeutic purposes. None of the promotions for therapeutic use in the record was attributed to the manufacturers or vendors.

The main issue on this appeal is whether the evidence of the extensive use of large doses of Vitamins A and D to treat or prevent diseases and the promotion of such usage by persons not associated with the manufacturers or vendors establishes such widespread therapeutic use at the regulated levels as to overcome the plaintiffs' claim of the lack of an intended use to cure or prevent disease and thus justifies the Commissioner's determination.

The Commissioner admits that below the stated levels of potency, Vitamins A and D are foods. The evidence relied upon to show therapeutic intent, therefore, must be related to the potency level chosen to differentiate between the use of Vitamins A and D as foods and the use of these vitamins as drugs. The administrative record clearly establishes that the factors involved in choosing the levels at which Vitamins A and D become drugs were solely related to the Commissioner's fear of potential toxic effect and his belief that the ingestion of vitamins at levels above the U.S. RDA is not nutritionally useful. No further record evidence has been produced on the remand to show that the 10,000 IU and 400 IU levels were chosen because at those potencies, consumption of them is almost exclusively for therapeutic purposes. A sampling of the comments submitted to the FDA after publication of the proposed regulations reveals that people believe that a wide range of doses of these vitamins are therapeutically useful. A large group of individuals indicated that they ingested these vitamins at various dosages solely to supplement their daily diet in the belief that more Vitamins A and D were needed to maintain optimal health than the upper limits in the U.S. RDA. * * *

The Commissioner admitted in his affidavit that mere inclusion in the USP and NF is an insufficient basis for drug classification after the decision in *National Nutritional Foods Ass'n v. FDA*, 504 F.2d 761. He attempts to distinguish that case on the ground that Vitamins A and D are recognized at therapeutic dosages in the compendia and are regulated as drugs in this case only at levels in excess of the recognized food levels in the USP. Other articles, however, are recognized in the compendia at therapeutic levels and not regulated as drugs, for example Vitamin C. The Commissioner must, therefore, show that the conflicting treatment in the regulations of items similarly classified in the USP and NF is not arbitrary under the applicable criteria. The FDA regulates Vitamin C preparations at the USP's therapeutic level as food. To justify the regulation of Vitamins A and D as drugs by relying on § 201(g)(1)(A) the Commissioner would have to distinguish his treatment of Vitamin C as food.

In proposing and adopting these regulations for Vitamins A and D, the Commissioner did not rely upon or cite the recognition of these vitamins in the USP and NF. He may not at this late hour on appeal rely upon them as the basis for his drug classification because it is sheer post hoc rationalization. Inclusion in the USP or NF does not automatically establish that the classification of such an article as a drug is reasonable. To invoke the § 201(g)(1)(A) definition as justifying a drug classification, the Commissioner must conform with the rule-making procedure and, through a clear exposition of his rationale, state the justification for his reliance upon recognition in the USP and NF. * * *

PROBLEM #2. *JAVA JUNKIES*

Imagine that the FDA decides to tackle caffeine-containing foods as unapproved new drug products (after all, caffeine is an active ingredient in products currently regulated as drugs, consumers show mild signs of addiction (symptoms of withdrawal when cutting down), and it may cause chronic health risks). See Gwendolyn Prothro, The Caffeine Conundrum: Caffeine Regulation in the United States, 27 Cumb. L. Rev. 65, 70–74 (1996); see also Am. Psychiatric Ass'n, DSM–IV, at 213 (1994) (recognizing "caffeine intoxication" disorder). Sellers respond that they make no therapeutic (vascular headache) or structure-or-function (wakefulness) claims, it's formulated as a traditional food product (drink) rather than a pill, and there's no evidence of exclusive consumer use for a drug effect (many people like the taste, and it does provide calories). How would a court rule? What if, instead of coffee, the FDA went after a caffeine-containing syrup called Jolt® (sold by the same company that makes a soft drink under that brand name), which made no alertness claims and provided good flavor as well as calories?

NOTES AND QUESTIONS

1. *Drugs vs. food.* The agency also has used its food additive authority to regulate dietary supplements. See Lars Noah & Richard A. Merrill, Starting from Scratch?: Reinventing the Food Additive Approval Process, 78 B.U. L. Rev. 329, 346–49 (1998). In *NNFA*, the court left open the possibility that nearly exclusive consumer use may sustain the FDA's claim of an intended drug use. What if a company sold shark cartilage in health food stores without specifying its use but hoping that buyers would have heard from other sources its supposed value in treating various cancers? In one recent case, a court sustained the FDA's determination that Cholestin, a product derived from red yeast rice and intended to promote healthy cholesterol levels, was an unapproved new drug because it contained a natural substance that was chemically identical to the active ingredient pravastatin in a cholesterol-lowering prescription drug (Mevacor®). See Pharmanex v. Shalala, 221 F.3d 1151 (10th Cir.2000). In another case, a court sustained the FDA's claim that a vitamin supplement sold in a noningestible form was an unapproved new drug rather than either a food or a dietary supplement: "Although vitamin B–12 may commonly be used as a food, gels containing vitamin B–12 that are administered through the nose hardly meet the every day definition of food and are not commonly used as food, anymore than an enema containing vitamin B–12 meets the everyday definition of food." United States v. Ten Cartons ... Ener–B Nasal Gel, 888 F.Supp. 381, 391, 390–98 (E.D.N.Y.), aff'd, 72 F.3d 285, 287 (2d Cir.1995) (per curiam). Some products have recognized applications in the treatment of patients with special dietary needs, and the FDA has regulated such "medical foods" as a separate category. See 21 U.S.C. § 360ee(b)(3) ("The term 'medical food' means a food which is formulated to be consumed or administered enterally under the supervision of a physician and which is intended for the specific dietary management of a disease or condition for which distinctive nutritional requirements, based on recognized scientific principles, are established by medical evaluation."); Symposium, Medical Foods: Their Past, Present, and Future Regulation, 44 Food Drug Cosm. L.J. 461 (1989).

2. *Health claims.* Courts have sustained FDA enforcement actions based on its authority over drugs against vitamin products accompanied by therapeutic claims. See, e.g., United States v. "Vitasafe Formula M," 226 F.Supp. 266, 278 (D.N.J.1964), rev'd, 345 F.2d 864 (3d Cir.1965); see also United States v. Articles of Drug ... "Cal's Tupelo Blossom" ..., 344 F.2d 288, 289 (6th Cir.1965) (honey); United States v. Hohensee, 243 F.2d 367, 369–71 (3d Cir.1957) (tea). The FDCA now allows labels of food products to include limited health claims which otherwise would transform the article into a drug (e.g., foods high in calcium "may help reduce the risk of osteoporosis"). See 21 U.S.C. §§ 321(g)(1)(D), 343(r); see also United States v. Undetermined Quantities ... Exachol, 716 F.Supp. 787, 793–96 (S.D.N.Y.1989); Mara A. Michaels, Comment, FDA Regulation of Health Claims Under the Nutrition Labeling and Education Act of 1990: A Proposal for a Less Restrictive Scientific Standard, 44 Emory L.J. 319 (1995).

FDA, *Advance Notice of Proposed Rulemaking on Dietary Supplements*

58 Fed. Reg. 33,690 (1993).

    * * * Dietary supplements constitute a large and diverse class of products consumed in capsule, tablet, liquid, or powder form by a substantial portion of the American public. These supplements encompass a wide array of products that include vitamins, essential minerals, protein, amino acids, herbs, animal and plant extracts (e.g., garlic extracts and inert glandulars), fats and lipid substances (e.g., fish oils, sterols, and essential fatty acids), dietary fibers, and chemical compounds that may have biological activity but that are generally not recognized as nutrients under the traditional definition of that term (e.g., bioflavonoids, enzymes, nucleic acids, para-aminobenzoic acid, and rutin).

Many of the ingredients in dietary supplements are concentrated substances that occur naturally in plant and animal products that have a history of safe use as food. When these substances are prepared for incorporation into dietary supplements in tablet, capsule, or bulk powder form, significant differences from their conventional food forms may result. For example, a substance may be added to a supplement at a much higher concentration than naturally found in foods, making it easy to ingest the target substance in an amount that greatly exceeds the intake that is likely or possible from food in conventional food form. What is safe at low levels in foods may not necessarily be safe at higher levels or in more concentrated forms. The chemical form of the substance in dietary supplements may also differ from that commonly consumed in foods in conventional food form.

Supplement products are frequently sold in containers that look like, and that have label information resembling, drugs (e.g., expiration dates, lot numbers, cotton fillers, tamper proof caps). Product information leaflets bearing claims are often available on store shelves and at the point of purchase. Products or particular ingredients in products may also be promoted by sales person at health food and specialty nutrition stores.

Significant changes in the dietary supplement market and in consumers' use of supplements have occurred in recent years. Public interest in the potential effect of vitamins (e.g., vitamin E and other antioxidant vitamins) in lowering the risk of chronic disease, a wider marketing and promotion of amino acids (e.g., for body building), and a general growth in the herbal market have contributed to this changing market. * * * Dietary supplements are now readily obtainable at grocery stores, drug stores, health food stores, and specialty nutrition stores, as well as by mail order. These products are also widely advertised in health promotion or body building magazines. A recent survey of dietary supplement advertisements showed that 12 health and body building magazines contain advertisements for 311 dietary supplement products from 89 different companies.

At the same time that dietary supplement use is growing, there have been at least two recent significant outbreaks of public health problems associated with dietary supplements. In 1989, at least 1,500 cases of eosinophilia myalgia syndrome (EMS), including 38 deaths, were associated with the use of L-tryptophan-containing dietary supplements. Within the last year, there also have been a number of reports of serious illnesses associated with certain herbal and other botanical supplements. These developments have raised significant public health concerns. * * *

In May 1991, following the EMS outbreak associated with consumption of L-tryptophan-containing dietary supplements, the Commissioner of Food and Drugs established an internal FDA task force to review the agency's regulatory program for dietary supplements and to recommend improvements. Known as the Dietary Supplement Task Force, it was composed of agency staff with experience and expertise in regulatory, nutritional, legal, and medical issues related to supplements. The Commissioner asked the Task Force to examine a number of issues, including whether safety concerns exist regarding dietary supplements and, if so, to recommend a regulatory framework to distinguish supplements that raise safety concerns from those that do not.

The Task Force attempted to balance the agency's statutory mandate to protect the public health with some accommodation of the desire of a substantial segment of the public to obtain dietary supplements, including ones with possibly little or no documented nutritive value. The Task Force focused on products sold in capsule, tablet, liquid, and powder form. To facilitate its deliberations, the Task Force divided supplements into three categories: (1) Vitamin-and mineral-containing products; (2) amino acid-containing products; and (3) products containing all other ingredients, a category that included herbs without a history of documented traditional food use, plant and animal extracts, and certain other substances. * * *

In 1990, in the aftermath of the L-tryptophan-associated EMS outbreaks, FDA sought an objective and accurate scientific assessment by LSRO/FASEB [the Life Sciences Research Office of the Federation of American Societies of Experimental Biology] on the safety of amino acids. FDA sought this report to provide scientific information on the safety of amino acids. This information is needed by FDA in exercising its enforcement discretion with respect to supplements that contain these substances. * * * LSRO/FASEB recommended a systematic evaluation of certain effects of these substances, given the scarcity of safety data for the amino acids in dietary supplements. * * *

FDA's authority to regulate the safety and labeling of dietary supplements derives from both the food and the drug provisions of the Act. A product is legally a food or a drug based on its intended use. Products primarily consumed for their taste, aroma, or nutritive value are foods under section 201(f) of the Act. While many dietary supplements are foods under this definition, other products, although marketed as dietary supplements, fall within the drug definition because they are intended for use in the diagnosis, cure, mitigation, treatment or prevention of disease or to affect the structure or a function of the body. The intended use of a product may be determined from labeling, advertising, or other sources.

Because dietary supplements are subject to regulation as foods, drugs, or both, there are a variety of statutory provisions that come into play in the regulation of these products. * * * Fundamental to how the agency ensures the safety of foods, including dietary supplements, are the food additive provisions of the Act. Before 1958, a manufacturer could use an ingredient in food, and FDA had the burden of proving, subsequent to marketing, that the ingredient was harmful at some level. The 1958 Food Additives Amendment reflected a determination by Congress that marketers of processed foods should bear the burden of establishing the safety of the ingredients they use before exposing the public to them.

A food additive is broadly defined in section 201(s) of the Act as any substance, the intended use of which results, or may reasonably be expected to result, directly or indirectly, in its becoming a component or otherwise affecting the characteristics of food. Thus, ingredients incorporated into dietary supplements (vitamins, minerals, amino acids, herbs, and other similar nutritional substances that are processed in tablet, capsule, powder, or liquid form) are food additives unless they are generally recognized as safe (GRAS) * * * *

The broad spectrum of dietary supplement products present a range of safety and labeling issues. Most of the ingredients in dietary supplements, especially vitamins and essential minerals taken in moderate potencies, present few safety concerns. A smaller number of ingredients of dietary supplement products and of dietary supplement products themselves, however, do pose direct and indirect hazards. Direct hazards are those adverse health effects directly attributable to the components of dietary supplement products. They may be the result of effects of one or more of the ingredients (be it the desired ingredient or a binder or filler), an interactive effect of components of the product, or an effect of a contaminant in one or more of the ingredients of the dietary supplement.

The agency is concerned about potential direct hazards of some dietary supplements because information on the safety or the nature of many of the ingredients used in dietary supplements is not available. For example, there is considerable natural variability in the constituents of herbs and other botanicals and of glandular ingredients, and methods to characterize many of these products and their constituents do not exist (e.g., to determine the identity and bioavailability of active ingredients or to measure the levels of heavy metals, pesticides, or microbial contaminants). Furthermore, there apparently are no generally accepted current good manufacturing practices (CGMPs) that address how supplement products are to be manufactured to ensure that they have the claimed potency, appropriate purity, and other quality and performance attributes that help to ensure safety.

Indirect hazards may occur if the use of a supplement product delays the diagnosis or treatment of a health disorder. This is a particular concern when exaggerated or unfounded claims are made regarding the benefits of a product in treating or preventing serious diseases, such as cancer and AIDS. These indirect hazards are ordinarily dealt with through FDA's health fraud program. * * *

Vitamin and mineral dietary supplements have a long history of use at levels at the Recommended Dietary Allowances (RDAs), below the RDAs, or at low multiples of the RDAs, and are generally considered safe at these levels for the general population. Intakes above RDA levels, however, vary widely in their potential for adverse effects. For some nutrients, such as the mineral selenium, there is a small difference between intake levels that are safe and levels that can be harmful. Other nutrients such as vitamin C and thiamin have considerably larger ranges of safe intake. * * * [S]ome of these products are extremely high potency, containing 5,000 to about 55,000 percent of the U.S. RDA of one or more nutrients per tablet. * * *

The regulatory history of dietary supplements of vitamins and minerals goes back over 50 years. * * * In 1941, after passage of the Act, FDA issued regulations for vitamin and mineral dietary supplements expressed as minimum daily requirements. By the early 1960s, however, the agency felt that these regulations were outdated. The agency's concerns focused on high potency vitamins and on whether the potencies of vitamins and mineral supplements should be limited to nutritionally rational levels when these products were marketed as foods.

In 1973, FDA adopted new regulations to govern the labeling and composition of dietary supplements and other foods that purported to be, or were represented for, special dietary use because of their vitamin or mineral properties. The 1973 regulations set forth definitions, standards of identity, and labeling statements for vitamin and mineral dietary supplements. The standards permitted only five basic types of preparations; prescribed the vitamin, mineral, and other ingredient composition of multi-nutrient supplements; and specified maximum and minimum potencies for vitamins and mineral ingredients. A lawsuit was filed challenging this action, and the reviewing court remanded the regulations to FDA. In 1975, FDA held an administrative hearing on the regulations.

While FDA was in the process of completing the hearing and revising the vitamin and mineral regulations pursuant to the instructions of the court, Congress enacted legislation that became section 411 of the Act (21 U.S.C. § 350) (known as the "Proxmire Amendment"). This amendment prevents the agency from using the food standards or misbranding provisions of the Act to place maximum limits on the potency of vitamins or minerals in foods. It also prevents the agency from classifying any vitamin or mineral as a drug solely because it exceeds a potency level that is deemed to have a nutritionally sound rationale. * * *

FDA has identified certain public health issues related to dietary supplements of vitamins and minerals. These issues include: (1) The need for a comprehensive science-based evaluation of the potential toxicity of vitamins and minerals at various intake levels; and (2) in light of that review, the need to establish the levels of intake of vitamins and essential minerals that are safe. Certain vitamins and minerals are safe when consumed at low levels but may have adverse effects when consumed daily at higher levels. For example, consumption of as little as 25,000 international units (IUs) per day of preformed vitamin A (U.S. RDA is 5,000 IUs) for periods of several months or more can produce multiple adverse effects, including hepatic cirrhosis, increased intracranial pressure, and possibly birth defects. Especially vulnerable groups include children, pregnant women, and persons with liver pathology caused by a variety of factors including alcohol, viral hepatitis, and severe protein-energy malnutrition.

The preponderance of reports of adverse effects from excess vitamin B_6 (pyridoxine) supplementation have involved intakes above 200 milligrams per day (mg/day) and have been associated with symptoms of a sensory neuropathy. However, as little as 50 mg/day supplemental vitamin B_6 (U.S. RDA is 2 mg) has caused resumption of symptoms in an individual previously injured by higher intakes. Daily doses of 500 mg of niacin from a slow-release formulation and 750 mg from an unmodified niacin product have been associated with severe adverse effects. U.S. RDA is 20 mg. These severe side effects include gastrointestinal distress (burning pain, nausea, vomiting, bloating, cramping, and diarrhea) and mild to severe liver damage. Several reports have suggested that time-release formulations of niacin carry a higher risk of side effects than do unmodified niacin products. Ingestion of excess selenium can cause tissue damage, especially in tissues or organs that concentrate the element. The toxicity of selenium depends upon the chemical form of the ingested element. Human intoxications have occurred with high intakes after a period of a few weeks. * * *

The Task Force recommended that FDA use notice and comment rulemaking to establish safe levels of use for vitamins and essential minerals in dietary supplements. The Task Force recommended that these levels be the maximum daily safe supplemental intake for a given vitamin or essential mineral, called a "dietary supplement limit" (DSL). The Task Force discussed the consequences of regulating supplement products containing ingredients that are not GRAS. It stated that the agency generally has not been willing to pursue enforcement actions unless it could demonstrate some degree of toxicity or potential toxicity. The Task Force stated that FDA has declined to set safe levels for nutrients in dietary supplements because the industry has shown that setting such levels provides it with a cutoff point just below which FDA will not take action, even though such levels are high. Such levels then become the industry marketing norm. Nevertheless, the Task Force stated that setting such levels is appropriate to ensure safety. * * *

Amino acids are available in the marketplace as single compounds, in mixtures (containing two or more amino acids), as components of protein powders, as chelated single compounds, or in chelated mixtures. These products are marketed for a variety of uses. LSRO/FASEB found that amino acids in dietary supplements are primarily used for nonnutritional purposes, i.e., for specific therapeutic effects. * * * Amino acids are the individual structural units of proteins and are precursors for, or may function as, biologically active molecules such as some neurotransmitters and hormones. Nine amino acids, histidine, isoleucine, leucine, lysine, methionine, phenylalanine, threonine, tryptophan, and valine, must be supplied in the diet because they are not synthesized by humans or synthesized only in amounts inadequate for normal growth or maintenance and are thus considered essential. Other amino acids are nonessential because they are synthesized endogenously in amounts sufficient to support growth and nitrogen balance and are, therefore, not specifically required in the diet.

Most amino acids are supplied in the normal diet as constituents of protein, not as free amino acids. Consumption of foods containing intact proteins ordinarily provides sufficient amounts of amino acids for growth and development of children and maintenance of health of adults in the general U.S. population. Safety in these forms is generally not a concern. Some amino acids, such as L-tryptophan and L-arginine, have been promoted and used for their claimed pharmacologic effects. The use of dietary supplements containing these free amino acids appears to be a common practice among individuals interested in increasing muscle mass and strength.

In 1945, FDA issued a Trade Correspondence stating that a food to which an amino acid is added would ordinarily be regarded as a food for special dietary use and must be so labeled, but may also in some cases be subject to the drug provisions of the Act. Subsequently, the 1958 Food Additives Amendment required the premarket approval of any substance whose intended use could reasonably be expected to result in its becoming a component of food, unless the use of the substance were GRAS or subject to a prior sanction. In 1960, FDA proposed to list a number of amino acids as GRAS for their intended use as "nutrients and/or dietary supplements" with no limitations codified at that time under 21 C.F.R. § 121.101(d)(5). This proposal was finalized in 1961.

In the *Federal Register* of April 6, 1972, FDA proposed to revoke the GRAS status of all amino acids for use as nutrients in foods and for use in dietary supplements because of safety concerns based on studies showing that excessive intakes of certain amino acids produced adverse effects in animals. FDA concluded that the available information was insufficient to support the GRAS status of amino acids. * * * In the *Federal Register* of July 26, 1973, FDA published a final rule that revoked the GRAS status of amino acids for nutritive and dietary supplement purposes. FDA promulgated a food additive regulation that restricted the addition of amino acids as nutrients to foods only when needed to significantly improve the biological quality of the total protein in a food containing naturally occurring, primarily intact protein that is considered a significant dietary protein source. * * *

The outbreak of EMS from the use of L-tryptophan-containing dietary supplements has prompted FDA to reexamine its enforcement posture regarding amino acid containing supplements. EMS is a systemic connective tissue disease characterized by eosinophilia (an increase in one type of the white blood cells), myalgia (severe muscle pain), and cutaneous (skin) and neuromuscular manifestations. This illness, which occurred in epidemic fashion in the United States in the summer and fall of 1989, is associated with the use of dietary supplements containing L-tryptophan. To date, more than 1,500 cases, including 38 deaths, have met the Centers for Disease Control (CDC) case surveillance definition of the disease, although the true incidence of the disorder is thought to be much higher.

FDA first learned about problems with L-tryptophan in 1989, following a report from New Mexico about four cases of an illness manifested by myalgia and eosinophilia, in which the common denominator appeared to be the use of L-tryptophan. FDA subsequently issued a strong public warning on November 11, 1989, to discontinue the use of L-tryptophan. On November 17, 1989, in conjunction with CDC, FDA requested a nationwide recall of all over-the-counter dietary supplements containing 100 mg or more of L-tryptophan. The agency also issued an Import Alert to detain all foreign shipments of L-tryptophan. On March 22, 1990, the recall was extended to all marketed products containing added manufactured L-tryptophan because of a case of EMS in a patient consuming less than 100 mg daily. The net effect of the recall and import alert was a ban on the oral supplement forms of L-tryptophan because virtually all of the raw material used to formulate U.S. products was imported.

Despite recent intense research, the exact cause of EMS and an understanding of how it develops have not been established. Initial epidemiological studies implicated the L-tryptophan produced by a single Japanese manufacturer, Showa Denko K.K., and further noted that certain impurities were identifiable in batches of case-associated L-tryptophan. These findings suggested that some impurity or other component in these batches of L-tryptophan may have been responsible for EMS. However, both initial and subsequent epidemiological studies on the EMS epidemic have identified cases of EMS, and another related disease, eosinophilic fascitis, that occurred before the 1989 epidemic and that appear to be related to other batches or sources of L-tryptophan.

EMS and other related disorders are also reported to be associated with exposure to L–5–hydroxytryptophan, a related compound that is not manufactured using the biofermentation process that was used for production of L-tryptophan and is, therefore, not associated with the same impurities or contaminants. There is also some evidence for predisposing factors in some EMS patients. These data, as well as data from animal experiments, indicate that L-tryptophan, either alone or in combination with some other component in the supplement products, may be responsible for some of the pathological features in EMS. Taken together, these findings support previous suggestions that the L-tryptophan-associated EMS was caused by several factors and is not necessarily related to a contaminant in a single source of L-tryptophan. * * *

The Task Force recommended that amino acid-containing dietary supplements be regulated as drugs. This recommendation was based, in part, on information presented indicating that the primary intended use of these products is for therapeutic rather than nutritional purposes. The Task Force pointed to the wide marketing of amino acids for use in the diagnosis, cure, mitigation, treatment, or prevention of disease or to affect the structure of the body through such claims as "Nature's Tranquilizer," "stimulates the immune system," "reduce craving for alcohol and sweets," "used in the treatment of alcoholism," and "used in the treatment of schizophrenia and senility."

Based on the foregoing, it is clear that many amino acid products are being marketed in violation of the Act because they are unapproved food additives, and adequate scientific evidence to ensure their safe use does not exist, or because they are being marketed for therapeutic uses, and the drug requirements of the Act have not been satisfied for these uses. * * * FDA will consider whether the drug uses of particular amino acids are so well established and widespread as to justify rulemaking to establish as a matter of law that these products are drugs. * * *

Herbal and other botanical ingredients of dietary supplements include processed or unprocessed plant parts (bark, leaves, flowers, fruits, and stems) as well as extracts of essential oils. They are available in a variety of forms, such as teas, powders, tablets, capsules, and elixirs. Botanicals are marketed either as single substances or in combination with other materials, including vitamins and minerals, amino acids, and nonnutrient ingredients. * * * Many herbs and other botanical ingredients have been used in foods as flavoring agents. However, there are also many herbs that have no known history of food use and, even without drug claims, are used for medical purposes. Many of these herbs have a history of use as traditional medicines in many countries outside of the United States. * * *

While many ingredients in herbal dietary supplements have not been associated with specific health concerns, some components contained in these products have been associated with reports of adverse health effects or toxicities in animals and humans. For example, recently, at least six documented cases of toxic hepatitis have been associated with the consumption of chaparral (Larrea tridentata). There have been several cases of adverse reactions associated with the consumption of dietary supplements containing Lobelia inflata (lobelia, Indian tobacco). Germander (genus Teucrium) has been recently implicated in at least seven cases of acute nonviral hepatitis in France. Chronic renal failure has been reported to have occurred as the result of consumption of herbal powders containing Stephania tetrandra and Magnolia officinalis.

The use of yohimbe (Pausinystalia yohimbe) in dietary supplements such as body building products appears to be increasing. The known pharmacologically active components of yohimbe are yohimbine and related alkaloids. Yohimbine causes vasodilation, thereby lowering blood pressure. Other actions of yohimbine include antagonism of neurotransmitters and their precursors. Its use is contraindicated for certain medical conditions or with concurrent use of drugs or foods that exhibit monamine oxidase activity because of increased potential for adverse effects.

Human toxicity, including fatalities, have been associated with consumption of the Symphytum (comfrey and Russian comfrey), Heliotropium and Senecio species. The scientific literature documents the toxicity of these and other pyrrolizidine alkaloid (PA)-containing plants. Some of these plant materials are taken as teas or in capsules for a variety of suggested medical effects or simply as beverages. There are reports that PA causes liver injury and failure secondary to veno-occlusive disease (i.e., blocking the veins that remove blood from the liver). There have been sporadic cases reported, as well as reported epidemics, involving many thousand of people, of serious liver injury from consumption of flours contaminated with pyrrolizidine alkaloid. Toxicity associated with PA-containing plants can occur, and has occurred, after relatively short use (a few weeks and at relatively low doses). Liver failure, cirrhosis, and death (approximately 25 percent of 7,500 affected individuals in an outbreak in Afghanistan) can result. PA toxicity can even occur in newborns whose mothers have ingested PA-containing plant materials. Infants appear to be particularly sensitive to the effects of PAs, and fatal hepatic disease has been reported in a newborn infant whose mother consumed PA-containing products during pregnancy. Several animal studies have demonstrated that the toxicity of PAs and PA-containing plants, including comfrey, can cause cancer in test animals. * * *

[A final] category includes a broad array of substances that are offered for sale as components of dietary supplements, including fish and plant oils, fatty acids, fibers and vegetable gums, and carnitine. Some of the ingredients in this broad category are concentrated substances that occur naturally in plant and animal products. In addition, many of these substances have no recognized nutritive value or technical effects.

Fish and plant oil fatty acids and other lipids are available as ingredients in capsules or as oils. They include the ingredients menhaden oil, flax seed oil, black currant oil, oil of evening primrose, fish oils and omega–3–fatty acids, essential fatty acids, phytosterols, and others. A recent dietary supplement advertising survey found that lipid ingredients accounted for about 4 percent of the ingredients in products advertised in health magazines. Dietary fiber is available in products either singly or as mixtures. Major types of fiber include cellulose, hemicellulose, pectins, mucilages, gums, algal polysaccharides, and lignins. Common sources of some of these substances are wheat bran, psyllium, guar gum, and apple pectin. Products containing dietary fiber have been offered for nonfood uses, e.g., as an appetite suppressant. * * *

The agency has considered these products to be subject to the food provisions of the Act, except when therapeutic, disease prevention, or structure/function claims not related to nutritive value are made about the products. As food ingredients, these substances are subject to the food additive provisions of the Act. * * * The GRAS regulations list a number of vegetable gums, but the data that were used as the basis for most of these regulations were related to intended uses such as stabilizer, thickener, formulation aid, emulsifier, or firming agent and did not necessarily reflect the amounts or forms in which they are used as sources of fiber in dietary supplements. For many of these ingredients, there are no GRAS or food additive regulations in effect, and FDA has no basis on which to determine if the ingredient is GRAS.

Products in this "other" category are readily available in the marketplace, even though generally very little is known about their safety. * * * Some of these compounds have been associated with serious toxicity. For example, the compound gamma hydroxy butyrate (GHB) is ubiquitous in the human body, although its function is unknown. In the recent past, use of GHB in dietary supplements became popular as a sleep aid and also as a weightlifting aid. However, reports of serious adverse reactions observed in association with GHB became common throughout the country. These reports included respiratory depression, coma, seizures, and other serious reactions. As a result of these reports, FDA issued a consumer alert on this product. Toxicity from chronic use of germanium supplements includes nephrotoxicity that has resulted in death. In surviving patients, renal function has improved after discontinuation of germanium supplementation. However, in no case has recovery been complete. * * *

The Task Force recommended that the agency find an effective means of ensuring safe use of this "other" category of ingredients. Among the possible options suggested by the Task Force were to continue regulating these ingredients as food additives, to require a description of the nutrient value on the label of foods containing these ingredients, and to bring actions against these substances when they are represented as drugs. * * *

NOTES AND QUESTIONS

1. *Legislative relief.* In its infinite wisdom, Congress quickly reacted to the FDA's announcement (and aggressive lobbying by supplement manufacturers and consumers) by exempting dietary supplements from all but the most basic statutory requirements. In 1994, Congress enacted the Dietary Supplement Health and Education Act (DSHEA), Pub. L. No. 103–417, 108 Stat. 4325, in order to limit the agency's power to regulate dietary supplements as either food additives or new drugs. Although the FDA received numerous public comments in response to its 1993 notice, DSHEA rendered that initiative moot. See 60 Fed. Reg. 67,176 (1995). Indeed, Congress separately called on the agency to withdraw the Task Force's report. See S. Rep. No. 103–410, at 28 (1994). Although most commentators have criticized at least some aspects of DSHEA, a few vigorously defend its deregulatory approach as promoting consumer autonomy. See Michael H. Cohen, U.S. Dietary Supplement Regulation: Belief Systems and Legal Rules, 11 Hastings Women's L.J. 3 (2000); Joshua H. Beisler, Note, Dietary Supplements and Their Discontents: FDA Regulation and the Dietary Supplement Health and Education Act of 1994, 31 Rutgers L.J. 511 (2000).

2. *Deregulating market introduction.* In an enforcement proceeding alleging that a dietary supplement is adulterated, the agency now shoulders the burden of proving that it "presents a significant or unreasonable risk of illness or injury." 21 U.S.C. § 342(f)(1)(A). A company wishing to sell a supplement containing a "new dietary ingredient" (defined as one not marketed before October 15, 1994) must file a notification with the FDA 75 days prior to market introduction, which would have to demonstrate only that "[t]here is a history of use or other evidence of safety," id. § 350b(a)(2), but, if the agency found the notification inadequate, it could prevent marketing only by initiating formal enforcement proceedings. The term "dietary supplement" means a product "intended to supplement the diet that bears or contains one or more of the following dietary ingredients: (A) a vitamin; (B) a mineral; (C) an herb or other botanical; (D) an amino acid; (E) a dietary substance for use by man to supplement the diet by increasing the total dietary intake; or (F) a concentrate, metabolite, constituent, extract, or combination of any ingredient described" above. Id. § 321(ff)(1).

3.   *Permissible labeling claims.* In part, DSHEA grew out of the FDA's initial resistance to approving any health claims for dietary supplements as authorized by the NLEA in 1990. Congress therefore reminded the agency to issue regulations allowing supplement companies to make health claims that would otherwise trigger drug status. More significantly, DSHEA also authorized structure-or-function claims for dietary supplements so long as they included the disclaimer that the claims "have not been evaluated by the FDA" and that the "product is not intended to diagnose, treat, cure, or prevent any disease." See id. §§ 343(r)(6), 343–2; see also 65 Fed. Reg. 1000 (2000); Margaret Gilhooley, Deregulation and the Administrative Role: Looking at Dietary Supplements, 62 Mont. L. Rev. 85 (2001). Popular supplements now include gingko biloba (memory), glucosamine chondroitin ("may help promote healthy joints"), St. John's Wort (mental well-being), and echinacea ("may help promote a healthy immune system"). Although some research is emerging to suggest that certain dietary supplements may have therapeutic value, a number of other supplements seem to represent a return to the era of snake oil. See Rosanne M. Philen et al., Survey of Advertising for Nutritional Supplements in Health and Bodybuilding Magazines, 268 JAMA 1008, 1010 (1992) ("The claims of beneficial health effects made for many of these products are based only tenuously, if at all, on information from peer-reviewed research."); Shankar Vedantam, St. John's Wort Ineffective, Large Study Finds, Wash. Post, Apr. 18, 2001, at A2; Greg Winter, F.D.A. Review Likely for Herbal Tea Drink, N.Y. Times, Apr. 4, 2001, at C8. Even after DSHEA, however, dietary supplements making explicit or implicit therapeutic claims face drug regulation, as suggested by the previously noted decisions in *Pharmanex* and *Ener-B Nasal Gel.*

4.   *Safety concerns.* In addition to possibly representing economic frauds, some dietary supplements may pose serious health hazards. See Marcia Angell & Jerome P. Kassirer, Editorial, Alternative Medicine–The Risks of Untested and Unregulated Remedies, 339 New Eng. J. Med. 839 (1998); David A. Kessler, Editorial, Cancer and Herbs, 342 New Eng. J. Med. 1742 (2000); Carter Anne McGowan, Note, Learning the Hard Way: L–Tryptophan, the FDA, and the Regulation of Amino Acids, 3 Cornell J.L. & Pub. Pol'y 383 (1994); Jane E. Brody, Dietary Supplements May Test Consumers' Health, N.Y. Times, Sept. 22, 1998, at F17; Robert Pear, Tighter Rules Are Sought for Dietary Supplements, N.Y. Times, Apr. 17, 2001, at A10; Amanda Spake, Natural Hazards, U.S. News & World Rep., Feb. 12, 2001, at 43. At the FDA's request, the Institute of Medicine of the National Academy of Sciences recently convened a committee (with one of the authors of this casebook as a member) to develop a framework for evaluating the safety of dietary supplements.

5.   *Further commentary.* See Laura A.W. Khatcheressian, Regulation of Dietary Supplements: Five Years of DSHEA, 54 Food & Drug L.J. 623

(1999); Robert G. Pinco & Paul D. Rubin, Ambiguities of the Dietary Supplement Health and Education Act of 1994, 51 Food & Drug L.J. 383 (1996); Sean Harmon, Comment, Melatonin Mania: Can the FDA Regulate Hormonal Dietary Supplements to Protect Consumer Interests in Light of the Dietary Supplement Health and Education Act of 1994?, 22 U. Dayton L. Rev. 77 (1996); Kelly Ann Kaczka, Comment, From Herbal Prozac to Mark McGuire's Tonic: How the Dietary Supplement Health and Education Act Changed the Regulatory Landscape for Health Products, 16 J. Contemp. Health L. & Pol'y 463 (2000); Lauren J. Sloane, Note, Herbal Garden of Good and Evil: The Ongoing Struggles of Dietary Supplement Regulation, 51 Admin. L. Rev. 323 (1999); Jennifer J. Spokes, Note, Confusion in Dietary Supplement Regulation: The Sports Products Irony, 77 B.U. L. Rev. 181 (1997).

3. MEDICAL DEVICES

Alabama Tissue Center v. Sullivan

975 F.2d 373 (7th Cir.1992).

■ SHABAZ, DISTRICT JUDGE:

Six not-for-profit heart valve allograft processors filed a petition for review with this court contesting the "Notice of Applicability of a Final Rule" (NAFR) * * * stat[ing] that replacement heart valve allografts are subject to the final rule issued by the FDA on May 13, 1987, which requires the filing of a pre-market approval application (PMA) for all preamendment replacement heart valves and their equivalents. A heart valve allograft is a human heart valve which has been processed and preserved so it can be stored until needed for implantation into a human recipient. * * *

The FDC Act defines "device" as:

[A]n instrument, apparatus, implement, machine, contrivance, implant, in vitro reagent, or other similar or related article, including any component, part, or accessory, which is—

(1) recognized in the official National Formulary, or the United States Pharmacopeia, or any supplement to them,

(2) intended for use in the diagnosis of disease or other conditions, or in the cure, mitigation, treatment, or prevention of disease, in man or other animals, or

(3) intended to affect the structure or any function of the body of man or other animals, and

which does not achieve its primary intended purposes through chemical action within or on the body of man or other animals and which is not dependent upon being metabolized for the achievement of any of its principal intended purposes.

21 U.S.C. § 321(h). * * * The 1980 regulation defines "replacement heart valves" as:

[A] device intended to perform the function of any of the heart's natural valves. This device includes valves constructed of prosthetic materials, biologic valves (e.g., porcine valves), or valves constructed of a combination of prosthetic and biologic materials.

21 C.F.R. § 870.3925(a). * * *

In 1989, perhaps with some reason for doing so, the FDA began notifying the industry of its intent to subsequently regulate heart valve allografts, believing it to be within its authority pursuant to the prior regulation. For example, in October 1989 the Center for Devices and Radiological Health of the FDA participated in a workshop on human heart valves sponsored by the American Association of Tissue Banks. Further, on August 20 and 21, 1990, the Circulatory System Devices Panel, an advisory committee of the FDA, held a public hearing to assist the heart valve allograft processors in subsequently complying with the premarket approval. The FDA's proposed guidelines concerning the regulation of heart valve allografts were discussed at this meeting.

On June 26, 1991 the FDA published the NAFR. The summary of the NAFR states:

> The Food and Drug Administration (FDA) is issuing a notice to clarify that replacement heart valve allografts, devices, are subject to a final rule that was issued by FDA on May 13, 1987, requiring the filing of a premarket approval application (PMA) for all preamendment replacement heart valves, and those substantially equivalent to replacement heart valves. PMAs or investigational device exemptions (IDEs) will be required as described herein.

56 Fed. Reg. 29,177. * * *

Petitioners contend that a heart valve allograft is not a "device." This court, as reinforced by the Supreme Court, has allowed liberal construction of the FDC Act consistent with its purpose of protecting the public health. See United States v. 25 Cases, More or Less, of an Article of Device, 942 F.2d 1179, 1183 (7th Cir.1991). "The FDA has consistently interpreted 'device' in a very expansive manner." Id. at 1182.

Congress has provided a detailed definition of "device" at 21 U.S.C. § 321(h) to include an "implant." At issue is whether heart valve allografts are "implants." We are analyzing the term "implant" within the medical context, because our concern is with the provisions of the FDC Act which regulate medical devices. "Implant" is defined as "an object or material, such as an alloplastic or radioactive material or tissue, partially or totally inserted or grafted into the body for prosthetic, therapeutic, diagnostic, or experimental purposes." Dorland's Illustrated Medical Dictionary 824 (27th ed. 1988). Further, the act of implanting, or "implantation," is stated as:

> 2. the insertion of an organ or tissue, such as skin, nerve, or tendon, in a new site in the body.

> 3. the insertion or grafting into the body of biological, living, inert, or radioactive material.

Id. Heart valve allografts can reasonably be construed to be implants within these definitions. Petitioners argue that the definition of "device" was intended only to include man-made or artificial "implants." However, the ordinary meaning of "implant" does not support this argument. Further, a heart valve allograft is tissue which undergoes a cryopreservation process so that it has a considerable shelf life. Accordingly, heart valve allografts appear to be artificial "implants." We find that the FDA's interpretation of the statutory definition of "device" is permissible.

Further, petitioners contend that the definition of replacement heart valve in the 1980 regulation does not include heart valve allografts, because they are not "biologic valves." * * * The definition of "replacement heart valve" clearly encompasses matters relating to human organisms. Petitioners claim that "biologic valves" only refer to animal valves and not human valves primarily because the definition lists animal valves as an example of "biologic valves." The list and example contained in the definition are clearly not intended to be all inclusive. A reasonable inference cannot be drawn that the regulation sought to exclude human heart valve allografts particularly when such allografts have been in use for almost thirty years. Accordingly, the FDA's interpretation of its regulation is consistent with its regulation. * * *

United States v. Bowen

172 F.3d 682 (9th Cir.1999).

■ GRABER, CIRCUIT JUDGE:

Defendant repairs the SteriSafe Handpiece Sterilizer (SteriSafe), which is used to sterilize dental handpieces. He also manufactures the SteriDot High Purity Water Ampule (SteriDot), an accessory used with SteriSafe. The government brought this action, claiming that both products are adulterated * * * and that SteriDot also is misbranded in violation of the FDCA. The district court agreed and enjoined defendant from introducing into, or receiving from, interstate commerce any SteriSafes or SteriDots. * * *

Defendant argues that the district court erred by concluding that SteriSafe and SteriDot are "devices" as defined in 21 U.S.C. § 321(h). * * * Under the plain wording of the statute, an instrument that sterilizes dental handpieces satisfies the "device" requirement. Specifically, "[t]he sterilizing of a medium implies complete destruction of all germs in it." Webster's New Int'l Dictionary 2472 (unabridged 2d ed. 1954). A germ is "any microorganism, esp., any of the pathogenic bacteria; a microbe; a disease germ." Id. at 1051. Thus, a sterilization instrument's purpose is to destroy disease-causing germs. Because SteriSafe sterilizes dental handpieces, it is "an instrument ... which is ... intended for use in the ... mitigation ... or prevention of disease[] in man." Additionally, the term "device" includes any accessory to an instrument intended for use in the prevention of disease. * * *

Congress had two purposes in enacting the FDCA: (1) to regulate products that actually prevent disease, and (2) to regulate products that falsely claim that they prevent disease. Because of those dual concerns, the only question under the FDCA is whether the intended use of the product is to prevent disease, not whether the product actually prevents disease. See United States v. Article ... Consisting of 216 Cartoned Bottles, 409 F.2d 734, 739 (2d Cir.1969) ("Regardless of the actual physical effect of a product, it will be deemed a drug for purposes of the Act where the labeling and promotional claims show intended uses that bring it within the drug definition."). Accordingly, this court has applied the FDCA to instruments that do not actually prevent disease. See Church of Scientology of Cal. v. Richardson, 437 F.2d 214, 217 (9th Cir.1971) (holding that a Scientology "E-meter" was a device, even though the plaintiff admitted that "the devices are ineffective for any medical therapeutic purpose"); Drown v. United States, 198 F.2d 999, 1002–03, 1006 (9th Cir.1952) (holding that a machine that allegedly eliminated lumps from women's breasts was governed by the FDCA, even though "expert witnesses expressed the unanimous belief that appellant's instruments are useless for diagnosis or treatment of any human ailment"). * * *

United States v. An Undetermined Number of Unlabeled Cases

21 F.3d 1026 (10th Cir.1994).

■ MOORE, CIRCUIT JUDGE:

Clinical Reference Laboratory, Inc. appeals a grant of summary judgment holding certain urine and saliva specimen containers used in HIV-testing are adulterated "devices" subject to seizure * * * * CRL employs a series of laboratory protocols to help life insurance companies screen applicants for various health risks. One of these protocols detects HIV–1 antibodies in saliva and urine specimens. Formerly, to obtain the necessary samples, CRL purchased specimen containers, repackaged them into kits which included instruction sheets, and forwarded them along with consent forms to insurers to collect specimens. CRL reported its HIV findings to the insurance companies as either "non-reactive" for normal results or "inconclusive" for any other result.

The FDA maintains AIDS tests which do not use blood products or serum violate the Act. Furthermore, specimen containers used in these disapproved tests must receive premarket approval by the FDA. Accordingly, the FDA told CRL to cease distribution of the containers used in detecting HIV antibodies or face enforcement action. In response, CRL filed an action requesting declaratory and injunctive relief on the grounds the FDA lacked authority to regulate the containers. The FDA countered with its own action seeking to seize and condemn the containers. * * *

CRL contends the specimen containers do not qualify as devices regulated by the Act because CRL neither used them nor intended to use them for medical diagnosis as the containers were not part of a prelude to medical treatment. Essentially, CRL argues the containers' use for insurance risk assessment and CRL's subsequent actions removed the containers from the statute's reach. CRL maintains it did not provide a firm answer about the presence of HIV and reported findings only to the insurer. Moreover, CRL expressly informed applicants the test did not furnish a medical diagnosis. All of these actions, CRL claims, are inconsistent with the meaning of "diagnosis."

The Act includes in its definition of "device" an article "intended for use in the diagnosis of disease or other conditions, or in the cure, mitigation, treatment, or prevention of disease." 21 U.S.C. § 321(h)(2). To qualify as a device under the statute, an article must serve either a diagnostic or therapeutic purpose. The definition does not define the term "diagnosis" nor limit diagnostic devices to those used prior to medical treatment. * * * The plain meaning of "diagnosis" disregards context and bears no connection to medical treatment. A diagnosis is "the art or act of identifying a disease from its signs and symptoms" or alternatively an "investigation or analysis of the cause or nature of a condition, situation, or problem." Webster's Third New International Dictionary 622 (1981). Therefore, the Act regulates as a "device" an article intended for use in diagnosis regardless of whether medical treatment will follow.

CRL used the specimen containers as part of a protocol which seeks to identify the presence of HIV antibodies. The fact CRL's results were inconclusive does not eliminate the diagnostic nature of CRL's inquiry. Also, the fact insurance companies rather than health professionals considered CRL's findings to make business rather than medical decisions does not erase the diagnostic character of CRL's activities or the containers' use. Therefore, we conclude the specimen containers at issue are devices within the meaning of 21 U.S.C. § 321(h)(2) and subject to FDA regulation. * * * [The court held, however, that such devices were not properly subject to premarket approval requirements and, therefore, were not adulterated.]

■ COOK, SENIOR DISTRICT JUDGE (dissenting in part):

The statute in question provides that a device must be intended for use in the diagnosis of disease or in the cure, mitigation, treatment, or prevention of disease. The government concedes that it does not claim that a device which has no medical application could "qualify as a device under the FDCA." There is no evidence present in the record that the containers involved here had any medical application. They were used only to "transport the specimens to the lab for analysis." Again, the government characterizes them as "generic collection containers." They were used, along with other materials, merely to contain and transport the specimens from one location to another, where, upon arriving at their destination, a totally independent and separate testing protocol was applied. It is the testing protocol which is the diagnosis. Under the facts of this case, the containers played no part in the protocol of diagnosis. If an item's participation in the mere transportation and containment of a specimen means that the item constitutes a "device" under the statute and regulations, then it could be argued that all means of transportation and containment so used would also qualify as a "device." If the containers were required to be of special design as part of the protocol, a stronger argument could be made that they serve a use in diagnosis. From the evidence before us, these containers were perfectly ordinary. The conclusion that these ordinary containers were "used" in diagnosis can only be reached in the most attenuated sense, in the same way that a truck or airplane might be "used" in the transportation and/or containment process. The majority quite rightly says that the act must be liberally construed consistent with its overriding purpose to protect the public health. However, the majority's reading goes beyond liberality to all-inclusiveness.

NOTES AND QUESTIONS

1. *Heart valve allografts.* Another court found procedural flaws with the FDA's announcement that its PMA requirement for heart valves applied to allografts. See Northwest Tissue Ctr. v. Shalala, 1 F.3d 522, 536 (7th Cir.1993). The agency subsequently withdrew its notice. See 59 Fed. Reg. 52,078 (1994).

2. *Devices vs. biological products.* The court in *Alabama Tissue Center* interpreted the term "implant" in the definition of medical "device" rather broadly by referring to medical dictionaries. Are whole organs or tissue transplants potentially subject to FDA regulation as medical devices? In testifying before Congress one decade earlier, the FDA disclaimed having any such authority. See Hearing Before the Subcomm. on Investigations & Oversight of the House Comm. on Sci. & Tech., 98th Cong. (1983). The Public Health Service Act, which the FDA also implements and was revised substantially by FDAMA, defines the term "biological product" as "a virus, therapeutic serum, toxin, antitoxin, vaccine, blood, blood component or derivative, allergenic product, or analogous product ... applicable to the prevention, treatment, or cure of a disease or condition of human beings." 42 U.S.C. § 262(i); see also Loge v. United States, 662 F.2d 1268, 1272 (8th Cir.1981) (interpreting the scope of an earlier version of this definition); Gary E. Gamerman, Regulation of Biologics Manufacturing, 49 Food & Drug L.J. 213 (1994). Nowadays, the FDA regulates vaccines in a manner similar to new drugs. It regulates the blood supply in an entirely different fashion. See Linda M. Dorney, Comment, Culpable Conduct with Impunity: The Blood Industry and the FDA's Responsibility for the Spread of AIDS Through Blood Products, 3 J. Pharmacy & L. 129 (1994). Blood is sometimes referred to as a liquid organ, and one could interpret the reference to any "analogous product" as covering other types of human tissues (bone marrow, kidney, liver, skin, cornea, ova, etc.). See United States v. Loran Med. Sys., Inc., 25 F.Supp.2d 1082, 1085–86 (C.D.Cal.1997) (holding that the FDA could regulate fetal cells injected to stimulate insulin production as either a biological product or a drug, and explaining that "Congress conferred upon the FDA broad statutory authority to regulate products analogous to toxins, antitoxins, vaccines, blood, etc."). How would the agency classify an artificial blood substitute? And how about "xenotransplants" (i.e., organs and tissues from other animals)? To the extent that regulation in this area focuses on the potential transmission of viral agents, they would seem to fit more logically under the controls applicable to biologics than medical devices. The FDA's recent assertion of jurisdiction over human cloning, premised on the fact that reproductive tissues are manipulated in the process, seems dubious. See Gregory J. Rokosz, Human Cloning: Is the Reach of FDA Authority Too Far a Stretch?, 30 Seton Hall L. Rev. 464 (2000). These issues will be revisited in Chapter 11.

3. *Combination products.* Recognizing that some technologies would not fit neatly into just one of the statutory definitions, Congress amended the FDCA in 1990 to provide, among other things, that a "combination product" should be regulated according to its "primary mode of action." 21 U.S.C. § 353. Thus, transdermal nicotine patches or metered dose inhalers would be regulated as drugs even though their delivery mechanism would qualify as a medical device. In addition, courts have insisted that the FDA maintain consistency in the classification of comparable products sold by different companies. See Bracco Diagnostics, Inc. v. Shalala, 963 F.Supp. 20, 28 (D.D.C.1997) (enjoining inconsistent review of injectable contrast agents for use with ultrasound equipment, some as drugs and others as devices). Cosmetics that also qualify as drugs or devices must abide by the requirements applicable to both types of products. See 21 U.S.C. § 359. Thus, skin creams claiming protection against damaging UV rays must satisfy cosmetic ingredient labeling rules as well as the OTC drug monograph for sunscreens. See Patrick R. Jones, Note, Protecting the Consumer from Getting Burned: The FDA, the Administrative Process, and the Tentative Final Monograph on Over-the-Counter Sunscreens, 20 Am. J.L. & Med. 317 (1994).

4. *Some other atypical medical devices.* See United States v. 25 Cases, More or Less, of an Article of Device, 942 F.2d 1179, 1180–83 (7th Cir.1991) (breast self-examination devices); United States v. An Article of Device, 731 F.2d 1253, 1255–58 (7th Cir.1984) (chiropractic instrument that supposedly detected low levels of electromagnetic radiation emanating from the body); United States v. 23, More or Less, Articles, 192 F.2d 308, 310 (2d Cir.1951) (self-help phonograph records); United States v. One Unlabeled Unit . . . Thor of Genesis I, 885 F.Supp. 1025, 1027–28 (N.D.Ohio 1995) (vinyl covered bed with 24 audio speakers mounted on its sides and promoted as generating micro-massage for relaxation and various health benefits); United States v. Various Articles of Device, 814 F.Supp. 31 (E.D.Tenn.1992) (disinfectants); United States v. 22 Rectangular . . . MD–200, 714 F.Supp. 1159, 1164 (D.Utah 1989) (sterilizer machine for surgical instruments); 21 C.F.R. § 886.1150 (charts used by optometrists to test visual acuity). See generally Gary E. Gamerman, Note, Intended Use and Medical Devices: Distinguishing Nonmedical "Devices" from Medical "Devices" Under 21 U.S.C. § 321(h), 61 Geo. Wash. L. Rev. 806 (1993); Jay M. Zitter, Annotation, What Is "Device" Within Meaning of § 201(h) of Federal Food, Drug, and Cosmetic Act, 129 A.L.R. Fed. 343 (1996 & 2002 Supp.). Are items published in medical journals and textbooks subject to regulation as devices because they represent "articles" intended for use in the diagnosis and treatment of disease? Cf. Vincent Brannigan, The Regulation of Medical Expert Computer Software as a "Device" Under the Food, Drug, and Cosmetic Act, 27 Jurimetrics J. 370, 373–78 (1987) (questioning the FDA's assertion of jurisdiction in this area); Frank D. Nguyen, Comment, Regulation of Medical Expert Systems: A Necessary Evil?, 34 Santa Clara L. Rev. 1187, 1208–11, 1230–32 (1994) (proposing alternatives to FDA regulation of software as a medical device). Notice that the statutory definition, as amended in 1976, covers articles used to diagnose "conditions" as well as diseases, thereby resolving the regulatory status of pregnancy test kits left open in *Ova II*. See 44 Fed. Reg. 10,133 (1979); see also James W. Hulse et al., How Broad Is the FDA's Authority over Research and Investigational IVDs?, 48 Food & Drug L.J. 285 (1993). Note also that, while the statute only uses the term "devices," the legislative history and FDA officials routinely refer to "medical devices." Does that affect your reaction to the classification of specimen containers used solely for insurance underwriting purposes?

5. *Tobacco products as drugs and/or medical devices.* In a pair of early enforcement actions, the FDA successfully argued that cigarettes labeled with therapeutic or weight loss claims were unapproved new drugs. See United States v. 354 Bulk Cartons ... Trim Reducing–Aid Cigarettes, 178 F.Supp. 847, 851 (D.N.J.1959) (holding that cigarettes purporting to reduce appetite affect both the structure (body weight) and function (appetite) of the body); United States v. 46 Cartons ... Fairfax Cigarettes, 113 F.Supp. 336, 337 (D.N.J.1953) (holding that the FDA could regulate cigarettes as drugs where their labeling clearly suggested that they would reduce the risk of upper respiratory infections). In 1980, a court rejected an effort by a public interest group to force the FDA to regulate all tobacco products as drugs. See Action on Smoking & Health v. Harris, 655 F.2d 236, 240 (D.C.Cir.1980) (holding that cigarettes are not drugs simply because they affect the structure or function of the body unless they were intended to be used for this purpose, though leaving open the possibility that such intent could be inferred if consumers use cigarettes almost exclusively for such purposes).

In 1996, the FDA issued a rule restricting the advertising of tobacco products to minors. See 61 Fed. Reg. 44,396, 44,616–18 (1996). The agency claimed that nicotine qualified as a drug because the tobacco industry had intended to capitalize on its addictive potential, and it classified tobacco products as drug-delivery systems subject to regulation as "restricted" medical devices. For a summary and criticism of this assertion of jurisdiction, see Lars Noah & Barbara A. Noah, Nicotine Withdrawal: Assessing the FDA's Effort to Regulate Tobacco Products, 48 Ala. L. Rev. 1 (1996); Lars Noah, Regulating Cigarettes: (Non)sense and Sensibility, 22 S. Ill. U. L.J. 677 (1998); see also Symposium, Are the Risks Worth Regulating?: Tobacco v. the FDA, 47 Duke L.J. 1013 (1998). In the end, a closely divided Supreme Court declined to defer to the FDA's interpretation of the FDCA as allowing the agency to reach tobacco products given the fact that the agency had previously taken the position that it could not regulate such products absent therapeutic claims and the numerous statutes imposing restrictions on cigarettes that agencies other than the FDA enforced. See FDA v. Brown & Williamson Tobacco Corp., 529 U.S. 120 (2000); see also id. at 131–32 (declining to reach the industry's argument that only claims made to consumers could provide the basis for finding an intended drug or device use); Lars Noah, Interpreting Agency Enabling Acts: Misplaced Metaphors in Administrative Law, 41 Wm. & Mary L. Rev. 1463, 1529–30 (2000) (arguing that courts should not defer to agency interpretations of statutory ambiguities that expand jurisdiction). The Court left the tobacco issue for Congress to resolve, something that legislators had considered but failed to do while the challenges to the FDA's rule were pending. See Gregory D. Bassuck, Note, Advertising Rights and Industry Fights: A Constitutional Analysis of Tobacco Advertising Restrictions in a Federal Legislative Settlement of Tobacco Industry Litigation, 85 Geo. L.J. 715 (1997). Undeterred by the Supreme Court's ruling, public interest groups have urged the FDA to regulate new brands of "safer" cigarettes, but the agency appears to have conceded defeat for now. See Deirdre Davidson, Tobacco: The Next Fight, Legal Times, July 17, 2000, at 1. Meanwhile, one company has urged Congress to grant the agency limited authority over the industry. See Gordon Fairclough, Philip Morris Pushes for FDA Tobacco Regulation, Wall St. J., Apr. 11, 2001, at A2.

4.   NEW DRUGS

United States v. 50 Boxes More or Less

909 F.2d 24 (1st Cir.1990).

■ BREYER, CIRCUIT JUDGE:

The government has seized fifty boxes of a prescription drug called Cafergot P–B Suppository, a drug that contains two active ingredients (caffeine, ergotamine) designed to stop vascular headaches such as migraine and two other active ingredients (pentobarbital, bellafoline) designed to stop nauseous side effects resulting from the first two ingredients. The government has a legal right to seize these products if (1) the drug (which we shall call "CPB") is a "new drug" and (2) its manufacturer, Sandoz Pharmaceuticals, has failed to present "substantial evidence" that the drug is "effective." CPB is a "new drug" unless it is "generally recognized, among experts ... as safe and effective for use under the conditions prescribed ... in the labeling" (i.e., unless it is what drug regulators call "GRASE"). See 21 U.S.C. § 321(p)(1). The district court, concluding that CPB is a "new drug" (i.e., not GRASE) and that Sandoz has not presented "substantial evidence" of its effectiveness, granted the government's motion for summary judgment. Sandoz appeals.

Were the law to give ordinary English-language meanings to the statutory words quoted in the preceding paragraph, the record created for summary judgment purposes would strongly support Sandoz. CPB is not a new drug; Sandoz has sold it successfully for thirty-five years. The anti-headache ingredients in CPB are the same as those in another Sandoz product approved as safe and effective by both the Food and Drug Administration and the National Academy of Sciences, and Sandoz presents evidence that the anti-nausea ingredients in CPB are effective for that purpose. Six experts in the treatment of headache pain prepared affidavits attesting to the general medical consensus, based on published reports and clinical experience, that CPB is safe and effective for the treatment of vascular headache.

The law, however, does not give the quoted words their ordinary English meanings. For example, the term "new drug" means "any drug" that is not GRASE. The term "substantial evidence" does not mean what it means elsewhere in administrative law, namely, "such relevant evidence as a reasonable mind might accept as adequate to support a conclusion." *Universal Camera Corp. v. NLRB*, 340 U.S. 474, 477 (1951). It means "evidence consisting of adequate and well-controlled investigations, including clinical investigations, by experts," which "adequate and well-controlled investigations" must satisfy a host of technical scientific requirements, including "a valid comparison with a control" such as an "active treatment trial" that includes "randomization and blinding of patients or investigators" (double-blind studies). See 21 U.S.C. § 355(d); 21 C.F.R. § 314.126(b)(2)(iv) (1989). Finally, and perhaps most surprisingly, the exception for drugs "generally recognized as safe and effective" is not an exception at all. In *Weinberger v. Hynson, Westcott & Dunning*, the Supreme Court held that, to qualify as GRASE, a drug must meet the same elaborate, technical, scientific testing requirements that it would have to meet to win approval as a "new drug." The Court wrote that

> the hurdle of "general recognition" of effectiveness requires at least "substantial evidence" of effectiveness for approval of an NDA [i.e., "new drug" application]. In the absence of any evidence of adequate and well-controlled investigation supporting the efficacy of [a drug], a fortiori, [the drug] ... would be a "new drug" subject to the [new drug] provisions of the Act.

412 U.S. 609, 629–30 (1973). In sum, if we give the relevant statutory terms their special legal meanings, the statute permits the government to seize virtually any prescription drug by showing that the manufacturer has failed to conduct the technical scientific tests needed to obtain FDA "new drug" approval. And Sandoz concedes that neither it, nor anyone else, has tested CPB in the technical scientific manner specified in FDA regulations. This would seem sufficient basis for affirming the district court's grant of summary judgment.

Sandoz argues, however, that we should not accept the legal proposition that a drug is GRASE only if "adequate and well-controlled studies" demonstrate its "effectiveness." This legal proposition amounts to saying, in a sense, that a drug is exempt from "new drug" standards only if it meets "new drug" standards. Sandoz asks us to hold, instead, that a drug can be "generally recognized ... as ... effective" if the existing evidence to that effect, while not exactly the same as (and perhaps less costly than) technical, "well-controlled" studies, "is at least as scientifically convincing as 'substantial evidence' consisting of adequate and well-controlled studies." In support of this argument, Sandoz makes (or might make) several points.

First, its view of the meaning of GRASE makes better sense of the statute. The statute requires "substantial evidence" of "effectiveness" for approval of "new drugs," which it specifically defines as drugs that are not GRASE. Why would the statute define a category of drugs exempt from the "new drug" requirements and in the same breath make the exception virtually meaningless by applying the same requirements to drugs that are exempt?

Second, its view arguably avoids certain important policy risks. When Congress amended the drug statute in 1962, adding the requirement that all "new drugs" be proven "effective," approximately 4,000 approved "new drugs," and many times as many close imitations, were already on the market. Most of these drugs had not been proven effective by "substantial evidence" consisting of "adequate and well-controlled studies." From the perspective of health, should one read the statute to require the FDA to force all such drugs off the market, even those that were generally recognized by doctors as safe and effective (in the plain-English sense of those words) for their indicated use? If so, would those who needed such drugs not then be hurt? From the perspective of cost, should one read the statute to require the FDA to force the makers of all such drugs to undertake the special, expensive testing needed to satisfy the statutory (and FDA regulation) "substantial evidence" requirements, when a long history of safe and effective use (plus other scientific information) indicate both safety and effectiveness? Would the ultimate result not be unnecessary, and significant, increases in the price of drugs? From the perspective of law, should one read the statute to impose a requirement upon existing drugs that few could meet, thereby potentially granting to the FDA, through its discretionary power to enforce the law, the legal authority to pick and choose among existing drugs, keeping some on the market, removing others from the market, for reasons other than failure to meet the "substantial evidence" test?

Third, the Supreme Court itself has not read the law as rigidly as the above-quoted language from *Hynson* suggests. In *Weinberger v. Bentex Pharmaceuticals, Inc.*, a case decided the same day as *Hynson*, the Court wrote, "in some cases general recognition that a drug is efficacious might be made *without* the kind of scientific support necessary to obtain approval of an NDA." 412 U.S. 645, 652–53 (1973) (emphasis added). Sandoz argues that CPB is the very kind of drug the Court had in mind when it created this so-called *Bentex* exception to *Hynson*.

Fourth, the FDA itself has acted as if the GRASE exception was a genuine exception from the "substantial evidence" requirement. The FDA has promulgated regulations stating that it will certify over-the-counter (i.e., non-prescription) drugs as GRASE on the basis of evidence other than "adequate and well controlled studies," even though the statute does not distinguish between prescription and non-prescription drugs. See 21 C.F.R. § 330.10(a)(4)(ii) (1989); 37 Fed. Reg. 9469 (1972). Moreover, for at least a dozen years after the 1962 statute was enacted, the FDA took no action against many prescription drugs despite its knowledge that these drugs had not been proven "effective" by "adequate and well controlled studies." And the FDA conceded at oral argument that it still has not acted against some such drugs that were on the market before 1938. Of course, one could not reasonably expect drug manufacturers of several thousand existing drugs suddenly to produce complex, double-blind studies showing "effectiveness" nor expect the FDA to remove all such drugs from the market for lack of such studies. Yet, leaving administrative practicalities aside, the FDA's actions reveal that it did not believe the statute meant to impose the special "substantial evidence" of "effectiveness" requirement on all existing drugs, at least not immediately and not without exception.

Although we have set forth Sandoz's arguments as strongly as we can, we have done so to emphasize that even if those arguments are strong ones, we cannot accept them. For one thing, no drug manufacturer has ever won GRASE status for a drug that lacked "substantial evidence" of effectiveness by relying on the *"Bentex* exception." The *Hynson* Court, using absolute-sounding language, squarely rejected the argument that a drug could be GRASE despite a lack of "adequate and well-controlled studies" showing effectiveness. The contrary statement in *Bentex* was made in passing in a case presenting a different issue, namely, whether the FDA or the district courts have jurisdiction to determine whether a drug is a "new drug" within the meaning of the statute. This court, in an opinion written by (then senior) Justice Stewart, wrote that *Hynson* "foreclosed" the argument that Sandoz now makes. See United States v. Articles of Drug ... 5,906 Boxes, 745 F.2d 105, 116 (1st Cir.1984). Other circuits have written in the same vein. See, e.g., United States v. 225 Cartons ... Fiorinal, 871 F.2d 409, 418–19 (3d Cir.1989); Simeon Management Corp. v. FTC, 579 F.2d 1137, 1143 (9th Cir.1978).

For another thing, the passage of time has erased many of the anomalies growing out of the *Hynson* decision. Since 1972, the FDA, acting pursuant to a court order, has systematically been applying the "adequate and well-controlled studies" requirement to almost all of the drugs that were on the market in 1962. To change the requirements for GRASE status at this late date may serve little purpose.

Finally, insofar as *Bentex* creates an exception to *Hynson*'s interpretation of the statute's language, it would seem appropriate for the agency itself to work out the contours of that exception. The FDA has, in fact, created exceptions for non-prescription drugs, but those exceptions do not apply to CPB. We do not find the sentence in *Bentex* sufficient to undo settled law, or to overturn our own circuit precedent, a precedent created after the Supreme Court wrote *Bentex* itself. If the law is to change, Sandoz must look to the Supreme Court, not to this court, to bring that change about. In our view, the district court correctly applied governing precedent.

NOTES AND QUESTIONS

1. *Old vs. new drugs*. Courts have narrowly construed the GRASE exception, explaining for instance that, even if the active ingredients are GRASE, a combination not used previously would qualify as a "new drug." See United States v. 225 Cartons ... Fiorinal ..., 871 F.2d 409, 415–20 (3d Cir.1989); United States v. Article of Drug ... Promise Toothpaste, 826 F.2d 564, 566 (7th Cir.1987); United States v. Article of Drug ... "Myko-cert," 345 F.Supp. 571, 575–76 (N.D.Ill.1972); see also United States v. Atropine Sulfate 1.0 Mg., 843 F.2d 860 (5th Cir.1988) (same even if product contains a single active ingredient that qualifies as GRASE because of possible differences in inactive ingredients, dosages, or routes of adminis-tration). Occasionally, the FDA belatedly calls for a new drug application from the manufacturer of a drug sold before 1962 that slipped through the cracks of the retrospective review mentioned by the court. See Chris Adams, FDA Questions Safety and Efficacy of Abbott's Popular Thyroid Drug, Wall St. J., June 1, 2001, at B1. In addition, the GRASE exception was not designed to allow generic copies of previously approved new drugs to enter the market without securing separate FDA approval. See Tri–Bio Labs., Inc. v. United States, 836 F.2d 135, 141–42 (3d Cir.1987); Premo Pharm. Labs., Inc. v. United States, 629 F.2d 795, 802–05 (2d Cir.1980); United States v. Undetermined Quantities ... Anucort HC Suppositories, 709 F.Supp. 511, 513–18 (D.N.J.1987), aff'd mem., 857 F.2d 1466 (3d Cir.1988); see also United States v. Writers & Research, Inc., 113 F.3d 8, 11 (2d Cir.1997) (holding that a homeopathic drug promoted as a treatment for terminal illnesses was not exempt from new drug approval require-ments); United States v. Sandoz Pharms. Corp., 894 F.2d 825, 826–28 (6th Cir.1990) (preventing a manufacturer from relitigating a new drug issue resolved against it in a previous enforcement proceeding); United States v. Articles of Drug ... 5,906 Boxes, 745 F.2d 105, 113–17 (1st Cir.1984) (rejecting an effort to invoke a separate grandfather clause). See generally Jay M. Zitter, Annotation, What Is "New Drug" Within Meaning of § 201(p) of Federal Food, Drug, and Cosmetic Act, 133 A.L.R. Fed. 229 (1996 & 2002 Supp.). Subsequent chapters will discuss the approval mecha-nism for generic products based on findings of bioequivalence.

2. *It's all relative.* In *Ova II*, the district court made the following point:

> It should be observed in passing and for context that historically, a dispute on the question whether something is "safe and effective" was normally resolved on the basis of expert testimony adduced in the course of the litigation. Under the present scheme, that method is excluded and two new alternative methods are provided. One, if the item is one which has recognition in the technical and professional literature, in the form of papers by investigators competent in the field, it is accepted as being an "old drug" which may be marketed in interstate commerce without further proof that it is "safe and effec-tive." Two, if the item has no such body of published literature to support the proposition that it is "safe and effective," there must first be an administrative determination by FDA, as the disposition of a new drug application, that it is "safe and effective."

> The term "safe" and "effective," in some contexts, may be more or less absolute terms. Most people think of something as being "safe" when

its use or application under any conceivable set of circumstances is not likely to cause some kind of harm or damage. They will think of something as being "effective" when its use or application invariably achieve the desired result. But in real life it may be doubted whether these terms can have any absolute meaning and in most situations, if not all, the terms express relative concepts. Thus, everyone knows that plain water may be thought of as being safe and effective for the removal of a stain of cherry-colored sugar syrup from fabric. This will be true if the fabric is ordinary cotton, or linen, or polyester and the like. But if the fabric contains a "filler," or is colored with a water-soluble dye, the use of water may damage the fabric while removing the stain. In those conditions, while effective, the use of plain water will not be safe. Similarly, in cases where water will not harm the fabric, it will not be effective if the stain contains oil or grease. For them, a solvent such as alcohol, kerosene or benzene may be needed. These may be effective, but because they give off flammable fumes, care must be taken in using them. Oxalic acid is effective for the removal of rust stains, but it is a poison and must be used with great care. Are these products "safe"? Under what conditions? Thus, it is plain that the terms are relative and not absolute, and a designation that something is "safe" or "effective" involves collateral questions such as "to whom or what," and "for what purpose," and "compared to what"?

414 F.Supp. at 661–62. These questions recur in Chapter 3 when we consider new drug approval and medical device premarket review requirements.

3. *Proving GRASE.* In defending against an enforcement action alleging the sale of an unapproved new drug, the claimant apparently bears the burden of proving that the drug is generally recognized as safe and effective. See United States v. An Article of Drug . . . "Bentex Ulcerine," 469 F.2d 875, 878–80 (5th Cir.1972). A claimant cannot avoid the entry of summary judgment simply by offering doctors' testimonials about the safety and effectiveness of the drug in question. See United States v. Articles of Drug . . . Hormonin, 498 F.Supp. 424, 433–35 (D.N.J.1980), aff'd mem., 672 F.2d 902 (3d Cir.1981); United States v. Articles of Drug . . . "Colchicine," 442 F.Supp. 1236, 1242 (S.D.N.Y.1978). A claimant need not, however, prove that a consensus of favorable expert opinion exists. Even so, the FDA may respond by offering affidavits from experts who conclude that the drug is not safe and effective. See United States v. Undetermined Quantities of "Cal–Ban 3000," 776 F.Supp. 249, 256 (E.D.N.C.1991) ("If there is a dispute among experts as to a drug's safety and effectiveness, this demonstrates that there is no general recognition of its safety and effectiveness therefore making it a new drug under the FDCA."); United States v. 118/100 Tablet Bottles, 662 F.Supp. 511, 513 (W.D.La.1987). Even without introducing such affidavits, the FDA may be entitled to summary judgment on this issue by demonstrating that the absence of any studies about the drug published in the medical literature. See United States v. Seven Cardboard Cases . . . "Esgic with Codeine Capsules," 716 F.Supp. 1221,

1224–25 (E.D.Mo.1989). Thus, when the agency challenges an assertion of GRASE status, the seller faces long odds, but does the application of the "substantial evidence" standard render the exception from "new drug" approval requirements meaningless? Assuming that double-blind clinical trials exist to support the effectiveness of a long-used drug, doesn't GRASE status at least provide some procedural benefit?

4. *Material time and extent.* Even if expert agreement exists about the safety and effectiveness of a drug, as reflected in the medical literature, a product must also have been "used to a material extent or for a material time" to escape classification as a new drug. This scope and duration requirement ensures that the expert agreement will emerge from the test of time. See Kenneth C. Baumgartner, Getting a Grip on Material Time and Extent, 49 Food & Drug L.J. 433 (1994); Gary L. Yingling, Are We on the Road to a Single Drug Approval Process?, 45 Food Drug Cosm. L.J. 235 (1990).

5. *Over-the-counter drug monographs.* Manufacturers of OTC drugs must abide by the terms of "monographs" issued as regulations by the FDA. Unlike individual licenses for new drugs, OTC monographs emerge from lengthy reviews of the available safety and effectiveness information for entire classes of active ingredients, resulting in conclusions by the agency that nonprescription drug products were not "new drugs" under specified circumstances. Monographs dictate for particular categories of products—such as antacids or internal analgesics—permissible ingredients, dosages, and labeling claims. See 21 C.F.R. pt. 330; see also 64 Fed. Reg. 71,062 (1999) (counting foreign use); Cutler v. Hayes, 818 F.2d 879 (D.C.Cir.1987) (describing the OTC drug review); Cutler v. Kennedy, 475 F.Supp. 838, 853–55 (D.D.C.1979) (holding that, after it finalized an OTC monograph, the FDA could not authorize the continued marketing of a covered active ingredient for which it had found insufficient evidence of safety and effectiveness); Kenneth C. Baumgartner, A Historical Examination of the FDA's Review of the Safety and Effectiveness of Over-the-Counter Drugs, 43 Food Drug Cosm. L.J. 463 (1988); Stan Stringer, What Has Been Happening with Over-the-Counter Drug Regulation, 53 Food & Drug L.J. 633 (1998). Persons wishing to sell OTC drug products not covered by a monograph must file a new drug application. See Farquhar v. FDA, 616 F.Supp. 190, 192 (D.D.C.1985).

6. *Old medical devices.* The statutory definition makes no distinction between old and new devices, but devices that were introduced before May 28, 1976, or that are "substantially equivalent" to devices marketed before that date, may remain on the market, at least until the FDA issues a regulation that requires the filing of a premarket approval (PMA) application for a particular class of device (as it did for replacement heart valves). A person wishing to introduce a new device but asserting that it is substantially equivalent to a previously marketed device under FDCA § 510(k) must file a premarket notification (PMN) to advise the agency and demonstrate that the device has the same intended use and any changes in technological characteristics raise no new safety or effectiveness questions.

See 21 U.S.C. § 360(k); see also General Med. Co. v. FDA, 770 F.2d 214, 217 & n.1 (D.C.Cir.1985) (deferring to the agency's position that a switch from prescription to OTC labeling altered the intended use and prevented a finding of substantial equivalence); United States v. Article of Device ... "Stryker," 607 F.Supp. 990, 996–97 (W.D.Mich.1985) (seller was required to file a new PMN before introducing a modified device). This has become the primary mechanism for FDA review of new devices. See S. Rep. No. 101–513, at 15 (1990) ("Over 95% of the devices marketed since the passage of the [1976] Amendments have been found 'substantially equivalent' to a predicate device."); see also Chapter 3(B); Jonathan S. Kahan, Premarket Approval Versus Premarket Notification: Different Routes to the Same Market, 39 Food Drug Cosm. L.J. 510 (1984); Robert B. Leflar, Public Accountability and Medical Device Regulation, 2 Harv. J.L. & Tech. 1, 45–58 (1989) (arguing that § 510(k) has been used inappropriately to circumvent full approval requirements).

C. ADULTERATION, MISBRANDING, AND THE PRACTICE OF MEDICINE

Historically, the core provisions of the statute prohibited adulteration and misbranding of products subject to the FDA's jurisdiction. Under FDCA § 501(a), a drug or device would be deemed "adulterated" if, among other things, "it consists in whole or in part of any filthy, putrid, or decomposed substance," or "it has been prepared, packaged, or held under insanitary conditions whereby it may have been contaminated with filth, or whereby it may have been rendered injurious to health." Under FDCA § 502, a drug or medical device would be deemed "misbranded" if, among other things, "its labeling is false or misleading in any particular," its label failed to include with sufficient prominence certain identifying information (such as its established name, ingredients, identity of the seller, and quantity of contents), or its labeling failed to provide "adequate directions for use" and appropriate warnings.

Thus, in situations where the FDA finds bacterial contamination, it may allege that the drug violates the statutory prohibitions against adulteration. See United States v. Morton–Norwich Prods., Inc., 461 F.Supp. 760, 762–65 (N.D.N.Y.1978). In addition, if the product is labeled as "sterile," any such contamination would violate the misbranding prohibitions. See United States v. Torigian Labs., Inc., 577 F.Supp. 1514, 1524–25 (E.D.N.Y.), aff'd mem., 751 F.2d 373 (2d Cir.1984); see also Rheinecker v. Forest Labs., Inc., 813 F.Supp. 1307, 1311 (S.D.Ohio 1993) (holding that a drug of sub-standard quality could violate both the adulteration and misbranding prohibitions). Even without evidence that finished drugs or medical devices are contaminated or sub-potent, failures to implement good manufacturing practices (GMPs) required by the FDA would constitute adulteration. See United States v. Undetermined Quantities ... Proplast, 800 F.Supp. 499, 502 (S.D.Tex.1992); United States v. 789 Cases, More or Less, of Latex Surgeons' Gloves, 799 F.Supp. 1275, 1285–94 (D.P.R.1992), rev'd, 13 F.3d 12 (1st Cir.1993). The following cases focus on the misbranding provisions. Subsequent sections will revisit the adulteration issues in connection with agency efforts to implement GMP requirements.

United States v. An Article ... Acu-dot

483 F.Supp. 1311 (N.D.Ohio 1980).

■ LAMBROS, DISTRICT JUDGE:

This action is the result of a libel of information brought by the United States of America for the condemnation of numerous cases of an over-the-counter medical device called an Acu-dot, as provided for in 21 U.S.C. § 334. The American firm that markets the seized devices, Acu-dot Corp., was the sole claimant-intervenor responding to the published notice of the in rem action. The court has been very much aware throughout the pendency of this action that the economic viability of Acu-dot Corp. is exclusively founded on its ability to market the res of this action, and therefore granted claimant-intervenor's request for expedited trial. * * *

In simple terms, the Acu-dot is a small, pin-head sized magnet attached to the underside of a circular, adhesive patch. It is sold to the public in sheets of ten, packaged in a flat, cardboard box. Inside the box, in addition to the sheet of ten Acu-dots, can be found a four-page pamphlet, purporting to be instructions for the use of the device. The obverse of the cardboard box reads in this way:

ACU–DOT

Magnetic Analgesic Patch

For temporary relief of occasional minor aches and pains of muscles and joints.

Contains 10 Patches

The reverse is labelled in this way:

ACU–DOT

Magnetic Analgesic Patch

Mfg. for Acu–Dot Corp. Box F 598, Akron, Ohio 44308

Directions for use: Apply fingertip pressure to sensitive area to determine point or points of sharpest pain or discomfort. Thoroughly clean and dry area and apply an adhesive-backed ACU–DOT to each such point. Complete adhesion of the ACU–DOT is recommended. Leave ACU–DOT in place for a two- to five-day period, then procedure may be repeated as needed for continued symptomatic relief. If itching, rash or other skin irritation occurs, discontinue use. If pain or soreness persists for ten days or longer, discontinue use and consult a physician. Keep this and all medicines out of the reach of children.

FOR EXTERNAL USE ONLY

MADE IN U.S.A.

Manufactured under U.S.A. Patent No. 4162672

The pamphlet insert merely enlarges on the information presented by the outer packaging, adding, however, that the device is "Not a pill. Not a drug. Easy to use."

Libellant claims that the Acu-dots are "misbranded" * * *, specifically attack[ing] the descriptions of the devices as "magnetic analgesic patch(es)" and "for temporary relief of occasional minor aches and pains of muscles and joints." Libellant offered the testimony of three experts—one biophysicist and two medical doctors. These experts were adduced to show that none of the theories offered by claimant-intervenor were valid explanations for the mechanism by which the devices were to achieve their results. Further, each expert testified to his belief that the devices could not achieve the effect alleged by the labeling, other than through a placebo effect.

On behalf of the effectiveness of the res, claimant-intervenor presented several theories for the mechanism of the device. At various times, it was suggested that the magnetic action of the device "drew" blood to the affected area, which action had the therapeutic effect; that the blood, being composed in part of iron-based chemicals, produced an electromotive force within the body when passing through the field of the magnet, much in the way electric generators produce electricity by moving an electric wire through a magnetic field; that the pressure of the device against the skin creates therapeutic effects in a way analogous to acupuncture techniques; that the ionization of molecules in the skin area under the magnet caused the therapeutic effect claimed; and, finally, that the claimed beneficial effect of the device was achieved largely as a result of the psychosomatic placebo response.[3] These various theories were suggested by the teachings of the patent said to include the res (U.S. patent #4,162,672), by the theories presented in an article written by Kyoichi Nakagawa, M.D., one of a number of Japanese researchers attempting to analyze the mechanism of an identical device now in wide currency in Japan, and, most importantly, by the empirical results of an experiment conducted by Rocco Antenucci, M.D., an Akron area family physician who testified at the hearing.

The most impressive evidence on behalf of the res was the result of the Antenucci study. That study purported to be a double-blind comparison of the Acu-dots with non-magnetized facsimiles. Of the 70 patients receiving

---

3. * * * [A] placebo cannot be dismissed as "ineffective" simply because it works its effect in a way more oblique than standard therapeutic treatments. As is seen infra in this opinion, the real difficulty of this case is that a "placebo" can work only by means of the artifice of its presentation to the patient—the patient must be misled as to its inherent effectiveness. This artifice is the heart of the negative aspects of a placebo, for the composition of the placebo is largely irrelevant to its effectiveness, and a sugar pill of minimal cost to the patient should theoretically be as effective as a $500 device. The person marketing the $500 device is misleading the buyer because the seller claims that the $500 device relieves pain, when it is really the patient's belief in the device that relieves pain. The potential for abuse is obvious.

the facsimiles, 10 indicated some degree of pain relief. Of the 152 patients receiving the Acu-dots, 138 reported some degree of pain relief. These figures are impressive and argue strongly for the therapeutic claims.

However, each of the government witnesses was able to suggest major flaws in the conception and execution of the test protocol. Considerable doubt was also cast on the Nakagawa study and the court was finally left with this problem: libellant could demonstrate that the therapeutic claims of the device could not be explained by any reasonable theory that did not rely on a "placebo" explanation, but had no empirical evidence of the lack of efficacy; claimant-intervenor had very weak theoretical support for the mechanism of the device, and vested its claims in unexplained empirical evidence.

The lack of empirical evidence on the part of libellant is not an insurmountable deficiency. * * * After careful consideration of all of the evidence, this court finds that any therapeutic value of the res is the result of its placebo effect, and that this placebo effect is very strong in the case of ailments for which the device is claimed effective. Thus, the device often can achieve its claims of providing "temporary relief of occasional minor aches and pains of muscles and joints;" but this effect is the result of nothing more than sophisticated marketing chicanery.

This court hastens to affirm here its belief in the right of the American public to seek any treatment it wishes, especially when that treatment is a harmless, if ineffective, drug or device. * * * There is a difference, however, between the right to use a harmless, ineffective drug or device and a claimed right to promote and profit from the drug or device. * * *

This court resists the impulse to allow claimant to market a product that works only by means of a placebo effect on the basis that it nevertheless often achieves a relief of pain as claimed. The strong placebo effect may save the res from claims of "false labeling" under 21 U.S.C. § 352(a), but it does not protect the device from the charge that the labeling is "misleading" under 21 U.S.C. § 352(a), and that is all that is required to warrant condemnation of the res. The device's label is "misleading" because the device is not inherently effective, its results being attributable to the psychosomatic effect produced by the advertising and marketing of the device. A kiss from mother on the affected area would serve just as well to relieve pain, if mother's kisses were marketed as effectively as the Acu-dot device.

This court finds that the device is "misbranded" under 21 U.S.C. § 352, and properly subject to seizure and condemnation under 21 U.S.C. § 334, even though the claims are not technically false, because the claims are inherently misleading. * * *

NOTES AND QUESTIONS

1. *Policing against economic frauds.* Ineffective products violate the general prohibition against misbranding. See United States v. An Article of

Device ... "Toftness Radiation Detector," 731 F.2d 1253, 1259 (7th Cir. 1984) ("[A] prescription device is misbranded unless it can be used safely and effectively for the purposes for which it is intended. That is, the device has to work—if it does not work, it is misbranded."); see also United States v. Articles of Drug, 825 F.2d 1238, 1241–45 (8th Cir.1987) (passing off drugs containing caffeine as having other active ingredients); United States v. One Device Intended for Use as a Colonic Irrigator, 160 F.2d 194 (10th Cir.1947) (sustaining action against the "Tox–Eliminator"); Peter Barton Hutt, A History of Government Regulation of Adulteration and Misbranding of Medical Devices, 44 Food Drug Cosm. L.J. 99, 105 (1989) (recounting the FDA's early enforcement actions against quack devices). Scientists have begun to take the placebo effect seriously as a therapeutic mechanism. See Martin Enserink, Can the Placebo Be the Cure?, 284 Sci. 238 (1999); Rita Rubin, Kind Words and a Placebo Can Unleash a Powerful Effect, USA Today, Jan. 16, 2001, at 1D; Margaret Talbot, The Placebo Prescription?, N.Y. Times, Mag., Jan. 9, 2000, at 34. If a product is otherwise harmless, why should the FDA care that consumers may waste money on worthless treatments? Might ineffectiveness alone pose a risk to health? Note that, in these and other enforcement cases, the FDA must prove its case by a preponderance of the evidence. See United States v. 60 28–Capsule Bottles ... "Unitrol," 325 F.2d 513, 514 (3d Cir.1963); United States v. 4 Cases ... Slim–Mint Chewing Gum, 300 F.2d 144, 148–50 (7th Cir.1962); see also United States v. 43½ Gross Rubber Prophylactics ..., 65 F.Supp. 534, 535–37 (D.Minn.1946) (sustaining seizure of entire shipment of condoms based on limited sampling that identified defects in a small percentage). What substantiation is required to avoid misbranding (is it, like GRASE, "substantial evidence" of effectiveness)?

2. *Protecting gullible consumers.* In assessing promotional claims directed to laypersons, the courts often ask how an unsophisticated consumer would understand the message. See V.E. Irons, Inc. v. United States, 244 F.2d 34, 39–40 (1st Cir.1957); id. at 42 ("Bearing in mind the broadly remedial purposes of the Act in preventing deception, the Congress must be taken to have meant to strike not only at palpably false claims but also at clever indirection and ambiguity in the creation of misleading impressions."); United States v. 62 Packages ... Marmola Prescription Tablets, 48 F.Supp. 878, 887 (W.D.Wis.1943) (explaining, in the course of sustaining a misbranding charge against an anti-obesity drug, that the FDCA seeks "to protect the public, the vast multitude which includes the ignorant, the unthinking and the credulous who, when making a purchase, do not stop to analyze"). Disclaimers will not cure otherwise misleading claims. See Pasadena Research Labs. v. United States, 169 F.2d 375, 383 (9th Cir. 1948).

3. *Other types of misbranding violations.* The statute specifies a number of acts that may constitute misbranding. For instance, to provide "adequate directions for use," the labeling must identify the product's intended use(s). See Alberty Food Prods. v. United States, 194 F.2d 463, 464 (9th Cir.1952). In addition, courts have interpreted the basic prohibition to imply other specific requirements. See United States v. Dino, 919 F.2d 72,

75 (8th Cir.1990) ("While the statute does not specifically state that a drug in a container without this information is 'misbranded,' we think the language 'false or misleading in any particular' includes drugs received without lot numbers or expiration dates."). Labeling issues are addressed at greater length in Chapter 4.

United States v. Evers

643 F.2d 1043 (5th Cir.1981).

■ RANDALL, CIRCUIT JUDGE:

* * * Dr. H. Ray Evers is the owner and operator of Ra–Mar Clinic, a health facility which opened in 1976 in Montgomery, Alabama. Dr. Evers and his clinic specialize in the treatment of chronic degenerative diseases. Although the clinic is not a hospital, it has a 40–bed capacity and does accept patients for treatment on a resident basis for periods of up to three or four weeks. A central part of Dr. Evers' approach to the treatment of degenerative diseases is his use of "chemo-endartectomy therapy." Dr. Evers explains this therapy as "a special treatment given by licensed medical doctors for the relief of poor circulation that has been caused by hardening of the arteries (arteriosclerosis, atherosclerosis)." Dr. Evers' approach, which he describes as "holistic" and "preventative," seeks to alleviate circulatory disorders by creating the proper balance of metals, vitamins, enzymes and other substances in the body.

The most important part of Dr. Evers' chemo-endartectomy therapy is his use of "chelation." Chelation is a chemical reaction which occurs between certain drugs and various harmful metals which are in the bloodstream. These drugs, which Dr. Evers injects intravenously, form a bond with heavy metals in a form which allows them to pass out of the body through the kidneys. Chelating drugs are ordinarily used for the treatment of heavy metal poisoning, particularly lead poisoning. According to Dr. Evers, however, this process also removes from blood vessels build-ups of calcium which are blocking the vessels and causing hardening of the arteries. Dr. Evers claims that he has used chelation therapy with tremendous success in the treatment of circulatory disorders, and with little danger to his patients.

Whether this process actually has this beneficial effect is a serious question. Dr. Evers' claims for his therapy are not generally accepted by the medical profession, and, as discussed below, the FDA has not approved any chelating drug for use in the treatment of circulatory disorders. Moreover, chelating drugs bear a serious danger: if too many heavy metals are passed into the kidneys within too short a period of time, the patient may suffer kidney failure and may die as a result. An additional danger, of course, is that patients who could benefit from a more traditional mode of treatment (probably heart by-pass surgery) will be convinced by Dr. Evers' alternative to postpone that treatment until it is too late. * * *

The focus of the government's case against Dr. Evers is not, however, the potential danger in his use of chelation therapy. Instead, the government challenges his vigorous promotion and advertising of chelating drugs for a use which has not been approved by the FDA. * * * When the Ra–Mar Clinic opened in 1976, Dr. Evers placed a full two-page advertisement in the Montgomery Advertiser. Although the ad did not explain Dr. Evers' program in any detail, it specifically listed chemo-endartectomy therapy as one of his chief methods. The more important aspect of Dr. Evers' campaign, however, consists of a booklet describing the Ra–Mar Clinic. The booklet explains chemo-endartectomy and chelation in lay terms and describes the program employed by the Ra–Mar Clinic. The booklet claims remarkable success for chelation, cites Dr. Evers' extensive experience with the process, urges the reader to try chemo-endartectomy therapy before traditional modes of treatment, and underplays the serious dangers involved in the use of chelating drugs. This booklet was apparently given to patients and prospective patients of the clinic, both in person and through the mail. * * *

Although there exists a variety of lawful chelating drugs, the government has charged Dr. Evers in this suit with the misbranding of one particular chelating drug, calcium disodium edetate (Calcium EDTA). * * * [T]he FDA-approved labeling (commonly called the package insert) for Calcium EDTA does not indicate that the drug can be used to treat circulatory diseases and does not include any instructions for the use of the drug for such purposes. In fact, the sole purpose indicated on the label for Calcium EDTA is "the reduction of blood levels and depot stores of lead in lead poisoning (acute and chronic) and lead encephalopathy." The FDA is therefore correct in its assertion that, whether or not chelation is of any beneficial effect to a patient suffering circulatory diseases, the package insert in the Calcium EDTA used by Dr. Evers provided no direction whatsoever for that use of the drug. * * *

In response to this charge, Dr. Evers (as well as certain of his patients, as intervenors) argues that as a licensed physician he has a right to prescribe any lawful drug for any purpose, whether or not that purpose has been approved by the FDA. The district court agreed with Dr. Evers and held that no misbranding could result from a doctor's prescription of a lawful drug to his own patients. The court relied for this holding on the intent of the statute, which seeks to avoid interference with "the practice of medicine;" on supposed limitations on the powers of Congress; and on the patient's constitutional right to privacy in the context of medical care.

However, the analysis urged by Dr. Evers and adopted by the district court misapprehends the thrust of the government's case against Dr. Evers, for the FDA has at no point contended, and the government does not argue on appeal, that the misbranding provisions of the Act prohibit a doctor from prescribing a lawful drug for a purpose for which the drug has not been approved by the FDA. To the contrary, the FDA has explicitly informed Dr. Evers that he could legally prescribe chelating drugs for the treatment of circulatory disorders. When Dr. Evers inquired of the FDA in early 1974 whether he could use Calcium EDTA for that purpose, the agency responded by letter that "[u]se of a locally obtained drug for an indication which is not in the package insert is considered 'the practice of medicine,'" and that Dr. Evers therefore need not seek any exception to the regulations. This advice to Dr. Evers rested on a discussion of the Act which appears in a notice of proposed rulemaking which the FDA issued in 1972 but on which it has never acted. See 37 Fed. Reg. 16,503 (1972). As the agency explained in that notice:

> Once (an approved) new drug is in a local pharmacy after interstate shipment, the physician may, as part of the practice of medicine, lawfully prescribe a different dosage for his patient, or may otherwise vary the conditions of use from those approved in the package insert, without informing or obtaining the approval of the Food and Drug Administration. This interpretation of the Act is consistent with Congressional intent as indicated in the legislative history of the 1938 Act and the drug amendments of 1962. Throughout the debate leading to the enactment, there were repeated statements that Congress did not intend the Food and Drug Administration to interfere with medical practice and references to the understanding that the bill did not purport to regulate the practice of medicine as between the physician and the patient. Congress recognized a patient's right to seek civil damages in the courts if there should be evidence of malpractice, and declined to provide any legislative restrictions upon the medical profession.

Id. at 16,503.

Of course, while the Act was not intended to regulate the practice of medicine, it was obviously intended to control the availability of drugs for prescribing by physicians. In order to extend this control to situations like the one before us, the FDA has proposed regulations and actively has sought legislation which would restrict the availability of lawful drugs for uses for which the drugs have not been approved by the FDA. Nevertheless the government agrees with Dr. Evers that the provisions of the Act and the regulations of the FDA that are now in force do not prevent him from prescribing for uses not approved by the FDA drugs which have been approved by the FDA for some other purpose. * * *

Since the government relies for its case on Dr. Evers' promotion and advertising of chelating drugs for an unapproved use, and since the FDA itself interprets the Act to allow physicians to prescribe (while not promoting or advertising) lawful drugs for unapproved uses, we need not decide whether, as the district court apparently concluded, the Constitution prohibits federal interference with prescriptions by licensed physicians. The question before us is the narrower issue of whether Dr. Evers violated section 301(k) of the Act. In order to establish such a violation, the government must demonstrate the two elements required by that section. In terms of this case, we must find (1) that Dr. Evers held Calcium EDTA for sale after its shipment in interstate commerce, and (2) that Dr. Evers' promotion and advertising of Calcium EDTA without providing any more information than was contained on the drug's label and in the clinic's pamphlets failed to provide "adequate directions for use" and therefore constitutes misbranding under section 502(f)(1) of the Act.

The Act was intended, inter alia, to keep misbranded drugs out of the channels of interstate commerce. The flow of commerce begins with the manufacturer of the drug and ends with the consumer, that is, the patient. Accordingly, section 301 of the Act is designed to prevent misbranding at each stage of the distribution process. * * * Section 301(k) extends the Act's protection to the entire distribution process for drugs moving in interstate commerce by covering what is often the final stage in that process: the distribution by a person not himself a party to the interstate transportation of the drug. * * * A serious gap would be left in the statute if doctors who had received drugs in an intrastate transaction from a party who had in turn received them from interstate commerce were allowed to misbrand the drugs and then distribute them to their patients. Doctors holding drugs for use in their practice are clearly one part of the distribution process, and doctors may therefore hold drugs for sale within the meaning of section 301(k) of the Act.

We now turn to the second requirement of section 301(k) in the context of this case: the drug at issue must have been misbranded. In order to establish that Dr. Evers misbranded Calcium EDTA, the government relies on section 502(f)(1) of the Act. As discussed above, that section deems a drug to be misbranded "unless its labeling bears ... adequate directions for use." * * * [I]nterpretation begins with 21 C.F.R. § 201.5 (1980), which defines "adequate directions for use" as "directions under which the layman can use a drug safely and for the purposes for which it is intended." The "intended use" of the drug is the "objective intent of the persons legally responsible for the labeling of the drug," and may be determined, for example, by "labeling claims, advertising matter, or oral or written statements by such persons or their representatives." 21 C.F.R. § 201.128. Since Dr. Evers clearly intended to use Calcium EDTA for the treatment of arteriosclerosis, these provisions would seem to require him to provide adequate directions in lay terms to his patients for the use of Calcium EDTA in the treatment of arteriosclerosis. However, * * * since Calcium EDTA is a prescription drug, there is no conceivable explanation which Dr. Evers could have given to his patients which would have complied with section 502(f)(1)'s requirement of adequate directions for lay use.

However, this does not mean that drug distributors misbrand each prescription drug which they hold for sale, for the statute provides for two important exceptions to section 502(f)(1) of the Act. In the first place, the section itself authorizes the FDA to create a regulatory exemption. The FDA has exercised this authority by creating an exception for prescription drugs. See 21 C.F.R. §§ 201.100, 201.115. In order to qualify for the prescription drug exception under these regulations, the drug's labeling must meet a number of specific full disclosure requirements. The labeling must include, for example: certain information regarding dosage, administration, and the drug's active ingredients; a warning that the drug cannot lawfully be dispensed without a prescription; an identifying number from which one may determine the manufacturing history of the particular package of the drug; a statement directed to the pharmacist specifying the type of container to be used in dispensing the drug; and, if the drug is a "new drug" within the meaning of the Act, a label which has been approved by the FDA pursuant to a new drug application under the Act. If these extensive requirements are met, the drug is completely exempt from the reach of section 502(f)(1) of the Act, and the distributor of the drug therefore need not provide "adequate directions for use" to the layman.

In the second place, the statute itself provides for an exception in section 503(b)(2) of the Act. This section states that if certain basic information is provided on the label a prescription drug shall be exempt from most of the requirements of section 502 of the Act, including that of section 502(f)(1). While the requirements of this section are somewhat more lenient than those of the regulatory exception, it provides a much narrower protection for the distributor of the drug, for it exempts the provisions of section 502 of the Act only at the point at which the drug is actually prescribed and dispensed by a licensed physician. The regulatory exemption, on the other hand, protects any person who holds the drug for sale at any point in the distribution process. * * *

The purpose of this scheme is, in brief, to require that adequate information be provided to the person who must decide whether and how to administer the drug. Where non-prescription drugs are involved, the "adequate directions for use" requirement insures full disclosure to the layman purchasing the drugs for self-treatment. But prescription drugs depend for their safety and effectiveness on the professional judgment of a licensed physician. Accordingly, the prescription drug exceptions to the "adequate directions for use" requirement contain conditions requiring adequate information for prescribing doctors. * * * It is undisputed that Dr. Evers did in fact fail to provide adequate directions for either lay or professional use; Dr. Evers does not contend that his booklets contained "adequate directions for lay use" within the meaning of the regulations, and he does not appear to have made any attempt to meet the terms of either the regulatory or the statutory exception for prescription drugs.

When each of the two elements of the offense with which Dr. Evers is charged is examined individually, Dr. Evers does indeed seem to have violated the statute. A different picture emerges, however, when the two elements are considered together. Since Calcium EDTA is a prescription drug, the FDA can establish an act of misbranding under section 502(f)(1) of the Act only by proving that Dr. Evers did not provide adequate information for use by physicians, as is required by the exceptions to that section * * * [, but] the government does not contend that Dr. Evers was distributing Calcium EDTA to other licensed physicians. The government therefore must find itself in an awkward position: while the misbranding violation it urges is based on Dr. Evers' failure to provide adequate information to licensed physicians, it seeks to include his actions within the reach of section 301(k) of the Act by virtue of his distribution to patients.

The requirement which the FDA seeks to impose is nonsensical. Since Calcium EDTA is a prescription drug, the misbranding provision under which Dr. Evers was charged requires him to provide adequate information for use by prescribing physicians. However, Dr. Evers was the only physician who used the Calcium EDTA in question. The government's application of the statute may therefore be reduced to the following proposition: Dr. Evers did not provide adequate information to himself. * * *

Although Dr. Evers was holding Calcium EDTA for sale in the sense that he was distributing it to his own patients, he was not holding it for sale to physicians. Section 301(k) of the Act cannot reasonably be read to require a physician who is holding a drug for sale only to patients to provide adequate information to physicians to whom he is not distributing the drug. * * * No legitimate purpose is served when a statutory provision requiring disclosure to one particular group of purchasers is invoked on the basis of sales made to a different group. Since Dr. Evers was holding Calcium EDTA, a prescription drug, for sale only to his patients, and since section 502(f)(1) of the Act does not require any disclosure to patients regarding prescription drugs, we conclude that Dr. Evers did not violate section 301(k) of the Act.[16] We have not been called upon in this case to consider the safety and effectiveness of Dr. Evers' use of chelation therapy; accordingly, we neither approve nor criticize his medical practices. * * *

NOTES AND QUESTIONS

1. *Prescription labeling.* See United States v. Articles of Drug, 625 F.2d 665, 672–75 (5th Cir.1980) (accepting the FDA's interpretation of the statute as requiring that prescription drugs satisfy regulatory exemptions to avoid a misbranding charge for failure to provide adequate directions for lay use); United States v. El–O–Pathic Pharmacy, 192 F.2d 62, 74–78 (9th Cir.1951). These same issues may arise with respect to medical devices. See United States v. Articles of Device ... "Diapulse," 527 F.2d 1008, 1011–12 (6th Cir.1976); United States v. Articles of Device ... Acuflex, 426 F.Supp.

16. One might argue that although Dr. Evers did not distribute Calcium EDTA to other physicians, he nevertheless "labeled" the drug to the medical community at large through his public promotional and advertising efforts, and that he therefore caused the drug to be "misbranded" because the drug's label did not meet the full disclosure requirements of the regulatory exception to section 502(f)(1) with respect to the new use advocated for the drug by Dr. Evers. * * * This approach relies on the promotion per se of the drug, and seems to ignore altogether the fact that misbranding under section 301(k) of the Act can occur only with respect to particular drugs "held for sale after shipment in interstate commerce." At base, this theory equates promotion with sale, and therefore brings into question the legality of a physician's advocacy of any medical program involving drugs not approved for the advocated use by the FDA, even when the physician does not himself sell or even dispense the drug. But the Act was intended to regulate the distribution of drugs in interstate commerce, not to restrain physicians from public advocacy of medical opinions not shared by the FDA. We believe, therefore, that a doctor who merely advocates to other doctors a lawful prescription drug for a use not approved by the FDA, and does not distribute that drug to other doctors, is not holding that drug for sale within the meaning of the statute and therefore is not in violation of section 301(k) of the Act.

366 (W.D.Pa.1977); see also United States v. An Article of Device ...
"Toftness Radiation Detector," 731 F.2d 1253, 1260–62 (7th Cir.1984)
(holding that the claimant had the burden of proving compliance with the
prescription labeling exemption). See generally Richard P. Shafer, Annotation, Exemption from Provision of § 502(f) of the Federal Food, Drug, and
Cosmetic Act (21 U.S.C. § 352(f)) That Drug or Device Is Misbranded
Unless Its Label Bears "Adequate Directions for Use," 65 A.L.R. Fed. 725
(1983 & 2002 Supp.). Chapter 4(A)(1) will revisit some of these questions.

2. *Interstate commerce.* The FDA's jurisdiction extends only to products
that have moved in interstate commerce, but it generally has no difficulty
satisfying this requirement. See Baker v. United States, 932 F.2d 813, 814–
16 (9th Cir.1991) (holding that the interstate movement of ingredients used
in a drug manufactured and sold only intrastate would create a sufficient
connection to interstate commerce). With regard to medical devices, Congress eliminated the need to demonstrate any movement in interstate
commerce. See United States v. Two Units ... of a Power Unit and a
Chair, 49 F.3d 479, 481 (9th Cir.1995); see also FDAMA, Pub. L. No. 105–
115, § 419, 111 Stat. 2296, 2379 (1997) (codified at 21 U.S.C. § 379a)
(extending this presumption to all FDA regulated products). A drug or
device is "held for sale" by a health care provider even if not resold to
patients but used in the course of treatment. See United States v. Diapulse
Corp. of Am., 514 F.2d 1097, 1098 (2d Cir.1975); United States v. Article of
Drug ... Reserpine Tablets, 568 F.Supp. 29, 31 (D.N.J.1983); United States
v. Article of Device ... Cameron Spitler, 261 F.Supp. 243, 246 (D.Neb.
1966); see also John J. Smith, Physician Modification of Legally Marketed
Medical Devices: Regulatory Implications Under the FDCA, 55 Food &
Drug L.J. 245 (2000).

3. *Practice of medicine.* As mentioned in *Evers*, once a product reaches a
health care professional, the FDA has no power to regulate its use, not
because the product lacks the necessary connection with interstate commerce, but because of the agency's longstanding policy against interfering
with the practice of medicine. See FTC v. Simeon Management Corp., 391
F.Supp. 697, 705–07 (N.D.Cal.1975) (holding that the promotion of a
treatment program by a weight loss clinic based on off-label uses of drugs
did not violate the FDCA), aff'd, 532 F.2d 708, 717 (9th Cir.1976); see also
Chapter 4(B)(1) (discussing the legitimacy of off-label uses). Historically,
states exercised primary authority over medical practitioners. See Hearing
Before the House Subcomm. on Oversight & Investigations, 106th Cong.
(1999) (statement of Dr. Janet Woodcock, Director of the Center for Drug
Evaluation and Research, FDA) ("FDA does not generally regulate the
practice of pharmacy or the practice of medicine—the States traditionally
have regulated both the prescribing and dispensing of drugs."); Timothy
Stolzfus Jost, Oversight of the Quality of Medical Care: Regulation, Management, or the Market?, 37 Ariz. L. Rev. 825, 827–41 (1995). Is this
sufficient oversight? Note that some physicians still use chelation therapy
even though it does not appear to work. See Researchers Debunk Fringe
Heart Therapy, Hous. Chron., Mar. 22, 2001, at A25.

4. *Commercialization.* What if Dr. Evers had sold Calcium EDTA to other physicians for use in the treatment of arteriosclerosis along with detailed instructions and warnings (would he have anything to fear from the FDA)? See United States v. Burzynski Cancer Research Inst., 819 F.2d 1301, 1304–05 (5th Cir.1987) (recounting FDA enforcement action against a clinic selling unapproved new drugs in interstate commerce); United States v. Hoxsey Cancer Clinic, 198 F.2d 273, 281 (5th Cir.1952) (same); see also Cowan v. United States, 5 F.Supp.2d 1235, 1240 (N.D.Okla.1998) (explaining, in the course of rejecting a terminally ill patient's effort to secure access to an unapproved AIDS drug containing goat neutralizing antibodies, that "[n]othing in the FDCA or the case law suggests that the exception [for physicians from the statute's registration requirements] was intended to be expanded to permit doctors to test unapproved drugs").

Retkwa v. Orentreich

579 N.Y.S.2d 577 (Sup.Ct.1991).

■ SKLAR, JUSTICE:

Defendants Norman Orentreich, MD and Orentreich Medical Group move for an order vacating a medical malpractice panel's unanimous finding of liability against the defendants, on the ground that the panel erroneously considered evidence on the issue of whether defendants violated the Federal Food, Drug and Cosmetic Act by compounding liquid silicone for injection into plaintiff's face. * * *

Defendants readily admit that the microdroplet liquid silicone which was compounded by Dr. Orentreich's staff was a class III "device" without premarket approval and was therefore deemed to be an adulterated device within the meaning of the Act. The defendants allege, however, that the nonmedical grade base silicone which was shipped by Dow Chemical [from Delaware to New York] was not such a device when shipped interstate and that therefore the requisite contact with interstate commerce was absent. Defendants further allege that the Act was not intended to regulate physicians within their own practices, whether or not the device being used was approved * * * *

It is not necessary under [21 U.S.C. § 331(k)] to show that a device was adulterated when it left the interstate sender's hand or that it became adulterated while still in interstate commerce. Nor is there a necessity to show any wrongful motive or intent on the part of the sender. Indeed, it is not even necessary that the individual or entity receiving the article in interstate commerce be involved in the misbranding or adulteration. Rather, it is sufficient if the device was held for sale after shipment in interstate commerce and then was adulterated. A device is "held for sale" within the meaning of the Act if it is, inter alia, held by a practitioner for treatment of patients.

Defendants' assertion that the nonmedical grade base silicone which was shipped interstate by Dow is not a device within the meaning of the

Act is without merit. * * * It is readily apparent from the definition of the word "device" that it applies to any component of a device which was intended to affect the structure or functions of the body. Clearly defendants intended such result when the base silicone was ordered from Dow and when they compounded it and injected it. Moreover, analogous case law involving drugs supports the conclusion that the base silicone falls within the reach of the statute. For example, in *United States v. Dianovin Pharmaceuticals, Inc.*, 475 F.2d 100 (1st Cir.1973), the appeals court upheld the district court's determination that a drug manufacturer's use of the raw material vitamin K, which had been shipped in interstate commerce, in making the drug injectable vitamin K, solely for local consumption fell within the Act since articles intended for use as components of a drug were also defined as drugs * * * *

The defendants further urge that Congress did not intend that the Act interfere with the practice of medicine or prohibit the use by a physician of any product whether or not it was approved or adulterated. The defendants attempt to support their argument with case authority but a review of the cases cited reveals that the physicians in those cases were using approved drugs for unapproved uses. Indeed, I could find no authority for the proposition that the Act was inapplicable to physicians using a drug or device which was never approved for any purpose. * * * In *United States v. Algon Chem. Inc.*, 879 F.2d 1154, 1163 (3d Cir.1989), the United States Court of Appeals for the Third Circuit concluded that Congress intended nothing more than to preserve a physician's right to compound and prepare medicines which were legally obtained during the course of the physician's medical practice. * * *

I find that defendants' conduct in preparing and administering the silicone injections to the plaintiff falls within the "held for sale" provision of 21 U.S.C. § 331(k) and therefore has the requisite contact with interstate commerce to come within the operation of the Act. Further, the medical-practice exception to the Act does not pertain to a physician's compounding of an unapproved or illegal substance as any contrary result would defeat the intent of the protections afforded by the Act. Accordingly, the defendants' motion is denied.

United States v. Baxter Healthcare Corp.

901 F.2d 1401 (7th Cir.1990).

■ CUMMINGS, CIRCUIT JUDGE:

The federal Food and Drug Administration (FDA) challenges a program involving the reconstitution, repackaging, freezing, and distribution of already approved drugs without specific FDA approval for final products of the program as new drugs. The district court granted the FDA's motion for a preliminary injunction prohibiting Baxter Healthcare Corporation and intervenor Glaxo Specialties, Inc. from producing (so far as is relevant to this appeal) eight ready-to-use frozen antibiotic drug products pending trial on the merits. The FDA claims that Baxter and Glaxo must apply to the

FDA for separate approval to combine drug powders and liquids that have already been approved by the FDA into packages that are readily usable by the hospitals, clinics, and physicians to whom they are sold. * * * Baxter and Glaxo respond that the FDA unreasonably demands more than one approval for the same drug products. The companies assert that they do not violate the FDCA in acting without separate FDA approval because by the FDA's admission the drugs which are the components of the final products have already been approved by the FDA and, the companies assert, are being combined in FDA-approved containers in the detailed manner prescribed by the FDA through manufacturing practices open to inspection by the FDA. Baxter seeks to avoid submitting the products to the FDA's new drug approval system. * * *

Baxter is a large manufacturer and distributor of health-care products incorporated in Delaware originally as Travenol Laboratories, Inc. Since July 1982, Baxter has operated or attempted to operate a Travenol Regional Compounding Center (TRC), first opening a center in Morton Grove, Illinois, later adding a second in Bridgeport, New Jersey. Baxter created the TRC program because many drugs do not leave drug manufacturers in final form for administration to patients, but instead are purchased in either lyophilized (freeze-dried) or liquid concentrate form. Hospitals have commonly responded to the need to prepare the drugs for administration to patients by operating their own centralized drug preparation programs for the reconstitution, dilution, repackaging, and in some cases freezing, of antibiotics in batches. The TRC program is designed to transform such powders and concentrates on a large scale into dosage packages suitable for immediate use by health-care providers * * * *

The FDA alleges that the TRC activities violate the FDCA because, in essence, the drug packages produced at the TRCs are new drugs which must be separately tested for safety and efficacy. The FDA states that Baxter is inappropriately relying on a labeling system intended to be used in the best professional judgment of medical professionals in the context of hospitals and clinics, not by commercial manufacturers on a large scale. Baxter and Glaxo respond that the products at issue are in no sense new drugs because they are the direct result of the reconstitution of already approved component drugs in a manner which they assert is dictated by the FDA labels. The companies assert that they can follow the labels even more reliably and efficiently than can individual hospitals or doctors. * * *

Each of the eight component drugs at issue is subject to regulation under Section 507(a) of the FDCA as an antibiotic, the infection-fighting drug defined in the FDCA as that "produced by a microorganism and which has the capacity to inhibit or destroy microorganisms in dilute solution." * * * Under Section 507, the Commissioner of the FDA has the authority to certify every batch of antibiotic drug as safe and effective:

A batch of [antibiotic for human use] shall be certified if such drug has such characteristics of identity and such batch has such characteristics of strength, quality, and purity, as the Secretary prescribes in such regulations as necessary to adequately insure safety and efficacy of use, but shall not otherwise be certified. * * *

Section 507 of the FDCA authorizes the FDA to promulgate regulations requiring that each batch of antibiotic drug be certified. A batch is a specific homogenous quantity produced under a single order during one manufacturing cycle. In 1982, however, the FDA exempted all antibiotic drugs for human use from the batch certification requirement that had been authorized by Congress. See 21 C.F.R. § 433.1. This regulatory exemption was to apply so long as four conditions were met, only two of which are relevant here: (1) that the drug has been approved for marketing (pursuant to the approval procedures and requirements found in 21 C.F.R. Part 314), and (2) that the drug is packaged and labeled for dispensing in accordance with the applicable monograph, except where other labeling has been approved pursuant to an application. * * *

Baxter responds that it does not seek an exemption from Section 507(a) of the FDCA, but instead has complied fully with the FDCA because its drug products are in fact certified drugs. Thus the first and it would appear largely decisive question in this appeal is this: may the FDA permissibly interpret the term "antibiotic drug" in Section 507(a) as including the TRC drug products subject to a new round of certification? We conclude that it may. * * *

This may be the archetypal case calling for agency expertise. The FDA states that as a matter of science Baxter is "compounding" substances to produce drugs that differ in important, if sometimes subtle, ways from those component substances. In order to side with Baxter, we would need to find the authority to disagree with the following assertions solicited by the FDA in this case: (1) "leaching" (that is, movement of chemicals into the bag contents) from the plastic bags used as the final container for the TRC products may change the chemical composition of the TRC products with possibly harmful effects; (2) the longer than approved expiration dates for nafcillin, piperacillin, and ticarcillin may have the effect of altering the concentration of the drug, with possibly harmful effects; (3) similarly, the freezing of penicillin G and tobramycin without approval and use of an expiration date longer than that used in the insert might have the same effects; (4) a change in the method of manufacture of the component powders or liquids by their respective manufacturers "could result in the appearance of new impurities or degradation" of the TRC products, since adjustments might be required to be made by Baxter. In the view of the FDA, such concerns are not answered without adequate scientific testing to certify each drug product as a drug. Or, put in the terms of the FDCA, the drug products are "misbranded" pursuant to 21 U.S.C. § 352(*l*) because they are not antibiotics certified under 21 U.S.C. § 357(a) or exempt from certification pursuant to 21 U.S.C. § 357(c), (d). * * *

Congress has decided to treat commercial manufacturers of drugs differently from pharmacies and individual physicians in contexts closely related to that presented in this appeal. Therefore, to the extent Congress has addressed the issue, it has decided to focus governmental resources upon the commercial distributors of drugs rather than upon the trained pharmacists and physicians who must reconstitute drugs for patient use on a smaller scale. One sound argument for this choice is evident: A drug improperly compounded on a large scale will harm more patients than the same compounding mistake made on a smaller scale. * * *

As a policy choice, Congress has exempted pharmacies and physicians from the registration and inspection requirements that apply to all manufacturers of drugs. 21 U.S.C. §§ 360(g)(1), (2), 374(a)(1), (2). The FDA only follows that lead by focusing on the mass commercial distribution of drugs rather than at the individual level of hospitals and pharmacists. This does not suggest that the FDA has taken a path which is "manifestly contrary to the statute," but to the contrary suggests sound adherence to congressional intent. The methods used in small-scale drug admixture programs carried out by medical professionals may carry some of the same hazards complained of by the FDA regarding the TRC operations. But, as stated above, it is not illogical for Congress to suggest, and the FDA to effectuate the suggestion, that those hazards are most effectively met at the manufacturing level of the medical establishment. * * *

■ PELL, SENIOR CIRCUIT JUDGE (dissenting):

* * * When a single dose of an antibiotic, or a very small number of doses, are to be reconstituted, the reconstitution is done with a needle and syringe. An appropriate amount of sterile reconstituting fluid is drawn into the syringe, the needle is inserted through the stopper of the manufacturer's vial of lyophilized drug, and the reconstituting fluid is inserted into the vial. The powder and fluid are then agitated to form a solution. * * *

The single dose preparation technique for intravenous antibiotics is practiced at virtually all hospitals. Many larger hospitals, however, cannot meet their need for intravenous antibiotic drugs through the single dose preparation method. Many of these hospitals have established centralized drug preparation programs in which they reconstitute, dilute, and repackage the antibiotics in batches. It is not cost-effective for a hospital of more than 300 beds to engage in single dose reconstitution of antibiotics. Hospitals that engage in this type of centralized drug preparation do not necessarily reconstitute the antibiotics in response to an order for a specific patient. Some of these hospitals prepare batches of reconstituted antibiotics sufficient for one day's needs. Other hospitals prepare large batches intended to be used over a relatively long period of time. At least one hospital has prepared as many as 4,000 doses of reconstituted antibiotics at one time.

Hospitals that prepare single doses of reconstituted and/or diluted antibiotics may encounter numerous problems. These include: selection of the wrong drug, contamination during preparation, improper dosage, incorrect drug concentration, drug deterioration, labeling problems, and incompatible mixtures of drugs or fluids. Moreover, all hospitals experience critical care problems if prepared antibiotic drugs are not available.

Many reconstituted intravenous antibiotics have very short stability periods if maintained at room temperature, or even under refrigeration. In the 1960s and 1970s, research demonstrated that freezing could extend the stability period for most such drugs. * * * Virtually every hospital in the United States which has more than 300 beds has a pharmacy which operates an admixture program and many of these programs engage in the freezing of reconstituted antibiotics. Once freezing programs were developed, drug storage times were extended. The extensions were determined by reference to published literature, the institution's own studies, the manufacturer's labeling, or technical letters from manufacturers. Most hospitals, however, do not possess the facilities to engage in sophisticated analytical testing of these products. In fact, very few of these hospitals conduct stability testing on these frozen reconstituted antibiotics.

Baxter initiated its TRC program in 1982. The concept was that the TRC would perform the same functions as the hospital pharmacy, but more efficiently, more safely, and at a reduced price. * * * In the first seven years that the TRC has reconstituted and shipped these products, it has enjoyed an excellent safety record. During this time period, approximately seven million products have been produced at the TRCs, and there have been only 14 medical complaints. Moreover, none of these complaints have been attributed to the reconstitution and repackaging process at the TRC. * * * It is of interest to note that the FDA was informed of Baxter's intention to commence the TRC program even before it became operational. This was by letter to the district director of FDA in Chicago on June 16, 1982. FDA did not raise any regulatory objection to this program and Baxter began reconstituting drugs in July 1982. FDA investigators conducted inspections at the TRC in June 1983 and June 1985. Neither of these inspections resulted in any expressions of concern by the FDA. * * *

In the case at bar, the TRC products contain the same active and inactive ingredients as the approved product, and are of equal bioavailability and are bioequivalent to those approved products. Thus, it appears to me, the TRC products are the same "drug" as that which the FDA has approved. * * * [T]he TRC does not change anything about the product that would affect the rate and extent of absorption, and thus the TRC products are bioequivalent to the products that have already been approved by FDA. * * * They are not imitations or variations of the eight FDA antibiotics. They are the eight approved antibiotics now ready to be administered to a patient. They are simply brought farther along in their necessary preparation for use than were the drugs formerly. * * * Rather than employ this very extensive, expensive, and protracted [approval] procedure to deal specifically with the issues of stability in freezing and expiration dating, FDA is fully justified in utilizing the more specific and limited authority conferred by the CGMP regulations. * * *

I come away from reviewing this appeal with the unfortunate feeling that we have a case of bureaucratic overreaction to Baxter's declination to engage in a process which it did not deem legally necessary, in which position I fully concur. I do not intend to denigrate or minimize the importance of the [FDA] in protecting the interest of the public's safety in the use of drugs necessary in the continuation of good health. The diligence of FDA is testified to obviously by the periodic references in the media to drugs which are being administered in other parts of the world with effectiveness and apparent safety but which have not yet been approved for use in this country. I am putting aside in preparing this dissent any idea that the FDA in this case has succumbed to the necessities of its annual presentation of a budget to preserve, and ordinarily increase, that which Congress gives to it. Such budget requests, of course, are predicated to a considerable extent on justification of personnel needs, and I would be most disappointed in this respected governmental agency if it was devoting itself unnecessarily to an easily found target such as an established pharmaceutical company rather than to fly-by-night generic substitute operators. * * *

NOTES AND QUESTIONS

1. *Antibiotics*. In 1997, as part of FDAMA, Congress codified the FDA's regulatory exemption from batch certification for antibiotics by deleting § 507. See Pub. L. No. 105–115, § 125(b)(1), 111 Stat. 2296, 2325. Thus, antibiotic products are now regulated in precisely the same fashion as drugs.

2. *Practice of medicine and compounding*. In his dissenting opinion in *Baxter*, Judge Pell described large-scale admixture programs run by hospital pharmacies. Are these obviously lawful? The FDA has challenged physicians or pharmacists who compound drugs that they offer for general sale rather than solely in the treatment of a particular patient. See United States v. Sene X Eleemosynary Corp., 479 F.Supp. 970, 978–79 (S.D.Fla. 1979) (rejecting practice of pharmacy defense to misbranding charges associated with large-scale compounding); see also Cabiroy v. Scipione, 767 A.2d 1078 (Pa.Super.Ct.2001) (finding that a physician's injection of unapproved liquid silicone constituted negligence per se); cf. Federal Prescription Serv., Inc. v. American Pharm. Ass'n, 663 F.2d 253 (D.C.Cir.1981) (holding that the practice of pharmacy encompasses mail order); Sabin Russell, Independent Drugstores: Pharmacists Under Microscope, S.F. Chron., June 10, 2001, at A4 (noting safety concerns associated with a resurgence in pharmacy compounding). In one widely publicized recent case, federal prosecutors brought drug adulteration and misbranding charges against a pharmacist who had reconstituted substantially diluted chemotherapy agents for physicians. See Pam Belluck, Prosecutors Say Greed Drove Pharmacist to Dilute Drugs, N.Y. Times, Aug. 18, 2001, at A1 (adding that manslaughter charges may follow if the FBI traces any patient deaths to these subpotent drugs). In FDAMA, Congress explicitly authorized certain types of compounding. See Pub. L. No. 105–115, § 127, 111 Stat. 2296, 2328 (codified at 21 U.S.C. § 353a) (exempting a product from new drug approval and related requirements if, among other things, "the drug product is compounded [by a licensed pharmacist or physician] for an identified individual patient based on the unsolicited receipt of a valid prescription order," and defining compounding as not including "mixing, reconstituting, or other such acts that are performed in accordance with directions contained in approved labeling"). Congress also codified the

FDA's policy against interfering with the practice of medicine, though only with respect to devices. See id. § 214 (codified at 21 U.S.C. § 396).

3. *Reprocessing of single-use devices (SUDs).* As a cost-saving measure, hospitals increasingly reuse disposable medical devices (i.e., labeled for single-use only). Responding to concerns about inadequate sterilization and material degradation, the FDA has announced that it will regulate hospitals as device manufacturers when they engage in such reprocessing. See John J. Smith & Jennifer A. Agraz, Federal Regulation of Single–Use Medical Devices: A Revised FDA Policy, 56 Food & Drug L.J. 305 (2001).

D.   FDA PRACTICE AND PROCEDURES

Peter Barton Hutt, *The Transformation of United States Food and Drug Law*

J. ASS'N FOOD & DRUG OFFICIALS, Sept. 1996, at 1.

Neither the 1906 Act nor the 1938 Act is self-executing. Both have required FDA to implement very broad and general statutory provisions with more specific operating rules. Thus, FDA has spent the past century determining, and then making public, procedural and substantive policy statements designed to facilitate its administration of the organic statute. * * *

One of the major reasons for the use of rulemaking to replace individual court enforcement actions in the early 1970s was to achieve greater fairness and consistency in application of the law. Use of court enforcement, while clearly a permissible course of action, is inherently selective and can lead to the perception, and perhaps at times the reality, of invidious discrimination. Establishment of policy by promulgation of regulations, in contrast, assures that all affected companies have equal notice of FDA requirements and an equal opportunity for compliance. * * *

Prior to the 1970s, it was common practice simply to propose a regulation, obtain public comment and then publish a final regulation, without an explanation of the reasons for the proposal or why the changes recommended by the public comment were or were not accepted in the final regulations. FDA pioneered the use of explanatory preambles to both the proposed and the final regulations. The preamble to the proposal laid out in detail the need for the proposed regulation, any documentation appropriate for its specific provisions and an analysis of its intended interpretation and implementation. The preamble to the final regulation responded to each type of comment, stating the reasons why it was accepted or rejected. These preambles served and continue to serve to this day the purpose of educating FDA employees, the regulated industry and the general public about the important work of the agency. * * *

Because of the increasing burdens imposed by regulatory agencies on industry, Congress has responded with corresponding requirements for all federal agencies to justify their rulemaking. * * * As these requirements for the promulgation of regulations have increased, the number of regulations promulgated by FDA has decreased correspondingly. Issues that previously might have been resolved through regulations of the type promulgated by FDA during the 1970s increasingly have been handled by more informal approaches. * * * In the early 1990s, the use of guidelines by FDA * * * skyrocketed. Some courts have already found that these informal statements of policy are poorly disguised regulations and have invalidated or refused to enforce substantive guidelines implemented by FDA as though they were regulations. * * *

Under the 1906 Act, any violation constituted a misdemeanor punishable by a fine, imprisonment or both. Violative products were also subject to seizure. The 1938 Act expanded FDA's enforcement power. In addition to criminal liability and seizure, FDA was authorized to obtain a judicial injunction against any violation of the statute. FDA was also authorized to issue a written administrative notice or warning for minor violations in lieu of formal court proceedings, to conduct factory inspection and to issue publicity and other public information. FDA has not been satisfied with the enforcement powers specifically included within the 1938 Act. It has sought to expand these powers both through administrative action and through new legislation. * * *

Under the 1906 Act, FDA enforced the statute almost exclusively through seizure actions and criminal prosecution. * * * This pattern of enforcement continued under the 1938 Act but was profoundly affected by changes in statutory authority and FDA policy. First, as the 1938 Act was amended to require premarket approval for regulated products, FDA was able to enforce the statute informally through administrative decisions as part of the approval process rather than by formal court action. Second, as FDA realized that informal administrative sanctions such as regulatory/warning letters and recall requests were more efficient and effective, these informal actions also displaced formal court enforcement. Third, when FDA began to issue more and more of its policy in the form of regulations in the early 1970s and later guidelines in the early 1990s, violations by industry substantially decreased and thus the need for either informal or formal enforcement was diminished. As a result of all of these developments, the FDA enforcement statistics under the 1938 Act show an extraordinary shift from formal court action to informal administrative action * * * * FDA and the state agencies have always depended upon voluntary compliance by the vast majority of the regulated industry with food and drug laws and regulations. If there were any substantial noncompliance, neither FDA nor the state agencies would have sufficient resources to address the problem. * * *

[A]mendments to the 1938 Act represent a revolution in product regulation. From a policing role under the 1906 Act, FDA gradually undertook the role of sole gatekeeper to the marketplace. * * * This change in regulatory function has had the single most profound impact on FDA of any change in the history of the agency. For a product subject to premarket approval, no manufacturer may lawfully distribute the product and no member of the public has a right to obtain it unless and until FDA authorizes marketing.

This has also had a profound impact on the country. First, it severely limits individual freedom of choice. Citizens are simply precluded from obtaining products that they wish to purchase and have no recourse other than to await FDA approval. Personal autonomy is subjugated to government regulatory control. Second, premarket approval has enormous economic consequences. Particularly for small businesses, the investment required to obtain premarket approval of new products can be prohibitive. As FDA approval requirements and review times have increased, the cost of premarket approval has escalated. The average cost of an approved NDA for a new chemical entity now approaches a half billion dollars. The greater the investment required, the fewer the products that can be developed and marketed and the higher the price that must be charged to consumers for the ultimate approved products. Third, premarket approval under the 1938 Act includes no mechanism for public accountability. Citizens who wish to obtain a product have no right to participate in the process and no access to judicial review of whatever action is taken by FDA. Even the applicant is precluded from access to the courts until final action is taken on a product application. Because the premarket approval process is conducted in private without public participation and there is no right to judicial intervention or any other form of public accountability, it has become subject to increasing criticism. * * *

1.   ADJUDICATION

United States v. Alcon Laboratories

636 F.2d 876 (1st Cir.1981).

■ CAMPBELL, CIRCUIT JUDGE:

The United States appeals from orders of the district court for the District of Puerto Rico in two seizure actions and a suit for injunctive relief instituted by the Food and Drug Administration (FDA) against Alcon Laboratories, Inc. and one of its products pursuant to the Federal Food, Drug, and Cosmetic Act.

Alcon manufactures and markets in suppository dosage a prescription antiemetic drug called "WANS." The drug contains pyrilamine maleate (an antihistamine) and pentobarbital sodium (a barbiturate) and comes in three dosage strengths, WANS No. 1, WANS No. 2 and WANS Children. WANS has been used under medical supervision for approximately 25 years and did not become an object of FDA concern until 1978. * * *

Where the FDA believes that a drug is a "new drug" and is being marketed without approval of an NDA, it is empowered to institute seizure and injunction actions in federal district court to remedy the alleged violation of the Act. The agency may also seek criminal sanctions.

On March 17, 1978, the FDA sent Alcon a regulatory letter informing it of a report received from the agency's Neurological Drugs Advisory Committee ["that children aged 6 months to seven years who were treated for nausea and vomiting with drugs containing pyrilamine maleate and pentobarbital experienced severe and sometimes fatal reactions."] The Committee had concluded, the letter went on, "that there is no evidence of safety and efficacy for drugs containing pyrilamine maleate with or without a barbituate in the treatment of nausea and vomiting." Based on the Committee's report, "and because (the FDA was) unaware of substantial scientific evidence which demonstrates that a combination of these ingredients is generally recognized as safe and effective for the treatment of nausea and vomiting," the FDA advised Alcon that it considered Alcon's marketing of WANS to be in violation of the "new drug" provision of the Federal Food, Drug, and Cosmetic Act. * * * Alcon was told to reply within ten days and was warned that failure to discontinue marketing WANS would expose the company to seizure and injunction actions.

Alcon responded on April 3, 1978. It claimed that WANS was not a "new drug," objected to the FDA's departure from the ordinary sequence of its enforcement priorities on the basis of an "unsubstantiated, conclusionary indictment of the safety" of the active ingredients in WANS, and requested that it be allowed to "identify and review the data and information upon which the Agency relies, and to make a formal submission to the Agency...." The company also offered to revise the labeling of WANS consistent with the findings of its review. Subsequent to this letter, Alcon, on its own initiative, sent the FDA proposed new labeling for WANS and information supporting the safety and efficacy of the drug. Various company officials met with agency officials on July 10 and 18, 1978, to discuss WANS.

The FDA reviewed the materials provided by Alcon and in a letter of August 4, 1978, reaffirmed its position upon the "new drug" status of WANS: "the data submitted ... contains no adequate scientific data to support the safety and efficacy of the WANS products." Though the proposed relabeling was felt to be "an improvement," it could not substitute for "scientific evidence to establish that a fixed combination of pyrilamine maleate and pentobarbital sodium is either safe or effective for the treatment of nausea and vomiting." * * *

Alcon continued to manufacture WANS and on September 21, 1978, the FDA instituted a seizure action in federal district court alleging that the drug was a "new drug" being marketed in violation of section 505 of the Act. By court order, a large quantity of WANS suppositories (approximately 453,900) was seized. In its responsive pleadings in the seizure action, Alcon admitted that no approval of a new drug application was in effect for WANS or was being sought. The company nevertheless denied that WANS was being marketed in violation of section 505. Alcon argued that WANS is not subject to the "new drug" requirements of the Act

co. argument

because "it is generally recognized as safe for use under the conditions prescribed, recommended or suggested in its labeling"]* * * *

Despite seizure of the suppositories, Alcon continued to manufacture and distribute WANS, thus prompting the FDA, on November 28, 1978, to institute a further action, this time seeking a temporary restraining order, a preliminary injunction and a permanent injunction against continued marketing of WANS without FDA approval. On the next day, November 29, the district court denied the FDA's request for a temporary restraining order, and consolidated the injunctive suit with the earlier seizure action. * * *

No further action was taken in the case until January 28, 1980. On that date the FDA instituted a second seizure against WANS. Large quantities of the drug were again confiscated. A month later, on February 27, 1980, the district court consolidated the latest seizure action with the pending actions * * * * The United States presently attacks three aspects of the district court's order: [(1) its instruction that the FDA "defer regulatory action against the WANS preparation ... or against defendants" pending further administrative proceedings; (2) its decision to leave prior seizures of WANS "without effect;" and (3) its remand of the case to the agency.]* * *

FDA's claims

The order has the effect of forbidding the FDA from exercising in any forum its statutory power both to proceed against WANS and its producer and to seize the article pending condemnation. * * * This injunction exceeded the district court's authority. To prevent this sort of eroding of the agency's protective powers, the Supreme Court in *Ewing v. Mytinger & Casselberry, Inc.*, 339 U.S. 594 (1950), held that district courts lack jurisdiction to enjoin multiple seizure actions instituted by the FDA under the Act. * * * Alcon's argument that such a rule exposes a manufacturer to potentially devastating hardship and loss was disposed of in *Ewing*. * * *

It is the government's contention that the district court "ha(d) no authority simply to give back the seized property without determining ... whether or not the Act (was) violated." The Act provides that before trial the court shall "allow any party to a condemnation proceeding ... to obtain a representative sample of the article seized" and that after condemnation the court has discretion to order the goods sold or destroyed, 21 U.S.C. § 334(c), (d), but otherwise is silent upon the release of seized goods prior to a decision upon the FDA's claims. Rule E(5)(c) of the Supplemental Rules for Certain Admiralty and Maritime Claims, which were intended to inform seizure procedure under the Act, * * * provides for release of property if a plaintiff consents, or when "approved security as provided by law and these rules" is tendered. Neither circumstance exists here (and, indeed, in a new drug case, where the purpose of the seizure is to remove a possibly risky drug from public use, it is hard to see how the mere putting up of security would be a proper basis for release). In any event, we see little in Rule E(5) by way of a general grant of authority permitting courts to countermand administratively instituted seizures without first adjudicating the merits of the agency's claim. If the seizure is plainly frivolous, the

court can act rapidly and achieve justice in that manner, but its action *what District court should have done.*
should ordinarily follow, not precede, an adjudication. * * *

We conclude that the district court erred in dissolving the administrative seizures of WANS without first addressing the merits of the seizure proceedings initiated by the FDA, including, as part thereof, the agency's contention that WANS is a "new drug." We therefore vacate this portion of the district court's order. The district court believed that allowing "the continued retention of the material seized would be an abuse of judicial discretion" in light of its findings that WANS "has been used for years" and that "the information which prompted the FDA to initiate these actions was not only contradictory, but also insufficient to allow a causal relation." These preliminary and necessarily tentative and incomplete findings cannot serve as a substitute for a determination on the merits. It has been said that in pursuing a seizure action, the FDA must first allege sufficient facts to state a claim and must then prove its claim by a preponderance of the evidence. A decision by a district court as to whether the FDA has met those burdens would be the proper means for adjudicating the validity of the FDA's enforcement efforts; a seizure should only be dissolved thereafter, in event of the government's failure to do so. * * *

The district court premised its decision to remand to the FDA on interrelated procedural and substantive grounds. The court was troubled by the agency's failure to conduct "a formal administrative determination of the 'new drug' status of WANS" before instituting suit against Alcon. * * * [T]he court characterized itself as ill-suited to decide the "new drug" status of WANS or to determine whether "significant new information" existed that questioned WANS' safety. Citing lack of jurisdiction, the doctrine of primary agency jurisdiction and prudential considerations, the court decided that these questions were better left to "the Agency entrusted by Congress with the necessary expertise to make a responsible determination." Accordingly, it ordered the action "remanded to the Food and Drug Administration to hold a formal administrative hearing" * * * *

[T]he imposition of a pre-enforcement hearing requirement (coupled with preliminary relief, as, to be meaningful, it would have to be) is at odds with the language and intent of the Act. To be sure, in certain circumstances a formal administrative proceeding is a precondition to agency action. For example, when the FDA issues, pursuant to 5 U.S.C. § 554(e), a declaratory order governing all drugs covered by a particular new drug application, or when it withdraws approval of a new drug application pursuant to 21 U.S.C. § 355(e), it must first hold a hearing in compliance with section 554 of the Administrative Procedure Act * * * * By contrast, there is no statutory hearing requirement for FDA decisions to initiate seizure or injunction actions. Indeed, the probable cause determination necessary to institute multiple seizure actions against allegedly misbranded products is to be made "without hearing." 21 U.S.C. § 334(a)(1). As the Supreme Court has made abundantly clear, a manufacturer subjected to an FDA enforcement action has no right to raise objections in an administrative forum prior to the agency's institution of the action. This is because the imposition of any formal, pre-enforcement hearing requirement might seriously impair the effectiveness of the Act's enforcement provisions. * * *

NOTES AND QUESTIONS

1. *Seizures.* As mentioned in *Alcon*, one powerful enforcement tool available to the FDA allows it to seize violative products in a fashion that resembles arrest and pre-trial detention of a suspected criminal (this explains some of the odd captions in the case law). The manufacturer may appear in the condemnation proceeding as a claimant in order to challenge the agency's action, but it cannot ask a court to enjoin those proceedings. See Parke, Davis & Co. v. Califano, 564 F.2d 1200, 1205–06 (6th Cir.1977). But cf. United States v. Undetermined Quantities of Drugs, 675 F.Supp. 1113, 1114–17 (N.D.Ill.1987) (ordering release of seized drugs pending resolution of a condemnation proceeding, distinguishing *Alcon* as involving non-perishable and potentially harmful drugs). The courts generally have rejected constitutional objections to the FDA's exercise of its authority to seize adulterated or misbranded products. See Ewing v. Mytinger & Casselberry, Inc., 339 U.S. 594, 598–600 (1950) (rejecting a Fifth Amendment procedural due process objection to the initiation of multiple seizure actions without a prior hearing); United States v. Argent Chem. Labs., Inc., 93 F.3d 572, 574–78 (9th Cir.1996) (rejecting a Fourth Amendment objection to an FDA seizure made without first obtaining a warrant from a judicial officer based on a finding of probable cause because the drug industry is pervasively regulated and its members therefore have diminished expectations of privacy); cf. United States v. Proplast II, 946 F.2d 422, 423 (5th Cir.1991) ("To balance a claimant's constitutional right to due process in a post-deprivation procedure, while at the same time accommodating the public health protection policy embodied in the [FDCA], a hearing on the merits should be scheduled at the promptest date practicable. . . . ").

2. *Injunctions.* Seizures take violative products out of circulation but, if the manufacturer is obstinate and continues violating the statute, the FDA would have to bring repeated seizure actions. To deal with the problem of recurring infractions, the agency can request that a court issue an injunction against the manufacturer, as it did in *Alcon*. The government need not show irreparable harm or inadequacy of remedies at law in order to receive such equitable relief. See United States v. Vital Health Prods., Ltd., 786 F.Supp. 761, 770 (E.D.Wis.1992), aff'd, 985 F.2d 563 (7th Cir.1993). But cf. United States v. Nutri-cology, Inc., 982 F.2d 394, 396, 398 (9th Cir.1992) (affirming the denial of a preliminary injunction where the government had failed to demonstrate any likelihood of success on the merits or irreparable harm); David A. Levitt, Judicial Enforcement of the Federal Food, Drug, and Cosmetic Act: Are Injunctions Always Required to Remedy Ongoing Violations?, 48 Food & Drug L.J. 227 (1993) (arguing that the courts should still balance hardship to the parties). The government need only show a reasonable likelihood that identified violations of the statute will continue. For instance, courts may grant injunctions that effectively shut down manufacturers until they bring their operations into compliance with

GMPs. See United States v. Barr Labs., Inc., 812 F.Supp. 458, 487–91 (D.N.J.1993) (fashioning an injunction that directed the company to remedy several GMP violations with respect to a number of different product lines); United States v. Richlyn Labs., Inc., 827 F.Supp. 1145, 1150–52 (E.D.Pa.1992) (rejecting the defendant's argument that it was correcting problems and that the injunction was too harsh); see also United States v. Diapulse Corp., 457 F.2d 25, 29 (2d Cir.1972) ("Nor can appellant complain that the injunction is impermissible because it will put him out of business."). Courts also may craft injunctions that prohibit otherwise lawful conduct if necessary to cure the lingering effects of past transgressions such as inappropriate marketing. See United States v. Articles of Drug ... Doxylamine Succinate, 890 F.2d 1004, 1007–08 (8th Cir.1989). But cf. United States v. Diapulse Corp. of Am., 748 F.2d 56, 61–62 (2d Cir.1984) (rejecting such an injunction as overbroad).

United States v. Superpharm Corp.

530 F.Supp. 408 (E.D.N.Y.1981).

■ COSTANTINO, DISTRICT JUDGE:

This is an action under the Federal Food, Drug and Cosmetic Act to enjoin alleged violations of the Act and for other forms of relief. The suit, initiated in January, 1981, contends that Superpharm Corporation and Norman E. Rubin, president of Superpharm, engaged in the manufacture and distribution of a human drug, furosemide, in the absence of approval by the Food and Drug Administration. * * *

The Government maintains that this court has the authority pursuant to section 302 of the Act to order a recall. Section 302 provides in pertinent part that "the district courts of the United States ... shall have jurisdiction, for cause shown, to restrain violations of Section 301 of this Title." In addition, the Government contends that the court's general equitable power also authorizes the issuance of a recall order. * * *

An examination of the Act itself reveals that Congress specifically did not include a judicially ordered recall remedy when the Act was passed. It did, however, provide a threefold enforcement scheme: (1) injunctive relief; (2) criminal prosecution; and (3) seizure. Moreover, in reading the legislative history behind the Act when passed in 1938, it is clear that Congress considered seizures to be the most drastic remedy, and that the injunction remedy was included to temper the hardship inherent in seizures. * * * [G]iven this orientation, it is difficult to conclude that Congress intended section 302(a) to authorize judicial recalls.

In effect, the Government is asking this court to do something that the FDA itself cannot do. While there are provisions in the FDA regulations which provide for recalls, recalls cannot be ordered by the FDA as they are usually undertaken voluntarily at the request of the FDA. The authorized vehicle for FDA removal of goods from the marketplace is the seizure remedy. It is simply not within the FDA's stated authority to order a manufacturer to recall its own goods.

If for medical and public safety reasons the FDA believes the removal of the restrained pharmaceutical product is imperative, they have the seizure remedy at their disposal. To order a recall under the Act would be an unwarranted act of judicial legislation because the FDA * * * would have yet another method of attacking the allegedly illegal distributions of drugs without being restricted by either the Act or the regulations promulgated thereunder. Recalls are simply not within the enforcement powers of the Act, and the court perceives no reason to expand the remedies currently in effect by including such a remedy. * * *

In the instant case, resort to ancillary remedies through equitable powers is unnecessary to enforce the spirit, as well as the letter, of the Act. The FDA's statutory remedies provide for sufficient means to enforce the Act, and the legislative history and the Act itself manifest a reluctance to expand enforcement powers to the point where they are punitive. Moreover, the seizure remedy exists if the FDA perceives a potential public danger which must be rectified immediately, or if the manufacturer or distributor refuses to remove the illegal product from the market. Although the court's duty is heightened when, in a case such as this, the public interest is involved, the Government and the FDA have the tools at their disposal to solve the problem and there is no need to attempt to add to those powers when not necessary. No resort to, or expansion of, the court's equitable power is needed to remove these drugs from interstate commerce. Accordingly, the Government's request for an order recalling the drugs from the marketplace is denied.

United States v. Universal Management Services, Inc.

191 F.3d 750 (6th Cir.1999).

■ SUHRHEINRICH, CIRCUIT JUDGE:

* * * As part of their business, Appellants sell and distribute a product known as the Stimulator, and also a product that connects to the Stimulator known as the Xtender. The Stimulator is essentially an electric gas grill igniter, marketed as a pain relieving device. To produce the Stimulator, Appellants purchase gas grill igniters and outfit them with finger grips. A user then places the tip of the Stimulator on his body, presses with his thumb on a plunger, and an electric current passes into that part of the body. Appellants' advertising literature states that, when applied to certain acupressure points, the Stimulator can relieve numerous kinds of pain (e.g., migraine headaches, swollen joints, allergies). The Xtender is an accessory that allows an individual to use the Stimulator to reach areas of the body otherwise difficult to reach, such as the spine. In total, Appellants sold a total of 800,000 gas grill igniters, at a cost to the company of one dollar each, for $88.30 each.

In May 1995, U.S. Marshals seized over $1.2 million worth of Appellants' devices pursuant to seizure authority under the Federal Food, Drug & Cosmetic Act. Later that month, the Food and Drug Administration (FDA) informed Appellants that they considered the devices adulterated and subject to regulation, threatening further legal action if approval was not sought and distribution did not cease. Distribution did not cease and the Government sought the injunction that is the subject of this appeal. The district court granted summary judgment for the Government on December 30, 1997, and, in February 1998, rejected Appellants' Motion for Reconsideration. The resulting judgment placed a permanent injunction against the distribution of Appellants' products and ordered Appellants to offer full refunds to all customers who had purchased their devices after the May 1995 seizure. * * *

Below, the Government requested its costs and any such other relief the court deemed proper, including equitable disgorgement of profits. After finding disgorgement inappropriate, the district court found that restitution was a remedy available to the FDA and appropriate. The district court awarded restitution, finding that the FDCA does not contain a clear command indicating that restitution is not a remedy available to the district court. It supported its decision on the premise that the FDCA should receive liberal construction. The restitution ordered required Appellants to offer and provide refunds to all of their customers who requested them in writing. Appellants challenge the restitution order, arguing the FDCA does not permit restitution and, if it does, restitution was inappropriate in this case.

Issue here: injunction & restitution

The FDCA provides only three remedies for violations: (1) injunctive relief, 21 U.S.C. § 332; (2) criminal prosecution, 21 U.S.C. § 333; and (3) seizure, 21 U.S.C. § 334. To rule on Appellants' first contention, that the FDCA does not permit orders of restitution, we must consider the scope of injunctive relief authorized under § 332. The district court in this case was sitting as a court of equity. Restitution and disgorgement are part of courts' traditional equitable authority. Absent a clear command by Congress that a statute providing for equitable relief excludes certain forms of such relief, this court will presume the full scope of equitable powers may be exercised by the courts. * * *

[T]he remedy of seizure exists alongside an explicit authorization for injunctive relief to cure violations of the FDCA. The express provision for general equitable relief without the enumeration of any exceptions makes it difficult for this court to find any legitimate means for implicitly carving out such exceptions as we see fit. Even if Congress expressed some concern that seizure should remain the harshest relief available, there is no convincing argument that, in all cases, restitution creates a more harsh result than seizure, procedurally or substantively. Moreover, * * * these concerns are far from a clear statement of Congress's intent to exclude restitution, recalls, disgorgement, or any other traditional form of equitable relief. * * * Therefore, we hold that nothing in the FDCA precludes a court sitting in equity from ordering restitution in appropriate cases.

no gov't discretion for restitution / type of.

restitution is OK

Case Specific

Next, we must determine[whether restitution was an appropriate remedy on the facts of the case at bar.] We review an award of restitution for an abuse of discretion. Appellants first argue that the FDA's charge itself should preclude restitution. The FDA charge, they claim, was only that Appellants marketed a product without required approval, rather than that the product didn't perform as it was intended. If the performance is not questioned and no deficiency in the same is established, they contend that there has been no detriment to consumers justifying the restitution order. In other words, Appellants contend[that restitution was unwarranted because there is no evidence that consumers received anything less than what they bargained for.]

(∆'s argument)

The approval process exists to protect consumers' health and their pocketbooks. One of the primary goals of the FDCA is to protect consumers from economic harm. It is not the government's burden to prove that a product is not safe and effective. FDCA regulations exist to allow the public to assume that marketed devices have received the imprimatur of FDA approval. To circumvent the law by marketing illegally without approval is to deceive the public both as purchasers and users of the device. In such cases, restitution exists to make the consumer whole. Because restitution seeks to remedy the type of economic harm to consumers contemplated by the FDCA, it serves goals of the FDCA that are encompassed within the section the FDA charges Appellants violated. * * *

(not true for dietary supplements)

Appellants also claim that restitution is punitive because, unlike disgorgement which removes ill-gotten gain by forcing surrender of profits, restitution requires a return of the entire purchase price, included in which are costs and profits. Simply because disgorgement and restitution are different, however, does not make restitution punitive. Appellants, who disobeyed the law, should not have [their] expenses covered by consumers. To say that restitution is unavailable is to say that consumers must cover the costs of Appellants' production, advertising, and illegal distribution. Instead, the district court should have the discretion in a case such as this to make the consumers whole rather than allow the illegal activities to stand uncorrected to the consumer's detriment.

Despite Appellants' contentions, their violation was also more than a mere technicality. Congress set up a sophisticated statutory scheme for the regulation of medical devices, and the requirement that devices be approved or cleared by the FDA before marketing is at the heart of the scheme. Thus, Appellants' failure to achieve such clearance violates a key component of the regulatory scheme. And, in the context of public health and safety, the district court's equitable authority is broader and more flexible to support such a regulatory scheme than in ordinary litigation.

The district court did not abuse its discretion in determining restitution was appropriate in this case. The district court seemed to fairly balance the equities in the case. There is evidence that Appellants continued to distribute their product without seeking any approval even after they were put on notice of their violation by the FDA in May 1995, distributed after district court issued a preliminary injunction, and obstructed FDA inspections. Appellants were hardly mere flies caught in the web of technical government regulation. Appellants marketed a device to the consuming public, a public that the FDCA regulatory structure seeks to protect. Appellants marketed their product in clear violation of the FDCA. They continued to sell to the public even after the FDA notified them that their product could not be sold without FDA approval. For these reasons, the district court's order of restitution was well within its discretion. * * *

NOTES AND QUESTIONS

1. *Disgorgement hurts.* In the FDA's previous attempt to secure a restitution order, the court held that it lacked statutory authority to provide any such relief. See United States v. Parkinson, 240 F.2d 918, 922 (9th Cir.1956) ("The use of the extraordinary remedies of equity in governmental litigation should never be permitted by the courts unless clearly authorized by the statute in express terms."). For that reason, the decision in *Universal Management* sent chills through the FDA-regulated industries. Shortly afterward, the agency successfully negotiated a consent decree with Abbott Laboratories over longstanding GMP violations that included $100 million for disgorgement of profits from the sale of affected diagnostic products. See Deirdre Davidson, FDA Now Packs a Heavyweight Punch, Nat'l L.J., July 17, 2000, at B6.

2. *Civil penalties.* Congress expressly authorized the FDA to seek civil penalties from medical device manufacturers. See 21 U.S.C. § 333(f). One court accepted as reasonable a record plea agreement for $61 million in criminal and civil fines against a company that had sold cardiac catheters with unapproved design modifications that resulted in several deaths. See United States v. C.R. Bard, Inc., 848 F.Supp. 287, 294 (D.Mass.1994); id. at 291 (noting that this amount equalled the company's gross sales of the unlawful products); Barbara Carton, Bard Former Executives Are Convicted of Concealing Data on Heart Catheters, Wall St. J., Aug. 25, 1995, at B2. The FDA also can seek civil penalties for the unlawful distribution of prescription drug samples, 21 U.S.C. § 333(b), and for statutory violations by manufacturers of radiation-emitting products, id. § 360pp(b).

3. *Recalls.* Contrary to *Superpharm,* the *Universal Management* opinion hinted that courts also might use their equitable powers to order recalls, and a few lower courts had previously so concluded. See United States v. K–N Enters., Inc., 461 F.Supp. 988, 990–91 (N.D.Ill.1978); United States v. X–Otag Plus Tablets, 441 F.Supp. 105, 115 (D.Colo.1977), aff'd on other grounds, 602 F.2d 1387, 1391 (10th Cir.1979). In 1990, Congress amended the statute to authorize device recalls and other special forms of relief (such as administrative detention) against medical device manufacturers. See Safe Medical Devices Act, Pub. L. No. 101–629, § 8, 104 Stat. 4520 (codified at 21 U.S.C. § 360h(e)). Whether voluntary or mandatory, recalls of medical devices can raise some unusual issues not encountered with pharmaceutical products, particularly when dealing with implants. See Kenneth Chang, When Medical Devices Fail in the Body, N.Y. Times, Aug. 7, 2001, at D1 (describing the possible need to explant part of a hip prosthesis received by thousands of patients because of a flaw discovered in the manufacturing process that left an undetectable residue of machine lubricant that would interfere with fusion to the bone); see also Lawrence K. Altman & Denise Grady, Hospital Says a Faulty Recall May Have Put 400 in Danger, N.Y. Times, Mar. 5, 2002, at A1 (describing shortcomings in efforts to recall defective bronchoscopes).

John D. Copanos & Sons, Inc. v. FDA

854 F.2d 510 (D.C.Cir.1988).

■ GINSBURG, D., CIRCUIT JUDGE:

John D. Copanos & Sons, Inc., and Kanasco, Ltd., affiliated enterprises owned by John D. Copanos (hereinafter referred to collectively as Kanasco), manufacture and distribute human and veterinary drugs, including, until recently, a number of sterile injectable products. These injectable drugs were produced pursuant to a number of New Drug Applications (NDAs) and New Animal Drug Applications (NADAs) approved by the respondent Food and Drug Administration (FDA). On March 10, 1987, the FDA published a Notice of Opportunity for a Hearing (NOOH) in the *Federal Register*, proposing to withdraw Kanasco's NDAs and NADAs for sterile injectable products on the ground that the methods, facilities, and controls used to produce these drugs were inadequate to assure their identity, strength, quality, and purity. Kanasco responded to this Notice, and requested a hearing, but on August 6, 1987, the agency denied the hearing and summarily withdrew its approval of the company's applications, effectively barring Kanasco from producing the subject drugs. * * *

[The FDCA] establishes procedures whereby the FDA, "after due notice and opportunity for hearing to the applicant," can withdraw its prior approval. One of the statutory grounds for such withdrawal is that:

> the Secretary finds ... that on the basis of new information before him, evaluated together with the evidence before him when the application was approved, the methods used in, or the facilities and controls used for, the manufacture, processing and packing of such drug are inadequate to assure and preserve its identity, strength, quality, and purity and were not made adequate within a reasonable time after receipt of written notice from the Secretary specifying the matter complained of.

21 U.S.C. § 355(e) (NDAs); id. § 360b(e)(2)(B) (NADAs). The standards for determining whether a manufacturer's "methods[,] ... facilities and controls" are adequate "to assure and preserve [the] identity, strength, quality and purity" of its drugs are set forth in the FDA's "Current Good Manufacturing Practice" (CGMP) regulations. See 21 C.F.R. Part 211. Those regulations govern numerous aspects of the manufacturing process, including (1) the qualifications and responsibilities of personnel; (2) standards for the design and construction of buildings, facilities, and equip-

ment; (3) laboratory controls; and (4) requirements for record keeping, packaging and labeling. Drugs produced in violation of these CGMP regulations are deemed to be adulterated without the agency having to show that they are actually contaminated. 21 U.S.C. § 351(a)(2)(B).

FDA has rarely withdrawn its approval of an application for failure to comply with CGMP. Indeed, Kanasco maintains, without contradiction by the agency, that the only previous withdrawal actions based on this ground were uncontested and involved animal feed applications. * * *

From late August through early October 1984, the FDA conducted a CGMP inspection of Kanasco's oral dosage form manufacturing facility. This inspection revealed numerous deficiencies in the company's manufacturing and quality control procedures, including inaccurate and even falsified manufacturing records, failure to calibrate laboratory equipment, unsanitary conditions in the manufacturing area, and production of a subpotent and impure animal drug. At the conclusion of the inspection, the FDA left with the company a Form FDA–483 listing the deficiencies noted in the inspection. See 21 U.S.C. § 374(b).

Based on the results of this inspection, the United States sought to enjoin Kanasco from the further manufacture and shipment of pharmaceuticals. The complaint and the accompanying exhibits described in detail the CGMP deficiencies revealed in the August–October inspection, noting, in particular, that "[t]here is not an adequate number of qualified personnel to perform and supervise the manufacture, processing, packing, labeling, and holding of each product." Rather than contesting the allegations in this complaint, on November 2, 1984, Kanasco agreed that it would not manufacture or ship any drugs without the prior written authorization of the FDA, and the government dismissed the complaint without prejudice. In late November, Kanasco responded by letter to the observations in the Form FDA–483. This letter, for the most part, acknowledged the alleged deficiencies and promised corrective measures in the future. In January 1985, a consultant employed by Kanasco informed the FDA that the firm's injectable drug manufacturing operation was in compliance with CGMP.

In February and March 1985, the FDA returned to Kanasco to verify the consultant's assessment. Inspection of the facility once again revealed a variety of alleged deficiencies. * * * Kanasco again replied to the Form FDA–483 by letter, acknowledging the alleged deficiencies, disputing some of the agency's conclusions but promising improvements in the areas identified by the inspector. * * *

In May 1985, the FDA once again returned to Kanasco to evaluate the results of the company's recent media fills.* The FDA judged these tests unsatisfactory * * * * Then, in the summer of 1985, the FDA learned that, between January and June 1985, Kanasco had manufactured 23 lots—over

---

* [As the court explained: "A media fill is a test procedure in which product containers are filled with sterile growth media, run through the normal production procedures, incubated, and then examined for contamination; lack of contamination provides evidence that the filling process has been 'validated.'"]

one million vials—of injectable veterinary drugs, in violation of the 1984 Agreement. (FDA had authorized Kanasco to manufacture one batch of injectable product solely in order to test its manufacturing process.) Several thousand vials had been shipped to customers without FDA approval. In addition, the company withheld records that would have revealed the shipments.

In July 1985, FDA officials visited Kanasco to monitor the company's media fills. The Form FDA–483 prepared after this visit noted that flexible tubing had not been properly stored or sterilized, and that personnel in the aseptic fill room had touched exposed portions of their faces with gloved hands and reached across a conveyor holding previously sterilized bottles.

In the wake of these events, the government filed a second complaint for injunctive relief in the district court on August 7, 1985. On August 13, FDA returned to the company with a criminal search warrant. Based on this search, the FDA concluded that Kanasco had committed further violations of the CGMP record keeping requirements * * * *

On September 5, the district court by consent entered an interim order prohibiting Kanasco from making or distributing injectable drugs without prior judicial authorization. The court later ordered Kanasco to show cause why a permanent injunction should not be entered against it. Instead, however, on November 4, Kanasco agreed to a "Consent Decree of Permanent Injunction." Like the 1984 Agreement, the 1985 Decree prohibited the company from distributing any injectable drugs manufactured at its plant until the facility was operated and administered in accordance with CGMP. The Decree also required Kanasco to obtain the FDA's written approval of any personnel with supervisory responsibility to the manufacture of drugs. On the same day, the FDA authorized Kanasco to resume manufacturing injectable drugs "based upon the certification of [Kanasco's consultant that its manufacturing plants] appear to be in compliance with [CGMP]" as required by the Consent Decree. Three weeks later, however, an FDA inspection to verify the consultant's representations once again revealed potential violations of CGMP * * * *

On December 12, 1985, the FDA again sought a court order requiring Kanasco to cease the manufacture of all injectable drugs. Kanasco once again persuaded the agency, however, that the noted deficiencies had been, or would be, corrected. The FDA, again without conducting an on-site inspection, authorized the company to resume manufacturing and shipping injectable drugs, and so notified the court.

Ten months passed without incident—or inspection. When the FDA reinspected Kanasco's manufacturing facility in September 1986, it noted numerous potential violations of CGMP * * * * Kanasco's written response to the FDA's Form FDA–483 disputed a number of the agency's conclusions, particularly the determination that facilities and equipment were unvalidated. Kanasco nonetheless promised a number of improvements. The government again moved to enforce the 1985 Consent Decree. The court first temporarily enjoined Kanasco from manufacturing and shipping injectable drugs, and then by consent made the injunction permanent.

In December 1986 and January 1987, in an attempt to persuade the agency to allow its facility to reopen, Kanasco submitted to the FDA validation data relating to recent media fills. In February 1987, the FDA visited the Kanasco facility to collect data related to the recent submissions and to interview supervisory personnel. During its visits, the FDA encountered both new and familiar problems * * * *

Its patience finally exhausted, the FDA published a notice in the *Federal Register* on March 10, 1987, proposing to withdraw Kanasco's NDAs and NADAs for sterile injectable products. Seven of the NOOH's eight pages consisted of a "Regulatory History of Kanasco," recounting the above-stated chronology in greater detail. * * * * The NOOH required Kanasco, if it wanted a hearing, to submit "the data, information, and analyses relied on to justify a hearing, as specified in 21 C.F.R. § 312.200," and noted that the same regulation would govern any subsequent proceedings. The notice also warned that "[a] request for a hearing may not rest upon mere allegations or denials, but must present specific facts showing that there is a genuine and substantial issue of fact that requires a hearing." Failing that, "the Commissioner of Food and Drugs will enter summary judgment against the person(s) who request the hearing, making findings and conclusions, and denying a hearing."

Kanasco both requested a hearing and moved for summary judgment. The hearing request included a number of declarations and other exhibits that, according to the company, demonstrated that it was in compliance with CGMP and that it was committed to maintaining such compliance. The motion for summary judgment was based on the argument that the agency had not complied with the requirements in 21 U.S.C. §§ 355(e) and 360b(e)(2)(B) that it provide Kanasco with proper written notice "specifying the matter complained of" and "a reasonable time after receipt of written notice" within which to make adequate any deficiencies. By a Notice published August 6, 1987, the FDA denied both the hearing request and the motion for summary judgment, and ordered that Kanasco's NDAs and NADAs be withdrawn from the market. See 52 Fed. Reg. 29,274. * * *

Section 355(e) of 21 U.S.C., which governs the withdrawal of NDA approvals, requires the FDA to provide "due notice and opportunity for hearing to the applicant." It is well settled that this provision does not guarantee the applicant a hearing in all circumstances; the agency may by regulation provide for summary withdrawal of approvals when there is no "genuine and substantial issue of fact that requires a hearing." See 21 C.F.R. § 314.200(g); Weinberger v. Hynson, Westcott & Dunning, 412 U.S. 609, 621 (1973) ("[W]e cannot impute to Congress the design of requiring, nor does due process demand, a hearing when it appears conclusively from the applicant's 'pleadings' that the application cannot succeed."). * * *

Before 1962, NDAs were approved upon a showing that a drug was "safe." The 1962 amendments to the FDC Act directed the FDA to withdraw approval of an NDA if "there is a lack of substantial evidence" that the drug is also effective for its intended use. See Drug Amendments of 1962, Pub. L. No. 87–781, § 102(e), 76 Stat. 782. The amendments defined "substantial evidence" as "consisting of adequate and well-controlled investigations, including clinical investigations, by experts qualified by scientific training and experience to evaluate the effectiveness of the drug involved." Id. § 102(d) (codified as amended at 21 U.S.C. § 355(d)).

As a result of these amendments, the FDA was required to reevaluate more than 4000 outstanding NDAs for substantial evidence that the covered drugs were "effective." For help with this task, the FDA retained the National Academy of Sciences–National Research Council (NAS–NRC), which created expert panels to review the efficacy of all approved drugs. Holders of NDAs were invited to submit to the panels any data substantiating the efficacy of their drugs. If the FDA adopted the panel's conclusion that a particular drug had not been shown to be "effective," it would publish a notice indicating its intention to withdraw approval of the NDA, and offering the applicant the opportunity for a prior hearing. In order to avoid a large number of unnecessary proceedings, however, the FDA issued regulations establishing minimal standards for what it would accept as "adequate and well-controlled investigations" and limiting the right to a hearing to those applicants who could proffer at least some evidence meeting those standards. The agency's regulations provided that

> when it clearly appears from the data in the application and from the reasons and factual analysis in the request for the hearing that there is no genuine and substantial issue of fact which precludes . . . the withdrawal of approval of the application, . . . the Commissioner will enter an order on this data, making findings and conclusions on such data.

21 C.F.R. § 130.14(b) (1971).

In *Hynson*, the Supreme Court found that this administrative summary judgment procedure satisfied the Act's requirement of "due notice and opportunity for hearing" because the agency's regulations had reduced the statutory standard to "detailed guidelines," 412 U.S. at 617, giving "[t]he drug manufacturers . . . full and precise notice of the evidence they must present to sustain their NDAs," id. at 622, while making it possible for the agency to discern "at the threshold" whether the applicant had tendered any evidence which on its face met the statutory standards. Id. at 620. In a footnote, which Kanasco emphasizes, the court noted that summary judgment might not be appropriate if the agency's regulations were not "precise" but called for "the exercise of discretion or subjective judgment," such that it "may not be possible to tell from the face of a [submission] whether the standards have been met." Id. at 621 n.17.

We have not read *Hynson* to hold, however, that precise regulations specifying the type of evidence necessary to justify a hearing are a prerequisite to due notice whenever the agency is contemplating summary action. The requirements of "due notice" must depend upon the context of the agency's action. In *Hynson*, for example, the 1962 amendments to the Act placed on applicants the burden of producing "adequate and well-controlled investigations" demonstrating efficacy in order to retain their FDA approval. The success, vel non, of the applicant's submission therefore turned upon the types of evidence that would satisfy the statutory standard of "adequate and well-controlled." The agency's notice indicating its intent to withdraw approval, however, generally failed to explain why the information provided to the NAS–NRC panel did not meet this standard. See, e.g., USV Pharm. Corp. v. HEW, 466 F.2d 455, 461 (D.C.Cir.1972) (NAS–NRC reports upon which FDA notice relied were "cryptic and conclusory, without any statement of supporting facts"). Under those circumstances, particularized regulations were necessary to provide the applicant with notice of what its submission must contain in order to warrant continued authorization to market a drug.

By contrast, the petitioners here were not confronted with any significant ambiguity regarding the type of information that would warrant a hearing before the agency. The NOOH discussed in detail the facts and evidence that formed the basis for the agency's proposed withdrawal of approval. Read in conjunction with the record of prior proceedings and the CGMP regulations, this document provided adequate notice of the type of information that Kanasco would have to submit in order to command a hearing. To take but one example, the NOOH alleged that Kanasco manufactured a drug product for human use that was required to be penicillin-free in the same area and with the same equipment used to make products containing penicillin. See 52 Fed. Reg. at 7315; see also 21 C.F.R. § 211.42(d) ("Operations relating to the manufacture, processing, and packing of penicillin shall be performed in facilities separate from those used for other drug products for human use."). Due notice of the basis for the agency's action would hardly require the FDA to specify, in regulations or in the NOOH, what types of evidence Kanasco needed to submit to raise a material issue of fact about this allegation. The answer is self-evident: any competent evidence (e.g., affidavits or documentary exhibits) to the effect that (1) Kanasco did not in fact manufacture penicillin products using equipment also used for non-penicillin products; or (2) that the deficiency had been remedied within a reasonable time after receipt of written notice of the violation from the Secretary or his designee. We do not mean to suggest, of course, that an action withdrawing an NDA on CGMP grounds can never raise a genuine issue regarding the type of evidence that would be responsive. When the sorts of evidence that would be responsive appear to be obvious, however, as in this case, we think it is incumbent upon the petitioner to demonstrate how it was prejudiced by the lack of specific instructions telling it what to produce. Because Kanasco has failed to identify any evidence, or type of evidence, that it might have presented but for lack of notice as to its relevance, we reject the company's claim to any more specific notice than it received. * * *

The CGMP regulations on which the FDA based its withdrawal order in this case are "imprecise" in various places. See, e.g., 21 C.F.R. § 211.67 (equipment and utensils to be cleaned, maintained, and sanitized at "appropriate intervals"); id. § 211.25(a) (each employee to have the "education, training, and experience, or any combination thereof, to enable that person to perform the assigned functions"); id. § 211.46(b) (requiring equipment to assure "adequate control over air pressure" when "appropriate"). Moreover, the agency's "particularization" of these general standards has been explicitly challenged by Kanasco in a number of instances where Kanasco's non-compliance with the regulation's requirements cannot fairly be described as "manifest." There are, therefore, several "issues of fact" that are genuinely in dispute. * * * [But,] in order to warrant a hearing, it is not sufficient that Kanasco's submission raised questions of fact regarding some of the CGMP violations described in the agency's NOOH. Instead, that submission must raise a genuine issue about whether Kanasco is (1) in compliance with CGMP; and (2) corrected deficiencies within a "reasonable" time of their being brought to its attention. Kanasco's request for a hearing failed to make this showing. Turning to the second issue first, the record documents numerous instances where obvious or undisputed violations of CGMP were allowed to persist long after Kanasco had received appropriate notice from the FDA. * * * [In addition,] Kanasco failed to contest a number of "current" deficiencies noted by the FDA in its NOOH, and thus, has not shown that it brought itself, even temporarily, into compliance with CGMP. * * *

To demonstrate that it raised material issues of fact regarding these allegations, Kanasco points first to more than 1,000 pages of data documenting the numerous media fills it performed in October 1986. According to Kanasco, these data, which were incorporated by reference in its Request for Hearing, show that its manufacturing systems were properly validated. We note, however, that the agency's NOOH listed numerous methodological deficiencies in these validation data, including failure to mimic worst case, or even normal, production conditions, unexplained discrepancies regarding the order in which various procedures were alleged to have been performed, and missing raw data. The FDA further alleged that Kanasco had failed to validate a number of individual subsystems. Kanasco failed to respond to these specific allegations in its Request for Hearing. Instead, Kanasco offered only the general and unsupported statements of its experts to the effect that Kanasco's systems had in fact been validated. Because these statements fail to address the specific problems identified by the FDA, they do not create a genuine issue of fact.

Moreover, even if Kanasco's submission did create an issue of fact on the validation question, it would not be material since the company failed entirely to respond to a number of other allegations in the NOOH, including the failure to protect equipment during renovation of its plant, and the failure to store sterile containers in an appropriately classified environment. * * * In sum, the record demonstrates that in several respects Kanasco's methods, facilities and controls were "inadequate and were not made adequate within a reasonable time after receipt of written notice specifying the matter complained of." 52 Fed. Reg. at 29,307. The FDA was therefore entitled to withdraw Kanasco's NDAs and NADAs for injectable drugs without holding a hearing. * * *

NOTES AND QUESTIONS

1. *The regulatory dance.* The opinions in *Alcon, Universal,* and *Copanos* illustrate the difficulties that the FDA may encounter when attempting to enforce the statute. First, it must discover violations. For the most part, the agency's power to conduct inspections of drug and device establishments is well settled. See United States v. Jamieson–McKames Pharm., Inc., 651 F.2d 532, 536–40 (8th Cir.1981); Daniel H. White, Annotation, Validity of Inspection Conducted Under Provisions of the Federal Food, Drug, and Cosmetic Act (21 U.S.C. § 374(a)) Authorizing FDA Inspectors to Enter and Inspect Food, Drug, or Cosmetic Factory, Warehouse, or Other Establishment, 18 A.L.R. Fed. 734 (1974 & 2002 Supp.). The FDA's assertion of records inspection authority sometimes generates controversy. See In re Establishment Inspection Portex, Inc., 595 F.2d 84, 85–87 (1st Cir.1979); In re Establishment Inspection of Medtronic, Inc., 500 F.Supp. 536, 538–40 (D.Minn.1980). Resource constraints present a more serious obstacle to monitoring for compliance. Second, the FDA and the regulated entity usually both prefer resolving identified deficiencies through informal mechanisms. In some situations, however, a company will disagree with the agency's charge of noncompliance or simply wants to stall. Third, when the FDA decides that it must impose sanctions, it has to abide by various formal procedures that may consume significant time and energy, hence it will often look for short-cuts such as the summary judgment method discussed in *Copanos.* Overall FDA enforcement statistics for Fiscal Year 1999 (though not limited to drugs and devices) reveal the following:

Total inspections	15,161
Violations found	1,589
Warning letters issued	1,589
Recalls (inc. voluntary)	3,736
Seizures	25
Injunctions	8
Criminal prosecutions	373

Tamar Nordenberg, FDA Takes Action to Enforce the Law, FDA Consumer, May–June 2000, at 7; see also Mary Olson, Substitution in Regulatory Agencies: FDA Enforcement Alternatives, 12 J.L. Econ. & Org. 376, 404 (1996) (observing that, between 1972 and 1992, "budget reductions and increasing applications for product approval . . . led the agency to reduce its monitoring of FDA-regulated industries and to substitute less resource-intensive enforcement actions"); Mary K. Olson, Agency Rulemaking, Political Influences, Regulation, and Industry Compliance, 15 J.L. Econ. & Org. 573 (1999) (noting a decline in FDA inspections coupled with an increase in reported infractions); Marie A. Urban, The FDA's Policy on Seizures, Injunctions, Civil Fines, and Recalls, 47 Food & Drug L.J. 411 (1992).

2. *Enforcement discretion.* In *Heckler v. Chaney,* 470 U.S. 821 (1985), the Supreme Court rejected an effort by a group of death row inmates to force the FDA to take enforcement action against the use of lethal injection drugs because of alleged misbranding and new drug approval violations.

The Court held that agency nonenforcement decisions are presumptively unsuitable for judicial review:

> First, an agency decision not to enforce often involves a complicated balancing of a number of factors which are peculiarly within its expertise. Thus, the agency must not only assess whether a violation has occurred, but whether agency resources are best spent on this violation or another, whether the agency is likely to succeed if it acts, whether the particular enforcement action requested best fits the agency's overall policies, and, indeed, whether the agency has enough resources to undertake the action at all. An agency generally cannot act against each technical violation of the statute it is charged with enforcing. The agency is far better equipped than the courts to deal with the many variables involved in the proper ordering of its priorities.... The Act's enforcement provisions commit complete discretion to the Secretary to decide how and when they should be exercised.

Id. at 831–32; cf. Heterochemical Corp. v. FDA, 644 F.Supp. 271, 274–76 (E.D.N.Y.1986) (holding that the agency was not entirely free to decline enforcement action against companies that it had already found in violation of statute). Enforcement discretion does not, however, permit the FDA to treat similarly-situated products or persons differently. See United States v. Diapulse Corp. of Am., 748 F.2d 56, 61–62 (2d Cir.1984); Rhodia, Inc. v. FDA, 608 F.2d 1376, 1379 (D.C.Cir.1979); Bracco Diagnostics, Inc. v. Shalala, 963 F.Supp. 20, 28 (D.D.C.1997); United States v. Undetermined Quantities ... Exachol, 716 F.Supp. 787, 795 (S.D.N.Y.1989). But cf. United States v. Sage Pharm., Inc., 210 F.3d 475, 480 (5th Cir.2000) (holding that the FDA could target one firm for selling unapproved new drugs even though it had not yet acted against others who distributed substantially similar products).

3. *License withdrawal.* In *Copanos*, the FDA withdrew the companies' product licenses. As the court notes, the agency rarely does so to sanction noncompliance (the withdrawal of a license is more draconian than an injunction). The withdrawal of an NDA normally entails lengthy procedures. See Warner–Lambert Co. v. Heckler, 787 F.2d 147, 152, 162–63 (3d Cir.1986). How else might it have sanctioned a firm violating the statute (or what would it do next if Kanasco continued selling its now unapproved new drug products)?

United States v. Dotterweich

320 U.S. 277 (1943).

■ FRANKFURTER, JUSTICE:

This was a prosecution begun by two informations, consolidated for trial, charging Buffalo Pharmacal Company, Inc., and Dotterweich, its president and general manager, with violations of [the FDCA] * * * * Three counts went to the jury—two, for shipping misbranded drugs in interstate commerce, and a third, for so shipping an adulterated drug. The jury disagreed as to the corporation and found Dotterweich guilty on all three counts. * * *

The Food and Drugs Act of 1906 was an exertion by Congress of its power to keep impure and adulterated food and drugs out of the channels of commerce. By the Act of 1938, Congress extended the range of its control over illicit and noxious articles and stiffened the penalties for disobedience. The purposes of this legislation thus touch phases of the lives and health of people which, in the circumstances of modern industrialism, are largely beyond self-protection. Regard for these purposes should infuse construction of the legislation if it is to be treated as a working instrument of government and not merely as a collection of English words. The prosecution to which Dotterweich was subjected is based on a now familiar type of legislation whereby penalties serve as effective means of regulation. Such legislation dispenses with the conventional requirement for criminal conduct—awareness of some wrongdoing. * * *

If the 1938 Act were construed as it was below, the penalties of the law could be imposed only in the rare case where the corporation is merely an individual's alter ego. Corporations carrying on an illicit trade would be subject only to what the House Committee described as a "license fee for the conduct of an illegitimate business." A corporate officer, who even with "intent to defraud or mislead," introduced adulterated or misbranded drugs into interstate commerce could not be held culpable for conduct which was indubitably outlawed by the 1906 Act. This argument proves too much. It is not credible that Congress should by implication have exonerated what is probably a preponderant number of persons involved in acts of disobedience—for the number of non-corporate proprietors is relatively small. * * *

Hardship there doubtless may be under a statute which thus penalizes the transaction though consciousness of wrongdoing be totally wanting. Balancing relative hardships, Congress has preferred to place it upon those who have at least the opportunity of informing themselves of the existence of conditions imposed for the protection of consumers before sharing in illicit commerce, rather than to throw the hazard on the innocent public who are wholly helpless.

It would be too treacherous to define or even to indicate by way of illustration the class of employees which stands in such a responsible relation. To attempt a formula embracing the variety of conduct whereby persons may responsibly contribute in furthering a transaction forbidden by an Act of Congress, to wit, to send illicit goods across state lines, would be mischievous futility. In such matters the good sense of prosecutors, the wise guidance of trial judges, and the ultimate judgment of juries must be trusted. * * * For present purpose it suffices to say that in what the defense characterized as "a very fair charge" the district court properly left the question of the responsibility of Dotterweich for the shipment to the jury, and there was sufficient evidence to support its verdict.

■ MURPHY, JUSTICE (dissenting):

Our prime concern in this case is whether the criminal sanctions of the Federal Food, Drug, and Cosmetic Act of 1938 plainly and unmistakably apply to the respondent in his capacity as a corporate officer. He is charged with violating § 301(a) of the Act, which prohibits the introduction or delivery for introduction into interstate commerce of any adulterated or misbranded drug. There is no evidence in this case of any personal guilt on the part of the respondent. There is no proof or claim that he ever knew of the introduction into commerce of the adulterated drugs in question, much less that he actively participated in their introduction. Guilt is imputed to the respondent solely on the basis of his authority and responsibility as president and general manager of the corporation.

It is a fundamental principle of Anglo–Saxon jurisprudence that guilt is personal and that it ought not lightly to be imputed to a citizen who, like the respondent, has no evil intention or consciousness of wrongdoing. It may be proper to charge him with responsibility to the corporation and the stockholders for negligence and mismanagement. But in the absence of clear statutory authorization it is inconsistent with established canons of criminal law to rest liability on an act in which the accused did not participate and of which he had no personal knowledge. * * *

Moreover, the fact that individual liability of corporate officers may be consistent with the policy and purpose of a public health and welfare measure does not authorize this Court to impose such liability where Congress has not clearly intended or actually done so. Congress alone has the power to define a crime and to specify the offenders. It is not our function to supply any deficiencies in these respects, no matter how grave the consequences. Statutory policy and purpose are not constitutional substitutes for the requirement that the legislature specify with reasonable certainty those individuals it desires to place under the interdict of the Act.

Looking at the language actually used in this statute, we find a complete absence of any reference to corporate officers. There is merely a provision in § 303(a) to the effect that "any person" inadvertently violating § 301(a) shall be guilty of a misdemeanor. Section 201(e) further defines "person" as including an "individual, partnership, corporation, and association." The fact that a corporate officer is both a "person" and an "individual" is not indicative of an intent to place vicarious liability on the officer. Such words must be read in light of their statutory environment. Only if Congress has otherwise specified an intent to place corporate officers within the ambit of the Act can they be said to be embraced within the meaning of the words "person" or "individual" as here used.

Nor does the clear imposition of liability on corporations reveal the necessary intent to place criminal sanctions on their officers. A corporation is not the necessary and inevitable equivalent of its officers for all purposes. In many respects it is desirable to distinguish the latter from the corporate entity and to impose liability only on the corporation. In this respect it is significant that this Court has never held the imposition of liability on a corporation sufficient, without more, to extend liability to its officers who have no consciousness of wrongdoing. * * *

This fatal hiatus in the Act is further emphasized by the ability of Congress, demonstrated on many occasions, to apply statutes in no uncertain terms to corporate officers as distinct from corporations. The failure to mention officers specifically is thus some indication of a desire to exempt them from liability. In fact the history of federal food and drug legislation is itself illustrative of this capacity for specification and lends strong support to the conclusion that Congress did not intend to impose liability on corporate officers in this particular Act. * * *

[T]he framers of the 1938 Act had an intelligent comprehension of the inadequacies of the 1906 Act and of the unsettled state of the law. They recognized the necessity of inserting clear and unmistakable language in order to impose liability on corporate officers. It is thus unreasonable to assume that the omission of such language was due to a belief that the Act as it now stands was sufficient to impose liability on corporate officers. Such deliberate deletion is consistent only with an intent to allow such officers to remain free from criminal liability. Thus to apply the sanctions of this Act to the respondent would be contrary to the intent of Congress as expressed in the statutory language and in the legislative history.

The dangers inherent in any attempt to create liability without express congressional intention or authorization are illustrated by this case. Without any legislative guides, we are confronted with the problem of determining precisely which officers, employees and agents of a corporation are to be subject to this Act by our fiat. To erect standards of responsibility is a difficult legislative task and the opinion of this Court admits that it is "too treacherous" and a "mischievous futility" for us to engage in such pursuits. But the only alternative is a blind resort to "the good sense of prosecutors, the wise guidance of trial judges, and the ultimate judgment of juries." Yet that situation is precisely what our constitutional system sought to avoid. Reliance on the legislature to define crimes and criminals distinguishes our form of jurisprudence from certain less desirable ones. The legislative power to restrain the liberty and to imperil the good reputation of citizens must not rest upon the variable attitudes and opinions of those charged with the duties of interpreting and enforcing the mandates of the law.

NOTES AND QUESTIONS

1. *Strict criminal liability.* The Court in *Dotterweich* had split 5–4. In a subsequent case involving adulterated food, the Supreme Court reiterated its holding that the FDCA imposed strict criminal liability. See United States v. Park, 421 U.S. 658, 670–73 (1975) (conceding, however, that the defendant can claim that he or she was powerless to prevent or correct the alleged violation). Lower courts continue to uphold misdemeanor convictions of persons accused of violating the FDCA even though they lacked any criminal intent. See United States v. Torigian Labs., Inc., 577 F.Supp. 1514, 1529–31 (E.D.N.Y.), aff'd mem., 751 F.2d 373 (2d Cir.1984); see also United States v. Hodges X–Ray, Inc., 759 F.2d 557, 560–61 (6th Cir.1985) (extending this standard to another statute enforced by the FDA). But cf. United States v. Smith, 740 F.2d 734, 737–39 (9th Cir.1984) (affirming the dismissal of an indictment against clinical investigators for failing to maintain accurate records because the statutory provision authorizing the FDA to require recordkeeping by sponsors of clinical trials did not clearly apply to researchers).

2. *Misdemeanor penalties.* The statute calls for no more than one year in prison and/or a $1,000 fine in such cases. See 21 U.S.C. § 333(a)(1). Note, however, that caps on the sanctions available under the Act refer to individual transgressions and may cumulate. See V.E. Irons, Inc. v. United States, 244 F.2d 34, 45–46 (1st Cir.1957). Furthermore, sentencing reform legislation has dramatically raised the maximum fines for these and other federal crimes. See 18 U.S.C. § 3571. Thus, Genentech recently agreed to pay $50 million as part of a plea agreement to settle criminal charges that it had unlawfully promoted its human growth hormone product for unapproved uses. See Firm Fined for Improperly Promoting Drug, L.A. Times, Apr. 15, 1999, at C2; see also Melody Petersen, American Home to Pay U.S. for Production Violations, N.Y. Times, Oct. 4, 2000, at C18 (reporting that a vaccine manufacturer agreed to pay $30 million in fines for GMP violations).

3. *Felony for violations committed with an intent to defraud or mislead.* Courts uphold felony convictions of persons accused of violating the FDCA with criminal intent. See United States v. Haas, 171 F.3d 259, 265–67 (5th Cir.1999); United States v. Arlen, 947 F.2d 139, 142–44 (5th Cir.1991); United States v. Hiland, 909 F.2d 1114, 1127–31 (8th Cir.1990); see also United States v. Mitcheltree, 940 F.2d 1329, 1345–52 (10th Cir.1991) (reversing conviction for lack of sufficient evidence of specific intent to defraud). The statute calls for no more than three years in prison and/or a $10,000 fine in such cases. See 21 U.S.C. § 333(a)(2); see also Ruben Castaneda, Firm to Pay $33 Million in Defrauding of FDA, Wash. Post, Oct. 20, 2001, at B3. In addition, persons who willfully violate an FDA injunction may face criminal contempt sanctions. See United States v. Themy–Kotronakis, 140 F.3d 858, 861–64 (10th Cir.1998). Federal prosecutors also may bring charges against drug and device firms under general criminal statutes prohibiting false reports and conspiracies. See United States v. Serian, 895 F.2d 432 (8th Cir.1990); United States v. Automated Med. Labs., Inc., 770 F.2d 399, 400 (4th Cir.1985).

4. *Debarment.* In 1992, after a scandal involving bribes of FDA officials reviewing applications for the approval of generic drugs, Congress required that the agency permanently debar anyone convicted of a felony related to federal regulation of drug products from thereafter "providing services in any capacity to a person that has an approved or pending drug product application." 21 U.S.C. § 335a(a)(2); see also DiCola v. FDA, 77 F.3d 504 (D.C.Cir.1996) (rejecting constitutional challenges to a debarment order); Bae v. Shalala, 44 F.3d 489 (7th Cir.1995) (same); John R. Fleder, The History, Provisions, and Implementation of the Generic Drug Enforcement Act of 1992, 49 Food & Drug L.J. 89 (1994).

5. *Further commentary.* See John Braithwaite, Corporate Crime in the Pharmaceutical Industry (1984); John R. Fleder, The Role of the Department of Justice in Enforcement Matters Relating to the Food and Drug Administration, 46 Food Drug Cosm. L.J. 781 (1991); Dana H. Freyer, Corporate Compliance Programs for FDA–Regulated Companies: Incentives for Their Development and the Impact of the Federal Sentencing Guidelines for Organizations, 51 Food & Drug L.J. 225 (1996); Jeffrey S. Huang & Steven G. Rappaport, Survey, Federal Food and Drug Act Violations, 37 Am. Crim. L. Rev. 529 (2000).

2.   RULEMAKING

National Association of Pharmaceutical Mfrs. v. FDA

637 F.2d 877 (2d Cir.1981).

■ FRIENDLY, CIRCUIT JUDGE:

In 1962 Congress enacted various amendments to the Federal Food, Drug, and Cosmetic Act of 1938, to "strengthen and broaden existing laws in the drug field so as to bring about better, safer medicine and to establish a more effective system of enforcement of the drug laws." S. Rep. No. 1744, 87th Cong., 2d Sess. 8 (1962). Among the amendments was a section by which a drug is deemed adulterated if its packaging, processing, holding or manufacturing fail to conform to "current good manufacturing practice (CGMP) to assure that such drug meets the requirements of this chapter as to safety and has the identity and strength, and meets the quality and purity characteristics, which it purports or is represented to possess." 21 U.S.C. § 351(a)(2)(B). The Food and Drug Administration (FDA) issued its first regulations under this section in 1963. In February 1976, FDA announced a proposal to revise and update the then current CGMP regulations. * * *

The FDA received numerous comments both upon the substance of its requirements and upon its proposal that the new CGMP regulations should have the force of law. In an extensive preamble to the new regulations it set forth a legal analysis supporting its view that it had power to issue binding regulations and the reasons why it believed binding rather than merely interpretive regulations would be in the public interest. The regulations, now appearing at 21 C.F.R. Parts 210 and 211 (1980), were published on September 29, 1978, to be effective March 28, 1979. They cover a broad spectrum of affairs, including requirements for personnel practices, record keeping, building design, and procedures for the control of drug production, packaging and labeling. * * *

[T]he National Association of Pharmaceutical Manufacturers and the National Pharmaceutical Alliance, both trade associations, sought a declaration that FDA's attempt to give binding effect to the new CGMP regulations was beyond its authority. * * * Two different subsections of § 701 confer rulemaking authority upon the FDA. Section 701(a) provides:

The authority to promulgate regulations for the efficient enforcement of this chapter, except as otherwise provided in this section, is vested in the Secretary [of Health and Human Services].

The effect of § 4 of the Administrative Procedure Act of 1946 (APA), now 5 U.S.C. § 553, is to require that rulemaking under § 701(a), with certain exceptions, including "interpretative rules," follow an informal notice and comment procedure, which was done here. Section 701(e) provides that "[a]ny action for the issuance, amendment, or repeal of any regulation" under various sections of the Act of which § 501(a)(2)(B) is not one, shall follow a complex procedure which has been read to include a trial-type hearing; § 701(f) provides that review of any order resulting from such rulemaking lies in a court of appeals. See National Nutritional Foods Ass'n v. FDA, 504 F.2d 761, 771–74 (2d Cir.1974). Admittedly § 701(e) procedures were not followed here and the FDA's authority to give binding effect to the CGMP regulations at issue must rest on § 701(a).

Reading the language of that subsection, which comes from the Act of 1938, with the eyes of 1980, one would have little difficulty in concluding that the words suffice to empower the Commissioner of the FDA, to whom the Secretary has delegated his powers, 21 C.F.R. § 5.1(a)(1) (1980), to issue regulations, substantive as well as procedural, having the force of law. The comprehensive opinion of Judge J. Skelly Wright in *National Petroleum Refiners Ass'n v. FTC*, 482 F.2d 672 (D.C.Cir.1973), catalogued the many instances in which general statutory provisions not differing essentially from § 701(a) have been held to endow agencies with power to issue binding rules and regulations. In the interest of historical accuracy, it should be noted that at one time it was widely understood that generalized grants of rulemaking authority conferred power only to make rules of a procedural or an interpretative nature, and not binding substantive regulations, for which a specific delegation was thought necessary. * * * In 1953, however, the Court decided *American Trucking Ass'ns v. United States*, 344 U.S. 298, * * * [and] this generous construction of agency rulemaking authority has become firmly entrenched.

Beyond this there is formidable authority to the effect that § 701(a) itself is a grant of power to issue binding regulations. * * * [T]his court, in *National Nutritional Foods Ass'n v. Weinberger*, 512 F.2d 688, 696 (2d Cir.1975), characterized the 1973 quartet of Supreme Court decisions as having dispelled "[w]hatever doubts might have been entertained regarding the FDA's power under § 701(a) to promulgate binding regulations." The court said: "[o]ur attention has not been directed to anything in the legislative history of §§ 701(a) and (e) that militates against these conclusions," and correctly stated that "over the last decade rule-making has been increasingly substituted for adjudication as a regulatory technique, with the support and encouragement of the courts, at least where the regulation involves specialized scientific knowledge." * * * In *United States v. Nova Scotia Food Products Corp.*, 568 F.2d 240, 246–48 (2d Cir.1977), we again read the 1938 Act as authorizing the issuance of binding substantive regulations under § 701(a). * * *

NOTES AND QUESTIONS

1. *Formal vs. informal rulemaking.* FDCA § 701(e) granted the agency the authority to issue regulations governing certain subjects, but it also required that interested parties be allowed to request a public hearing as part of the rulemaking process. See Pharmaceutical Mfrs. Ass'n v. Gardner, 381 F.2d 271, 278 (D.C.Cir.1967); Annotation, Necessity of Formal Hearing Prior to Issuance of Regulations Under § 701 of the Federal Food, Drug, and Cosmetic Act, 43 A.L.R. Fed. 320 (1979 & 2002 Supp.). For instance, the FDA's power to promulgate prescription drug advertising regulations is subject to this "formal" rulemaking procedure. See 21 U.S.C. § 352(n). These procedures became a source of frustrating delays for the agency. See Robert W. Hamilton, Rulemaking on a Record by the Food and Drug Administration, 50 Tex. L. Rev. 1132, 1142 (1972) ("[T]he FDA has conducted two major [formal rulemaking] proceedings that have been the subject of wide criticism. Both proceedings have taken (or will take) more than ten years from the formulation of the original proposal to the actual effective date of the regulation."). For that reason, when the courts decided that the residual rulemaking authority in FDCA § 701(a) empowered the FDA to issue binding regulations on matters not specifically covered by § 701(e), the agency began to utilize "notice-and-comment" procedures for the promulgation of rules. The courts also, however, allowed parties to bring "pre-enforcement" challenges to such rules in some cases. See Abbott Labs. v. Gardner, 387 U.S. 136 (1967) (holding that an FDA drug labeling regulation was ripe for judicial review). Although "informal" rulemaking avoids the cumbersome hearings required with formal rulemaking, searching judicial review on the merits and increasing procedural demands added by all three branches of government have made it increasingly difficult, so the FDA and other agencies have experimented with short-cuts for issuing regulations. See Lars Noah, Doubts About Direct Final Rulemaking, 51 Admin. L. Rev. 401, 409–11 (1999) (describing the FDA's experience with one such technique, and arguing that it is unlawful). At one time, the FDA experimented with a system of underwriting public participation in its proceedings, but a court held that an agency lacked the authority to dispense public funds in this way. See Pacific Legal Found. v. Goyan, 664 F.2d 1221, 1224–27 (4th Cir.1981).

2. *Rulemaking vs. adjudication.* The FDA was one of the first federal agencies to make extensive use of its initially unclear rulemaking powers. In lieu of bringing enforcement actions under the open-ended provisions of the statute and generating adjudicatory precedent for future cases, the FDA began to promulgate more detailed rules to implement the statutory provisions. Although infractions would still require individual enforcement proceedings, the agency would simplify its burden of proof in those proceedings, which, coupled with the greater clarity of expectations, would help promote improved compliance. The FDA implemented some of its misbranding authorities in this fashion. See Pharmaceutical Mfrs. Ass'n v. FDA, 634 F.2d 106, 108 (3d Cir.1980) (per curiam) (sustaining the FDA's power to issue a regulation requiring patient package inserts warning of the risk of cancer for estrogen-containing drug products). In addition, as mentioned earlier, the agency utilized its rulemaking power to facilitate implementation of the Drug Amendments of 1962, for instance by specifying what would qualify as "substantial evidence" of effectiveness and then granting itself summary judgment whenever a manufacturer was not able to provide the requisite data from clinical trials, or by issuing monographs specifying the circumstances under which nonprescription drugs would be considered GRASE. See Charles C. Ames & Steven C. McCracken, Framing Regulatory Standards to Avoid Formal Adjudication: The FDA as a Case Study, 64 Cal. L. Rev. 14 (1976); David Selmer, Note, The FDA's Over-the-Counter Drug Review: Expeditious Enforcement by Rulemaking, 11 U. Mich. J.L. Reform 142 (1977).

3. *GMP regulations.* The implementation of the FDA's GMP authority illustrates some of the comparative advantages of rulemaking. In 1962, Congress amended the adulteration provision of the statute to impose a requirement that drug and device companies abide by good manufacturing practices. At first, the agency brought enforcement actions against firms thought to have violated this requirement, and it would have to persuade the court why a particular step in the production process failed to conform to GMPs. See United States v. Bel–Mar Labs., Inc., 284 F.Supp. 875, 882–84 (E.D.N.Y.1968). After some time, the FDA decided to issue a series of precise GMP requirements as binding regulations, which it first published as proposed rules and invited public comment. In addition to challenging the agency's statutory authority to issue any binding rules, an issue resolved in *NAPM v. FDA*, the drug industry attacked the GMP regulations on various other grounds. See National Ass'n of Pharm. Mfrs. v. HHS, 586 F.Supp. 740, 748–63 (S.D.N.Y.1984) (rejecting numerous substantive and procedural objections to these regulations). In subsequent enforcement actions, the courts would focus on questions of compliance with those precise requirements rather than on questions of whether the requirements amounted to GMPs under the statute (though some interpolation would remain necessary where the rules failed to address the precise issue in controversy):

> Current Good Manufacturing Practice (CGMP), explained in greater, but by no means sufficient, detail in regulations promulgated by the FDA, sets the minimum standards for drug manufacturers. Designed as a quality control measure to prevent super-and sub-potency, product mix-ups, contamination, and mislabeling, the CGMP regulations outline general rules for all aspects of drug manufacture including buildings and facilities, personnel, equipment, drug components and containers, production, packaging and labeling, and record-keeping. Failure to comply with CGMP regulations renders any resulting drug product "adulterated" and the drug product and its producer subject to regulatory action.

United States v. Barr Labs., Inc., 812 F.Supp. 458, 465 (D.N.J.1993); see also Freddy A. Jimenez, Enforcement of the Current Good Manufacturing Practices for Solid Oral Dosage Forms After United States v. Barr Laboratories, 52 Food & Drug L.J. 67 (1997). When the agency cites large companies for GMP violations, it may prompt compliance by delaying final approval of pending applications for any new drugs slated for manufacturing at the allegedly substandard facilities. See Melody Petersen, Faults Found at a Schering Plant, N.Y. Times, Mar. 2, 2001, at C3.

3. INFORMAL MECHANISMS

United States v. Bioclinical Systems, Inc.

666 F.Supp. 82 (D.Md.1987).

■ MOTZ, DISTRICT JUDGE:

The Government has brought this action under the Federal Food, Drug and Cosmetic Act, 21 U.S.C. § 332(a), seeking to enjoin alleged violations of the Act by Bioclinical Systems, Inc. (a manufacturer of plated culture media) * * * * [T]he FDA's April inspection identified 29 violations of the FDA's Good Manufacturing Practices (GMPs). Although they are to some extent interrelated, these violations may for present purposes be divided into two categories: those relating to Bioclinical's failure to attain a sterility assurance level (SAL) of 0.1% and those not relating to that standard. * * *

The fundamental question which divides the parties is whether or not the Compliance Office of the Division of Compliance Programs of the FDA may properly insist upon manufacturers of plated culture media meeting an SAL of 0.1%. It may not do so. Congress has mandated that a full and deliberate public process, including the making of recommendations by a broad-based advisory committee and the opportunity for public hearing, be followed before the FDA may establish a GMP. The FDA has bypassed that process here. Instead, the Office of Compliance has been imposing an 0.1% SAL as a de facto requirement during the course of its inspections since March 1986 (when a draft set of Inspectional Guidelines incorporating the standard was issued by the FDA's Center for Devices and Radiological Health).

The Government concedes that a GMP may not be properly established by adoption of a draft guideline. Rather, it argues that the 0.1% SAL constitutes a GMP independently of the draft guideline. This argument is conclusively rebutted by hard and concrete fact. A GMP must represent a "current good manufacturing process." See 21 U.S.C. § 360j(f)(1)(A). The evidence in this case is overwhelming that the in vitro diagnostic device industry (including manufacturers of plated cultural media) does not attain an 0.1% SAL. * * *

At bottom, what the Government is asserting here is that whatever the current industry practice may be, the SAL should be what the Office of Compliance dictates it to be. If the evidence demonstrated that the industry as a whole has been resisting in bad faith the adoption of a feasible good manufacturing practice in the face of a demonstrated hazard to the public health, there arguably would be merit in the Government's position. However, the evidence does not so demonstrate. Ideally, of course, plated culture media should be manufactured under sterile conditions. It may also be assumed (although the Government presented no evidence directly proving the fact) that technologically an 0.1% SAL could be met by the in vitro diagnostic device industry. However, the record does not establish that attainment of the 0.1% SAL is economically feasible. * * * More importantly, the record does not establish that the overriding interest of the public health requires the imposition of an 0.1% SAL. * * *

The question of whether or not an 0.1% SAL should be established as a GMP for the manufacture of plated culture media is not one which is within the expertise or the power of this court to resolve. However, it is equally not within the power of the FDA's Office of Compliance to impose the requirement unilaterally. Congress has specifically established the public review process which must be followed to resolve an issue of this magnitude, and it is through that process, not through enforcement actions, that the questions of public health and of technological and economic feasibility posed by the 0.1% SAL are to be decided.

Washington Legal Foundation v. Kessler

880 F.Supp. 26 (D.D.C.1995).

■ LAMBERTH, DISTRICT JUDGE:

* * * At issue in this case are activities of drug and medical device manufacturers which the FDA contends amount to improper labeling of medical products. Two practices in particular have attracted the attention of the FDA. The first involves the distribution by manufacturers to doctors of so-called "enduring materials" (such as medical journals, articles, and textbooks) which contain information regarding "off-label"[1] uses of the manufacturer's products. The distribution of enduring materials to health care professionals appears to be a common tool for manufacturers seeking to maintain good customer relations with those who purchase their products. The other practice with which the FDA has become concerned is manufacturer support of scientific or educational activities (such as medical symposia) at which off-label uses of the manufacturer's products are discussed or demonstrated. Again, sponsorship of medical symposia and the like is a common public relations practice for manufacturers of medical products.

According to WLF, the FDA has determined that each of these activities constitutes improper labeling and/or promotion when it involves the distribution of materials or sponsorship of activities in which off-label usage of one of the manufacturer's products is discussed. WLF further contends that this determination has taken the form of a specific agency

---

1. "Off-label" usage refers to the use of a drug or device in a manner not approved by the FDA and not set forth in the product's labeling materials. While manufacturers may not themselves promote such uses, it is not unlawful for doctors to employ or pre- scribe medical products for "unapproved" uses. Indeed, the FDA claims that it has "long recognized the important role that some unapproved uses may play in the practice of medicine."

policy which the FDA has been enforcing for several years against medical product manufacturers, and which it intends to continue to enforce in the future. * * * The FDA contends that so long as the agency has not released a formal policy statement or instituted an enforcement action against a manufacturer, there is no "final agency action" reviewable in this court. * * *

The FDA claims that it is in the process of revising its policies on industry-supported promotion of off-label uses of medical products. As part of this process, the FDA published a "Draft Policy Statement on Industry–Supported Scientific and Educational Activities." 57 Fed. Reg. 56,412 (1992). By its terms, this Draft Policy Statement represents a tentative agency position concerning how the FDA intends to distinguish between manufacturer-supported activities "that are otherwise independent from the promotional influence of the supporting company [and are therefore permissible] and those that are not [and therefore violate the Federal Food, Drug and Cosmetic Act]." Id. The Draft Policy Statement sets forth a number of criteria that the FDA considers useful in distinguishing between independent and impermissibly manufacturer-influenced activities. * * * The FDA maintains that the policies and procedures described in the Draft Policy Statement have not yet been adopted as official FDA policy, and that the agency is still in the process of formulating its final policy statement.

In October of 1993, plaintiff WLF filed a Citizen Petition with the FDA * * * request[ing] that the FDA formally withdraw its Draft Policy Statement * * * *

At the heart of the motion to dismiss is defendants' contention that WLF's dispute is not yet ripe for judicial review. Specifically, FDA asserts that (1) because FDA is still considering how to respond to WLF's Citizen Petition, WLF's suit is "premature"; (2) this dispute is not ripe for review, inasmuch as FDA has not adopted an official policy concerning manufacturer-supported distribution of off-label usage information; and (3) resolution of the dispute in its present posture would improvidently require the court to step into the FDA's role as a formulator of public health policy. * * *

[W]ith regard to WLF's Citizen Petition, the FDA failed to follow the procedures set forth in its own regulations whereby the agency must respond to such petitions within 180 days of receiving them. FDA did not respond to WLF's petition for 270 days, and then only several weeks after the filing of the present lawsuit. At oral argument, counsel for the defendants explained that WLF's petition had "slipped through the cracks," and that the agency's failure to respond to the petition within the 180 day time period was wholly inadvertent. The court accepts this explanation, and also agrees with FDA that the agency's failure to respond timely to WLF's petition should not itself constitute a formal denial of the petition, for purposes of determining whether there has been final agency action. At the same time, however, the FDA's handling of WLF's Citizen Petition, as well as the statements in its filings and at oral argument, evidence a somewhat less vigilant concern for the doctors' First Amendment rights than this court would hope to see. * * *

[I]n light of the two and one-half year time period that FDA estimates will be required to resolve WLF's dispute, WLF's decision to seek judicial review cannot be described as an attempt to "flout" any "established administrative process." * * * [G]iven plaintiff's allegations that FDA has not only promulgated, but has also sought to enforce (albeit somewhat informally) a final agency policy, the court doubts very much that WLF is likely to "successfully vindicate [its] claims" in an administrative proceeding before the FDA. In light of these conclusions, the court finds that WLF is not barred by the exhaustion doctrine from maintaining the present suit. * * *

FDA maintains that it has not yet adopted an official policy concerning manufacturer-supported off-label usage information, and therefore an attempt by this court to resolve the dispute at this stage would be premature and would usurp the FDA's role as a formulator of administrative policy. The court is mindful of the serious prudential concerns raised by FDA's ripeness argument. * * *

Whether FDA has officially adopted a final policy, however, is not determinative. In the context of a ripeness inquiry, it is the effect of the agency's conduct which is most important in determining whether an agency has adopted a final policy. And this case illustrates why this must be so: If an agency's own characterization of the finality of its policy were determinative, that agency could effectively regulate industry without ever exposing itself to judicial review. A powerful agency such as FDA could achieve this result through the simple expedient of (1) never formally declaring the policy to be "final," and (2) threatening (but never actually initiating) enforcement procedures against companies which failed to comply with the agency's de facto policy. Indeed, this is precisely what plaintiff has alleged.

WLF's complaint alleges that the FDA has sought to enforce a final agency policy concerning manufacturer-supported dissemination of off-label usage information. With regard to manufacturers' distribution of "enduring materials" containing such information, WLF describes a number of different instances in which representatives of the FDA sent warning letters and followed up with telephone calls to manufacturers which had planned to distribute medical textbooks and other enduring materials to doctors. * * *

In addition to sending warning letters to individual companies, high-ranking officers of the FDA are alleged to have made general remarks which plaintiff contends reveal the existence of a definitive agency position concerning off-label usage information. The Commissioner of the FDA himself, defendant David Kessler, allegedly made the following statement in June of 1991: "I would urge all members of the pharmaceutical industry to take a long hard look at their promotional practices. I do not expect companies to wait until this guidance becomes final to put their advertising and promotional houses in order." More recently, David Adams, Director of the Policy Development and Coordination Staff in Commissioner Kessler's office is alleged to have written the following statement regarding the FDA's Draft Policy Statement:

> Although this document was published as a draft policy statement with an invitation to submit comments, it reflects actual agency policy. It tells you how the agency makes decisions from day to day in determining whether activities are subject to regulation and are potentially illegal under the Food, Drug and Cosmetic Act.

Other FDA officials are alleged to have made similar comments at various times.

FDA maintains that these letters and comments do not amount to "final agency action." According to FDA, the "regulatory letters" described above merely "reflect views of particular individuals, not the institutional decision of the agency." As such, defendants argue that this "informal advice given by specific employees of FDA" should not suggest the existence of any formal agency policy. Likewise, because neither the Draft Policy Statement nor the comments of Commissioner Kessler constitute "coercive imperatives" which the FDA is bound to adhere to, these are not evidence of a final policy either, according to FDA. Unfortunately, by focusing exclusively on the individual trees, FDA appears to have lost sight of the forest. The question here is not whether any single act on the part of the FDA signifies the existence of a final agency policy; rather, the aggregate effect of these acts must be analyzed to determine whether the agency by its conduct has objectively demonstrated the existence of such a policy. * * *

Although the FDA characterizes the "regulatory letters" and other statements of FDA officials as merely "advisory," the court must not be blind to the practical effects of these letters and other statements. As alleged in plaintiff's complaint, the collective effect of FDA's conduct has been to discourage manufacturers from disseminating information that they would otherwise have chosen to distribute. The result is that doctors, including WLF's member-doctors, have been prevented from receiving information which they claim to have an interest in receiving. Contrary to FDA's protestations, the plaintiff's allegations clearly set forth a causal connection between FDA's conduct and the decision of various companies to stop disseminating certain kinds of information and to stop supporting certain scientific and educational activities.

It may be true, as FDA argues, that a company which disagrees with the "advice" contained in FDA's regulatory correspondence may disregard this advice, go ahead with its planned activities, and then challenge the constitutionality of any adverse FDA action in an enforcement proceeding. However, the reality of the situation, as alleged by plaintiff, is that few if any companies are willing to directly challenge the FDA in this manner. In the first instance, the company must expose itself to the FDA's power to seize an entire product line if the FDA finds the products to be "misbranded." Although the company can then litigate the validity of the seizure (and therefore the policy pursuant to which the seizure was made), the prospect of lost sales and protracted litigation is understandably discouraging to these companies. In addition, the FDA wields enormous power over drug and medical device manufacturers through its power to grant or deny new product applications. It is evident that manufacturers are most reluctant to arouse the ire of such a powerful agency. The result, according to plaintiff, is that "FDA has been able to effectuate its policies without having to resort regularly to formal rulemaking." As evidence of this, the complaint describes a substantial reduction in the distribution of enduring materials to doctors and in the willingness of manufacturers to sponsor scientific and educational activities since the alleged implementation of FDA's off-label usage policy. * * *

Under such circumstances the presumption of reviewability attaches with particular force. The fact that this suit is being brought by doctors who have been prevented from receiving information rather than the manufacturers with whose conduct the FDA policy primarily interferes lends further credence to plaintiff's contention that the FDA's power over industry is such that it is able to implement de facto regulatory policies without formally adopting final agency positions. As a general proposition, the court finds the possibility of such a practice disturbing; in the context of the plaintiff's constitutional allegations, the court finds the possibility of such a practice intolerable. Thus, the court concludes that the allegations contained in the plaintiff's amended complaint clearly raise a question of fact as to whether the FDA has been enforcing a de facto policy concerning manufacturer-supported distribution of off-label usage information. * * *

NOTES AND QUESTIONS

1. *Round one in the WLF skirmish.* The federal courts' resolution of the merits of WLF's constitutional challenge is discussed at length in Chapter 4(C). Note, however, that most courts have declined to review the agency's regulatory letters for lack of ripeness or failure to exhaust administrative remedies. See Dietary Supplemental Coalition, Inc. v. Sullivan, 978 F.2d 560, 563 (9th Cir.1992); Biotics Research Corp. v. Heckler, 710 F.2d 1375, 1376–78 (9th Cir.1983); Professionals & Patients for Customized Care v. Shalala, 847 F.Supp. 1359, 1365 (S.D.Tex.1994), aff'd, 56 F.3d 592, 599 (5th Cir.1995); Estee Lauder, Inc. v. FDA, 727 F.Supp. 1, 4–7 (D.D.C.1989).

2. *Guidance documents.* As informal rulemaking became increasingly cumbersome, the FDA shifted from promulgating binding rules to issuing nonbinding guidelines. First, as happened in *WLF*, these informal announcements may operate as de facto rules but escape normal procedural safeguards for their promulgation or review. See James Hunnicutt, Note, Another Reason to Reform the Federal Regulatory System: Agencies' Treating Nonlegislative Rules as Binding Law, 41 B.C. L. Rev. 153 (1999). Second, they allow the FDA to take positions that do not even constrain agency officials, which leaves regulated entities guessing about their rights and obligations. See Lars Noah, The FDA's New Policy on Guidelines: Having Your Cake and Eating It Too, 47 Cath. U. L. Rev. 113 (1997). Notwithstanding these concerns, in FDAMA Congress sanctioned (subject to certain limitations) this shift to greater reliance on guidance documents. See 21 U.S.C. § 371(h).

Lars Noah, *Administrative Arm–Twisting in the Shadow of Congressional Delegations of Authority*

1997 WIS. L. REV. 873 (1997).

The typical subjects of administrative law scholarship, rulemaking and adjudication, represent only a small fraction of agency activity. This distortion in emphasis is not surprising given the well understood fact that most agency activity inevitably occurs behind the scenes and beyond the reach of the Administrative Procedure Act (APA). Exactly fifty years ago, the Attorney General's Manual on the APA recognized that agency "settlement of cases and issues by informal methods is nothing new," adding that "even where formal proceedings are fully available, informal procedures constitute the vast bulk of administrative adjudication and are truly the lifeblood of the administrative process." Half a century later, this observation continues to hold true, as does the seemingly intractable problem of controlling the exercise of such wide-ranging discretionary power.

Arm-twisting represents one broad and important category of informal agency activity. As used in this Article, administrative "arm-twisting" refers to a threat by an agency to impose a sanction or withhold a benefit in hopes of encouraging "voluntary" compliance with a request that the agency could not impose directly on a regulated entity. Although it provides agencies with significant flexibility, arm-twisting differs from many of the newfangled regulatory approaches that are designed primarily to benefit the targets of administrative control. Indeed, arm-twisting often saddles parties with more onerous regulatory burdens than Congress had authorized, accompanied by a diminished opportunity to pursue judicial challenges.

This phenomenon may be even more insidious than the frequently discussed tendency of agencies to develop informal but essentially binding policies without adhering to notice and comment rulemaking procedures. The use of informal mechanisms to evade increasingly burdensome procedural requirements and searching judicial scrutiny—the so-called "ossification" of the informal rulemaking process—has attracted significant attention in recent years. In contrast, the use of informal mechanisms to evade the substantive limitations on an agency's delegated authority has gone largely unnoticed. Although a few commentators have touched upon discrete aspects of this seemingly troublesome phenomenon, no one has evaluated arm-twisting as such. * * *

As suggested in the sections that follow, administrative agencies have numerous opportunities to pursue indirectly ends that they could not impose directly. Arm-twisting may occur during licensing, government contracting, and enforcement proceedings. It may reflect formally announced agency policy or instead result from informal, ad hoc bargaining.

Agencies may threaten to deny licenses, refuse to enter into procurement agreements, disseminate adverse publicity, or impose other sanctions against uncooperative parties. Often such threats simply represent a more efficient method of achieving ends explicitly authorized by Congress, but in some cases they may allow agencies to pursue extrastatutory goals, seemingly in contravention of the limits on their delegated authority.

A. *Conditions Imposed During Licensing*

* * * In 1992, in response to complaints about excessive delays in approving drugs to treat AIDS and other life-threatening conditions, the [FDA] promulgated regulations to establish an accelerated approval procedure for new drugs and biologics intended to treat serious or life-threatening illnesses. Before approving a new drug, the FDA must find that it is both safe and effective, but, under the accelerated approval procedures, it will demand weaker evidence of effectiveness than it normally requires. The agency has succeeded in rapidly approving important new therapies during the last few years.

If a pharmaceutical company wishes to utilize this expedited licensing procedure, it must agree to several conditions on approval not explicitly authorized by Congress [until 1997]. For example, an applicant would have to accept any necessary postmarketing restrictions, including distribution only through certain medical facilities or by specially-trained physicians; distribution conditioned on the performance of specified medical procedures; and advance submission of all promotional materials for FDA review. The governing statute d[id] not, however, authorize the imposition of any of these conditions. Moreover, the FDA demands that the company waive its right to demand an evidentiary hearing in the event that the agency chooses to withdraw the approval. In response to industry complaints about such conditions, the agency explained that any "applicants objecting to these procedures may forego approval under these regulations and seek approval under the traditional approval process." However, with potentially millions of dollars in lost revenue for each additional month awaiting FDA approval, eligible drug companies cannot afford to forego these accelerated procedures, and so far the industry has opted not to challenge the rules in court. * * *

One may well ask how far an agency might go in conditioning licenses. In addition to postmarketing studies and the waiver of hearing rights, for example, could the FDA condition product approvals on agreements not to engage in broadcast advertising or not to raise drug prices faster than the rate of inflation? Could the agency demand waivers of patent rights or promises to contribute some percentage of profits to a public health agency (or perhaps the Republican National Committee)? * * *

B. *Government Contracting*

* * * In a few instances, threats to stop dealing with a firm accompany an allegation of some regulatory infraction. For example, "warning letters" issued by the FDA identify the supposed violation, provide the recipient

with a limited period of time to take corrective action (coupled with a threat of formal enforcement proceedings), and, in the case of drugs and medical devices, explain that government purchasing entities have been advised to stop dealing with the company in the meantime. Again, because the federal government represents the single largest purchaser of prescription drugs in this country, few manufacturers would dare risk losing these contracts. If a company voluntarily corrects the alleged violations of federal law, it never gets an opportunity to challenge the legal basis for the FDA's objections. Should a company disagree with the agency's allegations and choose to pursue a judicial challenge rather than accede to its demands, the FDA invariably argues that the controversy is not yet ripe for review, and so far only a single court has held that a challenge was justiciable on the basis of such an interim procurement freeze.

C. *Voluntary Recalls and Adverse Publicity*

The [FDA] generally lacks the statutory authority to order a recall of potentially dangerous products subject to its regulatory jurisdiction. Although Congress has granted the agency such authority with regard to limited classes of products, and others have recommended providing it with broader recall powers, the FDA generally has resisted suggestions that the statute be amended to provide it with recall authority. Instead, the agency prefers encouraging voluntary recalls, and it has even promulgated detailed regulations setting forth its recall procedures and policies. * * *

This strategy has succeeded because firms know that a failure to cooperate with an agency's request risks more serious enforcement measures authorized by statute, such as product seizures, injunctions, and even criminal penalties. Because these measures require somewhat cumbersome judicial proceedings, however, the issuance of adverse publicity may be a more effective means of inducing prompt action. Companies often prefer a voluntary recall because it allows them to exercise greater control over the nature and extent of public notification regarding any hazards associated with their particular product.

The [FDCA] expressly authorizes the issuance of adverse publicity by the FDA, though only in limited circumstances. Even when Congress has delegated such power, however, some controversy surrounds the use of adverse publicity. In particular, targets of an information campaign often have no meaningful opportunity to respond to the charges or seek judicial review. In recognition of the risk of improper use, the FDA once proposed a policy to limit the issuance of such publicity. The agency never finalized this proposal, and it continues to rely on explicit or implicit threats of disseminating adverse publicity as a method of encouraging voluntary compliance with its various demands. * * *

D. *Consent Decrees in Enforcement Proceedings*

As is true with most civil lawsuits and criminal prosecutions, the vast majority of all administrative enforcement proceedings result in settlements. Although sometimes simply reflected in private agreements, these settlements often lead to the entry of judgment by a court in the form of a consent decree, which gives the court continuing jurisdiction over the dispute and the power to enforce the agreement by fashioning appropriate equitable remedies. In the course of settling enforcement actions, agencies sometimes manage to extract concessions from the companies suspected of violating statutory requirements, and they frequently include regulatory provisions in these administrative consent decrees that they could not impose directly on a regulated entity.

Again, the FDA provides some prime recent examples. In the early 1990s, the agency negotiated consent decrees with pharmaceutical companies that it had accused of unlawfully promoting certain prescription drug products. In one of these cases, a manufacturer agreed to undertake an extensive corrective advertising campaign and also to preclear all of its promotional materials with the FDA for a period of two years, even though the statute generally prohibits such mandatory preclearance of pharmaceutical advertising. In another case, a company agreed to establish an FDA-approved training program for its pharmaceutical sales representatives, even though the agency does not appear to have the power to regulate such communications. In these and other cases, explicit FDA threats of especially burdensome product seizures or injunctions prompted the drug companies to accept these unprecedented requirements. * * *

[*Discussion*:]

One may applaud some of these agency initiatives as refreshingly innovative alternatives to the typically inflexible and occasionally counterproductive regulations and enforcement policies of the federal government. Indeed, some of the approaches represent responses to past complaints by regulated firms about undue rigidity in administrative decisionmaking, and companies no doubt prefer negotiated outcomes (with strings attached) to the denial of a license, the rejection of a contract bid, or the imposition of a formal sanction. This same flexibility, however, carries with it opportunities for abuse. * * *

During the last quarter of a century, for instance, the FDA has been notoriously creative in construing its own statutory authority. In the early 1970s, agency officials expressed the view that their enabling statute represents a broad "constitution" authorizing the FDA to protect the public health by any necessary and proper means, rather than a limited and precise delegation of power from Congress. Some might congratulate the agency for its adaptability to changing circumstances, but others have credibly accused it of overreaching and arbitrariness. * * * When private parties settle disputes, they bargain in the "shadow" of the law, with the prospect of judicial review serving to constrain the range of potential outcomes. When administrative agencies bargain with regulated entities, it is less clear that they operate in the shadow of the law, in particular the constraints on the power delegated by Congress. * * *

Arm-twisting succeeds, and evades judicial or other scrutiny, in part because companies in pervasively regulated industries believe that they cannot afford to resist agency demands. For instance, some critics have accused the FDA of retaliating against firms that fail to cooperate. Whether or not such charges are accurate, the perception leads companies to accede to the agency's demands even though they may lack any basis in law or fact. * * *

Consider again the product approval examples discussed at the outset. Congress has authorized the FDA to impose certain conditions on * * * new drug approvals (e.g., warning requirements); it has not explicitly authorized other requirements (e.g., recalls or postmarketing surveillance); and it implicitly or explicitly forbade the imposition of still other requirements (e.g., preclearance of drug advertising). The latter category should be off limits, leaving parties at most to bargain over commitments about which Congress expressed no intent one way or another, though even that intermediate category could raise ultra vires concerns.

Perhaps the power to license implies a power to impose conditions on approval, but, to ameliorate the risk that regulators may impose ultra vires demands, one might insist that Congress explicitly authorize agencies to deviate from statutory directives. Congress has, for instance, invited the FDA to impose such other conditions on product approvals as it may deem necessary in certain limited circumstances. Beyond such situations, however, courts should hold agencies to the limits of their enabling statutes. * * *

Administrative arm-twisting hardly represents a new phenomenon, but it has received very little critical attention to date. Arm-twisting also is not a unitary, easily identified practice. Instead, federal officials have exerted their leverage across numerous regulatory programs and through a variety of mechanisms, including licensing, contracting, and enforcement monitoring. State and local officials also engage in forms of arm-twisting, in the context of land use planning and criminal plea bargaining, as have regulatory officials in Japan and elsewhere.*

The one feature common to all of these examples is the use of negotiation and indirection by government officials eager to stretch the outer boundaries of their delegated powers. Even when agencies pursue laudable goals, such a practice poses serious concerns about sacrificing fairness and accountability. This Article has suggested a range of potential constraints on administrative arm-twisting to minimize the risks associated with this exercise of largely unchecked discretion, including heightened judicial supervision to ensure that Congress has explicitly authorized (or at least not prohibited) both the means used and the ends pursued by the agency, as well as greater openness by regulatory officials in describing what they regard as permissible subjects for negotiation. In addition, Congress must try to watch for and, where necessary, respond to administrative arm-twisting in order to prevent agencies from inappropriately aggrandizing their power. Although these are partial solutions at best,

---

* See, e.g., Willem Wassenaar, Canada: Evolution of Drug Regulation Within the   Health Protection Branch, 35 Food Drug Cosm. L.J. 451 (1980).

some effort must be made to push administrative bargaining out of complete darkness and, if not into the sunshine, at least into the shadow of the law.

E. OTHER ACTORS

1. FEDERAL AGENCIES

American Pharmaceutical Association v. Weinberger

377 F.Supp. 824 (D.D.C.1974), aff'd, 530 F.2d 1054 (D.C.Cir.1976).

■ PRATT, DISTRICT JUDGE:

This is an action for judicial review of a regulation of the Food and Drug Administration (FDA) which restricts the distribution of methadone to certain specified outlets as set forth in the regulation. In effect, it prohibits virtually all licensed pharmacies from dispensing this drug when lawfully prescribed by a physician, despite the fact that methadone was invented and was first used as a safe, useful and effective agent in the treatment of severe pain and for antitussive purposes. Decision is not made easier by the fact that in recent years methadone has become a widely known maintenance agent in the treatment of heroin addicts and there is evidence of serious abuses in the distribution of this drug. In their efforts to control improper distribution of methadone, there are strong public policy arguments on the side of defendants. At the same time, the popularity of methadone for use as a pain killer has declined because of the introduction of effective new drugs * * * *

Plaintiffs object to those parts of the regulations which purport to restrict the distribution of methadone to direct shipments from the manufacturer to (a) approved maintenance treatment programs, (b) approved hospital pharmacies, and (c) in cases where hospital pharmacies are unavailable in a particular area, to selected community pharmacies. * * * They argue that the restrictions imposed on the channels of distribution exceed the limits of FDA's authority, were promulgated on the basis of an inadequate record and, being discriminatory in several respects, violate the due process clause of the Fifth Amendment. * * * Since the court concludes that the regulation exceeds the limits of FDA's statutory authority insofar as it purports to restrict the channels of distribution for a drug which is not deemed solely investigational, the court need not address plaintiffs' latter two arguments.

The drug methadone, a synthetic substitute for morphine, is a "new" drug * * * first approved by FDA in the 1950s as safe for use as an analgesic and antitussive agent as well as for short-term detoxification of persons addicted to heroin. Subsequently, investigation of methadone for use in long-term maintenance of narcotic addicts (methadone maintenance) was approved by FDA pursuant to its authority under 21 U.S.C. § 355(i), the investigational new drug (IND) exemption. Section 355(i) of the Act empowers FDA to exempt from NDA approval requirements those new drugs "intended solely for investigational use by experts qualified by scientific training and experience to investigate the safety and effectiveness of drugs." Final guidelines for long-term maintenance programs were promulgated by FDA in 1971. A year later FDA determined that "retention of the drug (methadone) solely on an investigational status appears to be no longer warranted" and published a notice of proposed rulemaking which resulted, with certain modifications, in the regulations now in question.

The final regulation gave notice that pursuant to FDA's authority under 21 U.S.C. § 355(c), the Commissioner was withdrawing approval of all outstanding NDAs because of "a lack of substantial evidence that methadone is safe and effective for detoxification, analgesia, or antitussive use under the conditions of use that presently exist." 37 Fed. Reg. 26,794 (1972). Having withdrawn all approved NDAs, the [FDA]'s new regulatory scheme is presently the exclusive means of distribution for the drug methadone. The Commissioner has thereby created an admittedly unique classification for methadone since on the one hand he has determined that methadone should not be limited solely to investigational status while at the same time concluding that the drug is inappropriate for regular NDA approval. As statutory support for this novel solution to the methadone dilemma, defendants rely on an expansive interpretation of the Commissioner's NDA authority under § 355 of the Act. * * *

Congress apparently intended that the Secretary, or his delegate, FDA, be responsible for the adequacy of premarketing methods and controls inasmuch as the provision delineates the scope of the provision to the manufacturing, processing and packaging stage of a drug's genesis. The defendants point out, however, that § 355(d) also gives the Secretary the authority to refuse to approve an NDA where the reports of the investigations submitted do not include adequate tests showing whether the new drug is "safe for use under the conditions prescribed, recommended, or suggested in the proposed labeling thereof." Defendants argue that the term "safe" should be interpreted with reference not only to the inherent qualities of the drug under consideration but also in the sense of the drug's being secure from possible misuse. Such a broad interpretation would, according to defendants' theory, serve as the statutory foundation for FDA's exercise of authority in restricting methadone's channels of distribution because FDA's principal rationale for restricting distribution was "to help reduce the likelihood of diversion." 37 Fed. Reg. 26,790 (1972). * * *

[T]he context of the statute indicates that the term "safe" was intended to include only the inherent safety of the drug when used in the manner intended. Moreover, as also noted above, the subject of "controls" is specifically covered in provision (3) of the same subsection (d) wherein the term "safe" appears. Provision (3) extends the Secretary's authority to pass on the adequacy of methods, facilities and controls only with respect to manufacturing, processing and packaging. Under the doctrine of "expressio unius est exclusio alterius" any stage of the drug's genesis not specifically mentioned in provision (3) was presumably intended to be excluded from the Secretary's authority. Thus by examining the term "safe" in the context of those provisions of the Act in which it appears as well as in relationship to the provision of the Act which specifically deals with controls, the court concludes that the term "safe" was intended to refer to a determination of the inherent safety or lack thereof of the drug under consideration when used for its intended purpose.[9]

Finally, the legislative history of the Act fully supports this conclusion. In enacting the Comprehensive Drug Abuse Prevention and Control Act of 1970, Congress was presented with a conscious decision as to how the lines of authority should be drawn with respect to the regulation of dangerous drugs. Congress decided to continue all control authority over the distribution of dangerous drugs in the Justice Department despite a recommendation of the Prettyman Commission that this function be transferred to HEW. The House Committee on Interstate and Foreign Commerce in their report on the Comprehensive Drug Abuse Prevention and Control Act of 1970 indicated that Title II of that Act, known as the Controlled Substances Act, was designed to "provide authority for the Department of Justice to keep track of all drugs subject to abuse manufactured or distributed in the United States in order to prevent diversion of these drugs from legitimate channels of commerce." Although it is nowhere specifically stated that Congress contemplated that the Justice Department would have exclusive authority to prevent diversion, this result would appear logically to follow from a comparison of the functions delegated to the Secretary of HEW with those assigned to the Attorney General.

In addition to being a "new" drug and thus within the jurisdiction of the FDA, methadone is a controlled substance within Schedule II of the Controlled Substances Act. Under this Act the Attorney General is made responsible for the registration of any person who manufactures, distributes or dispenses any controlled substance. An applicant may be refused registration if the Attorney General makes a determination that registering the applicant would be inconsistent with the public interest. Congress has also provided the specific means for revoking or suspending the authority of a registrant to distribute controlled substances. * * * In addition, Congress has specified the precise procedure to be followed by the Attorney General in attempting to revoke or suspend a registration.

The court concludes that Congress intended to create two complementary institutional checks on the production and marketing of new drugs. At the production or pre-marketing stage, the FDA is given the primary responsibility in determining which new drugs should be permitted to enter the flow of commerce. The Commissioner must approve or deny every

---

9. Even if the court were to agree with defendant's interpretation of the term "safe," this alone would not provide a statutory basis for the regulations challenged herein. At most such an interpretation would authorize FDA to deny or withdraw any methadone NDA based on a finding that the drug could not be "safely" distributed. As outlined in the court's opinion, FDA's discretion under the Act's NDA provisions is limited to either approving or denying NDAs and nowhere is FDA empowered to approve an NDA upon the condition that the drug be distributed only through specified channels.

NDA, or he may determine that a particular new drug qualifies for IND status in order to permit additional experimentation. When an IND exemption is approved, the Commissioner may, of course, severely restrict the distribution of the exempted drug to bona fide researchers and clinicians. But once a drug is cleared for marketing by way of a NDA-approval, for whatever uses the Commissioner deems appropriate, the question of permissible distribution of the drug, when that drug is a controlled substance, is one clearly within the jurisdiction of the Justice Department. The diversion of the particular drug to a use not approved by the Commissioner would be grounds for revocation of the offending distributor's registration. FDA attempts to accomplish peremptorily by way of its challenged regulation, that which could only be accomplished, according to the scheme of the Controlled Substances Act, by way of show-cause proceedings initiated by the Attorney General, i.e., revoking the authority of otherwise duly-registered distributors with respect to the drug methadone. To allow the challenged portions of the methadone regulations to stand, therefore, would be to abrogate the collective judgment of Congress with regard to the appropriate means of controlling unlawful drug diversion.

This is particularly true of the regulations' denial of authority to the plaintiffs at bar. Although the Attorney General generally has discretion to register applicants wishing to distribute or dispense controlled substances, in the case of "practitioners" the Attorney General must register them "if they are authorized to dispense under the law of the State in which they regularly conduct business." 21 U.S.C. § 823(f). Congress has thereby specifically sanctioned the registration of all State-licensed practitioners with the clear intent of permitting them to dispense controlled substances on an equal basis with all other approved distributors. In the face of such clear-cut congressional intent, it would be anomalous to suggest that an agency, by the mere issuance of a regulation, could modify these mandated channels of distribution. Accordingly, the court concludes that FDA has overstepped the bounds of its authority in purporting to limit the distribution of methadone in the manner contemplated by its regulations.

It is undoubtedly true that methadone poses unique problems of medical judgment, law enforcement and public policy but this fact alone cannot justify a federal agency of specifically delimited jurisdiction from implementing equally unique control solutions not authorized by Congress. The problem of unlawful diversion is one presently consigned by Congress to the Drug Enforcement Administration (DEA, formerly the Bureau of Narcotics and Dangerous Drugs) of the Department of Justice. FDA, on the other hand, has the responsibility of making the initial decision, based on all available medical and scientific data, as to whether a particular new drug is safe and effective for its intended use. While the functions of FDA and DEA are not entirely exclusive of one another,[16] a certain division of

---

16. For example, the Attorney General, in exercising his authority under 21 U.S.C. § 811(a) to add or remove drugs from the schedules of controlled substances estab-lished by the Controlled Substances Act, must first call upon FDA for its recommendation. The recommendations of FDA, insofar as they concern "scientific and medical mat-

authority and responsibility was clearly intended by Congress and must be recognized by this court in order to preserve the integrity of the legislative scheme. Under these circumstances, the relative merits of FDA's plan to control the distribution of methadone, a controlled substance, must first be passed upon by Congress. * * *

NOTES AND QUESTIONS

1. *Role of the DEA.* The Controlled Substances Act includes a "schedule" of narcotics. See 21 U.S.C. § 812. Schedule I includes drugs with a high potential for abuse that have no medically accepted use, such as heroin. Schedule II includes drugs with a high potential for abuse and dependence that have a currently accepted medical use in treatment, such as opium. Schedule III includes drugs with a lower abuse potential that have a currently accepted medical use, such as amphetamine. Schedule IV includes drugs with a still lower abuse potential, such as phenobarbital. Schedule V includes drugs with the lowest abuse potential, such as limited concentrations of codeine, which are used in combination with non-narcotic active ingredients that have a separate medical use. In deciding whether a controlled substance has a currently accepted medical use, the DEA must consult with the FDA, which has received some criticism in the past for doing little more than rubber-stamping the DEA's scheduling recommendations. See Grinspoon v. DEA, 828 F.2d 881 (1st Cir.1987); see also Alliance for Cannabis Therapeutics v. DEA, 15 F.3d 1131 (D.C.Cir.1994) (upholding the agency's refusal to reschedule marijuana because it lacks a currently accepted medical use); Reckitt & Colman, Ltd. v. DEA, 788 F.2d 22 (D.C.Cir.1986) (reviewing a challenge brought by a drug manufacturer against a DEA scheduling decision); Douglas J. Behr, Prescription Drug Control Under the Federal Controlled Substances Act: A Web of Administrative, Civil, and Criminal Law Controls, 45 Wash. U. J. Urb. & Contemp. L. 41 (1994); Lars Noah, Challenges in the Federal Regulation of Pain Management Technologies, 30 J.L. Med. & Ethics (forthcoming 2002). In addition to making decisions about the appropriate scheduling for narcotics, the DEA supervises the manufacturing and distribution of legal narcotics. See United States v. Moore, 423 U.S. 122 (1975). The DEA requires that manufacturers register their operations, and it assigns aggregate and individual production quotas for Schedule II drugs. See 21 U.S.C. §§ 823(a), 826; see also Western Fher Lab. v. Levi, 529 F.2d 325, 330–32 (1st Cir.1976) (affirming challenged production quotas for phenmetrazine).

2. *Other federal agencies.* Under the Clinical Laboratory Improvement Amendments of 1988 (CLIA), HHS exercises responsibility for overseeing clinical laboratories that provide diagnostic services. See 42 U.S.C. § 263a; see also Consumer Fed'n of Am. v. HHS, 83 F.3d 1497 (D.C.Cir.1996) (reviewing a challenge to the agency's implementing regulations). The Secretary recently transferred to the FDA certain functions under CLIA.

ters" relating to the "appropriate schedule, if any, under which such drug or substance should be listed" are binding on the Attorney General.

See 64 Fed. Reg. 73,561 (1999). Other component agencies within HHS that perform primarily research rather than regulatory functions—namely, the National Institutes of Health (NIH) and the Centers for Disease Control and Prevention (CDC)—often work in tandem with the FDA. Finally, Chapter 4(B) mentions the division of regulatory authority over the advertising of drugs and medical devices between the FDA and the Federal Trade Commission (FTC).

3. *Antibiotic resistance.* The overuse and misuse of antibiotics has created drug-resistant strains of many bacteria. These may contribute to 70,000 deaths each year in the United States. See Justin Gillis & Ceci Connolly, Emphasis on Cipro Worries Officials, Wash. Post, Oct. 19, 2001, at A17. Until recently, vancomycin represented the last line of defense, but resistant strains have emerged. In 2000, the FDA approved Zyvox® (linezolid), the first of a new class of antibiotics called oxazolidinones. In order to maximize the useful life of this drug, could the FDA approve it only for use by infectious disease specialists in hospitals (trusting them to save it for vancomycin-resistant pathogens), or might the agency persuade the DEA to place the drug in Schedule II? See Scott B. Markow, Note, Penetrating the Walls of Drug–Resistant Bacteria: A Statutory Prescription to Combat Antibiotic Misuse, 87 Geo. L.J. 531, 542–43 (1998) (doubting the legality of either one of these approaches). Alternatively, could the FDA leave new antibiotics in quasi-permanent IND status, which would allow it to impose strict distribution controls? Cf. Note, The Open–Ended Investigation: A Method for Regulation of New Medical Services, 91 Yale L.J. 550 (1982). As it happens, just a year after approval one hospital reported a case of staph infection resistant to Zyvox.

4. *Distribution controls.* As explained in Chapter 4(A), the FDA does have clear authority to specify prescription status, though it does so primarily through labeling (and allows state authorities to decide which health care providers enjoy prescribing and dispensing privileges). The agency also can designate medical devices as "restricted" in order to limit their distribution. See 21 U.S.C. § 360j(e). Notwithstanding its apparent lack of broader statutory authority, the FDA has managed to place controls on the distribution of drugs that do not qualify as controlled substances. For instance, when it approved thalidomide for the treatment of leprosy patients, the agency conditioned approval on extremely strict distribution controls given the serious risk of birth defects: distribution only through specially-registered physicians and pharmacists, and tracking of patients who will have to use two forms of contraception and undergo frequent pregnancy tests. See Sheryl Gay Stolberg, Thalidomide Approved to Treat Leprosy, with Other Uses Seen, N.Y. Times, July 17, 1998, at A1. Until recently, the FDA had declined suggestions to require that the manufacturer of another potent teratogen, isotretinoin (Accutane®), accept restrictions designed to ensure that patients would not become pregnant while using this product to treat cystic acne. See Joan H. Krause, Accutane: Has Drug Regulation in the United States Reached Its Limits?, 6 J.L. & Health 1, 18–23 (1991); Rules Set on Acne Drug Prescriptions, L.A. Times, Nov. 1, 2001, at A33 (noting that over the last two decades, in spite of label warnings, more than 2000 women became pregnant while taking the drug, which prompted the FDA to require more comprehensive educational efforts); see also David B. Brushwood & Frederick H. Fern, Clozaril and the Threat of Product Liability: Defensive Drug Distribution Invites Regulatory Reform, 15 J. Prods. & Toxics Liab. 145 (1993). More controversially, the FDA suggested that the abortifacient mifepristone (commonly known as RU–486) be made subject to a variety of onerous distribution restrictions such as availability only through doctors who are trained to perform surgical abortions and have registered with the manufacturer. See Marie McCollough, Two Physicians Groups Denounce FDA Plan to OK RU486 Abortion Pill with Tight Restrictions on Use, Phil. Inquirer, Aug. 5, 2000. In the end, the agency did not condition approval of the drug (sold under the brand name Mifeprex®) on these restrictions. See Gina Kolata, U.S. Approves Abortion Pill, N.Y. Times, Sept. 29, 2000, at A1; see also Lars Noah, A Miscarriage in the Drug Approval Process?: Mifepristone Embroils the FDA in Abortion Politics, 36 Wake Forest L. Rev. 571 (2001).

2. STATE REGULATORS

Rayford v. State

16 S.W.3d 203 (Tex.Ct.App.2000).

■ ROSENBEG, JUSTICE:

* * * Erma Rayford, individually, and Baby Images, Inc. (collectively, Rayford) appeal an injunction granted to the State of Texas under the Texas Food, Drug and Cosmetic Act (FDCA) and the Texas Deceptive Trade Practices Act (DTPA) preventing her from possessing and using a medical device, a fetal ultrasound scanner, for nondiagnostic use. * * *

In 1989, Rayford, a qualified ultrasound sonographer, purchased an RT–50 fetal ultrasound scanner from General Electric (GE) and went into business as Baby Images, Inc. She provided ultrasound scanning of unborn babies and videotapes of the scan and advertised the videos as keepsakes through brochures she mailed and distributed by hand. She performed ultrasound scanning for nondiagnostic purposes and did not require that consumers have a prescription from a licensed physician.

The Texas Department of Health inspected Rayford's facilities several times between 1994 and 1997. On each occasion, the inspector issued a Notice of Detention. The inspector found that Rayford's possession and use of the RT–50 adulterated and misbranded it. In 1996, the State brought an action seeking an injunction and penalties under the FDCA and DTPA. * * *

Rayford challenges the entry of partial summary judgment for the violation of section 431.021(b) of the FDCA, which prohibits the adulteration or misbranding of any medical device in commerce. Rayford asserts her use of the RT–50 ultrasound device for a nonmedical purpose does not make the device adulterated or misbranded in commerce. The State responds that the federal and state legislative schemes apply to the ultimate

user of a device, not just the manufacturer, distributor, or seller of the device. The State argues Rayford's use of the ultrasound scanner for fetal imaging without a diagnostic purpose was a "new intended use," which gives the device a status as a class III device under the Federal Food Drug and Cosmetic Act (FFDCA), thereby making its use adulteration under the Texas Act. The State further argues the RT–50 was not properly labeled and Rayford's use without a prescription was misbranding in commerce.
* * *

Because ultrasound devices are class II devices, for Rayford's RT–50 to be a class III device, it must not be substantially equivalent to the ultrasound devices already approved. First, GE submitted a premarket notification for the RT–50 as a device substantially equivalent to one previously marketed, as required for a class II device. The notification described the technical aspects of the device as well as its intended use, stating, "The RT–50 is intended to be used for abdominal, obstetric and gynecological ultrasound examinations in hospitals and clinics where ultrasound exams are routinely performed." The notification also indicated the RT–50's intended diagnostic use was fetal imaging. The FDA found the RT–50 to be substantially equivalent to other approved ultrasound devices. In the hands of GE, the RT–50 remained class II.

Next, because Rayford used the RT–50 for nondiagnostic uses, we examine whether Rayford's use destroyed the RT–50's substantial equivalence to the ultrasound devices by changing the intended use. Rayford used the RT–50 for fetal imaging, but not for approved medical or diagnostic purpose. Rayford's unapproved nondiagnostic use is not the intended use of the RT–50 as established by GE. This nondiagnostic use is a new use. Whether this nondiagnostic use is a new intended use is determined by the person responsible for labeling the RT–50. The person who is responsible for labeling is the person who engages in the manufacture, preparation, propagation, or processing of the device, including actions in furtherance of the distribution of the device from the original manufacturer to the person who makes final delivery or sale to the ultimate user. Rayford bought the RT–50. She is a user and possessor, not a manufacturer or distributor, of the RT–50. Further, she did not sell the RT–50, that is, she did not sell or distribute the RT–50 to the ultimate user. While Rayford was selling a service in using the machine, the federal statutory scheme does not include a seller of a device's service as a person responsible for labeling. Therefore, Rayford does not have labeling responsibility, and Rayford's nondiagnostic use of the RT–50 did not "substantially alter" it and is not a "new intended use." Accordingly, Rayford's RT–50 continued its class II designation.

Finally, the summary judgment affidavits of Byron Tart, Director of Promotion and Advertising Policy and Staff for the Compliance Office of the FDA, show the FDA was aware of nonmedical use of the ultrasound device. Nevertheless, the FDA did not codify the nonmedical use to class III as is provided for in the regulations. Because Rayford is not the person with labeling responsibility and the FDA did not classify the known use as class III, the RT–50 remains class II. Because we have concluded the device is not a class III device, the State did not prove Rayford had an adulterated device in commerce under the FDCA. * * *

[A] device is misbranded if it is a restricted device that is used in violation of section 360j(e) of the FFDCA. See Tex. Health & Safety Code Ann. § 431.112(r). The FFDCA provides that a restricted device is only to be used on written or oral authorization of a physician. A restricted or prescription device is a device that cannot have adequate directions for lay use. See 21 C.F.R. § 801.109 (1999). These devices are exempt from the requirement of directions because they are required to be in the possession of physicians or used only on order of physicians. See id. § 801.110.

The summary judgment evidence demonstrates the RT–50 is exempt from labeling for adequate directions for lay use. That exemption makes the RT–50 a prescription device. It is undisputed that Rayford used the device without the supervision or order of a licensed practitioner. Therefore, Rayford's use was a violation of section 431.112(r), making the RT–50 misbranded in commerce as a matter of law, and the trial court was correct in granting the summary judgment on this misbranding ground. * * *

Virtually all states have their own versions of the FDCA, including similarly broad prohibitions against the adulteration and misbranding of drugs and medical devices. See Uniform State Food, Drug, and Cosmetic Bill, Food Drug Cosm. L. Rep. (CCH) ¶ 10,100. California goes further and operates an approval system. See Cal. Health & Safety Code § 111550(b); see also Summit Technology v. High–Line Med. Instruments, 922 F.Supp. 299, 317 (C.D.Cal.1996) (explaining that the "California FDCA is 'analogous' to the federal FDCA," and that both "statutes are comprehensive public health schemes administered by expert agencies"); James M. Gomez, Maker of HIV Test Kit Sues for State's O.K., L.A. Times, Sept. 28, 1993, at D2 (describing a dispute over an application filed with state regulators). But apart from an odd assortment of requirements for specific products, reflecting cither peculiar local conditions or the special concerns of state lawmakers, state requirements are quite limited. When states or localities decide to regulate, questions arise about possible conflicts with federal requirements.

Hillsborough County v. Automated Medical Labs., Inc.

471 U.S. 707 (1985).

■ MARSHALL, JUSTICE:

* * * Automated Medical Laboratories, Inc., is a Florida corporation that operates, through subsidiaries, eight blood plasma centers in the United States. One of the centers, Tampa Plasma Corporation (TPC), is located in Hillsborough County, Florida. Appellee's plasma centers collect

blood plasma from donors by employing a procedure called plasmapheresis. Under this procedure, whole blood removed from the donor is separated into plasma and other components, and "at least the red blood cells are returned to the donor." 21 C.F.R. § 606.3(e) (1984). Appellee sells the plasma to pharmaceutical manufacturers.

Vendors of blood products, such as TPC, are subject to federal supervision. Under § 351(a) of the Public Health Service Act, such vendors must be licensed by the Secretary of Health and Human Services (HHS). Licenses are issued only on a showing that the vendor's establishment and blood products meet certain safety, purity, and potency standards established by the Secretary. HHS is authorized to inspect such establishments for compliance.

Pursuant to § 351 of the Act, the Food and Drug Administration (FDA), as the designee of the Secretary, has established standards for the collection of plasma. The regulations require that a licensed physician determine the suitability of a donor before the first donation and thereafter at subsequent intervals of no longer than one year. A physician must also inform the donor of the hazards of the procedure and obtain the donor's consent, and must be on the premises when the procedure is performed. In addition, the regulations establish minimum standards for donor eligibility, specify procedures that must be followed in performing plasmapheresis, and impose labeling requirements.

In 1980, Hillsborough County adopted Ordinances 80–11 and 80–12. Ordinance 80–11 imposes a $225 license fee on plasmapheresis centers within the county. It also requires such centers to allow the County Health Department "reasonable and continuing access" to their premises for inspection purposes, and to furnish information deemed relevant by the Department. Ordinance 80–12 establishes a countywide identification system, which requires all potential donors to obtain from the County Health Department an identification card, valid for six months, that may be used only at the plasmapheresis center specified on the card. The ordinance incorporates by reference the FDA's blood plasma regulations, but also imposes donor testing and recordkeeping requirements beyond those contained in the federal regulations. Specifically, the ordinance requires that donors be tested for hepatitis prior to registration, that they donate at only one center, and that they be given a breath analysis for alcohol content before each plasma donation. The county has promulgated regulations to implement Ordinance 80–12. The regulations set the fee for the issuance of an identification card to a blood donor at $2. They also establish that plasma centers must pay the county a fee of $1 for each plasmapheresis procedure performed.

In December 1981, appellee filed suit in the United States District Court for the Middle District of Florida, challenging the constitutionality of the ordinances and their implementing regulations. Appellee argued primarily that the ordinances violated the Supremacy Clause, the Commerce Clause, and the Fourteenth Amendment's Equal Protection Clause. Appellee sought a declaration that the ordinances were unlawful and a permanent injunction against their enforcement. * * *

It is a familiar and well-established principle that the Supremacy Clause, U.S. Const., art. VI, cl. 2, invalidates state laws that "interfere with, or are contrary to," federal law. Gibbons v. Ogden, 9 Wheat. 1, 211 (1824) (Marshall, C.J.). Under the Supremacy Clause, federal law may supersede state law in several different ways. First, when acting within constitutional limits, Congress is empowered to preempt state law by so stating in express terms. In the absence of express preemptive language, Congress' intent to preempt all state law in a particular area may be inferred where the scheme of federal regulation is sufficiently comprehensive to make reasonable the inference that Congress "left no room" for supplementary state regulation. Preemption of a whole field also will be inferred where the field is one in which "the federal interest is so dominant that the federal system will be assumed to preclude enforcement of state laws on the same subject."

Even where Congress has not completely displaced state regulation in a specific area, state law is nullified to the extent that it actually conflicts with federal law. Such a conflict arises when "compliance with both federal and state regulations is a physical impossibility," or when state law "stands as an obstacle to the accomplishment and execution of the full purposes and objectives of Congress." We have held repeatedly that state laws can be preempted by federal regulations as well as by federal statutes. Also, for the purposes of the Supremacy Clause, the constitutionality of local ordinances is analyzed in the same way as that of statewide laws.

In arguing that the Hillsborough County ordinances and regulations are preempted, appellee faces an uphill battle. The first hurdle that appellee must overcome is the FDA's statement, when it promulgated the plasmapheresis regulations in 1973, that it did not intend its regulations to be exclusive. In response to comments expressing concern that the regulations governing the licensing of plasmapheresis facilities "would preempt State and local laws governing plasmapheresis," the FDA explained in a statement accompanying the regulations that "[t]hese regulations are not intended to usurp the powers of State or local authorities to regulate plasmapheresis procedures in their localities." 38 Fed. Reg. 19,365 (1973).

The question whether the regulation of an entire field has been reserved by the federal government is, essentially, a question of ascertaining the intent underlying the federal scheme. In this case, appellee concedes that neither Congress nor the FDA expressly preempted state and local regulation of plasmapheresis. Thus, if the county ordinances challenged here are to fail they must do so either because Congress or the FDA implicitly preempted the whole field of plasmapheresis regulation, or because particular provisions in the local ordinances conflict with the federal scheme. According to appellee, two separate factors support the inference of a federal intent to preempt the whole field: the pervasiveness of the FDA's regulations and the dominance of the federal interest in this area. Appellee also argues that the challenged ordinances reduce the number of plasma donors, and that this effect conflicts with the congressional goal of ensuring an adequate supply of plasma.

The FDA's statement is dispositive on the question of implicit intent to preempt unless either the agency's position is inconsistent with clearly expressed congressional intent, or subsequent developments reveal a change in that position. Given appellee's first argument for implicit preemption—that the comprehensiveness of the FDA's regulations evinces an intent to preempt—any preemptive effect must result from the change since 1973 in the comprehensiveness of the federal regulations. To prevail on its second argument for implicit preemption—the dominance of the federal interest in plasmapheresis regulation—appellee must show either that this interest became more compelling since 1973, or that, in 1973, the FDA seriously underestimated the federal interest in plasmapheresis regulation.

The second obstacle in appellee's path is the presumption that state or local regulation of matters related to health and safety is not invalidated under the Supremacy Clause. Through the challenged ordinances, Hillsborough County has attempted to protect the health of its plasma donors by preventing them from donating too frequently. It also has attempted to ensure the quality of the plasma collected so as to protect, in turn, the recipients of such plasma. * * * Of course, the same principles apply where, as here, the field is said to have been preempted by an agency, acting pursuant to congressional delegation. Appellee must thus present a showing of implicit preemption of the whole field, or of a conflict between a particular local provision and the federal scheme, that is strong enough to overcome the presumption that state and local regulation of health and safety matters can constitutionally coexist with federal regulation. * * *

We reject the argument that an intent to preempt may be inferred from the comprehensiveness of the FDA's regulations at issue here. As we have pointed out, given the FDA's 1973 statement, the relevant inquiry is whether a finding of preemption is justified by the increase, since 1973, in the comprehensiveness of the federal regulations. Admittedly, these regulations have been broadened over the years. When they were adopted in 1973, these regulations covered only plasma to be used in injections. In 1976, the regulations were expanded to cover also plasma to be used for the manufacture of "noninjectable" products. * * *

The FDA has not indicated that the new regulations affected its disavowal in 1973 of any intent to preempt state and local regulation, and the fact that the federal scheme was expanded to reach other uses of plasma does not cast doubt on the continued validity of that disavowal. Indeed, even in the absence of the 1973 statement, the comprehensiveness of the FDA's regulations would not justify preemption. * * * We are even more reluctant to infer preemption from the comprehensiveness of regulations than from the comprehensiveness of statutes. As a result of their specialized functions, agencies normally deal with problems in far more detail than does Congress. To infer preemption whenever an agency deals with a problem comprehensively is virtually tantamount to saying that whenever a federal agency decides to step into a field, its regulations will be exclusive. Such a rule, of course, would be inconsistent with the federal-state balance embodied in our Supremacy Clause jurisprudence.

Moreover, because agencies normally address problems in a detailed manner and can speak through a variety of means, including regulations, preambles, interpretive statements, and responses to comments, we can expect that they will make their intentions clear if they intend for their regulations to be exclusive. Thus, if an agency does not speak to the question of preemption, we will pause before saying that the mere volume and complexity of its regulations indicate that the agency did in fact intend to preempt. Given the presumption that state and local regulation related to matters of health and safety can normally coexist with federal regulations, we will seldom infer, solely from the comprehensiveness of federal regulations, an intent to preempt in its entirety a field related to health and safety. * * *

Appellee's second argument for preemption of the whole field of plasmapheresis regulation is that an intent to preempt can be inferred from the dominant federal interest in this field. We are unpersuaded by the argument. Undoubtedly, every subject that merits congressional legislation is, by definition, a subject of national concern. That cannot mean, however, that every federal statute ousts all related state law. Neither does the Supremacy Clause require us to rank congressional enactments in order of "importance" and hold that, for those at the top of the scale, federal regulation must be exclusive. * * *

Appellee's final argument is that even if the regulations are not comprehensive enough and the federal interest is not dominant enough to preempt the entire field of plasmapheresis regulation, the Hillsborough County ordinances must be struck down because they conflict with the federal scheme. Appellee argues principally that the challenged ordinances impose on plasma centers and donors requirements more stringent than those imposed by the federal regulations, and therefore that they present a serious obstacle to the federal goal of ensuring an "adequate supply of plasma." We find this concern too speculative to support preemption.

Appellee claims that "[t]he evidence at trial indicated that enforcement of the County ordinances would result in an increase in direct costs of plasma production by $1.50 per liter, and a total increase in production costs (including direct and indirect costs) of $7 per liter of plasma, an increase of approximately 15% in the total cost of production." Appellee argues that these increased financial burdens would reduce the number of plasma centers. In addition, appellee claims, the county requirements would reduce the number of donors who only occasionally sell their plasma because such donors would be deterred by the identification-card requirement.

On the basis of the record before it, the district court rejected each of appellee's factual assertions. * * * More importantly, even if the Hillsborough County ordinances had, in fact, reduced the supply of plasma in that county, it would not necessarily follow that they interfere with the federal goal of maintaining an adequate supply of plasma. Undoubtedly, overly restrictive local legislation could threaten the national plasma supply. Neither Congress nor the FDA, however, has struck a particular balance between safety and quantity; as we have noted, the regulations, which contemplated additional state and local requirements, merely establish minimum safety standards. Moreover, the record in this case does not indicate what supply the federal government considers "adequate," and we have no reason to believe that any reduction in the quantity of plasma donated would make that supply "inadequate."

Finally, the FDA possesses the authority to promulgate regulations preempting local legislation that imperils the supply of plasma and can do so with relative ease. Moreover, the agency can be expected to monitor, on a continuing basis, the effects on the federal program of local requirements. Thus, since the agency has not suggested that the county ordinances interfere with federal goals, we are reluctant in the absence of strong evidence to find a threat to the federal goal of ensuring sufficient plasma.

Our analysis would be somewhat different had Congress not delegated to the FDA the administration of the federal program. Congress, unlike an agency, normally does not follow, years after the enactment of federal legislation, the effects of external factors on the goals that the federal legislation sought to promote. Moreover, it is more difficult for Congress to make its intentions known—for example by amending a statute—than it is for an agency to amend its regulations or to otherwise indicate its position.

In summary, given the findings of the district court, the lack of any evidence in the record of a threat to the "adequacy" of the plasma supply, and the significance that we attach to the lack of a statement by the FDA, we conclude that the Hillsborough County requirements do not imperil the federal goal of ensuring sufficient plasma. * * *

Committee of Dental Amalgam Mfrs. v. Stratton

92 F.3d 807 (9th Cir.1996).

■ PREGERSON, CIRCUIT JUDGE:

The defendants, Dr. James Stratton, Acting Director of the California Office of Health Hazard Assessment, and Dan Lungren, the Attorney General of the State of California (collectively the "State"), and the intervening party, Environmental Law Foundation (ELF), appeal the district court's grant of summary judgment in favor of the plaintiffs, Committee of Dental Amalgam Alloy Manufacturers and Distributors and Dentsply International, Inc. (collectively the "manufacturers"). The district court held that, as applied to dental amalgam, the Medical Device Amendments to the federal Food, Drug and Cosmetics Act (MDA) preempt California's Safe Drinking Water and Toxic Enforcement Act of 1986 ("Proposition 65"). * * *

Proposition 65 was passed by the voters of California in 1986. Proposition 65 mandates that the public be informed about products that pose a health risk. Proposition 65 specifically states:

No person in the course of doing business shall knowingly and intentionally expose any individual to a chemical known to the state to cause cancer or reproductive toxicity without first giving clear and reasonable warning to such individual.

Cal. Health & Safety Code § 25249.6. * * * Dental amalgam is used by dentists to restore teeth. On July 1, 1990, pursuant to Proposition 65, the State of California listed mercury as a chemical known to cause reproductive harm. As a result, consumer warnings for dental amalgam are now required. * * *

[A]s a threshold matter, we must decide whether the district court was correct in holding that the MDA applied to dental amalgam. Congress defined the term "medical device" very broadly * * * * [W]e hold that dental amalgam does fall within the reach of the MDA. Dental amalgam is used in the treatment and prevention of tooth decay. Further, the FDA has already classified the component parts of dental amalgam [as medical devices]. * * *

Congress included an explicit preemption provision in the MDA. * * * In *Medtronic v. Lohr*, 518 U.S. 470 (1996) [excerpted in Chapter 5(B)(2)], the Supreme Court rejected a broad construction of this preemption provision. * * * [I]n determining what kind of federal "requirement" and what kind of state "requirement" trigger preemption, the Supreme Court in *Medtronic* deferred to the FDA's regulation that narrowly construes the MDA's preemption clause. Section 808.1(d) provides, in relevant part:

State or local requirements are preempted only when the Food and Drug Administration has established specific counterpart regulations or there are other specific requirements applicable to a particular device under the act, thereby making any existing divergent State or local requirements applicable to the device different from or in addition, the specific Food and Drug Administration requirement.

Based on this FDA regulation, a state or local "requirement" is preempted by the MDA only if specific counterpart requirements or regulations that are applicable to a particular device exist. * * * In addition, the Supreme Court in *Medtronic* specifically approved that part of the FDA regulation that provides that "[s]ection 521(a) does not preempt State and local requirements of general applicability where the purpose of the requirement relates either to other products in addition to devices ... or to unfair trade practices in which the requirements are not limited to devices." * * *

The district court held that, even though the FDA has not established "specific" regulations relating to dental amalgam, the MDA still preempts Proposition 65. First, the district court held that 21 C.F.R. § 801.109, the FDA regulation describing the manufacturing and labeling requirements, is "specific" enough to trigger preemption. Second, the district court held that the FDA's alleged refusal to impose reproductive toxicity requirements on dental mercury is by itself preemptive.

The district court was wrong on both counts. In *Medtronic*, the Supreme Court held that the FDA's manufacturing and labeling requirements were not "specific" enough to preempt state law. * * * Further, Proposition 65 is a state law of general applicability which was not enacted "with respect to" medical devices. Proposition 65 applies to all products and services that pose a health risk to the public. Except for identifying chemicals known to pose a health risk, Proposition 65 is not directed at any product or industry. Nor has the State of California adopted any specific regulation or requirement that relates to dental amalgam. The State of California has listed mercury as a product which causes reproductive harm. As a result, consumer warnings for dental amalgam are now required.

Thus, we hold that the consumer warning requirement under California's Proposition 65 is not "specific" enough to trigger preemption because it is "not the kind[] of requirement[] that Congress and the FDA feared would impede the ability of federal regulators to implement and enforce specific federal requirements." * * *

We also reject the district court's holding that the FDA's failure to impose a warning requirement on dental amalgam is by itself preemptive. Inherent in the term "requirement" is the idea that there be a positive enactment from the FDA before preemption can be triggered. * * * To hold that inaction by the FDA is sufficient to trigger preemption would mean that manufacturers would be free to ignore state laws that are intended to protect consumers, during the period that the FDA is considering whether to issue specific regulations relating to particular products, or after the FDA, for whatever reason, has "decided," through inaction, not to regulate particular products. Such a holding would contradict Congress's stated intent of providing consumer protection from unsafe medical devices when it enacted the MDA. * * *

NOTES AND QUESTIONS

1. *Proposition 65.* California's warning requirements had the dual purpose of educating consumers and discouraging the continued sale of suspected toxins. Although the warnings have not had much of a direct impact on consumer behavior, they have persuaded several manufacturers to reformulate their products. See Paulette L. Stenzel, Right-to-Know Provisions of California's Proposition 65: The Naiveté of the Delaney Clause Revisited, 15 Harv. Envtl. L. Rev. 493 (1991); Michael Barsa, Note, California's Proposition 65 and the Limits of Information Economics, 49 Stan. L. Rev. 1223 (1997). Warnings are not required for exposures to listed chemicals shown to pose either "no significant risk" of cancer or, in the case of reproductive toxicants, "no observable effect" at an exposure 1000 times higher than expected. "No significant risk" is defined as less than one excess cancer in a population of 100,000 exposed over a lifetime. Several other states have considered legislation modeled on Proposition 65, but all such proposals have been rejected to date. Even so, Proposition 65 affects how manufacturers convey warnings about chronic health risks. Because of the practical difficulties with separate systems for in-state labeling and distribution, Proposition 65 warnings appear on products sold outside of California. Proposition 65 has raised a number of difficult preemption issues. For instance, the broad array of options available for communicating a warning under Proposition 65 means that even specific federal labeling requirements will rarely preempt the California requirements entirely. See Chemical Specialties Mfrs. Ass'n v. Allenby, 958 F.2d 941, 947–50 (9th Cir.1992); D–Con Co. v. Allenby, 728 F.Supp. 605, 607 (N.D.Cal.1989). By state regulation, FDA-approved labeling for prescription drugs satisfies the warning requirement, but OTC products get no safe harbor. See Christopher Wanjek, Gee, Your Hair Smells Carcinogenic!, Wash. Post, Mar. 27, 2001, at T6 ("The [FDA] acknowledges that coal tar is carcinogenic but says that the over-the-counter coal-tar shampoos are safe.... But in California, where both hair and novel legal actions grow long and wild, ... [activists] are suing more than 20 manufacturers of coal-tar shampoos and ointments to require them to place warning labels on their products—and ultimately to sell them by prescription only.").

2. *Specific state requirements.* One early flashpoint for the preemption provision made applicable to medical devices in 1976 involved state regulation of hearing aids. The courts rejected preemption arguments to the extent that the state requirements addressed subjects that differed from the labeling requirements imposed by the FDA. See Smith v. Pingree, 651 F.2d 1021, 1023–25 (5th Cir.1981); Kievlan v. Dahlberg Elecs., 144 Cal. Rptr. 585, 590 (Ct.App.1978); see also Massachusetts v. Hayes, 691 F.2d 57, 60–64 (1st Cir.1982) (rejecting one state's challenge to the FDA's denial of a request for an exemption from preemption for a hearing aid requirement). See generally Morgan Downey, Laboratories or Puppets? The Challenge of Federal Preemption of State Legislation, 34 Food Drug Cosm. L.J. 334 (1979). In another context, a court rejected the argument that federal law impliedly preempted a state statute requiring pharmacists to substitute generic drugs for prescribed brand-name drugs under certain circumstances. See Pharmaceutical Soc'y of New York, Inc. v. Lefkowitz, 586 F.2d 953, 958 (2d Cir.1978). As states become more aggressive in trying to control drug prices (an issue taken up more fully in Chapter 9), these types of challenges will resurface in the future. See Tony Alexander & Gwendolyn Alexander, Maine's Price Control Law, Nat'l L.J., Sept. 25, 2000, at B9 (suggesting both supremacy and dormant commerce clause problems with such initiatives).

Could a state ban a drug approved by the FDA? Some states had banned sales of the diet drug fenfluramine before the FDA decided to withdraw approval, but this was done in response to the emerging safety concerns not known to the agency when it originally approved the drug. See Peggy Rogers, Florida Prohibits Diet Drug, Hous. Chron., Sept. 9, 1997, at A3 (adding that Tennessee also had done so previously); see also Boston Moves to Ban Mercury Thermometers, N.Y. Times, Nov. 16, 2000, at A25 (referring to "a nationwide push to remove [mercury thermometers] from

American medicine cabinets as a threat to lakes and streams"). In addition, responding to concerns about the hazards of certain dietary supplements in the wake of DSHEA, some states have stepped into the regulatory vacuum: several states have banned gamma hydroxybutyrate (GHB), in some cases by classifying it as a Schedule I controlled substance, and the same has happened with ephedra. See Iona N. Kaiser, Comment, Dietary Supplements: Can the Law Control the Hype?, 37 Hous. L. Rev. 1249, 1268–70 (2000).

3. *Express statutory preemption.* In contrast to medical devices, Congress has not expressly preempted state regulation of pharmaceutical products. On the contrary, when it enacted the Drug Amendments of 1962, Congress included a provision disavowing any intent to displace state control. See Pub. L. No. 87–781, § 202, 76 Stat. 780, 793 (1962) ("Nothing in the amendments made by this Act to the [FDCA] shall be construed as invalidating any provision of State law which would be valid in the absence of such amendments unless there is a direct and positive conflict between such amendments and such provision of State law."). In 1997, however, Congress amended the FDCA to preempt state regulation of OTC drugs. See 21 U.S.C. § 379r. Will that exempt nonprescription products from the warning requirements of Proposition 65?

4. *Administrative preemption.* As the Court explained in *Hillsborough*, even in the absence of express statutory preemption, an agency may issue regulations preempting state requirements. The FDA has done this in the case of three general OTC drug warnings. See 51 Fed. Reg. 8180, 8181 (1986) (Reye syndrome warning for drug products containing aspirin); 47 Fed. Reg. 54,750, 54,756–57 (1982) (general pregnancy warning for OTC products); 47 Fed. Reg. 50,442, 50,447–48 (1982) (tamper-resistant packaging and associated labeling requirements); see also 60 Fed. Reg. 16,962, 16,966 (1995) (protecting confidentiality in the reporting of adverse events). Courts may hold that agency requirements impliedly preempt inconsistent state laws, and agencies also can preempt state requirements for products that they have decided not to regulate. See Jack W. Campbell, IV, Regulatory Preemption in the Garcia/Chevron Era, 59 U. Pitt. L. Rev. 805 (1998); Amanda Frost, Judicial Review of FDA Preemption Determinations, 54 Food & Drug L.J. 367 (1999). More often, recent rules disclaim any intent to preempt, in compliance with an Executive Order requiring that all agencies assess the federalism impacts of their actions. See, e.g., 65 Fed. Reg. 81,082, 81,103 (2000) (proposing extensive revisions in the format and content of prescription drug labeling, and simply adding without any discussion that "this proposed rule does not preempt State law").

5. *Other constraints on state regulation.* State legislatures may react to the FDA's approval of mifepristone (Mifeprex®) by imposing restrictions on its availability. See Charles Ornstein, Abortion Pill's Foes Shift Focus, Dallas Morn. News, Sept. 30, 2000, at 1A. To the extent that recent Supreme Court cases have reinvigorated implied preemption in cases where state law stands as an "obstacle" to the achievement of federal purposes, would such state laws create an impermissible conflict? The Supreme

Court's latest decisions addressing indirect conflicts between federal and state law suggest a greater willingness to find implied preemption of more stringent state and local requirements. See Crosby v. National Foreign Trade Council, 530 U.S. 363 (2000) (invalidating sanctions imposed by Massachusetts against companies doing business with Burma because they differed from federal law); United States v. Locke, 529 U.S. 89 (2000) (invalidating state restrictions on the operation of oil tankers that differed from federal statute). See generally Caleb Nelson, Preemption, 86 Va. L. Rev. 225 (2000). In this respect, note that the Clinton administration actively encouraged the introduction of mifepristone in the U.S. market, and it took some unprecedented steps to facilitate FDA approval. See Margaret Talbot, The Little White Bombshell, N.Y. Times Mag., July 11, 1999, at 39.

When the FDA first approved oral contraceptives in 1960, some states restricted their availability, but the Supreme Court held these laws unconstitutional. See Griswold v. Connecticut, 381 U.S. 479, 485–86 (1965). Future state legislation preventing physicians from dispensing mifepristone may run afoul of the Court's abortion decisions. Because mifepristone only works early in pregnancy (pre-viability), the constitutional test asks whether a state's restriction on the use of the drug would "unduly burden" a woman's right to choose an abortion. See Planned Parenthood v. Casey, 505 U.S. 833, 873–901, 877 (1992) (plurality). Although limitations on the types of physicians who are authorized to dispense the drug (e.g., only those licensed to perform surgical abortions) might pass muster, see Mazurek v. Armstrong, 520 U.S. 968, 972–75 (1997), it does not appear that states could entirely prohibit access to a method for terminating pregnancy approved by federal officials. The Supreme Court recently invalidated a state prohibition on one surgical method of abortion because, by leaving only an arguably riskier method available, the law created hazards to maternal health for which it failed to provide any exception. See Stenberg v. Carhart, 530 U.S. 914, 930–38 (2000). To the extent that mifepristone offers demonstrated advantages over surgical abortion procedures, this would seem to prevent a state from prohibiting its use altogether. But what about other therapeutic agents that do not raise the constitutional questions in connection with procreative choices? If a state entirely prohibited sales within its borders of an FDA-approved product, and it had done so without any apparent safety rationale, would the Constitution forbid such an exercise of a state's police power?

Whalen v. Roe

429 U.S. 589 (1977).

■ STEVENS, JUSTICE:

The constitutional question presented is whether the State of New York may record, in a centralized computer file, the names and addresses of all persons who have obtained, pursuant to a doctor's prescription, certain drugs for which there is both a lawful and an unlawful market. The district

court enjoined enforcement of the portions of the New York State Controlled Substances Act of 1972 which require such recording on the ground that they violate appellees' constitutionally protected rights of privacy.
* * *

Many drugs have both legitimate and illegitimate uses. In response to a concern that such drugs were being diverted into unlawful channels, in 1970 the New York Legislature created a special commission to evaluate the State's drug-control laws. The commission found the existing laws deficient in several respects. There was no effective way to prevent the use of stolen or revised prescriptions, to prevent unscrupulous pharmacists from repeatedly refilling prescriptions, to prevent users from obtaining prescriptions from more than one doctor, or to prevent doctors from over-prescribing, either by authorizing an excessive amount in one prescription or by giving one patient multiple prescriptions. In drafting new legislation to correct such defects, the commission consulted with enforcement officials in California and Illinois where central reporting systems were being used effectively.

The new New York statute classified potentially harmful drugs in five schedules.[7] Drugs, such as heroin, which are highly abused and have no recognized medical use, are in Schedule I; they cannot be prescribed. Schedules II through V include drugs which have a progressively lower potential for abuse but also have a recognized medical use. Our concern is limited to Schedule II which includes the most dangerous of the legitimate drugs. With an exception for emergencies, the Act requires that all prescriptions for Schedule II drugs be prepared by the physician in triplicate on an official form. The completed form identifies the prescribing physician; the dispensing pharmacy; the drug and dosage; and the name, address, and age of the patient. One copy of the form is retained by the physician, the second by the pharmacist, and the third is forwarded to the New York State Department of Health in Albany. A prescription made on an official form may not exceed a 30–day supply, and may not be refilled.
* * *

A few days before the Act became effective, this litigation was commenced by a group of patients regularly receiving prescriptions for Schedule II drugs, by doctors who prescribe such drugs, and by two associations of physicians. * * * The district court found that the State had been unable to demonstrate the necessity for the patient-identification requirement on the basis of its experience during the first 20 months of administration of the new statute. There was a time when that alone would have provided a basis for invalidating the statute. *Lochner v. New York*, 198 U.S. 45 (1908), involved legislation making it a crime for a baker to permit his employees to work more than 60 hours in a week. In an opinion no longer regarded as authoritative, the Court held the statute unconstitutional as "an unreason-

---

7. These five schedules conform in all material aspects with the drug schedules in the Federal Comprehensive Drug Abuse Prevention and Control Act of 1970. 21 U.S.C. § 801 et seq. [For an update on state legislation in this area, see Richard L. Braun, Uniform Controlled Substances Act of 1990, 13 Campbell L. Rev. 365 (1991).]

able, unnecessary and arbitrary interference with the right of the individual to his personal liberty...." The holding in *Lochner* has been implicitly rejected many times. State legislation which has some effect on individual liberty or privacy may not be held unconstitutional simply because a court finds it unnecessary, in whole or in part. For we have frequently recognized that individual States have broad latitude in experimenting with possible solutions to problems of vital local concern.

The New York statute challenged in this case represents a considered attempt to deal with such a problem. It is manifestly the product of an orderly and rational legislative decision. It was recommended by a specially appointed commission which held extensive hearings on the proposed legislation, and drew on experience with similar programs in other States. There surely was nothing unreasonable in the assumption that the patient-identification requirement might aid in the enforcement of laws designed to minimize the misuse of dangerous drugs. For the requirement could reasonably be expected to have a deterrent effect on potential violators as well as to aid in the detection or investigation of specific instances of apparent abuse. At the very least, it would seem clear that the State's vital interest in controlling the distribution of dangerous drugs would support a decision to experiment with new techniques for control. For if an experiment fails—if in this case experience teaches that the patient-identification requirement results in the foolish expenditure of funds to acquire a mountain of useless information—the legislative process remains available to terminate the unwise experiment. It follows that the legislature's enactment of the patient-identification requirement was a reasonable exercise of New York's broad police powers. * * *

Appellees contend that the statute invades a constitutionally protected "zone of privacy." The cases sometimes characterized as protecting "privacy" have in fact involved at least two different kinds of interests. One is the individual interest in avoiding disclosure of personal matters, and another is the interest in independence in making certain kinds of important decisions. Appellees argue that both of these interests are impaired by this statute. The mere existence in readily available form of the information about patients' use of Schedule II drugs creates a genuine concern that the information will become publicly known and that it will adversely affect their reputations. This concern makes some patients reluctant to use, and some doctors reluctant to prescribe, such drugs even when their use is medically indicated. It follows, they argue, that the making of decisions about matters vital to the care of their health is inevitably affected by the statute. Thus, the statute threatens to impair both their interest in the nondisclosure of private information and also their interest in making important decisions independently. We are persuaded, however, that the New York program does not, on its face, pose a sufficiently grievous threat to either interest to establish a constitutional violation. * * *

Even without public disclosure, it is, of course, true that private information must be disclosed to the authorized employees of the New York Department of Health. Such disclosures, however, are not significantly different from those that were required under the prior law. Nor are they meaningfully distinguishable from a host of other unpleasant invasions of privacy that are associated with many facets of health care. Unquestionably, some individuals' concern for their own privacy may lead them to avoid or to postpone needed medical attention. Nevertheless, disclosures of private medical information to doctors, to hospital personnel, to insurance companies, and to public health agencies are often an essential part of modern medical practice even when the disclosure may reflect unfavorably on the character of the patient. Requiring such disclosures to representatives of the State having responsibility for the health of the community does not automatically amount to an impermissible invasion of privacy.

Appellees also argue, however, that even if unwarranted disclosures do not actually occur, the knowledge that the information is readily available in a computerized file creates a genuine concern that causes some persons to decline needed medication. The record supports the conclusion that some use of Schedule II drugs has been discouraged by that concern; it also is clear, however, that about 100,000 prescriptions for such drugs were being filled each month prior to the entry of the district court's injunction. Clearly, therefore, the statute did not deprive the public of access to the drugs.

Nor can it be said that any individual has been deprived of the right to decide independently, with the advice of his physician, to acquire and to use needed medication. Although the State no doubt could prohibit entirely the use of particular Schedule II drugs, it has not done so. This case is therefore unlike those in which the Court held that a total prohibition of certain conduct was an impermissible deprivation of liberty. Nor does the State require access to these drugs to be conditioned on the consent of any state official or other third party. Within dosage limits which appellees do not challenge, the decision to prescribe, or to use, is left entirely to the physician and the patient. * * *

The appellee doctors argue separately that the statute impairs their right to practice medicine free of unwarranted state interference. If the doctors' claim has any reference to the impact of the 1972 statute on their own procedures, it is clearly frivolous. For even the prior statute required the doctor to prepare a written prescription identifying the name and address of the patient and the dosage of the prescribed drug. To the extent that their claim has reference to the possibility that the patients' concern about disclosure may induce them to refuse needed medication, the doctors' claim is derivative from, and therefore no stronger than, the patients'. Our rejection of their claim therefore disposes of the doctors' as well.

A final word about issues we have not decided. We are not unaware of the threat to privacy implicit in the accumulation of vast amounts of personal information in computerized data banks or other massive government files. The collection of taxes, the distribution of welfare and social security benefits, the supervision of public health, the direction of our Armed Forces, and the enforcement of the criminal laws all require the orderly preservation of great quantities of information, much of which is personal in character and potentially embarrassing or harmful if disclosed. The right to collect and use such data for public purposes is typically accompanied by a concomitant statutory or regulatory duty to avoid unwarranted disclosures. Recognizing that in some circumstances that duty arguably has its roots in the Constitution, nevertheless New York's statutory scheme, and its implementing administrative procedures, evidence a proper concern with, and protection of, the individual's interest in privacy. We therefore need not, and do not, decide any question which might be presented by the unwarranted disclosure of accumulated private data whether intentional or unintentional or by a system that did not contain comparable security provisions. We simply hold that this record does not establish an invasion of any right or liberty protected by the Fourteenth Amendment.

NOTES AND QUESTIONS

1. *Access.* Doctors and drug companies continue to oppose such monitoring efforts. See Melody Petersen & Barry Meier, Few States Track Prescriptions As Way to Prevent Overdoses, N.Y. Times, Dec. 21, 2001, at A1. The Court's opinion in *Whalen* suggests that, in exercising their traditional police powers, states may limit patients' access to products approved by the FDA. Nonetheless, the recognition that patients enjoy some constitutional right of access to therapeutic agents seems to mean that a state could not prohibit access altogether, at least not absent some genuine public health concern. As explained in the next chapter, the courts have not read *Whalen* to protect any right of access to products not approved by the FDA.

2. *Medical records privacy.* The question at the heart of *Whalen* has, of course, become far more significant in the last few decades. See Lawrence O. Gostin, Health Information Privacy, 80 Cornell L. Rev. 451 (1995); Catherine Louisa Glenn, Note, Protecting Health Information Privacy: The Case for Self–Regulation of Electronically Held Medical Records, 53 Vand. L. Rev. 1605 (2000). In the waning days of the Clinton administration, HHS issued sweeping new rules designed to protect medical records privacy. See 65 Fed. Reg. 82,462 (2000).

3. INTERNATIONAL ACTORS

Richard A. Merrill, *The Importance and Challenges of "Mutual Recognition"*
29 SETON HALL L. REV. 736 (1998).

* * * In some ways we are, in 1998, at a stage of regulatory development comparable to that confronting Congress at the turn of the century. It was by then apparent that the production and marketing of food were no longer local activities. Meat packed in Chicago was being marketed in all of the nation's major cities. The same was increasingly true, but not so obvious, for the products of the fledgling pharmaceutical industry. Consumers could no longer rely exclusively, or indeed confidently, on local public

health officials to protect their health and welfare. * * * [T]he inexorable growth of interstate trade had shifted primary regulatory responsibility to the federal level before World War II, particularly for medical products.

At the end of the twentieth century, comparable practical challenges face policy-makers in the United States and across the world. International commerce in food and medicines has exploded in the last generation. Many of the major pharmaceutical firms are genuine multi-nationals. Medical devices firms generally owe their allegiance to a single country, but their customers, in increasing numbers, are distributed around the world. * * *

The circumstances facing the United States and its trading partners today, however, differ in one obvious and important respect from those that confronted members of the United States Congress in 1906. If those turn-of-the-century Senators and Representatives were prepared, as a political matter, to create a cross-jurisdictional regulatory authority, they had a constitutional—that is, a legal—basis for doing so. By contrast, today the international legal order would not afford a firm anchor for a multinational regulatory authority even if there were support for one—which there surely is not. National regulatory requirements for medicines and foods—particularly foods—have long embodied diverse policies and served multiple goals. No country has been more determined to preserve its autonomy in setting and enforcing health protection standards than the United States. And no doubt many of our trading partners believe we have been as guilty as they of adopting standards whose real objective is to protect or advantage domestic producers.

Accordingly, there are formidable obstacles to international harmonization of regulatory requirements for food and medical products. At the same time, there are mounting pressures on both producer and consuming countries to reach agreement on product and production standards. Even where harmonization does not seem possible, there are pressures—internally generated in part—to reach work-sharing arrangements that permit trading partners to make use of, and rely upon, the production-site activities of a partner's regulatory authorities. These latter pressures may prove irresistible simply because the alternatives to trusting the work of officials in other countries are unworkable—either accepting products based on physical examination or refusing their entry.

The recent Mutual Recognition Agreement with the European Community (EU MRA) is one expression of this reality. It is a cautious attempt by United States and European Union (EU) policy-makers to work out terms of reciprocal trust in which our regulatory officials accept the work, and sometimes the results, of their officials. The success of the venture—not yet demonstrated—will have important implications not only for international trade but also for protection of U.S. consumers. * * *

Essentially, I view mutual recognition agreements, such as the one currently under discussion, as contracts for service. The United States enters into an agreement with a trading partner under the expectation that the trading partner will take steps to help FDA perform its primary function of applying domestic legal standards to products imported into the

United States. The service contracted for may be the provision of information, such as sharing the report of an inspection, or it may be the evaluation of a medical device by a body recognized by the partner's regulatory authorities. In both cases, the assumption is that U.S. law provides the standards that ultimately determine the acceptability of an inspected facility or an imported product. In such an agreement, the role of the trading partner is not that of law maker but rather that of information source or service provider.

An agreement to harmonize standards, by contrast, * * * contemplates the establishment of a single common rule of conduct or single common measure of product compliance, i.e., establishment of a single standard that is observed in both countries. If we keep these descriptions in mind, we will have a clearer grasp of the requirements for domestic implementation of any agreement into which the United States enters and a better appreciation of the pace at which we are moving toward internationalization of regulation. * * *

[T]he Federal Food, Drug, and Cosmetic Act (FFDCA) now contains express legislative authorization for FDA to pursue certain types of international agreements. Indeed, Congress has sprinkled its authorization in a number of provisions, including two recently added by the FDA Modernization Act, passed in November 1997. * * * Assuring compliance with GMP requirements and facilitating inspections to verify compliance seem to be of particular concern to Congress. Other regulatory activities that might be the basis for international cooperation, and possible mutual recognition, are perhaps important but apparently less urgent.

The amended FFDCA adds an interesting geographic qualification to its instructions. FDA is specifically encouraged to reach mutual recognition agreements with the EU covering the regulation of all products within the agency's jurisdiction. Congress is thus on record as recognizing that there are some partners with whom we are more interested in cooperating than others. Maybe this is simply a reflection of the commercial importance of the trans-Atlantic trade. It may also demonstrate congressional acceptance of the proposition that the regulators in EU countries are as capable and vigorous as our own officials. * * *

United States FDA officials not only have a strong tradition of tough-minded regulation, but many share—though they do not often express—a conviction that they are more thorough and rigorous about regulation than their counterparts in other countries. They believe that U.S. standards are higher and, just as important, that their means of assuring compliance with those standards are more reliable and certainly less trusting. In their view, FDA regulation represents the "gold standard."

There is some evidence to support this self-assured view, but, whether or not it is fully justified, it is certainly genuine. This belief will almost certainly make harmonization more difficult and perhaps slow the drive toward mutual recognition. If United States regulatory officials start from the premise that FDA not only imposes the highest standards but also uses the most effective means for assuring compliance with those standards, "harmonization" appears to demand some relaxation of public health protection. At least it does so if other countries are not willing to adopt and enforce U.S. standards. This mindset may not ultimately impede FDA's willingness to enter into agreements of the mutual assistance variety, but it surely will be an impediment to efforts to achieve agreement on substantive standards. * * *

Another feature of the institutional culture at FDA is the widely-held conviction—or realization—that the agency is over-extended and under-resourced. The job that FDA has traditionally assumed is getting harder, not easier. * * * The realization that resources have not kept pace with workload, much less public expectations, helps explain the seriousness with which FDA officials seem prepared to entertain proposals for mutual recognition. If you can get other people to help you perform your functions—functions that you view as essential—this may help spread the cost of assuring compliance.

Another distinctive tradition has been reflected in the statute that FDA is responsible for administering. It can be described as paternalistic. Many U.S. officials—perhaps more in Congress than at FDA–have long contended that American firms regulated by FDA should not be able to market overseas products they cannot market in the United States. This conviction stems from language in the 1938 FFDCA, which FDA later interpreted as prohibiting the export of "new drugs" until they received FDA approval. FDA's policy made it impossible for a U.S manufacturer to ship a drug overseas that FDA had not approved—even if the drug had not been rejected for approval here and would be or had been approved by foreign authorities. The same premise was later incorporated in the somewhat weaker controls imposed on the export of unapproved medical devices by the 1976 Medical Devices Amendments to the FFDCA.

Congress relaxed these restrictions on the export of unapproved products in 1996. But it would still be incorrect to say that, under U.S. law, it is lawful to export any product that a receiving country is prepared to accept. * * * In short, FDA has historically been viewed by Congress—and has come to view itself—as having responsibility to protect citizens of other countries as well as citizens of our own. This tradition, too, may impede harmonization efforts, particularly if they appear to contemplate any relaxation of U.S. standards. * * *

NOTES AND QUESTIONS

1. *Harmonization efforts.* In 1998, the FDA issued a final rule implementing the mutual recognition agreement with the EU. See 63 Fed. Reg. 60,122 (1998) (codified at 21 C.F.R. pt. 26). Previously, the agency had involved itself in various international harmonization efforts. See 63 Fed. Reg. 49,583 (1998) (statistical principles for clinical trials); 60 Fed. Reg. 11,260 (1995) (publishing five International Conference on Harmonization (ICH) guidelines related primarily to different aspects of study designs appropriate for the review of drug safety); see also Paul M. Booth, FDA Implementation of Standards Developed by the International Conference on Harmonization, 52 Food & Drug L.J. 203 (1997); Joseph G. Contrera, Comment, The Food and Drug Administration and the International Conference on Harmonization: How Harmonious Will International Pharmaceutical Regulations Become?, 8 Admin. L.J. 927 (1995); Rosemarie Kanusky, Comment, Pharmaceutical Harmonization: Standardizing Regulations Among the United States, the European Community, and Japan, 16 Hous. J. Int'l L. 665 (1994); Ann E. Ryan, Comment, Protecting the Rights of Pediatric Research Subjects in the International Conference on Harmonisation of Technical Requirements for Registration of Pharmaceuticals for Human Use, 23 Fordham Int'l L.J. 848 (2000). As it revises various regulations, the FDA may choose to incorporate the ICH guidelines into domestic law. See 65 Fed. Reg. 81,082, 81,093–94 (2000) (proposing revisions in the format for prescription drug labeling, including a modified definition of "adverse event" that would conform to the ICH definition).

2. *Further commentary.* See Patricia I. Carter, Federal Regulation of Pharmaceuticals in the United States and Canada, 21 Loy. L.A. Int'l & Comp. L.J. 215 (1999); Michael J. Malinowski, Globalization of Biotechnology and the Public Health Challenges Accompanying It, 60 Alb. L. Rev. 119 (1996); Lars Noah, NAFTA's Impact on the Trade in Pharmaceuticals, 33 Hous. L. Rev. 1293 (1997); Harvey Teff, Drug Approval in England and the United States, 33 Am. J. Comp. L. 567 (1985); Brian L. Walser, Shared Technical Decisionmaking and the Disaggregation of Sovereignty: International Regulatory Policy, Expert Communities, and the Multinational Pharmaceutical Industry, 72 Tul. L. Rev. 1597 (1998); J. Michael Warner & Han Xiaoqing, The Chinese System of Administrative Protection for Pharmaceuticals, 31 John Marshall L. Rev. 1165 (1998); Mindy H. Chapman, Comment, Rx: Just What the Doctor Ordered: International Standards for Medical Devices, 14 Nw. J. Int'l L. & Bus. 566 (1994); Julie C. Relihan, Note, Expediting FDA Approval of AIDS Drugs: An International Approach, 13 B.U. Int'l L.J. 229 (1995); Note, FDA Reform and the European Medicines Evaluation Agency, 108 Harv. L. Rev. 2009 (1995).

CHAPTER 2

DEVELOPMENT AND TESTING OF EXPERIMENTAL THERAPIES

This chapter examines the regulatory mechanisms that govern human experimentation and participation in the development and testing of new medical products. This process requires the balancing of several competing concerns, including protecting human subjects who participate in experimental protocols, creating effective but not unwieldy systems of regulatory oversight, and avoiding potential conflicts of interest between investigators and the human subjects who volunteer to participate in research. These materials will explore a variety of questions that arise in the medical technology development process—such as what constitutes "research" triggering regulatory protections for human subjects; how to bridge the gap between the aspirations of the informed consent rules and the reality of their application; and what constraints exist on access to investigational medical technologies.

A. DRUG DISCOVERY AND TESTING

FDA, *From Test Tube to Patient: Improving Health Through Human Drugs*
<www.fda.gov/cder/about/whatwedo/testtube.pdf> (1999).

* * * The research process is a complicated, time-consuming, and costly one whose end result is never known at the outset. Discovering a new drug has been likened to searching for the proverbial needle in a haystack. Literally hundreds, and sometimes thousands, of chemical compounds must be made and tested to find one that can achieve the desirable result without too-serious side effects. * * * Such a complicated process costs vast amounts of time and money. FDA estimates that, on average, it takes eight-and-a-half years to study and test a new drug before the agency can approve it for the general public. That includes early laboratory and animal testing, as well as later clinical trials using human subjects. * * *

In some cases, a pharmaceutical company decides to develop a new drug aimed at a specific disease or medical condition. In others, company scientists may be free to pursue an interesting or promising line of research. And, in yet others, new findings from university, government, or other laboratories may point the way for drug companies to follow in their own research. Indeed, the process typically combines elements of all three avenues. New drug research starts by studying how the body functions, both normally and abnormally, at its most basic levels. * * * That, in turn, leads to a concept of how a drug might be used to prevent, cure, or treat a disease or medical condition. Once the concept has been developed, the researcher has a target to aim for.

Take cholesterol, a wax-like substance found naturally in the body. Too much cholesterol, either naturally or in the diet, can cause it to build up on the inside walls of blood vessels. This can clog the arteries that deliver blood to the heart muscle, blocking the flow of oxygen and nutrients, causing a heart attack. There have been few drugs that effectively cut cholesterol levels without either toxic or unpleasant side effects. This has limited their use. Others that were tested acted too late in the process by which the body makes cholesterol to lower its levels. What was needed * * * was a drug that would act earlier in the cholesterol making process. * * * To find one, scientists at Merck and elsewhere spent decades studying how the body makes and uses cholesterol. Along the way, they identified more than 20 biochemical reactions necessary for the body to make cholesterol, along with the enzymes required at each step to turn one chemical into the next one in the chain.

The research problem was to find the step where interference by a drug would effectively lower cholesterol production. By the 1970s, scientists had found a possibility. They had isolated a chemical, mevalonic acid, which was an early link in the cholesterol chain, and an enzyme called HMG–CoA reductase, which produced mevalonic acid. What was needed, then, was a drug that could either inhibit HMG–CoA reductase or prevent cells from correctly using the enzyme.

Sometimes, scientists are lucky and find the right compound quickly. More often, hundreds or even thousands must be tested. In a series of test tube experiments called assays, compounds are added one at a time to enzymes, cell cultures, or cellular substances grown in a laboratory. The goal is to find which additions show some chemical effect. * * * A more high-tech approach is to use computers to simulate an enzyme or other drug target and to design chemical structures that might work against it. Enzymes work when they attach to the correct site on a cell's membrane. A computer can show scientists what the receptor site looks like and how one might tailor a compound to block an enzyme from attaching there. * * *

Yet a third approach involves testing compounds made naturally by microscopic organisms. Candidates include fungi, viruses, and molds, such as those that led to penicillin and other antibiotics. Scientists grow the microorganisms in what they call a fermentation broth, one type of organism per broth. Sometimes 100,000 or more broths are tested to see whether any compound made by a microorganism has a desirable effect. In the search for a new cholesterol drug, scientists found a fungus that inhibited the HMG–CoA reductase enzyme in a test tube. Chemists then had to identify which of the fungus's dozens of chemical by-products was actually inhibiting the enzyme. Once that was done, the chemical's structure was analyzed and improved to enhance its effects.

To this point, the search for a new drug has been confined to a laboratory test tube. Next, scientists have to test those compounds that have shown at least some desired effects in living animals. * * * Two or more species are typically tested because a drug may affect one differently from another. Such tests show whether a potential drug has toxic side effects and what its safety is at different doses.

So far, research has aimed at discovering what a drug does to the body. Now, it must also find out what the body does to the drug. So, in animal testing, scientists measure how much of a drug is absorbed into the blood, how it is broken down chemically in the body, the toxicity of its breakdown products (metabolites), and how quickly the drug and its metabolites are excreted from the body. Sometimes, such tests find a metabolite that is more effective than the drug originally picked for development.

Of particular concern is how much of the drug is absorbed into the blood. Scientists may add other chemicals to the drug to help the body absorb it or, on the other side, to prevent it from being broken down and excreted too soon. Such changes in the drug's structure mean even more testing. Absorption rates can cause a host of problems. For example, for a certain drug to be effective, 75 percent of it may need to reach the blood-stream. But absorption rates can vary among individuals from, say, 10 to 80 percent. So, the drug must be able to produce the desired effects in those who absorb only 10 percent, but not cause intolerable side effects in people who absorb 80 percent.

By this time in the testing process, many drugs that had seemed promising have fallen by the wayside. More often than many scientists care to admit, researchers just have to give up when a drug is poorly absorbed, is unsafe, or simply doesn't work. Nevertheless, progress may yet be made. Occasionally, a stubborn scientist keeps looking and finds a usable compound after others had given up. In other cases, compounds may be put aside because they failed to work on one disease, only to be taken off the shelf years later and found to work on another. Such was the case with Retrovir (zidovudine, also known as AZT), the first drug approved for treatment of AIDS. The drug was first studied in 1964 as an anticancer drug, but it showed little promise. It was not until the 1980s, when desperate searches began for a way to treat victims of the AIDS virus, that scientists at Burroughs Wellcome Co., of Research Triangle Park, N.C., took another look at zidovudine. After it showed very positive results in human testing, it was approved by FDA in March 1987.

The organization Pharmaceutical Research and Manufacturers of America estimates that only five in 5,000 compounds that enter preclinical testing make it to human testing, and only one of those five may be safe and effective enough to reach pharmacy shelves.

The role of FDA in the early stages of drug research is small. FDA determines whether the drug is safe enough to test in humans and, if so—

after all human testing is completed—decides whether the drug can be sold to the public and what its label should say about directions for use, side effects, warnings, and the like. FDA first becomes involved when a drug company has completed its testing in animals and is ready to test a drug on humans. (Actually, some animal testing continues after human tests begin to learn whether long-term use of the drug may cause cancer or birth defects. Also, more animal data may be needed if human tests turn up unexpected effects. And new therapeutic uses may be found by continued animal studies.) Although FDA usually does not tell drug companies what specific laboratory or animal tests to run, the agency does have regulations and guidelines on the kinds of results FDA expects to see in any request to conduct human testing.

International Primate Protection League v. Institute for Behavioral Research

799 F.2d 934 (4th Cir.1986).

■ WILKINSON, CIRCUIT JUDGE:

In this case we must decide whether a group of private individuals may challenge a medical researcher's compliance with federal standards for the care of laboratory animals. Because we find that the plaintiffs lack standing to bring such a lawsuit, we affirm the judgment of the district court in its dismissal of this action.

To imply a cause of action in these plaintiffs might entail serious consequences. It might open the use of animals in biomedical research to the hazards and vicissitudes of courtroom litigation. It may draw judges into the supervision and regulation of laboratory research. It might unleash a spate of private lawsuits that would impede advances made by medical science in the alleviation of human suffering. To risk consequences of this magnitude in the absence of clear direction from the Congress would be ill-advised. In fact, we are persuaded that Congress intended that the independence of medical research be respected and that administrative enforcement govern the Animal Welfare Act.

The principal complainant in this case, Alex Pacheco, first met the principal defendant, Dr. Edward Taub, in May 1981. Pacheco, an undergraduate student in the program of Environmental Studies at George Washington University in Washington, D.C., had worked frequently for the protection of animals * * * * He had founded the Ohio Animal Rights Committee and, in Washington, D.C., had founded People for the Ethical Treatment of Animals, Inc. (PETA), on which he continued to serve as director. Taub, the chief of the Behavioral Biology Center of the Institute for Behavioral Research (IBR), was studying the capacity of monkeys to learn to use a limb after nerves had been severed. Funded by the National Institutes of Health (NIH), the project amplified Taub's earlier research in this area and attempted to discover benefits for the rehabilitation of human patients suffering from a serious neurological injury such as a stroke.

Pacheco offered to work as a volunteer for Taub on the neurological study at an IBR facility in Silver Spring, Maryland. Taub gave Pacheco the keys to the premises and permission to enter at any time, and Pacheco came regularly to the laboratory during the summer of 1981. He concluded from his observations that IBR did not provide the monkeys with sufficient food or water, a sanitary environment, or adequate veterinary care. On several nights during the week of August 27, 1981, Pacheco brought other researchers to IBR to confirm his impressions. * * * [T]he Assistant State's Attorney for Montgomery County filed criminal charges against Taub in the county district court, alleging seventeen violations of the animal cruelty statute.

On October 9 the Circuit Court for Montgomery County, without opposition from IBR, instructed Sgt. Swain and Dr. James Stunkard, a veterinarian, to supervise the transfer of the monkeys to an NIH facility in Poolesville, Maryland that Swain and Stunkard had chosen as the best place for temporary care and custody. * * * Dr. Taub stood trial in November 1981 in the District Court for Montgomery County, which on December 2 entered orders of conviction on six of the seventeen counts and acquittal on the other eleven counts. Fearing that the court order on custody of the monkcys would partially expire with the acquittals, PETA acted quickly to prevent the return of any animals to IBR. * * *

The plaintiffs in the former case, including PETA, hoped to require the Secretary of Agriculture to enforce against Taub and IBR the provisions of the Animal Welfare Act. The plaintiff in the latter case sought a more general declaration of the duties of Secretary Block and NIH to control the research treatment of animals and also requested an injunction to prevent the return of the seized monkeys to Taub and IBR. * * * The Court of Appeals of Maryland then granted a writ of certiorari and in August 1983 reversed the conviction, holding that Article 27, § 59 of the Maryland Code did not apply to an institution conducting medical research pursuant to a federal program. * * *

Not only do plaintiffs fail to allege cognizable injuries; they fail also to prove that the implicated federal statute authorizes their right to seek relief. The two shortcomings provide related, though alternative, bases for dismissal of this action.

The Animal Welfare Act is the federal statute on which plaintiffs rely in defining their allegations of mistreatment. The Act seeks to insure that "animals intended for use in research facilities . . . are provided humane care and treatment." 7 U.S.C. § 2131(1). There is no indication, however, that Congress intended this goal to come at the expense of progress in medical research. To the contrary, both the language of the statute and the means chosen by Congress to enforce it preserve the hope that responsible primate research holds for the treatment and cure of humankind's most terrible afflictions. The statutory design is, in turn, inconsistent with the private right of action that plaintiffs assert.

The administrative enforcement that Congress envisioned for this statute is readily apparent.[4] The Act directs the Secretary of Agriculture to "promulgate standards to govern the humane handling, care, treatment, and transportation of animals," but cautions that "nothing in this chapter shall be construed as authorizing the Secretary to promulgate rules, regulations, or orders with regard to design, outlines, guidelines, or performance of actual research or experimentation by a research facility as determined by such research facility." 7 U.S.C. § 2143. * * * The Secretary may also remove an animal found to be suffering through the non-compliance of a laboratory—but only if the animal "is no longer required by the research facility to carry out the research, test, or experiment for which such animal has been utilized." Id. § 2146(a).

A review of the Act thus underscores two points. One is a commitment to administrative supervision of animal welfare. The other is the subordination of such supervision to the continued independence of research scientists. The Secretary's rulemaking authority does not extend to the design of experiments; the Secretary's enforcement authority does not extend to the confiscation of animals in use. In the words of Congress, "Under this bill the research scientist still holds the key to the laboratory door." H.R. Rep. No. 91–1651 (1966).

The amicus curiae brief of sixty-eight scientific and medical organizations reviews the history underlying these priorities. Research with primates helped to lead, for example, to the development of the polio vaccine, and other animal research has contributed to the discovery of insulin, the invention of transplantation techniques, and the improvement of cancer therapies. Amici predict that animal research will play some part in the prevention and treatment of such illnesses as multiple sclerosis, AIDS, and Alzheimer's disease. Recent amendments to the Animal Welfare Act have accordingly reaffirmed the congressional finding that "the use of animals is instrumental in certain research and education or for advancing knowledge of cures and treatments for diseases and injuries which afflict both humans and animals." H. Conf. Rep. No. 99–447 (1985).

Consistent with this purpose, Congress crafted a comprehensive plan for the regulation, inspection, and sanction of medical facilities that utilize animals in research. It is clear that the supervisory goals of the statute were to be realized through a regime of administrative enforcement, with a right of judicial review for an aggrieved facility. It is equally clear that these goals were not to be realized through a succession of private lawsuits. * * *

---

4. Under the revised statute, enforcement by the Secretary of Agriculture will be supplemented by the requirement that each research facility appoint an Institutional Animal Committee, including at least one veterinarian and one person not affiliated with the facility, to monitor the treatment of animals. The committee will report unconnected violations to the Department of Agriculture and to any federal agency that funds the research facility. 7 U.S.C. § 2143. This additional administrative system adopts for the Animal Welfare Act an approach that has been followed for many years by NIH.

The uniformity and specialization normally thought to accompany regulatory oversight, in this case that of the Secretary, would not inhere in enforcement of the statute through private rights of action. Judges and juries possess limited acquaintance with the problems and requirements of biomedical research. Their judgments and verdicts may fail to provide that modicum of consistency and predictability without which laboratory scientists would find it difficult to operate. To add extensive pre-trial discovery of a facility's practices to the administrative inspections already authorized by Congress would impose a gratuitous burden upon federally funded research. Finally, the prospect of damage awards in excess of the prescribed statutory penalties might discourage scientists from entering many lines of medical inquiry. * * * [W]e are convinced that Congress intended the administrative remedy to be the exclusive remedy. To accord plaintiffs standing to sue by virtue of a private cause of action would not conform to the aims of Congress in the Animal Welfare Act. * * *

NOTES AND QUESTIONS

1. *Other standing cases.* Interestingly, the Federal Laboratory Animal Welfare Act, as implemented, covers guinea pigs and hamsters, but not birds, mice, or rats. See Animal Legal Defense Fund, Inc. v. Espy, 23 F.3d 496 (D.C.Cir.1994) (concluding that plaintiffs lacked standing to challenge the USDA's implementing regulation); Animal Legal Defense Fund, Inc. v. Espy, 29 F.3d 720 (D.C.Cir.1994) (same); see also Alternatives R&D Fdn. v. Glickman, 101 F.Supp.2d 7 (D.D.C.2000); cf. Animal Legal Defense Fund v. Shalala, 104 F.3d 424 (D.C.Cir.1997) (holding that the NAS committee responsible for revising the "Guide for the Care and Use of Laboratory Animals," which must be used by entities receiving NIH funding, was subject to the requirements of the Federal Advisory Committee Act). See generally Joshua E. Gardner, At the Intersection of Constitutional Standing, Congressional Citizen–Suits, and the Humane Treatment of Animals: Proposals to Strengthen the Animal Welfare Act, 68 Geo. Wash. L. Rev. 330 (2000).

2. *Further commentary.* See National Research Council, Use of Laboratory Animals in Biomedical and Behavioral Research (1988); Vaughn Monamy, Animal Experimentation: A Guide to the Issues (2000); Deborah Rudacille, The Scalpel and the Butterfly: The War Between Animal Research and Animal Protection (2000); Steven M. Wise, Rattling the Cage: Toward Legal Rights for Animals (2000); Mimi Brody, Animal Research: A Call for Legislative Reform Requiring Ethical Merit Review, 13 Harv. Envtl. L. Rev. 423 (1989); Rebecca Dresser, Research on Animals: Values, Politics and Regulatory Reforms, 58 S. Cal. L. Rev. 1147 (1985); Estelle A. Fishbein, What Price Mice?, 285 JAMA 939 (2001); Gary Francione, The Constitutional Status of Restrictions on Experiments Involving Nonhuman Animals, 40 Rutgers L. Rev. 797 (1988); Karen L. McDonald, Creating a Private Cause of Action Against Abusive Animal Research, 134 U. Pa. L. Rev. 399 (1986); Carole Lynn Nowicki, The Animal Welfare Act: All Bark and No Bite, 23 Seton Hall Legis. J. 443 (1999); Martha C. Nussbaum, Animal

Rights: The Need for a Theoretical Basis, 114 Harv. L. Rev. 1506 (2001) (book review); Richard C. Posner, Animal Rights, 110 Yale L.J. 527 (2000) (book review); Cass R. Sunstein, A Tribute to Kenneth L. Karst: Standing for Animals (with Notes on Animal Rights), 47 UCLA L. Rev. 1333 (2000); Symposium, Progress Without Pain: The Argument for Humane Treatment of Research Animals, 31 St. Louis U. L.J. 513 (1987); Symposium, Animals in Research, 13 J. Med. & Phil. 121 (1988); D. Richard Joslyn, Annotation, Validity, Construction, and Application of Animal Welfare Act, 36 A.L.R. Fed. 627 (1978 & 2002 Supp.); Alan M. Goldberg & John M. Frazier, Alternatives to Animals in Toxicity Testing, Sci. Am., Aug. 1989, at 24; Michael Waldholz, Liberating Animals from Drug Testing, Wall St. J., Nov. 13, 1989, at B1.

The FDA has issued good laboratory practice (GLP) regulations that govern pre-clinical research. See 21 C.F.R. pt. 58. If the pre-clinical results are promising, the sponsor may then seek to test the investigational compound in humans. Because the FDCA prohibits the shipment of unapproved drugs in interstate commerce, pharmaceutical companies wishing to test investigational drugs must seek an exemption under the investigational new drug (IND) provision of the Act:

(1) The Secretary shall promulgate regulations for exempting from the operation of the foregoing subsections of this section drugs intended solely for investigational use by experts qualified by scientific training and experience to investigate the safety and effectiveness of drugs. Such regulations may, within the discretion of the Secretary, among other conditions relating to the public health, provide for conditioning such exemption upon—

(A) the submission to the Secretary, before any clinical testing of a new drug is undertaken, of reports, by the manufacturer or the sponsor of the investigation of such drug, of preclinical tests (including tests on animals) of such drug adequate to justify the proposed clinical testing;

(B) the manufacturer or the sponsor of the investigation of a new drug proposed to be distributed to investigators for clinical testing obtaining a signed agreement from each of such investigators that patients to whom the drug is administered will be under his personal supervision . . .; and

(C) the establishment and maintenance of such records, and the making of such reports to the Secretary, by the manufacturer or the sponsor of the investigation of such drug of data (including but not limited to analytical reports by investigators) obtained as the result of such investigational use of such drug. . . .

(4)   . . . Such regulations shall provide that such exemption shall be conditioned upon the manufacturer, or the sponsor of the investiga-

tion, requiring that experts using such drugs for investigational purposes certify to such manufacturer or sponsor that they will inform any human beings or their representatives that such drugs are being used for investigational purposes and will obtain the consent of such human beings or their representatives. . . . Nothing in the subsection shall be construed to require any clinical investigator to submit directly to the Secretary reports on the investigational use of drugs.

21 U.S.C. § 355(i). The FDA's implementing regulations cover issues such as control of the investigational drug, recordkeeping requirements and investigator reports, and assurance of institutional review board (IRB) review. See 21 C.F.R. pt. 312; see also Richard Kingham, History of FDA Regulation of Clinical Research, 22 Drug Info. J. 151 (1988). "FDA's primary objectives in reviewing an IND are, in all phases of the investigation, to ensure the safety and rights of subjects, and in Phase 2 and 3, to help assure that the quality of the scientific evaluation of drugs is adequate to permit an evaluation of the drug's effectiveness and safety." 21 C.F.R. § 312.22(a). Unless the FDA raises an objection within 30 days of filing, the IND becomes effective.

Once a sponsor has secured an IND, it may lawfully conduct the three phases of pre-approval clinical trials to test the investigational drug unless the FDA places a "clinical hold" on the IND after the trials have begun. See id. § 312.42. The regulations describe the phases of testing as follows:

The clinical investigation of a previously untested drug is divided into three phases. Although in general the phases are conducted sequentially, they may overlap. These three phases of an investigation are as follows:

(a) *Phase 1.*

(1) Phase 1 includes the initial introduction of an investigational new drug into humans. Phase 1 studies are typically closely monitored and may be conducted in patients or normal volunteer subjects. These studies are designed to determine the metabolism and pharmacologic actions of the drug in humans, the side effects associated with increasing doses, and, if possible, to gain early evidence on effectiveness. During Phase 1, sufficient information about the drug's pharmacokinetics and pharmacological effects should be obtained to permit the design of well-controlled, scientifically valid, Phase 2 studies. The total number of subjects and patients included in Phase 1 studies varies with the drug, but is generally in the range of 20 to 80.

(2) Phase 1 studies also include studies of drug metabolism, structure-activity relationships, and mechanism of action in humans, as well as studies in which investigational drugs are used as research tools to explore biological phenomena or disease processes.

(b) *Phase 2.* Phase 2 includes the controlled clinical studies conducted to evaluate the effectiveness of the drug for a particular indication or indications in patients with the disease or condition under study and to determine the common short-term side effects and risks associated with the drug. Phase 2 studies are typically well-controlled, closely monitored, and conducted in a relatively small number of patients, usually involving no more than several hundred subjects.

(c) *Phase 3*. Phase 3 studies are expanded controlled and uncontrolled trials. They are performed after preliminary evidence suggesting effectiveness of the drug has been obtained, and are intended to gather the additional information about effectiveness and safety that is needed to evaluate the overall benefit-risk relationship of the drug and to provide an adequate basis for physician labeling. Phase 3 studies usually include from several hundred to several thousand subjects.

Id. § 312.21; see also Walter Sneader, Drug Discovery: The Evolution of Modern Medicines (1985); John P. Swann, Academic Scientists and the Pharmaceutical Industry: Cooperative Research in Twentieth Century America (1988); Richard J. Findlay, Originator Drug Development, 54 Food & Drug L.J. 227 (1999) (describing the drug development process, and providing estimates for the length of time typically required to complete each clinical trial phase); Robert D. Rosenberg, Redesigning Heparin, 344 New Eng. J. Med. 673 (2001) (describing the anticoagulant's history, including the synthesis of a related molecular version of the substance, and predicting future developments based on a better understanding of heparin's properties and function); Justin A. Zivin, Understanding Clinical Trials, Sci. Am., Apr. 2000, at 69. The testing of experimental biological products must abide by the same regulatory requirements as other investigational drugs. See 21 C.F.R. § 601.25.

The relatively short duration, narrow subject population, and small size of pre-approval clinical trials limit the ability of these studies to uncover rare or delayed adverse reactions associated with new drugs. In order to have a 95% chance of detecting an adverse drug reaction with an incidence of 1–in–1,000, a study must enroll at least 3,000 patients. Because clinical trials typically enroll no more than 4,000 total individuals and may last a year or two, the studies will only detect acute adverse reactions that occur at a rate of 1–in–1,000 or higher. See Reporting Adverse Drug and Medical Device Events: Report of the AMA's Council on Ethical and Judicial Affairs, 49 Food & Drug L.J. 359, 360 (1994). Wholly apart from the problems associated with the relatively small numbers of subjects, pre-approval clinical trials historically have enrolled unrepresentative samples of patient populations. Researchers traditionally have excluded—or included only in very limited numbers—women, minorities, children, and the elderly in clinical trials of new drugs. See Barbara A. Noah, Racial Disparities in the Delivery of Health Care, 35 San Diego L. Rev. 135, 152–54 (1998) (describing the difficulties of extrapolating information about a drug's safety or effectiveness for the general population from data derived largely from white males); see also R. Alta Charo, Protecting Us to Death: Women, Pregnancy, and Clinical Research Trials, 38 St. Louis U. L.J. 135 (1993); L. Elizabeth Bowles, Note, The Disenfranchisement of Fertile Women in Clinical Trials: The Legal Ramifications of and Solutions for Rectifying the Knowledge Gap, 45 Vand. L. Rev. 877 (1992); Seminar on

Women in Clinical Trials of FDA–Regulated Products: Who Participates and Who Decides?, 48 Food & Drug L.J. 161 (1993). The FDA has now issued a series of guidelines to encourage the inclusion of so-called "special populations" in clinical trials in order to combat this problem.

United States v. Garfinkel

29 F.3d 451 (8th Cir. 1994).

■ MAGILL, CIRCUIT JUDGE:

In this appeal, the government challenges the district court's order dismissing two counts of the indictment brought against Barry Garfinkel. The two dismissed counts charged Garfinkel with the violation of Food and Drug Administration (FDA) regulations. We reverse and remand to the district court for further proceedings. * * *

Garfinkel, the principal investigator for an experimental drug study, was responsible for the clinical treatment and follow-up of patients receiving the experimental drug, Anafranil. The indictment charged Garfinkel * * * with failing to establish and maintain accurate drug-protocol records required by FDA regulations. *[handwritten:] charge*

The use of experimental drugs is regulated by FDA, pursuant to the authority of the Food, Drug, and Cosmetic Act. Drug manufacturers must apply for an exemption from the otherwise applicable premarketing approval requirements * * * by submitting an investigational new drug application (IND). An IND allows qualified experts or investigators, such as Garfinkel, to conduct investigations on the safety and effectiveness of the experimental drug. The pharmaceutical company filing an IND is referred to as the sponsor of the proposed new drug.

Prior to commencing any clinical study, FDA regulations require a sponsor to provide FDA with extensive information regarding the proposed study, including a detailed investigation plan known as the study protocol. All physicians participating in a study as investigators must adhere to the study protocol. Pursuant to § 355(i) of the Act, FDA regulations impose explicit recordkeeping requirements upon protocol investigators such as Garfinkel.

Garfinkel's motion to dismiss * * * argued (1) that § 355(i), the relevant subsection of the Act, places the entire recordkeeping burden upon the manufacturer and sponsor rather than the clinical investigator; and (2) that executive agencies do not have the authority to establish regulations enforceable by criminal penalties in the absence of sufficient congressional guidelines and standards for the exercise of that authority. * * * *[handwritten: Π's claim]*

The statute suggests, but does not require, that FDA promulgate specific types of regulations pertaining to sponsors and manufacturers. The statute, in fact, does not require that FDA promulgate any recordkeeping regulations at all. FDA, however, is required to promulgate regulations which will allow for exemptions from the new drug application process. Those exemptions may apply only to "drugs intended solely for investigational use," by experts "to investigate the safety and effectiveness of drugs," and those exemptions must be conditioned on the imposition of certain informed-consent provisions upon manufacturers or sponsors.

Urging this court to construe § 355(i) narrowly to avoid the constitutional question, Garfinkel argues that § 355(i) only authorizes FDA to promulgate regulations pertaining to the sponsors and manufacturers of new drugs. In turn, the government contends that the statute, as evidenced by its language and legislative history, authorizes FDA to promulgate regulations pertaining to clinical investigators. * * * Specifically, we must determine whether the language "among other conditions relating to the protection of the public health" authorizes FDA to impose recordkeeping requirements on clinical investigators.

The obligations imposed by FDA on clinical investigators mandate the maintenance and retention, as well as the provision to the sponsor, of reports and data relating to the underlying drug trials of investigational drugs. A clinical investigator who falsified or destroyed original records of a drug study, and who then submitted false records to a sponsor, would clearly cause the sponsor to maintain false records and to make false reports to FDA. Moreover, were an investigator not required to maintain his or her own records (as distinct from those maintained by the sponsor), FDA would in those cases frequently be precluded from even discovering the falseness of the reports and would then review and perhaps approve drug products on the basis of false data.

We hold that in light of the dangers incumbent in the receipt of false data, mandating the maintenance and retention of protocol records is in the interest of the protection of the public health. We nonetheless hold that the language of the statute is ambiguous at least as it relates to FDA's authority over clinical investigators. * * *

Because the statutory language is ambiguous on this precise issue, we examine the legislative history to determine whether FDA's interpretation conflicts with Congress's expressed intent. We find support in the legislative history for FDA's interpretation of the statute. Although the House of Representatives' version of the 1962 Amendments to the Act originally included several prescribed conditions to be imposed by FDA regulations, the Conference Report makes clear that "these are not the sole conditions imposed for the protection of the public interest." We agree with Garfinkel that the legislative history indicates Congress's focus was on the manufacturers and sponsors of investigational drugs, but we find nothing in the legislative history to indicate that Congress intended to limit FDA's authority to the sponsors and manufacturers. To the contrary, we learn that Congress was concerned that any regulations promulgated by FDA have due regard for the professional ethics of the medical profession, thus indicating that Congress perceived that regulations could impact upon the physician/patient relationship. Finding that § 355(i)'s legislative history is ambiguous as to FDA's authority to impose recordkeeping obligations on clinical investigators, we hold that FDA's interpretation of the statute does not conflict with Congress's expressed intent.

Lacking an expression of contrary intent by Congress, we cannot disturb the Secretary's construction of the statute if it reflects a permissible interpretation of the statute. * * * According FDA's interpretation substantial deference, we hold that § 355(i) authorizes the promulgation of clinical-investigator recordkeeping regulations.

NOTES AND QUESTIONS

1. *Keeping tabs on investigators.* Recall from *APhA* the court's concession that the FDA has the authority to impose distribution controls on investigational products. Are criminal proceedings against investigators the most appropriate response to failures to abide by FDA regulations? Cf. United States v. Keplinger, 776 F.2d 678 (7th Cir.1985) (prosecution for fraudulent animal testing of drugs). One alternative is to disqualify clinical investigators who have violated IND requirements. See 21 C.F.R. § 312.70. Can't the agency also accomplish its purpose by targeting the sponsor in cases of noncompliance by investigators? Doesn't it otherwise risk unduly interfering in the practice of medicine?

2. *Constitutional rights of researchers.* Recall the *Whalen* Court's rejection of the physicians' argument that New York's recordkeeping requirements violated their privacy-based right to practice medicine without interference. Commentators have debated the claim that scientists enjoy constitutional protection derived from the First Amendment against governmental interference with their right to engage in research. See Richard Delgado & David R. Millen, God, Galileo, and Government: Toward Constitutional Protection for Scientific Inquiry, 53 Wash. L. Rev. 349 (1978); James R. Ferguson, Scientific Inquiry and the First Amendment, 64 Cornell L. Rev. 639 (1979); Gary L. Francione, Experimentation and the Marketplace Theory of the First Amendment, 136 U. Pa. L. Rev. 417 (1986); Robert M. O'Neil, Scientific Research and the First Amendment: An Academic Privilege, 16 U.C. Davis L. Rev. 837 (1983); John A. Robertson, The Scientist's Right to Research: A Constitutional Analysis, 51 S. Cal. L. Rev. 1203 (1977).

3. *Medical devices.* For investigational devices, a process roughly parallel to the IND approach described above governs how manufacturers may begin the testing process in humans. As explained in Chapter 3, different categories of medical devices require different levels of pre-market investigation. To the extent that human testing is required for an application to market a new medical device, the manufacturer must request an investigational device exemption (IDE) permitting limited distribution of the new device for use in clinical trials. See 21 U.S.C. § 360j(g); see also Marc H. Bozeman, The Clinical Investigation of Medical Devices–A Preliminary Guide for Manufacturers, 34 Food Drug Cosm. L.J. 289 (1979). However, IDEs for devices that do not pose a significant risk need not be reviewed by the FDA—a sponsor need only secure IRB approval.

The IDE requires the manufacturer to comply with a variety of regulations designed to protect patients who participate as test subjects. See 21 C.F.R. pt. 812.

> [I]nvestigational devices are ... subject to a ... set of complex and comprehensive regulations which set forth detailed procedures for determining whether investigational devices are safe and effective. To obtain approval of a device under the IDE, a manufacturer must submit an application to the FDA containing an abundance of information.... [T]he manufacturer must submit a detailed statement regarding the intended use of the device and the objectives and planned duration of the investigational study; a written protocol describing the methodology to be used and an analysis of the protocol demonstrating that the investigation is scientifically sound; an analysis of all risks involved; a description of each component, ingredient, property, and principle of operation of the device; a detailed description of the methods, facilities and controls used for manufacturing, processing, packing, storing and installing the device; sample agreements between the manufacturers and all proposed investigators; detailed information about the health care professionals and institutions participating in the investigation; proposed labeling; proposed informed consent forms; and a full set of written procedures for monitoring the investigation, including record and report maintenance. Pursuant to 21 C.F.R. § 812.27, the manufacturer must submit a bibliography of every publication relevant to the evaluation of the device and information from non-clinical testing. Based on the information submitted, the FDA will approve the device under the IDE unless "the risks to the subjects are not outweighed by the anticipated benefits to the subjects and the importance of the knowledge to be gained, or informed consent is inadequate, or the investigation is scientifically unsound, or there is reason to believe that the device as used is ineffective."

Martin v. Telectronics Pacing Sys., Inc., 105 F.3d 1090, 1095–96 (6th Cir.1997). As demonstrated below, even this complex and well-developed regulatory process for the testing of experimental products poses some challenges for all parties concerned—manufacturers, prospective beneficiaries of the new products, regulatory agencies, and the courts.

Femrite v. Abbott Northwestern Hospital

568 N.W.2d 535 (Minn.Ct.App.1997).

■ HARTEN, JUSTICE:

Appellants Cary Femrite and Ruth Perkl underwent spinal fusion surgery that involved implantation with pedicle screw devices at respondent Abbott Northwestern Hospital. In December 1989, Femrite was implanted with a screw device known as the "VSP" or "Stefee" system manufactured by AcroMed. In February 1990, Perkl was implanted with a screw device known as the "Cotrel Dubousset" manufactured by Sofamor Danek. At the time of surgery, neither appellant was informed that the surgery was experimental or that implantation of the screw device in pedicles was investigational. Both appellants experienced complications and medical problems after receiving the implants. * * *

To enable a manufacturer to obtain necessary clinical data for FDA premarket approval, the FDA grants an Investigational Device Exemption (IDE), which permits a device (that would ordinarily require premarket approval) to be "shipped lawfully for the purpose of conducting investigations of that device." An "investigation" is defined as "a clinical investigation or research involving one or more subjects to determine the safety and effectiveness of a device." A hospital may not initiate investigational studies under an IDE without approval and oversight by a hospital's institutional review board (IRB). An IRB is a committee designed to review biomedical research involving patients. * * *

Appellants argue that the district court erred when it dismissed their claims based on Abbott's alleged negligence in performing its administrative functions. Appellants contend that Abbott allowed physicians to make spinal implantation of screw devices outside an approved IDE in violation of federal law, that Abbott violated state law by failing to obtain informed consent, and that Abbott failed to comply with its own internal case management policies. All of appellants' claims, however, depend on the single premise that it was unlawful for Abbott to allow physicians to use the screw devices in appellants' spinal surgeries. Thus, our determination hinges on whether federal law limited implantation of the screw device in spinal surgeries to investigational usage or simultaneously permitted it to be implanted into spinal pedicles as an "off-label" use. * * *

The district court determined that appellants failed to state a cause of action for negligence per se because appellants "were not participants in a clinical investigation or a research study." Appellants insist that the district court's disposition of this claim "begs the question" because they contend the screw device was an investigational device that could be used only within the context of a clinical investigation. * * * [T]he record is devoid of evidence to support appellants' assertion that in 1986 the FDA approved use of the screw devices for arms and legs, but specifically prohibited their use in spines.

Appellants also submit a 1995 FDA letter authorizing the use of the screw device * * * only for patients with severe spondylolisthesis. Appellants point out that the FDA letter authorizing use of the device for spondylolisthesis indicates that other uses of the device are considered investigational and could occur lawfully only pursuant to an approved IDE. Thus, appellants suggest that if spondylolisthesis is absent, the screw device may be implanted into spinal pedicles only within clinical investigations.

Abbott, on the other hand, argues that the use of the screw devices here was an "off-label" use because the FDA had already approved the device for use in long and flat bones. Abbott contends that implantation of the screw device in spinal fixation surgeries is an "off-label" use, and as such, involves medical discretion, which is beyond FDA regulation. * * *

To support their argument that "off-label" use of the screw devices was permitted, Abbott submitted an affidavit of James Benson, former Acting FDA Commissioner and Deputy Commissioner. Benson's affidavit states that "off-label" use is a "longstanding and common practice which has been acknowledged by the FDA." Benson's affidavit also states that use of screw devices in the pedicles of the spine did not violate FDA regulations or policy as of December 1992 (when he left the FDA).

Appellants nevertheless contend that it is anomalous to suggest that the screw device could be implanted in patients within the scope of clinical investigations—which were being conducted at Abbott at the time of appellants' surgeries—and at the same time lawfully be implanted into other patients who were not participating in the investigations. Appellants deny that physicians could consider "off-label" usage to be a standard of care in some cases and simultaneously investigational in others.

The record, however, demonstrates otherwise. In 1986, AcroMed received 510(k) approval to market bone screws or plates as a Class II device for use in long bones such as those in arms and legs. Given that approval, physicians could permissibly implant the screw device elsewhere in the body as an "off-label" use, albeit the approval was for use in arms and legs; nevertheless, manufacturers were not permitted to market the device for such usage because of the 1984 and 1985 FDA classification of the device as Class III investigational for pedicle spine usage. Manufacturers of the screws and plates for long, flat bones apparently sought authority to market these products for use as pedicle screw devices. To that end, the same manufacturers that received 510(k) approval to market their screw device for one purpose (long and flat bones) also requested FDA approval to conduct clinical investigations in their quest for eventual FDA approval to market the same screw device as a pedicle screw device. Therefore, a hospital could acquire the same device from a manufacturer either through routine commercial means for "off-label" use or as an investigational device under an IDE. * * * FDA "encourages surgeons using pedicle screw devices to enroll their patients in such approved clinical investigations." There is no evidence, however, that such enrollment is required. * * * [W]e conclude as a matter of law that the physicians' implantation of the screw devices in appellants' surgeries was a permissible "off-label" use not in violation of FDA regulations. Accordingly, we affirm summary judgment on appellants' FDA regulation negligence per se claims. * * *

NOTES AND QUESTIONS

1. *Informed consent at common law.* Might the conduct described in *Femrite* still amount to negligence even if not forbidden by the FDA? Although some courts require that physicians disclose to patients the fact that a treatment remains experimental, others have rejected informed consent claims premised on the failure to reveal a product's regulatory status. See, e.g., Southard v. Temple Univ. Hosp., 781 A.2d 101, 107–08 (Pa.2001).

2. *The fine line between research and the practice of medicine.* Consider this definition in the IND regulations: *"Clinical investigation* means any experiment in which a drug is administered or dispensed to, or used involving, one or more human subjects. For purposes of this part, an experiment is any use of a drug except for the use of a marketed drug in the course of medical practice." 21 C.F.R. § 312.3(b). Recall from Chapter 1 that the court in *Evers* rejected an FDA misbranding action against a physician who engaged in the off-label use of Calcium EDTA for the treatment of arteriosclerosis, while the court in *Retkwa* sustained a negligence per se claim in a medical malpractice case against a cosmetic surgeon for injecting liquid silicone, which had not received FDA approval for any use in patients. Should the existence of an IND or IDE for a new use of a previously approved product alter the FDA's usual policy of tolerating off-label uses? Why is an IND or IDE even required before undertaking clinical trials of a new use if the product already may lawfully move in interstate commerce? What if the agency had specifically rejected an application for an investigational exception for that use?

B. INSTITUTIONAL REVIEW BOARDS

Institutional review boards function primarily as protectors of human subjects who participate in medical research of all sorts. At the same time, IRBs play an essential role in the approval process for new medical products. By overseeing research protocols to test the safety and effectiveness of experimental drugs and medical devices, IRBs enable clinical researchers to collect the data necessary for a thorough FDA assessment of new products. IRBs review and then supervise protocols involving the use of investigational drugs and medical devices, as well as other types of clinical research.

Several ethical codes provide guidance for clinical researchers. The Nuremberg Code, which emerged out of the trials of Nazi physicians after World War II, sets out a series of essential principles for permissible medical experiments. See 276 JAMA 1691 (1996). In 1964, the World Medical Association adopted the Declaration of Helsinki, which provides additional guidance. See 277 JAMA 925 (1997); see also Jay Katz, Human Sacrifice and Human Experimentation: Reflections at Nuremberg, 22 Yale J. Int'l L. 401 (1997). The American Medical Association also has issued guidelines on clinical research. Recent international research projects have tested the reach and effectiveness of these guidelines. See Joe Stephens, The Body Hunters: As Drug Testing Spreads, Profits and Lives Hang in Balance, Wash. Post, Dec. 17, 2000, at A1 (first of a six article series on international clinical research abuses).

These codes and guidelines provided the underpinnings for the first formal regulations governing human research, which were originally issued by the Department of Health, Education, and Welfare (the predecessor of HHS) in 1974. See 30 Fed. Reg. 18,914 (1974) (codified as amended at 45 C.F.R. pt. 46). Seven years later, the FDA promulgated its regulations, which are excerpted below. See 46 Fed. Reg. 8942 (1981) (codified as amended at 21 C.F.R. pts. 50 & 56). In 1977, even before its regulations were in place, the FDA developed its Bioresearch Monitoring Program and began to review the activities of IRBs in earnest. Under this program, the agency regularly conducts on-site inspections of IRBs to review compliance with FDA regulations and internal procedures. Both the FDA and the NIH's Office of Human Research Protections (OHRP) have the authority to inspect and suspend research activities at institutions that receive federal funding.

The FDA's regulations apply to all studies of investigational drugs, medical devices, and biological products. HHS's regulations apply to all types of research conducted at institutions that receive federal funds. The two sets of regulations are for the most part co-extensive, and, because most research institutions receive federal funding for at least some of the work being done under their roofs, IRBs generally hold all research protocols to the standards set out in these regulations. All institutions that receive HHS funding must provide the Department with an "assurance" that all research conducted at the institution, regardless of the source of funding, will protect human subjects according to the principles in the regulations. See 45 C.F.R. § 46.103; see also Jesse A. Goldner, An Overview of Legal Controls on Human Experimentation and the Regulatory Implications of Taking Professor Katz Seriously, 38 St. Louis U. L.J. 63 (1993). But cf. R. Alta Charo, Human Subjects Have It Worse Than Guinea Pigs, Chron. Higher Educ., June 25, 1999, at A64 (noting significant gaps in coverage).

NOTES AND QUESTIONS

1. *Reviewing the reviewers.* A recent study reviewed 1,000 spot checks carried out by the FDA. See Sheila Kaplan & Shannon Brownlee, Dying for a Cure, U.S. News & World Rep., Oct. 11, 1999, at 36. In the protocols examined, 213 researchers failed to obtain informed consent from research subjects; 364 researchers deviated from their approved research protocols; and 140 failed to report adverse reactions in their study subjects. Other surveys have also found major deficiencies in IRB review and oversight at major research institutions. See Jon Cohen, Clinical Trial Monitoring: Hit or Miss?, 264 Science 1534, 1536 (1994) (explaining that, in over 3,000 IRB site inspections conducted between 1977 and 1994, the FDA found informed consent problems at over half of the inspected sites and deviations from approved study protocols at 29% of the sites). The HHS Office of the Inspector General (OIG) recently issued a series of reports that criticized the operation of IRBs and OHRP's supervision of human research more generally. The reports focused on several problems endemic to IRB operations, such as overwhelming workload, lack of expertise, and conflicts of interest that interfered with proper review of research protocols. See OIG, HHS, Institutional Review Boards: Their Role in Reviewing Approved Research, OEI–01–97–00190 (1998); OIG, HHS, Institutional Review Boards: Promising Approaches, OEI–01–97–00191 (1998); see also David M.

Cocchetto, Practical Considerations in Direct Interactions Between Sponsors and IRBs, 49 Food & Drug L.J. 77 (1994). Recognizing that IRBs may lack critical expertise to review certain types of highly complex medical research, the NIH recently issued guidelines requiring that all research involving recombinant DNA that receives NIH funding be approved by an Institutional Biosafety Committee with relevant experience. See NIH Guidelines Involving Recombinant DNA Molecules (1999), available at <www.nih.gov>; see also Michael A. Morse et al., Monitoring and Ensuring Safety During Clinical Research, 285 JAMA 1201 (2001); Mark Barnes & Patrick Florencio, IRBs Tend to Grow Short of Needed Skills, Nat'l L.J. Sept. 4, 2000, at B1. Don't forget that most IRBs are not federal government entities. Apart from the NIH's in-house IRBs, most of these Boards are affiliated with state-run or private hospitals. Is it appropriate for the FDA to delegate quasi-regulatory functions to such entities? The inevitable ambiguities in the regulations result in potentially inconsistent and inexpert interpretations by IRBs.

2. *Cracking down.* In the past several years, a number of research institutions have seen their activities suspended or restricted due to agency concerns about compliance with regulatory requirements governing human research. When inspectors suspend research activities at an institution, most projects in progress must cease immediately. See 21 C.F.R. § 56.121. The FDA has recently inspected and temporarily shut down a number of IRBs at well-regarded research institutions because of non-compliance with regulatory requirements governing human research. In one tragic example, an 18–year old research subject died while participating in a gene-therapy experiment at the University of Pennsylvania that FDA inspectors later concluded was inadequately monitored by the university's IRB. See Rick Weiss & Deborah Nelson, Gene Therapy's Troubling Crossroads, Wash. Post, Dec. 31, 1999, at A3. The FDA shut down all research at the university for a time, and many outraged politicians called for more stringent research controls. See Sheryl Gay Stolberg, Committee Considers Change in Reporting on Gene Therapies, N.Y. Times, Dec. 11, 1999, at A13. More recently, OHRP suspended all federally-funded research at the Johns Hopkins University School of Medicine after a 24–year old healthy volunteer died while participating in a study to understand the causes of asthma. See Gina Kolata, Johns Hopkins Death Brings Halt to U.S.-Funded Human Research, N.Y. Times, July 20, 2001, at A1. A letter from OHRP to Johns Hopkins cited numerous deficiencies in the institution's IRB processes in general, and particular problems with the IRB's approval and oversight of the study that caused the subject's death. See Patrick J. McNeilly, Letter to Johns Hopkins Univ. School of Medicine, July 19, 2001, available at <http://ohrp.osophs.dhhs.gov/detrm_letrs/jul01a.pdf>. OHRP lifted the suspension after it received a corrective action plan from the university.

3. *Pressures on academic medicine.* Financial connections between researchers and medical technology companies have generated increasing concern. See Marcia Angell, Editorial, Is Academic Medicine for Sale?, 342 New Eng. J. Med. 1516 (2000); Thomas Bodenheimer, Uneasy Alliance–Clinical Investigators and the Pharmaceutical Industry, 342 New Eng. J.

Med. 1539 (2000); Goldie Blumenstyk & David L. Wheeler, Academic Medical Centers Compete in the $3.2–Billion Drug–Testing Market, Chron. Higher Educ., Mar. 20, 1998, at A39 (describing university efforts to attract drug industry funding to conduct clinical trials at their institutions). New FDA regulations require that sponsors disclose their investigators' financial interests in products that are the subject of research protocols. See 21 C.F.R. § 54.4; Nina M. Gussack & Karen M. Suddath, Clinical Trial Conflicts Apply to Investigators, Nat'l L.J., May 14, 2001, at C3; see also Jesse A. Goldner, Dealing with Conflicts of Interest in Biomedical Research: IRB Oversight as the Next Best Solution to the Abolitionist Approach, 28 J.L. Med. & Ethics 379 (2000); Sidney A. Shapiro, Divorcing Profit Motivation from New Drug Research: A Consolidation of Proposals to Provide the FDA with Reliable Test Data, 1978 Duke L.J. 155. Might greater government involvement in the funding and execution of research be preferable?

4. *Finding a balanced response to research oversight deficiencies.* Commentators have recommended that Congress create an independent Human Subject Protection Agency with rulemaking and adjudicatory authority over all human research. See George J. Annas, Regs Ignored in Research, Nat'l L.J., Nov. 15, 1999, at A20; see also Marc Kaufman, Clinical Trial Sanctions Urged: HHS Plans to Tighten Controls to Protect Patients in Tests, Wash. Post, May 24, 2000, at A2 (reporting that the Clinton administration asked Congress to authorize fines of up to $250,000 against individual scientists who violate research regulations and fines of up to $1 million against non-compliant institutions, and that HHS wants to improve IRB training and direct monitoring of patients during in-progress clinical trials). Others urge caution, however, in considering additional layers of safeguards for clinical research, noting that research is by definition a risky undertaking and suggesting that researchers redouble their efforts to use sound scientific design for their research, to avoid conflicts of interest, and to obtain full informed consent from participants. See Arthur Caplan & David Magnus, Overregulating Research, Chi. Trib., Dec. 21, 1999, at 31.

5. *Public disclosure.* The FDA requires researchers and sponsors to report adverse events associated with any research protocol, but it does not disclose the information to the public in order to avoid compromising manufacturers' interests. See Public Citizen Health Research Group v. FDA, 185 F.3d 898, 903–06 (D.C.Cir.1999); Public Citizen Health Research Group v. FDA, 704 F.2d 1280, 1290–91 (D.C.Cir.1983). Some critics of the FDA's supervision of gene therapy trials argued that the agency should disclose to the public serious adverse events associated with these trials in order to maximize the information on which participants choose to continue or discontinue participation. The biotech industry, on the other hand, argues that the existing regulations already overburden research that will prove immensely beneficial to patients in the future. See Secrecy and Gene Therapy, Wash. Post, Dec. 18, 1999, at A26.

6. *"Commercial" IRBs.* Many in-house IRBs at research institutions are now charging a fee for the initial and continuing review of research protocols in order to offset the significant costs associated with regulatory compliance. Such arrangements appear to present few if any ethical concerns. However, independent commercial IRBs also exist, with no affiliation to any research institution, and they charge substantial fees. One of the largest commercial boards, Western IRB in Olympia, Washington, employs over 150 people and charges $550 to review a new protocol. See Paul T. Kefalides, Research on Humans Faces Scrutiny: New Policies Adopted, 132 Annals Internal Med. 513 (2000). What ethical difficulties might such a system create?

---

21 C.F.R. § 56.111. Criteria for IRB Approval of Research.

(a) In order to approve research covered by these regulations the IRB shall determine that all of the following requirements are satisfied:

(1) Risks to subjects are minimized: (i) by using procedures which are consistent with sound research design and which do not unnecessarily expose subjects to risk, and (ii) whenever appropriate, by using procedures already being performed on the subjects for diagnostic or treatment purposes.

(2) Risks to subjects are reasonable in relation to anticipated benefits, if any, to subjects, and the importance of the knowledge that may be expected to result. In evaluating risks and benefits, the IRB should consider only those risks and benefits that may result from the research (as distinguished from risks and benefits of therapies that subjects would receive even if not participating in the research). The IRB should not consider possible long-range effects of applying knowledge gained in the research (for example, the possible effects of the research on public policy) as among those research risks that fall within the purview of its responsibility.

(3) Selection of subjects is equitable. In making this assessment the IRB should take into account the purposes of the research and the setting in which the research will be conducted and should be particularly cognizant of the special problems of research involving vulnerable populations, such as children, prisoners, pregnant women, handicapped, or mentally disabled persons, or economically or educationally disadvantaged persons.

(4) Informed consent will be sought from each prospective subject or the subject's legally authorized representative, in accordance with and to the extent required by part 50.

(5) Informed consent will be appropriately documented, in accordance with and to the extent required by Sec. 50.27.

(6) Where appropriate, the research plan makes adequate provision for monitoring the data collected to ensure the safety of subjects.

(7) Where appropriate, there are adequate provisions to protect the privacy of subjects and to maintain the confidentiality of data.

(b) When some or all of the subjects, such as children, prisoners, pregnant women, handicapped, or mentally disabled persons, or economically or educationally disadvantaged persons, are likely to be vulnerable to coercion or undue influence additional safeguards have been included in the study to protect the rights and welfare of these subjects.

NOTES AND QUESTIONS

1. *IRB membership*. The regulations set out the minimum requirements for the composition of an IRB. See 21 C.F.R. § 56.107. If you were a subject participating in a clinical trial, what kinds of people would you like to have sit on the committee that evaluates the research protocol? The regulation requires that each IRB have at least five members, with varying backgrounds to promote complete review of research activities commonly conducted by the institution. In addition, it addresses issues of expertise and diversity, requiring that the IRB's membership reflect "consideration of race, gender, cultural backgrounds, and sensitivity to such issues as community attitudes, to promote respect for its advice and counsel in safeguarding the rights and welfare of human subjects." The regulation also refers to the need to include board members who are "able to ascertain the acceptability of proposed research in terms of institutional commitments and regulations, applicable law, and standards or professional conduct and practice" (lawyers, perhaps?). It requires the inclusion of persons knowledgeable about vulnerable categories of subjects, such as children, prisoners, pregnant women, or handicapped or mentally disabled persons, if the IRB will be reviewing research involving such subjects. Finally, IRBs must consist of members of more than one profession, must have members of both sexes, and must have at least one non-scientist member and one member who is not otherwise affiliated with the research institution. One member may, of course, fulfill several of these roles simultaneously on a small IRB. (One of the authors of this casebook has served on an IRB for several years.)

2. *Additional review by the parent institution and IRB authority*. Once an IRB has approved a research protocol, the parent institution has the authority to subject the protocol to additional review, if desired, but an institution may not approve research that has already been rejected by the IRB. See 21 C.F.R. § 56.112. If an IRB discovers that clinical investigators are not complying with IRB requirements, or have deviated from an approved IRB protocol, it has the authority to suspend or terminate approval of the project. If the board suspends or terminates approval under these circumstances, it must report its actions immediately to the principal investigator, institution officials, and the FDA. See id. § 56.113.

3. *Equipoise in clinical research*. When a researcher/physician designs a research protocol to test the relative effectiveness and safety of two different treatments for the same condition, the genuine uncertainty as to the relative merits of the two treatments is known as "equipoise." Commentators have noted that equipoise is an ethical necessity in order to justify clinical research of this kind. See Benjamin Freedman, Equipoise and the Ethics of Clinical Research, 317 New Eng. J. Med. 141 (1987); Don Marquis, How to Resolve an Ethical Dilemma Concerning Randomized Clinical Trials, 341 New Eng. J. Med. 691 (1999); see also Stuart L. Nightingale, Challenges in Human Subject Protection, 50 Food & Drug L.J. 493 (1995). Why do you think equipoise is essential for this sort of research?

4. *Placebo-controlled clinical trials.* The use of placebos in clinical trials allows researchers to measure efficacy of the studied drug or treatment and to compare the placebo response. Indeed, from the FDA's perspective when it comes time for reviewing a product approval application, placebo-controlled trials provide the clearest evidence of effectiveness. Most ethicists agree that placebo-controlled studies are appropriate when evaluating drugs to treat conditions for which there is no known effective treatment. However, when effective alternatives exist, even for treating a relatively mild medical condition, some ethicists argue that placebo-controlled designs are inappropriate. See C. Michael Stein & Theodore Pincus, Placebo–Controlled Studies in Rheumatoid Arthritis: Ethical Issues, 353 Lancet 400 (1999). Indeed, recent revisions to the Declaration of Helsinki adopt this view, but the U.S. National Bioethics Advisory Commission has indicated that it will not abide by this new directive. See Susan Okie, Health Officials Debate Ethics of Placebo Use, Wash. Post, Nov. 24, 2000, at A3 (noting that no one defends placebo controls where established therapies exist to treat serious and measurable conditions such as infections, diabetes and cancer); see also David P. Fidler, "Geographical Morality" Revisited: International Relations, International Law, and the Controversy over Placebo–Controlled HIV Clinical Trials in Developing Countries, 42 Harv. Int'l L.J. 299 (2001); Sharona Hoffman, The Use of Placebos in Clinical Trials: Responsible Research or Unethical Practice?, 33 Conn. L. Rev. 449 (2001); Asbjorn Hrobjartsson & Peter C. Gotzsche, Is the Placebo Powerless? An Analysis of Clinical Trials Comparing Placebo with No Treatment, 344 New Eng. J. Med. 1595 (2001); Timothy S. Jost, The Globalization of Health Law: The Case of Permissibility of Placebo–Based Research, 26 Am. J.L. & Med. 175 (2000); Robert Temple & Susan S. Ellenberg, Placebo–Controlled Trials and Active–Control Trials in the Evaluation of New Treatments: Ethical and Scientific Issues, 133 Annals Internal Med. 455 (2000). Suppose a protocol involves a randomized, double-blind, placebo-controlled approach with half of the patients randomized to the study medication, one-quarter to an approved medication for high blood pressure, and one-quarter to placebo. After two months of study results, the principal investigator suspects, based on the benefits and side-effects that the patients experience, that the study medication works significantly more safely and effectively than the standard medication or placebo. He wonders whether he should offer the study medication to the patients in the control groups who are not doing well. What should he do? Should the IRB have approved this study?

5. *Definition of "research."* A variety of sources define clinical research, some more broadly than others. See, e.g., Albert R. Jonsen et al., Clinical

Ethics 192 (4th ed. 1998) ("Clinical research is defined as any clinical intervention involving human subjects, patients or normal volunteers, performed in accord with a protocol designed to yield generalizable scientific knowledge."). The FDA regulations describe circumstances in which IRB review is required in a somewhat circular manner: "Clinical investigation means any experiment that involves a test article and one or more human subjects, and that either must meet the requirements for prior submission to the [FDA] under section 505(i) or 520(g) of the Act [which govern investigational new drugs and medical devices respectively], or need not meet [these requirements] . . . but the results of which are intended to be later submitted to . . . the [FDA] as part of an application for a research or marketing permit." 21 C.F.R. § 56.102(c). With very limited exceptions, "any clinical investigation which must meet the requirements for prior submission . . . to the [FDA] shall not be initiated unless that investigation has been reviewed and approved by, and remains subject to continuing review by, an IRB meeting the requirements of this part." Id. § 56.103(a). In most circumstances, the FDA will not consider clinical data derived from research that has not been approved and monitored by an IRB in support of an application for marketing permission for a new medical product. See id. § 56.103(b). In one curious recent case, plastic surgeons performed different face lift procedures on opposite halves of their patients' faces and then tracked them to see whether one technique provided better results over time, publishing their initial results in a professional journal. Because the study did not involve an FDA-regulated product and received no federal funding, IRB requirements did not apply. See Philip J. Hilts, Study or Human Experiment? Face–Lift Project Stirs Ethical Concerns, N.Y. Times, June 21, 1998, at A25.

6. *Distinguishing between "research" and "treatment."* Not all experimental treatments constitute research requiring IRB approval. The distinction between therapy and research, and thus between "patients" and "subjects," has generated a good deal of commentary. See, e.g., Lars Noah, Informed Consent and the False Dichotomy Between Standard and Experimental Therapy (forthcoming 2002). The National Commission for the Protection of Human Subjects of Biomedical and Behavioral Research issued its well-known "Belmont Report" in 1978. See U.S. Gov't Printing Office No. (OS) 78–0012 (1978), reprinted at 44 Fed. Reg. 23,192 (1979). The report thoughtfully explores a number of research-related issues, including the boundaries between practice and research, an introduction to basic ethical principles, and the complexities of applying these principles in the research context. It offered the following guidance:

> It is important to distinguish between biomedical and behavioral research, on the one hand, and the practice of accepted therapy on the other, in order to know what activities ought to undergo review for the protection of human subjects of research. The distinction between research and practice is blurred partly because both often occur together (as in research designed to evaluate a therapy) and partly because notable departures from standard practice are often called "experimental" when the terms "experimental" and "research" are not carefully

defined.... [T]he term "research" designates an activity designed to test a hypothesis, permit conclusions to be drawn, and thereby to develop or contribute to generalizable knowledge (expressed, for example, in theories, principles, and statements of relationships). Research is usually described in a formal protocol that sets forth an objective and a set of procedures designed to reach that objective. When a clinician departs in a significant way from standard or accepted practice, the innovation does not, in and of itself, constitute research. The fact that a procedure is "experimental," in the sense of new, untested or different, does not automatically place it in the category of research. Radically new procedures of this description should, however, be made the object of formal research at an early stage in order to determine whether they are safe and effective.... Research and practice may be carried on together when research is designed to evaluate the safety and efficacy of a therapy. This need not cause any confusion regarding whether or not the activity requires review; the general rule is that if there is any element of research in an activity, that activity should undergo review for the protection of human subjects.

Conversely, even the on-label use of FDA-approved products might have a research aspect to it insofar as physicians monitor and report unexpected adverse events in their patients that may trigger labeling revisions or product withdrawals by the FDA. Concerns about heart valve abnormalities with fenfluramine first surfaced because physicians at the Mayo Clinic decided to follow up a group of patients by ordering echocardiograms. See Michael A. Friedman et al., The Safety of Newly Approved Medicines: Do Recent Market Withdrawals Mean There Is a Problem?, 281 JAMA 1728, 1728 (1999) (describing a report from Mayo Clinic researchers of 24 cases of valvular disease and aortic and mitral valve regurgitation in patients taking fenfluramine in combination with the amphetamine phentermine).

7. *The tension between physician-as-caregiver and physician-as-scientist.* The traditional model of the doctor-patient relationship envisions a physician whose primary, indeed only, allegiance, is to the well-being of his or her patient. When physicians engage in research, this role is tested—some would say improperly:

> As medicine has become increasingly scientific and less accepting of unsupported opinion or proof by anecdote, the randomized controlled clinical trial has become the standard technique for changing diagnostic or therapeutic methods. The use of this technique creates an ethical dilemma. Researchers participating in such studies are required to modify their ethical commitments to individual patients and do serious damage to the concept of the physician as a practicing, empathetic professional who is primarily concerned with each patient as an individual. Researchers using a randomized clinical trial can be described as physician-scientists, a term that expresses the tension between the two roles. The physician, by entering into a relationship with an individual patient, assumes certain obligations, including the commitment always to act in the patient's best interests.... The role of the

scientist is quite different. The clinical scientist is concerned with answering questions—i.e., determining the validity of formally constructed hypotheses. Such scientific information, it is presumed will benefit humanity in general.

Samuel Hellman & Deborah S. Hellman, Of Mice but Not Men: Problems of the Randomized Clinical Trial, 324 New Eng. J. Med. 1585 (1991).

PROBLEM #3. *WHEN DOES TREATMENT BECOME RESEARCH?*

Frank Finagle, a plastic surgeon, chatted with a surgical colleague, Doris Dare, who told him about a different wound dressing material that she had been using with great success to speed the healing of large abdominal incisions. The FDA approved the wound dressing material for general surgical use, but only a few plastic surgeons have used it so far. Based on Dr. Dare's recommendation, Dr. Finagle decides to try the new wound dressing when he does tummy tucks and abdominal liposuction to see how he likes it. Hypothesizing that the material might work better than his usual choice, he resolves to use it on his next couple of cases and to look for any higher or lower than usual incidence of wound healing problems. Does Dr. Finagle's plan require IRB approval?

After liking the results in his initial surgical cases, Dr. Finagle decides to test the wound dressing in his next 20 patients to see whether these patients' incisions heal well. He resolves to keep a tally of the results in his pocket planner in addition to making the usual notations on his patients' charts, and to write an article for a medical journal about his results if they seem promising. Does this plan require IRB approval?

C.   SECURING INFORMED CONSENT

The informed consent process represents an essential safeguard for all clinical trial participants, including both patients who may benefit from the technology and healthy volunteers who sometimes provide necessary safety data for the approval process. This section will explore the basic requirements for obtaining informed consent in the clinical trial setting, examine some of the potential problems that IRBs may encounter when reviewing proposed research, and consider some situations in which the informed consent model may not work well.

In the past, individuals have been unwillingly or unknowingly subjected to medical research. See Robert J. Lifton, The Nazi Doctors (1986); Jonathan D. Moreno, Undue Risk: Secret State Experiments on Humans (1999). The materials below illustrate some of the problems and challenges associated with protecting human subjects from non-consensual research. Although the regulations provide guidance to IRBs, many boards struggle to understand and implement the underlying spirit of the regulations. Regulatory agencies can inspect IRB records to ensure compliance with the procedures for review, but it is more difficult to determine whether a particular IRB has fully advanced the goals behind these rules. See Kenneth C. Micetich, The IRB: Current and Future Challenges, in Health Care Ethics: Critical Issues for the 21st Century (John F. Monagle & David C. Thomasma eds.,1998).

———

21 C.F.R. Part 50. Protection of Human Subjects.

§ 50.20   General Requirements for Informed Consent.

Except as provided in Sec. 50.23, no investigator may involve a human being as a subject in research covered by these regulations unless the investigator has obtained the legally effective informed consent of the subject or the subject's legally authorized representative. An investigator shall seek such consent only under circumstances that provide the prospective subject or the representative sufficient opportunity to consider whether or not to participate and that minimize the possibility of coercion or undue influence. The information that is given to the subject or the representative shall be in language understandable to the subject or the representative. No informed consent, whether oral or written, may include any exculpatory language through which the subject or the representative is made to waive or appears to release the investigator, the sponsor, the institution, or its agents from liability for negligence.

§ 50.25   Elements of Informed Consent.

(a) *Basic elements of informed consent.* In seeking informed consent, the following information shall be provided to each subject:

(1) A statement that the study involves research, an explanation of the purposes of the research and the expected duration of the subject's participation, a description of the procedures to be followed, and identification of any procedures which are experimental.

(2) A description of any reasonably foreseeable risks or discomforts to the subject.

(3) A description of any benefits to the subject or to others which may reasonably be expected from the research.

(4) A disclosure of appropriate alternative procedures or courses of treatment, if any, that might be advantageous to the subject.

(5) A statement describing the extent, if any, to which confidentiality of records identifying the subject will be maintained and that notes the possibility that the [FDA] may inspect the records.

(6) For research involving more than minimal risk, an explanation as to whether any compensation and an explanation as to whether any medical treatments are available if injury occurs and, if so, what they consist of, or where further information may be obtained.

(7) An explanation of whom to contact for answers to pertinent questions about the research and research subjects' rights, and whom to contact in the event of a research-related injury to the subject.

(8) A statement that participation is voluntary, that refusal to participate will involve no penalty or loss of benefits to which the subject is otherwise entitled, and that the subject may discontinue participation at any time without penalty or loss of benefits to which the subject is otherwise entitled. * * *

PROBLEM #4. *PATIENT PROTECTION AND PROTOCOL DESIGN*

Erik Smith, a cardiologist and clinical researcher at Empire University, submits a research protocol to his institution's IRB for review. The protocol, which is sponsored by Pharmarama, Inc., involves the testing of an investigational drug ("XK–99") to treat hypertension. The planned research will require that human subjects with hypertension discontinue all of their regular medications in order to participate. The study is a randomized, double-blind, placebo-controlled trial. In other words, half of the subjects enrolled will receive the investigational drug; the other half will receive a placebo. Patients will be enrolled in one or the other "arm" of the trial at random, and neither the patients nor their treating physicians will know whether they are receiving the active drug or placebo. Dr. Smith, as principal investigator (PI), requests permission to enroll 300 patients in order to generate statistically significant data about the effectiveness of the drug. Previous studies of the drug suggest that most of its side effects are minor and infrequent, with the exception of a small risk of blood clotting that can lead to embolism or stroke. The informed consent form provides:

> You have been invited to participate in a research protocol to test the effectiveness of a promising new anti-hypertension compound called XK–99. The principal investigator of the protocol is Dr. Erik Smith. If you have questions concerning the research at any time, you may leave a message for him at (999) 555–1000.

> If you participate in this research, you will be randomized into one of two groups. One group will receive the experimental hypertension drug XK–99. The other group will receive a placebo drug. You will receive XK–99 free of charge for the duration of the study. When the research period has ended, you will have the opportunity to continue taking XK–99 if you wish.

> Before you begin taking the research drugs, you must have several tests, including blood pressure tests and blood screening tests. A nurse will draw blood from you at the first research visit, and at each of the three follow-up visits during the study. You may also be asked to take an exercise stress test using a treadmill at the beginning of the study to determine how your blood pressure responds to exertion. If you experience a significant increase in blood pressure during the treadmill test, you will be asked to repeat the test at each of the three follow-up visits while you are taking the experimental drug.

Risks of participation: There are always some minor risks associated with the testing of any new medication. The risks of XK–99 include dizziness, fainting, and very rarely blood clotting. You should not operate a vehicle or heavy machinery until you know how you respond to XK–99. You should not drink alcohol while taking XK–99. The risks from having your blood drawn are very small—you may feel dizziness or faintness, and occasionally you may experience infection at the site of the needle jab. The risks of the treadmill tests are minimal for most people.

Benefits of participation: You will receive no compensation for taking part in this study, but you will receive free medication while in the study. You may find that the study drug helps to reduce your high blood pressure. You have the right to withdraw from this research protocol at any time and receive ordinary standard treatment instead. You will not be able to continue taking XK–99 if you withdraw from the research protocol before completion.

The IRB discusses the proposed protocol and declines to grant approval. What concerns might the IRB members have about the study design? About the informed consent form? The IRB reports its decision, with a detailed explanation of its concerns, to the PI, who expresses dismay and exasperation. The PI phones his friend and colleague Prof. Samantha Jones, who is the Empire University Vice Provost for institutional research coordination. He complains that the IRB has rejected a "perfectly sound" research protocol and notes that without IRB approval, the university cannot receive the half million dollar grant from Pharmarama, Inc. to fund his research. What options, if any, are available to Dr. Smith and Prof. Jones?

Kus v. Sherman Hospital

644 N.E.2d 1214 (Ill.App.Ct.1995).

■ McLaren, Judge:

The plaintiff, Richard Kus, brought suit against the defendants, * * * alleging negligence and medical battery relating to the implantation of intraocular lenses [IOLs]. * * *

Prior to the plaintiff's intraocular lens implantations, pursuant to the medical staff bylaws of Sherman Hospital, an Institutional Review Board (IRB) was established at the hospital to protect the rights of patients who were human subjects of research. One of the functions of the IRB was to "require that a legally effective informed consent is obtained prior to conducting a research project." The bylaws of the IRB gave it "purview over all research or investigative activities" and reserved the right to "review the progress of all continuing studies ... for the purpose of safeguarding the rights of human subjects." Dr. Richard Fiedler chaired the Sherman IRB from 1978 to 1984 and testified that the purpose of the IRB was to make sure that the patient who was undergoing the procedure knew what he was getting into. Fiedler agreed that the IRB had the power to stop unsafe investigative practices. Specifically, Fiedler admitted that the IRB could stop a doctor from using consent forms which were not approved under the protocol for that specific research.

On March 5, 1980, Fiedler, on behalf of the IRB, issued a directive to all operating eye surgeons, including Dr. Vancil, which stated that "the original or a copy of the Informed Consent Form be on the chart of each patient undergoing an intraocular lens implant." On June 4, 1984, Fiedler issued a second directive to the same group of surgeons, which specified: "It is ... mandatory that prior to the insertion of one of these lenses that the hospital have a copy of the informed consent signed by the patient so that the lens can be implanted. Without the hospital's having the informed consent in its possession prior to the surgery, the surgery will not be allowed." The consent form referred to was the FDA-approved consent, detailed below.

The plaintiff's vision began to deteriorate in 1984, and he first went to see Dr. Vancil in January 1985. Vancil recommended cataract surgery and a lens implant, which, he allegedly told Kus, were "quite safe." Kus testified that Vancil never told him that the lens Vancil intended to implant was under investigation for safety and effectiveness. Indeed, Vancil gave Kus a booklet which described intraocular lens implant surgery as a "tried and true method" of vision correction after cataract surgery. Prior to surgery, in Vancil's office, Kus was presented with an informed consent document to read over and sign, which Kus did. The informed consent document which Kus signed had been modified from the FDA-approved and Sherman IRB-sanctioned consent form by the removal of a paragraph on "clinical investigation," which was meant to inform the patient that the lens was under investigation for safety and efficacy. The consent form which Kus signed was then placed in his chart at Sherman Hospital. Eye surgery proceeded on July 15, 1985. * * * Vancil implanted an intraocular lens manufactured by American into Kus' left eye. On that same day, July 15, 1985, a letter from American arrived in the office of the president of the hospital, John Graham. The letter was addressed to the IRB chairperson and indicated that, by order of July 3, 1985, the FDA had withdrawn American's investigational device exemption for a number of lenses, including the type implanted in Kus' left eye, and stated that, "FDA has ordered that further implantations of American's IOLs be stopped and returned to American as soon as possible." There was no evidence presented as to the time the letter was actually received. * * *

When the plaintiff's vision deteriorated in his right eye, Vancil again recommended the implantation of an intraocular lens, this time one manufactured by Surgidev, which at that point had not been recalled. When Kus questioned Vancil as to why Vancil did not recommend the American lens for the right eye, Vancil responded that American "did not keep up with their paperwork." Surgery on the right eye commenced on January 15, 1986, with allegedly no consent form in Kus' hospital chart. Kus claimed he signed the consent form 2 to 10 days after the surgery, and the form then appeared in his hospital chart. Similar to the form for the surgery on Kus' left eye, the consent form for the right eye surgery was also modified, and the form made no reference to the fact that the lens was being evaluated for safety and effectiveness.

A receptionist for Dr. Vancil testified that the reason the informed consent forms were missing the section on "clinical investigation" was that Vancil directed the office staff to remove language from the consent form approved by Sherman Hospital's IRB because "he didn't want it on there." This removal was done for all of Vancil's 43 patients who underwent intraocular lens surgery at Sherman Hospital. A subpoena was issued for Dr. Vancil to testify, but it was returned not served.

The Medical Device Amendments of 1976 (MDA) to the Food, Drug and Cosmetic Act of 1938 authorize the Secretary of Health and Human Services to promulgate a regulatory scheme for the clinical investigation of experimental devices under an investigational device exemption. The purpose of such exemptions is:

> To encourage, to the extent consistent with the protection of the public health and safety and with ethical standards, the discovery and development of useful devices intended for human use and to that end to maintain optimum freedom for scientific investigators in their pursuit of that purpose.

In the year following the enactment of the MDA, the FDA issued regulations providing for "Investigational Exemptions for Intraocular Lenses." (21 C.F.R. § 813.1 et seq. (1993)). The regulations detail the application process by which intraocular lenses can be implanted into human subjects. Under the terms of the regulations, Sherman Hospital was an "institution," which is defined as a hospital which "engages in the conduct of research on human subjects." The IRB of an "institution" is charged with the responsibility to review and monitor all investigational studies of intraocular lenses. Specifically, the IRB: "Shall assure that the rights of human subjects are properly protected, that legally effective informed consent is obtained, and that the method of obtaining consent properly informs the human subject of the significant aspects of the study in accordance with Part 50 of this chapter."

Part 50, dealing with IRBs, requires that each subject be provided with basic information, including: "A statement that the study involves research, an explanation of the purposes of the research and the expected duration of the subject's participation, a description of the procedures to be followed, and identification of any procedures which are experimental." Part 50 also requires that informed consent be "documented by the use of a written consent form approved by the IRB and signed by the subject." The IRBs are also required to conduct "continuing review of research" on at least an annual basis, which includes the duty to review the informed consent process. In the case at bar, the defense's expert witness, Earnest Prentice, admitted that, if Sherman Hospital's IRB had audited any of Dr. Vancil's charts in the 1½ years before Kus' surgery, the IRB would have discovered Vancil's use of the modified consent form. Additionally, Prentice admitted that a choice existed at Sherman Hospital by September 1, 1983, between an FDA-approved lens and the experimental lenses which were implanted into Kus' eyes.

After the implants in Kus' eyes allegedly caused difficulty and permanent damage due to their design, Kus filed suit against Sherman Hospital, alleging, in part: (1) medical battery, (2) negligence under a lack of informed consent theory, and (3) negligence for failing to respond adequately to a product recall involving the lens manufactured by American. The trial court dismissed the medical battery and negligence involving the recall claims by directed verdict. The jury returned a verdict for the hospital on the negligence count for the lack of informed consent. * * *

In the case at bar, we determine that a hospital, as well as a physician, may be held liable for a patient's defective consent in a case involving experimental intraocular lenses, and thus the plaintiff's claim is therefore viable. * * * [T]he general rule [is] that, unlike the physician, "a hospital generally has no duty to obtain a like informed consent from the same patient." * * * The rationale underlying this rule is that the physician has the " 'technical knowledge and training necessary to advise each patient of the risks,' " and that " 'the hospital does not know the patient's medical history, nor the details of the particular surgery to be performed.' " * * *

While we agree that generally a hospital is not in the best position to inform a patient of risks, here it is clear that Sherman Hospital undertook the responsibility to inform the plaintiff of the experimental nature of his surgery. Moreover, a participating institution in the intraocular lens study is required to conduct "continued review of research" under the federal guidelines which includes the duty to review the informed consent process. Thus, Sherman Hospital also had the minimal duty here of checking to ensure that the form its IRB had promulgated was being used. * * * [T]he particular facts in the case before us require a determination that a hospital, as well as a physician, may be liable for claims arising from the lack of informed consent in this instance. * * *

Evidence in the record indicates that here the consent form approved by Sherman Hospital's IRB was modified by Dr. Vancil so that Kus allegedly did not know that he was participating in an experiment. Whether those modifications amounted to Kus' consent being "substantially at variance" with the treatment he actually received—that of an experimental nature—or whether Kus did or did not know of the experimental nature of the treatment are issues which necessarily belong before the jury. The evidence we glean from the record here clearly does not so overwhelmingly favor the hospital that a contrary verdict could [n]ever stand, and granting a directed verdict on the medical battery count was therefore prejudicial error. * * *

NOTES AND QUESTIONS

1. *More informed consent follies. Kus* illustrates the important role that IRBs play in supervising research, whether with investigational drugs or devices. In large institutions with many research protocols in play simultaneously, IRBs may find it difficult to monitor compliance at the level needed in *Kus*. A combination of deference to physicians and large workload may prevent IRBs from discovering significant deviations from informed consent or protocol requirements in a timely fashion. See Frances O. Kelsey, The FDA's Enforcement of IRBs and Patient Informed Consent, 44 Food Drug Cosm. L.J. 13 (1989).

2. *IOLs*. When it enacted the MDA in 1976, Congress included a special provision applicable only to intraocular lenses. The statute provided that the investigational device exemption requirements for IOLs should be "applicable in such a manner that the device shall be made reasonably available to physicians meeting appropriate qualifications." 21 U.S.C. § 360j(*l*)(3)(D)(iii); see also 41 Fed. Reg. 38,802, 38,803 (1976); American Soc'y of Cataract & Refractive Surgery v. Sullivan, 772 F.Supp. 666, 673 (D.D.C.1991) (explaining that the statute "evidences a clear congressional intent to assure patients access to the most advanced IOL devices"). Consequently, under the agency's regulations, IOLs were governed by their own separate and detailed IDE requirements. See 21 C.F.R. pt. 813. This regulatory approach arguably granted IOLs a form of grandfather status rather than genuinely subjecting them to clinical trials. The FDA later revoked these special IOL provisions. See 62 Fed. Reg. 4164 (1997).

3. *IRB liability*. Although tort litigation against IRBs has been very limited to date, recent events suggest that such lawsuits will become more common. The increased volume of research has created tremendous pressure on IRBs and the institutions that house them. IRBs may not receive adequate institutional support or appropriate training for their members, and the volume of protocols under their supervision compounds the risk of errors and misjudgments. Does an IRB have a common law duty of care to research participants that will support a tort claim? Although physicians serve as members, their relationship to research participants differs substantially from the traditional doctor-patient relationship. Nevertheless, it is possible to argue the existence of a duty of care because IRBs undertake to protect an identifiable class of individuals (future enrollees in the approved protocol) and because the protected group relies on the IRB's capable supervision. A variety of failures by IRBs to abide by requirements for the review and supervision of research protocols may constitute breaches of a duty of care, including the failure to obtain appropriate informed consent, permitting research that is tainted by financial conflicts of interest, failure to oversee ongoing research appropriately and to shut down protocols that endanger human subjects, and errors of judgment concerning whether research comports with the ethical guidelines set out implicitly or explicitly in the regulations. See Barbara A. Noah, Bioethical Malpractice: Risk and Responsibility in Human Research (forthcoming 2002).

Only a few courts have addressed questions about the liability of IRBs or the institutions that house them. For example, in *Friter v. Iolab Corp.*, 607 A.2d 1111 (Pa.Super.Ct.1992), the plaintiff was injured by an intraocular lens implanted in his eye as part of an investigational protocol to determine the product's safety. The patient was never informed that the device was experimental or that his treatment was being delivered under the auspices of a research protocol. Although the court recognized that, under common law, the physician rather than the hospital has the duty to obtain informed consent for an investigational medical procedure, it added that "the facts of this case are quite different for we are not here addressing the duty owed by a physician to a patient but rather a duty owed by the hospital to the patient. In this instance, the hospital, as a participant in a clinical investigation ... specifically assumed a duty to ensure that informed consent was obtained by any patient participating in the study." Id. at 1113. Interestingly, the court used the federal regulations governing IRBs to imply a duty running to patients that did not exist at common law, even though the regulations themselves do not provide a right of action. The FDA's informed consent regulations do appear to contemplate the existence of a common law duty of care to research subjects. See 21 C.F.R. § 50.20 (providing in part that no exculpatory language may be used in an attempt "to waive any of the subject's legal rights" or to "release the investigator, the sponsor, the institution, or its agents from liability for negligence"); see also 46 Fed. Reg. 8942 (1981).

In another case, a federal district court denied a hospital's motion for summary judgment in a lawsuit brought by a patient injured after undergoing laser eye surgery on both eyes, where the protocol governing the experimental procedure prohibited operations on fellow eyes and on patients with a high degree of myopia. See Gregg v. Kane, 1997 WL 570909 (E.D.Pa.1997). In discussing potential liability for the patient's injury, the opinion referred to the hospital and its IRB interchangeably. The court noted deficiencies in the IRB's review: "[N]either the IRB statement granting unconditional approval nor the minutes of the IRB meetings discussing the protocol contain any indication that [an independent] risk assessment was done." Id. at *9. The court concluded that, although the protocol clearly did not permit operations for the plaintiff's type of eye problem, she was permitted to undergo the operation anyway, "apparently under the auspices of the protocol" and that the departures from the protocol guidelines "could be seen as examples of negligent, even reckless, conduct on behalf of [the hospital]." Id. at *10. Finally, one state court, finding that the Johns Hopkins University IRB "abdicated [its] responsibility" to review "the potential safety and health hazard impact of a research project," chastised the board for "instead suggesting to the researchers a way to miscast the characteristics of the study in order to avoid the responsibility inherent in nontherapeutic research involving children." Grimes v. Kennedy Krieger Inst., 782 A.2d 807, 813 (Md.2001) (discussing negligent oversight of a study to compare different methods of lead paint abatement in housing).

Tivoli v. United States

1996 WL 1056005 (S.D.N.Y.1996).

■ Fox, District Judge:

* * * In July 1991 Laura Tivoli ("Plaintiff") was diagnosed as suffering from Cushings Syndrome, a disease of the endocrine system, and was referred by her treating physician to the NIH for evaluation and treatment. Cushings Syndrome is a condition in which the body overproduces cortisol. * * * There are four possible causes of Cushings Syndrome including a tumor on the pituitary gland, a condition which is called Cushings Disease and is treatable through surgical removal of the tumor. Plaintiff was referred to the NIH for evaluation for this surgical procedure. Every patient at the NIH Clinical Center is admitted pursuant to one or more protocols (studies) which are overseen by the Institutional Review Board (IRB) of the NIH.

On July 26, 1991, Plaintiff underwent [an experimental] diagnostic procedure called an Inferior Petrosal Sinus Sampling (IPSS) to assist the physicians in confirming her diagnosis of Cushings Disease by confirming the location of a tumor on her pituitary gland which was causing the problem, and by lateralizing the tumor, i.e., determining in which lobe of the pituitary gland the tumor was located. The IPSS procedure involved the insertion of a catheter into the femoral vein in Plaintiff's groin. The catheter was then manipulated through the body's venous system with the assistance of fluoroscopy to the base of the brain where, in the area close to the pituitary gland, a sampling of blood was to be taken. The analysis of that blood sample was expected to provide the sought after diagnostic information.

IPSS procedure

Unfortunately Plaintiff suffered a cerebral hemorrhage during the IPSS procedure resulting in a severe brain stem stroke syndrome (a stroke) which left her crippled and disfigured. Plaintiff's IPSS (and those of other patients and volunteers) was performed pursuant to protocol 90–CH–194 on which Dr. Jack Yanovsky was the principal investigator. Physicians at the NIH recognized that the protocols limited and restricted their activities in dealing with and performing procedures on patients. This is further confirmed in the testimony of Dr. Gilman Grave, Chairman of the IRB at the NIH, who testified that the protocols which were approved by the IRB controlled the manner or means in which the sampling procedure was conducted, including the designation of the catheter used. The IRB also limited the performance of IPSS procedures to only two physicians, Dr. Donald Miller and Dr. John Doppman, who were required to comply with the terms of the protocol in performing the procedure. * * *

The IRB at the NIH had the function of reviewing all protocols presented to assess the risk benefit ratio of each protocol. The process was explained by Dr. George Chrouoss, the Chief of Pediatric Endocrinology at the NIH. The protocol itself is written by the principal investigator (PI). * * * The IRB can then approve the protocol, reject it, or add additional stipulations or requirements for its performance. * * *

[A] member of the IRB expressed concerns that the protocol which was being reviewed in July 1990 did not list all of the rare complications of venography. Drs. Miller and Doppman stated that the risk of serious complications or death in IPSS exists, but is, at most 0.9% based upon statistical analysis, as they set forth in their published article in the *Journal of Radiology* entitled "Petrosal Sinus Sampling: Technique and Rationale." * * * The IPSS is a specialized application of venography. While this application of venography was relatively new and still under study in 1991, and no incidents of stroke had been reported during an IPSS at that time, the technique of venography was not new, and the risks attendant to it, including that of stroke, were well known. * * *

The only physician who came to Plaintiff's room to obtain any consent from her was Dr. Yanovsky, who was neither a radiologist nor, at that time, a Board Certified endocrinologist. He received her consent only to use some of the blood samples to be obtained during the IPSS for his protocol, and not for the performance of the IPSS procedure itself. It is particularly bizarre that this consent was obtained before Dr. Miller, the radiologist who was to perform the IPSS, had even met Plaintiff, much less obtained her consent.

The [NIH] requirement that the consent be discussed with the patient, in the patient's own room, well in advance of the performance of the procedure, and by the radiologist who would actually be performing the procedure, is understandable and appropriate since Cushings patients often exhibit emotional and cognitive difficulties. A meeting with the physician in the patient's room well before the procedure was scheduled would allow both the time and the privacy necessary and conducive to a full and complete explanation of the procedure to be performed as well as a discussion of the attendant risks and alternatives. Plaintiff, who had been exhibiting nervousness and anxiety * * * had no such opportunity to meet and confer deliberatively with the physician who performed her IPSS. In the very execution of Plaintiff's consent form the NIH deviated from its own procedures and policies. * * *

There was no discussion of the type of catheter to be used, or whether it was or was not the same catheter which had been used in all of the 400 or so prior IPSS procedures which had been mentioned to Plaintiff as having been performed at NIH without serious mishap. In fact Yanovsky, the Principal Investigator on the protocol, did not even know that the Mueller catheter, which had been used in most of the prior IPSS cases, had been discontinued by Dr. Miller who was then using the new and different Miller catheter to perform IPSS procedures. Since Yanovsky did not know about the change, and as PI it was his responsibility to keep the IRB advised, the IRB also did not know about the use of the Miller catheter until the catastrophic result of Plaintiff's IPSS. Dr. Yanovsky further stated that if he had known of the use of the Miller catheter the change was significant enough to have warranted its inclusion in his study. IRB Chairman Dr. Grave confirmed that he too remained unaware of any difference between the catheters used by Drs. Miller and Doppman until the IRB meeting subsequent to Plaintiff's IPSS. * * *

Dr. Yanovsky agreed that it is good medical practice to include and identify in the consent even remote risks of the procedure if of a life threatening nature. He further agreed that stroke or venous rupture is, and was at the time, a known complication of venography. Dr. Yanovsky conceded that the consent form itself does not contain the word stroke, or the phrase "like a stroke," and that the risk of stroke is a grave possibility as a complication of the IPSS.

The consent form contains no mention of a venous rupture or bleed as a possible complication of the IPSS. The only discussion of bleeding in the consent form is at the groin, the site of the incision which is hardly the same risk or complication as a stroke. [One expert] opined that the wording of the Yanovsky consent, including the use of the phrases "theoretical possibility" and "like a stroke" were not sufficient to convey in common medical terms to a patient the potential risks in the IPSS procedure for stroke and attendant disability and death.

The Yanovsky consent is signed by Plaintiff and Yanovsky on page 7. On that same page the document lists and identifies several physicians to whom Plaintiff could address questions or problems. It is noteworthy that the names of Drs. Miller and Doppman, the only two radiologists authorized to perform the IPSS procedure, are not among them, confirming Yanovsky's position that this consent form was not addressed to the IPSS procedure itself, but rather was limited to the use of Plaintiff's blood samples obtained during the procedure in his study.

A consent to the performance of the IPSS procedure was obtained from Plaintiff by Dr. Miller, the radiologist who performed the procedure. * * * As to risks and complications, the only information he provided to Plaintiff which is at all significant here is "when you put a catheter in the vein at the base of the skull there is always a risk of clot forming in the cavernous sinus what we call cavernous sinus thrombosis, that's very serious, like a stroke . . . . That's never actually happened; we worry about it happening, but we've never seen it happen so it's theoretical." * * *

Plaintiff had no questions and signed the consent form which was witnessed by * * * a member of the team which was to perform the procedure. This too was a deviation from the normal practice and procedure at NIH as set forth on the very face of the NIH consent document which specifies that the execution of the consent should be witnessed by someone who was not a member of the operating team.

Plaintiff then made the previously mentioned remark which fixed her in Dr. Miller's memory. As she entered the procedure room she turned to Dr. Miller and said: "Nothing is going to happen, is it?" Miller responded: "Well you understand there aren't any guarantees, but as I told you, none of the Cushing patients have ever had any problems. The normal volunteers all went home okay. And they're fine. And that's really all I can tell you." * * *

Dr. Miller testified that there was nothing new about the catheter and that it contained no new material or device that had not received prior approval from the FDA. His testimony on that issue and the position taken by the government is patently absurd in the face of a medical journal article written by Dr. Miller, and submitted for publication to the *Journal of Radiology* on June 15, 1990. That article, entitled "Selective Catheterization of the Inferior Petrosal Sinuses: A New Catheter Design," is self explanatory as to Dr. Miller's position regarding the newness of the catheter design. The article goes on to describe in detail the draw backs of the previously used Mueller catheter, the reasons why "a new set of catheters was developed," and a brief description of the clinical trial in which IPSS procedures were performed on 22 patients in which "these new catheters" were used. Clearly Dr. Miller himself considered his new catheter to indeed be "new" when he submitted the article for publication in a professional journal, at least until Plaintiff's tragic complication caused him to rethink his position.

Once a treatment, an instrument, or a drug has been approved, it may be utilized for other applications or purposes without the necessity for further FDA approval. That principle does not apply to IRB approvals, however, as evidenced by the IRB action in prohibiting the use of the Miller catheter after Plaintiff's complication. * * *

Plaintiff was not told anything at all about the Miller catheter. She was not told that it was new or experimental or that it was different from the catheter which had been used in most of the 400 IPSS procedures which she was told had been performed without incident. She was also not told that the complications experienced by the two volunteer patients in January and February 1991 might plausibly have been catheter related neurologic episodes. She was not told of the risk of stroke in the IPSS procedure. * * *

Dr. Yanovsky mentioned nothing to Plaintiff about alternatives to the IPSS procedure since his consent was only addressed to using blood samples to be taken during the IPSS. Dr. Miller mentioned alternatives such as CT and MRI scans and endocrine studies, but advised her that these were not nearly as accurate as the IPSS. While the IPSS had been found to be 100% accurate in the diagnosis of Cushings Disease and in the lateralization of the tumor (determining in which lobe of the pituitary gland the tumor is located) there were other tests available * * * which, in combination, would have diagnosed the presence of a pituitary tumor with an accuracy of between 95 and 97%. * * *

Plaintiff was at the time of her IPSS a social worker holding an MSW degree. She had experience in dealing with patients with various emotional and behavioral disorders but no medical background or experience. She specifically recalls that she was not advised of the risk of stroke in the IPSS because she did not at that time know exactly what a stroke was although she knew that it occurred "like in older people." She had read the NIH booklet provided to her entitled "Preparing for Petrosal Sinus Sampling" and had not seen the word stroke. If that word had been in the booklet she would have asked to have it explained. * * * She further stated that if she had been told that there had been prior complications with the use of Dr. Miller's catheter she "would have withdrawn from the petrosal sinus sampling." Her testimony is supported by the proof of the great number of questions which Plaintiff had been asking of the physicians and nursing staff about her condition and the procedures, her previously noted anxiety, and most particularly by her hesitation and question to Dr. Miller as she entered the angio room for the IPSS procedure. * * *

Accordingly, since the physicians involved were Government employees, the consent was inadequate as to the risk of stroke, the Plaintiff suffered a stroke as a consequence of the IPSS procedure, and a reasonable patient in Plaintiff's position would have considered the missing data significant and would not have consented to the procedure if the data had been provided, I find that the Government is liable to the Plaintiff for the injuries which she suffered during the IPSS procedure. * * *

NOTES AND QUESTIONS

1. Tivoli *transgressions.* The plaintiff in *Tivoli* sued the physicians who treated her under the umbrella of an NIH-supervised protocol; she did not sue the supervising IRB. The case does not involve a typical research protocol to evaluate the usefulness of an investigational device; instead, it is a protocol to evaluate an experimental procedure (which happens to involve the use of a device). The case is nonetheless useful as an illustration of how an individual physician-patient relationship can fail to conform to the ideals of the informed consent process in an experimental medical procedure. How many violations of the informed consent regulations or NIH policies can you identify in the *Tivoli* opinion? To what do you attribute these violations—carelessness, failure of the institution to educate its researchers properly about patient-protective policies, inadequate IRB oversight, or something else?

2. *The patient/subject perspective.* A 1995 survey of 371 research subjects found that nearly 20% of those questioned believed incorrectly that they were not and never had been research subjects. See Laura C. McBride & Mark R. Yessian, IRBs and Continuing Review: Regulatory Interference or Vital Safeguard?, Food Drug Cosm. & Med. Dev. L. Dig., Mar. 1999, at 13; see also Bartolo, Tales of Informed Consent: Four Years on an Institutional Review Board, 2 Health Matrix 193 (1992). Many patients apparently fail to understand that they have agreed to participate in a research protocol rather than or in addition to receiving standard therapy. Despite the fact that many IRBs have interpreted the "language understandable to the subject" clause in 21 C.F.R. § 50.20 to require informed consent forms to be written at an 8th grade reading level (what some have referred to as the Homer Simpson standard), comprehension problems persist.

3. *Remuneration and other arguably coercive methods for enrolling research subjects.* For many years, recruitment of research subjects has involved payment for participation, although most IRBs agree that this practice poses difficult ethical problems. More recently, some protocols to test drugs in pediatric populations have offered gift certificates to toy stores as well as cash. What concerns might patient advocates have about research protocols that recruit subjects through offers of money or gifts? Federal guidelines offer little assistance in dealing with this thorny issue, and the research community so far has failed to reach a consensus about it. Nevertheless, the research community, patient advocates, and ethicists appear to agree on some basic principles. IRBs tend to prefer payments that compensate for travel expenses and lost time at work but that are not so large as to be unduly influential. See Neal Dickert & Christine Grady, What's the Price of a Research Subject? Approaches to Payment for Research Participation, 341 New Eng. J. Med. 198 (1999) (discussing the relative merits of the market model, the wage-payment model, and the reimbursement model for compensating research subjects, and concluding that the wage-payment model most effectively reduces concerns about inappropriate inducement).

4. *Expanding categories of research for which IRBs could waive the informed consent requirement.* The FDA's regulations exempt certain types of "minimal risk" studies from the informed consent requirements. See 21 C.F.R. § 56.110. Some commentators controversially proposed expanding these exempt categories, arguing that patients are often over-protected in the context of clinical trials that involve very little risk while paradoxically receiving little or no protection from physicians who wish to try experimental treatments as "therapeutic innovation." See Robert D. Truog et al., Is Informed Consent Always Necessary for Randomized, Controlled Trials?, 340 New Eng. J. Med. 804 (1999).

Doe v. Sullivan

756 F.Supp. 12 (D.D.C.1991).

■ HARRIS, JUDGE:

* * * In August 1990, the United States began deploying troops to Saudi Arabia in response to Iraq's unprovoked invasion of Kuwait. As Operation Desert Shield progressed toward the United Nations' deadline of January 15, 1991, for Iraq to withdraw from Kuwait, the DOD began planning for a possible war with Iraq. Because of well-publicized reports that Iraq has storehouses of chemical and biological weapons, the DOD developed plans to use certain drugs believed to have the ability to counteract the effects of such weapons on the troops. Some of the drugs have not yet received approval from the Food and Drug Administration (FDA) for distribution in the United States and, therefore, remain under the FDA classification of "investigational new drugs." Plaintiffs, a serviceman in the United States Army and his wife, seek an injunction preventing the DOD from using these unapproved drugs without first obtaining the informed consent of the military personnel taking part in the mission which is now known as Operation Desert Storm.

Shortly after Operation Desert Shield began, the DOD asked the FDA to recognize in its regulations that obtaining informed consent from military personnel before administering unapproved drugs is not feasible under circumstances of military exigency. On December 21, 1990, the FDA published an interim rule that authorizes the Commissioner of Food and Drugs to determine that obtaining informed consent is not feasible in specific situations involving combat or the immediate threat of combat. Since the FDA adopted that interim rule, § 50.23(d), the Commissioner has concurred with the DOD's plans to administer two unapproved drugs to the troops in Operation Desert Storm. One of the drugs is a pretreatment to counteract the effects of organophosphate nerve agents. The other unapproved drug is a vaccine to prevent bacterial poisoning from biological warfare.

Plaintiffs challenge § 50.23(d) and the DOD's plans to administer unapproved drugs under the rule. Plaintiffs contend that § 50.23(d) violates the Food, Drug and Cosmetic Act's limitations on using unapproved drugs on unconsenting humans. Plaintiffs further argue that § 50.23(d) marks a sharp departure from the FDA's longstanding regulations regarding the feasibility of obtaining informed consent. Citing the 1985 Department of Defense Authorization Act (DOD Act), which prohibits the use of DOD funds for research on involuntary human subjects, plaintiffs contend that the DOD plans exceed the scope of its authority. Finally, plaintiffs argue that the use of unapproved drugs on military personnel without their informed consent constitutes a violation of their Fifth Amendment right to due process. * * *

The DOD's decision to use unapproved drugs is precisely the type of military decision that courts have repeatedly refused to second-guess. The DOD has elected to administer the drugs because of its determination that the drugs will improve the survival rate of troops that may encounter chemical and biological weapons. The DOD believes that protecting each individual serviceman, in turn, will increase the safety of other servicemen in the field and will decrease the medical burden of treating victims of chemical and biological weapons. Clearly, judicial interference in this type of strategic decision would not be proper. For this reason, plaintiffs' claim must be dismissed. * * *

The DOD's plans to administer unapproved drugs to the troops in Operation Desert Storm do not violate its authority under the DOD Act. The DOD Act prohibits the use of DOD funding "for any research involving a human being as an experimental subject," unless the subject's informed consent is obtained first. The statute expressly requires informed consent even when the research is meant to be beneficial to the subject. Plaintiffs argue that the DOD's use of unapproved drugs constitutes "research." They stress that, under FDA regulations, the DOD must collect data on the efficacy of the unapproved drugs. In addition, they contend that any use of unapproved drugs is research per se, despite the fact that the drugs are meant to be beneficial.

Plaintiff's definitional argument is not persuasive in light of the DOD Act's plain meaning. The DOD's use of unapproved drugs does not involve the type of scientific investigation under controlled circumstances that "research" connotes. On the contrary, the DOD has responded to very real circumstances and chosen what it views as the best alternative given current knowledge. The primary purpose of administering the drugs is military, not scientific. The fact that the DOD will collect information on the efficacy of the drugs does not transform the strategic decision to use the unapproved drugs in combat into research. Furthermore, the FDA has interpreted the FDCA to permit using unapproved drugs in a "treatment-investigational setting" in the past. See 21 C.F.R. § 312.34–.35 (1990). The FDA, therefore, does not view every use of unapproved drugs as research, and nothing in the DOD Act suggests that Congress intended the term to have such a broad meaning. For this reason, the court would deny plaintiffs' claim under the DOD Act.

Plaintiffs challenge to the FDA's interim rule under the FDCA also must be denied. The FDCA requires the FDA to set standards for approving new drugs and to regulate the use of unapproved drugs. The Act states that investigators must obtain informed consent before administering unapproved drugs to human subjects, "except where they deem it not feasible or, in their professional judgment, contrary to the best interests of such human beings." 21 U.S.C. § 355(i). The FDA adopted § 50.23(d) under the statutory exception for circumstances in which obtaining informed consent is not feasible. Plaintiffs challenge § 50.23(d) on the grounds that it allows a waiver of the informed consent requirement when, in fact, obtaining informed consent is feasible.

Before the FDA adopted § 50.23(d), longstanding FDA regulations stated that obtaining informed consent is "deemed feasible" unless the subject is unable to communicate, unconscious, or incompetent. See 21 C.F.R. § 50.23 (1990). The FDA added § 50.23(d) to its regulations to allow the Commissioner of Food and Drugs, at the DOD's request, to determine that obtaining informed consent is not feasible in specific combat circumstances. Section 50.23(d) requires the DOD to limit its request to "a specific military operation involving combat or the immediate threat of combat." The circumstances must be such that accomplishing the military mission and ensuring the safety of others requires using the drug "without regard to what might be any individual's personal preference for no treatment or for some alternative treatment."

Plaintiffs argue that § 50.23(d) is not premised on the possibility or practicability of informing troops and requesting consent. Rather, the rule is designed to preclude the possibility that some military personnel may refuse to take the unapproved drugs. Plaintiffs also point out that the two drugs for which the DOD already has received clearance are pretreatments for which the DOD could supply information and consent forms. Thus, plaintiffs argue, the interim rule violates the FDCA both on its face and in its actual application to the troops in Operation Desert Storm.

The FDA's interpretation of the term "feasible" in the FDCA is entitled to deference unless it is "arbitrary, capricious, or manifestly contrary to the statute." In § 50.23(d), the FDA recognized that certain military concerns may make obtaining informed consent from military personnel in combat impracticable. The impracticability arises out of concern for the safety of the servicemen and the success of the mission. Although infeasibility in this situation differs from the form of infeasibility recognized in the FDA's previous regulations, it is well within the ordinary meaning of the term and the statute. Plaintiffs argue that the FDA's traditional interpretation of feasible, which focused on the subject's condition, marked the limits of infeasibility under the statute. Plaintiff's interpretation would excuse informed consent only in circumstances when obtaining informed consent is impossible. The statute itself, however, does not dictate such a narrow construction of the term. * * *

The third basis for the plaintiffs' claim is that administering unapproved drugs to troops without first obtaining their informed consent deprives the troops of a liberty interest without due process of law in violation of the Fifth Amendment. The ordinary standard of scrutiny for alleged violations of substantive due process is whether the law or regulation is rationally related to a legitimate government purpose. The DOD has asserted several interests underlying its decision to use the unapproved drugs. First, the drugs have as their goal protecting individual servicemen from the effects of chemical and biological weapons. Second, administering the drugs uniformly prevents unnecessary danger to troops and medical personnel from injury to, or the death of, fellow military personnel in battle. Finally, the DOD has an interest in successfully accomplishing the military goals of Operation Desert Storm. The last two concerns certainly constitute legitimate government interests that may counterbalance an individual's interest in being free from experimental treatment without giving informed consent.

Administering unapproved drugs to troops without first obtaining informed consent must bear "a real and substantial relation" to the legitimate goals the DOD has asserted. If individual servicemen were allowed to refuse the unapproved drugs, the DOD would be forced to decide whether to excuse unconsenting servicemen from battle conditions in which they might encounter chemical or biological weapons. A decision not to send military personnel who refuse the drugs into battle could have a significant impact on battle strategy and the success of the mission. On the other hand, a decision to send military personnel into battle without the protection of the drugs could affect the safety of the individual servicemen and others in the field. As the government also argues, if an unprotected serviceman suffers nerve gas or bacterial poisoning, that serviceman will require the attention of other servicemen in the field, distracting them from the goals of the mission. To this distraction may be added the increased risk to military personnel running rescue missions and the increased burden on medical personnel and supplies. Uniformly administering the unapproved drugs avoids the dilemma posed by unconsenting individuals, advances the safety of the troops as a group, and promotes the DOD's overall goal of military success. The court, therefore, finds that waiving the informed consent requirement is a rational means for the DOD to accomplish its legitimate goals. For this reason, the court would deny plaintiffs' constitutional claim. * * *

NOTES AND QUESTIONS

1. *Subsequent history.* The district court's decision was affirmed on appeal, though on other grounds. See Doe v. Sullivan, 938 F.2d 1370, 1371,

1381–83 (D.C.Cir.1991) ("Operation Desert Storm ended during the pendency of this appeal. The challenged FDA regulation, however, remains in place. Neither the DOD nor the FDA has proposed its withdrawal. The named plaintiffs therefore persist in urging adjudication of their facial challenge to the FDA's regulation.... While we further conclude that the consistency of the regulation with the governing law is justiciable, we agree with the district court that the regulation is within the FDA's statutory authority under the FDC Act, and does not transgress any other legal constraint. For that reason, we affirm the order dismissing the complaint."); see also Robyn P. Ryan, Should Combat Troops Be Given the Option of Refusing Investigational Drug Treatment?, 52 Food & Drug L.J. 377 (1997). Suspicion now exists that these drugs caused or contributed to the development of mysterious symptoms labeled as Gulf War syndrome. See Claire A. Milner, Comment, Gulf War Guinea Pigs: Is Informed Consent Optional During War?, 13 J. Contemp. Health L. & Pol'y 199, 205–06 (1996). The military has a checkered history when it comes to human experimentation. Between 1960 and 1972, at the height of the Cold War, the DOD sponsored experiments in which cancer patients and prisoners were exposed to total body radiation or were administered plutonium in order to test the body's response. A majority of the cancer patients selected to participate in the hospital-based experiments were African–Americans. The "Human Radiation Experiments" failed to use consent forms for the first five years; later, the consent forms greatly understated the risks involved. See In re Cincinnati Radiation Litig., 874 F.Supp. 796 (S.D.Ohio 1995); Advisory Cmte. on Human Radiation Experiments, Research Ethics and the Medical Profession, 276 JAMA 403 (1996); see also United States v. Stanley, 483 U.S. 669 (1987) (Army's secret LSD experiments). Does the uniqueness of the battlefield context justify the diminution of individual rights to refuse unwanted medical treatment? What if the DOD sought to vaccinate civilians in a combat zone without securing their informed consent? What if a public school board wanted to inoculate all of its students with an experimental drug without consent in order to prevent an outbreak of meningitis?

2. *Other exceptions to the informed consent requirement.* In other limited circumstances, laws or courts have required patients to submit to treatment without their informed consent, but these treatments are generally not experimental (and hence not governed by FDA or NIH regulations). For example, courts have upheld public health laws that mandate vaccination in order to prevent the spread of certain common diseases. See, e.g., Jacobson v. Massachusetts, 197 U.S. 11 (1905) (upholding a city regulation requiring vaccination against smallpox). But see Lewis v. Sobol, 710 F.Supp. 506 (S.D.N.Y.1989) (issuing an injunction permitting a child to attend school without vaccination based on a statutory religious exemption to mandated vaccination program for school attendance). Courts have also ordered patients to remain hospitalized for lengthy periods of time to treat contagious diseases such as tuberculosis. See, e.g., City of New York v. Antoinette R., 630 N.Y.S.2d 1008 (Sup.Ct.1995) (ordering a woman with tuberculosis who refused to complete her course of treatment to remain in a hospital for up to seven months until she finished her antibiotics or demonstrated that she would comply with the medication regime outside of the hospital).

3. *The emergency research exception to general informed consent rules.* The FDA regulations recognize that, in some emergency situations, it may not be feasible to secure informed consent before using an experimental product:

(a) The obtaining of informed consent shall be deemed feasible unless, before use of the test article (except as provided in paragraph (b) of this section), both the investigator and a physician who is not otherwise participating in the clinical investigation certify in writing all of the following:

(1) The human subject is confronted by a life-threatening situation necessitating the use of the test article.

(2) Informed consent cannot be obtained from the subject because of an inability to communicate with, or obtain legally effective consent from, the subject.

(3) Time is not sufficient to obtain consent from the subject's legal representative.

(4) There is available no alternative method of approved or generally recognized therapy that provides an equal or greater likelihood of saving the life of the subject.

(b) If immediate use of the test article is, in the investigator's opinion, required to preserve the life of the subject, and time is not sufficient to obtain the independent determination required in paragraph (a) of this section in advance of using the test article, the determinations of the clinical investigator shall be made and, within 5 working days after the use of the article, be reviewed and evaluated in writing by a physician who is not participating in the clinical investigation. . . .

21 C.F.R. § 50.23. In some studies, researchers can predict the recurrence of this problem because the investigational products are designed to treat emergency medical conditions, such as heart attack, stroke, or trauma. It is often difficult or impossible to design traditional research protocols that will capture needed data because the relevant pool of potential subjects cannot consent to treatment in these situations. The applicable regulation provides, in part, as follows:

(a) The IRB responsible for the review, approval, and continuing review of the clinical investigation described in this section may approve that investigation without requiring that informed consent of all research subjects be obtained if the IRB (with the concurrence of a licensed physician who is a member of or consultant to the IRB and who is not otherwise participating in the clinical investigation) finds and documents each of the following:

(1) The human subjects are in a life-threatening situation, available treatments are unproven or unsatisfactory, and the collection of

valid scientific evidence, which may include evidence obtained through randomized placebo-controlled investigations, is necessary to determine the safety and effectiveness of particular interventions.

(2) Obtaining informed consent is not feasible because: (i) The subjects will not be able to give their informed consent as a result of their medical condition; (ii) The intervention under investigation must be administered before consent from the subjects' legally authorized representatives is feasible; and (iii) There is no reasonable way to identify prospectively the individuals likely to become eligible for participation in the clinical investigation.

(3) Participation in the research holds out the prospect of direct benefit to the subjects because: (i) Subjects are facing a life-threatening situation that necessitates intervention; (ii) Appropriate animal and other preclinical studies have been conducted, and the information derived from those studies and related evidence support the potential for the intervention to provide a direct benefit to the individual subjects; and (iii) Risks associated with the investigation are reasonable in relation to what is known about the medical condition of the potential class of subjects, the risks and benefits of standard therapy, if any, and what is known about the risks and benefits of the proposed intervention or activity....

(6) ... The IRB has reviewed and approved procedures and information to be used when providing an opportunity for a family member to object to a subject's participation in the clinical investigation....

(7) Additional protections of the rights and welfare of the subjects will be provided, including, at least: (i) Consultation (including, where appropriate, consultation carried out by the IRB) with representatives of the communities in which the clinical investigation will be conducted and from which the subjects will be drawn; (ii) Public disclosure to the communities in which the clinical investigation will be conducted and from which the subjects will be drawn, prior to initiation of the clinical investigation, of plans for the investigation and its risks and expected benefits; (iii) Public disclosure of sufficient information following completion of the clinical investigation to apprise the community and researchers of the study, including the demographic characteristics of the research population, and its results; (iv) Establishment of an independent data monitoring committee to exercise oversight of the clinical investigation....

Id. § 50.24(a); see also 50 Fed. Reg. 42,866 (1985) (announcing the availability of an FDA guideline for the emergency use of unapproved medical devices); Richard S. Saver, Critical Care Research and Informed Consent, 75 N.C. L. Rev. 205 (1996). What concerns do the regulation leave unresolved? Compare this regulation's use of the concept of feasibility with the approach suggested in *Doe v. Sullivan*.

D. Access to Experimental Products

Patients often desire access to experimental drugs, biological products, and medical devices before these products receive final marketing approval from the FDA. A number of regulations pertaining to investigational new drugs and medical devices, and to research employing these investigational drugs and devices, impact patients' access to these products prior to formal marketing approval. Some patients with severe or life-threatening medical conditions may also wish to utilize unapproved medical technologies that do not even have the imprimatur of official "investigational" status that comes with an IND or IDE. As illustrated by the following litigation concerning access to Laetrile (amygdalin), some courts may recognize individual choice in medical decisionmaking as paramount, but ultimately the FDA and courts have little sympathy for individuals who wish to forego standard treatments in favor of such remedies.

Rutherford v. United States

438 F.Supp. 1287 (W.D.Okla.1977).

■ Bohanon, District Judge:

* * * On July 29, 1977, the Commissioner of Food and Drugs announced that: (1) Laetrile is not generally recognized by qualified experts as a safe and effective cancer drug and (2) Laetrile is not exempt from the pre-market approval requirement for new drugs by virtue of the "grandfather" provisions of the Act. Distribution of Laetrile in interstate commerce, the Commissioner concluded, is thus illegal and subject to regulatory activity by the Food and Drug Administration. Plaintiffs challenge such administrative decision and urge that Laetrile is not a "drug," that in any event it is not a "new drug," and that FDA's enforcement procedures against the interstate transportation and use of the substance violate plaintiffs' constitutional rights. * * *

In plaintiffs' constitutional challenge of FDA's proscription they invoke rights fundamental to a free society and inextricably related to enumerated constitutional concepts. While the Constitution does not explicitly mention a right of personal privacy, it is unchallengeable "that a right of personal privacy, or a guarantee of certain areas or zones of privacy, does exist under the Constitution." Roe v. Wade, 410 U.S. 113, 152 (1973). This right has been discerned within the penumbras of the Bill of Rights, and specifically within the language of the First, Fourth, Fifth, Ninth and Fourteenth Amendments to the Constitution * * * .

Mr. Justice Douglas referred to "the freedom to care for one's health and person" as coming within the purview of this right. Doe v. Bolton, 410 U.S. 179, 213 (1973) (concurring opinion). "The right of privacy," Justice Douglas proceeded, "has no more conspicuous place than in the physician-patient relationship." Id. at 219. He concluded: "The right to seek advice on one's health and the right to place reliance on the physician of one's choice are basic. . . ." This right of privacy has been characterized more than once as simply the right "to be let alone." That right includes the privilege of an individual to plan his own affairs, for " 'outside areas of plainly harmful conduct, every American is left to shape his own life as he thinks best, do what he pleases, go where he pleases.' "

Many knowledgeable and concerned individuals are questioning the effectiveness and wisdom of our orthodox approaches to combating cancer. The correctness of their criticisms may not be determined for many years, and in any event such discussion provokes controversies largely beyond the realm of the courts' function. Nonetheless, it appears uncontrovertible that a patient has the right to refuse cancer treatment altogether, and should he decide to forego conventional treatment does he not possess a further right to enlist such nontoxic treatments, however unconventional, as he finds to be of comfort, particularly where recommended by his physician? We must carefully distinguish between the constitutional standards applicable to the use of an innocuous substance as a health-care aid, and those standards which apply to the promotion or advertisement of that same substance.

Plaintiffs seek to exercise final control over the handling of their own individual health-care problems. Numerous cancer patients possess extensive first-hand experience with Laetrile which has led them to believe, correctly or not, that the substance has eased their pain and prolonged their lives. Such personal convictions are not readily dispelled by government pronouncements or affidavits to the contrary. When deprived of treatment in this country, they go elsewhere, and in so doing are denied close contact with their families and family doctors. Unintentionally FDA has wrought needless hardship and expense to countless individuals required to travel to Mexico or Germany in order to utilize Laetrile. If it were more readily available in this country, perhaps many patients currently obtaining the treatment abroad could be persuaded to remain under their doctor's care here and use the substance in conjunction with conventional treatments.

The final consequences are ultimately borne by those whose bodies are the battleground on which cancer's war is waged. Many perceive the drug's acquisition as a life and death matter, and are understandably frustrated and enraged over attempts by their own government to deny them the right to decide for themselves questions of such a personal and grave nature. Doubtless FDA desires to protect the public. Such good intention, however, is not the overriding issue. Many of us allocate time and money and other resources in ways susceptible to just criticism by many standards. Nonetheless, our political ideals emphasize that the right to freely decide is of much greater significance than the quality of those choices actually made. It is never easy for one who is concerned and feels himself particularly knowledgeable to observe others exercise their freedom in ways that to him appear unenlightened.

As a nation, however, historically and continuously, we are irrevocably committed to the principle that the individual must be given maximum latitude in determining his own personal destiny. To be insensitive to the very fundamental nature of the civil liberties at issue in this case, and the fact that making the choice, regardless of its correctness, is the sole prerogative of the person whose body is being ravaged, is to display slight understanding of the essence of our free society and its constitutional underpinnings. This is notably true where, as here, there are no simple answers or obvious solutions, uncertainty is pervasive, and even the best efforts leave so much to be desired.

When certain "fundamental rights" are invoked, such as the right of privacy involved herein, regulation may be justified only by a "compelling state interest," and legislative enactments "must be narrowly drawn to express only the legitimate state interests at stake." *Roe v. Wade*, 410 U.S. at 155. By denying the right to use a nontoxic substance in connection with one's own personal health-care, FDA has offended the constitutional right of privacy. * * *

strict scrutiny for right of privacy

This court's decision in this case in no way portends the return of the traveling snake oil salesman. As emphasized earlier, the right to use a harmless, unproven remedy is quite distinct from any alleged right to promote such. FDA is fully empowered under other statutory provisions to combat false or fraudulent advertising of ineffectual or unproven drugs.

NOTES AND QUESTIONS

1. *The final word on Laetrile.* On appeal, the court held that the new drug provisions of the FDCA did not apply to treatments sought by terminally ill patients. See Rutherford v. United States, 582 F.2d 1234, 1237 (10th Cir.1978). The United States Supreme Court reversed:

> [W]e have no license to depart from the plain language of the Act, for Congress could reasonably have intended to shield terminal patients from ineffectual or unsafe drugs.... [T]he Commissioner generally considers a drug safe when the expected therapeutic gain justifies the risk entailed by its use. For the terminally ill, as for anyone else, a drug is unsafe if its potential for inflicting death or physical injury is not offset by the possibility of therapeutic benefit.... To accept the proposition that the safety and efficacy standards of the Act have no relevance for terminal patients is to deny the Commissioner's authority over all drugs, however toxic or ineffectual, for such individuals.

United States v. Rutherford, 442 U.S. 544, 555–58 (1979). The Court declined to address the constitutional issue. On remand, the appellate court rejected the constitutional argument:

> It is apparent in the context with which we are here concerned that the decision by the patient whether to have a treatment or not is a protected right, but his selection of a particular treatment, or at least a medication, is within the area of governmental interest in protecting public health. The premarketing requirement of the [FDCA] is an exercise of congressional authority to limit the patient's choice of

medication. . . . The use of Laetrile is sought to be prevented because in the opinion of the Commissioner the proponents have not met the burden imposed by the agency procedures and by the statute to fulfill the premarketing requirements.

Rutherford v. United States, 616 F.2d 455, 457 (10th Cir.1980); see also Rutherford v. United States, 806 F.2d 1455 (10th Cir.1986) (rejecting the petitioners' collateral attack on the FDA's conclusion that Laetrile is a "new drug"); New York State Opthalmological Soc'y v. Bowen, 854 F.2d 1379, 1390 (D.C.Cir.1988) ("[S]uch a principle cannot justify a blanket right to obtain without any government interference every and any kind of treatment that might be available and that a physician might recommend."); Carnohan v. United States, 616 F.2d 1120, 1121 (9th Cir.1980) ("Constitutional rights of privacy and personal liberty do not give individuals the right to obtain laetrile free of the lawful exercise of government police power."); Scott H. Power, Comment, The Right of Privacy in Choosing Medical Treatment: Should Terminally Ill Persons Have Access to Drugs Not Yet Approved by the Food and Drug Administration?, 20 John Marshall L. Rev. 693 (1987); Don G. Rushing, Comment, Picking Your Poison: The Drug Efficacy Requirement and the Right of Privacy, 25 UCLA L. Rev. 577 (1978); Note, Laetrile: Statutory and Constitutional Limitations on the Regulation of Ineffective Drugs, 127 U. Pa. L. Rev. 233 (1978).

The constitutional claim in *Rutherford* was at least colorable, given the decisions in the abortion cases *Roe v. Wade* and *Doe v. Bolton*. Nonetheless, in the two decades since *Rutherford* was decided, the Supreme Court's right to privacy jurisprudence has become even less likely to assist patients demanding access to experimental therapies. See, e.g., Washington v. Glucksberg, 521 U.S. 702 (1997) (holding that a prohibition on physician-assisted suicide does not violate the due process rights of competent, terminally ill adults who want to obtain medication to hasten their deaths); Cruzan v. Director, Missouri Dept. of Health, 497 U.S. 261 (1990) (holding that the due process clause does not forbid a state from requiring clear and convincing evidence of an incompetent patient's wishes regarding the withdrawal of life-support in order to prevent potential abuses by surrogate decisionmakers and to safeguard the state's interest in preserving life). The FDA has taken a similar position on other unapproved new drugs intended to treat cancer. See, e.g., Durovic v. Richardson, 479 F.2d 242 (7th Cir. 1973) (affirming judgment for the FDA finding that Krebiozen was an unapproved new drug); Tutoki v. Celebrezze, 375 F.2d 105 (7th Cir.1967) (affirming dismissal of cancer patients' appeal seeking access to the unapproved new drug Krebiozen).

2. *State responses.* State courts have also examined the Laetrile question and have considered the problems associated with physicians' and patients' assertions that the constitutional right of privacy protects the decision to obtain drugs not generally recognized as effective by the FDA. In *People v. Privitera*, 591 P.2d 919 (Cal.1979), the court concluded that a fundamental right of privacy, which ordinarily involves matters relating to marriage, procreation, contraception, family relationships and child rearing, was not implicated in decisions about medical treatment: "If the state has the power to ban a drug with a recognized medical use because of its potential for abuse, then—given a rational basis for doing so—the state clearly has the power to ban a drug not recognized as effective for its intended use." Id. at 923. The dissent in the case noted that "[t]he right to control one's own body is not restricted to the wise; it includes the 'foolish' refusal of medical treatment.... Without specific reference to a constitutional basis, the right to choose what may be a suicidal medical course has been upheld." Id. at 932 (Bird, J., dissenting) (referring to decisions permitting Jehovah's Witnesses to refuse life-saving blood transfusions); see also Bouvia v. Superior Court, 179 Cal.App.3d 1127 (1986); In re Conroy, 486 A.2d 1209 (N.J.1985). After the *Rutherford* litigation, approximately half the states passed laws legalizing the use of Laetrile for terminal cancer treatment. See, e.g., Alaska Stat. § 08.64.367; Ariz. Rev. Stat. § 36–2452; Col. Rev. Stat. § 12–30–113; Del. Code Ann. § 4901.

3. *Paternalism or good policy.* The FDA expressed concern that allowing terminal patients to use Laetrile could lead to needless deaths, because such access might mislead patients or prevent them from seeking legitimate and efficacious therapy. Subsequent research concluded that Laetrile was ineffective in the treatment of cancer. See Charles G. Moertel et al., A Clinical Trial of Amygdalin (Laetrile) in the Treatment of Human Cancer, 306 New Eng. J. Med. 201, 203–04 (1982) (noting also that it was sometimes associated with high levels of blood cyanide); see also David M. Greenberg, Vitamin Fraud in Cancer Quackery, 122 W.J. Med. 345, 345–46 (1975) (debunking several hypotheses about the supposed cancer-fighting mechanism of Laetrile). Can you think of other situations in which concerns about public health more convincingly trump concerns about individual choice? Is there any non-medical value in permitting patients without other effective medical options to pursue a last hope for treatment, even without proof of efficacy?

4. *Importation of unapproved drugs for personal use.* FDA guidelines permit individuals to import up to a three-month supply of an unapproved new drug for personal use under two sets of circumstances: (1) the intended use is appropriately identified and is not for the treatment of a serious condition, and the product is not known to be a serious threat to health; or (2) the intended use is unapproved and for a serious condition for which treatment may not be available domestically, there is no known commercialization or promotion to persons residing in the U.S. by those involved in distribution of the product, the product does not represent an unreasonable risk, and the individual seeking to import the product provides the name of a doctor responsible for treatment in the U.S. or provides evidence that the product is for continuation of a treatment begun abroad. See Peter S. Reichertz & Melinda S. Friend, Hiding Behind Agency Discretion: The FDA's Personal Use Drug Importation Policy, 9 Cornell J.L. & Pub. Pol'y 493, 501–02 (2000); see also Sifre v. Robles, 917 F.Supp. 133 (D.P.R.1996) (holding that the plaintiff, an individual seeking to import "memory and intelligence enhancement drugs" for personal use, did not meet the FDA's informal standards for such imports).

[handwritten margin note: re-importation allowed]

The FDA first adopted a more permissive version of this policy in 1988 so that patients suffering from AIDS and cancer could import limited quantities of unapproved drugs. The agency soon expanded the policy, but it specifically prohibited personal use importation of the French abortion pill RU–486, triggering a judicial challenge. See Benten v. Kessler, 799 F.Supp. 281, 289 (E.D.N.Y.1992) (granting a preliminary injunction because of the petitioner's likelihood of success on the merits of her claim that this limitation should have undergone notice-and-comment rulemaking procedures). The court of appeals stayed the preliminary injunction pending appeal, and the Supreme Court denied a petition to vacate that stay. See Benten v. Kessler, 505 U.S. 1084, 1085 (1992) (per curiam). In dissent, Justice Stevens argued that the FDA had impermissibly burdened the woman's liberty interest in selecting a method for terminating her pregnancy. See id. at 1086 (Stevens, J., dissenting); see also Debora C. Fliegelman, Comment, The FDA and RU486: Are Politics Compatible with the FDA's Mandate of Protecting Public Health and Safety?, 66 Temp. L. Rev. 143 (1993); Elizabeth A. Silverberg, Looking Beyond Judicial Deference to Agency Discretion: A Fundamental Right of Access to RU486?, 59 Brook. L. Rev. 1551 (1994).

5. *Medical marijuana.* Patient demands to use marijuana for medical purposes raise a similar set of issues. See, e.g., Pearson v. McCaffrey, 139 F.Supp.2d 113 (D.D.C.2001); Seeley v. State, 940 P.2d 604 (Wash.1997); Marsha N. Cohen, Breaking the Federal/State Impasse over Medical Marijuana: A Proposal, 11 Hastings Women's L.J. 59 (2000); J. Ryan Conboy, Smoke Screen: America's Drug Policy and Medical Marijuana, 55 Food & Drug L.J. 601 (2000); Andrew J. LeVay, Note, Urgent Compassion: Medical Marijuana, Prosecutorial Discretion and the Medical Necessity Defense, 41 B.C. L. Rev. 699 (2000); Erik R. Neusch, Comment, Medical Marijuana's Fate in the Aftermath of the Supreme Court's New Commerce Clause Jurisprudence, 72 U. Colo. L. Rev. 201 (2001); Annaliese Smith, Comment, Marijuana as a Schedule I Substance: Political Ploy or Accepted Science?, 40 Santa Clara L. Rev. 1137 (2000); Marcia Tiersky, Comment, Medical Marijuana: Putting the Power Where It Belongs, 93 Nw. U. L. Rev. 547 (1999); Mark Robichaux, Would Marijuana Be OK by Prescription If You Didn't Get High?, Wall St. J., Feb. 28, 2001, at A1.

United States v. Oakland Cannabis Buyers' Cooperative

532 U.S. 483 (2001).

■ THOMAS, JUSTICE:

* * * In November 1996, California voters enacted an initiative measure entitled the Compassionate Use Act of 1996. Attempting "[t]o ensure that seriously ill Californians have the right to obtain and use marijuana for medical purposes," Cal. Health & Safety Code Ann. § 11362.5, the statute creates an exception to California laws prohibiting the possession and cultivation of marijuana. These prohibitions no longer apply to a patient or his primary caregiver who possesses or cultivates marijuana for

the patient's medical purposes upon the recommendation or approval of a physician.

In the wake of this voter initiative, several groups organized "medical cannabis dispensaries" to meet the needs of qualified patients. United States v. Cannabis Cultivators Club, 5 F. Supp. 2d 1086, 1092 (N.D.Cal. 1998). Respondent Oakland Cannabis Buyers' Cooperative is one of these groups. The Cooperative is a not-for-profit organization that operates in downtown Oakland. A physician serves as medical director, and registered nurses staff the Cooperative during business hours. To become a member, a patient must provide a written statement from a treating physician assenting to marijuana therapy and must submit to a screening interview. If accepted as a member, the patient receives an identification card entitling him to obtain marijuana from the Cooperative.

In January 1998, the United States sued the Cooperative and its executive director, respondent Jeffrey Jones, in the United States District Court for the Northern District of California. Seeking to enjoin the Cooperative from distributing and manufacturing marijuana, the United States argued that, whether or not the Cooperative's activities are legal under California law, they violate federal law. * * *

The Controlled Substances Act provides that, "[e]xcept as authorized by this subchapter, it shall be unlawful for any person knowingly or intentionally . . . to manufacture, distribute, or dispense, or possess with intent to manufacture, distribute, or dispense, a controlled substance." 21 U.S.C. § 841(a)(1). The subchapter, in turn, establishes exceptions. For marijuana (and other drugs that have been classified as "schedule I" controlled substances), there is but one express exception, and it is available only for Government-approved research projects, § 823(f). Not conducting such a project, the Cooperative cannot, and indeed does not, claim this statutory exemption. The Cooperative contends, however, that notwithstanding the apparently absolute language of § 841(a), the statute is subject to additional, implied exceptions, one of which is medical necessity. According to the Cooperative, because necessity was a defense at common law, medical necessity should be read into the Controlled Substances Act. * * *

Under any conception of legal necessity, one principle is clear: The defense cannot succeed when the legislature itself has made a "determination of values." In the case of the Controlled Substances Act, the statute reflects a determination that marijuana has no medical benefits worthy of an exception (outside the confines of a Government-approved research project). Whereas some other drugs can be dispensed and prescribed for medical use, see 21 U.S.C. § 829, the same is not true for marijuana. Indeed, for purposes of the Controlled Substances Act, marijuana has "no currently accepted medical use" at all. See id. § 811. * * *

The Cooperative points out, however, that the Attorney General did not place marijuana into schedule I. Congress put it there, and Congress was not required to find that a drug lacks an accepted medical use before including the drug in schedule I. We are not persuaded that this distinction has any significance to our inquiry. Under the Cooperative's logic, drugs that Congress places in schedule I could be distributed when medically necessary whereas drugs that the Attorney General places in schedule I could not. Nothing in the statute, however, suggests that there are two tiers of schedule I narcotics, with drugs in one tier more readily available than drugs in the other. On the contrary, the statute consistently treats all schedule I drugs alike. Moreover, the Cooperative offers no convincing explanation for why drugs that Congress placed on schedule I should be subject to fewer controls than the drugs that the Attorney General placed on the schedule. Indeed, the Cooperative argues that, in placing marijuana and other drugs on schedule I, Congress "wishe[d] to assert the most restrictive level of controls created by the [Act]." If marijuana should be subject to the most restrictive level of controls, it should not be treated any less restrictively than other schedule I drugs.

group argument

The Cooperative further argues that use of schedule I drugs generally—whether placed in schedule I by Congress or the Attorney General—can be medically necessary, notwithstanding that they have "no currently accepted medical use." According to the Cooperative, a drug may not yet have achieved general acceptance as a medical treatment but may nonetheless have medical benefits to a particular patient or class of patients. We decline to parse the statute in this manner. It is clear from the text of the Act that Congress has made a determination that marijuana has no medical benefits worthy of an exception. The statute expressly contemplates that many drugs "have a useful and legitimate medical purpose and are necessary to maintain the health and general welfare of the American people," id. § 801(1), but it includes no exception at all for any medical use of marijuana. Unwilling to view this omission as an accident, and unable in any event to override a legislative determination manifest in a statute, we reject the Cooperative's argument.[6]

Next group argument

Finally, the Cooperative contends that we should construe the Controlled Substances Act to include a medical necessity defense in order to avoid what it considers to be difficult constitutional questions. In particular, the Cooperative asserts that, shorn of a medical necessity defense, the statute exceeds Congress' Commerce Clause powers, violates the substantive due process rights of patients, and offends the fundamental liberties of the people under the Fifth, Ninth, and Tenth Amendments. As the Cooperative acknowledges, however, the canon of constitutional avoidance has no application in the absence of statutory ambiguity. Because we have no

---

6. The Government argues that the 1998 "sense of the Congress" resolution, 112 Stat. 2681–760, supports its position that Congress has foreclosed the medical necessity defense. Entitled "Not Legalizing Marijuana for Medicinal Use," the resolution declares that "Congress continues to support the existing Federal legal process for determining the safety and efficacy of drugs and opposes efforts to circumvent this process by legalizing marijuana, and other Schedule I drugs, for medicinal use without valid scientific evidence and the approval of the Food and Drug Administration." Because we conclude that the Controlled Substances Act cannot sustain the medical necessity defense, we need not consider whether the 1998 "sense of the Congress resolution" is additional evidence of a legislative determination to eliminate the defense.

doubt that the Controlled Substances Act cannot bear a medical necessity defense to distributions of marijuana, we do not find guidance in this avoidance principle. Nor do we consider the underlying constitutional issues today. * * *

■ STEVENS, JUSTICE (concurring in the judgment):

* * * Apart from its limited holding, the Court takes two unwarranted and unfortunate excursions that prevent me from joining its opinion. First, the Court reaches beyond its holding, and beyond the facts of the case, by suggesting that the defense of necessity is unavailable for anyone under the Controlled Substances Act. Because necessity was raised in this case as a defense to distribution, the Court need not venture an opinion on whether the defense is available to anyone other than distributors. Most notably, whether the defense might be available to a seriously ill patient for whom there is no alternative means of avoiding starvation or extraordinary suffering is a difficult issue that is not presented here. * * *

The overbroad language of the Court's opinion is especially unfortunate given the importance of showing respect for the sovereign States that comprise our Federal Union. That respect imposes a duty on federal courts, whenever possible, to avoid or minimize conflict between federal and state law, particularly in situations in which the citizens of a State have chosen to "serve as a laboratory" in the trial of "novel social and economic experiments without risk to the rest of the country." New State Ice Co. v. Liebmann, 285 U.S. 262, 311 (1932) (Brandeis, J., dissenting). In my view, this is such a case. By passing Proposition 215, California voters have decided that seriously ill patients and their primary caregivers should be exempt from prosecution under state laws for cultivating and possessing marijuana if the patient's physician recommends using the drug for treatment.[4] This case does not call upon the Court to deprive all such patients of the benefit of the necessity defense to federal prosecution, when the case itself does not involve any such patients. * * *

DeVito v. HEM, Inc.

705 F.Supp. 1076 (M.D.Pa.1988).

■ RAMBO, DISTRICT JUDGE:

Defendants HEM, Inc., and Du Pont, Inc. are the "sponsors" of "clinical investigations" of an "investigational new drug" called Ampligen. * * * Plaintiff is a 38 year old man who has Acquired Immunodeficiency Syndrome (AIDS). He participated in three clinical investigations sponsored

---

4. Since 1996, six other States—Alaska, Colorado, Maine, Nevada, Oregon, and Washington—have passed medical marijuana initiatives, and Hawaii has enacted a similar measure through its legislature. See Alaska Stat. Ann. §§ 11.71.090, 17.37.010–.080; Colo. Const., art. XVIII, § 14; Haw. Rev. Stat. §§ 329–121 to 329–128; Me. Rev. Stat. Ann., tit. 22, § 2383–B(5); Nev. Const., art. 4, § 38; Ore. Rev. Stat. §§ 475.300–.346; Wash. Rev. Code §§ 69.51A.005–.902.

by HEM and Du Pont which were designed to test the efficacy of Ampligen in treating AIDS.

The first of these investigations was called AMP101. All of the participants in AMP101 had been diagnosed as having AIDS Related Complex (ARC). The actual drug was administered to about half of the participants. The investigation was "double-blind," i.e., neither the patients nor the doctors conducting the investigation knew which patients were receiving Ampligen and which were receiving the placebo. As it turns out, plaintiff received the placebo and, unfortunately, progressed to AIDS by the end of the AMP101 investigation.

The second and third clinical investigations in which plaintiff participated were called AMP101a and AMP101e, respectively. In those investigations, patients from the AMP101 investigation who had progressed to AIDS were given Ampligen. In mid-October 1988, while the AMP101e investigation was still being conducted, conclusions as to the results of the AMP101 investigation were reached by HEM and Du Pont. Those conclusions were that Ampligen had no proven efficacy whatsoever for the treatment of AIDS and that all testing of the drug should be terminated. Plaintiff received notice of the decision to terminate the clinical investigations in a letter given to him by one of the doctors at Hahnemann [Hospital]. * * *

At [a preliminary hearing on his request for a temporary restraining order], plaintiff testified that while he was receiving Ampligen his condition improved and stabilized. Plaintiff also testified that he cannot resort to treatment with the drug AZT—which has been used in treatment of other AIDS patients—because the drug is too toxic for his system to tolerate. Despite the findings of HEM and Du Pont with respect to Ampligen, plaintiff is convinced the drug is keeping him alive. * * *

Plaintiff's claim against the FDA is that FDA has not intervened to stop the use of Ampligen and has not considered whether plaintiff should remain on the drug in the interest of his safety. This claim is without merit. The regulations which plaintiff argues require FDA to consider whether plaintiff should remain on the drug in the interest of his safety apply only when FDA has placed an investigation on "clinical hold." Here, there has been no clinical hold imposed by FDA.

Plaintiff has not cited, and this court cannot find, any authority requiring FDA to take any action whatsoever when a sponsor decides to terminate a clinical investigation. But even if FDA had taken some action with regard to the termination of the Ampligen investigation, plaintiff would be required to exhaust his administrative remedies with the FDA before seeking relief in this court. It does not appear that plaintiff has taken any steps to, for example, seek FDA approval for Ampligen on his own behalf. In any event, plaintiff has not shown any putatively illegal conduct of FDA likely to be redressed by a favorable decision. Therefore, this court lacks subject matter jurisdiction over plaintiff's claim against FDA.

Plaintiff next argues that, if this court does not have jurisdiction over his claim against FDA, "the other Defendants have made an unreasonable determination without recourse to the procedures required under the FDA Act and regulations." However, neither the Act nor the regulations address the circumstances under which the sponsors of an IND may terminate clinical investigations. It appears that decision is left to the discretion of the sponsors. The only applicable regulation provides: "At any time a sponsor may withdraw an effective IND without prejudice. If an IND is withdrawn, FDA shall be so notified, [and] all clinical investigations conducted under the IND shall be ended...." Testimony at the hearing indicated that FDA was notified of the decision to stop the investigation of Ampligen. Rather than having acted "without recourse to the procedures required," it appears the defendants fully complied with the appropriate regulations.

In addition, plaintiff attached as exhibits to his memorandum the consent agreements he entered into with Hahnemann prior to his participation in the investigations. Each of those exhibits indicates plaintiff's understanding that his involvement in the clinical investigations might be stopped "if all or part of [the studies were] discontinued by the sponsor or governmental agencies." The consent agreement for AMP101e—the most recent investigation in which plaintiff participated—also indicates plaintiff's understanding that he would continue to receive Ampligen in that investigation unless "data analysis of AMP101 indicates lack of efficacy of Ampligen." These exhibits, coupled with plaintiff's inability to cite any authority for his claim that the Act requires HEM, Du Pont or Hahnemann to supply him with Ampligen, make it clear that plaintiff has not shown any putatively illegal conduct on the part of those defendants which is likely to be redressed in a favorable decision. Accordingly, this court lacks subject matter jurisdiction over plaintiff's claim against HEM, Du Pont and Hahnemann. * * *

In support of his allegation of federal question jurisdiction plaintiff stated, "the termination of Ampligen under these circumstances violates his Fourteenth Amendment due process rights as well as his rights under the First, Fourth, Fifth and Ninth Amendments to the United States Constitution." This argument obviously was gleaned from the district court opinion in *Rutherford v. United States*, 438 F.Supp. 1287 (W.D.Okla.1977). Plaintiff's argument seems to be that the part of the *Rutherford* opinion he quoted stands for the proposition that he has a right of personal privacy which includes the rights to care for and seek advice on his health and to place reliance on the physician of his choice. None of the defendants in this case dispute plaintiff's rights to privacy, to care for and seek advice on his health or to place reliance on the physician of his choice. All of the defendants have noted, however, that plaintiff has cited no authority for the implicit proposition that his right to privacy requires the defendants to provide him with Ampligen.

Moreover, although the district court decision in *Rutherford* cited above was affirmed by the Tenth Circuit, the United States Supreme Court later reversed and remanded the case. Ultimately, the case was dismissed and all injunctions entered were dissolved. See Duncan v. United States, 590 F.Supp. 39, 42 n.1 (W.D.Okla.1984). Most significantly, the Supreme Court held that there is no exemption, express or implied, from the Act's drug approval provisions for terminally ill patients who desire to receive a drug. Unfortunate as it might seem, the Court's holding in *Rutherford* makes it clear that plaintiff's claim cannot succeed. * * *

NOTES AND QUESTIONS

1. *Related litigation.* Another group of patients who were receiving Ampligen in a clinical trial to treat chronic fatigue syndrome sued HEM Pharmaceuticals to enforce a provision in the informed consent form that promised an additional year of access to treatment with the drug in an open-label trial if they completed the placebo-controlled, double-blind trial. Although the drug caused some serious adverse reactions in the original study, the FDA had granted permission for the open-label study but denied the company's request for a treatment IND. Observing that "[s]omehow the category of unilateral contracts appears to have escaped HEM's notice," the court reminded the company that "the petitioners performed by submitting to the double-blind tests. They incurred the detriment of being tested upon for HEM's studies in exchange for the promise of a year's treatment of Ampligen. Upon completion of the . . . tests, there was a binding contract." Dahl v. HEM Pharm. Corp., 7 F.3d 1399, 1404–05 (9th Cir.1993) (affirming a preliminary injunction requiring the company to supply the drug).

2. *Treatment INDs.* The FDA has recognized that in certain situations where no satisfactory alternative treatment exists, physicians may wish to use an investigational new drug to treat an individual patient or small class of patients but not as part of a clinical trial. Recall from *Femrite* that they may do so as an off-label use when the product has already been approved for a different indication. If, however, a product has not received any prior approval, it will be available only pursuant to an IND. Regulations promulgated in 1987 allow a manufacturer to supply an investigational drug for treatment use in very ill patients. The criteria for treatment use include: (1) the drug is intended to treat a serious or immediately life-threatening disease; (2) there is no comparable or satisfactory alternative drug or other therapy available to treat that disease in the particular patient population; (3) the drug is being studied in a controlled clinical trial under an IND or clinical trials have been completed for the drug; and (4) the drug's sponsor is actively pursuing marketing approval. See 52 Fed. Reg. 19,466 (1987) (codified as amended at 21 C.F.R. § 312.34(b)(1)); see also AIDS Amendments of 1988, Pub. L. No. 100–607, § 201(4), 102 Stat. 3048, 3066–67 (codified as amended at 42 U.S.C. § 300cc–12) (endorsing the use of treatment INDs for investigational AIDS drugs). The regulations require that an IRB review the treatment IND protocol and that patients give informed consent under the usual consent criteria. A separate regulation allows for the use of investigational drugs in emergency situations where physicians may not have time to submit a request for a treatment IND. See

21 C.F.R. § 312.36; see also Dale L. Moore, An IRB Member's Perspective on Access to Innovative Therapy, 57 Alb. L. Rev. 559 (1994); Beth E. Myers, The Food and Drug Administration's Experimental Drug Approval System: Is It Good for Your Health?, 28 Hous. L. Rev. 309 (1991); Myron L. Marlin, Comment, Treatment INDs: A Faster Route to Drug Approval, 39 Am. U. L. Rev. 171 (1989).

3. *Patient demand for new therapies.* In the early 1990s, the AIDS crisis triggered an outcry against the FDA's often painstakingly slow and rigid new drug approval process. Usually, only patients enrolled in clinical trials can receive experimental drugs. Others must wait for the approval process to run its course. AIDS activists (and those who lobby in favor of early access to experimental therapies for other life-threatening diseases) pointed out that people afflicted with diseases for which no effective treatment exists are often willing to tolerate higher degrees of risk in exchange for the chance at prolonging or improving the quality of life. For more on access to experimental drugs and the history of the AIDS activist movement, see Loretta M. Kopelman, AIDS Activists and Their Legacy for Research Policy, in Health Care Ethics: Critical Issues for the 21st Century (John F. Monagle & David C. Thomasma eds., 1998); Mary T. Griffin, AIDS Drugs and the Pharmaceutical Industry: A Need for Reform, 17 Am. J.L. & Med. 363 (1991); Matthew C. Lovell, Second Thoughts: Do the FDA's Responses to a Fatal Drug Trial and the AIDS Community's Doubts About Early Access to Drugs Hint at a Shift in Basic FDA Policy?, 51 Food & Drug L.J. 273 (1996); Steven R. Salbu, Regulation of Drug Treatments for HIV and AIDS: A Contractarian Model of Access, 11 Yale J. on Reg. 401 (1994); Philip A. Leider, Comment, Domestic AIDS Vaccine Trials: Addressing the Potential for Social Harm to the Subjects of Human Experiments, 88 Cal. L. Rev. 1185 (2000); Louis K. Perrin, Note, The Catch–22 for Persons with AIDS: To Have or Not to Have Easy Access to Experimental Therapies and Early Approval for New Drugs, 69 S. Cal. L. Rev. 105 (1995); see also John J. Smith, Science, Politics, and Policy: The Tacrine Debate, 47 Food & Drug L.J. 511, 525 (1992) ("The potential impact of interest group advocacy goes far beyond HIV/AIDS and the Alzheimer's lobbies.").

4. *"Parallel track" access to investigational new drugs.* In response to complaints from AIDS patients, the FDA adopted accelerated approval procedures, which will be discussed in Chapter 3. It also developed a parallel track policy to promote earlier and broader access to investigational AIDS drugs than is possible under a treatment IND. Only patients who do not otherwise meet the enrollment criteria of the parallel clinical trial may receive treatment under a parallel track IND:

> Under this policy, expanded availability protocols might be approved for promising investigational drugs when the evidence for effectiveness is less than that generally required for a Treatment IND. The expanded availability protocol may include one or more studies without concurrent control groups and may be accompanied by a Treatment IND protocol. All drugs distributed under the parallel track mechanism will be under a study protocol. Data, particularly pertaining to side

effects and safety will be collected under these studies. However, most of the data essential for market approval will come from the controlled clinical trials.... In general, the investigational drug should meet a serious unfulfilled health need such that the potential benefits justify the considerable risks of very early expansion of use.

57 Fed. Reg. 13,250 (1992).

5. *Finding clinical trials.* Many patients whose disease does not respond to standard therapy may want to participate in a clinical trial of an experimental product. In 1997, Congress required that the Director of the National Institutes of Health establish and operate a data bank of information about clinical trials for drugs intended to treat serious or life-threatening diseases. See FDAMA, Pub. L. No.105–115, § 113, 111 Stat. 2296 (1997). The clinical trials database maintained by NIH can be found at <http://clinicaltrials.gov/ct/gui/c/r>. One decade earlier Congress had directed the agency to establish a similar registry of clinical trials of investigational AIDS drugs. See 42 U.S.C. § 300cc–17. Historically, patients would learn of such opportunities only if their regular physician happened to know of a potentially useful trial. Increasingly, investigators and sponsors advertise their clinical trials (sometimes on television), and Internet-savvy patients may locate clinical trials on their own.

Wendy K. Mariner, *Equitable Access to Biomedical Advances: Getting Beyond the Rights Impasse*

21 CONN. L. REV. 571 (1989).

* * * Demands for access to new biomedical advances surface abruptly and are asserted with great emotional force by identifiable people. But existing legal rights simply do not embrace entitlement to particular medical services or products. * * *

Among the most difficult questions of government responsibility for access to new drugs are those that concern drugs that have not been approved for public distribution. They pit traditional American values like freedom of choice against government's role as protector and preserver of the public's health. The claim by AIDS patients that they should be entitled to whatever kind of therapy they wish is especially appealing because orthodox medicine offers no cure for AIDS. Yet existing law offers little support for any claim of entitlement to unapproved drugs. Claims of entitlement to unapproved drugs for AIDS strongly resemble cancer patients' efforts to obtain laetrile. * * *

Does *Rutherford* foreclose the claim of patients with AIDS to use unapproved drugs? Patients with AIDS may be considered terminally ill, to the degree that that term has meaning. While the disease often progresses over many years, allowing people widely varying levels of activity and suffering, it has proved fatal in the majority of cases and is currently presumed to be uniformly fatal. While *Rutherford* may have involved some patients whose conditions might have improved at least temporarily with conventional therapy, one could reasonably assume that most of the plaintiffs sought laetrile because conventional therapy had been unsuccessful for them. Thus, there appears to be little difference between the circumstances of persons with AIDS and the cancer patients in *Rutherford*.

Of course, in *Rutherford*, the Court did not consider any constitutional claims of entitlement to specific forms of therapy. Few cases have. In *Duncan v. United States*, parents sought to obtain the "U" Series "drug" for their child with Down syndrome. Dr. Henry Turkel, the drug's developer, had filed two new drug applications for the drug; both were denied and the denials affirmed by the court of appeals. The district court had little difficulty denying the parents' claims on the basis of *Rutherford* and its few progeny. It found no merit in the claim that compliance with the Act's requirements for filing an NDA were too burdensome, even though they could not realistically be met by individuals. No new drug could be used without satisfying the statutory requirements for FDA approval. The parents also claimed that they were denied equal protection. The court disposed of the claim in a few sentences, saying that the Act does not single out any class for distinctive treatment. Since all persons are treated in the same way, there can be no claim of discrimination. * * *

The FDCA prohibits the distribution of drugs unless they are shown to the satisfaction of the FDA to be safe and effective. This prohibition is a textbook example of congressional delegation of authority to make scientific determinations. There is, however, no absolute scientific answer to the question of whether a drug is safe. All drugs have side effects or can produce adverse reactions. Minor side effects and rare adverse reactions are often considered acceptable when the drug provides sufficient benefit to outweigh the risks of harm. Thus, the question is whether a particular drug is safe enough or effective enough? Yet safe enough for whom? By whose standards? * * *

The statute itself provides no criteria for measuring acceptable levels of safety or effectiveness. The choice of standards is fundamentally a political one that varies with the values of the decisionmaker. The FDA most certainly recognizes the absence of statutory guidance. Generally, it must decide that something is safe and effective enough by balancing the nature and degree of risks against the benefit to be gained from reasonably effective products. Perhaps little more can be asked of the agency. After all, it is impossible to list the risks and benefits of all drugs to be studied in the future, much less measure such risks and benefits. Even if a list could be prepared, exceptions would be immediately necessary for the first new drug intended to treat a now incurable disorder. After all, isn't something better than nothing? This is surely what desperate AIDS patients believe. What does it matter that the drug might cause loss of hair and even bone marrow depression if it eliminates most of the virus from one's system? Isn't that a choice a patient is entitled to make? * * *

CHAPTER 3

PREMARKET APPROVAL AND POSTMARKET SURVEILLANCE

A. PHARMACEUTICAL PRODUCTS

1. NEW DRUG APPROVAL APPLICATIONS

Edison Pharmaceutical Co. v. FDA

600 F.2d 831 (D.C.Cir.1979).

■ TAMM, CIRCUIT JUDGE:

* * * In the 1950s, Dr. Murray Israel developed Cothyrobal, an injectable drug intended to treat hypercholesterolemia and hypothyroidism. Cothyrobal is a combination of the thyroid extract, sodium levothyroxine, and cyanocobalamin (vitamin B_{12}). Levothyroxine is a cholesterol lowering substance with some toxic side effects. Proponents of Cothyrobal claim that vitamin B_{12} inhibits the toxicity of levothyroxine while retaining its medicinal benefits.

In May 1969, Edison filed the NDA for Cothyrobal that is the subject of this appeal. The Commissioner found the information offered in support of the application deficient. * * * The basis for the Commissioner's decision was Edison's failure to submit double-blind controlled studies comparing the effects of Cothyrobal and levothyroxine which he determined were necessary to prove the efficacy of the drug. Edison appealed that ruling to this court, contending that the studies it had submitted were as scientifically sound as humanly possible. A panel of this court reversed and ordered the Commissioner to hold "a full evidentiary hearing" to determine whether double-blind testing comparing the effects of levothyroxine and Cothyrobal could be conducted safely and to determine "*all* relevant issues relating to the approvability of (Edison's) application."

The FDA held the required hearings in December 1975 and January 1976. The administrative law judge (ALJ) concluded that limited double-blind testing could be performed safely. He further found that the studies submitted with the NDA failed to demonstrate the safety and efficacy of Cothyrobal, as required by section 505(d) of the Act * * * * Accordingly, the ALJ refused approval of the NDA. That decision was affirmed by the Commissioner * * * *

Under section 505(d)(5) of the Act, an NDA must be denied if there is a lack of "substantial evidence that the drug will have the effect it purports or is represented to have under the conditions of use" contained in the proposed labeling. Substantial evidence is "evidence consisting of adequate and well-controlled investigations, including clinical investigations, by experts qualified by scientific training and experience to evaluate the effectiveness of the drug involved." 21 U.S.C. § 355(d). Uncontrolled studies or partially controlled studies alone are insufficient proof of a drug's efficacy. 21 C.F.R. § 314.111(a)(5)(ii)(c) (1978). "Isolated case reports, random experience, and reports lacking details which permit scientific evaluation will not be considered." Id. An "adequate and well-controlled investigation * * * [p]rovides a comparison of the results of treatment or diagnosis with a control in such a fashion as to permit quantitative evaluation."

Clinically controlled testing usually involves administration of treatment to two groups of comparable subjects afflicted with the same condition. The first group receives the test drug; the second group, the control group, receives either an inactive preparation known as a placebo or a known drug to which the test drug is being compared. The results of the two groups are then analyzed. Since human reaction to disease treatment may be influenced by a patient's expectations, and since observation of symptoms, particularly subjective symptoms, may be influenced by an observer's expectations, controlled investigations are usually conducted so neither subject nor observer knows which patient is part of the control group. This technique is called double-blinding. Double-blinding techniques are generally required to assure the formation of a scientifically valid judgment as to the therapeutic efficacy of a particular treatment. In certain circumstances, however, such as those involving diseases with high and predictable mortality rates, or signs and symptoms of predictable duration or severity, the regulations permit the use of historical controls. In an historically controlled study, the effects of the medication on a test population are compared with adequately documented accounts of the natural history of the disease instead of with control groups.

A double-blind controlled clinical investigation of Cothyrobol would require comparison of effects of Cothyrobol with those of levothyroxine. * * * [T]he Commissioner assumed arguendo that concurrent control group testing of Cothyrobal and levothyroxine was too dangerous to perform and examined each study submitted with the NDA to determine the approvability of the application. The Commissioner found these studies uniformly replete with inaccuracies and ambiguities, lacking protocol and statistical analysis. Specifically, the Commissioner set out in detail the substantive deficiencies of each. The Commissioner concluded, and we agree, that the studies were not "adequate and well-controlled" within the meaning of section 505(d) and did not establish the efficacy of Cothyrobal. On appeal, Edison does not dispute the specific inadequacies of the studies found by the Commissioner. * * *

Section 505(d)(1) of the Act requires that an NDA include "adequate tests by all methods reasonably applicable to show whether or not such drug is safe for use under the conditions prescribed, recommended, or suggested in the proposed labeling thereof." The Commissioner concluded that Edison failed to prove the safety of Cothyrobal. The Commissioner noted that Edison's own attempt to avoid the usual double-blind studies places the safety of the Cothyrobal in question. Because Edison argues that the toxic effects of levothyroxine make it humanly impossible to administer that drug in controlled testing, patients receiving Cothyrobal may be subject to the same risks as those receiving levothyroxine, absent a showing of the claimed ability of vitamin B_{12} to mitigate the antithyrotoxic effects of levothyroxine. * * *

Although the Commissioner recognized that studies showing the safety of a drug need not be adequate and well-controlled * * * he properly ruled that they "must be adequately constructed so that scientists can draw reasonable conclusions from them." The Commissioner, relying on testimony of three expert witnesses, concluded that both the animal studies and clinical testing offered by Edison were deficient and failed to demonstrate the safety of Cothyrobal. In addition, a number of witnesses, including some called by Edison, testified to adverse side effects, such as tachycardia and insomnia, which may have resulted from treatment with Cothyrobal. Edison failed to rebut this evidence. The Commissioner therefore concluded that Edison did not carry its burden of proving the safety of the drug. In view of the foregoing, we find the Commissioner's decision supported by substantial evidence. * * *

Edison next objects to the exclusion of testimonial evidence which it alleges demonstrates the efficacy of Cothyrobal. Edison argues that because the symptoms of hypothyroidism are difficult to recognize, efficacy can be assessed most accurately through the degree of relief experienced by the patients. Thus, according to Edison, the "best way" to prove that the drug works "is to bring the patients in themselves" and allow them to testify. Similarly, Edison contends that the most relevant expert testimony is that of doctors who have administered Cothyrobal and can relate their clinical impressions of the ability of the drug to relieve pain. Edison, therefore, characterizes the testimony of non-clinical FDA experts, despite their impressive credentials and scientific experience, as "meaningless," and suggests that the ALJ erred when he considered their criticisms of the studies submitted with the NDA.

Edison's attempt to replace evidence of "controlled" investigation with testimony relating personal experiences or clinical impressions is inconsistent with the Act, the accompanying regulations, and explicit Supreme Court precedent. Personal testimonials simply do not meet the exacting standards required by the Act and the regulations. [In *Weinberger v. Hynson, Westcott & Dunning, Inc.*, 412 U.S. 609 (1973), the Supreme] Court explained that the statutory and regulatory criteria

> express well-established principles of scientific investigation. Moreover, their strict and demanding standards, barring anecdotal evidence indicating that doctors "believe" in the efficacy of a drug, are amply justified by the legislative history. The hearings underlying the 1962 Act show a marked concern that impressions or beliefs of physicians, no matter how fervently held, are treacherous.

Id. at 619. Subjective evaluations by selected patients are even more suspect. We therefore conclude that the ALJ's rulings excluding personal testimonials accord with applicable law. We further find the admission of non-clinical FDA expert testimony entirely proper. * * *

SmithKline Corp. v. FDA

587 F.2d 1107 (D.C.Cir.1978).

■ BAZELON, CIRCUIT JUDGE:

Smith, Kline & French Laboratories (SKF), a Division of SmithKline Corporation, has since 1950 produced and marketed Dexamyl, a prescription drug used as an anorectic in the treatment of obesity. Dexamyl is a combination drug containing Dexedrine (dextroamphetamine sulfate), an appetite suppressant, and amobarbital, a barbiturate designed to reduce the possible adverse side effects of Dexedrine. On August 24, 1976, the Acting Commissioner of Food and Drugs published an order denying SKF a hearing and refusing to approve the pending new drug applications (NDAs) for Dexamyl. 41 Fed. Reg. 35,741 (1976). SKF petitions this court to reverse the Acting Commissioner's summary judgment order and to remand to the Food and Drug Administration for an evidentiary hearing pursuant to 21 U.S.C. § 355(c). * * *

FDA has promulgated regulations implementing this statutory scheme. It has required that for a fixed combination prescription drug such as Dexamyl substantial evidence must be presented both that the drug is effective for its intended use and that each constituent component contributes to the claimed effects. In addition, FDA has specified criteria for the "adequate and well-controlled investigations" acceptable as substantial evidence of effectiveness. Although the Act appears to contemplate a hearing if FDA does not approve an NDA, FDA has developed summary judgment procedures in cases where an applicant has failed to submit substantial evidence of drug efficacy sufficient to meet regulatory standards. The Supreme Court has in principle approved such procedures, stating that, "(w)e cannot impute to Congress the design of requiring, nor does due process demand, a hearing when it appears conclusively from the applicant's 'pleadings' that the application cannot succeed." Weinberger v. Hynson, Westcott & Dunning, Inc., 412 U.S. 609, 621 (1973). * * *

On August 6, 1971, SKF submitted NDAs for Dexamyl * * * * FDA informed SKF by letter on January 15, 1973, that these NDAs were not approvable because "(t)he studies submitted fail to demonstrate the contribution of the sedative-tranquilizer constituent to the total effect of the drug." * * * On July 11, 1973, SKF submitted to FDA the results of five, new, double-blind, clinical trials testing the efficacy of Dexamyl (multi-investigator clinical trials). Two weeks later, on July 27, 1973, FDA informed SKF by letter that the record regarding Dexamyl was closed as of that date, and that no further data would be accepted from SKF.

Three years later, on August 24, 1976, FDA published an order denying a hearing and refusing to approve the pending NDAs for Dexamyl. * * * The Acting Commissioner based his holding on the fact that none of the evidence submitted by SKF met the regulatory standards for adequate and well-controlled clinical studies. * * * Prior to August 24, SKF had received no criticism from FDA of SKF's multi-investigator clinical trials. After reviewing FDA's August 24 order, SKF asked Herbert Solomon, Ph.D., Professor of Statistics at Stanford University, and William M. Wardell, M.D., Ph.D., Associate Professor of Pharmacology and Toxicology at the University of Rochester Medical Center, to review these studies. These two experts prepared affidavits averring that the studies were adequate and well-controlled clinical investigations under applicable scientific and regulatory standards. * * *

[T]he FDA regulations defining "well-controlled investigations" * * * for the most part express general norms of scientific research rather than exact rules of procedure. The task of a court of appeals reviewing an FDA grant of summary judgment thus becomes, at least in those cases which do not involve the violation of a manifestly "precise" regulation, the determination of whether the applicant's submission on its face is so conclusively deficient in light of these norms that no issue of fact remains whether "experts qualified by scientific training and experience" could "fairly and responsibly" conclude, on the basis of the submission, that "the drug will have the effect it purports or is represented to have under the conditions of use prescribed, recommended, or suggested in the labeling or proposed labeling thereof."

The difficulties besetting this enterprise are formidable. The issues entail complicated questions of scientific methodology, an area in which courts have little institutional competence. These questions must be confronted, moreover, in the absence of an evidentiary record. * * * Although courts will ordinarily exercise considerable deference to an "agency's technical expertise and experience," particularly with respect to questions involving " 'engineering and scientific' considerations," it is not clear how far that deference should extend when an agency has deliberately prevented the creation of a record by which its determinations can be probed for their underlying "basis in fact." * * * [W]hen a record is barren concerning an issue presented in a petition for review in this case the issue of whether an applicant's studies are methodologically adequate in light of the pertinent regulations we are asked to perform even this limited function on the basis of faith alone.

The instant case amply illustrates these difficulties. SKF strenuously urges that FDA's criticisms of its multi-investigator clinical trials are based upon "imprecise" regulations and are scientifically fallacious. Since FDA refused to consider these contentions, however, the record before us consists chiefly of SKF's NDA, together with its multi-investigator clinical trials, and FDA's August 24, 1976 order. We are thus confronted on one side by the arguments of lawyers, and on the other by the untested conclusions of FDA. To decide the scientific merit of these disputes, on the basis of the record now before us, would certainly be to risk the dangerous unreliability likely to occur when "technically illiterate judges" attempt substantively to review mathematical and scientific questions.

That risk may, in the end, prove inescapable, but it can perhaps be minimized if it is kept firmly in mind that we need not resolve the *scientific* question of the methodological adequacy of SKF's multi-investigator clinical trials, but the *legal* question of whether they are on their face conclusively inadequate in light of the pertinent regulations. The manner in which we resolve this latter question involves policy considerations: we must take account of both fairness to the petitioner and the public interest in effective drug regulation. Since FDA has precluded SKF from establishing on the record the factual predicates for its arguments that FDA's criticism of the multi-investigator clinical trials are scientifically inaccurate, rudimentary fairness requires that we at least give the factual claims underlying SKF's arguments the benefit of the doubt. * * *

SKF rests its claim to a hearing chiefly on its multi-investigator clinical trials. SKF argues that these trials establish both that Dexamyl is effective as an anorectic and that each of its components contributes to the effects claimed; i.e., that the Dexedrine in Dexamyl performs its weight-loss function undiminished by the presence of amobarbital, and that the amobarbital makes its own contribution by reducing adverse side effects experienced by patients who take Dexedrine alone. The trials tested Dexamyl tablets against Dexedrine. The studies were double-blind; neither investigators nor patients knew which of the two drugs had been prescribed to any particular patient. There were five investigators, scattered throughout the country; each was a physician who treated patients in his private medical practice for obesity. All followed the same protocol, under which 30 patients were selected for each study, 15 of whom were assigned randomly to one drug, and 15 to the other. The trials lasted eight weeks.

In its August 24, 1976 order, FDA noted numerous deficiencies which, it claimed, rendered the trials conclusively inadequate in light of the pertinent regulations. Before this court, however, FDA has chosen to press only six of these deficiencies. Should even a single one of these six deficiencies prove valid, we must sustain FDA's summary judgment order.

The subjects of the trials were selected from among patients between the ages of 18 and 60 who were at least 20 percent overweight, and who scored four or more on a prescribed Anxiety Manifestation Index. No patients were included if, among other things, they suffered from a number of specified diseases or had a history of drug abuse. The protocol also required that patients selected for a trial not have received any anorectic or tranquilizing medication for at least two weeks prior to their participation in the study, and tranquilizers, sedatives and other anorectic agents or measures for weight control were prohibited during the trial. Patients were placed on a 1200 calorie diet. * * *

Dexamyl's present labeling indicates use with obese patients, but the subjects of the trials were anxious, obese patients. Since anxiety was one of the side effects of Dexedrine that amobarbital was designed to remedy,

FDA argues that it is impossible to generalize the results obtained in the subpopulation of patients studied by the trials. Its point appears to be that the trials do not demonstrate whether Dexedrine produces in non-anxious obese patients side-effects that can be remedied by amobarbital. If no such side effects are produced, the prescription of amobarbital would be superfluous. FDA's contention is well grounded in its regulations. The trials provide no "assurance" that Dexedrine, in the amounts contained in Dexamyl, produces in non-anxious obese patients side effects capable of being remedied by amobarbital. This conclusion is not fatal to SKF, however, since it implies only that Dexamyl's labeling be altered to recommend Dexamyl for use with anxious, obese patients. SKF implies that it would accept such an alteration, and we must therefore examine the other deficiencies alleged by FDA to determine whether the trials are conclusively inadequate despite such an alteration in labeling.

The trials were conducted by physicians whose private medical practices included obese patients, and each physician-investigator was aware that the trials were testing the side-effect potential of the two drugs involved. The physicians were expected to use their normal but trained powers of observation, supplemented by specific inquiry where they deemed it appropriate. They completed forms recording extensive data for all patients. Particular attention was paid to adverse effects, which were detailed as to dates (onset and termination), severity, and relationship to the drug prescribed. The supervising physicians recorded whatever action they took as the result of such an adverse effect, including any reduction of dosage or outright discontinuance of the drug involved.

FDA regulations require a well-controlled study to explain its "methods of observation and recording of results, including the variables measured, quantitation, assessment of any subjects response, and steps taken to minimize bias on the part of the subject and observer." 21 C.F.R. § 314.111(a)(5)(ii)(a)(3). FDA contends that the trials are conclusively inadequate in light of this regulation since they nowhere describe what procedure (observation, general questions or specific inquiries) was actually used by each investigator to elicit adverse reaction data, whether specific inquiry was resorted to under the same circumstances or whether each of the investigators asked their subjects the same questions. * * *

We must ask, that is, whether the trials are so conclusively deficient in light of the norm of scientific research expressed by the regulation that no question of fact remains whether qualified experts could fairly and responsibly conclude from the trials whether Dexamyl was effective for its intended uses. SKF argues that such a question of fact exists. The trials were conducted in a double-blind fashion. Since neither investigators nor subjects knew which patients were receiving Dexamyl and which Dexedrine, SKF concludes that the possible irregularities in observation noted by FDA would not bias the trials' results. Whether the level of "explanation" offered by SKF was sufficient under the regulation thus involves a complex question of scientific methodology. We, of course, have neither the knowledge nor the competence to ourselves resolve this question. Giving petitioner's version of the facts the benefit of the doubt, however, we must agree that the question is presently unsettled. But we will not so abandon the public interest in the expeditious enforcement of the drug laws as to assume, in the absence of a more developed record, that SKF's contentions have truly raised a genuine issue of fact requiring an adjudicatory hearing.

The trials compared a "test" group of patients who received Dexamyl against a "control" group who received Dexedrine. FDA regulations require that a well-controlled study must include "(a) method of selection of the subjects that ... (iii) Assures comparability in test and control groups of pertinent variables." 21 C.F.R. § 314.111(a)(5)(ii)(a)(2). FDA argues that the trials are conclusively inadequate in light of this regulation because they fail to demonstrate the comparability of test and control subjects regarding the incidence and degree of anxiety. SKF vigorously contests this characterization of the trials, contending that they did indeed include a method of selection assuring comparability. The subjects were assigned to test and control groups on a random basis, and a statistical analysis of the Anxiety Manifestation Index for both groups indicated a random distribution of anxiety. FDA discounts this analysis, however, stating that the regulations require a check on the results of randomization at the conclusion as well as at the beginning of a study. In this FDA appears to be improperly elaborating on its own regulations, which require only that a study provide a "method of selection of the subjects" that would ensure comparability. * * *

FDA argues that the trials also failed to assure comparability between test and control groups with respect to the past use of amphetamines. This is important, FDA stresses, because "amphetamines as a class can produce both tolerance and dependence," and because "a subject's prior history of amphetamine use may affect ... the incidence of various side effects." 41 Fed. Reg. at 35,746. SKF contends, however, that these factors are irrelevant because no subject was included in the trials who had used amphetamines during the two weeks immediately prior to the commencement of the studies and because this two week "washout" period was sufficient to eliminate any interference that might be caused by a subject's prior history of amphetamine use. The issue of whether the two week washout period is sufficient to assure comparability in the selection of test and control groups appears to raise a question of fact. Whether this appearance is genuine, however, depends upon the state of opinion in the scientific community, a circumstance concerning which we are at present entirely ignorant. * * *

The trials analyzed data compiled by each of the five individual investigators. This data was then pooled or aggregated for further statistical analysis. FDA concluded that this pooling failed to provide the necessary assurance of comparability between test and control groups with respect to pertinent variables. SKF argues that FDA's conclusion overlooks the fact that all five investigators used the same experimental protocol, including the two week washout period for prior amphetamine use, the random assignment of subjects to test and control groups, and the double-blind administration of the trials. Thus, for example, if the washout period were effective in assuring comparability between test and control groups for a single investigator, it would also be so with respect to the aggregated data.

Since we have already concluded that the effectiveness of the washout period is an open question, we must also consider this aspect of the issue of pooling as unsettled. * * * The fact that different investigators used different techniques for soliciting or recording the data, for example, may present a bar to the statistical pooling of their results. But this is an intricate scientific question concerning which we cannot exercise independent judgment, and FDA has offered neither evidence nor explanation. Extending the benefit of the doubt to petitioner's general claim that the protocol was in fact sufficiently detailed to permit pooling, we must conclude that the question of whether a genuine issue of fact here exists remains open.

The trials compared Dexamyl to Dexedrine. FDA regulations state that a well-controlled study must provide "a comparison of the results of treatment or diagnosis with a control in such a fashion as to permit quantitative evaluation.... An effective regime of therapy may be used for comparison...." 21 C.F.R. § 314.111(a)(5)(ii)(a)(4)(iii). FDA concluded that the trials were conclusively inadequate in light of this regulation "since the active control used, dextroamphetamine, does not permit a quantitative evaluation of the effects of Dexamyl."

> Because the anorectic effect of dextroamphetamine is only marginal to begin with (i.e., its advantage over placebo is small), and because its anorectic effect is highly variable, its effectiveness is not demonstrable in every study. * * * Accordingly, a finding of "no difference" between Dexamyl and dextroamphetamine in a particular study can mean either that both were effective or that neither was effective in that study.

41 Fed. Reg. at 35,750. * * *

SKF argues, if FDA recognizes Dexedrine as effective, the trials were not on their face deficient to use the drug as an active control. We agree with SKF in this matter. FDA's endorsement of Dexedrine as effective for the short term management of exogenous obesity provides at least prima facie support for SKF's view of the appropriateness of Dexedrine as an active control. Since, in contrast to other issues we have heretofore considered, SKF's position is supported by evidence, we conclude that there is a genuine issue of fact whether Dexedrine, although effective, is so unpredictable as to foreclose the possibility of quantitative evaluation. Such issues are not to be decided at summary judgment.

FDA requires that a well-controlled investigation explain "the methods used to minimize bias on the part of the observers and the analysts of the data." 21 C.F.R. § 314.111(a)(5)(ii)(a)(4). FDA concluded that the trials were conclusively deficient in light of this regulation. * * * SKF rejects this argument, noting that the steps taken in the trials to minimize analyst bias are stated in the protocol and final report. These include a multiple covariance quantitative analysis, a Chi–Square analysis of qualitative re-sults, a report of the details and results of these analyses, and an analysis both of all subjects and of only those subjects who completed the entire eight week program.

Since it is impossible to determine, in the abstract, whether the information provided in the trials' protocol constitutes a sufficient "expla-nation" for purposes of the regulation, we must ask, once again, whether the trials are so conclusively deficient with respect to the norm of scientific research expressed by the regulation that no issue of fact remains whether qualified experts could fairly and responsibly conclude from the trials whether Dexamyl was effective for its intended uses. We have no way of answering this question in the absence of a more developed record. Giving the benefit of the doubt to petitioner, we conclude that the question remains open.

If Dexamyl's labeling were altered to recommend its use for anxious, obese patients, FDA's summary judgment order cannot be sustained. It remains an open question, however, whether the trials are conclusively deficient in light of FDA regulations requiring comparability of test and control groups, an explanation of the methods used to observe and record results, and an explanation of the methods used to minimize analyst bias. These issues cannot be resolved in the absence of an evidentiary record. * * * Since we cannot sustain FDA's summary judgment order and since, at the same time, we have no assurance that there is presently a genuine issue of fact to be aired at an adjudicatory hearing, this record should be remanded to FDA for a proceeding to determine whether such a genuine issue of fact exists. The extent of this proceeding should be as limited as its circumscribed purpose. Were this proceeding to become too lengthy or elaborate, it would create precisely the drain on FDA's resources [that] FDA's summary judgment regulations were designed to prevent. * * *

NOTES AND QUESTIONS

1. *Industry challenges to FDA decisionmaking.* Pharmaceutical manufac-turers rarely pursue judicial challenges to an FDA denial of an NDA, no doubt in recognition of the fact that courts show significant deference to the agency's expertise. See, e.g., Unimed, Inc. v. Richardson, 458 F.2d 787, 789 (D.C.Cir.1972) ("[W]e remind ourselves that our role in the congres-sional scheme is not to give an independent judgment of our own, but rather to determine whether the expert agency entrusted with regulatory responsibility has taken an irrational or arbitrary view of the evidence assembled before it. We are unable to say that it has. . . ."); Ubiotica Corp. v. FDA, 427 F.2d 376 (6th Cir.1970). The Cothyrobal NDA at issue in *Edison* had a checkered history. The inventor of the drug previously filed an antitrust lawsuit charging that a pair of his competitors had conspired with the FDA to block approval of Cothyrobal, a claim that the court remanded to the district court but not without first warning the agency to use an "unimpeachable review process." See Israel v. Baxter Labs., Inc., 466 F.2d 272, 283 (D.C.Cir.1972).

2. *The shift from passive to active premarket review.* Since 1938, the FDA's governing statute has required that the agency review all new drugs for safety prior to marketing. See 21 U.S.C. § 355. Under the original provision, applications for approval automatically went into effect after 60 days, unless the agency extended the review period and notified the applicant. In 1962, Congress amended the FDCA to create a pre-approval system for new chemical entities under which the NDA sponsor must demonstrate both the safety and effectiveness for the new drug's intended use(s) and await FDA clearance for marketing. The agency also subjected drugs first marketed prior to 1962 to a complex retrospective review procedure as a prerequisite for continued marketing. In implementing the Drug Amendments of 1962, the FDA routinely disregarded testimonials as evidence of safety and effectiveness. See Upjohn Co. v. Finch, 422 F.2d 944, 951–52 (6th Cir.1970); see also Richard A. Merrill, The Architecture of Government Regulation of Medical Products, 82 Va. L. Rev. 1753, 1761–76 (1996) (providing a detailed discussion of how the current new drug approval process evolved from earlier approaches).

3. *Time and effort required for approval.* Pharmaceutical manufacturers expend tremendous resources in the preparation of applications for the approval of new drugs. The development process now takes almost twelve years on average, from early research and pre-clinical testing through the multi-stage clinical trials process and FDA review. After investing a substantial amount of time and resources in animal studies and other preliminary data gathering, a pharmaceutical company must see the drug through controlled clinical trials as required by the FDA's new drug approval process. See Richard J. Findlay, Originator Drug Development, 54 Food & Drug L.J. 227 (1999); Symposium, Drug Development: Who Knows Where the Time Goes?, 52 Food & Drug L.J. 141 (1997). As mentioned in Chapter 2(A), out of 5000 candidates that enter pre-clinical testing, only five may enter clinical trials, and only one of those may reach the market. If one accounts for the numerous failures along the way and the cost of capital, estimates place the average investment for an approved new drug at more than $800 million. See Ceci Connolly, Price Tag for a New Drug, Wash. Post, Dec. 1, 2001, at Λ10 (adding that the figure had more than tripled in the space of a decade, largely because of demands for larger and more complex clinical trials). But cf. Alice Dembner, Public Handouts Enrich Drug Makers, Scientists, Boston Globe, Apr. 5, 1998, at A1 (describing a government study that concluded that the average out-of-pocket cost to develop a drug, after factoring in tax breaks, was just $65.5 million); Sarah Lueck, Drug Industry Exaggerates R&D Costs to Justify Pricing, Consumer Group Says, Wall St. J., July 24, 2001, at B6 (noting that "taxpayer-funded scientists conducted 55% of the studies that led to the ... development of the top-five selling drugs in 1995"). (In some ways, the motion picture industry operates in a similar fashion, with blockbuster movies dwarfed by flops and reportedly substantial expenditures sunk into the production process.) In 1998, analysts estimated that the pharmaceutical industry spent approximately $21 billion on R&D, though some critics pointed out that companies inappropriately count marketing efforts in this figure.

4. *Drug lag.* For years, critics blamed the FDA's lengthy pre-approval process for creating a "drug lag" that delayed drugs already approved in Europe and elsewhere from reaching the U.S. market. See General Accounting Office, FDA Drug Approval—A Lengthy Process that Delays the Availability of New Drugs (1980); General Accounting Office, FDA Drug Approval: Review Time Has Decreased in Recent Years (1995); Richard Dorsey, The Case for Deregulating Drug Efficacy, 242 JAMA 1755 (1979); Louis Lasagna, The Development and Regulation of New Medications, 200 Science 871 (1978); Barry S. Roberts & David Z. Bodenheimer, The Drug Amendments of 1962: The Anatomy of a Regulatory Failure, 1982 Ariz. St. L.J. 581; see also National Academy of Sciences, The Competitive Status of the U.S. Pharmaceutical Industry (1983); Peter Huber, Safety and the Second Best: The Hazards of Public Risk Management in the Courts, 85 Colum. L. Rev. 277 (1985) (explaining that delays in marketing risky but useful drugs may harm a greater number of patients); Peter Huber, The Old–New Division in Risk Regulation, 69 Va. L. Rev. 1025 (1983); Mary K. Olson, Regulatory Agency Discretion Among Competing Industries: Inside the FDA, 11 J.L. Econ. & Org. 379 (1995) (identifying conflicting pressures that may affect approval decisions); C. Frederick Beckner, III, Note, The FDA's War on Drugs, 82 Geo. L.J. 529 (1993); Mark A. Kassell, Note, Getting There First with the Best: The Need to Shorten the Prescription Drug Approval Process, 27 Val. U. L. Rev. 95 (1992). Might something else account for delayed marketing? Whatever the explanation, this lag created an unintended safety benefit because applicants must include any available foreign marketing data with the NDA. See 21 C.F.R. § 314.50(c)(2)(iii). Consequently, the FDA received a greater quantum of data on which to base its review than it would have if relying solely on pre-approval clinical trials. For a look at the European Union's approach to the drug approval process, see Evelyne Friedel & Michael Freundlich, European Community Harmonization of the Licensing and Manufacturing of Medicinal Products, 49 Food & Drug L.J. 141 (1994); Richard F. Kingham et al., The New European Medicines Agency, 49 Food & Drug L.J. 301 (1994).

5. *Accelerating drug approval.* Starting in the 1980s, in response to the previously mentioned demands from AIDS activists, the FDA developed mechanisms for accelerated approval. First, under expedited approval procedures, new drugs intended to treat life-threatening and seriously-debilitating illnesses (such as AIDS or cancer) could receive marketing approval with a weaker body of evidence demonstrating effectiveness than is normally required in the NDA process. Qualifying drugs might reach the market after two, instead of three, phases of human clinical trials, though the agency could then demand post-approval studies to discover additional information about the drug's safety and optimal use. See 21 C.F.R. §§ 312.80–.82 (setting out procedures to expedite the development, testing, and marketing of new drugs). This approach reflected a willingness to accept less data demonstrating effectiveness in circumstances where patients desperately needed new therapies to survive. The FDA focused primarily on assuring safety, with the hope that the drugs will prove effective as well. Foregoing Phase III trials, however, also reduces the quantum of safety data.

In 1992, the agency began to accept "surrogate marker" evidence in these cases—clinical indicators that can be used to predict the ultimate effectiveness of a given drug therapy for a targeted condition. See 21 C.F.R. §§ 314.510, 601.41; see also 57 Fed. Reg. 58,942 (1992). For example, in the case of new AIDS drugs, the reduction of CD4 cell counts in HIV-infected patients might serve as a surrogate marker for control of disease progression, the clinical endpoint. See Steven R. Salbu, The FDA and Public Access to New Drugs: Appropriate Levels of Scrutiny in the Wake of HIV, AIDS, and the Diet Drug Debacle, 79 B.U. L. Rev. 92 (1999); Sheila R. Shulman & Jeffrey S. Brown, The Food and Drug Administration's Early Access and Fast–Track Approval Initiatives: How Have They Worked?, 50 Food & Drug L.J. 503 (1995). In 1997, Congress belatedly codified these "fast track" procedures. See 21 U.S.C. § 356; see also Deborah G. Parver, Comment, Expediting the Drug Approval Process: An Analysis of the FDA Modernization Act of 1997, 51 Admin. L. Rev. 1249 (1999).

6. *Altering the substantial evidence standard.* The Food and Drug Administration Modernization Act of 1997 (FDAMA) also relaxed the "substantial evidence" standard. If the FDA concludes that the data from one clinical trial are sufficient to establish substantial evidence of effectiveness, the statute now permits the agency to approve an NDA on this basis. The FDA retains the discretion, however, to require the traditional two adequate and well-controlled clinical trials. See 21 U.S.C. § 355(d); see also 62 Fed. Reg. 13,650 (1997); Jennifer Kulynych, Will FDA Relinquish the "Gold Standard" for New Drug Approval? Redefining "Substantial Evidence" in the FDA Modernization Act of 1997, 54 Food & Drug L.J. 127 (1999); Michael P. Van Huysen, Comment, Reform of the New Drug Approval Process, 49 Admin. L. Rev. 477 (1997). Although a single large multi-center trial may have enough statistical power to confirm effectiveness, the amendment may lead to the enrollment of fewer total subjects, making these pre-approval studies even less likely to uncover low frequency or longer latency adverse drug reactions.

7. *User fees.* Under the Prescription Drug User Fee Act of 1992 (PDUFA), Pub. L. No. 102–571, 106 Stat. 4491 (codified at 21 U.S.C. § 379g-h), sponsors of NDAs pay a substantial user fee, up to $309,647, to the FDA for review of their applications. See FDA, User Fee Schedule for Fiscal Year 2001, available at <www.fda.gov/oc/oms/ofm/userfees/userfees.htm>. In exchange for the authority to collect user fees, the agency agreed to spend the proceeds on hiring and training new personnel to participate in the NDA review process, informally promising to reduce the NDA processing times significantly. See Bruce N. Kuhlik, Industry Funding of Improvements to the FDA's New Drug Approval Process: The Prescription Drug User Fee Act of 1992, 47 Food & Drug L.J. 483, 485–91 (1992); see also Mary K. Olson, Regulatory Reform and Bureaucratic Responsiveness to Firms: The Impact of User Fees in the FDA, 9 J. Econ. & Mgmt. Strategy (2000). In the first five years, the FDA received over $325 million in user fees and hired more than 240 new reviewers. Since the enactment of PDUFA, the average time from submission to approval of new drug applications has dropped from approximately 30 months to 12 months, though recently it began to creep up again. See Chris Adams & Scott Hensley, Drug Makers Want FDA to Move Quicker, Wall St. J., Jan. 29, 2002, at B12. Although the user fee amendments expired in October 1997, Congress extended the program for five additional years. See FDAMA, Pub. L. No. 105–115, § 103, 111 Stat. 2296, 2299–304 (1997).

E.R. Squibb & Sons, Inc. v. Bowen
870 F.2d 678 (D.C.Cir.1989).

■ GINSBURG, D.H., CIRCUIT JUDGE:

* * * During the 1950s, Squibb received FDA approval for, and began marketing, four oral combination drugs (referred to collectively as Mysteclin), each of which contained both the antibiotic tetracycline and one of two antifungal agents, nystatin or amphotericin B. Squibb included the antifungal agents on the theory that ingestion of tetracycline could lead to an overgrowth of the organism *Candida albicans*, a fungus that is commonly present in the human body but that can in some circumstances cause infection.

In 1962, Congress amended the FDCA to require proof that, in addition to being "safe for use," a drug is "effective in use." 21 U.S.C. § 355(b). * * * In accordance with the 1962 amendments, the FDA undertook a review of drugs that it had approved under the pre–1962 standard. In order to accomplish this task, it called upon the National Academy of Science–National Research Council (NRC) to perform preliminary evaluations of the effectiveness of pre–1962 drugs.

In 1969, the FDA announced that it would delete from the list of certifiable drugs in its regulations those drugs containing the combination of antibiotic and antifungal agents found in the various forms of Mysteclin, and that it would withdraw approval of all certifications granted pursuant to those regulations. The agency based this decision on the NRC's conclusion that "substantial evidence is lacking that each of these combination drugs will have the effect it purports or is represented to have." Squibb filed objections to this decision, which was then stayed pending the outcome of an evidentiary hearing in which manufacturers of the affected drugs were invited to demonstrate that their products met the statutory standards for effectiveness.

As of the time of the hearing, Squibb used two types of labeling for Mysteclin, depending upon the antifungal agent involved: for Mysteclin products containing amphotericin B, the labeling claimed effectiveness in preventing candidal disease attributable to antibiotic therapy; for products containing nystatin, the labeling claimed effectiveness only in suppressing candidal overgrowth. During the hearing, Squibb introduced several alternative forms of labeling for Mysteclin products containing amphotericin B, apparently in order to conform its labeling to what it hoped the evidence would show. The new labeling, like the labeling for the products containing nystatin, claimed effectiveness only against the possibility of candidal overgrowth in the intestinal tract. Although Squibb introduced evidence in support of both the disease and the suppression claims, it limits its current petition for review to the FDA's rejection of the suppression claim, and we tailor our discussion accordingly.

Following the hearing, the Administrative Law Judge held that Squibb had failed to show that Mysteclin is "effective in use" and ordered its certification withdrawn. Squibb appealed that decision to the Commissioner, who affirmed the ALJ in all relevant respects. Specifically, the Commissioner held that (1) in order to show that a drug is "effective in use," the manufacturer must demonstrate not only that it has the effect claimed on its label, but also that the claimed effect is of some medical significance; (2) Squibb had failed to establish "that suppression of gastrointestinal candida is itself a medically significant effect;" (3) the record evidence in fact showed that "candida overgrowth is not itself a disease" and that its suppression "is a pharmacologic, not necessarily a therapeutic, effect, i.e., it is a physiologic effect of no proven benefit to the patient;" and (4) in any event, the studies submitted by Squibb failed to establish that Mysteclin is effective in suppressing candidal overgrowth. The FDA then announced its final decision to withdraw approval for Mysteclin.

Squibb's primary contention is that the Commissioner erroneously required it to show that the suppression effect claimed for Mysteclin on its labeling is itself medically significant. As Squibb reads the 1962 amendments, a manufacturer, in order to satisfy the "effective in use" standard, need show only that a drug does what its label says it does, not that the claimed effect produces any particular medical benefit. Although no provision of the FDCA defines the term "effective in use," Squibb argues that both the plain language and the legislative history of the amendments evince a clear congressional intent compelling its interpretation, and that we must therefore reject the Commissioner's contrary reading. * * *

In support of its "plain language" argument, Squibb points to (1) the statutory provision for withdrawal of FDA approval if "there is a lack of substantial evidence that [a] drug will have the effect it purports or is represented to have under the conditions of use prescribed, recommended, or suggested in the labeling thereof," and (2) the definition of "substantial evidence" as "evidence . . . that the drug will have the effect it purports or is represented to have under the conditions of use prescribed, recommended, or suggested in the labeling . . . thereof." Squibb reads these provisions as clearly indicating that as long as the "effect" claimed for a drug in its labeling is not harmful (since, if it were, it would fail the Act's requirement that a drug be proven "safe for use") and as long as that claim is accurate, the Commissioner may not withdraw approval of the drug. In other words, Squibb interprets the Act as erecting, under the head of effectiveness, only a truth-in-labeling requirement.

The statutory language does not compel Squibb's reading, however. The cited provisions are directed primarily at the evidentiary standard that a manufacturer must meet in order to demonstrate that a drug is "effective in use;" they do not address the question whether any claimed "effect," however innocuous, is sufficient. * * *

Although the 1962 amendments are silent as to the precise meaning of "effective in use," the FDCA read as a whole would appear, if anything, to preclude the reading advanced by Squibb. The pre-marketing approval provisions here at issue apply, by their terms, only to "drugs," which the FDCA defines, insofar as relevant here, as "articles intended for use in the diagnosis, cure, mitigation, treatment, or prevention of disease in man," or "to affect the structure or any function of the body of man." The former provision plainly applies only to drugs whose intended effect is in some way related to disease. It would appear to foreclose Squibb's argument that Mysteclin is "effective in use" so long as it has only a safe use that is not disease-related. The latter provision, in contrast, appears to contemplate that a substance will be approved as a "drug" even though it has only a physiologic, rather than a therapeutic, effect. * * *

Squibb contends that because it has removed all therapeutic claims from its labeling for Mysteclin, the drug now falls solely within the "structure or . . . function" definition, and thus must be approved if it is safe (which is not disputed) and it has the physiologic effect claimed for it. * * * In support of this view, Squibb notes that the FDA has approved several articles, most notably birth control pills and weight reduction remedies, as to which only physiologic claims are made and which have not been proven medically beneficial.

Whatever the merits of Squibb's argument with respect to drugs that are properly characterized as "structure or . . . function" drugs, we do not think that Mysteclin is such a drug. First, it is questionable whether a drug that acts only upon non-human organisms that happen to reside within the human body can properly be understood as affecting the "body of man" (as opposed to the "prevention of disease in man") within the meaning of the definition. Second, assuming that such organisms could be understood as part of the human body, a drug that suppresses their growth does not affect the "structure" or "function" of the human body as the courts have construed those terms. * * *

[T]he "structure or . . . function" definition, unlike the "disease in man" definition, is relatively narrow, and was not intended to encompass all articles that might have some remote physical effect upon the body. * * * Given Congress's intent, in adding the "structure or . . . function" definition, specifically to bring "anti-fat" remedies within the regulatory framework, there is no doubt that articles intended to reduce weight, thus affecting the structure of the human body, fall within that definition. Similarly, articles intended to prevent pregnancy, thus affecting the reproductive function of the human body, fall within that definition. The suppression effect Squibb claims for Mysteclin, in contrast, would simply reduce the number of non-human organisms residing within the intestinal tract. Candida organisms are hardly part of the physical "structure" of the human body, nor does their suppression affect any "function" of the body in the sense that articles that induce sleep or inhibit digestion do.

Mysteclin's undisputed status as a drug, therefore, appears to depend upon its being an article "intended for use in the diagnosis, cure, mitigation, treatment, or prevention of disease in man." As such, the statutory mandate that it be shown "effective in use" would appear plainly to require a showing that, consistent with its identity as a "disease in man" drug, it has some disease-related effect. It is inconceivable that Congress meant for a drug to be approved without some showing of effectiveness in the intended use (i.e., relating to disease) that made it subject to regulation in the first place.

Nonetheless, we are reluctant for two reasons to rule, on the basis of the distinction between disease-related drugs and "structure or ... function" drugs, that the statute unambiguously precludes the reading advanced by Squibb. First, and most important, the FDA does not argue that anything turns on the definitional distinction discussed above. Rather, in response to Squibb's argument that Mysteclin is a drug only by virtue of the "structure or ... function" definition of drug (and as such need not be shown effective in any medically significant way), which it raised for the first time in its reply brief, the agency, at oral argument, offered only the broad rejoinder that some showing of therapeutic significance is required for all drugs—even those falling within the "structure or ... function" definition. Absent an explicit reference to "disease in man" in the latter definition, however, it is not clear to us that the statutory language compels the agency's broad reading. Moreover, in light of our conclusion that Mysteclin falls within the "disease in man" definition of drug, the agency's broad argument need not be decided in this case. * * *

As noted above, the FDA's reading of the 1962 amendments to require proof of some therapeutic effect finds strong support in the FDCA as a whole, at least for drugs falling within the "disease in man" definition. In this case, the Commissioner found that Squibb had failed to show that the suppression effect claimed for Mystesclin is of any therapeutic significance at all. Assuming for the moment the correctness of that finding for the purpose of evaluating the Commissioner's legal determination, we hold that the agency's reading of the statute as requiring it to withdraw approval for Mysteclin is a permissible interpretation of the statute. * * *

Squibb next challenges the Commissioner's conclusion that "the record contains no evidence to support Squibb's argument that suppression of gastrointestinal candida is itself a medically significant effect." Squibb asserts that it met its evidentiary burden on this point with the testimony of experts who stated that, in their view, suppression of candidal overgrowth is of some medical significance. One of the FDA's own witnesses, for example, testified that candidal overgrowth in the intestine is to be avoided because "the Candida can be an important cause of disease," including "Candida infections or disease, thrush, of the mouth or the esophagus or of the vagina or of the bowel, or of the skin." Squibb's witnesses testified to like effect, one also noting that in his opinion, "a drug with this [suppression] effect is of value in the practice of medicine."

According to Squibb, the Commissioner must defer to the opinions of these experts as long as their opinions are based upon substantial evidence. Squibb does not challenge, however, the Commissioner's conclusion that its studies failed to show that suppression of candidal overgrowth is of any disease-related significance. Squibb asserts that (1) both its studies and the testimony of its experts showed that Mysteclin does produce the claimed suppression effect; and (2) the Commissioner is required to defer to the experts on the medical significance of that effect. Because we reject Squibb's second argument, we need not address its first. * * *

In light of our holding that the Commissioner permissibly required Squibb to show some medical significance for its suppression claim, it follows that such a showing must meet the substantial evidence standard set forth in the 1962 amendments. Thus, Squibb was required to come forward with substantial evidence demonstrating not just that Mysteclin produces the claimed suppression effect, but also that effect is of some medical value. Since Squibb has adduced only anecdotal evidence to support its claim of medical efficacy—evidence that cannot constitute "substantial evidence" under either the statutory standard or the FDA's regulations— we find that the Commissioner's withdrawal of approval for Mysteclin is supported by the record. * * *

NOTES AND QUESTIONS

1. *Intended use and effectiveness.* After the court sustained the FDA's withdrawal of the NDAs for Mysteclin, can Squibb continue selling the product on the theory that it's not really a drug because the labeling only refers to non-therapeutic uses? Presumably it would continue making therapeutic claims for the tetracycline, but what if it sold the antifungal alone, claiming only to suppress candidal overgrowth? In fact, one company attempted to do just that, arguing that a veterinary product containing subtherapeutic levels of antibiotics and intended to reduce odors caused by bacteria in the digestive tract did not qualify as a "drug" because it served no therapeutic purpose and also did not directly affect the structure or function of the body. Nonetheless, the FDA succeeded in bring an unapproved new drug charge against this product. See United States v. Undetermined Quantities of Bottles ... "Pets Smellfree," 22 F.3d 235, 240 (10th Cir.1994) (rejecting the claimant's reliance on the holding in *Squibb*). If, instead, it continued selling the combination, could Squibb make no claim for the antifungal (effectively recharacterizing it as an inactive ingredient)?

2. *Therapeutic benefit.* Other courts have sustained the FDA's demand that drugs serve a therapeutic purpose. See Warner–Lambert Co. v. Heckler, 787 F.2d 147, 154–56 (3d Cir.1986) (rejecting the plaintiff's claim that " 'effectiveness' as used in the Act means only that the drug will have the effect the manufacturer claims for it," and concluding that the demonstration of effectiveness must include evidence of a therapeutic level of action compared with placebo). Recall, however, the FDA's limited recent willingness to accept surrogate markers for clinical endpoints. Should the reduction of blood pressure (or cholesterol) qualify? Cf. Denise Grady, As Silent Killer Returns, Doctors Rethink Tactics to Lower Blood Pressure, N.Y. Times, July 14, 1998, at F1 (reporting that "it is not known whether all drugs that lower blood pressure also protect against heart attack and stroke"). Even when a drug effectively treats a particular condition, controversy may arise about the consequences of using medications (e.g., psychotropic drugs) for that purpose. For example, many have criticized the escalating use of Ritalin® (methylphenidate hydrochloride) to treat "attention deficit disorder" in children. See Richard DeGrandpre, Ritalin Nation (1999); Larry S. Goldman et al., Diagnosis and Treatment of Attention–Deficit/Hyperactivity Disorder in Children and Adolescents, 279 JAMA 1100 (1998); Victor W. Henderson, Stimulant Drug Treatment of the Attention Deficit Disorder, 65 S. Cal. L. Rev. 397, 405–09 (1991). Should the FDA take such contentious questions into account when it reviews an NDA?

3. *Risk-benefit balancing.* The information derived from Phase III studies provides the data that the FDA reviewers use to evaluate the risk-benefit ratio for a drug. See 21 C.F.R. § 312.21. In performing the risk-benefit calculus, the agency recognizes that even effective drugs carry the risk of side effects for some patients, but that a small overall risk may be justified if the new drug promises significant potential benefits to the targeted class of patients. If Mysteclin serves no medically-significant purpose, won't its approval fail on lack of safety grounds (assuming that it's not completely benign)? Or is it better to view these as two separate inquiries with the final risk-benefit judgment left to the individual physician and patient? See Henry G. Grabowski & John M. Vernon, The Regulation of Pharmaceuticals: Balancing the Benefits and Risks (1983); John C. Ballin, Who Makes the Therapeutic Decisions?, 242 JAMA 2875 (1979); Denise Grady, Calculating Safety in Risky World of Drugs, N.Y. Times, Mar. 6, 2001, at F1. Consider this example:

> [L]idoflazine, an anti-anginal drug that is effective but has a tendency to cause potentially fatal heart rhythm abnormalities, was rejected [by the FDA] because it had not been shown to work in people unresponsive to other agents, so that there were no patients in whom the drug's excess risk was known to be worth taking. At almost the same time, however, another anti-anginal drug called bepridil, with risks similar to those of lidoflazine, *was* approved for people unresponsive to other agents when it was shown to be effective in such patients.

Robert M. Temple, Commentary on "The Architecture of Government Regulation of Medical Products," 82 Va. L. Rev. 1877, 1887 (1996). "For serious diseases, especially those poorly treated by available therapy, considerable toxicity is acceptable, and labeling is used to attempt to guide physicians in detecting and mitigating harm. In some cases, a relatively toxic drug will be identified as a 'second-line,' a drug to be used only in people who cannot tolerate, or do not respond to, safer agents." Id. at 1888.

Recall from Chapter 2 the issues associated with Laetrile, which the FDA refused to approve because it was not effective in treating cancer. See Rutherford v. American Med. Ass'n, 379 F.2d 641, 644 (7th Cir.1967) (noting that lack of "toxicity is not the sole criterion to be applied by the FDA to new drugs. Effectiveness of the drug as well as its safety ... is a relevant criterion."); see also Tutoki v. Celebrezze, 375 F.2d 105, 107 (7th Cir.1967) (affirming the district court's dismissal of a challenge to the FDA's action in prohibiting the distribution of Krebiozen). If it does serve a therapeutic purpose, though one that the FDA regards as inconsequential, how does the NDA fare? Cf. Laura Johannes & Steve Stecklow, Dire Warnings About Obesity Rely on Slippery Statistic, Wall St. J., Feb. 9, 1998, at B1 ("[T]he FDA's bar for approving new drugs is lower for disease treatments than for other problems, such as baldness or skin wrinkles. The agency is less likely to approve a drug for a nondisease condition when it is shown to have serious side effects—such as those that diet drugs produce."). For example, one of the casebook authors helped persuade the FDA to approve Claritin® (loratidine) to treat seasonal allergies notwithstanding evidence of carcinogenicity from rodent studies. Moreover, the drug's special utility as a nonsedating antihistamine evidently flowed in part from the fact that it contains a barely therapeutic (and therefore often ineffective) level of active ingredient. See Stephen S. Hall, Prescription for Profit, N.Y. Times Mag., Mar. 11, 2001, at 40.

What if a drug serves a medically-significant purpose but at high risk? Should the fact that other approved drugs accomplish the same purpose at a lower risk alter the analysis? And how does uncertainty factor into the equation? One commentator offered the following observations:

> Assume one study shows that twenty-five out of thirty people who took a new drug for AIDS lived at least five years, while all thirty of those who received nothing died within two years. Would this be sufficient evidence of effectiveness to permit approval of the drug without replicating the study? Assume that the study is repeated with a second group of patients, but that this time twenty-five out of thirty who took the drug died within twelve months, while all those who received nothing died after eighteen months. Which results show the actual effects of the drug? Did one study use an inappropriate population or other procedures that could produce misleading results? Should a third study be required before a decision on approval is made? What if two out of three studies find that patients who took the new drug lived several years longer than those who did not, with the third showing the reverse?

> The sufficiency of the evidence is inextricably bound to the adequacy of the clinical (and laboratory) trials. Thus, the proposal that certain new drugs should be approved without undergoing Phase Three trials may rest on a claim that Phase Three trials do not produce useful information on the effectiveness (and possibly the safety) of the drug. If they do not, perhaps the FDA has been requiring unnecessary studies, delaying the availability of beneficial drugs. Alternatively, the proposal could suggest accepting less evidence of effectiveness, so that

new drugs should be approved if they work at all in some people. This amounts to a new, lower standard of effectiveness.

A third, perhaps more plausible, interpretation is that the FDA is willing to accept a high probability of safety and effectiveness without pursuing additional trials that could demonstrate more clearly the level of effectiveness or risk. Most would argue that a probability of success is all that can be established by scientific methods. After all, the precise mechanisms by which even some widely accepted drugs operate has not been identified. We can only speak of the effectiveness of aspirin in reducing pain in terms of its probable effect on the nervous system. A paradox of scientific progress is that the deeper our knowledge, the greater must be our acceptance of uncertainty, including uncertainty about the truth of our beliefs.

Under these circumstances, a decision to approve drugs on lesser or different evidence than accepted in the past could be either a rational effort to restrict the evidence required to that absolutely necessary and no more, or an abdication of statutory responsibility not to permit drugs that are not shown to be sufficiently safe and effective onto the market. The position one takes on this point depends largely on one's values and the levels of safety and effectiveness such values suggest.

Wendy K. Mariner, Equitable Access to Biomedical Advances: Getting Beyond the Rights Impasse, 21 Conn. L. Rev. 571, 595–97 (1989). Finally, what role should foreign marketing data play in the review process? See Robert G. Pinco, Implications of FDA's Proposal to Include Foreign Marketing Experience in the Over-the-Counter Drug Review Process, 53 Food & Drug L.J. 105 (1998).

4. *The role of politics in new drug approvals.* Usually, the FDA reviews whatever product applications happen to come in the door, but on occasion it will beat the bushes looking for a company willing to seek approval for a drug that the agency wants brought to the market. See 40 Fed. Reg. 5351 (1975) (urging manufacturers to seek approval of DES for contraception), withdrawn, 54 Fed. Reg. 22,585 (1989); Ralph T. King, Jr., The Pill U.S. Drug Companies Dare Not Market, Wall St. J., June 26, 1998, at B1 ("In an unusual role reversal, the companies are resisting pressure from the FDA to market their birth-control pills as emergency contraception."); Tamar Lewin, U.S. Agency Wants the Pill Redefined, N.Y. Times, July 1, 1996, at A1 (same); Katharine Q. Seelye, Accord Opens Way for Abortion Pill in U.S. in Two Years, N.Y. Times, May 17, 1994, at A1 (describing high-level pressure exerted by the Clinton administration on the French manufacturer of RU–486 to apply for FDA approval, and the manufacturer's decision to grant its rights to the Population Council to sponsor an NDA).

5. *Supplemental NDAs.* After a new drug has been approved, a sponsor wishing to add another indication to the labeling must submit an NDA supplement (frequently referred to as an "efficacy supplement") containing the results of additional clinical testing to demonstrate the drug's effectiveness for that new use. There are several reasons why companies frequently choose not to seek supplemental approval. For instance, ethical constraints may complicate efforts to test approved drugs for unapproved but widely accepted medical uses. See David A. Kessler, Regulating the Prescribing of Human Drugs for Nonapproved Uses Under the Food, Drug, and Cosmetic Act, 15 Harv. J. Legis. 693, 730 (1978). Even if physicians could be found to supervise clinical investigations, companies must make trade-offs in allocating their limited research and development budgets, choosing between investigations of new chemical entities that might represent important therapeutic breakthroughs and conducting clinical trials to seek approval for secondary indications. See Martin D. Abeloff, Letter, Off–Label Uses of Anticancer Drugs, 267 JAMA 2473, 2474 (1992) ("Due to the rigorous, time-consuming, and expensive process of approving drugs for secondary indications, pharmaceutical companies have been reluctant to apply to the FDA for new labeled indications."). Indeed, the average agency review times for efficacy supplements were not significantly shorter than the two years previously required to review full NDAs. See Joseph A. DiMasi et al., New Indications for Already–Approved Drugs: An Analysis of Regulatory Review Times, 31 J. Clinical Pharmacol. 205 (1991). Nonetheless, some manufacturers choose to file such supplements for new uses of already approved drugs so that they can promote their products for these additional uses. See, e.g., F–D–C Rep. ("The Pink Sheet"), Feb. 14, 1994, at 10 (describing Pfizer's pending NDA supplement for the use of the antihypertensive drug Cardura® in the treatment of benign prostatic hypertrophy). As explained in Chapter 10(B), they also may receive an additional period of marketing exclusivity.

6. *Pediatric studies requirement.* The FDA has recognized that children metabolize and excrete prescription drugs differently than adults. In order to maximize the potential benefit of the products for children, Congress included a requirement in FDAMA that the agency identify, publish, and annually update a list of approved drugs for which additional information about safety and effectiveness in pediatric populations might prove useful. See 21 U.S.C. § 355a(b). The FDA can request that sponsors of pending or approved NDAs conduct pediatric studies. See id. § 355a(c); see also Kurt R. Karst, Comment, Pediatric Testing of Prescription Drugs: The Food and Drug Administration's Carrot and Stick for the Pharmaceutical Industry, 49 Am. U. L. Rev. 739 (2000). Recent concerns about pediatric use of certain medical devices, such as CAT scanners, suggest that pediatric studies for devices might also prove useful. See David J. Brenner et al., Estimated Risks of Radiation–Induced Fatal Cancer from Pediatric CT, 176 Am. J. Roentgenology 289 (2001) (explaining that "larger [radiation] doses and increased lifetime radiation risks in children produce a sharp increase, relative to adults, in estimated . . . lifetime cancer mortality risks").

2. Generic Drugs and Bioequivalence Issues

Serono Laboratories, Inc. v. Shalala

158 F.3d 1313 (D.C.Cir.1998).

■ Garland, Circuit Judge:

* * * To obtain FDA approval, the first applicant to market a drug, known as the "pioneer," must submit a new drug application (NDA)

containing, among other things, "full reports of investigations" made "to show whether or not such drug is safe for use and whether such drug is effective in use." 21 U.S.C. § 355(b)(1). Recognizing that the NDA process is costly and time-consuming, and seeking "to make available more low cost generic drugs," Congress amended the Act. * * * The Drug Price Competition and Patent Term Restoration Act of 1984 (known as the "Hatch–Waxman Amendments"), permits a manufacturer of a generic alternative to a pioneer drug to seek FDA approval by submitting an abbreviated new drug application (ANDA) that need contain only the more limited information specified in 21 U.S.C. § 355(j)(2).

Two aspects of the ANDA process, corresponding to two kinds of drug ingredients, are relevant to this case. First, with respect to "active ingredients," the statute provides that the Secretary of Health and Human Services shall approve an application for a generic drug unless the Secretary finds, among other things, that "information submitted with the application is insufficient to show that the active ingredients are the same as the active ingredients of the listed [pioneer] drug." 21 U.S.C. § 355(j)(3)(C)(ii). * * * Second, with respect to "inactive ingredients," the statute provides that the Secretary shall approve an application unless she finds that "information submitted in the application or any other information available to the Secretary shows" that "the inactive ingredients of the drug are unsafe" or "the composition of the drug is unsafe ... because of the type or quantity of inactive ingredients included or the manner in which the inactive ingredients are included." 21 U.S.C. § 355(j)(3)(H). * * *

In 1969, the FDA approved an NDA submitted by plaintiff Serono Laboratories, Inc. for Pergonal, a pioneer drug. Pergonal is a "menotropins" product administered by intramuscular injection and used to treat male and female infertility. A menotropins product is extracted from the urine of post-menopausal women, and contains two active ingredients: follicle-stimulating hormone (FSH) and luteinizing hormone (LH). FSH and LH make up less than five percent of Pergonal, with lactose and uncharacterized urinary proteins (UUPs) constituting the remainder.

In 1990, Lederle Parenterals, Inc. submitted an ANDA to the FDA seeking approval of a generic version of Pergonal, now known as Repronex. Defendant-intervenor Ferring Pharmaceuticals Inc. acquired the rights to Lederle's ANDA while it was pending. In December 1992, Serono filed a "citizen petition," * * * urging the FDA to withhold approval of the ANDA. Serono argued, among other things, that the UUPs in the proposed generic drug were "inactive ingredients" that differed from those in Pergonal and had not adequately been demonstrated to be safe. * * *

Serono also argued that the active ingredient FSH in the proposed generic drug was not, as required by statute, "the same as" the FSH in Pergonal because of differences in "isoforms" of the two products. FSH is a protein-based hormone consisting of two protein chains in a backbone-like configuration, with carbohydrate side chains. Natural variation in the carbohydrate elements leads to different isoforms of the hormone. Serono argued that this isoform variation in FSH rendered Repronex different from Pergonal, and hence ineligible for an ANDA.

On January 30, 1997, the FDA approved the ANDA for Repronex. The FDA gave Repronex an "AB" rating in its publication, Approved Drug Products with Therapeutic Equivalence Evaluations (known as the "Orange Book"), meaning that physicians and pharmacists could substitute Repronex for Pergonal. * * *

[After Serono sued the FDA in district court and moved for a preliminary injunction, the] FDA issued its final decision denying Serono's citizen petition. Dr. Janet Woodcock, Director of the FDA's Center for Drug Evaluation and Research, rejected Serono's claim that the isoform variation in the active ingredient FSH meant that the FSH in Repronex was not the "same as" the FSH in Pergonal. Dr. Woodcock acknowledged the isoform variation, but concluded that it was not "clinically significant for the product's intended uses" and therefore did not preclude a "sameness" finding for purposes of 21 U.S.C. § 355(j). Dr. Woodcock further concluded that the differing lactose concentrations in the two products, as well as the differing UUP profiles, did not affect the safety of Repronex. She also rejected the characterization of the UUPs as "inactive ingredients," classifying them instead as "impurities." * * *

[T]he district court granted Serono's motion for a preliminary injunction, barred the FDA "from approving the Ferring ANDA," and ordered it to "rescind immediately its designation of an 'AB' rating [for Repronex] in the Orange Book." * * * Serono argues, and the district court agreed, that "same as" under the statute, and "identical" under the regulation, must mean absolute "chemical" identity. The court rejected the FDA's view that "clinical" identity is sufficient for a menotropins product as long as the above-described conditions are met, and therefore concluded that Serono was likely to prevail on the merits of its claim that the FSH in Repronex and Pergonal is not the same. Since the district court's conclusion rests on issues of statutory and regulatory interpretation, we review that conclusion de novo. * * *

In this case, the statute does not define the term "same as," and does not indicate whether chemical or clinical identity was contemplated. We need to consider, therefore, what the terms mean in context. What the statute requires to be the "same" are the two drugs' "active ingredients," and FDA regulations pre-dating the Hatch–Waxman Amendments define an "active ingredient" as "any component that is intended to furnish a pharmacological activity or other direct effect." Hence, the ingredients that are to be compared for "sameness" are themselves defined in terms of pharmacological activity, adding credibility to the FDA's view that chemical identity is not the only way to read the statutory language. * * * Indeed, the statute says nothing at all about the type of information an applicant must submit to demonstrate "sameness," nor about the type of information upon which the FDA may rely. It says only that the information must not be "insufficient" to show that the active ingredients are the same. If anything, this broad grant of discretion to the agency with respect to the information it may consider in making a finding of "sameness" indicates that Congress did not have one precise definition of the term in mind.

Moreover, the statutory phrase must be read in the context of the kind of drug at issue. As Dr. Woodcock noted, "it is usually not possible to assure by chemical analysis that different batches of [a protein product like FSH] are identical at the level of the carbohydrate side chains." For the same reason, "batch to batch variability in isoform patterns" exist for Pergonal itself. This means that if absolute chemical identity were required, it would not be possible to say any generic was the "same as" Pergonal, because the "batch to batch variability" would make the target of the comparison (not just Pergonal, but the specific batch of Pergonal) indeterminate. Indeed, the Woodcock Letter indicates that if absolute chemical identity were required, not only menotropins but other categories of protein products would be excluded from the ANDA process as well. Yet, it seems likely—although by no means certain—that if Congress had intended to exclude entire categories of drugs from the scope of the Hatch–Waxman Amendments, which were passed to "facilitate the approval of generic copies of drugs," there would be some mention of that fact in the statute or legislative history. Instead, both are wholly silent on the subject. We thus conclude that the statute does not unambiguously require the term "same as" to be defined as complete chemical identity. * * *

The FDA concluded that "to be considered to have the same active ingredients as the reference listed drug, generic FSH products based on Pergonal ... must have the same primary structure, i.e., the same protein backbone and amino acid sequence as Pergonal (assured by using the same natural source material), the same potency, and the same degree of batch-to-batch uniformity." The agency thus endeavored to guarantee the greatest degree of "sameness" possible for this kind of product, by ensuring an identical chemical structure where possible (in the primary structure), while reducing natural batch-to-batch variance (in the carbohydrate side chains) to the same degree as that found in the pioneer drug. To accomplish the latter, the FDA observed that Serono controls the batch-to-batch uniformity of Pergonal by using USP rat potency tests, and that Ferring does the same for Repronex. The agency concluded that "it would be unreasonable to hold the generic menotropins product to a higher standard of uniformity than the standard used for Pergonal." * * *

The FDA's determination of what is required to establish "sameness" for purposes of the Act rests on the "agency's evaluations of scientific data within its area of expertise," and hence is entitled to a "high level of deference" from this court. * * * We conclude that the district court erred as a matter of law in ruling that the FDA's interpretation of the statute and regulations was impermissible. As that ruling was the principal basis for the court's conclusion that Serono was likely to succeed on the merits of its claim that the active ingredient FSH in Repronex was not the "same as" that in Pergonal, the court erred in that conclusion as well.

Lactose is an inactive ingredient in both Repronex and Pergonal. With regard to inactive ingredients, the Act directs the FDA to approve an ANDA for a generic drug unless the agency finds the inactive ingredients are "unsafe for use" or the composition of the drug is unsafe "because of the type or quantity" of the inactive ingredients. Although the statute itself contains no other limitation, an FDA regulation that became effective in 1992 provides that the agency will not grant an ANDA for a generic drug intended for parenteral (injectable) use, "unless it contains the same inactive ingredients ... in the same concentration as the listed drug." * * * [I]t is conceded that the concentration of lactose in the two drugs is different. Repronex contains twice as many milligrams of lactose per vial as Pergonal. Deputy Director Johnston addressed this issue, * * * determining that because the ANDA for Repronex was filed in 1990, the regulations that were in effect in that year rather than those that went into effect in 1992 should apply. * * *

The district court rejected Johnston's determination. * * * [I]t pronounced itself "dumb-founded" by the contention that a new drug could "come to market on a more lenient basis than required by existing law." * * * We do not find the FDA's policy so dumbfounding. First, the agency's decision not to apply the 1992 "same concentration" rule did not free the agency to disregard safety considerations. The statute's bottom line—that the agency must be satisfied that the lactose in the generic is not unsafe—still holds. Second, as long as the agency continues to ensure an ingredient's safety on a case-by-case basis, the decision not to retroactively apply a per se rule regarding concentration is not irrational. The application process for new drugs can be a long one—even the "abbreviated" ANDA process utilized here took more than six years for an agency decision. If every pending application had to be revised each time the FDA changed its regulations, the process would become much more lengthy—even Sisyphean if the rules of the game changed each time the application neared the finish line. Indeed, if complete retroactivity were required, the unintended consequence might well be to force the agency to limit its revision of regulations, in order to prevent the process from becoming unworkable. * * *

Although the Hatch–Waxman Amendments authorized the FDA to promulgate regulations to implement its new ANDA provisions, and one such regulation was the 1992 "same concentration" rule, the Amendments also expressly stated that ANDAs "may be submitted in accordance with" the FDA's existing regulations until the new regulations "take effect." As the FDA rightly points out, for this provision to have any meaning, the FDA must also be permitted to review applications under the regulations in effect at the time of the submission. Accordingly, the district court erred as a matter of law in concluding that Serono was likely to succeed on the merits because the FDA had failed to apply its 1992 regulation to the Repronex ANDA. * * *

If, as we have held, Serono is not likely to establish that Ferring's ANDA was wrongly approved, then public interest considerations weigh against an injunction. The purpose of the Hatch–Waxman Amendments was, after all, "to increase competition in the drug industry by facilitating the approval of generic copies of drugs." Congress expected that competition "to make available more low cost generic drugs." Congress' purpose is directly implicated here, the FDA argues, because Ferring has priced Repronex to sell at 40% below the price of Pergonal, and because there has been a shortage of this type of fertility drug. * * *

Zeneca, Inc. v. Shalala

213 F.3d 161 (4th Cir.2000).

■ HAMILTON, SENIOR CIRCUIT JUDGE:

* * * Once the FDA has "listed" a pioneer drug as approved, the FFDCA allows any person or entity desiring to market a generic copy of the pioneer drug to seek FDA approval of its generic version through an Abbreviated New Drug Application (ANDA). The ANDA procedure "permits generic drug applications to piggy-back on clinical findings that [the] FDA has already embraced" in the NDA, *In re Barr Labs., Inc.*, 930 F.2d 72, 73 (D.C.Cir.1991), and thus, the ANDA applicant need not duplicate the clinical safety studies that supported the pioneer drug's NDA. The ANDA process, however, does not absolve the generic drug manufacturer from its burden of establishing that its generic drug is the bioequivalent of the pioneer drug and is safe and effective.

In order to obtain approval of a generic drug, a manufacturer must provide information sufficient to establish that, among other things: (1) the generic drug is "bioequivalent" to the pioneer drug; (2) its active ingredients, route of administration, strength and dosage form are "the same as" those of the pioneer drug; and (3) the inactive ingredients are not "unsafe for use under the conditions prescribed, recommended, or suggested in the labeling proposed for the drug." With respect to the substitution of inactive ingredients in a parenteral [e.g., injectable] drug, the FDA's regulations require that most of the generic drug's inactive ingredients be the same as the inactive ingredients of the pioneer drug. Differences in inactive ingredients that are preservatives, buffers, or antioxidants are permitted as long as those differences do not affect the safety of the drug. Manufacturers of generic drugs are also required to show that "the labeling proposed for the new [generic] drug is the same as the labeling approved for the listed drug ... except for changes required ... because the new drug and the listed drug are produced or distributed by different manufacturers." * * *

Zeneca manufactures the pioneer drug Diprivan (a form of propofol), which the FDA approved in 1989 based on Zeneca's submission of an NDA. Diprivan is a parenteral drug used for inducing and maintaining anesthesia and for support of mechanical ventilation and sedation. Diprivan has a pH range of 7.0 to 8.5. Shortly after Zeneca introduced Diprivan in the United States, post-operative fevers and infections were documented and associated with its use. These post-operative fevers and infections were determined to be the result of microbial contamination caused by mishandling of the drug by medical personnel. With the FDA's encouragement, Zeneca decided to reformulate Diprivan by adding the preservative disodium edentate (EDTA) in order to prevent microbial contamination. Zeneca performed clinical studies on the safety of the reformulated Diprivan and, in return, was awarded three years of exclusivity for the reformulated Diprivan when it was approved in 1996.

In March 1997, Gensia submitted an ANDA to the FDA for approval of a generic propofol product with EDTA, the same composition as Diprivan. In July 1997, Gensia informed the FDA that it was evaluating the development of propofol using the preservative sodium metabisulfite (sulfite) instead of EDTA. In its July 1997 letter, Gensia provided preliminary data on a propofol product with sulfite that would have a pH range of 6.0 to 7.5. Gensia asked the FDA to review the preliminary data and consider, in particular, the proposed lower pH of Gensia's formulation and the safety of sulfite as a preservative. The Office of Generic Drugs (the OGD) undertook a review of the preliminary data. In addition, the FDA's Division of Anesthetic, Critical Care and Addiction Products, the division that reviewed and approved the NDA for Diprivan, provided consultation to the OGD about the proposed propofol product containing sulfite. On January 16, 1998, Gensia withdrew its ANDA for propofol with EDTA and submitted an ANDA for propofol with sulfite with a new proposed pH range of 4.5 to 6.4.

On April 7, 1998, after learning that the FDA was considering an ANDA for generic propofol, Zeneca filed an administrative petition for a stay of action pursuant to 21 C.F.R. § 10.35 (1999). Zeneca's petition requested, among other things, that the FDA decline to approve any generic version of Diprivan that "contains an antimicrobial additive other than [EDTA], the safety of which is not supported by preclinical, clinical, or other scientific investigative studies." Zeneca contended that the substitution of sulfite for EDTA and the lower pH of Gensia's propofol with sulfite raised safety issues; specifically, issues of allergenicity, toxicity, antimicrobial effectiveness, and product stability. Further, Zeneca argued that the addition of a sulfite warning required by 21 C.F.R. § 201.22 to the label of Gensia's propofol with sulfite would violate the statutory "same labeling" requirement for generic drugs.

On January 4, 1999, the FDA approved Gensia's ANDA for propofol with sulfite. On the same day, the FDA denied Zeneca's petition. The FDA noted that it "did not require clinical studies to establish the safety of [Gensia's] drug product; instead, the Agency found that sufficient information was available both in the ANDA and before the Agency to address whether changing the preservative to sodium metabisulfite compromised the safety of the propofol injectable emulsion product." The FDA concluded that it "had substantial data to evaluate the possible effects of sodium metabisulfite in propofol because sodium or potassium metabisulfite is present in concentrations ranging from 0.1 mg/ml to 10 mg/ml in more than 50 approved drug products." Based on the information in the administrative record and its scientific expertise, the FDA determined that the presence of sulfite in Gensia's propofol did not affect the safety profile of the drug.

The FDA also concluded that Gensia's propofol with sulfite was safe and therapeutically equivalent to Diprivan. Of particular note, the FDA acknowledged that "patients with sulfite allergies should not be administered a formulation of propofol with [sulfite]. Appropriate labeling, however, is sufficient to protect against improper use of the product." Accordingly, the FDA required Gensia's propofol with sulfite product to include a "statement in the insert labeling informing practitioners of precautions related to the presence of sulfites," and to "highlight prominently on the container label that the product contains [sulfite]." The FDA concluded that these warnings "serve to alert practitioners of the potential for allergic reactions and are adequate to ensure safe use of the drug." Based on the addition of these warnings to the label of Gensia's propofol with sulfite, the FDA concluded that Gensia's propofol with sulfite was a safe generic drug when properly administered to the majority of the population, which has no allergic reaction to sulfites. * * *

On appeal, Zeneca makes three substantive arguments in support of its claim that the FDA's approval of Gensia's ANDA for propofol with sulfite was arbitrary and capricious, and must therefore, be declared invalid and permanently enjoined. First, Zeneca argues that the FDA's approval of Gensia's ANDA for propofol with sulfite violated two FDA regulations prohibiting the FDA from approving an ANDA for a generic drug with a different preservative than the pioneer drug where the information submitted by the generic drug manufacturer fails to show that the substitute preservative does not affect the safety of the proposed generic drug. Second, Zeneca argues that the FDA violated its own regulation requiring a generic drug's labeling to be the same, with some exceptions, as its pioneer counterpart. Finally, Zeneca argues that the FDA approved Gensia's ANDA for propofol with sulfite based upon a flawed medical review of the safety of Gensia's propofol with sulfite. * * *

Zeneca first argues that the FDA violated 21 C.F.R. §§ 314.94(a)(9)(iii) and 314.127(a)(8)(ii)(B) by approving Gensia's ANDA for propofol with sulfite without requiring Gensia to adequately show that the substitution of sulfite for EDTA as a preservative did not affect the safety of the drug formula based on Diprivan. Therefore, Zeneca argues, the FDA's approval was arbitrary and capricious. We conclude that Zeneca's argument is without merit.

Section 314.94(a)(9)(iii) permits substitution of preservatives in parenteral drugs "provided that the applicant identifies and characterizes the differences and provides information demonstrating that the differences do not affect the safety of the proposed drug product." Similarly, section 314.127(a)(8)(ii)(B) provides, in relevant part, that the FDA will not approve an ANDA for a generic drug product "unless it contains the same inactive ingredients, other than preservatives . . . and, if it differs from the listed drug in a preservative . . . the application contains sufficient information to demonstrate that the difference does not affect the safety of the drug product." Collectively, these regulatory sections establish that prior to approving an ANDA for a generic drug with a preservative that differs from the listed pioneer drug, the FDA must determine that the preservative does not affect the safety of the drug. In this case, the FDA concluded that the substitution of sulfite for EDTA as a preservative did not affect the safety of Gensia's propofol because warnings on the product's container and labeling would "serve to alert practitioners of the potential for allergic reactions and are adequate to ensure safe use of the drug."

As an initial matter, we note that the use of sulfites in prescription drugs is widespread. See Sulfiting Agents; Labeling in Drugs for Human Use; Warning Statement, 50 Fed. Reg. 47,558, 47,558 (1985) (proposed rule) (noting that, at that time, sulfites were present "in more than 1,100 oxygen-sensitive prescription drug products"). Moreover, the "FDA has not found evidence in the available information on sulfites in human drugs that demonstrates a significant health hazard to the general population." Id. at 47,560. Zeneca does not challenge this finding nor does it contest the FDA's determination that "sulfites serve a necessary public health function by maintaining the potency of certain medications." Sulfiting Agents; Labeling in Drugs for Human Use; Warning Statement, 51 Fed. Reg. 43,900, 43,903 (1986) (final rule). Accordingly, the issue before us is not whether sulfites, in and of themselves, are safe. They are. Rather, the issue is whether the substitution of sulfite for EDTA in Gensia's propofol with sulfite affects the safety of Gensia's propofol with sulfite. The FDA concluded that the substitution of sulfite for EDTA in Gensia's propofol with sulfite did not affect the safety of Gensia's propofol with sulfite because warning labels obviated any potential risks.

Zeneca argues that the FDA's reliance upon warnings on the product's container and labeling in making its decision as to whether Gensia's propofol with sulfite is safe for use is prohibited under the plain language of sections 314.94(a)(9)(iii) and 314.127(a)(8)(ii)(B). In other words, Zeneca argues, under the plain language of these two regulations, the FDA may not rely on an enhanced warning label to obviate the safety concerns associated with different preservatives.

In response, the FDA contends that Zeneca's argument is without merit, because it places an unreasonably narrow construction on the regulations at issue, regulations promulgated by the FDA. In support of its contention, the FDA points to the plain language of 21 U.S.C. § 355(j)(4)(H), the statute the two regulations at issue were promulgated to implement, which expressly provides that under the ANDA process, the FDA's consideration of the safety of inactive ingredients in generic drugs is dependent upon: (1) the "conditions prescribed, recommended, or suggested in the labeling"; and (2) the "type or quantity of inactive ingredients included or the manner in which the inactive ingredients are included."

Zeneca's argument challenges the FDA's interpretation of its own regulations, which interpretation "is entitled to 'substantial deference' and will be sustained unless it is plainly erroneous or inconsistent with the regulation[s]." We find the FDA's interpretation * * * to be consistent with the language of these regulations and not plainly erroneous. Specifically, the language of sections 314.94(a)(9)(iii) and 314.127(a)(8)(ii)(B) is broad enough to encompass the FDA's interpretation. Furthermore, the FDA's interpretation is completely faithful to the statute that these two regulations were promulgated to implement. * * *

Next we address Zeneca's argument that the FDA violated its own regulation requiring a generic drug's labeling to be the same as its pioneer counterpart. Section 355(j)(2)(A)(v) of the FFDCA allows labeling differences that are necessary "because the new [generic] drug and the listed [pioneer] drug are produced or distributed by different manufacturers." The FDA has interpreted § 355(j)(2)(A)(v) to permit changes in labeling because of "differences in expiration date, formulation, bioavailability, or pharmacokinetics, [or] labeling revisions made to comply with current FDA labeling guidelines or other guidance." In this case, the FDA interpreted 21 C.F.R. § 314.94(a)(8)(iv) to find that the sulfite warning for Gensia's propofol with sulfite fit squarely within the exceptions for (1) formulation differences and (2) differences required to comply with the labeling guidelines in the FDA's sulfite warning regulation. * * *

We find the FDA's interpretation of 21 C.F.R. § 314.94(a)(8)(iv) to be consistent with the language of the regulation and not plainly erroneous. The sulfite safety warning in Gensia's labeling is a direct result of the difference in formulation between Gensia's propofol with sulfite and Diprivan. Gensia was fully authorized to formulate its generic drug with a different preservative than is contained in Diprivan. Because a difference in preservative is a permitted variation in formulation, it is reasonable for the FDA to interpret its own regulation to allow corresponding differences in labeling to identify the preservative and provide any appropriate warnings.

In addition to permitting labeling changes based on differences in formulation, section 314.94(a)(8)(iv) permits changes in order "to comply with current FDA labeling guidelines and guidance." Section 201.22(b) of the FDA's regulations requires that prescription drugs containing sulfites

> shall bear the warning statement "Contains (insert the name of the sulfite, e.g., sodium metabisulfite), a sulfite that may cause allergic-type reactions . . . in certain susceptible people. The overall prevalence of sulfite sensitivity in the general population is unknown and probably low. Sulfite sensitivity is seen more frequently in asthmatic than in nonasthmatic people."

The FDA interpreted section 314.94(a)(8)(iv) to permit Gensia to include in its labeling the "warning statement" required by section 201.22, a current FDA labeling guideline. This interpretation is consistent with the language of section 314.94(a)(8)(iv). Furthermore, we see no merit to Zeneca's argument that the exception permitting revisions in labeling to comply with the FDA's current labeling guidelines only applies in situations in which the guidelines are issued after approval of the pioneer drug but before approval of the generic. * * *

Finally, Zeneca argues that the FDA's approval of Gensia's propofol with sulfite as a generic drug must be declared invalid and permanently enjoined because in determining that Gensia's propofol with sulfite is safe the FDA relied upon safety evaluations that analyzed the wrong pH range. In this regard, Zeneca contends that the FDA conducted its safety evaluations of Gensia's propofol with sulfite based on the initially proposed pH range of 6.0–7.5 rather than the lower pH range of 4.5–6.4 actually used in Gensia's ANDA for propofol with sulfite.

In considering Zeneca's argument, we are mindful that the "FDA's 'judgments as to what is required to ascertain the safety and efficacy of drugs fall squarely within the ambit of the FDA's expertise and merit deference from us.'" A.L. Pharma, Inc. v. Shalala, 62 F.3d 1484, 1490 (D.C.Cir.1995). Our review of the record reveals that Zeneca's argument, that the FDA relied upon the wrong pH range in determining that Gensia's propofol with sulfite is safe, is without merit. * * * [T]he FDA's safety determination regarding Gensia's propofol with sulfite included its assessment of the actual lower pH range used in Gensia's final proposed version of propofol with sulfite. * * *

NOTES AND QUESTIONS

1. *Establishing bioequivalence.* Subject to the patent and market exclusivity constraints discussed in Chapter 10, the FDA may approve an ANDA if the applicant demonstrates that its generic product is "bioequivalent" to (meaning that it has essentially the same rate and extent of absorption as) the innovator drug, a showing that substitutes for the much costlier clinical trials demanded as part of an NDA to demonstrate safety and effectiveness of the innovator drug. See, e.g., Somerset Pharm., Inc. v. Shalala, 973 F.Supp. 443, 453–54 (D.Del.1997) (deferring to the FDA's scientific judgment that metabolite testing could serve as an indicator of bioequivalence of generic versions of the drug selegiline hydrochloride indicated for the treatment of Parkinson's disease). It may take 3–5 years and an initial investment of $1 million to secure FDA approval of an ANDA for a generic drug product. See Richard J. Findlay, Originator Drug Development, 54 Food & Drug L.J. 227, 229 (1999); see also Justina A. Molzon, The Generic Drug Approval Process, 5 J. Pharmacy & L. 275 (1996); Ralph A. Lewis, Comment, The Emerging Effects of the Drug Price Competition and Patent Term Restoration Act of 1984, 8 J. Contemp. Health L. & Pol'y 361 (1992). Sometimes, the FDA does not respond quickly to ANDA submissions. See, e.g., In re Barr Labs., Inc., 930 F.2d 72 (D.C.Cir.1991). On the other hand, when the FDA takes shortcuts in assessing bioequivalence before ANDA approval, serious safety and effectiveness problems may arise. See Thomas M. Burton, Doctors Raise Warnings About a Form of Clozapine, Wall St. J., Oct. 24, 2000, at B1 (describing the FDA's decision to test the generic psychiatric drug's bioequivalence using very low doses, and detailing clinical data suggesting that the generic drug's absorption rate and efficacy differ from that of the innovator); cf. Jill D. Deal, Some FDA Applications Can Escape Full Testing, Nat'l L.J., May 22, 2000, at B18 (describing an

FDA draft guidance document that permits sponsors of applications for generic drug approval to use studies conducted on similar but not identical innovator products to establish the generic product's safety and effectiveness, and suggesting that this exception may also speed the market entry of generic biological products).

2. *Battling generic competition.* NDA holders may raise bioequivalence objections in an effort to stall generic competition. In some instances, these are broad-based assaults on the standards used by the FDA. See Schering Corp. v. Shalala, 995 F.2d 1103, 1104 (D.C.Cir.1993) (per curiam) (describing one drug company's efforts to challenge the FDA's bioequivalence criteria for non-systemic drugs); Fisons Corp. v. Shalala, 860 F.Supp. 859, 861 (D.D.C.1994) (same); Glaxo, Inc. v. Heckler, 623 F.Supp. 69 (D.N.C. 1985); F–D–C Rep. ("The Pink Sheet"), Feb. 6, 1995, at T&G–12 (describing incumbent firm's petition to the FDA asserting bioequivalence problems with generic version of arthritis drug); F–D–C Rep. ("The Pink Sheet"), May 16, 1994, at T&G–6 (describing petitions submitted by two companies with approved albuterol metered dose inhalers (MDIs) challenging the FDA's guidelines for bioequivalence testing and arguing that generic albuterol MDIs should not be approved without more stringent testing); F–D–C Rep. ("The Pink Sheet"), Mar. 4, 1991, at 9 (describing Wyeth–Ayerst's success in persuading the FDA to establish more stringent bioequivalence requirements for conjugated estrogens); Andrew Pollack, Biotechnology Companies Try to Ward Off Generic Drugs, N.Y. Times, Dec. 28, 2000, at C1; Sheryl Gay Stolberg & Jeff Gerth, Keeping Down the Competition: How Companies Stall Generics and Keep Themselves Healthy, N.Y. Times, July 23, 2000, at A1. In other cases, as happened in *Serono*, brand-name companies object to the agency's approval of a particular ANDA. See, e.g., Upjohn Mfg. Co. v. Schweiker, 681 F.2d 480, 482–84 (6th Cir.1982) (upholding the FDA's decision to reject Upjohn's citizen petition challenging the agency's authority to approve a generic version of ibuprofen, and commenting that "Upjohn does not contend that the drug is not safe and effective. Instead, it has mounted a technical assault on the FDA's approval of the Boots application, in an effort to preserve its monopoly."); see also Peter O. Safir, Current Issues in the Pioneer Versus Generic Drug Wars, 50 Food & Drug L.J. 335 (1995).

3. *Identical labeling.* In addition to containing the same active ingredient, a generic drug product must use the same labeling, subject to the exceptions discussed in *Zeneca*. The FDA may, however, approve an ANDA even if its labeling includes only a subset of the indications approved for the pioneer drug. See Bristol–Myers Squibb Co. v. Shalala, 91 F.3d 1493, 1500 (D.C.Cir.1996).

B. Medical Devices

All new drugs must undergo premarket approval, prescription and OTC products alike (though recall that the FDA treats most nonprescription drugs as not new (GRASE) if they comply with the terms of an OTC monograph). The agency takes a somewhat different approach to medical devices. Although substantial equivalence to a pre–1976 device operates much like a GRASE determination, some post–1976 devices that are not substantially equivalent may remain exempt from premarket approval and some pre–1976 devices eventually may undergo premarket approval. It all depends on how the FDA classifies the device. In a recent tort preemption decision, which is excerpted more fully in Chapter 5(B)(2), the Supreme Court provided the following summary of the different routes to market.

Medtronic, Inc. v. Lohr

518 U.S. 470 (1996).

■ STEVENS, JUSTICE:

* * * While the FDCA provided for premarket approval of new drugs, it did not authorize any control over the introduction of new medical devices. As technologies advanced and medicine relied to an increasing degree on a vast array of medical equipment "[f]rom bedpans to brain-scans," including kidney dialysis units, artificial heart valves, and heart pacemakers, policymakers and the public became concerned about the increasingly severe injuries that resulted from the failure of such devices. In 1970, for example, the Dalkon Shield, an intrauterine contraceptive device, was introduced to the American public and throughout the world. Touted as a safe and effective contraceptive, the Dalkon Shield resulted in a disturbingly high percentage of inadvertent pregnancies, serious infections, and even, in a few cases, death. * * *

In response to the mounting consumer and regulatory concern, Congress enacted the statute at issue here: the Medical Device Amendments of 1976 (MDA or Act). The Act classified medical devices in three categories based on the risk that they pose to the public. Devices that present no unreasonable risk of illness or injury are designated Class I and are subject only to minimal regulation by "general controls." Devices that are potentially more harmful are designated Class II; although they may be marketed without advance approval, manufacturers of such devices must comply with federal performance regulations known as "special controls." Finally, devices that either "present a potential unreasonable risk of illness or injury," or which are "purported or represented to be for a use in supporting or sustaining human life or for a use which is of substantial importance in preventing impairment of human health," are designated Class III. Pacemakers are Class III devices.

Before a new Class III device may be introduced to the market, the manufacturer must provide the FDA with a "reasonable assurance" that the device is both safe and effective. Despite its relatively innocuous phrasing, the process of establishing this "reasonable assurance," which is known as the "premarket approval" or "PMA" process, is a rigorous one. Manufacturers must submit detailed information regarding the safety and efficacy of their devices, which the FDA then reviews, spending an average of 1,200 hours on each submission.

Not all, or even most, Class III devices on the market today have received premarket approval because of two important exceptions to the PMA requirement. First, Congress realized that existing medical devices could not be withdrawn from the market while the FDA completed its PMA analysis for those devices. The statute therefore includes a "grandfathering" provision which allows pre–1976 devices to remain on the market without FDA approval until such time as the FDA initiates and completes the requisite PMA. Second, to prevent manufacturers of grandfathered devices from monopolizing the market while new devices clear the PMA hurdle, and to ensure that improvements to existing devices can be rapidly introduced into the market, the Act also permits devices that are "substantially equivalent" to pre-existing devices to avoid the PMA process.

Although "substantially equivalent" Class III devices may be marketed without the rigorous PMA review, such new devices, as well as all new Class I and Class II devices, are subject to the requirements of § 360(k). That section imposes a limited form of review on every manufacturer intending to market a new device by requiring it to submit a "premarket notification" to the FDA (the process is also known as a "§ 510(k) process," after the number of the section in the original Act). If the FDA concludes on the basis of the § 510(k) notification that the device is "substantially equivalent" to a pre-existing device, it can be marketed without further regulatory analysis (at least until the FDA initiates the PMA process for the underlying pre–1976 device to which the new device is "substantially equivalent"). The § 510(k) notification process is by no means comparable to the PMA process; in contrast to the 1,200 hours necessary to complete a PMA review, the § 510(k) review is completed in an average of only 20 hours.

Congress anticipated that the FDA would complete the PMA process for Class III devices relatively swiftly. But because of the substantial investment of time and energy necessary for the resolution of each PMA application, the ever-increasing numbers of medical devices, and internal administrative and resource difficulties, the FDA simply could not keep up with the rigorous PMA process. As a result, the § 510(k) premarket notification process became the means by which most new medical devices–including Class III devices—were approved for market. In 1983, for instance, a House Report concluded that nearly 1,000 of the approximately 1,100 Class III devices that had been introduced to the market since 1976 were admitted as "substantial equivalents" and without any PMA review. This lopsidedness has apparently not evened out; despite an increasing effort by the FDA to consider the safety and efficacy of substantially equivalent devices, the House reported in 1990 that 80% of new Class III devices were being introduced to the market through the § 510(k) process and without PMA review. * * *

Lake v. FDA

1989 WL 71554 (E.D.Pa.1989).

■ CAHN, DISTRICT JUDGE:

Mr. Lake was the inventor of the Inductive Nasal Device (IND) [not to be confused with the acronym for an investigational new drug], which he maintained could cure the common cold and allergies. Despite these extraordinary claims and the appropriately august name attached to the invention, the IND is, essentially, a nose clip. Mr. Lake repeatedly attempted to obtain Food and Drug Administration (FDA) approval to market the IND. The FDA, however, was unconvinced of the efficacy of the invention and refused to approve its sale as a cure for colds and allergies. * * *

The FDA was first called on to review the IND in 1979. The invention was automatically considered a class III device pursuant to 21 U.S.C. § 360c(f)(1). Class III devices can only be marketed after the FDA has granted a premarket approval application (PMA). In order to sell the IND, Mr. Lake either had to procure approval of the PMA or get the IND reclassified out of class III. * * * Mr. Lake filed a PMA, but the FDA denied his application. The FDA cited numerous deficiencies, including a lack of scientific evidence demonstrating the safety and effectiveness of the device. Mr. Lake amended the PMA, but the FDA still found the petition lacking because no clinical trials had been held.

Realizing that the first route to market, the PMA process, had been foreclosed, Mr. Lake tried the second route; he filed a reclassification petition. He asserted the IND was properly a class I device. Under 21 U.S.C. § 360c(f)(2), the Secretary is empowered to review reclassification petitions for "deficiencies," and if none are found, then the Secretary must refer the petition to a panel of experts for consideration. The FDA rejected Mr. Lake's original petition because it failed to conform with several agency form and content requirements set out at 21 C.F.R. § 860.123, including a failure to provide valid scientific evidence of the safety and effectiveness of the device. * * *

Plaintiff first argues that the FDA acted arbitrarily and capriciously because the letter stating that "no device will prevent or cure the common cold" demonstrates FDA officials had a closed mind and that plaintiff could not get a fair hearing. * * * I find this line of argument unpersuasive.

It would be an abuse of discretion for the FDA to refuse to consider scientific evidence of the efficacy of the IND based on an unsubstantiated belief that no device could ever cure the cold. In this case, however, the FDA was merely stating its view of the current state of scientific knowledge. There is no evidence that Mr. Lake presented valid scientific evidence which the FDA ignored because of its predisposition against believing a device could cure the cold. To the contrary, the FDA patiently answered the correspondence, questions, and petitions of Mr. Lake. It suggested methods of testing and provided Mr. Lake with the information necessary to guide him through the application process. If the FDA evinced some skepticism with respect to Mr. Lake's claims, it was only because after numerous communications the plaintiff still had failed to provide any evidence of the efficacy of the IND. The agency is to be commended, not censured, for applying caution in evaluating unproven medical treatments.

The second argument raised by the plaintiff is that the FDA violated the Medical Device Amendments of 1976 by making it too difficult to procure reclassification into class I. * * * Plaintiff takes the position that the IND falls within [class I] because it presents no unreasonable risk of illness or injury. Defendant maintains that when there is no valid scientific evidence of benefit, the risk is per se unreasonable.

Plaintiff raises an interesting question of statutory interpretation. Section 360(a)(1)(A)(ii) provides for the marketing of devices which are unproven to be "safe and effective" and which do not provide an "unreasonable risk of illness or injury." Thus, it is possible that a small class of devices unproven as safe, but without demonstrable risks could be reclassified into class I. As one court has recognized: "Congress contemplated that a device not both safe and effective might be able to enter the stream of commerce, although such a device has to meet conditions so narrow that no actual device may fall into the category." General Medical Co. v. FDA, 770 F.2d 214, 222 (D.C.Cir.1985). * * * The court concluded that Congress intended to provide that certain devices which were unproven as to safety and effectiveness, did not purport to be of importance in improving human life, and presented no potential unreasonable risk of injury could avoid the PMA process. In applying this rule to the facts of the case [involving the "Drionic" antiperspirant device], the *General Medical* court held that because there was some minimal evidence of minor harm and no benefits, the harm outweighed the benefits, and the risk of injury was therefore unreasonable.

The case at bar, however, goes one step beyond *General Medical*. There is nothing in the record demonstrating even minor harm from the IND. The FDA stands solely on its interpretation of the statute that a lack of evidence presents an unreasonable risk. The FDA's interpretation is valid. It could not have been the intent of Congress to allow the marketing of unproven medical devices about which no scientific evidence is available. To hold otherwise would allow people to market all manner of fraudulent devices. We are long past the day when snake oil can be sold with impunity. Plaintiff's reading of the statute would shift the burden of proof to the FDA and that is not how our public health laws are designed to work. When there is no valid scientific evidence of efficacy, and the risks are unknown, the risk is unreasonable.

The FDA interpretation does not, as plaintiff argues, read § 360c(a)(1)(A)(ii) out of existence. There are devices which may still fall into the category. The relevant subsection refers to devices about which there is insufficient evidence that the various controls of the Act guarantee safety and effectiveness. There may well be devices about which some valid evidence of efficacy and safety exists, but the evidence is inconclusive. The controls may, therefore, not "guarantee" safety and effectiveness. However, there may be no evidence of any risks associated with use. In such a situation, the FDA may find that the minimal benefits, when combined with the lack of known risk, qualify the device for class I status.

The purpose of including § 360c(a)(1)(A)(ii) was to "assure that premarket approval does not become a routine requisite for all devices, while still providing the Secretary with ample latitude to classify a device into class III in instances in which its use poses public health concerns." Congress did not want the PMA process to be the only way a device could get to market because the required clinical studies are expensive and time-consuming. If a device has some demonstrated benefits and no risks, there is no reason to force it to jump through restrictive regulatory hoops. However, Congress did not intend that devices with no proven benefit could be marketed. Indeed, the legislative history defined "potential unreasonable risk of illness or injury" as a risk which is "simply foreseeable" and "[t]he fact that a device is being marketed without sufficient testing is an adequate basis for the Secretary's conclusion that the device presents a potential unreasonable risk to health." In this case the Secretary made a determination that the lack of sufficient testing presented a potential health risk. * * *

Thus, valid scientific evidence must be available in order for a device to be reclassified. It is not difficult to conclude from this that the FDA has the power to require such evidence in reclassification petitions. * * * Nor did the FDA demand too much evidence of the plaintiff. If the requirements were too stringent, the plaintiff might have an argument that the FDA was doing more than assessing "deficiencies," however, an examination of the evidentiary requirements shows that the rules are only designed to make sure a panel of experts has something other than conjecture upon which to base its decision. * * *

Plaintiff also argues that even if the statute requires the provision of valid scientific evidence, Mr. Lake did so. The evidence presented by plaintiff in support of his claim that the IND can cure the common cold is underwhelming. Plaintiff relies heavily on the argument that the swimmer's nose clip and nose clip used for certain diagnostic procedures is substantially equivalent to his device. While the devices are similar physically, the claims which are made about his nose clip are much different. Plaintiff wants to label his device as curing the common cold and allergies. The fact that the nose clip may be safe and effective for use in hospitals or for swimming proves little. New uses may well present new risks. * * *

In this case it is not hard to see why additional proof of safety is required. The closing of an infected or irritated nose may well have negative, not positive effects on the course of illness. In addition, anyone who fails to see an allergist because he believes the IND will help, may harm himself. Anyone who avoids bed rest believing the IND will cure him, may suffer all manner of subsequent illnesses caused by inattention to a cold. * * * I will defer to the FDA * * * *

Lawrence S. Makow, Note, *Medical Device Review at the Food and Drug Administration: Lessons from Magnetic Resonance Spectroscopy and Biliary Lithotripsy*

46 STAN. L. REV. 709 (1994).

* * * Renal lithotripsy—a dramatic nonsurgical solution for removing kidney stones—was first reported in 1980. Surgical removal of kidney

stones had always been a risky operation because the injury to the body of the kidney can be significant, and kidney failure has major consequences. Treatment with extracorporeal shock wave lithotripsy [ESWL] therefore represented a significant breakthrough. Almost overnight, ESWL changed the face of kidney stone treatment: Operations to excise kidney stones rapidly dropped from 30 percent of all urological procedures to 2 percent.
* * *

Lithotripsy is based on the principle that high pressure sonic energy can fragment rigid objects while leaving less rigid tissues virtually undisturbed. A lithotripter generates sound waves electrically by means of a spark plug or a metal plate. As the waves pass the speed of sound, they become shock waves, and an "acoustic lens" focuses the waves in the body at the point of the kidney stone. Because the stone is much more rigid than the surrounding body tissue, the focused shock waves destroy the stone without irreversibly damaging the surrounding environment. Repeated applications pulverize the stone into a sandy powder, which the patient can then pass through normal urination.

Common side effects of renal lithotripsy include transient injury to the renal parenchyma, subcutaneous bruising, short-lived pain, and in some cases an accumulation of stone dust in the ureter. Modern lithotripter technology, however, has reduced the occurrence of such problems. On balance, renal lithotripsy is widely considered a tremendous success.

The success of renal lithotripsy prompted investigators to examine applying the technology to gallstones. The incidence of symptomatic gallstones is far higher than that of kidney stones. Gallstone patients also suffer from serious and frequently debilitating pain. The standard treatment for gallstones has traditionally been severe—the complete removal of the gallbladder through an abdominal incision (cholecystectomy). The gallbladder is primarily a warehouse for bile, which the body needs to break down fatty foods; the gallbladder continuously stores and releases bile as needed into the intestines through the common bile duct.

As part of the adjustment to post-operative life without a gallbladder, cholecystectomy patients must follow low-fat diets for the balance of their lives. In addition, the operation itself can cause patients considerable trauma. Because the operation requires a large incision that dissects the abdominal muscles, patients are often incapacitated for several weeks following surgery and may be weak for much longer. And like most major surgery, traditional cholecystectomy involves the risks of general anesthesia.

Although a number of treatments for gallstones exist, cholecystectomy was the most common procedure until recently. Other methods include percutaneous transhepatic cholecystolitholysis (contact dissolution) with methyl tertbutyl ether (MTBE), and oral dissolution therapy, by ingesting salts of bile acids such as ursodeoxycholic acid (ursodiol). But serious limitations make these techniques less attractive than ESWL. Contact dissolution remains highly experimental and may cause necrosis of surrounding tissues. Oral dissolution techniques generally work slowly and do not give immediate symptomatic relief from the pain accompanying gallstones. Persistent pain forces many patients to seek cholecystectomies. Furthermore, the greater the mass of stone material in the gallbladder, the less effective dissolution techniques become. As a result, the FDA had approved ursodiol therapy only for patients who could not undergo surgery. For the majority of gallstone sufferers, there was no nonsurgical alternative.

While renal lithotripsy received rather expeditious approval by the FDA, biliary lithotripsy has been bogged down in the regulatory process. The discrepant treatment stems partially from the physiological differences between biliary and renal lithotripsy. The biliary treatment has been slightly less successful in completely fragmenting the stones. Although fragmentation rates routinely approach 95 percent for cholesterol gallstones, calcified stones are not as easily pulverized. The biggest concern about biliary lithotripsy, however, has been debris clearance—the patient's ability to get rid of the fragments once the stone is successfully crushed.

The clinical objective of renal lithotripsy is not merely relief from the symptoms of kidney stones, but complete stone clearance. The measure of success is the number of "stone-free" patients at the end of a given time period following therapy. Naturally, this same standard was applied to biliary lithotripsy, even though the gallbladder does not flush its contents as thoroughly as does the kidney. Designers of early clinical studies therefore expected stone clearance to be better achieved by using ESWL in conjunction with a dissolution agent, such as ursodiol. Unfortunately, ursodiol may also tend to inhibit stone clearance by further diminishing the gallbladder's ability to contract and squeeze out its contents. Thus, although lithotripsy can often reduce gallstones to a fine sludge, in some patients that sludge will not clear from the gallbladder for six to twelve months, or may persist indefinitely. In contrast, kidney stone fragments usually clear completely in a much shorter time.

When measured against the benchmark established by renal lithotripsy, the relatively modest stone clearance rates of biliary lithotripsy were initially disappointing. Still, biliary ESWL remains the only nonsurgical technique to provide rapid and ongoing symptomatic relief from the severe pain caused by gallstone disease. Although some physicians believe that any lingering sludge presents an unacceptable risk of stone recurrence, other physicians counter that recurrence is always possible in a gallstone patient because the factors that originally led to stone formation remain. If absolute certainty of nonrecurrence is the sine qua non for a therapy's success, no treatment that leaves the gallbladder in place would ever be acceptable despite eliminating symptoms.

A second factor that has reduced the perceived need for biliary ESWL has been the contemporaneous development of laparoscopic cholecystectomy—a new and less invasive surgical alternative. The laparoscope, a surgical device that allows physicians to peer inside the body with a tiny television camera, obviates the need for direct visual inspection through a large, open incision. Using the laparoscope, surgeons can remove the gallbladder without making a large incision. Instead, doctors manipulate surgical instruments in front of the fiber-optic camera and remove the gallbladder through a much smaller opening. The laparoscopic procedure has spread quickly and is now a standard technique. Although surgical treatment for gallstones still requires the removal of the gallbladder, such surgery is no longer nearly as debilitating as before. But laparoscopic cholecystectomy is still complex and involves serious risks, which have been exacerbated by surgeons who have rushed to learn the method in abbreviated seminars. Thus, the need for a more effective nonsurgical elimination of gallstones remains. * * *

In 1984, Dornier Medical Systems received premarket approval for a kidney ESWL system—a class III device. ESWL quickly became the favored technique for treating kidney stones. The success of renal ESWL prompted investigators to apply the technique to gallstones. In 1988, manufacturers initiated clinical trials intended to earn premarket approval for biliary lithotripsy. To optimize the study results, the applicants combined biliary ESWL with the adjuvant use of ursodiol based on the perceived synergy of the treatments: ESWL would cause stone fragmentation and create more stone surface area upon which the ursodiol could act, resulting in more rapid and complete clearance than either therapy alone. At an October 1989 hearing, an FDA panel considered the completed PMA applications of the biliary lithotripter manufacturers. The panel noted deficiencies in the applications and denied premarket approval.

A major reason for the failure of these initial applications was the study design. First, following the model of renal lithotripsy, researchers defined the therapeutic endpoint as a gallbladder free of all stones and debris. In retrospect, this objective probably created overly optimistic expectations. Although almost all patients undergoing gallstone lithotripsy enjoy immediate relief from pain, such symptomatic relief was overlooked in favor of complete stone clearance. Because of the gallbladder's physiological dissimilarity to the kidney, most patients in the original studies did not show stone-free gallbladders.

A second error was including patients with various stone types. After detailed examination of the clinical results, researchers found that ESWL was most effective (as measured by stone-free rates) for solitary stones of 20 millimeters in diameter or smaller and gradually less effective as the stone burden increased. Because ursodiol therapy alone was effective in treating these small solitary stones, the panel understandably doubted that the initial clinical studies demonstrated that ESWL added anything. Furthermore, the data lacked clarity in a number of areas, including how long the patients received treatment and how the manufacturers calculated certain statistical results. Based on these factors, the panel's recommendation against approval was clearly justified.

On August 2, 1990, the FDA issued "FDA Guidance to Firms on Biliary Lithotripsy Studies." The letter outlined the design of an acceptable study, requiring a separate control group of prospectively randomized patients who would be treated with ursodiol alone. This requirement essentially mandated that all clinical studies be redone. The FDA Guidance also announced that ursodiol had not been specifically approved for use with ESWL and that such use would require applicants to file a new drug approval supplement—adding an entirely new regulatory hurdle. The agency reasoned that ursodiol's efficacy had been shown only for intact stones, not stone fragments, but the FDA was probably more concerned with the uncertainty of ursodiol's safety in the postlithotripsy gallbladder.

The FDA's announcement hit the research community like a bombshell. For firms that had already submitted data or that were well into their clinical studies, the Guidance meant that those firms could not use the earlier studies unless CDRH [FDA's Center for Devices and Radiological Health] accepted their historical data. One firm left the industry within three months. The sheer expense of duplicating the studies was merely one of the problems facing manufacturers. Ursodiol therapy had been approved as an alternative treatment to open cholecystectomy for patients with light stone burdens, but the advent of the much less invasive laparoscopic cholecystectomy raised serious ethical questions about randomly assigning patients to an ursodiol-only experimental group. The surgical alternative was now open to a wider range of patients and caused fewer side effects. As a result, ursodiol monotherapy, with its marginal effectiveness, was widely considered obsolete. Yet the FDA Guidance required manufacturers seeking approval of biliary ESWL to conduct studies in which sick patients received much less effective treatment.

Although the panel's rejection of the original PMA applications was probably justified, the FDA's subsequent refusal to recognize the results of several well-designed studies remains unexplained. On September 16, 1992, a National Institutes of Health (NIH) panel issued a "consensus" statement on gallstone treatment. The panel cited ESWL-ursodiol stone-free rates of 95 percent in patients with solitary stones of less than 20 millimeters in diameter, and 80 percent in patients with up to three stones of 20 to 30 millimeters in diameter. Such results far exceed any claim for ursodiol monotherapy and should dispel any lingering doubt as to the superiority of ESWL and ursodiol combined.

Armed with the knowledge of biliary ESWL's clinical performance, which the NIH would later recognize, investigators remained convinced that combination therapy was more effective than ursodiol monotherapy, especially for solitary stones of 20 millimeters or smaller. To avoid what they considered a superfluous repetition of an entire clinical study, the investigators publicly confronted the FDA over its position. They objected to the agency changing the approval requirements midstream by requiring the ursodiol-only patient group and argued that historical controls should suffice to show the effectiveness of ursodiol alone. In response, the FDA defended its Guidance letter, arguing that despite the letter's late issuance, manufacturers had been on notice of its requirements for some time. The FDA further indicated that using historical controls would be "difficult, but we have not ruled out that possibility." The agency still has not granted PMA to any biliary lithotripter, despite receiving substantial data demonstrating biliary ESWL's superiority to the historical ursodiol monotherapy controls.

To gather historical data on ursodiol monotherapy, the remaining lithotripter manufacturers, together with physicians investigating the technology, pooled their ursodiol-only data. The FDA, however, responded by requesting more information. Specifically, the agency required the previously submitted new drug application (NDA) data about ursodiol from Ciba–Geigy, the only firm with an approved ursodiol formulation [Actigall®]. But Ciba–Geigy refused to provide the data to the lithotripter manufacturers or to the FDA. Understandably, the manufacturers are exasperated: "If FDA maintains its current position, manufacturers are likely to drop their efforts to obtain approval of lithotripsy for biliary use." The FDA recently refused even to file the PMA applications of two biliary lithotripter manufacturers based on their lack of data from patients randomized prospectively to ursodiol-only treatment.

At the same time, a series of additional studies has demonstrated the superior effectiveness of combination therapy. Even surgeons, who would be economic competitors of biliary ESWL users, have recently recognized that the proper management of gallstones requires a flexible, interdisciplinary approach, with biliary ESWL as the favored therapy for certain patients. Nothing in the statute prevents the FDA from acknowledging this new data; in fact, the agency is explicitly empowered to do so.

Manufacturers have attempted to comply with the FDA's requirement of prospective randomized studies of ESWL-plus-ursodiol and ursodiol monotherapy. Given the serious ethical concerns about the drug monotherapy, researchers are apparently unwilling or unable to recruit patients for such studies. The situation appears deadlocked: The manufacturers cannot generate the required studies, and the FDA has not renounced its guidelines. Although most of the available data show biliary ESWL to be safe and effective for a readily identifiable segment of patients, the treatment remains frozen in an unapproved state. * * *

The atmosphere of uncertainty currently surrounding medical device approval creates real social costs. FDA approval is an absolute necessity to market medical devices in the United States, so any agency inconsistency makes manufacturers' product development plans more risky. This riskiness in turn increases the cost of capital that corporations allocate to device development, and therefore raises the profit threshold at which any project has a positive net present value. If the FDA's decisionmaking remains volatile, an increasing number of marginally profitable, yet socially desirable, technologies will not reach patients. * * *

The FDA should not require a new device to represent an improvement over existing treatments for all patients. Rather, the agency should only demand reasonable scientific evidence that the device does what its makers claim. The FDA may choose, through its power to approve labeling and restrict the scope of a device's use, to narrow the approval accordingly. But the agency should not completely block the commercial distribution of a proven safe device for which there is reasonable evidence of effectiveness.

* * * If such a device meets the high safety standard, more of the efficacy judgment should be shifted from the agency to the medical community. * * *

The correlation between safety and efficacy varies among devices. Safety and efficacy are strongly linked where the device's failure would expose a patient to danger and weakly linked where the primary safety concerns are unrelated to how well the device accomplishes its intended effect. An example of a device exhibiting a strong linkage is a cardiac defibrillator. A primary safety concern is the reliability of the delivered shocks. A defibrillator is used exclusively in lifesaving situations. Thus, in reviewing the defibrillator, the FDA could not evaluate efficacy independently from safety concerns. To the extent that efficacy merges with safety, the rigorous standard for safety must also be applied to those aspects of efficacy.

The biliary lithotripter, in contrast, exemplifies weak linkage. The device's principal short-term safety concern—the effect of shock waves on tissue surrounding the treated area—is independent from whether the lithotripter is ultimately effective in breaking up stones. This major safety risk arises from a side effect of the system's operation. In cases of such weak linkage between safety and efficacy, the FDA should apply an asymmetric standard: While the manufacturer must still make a strong showing of the device's safety, the agency should approve the product even given only limited effectiveness in achieving its intended clinical outcome. Here, the FDA's role should primarily be to assure full disclosure of the device's efficacy data to the medical community.

In the case of biliary lithotripsy, such an "inform the market" approach would have two significant benefits. First, this approach would allow the FDA to recognize biliary ESWL studies that are not formally part of the data submitted by the manufacturers. Second, this approach would allow the FDA to approve biliary ESWL without conclusive proof that combination therapy of ESWL-plus-ursodiol is more effective than drug therapy alone. Given adequate assurances of safety, that decision would be left to the medical community. * * * By adhering to higher than threshold effectiveness standards, the FDA substitutes its decisions for the clinical choice of the physician. If a device is safe and sufficiently reliable data supports its effectiveness, the FDA has no reason to prohibit the device simply because the clinical role of the technology remains controversial.

Some analysts might argue that relaxing the standard for efficacy would flood the market with "snake oil" devices—products that, although safe, serve no real function and are essentially consumer scams. Despite this legitimate concern, a relaxed efficacy standard would not likely exacerbate the problem. First, even a highly effective device can easily be used on a patient who does not need it. In other words, a device's efficacy in any particular application will always ultimately depend on the clinical judgment of the patient's physician. Second, the makers of truly quack devices are not likely to seek FDA approval of their products. Rather, these manufacturers remain largely outside the regulatory system, and any additional stringency in the efficacy requirement would not deter such charlatans. Finally, several external restraints in the health care system limit the use of marginally effective technologies. These include the Medicare prospective payment system, which rewards efficient patient treatment, the separate requirement of approval of Medicare reimbursement by the Health Care Financing Administration (HCFA), utilization review by insurance companies, and the threat of medical malpractice liability. In particular, HCFA's separate review of a device's effectiveness in the actual practice setting may render the FDA's broad efficacy inquiry redundant.

Even if one could safely relegate the problem of fraudulent cures to a curiosity of a bygone era (and unfortunately that is not true), the problem of the subtlety and complexity of modern medical devices would remain. Practitioners may be unable to discern the effectiveness of a device prior to its use. Certainly, efficacy should remain an essential prong of the FDA's test for device approval. But the agency should only require reliable studies to establish the device's effectiveness in an identifiable group of patients. The FDA should not force manufacturers to prove that a device meets some substantive standard of efficacy relative to other therapeutic options. Once the threshold showing of efficacy has been made, and safety is clearly established, the medical community—not the FDA—should define the precise place of the technology in the existing array of treatment options.

The excessive involvement of the FDA presents several potential social costs. Overly stringent device review may deprive a physician of a diagnostic or therapeutic choice that may be optimal for a particular patient, thereby resulting in lower quality or more expensive care. Furthermore, excessive regulation discourages innovation and development; a prolonged battle with the FDA may deprive a manufacturer of the financial resources necessary to bring the technology to market. Nascent and incompletely proven technologies with the potential to blossom into medical staples may die prematurely. Even if the manufacturer has the financial resources to finish development, the potential for the device may be stunted. The FDA's denial of premarket approval—or an excessive delay in granting approval—broadcasts to the medical community that the technology is suspect, chilling the potential market. When safe and effective devices are squelched in this manner, society suffers a net loss. * * *

There is a final reason for extending PMA to safe devices when there is substantial, although vigorously debated, evidence of clinical efficacy. In the 1990 Act, Congress significantly enhanced the FDA's postmarket enforcement powers. The agency is therefore much more capable of correcting any error of mistaken approval. * * * In light of the FDA's power to monitor the use of devices and its authority to prohibit such use should problems emerge, the preemptive exclusion of a safe but controversially effective technology like biliary ESWL is even less justified. In such situations, no sound reason exists for the FDA to limit access to the device. * * *

United States v. Snoring Relief Labs Inc.

210 F.3d 1081 (9th Cir.2000).

■ NELSON, CIRCUIT JUDGE:

* * * Snoring Relief tried to become the first company to market a self-fitting, anti-snoring mouthpiece without a prescription. SnorBan requires the patient to self-fit the device by placing it in boiling water, advancing her jaw forward, and inserting the device. The patient determines how far forward to advance her jaw, and then takes a dental impression. Advancing the jaw forward apparently improves the patient's airway and prevents snoring.

Snoring Relief did not seek pre-market approval or notification for SnorBan from FDA. On September 7, 1995, FDA notified Snoring Relief that it was violating the FDC Act by selling SnorBan without having submitted pre-market notification or receiving pre-market approval. On October 16, 1995, Snoring Relief submitted pre-market notification in the form of a letter from Snoring Relief's president; a journal article about anti-snoring mouthpieces; SnorBan fitting instructions; and a brochure written by Snoring Relief's president. Snoring Relief contended that its product was substantially equivalent to two other anti-snoring mouthpieces, both of which are available by prescription only. Snoring Relief wanted to make SnorBan available over-the-counter, and compared its self-fitting device to athletic mouth guards. Also, its application contended that there was not an increased risk of undiagnosed sleep apnea.

On April 1, 1996, FDA denied Snoring Relief's request to market SnorBan over-the-counter. FDA's Dental Devices Branch of the Office of Device Evaluation enlisted Dr. Susan Runner, a doctor of dental surgery and the Senior Regulatory Review Officer, to compare SnorBan to the prescription-only, anti-snoring mouthpieces. Dr. Runner concluded that marketing SnorBan without a prescription raised two new questions about safety and effectiveness: (1) It would require the patient to distinguish between simple snoring and obstructive sleep apnea, a potentially life-threatening condition; and (2) it would require the patient to determine if she has any temporomandibular joint (TMJ) disease that would not permit the use of an oral appliance. If the patient advances her jaw too far forward in fitting the device, she could suffer TMJ. Dr. Runner concluded that "selection of which patients are appropriate for oral appliance therapy should always be made by the health professional." Based on this evaluation, FDA denied SnorBan's request for an exemption and found that SnorBan is a Class III device requiring pre-market approval before it can be legally marketed.

Before and after FDA's final decision, Snoring Relief marketed SnorBan without pre-market approval. On February 22, 1996, FDA sent Snoring Relief a warning letter about this continued violation. On April 15, 1996, Snoring Relief responded not by asking to market SnorBan with a prescription, but by asking for a waiver from the pre-market notification requirement. Snoring Relief said its product was similar to the Stop Snore

Collar, a pillow-like anti-snoring device that only required an apnea warning label. FDA disagreed, and in a May 9, 1996, letter distinguished mouthpieces from anti-snoring devices used externally such as pillows or nasal strips.

In a July 8, 1996, letter to FDA, Snoring Relief dismissed the distinction between intra-oral and extra-oral anti-snoring devices, and offered to provide a warning label about sleep apnea with its product. On July 23, 1996, FDA rejected Snoring Relief's continued attempts to market SnorBan without a prescription. FDA also warned against the illegal marketing of SnorBan. Snoring Relief continued to distribute its unapproved device without a prescription. On August 14, 1997, the government filed an in rem seizure action alleging that SnorBan is an adulterated, Class III device because it lacked pre-market approval * * * *

Snoring Relief did not contest that SnorBan was a "device" pursuant to the language of the FDC Act, nor did it petition for reclassification. * * * Snoring Relief claims to be exempt from FDA regulations (or be cleared for marketing) based on its pre-market notification to FDA that SnorBan is "substantially equivalent" to anti-snoring pillows, collars, and nasal strips. FDA repeatedly rejected these contentions. Initially, FDA compared Snor-Ban to other anti-snoring mouthpieces available by prescription only, concluding that a non-prescription anti-snoring mouthpiece presented new safety and effectiveness concerns about undiagnosed sleep apnea and TMJ. On two subsequent occasions, FDA rejected Snoring Relief's comparisons of SnorBan to anti-snoring pillows, collars, and nasal strips. These agency decisions should be narrowly reviewed under the APA's arbitrary and capricious standard. * * *

What Snoring Relief really wants is for the district court (and this court) to review FDA's decision de novo. But, as the government said, "the issue is an agency decision not to exercise its enforcement discretion to waive the pre-market notification requirement for SnorBan. FDA is entitled to decide how to exercise its discretion, and the court only reviews that decision under the arbitrary and capricious standard." We agree. * * *

The district court reviewed FDA's safety and effectiveness concerns about SnorBan regarding undiagnosed sleep apnea and potential TMJ, and concluded that Snoring Relief did not submit any new evidence to FDA suggesting that anti-snoring mouthpieces should be available without a prescription. The two articles that Snoring Relief submitted about anti-snoring mouthpieces both suggest that the mouthpieces should be fitted by medical personnel. Snoring Relief's two experts did not indicate whether they had any clinical experience with SnorBan. Furthermore, Snoring Relief submitted no medical studies suggesting that anti-snoring mouthpieces were safe for non-prescription use.

Snoring Relief argues that warning labels about sleep apnea and TMJ would have been sufficient, and that FDA allows such warnings with other anti-snoring products such as anti-snoring pillows, collars, and nasal strips. * * * FDA was not arbitrary and capricious in finding SnorBan was not substantially equivalent to these products—the agency consistently has found that extra-oral anti-snoring devices such as nasal strips present "no real safety concerns." Given the narrow arbitrary and capricious standard of review and the lack of contrary evidence presented by Snoring Relief, FDA's distinctions among these products were reasonable. * * *

NOTES AND QUESTIONS

1. *Gallstone update.* On September 6, 2000, the FDA finally approved a biliary lithotripsy device. See PMA Approval Order <http://www.fda.gov/cdrh/pdf/p970042.html>; see also Medstone STS Lithotripter Approvable for Gallstone Treatment in Combination with Novartis' Actigall, FDA Panel Says: Postmarket Studies Recommended, Health News Daily, May 1, 1998, at 2.

2. *Home test kits.* The FDA has approved several diagnostic devices for home use, including tests for pregnancy, blood sugar, and cholesterol. See Judy Mann, In the Privacy of Your Own Home, Wash. Post, Apr. 22, 1994, at E3. In some instances, political factors have played a role in agency decisions to reject home test kits. For instance, until 1994 the FDA categorically refused to review PMAs for home-use HIV in vitro diagnostic devices without reference to their particular safety for consumer use and effectiveness (i.e., reliability). See Graeme Browning, A Bold Step into the AIDS Debate, 26 Nat'l J. 2053 (1994); see also Steven R. Salbu, HIV Home Testing and the FDA: The Case for Regulatory Restraint, 46 Hastings L.J. 403, 454–55 (1995) ("[T]he FDA should not assess evidence that is not relevant to the evaluation of the primary safety and effectiveness of a medical device.... Accordingly, it is inappropriate for the FDA to consider ... whether [HIV] home testing reduces the likelihood that recipients of positive will receive effective counseling."); William O. Fabbri, Note, Home HIV Testing and Conflicts with State HIV Testing Regulations, 21 Am. J.L. & Med. 419 (1995). A similar set of arguably irrelevant policy issues arose when the agency undertook to review home test kits intended to screen children for illicit drug use.

3. *Initial classifications.* A dozen years after Congress enacted the Medical Device Amendments of 1976, the FDA finished issuing rules classifying medical devices. Of the almost 2000 types identified, approximately 30% were assigned to Class I (such as bandages), 60% to Class II (such as blood pressure monitoring devices), and 10% to Class III (such as artificial heart valves). In 1990, Congress further amended the statute by directing the FDA to consider down-classifying Class III devices marketed before 1976. See 21 U.S.C. § 360e(i). In practice, the difference in the degree of control over Class I and Class II devices (or for that matter Class III devices not yet subject to PMA requirements) is small. Class I devices need only comply with general controls applicable to all medical devices such as GMPs and labeling requirements. The FDA has exempted many low-risk Class I devices from PMN requirements. See 59 Fed. Reg. 63,005 (1994). In addition to general controls and premarket notification, Class II devices must also comply with special controls such as performance standards (though the FDA has yet to finalize any) or postmarket surveillance.

4. *Comparing premarket clearance and premarket approval.* As the Supreme Court noted in *Medtronic*, the vast majority of new devices have been introduced after the filing of a premarket notification (PMN) under § 510(k) of the Act. See S. Rep. No. 101–513, at 14 (1990) (noting that over 95% of the devices first marketed after 1976 have been found to be "substantially equivalent" to a pre-MDA device); see also Benjamin A. Goldberger, The Evolution of Substantial Equivalence in FDA's Premarket Review of Medical Devices, 56 Food & Drug L.J. 317 (2001). A PMN must contain proposed labeling and an explanation of how the device is substantially equivalent in intended use and technological characteristics to a particular predicate device. In addition to having the same intended use, the device (1) must have the same technological characteristics as the predicate device, or (2) must not raise different questions of safety and effectiveness than the predicate device if it has different technological characteristics. A PMN must either (1) contain an adequate summary of any information concerning safety and effectiveness, including adverse health effects, or (2) state that such information will be made available to any person upon request. In addition, the agency increasingly has demanded that manufacturers provide clinical data to support their claims that any technological changes did not impact safety and effectiveness. If a seller subsequently makes significant changes to the device, it must file either a supplement to the original PMN or a brand new PMN. See United States v. An Article of Device . . . "Stryker," 607 F.Supp. 990, 996–97 (W.D.Mich. 1985); see also United States v. Prigmore, 243 F.3d 1 (1st Cir.2001) (reversing felony convictions for a conspiracy to defraud the FDA by failing to file PMA supplements for substantial modifications to previously approved catheters that only affected their safety and effectiveness during an off-label use). The PMN process vaguely resembles the FDA's passive approach to reviewing NDAs for safety prior to 1962. For a criticism that § 510(k) has been used inappropriately to circumvent full approval requirements, see Robert B. Leflar, Public Accountability and Medical Device Regulation, 2 Harv. J.L. & Tech. 1 (1989); see also Susan Bartlett Foote, Loops and Loopholes: Hazardous Device Regulation Under the 1976 Amendments to the Food, Drug and Cosmetic Act, 7 Ecol. L.Q. 101 (1978); Jonathan S. Kahan, Premarket Approval Versus Premarket Notification: Different Routes to the Same Market, 39 Food Drug Cosm. L.J. 510 (1984).

5. *Device reclassification.* The FDA requires that reclassification petitions provide:

> [E]vidence from well-controlled investigations, partially controlled studies, studies and objective trials without matched controls, well-documented case histories conducted by qualified experts, and reports of significant human experience with a marketed device, from which it can fairly and responsibly be concluded by qualified experts that there is reasonable assurance of the safety and effectiveness of a device under its conditions of use. The evidence required may vary according

to the characteristics of the device, its conditions of use, the existence and adequacy of warnings and restrictions and the extent of experience with its use. Isolated case reports, random experience, reports lacking sufficient details to permit scientific evaluation, and unsubstantiated opinions are not regarded as valid scientific evidence to show safety and effectiveness.

21 C.F.R. § 860.7(c)(2).

Contact Lens Manufacturers Association v. FDA

766 F.2d 592 (D.C.Cir.1985).

■ Ginsburg, Ruth Bader, Circuit Judge:

* * * Congress itself was not positioned to determine the appropriate classification of every medical device then in existence or yet to be invented; nor could it describe the statutory categories with sufficient precision to ensure that each device would simply fall into the proper class of its own accord. The legislators therefore charged the FDA with the task of implementing the Amendments, and thus of essaying judgments appropriate to ensure safe and effective medical devices without stifling innovative technology.

Congress drew several initial bright lines, however, that significantly affected the classification process. * * * [U]nder provisions labeled "transitional," class III ranking automatically attached to "any device intended for human use ... which the [FDA] in a notice published in the Federal Register before the enactment date has declared to be a new drug." 21 U.S.C. § 360j(*l*)(1)(E). The FDA could later reclassify any device that, for whatever reason, had been "overclassified," but this remedy required a proffer of "new information," id. § 360c(e)—or, as the FDA formulated the standard, "valid scientific evidence" of safety and effectiveness. 21 C.F.R. §§ 860.7, 860.123(a)(6). The instant petition concerns the first attempt ever to reclassify a medical device committed to class III by the Amendments' "transitional provisions." Contact Lens Manufacturers Association (CLMA) challenges the FDA's withdrawal of the agency's own proposal to transfer certain rigid gas permeable (RGP) contact lenses from class III to class I. * * *

Contact lenses consisting almost entirely of polymethylmethacrylate (PMMA)—"hard" lenses—have been marketed in the United States since the early 1950s. Because the public's pre-Amendments experience with PMMA lenses was broad and substantially injury-free, these lenses will remain outside the Amendments' classification scheme until the FDA formally decides where to place them. That decision has not yet been made; three years ago, however, the FDA proposed to regulate PMMA lenses as class II devices. Hydroxyethylmethacrylate (HEMA) lenses—"soft" lenses—are a more recent development. The FDA first approved a HEMA lens in 1971. In September 1975, citing their relative novelty, the FDA announced that HEMA lenses—indeed all lenses "other than those consisting [almost wholly] of PMMA''—had been and would continue to be regarded as ''new drugs'' * * * *

The product at issue in this case is said to combine attractive features of both lens types described above. ''RGP lenses'' (like ''PMMA lenses'' or ''HEMA lenses'') is a generic term that indicates no single mix of polymers or manufacturing process; but all lenses properly called RGP share certain salient characteristics. The ideal RGP lens permits both the superior visual acuity attainable with a hard lens and the ''direct transmission of oxygen to corneal tissue'' that the hard lens regrettably prevents. Nearly a million people in the United States wore RGP lenses in 1982. As of 1975, however, RGP lenses, like soft lenses, were comparatively new and untested; since enactment of the Amendments the FDA has regarded RGP lenses as ''transitional'' class III devices by reason of the same September 1975 *Federal Register* announcement that resulted in placement of HEMA lenses in the class III category.

Consequently, before a manufacturer can market a particular RGP lens to the public, the manufacturer must demonstrate the safety and effectiveness of that lens convincingly enough to gain the FDA's pre-market approval. ''In effect,'' the manufacturer must obtain ''a license to market the device.'' (If RGP lenses were class I devices, the manufacturer would be required to make the showing CLMA regards as less burdensome that the lens was ''substantially equivalent'' to another RGP lens already on the market.) The expense of obtaining a class III device license—''estimated at $750,000–$1,000,000 (over and above development costs),'' the bulk of which goes to clinical investigation—constitutes a significant barrier to entry. * * *

CLMA petitioned the FDA to reclassify RGP lenses from class III to class II. Pursuant to 21 U.S.C. § 360c(b) (1982), the FDA referred the petition to an expert advisory committee, the Ophthalmic Section of the Ophthalmic; Ear, Nose, and Throat; and Dental Devices Panel, which recommended the following month that the petition be granted on the condition that CLMA submit additional materials. * * * [T]he FDA announced that, although CLMA's upgraded submissions continued to be inadequate, ''CLMA's objectives are meritorious,'' and therefore the FDA intended to adopt the reclassification proposal as the agency's own. * * *

[One] year after the FDA's initial indication of interest, the reclassification proposal emerged. ''Based on a careful review of new, publicly available, valid scientific evidence,'' the proposal stated, ''FDA has tentatively concluded that ... certain [RGP lenses] should be reclassified into class I.'' * * * The proposal extensively and favorably discussed the clinical data cited by reclassification proponents. Nevertheless, the FDA invited comment on a range of issues. * * * [After several extensions of the comment period and a public hearing,] CLMA's once high expectations for the RGP proposal ended: the FDA repudiated its ''tentative conclusions'' and withdrew its reclassification proposal altogether.

The FDA attributed its changed view to ''comments and oral and written testimony that required it to reevaluate the evidence upon which it relied in the proposal, and to evaluate additional information." First, the agency explained, various commenters had demonstrated that the clinical studies cited as proof of the safety and effectiveness of CAB and polyacrylate-silicone lenses then on the market did not, after all, add up to "valid scientific evidence." Second, even if the studies did constitute such evidence, they were "insufficient to justify reclassification" because they "failed to establish the safety and effectiveness of [RGP] lenses as a generic type of device." Given the countless conceivable combinations of "polymer formulation and manufacturing processes," and the corresponding variations in lenses' "nontoxicity, biocompatibility, [and] light transmission," the FDA could not conclude that mere membership in the family of "RGP lenses" clinched any particular lens' safety and effectiveness.

The FDA thus determined that no reclassification of RGP lenses could provide reasonable assurance of safety and effectiveness: class I status was not feasible because the FDA could not determine whether a new lens was "substantially equivalent" to an already-marketed lens without securing a wealth of detailed information about both lenses' composition and manufacture; and class II status was not in order because, even if such information could be gathered for the purpose of establishing a "performance standard" and measuring new lenses against it, conformity with the standard would not guarantee that a lens would function safely and effectively in the human eye. "In short, FDA learned that at this stage in [RGP lens] development, there is no substitute for clinical trials [i.e., class III status] to provide reasonable assurance of the safety and effectiveness of these lenses."

CLMA complains, in petitioning for review, that the FDA has disregarded a medical consensus favoring reclassification and has rendered insensible the requirement of "valid scientific evidence." We recognize substantial merit in CLMA's argument that RGP lenses should not be locked within so tight a regulatory regime. Nonetheless, we cannot disturb the FDA's decision. The agency acted within an area of its expertise, it ruled in a manner at least arguably consistent with the statutory scheme, and it considered the matter in a detailed, adequately reasoned fashion. We therefore defer to the agency and affirm its judgment. * * *

The FDA has consistently maintained that proponents of reclassification assume the burden of demonstrating—through "publicly available, valid scientific evidence"—that the device's present classification is inappropriate and that the proposed classification will provide reasonable assurance of the device's safety and effectiveness. We cannot fault the FDA's assignment of the burden of proof to those seeking to change the status quo. Thus, CLMA's claim that maintenance of class III status for RGP lenses lacks record support, even if true, is off target. More to the point, CLMA asserts that the FDA in these proceedings has adopted an unreasonably strict view of what constitutes "valid scientific evidence." Though CLMA presses this argument with vigor, we are mindful that in such matters generalist courts see through a glass darkly and should be especially reluctant to upset an expert agency's judgment that a party has failed to adduce sufficient scientific proof of safety and effectiveness.

The FDA's rationale for withdrawing its reclassification proposal opens with the rather belated assertion that nothing in the record establishes the safety and effectiveness of RGP lenses now on the market. Facets of this position are unsettling. In justification of its current stance, the FDA disparaged the same studies it had once acclaimed, and retracted its earlier assertion that "the safety of the device also is shown by the absence of reports in the literature of serious, irreversible adverse effects on health presented by the device." But the reclassification proposal specifically asked for comment on whether "the data ... constitute sufficient 'valid scientific evidence.'" We would be denying the value of notice-and-comment rulemaking were we to condemn the FDA for altering its outlook on the basis of submissions it received.

Citing its regulation declaring that "isolated case reports, random experience, reports lacking sufficient details to permit scientific evaluation, and unsubstantiated opinions are not regarded as valid scientific evidence to show safety or effectiveness," the FDA discounted the praises sung by dozens of "contact lens professionals" who favored reclassification and who reported that none of their patients had ever experienced serious problems with RGP lenses. We find the FDA's categorical belittlement of these eyewitness comments somewhat numbing, but we cannot gainsay the FDA's judgment that although such testimonials may suffice to disprove safety and effectiveness, they fail to establish with scientific rigor the absence of danger.

The FDA's ultimate resistance to conceding the safety and effectiveness of lenses now on the market is perhaps most remarkable because these are the very lenses already granted premarket approval on the application of particular manufacturers. The agency's demand for compelling proof on matters presumably demonstrated to it convincingly by the licensed manufacturers, however, is a conundrum the statute itself sets up. Under the Amendments, trade secret information that a manufacturer submits to secure premarket approval may not be cited by the FDA or any third party in aid of reclassification proposals. Much as in patent law, Congress has determined that free riding is too high a price to pay for vigorous competition among medical device manufacturers; the FDA is not at liberty to disregard this determination. * * *

Of decisive importance, however, the FDA's refusal to reclassify RGP lenses does not stand or fall with the FDA's limited-purpose agnosticism about the safety and effectiveness of lenses currently on the market. Independently sufficient and far more persuasive is the FDA's determination that all reclassification proposals to date "inadequately characterize" the class of RGP lenses. That is, even if the available evidence demonstrates the safety and effectiveness of lenses already on the market, this evidence cannot be taken as proof that any RGP lens a manufacturer might create will meet the statutory requirements; thus, at least for the present, the premarket approval process is unavoidable. "The safety and effectiveness of a contact lens is a function of the complex interrelationship of material, design, and manufacture that results in a unique set of physical, chemical, mechanical, and optical characteristics." Alter any one of these variables, the FDA now maintains, and you have a unique new lens whose safety and effectiveness are unknown and, without thorough clinical testing, unknowable. * * * The inadequacy of generic characterization of RGP lenses thus emerges as a mainstay of the FDA's contention that nothing short of lens-by-lens clinical testing and premarket approval will ensure safety and effectiveness. * * *

We are cognizant of the ironies effected by the statute and the FDA's initially insecure administration of it. Considering the difficulty of the assignment Congress entrusted to the agency, and the respect we owe to the FDA's expert judgment, however, we cannot say that the action we have been asked to review is unlawful. * * * We hold simply and only that at this juncture, the FDA has not been shown to have proceeded without reason or regard for the statute in withdrawing its proposal to reclassify RGP lenses. The petition for review is accordingly dismissed and the challenged decision is affirmed.

Ethicon, Inc. v. FDA

762 F.Supp. 382 (D.D.C.1991).

■ GREEN, DISTRICT JUDGE:

* * * Plaintiff Ethicon, Inc. manufactures Vicryl poly(glycolide/L-lactide) absorbable surgical sutures ("poly (g/l) sutures"). Ethicon challenges the decision by defendants Food and Drug Administration (FDA) and Secretary of Health and Human Services Dr. Louis W. Sullivan to reclassify a generic class of poly (g/l) sutures from Class III to Class II under the Medical Device Amendments to the Federal Food, Drug, and Cosmetic Act. Ethicon seeks a judgment declaring the reclassification decision null and void for FDA's alleged failure to fulfill both substantive and procedural statutory requirements for the reclassification of medical devices. * * *

[D]efendant-intervenor United States Surgical Corporation (USSC) petitioned FDA to reclassify a generic class of poly (g/l) sutures from Class III to Class II. FDA referred the petition to its Administrative Panel on General and Plastic Surgery Devices, and a notice of the Panel's meeting was duly announced. The Panel received written testimony and held a hearing. * * * At the close of the hearing, the Panel unanimously recommended that poly (g/l) sutures be reclassified from Class III to Class II. * * *

FDA issued a letter ruling granting USSC's petition and reclassifying the generic class of poly (g/l) sutures. FDA found that sufficient publicly available scientific evidence existed to enable development of a performance standard for poly (g/l) sutures, the generic class of poly (g/l) sutures was well-characterized, and reclassification was warranted. It specifically commented that "a class III designation for absorbable poly (g/l) surgical sutures constitutes overregulation." FDA defined the generic class as including any "absorbable sterile, flexible strand as prepared and synthesized from homopolymers and copolymers made from glycolide and/or L-lactide." It thus determined that the generic class encompasses Vicryl and Dexon and any other poly (g/l) sutures that in the future could be shown to be substantially equivalent to either of them. * * *

Ethicon petitioned FDA to reconsider the reclassification decision and asked for a stay pending the decision on its petition. * * * FDA issued a letter ruling denying Ethicon's motion for a stay and petition for reconsideration. * * * Ethicon argues that FDA reached its reclassification decision improperly by failing to satisfy both the substantive and procedural statutory requirements for reclassification. * * *

Ethicon's first set of arguments centers on its contention that FDA's decision was grounded in an "inadequate characterization of the generic class" of poly (g/l) sutures. Ethicon faults FDA for wrongly generalizing from existing information, for assuming that all poly (g/l) sutures with the same glycolide-L-lactide ratios as the two on the market are "essentially identical." Ethicon alleges that by basing the reclassification on published evidence limited to Vicryl and Dexon, FDA contradicted the approach it followed in the *Contact Lens* case, where FDA denied reclassification because it determined that insufficient information existed to assure safety and effectiveness of certain contact lenses or to identify a generic class of such lenses for the purpose of reclassification. Finally, Ethicon claims that "the few paragraphs found in the publicly available literature that do discuss the manufacturing processes of poly (g/l) sutures are no substitute for the detailed description ... necessary to adequately understand the manufacturing variables and conditions that may affect the safety and effectiveness of any particular suture."

A review of the regulatory structure governing the determination of generic classes, briefly described above, and of *Contact Lens* reveals the lack of merit in Ethicon's arguments. First of all, there is no requirement that a device in a generic class be "essentially identical" to all others in its class. Rather, the device need only be "substantially equivalent." * * * The agency's characterization of a generic class or type of device is fact-specific, as is evident from the factors FDA's regulations require it to consider in making the determination that a device is safe and effective. The Panel must consider, inter alia, the persons for whose use the device is intended, the conditions and intended conditions of use of the device, the probable benefit to health from use weighed against probable injury or illness from use, and the reliability of the device. Inevitably the requisite evidence will vary, according to "the characteristics of the device, its conditions of use, the existence and adequacy of warnings and other restrictions, and the extent of experience with its use." * * *

[T]he instant controversy ultimately turns on a disagreement between the parties as to the interpretation of the statutory definition of a Class II device—in other words, what constitutes "sufficient information to establish a performance standard" that will "provide reasonable assurance of the safety and effectiveness of the device." In essence, Ethicon is disputing the quantity and quality of the evidence FDA considered—it is disagreeing with the conclusion that the evidence supports a finding of safety and effectiveness.

In FDA's view, "sufficient information" for evaluating a device requires that valid scientific evidence in the record correlates the control of performance parameters to safe and effective use of the device. Thus, the question is whether the administrative record contains sufficient information for the agency to understand the device and sufficient evidence to demonstrate that factors determining the device's safety and effectiveness are controllable. An examination of the two letter rulings and of the supporting administrative record, make clear that FDA more than satisfied its mandate. * * *

After four years of study and after the unanimous recommendation of an independent panel composed of eminent physicians and researchers, FDA determined that poly (g/l) sutures posed no threat to the health or safety of the public that would prevent them from being more than adequately regulated as Class II devices under the Act. The court finds that "FDA has permissibly exercised its considerable discretion," and indeed reasonably acted, and therefore defers to the agency's decision. * * *

NOTES AND QUESTIONS

1. *Competition by other means.* Why would Ethicon resist an effort to partially deregulate a class of products that it sells? Should that in any way influence the court's analysis?

2. *Comparing devices to drugs.* Although the PMA process looks comparable to the NDA process, significant differences exist in the type of safety and effectiveness evidence required for approval. For instance, sponsors cannot conduct double-blind controlled trials of effectiveness in most cases because both the investigator and the patient will know whether or not the treatment uses the experimental device. Cf. Marlene Cimons, Fetal Cell Implants Improve Parkinson's Patients, L.A. Times, Feb. 1, 2001, at A16 (describing the controversial use of sham brain surgery including phony incisions to serve as a placebo control in a clinical trial). What kind of studies might the FDA have suggested Mr. Lake perform with his noseclip? Moreover, unlike metabolized drugs whose mode of action may remain something of a mystery, medical devices have clear mechanical properties that one can assess without the same need for clinical trials. For instance, engineers usually can test durability of materials by subjecting prototypes to simulated use in the lab, though failure analysis after actual use in patients may provide important additional information about questions such as biocompatibility. In addition, fundamental differences exist in the way drugs and devices are developed and used:

1. Medical devices are subject to frequent incremental innovations;

2.   Devices generally are used by health professionals, while drugs are used primarily by patients;

3.   New devices generally originate with physicians, whereas new drugs originate within industry;

4.   The annual sales volume for a medical device is typically only a fraction of the sales volume for a drug, and often could not sustain the cost of a preapproval application;

5.   Many devices are developed by small companies working with physicians. The viability of these companies depends on their ability to react promptly to advancements in technology and the changing needs of the physician. Complex or prolonged review would jeopardize their survival.

See Peter Barton Hutt et al., The Standard of Evidence Required for Premarket Approval Under the Medical Device Amendments of 1976, 47 Food & Drug L.J. 605, 612–13 (1992); see also id. at 625 ("[U]nlike drugs, many devices are not therapeutic in themselves, but instead are used as tools of a health professional. Therefore, their safety and effectiveness largely depends on the skill of the professional user."); Richard A. Merrill, The Architecture of Government Regulation of Medical Products, 82 Va. L. Rev. 1753, 1800 (1996) ("The Medical Device Amendments represented a conscious legislative attempt to avoid what some viewed as the innovation-stifling effects of FDA's drug approval system."); id. at 1808 ("[T]he Amendments were promoted as a new type of regulatory statute, one that would assure careful review of the few high risk technologies but permit less intrusive, less costly regulation of most devices.").

For these reasons, the FDCA provision governing PMAs, which by definition would be required only for the most innovative of medical devices, differs in important respects from the counterpart provision governing NDAs: it calls for something less than "substantial evidence" of effectiveness, and it explicitly provides for risk-benefit balancing when deciding whether a device is safe and effective. See 21 U.S.C. § 360c(a); see also David A. Kessler et al., The Federal Regulation of Medical Devices, 317 New Eng. J. Med. 357, 359 (1987) ("This statutory standard is less rigorous than the standard for the approval of new drugs. . . . For devices, data from well-controlled scientific studies are acceptable, but so is 'valid scientific evidence' from which experts can reasonably conclude that the device will be effective.").

3. *Advisory committees and third party reviews.* Recall that the FDA sought assistance from the NAS when it undertook the "DESI" reviews of drugs approved before 1962. Even today, the agency maintains a large network of advisory committees composed of independent experts that will meet periodically to consider the merits of NDAs undergoing final review, and the FDA typically abides by the advice that it receives. In the case of medical devices, Congress mandated that similar advisory panels review PMAs as well as reclassification proposals. See 21 U.S.C. § 360c(b), (c), (f)(2)(B); see also Hutt et al., 47 Food & Drug L.J. at 618 n.69 ("In part, these provisions were an attempt to address medical practitioners' concerns that determinations of device safety and effectiveness, if left solely to the FDA, would be influenced by the FDA's institutional propensity to be too demanding of new technologies."). See generally Lars Noah, Scientific "Republicanism": Expert Peer Review and the Quest for Regulatory Deliberation, 49 Emory L.J. 1033, 1054–57 (2000). Critics of FDA delays in approving medical technologies have urged greater reliance on reviews conducted by non-governmental entities. See Elizabeth C. Price, Teaching the Elephant to Dance: Privatizing the FDA Review Process, 51 Food & Drug L.J. 651 (1996); Charles J. Walsh & Alissa Pyrich, Rationalizing the Regulation of Prescription Drugs and Medical Devices: Perspectives on Private Certification and Tort Reform, 48 Rutgers L. Rev. 883, 987–1016 (1996). In FDAMA, Congress authorized a limited system of third party reviews for certain PMNs. See 21 U.S.C. § 360m; see also M–D–D–I Rep. ("The Gray Sheet"), June 19, 2000, at 5 (noting difficulties with implementation); Lauren Neergaard, FDA Reverses Surgical Gel Denial: Manufacturer Was First to Use Independent Appeals Process, Wash. Post, Nov. 20, 2001, at A6. For a look at other countries' approaches to medical device regulation, see John Y. Chai, Medical Device Regulation in the United States and the European Union: A Comparative Study, 55 Food & Drug L.J. 57 (2000); Sharon Frank, An Assessment of the Regulations on Medical Devices in the European Union, 56 Food & Drug L.J. 99 (2001).

C. POSTMARKET SURVEILLANCE SYSTEMS

The FDA's premarket review and approval processes cannot possibly identify all risks associated with medical technologies. See General Accounting Office, FDA Drug Review: Post Approval Risks 3 (1990) (concluding that more than half of all drugs approved between 1976 and 1985 had serious risks that were discovered only after approval). In part this represents an unavoidable limitation in conducting clinical trials. It also poses important questions about the relative costs and benefits of a regulatory process that focuses resources on premarket review.

1. SPONTANEOUS ADVERSE EVENT REPORTING

For prescription drugs, the FDA has created a system of mandatory adverse drug experience or reaction (ADE or ADR) reporting by manufacturers, coupled with voluntary health care professional reporting, to monitor the safety of products after they enter the market. The agency defines an "adverse drug experience" as "any adverse event associated with the use of a drug in humans, whether or not considered drug related." 21 C.F.R. § 314.80(a). Within 15 days of discovery, manufacturers must submit a report to the FDA of any adverse drug experience that is both "serious" and "unexpected," and they must "promptly investigate" such adverse experiences. See id. § 314.80(c)(1).

By contrast, manufacturers need only submit periodic reports for non-serious or expected adverse events. The periodic reports must contain summaries of all 15–day reports, along with reports of other adverse experiences, and explanations of any action that the manufacturer has taken in response to the reported information. See id. § 314.80(c)(2)(i)-(ii). The regulations also require that holders of an approved NDA submit quarterly adverse drug experience reports for at least the first three years of marketing and annual reports thereafter. See id. § 314.80(c)(2)(i). The initial close scrutiny reflects an understanding that, during the first three years, physicians are less familiar with the product and its known side effects and that the drug's safety profile will continue to develop as more patients take the product.

The agency's post-approval risk monitoring programs attempt to (1) detect previously unknown adverse reactions associated with a drug product; (2) evaluate in more detail the product's known risks; (3) uncover adverse reactions that arise from product interactions; and (4) uncover adverse reactions peculiar to particular segments of the patient population. See FDA, Managing the Risks from Medical Products Use: Creating a Risk Management Framework 52 (1999); see also 50 Fed. Reg. 7471 (1985) (noting that the ADR system was created as a mechanism to warn the FDA and health care professionals about significant safety problems associated with prescription drugs). The FDA enters information gathered from mandatory and voluntary reporting into a database, and a "postmarketing safety evaluator" processes the information. Based on the apparent gravity of the risk, the agency may issue a medical alert to health professionals, require labeling changes to reflect new information, require boxed warnings in labeling to emphasize particularly important warnings, or require that the product be withdrawn from the market altogether. Although the system is hampered by the low rate of voluntary reporting by physicians, the agency appears willing, for now, to accept the system's limitations because of its heavy allocation of regulatory resources on safety evaluation during the premarket approval process for drugs.

For medical devices, the FDA's more rigorous postmarket surveillance system appears designed to compensate for a more relaxed, multi-level premarket review system. Because few medical devices are subjected to a full premarket evaluation, the postmarketing surveillance process becomes more significant. The Medical Device Amendments of 1976 required that all manufacturers submit medical device reports (MDRs) to the FDA whenever deaths, serious injuries, or dangerous malfunctions occurred in association with the use of a medical device. Initially, reporting rates for medical devices were disappointing. See General Accounting Office, Medical Devices: Early Warning of Problems Is Hampered by Severe Underreporting 3 (1986) (finding that less than 1% of adverse events associated with the use of medical devices in hospitals were reported to the FDA and that more serious events were less likely to be reported). In 1990, Congress expanded MDR requirements to impose reporting obligations on distributors and user facilities, and it mandated more structured postmarket surveillance for many high risk devices. In recent years, the FDA has received more than 100,000 MDRs annually.

Nelson v. American Home Products Corp.

92 F.Supp.2d 954 (W.D.Mo.2000).

■ WHIPPLE, DISTRICT JUDGE:

Rodger Nelson lost his eyesight while he was taking Cordarone, a prescription heart medication manufactured and sold by American Home Products Corporation and Wyeth–Ayerst Laboratories Company (collectively referred to as "Defendants"). This products liability lawsuit followed. To recover damages from Defendants, Plaintiffs Rodger and Lou Nelson must prove, among other things, that Defendants' drug caused Nelson's lost eyesight. Defendants have moved for summary judgment on grounds that the Nelsons have failed to generate any issues of material fact that would permit a reasonable inference in their favor on the issue of causation. Specifically, Defendants argue that the Nelsons have failed to produce any admissible evidence that would entitle a reasonable trier of fact to infer that Defendants' drug caused Nelson's lost eyesight. * * *

The requisite proof for causation must go beyond that which is required by the Food and Drug Administration for reporting adverse drug effects or re-labeling to warn of the potential for adverse drug effects. The FDA requires such reporting and re-labeling regardless of whether a causal connection has been proved. * * * [I]nformation that Defendants are required to report without regard to proof of causation cannot be cited later as an admission of causation. * * *

Defendants' labeling changes and notification letters merely relayed information about a possible association between their drug and optic neuropathy. Spontaneous reporting by a pharmaceutical company should be encouraged; it serves "as a signaling system for adverse drug reactions that may not have been detected during pre-market testing." Haggerty v. Upjohn Co., 950 F. Supp. 1160, 1164 (S.D.Fla.1996). Such reporting does not, however, indicate causation. Id.; see also Adverse Drug Reaction Monitoring, 314 New Eng. J. Med. 1589, 1591 (1996) ("Despite their usefulness, one or even many reports of adverse reactions often do not provide sufficient information to confirm that a drug caused the reaction. A reaction may be caused by the suspect drug, another drug that a patient is taking, or the underlying diseases for which the drug was prescribed; it may also be entirely coincidental."). Evidence of an association may be sufficient for formulation of a hypothesis that can later be tested and confirmed, but it is not proof of causation in the courtroom or the scientific community.

In this respect, it is important to note that the literature on which the Nelsons' experts rely consists solely of anecdotal case reports. While such case reports may be relevant to the question of whether Defendants had notice of the possible ocular side effects of Cordarone, they are not, without more, reliable evidence of causation. The case reports cited by the Nelsons' experts simply inform their readers about a noted temporal association between Amiodarone and optic neuropathy and the authors' hypotheses about the methodology of causation. The reports are mere compilations of reported occurrences. The authors did not attempt to isolate and investigate the effects of alternative causative agents. The reports themselves do not contain a testable and systemic inquiry into the mechanism of causation. At most, these case reports relay a basis for scientific hypotheses; they do not demonstrate a causal link sufficient for admission to a finder of fact in court.

United States v. Laerdal Manufacturing Corp.

853 F.Supp. 1219 (D.Or.1994).

■ FRYE, DISTRICT JUDGE:

* * * Under the MDR regulations, the manufacturer of a medical device who receives information that reasonably suggests that the device may have caused or contributed to a death or serious injury is required to notify the FDA by telephone within five calendar days of receiving the information and is required to file a written report concerning the death or serious injury within fifteen working days of receipt of such information. The MDR regulations further provide that the manufacturer of a medical device is required to submit a written report to the FDA within fifteen working days of receipt of information that reasonably suggests that the device may have malfunctioned and that, if the malfunction was to recur, it is likely that the device may cause or contribute to a death or serious injury. 21 C.F.R. § 803.24.

The United States presented evidence at trial that during the summer of 1993 personnel of Laerdal Manufacturing became aware of the Grand Rapids incident which occurred on June 16, 1993 and became aware that the Grand Rapids incident involved a death. [The Grand Rapids fire department had responded to an emergency call in which the patient was experiencing cardiac difficulties. The Laerdal automated external defibrillator apparently failed to detect that the patient's heart was fibrillating, and therefore indicated that a shock to the heart was not warranted. Upon investigation, the tape of the patient's heart rhythm indicated fibrillation, according to experts; therefore, the device should have delivered a shock to the patient's heart.]

Laerdal Manufacturing contends that the United States did not show that it had violated the MDR regulations by not filing a report on the Grand Rapids incident because * * * the FDA investigator concluded during the inspection conducted in October and November of 1993 that the information regarding the death in the Grand Rapids incident was "indefinite." Laerdal Manufacturing asserts that it did not have information reasonably suggesting that its automated external defibrillator "caused or contributed to" the death. * * *

The regulation and the reporting procedure adopted by Laerdal Manufacturing do not require that the findings be more than "indefinite" when reported. The MDR regulations require Laerdal Manufacturing to submit an MDR report when any of the various company personnel are informed of events which "may have caused or contributed to a death." In the case of the Grand Rapids incident, the clinical investigator and the QA reliability engineer were informed in the summer of 1993 that a device manufactured by Laerdal Manufacturing was involved in treatment events in which a death occurred; that the device did not shock the patient during the incident; and that the device did commit to shock in five out of five replays into a quality assurance device after the incident. This information supports the conclusion that the device "may have caused or contributed to a death." An MDR report was not submitted until February 4, 1994, and then only to be cooperative with the FDA because the Director of Quality Assurance still felt that a report was not required.

There is testimony in the record that Laerdal Manufacturing has had other reported complaints of devices that have allegedly delivered shocks when they should not have and complaints where the device failed to detect and to treat ventricular fibrillation. * * * [The court enjoined the company from further noncompliance with MDR requirements.]

NOTES AND QUESTIONS

1. *Injunctions to secure compliance.* On appeal, the Ninth Circuit affirmed the ruling in *Laerdal*. Noting that 21 C.F.R. § 803 is a strict liability provision, the court concluded that the corporation's continued insistence that its violation of the reporting regulation was an unintentional, "good faith error" provided evidence of likely future violations:

> Laerdal cites as support for its failure to file a report "the ambiguous language of the regulation." ... At trial and on appeal, Laerdal has attempted to demonstrate the "foibles of the MDR system." It claims that "MDR reports languish for several months in a bureaucratic limbo" and that the consequences of its Grand Rapids violation were "merely trifling." ... Even if Laerdal had not intended to violate the regulation, its continued insistence on justifying its actions in committing the violation "is an important factor in deciding whether future violations are sufficiently likely to warrant an injunction." ... That Laerdal's self-justification extends to indicting the MDR system itself reflects "the sort of extraordinary intransigence and hostility" toward the FDA and the MDR regulations that support the inference of a likelihood to commit future violations.

United States v. Laerdal Mfg. Corp., 73 F.3d 852, 856 (9th Cir.1995).

2. *The magnitude of underreporting of adverse events.* The FDA mandates that pharmaceutical companies submit adverse experience reports whenever a health care professional or consumer notifies it of "any adverse event associated with the use of a drug in humans, whether or not considered drug-related." 21 C.F.R. § 314.80. The regulations do not require that drug manufacturers actively seek out safety information about their products. Thus the "mandatory" system is only as effective as the degree of voluntary participation permits. Even if manufacturers comply fully with mandatory adverse event reporting requirements, these reports represent only the proverbial tip of the iceberg. Pharmaceutical companies only submit reports of adverse events based on what physicians and other health professionals send to them, and these reports comprise only a small fraction of the total number of adverse drug reactions that occur. The full extent of underreporting of adverse reactions remains unknown, but several estimates suggest that the underreporting problem is enormous. See H.D. Scott et al., Rhode Island Physicians' Recognition and Reporting of Adverse Drug Reactions, 70 R.I. Med. J. 311, 311–316 (1987) (concluding that physicians report less than 1% of serious ADRs). In Britain, estimates suggest that no more than 10% of serious ADRs and 2–4% of non-serious ADRs are processed through the spontaneous reporting system there. See FDA, Center for Drug Eval. & Research, The Clinical Impact of Adverse Drug Event Reporting, at 5 (1996), available at <http://www.fda.gov/medwatch>; see also Brian L. Strom & Peter Tugwell, Pharmacoepidemiology: Current Status, Prospects, and Problems, 113 Annals Internal Med. 179, 179–81 (1990). When it enacted the Best Pharmaceuticals for Children Act, Congress included a separate requirement that the FDA promulgate a rule to require that drug labeling include a toll-free number for consumers to report adverse events to the agency. See Pub. L. No. 107–109, § 17(a), 115 Stat. 1408 (2002).

3. *Frequency of adverse events associated with a product.* Because the spontaneous reporting numerator represents only a tiny fraction of the actual number of ADRs, it remains difficult to estimate accurately the incidence of safety problems with many prescription drugs. To further complicate the drug safety picture, the FDA lacks useful data about the number of patients who take particular drugs as well as about the length and degree of exposure to these drugs. These data are necessary to determine the denominator for purposes of calculating the incidence of drug safety problems. Until recently, NDA holders were required to submit periodic reports of the frequency of ADRs associated with their products, as well as reports within 15 working days of "any significant increase in frequency" of ADRs. See 21 C.F.R. § 314.80(c)(1)(ii) (1996). The FDA revoked the increased frequency reporting requirement, stating that it had not generated additional useful information on which the agency could base post-approval safety decisions. See 62 Fed. Reg. 34,166 (1997). Separately, the FDA required reports of any significant increases in "therapeutic failure (lack of effect)" detected by a manufacturer, see 57 Fed. Reg. 17,950, 17,960 (1992) (codified at 21 C.F.R. § 314.80(c)(1)(ii)), but has since revoked that reporting requirement as well. See 62 Fed. Reg. at 34,168.

4. *Securities law and ADRs.* The failure to disclose relevant information about ADRs may raise an issue of securities fraud. See In re Carter–Wallace, Inc. Securities Litig., 150 F.3d 153 (2d Cir.1998). In that case, the plaintiffs alleged that advertisements promoting a new epilepsy drug in medical journals affected the price of the company's stock and were statements "in connection with" a securities transaction. The advertisements recited the drug's safety record and stated that no life-threatening side effects had been attributed to the drug. In fact, during the time period in which the advertisements ran, the company received reports of ten deaths associated with the drug; the company then issued a "Dear Doctor" letter recommending that physicians discontinue the drug therapy for their patients. The court remanded the case for consideration of whether the company had accumulated sufficient information about the adverse events associated with the product to have disclosed the ADR problem prior to the point that it issued the "Dear Doctor" letter. In another recent case, the court affirmed the lower court's dismissal of a complaint alleging that American Home Products (AHP) had made material misrepresentations regarding the safety of its weight-loss drugs Pondimin® and Redux® and that these statements caused plaintiffs to suffer financial loss when the company's stock prices fell following public disclosure of the information:

> Plaintiffs do not allege that the European data and adverse reaction reports, taken by themselves, established any statistically significant relationship between AHP's products and valvular heart disease.... Because the link between the two drugs and heart-valve disorders was never definitively established during the relevant period even after the withheld data is taken into account, AHP's failure to disclose this data cannot render its statements about the inconclusiveness of the relationship materially misleading. AHP characterized the Mayo data as inconclusive. Had it simultaneously disclosed the European data and the adverse reaction reports, the aggregate of available information would nevertheless have led a reasonable investor to the same conclusion—that the relationship between the two drugs and heart valve disorders was still inconclusive.

Oran v. Stafford, 226 F.3d 275, 283–84 (3d Cir.2000). The court also concluded that the company's statements regarding the FDA's approval of the drug did not constitute any material misrepresentation or omission: "AHP did not make any 'affirmative characterization' that the FDA's approval was based on a complete review of every piece of relevant medical information. Rather, AHP made a simple (and accurate) factual assertion that the FDA had found that Redux had an 'acceptable safety profile' following a 'thorough review of more than 17 clinical trials.'" Id. at 285; see also San Leandro Emergency Med. Group v. Philip Morris Cos., 75 F.3d 801, 811 (2d Cir.1996) (holding that drug companies need not disclose to investors isolated reports of illnesses suffered by users of their drugs until those reports provide statistically significant evidence that the ill effects may be caused by—rather than randomly associated with—use of the drugs and are sufficiently serious and frequent to affect future earnings).

Barbara A. Noah, *Adverse Drug Reactions: Harnessing Experiential Data to Promote Patient Welfare*

49 CATH. U. L. REV. 449 (2000).

* * * [T]he problem of adverse drug reactions is pervasive and long-standing. A 1998 study concluded that over 100,000 people die in the

United States each year from adverse reactions to medications, making them the fourth leading statistical cause of death in this country. Many of these reactions can be attributed to the expected side effects of potent therapeutic agents, but some of these adverse reactions come as a surprise. In addition to causing significant rates of morbidity and mortality, adverse drug reactions tend to prolong hospital stays, resulting in increased economic burdens on patients and on the health care system. * * *

[T]he product's labeling at the time of marketing approval only represents what is known about the drug's risks and side effects based on the narrow parameters of relatively small clinical trials. The FDA, industry, and health care providers obviously must monitor new drugs carefully and track adverse events associated with these drugs once they become generally available. As experience accumulates, the FDA may demand labeling revisions to reflect newly-discovered side effects or interactions with other prescription or nonprescription drugs, including disclosure of side effects occurring at much lower frequencies. Although the American public predictably recoils at any suggestion that patients continue to act as "guinea pigs" after new drug approval, real world use by a large and diverse patient population over a longer period of time provides the only true test of a drug's safety. * * *

The FDA acknowledges that pre-marketing human clinical studies have inherent limitations. Their relatively short duration, narrow subject population, and small size, among other things, limit the ability of these studies to uncover rare or delayed adverse reactions or drug interactions. "It is simply not possible to identify all the side effects of drugs before they are marketed. The difficulty is not a failure of the ... drug approval process; it is the expected consequence of the biologic diversity of humans...." The FDA's regulations classify side effects as "rare" if they occur at a frequency of less than 1–in–1000. According to the FDA's statistics, in order to have a ninety-five percent chance of detecting an adverse reaction with an incidence of 1–in–1000, a study must enroll at least 3000 patients. Because clinical trials typically involve no more than 3000 to 4000 individuals prior to marketing, the studies will only detect adverse reactions that occur at a rate of 1–in–1000 or higher.

Critics suggest that the FDA's traditional emphasis on pre-approval review comes at the expense of adequate post-approval surveillance. Each year, the FDA receives approximately 230,000 reports of possible adverse drug reactions, and approximately ten percent of these reports raise concerns about serious reactions that pre-approval clinical trials failed to detect. Yet the FDA only devotes the equivalent of fifty-five full-time employees to post-approval surveillance, as compared with over 1700 full-time equivalents engaged in pre-market review of new drug applications. Moreover, only a small percentage of those employees responsible for post-approval review have advanced degrees in a specialty relevant to the surveillance of pharmaceutical products, such as epidemiology or biostatistics.

Another recent development may magnify the drug surveillance problem. Even if this allocation of scarce regulatory resources worked relatively well in the past, the FDA has responded to pressures from patient advocates and the pharmaceutical industry to accelerate the drug approval process. The new fast-track approval system, combined with new user fees that provide an economic incentive to approve new drugs more quickly, has increased the pressure on an already inadequate adverse drug reaction monitoring system. Although many new drug applications now pass through the FDA review process in significantly less time, and sometimes under relaxed regulatory standards, Congress has not provided for any enhanced post-approval resources to monitor the safety of the rapidly increasing stream of new drugs entering the market. * * *

The debate over the tradeoff between lengthy scrutiny of NDAs and the consequent delay in market availability is not a new one, but these recent statutory changes increase the frequency with which new drugs reach the market after shorter review periods, and with lower levels of foreign marketing data or reduced data from clinical trials. * * * In contrast to the FDA, which allocates very limited resources to the task of post-approval monitoring, many foreign drug approval systems [including England and other members of the European Community] provide significant resources for detecting problems with drugs during the post-approval stage, in recognition of the fact that it often takes widespread use to uncover serious, but less common, problems associated with drug products. * * *

[T]he obligation to file ADR reports, in theory, does not depend on a causality assessment. The FDA's regulations make it clear that manufacturers should not report only those adverse events "caused" by their drug; a suspected association will suffice. However, the FDA's guidance on the causation assessment may create more confusion than illumination. One of the most problematic aspects of both the required reporting system and the voluntary MedWatch system is the process of determining whether a particular symptom or effect arises from the patient's medication, from the underlying disease, or from some other, extraneous cause, such as diet or alcohol intake. When the FDA states that no proof of causation is needed to trigger the obligation to report, in effect, the agency assumes that health professionals have already made a rough assessment of causality. In other words, the FDA assumes it is likely that the physician concluded that the drug in question may have caused the patient's problem because the physician would not otherwise have reported the suspected adverse reaction to the manufacturer or the FDA. * * *

Manufacturers have an incentive to underestimate the likelihood of a causal relationship between their products and patient ADRs. Premature assessments of causality (or lack of causality) can, however, potentially distort the statistics relating to how frequently the ADR occurs in the patient population using the drug. Further complicating the causation question, some adverse reactions occur at just slightly above the background rate (the rate at which a condition manifests itself in a given population without exposure to the drug in question) in the treated population. Because frequency analysis contributes to a population-wide causality assessment, it is important not to discard suspected individual ADRs prematurely. * * *

Health care providers have an ethical, though not legal, obligation to identify and report adverse drug reactions to the FDA. The American Medical Association (AMA) has emphasized the importance of continued physician participation in the ADR reporting system, noting that the FDA pays particular attention to reports received directly from physicians (as opposed to reports from patients). Because a substantial number of physician reports concern serious reactions resulting in hospitalization or death, these voluntary physician reports tend to generate the highest proportion of drug labeling changes. * * *

In 1993, the FDA created a system to bypass the pharmaceutical manufacturer and encourage direct reporting to the agency of suspected adverse reactions. To facilitate provider reporting of suspected medical product problems (including problems with drugs, biologics, medical devices and medical foods), the FDA established the "MedWatch Medical Products Reporting Program." The MedWatch program represents the FDA's first concerted effort to involve physicians more formally in the post-approval drug monitoring process. * * * The early returns paint a moderately favorable picture about the effectiveness and quality of physician participation in the MedWatch program. Overall, the quantity of adverse drug reaction reports to the FDA has increased dramatically, from approximately 40,000 in 1985 to nearly 160,000 in 1996. Health professionals submitted 58% of the total reports received in 1996, though only 9% of these were reported directly to the FDA. * * *

In comparison to prescription drug surveillance, the FDA's approach to market surveillance of medical devices generally represents a more proportionate response to the relative risks posed by this category of products than its approach to prescription drugs. * * * A number of differences exist between the systems that regulate safety of drugs and medical devices. For approved medical devices, the statute until recently required structured post-marketing surveillance for certain devices that may cause serious adverse consequences. FDAMA relaxed some of these reporting requirements, however, by repealing mandatory safety surveillance for certain devices and giving the FDA discretion over the decision about whether to order safety monitoring.

The medical device statute also requires spontaneous reporting. A device manufacturer must file a Medical Device Report (MDR) whenever it receives information that suggests that its device "may have caused or contributed to a death or serious injury, or has malfunctioned" in a way that might cause serious injury. In addition, the medical device reporting provision requires reporting from both device manufacturers and certain device user facilities, such as hospitals. Whenever a user facility becomes aware that a device may have caused or contributed to the death or serious injury of a patient in the facility, the user must submit a report to the FDA within ten working days. In contrast, the ADR system requires reporting from manufacturers, but it only requests reports from physicians * * * * Overall, the medical device reporting requirements appear better suited to the task of monitoring medical device safety, in large part because the FDA has the regulatory authority to require that users of high-risk devices, as well as manufacturers of such devices, submit timely reports of adverse events. * * *

As the volume of new drugs entering the market continues to grow, the pressure on the FDA's limited post-approval surveillance resources will no doubt increase. * * * Many of the recently-approved drugs for which the FDA has opted to withdraw marketing approval enjoyed phenomenal sales during their brief periods of availability. Consumer demand for some of the newer diet drugs, for example, predictably led to widespread prescribing for patients who did not meet the physiological criteria for which the FDA approved the drugs. Other recently withdrawn drugs appeared safe at the time of their approval but showed an alarming tendency to interact with other commonly prescribed drugs, causing adverse events in a significant number of patients. Another group of drugs caused serious and permanent liver damage in some patients, despite appearing relatively safe during clinical trials. * * *

A. *Weight-Loss Medications*

In September 1997, the FDA recalled the popular diet drug Redux (dexfenfluramine) from the market after physicians and the agency linked it with heart valve abnormalities in a substantial percentage of women who took the drug. As part of the pre-approval process, an independent panel of scientific experts typically evaluates the drug's safety and effectiveness and votes whether to recommend approval to the FDA. In the case of Redux, the FDA and members of its advisory committee initially expressed reluctance about approving Redux because clinical studies demonstrated an association between the drug and primary pulmonary hypertension. At a second meeting in April 1996, the advisory committee recommended marketing the drug. After the drug received marketing approval, the FDA discovered that the drug's manufacturer had received reports of prior marketing experience in Europe that appeared to implicate the drug in a series of unexplained heart valve problems, and that the manufacturer had not conveyed this information to the FDA.

The weight-conscious American society created a substantial demand for the drug. Some physicians began to prescribe Redux for long-term use despite label warnings about the dangers of exceeding the usage periods tested in the pre-approval trials. As ominous data about side effects began to accumulate, the FDA grew increasingly concerned. Citing the previously understood link between Redux and pulmonary hypertension, as well as severe heart problems and brain damage, the FDA requested a voluntary withdrawal of the drug.

The term "fen-phen" refers to a frequently-prescribed combination of one of two diet drugs, Pondimin (fenfluramine) or Redux (dexfenfluramine), with the amphetamine phentermine. Although the two drugs received approval individually, the FDA never reviewed the combination, which makes it an "off-label," though lawful, use. During the same period in 1997 when problems with Redux (used alone) became apparent, physicians at the Mayo Clinic noted that women taking Pondimin or Redux in combination with phentermine were developing serious and unusual heart valve problems. The physicians reported their findings to the FDA, which then called for reports of similar cases and received nearly 100 responses. Additional studies conducted at five separate universities found that one-third of patients taking the drug combination had heart valve damage, though subsequent reports suggested lower frequencies. The FDA then requested voluntary withdrawal of Pondimin from the market.

The eventual detection of heart valve defects associated with fen-phen prompted concern within the medical community. Because the FDA knew prior to approval that both Pondimin and Redux could cause pulmonary hypertension, a rare but deadly side-effect, critics of the post-approval monitoring system questioned why the agency had not required, as a condition of its marketing, that physicians and epidemiology centers more closely monitor and report problems with the drug. The clinical experience and professional intuition of health care providers treating their obese patients appear to have been the primary factor leading to the discovery of the link between these diet drugs and heart valve damage. Although the FDA received the initial voluntary physician reports and then called for more information that eventually led to the drugs' removal from the market, the regulatory system that mandates manufacturer reporting seems to have played only a minor role in the ultimate outcome. It may be reasonable, therefore, to question whether the FDA's heavy reliance on voluntary physician reporting makes sense, or whether some restructuring of the system might represent a more appropriate approach.

B. *Liver Toxicity Problems*

Measures of liver function are a significant indicator of how the body metabolizes many types of medications. When the liver cannot, for some reason, properly break down a drug, the patient may experience some form of liver failure. More typically, a patient experiences a problem with liver function such as an elevated level of liver transaminase enzymes, or symptoms such as jaundice, nausea, vomiting, abdominal pain, loss of appetite, or dark urine. In severe cases, the liver may fail completely and require transplantation. Because of the serious risks associated with drugs that affect liver function, researchers use metabolic studies and clinical trials to detect liver problems associated with new drugs so that physicians can prescribe these products safely.

The painkiller Duract (bromfenac sodium) first entered the market in July 1997. By the time the FDA withdrew approval for marketing in June 1998, the drug apparently had caused four deaths due to liver toxicity and required liver transplants in eight other patients. During clinical trials of Duract, researchers discovered an unexpectedly high incidence of elevated liver enzymes in patients who took the drug for relatively long periods, but experts disagreed about the significance of these problems. One FDA medical officer expressed serious concerns about the drug's potential to produce liver toxicity, and he argued in favor of attaching the agency's most stringent warnings to the drug's labeling at the outset. The FDA chose to approve the product only for short-term use (ten days or less), and included information about elevated liver enzymes in the product labeling.

As the FDA became aware of liver problems in patients taking Duract during the year that the drug was available, it took interim steps to notify physicians of emerging safety problems. Despite the labeling information, some physicians prescribed Duract for longer than ten days, and the agency began receiving reports of liver failure. The FDA responded by requiring prominent boxed warnings in the drug's labeling, and the manufacturer issued a "Dear Doctor" letter emphasizing the drug's dangers and describing the parameters for proper use. These efforts did not completely prevent the inappropriate prescribing of Duract for long-term use. Thus, in June 1998, after the FDA concluded that it could not impose effective restrictions on the duration of use, the manufacturer voluntarily withdrew the drug from the market. * * *

C. Unexpected Drug Interactions

Recent reports have uncovered serious and unexpected drug interaction problems with a number of prescription drugs. Practically speaking, it is virtually impossible for a manufacturer to test a new chemical entity with every other medication that might create an adverse interaction. During the clinical trials process, a sponsor of an NDA must select, with input from the FDA, likely drugs to test in combination with its new drug in order to uncover potential drug interactions. Those who evaluate drug safety find it particularly difficult to predict drug interactions at the clinical trials phase of the new drug evaluation process because many variables, such as particular patient sensitivities and lifestyle habits, confound the causation assessment.

For example, in pre-approval trials for the blood pressure and angina medication Posicor (mibefradil), the sponsor tested the new drug with drugs selected as likely combinations, including drugs that the sponsor believed would create adverse interactions. The FDA advisory committee voted five to three to approve Posicor, with the dissenters expressing serious concerns about the drug's safety based on the clinical studies. Although at the time of approval the agency was aware that Posicor tended to interact badly with other commonly-prescribed drugs, it took the widespread use of the drug after approval to demonstrate the magnitude of the problem. The reported ADRs suggested that Posicor interacts negatively with as many as two dozen other prescription drugs. Furthermore, the patients for whom doctors prescribe the drug are mainly elderly and often have multiple health problems; thus, these patients tended to take a variety of prescription drugs concurrently, thereby increasing the odds of a negative interaction. Numerous reports of adverse drug interactions, including low heart rates, irregular heartbeats, kidney damage, and twenty-four reported deaths, convinced the FDA to withdraw its approval of the drug. After less than one year on the market, the manufacturer discontinued the sale of Posicor. * * *

Possible Solutions:

In the last two years, patients have encountered a number of unanticipated drug-related hazards including pulmonary hypertension and heart valve damage from diet drugs, liver toxicity from several different drugs, and a series of dangerous interactions involving prescription medications. This constellation of drug hazards has led some critics to question both the effectiveness of the pre-approval system, and the ability of the post-approval safety surveillance system to detect and respond quickly to previously-unknown drug risks. Conversely, to the extent that the FDA feels insecure about the effectiveness of its post-approval monitoring system, there is a risk that it may overreact to an apparent crisis. * * *

Increased FDA resources represent one obvious response to the problem of identifying and dealing with adverse drug reactions. Additional regulatory staff are already available at the pre-approval stage to meet the public demand that NDAs be reviewed in a timely fashion. The agency also needs additional staff to implement a more effective post-approval monitoring process in response to the problems arising from the increasing stream of newly-approved drugs. Congress and the FDA clearly recognize the need for increased funding, and they appear to be taking steps in the right direction. In addition to increased appropriations, Congress should consider amending the statutory provisions authorizing user fees and targeting a percentage of fees specifically for adverse drug reaction monitoring, instead of directing all of the user fee proceeds towards increasing personnel to review NDAs.

Separately, the FDA should continue its effort to improve the clarity of its existing post-approval reporting requirements. The agency might accomplish this goal by amending its existing regulations, or it might issue additional guidelines to aid in the interpretation of the regulations. Because current regulations provide manufacturers some leeway to make judgments about whether to forward ADRs to the FDA, commentators have expressed concern that the FDA sees only a fraction of the reports that physicians forward to manufacturers. Clarifying reporting requirements may help to diminish the underreporting that arises from a lack of understanding of certain key regulatory terms. Past regulatory amendments and guidance documents, however, have proven somewhat ineffective at increasing the rate of ADR reporting. * * *

Additional resources and clearer regulatory requirements alone will not, however, provide an adequate response to the problem of identifying unexpected adverse drug events. Several approaches might help to improve the quality and quantity of data on which health care professionals base their prescribing decisions. Congress should consider authorizing explicit Phase IV study requirements for all newly-approved drugs, not just for those approved under an accelerated review process. In contrast to the current approach of passively waiting for additional information about new drugs from manufacturers and health care providers, required Phase IV post-approval studies or other special post-market surveillance conditions could more readily generate additional information early in the marketing process and in a more systematic fashion. The FDA and the industry should make better use of the opportunities that Phase IV studies present in order to uncover serious or rare adverse drug reactions and interactions more quickly. Simple post-approval safety trials will detect rarer adverse reactions by studying a large, diverse group of patients. * * *

[C]ommentators have recommended the creation of a completely independent drug safety board to compile and review drug product safety and efficacy data. Such a board would bypass manufacturer tendencies to discount negative safety information and would counteract the FDA's natural hesitancy to confess error when a drug it just approved generates unusual and unexpected rates of adverse reactions. The independent board might oversee a requirement for mandatory postmarket data collection among a representative population of patients with typical conditions and duration of treatment for the particular drug. In addition, the independent board could investigate specific instances or patterns of ADRs, and it could make regulatory reform or policy recommendations to the FDA so that the agency could reduce the risk of similar events in the future. * * *

[The Centers for Disease Control and Prevention (CDC)] might undertake the role of a disinterested "drug safety board." Because the FDA would remain responsible for the initial pre-approval safety evaluation for all new drugs, the CDC, in the role of safety monitor, could provide an independent analysis of safety data as it becomes available. Moreover, the CDC has the requisite biostatistical and epidemiological expertise to perform the task effectively, and the capability to conduct quick follow-up investigations in the field. Commentators have called for greater epidemiological expertise at the FDA, noting that the number of trained epidemiologists at the agency has declined in recent years and suggesting that the FDA utilize outside resources. The FDA and CDC are ideally situated to play the independent and complementary roles necessary to improve prescription drug safety and the overall quality of patient care. * * *

Forsham v. Califano

442 F.Supp. 203 (D.D.C.1977).

■ CORCORON, DISTRICT JUDGE:

Plaintiffs are seven physicians who specialize in the treatment of diabetes and six diabetic patients taking phenformin hydrochloride prescribed by their physicians as part of their diabetic therapy. Phenformin is an orally administered drug designed to control blood sugar levels in patients with adult-onset diabetes who are not dependent on insulin and who cannot or will not reduce their daily caloric intake. Phenformin allows such diabetics to control their condition with fewer dietary restrictions and to delay the time when they must begin taking insulin.

The defendant is the Secretary of Health, Education and Welfare who, pursuant to Section 505(e) of the Federal Food, Drug and Cosmetic Act has suspended new drug applications for phenformin on grounds that the drug poses an "imminent hazard." The pertinent language of 21 U.S.C. § 355(e) states:

> That if the Secretary . . . finds that there is an imminent hazard to the public health he may suspend the approval of such [new drug] application immediately and give the applicant prompt notice of his action and afford the applicant the opportunity for an expedited hearing under this subsection; but the authority conferred by this proviso to suspend the approval of an application shall not be delegated.

Plaintiffs seek to enjoin the Secretary from implementing his suspension order. * * *

While acknowledging the existence of "conflicting testimony" on the incidence of lactic acidosis among phenformin patients and the view expressed by the manufacturers that labeling changes made in January 1977 would reduce the incidence of phenformin-related lactic acidosis, the Secretary nonetheless deemed that the following factors necessitated his decision to suspend:

1. The discontinued marketing of phenformin in Norway and Canada based on the experience in those countries with phenformin-related lactic acidosis cases.

2. Adverse reports of phenformin-related lactic acidosis in Finland, Sweden, New Zealand, and Australia.

3. The discontinued use of phenformin by several diabetes clinics in major U.S. hospitals.

4. The unanimous October 1976 recommendation by the FDA Endocrinology and Metabolism Advisory Committee that phenformin be removed from the market.

5. The May 6, 1977, decision by the FDA's Bureau of Drugs to seek withdrawal of approval of NDAs for phenformin.

6. Calculations submitted by the FDA's Bureau of Drugs based on information it had received from phenformin manufacturers, research conducted in other countries, studies conducted in a group of university based medical centers and reports from individual hospitals. Those calculations indicated that * * * the estimated incidence of death due to lactic acidosis in phenformin users is between 0.125 and 2 deaths annually per 1,000 patients—a rate 5 to 80 times higher than that of other widely used drugs known to cause fatalities even when properly used * * * [and] that final administrative action on withdrawal of the NDAs for phenformin could take from six to twelve months during which time anywhere from 10 to 700 people could die from phenformin associated lactic acidosis.

Plaintiffs do not ask the court at this juncture to evaluate the relative merits of the conflicting medical views on the hazards posed by phenformin. Rather they assert (1) that the Secretary employed an improper standard in determining that phenformin posed an imminent hazard; (2) that the long standing availability of the data relied on by the Secretary and the chronology of events preceding his decision demonstrate a lack of the immediacy required to support such a determination; and (3) that the procedural mechanism employed by the Secretary in implementing his decision was arbitrary, capricious, and ultra vires. * * *

[W]e are not inclined to adopt plaintiff's "crisis" interpretation of imminent hazard. Rather we are more persuaded by defendant's suggested analogy to cases interpreting the imminent hazard provisions of the Federal Insecticide, Fungicide and Rodenticide Act which caution "against any approach to the term imminent hazard ... that restricts it to a concept of crisis" and adopt the view that "it is enough that there is substantial likelihood that serious harm will be experienced during ... any realistic projection of the administrative process."

We decide accordingly that the Secretary's criteria for evaluating the existence of an imminent hazard were not improper. There remains to be determined whether a rational connection exists between the facts on which he relied and his decision to suspend. Keeping in mind that "invocation of this emergency power is a matter which is peculiarly one of judgment," this court cannot say that the facts on which the Secretary relied, particularly the calculations provided by the Bureau of Drugs, do not adequately support his decision to suspend. * * * The mere fact that respectable scientific authority can be found on both sides of this question does not render the Secretary's decision arbitrary and capricious. Similarly, the fact that much of the raw data used by the Bureau in arriving at its conclusion had been available for some length of time does not preclude its use in finding an imminent hazard when, as the FDA alleged happened in this case, the magnitude of phenformin's risk was determined only after an extensive re-evaluation of the data following the May 13th hearing.

In view of the facts used by the Secretary to support his decision we are also not persuaded by plaintiffs' arguments that his decision was arbitrary because allegedly less drastic means such as the use of accepted labeling procedures might eventually result in reducing phenformin's hazards or that the decision was arbitrary because other drugs currently available might be equally as hazardous. Assuming, as we must at this juncture, the validity of the Bureau of Drug's projection of between four and 60 phenformin related deaths each month, we cannot find that the Secretary's conclusion that labeling changes "cannot be expected to achieve a needed reduction in the usage of phenformin within any reasonable time frame ... with so many lives at stake," was either arbitrary or unreasonable. Nor was it made so by his decision to act first on phenformin rather than some other drug which may pose a hazard of similar magnitude. * * *

NOTES AND QUESTIONS

1. *Imminent hazard.* The first section of this chapter described the risk/benefit calculus that FDA reviewers use to determine whether it is appropriate to grant marketing approval for a new drug. When it receives post-marketing risk information, should the agency simply redo its original calculus under the approval criteria or should different factors influence regulatory judgments at this stage? The FDA never again invoked its imminent hazard authority. This expedited withdrawal procedure raises procedural due process questions because it deprives the pharmaceutical manufacturer of a valuable property interest without affording a prior hearing. In connection with medical devices, the FDA has used a comparable power to demand recalls. See, e.g., Kim A. Eagle, Safety Alerts Involving Device Therapy for Arrhythmias, 286 JAMA 843 (2001).

2. *Informal action to withdraw a product.* The FDA more frequently obtains voluntary agreement from manufacturers to withdraw drugs when safety concerns emerge. See Naomi Aoki, A Question of Speed and Safety, Boston Globe, Nov. 28, 2001, at G1 (noting "the growing number of drugs that have been recalled in the past three years—nearly a dozen implicated in more than 1,000 deaths"). For example, in November 2000, the manufacturers of Lotronex® (alosetron), a drug used to treat irritable bowel syndrome (IBS), withdrew it from the market less than ten months after approval. Of the 300,000 patients who had taken the drug during that brief period, seventy developed severe constipation or ischemic colitis (a lack of blood flow to the colon); some cases required surgical intervention, and five people died. Those who favored withdrawing Lotronex argued that its risks were unacceptable because it only treated a non-life-threatening condition, but the majority of patients on the drug who suffered no serious side effects protested the withdrawal because it helped them to cope with a condition that significantly interfered with their daily life activities. See Denise Grady, FDA Pulls a Drug, and Patients Despair, N.Y. Times, Jan. 30, 2001, at F1. In negotiations over returning the drug to the market, the manufacturer rejected FDA proposals to limit prescribing to gastroenterologists who had been "certified" to prescribe the drug, and to prevent off-label prescribing (the drug was only approved for use in women based on the proof of effectiveness in clinical trials, but physicians also regularly prescribed it for men suffering from IBS). Another option under consideration would provide the drug under an IND, allowing patients who meet particular medical criteria to obtain Lotronex through participation in a clinical trial. See id.; see also Chris Adams, FDA Weighs Requests to Return Lotronex to Consumer Market, Wall St. J., Apr. 19, 2001, at B2. The FDA also sometimes convinces companies to withdraw nonprescription drug products containing ingredients of questionable safety. For example, manufacturers of OTC cold remedies containing phenylpropanolamine (PPA) recently reformulated their products to remove the ingredient after studies demonstrated that it was associated with an increased risk of stroke in certain users. See Jeff Gerth & Sheryl Gay Stolberg, Another Part of the Battle: Keeping a Drug in the Store, N.Y. Times, Dec. 13, 2000, at A1 (describing

PPA's long marketing history and growing evidence of safety concerns associated with the OTC ingredient).

3. *Intermediate responses.* Short of withdrawing a drug, the FDA has several less draconian measures at its disposal to reduce the risks associated with approved prescription drugs. For example, the agency can require relabeling with stronger warnings and/or clearer directions for use, can require mandatory education programs for prescribers, and can try to place restrictions on distribution or use. See Thomas M. Burton & Gardiner Harris, Bristol–Myers Squibb Must Label Serzone with Liver Warning, Wall St. J., Dec. 7, 2001, at B4 (describing the FDA's requirement of a black box warning in response to a serious but rare side effect associated with an antidepressant). The FDA also has proposed a rule that would require placement of an inverted solid black triangle on the labels of drugs approved for fewer than three years and that contain a new molecular entity, a new active ingredient combination, are indicated for a new population, or utilize a different delivery system. See 65 Fed. Reg. 81,082, 81,088 (2000).

4. *Drug safety issues and impact on the elderly.* For a variety of physiological and socio-medical reasons, the elderly are particularly susceptible to adverse drug reactions. Age-related responses to drugs can result from pharmacokinetic differences, such as variations in the way a drug is absorbed, excreted, or otherwise metabolized. In addition, two-thirds of people over the age of sixty-five use one or more drugs daily, and many people in this age group use multiple prescription drugs concurrently, putting this population at a substantially higher risk of adverse drug reactions and interactions. See Barbara A. Noah & David B. Brushwood, Adverse Drug Reactions in Elderly Patients: Alternative Approaches to Postmarket Surveillance, 33 J. Health Law 383, 404–05 (2000).

5. *Sentinel system for medical devices.* FDAMA reiterated a preference for postmarket rather than premarket controls for medical devices. In amendments to provisions governing the review of both PMAs and PMNs, Congress urged the agency to consider increased reliance on postmarket controls to facilitate premarket clearances. Ironically, however, at the same time that FDAMA exempted more devices from premarket approval or notification, it also seemingly weakened some of the postmarket controls, for instance by leaving the imposition of postmarket surveillance requirements to the FDA's discretion, and by excluding distributors from MDR requirements. See 21 U.S.C. § 360*l*(a). Arguably, these revisions do not rachet down postmarket reviews so much as shift the emphasis from quantity to quality. Congress directed the FDA to establish a "sentinel system" that will facilitate efficient reporting by requiring that only a subset of user facilities file device reports. The selected facilities must constitute a "representative profile of user reports for device deaths and serious ... injuries." Id. § 360i(b)(1)(D)(5). A one-year pilot study (called "DeviceNet") was completed recently, and it generated dramatic increases in reporting rates over what one would have expected for user facilities. The FDA hopes to build on this success with its proposed "Medical Device

Surveillance Network" (MeDSuN). See M–D–D–I Rep. ("The Gray Sheet"), Oct. 25, 1999, at 12. The agency intends to use the representative subset of user facilities to perform a more targeted and thorough collection and investigation of MDRs, including near misses, but the necessary funding for this resource-intensive activity remains uncertain, and it may be difficult to recruit the various facilities needed to participate in this nationwide sentinel system.

2.   POSTAPPROVAL STUDY REQUIREMENTS

The FDA enjoys only limited statutory authority to require postapproval studies of approved drug products. See Robert L. Fleshner, Post–Marketing Surveillance of Prescription Drugs: Do We Need to Amend the FDCA?, 18 Harv. J. Legis. 327 (1981). As described previously, the fast-track regulations create an accelerated approval process for drug and biological products intended to treat serious or life-threatening illness pursuant to which the FDA may require postapproval studies to establish a firmer connection between the initial efficacy data and the products' ultimate clinical benefits. See 21 C.F.R. §§ 314.510, 601.41 (noting that the applicant must carry out the studies "with due diligence"). In codifying these procedures, FDAMA required that sponsors make annual progress reports to the FDA on the status of their required Phase IV studies. See 21 U.S.C. § 356(b)(2)(A), (b)(3)(A).

The FDA long ago issued regulations that contemplated approving NDAs for certain types of drugs based on a commitment to conduct additional post-marketing research:

> A new drug may not be approved for marketing unless it has been shown to be safe and effective for its intended use(s). After approval, the applicant is required to establish and maintain records and make reports related to clinical experience or other data or information necessary to make or facilitate a determination of whether there are or may be grounds under section 505(e) of the act for suspending or withdrawing approval of the application. Some drugs, because of the nature of the condition for which they are intended, must be used for long periods of time—even a lifetime. To acquire necessary data for determining the safety and effectiveness of long-term use of such drugs, extensive animal and clinical tests are required as a condition of approval. Nonetheless, the therapeutic or prophylactic usefulness of such drugs may make it inadvisable in the public interest to delay the availability of the drugs for widespread clinical use pending completion of such long-term studies. In such cases, the Food and Drug Administration may approve the new drug application on condition that the necessary long-term studies will be conducted and the results recorded and reported in an organized fashion.

35 Fed. Reg. 14,784 (1970) (codified as amended at 21 C.F.R. § 310.303(a)); see also Nancy Mattison & Barbara W. Richard, Postapproval Research Requested by the FDA at the Time of NCE Approval, 21 Drug Info. J. 309, 323 (1987) (finding that the FDA had conditioned its approval of one-third

to one-half of new drugs on the NDA sponsor's conducting additional postapproval studies).

Whether the agency mandates Phase IV studies or persuades companies to undertake such research voluntarily, it may have difficulty ensuring that the additional work is completed. A recent survey conducted by Public Citizen found that NDA sponsors often disregard postapproval study commitments and that the FDA has failed to follow up by demanding the additional data. See Larry D. Sasich et al., The Drug Industry's Performance in Finishing Postmarketing Research (Phase IV) Studies, tbl.1 (2000). The survey found that the FDA approved a total of 122 new drugs between 1990 and 1994; 72 percent of these approvals included a commitment to conduct at least one Phase IV study. As of December 1999, only 13 percent of the sponsors in this group had actually completed their promised studies. For the 107 new drugs approved after 1994 which had made Phase IV commitments, none of the promised studies were complete as of December 1999.

D. THE PERILS OF BAD REGULATORY ADVICE

PROFESSIONAL RESPONSIBILITY EXERCISE*

Amy Taylor was a fourth year associate at Beckham, Caplin & Kramer (BCK), a small law firm in Washington, D.C., that specialized in food and drug law. Taylor enjoyed this specialty—it was both intellectually challenging and dealt with important public health issues.

One of the most interesting projects that Taylor had worked on thus far at BCK was on behalf of the Nonprescription Drug Manufacturers Alliance (NDMA), a trade association with more than 100 members. In 1988, the FDA had issued a final OTC monograph for nighttime sleep-aid products, which allowed for the use of 50 mg of diphenhydramine hydrochloride or doxylamine succinate as active ingredients. See 21 C.F.R. pt. 338. A few years later, the consumer advocacy group GadFly had filed a citizens petition asking the agency to remove doxylamine from the monograph. GadFly made a pair of arguments in contending that doxylamine was not generally recognized as safe and effective (GRASE): (1) newly completed animal studies with a chemical similar to doxylamine revealed a statistically significant increase in congenital abnormalities in the offspring; and (2) the clinical trials originally submitted by the manufacturers to demonstrate efficacy were conducted by a principal investigator later convicted of scientific fraud. After reviewing the material submitted with the petition, the FDA concluded that no grounds existed for concerns about the ingredient's safety, but it agreed that questions about the validity of the clinical trials cast doubt on its original finding that doxylamine qualified as GRASE.

---

* Adapted from a fictional case study involving the FDA's regulation of caffeine as a food additive. See Philip B. Heyman & Lance Liebman, The Social Responsibilities of Lawyers 216–34 (Foundation Press 1988).

NDMA wanted to object to the proposed amendment of the monograph, both on behalf of those member companies that used doxylamine and also on behalf of the entire industry insofar as this rule could set a dangerous precedent of revisiting previously concluded monograph proceedings. NDMA came to BCK for assistance, and the partner in charge of the account asked Taylor to draft comments in opposition to the FDA's proposal. A few manufacturers transmitted anecdotal evidence to confirm the ingredient's effectiveness, but it would take significant time and money to conduct new clinical trials. Because the notice of proposed rulemaking had not identified any safety concerns as the basis for withdrawing doxylamine, the comments argued that the FDA should postpone any final action until the industry had an opportunity to undertake the additional research.

A few months after completing the comments for NDMA, Taylor attended her tenth college reunion and struck up a conversation with Melanie Gruter, an old roommate who was finishing up a post-doc at the Harvard School of Public Health. In the course of comparing notes about their respective jobs, Taylor mentioned the NDMA project. Gruter replied that her lab had just completed an epidemiological study on the subject, which found an apparent increase in the rate of birth defects among women exposed to an average 100 mg of doxylamine a day during the first trimester of pregnancy. From her background research, Taylor knew that this study directly conflicted with prior work in the field. Although she lacked any real details about the research, much less the expertise to evaluate the study, Taylor trusted her old friend and began to wonder whether she had an ethical obligation to notify the FDA.

The following week, Paul Hadley, a senior partner at the firm, asked Taylor to join in a meeting with a new client that had just gotten underway in his office. When she arrived, Mr. Hadley introduced her to Steven Malone, director of regulatory affairs at Radford Drugs, Inc. The company produced a wide variety of OTC drug products in the U.S., and it wanted to introduce a new and powerful sleep-aid. Although they have no doubt that doxylamine works as claimed (and is more effective than 50 mg of diphenhydramine), the sudden uncertainty about the regulatory status of doxylamine led Radford's product development team to formulate a product containing 50 mg of diphenhydramine (as allowed by the monograph) along with 10 mg of doxylamine. Because the monograph would not allow such a combination in any event (even if the FDA relents on its proposal to withdraw doxylamine), the company wants to characterize doxylamine as an "inactive" ingredient. Mr. Malone wanted to know whether this strategy would allow the company to continue using doxylamine, even if the FDA decided to remove it from the monograph, but also avoid listing it on the label. Mr. Hadley asked Taylor to research the question and have a response by Monday morning.

A weekend spent with the applicable sections of the *Code of Federal Regulations* and a variety of *Federal Register* notices revealed the following: a regulation mandating that an OTC "product contains only suitable inactive ingredients which are safe in the amounts administered and do not interfere with the effectiveness of the preparation," 21 C.F.R. § 330.1(e); a regulation listing non-GRASE substances (to which doxylamine would be added if the FDA eventually finalizes its proposed withdrawal) and providing that "[a]ny OTC drug product ... containing any active ingredient(s) as specified in paragraph (a) of this section is regarded as a new drug," id. § 310.545(b); a regulation defining "active ingredient" for GMP purposes as "any component that is intended to furnish pharmacological activity or other direct [drug] effect," id. § 210.3(b)(7); and a boilerplate FDA comment that appeared in several final monographs for other OTC product categories recognizing that non-monograph active ingredients may still have legitimate uses as inactive ingredients, see, e.g., 56 Fed. Reg. 37,792 (1991); see also 42 Fed. Reg. 19,156, 19,157 (1977) ("[T]his proposal [which was never finalized] is intended to preclude the retention and redesignation of an active ingredient as an inactive ingredient unless it serves an acceptable function as an inactive ingredient.").

In addition, in the course of running an on-line search for commentary about the agency's definition of active ingredient, Taylor came across the following discussion in an opinion resolving private litigation under the Lanham Act for false or misleading advertising:

> Sandoz's counsel argued to the district court that "[i]f [the demulcents] relieve coughs they're active. That's true as a matter of common sense and normal English." Such an interpretation of FDA regulations, absent direct guidance from the promulgating agency, is not as simple as Sandoz proposes. The FDA has not found conclusively that demulcents must be labeled as active or inactive ingredients within the meaning of 21 C.F.R. § 210.3(b)(7). We decline to find and do not believe that the district court had to find, either "as a matter of common sense" or "normal English," that which the FDA, with all of its scientific expertise, has yet to determine. Because "agency decisions are frequently of a discretionary nature or frequently require expertise, the agency should be given the first chance to exercise that discretion or to apply that expertise." Thus, we are unable to conclude that Vicks's labeling of Pediatric 44's demulcents as inactive is literally false, even if Vicks concurrently claims that these ingredients enable its medicine to work the instant it is swallowed. Sandoz's position would require us to usurp administrative agencies' responsibility for interpreting and enforcing potentially ambiguous regulations.

Sandoz Pharm. Corp. v. Richardson–Vicks, Inc., 902 F.2d 222, 231 (3d Cir.1990). Taylor also read an article recommending that the FDA revise its existing labeling rules to require the listing of all inactive ingredients. See Holly A. Brown, Comment, The Need for Regulation Mandating the Labeling of Inactive Ingredients in Pharmaceuticals, 8 Admin. L.J. 291 (1994).*

---

* Note that in 1997, several years after the events described in this hypothetical case, Congress mandated such ingredient labeling. See FDAMA § 412(c) (codified at 21 U.S.C. § 352(e)(1)(A)(iii)). The FDA issued implementing regulating two years later. See 64 Fed. Reg. 13,254, 13,288 (1999) (codified at 21 C.F.R. § 201.66(c)(8)).

On Monday, Taylor was prepared to present her findings. She went through the possible legal arguments before concluding that Radford could not add doxylamine as an inactive ingredient because it did not serve a legitimate secondary (e.g., preservative or flavoring) function but instead had a pharmacological effect. She was somewhat taken aback, however, when Mr. Hadley quickly jumped in after she presented her conclusion: "Wait a minute, Amy," he said. "It's not so clear to me that Radford can't do so. I think that the company would have a solid basis in the law for going the inactive ingredient route." Taylor tried to disagree, but Malone broke in: "It sounds like we have a pretty good legal argument. Besides, what would the FDA do to me if the argument does not hold up? And how likely would it be that they would find out in the first place?"

Mr. Hadley explained that, if it was not listed on the label, the agency would indeed have difficulty in finding out whether doxylamine was, in fact, present in the product. Mr. Malone then asked what the FDA would do if it did decide to issue a final rule prohibiting the use of doxylamine as an active ingredient. "First of all," Mr. Hadley replied, "if it were able to put together some evidence that Radford had added doxylamine, the agency would send you a 'warning letter,' threatening to impose sanctions unless you immediately undertake some corrective action." "But how likely is it that the FDA would require us to recall the product?" Mr. Malone asked. "Based on my experience with the agency, not very likely," Mr. Hadley responded.

But Taylor did not agree with his assessment at all: "I'm not so sure that's true in this case. Given the recent public criticism over the need to withdraw several newly approved prescription drugs, the FDA might over-react and insist on a recall. In addition," she continued, "consumer groups might bring suit for fraud or make adverse public statements about the product. Recently, several consumer groups have been analyzing other FDA-regulated products and publicizing the results." She failed to mention the soon-to-be-published findings from the new epidemiological study.

"But, Amy," Mr. Hadley countered, "there is a strong legal argument that low dose doxylamine serves a legitimate function as an inactive ingredient, and as such need not be included by name on the label." Before Taylor could respond, Mr. Malone broke in: "I agree with you, Paul. It sounds to me like we have a good legal basis for not including doxylamine on the label, and I'd like a letter from your firm on that for my files." "Sure, Steve," he responded, and turned toward Taylor. "Amy, I'll leave it to you to work something out with Steve. I suggest you put together a draft for him to look at sometime this week." Taylor went back to her office, but she did not feel comfortable about writing the letter.

DISCUSSION QUESTIONS

1. Before being assigned to work on the Radford problem, Amy Taylor prepared comments to the FDA arguing that it should not yet remove doxylamine from the OTC monograph. In one sense, Taylor's task presented no ethical dilemma. She was expressing the position of her client, the NDMA, and it is plainly a respectable argument under the law. But what if she believes that some consumers might develop serious side effects, as the unpublished Harvard School of Public Health study seems to suggest? This would be a result of the delay she is advocating. If an attorney knew that there had been a number of deaths during the early use of a new prescription drug in Europe but that there was no requirement that these be made known to the FDA, could she file the papers necessary for obtaining approval for use of the drug in the United States? Is this a different case? What could Taylor do if she believed there was great danger in the actions her client proposed? Perhaps she could raise the issue directly with the client or urge the supervising partner to do this. What factors would enter into a decision to take one of these steps? Is it any consolation that an existing FDA regulation mandates that the labels of all OTC drugs intended for systemic absorption caution pregnant or nursing women to "seek the advice of a health professional before using this product," 21 C.F.R. § 201.63(a)?

2.   An equally difficult question is what advice a lawyer should give to her client when she thinks what the client wants to do would, in all likelihood, be deemed unlawful by a regulatory agency or court, but there is room for doubt. Is there any obligation to go beyond informing the client of the attorney's view of the law and the attorney's prediction as to how the relevant tribunals would handle a dispute about the issue? If the client indicates that he intends to proceed despite advice that the proposed action is almost certainly illegal, does the lawyer have an obligation to remind the client of the impropriety of ignoring the law in that way or is it sufficient that the client is aware of the likely consequences? What if the lawyer will be expected to prepare documents or otherwise assist in the transaction? Is it at least proper for the lawyer to take these steps if she believes there is a "presentable" argument for the legality of what the client is proposing to do or should she impose a higher standard?

Even if any illegality is purely technical, i.e., it has no significant economic or health consequences, does Taylor have an obligation to try to persuade Malone that his company nonetheless should include doxylamine on the label? Would Taylor be wrong to continue to participate in and assist the transaction (e.g., by such further steps as negotiating to purchase product labels which she knew did not mention doxylamine) if she believed she was furthering a plain violation of the law?

3.   Should Taylor draft the letter? Here, in contrast to negotiating with the seller of labels, there is the further issue that she is being asked to state as her own opinion legal views that she does not hold. And the very purpose of the opinion letter is to persuade private associates of Mr. Malone and regulatory officials that the company is acting in good faith. There are three types of letters that Taylor could write in this situation:

(a) An "Opinion Letter" stating that in her opinion the law does not require Radford to include doxylamine on the label. If she drafts such a letter she will be putting her (or Paul Hadley's) name and the name of the firm behind it.

(b) A letter specifying the legal risks of not including doxylamine on the label without stating whether she thinks the action is legal or not.

(c) A letter defending the client's failure to include doxylamine on the label. (This letter is a bit closer to the Opinion Letter, except that, as in option (b), an attorney need not say that she agrees with her client's position.)

Which type of letter would you draft if you were in Taylor's position? None of the letters would help Radford much in a court proceeding, but an Opinion Letter or a letter such as that listed above as option (c) might help the company in negotiations with the regulatory agency (as evidence of a good faith mistake) if the company tried to convince the FDA not to sanction the company. What are the implications of preparing a draft to be worked out with the client? Is this ever proper?

4. Another troublesome issue raised by this case is what an attorney should do if she thinks that what her client wants to do is illegal but also thinks that the client is not likely to get caught. A particularly difficult variation of this issue is how candid an attorney should be when a client asks her concerning the likelihood of being discovered or the probability of various fines and penalties. Do you agree with the way Mr. Hadley handled the question? What else could he have done? How much does your response turn on the possible harmful consequences to others of the apparently proscribed conduct?

5. Obviously, Taylor doesn't agree with Mr. Hadley's response to Mr. Malone regarding the problem. As a junior attorney in a law firm, what are her options? What would you do in such a situation? How would your responses to the previous questions affect your decision (i.e., your perspective as to how harmful the consequences to consumers might be if doxylamine were not listed on the label, whether the act was illegal, how likely you think it is that the FDA would bring an enforcement action)?

Is it relevant that Taylor's law firm is known as a specialist in the food and drug law field? Does this give her an additional responsibility to avoid signing her name to views about FDA regulatory matters that she does not believe to be her best sense of correct law? Does she have a duty to her law firm to act so as to preserve their reputation as "wise" and "sound" lawyers in this field? If so, was she required to tell the client that this concern would influence her?

At what point would you refuse to work any longer on the case? What if you were a junior attorney in a government agency and disagreed with the way a senior attorney dealt with a matter? For example, suppose that you worked for the FDA and the Chief Counsel (your boss) advised the Commissioner to withdraw the proposed amendment without first considering the results of the just released Harvard School of Public Health study?

The following provisions of the *D.C. Rules of Professional Conduct* (patterned on the ABA's *Model Rules of Professional Conduct*) may offer some relevant guidance in considering these questions:

Rule 1.2(e): A lawyer shall not counsel a client to engage, or assist a client, in conduct that the lawyer knows is criminal or fraudulent, but a lawyer may discuss the legal consequences of any proposed course of conduct with a client and may counsel or assist a client to make a good-faith effort to determine the validity, scope, meaning, or application of the law.

comment 6: The fact that a client uses advice in a course of action that is criminal or fraudulent does not, of itself, make a lawyer a party to the course of action.... There is a critical distinction between presenting an analysis of legal aspects of questionable conduct and recommending the means by which a crime or fraud might be committed with impunity.

Rule 1.6(c): A lawyer may reveal client confidences and secrets, to the extent reasonably necessary: (1) to prevent a criminal act that the lawyer reasonably believes is likely to result in death or substantial bodily harm absent disclosure of the client's secrets or confidences by the lawyer....

comment 17: The lawyer's exercise of discretion in determining whether to make disclosures that are reasonably likely to prevent the death or substantial bodily injury of another requires consideration of such factors as the client's tendency to commit violent acts or, conversely, to make idle threats.... A lawyer's decision not to take preventive action permitted by subparagraph (c)(1) does not violate this Rule.

Rule 2.1: In representing a client, a lawyer shall exercise independent professional judgment and render candid advice. In rendering advice, a lawyer may refer not only to law but to other considerations such as moral, economic, social, and political factors, that may be relevant to the client's situation.

Rule 5.2: (a) A lawyer is bound by the Rules of Professional Conduct notwithstanding that the lawyer acted at the direction of another person. (b) A subordinate lawyer does not violate the Rules of Professional Conduct if that lawyer acts in accordance with a supervisory lawyer's reasonable resolution of an arguable question of professional duty.

comment 2: When lawyers in a supervisor-subordinate relationship encounter a matter involving professional judgment as to ethical duty, the supervisor may assume responsibility for making the judgment. Otherwise a consistent course of action or position could not be taken.

Rule 8.3(a):   A lawyer having knowledge that another lawyer has committed a violation of the Rules of Professional Conduct that raises a substantial question as to that lawyer's honesty, trustworthiness, or fitness as a lawyer in other respects, shall inform the appropriate professional authority.

In addition, consider comment 4 to Rule 1.13: "When constituents of the organization make decisions for it, the decisions ordinarily must be accepted by the lawyer even if their utility or prudence is doubtful.... [W]hen a lawyer knows that the organization may be substantially injured by tortious or illegal conduct by a constituent member of an organization that reasonably might be imputed to the organization ..., it may be reasonably necessary for the lawyer to ask the constituent to reconsider the matter. If that fails, or if the matter is of sufficient seriousness and importance to the organization, it may be reasonably necessary for the lawyer to take steps to have the matter reviewed by a higher authority in the organization." Elaborating on this idea, one scholar offered the following illustration: "A law violation, such as the illegal manufacture of a defective product, that threatens injury to nonclient third parties could still result in injury to the organization because of the threat of suits." Charles W. Wolfram, Modern Legal Ethics 744 (1986); see also id. at 692–710 (discussing the ethical problems that may arise in counseling clients and preparing opinion letters); Geoffrey C. Hazard, Jr., How Far May a Lawyer Go in Assisting a Client in Legally Wrongful Conduct?, 35 U. Miami L. Rev. 669, 682–83 (1981).

Stanton v. Astra Pharmaceutical Products, Inc.

718 F.2d 553 (3d Cir.1983).

■ BECKER, CIRCUIT JUDGE:

* * * Pursuant to [21 U.S.C. § 355(j)(1), a provision that Congress added to the FDCA in 1962 authorizing the FDA to mandate the filing of certain reports], the Secretary promulgated regulations on May 28, 1964. These regulations require companies marketing registered drugs to submit to the FDA annual reports, 21 C.F.R. § 130.35(e) (1971), as well as immediate reports of all unexpected adverse reactions to those drugs, id. § 130.35(f).

Between May 28, 1964, and the end of 1970, Astra received 202 reports of adverse reactions allegedly related to Xylocaine. These reactions ranged from minor, temporary effects to death. Yet Astra forwarded none of these reports to the FDA, relying upon the advice of its counsel, Alan H. Kaplan, that Xylocaine was not a "new drug" and therefore was exempt from the reporting requirements embodied in 21 C.F.R. § 130.35(e) and (f). However, the company prepared the reports and made them a part of the Establishment Inspection Reports seen by non-medical FDA inspectors who came to inspect Astra's facilities between 1964 and 1971.

In deciding not to file the reports ostensibly required by section 130.35, Astra also relied on a letter, dated October 2, 1963, from John F. Palmer, M.D., the Chief of the Department of Health, Education and Welfare's (HEW's) New Drug Status Branch, in which Dr. Palmer advised Astra that two-percent Xylocaine was "not now regarded" by the Division of Drugs as a "new drug" within the meaning of 21 U.S.C. § 321(p). On April 25, 1968, however, Arthur M. West, M.D., Acting Director of HEW's Division of Surgical Dental Drugs and Adjuncts, wrote to Astra and requested that the company file all reports prescribed in regulations promulgated pursuant to 21 U.S.C. § 355(j).

Upon receipt of this letter, Astra wrote back and reminded the FDA of both the 1963 letter from Dr. Palmer and the FDA's announcement on September 12, 1964, postponing the effective date of § 130.35(b)'s reporting requirements, see 29 Fed. Reg. 12,872 (1964). Dr. West responded in July 1969 by referring Astra to a statement published in the *Federal Register* on May 20, 1968, in which the FDA formally had revoked "all opinions previously given by the [FDA] to the effect that an article is 'not a new drug' or is 'no longer a new drug.'" Dr. West further informed Astra that, "since these drugs are presently under review by the National Academy of Sciences–National Research Council, we are deferring any final decision on the new drug status until the findings of the review are published." Thus, Astra knew, or should have known, by May 20, 1968, three and one-half years before [plaintiff] Harrikah Stanton's adverse reaction, that the FDA deemed Xylocaine to be a "new drug" for purposes of compliance with the reporting requirements of 21 U.S.C. § 355(j) and 21 C.F.R. § 130.35.

Despite the above exchanges between Astra and the FDA, Astra contends that 21 U.S.C. § 355(j) and 21 C.F.R. § 130.35(f) apply only to "new drugs" and not to "old drugs" or drugs that are generally recognized by experts as safe and effective; Astra further claims that Xylocaine had achieved such recognition by 1964. * * * [S]ection 130.35 does not admit of the exclusion urged by Astra. Section 130.35 applies to "[e]ach applicant for whom a new-drug application or supplement ... became effective or was approved *at any time* prior to June 20, 1963." 21 C.F.R. § 130.35(a), (b) (emphasis added). This language appears to encompass Xylocaine, which was approved by the FDA in 1948. Moreover, application of section 130.35 to a drug approved in 1948 would seem essential in light of the FDA's statutory obligation continually to monitor drugs already on the market in order to determine whether to withdraw FDA approval pursuant to 21 U.S.C. § 355(e).

Astra relies both on the 1963 letter from the FDA, in which the agency advised Astra that it did not consider Xylocaine to be a new drug, as well as on the FDA's 1964 suspension of the effectiveness of certain regulations pending the resolution of a court challenge. But neither the 1963 letter nor the 1964 suspension can avail Astra. While we concede that Astra initially was entitled to rely on the 1963 letter, the FDA effectively nullified the assertions contained in that letter when it announced in 1968, well before Harrikah Stanton's bone-marrow test in 1971, that "all opinions previously given by the [FDA] to the effect that an article is 'not a new drug' or is 'no longer a new drug' are hereby revoked," 33 Fed. Reg. 7758 (1968). And as for the 1964 suspension: that declaration stayed the enforcement of only 21 C.F.R. § 130.35(b), without any mention of subsections 130.35(e) and (f). * * * Thus, at least as of 1968, Astra knew, or should have known, that the FDA expected Astra to file the reports prescribed by section 130.35.

Second, the mere fact that Astra's attorneys interpreted section 130.35 incorrectly does not negate Astra's negligence in failing to comply with the regulations. Astra took a chance, and it is liable for the consequences of its acts. And even assuming that advice of counsel does constitute a legally cognizable excuse, that excuse could insulate Astra from liability only between the time that the FDA promulgated the regulations in 1964 and the time that the agency revoked all private letter-rulings as to new-drug status in 1968. Astra still had three and one-half years before the December 1971 tragedy to file the reports. * * *

Florida Breckenridge, Inc. v. Solvay Pharmaceuticals

174 F.3d 1227 (11th Cir.1999).*

■ Per curiam:

* * * In 1962, the FDCA was amended to require proof that the product was effective as well as safe. Congress made this new efficacy requirement retroactive to apply to all drugs that already had approved NDAs based on safety. The companies producing these drugs were given a two year window to submit revisions of their NDAs to prove their efficacy. In order to facilitate the efficacy evaluations of these drugs, the FDA set up the Drug Efficacy Study Implementation (DESI) program. Under this program, groups of drugs with approved NDAs were evaluated by an independent panel. If the panel found that the drugs met a certain standard for efficacy, the evidence was submitted to the FDA. If the FDA concurred with the DESI determination, a notice was published in the *Federal Register* and a supplemental NDA would be approved for these drugs. Under the FDCA, all drugs are new drugs and therefore require an approved NDA or ANDA before marketing unless they are generally recognized among experts as safe and effective for their labeled use (the "GRASE" exception) or are grandfathered.

By its terms, the DESI program applied only to drugs that already had approved NDAs as of 1962. In conjunction with the DESI program, the FDA developed a policy whereby drugs that were identical, similar or related ("ISR drugs") to an approved drug in the DESI review program

---

* The opinion, which was published in the advance sheets of the Federal Reporter, was withdrawn from the bound volume at the request of the court.

could "piggy-back" off of the DESI review by submitting an ANDA after the DESI review established the efficacy of the pioneer drug. For a time, FDA policy allowed a drug manufacturer to market an ISR drug after filing, but before approval of an ISR drug's ANDA. This policy was challenged in court and overturned in 1975. Hoffmann–LaRoche, Inc. v. Weinberger, 425 F.Supp. 890, 894 (D.D.C.1975) ("[T]he Court holds that the FDA's policy of permitting new drugs to be marketed without an approved new drug application contravenes the clear statutory requirement of preclearance mandated by 21 U.S.C. § 355."). In response to this case, the FDA published a revision to its policy guidelines that "clarified" the agency's position. CPG 7132c.02, which Breckenridge submitted as an appendix to its brief, reads in part:

> The agency has decided to reaffirm that all products marketed as drugs under the DESI program are new drugs, and therefore, require an approved NDA or ANDA for marketing. In view of the reaffirmation of this policy, the agency must proceed to remove from the market all current DESI-effective prescription products that are not subjects of approved NDAs or ANDAs, and to prevent in the future the marketing of such unapproved products.

FDA Compliance Policy Guidelines § 440.100. This policy guideline document goes on to create priorities for the removal of unapproved drugs from the market. According to the FDA, there were so many unapproved drugs on the market that they needed to establish a triage system: "Considering the magnitude of the problem, the limitation on FDA's resources, and the resulting long time period before compliance can be fully attained, the agency has developed a strategy to handle unapproved products on a priority basis." Id. In stunning testament to the efficiency of the FDA's strategy, this policy is still in effect today because twenty-four years later, and thirty-six years after the 1962 amendments to the FDCA, there are still thousands of these unapproved drugs on the market. One of these drugs is Estratest, produced by Solvay.

Although the record contains conflicting dates, Solvay began marketing its Estratest drug in 1964 at the earliest. Estratest is a hormone supplement, consisting of esterified estrogens and methyltestosterone, that is widely prescribed to women who are suffering from the physical symptoms associated with menopause and who do not obtain relief from estrogen therapy alone. At the time of Estratest's entry into the marketplace, Solvay did not have, nor has it ever had over the past thirty-five years, an NDA or ANDA approved by the FDA. Obviously, Estratest could not have been directly subject to DESI review because it was not marketed, nor was it the subject of an approved NDA based on its safety, before the 1962 amendments to the FDCA became effective.

As part of the DESI process, a study evaluated the efficacy of a class of drugs that combined estrogens and androgens. The drugs under review all had approved NDAs from before 1962. None of these drugs contained Estratest's combination of esterified estrogens and methyltestosterone. The drugs were evaluated in a published notice, DESI 7661. On November 22,

1972, as noted in the correspondence log submitted by Solvay in their reply brief, Solvay's predecessor corporation contacted the FDA to determine whether Estratest could be considered ISR under the DESI 7661 notice. After an undescribed response from the FDA, there is a gap in the log until a letter from the FDA in July of 1979, which indicates that the FDA notified Solvay that Estratest was under legal review and that temporarily no action relating to the NDA requirement would be taken but that any continued marketing of Estratest was at Solvay's risk. Since that time and to this date, Solvay, while continuing to market Estratest, has been trying to get approval of NDAs for Estratest, but has gotten a series of not-approvable letters.

In the spring of 1997, Breckenridge introduced a drug, Menogen, into the marketplace. This drug contained esterified estrogens and methyltestosterone in the same dosages as Estratest and was marketed as the generic equivalent of Estratest. Breckenridge did not obtain approval of an NDA or ANDA before marketing Menogen, and has not obtained approval to this date. Breckenridge relies on Solvay's contention that Estratest is legally on the market without approval to extend also to Menogen. Shortly after Breckenridge began marketing Menogen, they received notification from Solvay that they believed Menogen infringed on Estratest's trade dress and that the generic equivalency claims constituted false advertising. In response, Breckenridge filed this suit for a declaratory judgment that their marketing of Menogen did not infringe the Estratest trade dress or constitute false advertising under the Lanham Act. Solvay counterclaimed, asserting claims for trade dress infringement and false advertising under the Lanham Act, the Florida Deceptive and Unfair Trade Practices Act and common law unfair competition law.

After discovery, both parties moved for summary judgment. The district court granted summary judgment for Breckenridge. On the trade dress infringement claim, the court held that no reasonable fact-finder could find a likelihood of confusion as to source between Estratest and Menogen. On the false advertising claim, the court held that because both parties were allowed on the market without FDA approval, the false advertising analysis was not governed by the FDA regulations regarding generic drugs and that in this world of non-regulated pharmaceuticals, a lower standard of equivalence was sufficient to render Breckenridge's claims literally true.

Solvay appealed the summary judgment to this court, arguing that the district court erred in its likelihood of confusion analysis and that drugs allowed on the market without FDA approval should still be subject to the FDA equivalency standards for advertised claims of generic equivalency. After Solvay filed its initial brief, the Department of Justice and the FDA filed an amicus curiae brief to address what they perceived as errors in the district court's opinion regarding the regulatory status of Estratest and Menogen and the resulting use of a different equivalency standard for generic drugs than is specified in the FDCA and FDA regulations. The government pointed out that the FDA's position is that neither drug is lawfully on the market because both require an approved NDA or ANDA before they may be legally sold, raising the point that unclean hands might bar either party from benefitting from trade law protection. The government did not explain why the FDA failed, for well over thirty years, to enforce the law and remove Estratest from the market. In response to the government's brief, both Solvay and Breckenridge harshly criticized the government for not reading the record, claiming that neither party ever told the court that they weren't subject to FDA regulation. Both parties continued to maintain, however, that although regulated they were not subject to FDA approval.

At oral argument, both parties continued to assert that they were lawfully on the market, although they could not articulate consistent or specific reasons why. They claimed to be surprised by the issue, claiming that it was never raised before the district court. At the end of oral argument, both parties agreed to submit supplemental briefs on the issue of whether protection was available under the Lanham Act for drugs sold in violation of the FDCA. Instead, two days before their supplemental brief was due, Solvay filed this motion to dismiss their appeal with prejudice. Breckenridge responded by requesting sanctions for a frivolous appeal pursuant to Fed. R. App. P. 38, and in the process executed a head-snapping reversal of position regarding Solvay's representations to the district court about Estratest's regulatory status. They did not, however, oppose Solvay's motion to dismiss.

It seems obvious to this court that this last-moment motion to dismiss, after the completion of oral arguments and without a settlement agreement, resulted from Solvay's realization that it was caught misrepresenting Estratest's regulatory status and wishes to avoid a published opinion that would alert the world to its misdeeds. This case comes right up to the line where the interests of justice would require us to deny Solvay's motion. Especially in light of the fact that the motion is unopposed, we will grant it. In our supervisory capacity, however, we feel that we must review the attorneys' conduct before this court and the district court and determine whether a disciplinary referral is appropriate.[2] Careful review of the record has uncovered a pattern of conduct by both parties' attorneys designed to

---

2. Although this order focuses on the conduct of the attorneys for Solvay and Breckenridge, we note that the FDA is also due a share of criticism. It is incomprehensible that Estratest has been allowed on the market without approval for thirty-five years. It seems reasonable that most patients undergoing treatment for menopause fairly assume that any medication freely available and prescribed by their doctor has been proven safe and effective to the satisfaction of the FDA. They have a right to expect that the laws, as passed by Congress to protect them, are being enforced. To this date, Estratest has failed to satisfy the FDA that it is safe or effective as required by the FDCA, and yet the FDA has taken no action to remove the drug from the market. We are accustomed to hearing arguments in situations like this bemoaning scarce governmental resources and the like, but there can be no good excuse for allowing a company to violate the law for thirty-five years. If the drug is not safe or effective enough to be approved, thirty-five years seems like sufficient time to get around to taking some action. Certainly, Solvay was on notice that they were violating the law, and the FDA's inaction in no way excuses Solvay's conduct, but neither does Solvay's notice excuse the FDA's inaction.

mislead and confuse the court regarding the regulatory status of Estratest and Menogen. Unfortunately, we must remind these attorneys that they are officers of the court. As such, they "owe duties of complete candor and primary loyalty to the court before which they practice." These duties are never subservient to a lawyer's duty to advocate zealously for his or her client. In this case, the attorneys for both parties have frustrated the system of justice, which depends on their candor and loyalty to the court, because they wanted to avoid an unpleasant truth about their clients' conduct. "In short, they have sold out to the client."

Normally, this sort of conduct is caught before it can do much harm by the adversarial nature of our system of justice. In this case, however, the adversarial parties both had an interest in hiding the fact that they needed FDA approval from the court. In Solvay's case, admitting that Estratest was not legally on the market would be fatal to their claims because the Lanham Act only protects parties engaged in lawful commerce. * * * Likewise, Breckenridge had an interest in hiding the FDCA violations from the court. Since this litigation began, the FDA has taken action against Breckenridge for, among other things, marketing Menogen without FDA approval.[4] Naturally, they would like to avoid making any admissions in this case. Furthermore, Breckenridge based its entire defense to the false advertising claim on the theory that there is a segment of the pharmaceutical market that is not subject to FDA approval, and that these drugs should be subject to a less stringent equivalency standard for the purposes of advertising generic equivalency. This theory is entirely dependent on misleading the court into believing that neither Estratest nor Menogen require FDA approval.

As discussed above, we believe that there is no magical exception that allows Solvay or Breckenridge to opt out of the FDA approval process. As the government's brief points out, both Estratest and Menogen are "new drugs" under the FDCA and require approved NDAs or ANDAs before they may be lawfully marketed. Because both parties had incentives to avoid addressing this threshold issue, the attorneys on both sides actively attempted to mislead and confuse the district court and this court regarding the regulatory status of both drugs. * * *

On several separate occasions, [District] Judge Ryskamp inquired about why neither drug needed FDA approval. When confronted with these questions, the attorneys either changed the subject without answering or gave a vague explanation claiming that for historical reasons the drugs were either not subject to FDA regulation or did not require FDA approval. * * * The attorneys effectively misled Judge Ryskamp into believing that Estratest's legal status had been established under a grandfather provision

---

4. Once again, we are baffled as to why the FDA decided to go after the generic manufacturer, which had been marketing the drug for approximately one year, while ignoring Solvay's violations, which had been ongoing for thirty-five years. If we understand the government's argument, Breckenridge had violated other provisions of the FDCA, which made the enforcement action more urgent. Nonetheless, this seems insufficient to explain an enforcement differential of thirty-four years.

that caused them not to be regulated by the FDA. As previously discussed, there is no possibly valid legal argument that would make this characterization true. Both parties admit that they are not subject to the grandfather provisions of the FDCA, and both drugs were introduced after the 1962 amendments. The judge clearly relied on the attorney's representations, and, in fact, based his decision on the false advertising claims on these misrepresentations.

In their briefs, the parties continued to make the general assertion that they were allowed on the market without approval. After the government filed its amicus brief, pointing out that both products were marketed unlawfully and that the attorneys had misrepresented the drugs' regulatory status, both parties responded by misrepresenting their own conduct at the trial level. Breckenridge accused the government of not reading any portion of the record below and of fabricating its charge, claiming that neither party ever represented to the court that the drugs were not subject to FDA regulation: "[N]either Solvay nor Breckenridge ever referred to Menogen or Estratest as 'unregulated.' " Solvay then jumped on the government-bashing bandwagon, claiming that "neither party made any such representation," and claiming to be "perplexed by the district court's statement that the drugs were not 'regulated' by the FDA." These assertions are outrageous. As quoted above, Mr. Jameson [counsel for Solvay] specifically told the court on two occasions that the drugs were "not subject to FDA regulation." Such mischaracterizations of the record are particularly egregious, considering that both attorneys made them while accusing the government of lying about the record.

At oral argument, the misconduct continued. Jameson first argued that Estratest was lawfully on the market as a direct result of the DESI review process. Jameson's statements give the impression that Estratest, itself, was subject to DESI review. It was not. As discussed above, Estratest was not even on the market in 1962, nor did it ever have an approved NDA. Further, his description of the purpose of DESI as being to examine drugs on the marketplace to see if they should remain on the marketplace is very misleading. The purpose was to examine drugs already approved as safe by the FDA, and to help drug companies provide the FDA with an evaluation of their efficacy. Estratest has never, to this date, been approved by the FDA as safe or effective. Jameson further misled the court by characterizing the DESI process as an "alternative to the 'formal' approval process." In fact, there are no alternatives to the "formal" approval process for DESI or ISR drugs. All DESI and ISR drugs are "new drugs" under the FDCA and require approval of an NDA or ANDA before lawful marketing. DESI never operates as an alternative to such approval. The falsity of this characterization is further proved by the fact that, subsequent to the publication of the DESI 7661 notice, Solvay filed an ANDA in an attempt to get approval and was warned by the FDA that marketing of the drug was at Solvay's risk. Jameson knew this—the information is all in papers that he appended to his reply brief as evidence that FDA knew that Estratest was on the market.

After realizing that this court would not be so easily bamboozled, Jameson attempted to refine his argument, arguing that the DESI review somehow operated as conclusive proof that Estratest falls under an exception under the FDCA known as the GRASE exception. Because we dismiss this appeal, we are precluded from ruling definitively on this claim. However, our review of the law, at this stage, points to the conclusion that it is wholly without merit. If a drug is generally recognized among qualified experts as safe and effective, it is not a new drug under the FDCA and therefore does not need an NDA. However, GRASE is a term of art, and the Supreme Court has explained that it really is not much of an exception because it requires at least the same exacting proof that NDA approval requires. Furthermore, GRASE cannot be construed to provide a way to evade the regulatory process by allowing a firm that has repeatedly failed to gain approval of an existing NDA to opt out of the approval process. Consequently, it would appear that Estratest cannot satisfy the GRASE exception.

Finally, Jameson argued that the FDA's failure to take action to remove them from the market proves that they are GRASE. Obviously, this is nonsense. Courts have already held that the FDA policy of deferring the removal of ISR drugs from the marketplace is not a defense, even to criminal prosecution for marketing a new drug without an approved NDA. In order to fall under the GRASE exception, a drug must meet requirements at least as stringent as those for NDA approval. Solvay has continually failed to obtain approval based on the evidence it has provided the FDA. They may not, then, circumvent the approval process merely by marketing their drug in defiance of the FDA for thirty-five years. Solvay has been attempting to get approval of its ANDA/NDA for 27 years, and has gotten a continual stream of not-approvable letters. The very fact that they are seeking approval indicates that they do not honestly believe that they fall under the GRASE exception. Furthermore, the exception cannot be used to succeed where the FDA screening process has specifically denied approval. This would pervert the statute, as the Supreme Court noted. Finally, even if Estratest could be said to now, in 1999, to have gained GRASE status, that status would not retroactively render the past thirty-five years of illegal marketing lawful. * * *

During the course of this litigation, Mr. Jameson and Ms. Allison * * * engaged in a pattern of practice designed to mislead and confuse the court regarding the regulatory status of their clients' drugs. Although we grant the unopposed motion, we are referring this matter to the disciplinary committee of this court for further consideration.

NOTES AND QUESTIONS

1. *Candor to the tribunal.* The *Solvay* court expressed outrage at the conduct of the lawyers during litigation. Do you think that they actually comprehended the byzantine FDA regulatory history? Did they have an

obligation to seek counsel from lawyers who specialize in the area and better understand these complexities?

2.   *Questionable regulatory advice?* The *Stanton* court, by contrast, dealt with a problem that arose from poor regulatory advice given to a company by a lawyer who specialized in FDA matters (one of the authors of this casebook previously worked for him, though many years after the *Stanton* case). Apart from the possibility that the company risked agency sanctions for its failure to comply (and also a negligence per se charge in a tort action), does the lawyer violate ethical norms? Consider the following excerpt:

> Attorneys representing clients before agencies are subject to the same ethical obligations that govern their conduct before courts. In most jurisdictions, these include duties of candor to the tribunal, with correlative prohibitions against unnecessary delays or harassment of other parties. Rule 3.1 of the ABA's Model Rules of Professional Conduct directs that "a lawyer shall not bring or defend a proceeding, or assert or controvert an issue therein, unless there is a basis for doing so that is not frivolous." In addition, under the Model Code of Professional Responsibility "a lawyer shall not ... delay a trial ... when he knows or when it is obvious that such action would serve merely to harass or maliciously injure another." Although these rules are framed in terms of conduct during the course of litigation before courts, they have equal application to adjudicatory proceedings before agencies.

> Attorneys enjoy somewhat greater latitude in administrative proceedings that are not regarded as adjudicatory. Rule 3.9 of the Model Rules directs advocates in nonadjudicative proceedings before agencies to conform to the duties regarding candor to the tribunal, fairness to the opposing party and counsel, and the impartiality and decorum of the tribunal. Notably missing from Rule 3.9, however, are cross-references to Rules 3.1 and 3.2, which respectively proscribe frivolous claims and other conduct designed to delay or harass. Nonetheless, Rule 3.9 does not countenance conduct by lawyers in nonadjudicative proceedings that would be regarded as objectionable in adjudicative proceedings. As explained in the accompanying Comment, agencies "should be able to rely on the integrity of submissions made to it."

> Although the precise contours of these ethical duties may vary depending on whether the agency proceeding is considered adjudicative or legislative, an attorney generally is expected to act no differently than he or she would act when representing a client in court. In practice, however, these rules of professional responsibility may be viewed as somewhat less stringent in the administrative context than in the judicial.... In fact, some have suggested that Rule 3.9 might apply only to conduct during trial-type hearings in nonadjudicative proceedings before agencies, an interpretation that would leave a large class of regulatory submissions prepared by attorneys wholly exempt from the rules of professional responsibility. Other commentators have

argued that conduct during informal, nonadjudicative proceedings should be governed by stricter rather than lesser ethical standards precisely because of the absence of any opportunity for testing through an adversarial presentation of evidence and arguments. . . .

Finally, it must be remembered that the rules of professional responsibility only set the outer boundaries for ethical behavior where transgressions may trigger severe disciplinary sanctions. In recognition of this limitation, courts have chosen to establish more demanding rules of conduct designed to preserve the integrity of the litigation process, most notably Rule 11. A similar approach may be necessary in the agency context.

Lars Noah, Sham Petitioning as a Threat to the Integrity of the Regulatory Process, 74 N.C. L. Rev. 1, 49–53 (1995). Citing this article, the FDA proposed revising its citizen petition procedures to, among other things, strengthen existing certification requirements. See 64 Fed. Reg. 66,822 (1999) (to be codified at 21 C.F.R. § 10.30(b)); see also Ubiotica Corp. v. FDA, 427 F.2d 376, 382 (6th Cir.1970) (stating that counsel was properly excluded from further participation in an agency hearing for conduct deemed "dilatory, recalcitrant, obstructive of orderly process, and contemptuous").

CHAPTER 4

DISSEMINATION OF PRODUCT INFORMATION

The FDA comprehensively regulates product composition as well as product information, and it controls the latter both directly—by imposing limitations on permissible labeling and advertising—and indirectly—by subjecting products to more stringent controls based on the intended uses reflected in the product information. It's hardly the only federal agency that regulates by controlling information (just think of the Securities and Exchange Commission), and it's hardly a recent development (the FDA's misbranding authority goes back almost a century). This chapter discusses the reach of the agency's statutory power over the labeling and advertising of therapeutic products, directed to both physicians and patients, and then it considers the effect of constitutional limitations on the FDA's ability to exercise that authority.

A. LABELING

Kordel v. United States

335 U.S. 345 (1948).

■ DOUGLAS, JUSTICE:

* * * Kordel writes and lectures on health foods from information derived from studies in public and private libraries. Since 1941 he has been marketing his own health food products, which appear to be compounds of various vitamins, minerals and herbs. The alleged misbranding consists of statements in circulars or pamphlets distributed to consumers by the vendors of the products, relating to their efficacy. The petitioner supplies these pamphlets as well as the products to the vendors. Some of the literature was displayed in stores in which the petitioner's products were on sale. Some of it was given away with the sale of products; some sold independently of the drugs; and some mailed to customers by the vendors.

It is undisputed that petitioner shipped or caused to be shipped in interstate commerce both the drugs and the literature. Seven of the counts charged that the drugs and literature were shipped in the same cartons. The literature involved in the other counts was shipped separately from the drugs and at different times—both before and after the shipments of the drugs with which they were associated. The question whether the separate shipment of the literature saved the drugs from being misbranded within the meaning of the Act presents the main issue in the case.

Section 301(a) of the [FDCA] prohibits the introduction into interstate commerce of any drug that is adulterated or misbranded. It is misbranded according to § 502(a) if its "labeling is false or misleading in any particular" and unless the labeling bears "adequate directions for use." § 502(f). The term labeling is defined in § 201(m) to mean "all labels and other written, printed, or graphic matter (1) upon any article or any of its containers or wrappers, or (2) accompanying such article." Section 303 makes the violation of any of the provisions of § 301 a crime.

In this case the drugs and the literature had a common origin and a common destination. The literature was used in the sale of the drugs. It explained their uses. Nowhere else was the purchaser advised how to use them. It constituted an essential supplement to the label attached to the package. Thus the products and the literature were interdependent, as the court of appeals observed.

It would take an extremely narrow reading of the Act to hold that these drugs were not misbranded. A criminal law is not to be read expansively to include what is not plainly embraced within the language of the statute, since the purpose fairly to apprise men of the boundaries of the prohibited action would then be defeated. But there is no canon against using common sense in reading a criminal law, so that strained and technical constructions do not defeat its purpose by creating exceptions from or loopholes in it.

It would, indeed, create an obviously wide loophole to hold that these drugs would be misbranded if the literature had been shipped in the same container but not misbranded if the literature left in the next or in the preceding mail. The high purpose of the Act to protect consumers who under present conditions are largely unable to protect themselves in this field would then be easily defeated. The administrative agency charged with its enforcement has not given the Act any such restricted construction. The textual structure of the Act is not agreeable to it. Accordingly, we conclude that the phrase "accompanying such article" is not restricted to labels that are on or in the article or package that is transported.

The first clause of § 201(m)—all labels "upon any article or any of its containers or wrappers"—clearly embraces advertising or descriptive matter that goes with the package in which the articles are transported. The second clause—"accompanying such article"—has no specific reference to packages, containers or their contents as did a predecessor statute. It plainly includes what is contained within the package whether or not it is "upon" the article or its wrapper or container. But the second clause does not say "accompanying such article in the package or container," and we see no reason for reading the additional words into the text.

One article or thing is accompanied by another when it supplements or explains it, in the manner that a committee report of the Congress accompanies a bill. No physical attachment one to the other is necessary. It is the textual relationship that is significant. The analogy to the present case is obvious. We need not labor the point.

The false and misleading literature in the present case was designed for use in the distribution and sale of the drug, and it was so used. The fact that it went in a different mail was wholly irrelevant whether we judge the transaction by purpose or result. And to say that the prior or subsequent shipment of the literature disproves that it "is" misbranded when introduced into commerce within the meaning of § 301(a), is to overlook the integrated nature of the transactions established in this case. Moreover, the fact that some of the booklets carried a selling price is immaterial on the facts shown here. * * * [T]he booklets and drugs were nonetheless interdependent; they were parts of an integrated distribution program. The Act cannot be circumvented by the easy device of a "sale" of the advertising matter where the advertising performs the function of labeling.

Petitioner points out that in the evolution of the Act the ban on false advertising was eliminated, the control over it being transferred to the Federal Trade Commission. We have searched the legislative history in vain, however, to find any indication that Congress had the purpose to eliminate from the Act advertising which performs the function of labeling. Every labeling is in a sense an advertisement. The advertising which we have here performs the same function as it would if it were on the article or on the containers or wrappers. As we have said, physical attachment or contiguity is unnecessary under § 201(m)(2). * * *

United States v. Urbuteit

335 U.S. 355 (1948).

■ Douglas, Justice:

* * * Respondent Urbuteit terms himself a naturopathic physician and conducts the Sinuothermic Institute in Tampa, Florida. The machines against which the libel was filed are electrical devices allegedly aiding in the diagnosis and cure of various diseases and physical disorders such as cancer, diabetes, tuberculosis, arthritis, and paralysis. The alleged cures effected through its use are described in the allegedly false and misleading leaflet, "The Road to Health," published by Urbuteit and distributed for use with the machines.

Urbuteit shipped from Florida a number of these machines to one Kelsch, a former pupil of his who lives in Ohio. Kelsch used these machines in treating his patients and, though he did not receive them as a merchant, he sold some to patients. As part of this transaction Urbuteit contracted to furnish Kelsch with a supply of leaflets, which were sent from Florida to Ohio at a different time than when the machines were forwarded. Kelsch used the leaflets to explain the machines to his patients.

The leaflets seem to have followed the shipment of the machines. But as *Kordel v. United States* holds, that is immaterial where the advertising matter that was sent was designed to serve and did in fact serve the purposes of labeling. This machine bore only the words, U.S. Patent Sinuothermic Trade Mark. It was the leaflets that explained the usefulness of the device in the diagnosis, treatment, and cure of various diseases. Measured by functional standards, as § 201(m)(2) of the Act permits, these leaflets constituted one of the types of labeling which the Act condemns.

The power to condemn is contained in § 304(a) and is confined to articles "adulterated or misbranded when introduced into or while in interstate commerce." We do not, however, read that provision as requiring the advertising matter to travel with the machine. The reasons of policy which argue against that in the case of criminal prosecutions under § 303 are equally forcible when we come to libels under § 304(a). Moreover, the common sense of the matter is to view the interstate transaction in its entirety—the purpose of the advertising and its actual use. In this case it is plain to us that the movements of machines and leaflets in interstate commerce were a single interrelated activity, not separate or isolated ones. The Act is not concerned with the purification of the stream of commerce in the abstract. The problem is a practical one of consumer protection, not dialectics. The fact that the false literature leaves in a separate mail does not save the article from being misbranded. Where by functional standards the two transactions are integrated, the requirements of § 304(a) are satisfied, though the mailings or shipments are at different times. * * *

NOTES AND QUESTIONS

1. *Common origin.* The manufacturer need not also have authored the written material for it to qualify as labeling if used in connection with the sale of a product. See United States v. Diapulse Mfg. Corp., 389 F.2d 612 (2d Cir.1968) (holding that reprints of medical articles distributed with a device qualified as labeling); United States v. Vital Health Prods. Ltd., 786 F.Supp. 761 (E.D.Wis.1992) (same for newsletters published by third parties distributed with a product), aff'd mem., 985 F.2d 563 (7th Cir.1993). Where the written material is not so used, however, courts have rebuffed FDA claims that the mere placement at retail of a product near a book turns the latter into product labeling. See United States v. Article of Drug for Veterinary Use, 50 F.3d 497 (8th Cir.1995); United States v. 24 Bottles "Sterling Vinegar & Honey," Etc., 338 F.2d 157 (2d Cir.1964).

2. *Prescription drugs.* Product information for prescription drugs rarely accompanies the product itself. Although physicians do not purchase prescription drugs for their patients, they do control the decision to use a particular drug. The physician acts as a proxy for the purchaser, and the FDA has classified any product-related literature given to physicians as labeling. See 21 C.F.R. § 202.1(*l*)(2). In fact, the agency has proposed eliminating some of the information that currently must appear on the package label itself in order to minimize overcrowding and reduce the risk of mix ups by pharmacists. See 65 Fed. Reg. 81,082, 81,099–100 (2000).

3. *What's in a name?* The FDCA requires that labeling include the "established name" immediately after the brand name. See 21 U.S.C.

§ 352(e)(2); see also Abbott Labs. v. Gardner, 387 U.S. 136, 138 (1967) ("The underlying purpose of the 1962 amendment was to bring to the attention of doctors and patients the fact that many of the drugs sold under familiar trade names are actually identical to drugs sold under their 'established' or less familiar trade names at significantly lower prices."). Reacting to recent concerns about prescribing errors that result from confusingly similar brand names, the FDA has begun to consider drug nomenclature issues when approving a new drug. See Tracy–Gene G. Durkin & Julie D. Shirk, Drug Name Dilemma: A Pharmaceutical Trademark Must Pass Muster with FDA for Safety As Well As with PTO, Nat'l L.J., May 14, 2001, at C1; see also Danielle A. Gentin, You Say Zantac, I Say Xanax: A Critique of Drug Trademark Approval and Proposals for Reform, 55 Food & Drug L.J. 255 (2000). The agency also has proposed requiring the use of bar codes on the labels of prescription drugs administered in hospital settings.

4. *Misbranding authority*. As discussed in Chapter 1(C), the FDCA enumerates a series of conditions that could cause products to be misbranded. For example, a drug or medical device is deemed to be misbranded unless its labeling bears "such adequate warnings against use in those pathological conditions or by children where its use may be dangerous to health, or against unsafe dosage or methods or duration of administration or application, in such manner and form, as are necessary for the protection of users." 21 U.S.C. § 352(f)(2).

United States v. Article of Drug . . . Decholin

264 F.Supp. 473 (E.D.Mich.1967).

■ Freeman, District Judge:

* * * The only substantive provision of concern is Federal Food, Drug and Cosmetic Act, § 503, as amended, 21 U.S.C. § 353, reading in pertinent part:

(b)(1) A drug intended for use by man which . . .

(B) because of its toxicity or other potentiality for harmful effect, or the method of its use, or the collateral measures necessary to its use, is not safe for use except under the supervision of a practitioner licensed by law to administer such drug . . .

(C) . . . shall be dispensed only (i) upon a written prescription of a practitioner licensed by law to administer such drug, or (ii) upon an oral prescription of such practitioner which is reduced promptly to writing and filed by the pharmacist, or (iii) by refilling any such written or oral prescription if such refilling is authorized by the prescriber either in the original prescription or by oral order which is reduced promptly to writing and filed by the pharmacist. . . .

(4) A drug which is subject to paragraph (1) of this subsection shall be deemed to be misbranded if at any time prior to dispensing its label fails to bear the statement "Caution: Federal law prohibits

dispensing without prescription." A drug to which paragraph (1) of this subsection does not apply shall be deemed to be misbranded if at any time prior to dispensing its label bears the caution statement quoted in the preceding sentence.*

It is agreed that Decholin is a drug within the meaning of the Act and that the seized tablets had moved in interstate commerce. It is also undisputed that the labels on the libeled packages give no indication that Decholin may not lawfully be dispensed without prescription. The precise legal consideration raised by these motions is whether amended section 503 causes Decholin to be misbranded because its containers fail to carry such a precautionary statement. * * *

There is only one fundamental issue presented by these motions: is Decholin unsafe as a drug intended for human use without a prescription? Nevertheless, recognizing that in section 503(b)(1)(B) Congress listed a number of ostensibly different reasons why a drug may be unsafe for self-medication and attempting to deal with the parties' arguments in an organized fashion, the motions will be viewed as raising two issues. First, is the pharmacological effect of Decholin such that, unless it is taken pursuant to and in accordance with a physician's directions, reactions sufficient to cause the product to be unsafe may result from its ingestion? This will be called the "toxicity question." Second, does the fact that Decholin may be taken by a person who, although experiencing the indications set out on the label, has an ailment which Decholin cannot cure, coupled with the fact such an individual may postpone a visit to his physician in reliance upon the over-the-counter availability of Decholin, cause the drug to be unsafe? Because the gist of the Government's argument on this issue is that an immediate professional diagnosis to detect the underlying cause of the symptoms in a particular case is a step which must precede or accompany use in order for the drug to be considered safe, this point will be called the "collateral measures question." Unfortunately, some of the subissues and contentions underlying each of these two topics are so similar that the effort to pinpoint two distinct inquiries will not be totally successful.

At the basis of both questions lies the fact that the indications mentioned on the Decholin container can stem from any one of what, for present purposes, will be considered as three types of causes: biliary tract obstruction, organic disease and various minor factors. These last include a host of elements ranging from pregnancy through dietary indiscretions, such as skipping meals, and on to old age. Claimant willingly agrees with the Government that Decholin would not be prescribed by a physician to cure either a tract obstruction or an organic disease.

Toxicity Question

If the record showed clearly why a practitioner would not order Decholin for a person suffering from an obstruction or an organic disease,

---

* In 1997, Congress amended this provision to replace the cautionary statement with a simple "Rx only" label designation. See 21 U.S.C. § 353(b)(4)(A).

the toxicity question could be in a better posture for summary disposition. However, the affidavits of the experts suggest different reasons which may be grounded upon conflicting views on a factual issue, the pharmacological effect of the drug. The statements of claimant's authorities suggest that they would not prescribe Decholin in the presence of one of these major ailments primarily, if not exclusively, just because the drug would do no good for the patient. However, these experts are quick to point out that they have never heard of an instance in which a person with either an obstruction or an organic disease sustained any ill effect from self-medication with Decholin; and at least several of them doubt that harm would ever come to an individual who takes the drug under these circumstances. Therefore, Ames [the manufacturer appearing as the claimant] would consider Decholin safe for unrestricted distribution. * * *

There remain the opposing contentions why a practitioner would not recommend Decholin in some cases, and beneath these antagonistic positions lies another and more subtle conflict which has great significance with regard to the proper interpretation of section 503(b)(1)(B). Although this dispute is not formally expressed in the record, a critical study of the affidavits leaves little doubt that it is nonetheless real. Broadly speaking, it could be said to center around the issue whether a drug's potentiality for causing harm if taken without prescription should be considered from a theoretical or a practical viewpoint.

Even the Government's most helpful spokesman, Dr. Sklar, did not mention that he knew or had heard of a case in which Decholin or any article of similar composition had done harm in any perceptible degree to a layman who had taken the preparation, without consulting a physician, upon experiencing the indications listed on the Decholin label. This is not surprising since the Government admitted in answer to interrogatories that it knew of no actual cases of harm attributable to the product. On the other hand, statements made by three of claimant's experts leave the strong impression that the principal reason why they would consider Decholin safe for self-medication is the fact that their experiences have taught them that a person suffering from an organic disease or a biliary tract obstruction will feel so ill that, as a matter of course, he will seek professional help. Therefore, claimant's experts do not seem to be so much of the opinion that home treatment with Decholin cannot cause harm as they do of the view that it will not; whereas the Government's affiants stress that Decholin could cause harm to the uninformed lay user, while the Government itself all but concedes that if future unadvised laymen act as their predecessors have, the drug will not be responsible for any serious consequences. * * *

The legislative history of the 1951 amendment, which gave birth to section 503(b)(1)(B), shows that Congress did not desire to proscribe self-medication with a product just because under some set of circumstances— and especially hypothetical conditions—the drug may be harmful if taken without professional supervision. * * * In fact, throughout the entire House debate runs the theme that "common household remedies" were not meant to be taken off the over-the-counter market * * * articles which most physicians would consider perfectly harmless when taken in the normal course of events by a person with a modicum of common sense. Nevertheless, it is hard to imagine that under no circumstances could any of these drugs do serious harm to an individual who does not appreciate the nature of the cause which lies at the root of his symptoms. * * *

If, in attempting to evaluate a drug, a court were to consider every contingency and take account of the immaturity or stupidity of every potential user, it would not be paying heed to the [Senate] Committee's desire that it give to the word "safe" the ordinary meaning. Similarly, it seems that the Government, in order to prevail in this case, must establish that Decholin has a potentiality for causing consequences for an unadvised layman which can actually be called harmful; for in common usage the term "safe" is not inapplicable to an article merely because the product may give rise to some effects which are uncomfortable or cause inconvenience. * * *

Without presuming to list all the factors which may merit consideration in a section 503(b)(1)(B) action, the following seem especially pertinent here. Probably the single most important element is the seriousness of the effect likely to result under the Government's theory from unsupervised lay use of Decholin. The Government's answers to interrogatories state that the possible aftermath of self-medication by a person suffering from a tract obstruction is jaundice or even death. If it can prove its contention in this regard, no one could maintain that the harm attributable to the drug is not serious. However, in order that the product's true danger can be understood—in order that its theoretical and practical potentials for causing injury can be more clearly distinguished—it would be necessary to know in much more detail the circumstances under which jaundice or death will follow the ingestion of Decholin. For instance, it would be at least helpful, if not actually essential, to understand whether a normal dosage or only a quantity which the reasonable layman is likely to realize constitutes an excessive amount of self-medication will produce these effects. Similarly, a decision would be easier to reach if the record indicated the immediacy of the harmful consequences. Will jaundice or worse result only if a person suffering from an obstruction prolongs his reliance upon Decholin past the point at which the typical individual in his condition would have become convinced of the futility of self-help and have sought professional diagnosis and treatment? If this is the case, what effect would the drug have on the average man? During the period in which he could be expected to take the tablets, would Decholin result in a worsening of his condition to any significant extent beyond the point to which it would have progressed during the time from the onset of the indications until he would probably have consulted a physician had the drug not been available without prescription? If so, would this deterioration actually represent a more serious threat to his life or simply require additional treatment? It would also seem significant if the effects allegedly produced by Decholin cause a noticeable change in a victim's condition with the result that he could be expected to appreciate that the drug is doing him no good and discontinue its use before real harm occurs.

Collateral Measures Question

In support of its position that it should be granted summary judgment on the basis of this issue regardless of the outcome of the toxicity question, the Government relies upon the fact that both it and Ames agree that the Decholin indications may be caused by a disease or a disorder (e.g., biliary tract obstruction) which the drug cannot cure. The Government argues that a person suffering from such an obstruction, for instance, is likely to go to the pharmacy, compare his symptoms with the Decholin label, purchase the drug, medicate himself and thereby postpone visiting a physician. Therefore, according to the Government, Decholin is unsafe as a matter of law because the layman is unable to detect the true cause of his discomfort when a differential diagnosis is essential to his well-being, and because his easy access to Decholin is responsible for delaying recourse to the expert qualified to make this all-important determination. * * *

While Ames is probably correct in saying that the distribution of a drug was not intended by Congress to be restricted just because it will not serve as a cure in all instances in which it may be taken by a person following the manufacturer's recommendations, the fact that a particular product may be an ineffectual remedy under some circumstances could certainly be a substantial consideration in finding that it is unsafe for self-medication. Conversely, a showing that a drug has a tendency to cause laymen to delay seeking help in determining the natures of their illnesses is not per se sufficient to warrant removing it from the over-the-counter market.

Both of these observations find support in the legislative history surrounding the 1951 amendment. * * * [N]o Representative wished to prevent the free sale of common household remedies. Nevertheless, any of these articles—aspirin, seltzers and mouthwashes—have certainly been taken on countless occasions by people suffering from ailments which these products could not cure when the users' best interests would have been served by professional consultation in lieu of self-medication.[9] * * * If merely establishing that the easy availability of a medicine has the tendency to postpone a differential diagnosis in a case in which the drug alone cannot provide a cure were enough to compel the removal of the product from a druggist's public shelves, there would be few drugs left on the over-the-counter market once the Government saw fit to wage a full-scale assault on self-medication.

Assuming, therefore, that efficacy is not totally unrelated to the question of safety but that the simple fact that inefficacy will result in a postponement in seeking professional assistance is not sufficient to warrant a finding that a product is a prescription drug, the question remains regarding the circumstances in which ineffectiveness, coupled with the

9. During oral argument on these motions, Government counsel was asked whether its view would not serve to make aspirin a prescription drug. His equivocal reply tended toward the negative, apparently because of his belief that Decholin, unlike aspirin, has the potential for being taken by a person who has a serious ailment that the drug cannot cure. This attempted distinction overlooks the fact that at the root of a headache may lie anything from nervous tension to a malignant brain tumor.

likelihood of delay, would serve as the basis for considering a remedy dangerous for unsupervised lay use. The first factor would be the seriousness of the effect that a delay might cause, with the Government's case becoming stronger as its proof tends to show that the consequences of a postponed diagnosis do not merely border on inconvenience as opposed to actual harm. It also seems essential to know how much of a delay will be detrimental, for, in light of the legislative history, it is improper to view the 1951 enactment as a measure designed to protect the stubborn individual who continues to put his trust in self-medication long after the average person would have sought out a physician.

A third concern would certainly be the quality of the advice, invariably contained on a drug label, cautioning users to consult a practitioner if certain symptoms develop in addition to those for which the medicine has been recommended by its manufacturer. * * * [T]he pertinent question is not whether an individual is able to detect the cause of his ailment, but rather whether the symptoms described on the package as reasons for him to visit a physician are sufficient to alert him to the possibility that his illness may require professional attention. In other words, if a serious disease which Decholin cannot cure is the crux of the trouble, will nausea or severe abdominal pain appear along with excessive belching and constipation?

A fourth consideration is closely related to the third because an over-the-counter drug will probably carry, as Decholin does, a warning on its container to the effect that if the indications continue, a physician should be consulted. The issue is whether in a case where a particular drug will not alleviate the cause of an ailment it will, nevertheless, effect a disappearance of the indicative symptoms with the result that a user may have every reason to feel that he has been cured when, in fact, he has not been. * * *

FDA, *Notice of Public Hearing on Over-the-Counter Drug Products*

65 Fed. Reg. 24,704 (2000).

* * * In 1972, FDA initiated rulemaking procedures (the OTC Drug Review) to determine which OTC drugs can be generally recognized among qualified experts as safe and effective and not misbranded under prescribed, recommended, or suggested conditions of use. Through the OTC Drug Review, FDA establishes monographs for classes of OTC drug products (e.g., antacids, skin protectants) that are found to be generally recognized as safe and effective and not misbranded when the products contain the ingredients and are labeled according to the monograph. OTC drug monographs describe the active ingredients, amount of drug, formulation, labeling, and other general requirements for drugs to be lawfully sold OTC. * * *

Safety for OTC use means a low incidence of adverse reactions or significant side effects under adequate directions for use and warnings against unsafe use, as well as low potential for harm which may result from abuse under conditions of widespread availability. Effectiveness means a reasonable expectation that, in a significant proportion of the target population, the pharmacological effect of the drug, when used under adequate directions for use and warnings against unsafe use, will provide clinically significant relief of the type claimed. The benefit-to-risk ratio of a drug must be considered in determining both safety and effectiveness. * * *

During the course of the OTC Drug Review, advisory review panels of nongovernment experts evaluated the various classes of OTC drug products and recommended that a number of drugs be switched from prescription to OTC status. FDA acted on these recommendations and switched a number of products to OTC status, including antihistamines (e.g., diphenhydramine hydrochloride (HCl), doxylamine succinate), topical nasal decongestants (e.g., oxymetazoline HCl, xylometazoline HCl), topical hydrocortisone, topical antifungals (e.g., haloprogin, miconazole nitrate), an anthelmintic (pyrantel pamoate), an oral anesthetic (dyclonine HCl), and various fluoride dental rinses.

FDA has also approved the switch of a number of drugs from prescription to OTC status under new drug applications. These include an antidiarrheal (loperamide), topical antifungals (e.g., clotrimazole, terbinafine HCl), antihistamines (e.g., clemastine fumarate), a pediculicide (permethrin), an ocular vasoconstrictor (oxymetazoline HCl), vaginal antifungals (e.g., clotrimazole, miconazole nitrate), analgesics (e.g., ketoprofen, naproxen sodium), acid reducers (e.g., cimetidine, famotidine), a hair growth treatment (minoxidil), and smoking cessation drugs (e.g., nicotine polacrilex).

In allowing these drugs to be sold OTC, the agency considered the safety and effectiveness criteria stated above, the benefit-to-risk ratio, and whether clear and understandable labeling could be written for self-medication without the intervention of a health professional. In some cases, manufacturers were required to conduct labeling comprehension studies to determine if consumers would understand the proposed OTC labeling for the products.

FDA has received comments in the past suggesting that a number of other types of drugs should be considered for OTC status. These types of products include diuretics, antihypertensive agents, cholesterol-lowering drugs, antidiabetic drugs, treatments for osteoporosis, topical agents for the treatment of perioral herpetic lesions, drugs for problems of the stomach and intestines, asthma treatments, and oral contraceptives.

Drugs found appropriate for OTC sale have an increasingly vital role in the U.S. health care system by providing consumers easy access to certain drugs that can be used safely for conditions that consumers can self-treat without the help of a health care practitioner. Consumers have access to more than 100,000 OTC drug products encompassing more than 800 active ingredients and covering more than 100 therapeutic categories or classes.

In light of the continuously changing health care environment, including the growing self-care movement, the agency continues to examine its overall philosophy and approach to regulating OTC drug products. FDA is soliciting information from, and the views of, interested persons, including health professional groups, scientists, industry, and consumers, on the agency's regulation of OTC drug products. * * * Issues that are of specific interest to the agency include the following:

A. Criteria

  ● In the context of the present environment, what criteria should FDA consider in rendering decisions on OTC availability of drug products?

  ● What types of drugs are or are not appropriate for OTC distribution?

  ● What types of diseases are or are not suitable for treatment with products marketed OTC (e.g., chronic illnesses; diseases that require initial diagnosis by a physician; diseases that if left untreated, or are inadequately treated, can lead to serious morbidity or mortality)?

  ● How should the risks and benefits to individuals and risks and benefits to the public health be assessed and weighed in any decision on OTC marketing? For example, how should the agency balance the potential benefits of OTC antimicrobial agents with the potential risks to society at large of the development of resistant organisms associated with increased, and potentially improper, use?

B. Classes of Products

  ● Are there specific classes of products that are not currently marketed OTC that should be available OTC? If so, which ones and why? What specific evidence should be required to support such approvals?

  ● Are there specific classes of products that should not be available OTC? What specific concerns do these classes raise? * * *

C. Consumer Understanding

  ● How can FDA be assured of consumer understanding of the benefits and risks of specific drug products and the ability of consumers to use products safely and effectively were the drug products to be marketed OTC? Issues that may be discussed include: (1) sampling criteria for comprehension studies; (2) language barriers; (3) appropriate use and interpretation of self-administered diagnostic tests; (4) ramifications of misdiagnosis; (5) ability of consumers to appreciate, without required intervention by a physician, the need for continuous (sometimes life-long) treatment, appropriate followup, and need for other treatment; (6) consumer confusion between trade names and generic/chemical names; and (7) consumer confusion with brand extensions (e.g., when the active ingredients generally associated with a brand are not present in some of the brand's extended product line).

  ● What methodologies can be employed to demonstrate consumer understanding?

- How can information on efficacy be adequately conveyed to consumers through labeling? For example, how can the label adequately convey this efficacy information for: (1) therapies with marginal benefit, or (2) therapies with preventive claims that may provide benefit to a specific population but the benefit to the individual consumer is unclear?

- Can prevention claims encourage ill-advised behavior, and if so, how could this potential be minimized? For example, would use of a cholesterol-lowering drug allow patients to ignore other needed interventions such as smoking cessation, dietary discretion, and management of other risk factors?

D. Selection of Treatment

- With regard to the choice of treatment regimens, how can rational selection be ensured when there are coexisting prescription and OTC therapies for a given disease?

- In an environment with coexisting products, what are the most effective means to ensure that patients know the best ways to treat their illnesses?

- How should the availability of OTC options and prescription options for the same indication be reconciled? Are there examples where this dichotomy would raise public health concerns?

- Within a therapeutic class, should the first drug to enter the OTC market be the "best" drug, in terms of the benefit-to-risk ratio? How should the availability of a "better" OTC product, in terms of efficacy or safety, affect the status of products already on the OTC market for treatment of the same condition? Should older therapies that may provide less benefit or more risk be removed from the OTC market, or should the labeling be revised? Suppose the more effective drug is more difficult to use and must remain prescription— might that encourage use of the less satisfactory drug?

E. OTC Marketing System

- Is the current structure for marketing OTC products in the United States adequate? What lessons can we learn from different OTC marketing systems? For example, what can be learned from the countries and those U.S. states where some nonprescription drug products are sold OTC and others are sold "behind the counter"?

F. FDA's Role in Switches

- Under what circumstances should FDA actively propose OTC marketing for a drug in the absence of support from the drug sponsor?

- Should FDA be more active in initiating switches of prescription products to OTC use? * * *

PROBLEM #5. *FIGHTING AN OTC SWITCH TOOTH AND NAIL*

You represent a pharmaceutical company that sells an immensely successful non-sedating antihistamine for prescription use. Acting on a petition filed by a group of health insurers who provide prescription drug benefits but would prefer not having to pay for the use of this particular drug (not to mention the physician visits necessary to receive a prescription), the FDA has decided to switch this drug to nonprescription status because it has a relatively favorable safety profile and is intended only for symptomatic relief. Your client is outraged. Not only will it have to reduce the price of the drug dramatically or risk losing volume (because few health insurers reimburse patients for OTC products), but it also may face greater tort liability for any injuries that occur. Is there any basis for challenging the agency's decision in court? What other information would you need?

NOTES AND QUESTIONS

1. *Rx-to-OTC switches.* Before passage of the Durham–Humphrey Amendment in 1951, the FDA generally deferred to a manufacturer's choice of prescription or nonprescription status. Nowadays, although the agency may approve some new drugs as nonprescription from the outset, see Stephen Paul Mahinka & M. Elizabeth Bierman, Direct-to-OTC Marketing of Drugs: Possible Approaches, 50 Food & Drug L.J. 49 (1995), it usually waits until a prescription drug has been on the market for several years without any serious adverse events before agreeing to switch the product to nonprescription status. In addition to requiring a favorable safety profile, the FDA focuses on whether one can formulate labeling that will allow for safe self-medication. See Peter Barton Hutt, A Legal Framework for Future Decisions on Transferring Drugs from Prescription to Nonprescription Status, 37 Food Drug Cosm. L.J. 427 (1982); see also Peter Temin, The Origin of Compulsory Drug Prescriptions, 22 J.L. & Econ. 91, 103 (1979) ("[T]he FDA assumed that adequate directions for laymen could not be written for some drugs."); cf. World Health Organization, Guideline for the Regulatory Assessment of Medicinal Products for Use in Self–Medication (2000). In *Decholin*, the manufacturer sought to defend nonprescription marketing. Sometimes one finds the roles reversed, with the manufacturer wanting to retain prescription status, while the FDA may urge a switch to OTC labeling, and the issues may have more to do with economics than the factors identified in the statute. See Ceci Connolly, Panel: Reclassify Allergy Pills, Wash. Post, May 12, 2001, at A1 (reporting that an advisory committee recommended that the FDA grant a citizen petition submitted by a health insurance company requesting that the agency switch three non-sedating prescription antihistamines to OTC status); Melody Petersen, Delays Possible for Over-the-Counter Allergy Drugs, N.Y. Times, May 16, 2001, at C1 (explaining that, for a variety of reasons, the FDA is unlikely to act on the committee's recommendation); Sheryl Gay Stolberg, FDA Considers Switching Some Prescription Drugs to Over-the-Counter Status, N.Y. Times, June 28, 2000, at A18 (adding, however, that for drugs about to face generic competition, an OTC switch may offer an additional period of market exclusivity for the brand-name manufacturer).

2. *Contraceptives.* The agency is considering a petition to allow nonprescription marketing of emergency contraceptive products in light of their short (72 hour) window for effective use. See Rita Rubin, Easier "Morning After" Access: Groups Request Over-the-Counter Status from FDA, USA Today, Feb. 14, 2001, at 10D. A few states have considered making morning after pills available without a prescription, though a pharmacist would have to dispense them. See Lisa Rein & Craig Timberg, Emergency Birth Control Approved, Wash. Post, Feb. 21, 2001, at A1 (describing a pilot program in Washington); see also Gregory M. Fisher, Third Class of Drugs–A Current View, 46 Food Drug Cosm. L.J. 583 (1991) (suggesting the creation of an intermediate category modeled on Canada's approach); cf. GAO, Nonprescription Drugs: Usefulness of a Restricted Sale Class Has Not Been Demonstrated, PEMD–95–12 (1995). Wouldn't federal law preempt switches accomplished by individual states?

3. *Prescription restrictions in the new economy.* Traditionally, states regulated the practice of medicine and pharmacy, and they defined who could issue prescriptions. See Idaho Ass'n of Naturopathic Physicians, Inc. v. FDA, 582 F.2d 849 (4th Cir.1978). Although filling prescriptions by mail-order raised some eyebrows in the early 1990s, the FDA did not react. With the advent of the Internet, however, on-line prescribing has spread, blurring the distinction between prescription and OTC products and raising concerns that patients could receive hazardous pharmaceuticals without any meaningful supervision by physicians. The FDA announced an effort to control Internet prescribing of drugs. See Steve Sternberg, Clinton Wants FDA to Control Drug Sales Online, USA Today, Dec. 29, 1999, at 6D. See generally Kelly K. Gelein, Note, Are Online Consultations a Prescription for Trouble? The Uncharted Waters of Cybermedicine, 66 Brook. L. Rev. 209 (2000); Sean P. Haney, Note, Pharmaceutical Dispensing in the "Wild West": Advancing Health Care and Protecting Consumers Through the Regulation of Online Pharmacies, 42 Wm. & Mary L. Rev. 575 (2000); Eric M. Peterson, Comment, Doctoring Prescriptions: Federal Barriers to Combating Prescription Drug Fraud Against On-line Pharmacies in Washington, 75 Wash. L. Rev. 1331 (2000); Kerry Toth Rost, Note, Policing the "Wild West" World of Internet Pharmacies, 76 Chi.-Kent L. Rev. 1333 (2000); Patricia Stolfi, Comment, Caveat Emptor: Regulating the On-line Medicine Man in the New Frontier, 17 J. Contemp. Health L. & Pol'y 377 (2000).

1. PROFESSIONAL LABELING

Medications that cannot be used safely by consumers without the diagnosis and supervision of a physician are designated as prescription drugs and can be dispensed only on the order of a licensed medical practitioner. See 21 U.S.C. § 353(b). As one would expect, physician labeling contains far more detailed risk information than is generally possible in the labeling of most consumer products, and it includes information about both acute and chronic risks.

Prescription drugs are potent medications that unavoidably are associated with adverse effects, but the benefits of using such drugs outweigh the accompanying risks so long as the expert judgment of a trained professional is first applied in the decision to use a drug for a particular patient. Regulators traditionally have asserted that the best mechanism for achieving these ends is detailed labeling that includes all pertinent risk information. The labeling for prescription drugs provides comprehensive information to help physicians in making therapeutic risk-benefit decisions in individual cases. When it reviews new drug applications, the FDA carefully considers all aspects of proposed labeling. In promulgating regulations governing the content and format of "package inserts," it emphasized that "the decision as to whether a warning is legally required for the labeling of a drug must rest with the agency." 44 Fed. Reg. 37,434, 37,453 (1979). Although decisions are made for each new drug independently at the time of their approval, the agency does attempt to achieve consistency in the labeling required for similar prescription drugs.

In the labeling for any prescription drug, the FDA demands that cautionary information be categorized according to the relative severity of the hazard and the degree to which the risk has been substantiated. Package inserts contain many detailed paragraphs of information about indications for use and side effects to assist physicians in making prescribing decisions for individual patients. Topic headings in prescription drug labeling should include: Clinical Pharmacology, Indications and Usage, Contraindications, Warnings, Precautions, and Adverse Reactions. The placement of risk information into one of the latter several categories depends on the relative severity of a hazard, ranging from situations where risks "clearly outweigh any possible benefit" (to be noted as contraindications), to non-serious side effects that occur with a frequency of less than one in a thousand (to be noted as "rare" adverse reactions). This hierarchy stands in marked contrast to the agency's largely undifferentiated approach for OTC drug labeling.

The Warnings section of the package insert is reserved for risks that are more serious than adverse reactions but are not so serious as to clearly outweigh possible benefits of a drug, and particularly serious risks may have to be highlighted as a "boxed warning." In certain cases, information concerning uncommon but potentially serious allergic reactions may have to appear in the Warnings section. For example, prescription drugs made with sulfiting agents must include a lengthy warning. See 21 C.F.R. § 201.22(b). A similar statement concerning possible allergic reactions to Yellow No. 5 is required, but only in the Precautions section of prescription drug labeling. See id. § 201.20(b). Such detailed precautionary information contrasts with the simple ingredient declarations that the FDA requires when these additives are present in food and OTC drug products.

Whatever category is appropriate for the disclosure of hazard information in the package insert, the FDA demands that the risk be substantiated.

The regulations provide, for instance, that only "[k]nown hazards and not theoretical possibilities shall be listed" as contraindications. Id. § 201.57(d). The agency explained in the preamble to this rule that "including theoretical hazards as contraindications in drug labeling would cause that very important section of the labeling to lose its significance." 44 Fed. Reg. at 37,447. As several commentators have emphasized, over-warning of prescription drug side effects may adversely affect prescribing decisions:

> [The FDA] has an interest in "rational prescribing," i.e., ensuring that the risks and benefits of a particular drug be fairly presented so that a physician can compare them with other available therapies. That goal is not advanced if a drug is made to appear riskier than other drugs and other therapies due to the over-dramatization of risk information. To allow a warning based on inconclusive evidence or scientific hunches results in doctors not prescribing effective drugs to a patient because of the erroneous belief that a side-effect might occur.

Feldman v. Lederle Labs., 592 A.2d 1176, 1200 (N.J.1991) (Garibaldi, J., dissenting); see also Richard M. Cooper, Drug Labeling and Products Liability: The Role of the Food and Drug Administration, 41 Food Drug Cosm. L.J. 233, 238 (1986) ("This point has additional force where there is no similar collection of risk information about alternative therapies, such as surgical procedures."); Thomas Scarlett, The Relationship Among Adverse Drug Reaction Reporting, Drug Labeling, Product Liability, and Federal Preemption, 46 Food Drug Cosm. L.J. 31, 36 (1991) ("[O]verstated warnings could tip the judgment of the medical profession in an undesirable direction.").

A statement in the Warnings section is only appropriate after "reasonable evidence of an association of a serious hazard with a drug" is found, though "a causal relationship need not have been proved." 21 C.F.R. § 201.57(e). Evidence from long-term animal studies normally should be included in the Precautions section, together with an explanation of species and bioassay results, though in some cases "serious animal toxicity data may require warnings in drug labeling." See id. § 201.57(e), (f)(5). The FDA even requires that the Adverse Reactions section, which contains some of the least serious risk information in the package insert, only include those side effects that are "reasonably associated" with use of the drug. See id. § 201.57(g). Although all adverse experiences with a new drug must be reported to the agency, whether or not reasonably associated with use of the drug, for purposes of labeling an adverse reaction "would not include unsubstantiated reactions." 44 Fed. Reg. at 37,453. When substantiated hazards are discovered, however, manufacturers have a duty to alert the agency and to add the new risk information to drug labeling. See id. at 37,447.

The FDA's rules governing the disclosure of potential risks of use by pregnant women illustrate the interplay between categorization and substantiation. A "Pregnancy category" designation, accompanied by a specified explanation and any additional information concerning the risk of birth defects, must appear in the Precautions section of most package inserts, depending on the available evidence of a drug's potential teratogenicity. See 21 C.F.R. § 201.57(f)(6)(i); see also Francesca Kritz, Ending Guesswork on Drugs in Pregnancy, Wash. Post, Feb. 26, 2002, at Z1 (reporting that the FDA may soon revamp this rating system). If adequate and well-controlled clinical studies have failed to demonstrate any risk to the fetus, the drug is to be designated as Pregnancy category A. Pregnancy category B is appropriate in cases where clinical studies have not been performed in pregnant women but the data from animal testing fail to demonstrate a risk to the fetus, and Pregnancy category C should be used if the animal test results were unfavorable but the benefits of use outweigh the possible risk of birth defects. In the event that there is positive human evidence of a risk to the fetus, but the potential benefits from use of the drug by pregnant women may be acceptable, Pregnancy category D should appear in the Precautions section of the package insert along with a cross-reference to the Warnings section which must include a specified hazard statement. Finally, if evidence from use in humans or animals discloses a risk of birth defects which clearly outweighs any possible benefit of using the drug during pregnancy, Pregnancy category X is appropriate, along with a cross-reference to the Contraindications section. Although the use of different letters for each category is unique, the scheme used for teratogenic risk information reflects the FDA's general categorization and substantiation requirements applicable to other prescription drug hazards.

The labeling of prescription medical devices must bear information concerning "any relevant hazards, contraindications, side effects, and precautions." 21 C.F.R. § 801.109(c). Although these elements are not spelled out in the same detail contained in the regulations governing package inserts for drugs, the FDA's guidelines set forth identical categorization and substantiation requirements for device labeling. Class labeling requirements for certain products such as intrauterine devices (IUDs) contemplate the same level of detail as found in prescription drug package inserts. See id. § 801.427(b)(1). In addition, through premarket approval of Class III devices, the FDA establishes detailed requirements regarding the design, manufacture, and labeling of a device in advance of sale. Most Class I devices and Class II devices, as well as some Class III devices for which premarket approval has not yet been required, are subject to premarket notification requirements, and the FDA does review labeling when deciding whether a device is "substantially equivalent" to a previously marketed device. See 21 U.S.C. § 360(k); 21 C.F.R. §§ 807.81–807.97.

In recognition of the problems with excessive detail and physician inattention, the FDA recently announced plans to revise the format of package inserts in order to highlight the most significant information. See 65 Fed. Reg. 38,563, 38,564 (2000) (announcing that the agency has "engaged in several initiatives to make prescription drug labeling a better information source for health care practitioners—clearer, more informative, more accessible, and more consistent"); Sarah Lueck, FDA Frames Plan to Revamp Rules for Drug Labeling, Wall St. J., June 26, 2000, at B12 ("The agency envisions drug labels resembling nutrition labels found on packaged foods, which look similar and contain the same types of data across product categories."). At the center of this effort is a proposal to revise the format and content of the package insert.

The agency's notice of proposed rulemaking, published in the Clinton administration's waning days, begins by explaining that labeling "is the primary mechanism through which FDA and drug manufacturers communicate essential, science-based prescribing information to health care professionals." 65 Fed. Reg. 81,082, 81,082 (2000); see also id. at 81,083 ("This information is intended to help ensure that health care practitioners are provided with a complete and accurate explanation of prescription drugs to facilitate their safe and effective prescribing. Thus, the [existing] regulations require prescription drug labeling to contain detailed information on various topics that may be important to practitioners."). The notice then asserts that the recent "increase in the amount, detail, and complexity of labeling information . . . has made it harder for health care practitioners to find specific information and to discern the most critical information in product labeling." Id. at 81,083; see also id. ("[P]ractitioners expressed concern about the lack of ease in locating specific information among the extensive information presented."). According to the FDA, several developments account for this increasing length and complexity, including technological advances in the products and the need for information about drug interactions and use in special populations. In addition, the agency blames the threat of tort liability for cluttering the package insert with unnecessary warnings.

In an effort to help physicians cope with these changes, the FDA proposes significant modifications to the package insert. See id. at 81,104 ("The objective of the proposed rule is to make it easier for health care practitioners to find, read, and use information important to the safe and effective prescribing of prescription pharmaceuticals (drugs and biologics) for patient treatment."). First, it plans to add a relatively short "highlights" section at the outset. Second, the agency proposes including an "index" (more accurately a table of contents) before the comprehensive prescribing information. Third, it wants to reorder the required sections in the package insert to move the most important and frequently referenced information closer to the beginning. Fourth, the FDA proposes changing type face, such as requiring bold type in order to highlight subheadings and a minimum font size in order to improve readability. An exemplar of a reformatted package insert appears as an appendix to this chapter.

The FDA's proposal nowhere suggests that it may have placed excessive faith in the capacity of labeling to ensure rational prescribing. To the contrary, the agency assumes that physicians regularly refer to package inserts, particularly those accompanying new and unfamiliar products, and that a more user-friendly format will reduce the time currently wasted in searching for particular information, facilitate the selection of the most effective therapies and dosages, and reduce the occurrence of preventable side effects as well as other prescribing errors. See id. at 81,104–05. A few critics warned that adding the proposed highlights section might lead some physicians to rely on this abridged drug information, but they assume that prescribers would otherwise attentively read the long version. As the FDA correctly pointed out in responding to this concern, "[i]t is unrealistic to expect practitioners to read every word of product labeling each time they reference it, regardless of how desirable it may be for them to do so." Id. at 81,087. Although likely to represent an improvement at the margins, the agency's optimistic assumption that most physicians rely on the package insert seems naive. If one started from the opposite premise, then the risk-benefit judgments made by the agency when it decides whether to approve new medical technologies might turn out differently.

It appears that physicians rarely bother to read the package insert closely or at all. New information may require multiple avenues of dissemination and the passage of time before it sinks into to collective consciousness and alters prescribing behavior. See Lars Noah, Medicine's Epistemology: Mapping the Haphazard Diffusion of Knowledge in the Biomedical Community, 44 Ariz. L. Rev. (forthcoming 2002). One recent study sponsored in part by the FDA found that labeling revisions and other efforts to communicate new risk information to physicians have essentially no effect on prescribing behavior. See Walter Smalley et al., Contraindicated Use of Cisapride: Impact of Food and Drug Administration Regulatory Action, 284 JAMA 3036 (2000). Two years after the heartburn remedy Propulsid® (cisapride) entered the market, the FDA revised the labeling in response to reports of serious cardiac side effects, but this had no apparent effect on its use. Three years later, in the face of accumulating adverse event information, the FDA again revised the labeling to strengthen the black-box warning, and it ordered the manufacturer to send 800,000 copies of a letter designed to draw attention to this information. The study attempted to quantify to what extent the second effort to disseminate clinically-relevant information altered prescribing behavior in the first year after publication, and it found "no material reduction" in the contraindicated uses of the drug. The authors concluded that "[t]he exposure of [hundreds of thousands of] patients to inappropriate cisapride use, despite the prominent publication of case reports, label changes, and Dear Health Care Professional letters, highlights the need to develop more effective methods for modifying practice to reflect new information about a drug's risks and benefits." Id. at 3039.

A commentary accompanying this study decried the loss of safe and effective drugs prompted by such prescribing errors, and it blamed these sorts of errors on "the overwhelming amount of information on drugs." Raymond L. Woosley, Drug Labeling Revisions–Guaranteed to Fail?, 284 JAMA 3047, 3047 (2000); see also id. at 3048 ("In the last 25 years, the package inserts for new drugs have increased in length more than 5–fold. For example, the 2–page package insert for cisapride, when printed in 12–point font on 8.5 x 11 paper, is more than 10 pages long and contains more than 470 facts about the drug. Practicing physicians would have difficulty mastering all of this information for even one drug, much less the 40 to 100 medications that they regularly prescribe."). The FDA has recognized that a problem exists. Recently, for example, agency officials openly chastised physicians for disregarding instructions in the labeling for newly approved drugs, and they warned that the agency might have to become more cautious in approving medical technologies because physicians seem incapable of following directions:

> Errors involving pharmaceutical use are influencing our benefit-risk assessments. The recent market withdrawals of terfenadine, astemizole, mebefradil, bromphenac, and cisapride resulted, in part, from the health care system's inability to manage the known and preventable risks associated with these products. These experiences have catalyzed an evolution in our thinking on risk management and the evaluation of new drugs for approval. The FDA's risk assessment must evaluate both a drug's intrinsic safety profile as well as the ability of the health care system to adequately manage known toxicities. Unless effective risk management strategies and methods are brought to bear, additional effective drugs are likely to be withdrawn, and some drugs may never become available in the first place.

Peter Honig et al., Letter, How Many Deaths Are Due to Medical Errors?, 284 JAMA 2187, 2188 (2000); see also Banned Medicines Riskier for Women, Hous. Chron., Feb. 9, 2001, at 3 ("[I]ncreasingly frustrated FDA scientists say the main problem is that doctors ignored or never read warning labels that could have prevented deaths.").

Bradley v. Weinberger

483 F.2d 410 (1st Cir.1973).

■ COFFIN, CHIEF JUDGE:

Plaintiffs, 178 physicians who treat diabetes and one diabetes patient who use oral hypoglycemic agents to control the disease by lowering the blood sugar level, brought suit to enjoin the defendants Secretary of Health, Education and Welfare and the Commissioner of the Food and Drug Administration (FDA) from enforcing and the defendant drug companies from complying with the FDA's proposal for altering the labeling of those drugs. The district court granted a preliminary injunction, being persuaded that there was a reasonable likelihood of success in showing that the FDA had failed to comply with the statutes and its own regulation requiring that under some circumstances labeling make reference to the existence of a serious medical controversy. We vacate the injunction for reasons important to the proper judicial role in reviewing administrative actions.

This controversy revolves around a long-term, federally funded study undertaken by the University Group Diabetes Program (hereafter the UGDP study) to determine the effects of oral hypoglycemic agents on vascular complications in patients with adult-onset diabetes. The study, involving twelve clinics and 1200 patients, consisted of four treatment groups: diet alone, diet plus regular insulin doses, diet plus varying insulin doses, and diet plus fixed doses of either tolbutamide or phenformin (two hypoglycemic agents). After monitoring the patients for from five to eight years, the study concluded that the combination of diet and either tolbutamide or phenformin was no more effective than diet alone in prolonging life but that those oral agents might be more hazardous than diet or diet plus insulin insofar as cardiovascular mortality was concerned. The latter conclusion, which led the investigators to discontinue use of the agents in the study as an unethical risk, was based on findings that patients treated with the two agents used in the study suffered more than twice as many cardiovascular deaths than patients receiving the other treatments.

After the study received much publicity and criticism, the FDA convened an ad hoc committee of experts on May 21, 1970, to evaluate the study's findings and the following day issued a press release agreeing with the UGDP study's conclusions and indicating that the agency would require labeling changes to reflect those views. After more extensive evaluation, the FDA concluded that protection of the public required a strong warning to physicians recommending use of an oral agent only if other treatments were inadvisable and noting the UGDP's findings regarding the apparently increased danger of cardiovascular mortality. This evaluation and proposed labeling change was first formally published in the FDA *Drug Bulletin* of June, 1971.

On October 7, 1971, the Committee on the Care of the Diabetic, consisting of eminent doctors and experts in the field including some of the plaintiff doctors, submitted through its counsel a petition to the FDA. It asked the FDA to rescind its labeling recommendation, insure that all future FDA comments on the UGDP study include references to its alleged deficiencies and controversial nature, provide petitioners with the complete raw data of the study, and, "in accord with its policy of fair balance," disseminate with equal emphasis and frequency studies and individual expert opinions differing with the study. The petition was accompanied by a detailed scientific critique of the UGDP study and some 250 pages of scientific studies, papers and comments illustrating the nature and extent of the opposition viewpoint. The study was primarily criticized for inadequate patient selection controls and use of fixed, rather than variable, doses of the drugs, contrary to allegedly accepted medical practice. The FDA proposal was attacked for extending the study's findings to all oral agents and patients despite the study's own warning that such extrapolation could not be made on a statistical basis. The petition also referred to two smaller studies which indicated no cardiovascular complications from oral agents. It was supplemented in January, 1972, by another 220 pages of scientific materials.

In the May, 1972, *Drug Bulletin*, the FDA published the "Final Labeling Approved for Oral Hypoglycemic Drugs," which proposed changes in the "indications" section of the label and the addition of a "special warning" section. The proposal speaks of "the increased cardiovascular hazard which appears to be associated with oral hypoglycemic agents," notes that the UGDP study was the basis for the change, recites its findings, states that these conclusions apply to all oral agents, not just those employed in the study, and ends with the comment that "further studies are being undertaken to shed additional light on the role" of the oral agents. On June 5, 1972, the Commissioner formally replied to the Committee's petition with an eleven-page, single-space letter addressing generally the legal and medical issues and with a 100 page appendix dealing specifically with the scientific criticisms of the study, criticizing the two contrary studies referred to by the petition, and appending the comments of major medical groups and various scientific papers supportive of the FDA's position. * * *

[T]here appears to be no prior case in which an FDA drug labeling decision was challenged not by the producer but by concerned medical practitioners, and no case in which the misbranding statutes and regulations were sought to be applied not to the manufacturer's label but to the FDA's proposal for alteration of the label in light of new information. * * *

The definitional statute (21 U.S.C. § 321(n)) provides: "If an article is alleged to be misbranded because the labeling is misleading, then in determining whether the labeling is misleading there shall be taken into account (among other things) not only representations made or suggested . . . but also the extent to which the labeling fails to reveal facts material in light of such representations or material with respect to consequences which may result from the use of the article to which the labeling relates." Implementing the latter definition is regulation 1.3:

> The existence of a difference of opinion, among experts qualified by scientific training and experience, as to the truth of a representation made or suggested in the labeling is a fact (among other facts) the failure to reveal which may render the labeling misleading, if there is a material weight of opinion contrary to such representation.

One reading of this regulation would suggest that unsubstantiated individual clinical opinions of qualified experts, which are insufficient under the "substantial evidence" test enacted in the effectiveness section, might be sufficient to create a fact omission of which might render the labeling misleading.

The Commissioner never considered the meaning of this regulation, its relationship to the substantial evidence test, the intersection of the safety, effectiveness, and misbranding requirements, or the applicability of the misbranding requirements, both statutory and regulatory, to an FDA proposal for re-labeling, for the simple reason that the issue was not presented to him. Arguably these are simply issues of law which we are fully capable of resolving without administrative assistance. But as the Supreme Court has very recently noted in similarly resolving a closely analogous case, the interpretation of even definitional sections in the drug law will often involve expert knowledge and the ability to evaluate the scientific evidence that becomes relevant. * * *

Because the plaintiffs failed to exhaust their administrative remedies regarding the issues they now present and, consequently, the district court reviewed the agency decision on something other than the administrative record, we must vacate the injunction.

NOTES AND QUESTIONS

1. *Making a federal case out of it.* The dispute over the UGDP study continued, including a FOIA request appealed to the Supreme Court. See Forsham v. Harris, 445 U.S. 169 (1980) (sustaining the government's refusal to provide original study records over which it had no custody); see also Gina Kolata, Controversy over Study of Diabetes Drugs Continues for Nearly a Decade, 203 Science 986 (1979). After some further skirmishing, the FDA issued a warning requirement based on the disputed study. See 49 Fed. Reg. 14,303 (1984) (codified at 21 C.F.R. § 310.517). Given the well-accepted practice of off-label prescribing, why did the group of physicians go to such lengths in challenging the FDA's new labeling requirements?

2. *Prohibitions against identifying disagreements with FDA labeling requirements.* The agency revised its regulation in the wake of the *Bradley* decision to clarify that it does not allow any "statement of differences of opinion with respect to warnings (including contraindications, precautions, adverse reactions, and other information relating to product hazards) required in labeling for food, drugs, devices, or cosmetics." 21 C.F.R. § 1.21(c)(1). In the course of rejecting suggestions that labels communicate dissenting opinions, the agency emphasized that "labeling is not intended to be a dispositive treatise of all possible medical opinion. . . . The opinions of individual physicians on such matters can be, and are, thoroughly and adequately discussed through medical journals, treatises, meetings of professional associations, and other similar events." 40 Fed. Reg. 28,582, 28,583 (1975). As explained in the preamble to the proposed regulation, the agency feared that including disclamatory opinions in warnings would "be confusing and misleading." 39 Fed. Reg. 33,229, 33,231–32 (1974) (adding that "disagreement is properly the subject of scientific discussion in professional journals and symposia, but not in drug labeling").

3. *Influencing the practice of medicine.* The FDA has recognized that labeling should not provide the sole source of information relevant to prescribing decisions. In issuing a rule governing the format of package inserts, the FDA rejected suggestions calling for the inclusion of general statements about good professional practice: "There are potentially many such statements, which, if all are included in drug labeling, would transform labeling into small textbooks of medicine." 44 Fed. Reg. 37,434, 37,436 (1979) ("Physicians are always in a position to pursue additional information through normal educational sources, such as treatises and medical journals."). As explained in the preamble to the proposed regulation, the agency hoped to improve package inserts in part by "eliminating extraneous information which can best be obtained from the published literature." 40 Fed. Reg. 15,392, 15,392 (1975). Even so, the FDA recently proposed mandating a best practices statement in the labeling of antibiotics, reminding physicians against overprescribing them because of the public health consequences associated with growing drug-resistance. See 65 Fed. Reg. 56,511, 56,518 (2000). In part, the agency's concession that package inserts should not provide the sole source of prescribing information grows from the inevitable obsolescence of the labeling as well as the variable appropriate uses to which physicians may put approved products. The FDA also uses other avenues to communicate with health care providers, including regular columns in prominent medical journals as well as a newsletter that it mails to physicians. In addition to publicizing new risk information, it may use these fora to influence best practices. See Lawrence K. Altman, Risk of Death Found in Use of Heart Drug, N.Y. Times, Nov. 1, 1995, at A16; see also Jerry Avorn & Stephen B. Soumerai, Improving Drug–Therapy Decisions Through Educational Outreach: A Randomized Controlled Trial of Academically Based "Detailing," 308 New Eng. J. Med. 1457 (1983); Stephen B. Soumerai & Jerry Avorn, Changing Prescribing Practices Through Individual Continuing Education, 257 JAMA 487 (1987).

4. *Avenues for airing differences of opinion.* Just before the controversial abortion drug Mifeprex® (mifepristone) reached the U.S. market, pro-choice groups sent letters to physicians recommending a less cumbersome treatment regimen in an effort to expand use, see Sarah Lueck, Groups Offer Abortion–Drug Variations, Wall St. J., Oct. 30, 2000, at B2, while pro-life groups sent letters to physicians providing more dramatic risk information in an effort to discourage use, see Rachel Zimmerman, Wrangling over Abortion Intensifies as RU486 Pill Nears the Market, Wall St. J., Nov. 14, 2000, at B1 (reporting that one group "sent 150,000 letters to obstetrician/gynecologists and family-practice physicians warning of possible adverse effects"). In addition, just prior to the approval, the manufacturer of the ulcer drug Cytotec® (misoprostol), which doctors widely prescribe for off-label use to induce labor and is specifically identified in the labeling for Mifeprex® as needed to complete the abortion, sent a letter to health care providers warning that its drug should never be administered to pregnant women, a position that the company clarified a few months later under pressure from the FDA. See Ralph W. Hale & Stanley Zinberg, Editorial, Use of Misoprostol in Pregnancy, 344 New Eng. J. Med. 59, 60 (2001) ("The timing of the letter, just weeks before the FDA announced its approval of mifepristone, left many people wondering whether there were other motivations for Searle's actions."). It seems unlikely that any other drug will generate similar efforts to influence prescribing behavior, but this episode demonstrates that physicians may receive conflicting off-label drug information from a variety of sources.

5. *Mandating misleading risk information.* Some warnings are designed to serve a collateral purpose. For instance, the FDA requires that products containing CFC propellants include the following warning on their label: "Contains a chlorofluorocarbon that may harm the public health and environment by reducing ozone in the upper atmosphere." 21 C.F.R. § 369.21 (OTC drugs); id. § 801.425(a) (medical devices). The warning is designed to promote environmentally conscious purchasing decisions rather than convey information about risks to the user. See Lars Noah, The Imperative to Warn: Disentangling the "Right to Know" from the "Need to

Know" About Consumer Product Hazards, 11 Yale J. on Reg. 293, 313–14, 398 (1994) (criticizing this approach).

2. PATIENT LABELING

Prescription drug warning requirements have not been confined to physician labeling. Over the last three decades, the FDA has proposed requiring that information be given directly to patients. In 1970, the agency required that sellers of oral contraceptives supply a "patient package insert" (PPI). The insert included the following cautionary information: "Do Not Take This Drug Without Your Doctor's Continued Supervision. The oral contraceptives are powerful and effective drugs which can cause side effects in some users and should not be used at all by some women. The most serious known side effect is abnormal blood clotting which can be fatal." 21 C.F.R. § 130.45(d)(1) (1970). The FDA revised this requirement several times since then to include far more detailed warnings. In addition, the agency has required PPIs on a case-by-case basis as a condition of NDA approval.

Pharmaceutical Manufacturers Association v. FDA

484 F.Supp. 1179 (D.Del.), aff'd, 634 F.2d 106 (3d Cir.1980).

■ STAPLETON, DISTRICT JUDGE:

In this case, plaintiffs * * * challenge the validity of a regulation promulgated by the Food and Drug Administration which requires certain information to be provided to patients for whom drugs containing estrogens are prescribed. * * * The regulation in question, codified in 21 C.F.R. § 310.515, is one of only four regulations which require patient labeling to be dispensed with a prescription drug.[1] The regulation was proposed on September 29, 1976, with a notice of proposed rulemaking published in the *Federal Register* (41 Fed. Reg. 43,108) permitting sixty days for comments. The regulation as proposed and as promulgated outlined several categories of information which must be included in a patient package insert, and required that such an insert be provided to a patient every time the drug was dispensed or administered (i.e., injected). Thus, physicians as well as pharmacists are required to provide the labeling when they act as dispensers of the medication.

The agency's action came a a result of several studies published in 1975 which indicated an association between the use of conjugated estrogens and an increased risk of endometrial cancer in women. The FDA convened its Obstetrics and Gynecology Advisory Committee to review the studies, and that Committee proposed changes in the physician labeling provided by manufacturers of estrogen. * * * The final rule, published July

---

1. The others apply to oral contraceptives, 21 C.F.R. § 310.501, to progestational drug products, id. § 310.516, and to isoproterenol inhalation preparations, id. § 201.304. The agency's authority to require patient labeling on prescription drugs has never been subject to a court challenge.

22, 1977, was accompanied by a lengthy preamble which attempted to deal with the comments the agency had received and to explain the purpose and effect of the rule. * * *

Plaintiffs and plaintiff-intervenors raise a number of challenges to the regulation. First, they contend that the FDA lacks statutory authority to require patient packaging inserts for prescription drugs. They next assert that such a requirement is an unconstitutional interference with the practice of medicine. Finally, they challenge the adequacy of the FDA's findings and conclusions embodied in the preamble to the regulation and argue that, based on the administrative record, the regulation is "arbitrary, capricious, an abuse of discretion, or otherwise not in accordance with law." 5 U.S.C. § 706(2)(A). * * *

The primary objective of the Federal Food, Drug and Cosmetic Act is the protection of the public health. As such, its rulemaking authority under Section 701(a) has been broadly construed to uphold a wide variety of assertions of regulatory power. * * * At the same time, the broad language of Section 701(a) does not give the FDA unlimited regulatory powers; regulations issued under that section must effectuate a congressional objective expressed elsewhere in the Act. In the instant case, the agency maintains that it has promulgated the challenged regulation pursuant to Section 701(a) in order to effectuate the objectives reflected in Sections 502(a) and 505(d) of the Act. * * *

These statutory provisions, combined with Section 701(a), provide direct support for the challenged regulation. Among other things they reflect a clear congressional objective that the users of drugs, whether prescription or non-prescription, shall receive facts "material ... with respect to consequences which may result from the use of the ... (drug) under the conditions of use prescribed in the labeling thereof or under such conditions of use as are customary or usual." 21 U.S.C. § 321(n). The Commissioner, in furtherance of this objective, has seen fit in the challenged regulation to require that information concerning consequences which may result from the use of estrogen drugs be provided to the users thereof on their labeling. I think it clear that Section 701(a) authorizes him to do so.

The plaintiffs acknowledge that Sections 201 and 502 may be read in this manner, but maintain that this reading is contrary to the legislative history of the 1938 Act and is specifically precluded by the enactment of the Durham–Humphrey amendments to the Act in 1951.

Relying on the legislative history of the 1938 Act, the plaintiffs assert that Section 502(a) was never intended to apply to drugs dispensed on prescription. I find nothing in that legislative history to support this position. Indeed, all the evidence persuades me that the opposite is true. Despite a number of requests from representatives of the medical profession that prescription drugs be exempted from all labeling requirements, the final version of the Act provided an exemption only with respect to certain identified requirements. Section 503(b) exempted any drug dispensed on a written prescription from the labeling requirements of Section

502(b) (relating to quantity of contents) and 502(e) (relating to common names), and exempted prescription narcotics from the requirement that the label carry a warning that the drug may be habit forming, so long as the prescription was not refillable. It did not, however, exempt prescription drugs from the requirements of either 502(a) or 502(f), and both were understood to apply fully to all drug preparations.[9] * * *

Finally, plaintiffs argue that any authority which the FDA may have had under the 1938 Act with respect to patient labeling of prescription drugs was withdrawn by Congress in 1951. One of the amendments adopted in that year exempted prescription drugs from the "warnings against misuse" requirement and the "adequate directions for use" requirement of Section 502(f) in those situations where the label contains certain specified information, including whatever warnings or directions for use are specified by the physician in the prescription. According to plaintiffs, the adoption of this exemption as Section 503(b)(2) of the Act was intended by Congress to deprive the Secretary of authority to require that patient labeling for prescription drugs contain information regarding possible undesirable effects of the prescribed use. * * *

[W]hile plaintiffs are correct in pointing out that the effect of the Section 503(b)(2) exemption as enacted in 1951 was to make the prescribing physician the primary source of information available to a consumer of a prescription drug, this does not mean that Congress intended to leave this matter to the unregulated discretion of the prescribing physician. The retention of Section 502(a) as a regulatory provision applicable to prescription drugs precludes one from attributing that intention to Congress. * * * [W]hen the Commissioner determines that the possible side effects of a drug when used as customarily prescribed are sufficiently serious as to be material to the patient's decision on use of the drug, he or she may require disclosure of those side effects on the labeling pursuant to Section 701(a). * * *

I next turn to the question of whether requiring patient package inserts to be dispensed with prescription drugs interferes with any constitutionally protected right of physicians. Plaintiffs argue that the mandatory nature of the regulation interferes with the doctor-patient relationship, and thus with the practice of medicine, by requiring the physician to communicate information emanating from Washington without regard to his or her professional judgment concerning the accuracy of the advice or the desirability of the patient being exposed to it.

The plaintiffs' argument is founded in part on their conception of the appropriate distribution of regulatory authority between the states and the federal government and in part on their view that a licensed physician's

---

9. Section 502(f) authorized the Secretary to exempt any drug from the "adequate directions for use" requirement if such directions are not necessary for the protection of the public health, but did not authorize an exemption from the warnings requirement of that subsection. After the passage of the 1938 Act, the Administrator did exempt drugs dispensed by prescription from the directions for use requirement. 21 C.F.R. § 1.106, 3 Fed. Reg. 3168 (1938).

professional judgment may not be subjected to prior restraint and that society's interest in regulating the practice of medicine can be satisfactorily served by review of physician conduct in the context of malpractice or professional censure proceedings.

To the extent that the plaintiffs' claim of unconstitutional interference with the right to practice medicine is founded on a notion of federalism which reserves all rights over such regulation to the states, it is without merit. It is undisputed that the practice of medicine is subject to the exercise of state police power where such regulation furthers a legitimate state interest. But that assumption does not imply an absence of federal jurisdiction over the same area, where the federal regulation constitutes a reasonable exercise of a power vested in Congress under the Constitution. * * * The fact that the practice of medicine is an area traditionally regulated by the states does not invalidate those provisions of the Act which may at times impinge on some aspect of a doctor's practice.

Turning to plaintiff's view of a physician's right to exercise professional judgment, it is important to focus on what the challenged regulation does not do. The regulation at issue here does not forbid a physician from prescribing conjugated estrogen drugs, or limit the physician's exercise of professional judgment in that regard. Nor does it limit the information the physician may impart to his or per patients concerning estrogens. If the physician disagrees with a perceived "slant" of the labeling provided by the manufacturer, or with the facts stated therein, he or she is free to discuss the matter fully with the patient, noting his own disagreement and views. The sample labeling encourages the patient to have this kind of open discussion with her doctor.

When these limitations on the effect of the challenged regulation are considered, it becomes apparent that the plaintiffs urge recognition not of a right to exercise judgment in prescribing treatment, but rather of a right to control patient access to information. * * * [L]abeling is only one of many sources from which patients receive information about drugs and the control which the plaintiffs claim to have possessed prior to the challenged regulation is largely illusory. But there is a more fundamental problem with their position. There simply is no constitutional basis for recognition of a right on the part of physicians to control patient access to information concerning the possible side effects of prescription drugs. The cases cited by plaintiffs do contain language referring to a doctor's right to practice medicine, but the rights there recognized were only those necessary to facilitate the exercise of a right which patients were found to possess. The physician rights discussed are thus derivative of patient rights and do not exist independent of those rights. * * *

The patient rights recognized in the line of cases relied upon by plaintiffs flow from a constitutionally protected right of privacy. * * * To the extent these cases have any bearing on the present issue, then, their rationale would appear to support the challenged regulation. The objective of that regulation is to provide the patient with the facts relevant to a choice about the use, and manner of use, of estrogen drugs. The asserted right to limit patient access to such information can hardly be said to facilitate the patient's "interest in independence" in decision making.

By holding that physicians do not possess the constitutional right which plaintiffs claim, I do not overlook the affidavits of numerous experienced physicians who foresee patient anxiety and ruptured physician-patient relationships as a result of the implementation of the regulation. These matters are clearly relevant to an evaluation of the wisdom of the regulation. They do not, however, render it constitutionally infirm. * * *

The preamble to the challenged regulation provides a concise general statement of its basis and purpose. The evidence supporting the decision to require patient labeling is reviewed and the major concerns addressed in the comments are noted and responded to. In particular, the Commissioner notes that he had considered whether to allow the prescribing physician to determine that the labeling should not be given to a particular patient, but that "such (an) option is not provided in this regulation." 42 Fed. Reg. 37,636, 37,639–40 (1977).

The reasons for the denial of such an option are also sufficiently articulated to permit a determination that it has a rational basis. Given the purposes of the Act and its mislabeling provisions, the touchstone of any decision of the Commissioner is the safety and health of the patient. With this touchstone in mind, the primary factors to be weighed in deciding to grant or deny the option for which plaintiffs press are (1) the extent and character of the risk involved in using estrogen drugs, (2) the efficacy of, or the benefit to be derived from, providing patients with information concerning that risk, and (3) the extent and character of any risk involved in exposing all patients to that information. The Commissioner explains his views in each of these areas. First, it is apparent that he considers the risk associated with the use of estrogen drugs to be great, in terms of both the number of users and the gravity of the consequences to those who are adversely affected. Second, he explains that he finds this to be an area where patients are capable of understanding the advantages and risk of use and where most patients, because of the nature of the condition for which the drug is prescribed, have a real option to use or not to use it. And, finally, on the other side of the balance, the Commissioner states that, unlike the situation with respect to some other drugs, he finds no likelihood of a substantial adverse effect on patients from exposure to the information provided by the labeling. Based on these considerations, the decision was made against affording the option.

I do not understand plaintiffs to contend that a reasonable person could not have assessed the risk of use and the efficacy of providing information to patients in the way the Commissioner did. They vigorously dispute his finding, however, with respect to the absence of substantial adverse effect from use of the labeling. Specifically, they point to affidavits filed in this case in which experienced physicians note their concerns that for some patients exposure to the labeling information will result in unnecessary anxiety, failure to follow prescribed treatment, ruptured doctor-patient relationships, self-diagnosis, and symptoms by suggestion.

The question before the court, however, is not whether evidence exists which would tend to support an approach different from that taken by the Commissioner; the question is whether the record affirmatively demonstrates that the Commissioner's action had a rational basis. As earlier noted, I conclude that the preamble provides such assurance. In addition to the material already described, the preamble expressly addresses and evaluates the possibility of discontinued treatments, suggestion-induced symptoms, self-diagnosis, and strained doctor-patient relations. With respect to the patient compliance with prescribed dosage regimen and suggestion-induced side effects, for example, the Commissioner commented:

The factors behind patient adherence to agreed medication regimens are complex. With the present state of knowledge it is impossible to predict accurately the influence that patient labeling will have on adherence to agreed medication regimens. Experience with oral contraceptive patient labeling suggests, however, that patient experience with drug therapy, rather than written information, primarily determines discontinuation of drug therapy. Furthermore, in the case of estrogens, the Commissioner firmly believes patients should take these drugs for as brief a period as possible and that women should be appraised of the reasons why this is the case. In the suggested wording of the patient labeling, patients are consistently referred to their physician so that decisions can be made in the context of appropriate medical advice. If a patient decides to follow the instruction of her physician, the Commissioner does not believe that patient labeling will significantly increase the incidence of suggestion-induced side effects. Suggestion effects, moreover, seem to play a minimal role in determining serious adverse reactions. It is, in any event, possible to hypothesize beneficial as well as negative effects of suggestion. Clear expectations about the effects of drug therapy, reinforced by patient labeling, may make patients more sensitive and aware of certain physical or psychological reactions. Effects which might otherwise go unnoticed may be identified as drug related. Although this may have the effect of nominally increasing the reported incidence of less serious adverse reaction it also may have beneficial results. Patients may be more sensitive to "warning signals" of serious adverse effect.... It is the Commissioner's opinion that the possible positive effects of supplying accurate side-effect information outweigh the possible negative effects.

While reasonable minds might reach different conclusions, this explication of the Commissioner's reasoning is sufficient to demonstrate that the challenged regulation is the product of a rational process.

Plaintiffs complain, however, that, even if the Commissioner has provided a sufficient explanation of his reasoning and analysis, the absence from the administrative record of a factual basis for that reasoning and analysis renders his action arbitrary and capricious. They point specifically to the absence of any clinical or expert opinion evidence to support the Commissioner's view that no substantial adverse consequence can be expected to flow from the receipt by patients of the labeling information.

To be rational, informal agency decisionmaking must have a factual basis. This does not mean, however, that the administrative record must contain evidence to support each step in the agency's reasoning process. A determination of whether an agency action is rendered arbitrary and capricious by the absence of record evidence in a particular area necessarily depends on the circumstances, including such things as the character of the finding or conclusion said to be lacking in support, its importance in the deliberative process, whether it is a matter with which the agency has regular experience and expertise, the availability of competent evidence on the issue, and the character of any contrary evidence offered by commentors.

Here, in order to pass upon the contention that a physician option should be provided, the Commissioner was called upon to forecast possible patient reaction to the labeling information. This was a matter with respect to which the agency had had some relevant prior experience. At the same time, patient labeling was a relatively new phenomenon, and the record suggests that clinical data on its effect was not yet available. Moreover, the issue was one as to which a rational judgment could be made based on the Commissioner's specific knowledge of the information to be conveyed and his general knowledge of human nature, at least in the absence of any evidence suggesting that patterns of common experience were likely to be misleading. In this context, I believe the Commissioner was entitled to make a forecast without supporting clinical data or expert opinion.

The challenged regulation is not arbitrary, capricious, or otherwise contrary to law and defendants' motion for summary judgment will be granted.

Henley v. FDA

77 F.3d 616 (2d Cir.1996).

■ McLaughlin, Circuit Judge:

* * * The FDA regulates the labeling of oral contraceptives, including the package inserts. Before 1989, the FDA's oral contraceptive labeling regulations required a specific warning in the package insert that estrogen, a component of oral contraceptives, has "been shown to cause cancer in animals, which showing justifies the inference that estrogens may cause cancer in humans." 21 C.F.R. § 310.501 (1989).

In 1989, after notice and comment proceedings, the FDA revised the requirements for patient package inserts for oral contraceptives (the "1989 Ruling"). See 54 Fed. Reg. 22,585 (1989). The new regulations required the inclusion of general categories of information—e.g., the effectiveness of the drug, its side effects, risks associated with cigarette smoking, potential adverse reactions, etc. Significantly, the FDA no longer mandated the use of any specific wording, including the animal carcinogen warning. The change from a specific warning to a general description was purportedly made so that information on the risks and benefits of the drug could thereafter be updated on a more timely basis without having to engage in protracted notice and comment rule-making procedures.

Elizabeth Henley, on behalf of * * * a women's health organization, filed a citizen petition with the FDA, requesting the FDA to amend the warning label requirements for oral contraceptives. * * * Henley asserted that many women do not want to rely solely on early detection, but, rather, on early prevention, i.e., eliminating or reducing their exposure to animal or human carcinogens. * * * Henley's petition further listed thirteen human studies that allegedly established a correlation between long-term oral contraceptive use and breast cancer. Thus, Henley argued, "[w]omen have the right to all the information necessary to make their own choice as to whether or not the benefits of using the pill outweigh the risk."

The FDA denied Henley's petition. It maintained that recent scientific studies involving women and oral contraceptives indicated no increased risk of cancer in humans. * * * In addition, the FDA explained that it continually monitors scientific information pertaining to the use of oral contraceptives, and updates, when appropriate, the guidance texts that it provides to drug companies. It further claimed that the 1989 Ruling made it possible to update package inserts more promptly because revisions would not be subject to notice and comment rule-making. * * *

The Administrative Procedure Act (APA) provides that a district court may set aside an agency's findings, conclusions or actions only if they are "arbitrary, capricious, an abuse of discretion, or otherwise not in accordance with law." 5 U.S.C. § 706(2)(A). * * * An agency rule may be deemed arbitrary, capricious or an abuse of discretion "if the agency has relied on factors which Congress has not intended it to consider, entirely failed to consider an important aspect of the problem, offered an explanation for its decision that runs counter to the evidence before the agency, or is so implausible that it could not be ascribed to a difference in view or the product of agency expertise." Motor Vehicle Mfrs. Ass'n v. State Farm Mut. Auto. Ins. Co., 463 U.S. 29, 43 (1983).

Although the scope of judicial review under this standard is narrow and deferential, "a reviewing court must be certain that an agency has considered all the important aspects of the issue and articulated a satisfactory explanation for its action, including a rational connection between the facts found and the choice made." But, a reviewing court cannot "substitute its judgment for that of the agency," Citizens to Preserve Overton Park, Inc. v. Volpe, 401 U.S. 402, 416 (1971), particularly when that determination is propelled by the agency's scientific expertise, see Baltimore Gas & Elec. Co. v. Natural Resources Defense Council, Inc., 462 U.S. 87, 103 (1983).

Obviously, as [the district court] noted, "the FDA's determination of what labeling best reflects current scientific information regarding the risks and benefits of oral contraceptives involves a high degree of expert scientific analysis." The regulations prior to the 1989 Ruling were based on research from 1978. According to the FDA, studies performed on women after 1978 have failed to establish an increase in the risk of cancer for women taking the oral contraceptive formulations that are currently in use. Although acknowledging that animal studies indicate a link between estrogen and cancer, the FDA maintains that those results are simply not as probative as the results of recent human studies. Specifically, the FDA noted that animal studies employed higher doses of estrogen than those currently contained in oral contraceptives, and that data from human studies are more directly applicable to women than data from animal studies.

Based on the information and studies cited by the FDA and the reasons proffered for its determination, we cannot say that its labeling decision was irrational, unsupported by relevant factors, counter to the evidence, or "so implausible that it could not be ascribed to a difference in view or the product of agency expertise." Certainly, neither the outside of a drug package nor its insert can contain the entire body of scientific research, and the average consumer cannot be expected to analyze and weigh each conflicting study. The FDA possesses the requisite know-how to conduct such analyses, by sifting through the scientific evidence to determine the most accurate and up-to-date information regarding a particular drug, and how those data affect human usage. We therefore defer to its reasonable findings in this case. See, e.g., Schering Corp. v. FDA, 51 F.3d 390, 399 (3d Cir.1995) (finding that FDA's "judgments as to what is required to ascertain the safety and efficacy of drugs fall squarely within the ambit of the FDA's expertise and merit deference from us").

Henley also argues that the FDA's approved labeling is "misleading," because its content does not disclose that animal studies reveal a relationship between estrogen use and cancer. Consequently, she contends that the FDA's decision is contrary to law. We disagree. * * * As discussed above, the FDA has rationally concluded, based on its expertise, that the inclusion of an animal carcinogen warning is not warranted in light of current scientific studies performed on humans. The pertinent animal studies in this case—showing a connection between estrogen and cancer—are not necessarily applicable to humans, particularly where the animal studies used relatively higher dosages than would normally be ingested by humans. We therefore find that the FDA did not fail to reveal facts material to the use of the drug, see 21 U.S.C. § 321(n), and conclude that its labeling decision was not misleading. * * *

Henley has presented sound and cogent arguments for the inclusion of cautionary information, and we might not have chosen the FDA's course had it been our's to chart. But that is hardly the point. Where, as here, an agency's determination cannot be characterized as arbitrary, capricious, an abuse of discretion, or contrary to law, the APA precludes us from substituting our judgment for that of the agency.

NOTES AND QUESTIONS

1. *Practice of medicine objections.* In the challenge brought by the PMA, what exactly was the basis for the industry's claim of an unconstitutional interference with the practice of medicine? Apart from the federalism issue, did it suggest that physicians enjoyed a First Amendment right to communicate freely with patients? Imagine that a PPI advocated that the patient undergo an abortion if she became pregnant while taking a drug known to cause birth defects—could the FDA force a health care provider morally opposed to abortion to hand out this leaflet (especially in one of the states that protects so-called "conscientious objectors"), or does the patient's right to receive such information trump? Cf. Planned Parenthood v. Casey, 505 U.S. 833, 884 (1992) (plurality) ("All that is left of petitioners' argument is an asserted First Amendment right of a physician not to provide information about the risks of abortion, and childbirth, in a manner mandated by the State. To be sure, the physician's First Amendment rights not to speak are implicated, but only as part of the practice of medicine, subject to reasonable licensing and regulation by the State. We see no constitutional infirmity in the requirement that the physician provide the information mandated by the State here."); Paula Berg, Toward a First Amendment Theory of Doctor–Patient Discourse and the Right to Receive Unbiased Medical Advice, 74 B.U. L. Rev. 201 (1994); Bruce D. Weinstein, Do Pharmacists Have a Right to Refuse to Fill Prescriptions for Abortifacient Drugs?, 20 Law Med. & Health Care 220 (1992).

2. *PPIs for everyone?* In 1979, based on studies indicating the usefulness of supplying written information directly to patients, the FDA proposed regulations that would have required PPIs for most prescription drug products. See 44 Fed. Reg. 40,016, 40,020–21 (1979). Although the agency recognized that consumers may have difficulties understanding some of the concepts and information described in professional labeling, the proposed PPIs would have differentiated between Contraindications, Warnings, Precautions, and Adverse Reactions in much the same way as the package insert directed to physicians. After receiving various complaints about the costs of such an undertaking, the FDA instead established a three-year pilot program mandating the distribution of PPIs for ten classes of drugs. See 45 Fed. Reg. 60,754, 60,773 (1980). Even this scaled-down program was stayed by the agency in 1981, shortly after Ronald Reagan became President, and it was revoked the following year. See 46 Fed. Reg. 23,739, 23,815 (1981); 47 Fed. Reg. 39,147 (1982); see also Public Citizen v. HHS, 671 F.2d 518 (D.C.Cir.1981) (reviewing a procedural challenge to the stay); Rosalind M. Kendellen, The Food and Drug Administration Retreats from Patient Package Inserts for Prescription Drugs, 40 Food Drug Cosm. L.J. 172 (1985).

3. *Voluntary PPIs.* Pharmaceutical manufacturers sometimes voluntarily provide separate information for patients, and the FDA has expressed renewed interest in requiring the distribution of prescription drug information directly to patients. In the early 1990s, as part of its "MedGuide" initiative, the agency proposed guidelines for the development of PPIs for all prescription drug products. See 60 Fed. Reg. 44,182 (1995); see also Howard M. Rowe, Patient Package Inserts: The Proper Prescription?, 50 Food & Drug L.J. 95 (1995). Congress intervened, however, by placing a temporary moratorium on finalization of this proposal in order to allow the industry to develop its own voluntary program to replace the FDA's initiative. See Pub. L. No. 104–180, § 601, 110 Stat. 1569, 1593 (1996); see also Charles Marwick, MedGuide: At Last a Long–Sought Opportunity for Patient Education About Prescription Drugs, 277 JAMA 949 (1997); Sheryl Gay Stolberg, Faulty Warning Labels Add to Risk in Prescription Drugs, N.Y. Times, June 4, 1999, at A27. In recent years, pharmacists have experimented with computer-generated information sheets to accompany prescriptions, sometimes but not always with assistance from pharmaceutical manufacturers or medical associations. See 60 Fed. Reg. at 44,193–95. For the most part, however, prescription drug labeling still remains geared toward providing physicians with the information that may be relevant in deciding whether to prescribe a medication for a particular patient. Contrast the FDA's requirements, discussed in Chapter 2(C), for the documentation of informed consent from patients when they serve as subjects in clinical trials.

4. *OTC labeling.* For nonprescription products, the FDA has demanded detailed warning statements for acute risks, with an emphasis on providing directions for safe use or highlighting the consequences of misuse. The whole premise of making drugs available to consumers without a prescription is that self-diagnosis of certain conditions and self-treatment with these medications does not create safety concerns. Because few drugs are entirely risk free, OTC drug products can be marketed only if consumers are given information adequate to minimize the danger of any side effects. In 1999, the FDA substantially reformatted the labeling of nonprescription drugs in order to enhance the readability of the required information. See 64 Fed. Reg. 13,254, 13,286 (1999) (codified at 21 C.F.R. § 201.66).

In addition to risk labeling requirements for particular drugs, general warnings mandated for all OTC drug products include "Keep this and all drugs out of the reach of children," and "In case of accidental overdose seek professional assistance or contact a poison control center immediately." 21 C.F.R. § 330.1(g). Another general warning required for OTC drug products intended for systemic absorption cautions pregnant and nursing women to "seek the advice of a health professional before using this product." Id. § 201.63(a). Nonprescription drug products containing aspirin must warn that "Children and teenagers should not use this medicine for chicken pox or flu symptoms before a doctor is consulted about Reye syndrome, a rare but serious illness reported to be associated with aspirin." Id. § 201.314(h)(1). In response to the number of accidents caused by operators of vehicles who become drowsy while taking certain OTC medications, the National Transportation Safety Board has urged the FDA to strengthen warnings of such effects. See Jeff Zeleny, NTSB Says Drugs Need More Label Warnings, Chi. Trib., Nov. 15, 2001.

A few nonprescription medical devices are subject to specific FDA risk labeling requirements. For example, every tampon package must at a minimum include the following statement: "Tampons are associated with Toxic Shock Syndrome (TSS). TSS is a rare but serious disease that may cause death. Read and save the enclosed information." 21 C.F.R. § 801.430(c). The accompanying package insert must include a number of detailed statements describing the precise risks of TSS and instructions for minimizing the risk.

B. ADVERTISING

As mentioned in *Kordel*, Congress initially lodged authority over advertising in the Federal Trade Commission (FTC). Subsequent amendments to the FDCA gave the FDA limited power to regulate the advertising of prescription drugs and so-called "restricted" medical devices. See 21 U.S.C. § 352(n), (q) & (r). The FTC retains authority over the advertising for other FDA-regulated products, including OTC drugs. See 36 Fed. Reg. 18,539 (1971); Novartis Corp. v. FTC, 223 F.3d 783 (D.C.Cir.2000) (rejecting a challenge to a corrective advertising order for a nonprescription analgesic product); FTC v. Pantron I Corp., 33 F.3d 1088 (9th Cir.1994) (sustaining an enforcement action for false advertising against the seller of a baldness remedy); Thompson Med. Co. v. FTC, 791 F.2d 189, 192–93 (D.C.Cir.1986) (holding that the FDA's review of labeling claims for OTC drugs did not prevent an FTC enforcement action against OTC drug product advertising); Bristol–Myers Co. v. FTC, 738 F.2d 554 (2d Cir.1984); see also Removatron Int'l Corp. v. FTC, 884 F.2d 1489 (1st Cir.1989) (involving a medical device); Note, The FTC's Injunctive Authority Against False Advertising of Food and Drugs, 75 Mich. L. Rev. 745 (1977).

The statute provides that a prescription drug shall be deemed misbranded "unless the manufacturer, packer, or distributor thereof includes in all advertisements ... such other information in brief summary relating to side effects, contraindications, and effectiveness as shall be required in regulations." 21 U.S.C. § 352(n). The FDA does not, however, enjoy unlimited power to regulate prescription drug advertising. For instance, it can neither entirely prohibit nor routinely demand preclearance of proposed promotional campaigns. Moreover, in order to promulgate drug advertising regulations, the agency must utilize formal rulemaking procedures, which provide interested parties with a right to demand a hearing. See id.; see also Richard B. Ruge, Regulation of Prescription Drug Advertising: Medical Progress and Private Enterprise, 32 Law & Contemp. Probs. 650, 654–70 (1967).

Under the FDA's implementing regulations, advertising causes a prescription drug to be misbranded if it is false or misleading, fails to reveal material facts, or fails to present a fair balance of information. See 21 C.F.R. § 202.1(e)(5). Advertising claims concerning safety, effectiveness, and indications are limited to those appearing in FDA-approved labeling. See id. § 202.1(e)(4), (6). The agency interprets the statutory provision broadly to "include advertisements in published journals, magazines, other periodicals, and newspapers, and advertisements broadcast through media such as radio, television, and telephone communication systems." Id. § 202.1(*l*)(1). After originally promulgating its advertising regulations in the 1960s, the agency has preferred to issue technically nonbinding policy statements and guidelines, pursue individualized enforcement actions in this area, or recharacterize certain advertisements as promotional labeling. See, e.g., 62 Fed. Reg. 14,912, 14,913–16 (1997) (listing numerous FDA guidance documents concerning prescription drug advertising); Thomas A. Hayes, Drug Labeling and Promotion: Evolution and Application of Regulatory Policy, 51 Food & Drug L.J. 57 (1996); Thomas C. Morrison, Corrective Advertising as a Remedy for the False Advertising of Prescription Drugs and Other Professionally–Promoted Medical Products, 49 Food & Drug L.J. 385 (1994).

The FDA's authority to regulate restricted medical device advertising remained essentially dormant until it decided to assert regulatory control over tobacco products in order to restrict their marketing. See 61 Fed. Reg. 44,396 (1996) (codified at 21 C.F.R. pt. 897 (1997)). Although eventually invalidated on other grounds, see FDA v. Brown & Williamson Tobacco Corp., 529 U.S. 120 (2000), the agency's effort to invoke this statutory authority seemed far-fetched, especially because the legislative history and contemporaneous FDA interpretation of the term "restricted" equated it with the term "prescription." See Lars Noah & Barbara A. Noah, Nicotine Withdrawal: Assessing the FDA's Effort to Regulate Tobacco Products, 48 Ala. L. Rev. 1, 27–33 (1996). For further commentary on the scope of the agency's power to regulate the advertising of medical devices, see Edward M. Basile et al., Medical Device Labeling and Advertising: An Overview, 54 Food & Drug L.J. 519 (1999); Sandra J.P. Dennis, Promotion of Devices: An Extension of FDA Drug Regulation or a New Frontier?, 48 Food & Drug L.J. 87 (1993); Ronald M. Johnson, FDA Regulatory Actions and Future Plans for Medical Device Promotion and Advertising, 47 Food & Drug. L.J. 291 (1992).

1.   DETAILING AND CONTINUING MEDICAL EDUCATION PROGRAMS

Yarrow v. Sterling Drug, Inc.

263 F.Supp. 159 (D.S.D.1967).

■ NICHOL, CHIEF JUDGE:

* * * Sterling, as do others in the drug manufacturing industry, places its product information before the doctor by use of listings in a reference work, known as the *Physicians' Desk Reference* (PDR); by use of product cards mailed to the physician; by use of special letters mailed to the physician; and by use of "detail men," who call personally on the physician, orally give him information on new drugs being introduced, and who leave literature on such new drugs and samples thereof with the doctor.

The warnings published in the PDR on the side effects of the drug Aralen, from 1958 until 1961, refer to "visual disturbances." There was no listing of Aralen in the PDR in 1962. In 1963, the warning included blurring of vision, corneal changes, and retinal changes reported to be rare and largely irreversible. In 1964, the warning was largely the same, containing more specifics regarding retinal change, reported rare and irreversible.

The product card on Aralen, in 1957, included blurring of vision on the side effects. In 1959, the product card warned of temporary blurring of vision, corneal changes, and advised periodic eye examinations; in 1960, it warned of temporary blurring of vision, retinal vascular response, macular lesions, evidently irreversible, and advised periodic eye examinations. The same warning was given in 1961. In 1962, the Aralen product card warns of temporary blurring of vision, corneal changes and retinal changes. It suggests trimonthly examinations.

A letter mailed in 1963 advised doctors that "certain ocular complications have sometimes been reported during prolonged daily administration of chloroquine." It suggested trimonthly examinations, and asked that vision impairment and retinal change be reported.

The most significant and efficient means of presenting drug information to the doctor entails the use of detail men who make periodic personal calls on the individual doctor. In this case, Sterling's detail man introduced Mrs. Yarrow's doctor to Aralen, explained its uses and that it was the trade name for chloroquine phosphate. This was late in 1957, or early in 1958. From that time on, although the Sterling detail man called on the doctor at four to six week intervals, the detail man did not bring the side effects of Aralen to his attention.

The record shows that the detail men receive special training as to the various drugs, and that for the most part, they were pharmacists, chemists, or had a medical background. The detail men are kept up to date on the latest developments in drugs.

The doctor testified that he received great amounts of literature on the various drugs he was using; that it was impossible to read all of it; that he relied on detail men, medical conventions, various articles in medical journals, and conversations with other doctors for information on the drugs he was prescribing. * * *

Where the doctor is inundated with the literature and product cards of the various drug manufacturers, as shown here by the facts, a change in the literature or an additional letter intended to present new information on drugs to the doctor is insufficient. The most effective method employed by the drug company in the promotion of new drugs is shown to be the use of detail men; thus, the court feels that this would also present the most effective method of warning the doctor about recent developments in drugs already employed by the doctor, at no great additional expense. The detail men visit the doctors at frequent intervals and could make an effective oral warning, accompanied by literature on the development, that would affirmatively notify the doctor of side effects such as shown in the facts in this case. * * *

NOTES AND QUESTIONS

1. *Detailing in the courts.* The appellate court affirmed. See Sterling Drug, Inc. v. Yarrow, 408 F.2d 978, 992 (8th Cir.1969) ("This does not mean that every physician in the United States must have been given an immediate warning by a personal messenger. But it does mean that the trial court was justified in finding that it was unreasonable to fail to instruct the detail men, at least, to warn the physicians on whom they regularly called. . . ."); see also Stevens v. Parke, Davis & Co., 507 P.2d 653, 663 (Cal.1973); Love v. Wolf, 38 Cal.Rptr. 183, 195–97 (Ct.App.1964); Mahr v. G.D. Searle & Co., 390 N.E.2d 1214, 1232 (Ill.App.Ct.1979); cf. Wallace v. Upjohn Co., 535 So.2d 1110, 1117 (La.Ct.App.1988) (sales persons would not be personally liable for failing to warn physicians). Questions surrounding tort liability for failure-to-warn claims will be addressed at greater length in Chapter 7.

2. *Detailing today.* Pharmaceutical detailing goes back to 1850, and, even with the expansion in outlets for advertising, it remains an important and controversial promotional mechanism. See Abigail Zuger, Fever Pitch: Getting Doctors to Prescribe Is Big Business, N.Y. Times, Jan. 11, 1999, at A1 ("[T]he pharmaceutical sales force has exploded, from about 35,000 full-time sales representatives and supervisors in the top 40 pharmaceutical companies in 1994 to more than 56,000 in 1998. . . . That translates into nearly one drug salesperson and almost $100,000 for every 11 practicing physicians in the United States. . . ."); see also 65 Fed. Reg. 81,082, 81,108 (2000) (estimating that "23.7 million office and hospital calls per year [are] made by pharmaceutical representatives"). Although payola-style abuses of earlier decades have largely vanished, sales strategies have become more sophisticated, and detail representatives continue to wine and dine physicians. See Chris Adams, Doctors on the Run Can "Dine 'n' Dash" in Style in New Orleans, Wall St. J., May 14, 2001, at A1; Bill Brubaker, Drug Firms Still Lavish Pricey Gifts on Doctors, Wash. Post, Jan. 19, 2002, at E1; Sheryl Gay Stolberg & Jeff Gerth, High–Tech Stealth Being Used to Sway Doctor Prescriptions, N.Y. Times, Nov. 16, 2000, at A1 (noting the industry's defense that "physicians are hungry for information about" new drugs); see also American Medical Ass'n, Guidelines on Gifts to Physicians from Industry: An Update, 56 Food & Drug L.J. 27 (2001); Thomas N. Bulleit, Jr. & Joan H. Krause, Kickbacks, Courtesies, or Cost–Effectiveness?: Application of the Medicare Antikickback Law to the Marketing and Promotional Practices of Drug and Medical Device Manufacturers, 54 Food & Drug L.J. 279 (1999); Susan H. Fisher, Note, The Economic Wisdom of Regulating Pharmaceutical "Freebies," 1991 Duke L.J. 206.

3. *Detailing works.* One recent review of studies about promotional interactions between physicians and the pharmaceutical industry reached the following sober conclusion:

> [M]ost studies found negative outcomes associated with the interaction. These included an impact on knowledge (inability to identify wrong claims about medication), attitude (positive attitude toward pharmaceutical representatives; awareness, preference, and rapid prescription of a new drug), and behavior (making formulary requests for medications that rarely held important advantages over existing ones; nonrational prescribing behavior; increasing prescription rate; pre-

scribing fewer generic but more expensive, newer medications at no demonstrated advantage).

Ashley Wazana, Physicians and the Pharmaceutical Industry: Is a Gift Ever Just a Gift?, 283 JAMA 373, 378 (2000); see also Mary–Margaret Chren et al., Doctors, Drug Companies, and Gifts, 262 JAMA 3448 (1989); Jerome P. Kassirer, Financial Conflicts of Interest: An Unresolved Ethical Frontier, 27 Am. J.L. & Med. 149 (2001).

4. *Regulatory authority.* The FDA has limited authority to control detailing. See Bruce N. Kuhlik, The FDA's Regulation of Pharmaceutical Communications in the Context of Managed Care: A Suggested Approach, 50 Food & Drug L.J. 23 (1995); Lars Noah, Death of a Salesman: To What Extent Can the FDA Regulate the Promotional Statements of Pharmaceutical Sales Representatives?, 47 Food & Drug L.J. 309 (1992). The agency has taken action against companies when their detail representatives distribute home-made promotional materials that make misleading claims of superiority over a competitor's product. See Chris Adams, Arthritis–Drug Firms Warned over Marketing, Wall St. J., Dec. 12, 2000, at A4. Verbal statements do not, however, appear to qualify as "labeling" or "advertising" under the FDCA, though they may provide the basis for concluding that a product has a broader intended use than revealed in its labeling. See V.E. Irons, Inc. v. United States, 244 F.2d 34, 44 (1st Cir.1957) (holding that court was entitled to utilize oral representations made by authorized sales distributors); United States v. General Nutrition, Inc., 638 F.Supp. 556, 563–64 (W.D.N.Y.1986) (oral representations by store clerks caused misbranding); United States v. Articles of Drug, Etc., 263 F.Supp. 212, 215 (D.Neb.1967) ("The products involved here were orally represented to be an effective cure for everything from a backache to cancer."); cf. United States v. Various Articles of Device, 256 F.Supp. 894, 896–97 (S.D.Cal.1966) (holding that a "single oral sales 'pitch'" could not misbrand a medical device absent evidence that the claims "were part of a course of conduct instituted, participated in, or permitted" by the manufacturer).

———

Once a new drug has received FDA approval, physicians may prescribe it for any therapeutic use that they like, whether or not that indication appears in the labeling approved by the agency. See 59 Fed. Reg. 59,820, 59,821 (1994); 48 Fed. Reg. 26,720, 26,733 (1983) ("Once a drug product has been approved for marketing, a physician may, in treating patients, prescribe the drug for uses not included in the drug's approved labeling."); see also James M. Beck & Elizabeth D. Azari, FDA, Off–Label Use, and Informed Consent, 53 Food & Drug L.J. 71 (1998); Sidney A. Shapiro, Limiting Physician Freedom to Prescribe a Drug for Any Purpose: The Need for FDA Regulation, 73 Nw. U. L. Rev. 801 (1978). Until recently, however, companies could not promote their products for any uses not appearing in this approved labeling. See 21 C.F.R. §§ 201.100(c)(1), 202.1(e)(6)(i) & (xi); see also Lars Noah, Constraints on the Off–Label Uses of Prescription Drug Products, 16 J. Prods. & Toxics Liab. 139, 143–46 (1994). If new uses came to light after initial approval, a manufacturer wishing to promote such uses first would have to file a supplemental application seeking a labeling revision supported by clinical data demonstrating the safety and effectiveness of the drug for the additional use. See David A. Kessler, Regulating the Prescribing of Human Drugs for Nonapproved Uses Under the Food, Drug, and Cosmetic Act, 15 Harv. J. Legis. 693 (1978). Pursuing approval of new indications usually requires significant time and effort.

In the early 1990s, the FDA became concerned that some manufacturers were indirectly promoting off-label uses, for instance by sponsoring continuing medical education (CME) programs and scientific symposia featuring discussions about such uses of their products and by providing health care professionals with enduring materials (namely, textbooks or article reprints) mentioning such uses. In addition to bringing enforcement actions against particular companies, the FDA published what it characterized as a "Draft Policy Statement" to respond to industry-supported scientific and educational activities concerning drugs and medical devices. See 57 Fed. Reg. 56,412 (1992); David G. Adams, FDA Policy on Industry–Supported Scientific and Educational Activities: Current Developments, 47 Food & Drug L.J. 629 (1992). This document cautioned that CME programs funded by the pharmaceutical and medical device industries would be subject to regulation as promotional labeling or advertising for any products discussed during these programs except in limited circumstances where the sponsoring companies ensure that the program will be independent and objective.

FDA officials repeatedly have suggested that many industry-sponsored CME events are merely elaborate advertising opportunities and that the scientific information presented tends to be self-serving or even inaccurate. See David G. Adams, FDA Regulation of Communications on Pharmaceutical Products, 24 Seton Hall L. Rev. 1399 (1994); see also Nina A. Bickell, Drug Companies and Continuing Education, 10 J. Gen. Internal Med. 392 (1995); Robert M. Tenery, Jr., Interactions Between Physicians and the Health Care Technology Industry, 283 JAMA 391, 392 (2000) ("Unfortunately, while the need for CME for physicians has increased with rapidly expanding technology, the funding from independent sources has decreased proportionately."); Chris Adams, FDA Cites Firms for Improper Statements, Wall St. J., July 30, 2001, at B6 ("In at least nine recent cases, the [FDA] cited companies for improper statements or other presentations allegedly made by company representatives working the booths at medical conferences."); Gina Kolata, Where Marketing and Medicine Meet, N.Y. Times, Feb. 10, 1998, at A14 (reporting one cardiologist's description of a lavish conference indirectly funded by the industry as "one big infomercial"). But see Charles J. Walsh & Alissa Pyrich, FDA Efforts to Control the Flow of Information at Pharmaceutical Industry–Sponsored Medical Education Programs: A Regulatory Overdose, 24 Seton Hall L. Rev. 1325 (1994) (arguing that these concerns are overblown).

A few years later the agency softened its stance a bit when it published a guidance documents permitting the dissemination of article reprints and medical textbooks under limited circumstances. See 61 Fed. Reg. 52,800 (1996); 60 Fed. Reg. 62,471, 62,472 (1995). Although not technically binding, these documents expressed the FDA's policy of not enforcing prohibitions against the promotion of off-label uses when manufacturers distribute reprints of articles discussing one of the well-controlled studies that served as the basis for the FDA's approval (even if the article happens to mention other uses that the agency did not approve) and that are published in "bona fide peer-reviewed journals." However, this represented only a minor concession to manufacturers because it did not permit the dissemination of reprints describing clinical studies with the product that were not included in the original application for approval.

In 1997, Congress authorized manufacturers to disseminate enduring materials that discussed off-label uses of approved drugs, medical devices, and biological products under certain circumstances. See FDAMA, Pub. L. No. 105–115, § 401(a), 111 Stat. 2296, 2356–64 (1997) (codified at 21 U.S.C. § 360aaa). First, the information may be provided to health care professionals but not directly to patients. Second, the manufacturer must submit the information to the FDA at least sixty days before beginning distribution, and it must include a prominent disclaimer that the use has not been approved. Third, manufacturers may only distribute unabridged reprints or copies of peer-reviewed articles about scientifically sound clinical investigations with the product that have been published in a scientific or medical journal. The same provision authorizes the distribution of textbooks and other reference publications containing such information, so long as the publication was not prepared at the request of, or edited or substantially influenced by, the manufacturer. Fourth, the manufacturer must periodically supply the FDA with lists of any articles or reference publications disseminated under these provisions and the categories of persons who received them, and the manufacturer generally must file an application requesting supplemental approval of the off-label use described in the distributed information. If new information becomes available after dissemination of an article or text indicating that the off-label use is ineffective or poses a significant risk to public health, the FDA may order that the manufacturer cease dissemination of the material and perhaps distribute corrective information.

The recent experience with prescription weight loss drugs provides a cautionary tale about the potential hazards of encouraging physicians to make clinical judgments on the basis of new information about off-label uses reported in the scientific literature. Had these liberalized rules for off-label promotion existed five years earlier, Wyeth–Ayerst could have aggressively promoted the use of its drug Pondimin® (fenfluramine) in combination with phentermine by distributing reprints of a 1992 article reporting its effectiveness in weight reduction. See Gina Kolata, How Fen–Phen, A Diet "Miracle," Rose and Fell, N.Y. Times, Sept. 23, 1997, at F1. The off-label use of "fen-phen" became widespread anyway, and the FDA urged a recall of this and the chemically-related drug Redux® (dexfenfluramine) in

1997 because of reports of heart valve abnormalities and a higher than expected frequency of primary pulmonary hypertension. Other off-label uses of drugs reported in the scientific literature may catch on more slowly, at least without the widespread distribution of reprints by a manufacturer. See Jur Strobos, Stoning a Dead Bird: Advertising Limits on Approved New Drugs, 50 Food & Drug L.J. 533 (1995). Indeed, the time that it normally takes before physicians become aware of newly reported information represents one of the primary rationales for allowing manufacturers to disseminate such reprints, but it also suggests a hazard of premature responses to incomplete information.

For a skeptical assessment of the quality of some of the information appearing in the biomedical literature, see Lars Noah, Sanctifying Scientific Peer Review: Publication as a Proxy for Regulatory Decisionmaking, 59 U. Pitt. L. Rev. 677, 696–709 (1998). For instance, published articles often fail to provide information about toxicity identified during clinical trials investigating a therapy's effectiveness. See John P.A. Ioannidis & Joseph Lau, Completeness of Safety Reporting in Randomized Trials, 285 JAMA 437, 442 (2001). More significantly, biases may affect the outcome of studies financed by the industry. See United States ex rel. Cantekin v. University of Pittsburgh, 192 F.3d 402, 407 (3d Cir.1999) (crediting the explanation by the chair of an NIH review committee "that a researcher who receives substantial funding from a pharmaceutical company can be subtly biased in favor of finding that the company's drugs are effective"); Paula A. Rochon et al., A Study of Manufacturer–Supported Trials of Non–Steroidal Anti–Inflammatory Drugs in the Treatment of Arthritis, 154 Archives Internal Med. 157 (1994). For instance, a survey of seventy journal articles concerning calcium channel blockers found that 96% of the authors defending their safety had financial relationships with the manufacturers of these drugs, many of which had not been disclosed in the published articles. See Henry Thomas Stelfox et al., Conflict of Interest in the Debate over Calcium–Channel Antagonists, 338 New Eng. J. Med. 101, 103–04 (1998) (finding "a strong association between authors' published positions on the safety of calcium-channel antagonists and their financial relationships with pharmaceutical manufacturers").

Most journals require that authors disclose any potential conflicts of interest, and some of these disclosures reveal remarkable linkages between researchers and drug companies. See Cynthia Crossen, A Medical Researcher Pays for Challenging Drug–Industry Funding, Wall St. J., Jan. 3, 2001, at A1 ("Since the early 1980s, connections in biomedicine between academics and drug companies have become so pervasive that a recent footnote to an article on antidepressants in the New England Journal of Medicine disclosed more than 350 financial ties between the authors of the article and pharmaceutical companies that sell antidepressants."). Even so, problems persist. See Sheldon Krimsky & L.S. Rothenberg, Financial Interest and Its Disclosure in Scientific Publications, 280 JAMA 225, 226 (1998); Laura Johannes, Medical Editorialists May Have Failed to Disclose Tie to Obesity–Drug Maker, Wall St. J., Aug. 28, 1996, at B3 ("The New England Journal of Medicine is investigating whether two authors of a favorable editorial on a fast-selling new obesity drug inappropriately failed to disclose their consulting relationships with the companies that make and market the drug."); Janny Scott, Researcher to Clarify Ties to Drug Manufacturer, L.A. Times, Mar. 24, 1990, at B3 (describing the same type of incident at *JAMA*).

FDAMA did not address CME programs, and the agency published its final guidance on that subject just one month after enactment of the legislation. See 62 Fed. Reg. 64,074 (1997). FDAMA did, however, supersede the other enduring materials policies, and the agency subsequently promulgated implementing regulations. See 63 Fed. Reg. 64,556 (1998) (codified at 21 C.F.R. pt. 99). As explained later, these different restrictions were challenged on First Amendment grounds. Even with these liberalized rules in place, some companies apparently continue to run afoul of the FDA's restrictions on off-label promotion. See, e.g., Marc Kaufman, FDA Moves to Curb Ads for Thalidomide: Drug's Promotion as Cancer Fighter Blocked, Wash. Post, May 5, 2000, at A2.

United States v. American College of Physicians

475 U.S. 834 (1986).

■ MARSHALL, JUSTICE:

A tax-exempt organization must pay tax on income that it earns by carrying on a business not "substantially related" to the purposes for which the organization has received its exemption from federal taxation. The question before this Court is whether respondent, a tax-exempt organization, must pay tax on the profits it earns by selling commercial advertising space in its professional journal * * * *

[T]he American College of Physicians is an organization exempt from taxation under § 501(c)(3) of the Internal Revenue Code. The purposes of the College, as stated in its articles of incorporation, are to maintain high standards in medical education and medical practice; to encourage research, especially in clinical medicine; and to foster measures for the prevention of disease and for the improvement of public health. * * * In furtherance of its exempt purposes, respondent publishes *The Annals of Internal Medicine*, a highly regarded monthly medical journal containing scholarly articles relevant to the practice of internal medicine. Each issue of *Annals* contains advertisements for pharmaceuticals, medical supplies, and equipment useful in the practice of internal medicine, as well as notices of positions available in that field. Respondent has a longstanding policy of accepting only advertisements containing information about the use of medical products, and screens proffered advertisements for accuracy and relevance to internal medicine. * * *

Respondent has maintained throughout this litigation that the advertising in *Annals* performs an educational function supplemental to that of the journal's editorial content. Testimony of respondent's witnesses at trial tended to show that drug advertising performs a valuable function for doctors by disseminating information on recent developments in drug manufacture and use. In addition, respondent has contended that the role played by the Food and Drug Administration, in regulating much of the form and content of prescription-drug advertisements, enhances the contribution that such advertisements make to the readers' education. All of these factors, respondent argues, distinguish the advertising in *Annals* from standard commercial advertising. Respondent approaches the question of substantial relation from the perspective of the journal's subscribers; it points to the benefit that they may glean from reading the advertisements and concludes that that benefit is substantial enough to satisfy the statutory test for tax exemption. The Court of Appeals took the same approach. It concluded that the advertisements performed various "essential" functions for physicians and found a substantial relation based entirely upon the medically related content of the advertisements as a group.

The Government, on the other hand, looks to the conduct of the tax-exempt organization itself, inquiring whether the publishers of *Annals* have performed the advertising services in a manner that evinces an intention to use the advertisements for the purpose of contributing to the educational value of the journal. Also approaching the question from the vantage point of the College, the Claims Court emphasized the lack of a comprehensive presentation of the material contained in the advertisements. * * *

We believe that the Claims Court was correct to concentrate its scrutiny upon the conduct of the College rather than upon the educational quality of the advertisements. For all advertisements contain some information, and if a modicum of informative content were enough to supply the important contribution necessary to achieve tax exemption for commercial advertising, it would be the rare advertisement indeed that would fail to meet the test. * * *

[T]he advertising in *Annals* does not contribute importantly to the journal's educational purposes. This is not to say that the College could not control its publication of advertisements in such a way as to reflect an intention to contribute importantly to its educational functions. By coordinating the content of the advertisements with the editorial content of the issue, or by publishing only advertisements reflecting new developments in the pharmaceutical market, for example, perhaps the College could satisfy the stringent standards erected by Congress and the Treasury. * * *

■ BURGER, CHIEF JUSTICE (concurring):

Most medical journals are not comparable to magazines and newspapers published for profit. Their purpose is to assemble and disseminate to the profession relevant information bearing on patient care. The enormous expansion of medical knowledge makes it difficult for a general practitioner—or even a specialist—to keep fully current with the latest developments without such aids. In a sense these journals provide continuing education for physicians—a "correspondence course" not sponsored for profit but public health.

There is a public value in the widest possible circulation of such data, and advertising surely tends to reduce the cost of publication and hence the cost to each subscriber, thereby enhancing the prospect of wider circulation. Plainly a regulation recognizing these realities would be appropriate. Such regulations, of course, are for the Executive Branch and the Congress, not the courts. I join the opinion because it reflects a permissible reading of the present Treasury regulations.

NOTES AND QUESTIONS

1. *Promotion vs. education.* Notwithstanding the Court's decision, most biomedical journals continue to refuse advertisements from sellers of non-health care products or services on the view that advertisements can serve an educational function. See Robert H. Fletcher & Suzanne W. Fletcher, Editorial, Pharmaceutical Advertisements in Medical Journals, 116 Annals Internal Med. 951 (1992). Some commentators defend the educational value of such advertising. See John F. Beary, III, Editorial, Pharmaceutical Marketing Has Real and Proven Value: Characteristics of Materials Distributed by Drug Companies, 11 J. Gen. Internal Med. 635 (1996); Keith B. Leffler, Persuasion or Information? The Economics of Prescription Drug Advertising, 24 J.L. & Econ. 45 (1981). One review of pharmaceutical advertisements appearing in medical journals found significant discrepancies in the information provided. See Michael S. Wilkes et al., Pharmaceutical Advertisements in Leading Medical Journals: Experts' Assessments, 116 Annals Internal Med. 912 (1992). The study's suggestion that 92% of the advertisements violated FDA requirements, see id. at 917, generated legitimate criticism, see J. Howard Beales, III & William C. MacLeod, Assessments of Pharmaceutical Advertisements: A Critical Analysis of the Criticism, 50 Food & Drug L.J. 415, 443 (1995); Paul H. Rubin, Are Pharmaceutical Ads Deceptive?, 49 Food & Drug L.J. 7, 10–11 (1994). Even so, the finding that many drug ads provided incomplete information undermines claims that they serve primarily an educational rather than promotional function. However one chooses to characterize it, research indicates that advertising influences physician behavior. See Jerry Avorn et al., Scientific Versus Commercial Sources of Influence on the Prescribing Behavior of Physicians, 73 Am. J. Med. 4, 8 (1982) (concluding that "the predominance of nonscientific rather than scientific sources of drug information is consistent with what would be predicted from communications theory and marketing research data"); Flora Haayer, Rational Prescribing and Sources of Information, 16 Soc. Sci. Med. 2017 (1982); Mark A. Hurwitz & Richard E. Caves, Persuasion or Information? Promotion and the Shares of Brand Name and Generic Pharmaceuticals, 31 J.L. & Econ. 299 (1988).

2. *Editorial conflicts of interest.* Some commentators have expressed concerns that, by virtue of their tremendous expenditures for advertising in biomedical publications, pharmaceutical manufacturers may unduly influence the judgments of journal editors. See Lawrence K. Altman, The Doctor's World: Hidden Discord over Right Therapy, N.Y. Times, Dec. 24, 1991, at C3 (describing initial refusals to publish a researcher's dissent to the conclusions of his co-investigators that an antibiotic effectively treats ear infections, adding that "scientific journals profit handsomely from drug company advertisements, and the influence of industry on such publications has rarely been studied"); see also Richard A. Deyo et al., The Messenger Under Attack: Intimidation of Researchers by Special–Interest Groups, 336 New Eng. J. Med. 1176, 1179 (1997) (suggesting that journals may "need to set up defenses against potential threats of withholding advertising," adding that "[r]esearch on efficacy, safety, and cost effectiveness in the trillion-dollar health care industry frequently has important financial consequences"). Editors strenuously deny that their sources of advertising revenues have any impact on their judgments, but they have recognized the need to guard against such influence. See International Comm. of Med. Journal Editors, Uniform Requirements for Manuscripts Submitted to Biomedical Journals, 277 JAMA 927, 934 (1997) ("[A]dvertising must not be allowed to influence editorial decisions."); see also Drummond Rennie, Editors and Advertisements: What Responsibility Do Editors Have for the Advertisements in Their Journals?, 265 JAMA 2394 (1991); Phil B. Fontanarosa et al., Letter, Bioequivalence of Levothyroxine Preparations: Issues of Science, Publication, and Advertising, 278 JAMA 899 (1997). Some commentators have proposed that, in order to reduce real or perceived conflicts of interest, biomedical journals should adopt precisely the opposite of their current policy—namely, to accept advertising from sellers of health care products only as a last resort. See David Orentlicher & Michael K. Hehir, II, Advertising Policies of Medical Journals: Conflicts of Interest for Journal Editors and Professional Societies, 27 J.L. Med. & Ethics 113, 113–16, 118 (1999). Their proposal has fallen on deaf ears. In fact, responding to the loss of advertising revenue that resulted when drug companies shifted promotional campaigns to television, a group of biomedical journals recently touted the results of a study finding that print ads directed to health care professionals provide companies with the most cost-effective promotional outlet. See Vanessa O'Connell, Medical Journals Chase Drug–Ad Dollars, Wall St. J., May 22, 2001, at B8.

3. *Vanity press*. Industry unmistakably influences editorial choices when companies sponsor symposia or special issues of a medical journal. See Paula A. Rochon et al., Evaluating the Quality of Articles Published in Journal Supplements Compared with the Quality of Those Published in the Parent Journal, 272 JAMA 108, 111–12 (1994) (finding that supplements contained articles of inferior quality due to the lack of regular peer review). One study of the phenomenon found that "industry-sponsored symposiums are promotional in nature and that journals often abandon the peer-review process when they publish symposiums." Lisa A. Bero et al., The Publication of Sponsored Symposiums in Medical Journals, 327 New Eng. J. Med. 1135, 1137 (1992) ("Financial pressures on journals appear to contribute to the increasing publication of symposiums.").

2. DIRECT-TO-CONSUMER ADVERTISING

Twenty years ago, pharmaceutical companies engaged in essentially no prescription drug advertising to lay consumers. Traditionally, only persons who read the *Journal of the American Medical Association* and similar professional publications would see such promotional messages in print. By the early 1990s, drug advertisements became a common feature of weekly magazines and occasionally were broadcast on specialty cable television stations. Prescription drug advertisements now regularly also appear in newspapers and on the major television networks. (In contrast, the European Union has prohibited the advertising of prescription drugs to the general public. See Council Directive 92/28, 1992 O.J. (L113), art. 3. Indeed, only New Zealand allows such advertising, though Canada is considering it, and the EU has proposed relaxing some of its rules.) Perhaps spurred on by the rapid growth of direct-to-consumer advertising and the shortcomings of rules designed to control advertising directed to physicians, coupled with the emergence of brand new media such as the Internet for disseminating promotional messages, the FDA has begun to rethink its regulatory approach. See Lars Noah, Advertising Prescription Drugs to Consumers: Assessing the Regulatory and Liability Issues, 32 Ga. L. Rev. 141 (1997).

1. *History.* In 1963, the agency initially promulgated detailed regulations to control drug advertising, but these were designed naturally enough for promotions directed to medical professionals. See 28 Fed. Reg. 6375, 6376–77 (1963) (codified as amended at 21 C.F.R. § 202.1). The FDA first addressed direct consumer promotion in the mid–1970s, issuing a regulation that authorized advertising of prescription drug prices to consumers so long as a company made no representations about the safety or effectiveness of the product. See 40 Fed. Reg. 58,794, 58,799 (1975) (codified at 21 C.F.R. § 200.200). When pharmaceutical companies proposed to broaden promotional claims targeted to lay audiences in the early 1980s, the FDA initially imposed a moratorium on such advertising so that it could study the issue more carefully, but, in 1985, it lifted the moratorium, content to apply its existing regulations to this new practice. See 50 Fed. Reg. 36,677 (1985). To better supervise adherence to these requirements, the FDA persuaded the industry to submit all proposed consumer promotions for informal preclearance. See 61 Fed. Reg. 24,314, 24,314–15 (1996) (responding to misimpressions that the agency required rather than merely encouraged preclearance); 60 Fed. Reg. 42,581, 42,582 (1995) (describing the FDA's preclearance and case-by-case enforcement approach to controlling drug advertising directed to consumers). It took a full decade of regulating direct consumer advertising under the same regime used for promotions directed to medical professionals before the FDA officially announced an interest in revisiting this issue. In 1995 it published a notice announcing a public meeting and inviting comments, and, two years later, the FDA announced that it would finally attempt to craft regulations specifically designed to address direct consumer advertising of prescription drugs. See 62 Fed. Reg. 21,684, 21,685 (1997); see also Wayne L. Pines, A History and Perspective on Direct-to-Consumer Promotion, 54 Food & Drug L.J. 489 (1999).

2. *Motivations.* Drug companies may advertise directly to consumers for a variety of reasons, all of which ultimately seek to encourage patients to ask their physicians about prescribing the advertised product. First, direct

advertising may persuade consumers to visit physicians and request prescription drugs for previously untreated conditions. Second, such marketing may convince existing patients to inquire about new drug products more rapidly than their physicians might otherwise decide to switch their current prescriptions. Third, direct consumer advertising may create brand loyalty so that patients resist efforts by physicians or pharmacists to substitute less expensive generic versions of the prescribed drug. Finally, this brand loyalty may help a company retain its market share when a prescription product is switched to OTC status, an increasingly frequent occurrence. Advertising directed to consumers has, in fact, succeeded in dramatically increasing sales of prescription drugs. See Julie Appleby, Prescriptions Increase as Drugmakers Spend More on Ads, USA Today, Feb. 21, 2001, at 6B (reporting that companies spent more than $2 billion advertising prescription drugs directly consumers in 2000, and that sales increased to $145 billion); Melody Petersen, Increased Spending on Drugs Is Linked to More Advertising, N.Y. Times, Nov. 21, 2001, at C2; see also Meredith B. Rosenthal et al., Promotion of Prescription Drugs to Consumers, 346 New Eng. J. Med. 498 (2002); Robert Davis, Lilly Seeks a Lift with Weekly Prozac, USA Today, June 6, 2001, at 11D (describing the manufacturer's distribution of coupons offering a free month's supply of a new long-acting version of this antidepressant). In addition to traditional advertising, drug companies have come up with indirect methods for promoting their wares to consumers. Pharmaceutical manufacturers have paid former athletes to mention during interviews particular drugs that they have used to treat a condition. See Drug Makers Pay Sick Celebrities to Gain News Play, Wall St. J., Jan. 3, 2001, at B2.

3. *Existing restrictions.* The most significant limitation on direct consumer advertising under the existing regulations, requiring that manufacturers include a ''brief summary'' of all side effects and contraindications so as to provide fair balance for promotional claims, see 21 C.F.R. § 202.1(e)(4), (5), also seems to be the least meaningful restriction in the lay consumer context. This inaptly named brief summary has come to mean appending much of the package insert with the advertisement, often in small font sizes and on the back of the page. Although physicians may have sufficient interest and expertise to read the brief summary, it seems implausible that most lay consumers even try to make sense of this detailed information. The brief summary requirement previously had made non-print advertising nearly impossible, until the FDA announced guidelines in August 1997 that eased some of the restrictions on broadcast promotions.

4. *Pros and cons.* The FDA summarized the competing arguments concerning direct-to-consumer prescription drug advertising as follows:

> Proponents argue that direct-to-consumer promotion is of educational value and will improve the physician-patient relationship, increase patient compliance with drug therapy and physician visits, and lower drug prices. Opponents contend that consumers do not have the expertise to accurately evaluate and comprehend prescription drug advertising. Opponents also argue that such promotion is misleading

by failing to adequately communicate risk information, and that such promotion will damage the physician-patient relationship, increase drug prices, increase liability actions, and lead to over-medication and drug abuse.

60 Fed. Reg. 42,581, 42,582 (1995); see also id. at 42,583–84 (also noting questions about lay comprehension of the technical information currently used in the brief summary and in disclosure statements used with broadcast advertisements); American Medical Ass'n, Direct-to-Consumer Advertisements of Prescription Drugs, 55 Food & Drug L.J. 119 (2000); Caroline L. Nadal, Note, The Societal Value of Prescription Drug Advertisements in the New Millennium: Targeted Consumers Become the Learned, 9 J.L. & Pol'y 451 (2001); Lisa Rapaport, Pharmaceutical Ads Skip Important Details, Study Says, S.F. Chron., Dec. 4, 2000, at D5. In the wake of that public meeting, the FDA issued another notice to request the submission of additional comments. See 61 Fed. Reg. 24,314 (1996). In particular, the agency sought further reactions to suggestions that it simplify the brief summary requirement to demand that companies communicate information only about major risks but in non-technical language, provide only a generic disclosure statement that all prescription drugs entail significant risks, or vary the level of detail depending on the medium used.

5.   *Latest developments.* In 1999, the FDA finalized its guideline governing broadcast advertising of prescription drugs. See 64 Fed. Reg. 43,197 (1999). In relevant part, it provides:

> The prescription drug advertising regulations distinguish between print and broadcast advertisements. Print advertisements must include the brief summary, which generally contains each of the risk concepts from the product's approved package labeling. Advertisements broadcast through media such as television, radio, or telephone communications systems must disclose the product's major risks in either the audio or audio and visual parts of the presentation; this is sometimes called the major statement. This guidance does not address the major statement requirement. Sponsors of broadcast advertisements are also required to present a brief summary or, alternatively, may make "adequate provision . . . for dissemination of the approved or permitted package labeling in connection with the broadcast presentation" (21 CFR 202.1(e)(1)). This is referred to as the adequate provision requirement. The regulations thus specify that the major statement, together with adequate provision for dissemination of the product's approved labeling, can provide the information disclosure required for broadcast advertisements. The purpose of this guidance is to describe an approach that FDA believes can fulfill the requirement for adequate provision in connection with consumer-directed broadcast advertisements for prescription drug and biological products [but it does not cover restricted medical devices]. The approach presumes that such advertisements:
>
> • Are not false or misleading in any respect. For a prescription drug, this would include communicating that the advertised product is

available only by prescription and that only a prescribing healthcare professional can decide whether the product is appropriate for a patient.

- Present a fair balance between information about effectiveness and information about risk.

- Include a thorough major statement conveying all of the product's most important risk information in consumer-friendly language.

- Communicate all information relevant to the product's indication (including limitations to use) in consumer-friendly language.

A sponsor wishing to use consumer-directed broadcast advertisements may meet the adequate provision requirement through an approach that will allow most of a potentially diverse audience to have reasonably convenient access to the advertised product's approved labeling. This audience will include many persons with limited access to technologically sophisticated outlets (e.g., the Internet) and persons who are uncomfortable actively requesting additional product information or are concerned about being personally identified in their search for product information. One acceptable approach to disseminating the product's approved labeling is described below. This approach includes the following components:

A.   Disclosure in the advertisement of an operating toll-free telephone number for consumers to call for the approved package labeling. Upon calling, consumers should be given the choice of:

- Having the labeling mailed to them in a timely manner (e.g., within 2 business days for receipt generally within 4–6 days); or

- Having the labeling read to them over the phone (e.g., by offering consumers a selection of prerecorded labeling topics).

B.   Reference in the advertisement to a mechanism to provide package labeling to consumers.... One acceptable mechanism would be to provide the additional product information in the form of print advertisements appearing concurrently in publications that reach the exposed audience. The location of at least one of these advertisements would be referenced in the broadcast advertisement. If a print advertisement is part of an adequate provision procedure, it should supply a toll-free telephone number and an address for further consumer access to full package labeling....

C.   Disclosure in the advertisement of an Internet web page (URL) address that provides access to the package labeling.

D.   Disclosure in the advertisement that pharmacists, physicians (or other healthcare providers), or veterinarians (in the case of animal drugs) may provide additional product information to consumers. This statement should communicate clearly that the referenced professional is a source of additional product information....

When a broadcast advertisement is presented in a foreign language, the information sources that are part of the advertisement's "adequate provision" mechanism (i.e., print advertisements or brochures, web sites, toll-free telephone number recorded messages or operators) should be in the language of the broadcast ad. Regardless of the language used for the advertisement, current broadcast advertising regulations require the dissemination of approved product labeling, which, in most cases, must be in English, and is generally written in language directed to healthcare professionals. The Agency strongly encourages sponsors to consider the benefits of also providing consumers with nonpromotional, consumer-friendly product information in the language of the broadcast ad (e.g., FDA-approved patient labeling or accurate, consumer-friendly translations of product labeling information).

Evidently, these guidelines have not cut down on problems of industry failures to comply with the advertising rules, and the agency sometimes has issued multiple warning letters raising objections to the consumer marketing campaigns for particular drugs. See Chris Adams, FDA Scrambles to Police Drug Ads' Truthfulness, Wall St. J., Jan. 2, 2001, at A24 ("The FDA usually orders violators merely to halt their print or TV ads, or to cut offending material. Companies almost always comply, but then some wind up running afoul of FDA rules in a subsequent ad, or in another medium."); Chris Adams, Xenical Ads Avoid Listing Unpleasant Side Effects, Wall St. J., Apr. 3, 2001, at B1 (describing one company's creative effort to circumvent the rules). Stay tuned for further developments in this area. See Chris Adams, FDA to Review Policy Allowing Drug Ads on TV, Wall St. J., Mar. 28, 2001, at B1.

6. *Internet promotion.* In 1996, the FDA announced a public meeting to discuss the special difficulties posed by new communication technologies: for instance, how should a pharmaceutical company append a brief summary to any product-specific promotions included on its home page, can this site include hypertext links to other sites on the World Wide Web not sponsored by the company but that discuss the product or disease condition, and must a company sponsoring promotional Web sites in foreign countries abide by FDA restrictions simply because the same drug product received narrower approval in the United States? See 61 Fed. Reg. 48,707 (1996); see also Emilé L. Loza, FDA Regulation of Internet Pharmaceutical Communications, 55 Food & Drug L.J. 269 (2000); Nancy K. Plant, Prescription Drug Promotion on the Internet: Tool for the Inquisitive or Trap for the Unwary?, 42 St. Louis U. L.J. 89 (1998); Peter S. Reichertz, Legal Issues Concerning the Promotion of Pharmaceutical Products on the Internet to Consumers, 51 Food & Drug L.J. 355 (1996); Kristen Green, Note, Marketing Health Care Products on the Internet: A Proposal for Updated Federal Regulations, 24 Am. J.L. & Med. 365 (1998). Although companies may find that the Internet provides yet another powerful medium for disseminating promotional materials to consumers, one should not exaggerate the supposed uniqueness of these important questions. For instance, the FDA has never before suggested that print advertisements in foreign

publications should comply with its brief summary requirements simply because some consumers in the United States subscribe to these newspapers and magazines. A more serious concern relates to the ease with which information about prescription drugs and disease conditions circulates on the Internet, disseminated by persons not subject to FDA control. It remains unclear whether the agency will choose to address Internet promotional issues separately from the other forms of direct consumer advertising.

7. *Further commentary.* See Lance S. Gilgore, A Consideration of Direct-to-Consumer Advertising of Prescription Drugs and Potential Legal Problems with the Brief Summary Requirement: Is the FDA's Regulatory Authority Illusory?, 46 Food Drug Cosm. L.J. 849 (1991); James M. Johnstone, Direct-to-Consumer Advertising: An Industry Perspective, 47 Food & Drug L.J. 63 (1992); Wayne L. Pines, New Challenges for Medical Product Promotion and Its Regulation, 52 Food & Drug L.J. 61 (1997); Martin S. Roth, Patterns in Direct-to-Consumer Prescription Drug Print Advertising and Their Public Policy Implications, 15 J. Pub. Pol'y & Mktg. 63 (1996); Michelle D. Ehrlich, Note, Doctors Can "Just Say No": The Constitutionality of Consumer–Directed Advertising of Prescription Drugs, 12 Hastings Comm. & Ent. L.J. 535 (1990); Tamar V. Terzian, Note, Direct-to-Consumer Prescription Drug Advertising, 25 Am. J.L. & Med. 149 (1999).

Bober v. Glaxo Wellcome PLC

246 F.3d 934 (7th Cir.2001).

■ WILLIAMS, CIRCUIT JUDGE:

Mortimer Bober brought a class action lawsuit against the firms that manufacture and market Zantac 75 and Zantac 150, the over-the-counter and prescription strength forms of the stomach acid reliever ranitidine, on the ground that the firms provide consumers with false and misleading information about the substitutability of the two drugs, in violation of Illinois law. * * *

Zantac 150 is manufactured and sold by British drug company Glaxo Wellcome PLC and its American subsidiary Glaxo Wellcome, Inc. The Food and Drug Administration has approved it for use in the treatment of various digestive tract conditions, including certain kinds of ulcers and certain esophageal conditions. As its name suggests, it contains 150 milligrams of ranitidine, and it is available only with a prescription. Zantac 75 is manufactured by Glaxo Wellcome, Inc. and is sold by Warner–Lambert Consumer Healthcare, a joint venture formed by Glaxo Wellcome, Inc. and Warner–Lambert Company, another American drug company. According to its FDA-approved packaging, it is to be used for the relief and prevention of heartburn associated with acid indigestion and sour stomach. As its name too suggests, it contains 75 milligrams of ranitidine, but it may be purchased without a prescription.

Bober's complaint alleges that Glaxo Wellcome PLC and the other three defendants provide false and misleading information regarding whether Zantac 75 can be substituted for Zantac 150. The answer to that question was important to Bober because, at the time he filed this lawsuit, he was paying $1.47 per tablet for the Zantac 150 his doctor had prescribed for him, while an equivalent dose of Zantac 75 (two tablets) cost $.80. In an effort to obtain information on the substitutability of Zantac 75 and Zantac 150, Bober twice called a consumer hotline for Zantac 75 users set up by Warner–Lambert. When Bober first called the Zantac 75 consumer hotline, the hotline operator "told Mr. Bober that Zantac 75 and Zantac 150 were not the same medications, and that Mr. Bober could not substitute two Zantac 75 tablets for one Zantac 150 tablet." When Bober called the hotline a second time, a recorded message advised Bober, "If your doctor has directed you to take prescription Zantac, you should not substitute Zantac 75 for your prescription."

Bober's complaint also notes that Warner Lambert maintains a web site providing information about Zantac 75, although the complaint does not say whether Bober ever visited the web site. At the time Bober filed his complaint, a page on that web site answering frequently asked questions about Zantac 75 responded to a question about whether Zantac 75 could be substituted for Zantac 150 by informing visitors, "If your physician has prescribed a medicine, you should not substitute any other medicine for your prescription. You should always ask your physician any questions you may have about changing your medication."

In his complaint, Bober claims that the three quoted statements are false and misleading because, contrary to what the three statements imply, Zantac 75 and Zantac 150 contain the same medicine (ranitidine) and are therefore readily substitutable. On that basis, Bober's complaint alleges that the three statements violate the Illinois Consumer Fraud and Deceptive Business Practices Act ("CFA") and the similar laws of other states. * * * To establish a violation of the CFA's prohibition on deceptive acts or practices, a plaintiff must prove that: (1) the defendant engaged in a deceptive act or practice; (2) the defendant intended that the plaintiff rely on the act or practice; and (3) the act or practice occurred in the course of conduct involving a trade or commerce. Only the first of these requirements is at issue here. * * *

Bober's estate contends that the three statements at issue are deceptive in essentially three ways. First, Bober's estate asserts that the statements falsely claim that Zantac 75 and Zantac 150 do not contain the same medicine. None of the statements, however, expressly makes such a claim. The statements do claim that the two drugs are different medications, but that claim is completely true. The drugs are approved for very different maladies, went through different approval processes, and are sold in different ways. Moreover, to the extent that anyone could imply from the statements at issue that the drugs contain different medicine, information available to Zantac users, and in Bober's possession, would dispel any such implication. The web page that answers frequently asked questions about

Zantac 75 (a printout of which is attached to Bober's complaint) expressly states that Zantac 75 and Zantac 150 contain the same medicine. Likewise, the packaging information for Zantac 75 (which is also attached to Bober's complaint) strongly suggests the same fact when it explains that the active ingredient in Zantac 75 is ranitidine and promotes Zantac 75's safety by noting that prescription strength Zantac has an excellent safety record. Put simply, none of the three statements at issue can reasonably be read as falsely claiming or implying that Zantac 75 and Zantac 150 do not contain the same medicine.

Second, Bober's estate asserts that, in describing Zantac 75 and Zantac 150 as different medications and discouraging substitution of the former for the latter, the three statements at issue misrepresent the therapeutic equivalence of equal doses of the two drugs (an equivalence we assume exists in reviewing the sufficiency of Bober's complaint) by implying that Zantac 150 is more effective than Zantac 75 in treating the conditions for which Zantac 150 is prescribed. While it is clear that the statements at issue go out of their way to avoid any implication that equal doses of the drugs are therapeutically equivalent, we think that the statements also avoid any implication that the drugs are not therapeutically equivalent. In the context of all the information available to Bober and other Zantac users, including the three statements at issue, the packaging information for Zantac 75, and the Zantac 75 frequently asked question web page, it should have been clear to Bober and other Zantac users both that Zantac 75 and Zantac 150 contain the same active ingredient and that inquiries about substituting the former for the latter are properly directed to a user's treating physician. The available information, in our view, dispels any tendency to deceive that the statements at issue might otherwise have had. Accordingly, none of the three statements at issue can reasonably be read as misrepresenting the therapeutic equivalence of equal doses of Zantac 150 and Zantac 75.

Finally, Bober's estate asserts that the statements at issue both claim and imply that Zantac 75 simply cannot be substituted for Zantac 150, despite the fact that it would be perfectly appropriate for a doctor to recommend such a substitution. Again, the problem for Bober's estate is that examining the statements at issue, together and in the context of the other information available to Zantac users, eliminates any possibility of deception with regard to substitutability. From such a perspective, the statements discouraging substitution can only be read to discourage users from making a substitution without consulting their physicians. So read, the statements do not falsely claim or imply that Zantac 75 cannot be substituted for Zantac 150. As a matter of law, none of the three statements on which Bober based his CFA claims is deceptive.

Alternatively, Glaxo argues that all three of the statements are protected by section 10b(1) of the CFA, which excludes from liability "actions . . . specifically authorized by laws administered by any regulatory body or offices acting under statutory authority of this State or the United States." 815 Ill. Comp. Stat. 505/10b(1). It also argues that the statements were "labeling" specifically authorized by the FDA. The case law interpreting the relevant portion of the CFA's exemption provision is not entirely clear on the question of what is meant by "specifically authorized." * * * Taken together, the cases stand for the proposition that the state CFA will not impose higher disclosure requirements on parties than those that are sufficient to satisfy federal regulations. If the parties are doing something specifically authorized by federal law, section 10b(1) will protect them from liability under the CFA. On the other hand, the CFA exemption is not available for statements that manage to be in technical compliance with federal regulations, but which are so misleading or deceptive in context that federal law itself might not regard them as adequate.

The question is thus whether the statements Bober complains of are sufficiently within what is authorized by federal law that Glaxo is entitled to section 10b(1) protection. On this question, we limit our examination to the operator's statement—the only one that is even potentially misleading. The regulations implementing the FDCA are extensive and extremely detailed. Of particular relevance to the "different medications" part of the operator's statement are the regulations defining what constitutes a "new drug." A drug may be considered new based on "[t]he newness of use of such drug in diagnosing, curing, mitigating, treating, or preventing a disease . . . even though such drug is not a new drug when used in another disease or to affect another structure or function of the body." 21 C.F.R. § 310.3(h)(4). Before any "new drug" can be marketed, the manufacturer has to file a "new drug application" and meet the various testing, production, and labeling requirements set out in the Code. There is no dispute that Zantac 75 satisfies this definition of new drug. Even if we assume that in all other relevant respects it is identical to Zantac 150, Zantac 75 is marketed as a nonprescription treatment for acid indigestion, while Zantac 150 is a prescription drug treatment for duodenal and gastric ulcers (among other things). Indeed, Glaxo submitted a new drug application prior to marketing Zantac 75. * * * Given that for federal regulatory purposes Zantac 75 and Zantac 150 were indeed different "drugs," the express terms of the regulations taken as a whole specifically authorized Glaxo to say that they were different "medications," even if the statement may have led Mr. Bober as a layperson to misunderstand what was being said.

The second half of the operator statement is not so easily dealt with, but ultimately we believe that the Illinois courts would find that it too was specifically authorized. The situation here is not a common one. When Mr. Bober asked whether he could substitute Zantac 75 for Zantac 150, the operator said he "could not." In assessing whether this was a specifically authorized response, it is significant that the federal regulations governing drug labeling and advertising imposed competing constraints on Glaxo, such that Mr. Bober's question was particularly tricky to answer. The manufacturer of a drug may not recommend or even suggest uses for a drug that are not approved by the FDA or supported by sufficient medical evidence. 21 C.F.R. § 330.1(d) (OTC advertising); 21 C.F.R. § 202.1(e)(6) (prescription advertising). There is no dispute that Zantac 75 had not been tested for the use to which Mr. Bober sought to put it, which means that

Glaxo was prohibited from even suggesting that substitution would be appropriate. A drug is considered to be misbranded if its labeling or advertising makes any "statements comparing the safety or effectiveness, either greater or less of the drug with other agents for the same indication" if that statement is not supported by "adequate and well controlled studies." 21 C.F.R. § 201.57(c)(3)(v) (prescription labeling); 21 C.F.R. § 201.6(a) (general labeling). Glaxo concedes that it had not conducted any studies that would have allowed it to say that two Zantac 75 tablets would be less (or more) effective than one Zantac 150 tablet for treatment of Mr. Bober's illness. Glaxo's position was thus precarious. It had to answer Mr. Bober's question in a way that did not suggest he could use Zantac 75 for an "off-label" purpose, while at the same time it had to avoid the unsubstantiated suggestion that Zantac 150 would be superior to Zantac 75. * * *

Glaxo chose to reconcile its competing obligations by answering Bober's question with the statement "you cannot substitute" Zantac 75 for Zantac 150. This statement was technically accurate, because only Bober's doctor could approve an "off-label" use for Zantac 75 and the substitution of one drug for the other. The statement was also consistent with those federal regulations requiring Glaxo to refrain from suggesting "off-label" uses for Zantac 75. In protecting itself on that side, however, Glaxo predictably opened itself up to the claim Mr. Bober is now making, namely that the statement improperly suggested that Zantac 150 was superior to Zantac 75. While Glaxo could have added "ask your doctor" without being accused of suggesting an "off-label" use and thus perhaps struck a more perfect balance between its competing regulatory obligations, under the circumstances what it chose to say and not to say was a sufficiently careful compromise to fall within what is specifically authorized by federal law.

The pharmaceutical industry is highly regulated, both at the federal level and internationally. Technical requirements abound, and it is not only possible but likely that ordinary consumers will find some of them confusing, or possibly misleading as the term is used in statutes like Illinois's CFA. But, recognizing the primacy of federal law in this field, the Illinois statute itself protects companies from liability if their actions are authorized by federal law. * * *

■ WOOD, CIRCUIT JUDGE (concurring):

* * * Although the majority acknowledges that these were three representations made at three different times, it analyzes the Bober claim as if he either heard everything at once or as if no individual statement could be deceptive for CFA purposes if the aggregate of everything the defendants said about Zantac would ultimately have given an accurate picture. * * * Even if we can assume that consumers will assimilate all the information they are given on a given occasion, I find no Illinois case holding that a company can avoid potential liability for deceptive statements if it has buried further explanatory material on a web site or in a brochure that some consumers may never see. It is even worse if, as here, the absent information would only potentially save an otherwise misleading

statement. I am quite troubled by the implication one could draw from the majority's opinion that consumers have such an unbounded duty of inquiry. Such a holding would be inconsistent with Illinois's understanding of its own law, which requires that the statute be interpreted in a way consistent with its strong consumer protection purpose. What if Mr. Bober had stopped with the first telephone call, and never heard the recorded message? What if he had no access to a computer, or was not comfortable using one, and thus never visited the web site? The only answer that I can give to these questions is that Illinois law recognizes these risks and that is why it requires each separate statement to be assessed on its own. * * *

Looking at each of the statements individually, I agree with the majority that the recorded statement and the web site statement were not misleading. * * * Even if we approach this case as one in which two Zantac 75 tablets and one Zantac 150 tablet both deliver the same amount of ranitidine in the same way (which is a contested fact at this point), it remains true that prescription strength medication and non-prescription medication differ in important respects not related to the active ingredient. As the majority points out, there are different testing and approval procedures necessary for the different dosage levels of the identical medication. Perhaps more importantly, prescription medications as a practical matter give the patient a package of product and service: the product is the 150 mg. of ranitidine, and the service is a combination of the pharmacist's monitoring of dosage quality, amounts, potential interactions with other prescription drugs known to the pharmacy, and advice, and the doctor's ability to conduct similar medical monitoring, to the extent the patient needs to report back for prescription refills from time to time. Those kinds of services from the pharmacist cost money, just as any other retail-level service does. It is therefore not surprising that the version of the product that comes securely tied to a high level of service costs more than the "discount" version. A simple recorded message that tells the patient not to substitute until he or she finds out why the doctor made a particular choice is not misleading. * * *

The operator, however, gave Mr. Bober a different message. That message had two parts, both of which I find problematic. First, the operator said that Zantac 75 and Zantac 150 were not the "same medications"; second, he or she said that Mr. Bober "could not" substitute one for the other. From the layperson's point of view, which Illinois law requires us to use, both of these representations might be shown to be misleading. Even if someone who had spent a career in the pharmaceutical industry would recognize that as a matter of federal regulation the two forms of Zantac are different "medications," a trier of fact might well conclude that an average consumer, asking whether she could substitute the products, would be misled by the statement "they are different medications" into believing that Zantac 75 could in no circumstances be used to treat the illness for which she was taking Zantac 150. * * * The average consumer could also be misled by the flat statement that one "could not" substitute Zantac 75 for Zantac 150. Understood literally, this is simply not true. With the doctor's authorization, substitution certainly is possible, as both the recorded message and the web site conceded. But that qualification was not given by the operator. A more trusting caller might simply give up the quest and never even think to raise the subject with her doctor. * * *

Vess v. Ciba–Geigy Corp.

2001 WL 290333 (S.D.Cal.2001).

■ BREWSTER, SENIOR DISTRICT JUDGE:

* * * Plaintiff Todd D. Vess is a minor suing through his guardian ad litem, Deborah Vess, on behalf of himself, those similarly situated, and the general public of the state of California. * * * Plaintiff alleges that he was prescribed Ritalin in June 1994 when he was nine years old and that he purchased and ingested the drug for a non-specified period of time. The defendants are two non-profit groups and a manufacturer of Ritalin.

Defendant American Psychiatric Association [APA] is a nonprofit organization dedicated to the "advancement of knowledge, education and research in the field of psychiatry as well as to improvement of the diagnosis and treatment of the mentally ill." The APA publishes the *Diagnostic and Statistic Manual of Mental Disorders* ("DSM"). Plaintiff claims that the DSM contains false and misleading information about Attention Deficit Disorder, Attention Deficit Hyperactivity Disorder, and Ritalin.

Defendant CHADD [Children and Adults with Attention Deficit/Hyperactivity Disorder] is a nonprofit group that provides support to parents and individuals who have children or have personally been diagnosed as having Attention Deficit/Hyperactivity Disorder. CHADD describes itself as a "support and advocacy organization with over 200 local chapters and 20,000 members."

Defendant Novartis Pharmaceuticals Corp. is a Ritalin manufacturer. Novartis' predecessor, Ciba–Geigy Corp., began manufacturing methylphenidate under the brand name Ritalin in 1955. Ciba–Geigy's patent on Ritalin expired in the 1970s and there have been generic forms of the drug since. * * * Plaintiff alleges Ciba/Novartis has engaged in a variety of misconduct regarding Ritalin. Ciba/Novartis allegedly fails to warn Ritalin users that the full range of side effects has not yet been adequately studied. Ciba/Novartis allegedly failed to disclose the limited effectiveness of its product and misled clinicians and the public to believe Ritalin had positive benefits, despite the fact that the drug may not cause any benefits at all.

Plaintiff alleges that Ciba/Novartis conspired with the APA to "develop, promote, broaden, and confirm the diagnoses of Attention Deficit Disorder (ADD) and Attention Deficit Hyperactivity Disorder (ADHD)." Plaintiff claims that Ciba/Novartis and the APA have a financial relationship. According to plaintiff, the APA included ADD in the 1980 DSM, even though ADD did not meet the APA's own criteria for inclusion. Plaintiff complains that the current DSM contains further misrepresentations and omits dissenting opinions. In addition, plaintiff claims that the APA has fraudulently failed to disclose Novartis' role in the creation, promulgation, and revision of the DSM or the financial relationship between the APA and Ciba/Novartis.

Plaintiff claims that CHADD deliberately attempted to increase the sales of Ritalin, to increase the available supply, and to reduce or eliminate laws and restrictions on the use of Ritalin because of Ciba/Novartis' significant contributions to CHADD. Plaintiff complains that CHADD does not reveal on its website that it receives significant contributions from Ciba/Novartis.

Claims

The defendants are sued as co-conspirators. Plaintiff alleges violations of the Consumer Legal Remedies Act (CLRA), Cal. Code § 1770, for allegedly unlawful competition, and unfair and deceptive acts. Plaintiff sues under Cal. Bus. & Prof. § 17200 for unfair competition, and plaintiff sues under Cal. Bus. & Prof. § 17500 for false and misleading statements. Plaintiff seeks injunctive relief, disgorgement of revenues and profits, restitution, and punitive damages. * * *

Statute in Q

Cal. Code Civ. P. § 425.16 is California's anti-Strategic Lawsuits Against Public Participation, or "SLAPP" statute. It is intended to deter lawsuits brought primarily to chill the valid exercise of the constitutional rights of freedom of speech and petition for the redress of grievances. A SLAPP motion may be brought to strike a lawsuit based on a defendant's exercise of free speech. If a defendant prevails on a SLAPP motion, he is entitled to reasonable attorney's fees and costs. If a plaintiff prevails and the court finds the special motion to strike is frivolous or solely intended to cause delay, the court shall award costs and reasonable attorney's fees to plaintiff. The anti-SLAPP statute establishes a procedure for early dismissal of meritless lawsuits against public speech. * * *

Lawsuit deterring statute

According to the APA, plaintiff is asking this court to hold a nonprofit educational and scientific association liable in damages for developing and publishing a book about unquestionably important public health issues. * * * In addition, the APA argues that its efforts to educate state, national, and international governmental bodies about diagnostic categories and criteria is protected petitioning activity. The APA lists as examples its collaborative activities with the World Health Organization and other federal agencies.* * *

APA's arguments

CHADD publishes magazines and other printed materials, holds an annual conference, and conducts outreach efforts to governmental agencies and legislative bodies. CHADD argues that plaintiff is attacking its right to petition the government "to reduce and eliminate laws and restrictions concerning the use of Ritalin" and restrain its communications with its members and the public about ADHD and its effective treatment. CHADD argues that the anti-SLAPP statute protects these activities.

CHADD's arguments

Novartis argues that plaintiff's claims arise out of Novartis' participation in the public discussion and development of diagnostic criteria for the serious medical conditions of ADD and ADHD. FDA approval continues for the use of Ritalin in treating ADD/ADHD. Novartis does not diagnose ADD/ADHD or prescribe Ritalin to any patients. Thus, according to Novar-

Novartis argument

tis, plaintiff is only attacking Novartis' speech in connection with Ritalin. Novartis claims that all of plaintiff's allegations against Novartis involve speech. The claims include Novartis' alleged promotion, support, facilitation, failure to provide information, and misrepresentations in connection with Ritalin. Novartis argues that the speech relates to a public issue and a matter of public interest, as evidenced by plaintiff's own lawsuit. * * *

Novartis argues that plaintiff's claims are exactly the type the anti-SLAPP statute was designed to prevent. Plaintiff is attempting to impose his view on the way doctors practice medicine in California, rather than debating the current DSM standards and [FDA] approval in the available public fora. Novartis cites authority that this court may look at the litigation history in evaluating its anti-SLAPP motion and points out that the same plaintiff's attorneys have begun multiple class actions in multiple states with classes that overlap. Furthermore, some of the attorneys here sued in the late 1980s and early 1990s making some of the same fraud and conspiracy allegations present here. * * *

Plaintiff argues that his experts' testimony establishes that his case is not a strategic lawsuit against public participation, but is instead a lawsuit based on serious and substantial scientific problems. Plaintiff's expert Dr. Kirk reaches the conclusion that "39% of children who do not suffer from ADD/ADHD are diagnosed as having this mental disorder." Dr. Kirk goes on to attack the DSM as unscientific and reliable. In addition, plaintiff's expert Dr. Caplan concludes that the APA's process in revising the DSM is unscientific. Moreover, Dr. Kirk claims that his research uncovered a financial connection between Ciba–Geigy and the APA. * * *

Defendants have prima facie shown that the speech at issue is protected. Plaintiff's arguments to the contrary are unpersuasive. The anti-SLAPP law does not specify that it only applies to certain types of parties or specific causes of action. * * * In addition, allegations of a financial relationship between Novartis, CHADD, and the APA do not state an actionable claim. Plaintiff failed to plead any allegations of specific representations that were false, when the representations were made, where the representations were made, and by whom. Finally, plaintiff has not alleged any causal connection to the defendants or any damages. Plaintiff should be able to point out some specific misrepresentations to support plaintiff's claims but failed to do so. The court hereby grants defendants' Rule 9(b) motions [to dismiss]. * * *

The APA and CHADD argue that their activities are not the sort of "unlawful" or "unfair" consumer or business activity covered by the California consumer protection statutes under which plaintiff sues. The DSM states that it is not intended for consumers, but is instead to be applied by professional psychiatrists, physicians, and psychologists. Moreover, neither the APA nor CHADD actually markets or sells Ritalin. Nowhere does the amended complaint allege a transaction between the APA and plaintiff, CHADD and plaintiff, that plaintiff purchased or read the DSM, that plaintiff ever read any CHADD literature, or that plaintiff saw or relied on any APA or CHADD advertisements. * * *

The CLRA forbids certain unfair and deceptive practices that are "undertaken by any person in a transaction intended to result or which results in the sale or lease of goods or services to any consumer." Cal. Civ. Code § 1770. Transaction is defined as "an agreement between a consumer and any other person." Likewise, Section 17200 covers "business act[s] or practice[s]" designed to deceive consumers or competitors. "[T]he statute only applies to activities that can properly be called a business practice." The APA and CHADD argue that these provisions are limited to transactions between a buyer and seller in the sale of consumer goods. * * *

The CLRA applies to damages "as a result of the" unlawful practice, Cal. Civ. Code § 1780. The APA argues that plaintiff cannot maintain his claim unless he can link the APA's alleged activity with a specific injury, such as the misdiagnosis or wrong prescription of the named plaintiff caused by the DSM. The amended complaint does not contain any allegations of whether or how the DSM played a role in plaintiff's diagnosis. * * *

Plaintiff argues that the DSM is widely published and available and there is no language prohibiting consumers from using it, so it falls within the consumer protection statutes. Second, plaintiff argues that the sale of the DSM is the consumer transaction at issue, not the sale of Ritalin, so it is irrelevant that the APA does not sell Ritalin. Finally, plaintiff claims that the misrepresentation at issue is the DSM's misrepresentation that its diagnostic criteria for ADD is scientifically reliable. * * * Plaintiff alleges that CHADD sells its magazines and other printed materials. * * * Finally, plaintiff argues that virtually any representation made in any manner in connection with the sale of goods, services, or credit is advertising. Plaintiff argues that his allegations that CHADD and the APA made misrepresentations are sufficient to maintain his cause of action for false advertising. * * *

[handwritten margin note: P making "false advertising" claim vs. D's free speech claim]

Plaintiff does not allege that he, his doctor, or his parents ever read the DSM or any CHADD literature. Nor does he allege that he suffered damages that directly resulted from any alleged misstatements in the DSM or in CHADD literature. Plaintiff's late contention that the sale at issue in his claims against the APA is the sale of the DSM is disingenuous and found nowhere in the amended complaint. In any event, plaintiff alleges no misrepresentations in connection with the sale of the DSM or CHADD literature. If the issue is the APA's and CHADD's acceptance of donations, plaintiff has cited no APA or CHADD statement that it does not accept Novartis' contributions, or even any statement listing some donors, while omitting Novartis. Finally, plaintiff has not identified any advertisements. The court hereby grants the APA's and CHADD's 12(b)(6) motions to dismiss. * * *

Plaintiff is granted leave to amend. If he elects to do so, he must file his second amended complaint on or before April 16, 2001. If no amended complaint is filed by April 16, 2001, the court will dismiss plaintiff's first amended complaint with prejudice and grant each defendant's motion to strike pursuant to Cal. Code Civ. P. § 425.16 with reasonable attorney's fees and costs. * * *

NOTES AND QUESTIONS

1. *Ragging on Ritalin.* The diagnosis of attention deficit hyperactivity disorder, and the use of Ritalin® (methylphenidate hydrochloride, a Schedule II controlled substance) and other psychoactive drugs in its treatment, has long generated controversy. See Lawrence H. Diller, The Run on Ritalin: Attention Deficit Disorder and Stimulant Treatment in the 1990s, 26 Hastings Ctr. Rep. 12 (1996); Larry S. Goldman et al., Diagnosis and Treatment of Attention–Deficit–Hyperactivity Disorder in Children and Adolescents, 279 JAMA 1100 (1998); Victor W. Henderson, Stimulant Drug Treatment of the Attention Deficit Disorder, 65 S. Cal. L. Rev. 397 (1991). As mentioned in *Vess*, this class action lawsuit represented part of the latest wave of attacks. See Hernandez v. Ciba–Geigy Corp., 200 F.R.D. 285 (S.D.Tex.2001) (dismissing a similar complaint); Dawson v. Ciba–Geigy Corp., 145 F.Supp.2d 565 (D.N.J.2001) (rejecting a removal petition); Steven Keeva, No Deficit of Attention Here, ABA J., June 2001, at 28; Bob Van Voris, Ritalin Class Actions: Fast Start, Big Stumble, Nat'l L.J., Aug. 6, 2001, at A1.

2. *Atypical advertising.* Even if not actionable, the allegations that the manufacturer of Ritalin influenced the APA or sponsored a patient advocacy group may have some foundation and are hardly unique to this particular drug. See Lars Noah, Pigeonholing Illness: Medical Diagnosis as a Legal Construct, 50 Hastings L.J. 241, 290–94 (1999); Jeff Gerth & Sheryl Gay Stolberg, Medicine Merchants/Cultivating Alliances: With Quiet, Unseen Ties, Drug Makers Sway Debate, N.Y. Times, Oct. 5, 2000, at A1 (reporting that as part of their lobbying efforts companies have "also financed hundreds of existing patient advocacy groups"); Robert O'Harrow, Jr., FDA Eyes Drug Firm's Marketing, Wash. Post, Sept. 14, 2000, at E3 (describing one company's sponsorship of "grass roots groups to draw attention to hepatitis C and boost sales of the drugmaker's treatment"); cf. Andrea Peterson, Episodic Illness: How Rare Ailments Get on Prime Time, Wall St. J., Apr. 14, 1998, at A1 (reporting that some patient advocacy groups have worked to land "a 'product placement' for their illness in prime time"). Similar allegations have arisen concerning efforts to have the APA recognize premenstrual dysphoric disorder (PMDD) as distinct from premenstrual syndrome. Although the latest edition of the *DSM* left the question unresolved, Eli Lilly received approval from the FDA to market a version of Prozac for the treatment of PMDD and then engaged in an aggressive advertising campaign. See Tara Parker–Pope, Drug Companies Push Use of Antidepressants to Treat Severe PMS, Wall St. J., Feb. 23. 2001, at B1; Shankar Vedantam, Renamed Prozac Fuels Women's Health Debate, Wash. Post, Apr. 29, 2001, at A1; see also Kimberly A. Yonkers et al., Symptomatic Improvement of Premenstrual Dysphonic Disorder with Sertraline Treatment, 278 JAMA 983 (1997).

C. First Amendment Constraints on Regulating Information

Washington Legal Foundation v. Friedman

13 F.Supp.2d 51 (D.D.C.1998).

■ Lamberth, District Judge:

Plaintiff Washington Legal Foundation (WLF) is a non-profit public interest law and policy center that defends "the rights of individuals and businesses to go about their affairs without undue influence from government regulators." In this action, WLF seeks to enjoin the Food and Drug Administration (FDA) and the Department of Health and Human Services (HHS) from enforcing policies restricting certain forms of manufacturer promotion of off-label uses for FDA-approved drugs and devices. The policies at issue—expressed through Guidance Documents—concern manufacturer distribution of reprints of medical textbooks and peer-reviewed journal articles ("enduring materials"), and manufacturer involvement in continuing medical education seminars and symposia ("CME"). * * *

action

(note: the drug companies themselves are not generating the material in Q here)

FDA's first contention—that the Guidance Documents are a restraint upon conduct and not upon speech—may be addressed quickly. There is little question that the relevant "conduct" is the off-label prescription of drugs by physicians. The distribution of enduring materials and sponsorship of CME seminars addressing and encouraging that conduct is speech. * * * [T]he activities at issue in this case are only "conduct" to the extent that moving one's lips is "conduct," or to the extent that affixing a stamp and distributing information through the mails is "conduct." * * * This court is hard pressed to believe that the agency is seriously contending that "promotion" of an activity is conduct and not speech, or that "promotion" is entitled to no First Amendment protection. There may certainly be a "line" between education and promotion as regards a drug manufacturer's marketing activities, but that is the line between pure speech and commercial speech, not between speech and conduct. * * *

FDA argument

Drug promotion protected by 1st amendment

The FDA next asserts that the speech regulated by the Guidance Documents falls outside of the ambit of the First Amendment because of the federal government's extensive power to regulate the pharmaceutical industry * * * * First, the argument that a certain subset of speech may be considered completely outside of the First Amendment framework because the speech occurs in an area of extensive government regulation is a proposition whose continuing validity is at best questionable in light of the Supreme Court's most recent commercial speech cases. See Central Hudson Gas & Elec. Corp. v. Public Serv. Comm'n of New York, 447 U.S. 557 (1980). * * * Any lingering doubt as to whether the government may impose restrictions upon speech without offending the First Amendment merely because it has the authority to regulate the underlying activity was resolved in *44 Liquormart, Inc. v. Rhode Island,* 517 U.S. 484 (1996). In

FDA argument #2

that case, the Supreme Court expressly rejected the concept embodied in *Posadas de Puerto Rico Assoc. v. Tourism Co. of Puerto Rico*, 478 U.S. 328 (1986), that because the government had the power to extensively regulate in a certain area (casino gambling) it also had the authority to regulate speech without raising First Amendment concerns. * * *

Having concluded that manufacturer distribution of enduring materials and suggesting content or speakers for CME seminars in which the focus is on the sponsor's product is properly classified as commercial speech, this court will now analyze the constitutionality of the Guidance Documents under *Central Hudson*'s four-prong test.

Re: the constitutionality of the Guidance Documents in Q

1.   The Speech Is Neither Unlawful Nor Inherently Misleading.

FDA argument

* * * In claiming that the speech at issue involves "illegal activities," the FDA does not seriously press any argument that off-label prescriptions are illegal. Rather the agency directs attention to the statutory basis for the Guidance Documents and asserts that the speech cannot survive the first prong of the *Central Hudson* test because a drug or device is considered to be misbranded as a matter of law if it is promoted by the manufacturer for an off-label use. Therefore, when a manufacturer disseminates information about a drug product that diverges from the treatments included on the label, that manufacturer may be engaged in misbranding, which is illegal. However, the tautological nature of this argument exposes its shortcomings. The proper inquiry is not whether the speech violates a law or a regulation, but rather whether the conduct that the speech promotes violates the law. * * * Were the FDA's characterization of what constitutes "lawful activity" accurate, First Amendment protections for commercial speech could be all but eviscerated by the government: First Amendment challenges to speech restrictions would be defeated by noting that Congress had made the speech illegal, and therefore unlawful activity is at issue. The flaw in the FDA's reasoning is perhaps best demonstrated by example. In *Rubin v. Coors Brewing Co.*, 514 U.S. 476 (1995), the challenged statute prohibited the display of alcohol content on beer labels. Under the FDA's definition of "illegal activity," the statute would have been a satisfactory restriction on commercial speech because printing alcohol content on beer labels would render the product "misbranded."

It is clear that when the Supreme Court declares that the First Amendment does not protect illegal activity, it is referring to the conduct that the speech is promoting (e.g., prostitution, counterfeiting, narcotic use, and the like), and not the speech subject to the restriction. Therefore, only at such time as off-label prescriptions are proscribed by law could the FDA legitimately claim that speech at issue addresses "illegal activities."

re: potentially misleading

Whether the speech subject to the restrictions in the Guidance Documents is truthful and non-misleading presents a somewhat closer question. Notably, speech that is merely "potentially misleading" does not render it able to be proscribed under the commercial speech test without further analysis. "If the 'protections afforded commercial speech are to retain their force, we cannot allow rote invocation of the words "potentially misleading" to supplant (the government's burden).' " Ibanez v. Florida Dep't of

Business & Professional Reg., 512 U.S. 136, 146 (1994). In order to end the *Central Hudson* analysis on the first prong, the speech must be "inherently misleading" * * * *

In asserting that any and all scientific claims about the safety, effectiveness, contraindications, side effects, and the like regarding prescription drugs are presumptively untruthful or misleading until the FDA has had the opportunity to evaluate them, FDA exaggerates its overall place in the universe. It is certainly the case that by statute, no drug may be introduced or delivered into interstate commerce without FDA approval, and that the claims that a manufacturer may make about a drug through labeling, advertising and other forms of promotion are subject to FDA regulatory authority. However, the conclusions reached by a laboratory scientist or university academic and presented in a peer-reviewed journal or textbook, or the findings presented by a physician at a CME seminar are not "untruthful" or "inherently misleading" merely because the FDA has not yet had the opportunity to evaluate the claim. As two commentators astutely stated, "the FDA is not a peer review mechanism for the scientific community." Lars Noah & Barbara A. Noah, Liberating Commercial Speech: Product Labeling Controls and the First Amendment, 47 Fla. L. Rev. 63, 96 (1995). * * *

Interestingly, and quite significantly, the FDA has a categorically different view on whether article reprints or CME seminars addressing off-label treatments are "inherently misleading" when anyone other than the drug manufacturer is responsible for their dissemination. For example, in the Reprint Guidance, it cannot go unnoted that the FDA has no objection to manufacturer distribution pursuant to a request by a physician, or distribution from any source other than the drug manufacturer. * * * Obviously, the exact same journal article or textbook reprint cannot be inherently conducive to deception and coercion when it is sent unsolicited, yet of significant clinical value when mailed pursuant to a request. Additionally, the FDA makes no effort to regulate discussion of off-label uses at a CME seminar when there is no pharmaceutical company involvement, but a seminar in which a company does not suggest the content or the speakers could be just as convincing as to the possible benefits of an off-label use, if not more so, because an attendee is less likely to view such a presentation with a jaded eye. Whether or not the manufacturer plays a role in the dissemination, scientific and academic speech concerning off-label use is either "treacherous anecdotal evidence," or it is not. It is clear that it is not. Were the materials at issue here either actually or inherently misleading, one would have to conclude that the FDA would be derelict to not proscribe dissemination under all circumstances. * * *

To categorize the speech at issue here as "inherently misleading" is particularly unsupportable when one considers all the controls available to FDA to ensure that the information manufacturers wish to distribute is scientifically reliable, and therefore less likely to even be "potentially misleading." Pursuant to the order issued this day, the FDA may:

1. require conspicuous notifications that the uses under discussion have not been approved by the FDA;

2. require that for article reprints, that the reprint comes from a bona fide peer-review journal, with the term "bona fide peer-review" meaning "a journal that uses experts to objectively review and select, reject, or provide comments about proposed articles. Such experts should have demonstrated expertise in the subject of the articles under review, and be independent from the journal";

3. require that for textbook reprints, that the textbook is published by a "bona fide independent publisher," with the term "bona fide independent publisher" meaning "a publisher that has no common ownership or corporate affiliation with a pharmaceutical or medical device manufacturer and whose principal business is the publication and distribution of books through normal distribution channels";

4. require that for CME seminars and symposia, the sponsor must be an "independent program provider," with that term defined as "an entity that has no common ownership or other corporate affiliation with a pharmaceutical or medical device manufacturer, that engages in the business of creating and producing continuing medical educational seminars, programs or other symposia and that is accredited by a national accrediting organization pertinent to the topic of such seminars, programs or symposia";

5. require pharmaceutical and device manufacturers that sponsor or provide financial support for the dissemination or redistribution of articles or reference textbooks or for seminars and symposia that include references to uses of drugs or medical devices other than those approved by the FDA to disclose (i) its interest in such drugs or devices, and (ii) the fact that the use discussed has not been approved by the FDA;

6. enforce any rules, regulations, guidances, statutes or other provisions of law that sanction the dissemination or redistribution of material that is false or misleading.

These controls would greatly circumscribe the possibility that untruthful or misleading information would be disseminated by manufacturers. This court finds that the Guidance Documents address speech that is directed toward lawful activity and that is not misleading. Therefore, the first prong of the *Central Hudson* test is satisfied.

2. The Government's Interest Is Substantial.

Under *Central Hudson*, the second inquiry is whether the interest asserted by the government is substantial. The Supreme Court has consistently held that the government has a substantial interest in protecting the health and safety of its citizens. There are few, if any, more important functions performed by any regulatory agency than the function this case concerns—ensuring that when a citizen takes a prescription drug, that individual has absolute assurance that the product is safe and effective for the condition for which his physician has prescribed it. Any claim that the government's general interest is insufficient under *Central Hudson* is frivolous.

Within the general category of promoting health and safety, the government describes two more specific interests: 1) ensuring that physicians receive accurate and unbiased information so that they may make informed prescription choices, and 2) providing manufacturers with ample incentive to get previously unapproved uses on label. As one of these interests is legitimate and the other is not, they will be considered separately.

a. The Government Cannot Justify the Guidances out of the Fear that Information Will Be Misused by Physicians.

* * * The agency claims that "most physicians, well-educated and experienced though they may be, do not have the resources, experience, or education to critically evaluate evidence concerning off-label uses. While physicians may believe that they are in a better position than FDA to evaluate off-label claims, both the evidence and the law say otherwise." To the extent that the FDA is endeavoring to keep information from physicians out of concern that they will misuse that information, the regulation is wholly and completely unsupportable.

If there is one fixed principle in the commercial speech arena, it is that "a State's paternalistic assumption that the public will use truthful, nonmisleading commercial information unwisely cannot justify a decision to suppress it." *44 Liquormart*, 517 U.S. at 497; see also id. at 503 ("The First Amendment directs us to be especially skeptical of regulations that seek to keep people in the dark for what the government perceives to be their own good"). To endeavor to support a restriction upon speech by alleging that the recipient needs to be shielded from that speech for his or her own protection, which is the gravamen of FDA's claim here, is practically an engraved invitation to have the restriction struck.

In this instance, the government's notion that the scientific research product which the manufacturers seek to distribute needs to be withheld for the "good of the recipient" is even more unsupportable than usual. First, it must be noted that the manufacturers are not seeking to distribute this information to the general consumer public, who likely lack the knowledge or sophistication necessary to make informed choices on the efficacy of prescription drugs. Rather, they seek to disseminate this information exclusively to physicians. A physician's livelihood depends upon the ability to make accurate, life-and-death decisions based upon the scientific evidence before them. They are certainly capable of critically evaluating journal articles or textbook reprints that are mailed to them, or the findings presented at CME seminars. Furthermore, the FDA does not question a physician's evaluative skills when an article about an off-label use appears among a group of articles in the *New England Journal of Medicine*, or when one physician refers a peer physician to a published article he recently perused, or even when a physician requests a reprint from a manufacturer. Why the ability of a doctor to critically evaluate scientific findings depends upon how the article got into the physician's hands, or whether a manufacturer suggests speakers or content for a CME seminar, is unclear to this court.

In light of the fact that the Supreme Court has repeatedly rejected governmental attempts to equate less information with better decision-making, and in light of the fact that the FDA does not question a physician's evaluative skills when the information comes from a source other than a drug manufacturer, concerns about a physician's ability to critically evaluate materials presented to him is not a "substantial interest."

b. The Government Does Have a Substantial Interest in Compelling Manufacturers to Get Off–Label Treatments On–Label.

The other substantial interest that the regulations purportedly advance is that they provide an incentive for manufacturers to go through the strict FDA preclinical and clinical trial process to get off-label uses on-label. As explained previously, defendants have proved to this court's satisfaction that dissemination of scientific information on off-label uses is an effective means of influencing physicians to prescribe a drug for a given condition. Consequently, the dissemination of information demonstrating that a drug is effective has a positive effect upon sales of the drug. But, if the manufacturer's ability to disseminate any information on a new use for a previously approved drug is made wholly contingent upon FDA approval of that use, the manufacturer will be encouraged, if not compelled, to obtain FDA approval.

Plaintiff appears to take issue with the idea that the government has a substantial interest in requiring manufacturers to get new uses for previously approved drugs on-label. They assert that off-label uses are on the whole beneficial to the public health, contending that "the ability to prescribe off-label is essential to saving patients' lives." They cite the large number of off-label prescriptions written by physicians every year, and again state that, even by FDA's own admissions, off-label treatments may constitute the standard of care for some conditions. In sum, plaintiff argues that "the fact that a use is off-label rather than on-label has no necessary correlation to the benefits of that use." * * *

However, whether compelling manufacturers to get new uses on-label is wise government policy when considered against the backdrop of present day medical realities, financial constraints and procedural burdens is a policy question that must be addressed to Congress, not to this court. Congress has concluded that it benefits the public health to require manufacturers to get all uses approved by the FDA. The Supreme Court has held that the approval requirement is not subject to exceptions based upon the difficulty of obtaining approval, the cost, or even the conceded benefits of the unapproved use. In light of the fact that Congress has declared that all uses for a drug must be proven safe and effective by the FDA, and has recently reaffirmed that position through the 1997 Food and Drug Amendments, this court finds that this interest—that off-label uses of previously approved drugs are subjected to the FDA's evaluation process—

is of sufficient importance so as to constitute a "substantial government interest" as contemplated by *Central Hudson*.

3. The Guidance Documents Directly Advance a Substantial Government Interest in Requiring Manufacturers to Submit Supplemental Applications to Obtain Approval for New Uses.

Under the *Central Hudson* test, commercial speech restrictions must advance the government's interest in "a direct and material way." In *Edenfield v. Fane*, 507 U.S. 761 (1993), the Court held that, "this burden is not satisfied by mere speculation or conjecture; rather, a governmental body seeking to sustain a restriction on commercial speech must demonstrate that the harms it recites are real and that its restriction will in fact alleviate them to a material degree." Id. at 770–71. What the court must determine is whether the Guidance Documents directly advance the "subsequent approval" interest: do they encourage and/or compel a drug manufacturer to submit previously approved drugs to the FDA for approval of the off-label treatments? While defendants have not presented what this court considers to be substantial evidence on this point, the court still answers this question in the affirmative, in large part based upon the arguments of plaintiff.

That drug manufacturers often would like to avoid having to submit previously approved drugs to the FDA for subsequent approvals is clear. Plaintiff admits that among the reasons drug manufacturers wish to engage in the distribution of enduring materials and sponsorship of CME seminars concerning off-label uses is because of the slow pace of the FDA approval process. Furthermore, plaintiff notes that "economic considerations also may play a role in determining whether beneficial uses of drugs are submitted for approval." They explain (albeit consistently couched in the terms "FDA recognizes that") that manufacturers may be unwilling to pursue expensive and well-controlled clinical trials if subsequent sales of the drugs are insufficient to cover the costs. And, if a product is no longer protected by patent, a manufacturer will have little incentive to get the new use on-label because generic manufacturers could become instantaneous free-riders on the approval. Finally, even the pace of FDA approval has economic repercussions because during the time that it takes to get approval, a manufacturer is unable to market the product for the new use, and, given the correlation between marketing efforts and sales, that delay affects the manufacturer's bottom line.

It is clear that manufacturers have incentives to circumvent subsequent approval requirements, but one wonders what incentives they have to obtain them? For a brand-new drug, the incentive is simple: the pharmaceutical company cannot manufacture or introduce the drug into interstate commerce without FDA approval. However, the drugs subject to off-label prescriptions are already in interstate commerce, so the obvious restriction on conduct is unavailable. Therefore, one of the few mechanisms available to FDA to compel manufacturer behavior is to constrain their marketing options; i.e. control the labeling, advertising and marketing. If a manufacturer is proscribed from distributing enduring materials and/or sponsoring CME seminars that address that manufacturer's product absent FDA approval of that use, that proscription provides a strong incentive to get the use on-label, in light of the connection between marketing and sales.

Because the restrictions on the distribution of enduring materials and involvement with CME do provide an incentive for manufacturers to have previously approved drugs evaluated by the FDA for safety and effectiveness for an off-label use, this court finds that the restrictions in the Guidance Documents directly advance a substantial interest.

4. The Guidance Documents Are Unconstitutional Because They Are More Extensive than Necessary.

While commercial speech jurisprudence does not require the government to employ the least restrictive means of advancing an interest, the regulating body must make an effort to reasonably fit its means to its end sought. A commercial speech restriction will fail if it burdens "substantially more speech than necessary." United States v. Edge Broad. Co., 509 U.S. 418, 430 (1993). The court finds that the restrictions in the Guidance Documents are considerably more extensive than necessary to further the substantial government interest in encouraging manufacturers to get new uses on-label.

This determination is based in large part upon the fact that there exist less-burdensome alternatives to this restriction on commercial speech. The most obvious alternative is full, complete, and unambiguous disclosure by the manufacturer. Full disclosure not only addresses all of the concerns advanced by the FDA, but addresses them more effectively. It is less restrictive on speech, while at the same time deals more precisely with the concerns of the FDA and Congress.

First, it assuages concerns that the message communicated is inherently or potentially misleading, or that a physician would be deceived or misled by the speech. That the use discussed therein had not been approved by the FDA would be readily apparent. A physician would be immediately alerted to the fact that the "substantial evidence standard" had not been satisfied, and would evaluate the communicated message accordingly. And, the failure to provide such disclosure would render the communication subject to the full battery of FDA enforcement options, because not including such disclosure when required would clearly render the materials "inherently misleading."

Second, permitting this limited form of manufacturer communication still leaves more than adequate incentives compelling drug manufacturers to get new uses approved by the FDA. As plaintiffs noted at oral argument, it is a very narrow form of manufacturer communication upon which this court is ruling in enjoining enforcement of the Guidance Documents. There still are enormous differences between the permitted marketing of on-label as opposed to off-label uses. Manufacturers still are proscribed from producing and distributing any internally-produced marketing materials to physicians concerning off-label uses, or from involvement with seminars not conducted by an "independent program provider." Nor may the drug companies initiate person-to-person contact with a physician about an off-label use. Nor may they advertise off-label uses for previously approved drugs directly to the consumer. If a manufacturer wishes to engage in any of these or other marketing techniques, it cannot do so without first obtaining FDA approval of the off-label use. The fact that these adequate incentives still exist to get off-label treatments on-label is central to this court's finding that the First Amendment is violated by the Guidance Documents. Were manufacturers permitted to engage in all forms of marketing of off-label treatments, a different result might be compelled.

still can't market an off-label use

Third, to the extent that physicians look to FDA approval as an important (or the exclusive) indication of safety and effectiveness, and either will not prescribe or are reluctant to prescribe absent such approval, manufacturers will seek to obtain FDA approval to make their products more appealing to that market. And, to the extent that the tort regime looks to FDA approval as the definition of the "standard of care," the call to get new uses on-label will come from sources other than the FDA.

Fourth, the court must again note that off-label prescriptions, presently legal, do constitute the most effective treatment available for some conditions. Through the government's well-intentioned efforts to prevent misleading information from being communicated, a great deal of truthful information will also be embargoed. In this case, the truthful information may be life saving information, or information that makes a life with a debilitating condition more comfortable.

Finally, this alternative comports with the Supreme Court's preference for combating potentially problematic speech with more speech. In choosing between the dissemination of more or less information "it is precisely this kind of choice, between the dangers of suppressing information, and the dangers of its misuse if it is freely available, that the First Amendment makes for us." *Virginia State Board*, 425 U.S. at 770 (quoted in *44 Liquormart*, 517 U.S. at 497).

NOTES AND QUESTIONS

1. *Origins of the commercial speech doctrine.* Until the mid–1970s, so-called "commercial speech" received no constitutional protection. As it happens, the first decision extending the First Amendment to such speech arose in a prescription drug advertising case. In *Virginia State Board of Pharmacy v. Virginia Citizens Consumer Council*, 425 U.S. 748 (1976), the Court struck down a state prohibition against the advertising of prescription drug prices because even such purely commercial speech, bereft of all the other qualities typically associated with protected speech, still deserved some constitutional protection. The Court noted that the public's interest in the free flow of commercial information might be "as keen, if not keener by far" than its interest in political debate, and it added that the information at issue could have a profound impact on the consumer's quality of life. See id. at 763–64 ("When drug prices vary as strikingly as they do, information as to who is charging what becomes more than a convenience. It could mean the alleviation of physical pain or the enjoyment of basic necessities."). In *Bolger v. Youngs Drug Products Corp.*, 463 U.S. 60 (1983), another early commercial speech decision, the Court held that a federal law prohibiting unsolicited mailings was unconstitutional when applied to a pharmaceutical company distributing informational pamphlets that encouraged the use of contraceptives, emphasizing that such materials—containing information related to public health matters—deserved a high degree of protection under the Constitution. See id. at 69. For the Supreme Court's latest guidance on commercial speech, see Lorillard Tobacco Co. v. Reilly, 533 U.S. 525 (2001); United States v. United Foods, Inc., 533 U.S. 405 (2001).

2. *Rulemaking vs. adjudication.* Just before the U.S. Supreme Court began to extend First Amendment protections to commercial speech, the FDA started to utilize its authority to issue rules of general application as a more efficient means for exercising control than engaging in case-by-case enforcement of the broad substantive restrictions on product marketing set forth in the statute. The confluence of these two developments raised significant questions about the constitutionality of the FDA's promulgation of broad-based, prophylactic rules designed to reduce the potential for the dissemination of misleading information to consumers and health care professionals. This question was first broached in the early 1990s, in connection with the FDA's sweeping new rules governing the labeling of food and dietary supplements, especially restrictions on the use of health claims. In *Pearson v. Shalala*, 164 F.3d 650 (D.C.Cir.1999), the court invalidated some of these on First Amendment grounds because the FDA had declined to allow the use of disclaimers as a more tailored response to the potential for misleading consumers than the outright suppression of any unapproved health claims. See id. at 655–59; see also Pearson v. Shalala, 130 F.Supp.2d 105 (D.D.C.2001) (ordering the FDA to allow, with an appropriate disclaimer, a health claim for dietary supplements containing folic acid). The appellate court in *Pearson* also suggested, as had Judge Lamberth in his *WLF* opinion, that adjudication may be more apt a procedure than rulemaking for dealing with these issues. Before the Supreme Court first extended protections to commercial speech, lower courts had rejected constitutional objections to FDA *enforcement* actions seizing books that were used as product labeling. See United States v. Articles of Drug * * * Century Food Co., 32 F.R.D. 32 (S.D.Ill.1963); United States v. 8 Cartons * * * Molasses, 103 F.Supp. 626, 627 (W.D.N.Y.1951). Chapter 7(B)(3) revisits some of these issues in connection with the imposition of tort liability for failure to warn.

3. *Commercial vs. scientific speech.* Some commentators have argued that therapeutic information disseminated by drug and medical device manufacturers deserves more constitutional protection than simple product advertising. See Martin H. Redish, Product Health Claims and the First Amendment: Scientific Expression and the Twilight Zone of Commercial Speech, 43 Vand. L. Rev. 1433 (1990); Glenn C. Smith, Avoiding Awkward Alchemy in the Off–Label Drug Context and Beyond: Fully–Protected Independent

Research Should Not Transmogrify into Mere Commercial Speech Just Because Product Manufacturers Distribute It, 34 Wake Forest L. Rev. 963 (1999). Judge Lamberth rejected this argument as follows:

> Typical "commercial speech" is authored and/or uttered directly by the commercial entity that wishes to financially benefit from the message. A purveyor of goods or services makes claims about his products to order to induce a purchase. In this instance, by contrast, the speech that the manufacturers wish to "communicate" is the speech of others—the work product of scientists, physicians and other academics. It is beyond dispute that when considered outside of the context of manufacturer promotion of their drug products, CME seminars, peer-reviewed medical journal articles and commercially-available medical textbooks merit the highest degree of constitutional protection. Scientific and academic speech reside at the core of the First Amendment. Plaintiff claims that because this speech merits full protection when uttered by a scientist or academic, the level of constitutional scrutiny should not change merely because a corporation wishes to enhance the distribution of that message.... The mechanism by which a commercial transaction may be "proposed" can vary widely. In the consumer goods area, of course, the proposal usually involves a manufacturer making a claim about its product that encourages the purchase of the product. However, there are certainly instances in which a manufacturer promotes and induces the purchase of its product by directing attention to favorable information generated by wholly independent organizations.... [T]here can be little question that the reason that drug manufacturers wish to disseminate enduring materials and sponsor CME seminars is because they believe that such activity will increase the sales volume of their drugs.... Through distributing enduring materials and sponsoring CME seminars, drug manufacturers call a physician's attention to the subject drug product, showing that the drug effectively treats a certain condition (emphasize a desirable quality) in the hopes that the physician will prescribe (buy or patronize) the drug. The fact that an effective means for accomplishing that goal is through providing the academic research results generated by others does not mean that the activity is not an "advertisement." ... [T]he textbook excerpts, article reprints, and symposia presumptively refer to a specific product—the drug that is the subject of the off-label use. Were pharmaceutical manufacturers attempting to provide free yearly subscriptions to the Journal of American Medicine, or seeking to support CME regardless of whether their products would ultimately be addressed, a different conclusion might be compelled, as the speech would be closer to a public service. But, as long as the manufacturer seeks to disseminate information centered upon its product, this prong of the test is satisfied. Finally, the pharmaceutical companies clearly have an economic motivation for providing the information; as explained in some detail previously, the promotional efforts at issue have a positive effect on a physician's prescription practices and therefore on sales.

WLF v. Friedman, 13 F.Supp.2d at 62–64. Shouldn't it make a difference that this challenge had been mounted by the intended recipients (i.e., physicians) rather than the suppliers of the information (i.e., product manufacturers)? What if the FDA had decided instead to treat as promotional labeling or advertising any articles published in peer-reviewed journals and authored by academic scientists when they endorse an off-label use of a product manufactured by the company that had sponsored the research (but did nothing further to disseminate it)? See J. Howard Beales, III, Economic Analysis and the Regulation of Pharmaceutical Advertising, 24 Seton Hall L. Rev. 1370, 1395 n.111 (1994) ("[I]f financial support from a pharmaceutical manufacturer converts speech at scientific meetings into promotional pieces, it would appear to suffice to make journal articles by those same people promotional pieces as well."); David A. Kessler & Wayne L. Pines, The Federal Regulation of Prescription Drug Advertising and Promotion, 264 JAMA 2409, 2409–10 (1992) (explaining that the FDA "has defined its authority in this area to cover virtually any material issued by or sponsored by a drug manufacturer," but adding that "[a] person with no ties to a drug manufacturer can say anything he or she wants about a drug"); cf. FDA, Compliance Policy Guide No. 7132b.17 (Aug. 15, 1989) (declining to treat independently-authored articles as drug labeling or advertising). Would it violate the First Amendment for the agency to take enforcement action against drugs or devices misleadingly described in such materials?

4. *Continuation of the WLF litigation.* As mentioned earlier, FDAMA included a provision giving drug and device companies greater (though still limited) freedom to distribute enduring materials. After further briefing, Judge Lamberth held that this part of the statute also violated the First Amendment. See Washington Legal Found. v. Henney, 56 F.Supp.2d 81 (D.D.C.1999); see also Western States Med. Ctr. v. Shalala, 238 F.3d 1090 (9th Cir.2001) (holding that a different provision of FDAMA, which restricted the advertising of drugs compounded by pharmacists, violated the First Amendment), cert. granted, ___ U.S. ___, 122 S.Ct. 457 (2001). On appeal, the Justice Department lawyer (and former Deputy FDA Commissioner) who argued the case, offered a fanciful interpretation of the relevant FDAMA provision as creating no directly enforceable restrictions but instead a "safe harbor," suggesting that a company not moored in this safe harbor might still not run afoul of the pre-existing limitations on off-label promotion. Somewhat remarkably the court took the bait when it decided to dismiss the appeal and lift most of the injunction. See Washington Legal Found. v. Henney, 202 F.3d 331 (D.C.Cir.2000); see also Washington Legal Found. v. Henney, 128 F.Supp.2d 11, 15 (D.D.C.2000) (concluding that nothing remained of the injunction).

Although perhaps a plausible characterization of the agency's earlier guidance documents, this reading seemingly ignores the effect of FDAMA's provision making violations a distinct "prohibited act" under the statute that could trigger the imposition of sanctions, and it also disregards the practical consequences of any such safe harbor. Judge Lamberth understood those realities when, in the first phase of the litigation, he had rejected the FDA's claim that the challenge to the draft policy statement wasn't ripe for judicial review (recall from Chapter 1(C) that he had speculated that the FDA would "threaten[] (but never actually initiat[e]) enforcement procedures against companies which failed to comply with the agency's *de facto* policy"). Such a scenario would render hollow the D.C. Circuit's assurance that companies would remain free to raise their constitutional objections in subsequent enforcement actions. See id. at 336 n.6.

It's not entirely clear why the appellate court accepted the DOJ's quite different reading of the statute and implementing regulations. Normally, the litigating position adopted by lawyers when defending an agency will not trump the previously expressed position of agency officials, though here it gave the court a golden opportunity to avoid a dicey constitutional question (and, for those challenging these restrictions, the narrowed interpretation may have accomplished their goal). Although the government had reason to lack confidence about its prospects given the panel that it drew, there were serious flaws in Judge Lamberth's analysis. For instance, his earlier conclusion that the government lacks a substantial interest in protecting health care providers from misleading information seems indefensible. Instead, because physicians are a sophisticated audience, measures short of broadly prohibiting such communications rendered the FDA's original policies vulnerable under the final (nexus) prong of the commercial speech test (as Judge Lamberth noted in discussing disclaimers), but then FDAMA's more carefully drawn limitations probably should have survived on that score.

5. *Consequences for the future of FDA regulation.* Although the appellate court in *WLF* gave the FDA something of a reprieve, the agency's recent string of losses may force it to rethink its regulatory approach to controlling the dissemination of information. See John Kamp et al., FDA Marketing v. First Amendment: Washington Legal Foundation Legal Challenges to Off–Label Policies May Force Unprecedented Changes at FDA, 54 Food & Drug L.J. 555 (1999). One of the most compelling arguments against the agency's recent initiatives is that it should have proceeded by adjudication rather than by announcing sweeping prophylactic restrictions. Although case-by-case, after the fact enforcement—as done, for instance, by the FTC—is typically less efficient than broad-based, prospective rulemaking, the First Amendment may demand such a more particularized regulatory approach, especially given the risk of obsolescence where rules are predicated on evolving scientific information about dietary practices or therapeutic interventions.

6. *State and local interference with commercial speech.* San Francisco has considered prohibiting any print advertisements in bus shelters of drugs for the treatment of AIDS because of concerns that they convey an overly optimistic message about their safety and effectiveness and may undermine efforts to encourage safer sex. See John Ritter, Ads Linked to Rise in Rate of HIV Infections: City Considers Ban on Drug Billboards, USA Today, Apr. 6, 2001, at 4A; see also Sabin Russell, Deceptive AIDS Ads Must Stop, FDA Says, S.F. Chron., Apr. 28, 2001, at A1 (reporting that the agency sent warning letters to companies). Would such an ordinance pass muster under the First Amendment?

7. *Further commentary*. See Margaret Gilhooley, Constitutionalizing Food and Drug Law, 74 Tul. L. Rev. 815 (2000); Lars Noah, What's Wrong with "Constitutionalizing Food and Drug Law"?, 75 Tul. L. Rev. 137 (2000); Edmund Polubinski, III, Note, Closing the Channels of Communication: A First Amendment Analysis of the FDA's Policy on Manufacturer Promotion of "Off–Label" Use, 83 Va. L. Rev. 991 (1997); Caren Schmulen Sweetland, Note, The Demise of a Workable Commercial Speech Doctrine: Dangers of Extending First Amendment Protection to Commercial Disclosure Requirements, 76 Tex. L. Rev. 471 (1997).

PROBLEM #6. *STRETCHING THE FIRST AMENDMENT*

Emboldened by the recent decisions striking down statutory provisions and agency rules limiting the dissemination of therapeutic product information, the Nonprescription Drug Manufacturers Association (NDMA) has asked you about challenging the FDA's OTC drug labeling restrictions on First Amendment grounds. In particular, your client objects to the agency's prohibition against making any therapeutic claims that have not yet been approved in the applicable monograph or in a separate NDA. See 21 C.F.R. § 330.1(c)(2). For instance, when information about the advantages of using aspirin to reduce the risk of heart attacks first came to light in the 1980s, manufacturers could not make any cardio-protective claims in their labeling without running afoul of the FDA's rules. Only when the agency issued part of its monograph for internal analgesics a decade later could manufacturers provide "professional labeling" (essentially a package insert for physicians) that mentioned this use. See 63 Fed. Reg. 56,802, 56,814–15 (1998) (codified at 21 C.F.R. § 343.80) (allowing references to the use of aspirin in reducing the risk of stroke in patients who have had transient ischemia of the brain due to fibrin platelet emboli, and for reducing the risk of death and/or nonfatal myocardial infarction (MI) in patients with a previous infarction or unstable angina pectoris or a suspected acute MI). The FDA does not, however, allow any such labeling claims directed to consumers, see id. at 56,808–09, and it has proposed requiring a label warning that consumers should check with their physicians before using aspirin-containing OTC products for such a purpose. See 58 Fed. Reg. 54,224 (1993) (to be codified at 21 C.F.R. § 201.314(i)). What are your prospects of success in mounting such a constitutional challenge?

United States v. An Article ... "Hubbard Electrometer"

333 F.Supp. 357 (D.D.C.1971).

■ GESELL, DISTRICT JUDGE:

This is an action by the United States seeking nationwide condemnation of a gadget known as an E-meter and related writings * * * * This suit was originally tried to a jury before another judge of this court and the conviction there obtained was reversed on appeal after a long trial because of certain First Amendment problems suggested by the instructions and evidentiary rulings. See Founding Church of Scientology v. United States, 409 F.2d 1146 (D.C.Cir.1969). The present trial was conducted to the court without a jury * * * *

The E-meter is essentially a simple galvanometer using two tin cans as electrodes. It is crude, battery-powered, and designed to measure electrical skin resistance. It is completely harmless and ineffective in itself. A person using the meter for treatment holds the tin cans in his hands during an interview with the operator who is known as an auditor and who purports to read indicators from the galvanometer needle as it notes reactions to questions. * * *

L. Ron Hubbard, writing in a science fiction magazine in the 1940s, first advanced the extravagant false claims that various physical and mental illnesses could be cured by auditing. He played a major part in developing Scientology. Thereafter, commencing in the early 1950s, numerous Scientology books and pamphlets were written explaining how various illnesses can be and had been cured through auditing. These materials were widely distributed. Hubbard, who wrote much of the material, is a facile, prolific author and his quackery flourished throughout the United States and in various parts of the world. He was supported by other pamphleteers and adherents who also promoted the practice of Scientology and touted its alleged benefits.

Hubbard and his fellow Scientologists developed the notion of using an E-meter to aid auditing. Substantial fees were charged for the meter and for auditing sessions using the meter. They repeatedly and explicitly represented that such auditing effectuated cures of many physical and mental illnesses. An individual processed with the aid of the E-meter was said to reach the intended goal of "clear" and was led to believe there was reliable scientific proof that once cleared many, indeed most illnesses would automatically be cured. Auditing was guaranteed to be successful. All this was and is false—in short, a fraud. Contrary to representations made, there is absolutely no scientific or medical basis in fact for the claimed cures attributed to E-meter auditing.

Unfortunately the Government did not move to stop the practice of Scientology and a related "science" known as Dianetics when these activities first appeared and were gaining public acceptance. Had it done so, this tedious litigation would not have been necessary. The Government did not sue to condemn the E-meter until the early 1960s, by which time a religious cult known as the Founding Church of Scientology had appeared. This religion, formally organized in 1955, existed side-by-side with the secular practice of Scientology. Its adherents embrace many of Hubbard's teachings and widely disseminate his writings. The Church purports to believe that many illnesses may be cured through E-meter auditing by its trained ministers through an appeal to the spirit or soul of a man. As a matter of formal doctrine, the Church professes to have abandoned any contention that there is a scientific basis for claiming cures resulting from

E-meter use. The Church, however, continued widely to circulate Scientology literature * * * , which hold out false scientific and medical promises of certain cure for many types of illnesses.

In 1962, when the Government seized the E-meters involved in the present controversy, it took them from the premises of the Church, confiscating some E-meters which were actually then being used primarily by ministers of the Church to audit adherents or to train auditors for subsequent church activity. Thus the Government put itself in the delicate position of moving against not only secular uses of the E-meter but other uses purporting to be religious, and the court accordingly confronts the necessity of reconciling the requirements of the [FDCA] prohibiting misbranding and the requirements of the First Amendment protecting religious institutions and religious beliefs from governmental interference under the First Amendment.

The court of appeals has ruled that the evidence at the prior trial and reintroduced at this trial established prima facie that the Founding Church of Scientology, the principal claimant here, is a bona fide religion and that the auditing practice of Scientology and accounts of it are religious doctrine. No evidence to the contrary was offered by the Government on the second trial. Accordingly, for purposes of this particular case only, claimant must be deemed to have met its burden of establishing First Amendment standing for whatever significance the religious practice of Scientology may have on the outcome of this particular litigation. * * *

[I]t must first be determined whether the E-meter is a device within the meaning of the Act. It obviously meets the statutory definition of an apparatus or contrivance intended for use in the diagnosis, cure, mitigation or treatment of disease. Moreover, it is held out as such in the constant promotion of E-meter auditing, a process designed to effectuate cures of mental and physical illnesses. Claimants contend that the E-meter is harmless in itself, cures nothing by itself, and therefore cannot be a device since those who use it appreciate its ineffectiveness and cannot therefore have the requisite intent. This begs the question. The device plays a key part in both the secular and religious auditing process which is used and intended to be used in the cure, mitigation or treatment of disease. It need not be the only agent in an allegedly curative process to be a device within the definition. The E-meter is a device within the meaning of the Act.

Over 100 E-meters were seized. At the same time the Government seized some 200 separate pieces of literature containing approximately 20,000 pages, much of which it now contends demonstrates misbranding of the device by misrepresentation and lack of adequate directions for use under 21 U.S.C. §§ 334 and 352. The writings seized were located in a bookstore, or "Distribution Center," separately incorporated but owned by the Church, with offices in the basement of the Church premises. The Center advertised and sold for profit a long list of Scientology, Dianetics and other writings concerned with auditing in book, pamphlet, newsletter and other forms.

A few of these writings are primarily religious in nature. Others contain medical or scientific claims in a partially religious context. Most of the material, however, explains aspects of Scientology and Dianetics in purely matter-of-fact medical and scientific terms without any apparent religious reference. While the court of appeals concluded that literature setting forth the theory of auditing, including the claims for curative efficacy contained therein, is religious doctrine and hence as a matter of law not labeling, it recognized this was so only if the person charged with misrepresentation explicitly held himself out as making religious as opposed to medical, scientific or otherwise secular claims. The bulk of the material is replete with false medical and scientific claims devoid of any religious overlay or reference. * * * Thus the literature has all the necessary elements of labeling specified in 21 U.S.C. § 321(m) since it "accompanied" the device within the meaning of the Act. * * *

A single false scientific non-religious label claim is sufficient to support condemnation, and in fact there are many. Moreover, differentiation of individual documents as a practical matter is of little value when it comes to an overall resolution of the controversy. Realistically, the writings cannot only be viewed separately. They are available and distributed in infinite combinations. Whole books are involved which often ramble, contradict and are constructed to make diversified appeals that are basically secular and directed to varying temperaments, ages and attitudes of potential readers. Much of the material is skillful propaganda designed to make Scientology and E-meter auditing attractive in many varied, often inconsistent wrappings.

The food and drug laws are designed to protect the public. The literature disseminated by various Scientology groups is written for popular lay consumption. The words and thrust of the writings must accordingly be so considered. Claims as to the efficacy of the E-meter must be read to mean what they clearly purport to say to ordinary lay readers. The court notes that the task of determining whether a claim or representation is religious or non-religious, or whether a religious claim is genuine or merely "tacked on" to basically pseudo-scientific claims, is hardly less troublesome than the task of determining whether a religious claim is true or false. The court has attempted to resolve the difficulty thus presented by the court of appeals by refusing to consider the truth or falsity of any claim which, in the understanding of the average reader, could be construed as resting on religious faith. All doubts on this issue have been resolved in favor of the Claimants. But the overall effect of the many separate writings and the writings as a whole cannot be seriously questioned. Whether the documents are viewed singly or as a whole, the proof showed that many false scientific claims permeate the writings and that these are not even inferentially held out as religious, either in their sponsorship or context.

It should be kept in mind at all times that the Church is but one of several groups engaged in the promotion of Scientology; others include the Hubbard Guidance Center, that offers non-religious processing and auditing to the public for a fee; Hubbard Association of Scientologists International (HASI), a world-wide organization promoting Scientology among members of the organization who receive a monthly magazine ("Ability") and other benefits; and the Distribution Center, Inc., already mentioned. The combined effort of all these activities is to persuade the public to come forward for auditing with an E-meter for a fee, and while some may be motivated or attracted by religious considerations, others who audit or are audited are not.

An individual was not required to be either a Church member or a Scientologist to be audited at cost of $500 for 25 hours, with state of "clear" guaranteed for $5,000. The E-meter was available for sale to the public for a fee of $125. The benefits of auditing were extravagantly advertised. At the time this action was commenced, E-meters—perhaps as many as one-third the total supply—were being used by members of the public without any religious control or supervision. The writings were distributed to accompany the E-meter and intended to promote its use by members of the public; they were used by laymen for secular purposes; individually a great many contain false unqualified scientific claims without even a religious overlay or suggestion. Viewed as a whole the thrust of the writings is secular, not religious. The writings are labeling within the meaning of the Act. Thus, the E-meter is misbranded and its secular use must be condemned along with secular use of the offensive literature as labeling. The misbranding results not only from misrepresentation by reason of 21 U.S.C. § 352(a) but because the labeling failed to bear adequate directions for use required by 21 U.S.C. § 352(f)(1).

On the basis of these findings, the Government is entitled to some relief. It is only when the court confronts the question of appropriate remedy that serious difficulties arise. * * * A law designed to afford protection to the public against genuine evils may be used to regulate the activities of religion only if the regulation involved is the narrowest possible remedy to achieve the legitimate non-religious end, which in this case is only to protect the public against misrepresentation since the E-meter is harmless in itself. * * *

The literature held to make false representations, while in itself non-religious, nevertheless comprises for some, part of the writings, teachings, and history of a religion. Those who belong to the Church and accept its beliefs assert that many illnesses may be alleviated by religious counseling designed to free the spirit of encumbrances. They find in the rationale and procedures of Scientology satisfactory early explanations and techniques to implement what is essentially faith healing by use of the E-meter. Thus they purport to read the purely secular writings of Scientology with semantic interpretations fostered by their evolving religious doctrine. Purely scientific statements are given a theological slant by the initiated and the occasional theological indications in the writings are given enthusiastic exaggeration. What the layman reads as straight science fiction becomes to the believer a bit of early imperfect scripture. The result of all this is that what may appear to the layman as a factual scientific representation (clearly false) is not necessarily this at all when read by one who has embraced the doctrine of the Church.

Accordingly, the Government's protestations that it is not interfering with religious practice when it seeks to condemn the E-meter and related literature must be qualified. The Church is a religious institution protected by the First Amendment. The E-meter is used by its ministers as part of the ritual and practice of the Church. Serious interference indeed results if the Church is entirely prohibited from using the E-meter by condemnation or if the court orders the Food and Drug Administration to oversee a general rewriting of all the writings the Church purveys. Where there is a belief in a scientific fraud there is nonetheless an interference with the religion that entertains that belief if its writings are censored or suppressed. Similarly, if a church uses a machine harmless in itself to aid its ministers in communicating with adherents, the destruction of that machine intrudes on religion. The dilemma cannot be resolved by attempting to isolate purely false scientific claims from claims that have sufficient religious content to be outside the food and drug laws. There is a religious substance to everything when seen with the eyes of the believer.

For these reasons, the Church may not be wholly prevented from practicing its faith or from seeking new adherents. A decree of condemnation which ordered destruction of the device, with its necessary res judicata effect as to all E-meters in the country, would achieve this effect. On the other hand, a condemnation decree which allowed the FDA to reform the writings as is done in the usual commercial drug misbranding case would give a Government agency excessive power to interfere with the exercise of religion, fostering that Government "entanglement" with religion which has been recently condemned by the Supreme Court. Neither of these possible remedies is acceptable to the court.

Had the Government proceeded in equity to enjoin specific non-religious practices or representations which it believed to violate the Act, the court could have curtailed the purely commercial use of the E-meter while leaving the Church free to practice its belief under limited circumstances. An action in rem, however, acts only upon the device, and the court cannot fashion a remedy in libel which distinguishes with particularity between religious and non-religious uses. An equity proceeding is clearly the most satisfactory remedy in this and any similar future cases, and may in some instances be the only remedy which the Government may seek consistent with the First Amendment.

Dismissal of this libel after eight years of legal proceedings is not justified on the grounds that the Government has not used the most appropriate remedy. A decree of condemnation will therefore be entered, but the Church and others who base their use upon religious belief will be allowed to continue auditing practices upon specified conditions which allow the Food and Drug Administration as little discretion as possible to interfere in future activities of the religion. Pursuant to 21 U.S.C. § 334(d), upon the findings and conclusions contained in this Memorandum Opinion, relief in the following form shall be set out in an implementing order: * * *

The device may be used or sold or distributed only for use in bona fide religious counseling. No user, purchaser or distributee (other than the Founding Church of Scientology or an ordained practicing minister of the Church) shall be considered engaged in bona fide religious counseling unless and until such user, purchaser or distributee has filed an affidavit with the Secretary of the Food and Drug Administration stating the basis on which a claim of bona fide religious counseling is made, together with an undertaking to comply with all conditions of the judgment so long as the E-meter is used.

The device should bear a prominent, clearly visible notice warning that any person using it for auditing or counseling of any kind is forbidden by law to represent that there is any medical or scientific basis for believing or asserting that the device is useful in the diagnosis, treatment or prevention of any disease. It should be noted in the warning that the device has been condemned by a United States District Court for misrepresentation and misbranding under the food and drug laws, that use is permitted only as part of religious activity, and that the E-meter is not medically or scientifically capable of improving the health or bodily functions of anyone. Each user, purchaser, and distributee of the E-meter shall sign a written statement that he has read such warning and understands its contents and such statements shall be preserved.

Any and all literature which refers to the E-meter or to auditing, including advertisements, distributed directly or indirectly by the seller or distributor of the E-meter or by anyone utilizing or promoting the use of the E-meter, should bear a prominent notice printed in or permanently affixed to each item or such literature, stating that the device known as a Hubbard Electrometer, or E-meter, used in auditing, has been condemned by a United States District Court on the grounds that the literature of Dianetics and Scientology contains false and misleading claims of a medical or scientific nature and that the E-meter has no proven usefulness in the diagnosis, treatment or prevention of any disease, nor is it medically or scientifically capable of improving any bodily function. Where the notice is printed in or affixed to literature, it should appear either on the outside front cover or on the title page in letters no smaller than 11–point type.
* * *

NOTES AND QUESTIONS

1. *Free exercise.* The appellate court had reversed the original judgment in this case because it thought that the Supreme Court's free exercise decisions dictated a narrow interpretation of the term "labeling" when it related to the practice of religion:

[T]he E-meter has been condemned, not because it is itself harmful, but because the representations made concerning it are "false or misleading." And the largest part of those representations is contained in the literature of Scientology describing the process of auditing which appellants have claimed, without contest from the Government, is part of the doctrine of their religion and central to its exercise. Thus if their claims to religious status are accepted, a finding that the seized literature misrepresents the benefits from auditing is a finding that their religious doctrines are false. To construe the Food, Drug and Cosmetic Act to permit such a finding would, in the light of *United States v. Ballard*, 322 U.S. 78 (1944), present the gravest constitutional difficulties. . . . Were the literature here introduced clearly secular, we might well conclude that under existing law it constituted "labeling" for purposes of the Act. Such a conclusion might be justified by a broad reading of the statute, consistent with its high purpose of protecting the public health and pocketbook against health frauds. However, such broad readings are not favored when they impinge upon constitutionally sensitive areas, especially in the absence of a showing of legislative intent to regulate these areas. Nothing in the history or interpretation of the Act indicates that it was meant to deal with the special problem of religious healing, a problem often given legislative treatment separate from that imposed upon the general area of public health and medical practice. In light of these considerations, highlighted by the explicit holding of *Ballard*, we interpret the Act as not including within its concept of "labeling" the literature developing the doctrines of a religion.

Founding Church of Scientology v. United States, 409 F.2d 1146, 1156–57, 1159–60 (D.C.Cir.1969); see also Sheldon R. Shapiro, Annotation, Regulation Under Federal Food, Drug, and Cosmetic Act as Affected by Religious Guarantees of First Amendment, 13 A.L.R. Fed. 747 (1972). Note, however, that subsequent decisions of the Supreme Court seemingly have weakened the protection afforded the free exercise of religion in holding that the clause does not require that laws of general application provide special exceptions. See Employment Division v. Smith, 494 U.S. 872, 879 (1990) (rejecting free exercise claim by Native American employee fired after ingesting peyote, a Schedule I hallucinogenic substance); see also Olsen v. DEA, 878 F.2d 1458 (D.C.Cir.1989) (sustaining agency's refusal to exempt from the Controlled Substances Act the religious use of marijuana by members of the Ethiopian Zion Coptic Church); David E. Steinberg, Rejecting the Case Against the Free Exercise Exemption: A Critical Assessment, 75 B.U. L. Rev. 241 (1995); Carol M. Kaplan, Note, The Devil Is in the Details: Neutral, Generally Applicable Laws and Exceptions from *Smith*, 75 N.Y.U. L. Rev. 1045 (2000). Would the Church have more success today by asserting a free speech claim instead?

2. *The tax man cometh.* A different federal agency became a thorn in the side of the Church, rejecting its claims for tax-exempt status, as well as tax deductions claimed by persons who spent money on auditing, because the IRS viewed these as primarily commercial rather than religious activities. The courts upheld these determinations. See Hernandez v. Commissioner, 490 U.S. 680 (1989); Church of Scientology of California v. Commissioner, 823 F.2d 1310 (9th Cir.1987). See generally Paul Horwitz, Scientology in Court: A Comparative Analysis and Some Thoughts on Selected Issues in Law and Religion, 47 DePaul L. Rev. 85 (1997).

3. *Free speech redux.* Wholly apart from the free exercise concerns, does the district court's order present free speech problems (and is the speech that the order interferes with just commercial)? Is it in fact accurate to say that "the E-meter is not ... capable of improving the health or bodily functions of anyone"? Does such a definitive conclusion, to borrow Judge Lamberth's wonderfully sarcastic phrase, exaggerate the FDA's "overall place in the universe"? In *Bradley v. Weinberger*, could the sellers have argued that the agency's requirement for an unqualified warning in the labeling of all oral hypoglycemic drugs amounted to coerced speech in violation of the First Amendment?

Conant v. McCaffrey

2000 WL 1281174 (N.D.Cal.2000).

■ ALSUP, DISTRICT JUDGE:

This class action challenges the lawfulness of the federal government's policy to punish physicians who "recommend" marijuana to patients. * * * On November 5, 1996, the voters of California passed Proposition 215, the Compassionate Use Act of 1996, also known as the Medical Marijuana Initiative * * * * The Compassionate Use Act specifically protects physicians who recommend medical marijuana: "[No] physician in this state shall be punished, or denied any right or privilege, for having recommended marijuana to a patient for medical purposes." * * *

On December 30, 1996, less than two months after the Compassionate Use Act took effect, the Director of the Office of National Drug Control Policy issued "The Administration's Response to the Passage of California Proposition 215 and Arizona Proposition 200" (hereinafter the "Administration's Response"). The Administration's Response stated "that a practitioner's action of recommending or prescribing Schedule I controlled substances is not consistent with the 'public interest' (as that phrase is used in the federal Controlled Substances Act), and will lead to administrative action by the Drug Enforcement Administration to revoke the practitioner's registration." The Administration's Response focused on the term "recommend" in response to that term's inclusion in the Compassionate Use Act.

The Administration's Response stated that the Department of Justice and the Department of Health and Human Services would send a letter to national, state, and local practitioner associations and licensing boards, stating unequivocally that the DEA would seek to revoke the registrations of physicians who recommended or prescribed Schedule I controlled substances. The letter, according to the Administration's Response, would also outline the authority of the Inspector General for HHS to exclude specified individuals or entities from participation in the Medicare and Medicaid programs. * * *

On February 27, 1997, the Department of Justice and the Department of Health and Human Services sent a letter to national, state and local practitioner associations to clarify the government's position. That letter, the so-called Medical Leader Letter, assured, among other things, that "nothing in federal law prevents a physician, in the context of a legitimate physician-patient relationship, from merely discussing with a patient the risks and alleged benefits of the use of marijuana to relieve pain or alleviate symptoms." At the same time, the letter stated that physicians "may not intentionally provide their patients with oral or written statements in order to enable them to obtain controlled substances in violation of federal law." * * *

The named plaintiffs in this action include ten physicians, a physicians' organization, six patients with terminal illnesses, and an organization comprised of people with AIDS. * * * Dr. Marcus Conant, to take an example of the physician plaintiffs, has practiced medicine in San Francisco for over thirty years. Dr. Conant is the Medical Director of the Conant Medical Group, a large private AIDS practice. He is a Professor at the University of California medical center in San Francisco and is the author or co-author of over seventy publications on treatment of AIDS. He and his colleagues provide primary care for over 5,000 HIV infected patients, including approximately 2,000 patients with active AIDS.

In his AIDS practice, Dr. Conant prescribes aggressive treatments combining several different drugs that are recently emerging as the first effective treatment for AIDS. Dr. Conant has found, however, that these drugs often cause severe nausea and vomiting, a particular worry when the patient is suffering from AIDS wasting syndrome, which causes a steady, uncontrolled weight loss. For many patients, traditional anti-nausea drugs and appetite stimulants are effective. Dr. Conant believes, however, that for some patients medical marijuana proves to be the best if not the only viable treatment option. Prior to the Administration's Response, he recommended marijuana to some patients. In reaction to the Administration's Response, Dr. Conant limited his conversations with patients, curtailing information regarding the risks and benefits of medical marijuana. He directed his staff likewise to curtail their discussions with patients. * * *

Plaintiffs sought a preliminary and permanent injunction enjoining the government from enforcing or threatening to enforce any federal statute, regulation or other provision of law in a manner that would punish or penalize California physicians for communicating with their patients in the context of a bona fide physician-patient relationship regarding potential risks and benefits of medical use of marijuana. Plaintiffs further sought a declaration that the government's threats to enforce federal provisions of law in a manner that would punish or penalize physicians for communicating with their patients, using their best medical judgment in the context of a bona fide physician-patient relationship, regarding potential risks and benefits of medical use of marijuana violate the First Amendment on their face. * * *

The Controlled Substances Act vests power in the Attorney General to deny or revoke a physician's DEA registration to prescribe controlled substances. * * * One of the permissible grounds for revocation is a finding that the physician "has committed such acts as would render his registration under section 823 of this title inconsistent with the public interest as determined under such section." 21 U.S.C. § 824(a)(4). * * * Significantly, the government admits that revocation is *not* authorized where a doctor discusses the pros and cons of marijuana use with a patient. Yet the government claims the doctor crosses a statutory line when the discussion melds into a recommendation. Also of significance, both sides acknowledge that a doctor may not, under the statute, actually prescribe or dispense marijuana. Plaintiffs do not seek to do so. The focus is on "recommend" and whether a statutory line can really be drawn between discussions of pros and cons versus recommendations. * * *

Congress did not address whether the government may revoke a physician's registration based on the physician recommending a Schedule I drug to a patient. The term "recommend" does not appear in Section 824 of the statute. The legislative history is silent as to whether Congress intended that such conduct could constitute a ground for revocation. As stated, no case law addresses the point. No regulations have been issued. All that exist are statements by the government, including the Administration's Response, giving its current view of the statute.

Were it not for First Amendment considerations, the government's interpretation of the Controlled Substances Act might be permissible under *Chevron.* As the government notes, factor five's "[s]uch other conduct which may threaten the public health and safety" presumably includes conduct apart from that already listed in the previous four factors. That previously listed conduct includes convictions relating to controlled substances and violations of the law relating to controlled substances. Recommending the medical use of a prohibited substance might arguably fall within such "other conduct." As discussed below, however, the constitutional doubts raised by such an interpretation are most serious.

The practice of the learned professions such as medicine and law necessarily involve communications with patients, clients and others. While such communications implicate First Amendment concerns, no one would claim that the professions are immunized from regulation merely because speech is incident to the trade. For the professional, "[o]bedience to ethical precepts may require abstention from what in other circumstances might be constitutionally protected speech." In re Sawyer, 360 U.S. 622, 646–47 (1959) (Stewart, J., concurring). A lawyer, for example, may not counsel a client to violate the law or to commit perjury. The First Amendment would not prohibit the lawyer's disbarment for doing so. A doctor, to take another example, may not counsel a patient to rely on quack medicine. The First Amendment would not prohibit the doctor's loss of license for doing so. E.g., Shea v. Board Med. Examiners, 81 Cal.App.3d 564, 577 (1978). * * *

Still, there is First Amendment protection in the practice of the learned professions. As the government itself recognizes, when a governmental regulation of professional practice "implicates First Amendment rights, the court must balance those interests against the State's legitimate interest in regulating the activity in question." * * * [T]he Supreme Court has recognized the First Amendment interests in discussions between doctors and patients. In *Rust v. Sullivan*, 500 U.S. 173, 200 (1990), the Court suggested, but did not hold, that individual doctor-patient relationships, in contrast to family-planning clinics, might enjoy First Amendment protection even when subsidized by the government. Although the Court did not decide whether the doctor-patient relationship is entitled to special First Amendment protection from the state's purse strings, its discussion presupposed First Amendment interests in discussions between doctors and patients.

In *Planned Parenthood v. Casey*, 505 U.S. 833, 884 (1992), the Supreme Court again acknowledged the First Amendment interests in doctor-patient discussions, but suggested that a rational basis would justify regulation of speech as part of the practice of medicine. There, the petitioners challenged a provision that required doctors to inform abortion patients of the nature of the procedure, the health risks of the abortion and of childbirth, and the probable gestational age of the unborn child. A plurality rejected a First Amendment challenge to the informed-consent provision. The state may compel physicians to provide health-related information so long as it is true and reasonable. The *Casey* regulation merely compelled disclosure of information about a medical procedure, much like warning labels disclose the side effects and risks of pharmaceuticals. In this case, by contrast, the government would punish physicians for voicing their professional opinions based on their best medical judgment. * * *

In striking the appropriate balance in this case, the court recognizes that the government has a legitimate interest in suppressing and controlling the flow of dangerous drugs and controlled substances within the United States. A recommendation by a doctor may (or may not) be used by a patient to obtain marijuana under the Compassionate Use Act. On the other side of the scale, physicians have a legitimate need to discuss with and to recommend to their patients all medically acceptable forms of treatment. In California and seven other states, recommending marijuana to treat certain debilitating illnesses is recognized as legitimate in medically appropriate circumstances. The government itself would allow physicians to "discuss" the pros and cons of marijuana therapy with their patients. In some cases, however, it will be the professional opinion of doctors that marijuana is the best therapy or at least should be tried. If such recommendations could not be communicated, then the physician-patient relationship would be seriously impaired. Patients need to know their doctors' recommendations.

Contrary to the government's argument, it is not true that a mere recommendation will necessarily lead to the commission of a federal offense. To the contrary, such recommendations can lead to lawful and legitimate responses. First, a cancer or AIDS victim so advised may choose to honor the federal law but, armed with the doctor's recommendation, may urge the federal government to change that law. Petitioning Congress or federal agencies for redress of a grievance or a change in policy is a time-honored tradition. In the marketplace of ideas, few questions are more deserving of free-speech protection than whether regulations affecting health and welfare are sound public policy. In the debate, perhaps the status quo will (and should) endure. But patients and physicians are certainly entitled to urge their view. To hold that physicians are barred from communicating to patients sincere medical judgments would disable patients from understanding their own situations well enough to participate in the debate. As the government concedes, * * * many patients depend upon discussions with their physicians as their primary or only source of sound medical information. Without open communication with their physicians, patients would fall silent and appear uninformed. The ability of patients to participate meaningfully in the public discourse would be compromised. This factor alone persuades the court that the balance of considerations ought to be struck firmly on the side of protecting sincere medical recommendations.

Second, a cancer or AIDS victim may well be able to obtain medical marijuana without violating federal law. There are three possible ways. One is to enroll in a federally-approved experimental marijuana therapy program. Another is to travel to a country where marijuana is legally dispensed. * * * The point is that a recommendation for marijuana therapy does not translate, as night follows day, into a violation of federal law. To the contrary, a recommendation for marijuana may lead to actions by patients all of which are lawful under federal law and some of which are themselves protected, such as petitioning the government for a change in the prohibition itself, by the First Amendment.

To be sure, some patients may use sincere medical recommendations to obtain marijuana from cannabis clubs in circumstances illegal under federal law. A doctor, for example, may sincerely believe that a cancer victim, having exhausted other medications without success, should try marijuana. Such a circumstance may or may not qualify as a medical necessity. Even though the doctor warns of the illegal status of marijuana, the patient may use the doctor's recommendation to obtain marijuana under the Compassionate Use Act. If so, however, the acquisition of marijuana is committed by the patient, not the doctor. A sincere recommendation alone is not a federal crime, even if the doctor foresees it could be used to facilitate a federal crime. The federal interest in enforcing the marijuana prohibition in the United States is a legitimate concern, but it pales by comparison to the free speech concerns. * * *

When a doctor recommends marijuana, a patient who is accepting of the idea may well ask how to obtain it. Here, doctors must be honest. The First Amendment is not a license to circumvent the federal drug laws. If the doctor addresses the subject, he or she must be truthful and advise on the unavailability of marijuana under the present federal drug laws and on the availability of the federal experimental programs and overseas laws (to the extent the doctor is knowledgeable). * * *

[T]he government's construction of the Controlled Substances Act cannot stand. The government should be permanently enjoined from (i) revoking any physician class member's DEA registration merely because the doctor makes a recommendation for the use of medical marijuana based on a sincere medical judgment and (ii) from initiating any investigation solely on that ground. The injunction should apply whether or not the doctor anticipates that the patient will, in turn, use his or her recommendation to obtain marijuana in violation of federal law. * * *

NOTES AND QUESTIONS

1. *Physician prescribing of Schedule II controlled substances.* The DEA has threatened to revoke registrations of physicians who engage in off-label uses of certain Schedule II drugs. First, when it down-scheduled synthetic tetrahydrocannabinol (THC), the principal psychoactive component in marijuana, the agency prohibited any use beyond the FDA's approved labeling for the treatment of nausea in cancer patients. See 51 Fed. Reg. 17,476, 17,477 (1986). More recently, as part of an effort to undercut Oregon's Death with Dignity Act, the DEA has threatened to sanction physicians who assist in the suicide of terminally-ill patients using Schedule II drugs approved by the FDA for other purposes. See R. Steinbrook, Physician–Assisted Suicide in Oregon: An Uncertain Future, 346 New Eng. J. Med. 460 (2002).

HIGHLIGHTS OF PRESCRIBING INFORMATION

CAPOTEN® TABLETS   ▼ R$_x$
(captopril tablets)

WARNING: USE IN PREGNANCY

When used in pregnancy during the second and third trimesters, ACE inhibitors can cause injury and even death to the developing fetus. When pregnancy is detected, CAPOTEN should be discontinued as soon as possible. See WARNINGS/PRECAUTIONS: Fetal/Neonatal Morbidity and Mortality (5.5).

------------ RECENT LABELING CHANGES ------------

Indications (1.x)
Warnings/Precautions (5.x, 5.y, 5.z)
Adverse Reactions (8.x)

---------------- INDICATIONS AND USAGE ----------------

- **Hypertension** (caution in renally-impaired patients), alone or in combination with other anti-hypertensives (1.1)
- **Congestive Heart Failure**, usually in combination with diuretics and digitalis (1.2)
- **Left Ventricular (LV) Dysfunction after Myocardial Infarction** to improve survival and reduce morbidity in clinically stable patients with LV ejection fraction ≤ 40% (1.3)
- **Diabetic Nephropathy** (Type I IDD with proteinuria > 500 mg/day and retinopathy) (1.4)

------------ DOSAGE AND ADMINISTRATION ------------

General: Take 1 hour before meals. Individualize dosage.

Indication	Initiation of Therapy	Usual Daily Dose	Do Not Exceed
Hypertension	25 mg bid or tid	25-150 mg bid or tid*	450 mg/day
Heart Failure	25 mg tid	50-100 mg tid	450 mg/day
LV Dysfunction after MI	12.5 mg tid†	50 mg tid	
Diabetic Nephropathy		25 mg tid	

* Usual daily dosing does not exceed 50 mg BID or TID. Consider adding a thiazide-type diuretic. (2.2)
† A single dose of 6.25 mg should precede initiation of 12.5 mg therapy. (2.4)
Adjust dose in renal impairment (2.6, 5.7)

------------ HOW SUPPLIED ------------

Tablets: 12.5, 25, 50, 100 mg; scored (3)

------------ CONTRAINDICATIONS ------------

Known hypersensitivity (e.g., angioedema) to any ACE inhibitor.

------------ WARNINGS/PRECAUTIONS ------------

- Angioedema with possibility of airway obstruction (5.1)
- Neutropenia (<1000/mm³) with myeloid hypoplasia (5.2)
- Excessive hypotension (5.4)
- Fetal/Neonatal Morbidity and Mortality (5.5)
- Hepatic failure (5.6)
- Use with caution in renal impairment. (2.6, 5.7)
- Hyperkalemia (5.8)
- Cough (5.9)

Most Common Adverse Reactions (≥ n/100) (8)
- rash (sometimes with arthralgia and eosinophilia), taste impairment (diminution or loss), cough, pruritus, chest pain, palpitations, tachycardia, proteinuria

To report SUSPECTED SERIOUS ADRs, call (manufacturer) at (phone #) or FDA's MedWatch at 1-800-FDA-1088

------------ DRUG INTERACTIONS ------------

- Diuretics (6.1)
- Other vasodilators (6.2)
- Agents Causing Renin Release (6.3)
- Beta-Blockers (6.4)
- Agents Increasing Serum Potassium (6.5)
- Lithium (6.7)

------------ USE IN SPECIFIC POPULATIONS ------------

- Pregnancy: Fetal/Neonatal Morbidity and Mortality (5.5)
- Lactating Women: Potential for serious adverse reactions in nursing infants. (7.3)
- Pediatric Use: Safety and effectiveness not established. Use only if other measures ineffective. (7.4)
- Renal-impairment: Use with caution. (2.6, 5.7)

------------ See P for PATIENT COUNSELING INFORMATION ------------

These highlights do not include all the information needed to prescribe Capoten safely and effectively. See Capoten's comprehensive prescribing information provided below.

m/yy

COMPREHENSIVE PRESCRIBING INFORMATION: INDEX

COMPREHENSIVE PRESCRIBING INFORMATION

> ## ! WARNING: USE IN PREGNANCY
> When used in pregnancy during the second and third trimesters, ACE inhibitors can cause injury and even death to the developing fetus. When pregnancy is detected, CAPOTEN should be discontinued as soon as possible. See WARNINGS/PRECAUTIONS: Fetal/Neonatal Morbidity and Mortality (5.5).

1   INDICATIONS AND USAGE

1.1   **Hypertension:** CAPOTEN is indicated for the treatment of hypertension.

In using CAPOTEN, consideration should be given to the risk of neutropenia/agranulocytosis (see WARNINGS/PRECAUTIONS).

CAPOTEN (captopril) may be used as initial therapy for patients with normal renal function, in whom the risk is relatively low. In patients with impaired renal function, particularly those with collagen vascular disease, captopril should be reserved for hypertensives who have either developed unacceptable side effects on other drugs, or have failed to respond satisfactorily to drug combinations.

CAPOTEN is effective alone and in combination with other antihypertensive agents, especially thiazide-type diuretics. The blood pressure lowering effects of captopril and thiazides are approximately additive.

1.2   **Heart Failure:** CAPOTEN is indicated in the treatment of congestive heart failure usually in combination with diuretics and digitalis. The beneficial effect of captopril in heart failure does not require the presence of digitalis, however, most controlled clinical trial experience with captopril has been in patients receiving digitalis, as well as diuretic treatment.

1.3   **Left Ventricular Dysfunction After Myocardial Infarction:** CAPOTEN is indicated to improve survival following myocardial infarction in clinically stable patients with left ventricular dysfunction manifested as an ejection fraction ≤ 40% and to reduce the incidence of overt heart failure and subsequent hospitalizations for congestive heart failure in these patients.

1.4   **Diabetic Nephropathy:** CAPOTEN is indicated for the treatment of diabetic nephropathy (proteinuria >500 mg/day) in patients with type I insulin-dependent diabetes mellitus and retinopathy. CAPOTEN decreases the rate of progression of renal insufficiency and development of serious adverse clinical outcomes (death or need for renal transplantation or dialysis).

2   DOSAGE AND ADMINISTRATION

2.1   CAPOTEN (captopril) should be taken one hour before meals. Dosage must be individualized.

2.2   **Hypertension:** Initiation of therapy requires consideration of recent antihypertensive drug treatment, the extent of blood pressure elevation, salt restriction, and other clinical circumstances. If possible, discontinue the patient's previous antihypertensive drug regimen for one week before starting CAPOTEN.

The initial dose of CAPOTEN is 25 mg bid or tid. If satisfactory reduction of blood pressure has not been achieved after one or two weeks, the dose may be increased to 50 mg bid or tid. Concomitant sodium restriction may be beneficial when CAPOTEN (captopril) is used alone.

The dose of CAPOTEN in hypertension usually does not exceed 50 mg tid. Therefore, if the blood pressure has not been satisfactorily controlled after one to two weeks at this dose, (and the patient is not already receiving a diuretic), a modest dose of a thiazide-type diuretic (e.g., hydrochlorothiazide, 25 mg daily), should be added. The diuretic dose may be increased at one- to two-week intervals until its highest usual antihypertensive dose is reached.

If CAPOTEN is being started in a patient already receiving a diuretic, CAPOTEN therapy should be initiated under close medical supervision (see DRUG INTERACTIONS regarding hypotension (6.1)), with dosage and titration of CAPOTEN as noted above.

If further blood pressure reduction is required, the dose of CAPOTEN may be increased to 100 mg bid or tid and then, if necessary, to 150 mg bid or tid (while continuing the diuretic).

The usual dose range is 25 to 150 mg bid or tid. A maximum daily dose of 450 mg CAPOTEN should not be exceeded.

For patients with severe hypertension (e.g., accelerated or malignant hypertension), when temporary discontinuation of current antihypertensive therapy is not practical or desirable, or when prompt titration to more normotensive blood pressure levels is indicated, diuretic should be continued but other current antihypertensive medication stopped and CAPOTEN dosage promptly initiated at 25 mg bid or tid, under close medical supervision.

When necessitated by the patient's clinical condition, the daily dose of CAPOTEN may be increased every 24 hours or less under continuous medical supervision until a satisfactory blood pressure response is obtained or the maximum dose of CAPOTEN is reached. In this regimen, addition of a more potent diuretic, e.g., furosemide, may also be indicated.

Beta-blockers may also be used in conjunction with CAPOTEN therapy (see DRUG INTERACTIONS (6.4)), but the effects of the two drugs are less than additive.

2.3   **Heart Failure:** Initiation of therapy requires consideration of recent diuretic therapy and the possibility of severe salt/volume depletion. In patients with either normal or low blood pressure, who have been vigorously treated with diuretics and who may be hyponatremic and/or hypovolemic, a starting dose of 6.25 or 12.5 mg tid may minimize the magnitude or duration of the hypotensive effect (see WARNINGS/PRECAUTIONS: Hypotension (5.4)); for these patients, titration to the usual daily dosage can then occur within the next several days.

For most patients the usual initial daily dosage is 25 mg tid. After a dose of 50 mg tid is reached, further increases in dosage should be delayed, where possible, for at least two weeks to determine if a satisfactory response occurs. Most patients studied have had a satisfactory clinical improvement at 50 or 100 mg tid. A maximum daily dose of 450 mg of CAPOTEN should not be exceeded.

CAPOTEN should generally be used in conjunction with a diuretic and digitalis. CAPOTEN therapy must be initiated under very close medical supervision.

2.4   **Left Ventricular Dysfunction After Myocardial Infarction:** The recommended dose for long-term use in patients following a myocardial infarction is a target maintenance dose of 50 mg tid.

Therapy may be initiated as early as three days following a myocardial infarction. After a single dose of 6.25 mg, CAPOTEN therapy should be initiated at 12.5 mg tid. CAPOTEN should then be increased to 25 mg tid during the next several days and to a target dose of 50 mg tid over the next several weeks as tolerated (see CLINICAL PHARMACOLOGY (12.2)).

CAPOTEN may be used in patients treated with other post-myocardial infarction therapies, e.g., thrombolytics, aspirin, beta blockers.

2.5   **Diabetic Nephropathy:** The recommended dose of CAPOTEN for long term use to treat diabetic nephropathy is 25 mg tid.

Other antihypertensives such as diuretics, beta blockers, centrally acting agents or vasodilators may be used in conjunction with CAPOTEN if additional therapy is required to further lower blood pressure.

2.6   **Dosage Adjustment in Renal Impairment:** Because CAPOTEN is excreted primarily by the kidneys, excretion rates are reduced in patients with impaired renal function. These patients will take longer to reach steady-state captopril levels and will reach higher steady-state levels for a given daily dose than patients with normal renal function. Therefore, these patients may respond to smaller or less frequent doses.

Accordingly, for patients with significant renal impairment, initial daily dosage of CAPOTEN should be reduced, and smaller increments utilized for titration, which should be quite slow (one- to two-week intervals). After the desired therapeutic effect has been achieved, the dose should be slowly back-titrated to determine the minimal effective dose. When concomitant diuretic therapy is required, a loop diuretic (e.g., furosemide), rather than a thiazide diuretic, is preferred in patients with severe renal impairment. (See also WARNINGS/PRECAUTIONS: Hemodialysis (5.12))

3 HOW SUPPLIED

12.5 mg tablets in bottles of 100 and 1000, 25 mg tablets in bottles of 100 and 1000, 50 mg tablets in bottles of 100 and 1000, and 100 mg tablets in bottles of 100. Bottles contain a desiccant-charcoal canister.

Unimatic unit-dose packs containing 100 tablets are also available for each potency: 12.5 mg, 25 mg, 50 mg, and 100 mg.

The 12.5 mg tablet is a biconvex oval with a partial bisect bar; the 25 mg tablet is a biconvex rounded square with a quadrisect bar; the 50 and 100 mg tablets are biconvex ovals with a bisect bar. All captopril tablets are white and may exhibit a slight sulfurous odor.

Storage: Do not store above 86° F. Keep bottles tightly closed (protect from moisture).

4 CONTRAINDICATIONS

CAPOTEN (captopril) is contraindicated in patients who are hypersensitive to this product or any other angiotensin-converting enzyme inhibitor (e.g., a patient who has experienced angioedema during therapy with any other ACE inhibitor).

5 WARNINGS/PRECAUTIONS

To report SUSPECTED SERIOUS ADRs, call (manufacturer) at (phone #) or FDA's MedWatch at 1-800-FDA-1088

5.1 Angioedema

Angioedema involving the extremities, face, lips, mucous membranes, tongue, glottis or larynx has been seen in patients treated with ACE inhibitors, including captopril. If angioedema involves the tongue, glottis or larynx, airway obstruction may occur and be fatal. Emergency therapy, including but not necessarily limited to, subcutaneous administration of a 1:1000 solution of epinephrine should be promptly instituted.

Swelling confined to the face, mucous membranes of the mouth, lips and extremities has usually been resolved with discontinuation of captopril; some cases required medical therapy. (See PATIENT COUNSELING INFORMATION (P) and ADVERSE REACTIONS (8).)

5.2 Neutropenia/Agranulocytosis

Neutropenia (<1000/mm³) with myeloid hypoplasia has resulted from use of captopril. About half of the neutropenic patients developed systemic or oral cavity infections or other features of the syndrome of agranulocytosis.

The risk of neutropenia is dependent on the clinical status of the patient:

In clinical trials in patients with hypertension who have normal renal function (serum creatinine less than 1.6 mg/dL and no collagen vascular disease), neutropenia has been seen in one patient out of over 8,600 exposed.

In patients with some degree of renal failure (serum creatinine at least 1.6 mg/dL) but no collagen vascular disease, the risk of neutropenia in clinical trials was about 1 per 500, a frequency over 15 times that for uncomplicated hypertension. Daily doses of captopril were relatively high in these patients, particularly in view of their diminished renal function. In foreign marketing experience in patients with renal failure, use of allopurinol concomitantly with captopril has been associated with neutropenia but this association has not appeared in U.S. reports.

In patients with collagen vascular diseases (e.g., systemic lupus erythematosus, scleroderma) and impaired renal function, neutropenia occurred in 3.7 percent of patients in clinical trials. While none of the over 750 patients in formal clinical trials of heart failure developed neutropenia, it has occurred during the subsequent clinical experience. About half of the reported cases had serum creatinine ≥ 1.6 mg/dL and more than 75 percent were in patients also receiving procainamide. In heart failure, it appears that the same risk factors for neutropenia are present.

The neutropenia has usually been detected within three months after captopril was started. Bone marrow examinations in patients with neutropenia consistently showed myeloid hypoplasia, frequently accompanied by erythroid hypoplasia and decreased numbers of megakaryocytes (e.g., hypoplastic bone marrow and pancytopenia); anemia and thrombocytopenia were sometimes seen.

In general, neutrophils returned to normal in about two weeks after captopril was discontinued, and serious infections were limited to clinically complex patients. About 13 percent of the cases of neutropenia have ended fatally, but almost all fatalities were in patients with serious illness, having collagen vascular disease, renal failure, heart failure or immunosuppressant therapy, or a combination of these complicating factors.

Evaluation of the hypertensive or heart failure patient should always include assessment of renal function.

If captopril is used in patients with impaired renal function, white blood cell and differential counts should be evaluated prior to starting treatment and at approximately two-week intervals for about three months, then periodically.

In patients with collagen vascular disease or who are exposed to other drugs known to effect the white cells or immune response, particularly when there is impaired renal function, captopril should be used only after an assessment of benefit and risk, and then with caution.

All patients treated with captopril should be told to report any signs of infection (e.g., sore throat, fever). If infection is suspected, white cell counts should be performed without delay.

Since discontinuation of captopril and other drugs has generally led to prompt return of the white count to normal, upon confirmation of neutropenia (neutrophil count <1000/mm³) the physician should withdraw captopril and closely follow the patient's course.

5.3 Proteinuria

Total urinary proteins greater than 1 g per day were seen in about 0.7 percent of patients receiving captopril. About 90 percent of affected patients had evidence of prior renal disease or received relatively high doses of captopril (in excess of 150 mg/day), or both. The nephrotic syndrome occurred in about one-fifth of proteinuric patients. In most cases, proteinuria subsided or cleared within six months whether or not captopril was continued. Parameters of renal function, such as BUN and creatinine, were seldom altered in the patients with proteinuria.

5.4 Hypotension

Excessive hypotension was rarely seen in hypertensive patients but is a possible consequence of captopril use in salt/volume depleted persons (such as those treated vigorously with diuretics), patients with heart failure or those patients undergoing renal dialysis. (See DRUG INTERACTIONS (6.1).)

In heart failure, where the blood pressure was either normal or low, transient decreases in mean blood pressure greater than 20 percent were recorded in about half of the patients. This transient hypotension is more likely to occur after any of the first several doses and is usually well tolerated, producing either no symptoms or brief mild lightheadedness, although in rare instances it has been associated with arrhythmia or conduction defects. Hypotension was the reason for discontinuation of drug in 3.6 percent of patients with heart failure.

BECAUSE OF THE POTENTIAL FALL IN BLOOD PRESSURE IN THESE PATIENTS, THERAPY SHOULD BE STARTED UNDER VERY CLOSE MEDICAL SUPERVISION. A starting dose of 6.25 or 12.5 mg tid may minimize the hypotensive effect. Patients should be followed closely for the first two weeks of treatment and whenever the dose of captopril and/or diuretic is increased. In patients with heart failure, reducing the dose of diuretic, if feasible, may minimize the fall in blood pressure.

Hypotension is not *per se* a reason to discontinue captopril. Some decrease of systemic blood pressure is a common and desirable observation upon initiation of CAPOTEN (captopril) treatment in heart failure. The magnitude of the decrease is greatest early in the course of treatment; this effect stabilizes within a week or two, and generally returns to pretreatment levels, without a decrease in therapeutic efficacy, within two months.

5.5 Fetal/Neonatal Morbidity and Mortality

ACE inhibitors can cause fetal and neonatal morbidity and death when administered to pregnant women. Several dozen cases have been reported in the world literature. When pregnancy is detected, ACE inhibitors should be discontinued as soon as possible.

The use of ACE inhibitors during the second and third trimesters of pregnancy has been associated with fetal and neonatal injury, including hypotension, neonatal skull hypoplasia, anuria, reversible or irreversible renal failure, and death. Oligohydramnios has also been reported, presumably resulting from decreased fetal renal function; oligohydramnios in this setting has been associated with fetal limb contractures, craniofacial deformation, and hypoplastic lung development. Prematurity, intrauterine growth retardation, and patent ductus arteriosus have also been reported, although it is not clear whether these occurrences were due to the ACE inhibitor exposure.

These adverse effects do not appear to have resulted from intrauterine ACE inhibitor exposure that has been limited to the first trimester. Mothers whose embryos and fetuses are exposed to ACE inhibitors only during the first trimester should be so informed. Nonetheless, when patients become pregnant, physicians should make every effort to discontinue the use of captopril as soon as possible.

Rarely (probably less often than once in every thousand pregnancies), no alternative to ACE inhibitors will be found. In these rare cases, the mothers should be apprised of the potential hazards to their fetuses, and serial ultrasound examinations should be performed to assess the intraamniotic environment.

If oligohydramnios is observed, captopril should be discontinued unless it is considered life-saving for the mother. Contraction stress testing (CST), a non-stress test (NST), or biophysical profiling (BPP) may be appropriate, depending upon the week of pregnancy. Patients and physicians should be aware, however, that oligohydramnios may not appear until after the fetus has sustained irreversible injury.

Infants with histories of in utero exposure to ACE inhibitors should be closely observed for hypotension, oliguria, and hyperkalemia. If oliguria occurs, attention should be directed toward support of blood pressure and renal perfusion. Exchange transfusion or dialysis may be required as a means of reversing hypotension and/or substituting for disordered renal function. While captopril may be removed from the adult circulation by hemodialysis, there is inadequate data concerning the effectiveness of hemodialysis for removing it from the circulation of neonates or children. Peritoneal dialysis is not effective for removing captopril; there is no information concerning exchange transfusion for removing captopril from the general circulation.

When captopril was given to rabbits at doses about 0.8 to 70 times (on a mg/kg basis) the maximum recommended human dose, low incidences of craniofacial malformations were seen. No teratogenic effects of captopril were seen in studies of pregnant rats and hamsters. On a mg/kg basis, the doses used were up to 150 times (in hamsters) and 625 times (in rats) the maximum recommended human dose.

5.6 Hepatic Failure

Rarely, ACE inhibitors have been associated with a syndrome that starts with cholestatic jaundice and progresses to fulminant hepatic necrosis and (sometimes) death. The mechanism of this syndrome is not understood. Patients receiving ACE inhibitors who develop jaundice or marked elevations of hepatic enzymes should discontinue the ACE inhibitor and receive appropriate medical follow-up.

5.7 Impaired Renal Function

Hypertension—Some patients with renal disease, particularly those with severe renal artery stenosis, have developed increases in BUN and serum creatinine after reduction of blood pressure with captopril. Captopril dosage reduction and/or discontinuation of diuretic may be required. For some of these patients, it may not be possible to normalize blood pressure and maintain adequate renal perfusion.

Heart Failure—About 20 percent of patients develop stable elevations of BUN and serum creatinine greater than 20 percent above normal or baseline upon long-term treatment with captopril. Less than 5 percent of patients, generally those with severe pre-existing renal disease, required discontinuation of treatment due to progressively increasing creatinine; subsequent improvement probably depends upon the severity of the underlying renal disease.

See CLINICAL PHARMACOLOGY (12), DOSAGE AND ADMINISTRATION (2.6), ADVERSE REACTIONS: Altered Laboratory Findings (8.1).

5.8 Hyperkalemia

Elevations in serum potassium have been observed in some patients treated with ACE inhibitors, including captopril. When treated with ACE inhibitors, patients at risk for the development of hyperkalemia include those with: renal insufficiency; diabetes mellitus; and those using concomitant potassium-sparing diuretics, potassium supplements or potassium-containing salt substitutes; or other drugs associated with increases in serum potassium. In a trial of type I diabetic patients with proteinuria, the incidence of withdrawal of treatment with captopril for hyperkalemia was 2% (4/207). In two trials of normotensive type I diabetic patients with microalbuminuria, no captopril group subjects had hyperkalemia (0/116). (See PATIENT COUNSELING INFORMATION (P); DRUG INTERACTIONS (6.5); ADVERSE REACTIONS: Altered Laboratory Findings (8.1).)

5.9 Cough

Cough has been reported with the use of ACE inhibitors. Characteristically, the cough is nonproductive, persistent and resolves after discontinuation of therapy. ACE inhibitor-induced cough should be considered as part of the differential diagnosis of cough.

5.10 Valvular Stenosis

There is concern, on theoretical grounds, that patients with aortic stenosis might be at particular risk of decreased coronary perfusion when treated with vasodilators because they do not develop as much afterload reduction as others.

5.11 Surgery/Anesthesia

In patients undergoing major surgery or during anesthesia with agents that produce hypotension, captopril will block angiotensin II formation secondary to compensatory renin release. If hypotension occurs and is considered to be due to this mechanism, it can be corrected by volume expansion.

5.12 Hemodialysis

Recent clinical observations have shown an association of hypersensitivity-like (anaphylactoid) reactions during hemodialysis with high-flux dialysis membranes (e.g., AN69) in patients receiving ACE inhibitors. In these patients, consideration should be given to using a different type of dialysis membrane or a different class of medication.

6 DRUG INTERACTIONS

6.1 Hypotension—Patients on Diuretic Therapy

Patients on diuretics and especially those in whom diuretic therapy was recently instituted, as well as those on severe dietary salt restriction or dialysis, may occasionally experience a precipitous reduction of blood pressure usually within the first hour after receiving the initial dose of captopril.

The possibility of hypotensive effects with captopril can be minimized by either discontinuing the diuretic or increasing the salt intake approximately one week prior to initiation of treatment with CAPOTEN or initiating therapy with small doses (6.25 or 12.5 mg). Alternatively, provide medical supervision for at least one hour after the initial dose. If hypotension occurs, the patient should be placed in a supine position and, if necessary, receive an intravenous infusion of normal saline. This transient hypotensive response is not a contraindication to further doses which can be given without difficulty once the blood pressure has increased after volume expansion.

6.2 Agents Having Vasodilator Activity

Data on the effect of concomitant use of other vasodilators in patients receiving CAPOTEN for heart failure are not available; therefore, nitroglycerin or other nitrates (as used for management of angina) or other drugs having vasodilator activity should, if possible, be discontinued before starting CAPOTEN. If resumed during CAPOTEN therapy, such agents should be administered cautiously, and perhaps at lower dosage.

6.3 Agents Causing Renin Release

Captopril's effect will be augmented by antihypertensive agents that cause renin release. For example, diuretics (e.g., thiazides) may activate the renin-angiotensin-aldosterone system.

6.4 Agents Affecting Sympathetic Activity

The sympathetic nervous system may be especially important in supporting blood pressure in patients receiving captopril alone or with diuretics. Therefore, agents affecting sympathetic activity (e.g., ganglionic blocking agents or adrenergic neuron blocking agents) should be used with caution. Beta-adrenergic blocking drugs add some further antihypertensive effect to captopril, but the overall response is less than additive.

6.5 Agents Increasing Serum Potassium

Since captopril decreases aldosterone production, elevation of serum potassium may occur. Potassium-sparing diuretics such as spironolactone, triamterene, or amiloride, or potassium supplements should be given only for documented hypokalemia, and then with caution, since they may lead to a significant increase of serum potassium. Salt substitutes containing potassium should also be used with caution.

6.6 Inhibitors Of Endogenous Prostaglandin Synthesis

It has been reported that indomethacin may reduce the antihypertensive effect of captopril, especially in cases of low renin hypertension. Other nonsteroidal anti-inflammatory agents (e.g., aspirin) may also have this effect.

6.7 Lithium

Increased serum lithium levels and symptoms of lithium toxicity have been reported in patients receiving concomitant lithium and ACE inhibitor therapy. These drugs should be coadministered with caution and frequent monitoring of serum lithium levels is recommended. If a diuretic is also used, it may increase the risk of lithium toxicity.

6.8 Drug/Laboratory Test Interaction

Captopril may cause a false-positive urine test for acetone.

7 USE IN SPECIFIC POPULATIONS

7.1 Pregnancy Categories C (first trimester) and D (second and third trimesters) See **WARNINGS/PRECAUTIONS: Fetal/Neonatal Morbidity and Mortality (5.5).**

7.3 Lactating Women

Concentrations of captopril in human milk are approximately one percent of those in maternal blood. Because of the potential for serious adverse reactions in nursing infants from captopril, a decision should be made whether to discontinue nursing or to discontinue the drug, taking into account the importance of CAPOTEN (captopril) to the mother. (See USE IN SPECIFIC POPULATIONS: Pediatric Use (7.4).)

7.4 Pediatric Use

Safety and effectiveness in children have not been established. There is limited experience reported in the literature with the use of captopril in the pediatric population; dosage, on a weight basis, was generally reported to be comparable to or less than that used in adults.

Infants, especially newborns, may be more susceptible to the adverse hemodynamic effects of captopril. Excessive, prolonged and unpredictable decreases in blood pressure and associated complications, including oliguria and seizures, have been reported.

CAPOTEN (captopril) should be used in children only if other measures for controlling blood pressure have not been effective.

8 ADVERSE REACTIONS

Reported incidences are based on clinical trials involving approximately 7000 patients.

Renal: About one of 100 patients developed proteinuria (see WARNINGS/PRECAUTIONS (5.3)).

Each of the following has been reported in approximately 1 to 2 of 1000 patients and are of uncertain relationship to drug use: renal insufficiency, renal failure, nephrotic syndrome, polyuria, oliguria, and urinary frequency.

Hematologic: Neutropenia/agranulocytosis has occurred (see WARNINGS/PRECAUTIONS (5.2)). Cases of anemia, thrombocytopenia, and pancytopenia have been reported.

Dermatologic: Rash, often with pruritus, and sometimes with fever, arthralgia, and eosinophilia, occurred in about 4 to 7 (depending on renal status and dose) of 100 patients, usually during the first four weeks of therapy. It is usually maculopapular, and rarely urticarial. The rash is usually mild and disappears within a few days of dosage reduction, short-term treatment with an antihistaminic agent, and/or discontinuing therapy; remission may occur even if captopril is continued. Pruritus, without rash, occurs in about 2 of 100 patients. Between 7 and 10 percent of patients with skin rash have shown an eosinophilia and/or positive ANA

titers. A reversible associated pemphigoid-like lesion, and photo sensitivity, have also been reported.

Flushing or pallor has been reported in 2 to 5 of 1000 patients.

Cardiovascular: Hypotension may occur; see DRUG INTERACTIONS (6.1) for discussion of hypotension with captopril therapy. Tachycardia, chest pain, and palpitations have each been observed in approximately 1 of 100 patients.

Angina pectoris, myocardial infarction, Raynaud's syndrome, and congestive heart failure have each occurred in 2 to 3 of 1000 patients.

Dysgeusia: Approximately 2 to 4 (depending on renal status and dose) of 100 patients developed a diminution or loss of taste perception. Taste impairment is reversible and usually self-limited (2 to 3 months) even with continued drug administration. Weight loss may be associated with the loss of taste.

Angioedema: Angioedema involving the extremities, face, lips, mucous membranes, tongue, glottis or larynx has been reported in approximately one in 1000 patients. Angioedema involving the upper airways has caused fatal airway obstruction. (See PATIENT COUNSELING INFORMATION (P.).)

Cough: Cough has been reported in 0.5-2% of patients treated with captopril in clinical trials. (See WARNINGS/PRECAUTIONS: Cough (5.9).)

The following have been reported in about 0.5 to 2 percent of patients but did not appear at increased frequency compared to placebo or other treatments used in controlled trials: gastric irritation, abdominal pain, nausea, vomiting, diarrhea, anorexia, constipation, aphthous ulcers, peptic ulcer, dizziness, headache, malaise, fatigue, insomnia, dry mouth, dyspnea, alopecia, paresthesias.

Other clinical adverse effects reported since the drug was marketed are listed below by body system. In this setting, an incidence or causal relationship cannot be accurately determined.

Body as a whole: Anaphylactoid reactions (see WARNINGS/PRECAUTIONS: Hemodialysis (5.12)).

General: Asthenia, gynecomastia.

Cardiovascular: Cardiac arrest, cerebrovascular accident/insufficiency, rhythm disturbances, orthostatic hypotension, syncope.

Dermatologic: Bullous pemphigus, erythema multiforme (including Stevens-Johnson syndrome), exfoliative dermatitis.

Gastrointestinal: Pancreatitis, glossitis, dyspepsia.

Hematologic: Anemia, including aplastic and hemolytic.

Hepatobiliary: Jaundice, hepatitis, including rare cases of necrosis, cholestasis.

Metabolic: Symptomatic hyponatremia.

Musculoskeletal: Myalgia, myasthenia.

Nervous/Psychiatric: Ataxia, confusion, depression, nervousness, somnolence.

Respiratory: Bronchospasm, eosinophilic pneumonitis, rhinitis.

Special Senses: Blurred vision.

Urogenital: Impotence.

As with other ACE inhibitors, a syndrome has been reported which may include: fever, myalgia, arthralgia, interstitial nephritis, vasculitis, rash or other dermatologic manifestations, eosinophilia and an elevated ESR.

Fetal/Neonatal Morbidity and Mortality

See **WARNINGS/PRECAUTIONS: Fetal/Neonatal Morbidity and Mortality.**

8.1 Altered Laboratory Findings

Serum Electrolytes: Hyperkalemia: small increases in serum potassium, especially in patients with renal impairment (see WARNINGS/PRECAUTIONS (5.8)).

Hyponatremia: particularly in patients receiving a low sodium diet or concomitant diuretics.

BUN/Serum Creatinine: Transient elevations of BUN or serum creatinine especially in volume or salt depleted patients or those with renovascular hypertension may occur. Rapid reduction of longstanding or markedly elevated blood pressure can result in decreases in the glomerular filtration rate and, in turn, lead to increases in BUN or serum creatinine.

Hematologic: A positive ANA has been reported.

Liver Function Tests: Elevations of liver transaminases, alkaline phosphatase, and serum bilirubin have occurred.

10 OVERDOSAGE

Correction of hypotension would be of primary concern. Volume expansion with an intravenous infusion of normal saline is the treatment of choice for restoration of blood pressure.

While captopril may be removed from the adult circulation by hemodialysis, there is inadequate data concerning the effectiveness of hemodialysis for removing it from the circulation of neonates or children. Peritoneal dialysis is not effective for removing captopril; there is no information concerning exchange transfusion for removing captopril from the general circulation.

11 DESCRIPTION

CAPOTEN (captopril) is a specific competitive inhibitor of angiotensin I-converting enzyme (ACE), the enzyme responsible for the conversion of angiotensin I to angiotensin II.

CAPOTEN is designated chemically as 1-[(2S)-3-mercapto-2-methylpropionyl]-L-proline [MW 217.29].

Captopril is a white to off-white crystalline powder that may have a slight sulfurous odor; it is soluble in water (approx. 160 mg/mL), methanol, and ethanol and sparingly soluble in chloroform and ethyl acetate.

CAPOTEN is available in potencies of 12.5 mg, 25 mg, 50 mg, and 100 mg as scored tablets for oral administration. Inactive ingredients: microcrystalline cellulose, corn starch, lactose, and stearic acid.

12 CLINICAL PHARMACOLOGY

12.1 Mechanism of Action

The mechanism of action of CAPOTEN has not yet been fully elucidated. Its beneficial effects in hypertension and heart failure appear to result primarily from suppression of the renin-angiotensin-aldosterone system. However, there is no consistent correlation between renin levels and response to the drug. Renin, an enzyme synthesized by the kidneys, is released into the circulation where it acts on a plasma globulin substrate to produce angiotensin I, a relatively inactive decapeptide. Angiotensin I is then converted by angiotensin converting enzyme (ACE) to angiotensin II, a potent endogenous vasoconstrictor substance. Angiotensin II also stimulates aldosterone secretion from the adrenal cortex, thereby contributing to sodium and fluid retention.

CAPOTEN prevents the conversion of angiotensin I to angiotensin II by inhibition of ACE, a peptidyldipeptide carboxy hydrolase. This inhibition has been demonstrated in both healthy human subjects and in animals by showing that the elevation of blood pressure caused by exogenously administered angiotensin I was attenuated or abolished by captopril. In animal studies, captopril did not alter the pressor responses to a number of other agents, including angiotensin II and norepinephrine, indicating specificity of action.

ACE is identical to "bradykininase," and CAPOTEN may also interfere with the degradation of the vasodepressor peptide, bradykinin. Increased concentrations of bradykinin or prostaglandin E² may also have a role in the therapeutic effect of CAPOTEN.

Inhibition of ACE results in decreased plasma angiotensin II and increased plasma renin activity (PRA), the latter resulting from loss of negative feedback on renin release caused by reduction in angiotensin II. The reduction of angiotensin II leads to decreased aldosterone secretion, and, as a result, small increases in serum potassium may occur along with sodium and fluid loss.

The antihypertensive effects persist for a longer period of time than does demonstrable inhibition of circulating ACE. It is not known whether the ACE present in vascular endothelium is inhibited longer than the ACE in circulating blood.

12.2 Pharmacodynamics

Administration of CAPOTEN results in a reduction of peripheral arterial resistance in hypertensive patients with either no change, or an increase, in cardiac output. There is an increase in renal blood flow following administration of CAPOTEN and glomerular filtration rate is usually unchanged.

Reductions of blood pressure are usually maximal 60 to 90 minutes after oral administration of an individual dose of CAPOTEN. The duration of effect is dose related. The reduction in blood pressure may be progressive, so to achieve maximal therapeutic effects, several weeks of therapy may be required. The blood pressure lowering effects of captopril and thiazide-type diuretics are additive. In contrast, captopril and beta-blockers have a less than additive effect.

Blood pressure is lowered to about the same extent in both standing and supine positions. Orthostatic effects and tachycardia are infrequent but may occur in volume depleted patients. Abrupt withdrawal of CAPOTEN has not been associated with a rapid increase in blood pressure.

12.3 Pharmacokinetics

After oral administration of therapeutic doses of CAPOTEN, rapid absorption occurs with peak blood levels at about one hour. The presence of food in the gastrointestinal tract reduces absorption by about 30 to 40 percent; captopril therefore should be given one hour before meals. Based on carbon-14 labeling, average minimal absorption is approximately 75 percent. In a 24-hour period, over 95 percent of the absorbed dose is eliminated in the urine; 40 to 50 percent is unchanged drug; most of the remainder is the disulfide dimer of captopril and captopril-cysteine disulfide.

Approximately 25 to 30 percent of the circulating drug is bound to plasma proteins. The apparent elimination half-life for total radioactivity in blood is probably less than 3 hours. An accurate determination of half-life of unchanged captopril is not, at present, possible, but it is probably less than 2 hours. In patients with renal impairment, however, retention of captopril occurs (see DOSAGE AND ADMINISTRATION (2.6)).

Studies in rats and cats indicate that CAPOTEN does not cross the blood-brain barrier to any significant extent.

13 NONCLINICAL TOXICOLOGY

13.1 Carcinogenesis, Mutagenesis and Impairment of Fertility

Two-year studies with doses of 50 to 1350 mg/kg/day in mice and rats failed to show any evidence of carcinogenic potential. The high dose in these studies is 150 times the maximum recommended human dose of 450 mg, assuming a 50-kg subject. On a body-surface-area basis, the high doses for mice and rats are 13 and 26 times the maximum recommended human dose, respectively.

Studies in rats have revealed no impairment of fertility.

13.2 Animal Toxicology

Chronic oral toxicity studies were conducted in rats (2 years), dogs (47 weeks; 1 year), mice (2 years), and monkeys (1 year). Significant drug-related toxicity included effects on hematopoiesis, renal toxicity, erosion/ulceration of the stomach, and variation of retinal blood vessels.

Reductions in hemoglobin and/or hematocrit values were seen in mice, rats, and monkeys at doses 50 to 150 times the maximum recommended human dose (MRHD) of 450 mg, assuming a 50-mg subject. On a body-surface-area, these doses are 5 to 25 times maximum recommended human dose (MRHD). Anemia, leukopenia, thrombocytopenia, and bone marrow suppression occurred in dogs at doses 8 to 30 times MRHD on a body-weight basis (4 to 15 times MRHD on a surface-area basis). The reductions in hemoglobin and hematocrit values in rats and mice were only significant at 1 year and returned to normal with continued dosing by the end of the study. Marked anemia was seen at all dose levels (8 to 30 times MRHD) in dogs, whereas moderate to marked leukopenia was noted only at 15 and 30 times MRHD and thrombocytopenia at 30 times MRHD. The anemia could be reversed upon discontinuation of dosing. Bone marrow suppression occurred to a varying degree, being associated only with dogs that died or were sacrificed in a moribund condition in the 1 year study. However, in the 47-week study at a dose 30 times MRHD, bone marrow suppression was found to be reversible upon continued drug administration.

Captopril caused hyperplasia of the juxtaglomerular apparatus of the kidneys in mice and rats at doses 7 to 200 times MRHD on a body-weight basis (0.6 to 35 times MRHD on a surface-area basis); in monkeys at 20 to 60 times MRHD on a body-weight basis (7 to 20 times MRHD on a surface-area basis); and in dogs at 30 times MRHD on a body-weight basis (15 times MRHD on a surface-area basis).

Gastric erosions/ulcerations were increased in incidence in male rats at 20 to 200 times MRHD on a body-weight basis (3.5 and 35 times MRHD on a surface-area basis); in dogs at 30 times MRHD on a body-weight basis (15 times on MRHD on a surface-area basis); and in monkeys at 65 times MRHD on a body-weight basis (20 times MRHD on a surface-area basis). Rabbits developed gastric and intestinal ulcers when given oral doses approximately 30 times MRHD on a body-weight basis (10 times MRHD on a surface-area basis) for only 5 to 7 days.

In the two-year rat study, irreversible and progressive variations in the caliber of retinal vessels (focal sacculations and constrictions) occurred at all dose levels (7 to 200 times MRHD) on a body-weight basis; 1 to 35 times MRHD on a surface-area basis in a dose-related fashion. The effect was first observed in the 88th week of dosing, with a progressively increased incidence thereafter, even after cessation of dosing.

14 CLINICAL STUDIES

Congestive Heart Failure: In patients with heart failure, significantly decreased peripheral (systemic vascular) resistance and blood pressure (afterload), reduced pulmonary capillary wedge pressure (preload) and pulmonary vascular resistance, increased cardiac output, and increased exercise tolerance time (ETT) have been demonstrated. These hemodynamic and clinical effects occur after the first dose and appear to persist for the duration of therapy. Placebo controlled studies of 12 weeks duration in patients who did not respond adequately to diuretics and digitalis show no tolerance to beneficial effects on ETT; open studies, with exposure up to 18 months in some cases, also indicate that ETT benefit is maintained. Clinical improvement has been observed in some patients where acute hemodynamic effects were minimal.

Left Ventricular Dysfunction After Myocardial Infarction: The Survival and Ventricular Enlargement (SAVE) study was a multicenter, randomized, double-blind, placebo-controlled trial conducted in 2,231 patients (age 21-79 years) who survived the acute phase of a myocardial infarction and did not have active ischemia. Patients had left ventricular dysfunction (LVD), defined as a resting left ventricular ejection fraction ≤ 40%, but at the time of randomization were not sufficiently symptomatic to require ACE inhibitor therapy for heart failure. About half of the patients had had symptoms of heart failure in the past. Patients were given a test dose of 6.25 mg oral CAPOTEN (captopril) and were randomized within 3-16 days post-infarction to receive either CAPOTEN or placebo in addition to conventional therapy. CAPOTEN was initiated at 6.25 mg or 12.5 mg tid and after two weeks titrated to a target maintenance dose of 50 mg tid. About 80% of patients were receiving the target dose at the end of the study. Patients were followed for a minimum of two years and for up to five years, with an average follow-up of 3.5 years.

Baseline blood pressure was 113/70 mm Hg and 112/70 mm Hg for the placebo and CAPOTEN groups, respectively. Blood pressure increased slightly in both treatment groups during the study and was somewhat lower in the CAPOTEN group (119/74 vs. 125/77 mm Hg at 1 yr).

Therapy with CAPOTEN improved long-term survival and clinical outcomes compared to placebo. The risk reduction for all cause mortality was 19% (P = 0.02) and for cardiovascular death was 21% (P = 0.014). Captopril treated subjects had 22% (P = 0.034) fewer first hospitalizations for heart failure. Compared to placebo, 22% fewer patients receiving captopril developed symptoms of overt heart failure. There was no significant difference between groups in total hospitalizations for all cause (2056 placebo; 2036 captopril).

CAPOTEN was well tolerated in the presence of other therapies such as aspirin, beta blockers, nitrates, vasodilators, calcium antagonists and diuretics.

Diabetic Nephropathy: In a multicenter, double-blind, placebo controlled trial, 409 patients, age 18-49 of either gender, with or without hypertension, with type I (juvenile type, onset before age 30) insulin-dependent diabetes mellitus, retinopathy, proteinuria ≥ 500 mg per day and serum creatinine ≤ 2.5 mg/dL, were ran-

domized to placebo or CAPOTEN (25 mg tid) and followed for up to 4.8 years (median 3 years). To achieve blood pressure control, additional antihypertensive agents (diuretics, beta blockers, centrally acting agents or vasodilators) were added as needed for patients in both groups.

The CAPOTEN group had a 51% reduction in risk of doubling of serum creatinine (P < 0.01) and a 51% reduction in risk for the combined endpoint of end-stage renal disease (dialysis or transplantation) or death (P < 0.01). CAPOTEN treatment resulted in a 30% reduction in urine protein excretion within the first 3 months (P < 0.05), which was maintained throughout the trial. The CAPOTEN group had somewhat better blood pressure control than the placebo group, but the effects of CAPOTEN on renal function were greater than would be expected from the group differences in blood pressure reduction alone. CAPOTEN was well-tolerated in this patient population.

In two multicenter, double-blind, placebo controlled studies, a total of 235 normotensive patients with insulin-dependent diabetes mellitus, retinopathy and microalbuminuria (20-200 µg/min) were randomized to placebo or CAPOTEN (50 mg bid) and followed for up to 2 years. CAPOTEN delayed the progression to overt nephropathy (proteinuria ≥ 500 mg/day) in both studies (risk reduction 67% to 76%; P < 0.05). CAPOTEN also reduced the albumin excretion rate. However, the long term clinical benefit of reducing the progression from microalbuminuria to proteinuria has not been established

P PATIENT COUNSELING INFORMATION

Patients should be advised to immediately report to their physician any signs or symptoms suggesting angioedema (e.g., swelling of face, eyes, lips, tongue, larynx and extremities; difficulty in swallowing or breathing; hoarseness) and to discontinue therapy. (See WARNINGS/PRECAUTIONS (5.1).)

Patients should be told to report promptly any indication of infection (e.g., sore throat, fever), which may be a sign of neutropenia, or of progressive edema which might be related to proteinuria and nephrotic syndrome.

All patients should be cautioned that excessive perspiration and dehydration may lead to an excessive fall in blood pressure because of reduction in fluid volume. Other causes of volume depletion such as vomiting or diarrhea may also lead to a fall in blood pressure; patients should be advised to consult with the physician.

Patients should be advised not to use potassium-sparing diuretics, potassium supplements or potassium-containing salt substitutes without consulting their physician. (See WARNINGS/PRECAUTIONS (5.8); DRUG INTERACTIONS (6.5); ADVERSE REACTIONS (8).)

Patients should be warned against interruption or discontinuation of medication unless instructed by the physician.

Heart failure patients on captopril therapy should be cautioned against rapid increases in physical activity.

Patients should be informed that CAPOTEN (captopril) should be taken one hour before meals (see DOSAGE AND ADMINISTRATION (2.1)).

Pregnancy. Female patients of childbearing age should be told about the consequences of second- and third-trimester exposure to ACE inhibitors, and they should also be told that these consequences do not appear to have resulted from intrauterine ACE-inhibitor exposure that has been limited to the first trimester. These patients should be asked to report pregnancies to their physicians as soon as possible.

[FR Doc. 00-32375 Filed 12-21-00; 8:45 am]
BILLING CODE 4160-01-C

PART II

TORT LIABILITY

CHAPTER 5

PRODUCTS LIABILITY: PRELIMINARIES

To this point, we have focused on federal regulation of medical technologies. Although important, the FDA does not have a monopoly over the control drugs and medical devices. Tort litigation under state law generates significant, even if less direct, regulatory pressures on suppliers of such products. This chapter introduces several general features of products liability law as it applies to medical technologies, focusing in particular on the points of overlap between public and private law. The chapters that follow provide more detailed coverage of the different categories of tort liability applicable to the sale and use of defective medical products.

A. STRICT LIABILITY AND UNAVOIDABLY UNSAFE PRODUCTS

Products liability law, whether framed in terms of strict liability or negligence (or, for that matter, as a breach of implied warranty), allows consumers to recover damages caused by "defective" products sold by the defendant. Product manufacturers and others in the chain of distribution may face tort liability for (1) manufacturing defects (i.e., when a product comes off the assembly line out of specifications); (2) design defects (i.e., when the specifications themselves are deemed unreasonably unsafe because the risks associated with the design outweigh its utility when compared with reasonable alternative designs); or (3) inadequate warnings about inherent risks in the design that the defendant knew or should have known about but that consumers were unlikely to recognize. As explained in Chapter 6, the test for design defect used to (and in a few jurisdictions continues to) ask instead whether the product's performance disappointed the expectations of a reasonable consumer.

The earliest cases involved exploding glass bottles and defective automobiles. Although claims involving such products continue to occupy the courts, lawsuits against the manufacturers of drugs and medical devices have become increasingly important in the last few decades, both in their volume and in the conceptual challenges that they have presented. See Linda S. Svitak & Peter J. Goss, Drug and Device Litigation in the 21st Century, 27 Wm. Mitchell L. Rev. 271 (2000); Drugs in Litigation (1999 ed.). As a result, courts have created a variety of special rules to accommodate products liability litigation against the sellers and users of medical technologies. For some of the earliest commentary on the subject, see W.

Page Keeton, Some Observations About the Strict Liability of the Makers of Prescription Drugs: The Aftermath of MER/29, 56 Cal. L. Rev. 149 (1968); Richard A. Merrill, Compensation for Prescription Drug Injuries, 59 Va. L. Rev. 1 (1973); Paul Rheingold, Products Liability–The Ethical Drug Manufacturer's Liability, 18 Rutgers L. Rev. 947 (1964).

Restatement (Second) of the Law of Torts (American Law Inst. 1965):

§ 402A. Special Liability of Seller of Product for Physical Harm to User or Consumer

> Comment k: *Unavoidably unsafe products.* There are some products which, in the present state of human knowledge, are quite incapable of being made safe for their intended and ordinary use. These are especially common in the field of drugs. An outstanding example is the vaccine for the Pasteur treatment of rabies, which not uncommonly leads to very serious and damaging consequences when it is injected. Since the disease itself invariably leads to a dreadful death, both the marketing and use of the vaccine are fully justified, notwithstanding the unavoidable high degree of risk which they involve. Such a product, properly prepared, and accompanied by proper directions and warning, is not defective, nor is it unreasonably dangerous. The same is true of many other drugs, vaccines, and the like, many of which for this very reason cannot legally be sold except to physicians, or under the prescription of a physician. It is also true in particular of many new or experimental drugs as to which, because of lack of time and opportunity for sufficient medical experience, there can be no assurance of safety, or perhaps even of purity of ingredients, but such experience as there is justifies the marketing and use of the drug notwithstanding a medically recognizable risk. The seller of such products, again with the qualification that they are properly prepared and marketed, and proper warning is given, where the situation calls for it, is not to be held to strict liability for unfortunate consequences attending their use, merely because he has undertaken to supply the public with an apparently useful and desirable product, attended with a known but apparently reasonable risk.

Brown v. Superior Court (Abbott Labs.)

751 P.2d 470 (Cal.1988).

■ MOSK, JUSTICE:

* * * The doctrine of strict liability had its genesis in a concurring opinion by Justice Roger Traynor in *Escola v. Coca Cola Bottling Co.*, 150 P.2d 436 (Cal.1944). He suggested that a manufacturer should be absolutely liable if, in placing a product on the market, it knew the product was to be used without inspection, and it proved to have a defect that caused injury. The policy considerations underlying this suggestion were that the manufacturer, unlike the public, can anticipate or guard against the recurrence of hazards, that the cost of injury may be an overwhelming misfortune to the person injured whereas the manufacturer can insure against the risk and distribute the cost among the consuming public, and that it is in the public interest to discourage the marketing of defective products. This court unanimously adopted Justice Traynor's concept in *Greenman v. Yuba Power Products, Inc.*, 377 P.2d 897 (Cal.1963), holding a manufacturer strictly liable in tort and using the formulation of the doctrine set forth in *Escola*.

Strict liability differs from negligence in that it eliminates the necessity for the injured party to prove that the manufacturer of the product which caused injury was negligent. It focuses not on the conduct of the manufacturer but on the product itself, and holds the manufacturer liable if the product was defective. In 1965, soon after our decision in *Greenman*, the *Restatement Second of Torts* published section 402A, which set forth the strict liability doctrine. Almost all states have adopted some form of strict liability since that time. * * *

Even before *Greenman* was decided, the members of the American Law Institute, in considering whether to adopt a rule of strict liability, pondered whether the manufacturer of a prescription drug should be subject to the doctrine. During a rather confusing discussion of a draft of what was to become section 402A, a member of the Institute proposed that drugs should be exempted from strict liability on the ground that it would be "against the public interest" to apply the doctrine to such products because of "the very serious tendency to stifle medical research and testing." Dean Prosser, who was the reporter for the *Restatement Second of Torts*, responded that the problem was a real one, and that he had it in mind in drafting section 402A. A motion to exempt prescription drugs from the section was defeated on the suggestion of Dean Prosser that the problem could be dealt with in the comments to the section. However, a motion to state the exemption in a comment was also defeated. At the next meeting of the Institute in 1962, section 402A was approved together with comment k thereto.

The comment provides that the producer of a properly manufactured prescription drug may be held liable for injuries caused by the product only if it was not accompanied by a warning of dangers that the manufacturer knew or should have known about. * * * Comment k has been analyzed and criticized by numerous commentators. While there is some disagreement as to its scope and meaning, there is a general consensus that, although it purports to explain the strict liability doctrine, in fact the principle it states is based on negligence. * * * Comment k has been adopted in the overwhelming majority of jurisdictions that have considered the matter. * * *

[T]he fact that a drug with dangerous side effects may be characterized as containing a defect in design does not necessarily mean that its producer is to be held strictly liable for the defect. The determination of that issue depends on whether the public interest would be served by the imposition of such liability. As we have seen, the fundamental reasons underlying the imposition of strict liability are to deter manufacturers from marketing products that are unsafe, and to spread the cost of injury from the plaintiff to the consuming public, which will pay a higher price for the product to reflect the increased expense of insurance to the manufacturer resulting from its greater exposure to liability.

These reasons could justify application of the doctrine to the manufacturers of prescription drugs. It is indisputable, as plaintiff contends, that the risk of injury from such drugs is unavoidable, that a consumer may be helpless to protect himself from serious harm caused by them, and that, like other products, the cost of insuring against strict liability can be passed on by the producer to the consumer who buys the item. Moreover, as we observe below, in some cases additional testing of drugs before they are marketed might reveal dangerous side effects, resulting in a safer product.

But there is an important distinction between prescription drugs and other products such as construction machinery, a lawnmower, or perfume, the producers of which were held strictly liable. In the latter cases, the product is used to make work easier or to provide pleasure, while in the former it may be necessary to alleviate pain and suffering or to sustain life. Moreover, unlike other important medical products (wheelchairs, for example), harm to some users from prescription drugs is unavoidable. Because of these distinctions, the broader public interest in the availability of drugs at an affordable price must be considered in deciding the appropriate standard of liability for injuries resulting from their use.

Perhaps a drug might be made safer if it was withheld from the market until scientific skill and knowledge advanced to the point at which additional dangerous side effects would be revealed. But in most cases such a delay in marketing new drugs—added to the delay required to obtain approval for release of the product from the Food and Drug Administration—would not serve the public welfare. Public policy favors the development and marketing of beneficial new drugs, even though some risks, perhaps serious ones, might accompany their introduction, because drugs can save lives and reduce pain and suffering.

delays in research would not serve public welfare.

If drug manufacturers were subject to strict liability, they might be reluctant to undertake research programs to develop some pharmaceuticals that would prove beneficial or to distribute others that are available to be marketed, because of the fear of large adverse monetary judgments. Further, the additional expense of insuring against such liability—assuming insurance would be available—and of research programs to reveal possible dangers not detectable by available scientific methods could place the cost of medication beyond the reach of those who need it most.

Dean Prosser summed up the justification for exempting prescription drugs from strict liability as follows: "The argument that industries producing potentially dangerous products should make good the harm, distribute it by liability insurance, and add the cost to the price of the product, encounters reason for pause, when we consider that two of the greatest medical boons to the human race, penicillin and cortisone, both have their dangerous side effects, and that drug companies might well have been deterred from producing and selling them. Thus far the courts have tended to hold the manufacturer to a high standard of care in preparing and

justification for exemption

held to high standard for preparing & testing though.

testing drugs of unknown potentiality and in giving warning; but in the absence of evidence that this standard has not been met, they have refused to hold the maker liable for unforeseeable harm."

The possibility that the cost of insurance and of defending against lawsuits will diminish the availability and increase the price of pharmaceuticals is far from theoretical. Defendants cite a host of examples of products which have greatly increased in price or have been withdrawn or withheld from the market because of the fear that their producers would be held liable for large judgments. For example, according to defendant E.R. Squibb & Sons, Inc., Bendectin, the only antinauseant drug available for pregnant women, was withdrawn from sale in 1983 because the cost of insurance almost equalled the entire income from sale of the drug. Before it was withdrawn, the price of Bendectin increased by over 300 percent.

Drug manufacturers refused to supply a newly discovered vaccine for influenza on the ground that mass inoculation would subject them to enormous liability. The government therefore assumed the risk of lawsuits resulting from injuries caused by the [swine flu] vaccine. One producer of diphtheria-tetanus-pertussis vaccine withdrew from the market, giving as its reason "extreme liability exposure, cost of litigation and the difficulty of continuing to obtain adequate insurance." There are only two manufacturers of the vaccine remaining in the market, and the cost of each dose rose a hundred-fold from 11 cents in 1982 to $11.40 in 1986, $8 of which was for an insurance reserve. The price increase roughly paralleled an increase in the number of lawsuits from one in 1978 to 219 in 1985. Finally, a manufacturer was unable to market a new drug for the treatment of vision problems because it could not obtain adequate liability insurance at a reasonable cost.

There is no doubt that, from the public's standpoint, these are unfortunate consequences. And they occurred even though almost all jurisdictions follow the negligence standard of comment k. It is not unreasonable to conclude in these circumstances that the imposition of a harsher test for liability would not further the public interest in the development and availability of these important products. Our purpose is to demonstrate that there is a rational connection between the cost and availability of pharmaceuticals and the liability imposed on their manufacturers for injuries resulting from their use. We decline to hold, therefore, that a drug manufacturer's liability for injuries caused by the defective design of a prescription drug should be measured by the standard [of strict liability]
* * * *

One further question remains in this aspect of the case. Comment k, as we have seen, provides that the maker of an "unavoidably unsafe" product is not liable for injuries resulting from its use if the product is "properly prepared, and accompanied by proper directions and warning." With the few exceptions noted above, the courts which have adopted comment k have viewed all prescription drugs as coming within its scope. * * *

It seems unjust to grant the same protection from liability to those who gave us thalidomide as to the producers of penicillin.* If some method could be devised to confine the benefit of the comment k negligence standard to those drugs that have proved useful to mankind while denying the privilege to those that are clearly harmful, it would deserve serious consideration. But we know of no means by which this can be accomplished without substantially impairing the public interest in the development and marketing of new drugs, because the harm to this interest arises in the very process of attempting to make the distinction. * * * [T]he question of the superiority of one drug over another would have to be decided not in the abstract but in reference to the plaintiff, since the advantages of a drug cannot be isolated from the condition of a particular patient. Thus, in one case the drug that injured the plaintiff might be the better choice, while this would not be true as to another user. * * *

[T]he eligibility of each drug for favorable treatment must be tested at a trial, with its attendant litigation costs, and the drug must survive two risk/benefit challenges, first by the judge and then by the jury. In order to vindicate the public's interest in the availability and affordability of prescription drugs, a manufacturer must have a greater assurance that his products will not be measured by a strict liability standard * * * * [11]

In conclusion, and in accord with almost all our sister states that have considered the issue, we hold that a manufacturer is not strictly liable for injuries caused by a prescription drug so long as the drug was properly prepared and accompanied by warnings of its dangerous propensities that were either known or reasonably scientifically knowable at the time of distribution.[12]

---

* Ironically, one decade later, the FDA approved thalidomide for the treatment of Hansen's disease, though it conditioned approval on extremely strict distribution controls given the serious risk of birth defects. See Sheryl Gay Stolberg, Thalidomide Approved to Treat Leprosy, with Other Uses Seen, N.Y. Times, July 17, 1998, at A1.

11. * * * We concede that the language of the comment is unclear in this respect. Some portions suggest that it is to apply to all prescriptions drugs (the comment describes the products to which it applies as those which "in the present state of human knowledge, are quite incapable of being made safe for their intended and ordinary use"). Other passages distinguish among drugs ("many . . . drugs, vaccines and the like" are not "unreasonably dangerous" if they are "properly prepared, and are accompanied by appropriate warnings"). Nevertheless, we are of the view that the comment was intended to and should apply to all prescription drugs. As we note above, almost all jurisdictions

that have adopted the rule stated in the comment view its provisions as granting immunity from strict liability to all such drugs. In addition, * * * the benefit of the negligence standard stated in the comment would be greatly diminished if all drugs were required to run the gauntlet of a risk/benefit analysis in order to qualify for application of the standard.

12. Our conclusion does not mean, of course, that drug manufacturers are free of all liability for defective drugs. They are subject to liability for manufacturing defects, as well as under general principles of negligence, and for failure to warn of known or reasonably knowable side effects. It should also be noted that the consumers of prescription drugs are afforded greater protection against defects than consumers of other products, since "the drug industry is closely regulated by the Food and Drug Administration, which actively controls the testing and manufacture of drugs and the method by which they are marketed, including the contents of warning labels."

Grundberg v. Upjohn Co.

813 P.2d 89 (Utah 1991).

■ DURHAM, JUSTICE:

* * * Plaintiffs allege that Grundberg took a 0.5 milligram dose of Halcion the day she [fatally] shot her mother. They allege that this dose was recommended by her physician and was consistent with Upjohn's recommended dosage. Plaintiffs assert that Grundberg shot her mother while in a state of Halcion-induced intoxication, which allegedly included side effects such as depression, psychosis, depersonalization, aggressive assaultive behavior, and homicidal compulsion.

Plaintiffs' complaint states several causes of action, including common law negligence and strict liability. Plaintiffs claim that Upjohn failed to adequately warn about certain adverse side effects of Halcion and that Halcion was defectively designed. The failure-to-warn claim is scheduled for trial. The strict liability claim based on design defect is the subject of Upjohn's pending summary judgment motion, the outcome of which depends on this court's resolution of the certified question.

only strict liability claim considered here.

The parties agree that the *Restatement (Second) of Torts* section 402A, comment k (1965) and the principles it embodies provide an exemption from strict liability for a claimed design defect in the case of products that are "unavoidably unsafe." In moving for partial summary judgment, Upjohn argued that public policy supporting the research and development of new drugs requires a holding that _all_ FDA-approved prescription medications are "unavoidably unsafe" products under comment k and, as such, manufacturers of those drugs would not be liable for a claim based on defective design. Plaintiffs argue that whether a drug is "unavoidably unsafe" must be determined on a case-by-case basis, with a determination in each case of whether the specific drug's benefit exceeded its risk at the time it was distributed. The [federal] district court found this to be a controlling question of law and certified it to this court. * * *

Upjohn's argument

P's argument

We agree with comment k's basic proposition—that there are some products that have dangers associated with their use even though they are used as intended. We also agree that the seller of such products, when the products are properly prepared and marketed and distributed with appropriate warnings, should not be held strictly liable for the "unfortunate consequences" attending their use. Thus, we adopt comment k's basic policy as the law to be applied in this state and must now turn to the issue of how to apply that policy. * * *

By its terms, comment k excepts unavoidably unsafe products from strict liability only to the extent that the plaintiff alleges a design defect; comment k's immunity from strict liability does not extend to strict liability claims based on a manufacturing flaw or an inadequate warning. The purpose of comment k is to protect from strict liability products that cannot be designed more safely. If, however, such products are mismanufactured or unaccompanied by adequate warnings, the seller may be liable even if the plaintiff cannot establish the seller's negligence. * * * Both parties agree in this case that the prerequisite to a comment k exemption— that the drug was properly prepared and accompanied by warnings of its dangerous propensities—must be established on a case-by-case basis. This limitation on the scope of comment k immunity is universally recognized. * * *

In reviewing the approaches of other jurisdictions toward strict products liability for design defects in drug products, we are troubled by the lack of uniformity and certainty inherent in the case-by-case approach and fear the resulting disincentive for pharmaceutical manufacturers to develop new products. * * * We find the *Brown* result more in line with the public policy considerations in the important area of pharmaceutical product design. We do not agree, however, with the *Brown* court's apparent attempt to use the plain language of comment k as the vehicle for exempting all prescription drugs from strict liability rather than relying on the policies underlying that comment.

The American Law Institute's Restatements are drafted by legal scholars who attempt to summarize the state of the law in a given area, predict how the law is changing, and suggest the direction the law should take. The Restatement serves an appropriate advisory role to courts in approaching unsettled areas of law. We emphasize, however, that section 402A of the *Restatement (Second) of Torts*, as drafted in 1965, is not binding on our decision in this case except insofar as we explicitly adopt its various doctrinal principles. We agree with the principle comment k embodies, that manufacturers of unavoidably dangerous products should not be liable for a claim of design defect. We are persuaded that all prescription drugs should be classified as unavoidably dangerous in design because of their unique nature and value, the elaborate regulatory system overseen by the FDA, the difficulties of relying on individual lawsuits as a forum in which to review a prescription drug's design, and the significant public policy considerations noted in *Brown*. * * *

Because prescription drugs are chemical compounds designed to interact with the chemical and physiological processes of the human body, they will almost always pose some risk of side effects in certain individuals. Despite these risks, new drugs are continually approved by the FDA because of their social benefit in saving lives and alleviating human suffering. The health care system and general standard of living in this country, for example, would be seriously impaired without such essential drug products as antibiotics that allow quick recovery from ailments that were once debilitating or even fatal. * * *

Despite inherent risks, *and in contrast to any other product*, society has determined that prescription medications provide a unique benefit and so should be available to physicians with appropriate warnings and guidance as to use. The federal government has established an elaborate regulatory system, overseen by the FDA, to control the approval and distribution of these drugs. No other class of products is subject to such special restrictions or protections in our society. * * *

We find this extensive regulatory scheme capable of and appropriate for making the preliminary determination regarding whether a prescription drug's benefits outweigh its risks. The structured follow-up program imposed by law ensures that drugs are not placed on the market without continued monitoring for adverse consequences that would render the FDA's initial risk/benefit analysis invalid. Allowing individual courts and/or juries to continually reevaluate a drug's risks and benefits ignores the processes of this expert regulatory body and the other avenues of recovery available to plaintiffs. * * *

Finally, we do not believe that a trial court in the context of a products liability action is the proper forum to determine whether, as a whole, a particular prescription drug's benefits outweighed its risks at the time of distribution. In a case-by-case analysis, one court or jury's determination that a particular drug is or is not defectively designed has no bearing on any future case. As a result, differences of opinion among courts in differing jurisdictions leaves unsettled a drug manufacturer's liability for any given drug. Although the FDA may have internal differences of opinion regarding whether a particular new drug application should be approved, the individuals making the ultimate judgment will have the benefit of years of experience in reviewing such products, scientific expertise in the area, and access to the volumes of data they can compel manufacturers to produce. Nor is the FDA subject to the inherent limitations of the trial process, such as the rules of evidence, restrictions on expert testimony, and scheduling demands.[9] * * *

Although we do not accept the notion that courts are unsuited to address design defect claims in any products liability action, we do agree that prescription drug design presents precisely this type of "polycentric" problem. A drug is designed to be effectively administered to specific individuals for one or a number of indications. To determine whether a drug's benefit outweighs its risk is inherently complex because of the manufacturer's conscious design choices regarding the numerous chemical properties of the product and their relationship to the vast physiologic idiosyncracies of each consumer for whom the drug is designed. Society has recognized this complexity and in response has reposed regulatory authority in the FDA. Relying on the FDA's screening and surveillance standards

---

9. There is also a certain moral question to be addressed when determining whether a product's benefit outweighs its risk when faced with the reality of an injured plaintiff. For example, in the case of a vaccine, certain benefits of the drug's availability will accrue to group A, the individuals who are prevented from contracting the disease. A smaller number of individuals, however, may contract the disease and react violently to a component of the drug or, as some other result of the drug's properties, suffer terribly. Under a case-by-case approach, courts or juries must ask which is a more significant interest: efficacy with respect to group A versus harm to group B? The FDA must ask the same question: Does the benefit of this product outweigh its risk? The distinction is that the FDA is in a more objective and informed posture to make that determination.

enables courts to find liability under circumstances of inadequate warning, mismanufacture, improper marketing, or misinforming the FDA—avenues for which courts are better suited. Although this approach denies plaintiffs one potential theory on which to rely in a drug products liability action, the benefits to society in promoting the development, availability, and reasonable price of drugs justifies this conclusion.

In light of the strong public interest in the availability and affordability of prescription medications, the extensive regulatory system of the FDA, and the avenues of recovery still available to plaintiffs by claiming inadequate warning, mismanufacture, improper marketing, or misrepresenting information to the FDA, we conclude that a broad grant of immunity from strict liability claims based on design defects should be extended to FDA-approved prescription drugs in Utah. * * *

■ Stewart, Justice (dissenting):

The majority holds that a drug that is avoidably unsafe to human life or health is exempt from strict liability for design defects if approved by the FDA, even though alternative drugs can provide the same, or even better, therapy, with less risk to life or health. Thus, such FDA-approved drugs as various decongestants, expectorants, deodorants, hair growth stimulants, skin moisturizers, and cough and cold remedies, for example, have the same immunity as rabies or polio vaccines or medications essential in the treatment of cancer, heart disease, or AIDS. I see no basis for according drugs used to treat comparatively minor ailments a blanket immunity from strict liability for design defects if they are unreasonably dangerous to those who use them.

The limited immunity conferred by comment k on a few drugs was given only after thorough consideration by the American Law Institute. However, this court gives blanket immunity for design defects to all FDA-approved drugs on the basis of blind reliance upon the efficacy and integrity of FDA procedures, about which the majority knows almost nothing. * * * In truth, FDA safety procedures do not justify abdication of judicial responsibility. For example, the FDA does not require existing drugs to undergo newly developed tests which would increase the likelihood that a product is in fact safe. * * *

Numerous congressional investigations have demonstrated that the FDA has often approved drugs in complete ignorance of critical information relating to the hazards of such drugs which was contained either in its own files or in the published medical literature, or both. For example, the FDA approved Oraflex on April 19, 1982, for the treatment of arthritis. The manufacturer withdrew the drug from the market on August 4, 1982, because eleven deaths were reported to be associated with the drug's use in the United States and sixty-one deaths were reported in the United Kingdom. Of principal concern were reports of serious and sometimes fatal Oraflex-associated liver and kidney disease. * * * The FDA approved Merital for the treatment of depression on December 31, 1984. Merital was withdrawn from the market in January 1986 because of a large number of reports of serious immune-allergic or hypersensitivity reactions, including several fatalities, associated with its use. * * * The FDA approved Zomax on October 28, 1980, for the relief of mild to moderately severe pain. On March 4, 1983, marketing of the drug was halted by its manufacturer due to a large number of allergic reactions, including deaths, associated with its use. Eventually, more than 2,100 reactions were reported to the FDA. * * *

Although the FDA has a mechanism for the withdrawal of pharmaceutical agents which are found to be dangerous, the mechanism is slow and sometimes unreliable. For example, several studies were published in the early 1950s which should have put diethylstilbestrol (DES) manufacturers on notice that DES injured the reproductive systems of female fetuses whose mothers were exposed to the drug. However, it was not until 1971, nearly twenty years later, that the FDA finally banned the use of DES to prevent miscarriages, the most common use of the drug. * * * In relying on the efficacy of FDA approval procedures as the basis for dispensing with the judicial remedy of product liability, the majority simply ignores FDA failures to protect the public against unnecessary and unacceptable risks. * * *

Furthermore, not a shred of evidence has been presented to this court that indicates that liability under the tort system has deterred pharmaceutical companies from introducing new drugs. Even if that were the case, the question that must be answered, given the majority's holding, is why comment k does not provide a proper accommodation of all the competing policy interests involved in the issue before the court. Why should those who are seriously injured or suffer because of the death of another have to stand the expense of such losses to support the high profit margins in the drug industry? * * *

Certain drugs clearly qualify for comment k exemption, even though the drugs' risk may be comparatively great. A drug's social utility may be so great, for example, a chemotherapeutic agent used for treatment of cancer, that it would obviously qualify for comment k exemption. Other drugs, such as sleeping compounds or dandruff cures, whose social utility may not be of such a high order, would not automatically qualify. * * * The majority opinion states that a case-by-case analysis would leave drug companies uncertain regarding questions of immunity and would result in patchwork verdicts when a drug may be found to be subject to comment k exemption in one case but not subject to the exemption in another case. That consideration has little merit, in my view. We tolerate nonuniformity of result in negligence cases all the time. Nothing this court does can bring about uniformity of result with respect to drugs. The states are already divided on the issue of whether FDA approval of a drug should confer immunity from design defects, although it appears that no state has gone as far as Utah now does. Suffice to say, a number of courts apply comment k on a case-by-case basis—a task that cannot be avoided even under the majority's position if a strict liability claim is coupled with a negligence claim, as is usually the case.

Significantly, Congress has not shared this court's professed concern for uniformity. Whatever lack of uniformity there has been in drug cases has been insufficient to justify uniform national products liability legislation. Furthermore, the Legislature of this State thought that a presumption was sufficient protection for manufacturers rather than outright immunity. It is indeed ironic that the policy of uniformity weighs more heavily in this court than in the United States Congress or the Utah Legislature. We can only deal with the law in Utah, and the possibility of patchwork verdicts on a nationwide basis is simply beyond our power to affect. * * *

In this case, * * * [t]he majority ignores the fact that the FDA found Halcion to be neither unique nor particularly essential and presented no advancement over existing therapeutic alternatives. Perhaps not all would have been appropriate medications, but with so many possible alternatives, it is doubtful that Halcion should be immune from strict liability.

NOTES AND QUESTIONS

1. *Making sense of comment k.* At least one other jurisdiction applies comment k in a blanket fashion. See Young v. Key Pharm., 922 P.2d 59 (Wash.1996). A handful of courts apply comment k on a case-by-case basis. See Adams v. G.D. Searle & Co., 576 So.2d 728, 732 (Fla.Ct.App.1991); Toner v. Lederle Labs., 732 P.2d 297 (Idaho 1987); Savina v. Sterling Drug, Inc., 795 P.2d 915 (Kan.1990); Feldman v. Lederle Labs., 479 A.2d 374, 382–84 (N.J.1984); Castrignano v. E.R. Squibb & Sons, Inc., 546 A.2d 775 (R.I.1988); Collins v. Eli Lilly Co., 342 N.W.2d 37 (Wis.1984). A few courts reject comment k altogether. See Shanks v. Upjohn Co., 835 P.2d 1189, 1196–98 (Alaska 1992); Allison v. Merck & Co., 878 P.2d 948, 953–56 (Nev.1994). See generally Richard C. Ausness, Unavoidably Unsafe Products and Strict Products Liability: What Liability Rule Should be Applied to the Sellers of Pharmaceutical Products?, 78 Ky. L.J. 705 (1989–90); Joseph A. Page, Generic Product Risks: The Case Against Comment k and for Strict Tort Liability, 58 N.Y.U. L. Rev. 853 (1983); Victor E. Schwartz, Unavoidably Unsafe Products: Clarifying the Meaning and Policy Behind Comment k, 42 Wash. & Lee L. Rev. 1139 (1985); Joanne Rhoton Galbreath, Annotation, Products Liability: What Is an "Unavoidably Unsafe" Product, 70 A.L.R.4th 16 (1989 & 2002 Supp.). Another ambiguity concerns its application to investigational drugs. Comment k embraces experimental products, but would the *Grundberg* court exempt such products from design defect scrutiny even though the FDA has not yet approved them?

2. *Medical devices.* Although comment k referred only to prescription drugs and vaccines, several courts have applied it to comparable medical devices. See Tansy v. Dacomed Corp., 890 P.2d 881, 885 (Okla.1994) ("Most courts which have considered the question have found that comment k applies to medical devices, especially those which are implanted in the human body."); see also Hufft v. Horowitz, 5 Cal.Rptr.2d 377, 384 (Ct.App. 1992) (limiting the immunity to implantable devices). Is it really accurate to characterize implantable devices as "unavoidably unsafe"?

3. *Nonprescription products.* By its terms, comment k does not apply exclusively to prescription drugs, though courts routinely have read it in that fashion. See Ruiz–Guzman v. Amvac Chem. Corp., 7 P.3d 795, 803–04 (Wash.2000) (recognizing this tendency, but becoming the first jurisdiction to apply comment k to certain restricted pesticides). Indeed, most of the examples of trivial products referred to by the dissent in *Grundberg* were nonprescription drugs. With the advent of Rx-to-OTC switches, and the FDA's growing willingness to allow nonprescription marketing of drugs that offer genuine clinical utility accompanied by some risk, does any such distinction make sense today? In short, aren't at least some OTC drugs "unavoidably unsafe"? See Thomas M. Moore & Scott L. Hengesbach, Comment k: A Prescription for the Over-the-Counter Drug Industry, 22 Pac. L.J. 43 (1990); Daniel W. Whitney, Product Liability Issues for the Expanding OTC Drug Category, 48 Food & Drug L.J. 321 (1993). The new *Restatement* treats nonprescription drugs (and medical devices) as subject to the general provisions applicable to all other consumer products. See Rest. (3d) § 2 cmt. k.

4. *Blood and blood products.* Essentially all states exempt blood from strict products liability. See Michael J. Miller, Note, Strict Liability, Negligence and the Standard of Care for Transfusion–Transmitted Disease, 36 Ariz. L. Rev. 473, 488–90 (1994). These "blood shield" statutes also protect commercial suppliers of blood-derived products from strict liability claims. See McKee v. Cutter Lab., 866 F.2d 219, 221–22 (6th Cir.1989); Doe v. Travenol Labs., Inc., 698 F.Supp. 780 (D.Minn.1988); Rogers v. Miles Lab., 802 P.2d 1346, 1350–52 (Wash.1991); see also Rest. (3d) § 19(c) ("Human blood and human tissue, even when provided commercially, are not subject to the rules of this Restatement."); Christina Bohannan, Note, Product Liability: A Public Policy Approach to Contaminated Factor VIII Blood Products, 48 Fla. L. Rev. 263 (1996). But see JKB, Sr. v. Armour Pharm. Co., 660 N.E.2d 602, 605–06 (Ind.Ct.App.1996) (holding that state statute did not protect manufacturers). Does that extension to manufacturers of derivative products make sense? How will courts in the future respond to claims involving artificial blood?

Blood suppliers remain subject to tort liability in cases of negligence, though many courts define the standard of care as the relevant custom in the industry, which makes it difficult for plaintiffs to recover. See Smythe v. American Red Cross, 797 F.Supp. 147, 152–53 (N.D.N.Y.1992); Kozup v. Georgetown University, 663 F.Supp. 1048, 1055–60 (D.D.C.1987), aff'd in relevant part, 851 F.2d 437, 439 (D.C.Cir.1988); Ward v. Lutheran Hosps. & Homes Soc'y of Am., Inc., 963 P.2d 1031, 1036–37 (Alaska 1998); Spann v. Irwin Mem. Blood Ctrs., 40 Cal.Rptr.2d 360, 364–66 (Ct.App.1995); Brown v. United Blood Servs., 858 P.2d 391, 395–99 (Nev.1993). But see Doe v. Cutter Biological, Inc., 971 F.2d 375, 382–84 (9th Cir.1992) (denying the defendant's motion for summary judgment); Vuono v. New York Blood Ctr., Inc., 696 F.Supp. 743, 747–48 (D.Mass.1988); Doe v. American Nat'l Red Cross, 848 F.Supp. 1228, 1234 (S.D.W.Va.1994); United Blood Servs. v. Quintana, 827 P.2d 509, 521–27 (Colo.1992); Advincula v. United Blood Servs., 678 N.E.2d 1009, 1027–28 (Ill.1996); Hernandez v. Nueces County Med. Soc'y Community Blood Bank, 779 S.W.2d 867, 871–72 (Tex.App. 1989); cf. Snyder v. American Ass'n of Blood Banks, 676 A.2d 1036, 1048–

55 (N.J.1996) (allowing claim against trade association). See generally Ross D. Eckert, The AIDS Blood–Transfusion Cases: A Legal and Economic Analysis of Liability, 29 San Diego L. Rev. 203 (1992); Steven R. Salbu, AIDS and the Blood Supply: An Analysis of Law, Regulation, and Public Policy, 74 Wash. U. L.Q. 913 (1996); Jay M. Zitter, Annotation, Liability of Blood Supplier or Donor for Injury or Death Resulting from Blood Transfusion, 24 A.L.R.4th 508 (1982 & 2002 Supp.).

5. *Legislative responses.* In one instance, Congress decided to protect the manufacturers of especially valuable pharmaceutical products from the threat of tort liability. In 1986, in response to fears of critical vaccine shortages and the dramatic price increases mentioned by the *Brown* court, Congress enacted the National Childhood Vaccine Injury Act. See 42 U.S.C. § 300aa–1 et seq. Manufacturers of listed vaccines must pay an excise tax based on the risk of injury associated with particular components in order to fund an administrative compensation system, and the legislation adds procedural and substantive barriers that are designed to discourage the filing of tort claims. The Supreme Court described the basic contours of this mechanism, which loosely resembles workers' compensation systems, as follows:

> For injuries and deaths traceable to vaccinations, the Act establishes a scheme of recovery designed to work faster and with greater ease than the civil tort system. Special masters in the Court of Federal Claims hear vaccine-related complaints, which they adjudicate informally, within strict time limits, subject to similarly expeditious review. A claimant alleging that more than $1,000 in damages resulted from a vaccination after the Act's effective date in 1988 must exhaust the Act's procedures and refuse to accept the resulting judgment before filing any de novo civil action in state or federal court. The streamlining does not stop with the mechanics of litigation, but goes even to substantive standards of proof. While a claimant may establish prima facie entitlement to compensation by introducing proof of actual causation, she can reach the same result by meeting the requirements of what the Act calls the Vaccine Injury Table. The table lists the vaccines covered under the Act, together with particular injuries or conditions associated with each one. A claimant who meets certain other conditions not relevant here makes out a prima facie case by showing that she (or someone for whom she brings a claim) "sustained, or had significantly aggravated, any illness, disability, injury, or condition set forth in the Vaccine Injury Table in association with [a] vaccine ... or died from the administration of such vaccine, and the first symptom or manifestation of the onset or of the significant aggravation of any such illness, disability, injury, or condition or the death occurred within the time period after vaccine administration set forth in the Vaccine Injury Table." Thus, the rule of prima facie proof turns the old maxim on its head by providing that if the post hoc event happens fast, ergo propter hoc. The Secretary of Health and Human Services may rebut a prima facie case by proving that the injury or death was in fact caused by "factors unrelated to the administration of

the vaccine." If the Secretary fails to rebut, the claimant is entitled to compensation.

Shalala v. Whitecotton, 514 U.S. 268, 269–71 (1995); see also Beard v. HHS, 43 F.3d 659 (Fed.Cir.1994) (holding that an injury to a parent was not covered by the Act); Schafer v. American Cyanamid Co., 20 F.3d 1, 4–7 (1st Cir.1994) (same). See generally Richard L. Manning, Changing Rules in Tort Law and the Market for Childhood Vaccines, 37 J.L. & Econ. 247 (1994); Leonard D. Pertnoy, A Child's View of Recovery Under the National Childhood Vaccine Act or "He Who Hesitates Is Lost," 59 Mont. L. Rev. 275 (1998); Elizabeth C. Scott, The National Childhood Vaccine Injury Act Turns Fifteen, 56 Food & Drug L.J. 351 (2001); Lisa J. Steel, Note, National Childhood Vaccine Injury Compensation Program: Is This the Best We Can Do for Our Children?, 63 Geo. Wash. L. Rev. 144 (1994); Russell G. Donaldson, Annotation, Construction and Application of the National Childhood Vaccine Injury Act, 129 A.L.R. Fed. 1 (1996). Some commentators have suggested similar compensation systems for other types of vaccines. See Alison Joy Arnold, Comment, Developing, Testing, and Marketing an AIDS Vaccine: Legal Concerns for Manufacturers, 139 U. Pa. L. Rev. 1077 (1991); H. William Smith, III, Note, Vaccinating AIDS Vaccine Manufacturers Against Product Liability, 42 Case W. Res. L. Rev. 207 (1992); see also Gregory C. Jackson, Comment, Pharmaceutical Product Liability May Be Hazardous to Your Health: A No–Fault Alternative to Concurrent Regulation, 42 Am. U. L. Rev. 199 (1992) (suggesting such an approach for all drug products).

――――――

Restatement (Third) of the Law of Torts: Products Liability

(American Law Inst. 1998):

§ 6. Liability of Commercial Seller or Distributor for Harm Caused by Defective Prescription Drugs and Medical Devices

(a) A manufacturer of a prescription drug or medical device who sells or otherwise distributes a defective drug or medical device is subject to liability for harm to persons caused by the defect. A prescription drug or medical device is one that may be legally sold or otherwise distributed only pursuant to a health-care provider's prescription.

(b) For purposes of liability under Subsection (a), a prescription drug or medical device is defective if at the time of sale or other distribution the drug or medical device:

(1) contains a manufacturing defect as defined in § 2(a) [i.e., when the product departs from its intended design even though all possible care was exercised in the preparation and marketing of the product]; or

(2) is not reasonably safe due to defective design as defined in Subsection (c); or

(3) is not reasonably safe due to inadequate instructions or warnings as defined in Subsection (d).

(c) A prescription drug or medical device is not reasonably safe due to defective design if the foreseeable risks of harm posed by the drug or medical device are sufficiently great in relation to its foreseeable therapeutic benefits that reasonable health-care providers, knowing of such foreseeable risks and therapeutic benefits, would not prescribe the drug or medical device for any class of patients.

(d) A prescription drug or medical device is not reasonably safe due to inadequate instructions or warnings if reasonable instructions or warnings regarding foreseeable risks of harm are not provided to:

    (1) prescribing and other health-care providers who are in a position to reduce the risks of harm in accordance with the instructions or warnings; or

    (2) the patient when the manufacturer knows or has reason to know that health-care providers will not be in a position to reduce the risks of harm in accordance with the instructions or warnings.

(e) A retail seller or other distributor of a prescription drug or medical device is subject to liability for harm caused by the drug or device if:

    (1) at the time of sale or other distribution the drug or medical device contains a manufacturing defect as defined in § 2(a); or

    (2) at or before the time of sale or other distribution of the drug or medical device the retail seller or other distributor fails to exercise reasonable care and such failure causes harm to persons.

Subsequent chapters will address each of these categories of defect in greater detail. For present purposes just note that, instead of comment k immunity for design defect claims, the drafters chose to create a more manufacturer-protective standard for reviewing the design of prescription drugs and medical devices than applied to other types of products, where the test is risk-utility balancing that allows a finding of design defect if the plaintiff proves that a reasonable alternative design exists. See James A. Henderson, Jr. & Aaron D. Twerski, Drug Designs Are Different, 111 Yale L.J. 151 (2001). The standard for inadequate warnings also differs from that applied to other products insofar as this provision adheres to the "learned intermediary" rule, which generally requires warnings directed only to physicians. Only the manufacturing defect test is identical to that applied to other products.

B. The Relationship to Regulatory Standards

Restatement (Third) of the Law of Torts: Products Liability

(American Law Inst. 1998):

    § 4. Noncompliance and Compliance with Product Safety Statutes or Regulations

In connection with liability for defective design or inadequate instructions or warnings:

(a) a product's noncompliance with an applicable product safety statute or administrative regulation renders the product defective with respect to the risks sought to be reduced by the statute or regulation; and

(b) a product's compliance with an applicable product safety statute or administrative regulation is properly considered in determining whether the product is defective with respect to the risks sought to be reduced by the statute or regulation, but such compliance does not preclude as a matter of law a finding of product defect.

————

This asymmetrical treatment of noncompliance and compliance for all types of tort cases goes way back and certainly is reflected in litigation involving FDA-regulated products. See Jeffrey N. Gibbs & Bruce F. Mackler, Food and Drug Administration Regulation and Products Liability: Strong Sword, Weak Shield, 22 Tort & Ins. L.J. 194 (1987).

1. THE CONSEQUENCES OF NONCOMPLIANCE

Stanton v. Astra Pharmaceutical Products, Inc.

718 F.2d 553 (3d Cir.1983).

■ BECKER, CIRCUIT JUDGE:

* * * Harrikah Stanton was an eight-month-old infant on December 2, 1971, when she entered Harrisburg Hospital and submitted to a bone-marrow test to determine the cause of the hemolytic anemia from which she had suffered since birth. In performing the test, the hematologist, Dr. Herbert S. Bowman, injected a two-percent solution of Xylocaine into Harrikah's right posterior iliac crest to anesthetize the area from which he would aspirate bone marrow. The Xylocaine, known generically as lidocaine hydrochloride, was a local anesthetic manufactured by Astra.

Shortly after the procedure, Harrikah began convulsing and experienced cardiac and respiratory arrest. Dr. Marita Fabian, a senior resident at the hospital, and other hospital employees attempted to resuscitate her, but to little avail. The cardiac arrest resulted in severe and irreversible brain damage. Harrikah cannot walk, talk, or stand; her development has not progressed beyond that of a three- to four-month old child. She will require constant care for the rest of her life.

On October 24, 1973, plaintiffs commenced this negligence and product-liability action against Astra * * * * After an eight-week trial, the case was submitted to the jury on "special questions." On January 10, 1980, the jury returned a verdict against Astra alone. In response to the "special questions," the jury found that Harrikah had suffered an adverse reaction to Xylocaine; that Astra had acted negligently in failing to file the annual and adverse-reaction reports required by subsections 130.35(e) and (f); that the failure to file these reports rendered Xylocaine a defective product; and that Astra's negligence and the product's defective nature were substantial factors in causing Harrikah's injury. * * *

The verdict in plaintiffs' favor was predicated upon the jury's conclusion that Astra had acted improperly when it failed to file with the FDA the annual and adverse-reaction reports required by 21 C.F.R. § 130.35(e) & (f) (1972). Astra initially argues that section 130.35 does not apply to Xylocaine and that the company therefore had no obligation to file any of the specified reports. But even assuming that the regulation does apply, Astra contends, the company did not act negligently when it decided not to file the requisite reports, and the failure to file therefore did not render Xylocaine defective or unreasonably dangerous. Moreover, Astra argues, even if a jury could find that the company either had acted negligently in failing to file the reports or had marketed a defective product, neither the negligence nor the section 402A violation could have been a substantial factor in causing Harrikah's injuries.

We first will consider the question of the applicability of section 130.35; in the course of our discussion, we will outline the rather complex statutory and regulatory schema governing marketed drugs. Because we conclude that Astra had a duty to file the reports required by section 130.35, we then will proceed to the consequences of noncompliance. The jury determined that noncompliance with the FDA's regulations engendered liability based on negligence as well as strict liability under *Restatement (Second) of Torts* § 402A (1965). We will discuss separately each basis of liability. We conclude that the jury had sufficient evidence to find that Astra's conduct was negligent per se and that such conduct proximately caused Harrikah's injuries; we further conclude that the jury could find that Xylocaine was a defective product within the meaning of section 402A and that the defective product also was a proximate cause of the harm. * * *

Between May 28, 1964, and the end of 1970, Astra received 202 reports of adverse reactions allegedly related to Xylocaine. These reactions ranged from minor, temporary effects to death. Yet Astra forwarded none of these reports to the FDA, relying upon the advice of its counsel [as discussed in the excerpt of the court's opinion appearing in Chapter 3(D).] * * * Astra cannot seriously dispute that section 130.35 was promulgated to protect individuals such as Harrikah Stanton from precisely the type of harm that here occurred—an unexpected adverse reaction to Xylocaine. It thus would appear that Astra's failure to file the reports constituted negligence per se.

Astra points out, however, that noncompliance with safety regulations does not result inexorably in a finding of negligence because Pennsylvania law appears to follow the *Restatement (Second) of Torts* in recognizing a class of "excused violations." In particular, Astra argues that its failure to comply with the applicable statutes and regulations is excused by three circumstances: (1) Astra neither knew nor should have known of the need to comply; (2) Astra's counsel advised the company that there was no need to file the reports with the FDA; and (3) the reports actually had been prepared and were available to FDA plant inspectors. We agree that Pennsylvania law allows a defendant to offer excuses for a statutory or regulatory violation; however, the record permitted the jury to reject each of the excuses proffered by Astra.

First, even assuming that Astra at one time had reason to believe that 21 C.F.R. § 130.35 did not apply to Xylocaine, the FDA formally revoked in 1968 all previous opinions as to new-drug status and expressly informed Astra in 1969 that the FDA expected compliance with section 130.35. Thus, at least as of 1968, Astra knew, or should have known, that the FDA expected Astra to file the reports prescribed by section 130.35.

Second, the mere fact that Astra's attorneys interpreted section 130.35 incorrectly does not negate Astra's negligence in failing to comply with the regulations. Astra took a chance, and it is liable for the consequences of its acts. And even assuming that advice of counsel does constitute a legally cognizable excuse, that excuse could insulate Astra from liability only between the time that the FDA promulgated the regulations in 1964 and the time that the agency revoked all private letter-rulings as to new-drug status in 1968. Astra still had three and one-half years before the December 1971 tragedy to file the reports. Nor can we accept the availability of the reports to plant inspectors as an excuse for Astra's conduct. Plant inspectors are not physicians and do not possess the expertise necessary to facilitate a full evaluation of the reports. * * *

That Astra was negligent in failing to file the reports is not in itself sufficient to sustain the finding that Astra was liable. The negligence must also have been a proximate cause of Harrikah Stanton's injury. * * * [P]laintiffs attempted to establish causation by introducing evidence tending to show that the information withheld from the FDA was of great importance and that the agency could not properly perform its regulatory and supervisory roles without access to the unreported data, and that the FDA would have taken action had it been aware of Xylocaine's propensity to cause adverse reactions despite low dosage. Moreover, it was clear that Xylocaine had caused Harrikah's injuries: the jury found that Harrikah Stanton had experienced an adverse reaction, and Astra has never seriously argued that Xylocaine was not a "substantial factor" in causing that reaction.

Astra contends, however, as it did before the district court, that the evidence adduced by plaintiffs cannot support the jury's conclusion that the failure to file the reports was a substantial factor in causing Harrikah's injury because no witness stated expressly that, had those reports been filed, the FDA would have taken some action that would have saved this particular child from harm. It is true that the record does not contain such a statement, and that plaintiffs' evidence of causation is not very strong. On this point, the case thus is an extremely close one. * * *

The jury heard the testimony of four well qualified expert witnesses. They heard from these witnesses an analysis of the numerous adverse-reaction reports received by Astra, some of which described incidents of cardiac and respiratory arrest. They heard express testimony from these witnesses that Astra's conduct deprived the FDA and the medical community of important information, the lack of which would bias an evaluation of the safety of Xylocaine, and they heard testimony from which they could infer, keeping in mind the FDA's statutory duty continually to monitor marketed drugs for safety and effectiveness: (1) that had the FDA had these reports, it would have required notice to the medical community (through the package insert or PDR) of the critical information contained in the more than 200 adverse-reaction reports of the incidence of cardiac and respiratory arrest, notwithstanding low dosage of Xylocaine; and (2) that physicians receiving this information would have considered it in deciding how—and whether—to administer Xylocaine to their patients. Resolving every inference in plaintiffs' favor, we cannot conclude that the record was devoid of the requisite minimum quantum of evidence supporting the verdict. * * *

Plaintiffs' theory of strict liability is that the federal regulatory scheme creates an expectation on the part of the ordinary user of Xylocaine that the FDA would allow the continued marketing of the drug only after evaluating the information contained in reports required by regulations such as 21 C.F.R. § 130.35. By failing to file those reports, plaintiffs assert, Astra deprived the FDA and Harrikah Stanton's doctors of important information that people such as plaintiffs would have expected the agency and the physicians to have received and considered. * * *

In *Toole v. Richardson–Merrell Inc.*, 60 Cal.Rptr. 398 (Ct.App.1967), the California Court of Appeal confronted a section 402A claim similar to the one now before us and upheld a jury verdict holding a drug company strictly liable for injuries sustained by a plaintiff where the company had violated reporting provisions of the [FDCA]. Plaintiff had used the drug Triparanol (designed to treat arteriosclerosis), sold under the trade name "MER/29," and had developed cataracts in both eyes; Richardson Merrell's new-drug application had not disclosed the full extent of the company's knowledge regarding similar effects. Finding that the statutory violations rendered Triparanol a defective product because improperly prepared and marketed, the court declared:

> In light of the non-disclosure of significant facts which, if known to the FDA, would have enabled its scientists to make a more critical analysis of [the drug], it can hardly be said that the FDA's permission to market the drug was an informed judgment, based on all the known facts, or that it was uninfluenced by [defendant's] non-disclosure. * * *

We conclude that a Pennsylvania court applying Pennsylvania law would allow a jury to determine on the facts of this case that Xylocaine was a defective product within the meaning of section 402A. First, plaintiffs adduced evidence that, by failing to comply with 21 C.F.R. § 130.35, Astra deprived the FDA and, derivatively, the medical community at large of important information relating to the dangerousness of Xylocaine and that, without such information, the FDA could not make the professional and medical judgments that reasonable consumers rightfully expected it to make as a precondition of permitting the continued marketing of Xylocaine. Second, although plaintiffs' evidence was not particularly strong, we believe that plaintiffs presented sufficient evidence that the FDA would have acted had it received the unreported information. * * *

NOTES AND QUESTIONS

1. *Negligence (defectiveness) per se.* For other comparable decisions, see Orthopedic Equipment Co. v. Eutsler, 276 F.2d 455, 461 (4th Cir.1960); Lukaszewicz v. Ortho Pharm. Corp., 510 F.Supp. 961, 964–65 (E.D.Wis. 1981); see also Benedi v. McNeil–P.P.C., Inc., 66 F.3d 1378, 1387–89 (4th Cir.1995) (sustaining negligence claim and punitive damage award where manufacturer had delayed submitting adverse reaction reports to the FDA during an OTC drug monograph rulemaking); DiRosa v. Showa Denko K.K., 52 Cal.Rptr.2d 128, 133–34 (Ct.App.1996) (rejecting objection that the jury should not have decided whether dietary supplement failed to comply with FDA requirements). Questions have arisen about failures to disclose ADEs with drugs that the FDA subsequently withdrew from the market, which in any resulting tort litigation alleging negligence per se would simplify the causation difficulty discussed in *Stanton*. See David Willman, Risk Was Known as FDA OK'd Fatal Drug, L.A. Times, Mar. 11, 2001, at A1; Laura Johannes, Heart–Valve Problem That Felled Diet Pills Has Arisen Previously, Wall St. J., Dec. 11, 1997, at A1.

2. *Excuses, excuses.* The *Rest. (3d)* § 4 would recognize no excuses for noncompliance. See id. cmt. d. Is that position unduly restrictive? What if the FDA informally waived an obligation to comply in order to deal with unusual circumstances (e.g., critical vaccine shortages)? Or what if the agency's longstanding exercise of its prosecutorial discretion against demanding literal compliance with a particular requirement amounted to the de facto revocation of an obligation to comply? How would judges and juries presented with ambiguous regulations come to understand their application in practice? Cf. McNeil Pharm. v. Hawkins, 686 A.2d 567, 582–86 (D.C. 1996) (requiring plaintiffs to introduce expert testimony about the application of the statute and FDA regulations in order to support a negligence per se claim); Northern Trust Co. v. Upjohn Co., 572 N.E.2d 1030, 1040 (Ill.App.Ct.1991) (same).

3. *Private rights of action.* Courts have rejected suggestions that the FDCA creates an implied private right of action, which would allow litigants to recover damages directly from other parties in case they have violated this federal statute. See Bailey v. Johnson, 48 F.3d 965, 967–68 (6th Cir.1995); Brinkman v. Shiley, Inc., 732 F.Supp. 33, 35 (E.D.Pa.), aff'd mem., 902 F.2d 1558 (3d Cir.1989); see also Merrell Dow Pharms. Inc. v. Thompson, 478 U.S. 804, 814 (1986) (assuming, without deciding, that the FDCA lacks an implied private right of action as further support for holding that there was no federal question jurisdiction); James M. Beck & John A. Valentine, Challenging the Viability of FDCA–Based Causes of

Action in the Tort Context: The Orthopedic Bone Screw Experience, 55 Food & Drug L.J. 389 (2000). How might a private right of action under federal law differ from a negligence per se claim under state tort law premised on a violation of federal law?

2. COMPLIANCE AND FEDERAL PREEMPTION

Recall that *Restatement (Third)* § 4(b) makes compliance with safety standards relevant to but not dispositive of questions about product defectiveness. This black letter formulation accurately reflects case law involving drugs and medical devices. For instance, some courts have allowed juries to find that the specific warnings provided to patients by manufacturers of oral contraceptives were inadequate even though the labeling fully complied with the FDA's PPI regulation. See, e.g., Gurski v. Wyeth–Ayerst, 953 F.Supp. 412, 416–17 (D.Mass.1997); Stephens v. G.D. Searle & Co., 602 F.Supp. 379, 381–82 (E.D.Mich.1985); MacDonald v. Ortho Pharm. Corp., 475 N.E.2d 65, 66–67, 70–71 (Mass.1985); see also O'Gilvie v. International Playtex, Inc., 821 F.2d 1438, 1442–43 (10th Cir.1987) (same, for compliance with tampon warning label requirement). But see MacPherson v. Searle & Co., 775 F.Supp. 417, 420, 425 (D.D.C.1991) (granting summary judgment to the manufacturer because the required PPI adequately warned of the risk of injury suffered by the plaintiff); West v. G.D. Searle & Co., 879 S.W.2d 412, 414 (Ark.1994) (affirming same); see also Haddix v. Playtex Family Prods. Corp., 964 F.Supp. 1242, 1246 (C.D.Ill.1997) (same, for FDA-mandated warnings of toxic shock syndrome on tampon labels).

In the course of deciding that comment k should protect all prescription drugs from the threat of strict products liability for design defect, the *Brown* and *Grundberg* courts offered a series of policy arguments that might justify giving compliance with FDA requirements greater weight. A few courts have taken this additional step, though somewhat tentatively. See, e.g., Ramirez v. Plough, Inc., 863 P.2d 167, 172 (Cal.1993) (excerpted in Chapter 7(C)(2)) (rejecting an inadequate warning claim against the seller of an OTC drug labeled in conformity with FDA requirements); see also Peter H. Schuck, Multi–Culturalism Redux: Science, Law, and Politics, 11 Yale L. & Pol'y Rev. 1, 39 (1993) ("For better or for worse, the FDA is the agency that the public has empowered to make authoritative judgments of this kind on its behalf."). Such expressions of deference to administrative judgments about relative product safety remain rare, however.

———

Restatement (Third) of the Law of Torts: Products Liability

(American Law Inst. 1998):

§ 4. Noncompliance and Compliance with Product Safety Statutes or Regulations

Comment e. Occasionally, after reviewing relevant circumstances, a court may properly conclude that a particular product safety standard set by statute or regulation adequately serves the objectives of tort law and therefore that the product that complies with the standard is not defective as a matter of law. Such a conclusion may be appropriate when the safety statute or regulation was promulgated recently, thus supplying currency to the standard therein established; when the specific standard addresses the very issue of product design or warning presented in the case before the court; and when the court is confident that the deliberative process by which the safety standard was established was full, fair, and thorough and reflected substantial expertise. Conversely, when the deliberative process that led to the safety standard with which the defendant's product complies was tainted by the supplying of false information to, or the withholding of necessary and valid information from, the agency that promulgated the standard or certified or approved the product, compliance with regulation is entitled to little or no weight.

Lars Noah, *Rewarding Regulatory Compliance: The Pursuit of Symmetry in Products Liability*
88 GEO. L.J. 2147 (2000).

* * * Only after developing a proper appreciation of the rigors of the regulatory process of a particular agency can one decide whether an inevitably qualified government standards defense makes any sense. In addition to starting at the beginning (and not becoming distracted by highly visible regulatory failures such as breast implants or fenfluramine, which would not benefit from a compliance defense to tort claims in any event), I will emphasize regulatory standards that emerge from a structured and public rulemaking process. Such an emphasis differs from the individualized product licensing decisions that normally frame this debate * * * *

I.   *Contrasting Administrative and Judicial Regulation of Drug Labeling*

Imagine the following situation. The FDA promulgates a regulation specifying the risk information that must appear in the labeling of all prescription drugs of a certain therapeutic class. In order to promote labeling clarity and uniformity, the FDA also explicitly prohibits the inclusion of any additional warnings about this particular hazard. As happens with many regulatory initiatives, years elapse between the initial formulation of this proposal and its publication as a final rule. Under the Administrative Procedure Act (APA), agencies must, at a minimum, publish a notice of their proposed action, provide an opportunity for public comment, and issue an explanatory preamble to accompany the final text of the regulation. The issuance of a regulation represents the commitment of significant resources and reflects input by dozens of agency personnel from various disciplines.

Moreover, as observers of the administrative process know all too well, publication of a regulation in the *Federal Register* does not settle matters.

Nowadays, agencies must transmit their rules to Congress for fast-track consideration and a possible override resolution, and, more plausibly, agencies fear judicial scrutiny followed by a remand. For purposes of this hypothetical, assume that a public interest group files a petition to review the regulation in the U.S. Court of Appeals for the D.C. Circuit, claiming that the FDA's mandatory labeling statement is not sufficiently alarming given the nature of the hazard revealed by the administrative record, and that the prohibition on additional warnings of this particular risk amounted to arbitrary and capricious decisionmaking in light of the public health mandate underlying the agency's enabling statute. After considering these arguments and concluding that agency officials had taken the requisite hard look at the relevant comments and other information in the rulemaking record, the court denies the petition for review.

Even after running the gauntlet of these legislative and judicial checks, agencies cannot rest on their laurels. Often agencies must interpret and clarify the meaning of their regulations in the course of enforcement actions or through the issuance of guidelines. In addition, agencies may have to revisit regulations in light of changed circumstances, and they must respond to petitions urging the amendment or repeal of an existing rule, which then may trigger another round of judicial review. For example, the same group that unsuccessfully challenged the original rule in federal court may resurrect its objections by filing a citizen petition with the FDA requesting an amendment to the rule and then seeking judicial review of any agency decision to deny that request. As a number of administrative law scholars have noted in recent years, these numerous obstacles tend to discourage rulemaking altogether. When agencies do go to all of that trouble, however, their handiwork deserves more than the casual acknowledgment that the courts typically give it when resolving products liability litigation.

Now let us leave the comforting confines of the Beltway to discover how drug labeling is regulated in the heartland. Consider the fate of three pharmaceutical companies selling essentially identical products, but with differences in their labeling, which face tort litigation brought by patients who suffered precisely the side effect that the FDA's final rule sought to address. Company A blatantly failed to comply with the labeling regulation, and, among other things, the plaintiff pursues a negligence per se claim premised on the violation of this relevant safety requirement. Company B scrupulously complied with the labeling regulation; consequently, the company, emphasizing that it could not have provided additional risk information without running afoul of the FDA's rule, moves for summary judgment on the plaintiff's failure-to-warn claims. Company C, in a justified fit of paranoia, included both the FDA-mandated cautionary statement as well as additional language crafted by its legal staff and designed to make this— and all of the other hazard information—as alarming as possible; however, the plaintiff still pursues a failure-to-warn action premised on a theory of dilution by "overwarning" and, among other things, pursues a negligence per se claim for violating the agency's prohibition on additional risk information.

Under prevailing tort doctrines, all three plaintiffs will reach the jury, in two cases with the benefit of negligence per se instructions, and, in the suit against Company *B*, the trial judge will reject any suggestion that regulatory compliance conclusively establishes the absence of negligence or product defectiveness. As a consequence, often unsophisticated jurors in different parts of the country will make their own judgments about appropriate prescription drug labeling, effectively second-guessing the FDA's far more expert, accountable, and uniform determination that, in this hypothetical, has been affirmed by a federal court after reviewing the wealth of information compiled during the agency's rulemaking proceeding.

What accounts for this puzzling state of affairs? In most jurisdictions, the unexcused violation of a relevant safety statute or regulation constitutes negligence (or defectiveness) as a matter of law. In contrast, most jurisdictions consider proof of compliance with an applicable government safety standard at best as some relevant evidence when assessing allegations that a product is defective or that the defendant's conduct was negligent. Courts routinely note that government standards establish only "minimum" requirements, which a jury can decide a reasonable person should have exceeded under the circumstances. The statutory safety standards at issue in many of the earliest compliance cases were, however, quite limited in scope, often lacked any direct enforcement mechanism, and sometimes expressly preserved common-law tort remedies. In addition, the courts in these early cases emphasized that standards of this sort could not possibly have specified the safeguards appropriate for highly variable settings such as railroad crossings of differing types spread throughout the country.

In the century since the development of the common-law rule against recognizing a regulatory compliance defense, the focus of tort litigation has shifted from heavily context-dependent collision cases to recurring situations such as defects in mass-produced consumer goods, which are more readily subject to nationally uniform requirements for safeguards that should perform equally well anywhere in the land. At the same time, the sources and complexity of government safety regulations have changed dramatically—from vague commands issued by generalist legislatures to precise requirements formulated by specialist administrators. Modern regulatory systems typically represent legislative or administrative efforts to set optimal—not minimal—safety standards * * * *

Nonetheless, rejection of the government standards defense remains the prevailing rule by far. Courts continue to give little or no weight to compliance with today's far more intricate regulatory regimes, frequently dismissing the defense out of hand with the oft-repeated and largely unexamined premise that government safety standards are nothing more than minimum requirements. Although not formally obligated to adopt relevant federal regulations as particularizing the standard of care in tort litigation, at least absent preemption, courts should take them more seriously than they do at present.

II. *Accountable Regulation: Myths About Jury Competence and Agency Capture*

Wholly apart from the suggestion that government standards represent only minimum safety requirements, critics of the compliance defense denigrate the institutions that generate these requirements and applaud the independence and common sense of jurors in making judgments about appropriate levels of safety. But such a "grass roots" approach lodges profoundly important choices affecting society in our least representative, expert, or accountable institutions.

As the decisionmakers empowered by the citizenry to set safety standards, legislatures and regulatory agencies select the levels of product risk that they deem appropriate based on scientific, economic, and—yes—political considerations. When courts treat these standards as presumptively sub-optimal, they basically arrogate such important decisions for themselves and, in particular, juries. At some level, the longstanding rejection of a compliance defense appears to reflect a populist faith in laypersons and an accompanying distrust of distant federal bureaucracies.

Commentators who object to a regulatory compliance defense have identified various flaws in the administrative process, including claims that regulated entities have "captured" the agencies that oversee their activities. But, just as opponents of tort reform legitimately decry the lack of empirical evidence of a litigation crisis, proponents of the government standards defense should object to the agency capture thesis as supported by little more than anecdote and suspicion. To the extent that this turns on impressionistic assessments, let me suggest that health and safety agencies like the FDA have become more beholden to groups that purport to represent the public interest.

Although the dynamic surely differed in previous decades, and no one disputes the tremendous resources that industry can deploy to influence the legislative and regulatory processes even today, regulated entities operate at the mercy of powerful agencies such as the FDA, while consumer groups have nothing to lose by aggressively pursuing their agenda and vocally criticizing the agency when they fail to prevail. Indeed, without the persistent efforts of consumer interest organizations, a pair of important FDA warning regulations mentioned herein might never have seen the light of day because of industry resistance. When their arguments fail to move agency experts or otherwise lose out in the political process, however, should consumer activists get to keep waging what they regard as the good fight in the more congenial arena of tort litigation, addressing their gripes to receptive panels of jurors accountable to no one for decisions that have undoubted regulatory effects? Unless something indicates a profound failure of the regulatory process in a particular situation, I think not. * * *

III. *Distinguishing an FDA Compliance Defense from Preemption*

On rare occasions, courts have deferred to FDA determinations. For instance, in a 1993 decision involving an inadequate warning claim against the manufacturer of a nonprescription drug product, the California Supreme Court concluded that "there is some room in tort law for a defense of statutory compliance," in part because courts lack "the procedure and resources to conduct the relevant inquiries." Occasionally, legislatures adopt an FDA compliance defense, as Congress did for childhood vaccines in 1986, and as New Jersey did for all FDA-regulated products in 1987. Notwithstanding these limited pockets of protection, the recognition of an FDA compliance defense remains the exception. Courts still routinely ignore the agency's regulations and approval decisions in products liability litigation.

The primary rationale for disregarding the FDA's drug labeling decisions is that the agency has imposed only "minimum" standards open to supplementation by a lay jury's verdict enforcing a manufacturer's common-law duty to warn. As one former agency official commented several years ago, however, the "FDA surely does not regard its own prescription drug labeling decisions as merely establishing a floor." Nonetheless, the agency's formal pronouncements on the subject have contributed to the courts' confusion by disavowing any intent to influence tort litigation through its regulatory decisions. The FDA's apparent lack of opposition to judicial second-guessing in this context is difficult to fathom, though one commentator has suggested that public health agencies may not mind having the tort system serve as a "safety valve" for deflecting adverse publicity from themselves when hazards with a product subsequently come to light.

Preemption offers a blunter tool for securing judicial respect for federal standards. Under the rubric of federal preemption, Congress and the FDA may announce that their labeling or other requirements displace state authority to regulate. Over the course of the last decade, an increasing number of courts have interpreted such provisions as displacing state tort actions as well, primarily in medical device cases, and sometimes even in the absence of compliance with any particular federal safety standard. Because no statutory preemption clause applies in the case of drug regulation and implied preemption arguments rarely succeed in this context, pharmaceutical manufacturers can find little solace in these decisions.

Nonetheless, when the Supreme Court decided that provisions in other statutes displacing state authority to regulate also expressly preempted tort claims, it made a critical concession that should influence any debate about the advisability of adopting a government standards defense[:] * * * damage awards predicated on a manufacturer's departure from the common-law standard of reasonable care potentially have as much of a regulatory effect as positive law requirements reflected in state statutes or rules. Critics of the regulatory compliance defense respond that a tort judgment does not dictate any alteration of primary conduct, but in the next breath they emphasize the need to retain the threat of liability to serve a deterrent function given the often inconsequential administrative sanctions. They can't have it both ways. Although I agree that the regulatory impact of tort judgments does not necessarily establish an intent by Congress to preempt tort claims to the same extent as requirements imposed directly by state officials, juries indirectly—and inconsistently—but unmistakably do set product safety standards in this country. Once we accept the notion that jurors effectively regulate with their verdicts, one may ask whether this arrangement makes sense.

IV. *Blending Administrative and Judicial Regulation*

Professor Rabin emphasizes two comparative advantages enjoyed by the tort system: a superior capacity for ferreting out information about unscrupulous corporate behavior and attention to compensatory aims not taken into account by administrative agencies. Before evaluating these arguments separately, one must remember that manufacturers would continue to face the prospect of liability in most cases. Although a sweeping federal preemption defense would sacrifice the supposed virtues of the tort system, a regulatory compliance defense should have only a modest impact. Tort liability would remain in place to compensate plaintiffs and deter defendants insofar as genuinely defective products cause injuries. The government standards defense only goes to questions of breach and, in appropriate cases, provides a basis for concluding that a product manufactured, designed, and labeled in accordance with federal safety requirements was not in fact defective.

A. *Generating Information*

Professor Rabin's information-based argument does not seem terribly compelling. Although individual product approvals may depend upon licensing applicants for full disclosure, broad-based rulemaking initiatives give agencies access to a wealth of information, far more than typical in tort litigation. Where regulations dictate appropriate risk labeling for a range of similar products, much of this information will appear in refereed scientific journals, and the FDA can call on other health protection agencies, such as the Centers for Disease Control and Prevention, or prestigious scientific organizations, such as the National Academy of Sciences (NAS) and the Federation of American Societies for Experimental Biology (FASEB), to assist with compiling and reviewing the available research. The ad hoc panels of court-appointed experts that Professor Rabin describes, even in the highly unlikely event that they ever became widespread, could not possibly match the FDA's capacity for gathering and evaluating relevant risk information. Indeed, his use of tobacco as an illustration of the tort system's capacity for uncovering corporate misconduct is particularly inapt; the FDA first broke the story concerning the internal tobacco industry records and witnesses as a prelude to its rulemaking effort in this area. The lawyers who later capitalized on these disclosures might never have uncovered the documents or whistleblowers without the agency's initiative.

Ultimately, however, a regulatory compliance defense should not diminish whatever additional information that the tort system can supply. Plaintiffs will not have reduced incentives to discover fraud on an agency just because defendants get to assert a compliance defense, for which defendants would shoulder the burden of proof. On the contrary, plaintiffs may search more actively for evidence of corporate misconduct. If they do not already have an incentive to assert claims of negligence per se based on violations of relevant safety standards, plaintiffs will have every reason to find evidence of noncompliance, nondisclosure, or fraud in order to defeat the defense.

B. *Compensating Injured Victims*

Professor Rabin's compensatory argument also misses the mark. In effect, he suggests that some states have adopted a form of strict products liability that takes questions about defectiveness out of the equation. If true, then the compliance defense has nothing to say. In these jurisdictions, enterprises would know that they must pay for any product-related injuries to consumers, no matter the state-of-the-art, the clarity of risk information, or the social disutilities of the price increases that would have to accompany such a regime of compulsory insurance. The compliance defense would, however, remain of interest in those far more numerous jurisdictions that continue to inquire about defectiveness before spreading the costs of product-related injuries by imposing strict liability. Indeed, even in California, which Professor Rabin identifies as following a particularly strict version of products liability on the strength of yet another automobile case, the compliance defense would make a difference in prescription drug and medical device litigation because proof of some genuine product defect remains essential in that and most other jurisdictions so as not to deter the marketing of unavoidably unsafe therapeutic products.

As a related point, Professor Rabin explains that agencies set safety standards based on a comparison of risks and benefits but without any view toward the compensation of injuries. That might, however, actually argue in favor of borrowing such standards. Unlike jurors who may become fixated on awarding compensation to the needy plaintiff put before them, sometimes without any apparent regard to issues of defect or causation (or, indeed, aggregate compensatory questions), agency determinations appropriately focus on safety questions and have the advantage of taking a broader view of the inevitable tradeoffs involved in specifying appropriate product designs and disclosures of risk information. Moreover, it is not clear how agencies would react if they took compensatory issues into account when setting product safety standards. Professor Rabin implies that the range of covered injuries would expand, but that is hardly obvious.

One could offer a similar response to critics of the government standards defense who worry about regulatory obsolescence and administrative inertia. They assume uni-directionality, but this ignores the possibility that new scientific information may reveal excessive protectiveness in earlier standards formulated in the face of greater uncertainty. Indeed, obsolescence of this sort has not deterred courts from using *violations* of federal safety standards to assist plaintiffs in making negligence per se claims, and the often asserted difficulties in gauging compliance generally have not done so either. If federal product safety requirements appropriately set the standard of care when it helps plaintiffs, notwithstanding concerns that agencies may have set the requirements without considering compensatory issues or may have failed to keep them up-to-date, then compliance with those same requirements should satisfy the standard of care in products liability cases even though it happens to help defendants.

C. *Influencing Administrative Regulation*

In the highly unlikely event that an FDA compliance defense ever catches on with the courts, one should inquire whether this might filter back to alter the agency's standard-setting process in any way. To the extent that plaintiffs' lawyers and their close allies in the public interest community have not already become heavily involved in product safety rulemaking proceedings, they may have enhanced incentives to submit comments and provide any possibly relevant data to the FDA in the future. Although industry representatives will understand that the stakes have increased, they may, at the same time, prefer a more expeditious conclusion to the agency's rulemaking proceedings than in the past, when efforts to delay or derail finalization of rules typically worked to the industry's advantage (at least in a regime where a standard only serves to punish, whether in public or private litigation). The agency may proceed somewhat more deliberately, but the defense would not come into play in the absence of a final regulation. Moreover, after the promulgation of a rule, products liability defectiveness per se claims will remain available in cases of agency underenforcement, which will continue to promote industry compliance with FDA regulations notwithstanding scarce resources.

In short, the regulatory compliance defense might improve FDA standard-setting as much as it can help rationalize products liability litigation. Even if that assessment seems unduly optimistic, increased judicial deference to government standards in tort suits would not impede the administrative process. In any event, the debate about this question too frequently focuses on the private law half of the equation and underemphasizes or misunderstands the public law half. The regulatory dimension deserves at least as much attention as the perspective rooted in tort law.

Just as they malign proponents of the government standards defense for idealizing agencies and caricaturing the courts as inept, opponents of the defense inappropriately idealize the judiciary and caricature the regulatory process as corrupt. Both public and private law approaches to product risks suffer from imperfections, but that does not mean that each system somehow makes up for the other's limitations simply by operating in parallel, oblivious to their own weaknesses and the corresponding strengths of the other system of risk regulation. The FDA regulatory compliance defense does not put us to the stark all-or-nothing choice associated with federal preemption; instead, it appropriately attempts to blend the two systems in a manner that maximizes the strengths of each. Standards adopted by the FDA through rulemaking procedures provide the strongest case for the recognition of such a defense, and the courts should at least embrace the limited concession to this effect in the new *Restatement*, even if they remain doubtful about a broader compliance defense. * * *

NOTES AND QUESTIONS

1. *Precursors.* A study initiated one decade earlier by the ALI had recommended the recognition of a regulatory compliance defense, especially for prescription drugs. See 2 ALI, Reporters' Study, Enterprise Responsibility for Personal Injury: Approaches to Legal and Institutional Change 95–110 (1991). In an article published at the same time, the future reporters for the *Restatement (Third)* seemed dubious about the tendency to disregard compliance with FDA requirements. See James A. Henderson, Jr. & Aaron D. Twerski, Doctrinal Collapse in Products Liability: The Empty Shell of Failure To Warn, 65 N.Y.U. L. Rev. 265, 320 (1990) ("[F]or reasons that we find difficult to understand, courts have not deferred to the determinations of product safety agencies such as the Food and Drug Administration.... The analysis usually begins and ends with the statement that agency standards are minimum, not maximum, standards and that courts are therefore free to disregard them."). Although comment e to § 4 of the new *Restatement* provides an opening for the recognition of a regulatory compliance defense as a general matter, elsewhere it expresses only limited confidence in the FDA. See Rest. (3d) § 6 cmt. b, at 146 ("[U]nqualified deference to these regulatory mechanisms is considered by a growing number of courts to be unjustified. An approved prescription drug or medical device can present significant risks without corresponding advantages.").

2. *Standards vs. approvals.* One might distinguish compliance with generally applicable standards and individualized product approval decisions, in part because rulemaking is a more open and accountable decisionmaking process than licensing decisions that often occur behind the scenes and depend on the sponsor to provide all relevant information to the agency. Conversely, one might regard licensing decisions as more significant because they represent a more focused and tailored risk-benefit judgment about a particular product than rulemaking that generates broad and perhaps ambiguous regulations. Comment e is unclear on this score, though it seems to express a preference for safety standards embodied in agency regulations. In some instances, courts have noted their frustration when asked to untangle the meaning and application of FDA regulations in private litigation where the agency itself has not concluded that a manufacturer has either violated or complied with those requirements. See Florida Breckenridge, Inc. v. Solvay Pharms., Inc., 174 F.3d 1227, 1231–34 (11th Cir.1999); National Bank of Commerce v. Kimberly–Clark Corp., 38 F.3d 988, 996 (8th Cir.1994); Sandoz Pharms. Corp. v. Richardson–Vicks, Inc., 902 F.2d 222, 231 (3d Cir.1990). In a lengthy section of the *Stanton* opinion excluded from the above excerpt, the court undertook a detailed analysis of how the FDA's evolving rules for the reporting of adverse drug events applied to Astra Pharmaceuticals during the time period in question.

3. *Minimum standards vs. optimal standards.* The primary rationale for disregarding the FDA's drug and medical device risk-benefit decisions is that the agency has imposed only "minimum" standards open to supplementation by a lay jury's verdict enforcing a manufacturer's common law tort duty. See, e.g., Wells v. Ortho Pharm. Corp., 788 F.2d 741, 746 (11th Cir.1986); Plenger v. Alza Corp., 13 Cal.Rptr.2d 811, 819 n. 7 (Ct.App. 1992); Savina v. Sterling Drug, 795 P.2d 915, 931 (Kan.1990); Feldman v. Lederle Labs., 625 A.2d 1066, 1070 (N.J.1993); McEwen v. Ortho Pharm.

Corp., 528 P.2d 522, 533–35 (Or.1974); Lubbock Mfg. Co. v. Perez, 591 S.W.2d 907, 914 (Tex.Civ.Ct.App.1979); Washington State Physicians Ins. Exch. & Ass'n v. Fisons Corp., 858 P.2d 1054, 1069 (Wash.1993). Even if not conclusive, most courts will allow a manufacturer to introduce evidence of compliance with FDA requirements at trial. See, e.g., O'Gilvie v. International Playtex, Inc., 821 F.2d 1438 (10th Cir.1987); Foyle v. Lederle Labs., 674 F.Supp. 530, 533 (E.D.N.C.1987).

4. *Tort reform statutes.* In the National Childhood Vaccine Injury Act, Congress included an FDA compliance defense against tort liability for inadequate warnings and for punitive damages. See 42 U.S.C. §§ 300aa–22(b), 300aa–23(d). A few states have codified an FDA compliance defense. See Mich. Comp. Laws Ann. § 600.2946(5) (treating FDA drug approval as a conclusive defense absent evidence of fraud); N.J. Stat. Ann. § 2A:58C–4 (creating a rebuttable presumption of adequate warning); see also Taylor v. Gate Pharm., 639 N.W.2d 45 (Mich.Ct.App.2001) (invalidating the Michigan statute). A few other states provide an FDA compliance defense against only punitive damage claims. See Ariz. Rev. Stat. Ann. § 12–701(A); Ohio Rev. Code Ann. § 2307.801(C); Or. Rev. Stat. § 30.927 (1); Utah Code Ann. § 78–18–2(1); see also Bruce N. Kuhlik & Richard F. Kingham, The Adverse Effects of Standardless Punitive Damage Awards on Pharmaceutical Development and Availability, 45 Food Drug Cosm. L.J. 693 (1990). For a criticism of the latter version of the defense, see Teresa Moran Schwartz, Punitive Damages and Regulated Products, 42 Am. U. L. Rev. 1335 (1993).

5. *Further commentary.* See Steven Garber, Product Liability and the Economics of Pharmaceuticals and Medical Devices 192–93 (Rand 1993); Richard A. Epstein, Legal Liability for Medical Innovation, 8 Cardozo L. Rev. 1139, 1151–54, 1157–58 (1987); Margaret Gilhooley, Innovative Drugs, Products Liability, Regulatory Compliance, and Patient Choice, 24 Seton Hall L. Rev. 1481 (1994); Michael D. Green, Safety as an Element of Pharmaceutical Quality: The Respective Roles of Regulation and Tort Law, 42 St. Louis U. L.J. 163 (1998); Michael D. Green, Statutory Compliance and Tort Liability: Examining the Strongest Case, 30 U. Mich. J.L. Reform 461 (1997); Sylvia A. Law, Tort Liability and the Availability of Contraceptive Drugs and Devices in the United States, 23 N.Y.U. Rev. L. & Soc. Change 339 (1997); Richard L. Manning, Products Liability and Prescription Drug Prices in Canada and the United States, 40 J.L. & Econ. 203 (1997); Christopher Nedwick, The Impact of Licensing Authority Approval on Pharmaceutical Product Liability: A Survey of American and U.K. Law, 47 Food & Drug L.J. 41 (1992); Lars Noah, Civil Jury Nullification, 86 Iowa L. Rev. 1601 (2001); W. Kip Viscusi et al., Deterring Inefficient Pharmaceutical Litigation: An Economic Rationale for the FDA Regulatory Compliance Defense, 24 Seton Hall L. Rev. 1437 (1994); Note, A Question of Competence: The Judicial Role in the Regulation of Pharmaceuticals, 103 Harv. L. Rev. 773 (1990).

Even if courts refuse to credit compliance as a matter of common law, they might feel compelled to do so under the rubric of federal preemption. Manufacturers of pharmaceutical products have argued that sweeping FDA regulation impliedly preempts tort claims against them. In one of the rare cases to accept this argument, the court explained that "manufacturers cannot change the language in the product insert without FDA approval. It would be patently inconsistent for a state then to hold the manufacturer liable for including that precise warning when the manufacturer would otherwise be liable for not including it. Thus, assuming that the FDA has processed all the relevant and available information in arriving at the prescribed warning, its decision as to the proper wording must preempt by implication that of a state." Hurley v. Lederle Labs., 863 F.2d 1173, 1179 (5th Cir.1988). For the most part, however, this argument has met with little success. See Abbot v. American Cyanamid Co., 844 F.2d 1108, 1112 (4th Cir.1988); Mazur v. Merck & Co., 742 F.Supp. 239, 247 (E.D.Pa.1990); Tarallo v. Searle Pharm., Inc., 704 F.Supp. 653, 660 (D.S.C.1988); Feldman v. Lederle Labs., 592 A.2d 1176, 1185 (N.J.1991); see also David R. Geiger & Mark D. Rosen, Rationalizing Product Liability for Prescription Drugs: Implied Preemption, Federal Common Law, and Other Paths to Uniform Pharmaceutical Safety Standards, 45 DePaul L. Rev. 395 (1996); Beverly L. Jacklin, Annotation, Federal Preemption of State Common–Law Products Liability Claims Pertaining to Drugs, Medical Devices and Other Health–Related Items, 98 A.L.R. Fed. 124 (1990 & 2002 Supp.). The hesitancy to recognize an implied preemption defense to tort claims may, however, be changing.

A few of the federal statutes implemented by the FDA include preemption clauses, most notably the medical device provisions of the FDCA:

(a) General rule. Except as provided in subsection (b) of this section, no State or political subdivision of a State may establish or continue in effect with respect to a device intended for human use any requirement—

(1) which is different from, or in addition to, any requirement applicable under this chapter to the device, and

(2) which relates to the safety or effectiveness of the device or to any other matter included in a requirement applicable to the device under this chapter.

(b) Exempt requirements. Upon application of a State or a political subdivision thereof, the Secretary may, by regulation promulgated after notice and opportunity for an oral hearing, exempt from subsection (a) of this section, under such conditions as may be prescribed in such regulation, a requirement of such State or political subdivision applicable to a device intended for human use if—

(1) the requirement is more stringent than a requirement under this chapter which would be applicable to the device if an exemption were not in effect under this subsection; or

(2) the requirement—(A) is required by compelling local conditions, and (B) compliance with the requirement would not cause the device to be in violation of any applicable requirement under this chapter.

21 U.S.C. § 360k. This avenue for protection from tort liability has worked far better, especially after 1992 when the United States Supreme Court decided for the first time that federal statutes displacing nonidentical requirements expressly preempted state common law as well as positive law. See Cipollone v. Liggett Group, Inc., 505 U.S. 504, 518–30 (1992) (plurality opinion); see also Robert S. Adler & Richard A. Mann, Preemption and Medical Devices: The Courts Run Amok, 59 Mo. L. Rev. 895 (1994); Lars Noah, Amplification of Federal Preemption in Medical Device Cases, 49 Food & Drug L.J. 183 (1994); Roger W. Bivans, Note, Substantially Equivalent? Federal Preemption of State Common–Law Claims Involving Medical Devices, 74 Tex. L. Rev. 1087 (1996). In subsequent decisions, the Supreme Court interpreted preemption provisions found in other federal safety statutes in a similar fashion. See Freightliner Corp. v. Myrick, 514 U.S. 280 (1995); CSX Transp. Inc. v. Easterwood, 507 U.S. 658 (1993). Indeed, the courts had become so receptive to preemption arguments that an officer from one pacemaker company testified in opposition to a products liability bill before Congress, brashly announcing his belief "that tort reform has already arrived for medical device manufacturers," and worrying that the proposed legislation might weaken the industry's existing defense to liability! See Products Liability Standards: Hearings Before a Subcomm. of the House Comm. on Energy & Commerce, 103d Cong. 196 (1994) (statement of William Nealon, Vice Pres. & Gen. Counsel, Telectronics Pacing Sys.). The following decisions involving medical devices demonstrate, however, that the issue remains in substantial flux.

Medtronic, Inc. v. Lohr

518 U.S. 470 (1996).

■ Stevens, Justice (plurality opinion):

Congress enacted the Medical Device Amendments of 1976 [MDA], in the words of the statute's preamble, "to provide for the safety and effectiveness of medical devices intended for human use." The question presented is whether that statute preempts a state common-law negligence action against the manufacturer of an allegedly defective medical device. * * *

As have so many other medical device manufacturers, petitioner Medtronic took advantage of § 510(k)'s expedited process in October 1982, when it notified the FDA that it intended to market its Model 4011 pacemaker lead as a device that was "substantially equivalent" to devices already on the market. (The lead is the portion of a pacemaker that transmits the heartbeat-steadying electrical signal from the "pulse generator" to the heart itself.) On November 30, 1982, the FDA found that the model was "substantially equivalent to devices introduced into interstate commerce" prior to the effective date of the Act, and advised Medtronic that it could therefore market its device subject only to the general control provisions of the Act * * * *

Lora Lohr is dependent on pacemaker technology for the proper functioning of her heart. In 1987 she was implanted with a Medtronic pacemaker equipped with one of the company's Model 4011 pacemaker leads. On December 30, 1990, the pacemaker failed, allegedly resulting in a "complete heart block" that required emergency surgery. According to her physician, a defect in the lead was the likely cause of the failure. In 1993 Lohr and her husband filed this action in a Florida state court. Their complaint contained both a negligence count and a strict liability count. * * * Medtronic removed the case to federal district court, where it filed a motion for summary judgment arguing that both the negligence and strict liability claims were preempted by 21 U.S.C. § 360k(a). * * *

As in *Cipollone v. Liggett Group, Inc.*, 505 U.S. 504 (1992), we are presented with the task of interpreting a statutory provision that expressly preempts state law. While the preemptive language of § 360k(a) means that we need not go beyond that language to determine whether Congress intended the MDA to preempt at least some state law, we must nonetheless "identify the domain expressly preempted" by that language. * * *

IV

In its petition, Medtronic argues that the court of appeals erred by concluding that the Lohrs' claims alleging negligent design were not preempted by 21 U.S.C. § 360k(a). * * * Medtronic suggests that any common-law cause of action is a "requirement" which alters incentives and imposes duties "different from, or in addition to," the generic federal standards that the FDA has promulgated in response to mandates under the MDA. In essence, the company argues that the plain language of the statute preempts any and all common-law claims brought by an injured plaintiff against a manufacturer of medical devices.

Medtronic's argument is not only unpersuasive, it is implausible. Under Medtronic's view of the statute, Congress effectively precluded state courts from affording state consumers any protection from injuries resulting from a defective medical device. Moreover, because there is no explicit private cause of action against manufacturers contained in the MDA, and no suggestion that the Act created an implied private right of action, Congress would have barred most, if not all, relief for persons injured by defective medical devices. Medtronic's construction of § 360k would therefore have the perverse effect of granting complete immunity from design defect liability to an entire industry that, in the judgment of Congress, needed more stringent regulation in order "to provide for the safety and effectiveness of medical devices intended for human use," 90 Stat. 539 (preamble to Act). It is, to say the least, "difficult to believe that Congress would, without comment, remove all means of judicial recourse for those injured by illegal conduct," *Silkwood v. Kerr–McGee Corp.*, 464 U.S. 238, 251 (1984), and it would take language much plainer than the text of § 360k to convince us that Congress intended that result.

Furthermore, if Congress intended to preclude all common-law causes of action, it chose a singularly odd word with which to do it. The statute would have achieved an identical result, for instance, if it had precluded any "remedy" under state law relating to medical devices. "Requirement" appears to presume that the State is imposing a specific duty upon the manufacturer, and although we have on prior occasions concluded that a statute preempting certain state "requirements" could also preempt common-law damages claims, that statute did not sweep nearly as broadly as Medtronic would have us believe that this statute does.

The preemptive statute in *Cipollone* was targeted at a limited set of state requirements—those "based on smoking and health"—and then only at a limited subset of the possible applications of those requirements—those involving the "advertising or promotion of any cigarettes the packages of which are labeled in conformity with the provisions of" the federal statute. In that context, giving the term "requirement" its widest reasonable meaning did not have nearly the preemptive scope nor the effect on potential remedies that Medtronic's broad reading of the term would have in this suit. The Court in *Cipollone* held that the petitioner in that case was able to maintain some common-law actions using theories of the case that did not run afoul of the preemption statute. Here, however, Medtronic's sweeping interpretation of the statute would require far greater interference with state legal remedies, producing a serious intrusion into state sovereignty while simultaneously wiping out the possibility of remedy for the Lohrs' alleged injuries. Given the ambiguities in the statute and the scope of the preclusion that would occur otherwise, we cannot accept Medtronic's argument that by using the term "requirement," Congress clearly signaled its intent to deprive States of any role in protecting consumers from the dangers inherent in many medical devices.

Other differences between this statute and the one in *Cipollone* further convince us that when Congress enacted § 360k, it was primarily concerned with the problem of specific, conflicting state statutes and regulations rather than the general duties enforced by common-law actions. Unlike the statute at issue in *Cipollone*, § 360k refers to "requirements" many times throughout its text. In each instance, the word is linked with language suggesting that its focus is device-specific enactments of positive law by legislative or administrative bodies, not the application of general rules of common law by judges and juries. For instance, subsections (a)(2) and (b) of the statute also refer to "requirements"—but those "requirements" refer only to statutory and regulatory law that exists pursuant to the MDA itself, suggesting that the preempted "requirements" established or continued by States also refer primarily to positive enactments of state law. Moreover, in subsection (b) the FDA is given authority to exclude certain "requirements" from the scope of the preemption statute. Of the limited number of "exemptions" from preemption that the FDA has granted, none even remotely resemble common-law claims.

An examination of the basic purpose of the legislation as well as its history entirely supports our rejection of Medtronic's extreme position. The

MDA was enacted "to provide for the safety and effectiveness of medical devices intended for human use." 90 Stat. 539. Medtronic asserts that the Act was also intended, however, to "protect innovations in device technology from being 'stifled by unnecessary restrictions,' " and that this interest extended to the preemption of common-law claims. While the Act certainly reflects some of these concerns, the legislative history indicates that any fears regarding regulatory burdens were related more to the risk of additional federal and state regulation rather than the danger of pre-existing duties under common law. Indeed, nowhere in the materials relating to the Act's history have we discovered a reference to a fear that product liability actions would hamper the development of medical devices. To the extent that Congress was concerned about protecting the industry, that intent was manifested primarily through fewer substantive requirements under the Act, not the preemption provision; furthermore, any such concern was far outweighed by concerns about the primary issue motivating the MDA's enactment: the safety of those who use medical devices.

The legislative history also confirms our understanding that § 360(k) simply was not intended to preempt most, let alone all, general common-law duties enforced by damages actions. There is, to the best of our knowledge, nothing in the hearings, the committee reports, or the debates suggesting that any proponent of the legislation intended a sweeping pre-emption of traditional common-law remedies against manufacturers and distributors of defective devices. If Congress intended such a result, its failure even to hint at it is spectacularly odd, particularly since members of both Houses were acutely aware of ongoing product liability litigation. Along with the less-than-precise language of § 360k(a), that silence surely indicates that at least some common-law claims against medical device manufacturers may be maintained after the enactment of the MDA.

V

Medtronic asserts several specific reasons why, even if § 360k does not preempt all common-law claims, it at least preempts the Lohrs' claims in this suit. In contrast, the Lohrs argue that their entire complaint should survive a reasonable evaluation of the preemptive scope of § 360k(a). First, the Lohrs claim that the court of appeals correctly held that their negligent design claims were not preempted because the § 510(k) premarket notification process imposes no "requirement" on the design of Medtronic's pacemaker. Second, they suggest that even if the FDA's general rules regulating manufacturing practices and labeling are "requirements" that preempt different state requirements, § 360k(a) does not preempt state rules that merely duplicate some or all of those federal requirements. Finally, they argue that because the State's general rules imposing common-law duties upon Medtronic do not impose a requirement "with respect to a device," they do not conflict with the FDA's general rules relating to manufacturing and labeling and are therefore not preempted.

Design Claim. The court of appeals concluded that the Lohrs' defective design claims were not preempted because the requirements with which the company had to comply were not sufficiently concrete to constitute a preempting federal requirement. Medtronic counters by pointing to the FDA's determination that Model 4011 is "substantially equivalent" to an earlier device as well as the agency's continuing authority to exclude the device from the market if its design is changed. These factors, Medtronic argues, amount to a specific, federally enforceable design requirement that cannot be affected by state-law pressures such as those imposed on manufacturers subject to product liability suits.

The company's defense exaggerates the importance of the § 510(k) process and the FDA letter to the company regarding the pacemaker's substantial equivalence to a grandfathered device. * * * The design of the Model 4011, as with the design of pre–1976 and other "substantially equivalent" devices, has never been formally reviewed under the MDA for safety or efficacy.

The FDA stressed this basic conclusion in its letter to Medtronic finding the 4011 lead "substantially equivalent" to devices already on the market. That letter only required Medtronic to comply with "general standards"—the lowest level of protection "applicable to all medical devices," and including "listing of devices, good manufacturing practices, labeling, and the misbranding and adulteration provisions of the Act." It explicitly warned Medtronic that the letter did "not in any way denote official FDA approval of your device," and that "[a]ny representation that creates an impression of official approval of this device because of compliance with the premarket notification regulations is misleading and constitutes misbranding."

Thus, even though the FDA may well examine § 510(k) applications for Class III devices (as it examines the entire medical device industry) with a concern for the safety and effectiveness of the device, it did not "require" Medtronics' pacemaker to take any particular form for any particular reason; the agency simply allowed the pacemaker, as a device substantially equivalent to one that existed before 1976, to be marketed without running the gauntlet of the PMA process. In providing for this exemption to PMA review, Congress intended merely to give manufacturers the freedom to compete, to a limited degree, with and on the same terms as manufacturers of medical devices that existed prior to 1976. There is no suggestion in either the statutory scheme or the legislative history that the § 510(k) exemption process was intended to do anything other than maintain the status quo with respect to the marketing of existing medical devices and their substantial equivalents. That status quo included the possibility that the manufacturer of the device would have to defend itself against state-law claims of negligent design. * * * [T]he court of appeals properly concluded that the "substantial equivalence" provision did not preempt the Lohrs' design claims.

Identity of Requirements Claims. The Lohrs next suggest that even if "requirements" exist with respect to the manufacturing and labeling of the pacemaker, and even if we can also consider state law to impose a "requirement" under the Act, the state requirement is not preempted unless it is "different from, or in addition to," the federal requirement. Although the precise contours of their theory of recovery have not yet been defined (the preemption issue was decided on the basis of the pleadings), it is clear that the Lohrs' allegations may include claims that Medtronic has, to the extent that they exist, violated FDA regulations. At least these claims, they suggest, can be maintained without being preempted by § 360k, and we agree.

Nothing in § 360k denies Florida the right to provide a traditional damages remedy for violations of common-law duties when those duties parallel federal requirements. Even if it may be necessary as a matter of Florida law to prove that those violations were the result of negligent conduct, or that they created an unreasonable hazard for users of the product, such additional elements of the state-law cause of action would make the state requirements narrower, not broader, than the federal requirement. While such a narrower requirement might be "different from" the federal rules in a literal sense, such a difference would surely provide a strange reason for finding preemption of a state rule insofar as it duplicates the federal rule. The presence of a damages remedy does not amount to the additional or different "requirement" that is necessary under the statute; rather, it merely provides another reason for manufacturers to comply with identical existing "requirements" under federal law.

The FDA regulations interpreting the scope of § 360k's preemptive effect support the Lohrs' view, and our interpretation of the preemption statute is substantially informed by those regulations. The different views expressed by the courts of appeals regarding the appropriate scope of federal preemption under § 360k demonstrate that the language of that section is not entirely clear. In addition, Congress has given the FDA a unique role in determining the scope of § 360k's preemptive effect. Unlike the statute construed in *Cipollone*, for instance, preemption under the MDA does not arise directly as a result of the enactment of the statute; rather, in most cases a state law will be preempted only to the extent that the FDA has promulgated a relevant federal "requirement." * * * Congress explicitly delegated to the FDA the authority to exempt state regulations from the preemptive effect of the MDA—an authority that necessarily requires the FDA to assess the preemptive effect that the Act and its own regulations will have on state laws. FDA regulations implementing that grant of authority establish a process by which States or other individuals may request an advisory opinion from the FDA regarding whether a particular state requirement is preempted by the statute. The ambiguity in the statute—and the congressional grant of authority to the agency on the matter contained within it—provide a "sound basis" for giving substantial weight to the agency's view of the statute. See Chevron U.S.A. Inc. v. NRDC, 467 U.S. 837 (1984).

The regulations promulgated by the FDA expressly support the conclusion that § 360k "does not preempt State or local requirements that are equal to, or substantially identical to, requirements imposed by or under the act." 21 C.F.R. § 808.1(d)(2) (1995). At this early stage in the litigation, there was no reason for the court of appeals to preclude altogether the Lohrs' manufacturing and labeling claims to the extent that they rest on claims that Medtronic negligently failed to comply with duties "equal to, or substantially identical to, requirements imposed" under federal law.

Manufacturing and Labeling Claims. Finally, the Lohrs suggest that with respect to the manufacturing and labeling claims, the court of appeals should have rejected Medtronic's preemption defense in full. The court of appeals believed that these claims would interfere with the consistent application of general federal regulations governing the labeling and manufacture of all medical devices, and therefore concluded that the claims were preempted altogether. * * *

While admitting that these requirements exist, the Lohrs suggest that their general nature simply does not preempt claims alleging that the manufacturer failed to comply with other duties under state common law. In support of their claim, they note that § 360k(a)(1) expressly states that a federal requirement must be "applicable to the device" in question before it has any preemptive effect. Because the labeling and manufacturing requirements are applicable to a host of different devices, they argue that they do not satisfy this condition. They further argue that because only state requirements "with respect to a device" may be preempted, and then only if the requirement "relates to the safety or effectiveness of the device or to any other matter included in a requirement applicable to the device," § 360k(a) mandates preemption only where there is a conflict between a specific state requirement and a federal requirement "applicable to" the same device.

The Lohrs' theory is supported by the FDA regulations, which provide that state requirements are preempted "only" when the FDA has established "specific counterpart regulations or . . . other specific requirements applicable to a particular device." 21 C.F.R. § 808.1(d) (1995). They further note that the statute is not intended to preempt "State or local requirements of general applicability where the purpose of the requirement relates either to other products in addition to devices . . . or to unfair trade practices in which the requirements are not limited to devices." Id. § 808.1(d)(1). The regulations specifically provide, as examples of permissible general requirements, that general electrical codes and the Uniform Commercial Code warranty of fitness would not be preempted. The regulations even go so far as to state that § 360k(a) generally "does not preempt a state or local requirement prohibiting the manufacture of adulterated or misbranded devices" unless "such a prohibition has the effect of establishing a substantive requirement for a specific device." Id. § 808.1(d)(6)(ii). Furthermore, under its authority to grant exemptions to the preemptive effect of § 360k(a), the FDA has never granted, nor, to the best of our knowledge, even been asked to consider granting, an exemption for a state law of general applicability * * * *

The statute and regulations, therefore, require a careful comparison between the allegedly preempting federal requirement and the allegedly preempted state requirement to determine whether they fall within the intended preemptive scope of the statute and regulations. Such a comparison mandates a conclusion that the Lohrs' common-law claims are not preempted by the federal labeling and manufacturing requirements. The generality of those requirements make this quite unlike a case in which the federal government has weighed the competing interests relevant to the particular requirement in question, reached an unambiguous conclusion about how those competing considerations should be resolved in a particular case or set of cases, and implemented that conclusion via a specific mandate on manufacturers or producers. Rather, the federal requirements reflect important but entirely generic concerns about device regulation generally, not the sort of concerns regarding a specific device or field of device regulation that the statute or regulations were designed to protect from potentially contradictory state requirements.

Similarly, the general state common-law requirements in this suit were not specifically developed "with respect to" medical devices. Accordingly, they are not the kinds of requirements that Congress and the FDA feared would impede the ability of federal regulators to implement and enforce specific federal requirements. The legal duty that is the predicate for the Lohrs' negligent manufacturing claim is the general duty of every manufacturer to use due care to avoid foreseeable dangers in its products. Similarly, the predicate for the failure to warn claim is the general duty to inform users and purchasers of potentially dangerous items of the risks involved in their use. These general obligations are no more a threat to federal requirements than would be a state-law duty to comply with local fire prevention regulations and zoning codes, or to use due care in the training and supervision of a work force. These state requirements therefore escape preemption, not because the source of the duty is a judge-made common-law rule, but rather because their generality leaves them outside the category of requirements that § 360k envisioned to be "with respect to" specific devices such as pacemakers. As a result, none of the Lohrs' claims based on allegedly defective manufacturing or labeling are preempted by the MDA.

VI

In their cross-petition, the Lohrs present a final argument, suggesting that common-law duties are never "requirements" within the meaning of § 360k and that the statute therefore never preempts common-law actions. The Lohrs point out that our holding in *Cipollone* is not dispositive of this issue, for as Part IV, *supra*, suggests, there are significant textual and historical differences between the *Cipollone* statute and § 360k, and the meaning of words must always be informed by the environment within which they are situated. We do not think that the issue is resolved by the FDA regulation suggesting that § 360k is applicable to those requirements "having the force and effect of law" that are "established by ... court decision," 21 C.F.R. § 808.1(b); that reference, it appears, was intended to refer to court decisions construing state statutes or regulations. See 42 Fed. Reg. 30,383, 30,385 (1977).

Nevertheless, we do not respond directly to this argument for two reasons. First, since none of the Lohrs' claims is preempted in this suit, we need not resolve hypothetical cases that may arise in the future. Second, given the critical importance of device specificity in our (and the FDA's) construction of § 360k, it is apparent that few, if any, common-law duties have been preempted by this statute. It will be rare indeed for a court hearing a common-law cause of action to issue a decree that has "the effect of establishing a substantive requirement for a specific device." 21 C.F.R. § 808.1(d)(6)(ii). Until such a case arises, we see no need to determine whether the statute explicitly preempts such a claim. Even then, the issue may not need to be resolved if the claim would also be preempted under conflict preemption analysis * * * *

■ BREYER, JUSTICE (concurring in part and concurring in judgment):

This action raises two questions. First, do the Medical Device Amendments of 1976 (MDA) to the Federal Food, Drug, and Cosmetic Act ever preempt a state-law tort action? Second, if so, does the MDA preempt the particular state-law tort claims at issue here?

My answer to the first question is that the MDA will sometimes preempt a state-law tort suit. * * * One can reasonably read the word "requirement" as including the legal requirements that grow out of the application, in particular circumstances, of a State's tort law. Moreover, in *Cipollone v. Liggett Group, Inc.*, 505 U.S. 504 (1992), the Court made clear that similar language "easily" encompassed tort actions because "[state] regulation can be as effectively exerted through an award of damages as through some form of preventive relief." This rationale would seem applicable to the quite similar circumstances at issue here.

Finally, a contrary holding would have anomalous consequences. Imagine that, in respect to a particular hearing aid component, a federal MDA regulation requires a 2–inch wire, but a state agency regulation requires a 1–inch wire. If the federal law, embodied in the "2–inch" MDA regulation, preempts the state "1–inch" agency regulation, why would it not similarly preempt a state-law tort action that premises liability upon the defendant manufacturer's failure to use a 1–inch wire (say, an award by a jury persuaded by expert testimony that use of a more than 1–inch wire is negligent)? The effects of the state agency regulation and the state tort suit are identical. To distinguish between them for preemption purposes would grant greater power (to set state standards "different from, or in addition to," federal standards) to a single state jury than to state officials acting through state administrative or legislative lawmaking processes. Where Congress likely did not focus specifically upon the matter, I would not take it to have intended this anomalous result.

Consequently, I believe that ordinarily, insofar as the MDA preempts a state requirement embodied in a state statute, rule, regulation, or other administrative action, it would also preempt a similar requirement that takes the form of a standard of care or behavior imposed by a state-law tort action. It is possible that the plurality also agrees on this point, although it does not say so explicitly.

The answer to the second question turns on Congress' intent. Although Congress has not stated whether the MDA does, or does not, preempt the tort claims here at issue, several considerations lead me to conclude that it does not.

First, the MDA's preemption provision is highly ambiguous. That provision makes clear that federal requirements may preempt state requirements, but it says next to nothing about just when, where, or how they may do so. The words "any [state] requirement" and "any [federal] requirement," for example, do not tell us which requirements are at issue, for every state requirement that is not identical to even one federal requirement is "different from, or in addition to," that single federal requirement; yet, Congress could not have intended that the existence of one single federal rule, say, about a 2–inch hearing aid wire, would preempt every state law hearing aid rule, even a set of rules related only to the packaging or shipping of hearing aids. Thus, Congress must have intended that courts look elsewhere for help as to just which federal requirements preempt just which state requirements, as well as just how they might do so.

Second, this Court has previously suggested that, in the absence of a clear congressional command as to preemption, courts may infer that the relevant administrative agency possesses a degree of leeway to determine which rules, regulations, or other administrative actions will have preemptive effect. To draw a similar inference here makes sense, and not simply because of the statutory ambiguity. The Food and Drug Administration (FDA) is fully responsible for administering the MDA. That responsibility means informed agency involvement and, therefore, special understanding of the likely impact of both state and federal requirements, as well as an understanding of whether (or the extent to which) state requirements may interfere with federal objectives. The FDA can translate these understandings into particularized preemptive intentions accompanying its various rules and regulations. It can communicate those intentions, for example, through statements in "regulations, preambles, interpretive statements, and responses to comments," as well as through the exercise of its explicitly designated power to exempt state requirements from preemption.

Third, the FDA has promulgated a specific regulation designed to help. That regulation says: "State . . . requirements are preempted only when . . . there are . . . specific [federal] requirements applicable to a particular device . . . thereby making any existing divergent State . . . requirements applicable to the device different from, or in addition to, the *specific* [federal] requirements." 21 C.F.R. § 808.1(d) (1995) (emphasis added). The regulation does not fill all the statutory gaps, for its word "divergent" does not explain, any more than did the statute, just when different device-related federal and state requirements are closely enough related to trigger preemption analysis. But the regulation's word "specific" does narrow the universe of federal requirements that the agency intends to displace at least some state law. Insofar as there are any applicable FDA requirements here, those requirements, even if numerous, are not "specific" in any relevant sense. Hence, as the FDA's above-quoted preemption rule tells us, the FDA does not intend these requirements to preempt the state requirements at issue here. * * *

Fourth, ordinary principles of "conflict" and "field" preemption point in the same direction. Those principles make clear that a federal requirement preempts a state requirement if (1) the state requirement actually conflicts with the federal requirement—either because compliance with both is impossible, or because the state requirement "stands as an obstacle to the accomplishment and execution of the full purposes and objectives of Congress,"—or (2) the scheme of federal regulation is "so pervasive as to make reasonable the inference that Congress left no room for the States to supplement it."

It makes sense, in the absence of any indication of a contrary congressional (or agency) intent, to read the preemption statute (and the preemption regulation) in light of these basic preemption principles. The statutory terms "different from" and "in addition to" readily lend themselves to such a reading, for their language parallels preemption law's basic concerns. Without any contrary indication from the agency, one might also interpret the regulation's word "divergent" in light of these same basic preemption principles. Insofar as these basic principles inform a court's interpretation of the statute and regulation, they support the conclusion that there is no preemption here. I can find no actual conflict between any federal requirement and any of the liability-creating premises of the plaintiffs' state-law tort suit; nor, for the reasons discussed above, can I find any indication that either Congress or the FDA intended the relevant FDA regulations to occupy entirely any relevant field.

For these reasons, I concur in the Court's judgment. I also join the Court's opinion, but for Parts IV and VI. I do not join Part IV, which emphasizes the differences between the MDA and the preemption statute at issue in *Cipollone*, because those differences are not, in my view, relevant in this action. I do not join Part VI, because I am not convinced that future incidents of MDA preemption of common-law claims will be "few" or "rare."

■ O'CONNOR, JUSTICE (concurring in part and dissenting in part):

* * * Whether relating to the labeling of cigarettes or the manufacture of medical devices, state common-law damages actions operate to require manufacturers to comply with common-law duties. * * * If § 360k's language is given its ordinary meaning, it clearly preempts any state common-law action that would impose a requirement different from, or in addition to, that applicable under the FDCA—just as it would preempt a state statute or regulation that had that effect. Justice Breyer reaches the same conclusion.

The plurality's reasons for departing from this reading are neither clear nor persuasive. It fails to refute the applicability of the reasoning of *Cipollone*. Instead, in Part IV, the plurality essentially makes the case that the statute's language, purpose, and legislative history, as well as the consequences of a different interpretation, indicate that Congress did not intend "requirement" to include state common-law claims at all. The principal opinion proceeds to disclaim this position, however, in Parts V and VI and concludes, rather, that a state common-law action might constitute a requirement, but that such a case would be "rare indeed." The Court holds that an FDCA "requirement" triggers preemption only when a conflict exists between a specific state requirement and a specific FDCA requirement applicable to the particular device. The plurality emphasizes the "critical importance of device specificity" in its understanding of the preemption scheme.

To reach its particularized reading of the statute, the Court imports the interpretation put forth by the FDA's regulations. Justice Breyer similarly relies on the FDA regulations to arrive at an understanding of § 360k. Apparently recognizing that *Chevron* deference is unwarranted here, the Court does not admit to deferring to these regulations, but merely permits them to "infor[m]" the Court's interpretation. It is not certain that an agency regulation determining the preemptive effect of any federal statute is entitled to deference * * * * Where the language of the statute is clear, resort to the agency's interpretation is improper. * * * The Court errs when it employs an agency's narrowing construction of a statute where no such deference is warranted. The statute makes no mention of a requirement of specificity, and there is no sound basis for determining that such a restriction on "any requirement" exists. I conclude that a fair reading of § 360k indicates that state common-law claims are preempted, as the statute itself states, to the extent that their recognition would impose "any requirement" different from, or in addition to, FDCA requirements applicable to the device. From that premise, I proceed to the question whether FDCA requirements applicable to the device exist here to preempt the Lohrs' state-law claims.

I agree with the Court that the Lohrs' defective design claim is not preempted by the FDCA's § 510(k) "substantial equivalency" process. The § 510(k) process merely evaluates whether the Class III device at issue is substantially equivalent to a device that was on the market before 1976, the effective date of the MDA; if so, the later device may be also be marketed. Because the § 510(k) process seeks merely to establish whether a pre–1976 device and a post–1976 device are equivalent, and places no "requirements" on a device, the Lohrs' defective design claim is not preempted.

I also agree that the Lohrs' claims are not preempted by § 360k to the extent that they seek damages for Medtronic's alleged violation of federal requirements. Where a state cause of action seeks to enforce an FDCA requirement, that claim does not impose a requirement that is "different from, or in addition to," requirements under federal law. To be sure, the threat of a damages remedy will give manufacturers an additional cause to comply, but the requirements imposed on them under state and federal law do not differ. Section 360k does not preclude States from imposing different or additional *remedies*, but only different or additional *requirements*.

I disagree, however, with the Court's conclusion that the Lohrs' claims survive preemption insofar as they would compel Medtronic to comply with requirements different from those imposed by the FDCA. Because I do not subscribe to the Court's reading into § 360k the additional requisite of "specificity," my determination of what claims are preempted is broader. Some, if not all, of the Lohrs' common-law claims regarding the manufacturing and labeling of Medtronic's device would compel Medtronic to comply with requirements different from, or in addition to, those required by the FDA. The FDA's Good Manufacturing Practice (GMP) regulations impose comprehensive requirements relating to every aspect of the device-manufacturing process, including a manufacturer's organization and personnel, buildings, equipment, component controls, production and process controls, packaging and labeling controls, holding, distribution, installation, device evaluation, and recordkeeping. The Lohrs' common-law claims regarding manufacture would, if successful, impose state requirements "different from, or in addition to," the GMP requirements, and are therefore preempted. In similar fashion, the Lohrs' failure to warn claim is preempted by the extensive labeling requirements imposed by the FDA. These extensive federal manufacturing and labeling requirements are certainly applicable to the device manufactured by Medtronic. Section 360k(a) requires no more specificity than that for preemption of state common-law claims. * * *

PROBLEM #7. *PREEMPTION AND PREMARKET NOTIFICATION*

You represent Cardiotronics, Inc., the manufacturer of a pulse generator incorporating a new power source. After filing a premarket notification with the FDA in 1995, an agency reviewer demands that Cardiotronics provide additional information about the long-term reliability of this new power source as compared with traditional battery packs. Your client promptly submits this data. After further review, the FDA concludes that the pacemaker is substantially equivalent to a predicate device, but it insists that the pacemaker's labeling be revised to convey information about the possible risks of sudden failure associated with this new power source. In 1999, one unit inexplicably fails, causing serious injury to the user. Thereupon the patient sues Cardiotronics, asserting claims of design defect and inadequate warning. Assume that you are in a jurisdiction that requires plaintiffs in all design defect cases to prove that a "reasonable alternative design" existed. You file a motion for summary judgment, arguing that these claims are preempted. Will it work?

Buckman v. Plaintiffs' Legal Committee

531 U.S. 341 (2001).

■ REHNQUIST, CHIEF JUSTICE:

Respondent represents plaintiffs who claim injuries resulting from the use of orthopedic bone screws in the pedicles of their spines. Petitioner is a consulting company that assisted the screws' manufacturer, AcroMed Corporation, in navigating the federal regulatory process for these devices. Plaintiffs say petitioner made fraudulent representations to the Food and Drug Administration (FDA or Agency) in the course of obtaining approval to market the screws. Plaintiffs further claim that such representations were at least a "but for" cause of injuries that plaintiffs sustained from the implantation of these devices: Had the representations not been made, the FDA would not have approved the devices, and plaintiffs would not have been injured. Plaintiffs sought damages from petitioner under state tort law. * * *

It is not disputed that the bone screws manufactured by AcroMed are Class III devices. Class III devices must complete a thorough review process with the FDA before they may be marketed. * * * An exception to the PMA requirement exists for devices that were already on the market prior to the MDA's enactment in 1976. The MDA allows these "predicate" devices to remain available until the FDA initiates and completes the PMA process. * * * Demonstrating that a device qualifies for this exception is known as the "§ 510(k) process" * * * *

In 1984, AcroMed sought § 510(k) approval for its bone screw device, indicating it for use in spinal surgery. See In re Orthopedic Bone Screw Prods. Liab. Litig., 159 F.3d 817, 820 (3d Cir.1998). The FDA denied approval on the grounds that the Class III device lacked substantial equivalence to a predicate device. In September 1985, with the assistance of petitioner, AcroMed filed another § 510(k) application. "The application provided additional information about the ... device and again indicated its use in spinal surgery. The FDA again rejected the application, determining that the device was not substantially equivalent to a predicate device and that it posed potential risks not exhibited by other spinal-fixation systems." Id. In December 1985, AcroMed and petitioner filed a third § 510(k) application. "AcroMed and [petitioner] split the ... device into its component parts, renamed them 'nested bone plates' and '[cancellous] bone screws' and filed a separate § 510(k) application for each component. In both applications, a new intended use was specified: rather than seeking clearance for spinal applications, they sought clearance to market the plates and screws for use in the long bones of the arms and legs. AcroMed and Buckman claimed that the two components were substantially equivalent to predicate devices used in long bone surgery. The FDA approved the devices for this purpose in February 1986." Id. * * *

[T]he District Court for the Eastern District of Pennsylvania has been the recipient of some 2,300 civil actions related to these medical devices. Many of these actions include state-law causes of action claiming that petitioner and AcroMed made fraudulent representations to the FDA as to the intended use of the bone screws and that, as a result, the devices were improperly given market clearance and were subsequently used to the plaintiffs' detriment. The district court dismissed these "fraud-on-the-FDA" claims, first on the ground that they were expressly preempted by the MDA, and then, after our decision in *Medtronic*, on the ground that these claims amounted to an improper assertion of a private right of action under the MDA. * * *

Policing fraud against federal agencies is hardly "a field which the States have traditionally occupied," Rice v. Santa Fe Elevator Corp., 331 U.S. 218, 230 (1947), such as to warrant a presumption against finding federal preemption of a state-law cause of action. To the contrary, the relationship between a federal agency and the entity it regulates is inherently federal in character because the relationship originates from, is governed by, and terminates according to federal law. Cf. Boyle v. United Technologies Corp., 487 U.S. 500, 504–05 (1988) (allowing preemption of state law by federal common law where the interests at stake are "uniquely federal" in nature). Here, petitioner's dealings with the FDA were prompted by the MDA, and the very subject matter of petitioner's statements were dictated by that statute's provisions. Accordingly—and in contrast to situations implicating "federalism concerns and the historic primacy of state regulation of matters of health and safety," *Medtronic*, 518 U.S. at 485—no presumption against preemption obtains in this case.

Given this analytical framework, we hold that the plaintiffs' state-law fraud-on-the-FDA claims conflict with, and are therefore impliedly preempted by federal law.[2] The conflict stems from the fact that the federal statutory scheme amply empowers the FDA to punish and deter fraud against the Agency, and that this authority is used by the Agency to achieve a somewhat delicate balance of statutory objectives. The balance sought by the Agency can be skewed by allowing fraud-on-the-FDA claims under state tort law.

As described in greater detail above, the § 510(k) process sets forth a comprehensive scheme for determining whether an applicant has demonstrated that a product is substantially equivalent to a predicate device. * * * Admittedly, the § 510(k) process lacks the PMA review's rigor: The former requires only a showing of substantial equivalence to a predicate device, while the latter involves a time-consuming inquiry into the risks and efficacy of each device. Nevertheless, to achieve its limited purpose, the § 510(k) process imposes upon applicants a variety of requirements that are designed to enable the FDA to make its statutorily required judgment as to whether the device qualifies under this exception.

Accompanying these disclosure requirements are various provisions aimed at detecting, deterring, and punishing false statements made during this and related approval processes. The FDA * * * has at its disposal a variety of enforcement options that allow it to make a measured response to suspected fraud upon the Agency.[4]

---

2. In light of this conclusion, we express no view on whether these claims are subject to express preemption under 21 U.S.C. § 360k.

4. The FDCA leaves no doubt that it is the federal government rather than private litigants who are authorized to file suit for noncompliance with the medical device provisions: "[A]ll such proceedings for the enforcement, or to restrain violations, of this chapter shall be by and in the name of the United States." 21 U.S.C. § 337(a).

This flexibility is a critical component of the statutory and regulatory framework under which the FDA pursues difficult (and often competing) objectives. For example, with respect to Class III devices, the FDA simultaneously maintains the exhaustive PMA and the more limited § 510(k) processes in order to ensure both that medical devices are reasonably safe and effective and that, if the device qualifies under the § 510(k) exception, it is on the market within a relatively short period of time. Similarly, "off-label" usage of medical devices (use of a device for some other purpose than that for which it has been approved by the FDA) is an accepted and necessary corollary of the FDA's mission to regulate in this area without directly interfering with the practice of medicine. Indeed, a recent amendment to the FDCA expressly states in part that "[n]othing in this chapter shall be construed to limit or interfere with the authority of a health care practitioner to prescribe or administer any legally marketed device to a patient for any condition or disease within a legitimate health care practitioner-patient relationship." 21 U.S.C. § 396. Thus, the FDA is charged with the difficult task of regulating the marketing and distribution of medical devices without intruding upon decisions statutorily committed to the discretion of health care professionals.

State-law fraud-on-the-FDA claims inevitably conflict with the FDA's responsibility to police fraud consistently with the Agency's judgment and objectives. As a practical matter, complying with the FDA's detailed regulatory regime in the shadow of 50 States' tort regimes will dramatically increase the burdens facing potential applicants—burdens not contemplated by Congress in enacting the FDCA and the MDA. Would-be applicants may be discouraged from seeking § 510(k) approval of devices with potentially beneficial off-label uses for fear that such use might expose the manufacturer or its associates (such as petitioner) to unpredictable civil liability. In effect, then, fraud-on-the-FDA claims could cause the Agency's reporting requirements to deter off-label use despite the fact that the FDCA expressly disclaims any intent to directly regulate the practice of medicine, and even though off-label use is generally accepted.

Conversely, fraud-on-the-FDA claims would also cause applicants to fear that their disclosures to the FDA, although deemed appropriate by the Agency, will later be judged insufficient in state court. Applicants would then have an incentive to submit a deluge of information that the Agency neither wants nor needs, resulting in additional burdens on the FDA's evaluation of an application. As a result, the comparatively speedy § 510(k) process could encounter delays, which would, in turn, impede competition among predicate devices and delay health care professionals' ability to prescribe appropriate off-label uses. * * *

Respondent also suggests that we should be reluctant to find a preemptive conflict here because Congress included an express preemption provision in the MDA. To the extent respondent posits that anything other than our ordinary preemption principles apply under these circumstances, that contention must fail * * * *

We must also reject respondent's attempt to characterize both the claims at issue in *Medtronic* (common-law negligence action against the manufacturer of an allegedly defective pacemaker lead) and the fraud claims here as "claims arising from violations of FDCA requirements." Notwithstanding the fact that *Medtronic* did not squarely address the question of implied preemption, it is clear that the *Medtronic* claims arose from the manufacturer's alleged failure to use reasonable care in the production of the product, not solely from the violation of FDCA requirements. In the present case, however, the fraud claims exist solely by virtue of the FDCA disclosure requirements. Thus, although *Medtronic* can be read to allow certain state-law causes of actions that parallel federal safety requirements, it does not and cannot stand for the proposition that any violation of the FDCA will support a state-law claim.

In sum, were plaintiffs to maintain their fraud-on-the-agency claims here, they would not be relying on traditional state tort law which had predated the federal enactments in questions. On the contrary, the existence of these federal enactments is a critical element in their case. For the reasons stated above, we think this sort of litigation would exert an extraneous pull on the scheme established by Congress, and it is therefore preempted by that scheme. * * *

■ Stevens, Justice (concurring):

As the Court points out, an essential link in the chain of causation that respondent must prove in order to prevail is that, but for petitioner's fraud, the allegedly defective orthopedic bone screws would not have reached the market. The fact that the Food and Drug Administration (FDA) has done nothing to remove the devices from the market, even though it is aware of the basis for the fraud allegations, convinces me that this essential element of the claim cannot be proved. I therefore agree that the case should not proceed.[1]

This would be a different case if, prior to the instant litigation, the FDA had determined that petitioner had committed fraud during the § 510(k) process and had then taken the necessary steps to remove the harm-causing product from the market. Under those circumstances, respondent's state-law fraud claim would not depend upon speculation as to the FDA's behavior in a counterfactual situation but would be grounded in the agency's explicit actions. In such a case, a plaintiff would be able to establish causation without second-guessing the FDA's decisionmaking or overburdening its personnel, thereby alleviating the Government's central concerns regarding fraud-on-the-agency claims.

---

1. Though my analysis focuses on the failure of the plaintiffs to establish a necessary element of their claim, that failure is grounded not in the minutiae of state law but in the details of the federal regulatory system for medical devices. Therefore, while this case does not fit neatly into our pre-existing preemption jurisprudence, it is accurate, in a sense, to say that federal law "preempts" this state-law fraud-on-the-FDA claim because the FDA has not acknowledged such a fraud and taken steps to remove the device from the market.

If the FDA determines both that fraud has occurred and that such fraud requires the removal of a product from the market, state damages remedies would not encroach upon, but rather would supplement and facilitate, the federal enforcement scheme. Cf. Medtronic, Inc. v. Lohr, 518 U.S. 470, 495 (1996) (holding that the presence of a state-law damages remedy for violations of FDA requirements does not impose an additional requirement upon medical device manufacturers but "merely provides another reason for manufacturers to comply with ... federal law"); id. at 513 (O'Connor, J., concurring in part and dissenting in part) (same).

Under the preemption analysis the Court offers today, however, parties injured by fraudulent representations to federal agencies would have no remedy even if recognizing such a remedy would have no adverse consequences upon the operation or integrity of the regulatory process. I do not believe the reasons advanced in the Court's opinion support the conclusion that Congress intended such a harsh result. Cf. Silkwood v. Kerr–McGee Corp., 464 U.S. 238, 251 (1984) (declining to infer that a federal statutory scheme that affords no alternative means of seeking redress preempted traditional state-law remedies). For that reason, although I concur in the Court's disposition of this case, I do not join its opinion.

NOTES AND QUESTIONS

1. *Medical device preemption after* Medtronic *and* Buckman. Some commentators read *Medtronic* as signalling the demise of the preemption defense in medical device tort litigation. See Robert B. Leflar & Richard A. Mann, The Preemption Pentad: Federal Preemption of Products Liability Claims After Medtronic, 64 Tenn. L. Rev. 691 (1997); see also Robert J. Katerberg, Note, Patching the "Crazy Quilt" of Cipollone: A Divided Court Rethinks Federal Preemption of Products Liability in Medtronic, Inc. v. Lohr, 75 N.C. L. Rev. 1440 (1997). But see Lars Noah, The Preemption Morass, Legal Times, July 29, 1996, at S37 (arguing otherwise). Although the post-*Medtronic* case law has become decidedly more mixed, several lower courts continue to recognize a preemption defense in limited circumstances. See, e.g., Martin v. Medtronic, Inc., 254 F.3d 573 (5th Cir.2001) (PMA); Kemp v. Medtronic, Inc., 231 F.3d 216 (6th Cir.2000) (same); Mitchell v. Collagen Corp., 126 F.3d 902, 911–15 (7th Cir.1997) (same); Papike v. Tambrands Inc., 107 F.3d 737, 740–42 (9th Cir.1997) (labeling regulations); Oja v. Howmedica, Inc., 111 F.3d 782 (10th Cir.1997) (IDE); Chambers v. Osteonics Corp., 109 F.3d 1243 (7th Cir.1997) (same); Martin v. Telectronics Pacing Sys., Inc., 105 F.3d 1090, 1098–101 (6th Cir.1997) (same). But see Brooks v. Howmedica, Inc., 236 F.3d 956 (8th Cir.2001) (PMA does not preempt warning claim), vacated, 246 F.3d 1149 (8th Cir.2001) (en banc); Goodlin v. Medtronic, Inc., 167 F.3d 1367 (11th Cir.1999) (PMA). *Buckman* did nothing to clear up the confusion generated by *Medtronic*. Apart from the Court's willingness to engage in implied preemption analysis without seeming to pay any attention to an express preemption provision, is it suggesting that defectiveness per se claims might no longer exist (at least absent a specific FDA finding of noncompliance)? See Lars Noah, Inverting the Products Liability Preemption Defense, Health L. News, Sept. 2001, at 6.

2. *Preemption redux*. In the wake of *Medtronic*, the Supreme Court has decided similar cases involving other federal safety statutes, and it continues to accept the premise that preemption clauses expressly preempt state tort claims. See, e.g., Norfolk S. Ry. v. Shanklin, 529 U.S. 344 (2000) (railroad crossing safeguards). To the extent that the plurality in *Medtronic* suggested a return to pre-*Cipollone* days, these latest decisions confirm that a majority of the Court remains persuaded by the notion that tort judgments have the same potential regulatory effect as applications of other nonidentical state laws displaced by federal legislation. Perhaps this will inspire pharmaceutical companies to try resurrecting their previously unsuccessful implied preemption arguments, which courts routinely had rejected before the decision in *Cipollone*. One state court recently held that FDA approval of an AIDS screening test for use by blood banks impliedly preempted tort claims. See R.F. v. Abbott Labs., 745 A.2d 1174, 1187–88 (N.J.2000). In 1997, Congress amended the FDCA to preempt state regulation of nonprescription drugs, but it expressly saved products liability claims. See 21 U.S.C. § 379r; J. Warren Rissier, Note, The FDA's Proposed Labeling Rules for Over-the-Counter Drugs and Preemption of State Tort Law, 71 S. Cal. L. Rev. 1387 (1998). This would not, however, foreclose an implied preemption argument. Cf. Geier v. American Honda Motor Co., 529 U.S. 861 (2000) (rejecting express preemption because of statutory savings clause, but finding implied federal preemption of a tort claim premised on the failure to install airbags in an automobile).

3. *Distinguishing preemption from a compliance defense*. The new *Restatement* drew a sharp distinction between a regulatory compliance defense and federal preemption:

> When a court concludes that a defendant is not liable by reason of having complied with a safety design or warnings statute or regulation, it is deciding that the product in question is not defective as a matter of the law of that state. The safety statute or regulation may be a federal provision, but the decision to give it determinative effect is a state-law determination. In contrast, in federal preemption, the court decides as a matter of federal law that the relevant federal statute or regulation reflects, expressly or impliedly, the intent of Congress to displace state law, including state tort law, with the federal statute or regulation. The question of preemption is thus a question of federal law, and a determination that there is preemption nullifies otherwise operational state law. The complex set of rules and standards for resolving questions of federal preemption are beyond the scope of this Restatement. However, when federal preemption is found, the legal effect is clear. Judicial deference to federal product safety statutes or regulations occurs not because the court concludes that compliance with the statute or regulation shows the product to be nondefective; the issue of defectiveness under state law is never reached. Rather, the court defers because, when a federal statute or regulation is preemptive, the Constitution mandates federal supremacy.

Rest. (3d) § 4 cmt. e. Although quoted in part by both the majority and dissent in *Geier*, this passage seriously oversimplifies the matter. In the years before *Medtronic*, some lower courts had dismissed tort claims as preempted even in cases of failures to comply with FDA requirements. For instance, in *Talbott v. C.R. Bard, Inc.*, 865 F.Supp. 37 (D.Mass.1994), aff'd, 63 F.3d 25 (1st Cir.1995), cert. dismissed, 517 U.S. 1230 (1996), a manufacturer of cardiac catheters successfully invoked the preemption defense in a wrongful death action even though it had already pled guilty to numerous charges of filing false statements with the FDA and other statutory violations, infractions for which the company was ordered to pay $61 million in civil and criminal penalties. In the otherwise fractured *Medtronic* decision, all of the justices agreed that the statute would not preempt tort claims in cases of noncompliance with federal safety standards. Arguably, then, federal preemption is nothing more than a regulatory compliance defense that courts have read into federal statutes that expressly displace state law. See Lars Noah, Reconceptualizing Federal Preemption of Tort Claims as the Government Standards Defense, 37 Wm. & Mary L. Rev. 903 (1996). This is not just a semantic distinction. If preemption is really just a compliance defense, this may alter who has the burden of proof and limit defendants' opportunity to remove cases to federal court. Does *Buckman* alter this landscape?

4. *The FDA's position.* The FDA filed amicus briefs in some of these cases, arguing that the MDA did not preempt any tort claims. See, e.g., Duvall v. Bristol–Myers–Squibb Co., 65 F.3d 392, 401 n.9 (4th Cir.1995), vacated, 518 U.S. 1030 (1996); see also Margaret Jane Porter, The Lohr Decision: FDA Perspective and Position, 52 Food & Drug L.J. 7 (1997). Frustrated by its inability to persuade the courts in this way, the agency published a proposal to disclaim any intent to preempt tort claims against manufacturers of medical devices, see 62 Fed. Reg. 65,384 (1997), but it withdrew this notice after questions arose about the propriety of the FDA's decision to share a prepublication draft of the proposal with public interest groups closely aligned with plaintiffs' lawyers, see 63 Fed. Reg. 39,789 (1998). On one occasion, the agency announced that it would preempt state law in connection with tort litigation. See 60 Fed. Reg. 16,962, 16,966 (1995) (protecting confidentiality in the reporting of adverse events).

3.   TORT CLAIMS AGAINST THE FDA

In the event that a patient injured by a pharmaceutical product or medical device is unable to sue the manufacturer—whether because of preemption, a regulatory compliance defense, or bankruptcy—the FDA itself might become a target of tort litigation for authorizing the sale of an allegedly hazardous product.

Berkovitz v. United States
486 U.S. 531 (1988).

■ MARSHALL, JUSTICE:

The question in this case is whether the discretionary function exception of the Federal Tort Claims Act (FTCA or Act), 28 U.S.C. § 2680(a), bars a suit based on the Government's licensing of an oral polio vaccine and on its subsequent approval of the release of a specific lot of that vaccine to the public.

On May 10, 1979, Kevan Berkovitz, then a 2–month-old infant, ingested a dose of Orimune, an oral polio vaccine manufactured by Lederle Laboratories. Within one month, he contracted a severe case of polio. The disease left Berkovitz almost completely paralyzed and unable to breathe without the assistance of a respirator. The Communicable Disease Center, an agency of the federal government, determined that Berkovitz had contracted polio from the vaccine.

Berkovitz, joined by his parents as guardians, subsequently filed suit against the United States in federal district court.[1] The complaint alleged that the United States was liable for his injuries under the FTCA because the Division of Biologic Standards (DBS), then a part of the National Institutes of Health, had acted wrongfully in licensing Lederle Laboratories to produce Orimune and because the Bureau of Biologics of the Food and Drug Administration (FDA) had acted wrongfully in approving release to the public of the particular lot of vaccine containing Berkovitz's dose. According to petitioners, these actions violated federal law and policy regarding the inspection and approval of polio vaccines.

The Government moved to dismiss the suit for lack of subject-matter jurisdiction on the ground that the agency actions fell within the discretionary function exception of the FTCA. * * * [T]he discretionary function exception will not apply when a federal statute, regulation, or policy specifically prescribes a course of action for an employee to follow. In this event, the employee has no rightful option but to adhere to the directive. And if the employee's conduct cannot appropriately be the product of judgment or choice, then there is no discretion in the conduct for the discretionary function exception to protect.

Moreover, assuming the challenged conduct involves an element of judgment, a court must determine whether that judgment is of the kind that the discretionary function exception was designed to shield. The basis for the discretionary function exception was Congress' desire to "prevent judicial 'second-guessing' of legislative and administrative decisions grounded in social, economic, and political policy through the medium of an action in tort." United States v. Varig Airlines, 467 U.S. 797, 814 (1984). The exception, properly construed, therefore protects only governmental actions and decisions based on considerations of public policy. See Dalehite v. United States, 346 U.S. 15, 36 (1953) ("Where there is room for policy judgment and decision there is discretion"). In sum, the discretionary function exception insulates the Government from liability if the action

---

1. Petitioners also sued Lederle Laboratories in a separate civil action. That suit was settled before the instant case was filed.

challenged in the case involves the permissible exercise of policy judgment.
* * *

In restating and clarifying the scope of the discretionary function
exception, we intend specifically to reject the Government's argument,
pressed both in this Court and the court of appeals, that the exception
precludes liability for any and all acts arising out of the regulatory
programs of federal agencies. That argument is rebutted first by the
language of the exception, which protects "discretionary" functions, rather
than "regulatory" functions. The significance of Congress' choice of language is supported by the legislative history. As this Court previously has
indicated, the relevant legislative materials demonstrate that the exception
was designed to cover not all acts of regulatory agencies and their employees, but only such acts as are "discretionary" in nature. * * *

Petitioners' suit raises two broad claims. First, petitioners assert that
the DBS violated a federal statute and accompanying regulations in issuing
a license to Lederle Laboratories to produce Orimune. Second, petitioners
argue that the Bureau of Biologics of the FDA violated federal regulations
and policy in approving the release of the particular lot of Orimune that
contained Kevan Berkovitz's dose. We examine each of these broad claims
by reviewing the applicable regulatory scheme and petitioners' specific
allegations of agency wrongdoing. Because the decision we review adjudicated a motion to dismiss, we accept all of the factual allegations in
petitioners' complaint as true and ask whether, in these circumstances,
dismissal of the complaint was appropriate.

Under federal law, a manufacturer must receive a product license prior
to marketing a brand of live oral polio vaccine. In order to become eligible
for such a license, a manufacturer must first make a sample of the vaccine
product. This process begins with the selection of an original virus strain.
The manufacturer grows a seed virus from this strain; the seed virus is
then used to produce monopools, portions of which are combined to form
the consumer-level product. Federal regulations set forth safety criteria for
the original strain, the seed virus, and the vaccine monopools. Under the
regulations, the manufacturer must conduct a variety of tests to measure
the safety of the product at each stage of the manufacturing process. Upon
completion of the manufacturing process and the required testing, the
manufacturer is required to submit an application for a product license to
the DBS. In addition to this application, the manufacturer must submit
data from the tests performed and a sample of the finished product. * * *
These statutory and regulatory provisions require the DBS, prior to issuing
a product license, to receive all data the manufacturer is required to
submit, to examine the product, and to make a determination that the
product complies with safety standards.

Petitioners' first allegation with regard to the licensing of Orimune is
that the DBS issued a product license without first receiving data that the
manufacturer must submit showing how the product, at the various stages
of the manufacturing process, matched up against regulatory safety standards. The discretionary function exception does not bar a cause of action

based on this allegation. The statute and regulations described above require, as a precondition to licensing, that the DBS receive certain test data from the manufacturer relating to the product's compliance with regulatory standards. The DBS has no discretion to issue a license without first receiving the required test data; to do so would violate a specific statutory and regulatory directive. Accordingly, to the extent that petitioners' licensing claim is based on a decision of the DBS to issue a license without having received the required test data, the discretionary function exception imposes no bar.

Petitioners' other allegation regarding the licensing of Orimune is difficult to describe with precision. Petitioners contend that the DBS licensed Orimune even though the vaccine did not comply with certain regulatory safety standards. This charge may be understood in any of three ways. First, petitioners may mean that the DBS licensed Orimune without first making a determination as to whether the vaccine complied with regulatory standards. Second, petitioners may intend to argue that the DBS specifically found that Orimune failed to comply with certain regulatory standards and nonetheless issued a license for the vaccine's manufacture. Third, petitioners may concede that the DBS made a determination of compliance, but allege that this determination was incorrect. Neither petitioners' complaint nor their briefs and argument before this Court make entirely clear their theory of the case.

If petitioners aver that the DBS licensed Orimune either without determining whether the vaccine complied with regulatory standards or after determining that the vaccine failed to comply, the discretionary function exception does not bar the claim. Under the scheme governing the DBS's regulation of polio vaccines, the DBS may not issue a license except upon an examination of the product and a determination that the product complies with all regulatory standards. The agency has no discretion to deviate from this mandated procedure. Petitioners' claim, if interpreted as alleging that the DBS licensed Orimune in the absence of a determination that the vaccine complied with regulatory standards, therefore does not challenge a discretionary function. Rather, the claim charges a failure on the part of the agency to perform its clear duty under federal law. When a suit charges an agency with failing to act in accord with a specific mandatory directive, the discretionary function exception does not apply.

If petitioners' claim is that the DBS made a determination that Orimune complied with regulatory standards, but that the determination was incorrect, the question of the applicability of the discretionary function exception requires a somewhat different analysis. In that event, the question turns on whether the manner and method of determining compliance with the safety standards at issue involve agency judgment of the kind protected by the discretionary function exception. Petitioners contend that the determination involves the application of objective scientific standards, whereas the Government asserts that the determination incorporates considerable "policy judgment." In making these assertions, the parties have framed the issue appropriately; application of the discretionary function exception to the claim that the determination of compliance was incorrect hinges on whether the agency officials making that determination permissibly exercise policy choice. The parties, however, have not addressed this question in detail, and they have given us no indication of the way in which the DBS interprets and applies the regulations setting forth the criteria for compliance. Given that these regulations are particularly abstruse, we hesitate to decide the question on the scanty record before us. We therefore leave it to the district court to decide, if petitioners choose to press this claim, whether agency officials appropriately exercise policy judgment in determining that a vaccine product complies with the relevant safety standards.

The regulatory scheme governing release of vaccine lots is distinct from that governing the issuance of licenses. The former set of regulations places an obligation on manufacturers to examine all vaccine lots prior to distribution to ensure that they comply with regulatory standards. These regulations, however, do not impose a corresponding duty on the Bureau of Biologics. Although the regulations empower the Bureau to examine any vaccine lot and prevent the distribution of a noncomplying lot, they do not require the Bureau to take such action in all cases. The regulations generally allow the Bureau to determine the appropriate manner in which to regulate the release of vaccine lots, rather than mandating certain kinds of agency action. The regulatory scheme governing the release of vaccine lots is substantially similar in this respect to the scheme discussed in *Varig*.

Given this regulatory context, the discretionary function exception bars any claims that challenge the Bureau's formulation of policy as to the appropriate way in which to regulate the release of vaccine lots. In addition, if the policies and programs formulated by the Bureau allow room for implementing officials to make independent policy judgments, the discretionary function exception protects the acts taken by those officials in the exercise of this discretion. The discretionary function exception, however, does not apply if the acts complained of do not involve the permissible exercise of policy discretion. Thus, if the Bureau's policy leaves no room for an official to exercise policy judgment in performing a given act, or if the act simply does not involve the exercise of such judgment, the discretionary function exception does not bar a claim that the act was negligent or wrongful. Cf. Indian Towing Co. v. United States, 350 U.S. 61, 69 (1955) (holding that a negligent failure to maintain a lighthouse in good working order subjected the Government to suit under the FTCA even though the initial decision to undertake and maintain lighthouse service was a discretionary policy judgment).

Viewed in light of these principles, petitioners' claim regarding the release of the vaccine lot from which Kevan Berkovitz received his dose survives the Government's motion to dismiss. Petitioners allege that, under the authority granted by the regulations, the Bureau of Biologics has adopted a policy of testing all vaccine lots for compliance with safety standards and preventing the distribution to the public of any lots that fail to comply. Petitioners further allege that notwithstanding this policy, which allegedly leaves no room for implementing officials to exercise independent policy judgment, employees of the Bureau knowingly approved the release of a lot that did not comply with safety standards. Thus, petitioners' complaint is directed at a governmental action that allegedly involved no policy discretion. Petitioners, of course, have not proved their factual allegations, but they are not required to do so on a motion to dismiss. If those allegations are correct—that is, if the Bureau's policy did not allow the official who took the challenged action to release a noncomplying lot on the basis of policy considerations—the discretionary function exception does not bar the claim. Because petitioners may yet show, on the basis of materials obtained in discovery or otherwise, that the conduct challenged here did not involve the permissible exercise of policy discretion, the invocation of the discretionary function exception to dismiss petitioners' lot release claim was improper. * * *

PROBLEM #8. *PASSING THE BUCK*

Recall from Chapter 3(B) that the FDA has begun to allow third parties accredited by the agency to conduct reviews of premarket notifications for certain medical devices. See 21 U.S.C. § 360m. Imagine that one such organization, PMNs-r-Us, receives a § 510(k) submission from a manufacturer of resin casting tape (used to immobilize broken bones). After a brief debate between the engineering and medical experts over lunch, the organization concludes that a minor difference in the device's technological characteristics as compared to the predicate device does not render the product any less safe or effective, so it transmits a report to the FDA recommending premarket clearance. As the agency does with all such reports under its third party review program, an administrative assistant quickly checks the report for any obvious gaps before issuing a letter to the manufacturer. It turns out that review organization, in its hasty review, misjudged the potential risks associated with the design, and a patient is severely burned when his arm is put in a cast. In addition to bringing a products liability claim against the manufacturer, can he sue either the FDA or PMNs-r-Us for negligence?

NOTES AND QUESTIONS

1. *The record of tort litigation against the FDA.* After *Berkovitz*, lower courts concluded that the DBS had unjustifiably failed to implement the applicable requirements. See In re Sabin Oral Polio Vaccine Prods. Liab. Litig., 984 F.2d 124, 125–28 (4th Cir.1993). Courts routinely hold, however, that the FDA's product approval decisions fall within the FTCA's discretionary functions exception. See Forsyth v. Eli Lilly & Co., 904 F.Supp. 1153 (D.Haw.1995); Bailey v. Eli Lilly Co., 607 F.Supp. 660 (M.D.Pa.1985); Gelley v. Astra Pharm. Prods., Inc., 466 F.Supp. 182 (D.Minn.), aff'd, 610 F.2d 558 (8th Cir.1979); Gray v. United States, 445 F.Supp. 337 (S.D.Tex. 1978); see also Fisher Bros. Sales, Inc. v. United States, 46 F.3d 279 (3d Cir.1995) (rejecting, on the basis of the discretionary function exception, an

FTCA claim against the FDA for the agency's refusal to allow the importation of fruit from Chile that was incorrectly suspected of chemical contamination).

2. *The swine flu vaccine fiasco.* In 1976, responding to fears of an emerging influenza pandemic, the federal government initiated a mass immunization campaign, but pharmaceutical manufacturers refused to supply vaccines without protection from tort liability. Congress responded by amending the FTCA to allow the filing of tort claims against the government instead. See Pub. L. No. 94–380, 90 Stat. 1113 (1976) (codified at 42 U.S.C. § 247b); see also Thomas E. Baynes, Jr., Liability for Vaccine Related Injuries: Public Health Considerations and Some Reflections on the Swine Flu Experience, 21 St. Louis U. L.J. 44 (1977). After a number of vaccine recipients reported developing Guillain–Barre syndrome, the immunization program ceased, and the tort litigation against the United States commenced. See, e.g., Novak v. United States, 865 F.2d 718 (6th Cir.1989); Petty v. United States, 740 F.2d 1428 (8th Cir.1984); Unthank v. United States, 732 F.2d 1517 (10th Cir.1984); see also Mills v. United States, 764 F.2d 373, 378 (5th Cir.1985) (holding that a warning of the risk of anaphylactic shock was adequate); Ducharme v. Merrill–National Labs., 574 F.2d 1307, 1309–10 (5th Cir.1978) (rejecting constitutional objections to granting tort immunity to vaccine manufacturers); Arnold W. Reitze, Jr., Federal Compensation for Vaccination Induced Injuries, 13 B.C. Envtl. Aff. L. Rev. 169, 170–88 (1986). The government has paid out more than $100 million in claims.

3. *Vaccinating soldiers.* As discussed in *Doe v. Sullivan*, 756 F.Supp. 12 (D.D.C.), aff'd, 938 F.2d 1370 (D.C.Cir.1991) (excerpted in Chapter 2(C)), the Department of Defense inoculated military personnel during Operation Desert Storm with experimental vaccines against anthrax and other bio-warfare agents. It has been suggested that these treatments contributed to the development of Gulf War Syndrome. Even if soldiers could trace some injury to the use of these vaccines, the government would be immune (so to speak) to any tort litigation under another FTCA exception applicable to military operations and personnel. See 28 U.S.C. § 2680(j); United States v. Stanley, 483 U.S. 669 (1987) (Army's secret LSD experiments). Furthermore, any private companies supplying products to the military according to government specifications (e.g., BioPort Corp., which took over the production of anthrax vaccine from the government after Desert Storm) generally would be protected from tort claims under the government contractor defense. See Boyle v. United Technologies Corp., 487 U.S. 500 (1988).

C.   CAUSATION DIFFICULTIES

Although products liability claims against sellers of prescription drugs and medical devices will raise issues of actual and proximate causation that arise in other types of tort litigation, two stand out as peculiar to this class of cases. First, as products that often cause long latency diseases rather than acute injuries, pharmaceuticals have influenced the way courts deal with cause-in-fact problems, in prescription drug as well as toxic tort litigation. Second, in dealing with mass tort claims against the manufacturers of diethylstilbestrol (DES), courts have created special rules for the identification of responsible parties, which for the most part have remained unique to drug product litigation.

1. Epidemiological Data

Daubert v. Merrell Dow Pharmaceuticals, Inc.

509 U.S. 579 (1993).

■ Blackmun, Justice:

In this case we are called upon to determine the standard for admitting expert scientific testimony in a federal trial. Petitioners Jason Daubert and Eric Schuller are minor children born with serious birth defects. They and their parents sued respondent in California state court, alleging that the birth defects had been caused by the mothers' ingestion of Bendectin, a prescription antinausea drug marketed by respondent. Respondent removed the suits to federal court on diversity grounds.

After extensive discovery, respondent moved for summary judgment, contending that Bendectin does not cause birth defects in humans and that petitioners would be unable to come forward with any admissible evidence that it does. In support of its motion, respondent submitted an affidavit of Steven H. Lamm, physician and epidemiologist, who is a well-credentialed expert on the risks from exposure to various chemical substances. Doctor Lamm stated that he had reviewed all the literature on Bendectin and human birth defects—more than 30 published studies involving over 130,-000 patients. No study had found Bendectin to be a human teratogen (i.e., a substance capable of causing malformations in fetuses). On the basis of this review, Doctor Lamm concluded that maternal use of Bendectin during the first trimester of pregnancy has not been shown to be a risk factor for human birth defects.

Petitioners did not (and do not) contest this characterization of the published record regarding Bendectin. Instead, they responded to respondent's motion with the testimony of eight experts of their own, each of whom also possessed impressive credentials. These experts had concluded that Bendectin can cause birth defects. Their conclusions were based upon "in vitro" (test tube) and "in vivo" (live) animal studies that found a link between Bendectin and malformations; pharmacological studies of the chemical structure of Bendectin that purported to show similarities between the structure of the drug and that of other substances known to cause birth defects; and the "reanalysis" of previously published epidemiological (human statistical) studies.

The district court granted respondent's motion for summary judgment. The court stated that scientific evidence is admissible only if the principle upon which it is based is " 'sufficiently established to have general acceptance in the field to which it belongs.' " The court concluded that petitioners' evidence did not meet this standard. Given the vast body of epidemiological data concerning Bendectin, the court held, expert opinion which is not based on epidemiological evidence is not admissible to establish causation. Thus, the animal-cell studies, live-animal studies, and chemical-structure analyses on which petitioners had relied could not raise by themselves a reasonably disputable jury issue regarding causation. Petitioners' epidemiological analyses, based as they were on recalculations of data in previously published studies that had found no causal link between the drug and birth defects, were ruled to be inadmissible because they had not been published or subjected to peer review.

The United States Court of Appeals for the Ninth Circuit affirmed. Citing *Frye v. United States*, 293 F. 1013, 1014 (D.C.App.1923), the court stated that expert opinion based on a scientific technique is inadmissible unless the technique is "generally accepted" as reliable in the relevant scientific community. * * * The court emphasized that other courts of appeals considering the risks of Bendectin had refused to admit reanalyses of epidemiological studies that had been neither published nor subjected to peer review. Those courts had found unpublished reanalyses "particularly problematic in light of the massive weight of the original published studies supporting [respondent's] position, all of which had undergone full scrutiny from the scientific community." Contending that reanalysis is generally accepted by the scientific community only when it is subjected to verification and scrutiny by others in the field, the court of appeals rejected petitioners' reanalyses as "unpublished, not subjected to the normal peer review process and generated solely for use in litigation." The court concluded that petitioners' evidence provided an insufficient foundation to allow admission of expert testimony that Bendectin caused their injuries and, accordingly, that petitioners could not satisfy their burden of proving causation at trial. * * *

In the 70 years since its formulation in the *Frye* case, the "general acceptance" test has been the dominant standard for determining the admissibility of novel scientific evidence at trial. * * * The merits of the *Frye* test have been much debated, and scholarship on its proper scope and application is legion. Petitioners' primary attack, however, is not on the content but on the continuing authority of the rule. They contend that the *Frye* test was superseded by the adoption of the Federal Rules of Evidence [in 1975]. We agree. * * *

Here there is a specific Rule that speaks to the contested issue. Rule 702, governing expert testimony, provides: "If scientific, technical, or other specialized knowledge will assist the trier of fact to understand the evidence or to determine a fact in issue, a witness qualified as an expert by knowledge, skill, experience, training, or education, may testify thereto in the form of an opinion or otherwise." Nothing in the text of this Rule establishes "general acceptance" as an absolute prerequisite to admissibility. Nor does respondent present any clear indication that Rule 702 or the Rules as a whole were intended to incorporate a "general acceptance" standard. The drafting history makes no mention of *Frye*, and a rigid "general acceptance" requirement would be at odds with the "liberal thrust" of the Federal Rules and their "general approach of relaxing the traditional barriers to 'opinion' testimony." Given the Rules' permissive backdrop and their inclusion of a specific rule on expert testimony that does not mention " 'general acceptance,' " the assertion that the Rules somehow assimilated *Frye* is unconvincing. *Frye* made "general acceptance" the exclusive test for admitting expert scientific testimony. That austere standard, absent from, and incompatible with, the Federal Rules of Evidence, should not be applied in federal trials.

That the *Frye* test was displaced by the Rules of Evidence does not mean, however, that the Rules themselves place no limits on the admissibility of purportedly scientific evidence. Nor is the trial judge disabled from screening such evidence. To the contrary, under the Rules the trial judge must ensure that any and all scientific testimony or evidence admitted is not only relevant, but reliable.

The primary locus of this obligation is Rule 702, which clearly contemplates some degree of regulation of the subjects and theories about which an expert may testify. * * * The subject of an expert's testimony must be "scientific ... knowledge." The adjective "scientific" implies a grounding in the methods and procedures of science. Similarly, the word "knowledge" connotes more than subjective belief or unsupported speculation. The term "applies to any body of known facts or to any body of ideas inferred from such facts or accepted as truths on good grounds." Webster's Third New Int'l Dictionary 1252 (1986). Of course, it would be unreasonable to conclude that the subject of scientific testimony must be "known" to a certainty; arguably, there are no certainties in science. But, in order to qualify as "scientific knowledge," an inference or assertion must be derived by the scientific method. Proposed testimony must be supported by appropriate validation—i.e., "good grounds," based on what is known. In short, the requirement that an expert's testimony pertain to "scientific knowledge" establishes a standard of evidentiary reliability.

Rule 702 further requires that the evidence or testimony "assist the trier of fact to understand the evidence or to determine a fact in issue." This condition goes primarily to relevance. "Expert testimony which does not relate to any issue in the case is not relevant and, ergo, non-helpful." The consideration has been aptly described by Judge Becker as one of "fit." "Fit" is not always obvious, and scientific validity for one purpose is not necessarily scientific validity for other, unrelated purposes. The study of the phases of the moon, for example, may provide valid scientific "knowledge" about whether a certain night was dark, and if darkness is a fact in issue, the knowledge will assist the trier of fact. However (absent creditable grounds supporting such a link), evidence that the moon was full on a certain night will not assist the trier of fact in determining whether an individual was unusually likely to have behaved irrationally on that night. Rule 702's "helpfulness" standard requires a valid scientific connection to the pertinent inquiry as a precondition to admissibility.

That these requirements are embodied in Rule 702 is not surprising. Unlike an ordinary witness, see Rule 701, an expert is permitted wide latitude to offer opinions, including those that are not based on firsthand knowledge or observation. Presumably, this relaxation of the usual requirement of firsthand knowledge * * * is premised on an assumption that the expert's opinion will have a reliable basis in the knowledge and experience of his discipline.

Faced with a proffer of expert scientific testimony, then, the trial judge must determine at the outset, pursuant to Rule 104(a), whether the expert is proposing to testify to (1) scientific knowledge that (2) will assist the trier of fact to understand or determine a fact in issue.[11] This entails a preliminary assessment of whether the reasoning or methodology underlying the testimony is scientifically valid and of whether that reasoning or methodology properly can be applied to the facts in issue. We are confident that federal judges possess the capacity to undertake this review. Many factors will bear on the inquiry, and we do not presume to set out a definitive checklist or test. But some general observations are appropriate.

Ordinarily, a key question to be answered in determining whether a theory or technique is scientific knowledge that will assist the trier of fact will be whether it can be (and has been) tested. "Scientific methodology today is based on generating hypotheses and testing them to see if they can be falsified; indeed, this methodology is what distinguishes science from other fields of human inquiry." * * *

Another pertinent consideration is whether the theory or technique has been subjected to peer review and publication. Publication (which is but one element of peer review) is not a sine qua non of admissibility; it does not necessarily correlate with reliability, and in some instances well-grounded but innovative theories will not have been published. Some propositions, moreover, are too particular, too new, or of too limited interest to be published. But submission to the scrutiny of the scientific community is a component of "good science," in part because it increases the likelihood that substantive flaws in methodology will be detected. The fact of publication (or lack thereof) in a peer reviewed journal thus will be a relevant, though not dispositive, consideration in assessing the scientific validity of a particular technique or methodology on which an opinion is premised. Additionally, in the case of a particular scientific technique, the court ordinarily should consider the known or potential rate of error, and the existence and maintenance of standards controlling the technique's operation.

---

11. Although the *Frye* decision itself focused exclusively on "novel" scientific techniques, we do not read the requirements of Rule 702 to apply specially or exclusively to unconventional evidence. Of course, well-established propositions are less likely to be challenged than those that are novel, and they are more handily defended. Indeed, theories that are so firmly established as to have attained the status of scientific law, such as the laws of thermodynamics, properly are subject to judicial notice under Federal Rule of Evidence 201.

Finally, "general acceptance" can yet have a bearing on the inquiry. A "reliability assessment does not require, although it does permit, explicit identification of a relevant scientific community and an express determination of a particular degree of acceptance within that community." Widespread acceptance can be an important factor in ruling particular evidence admissible, and "a known technique which has been able to attract only minimal support within the community" may properly be viewed with skepticism.

The inquiry envisioned by Rule 702 is, we emphasize, a flexible one. Its overarching subject is the scientific validity—and thus the evidentiary relevance and reliability—of the principles that underlie a proposed submission. The focus, of course, must be solely on principles and methodology, not on the conclusions that they generate.

Throughout, a judge assessing a proffer of expert scientific testimony under Rule 702 should also be mindful of other applicable rules. Rule 703 provides that expert opinions based on otherwise inadmissible hearsay are to be admitted only if the facts or data are "of a type reasonably relied upon by experts in the particular field in forming opinions or inferences upon the subject." Rule 706 allows the court at its discretion to procure the assistance of an expert of its own choosing. Finally, Rule 403 permits the exclusion of relevant evidence "if its probative value is substantially outweighed by the danger of unfair prejudice, confusion of the issues, or misleading the jury." Judge Weinstein has explained: "Expert evidence can be both powerful and quite misleading because of the difficulty in evaluating it. Because of this risk, the judge in weighing possible prejudice against probative force under Rule 403 of the present rules exercises more control over experts than over lay witnesses."

We conclude by briefly addressing what appear to be two underlying concerns of the parties and *amici* in this case. Respondent expresses apprehension that abandonment of "general acceptance" as the exclusive requirement for admission will result in a "free-for-all" in which befuddled juries are confounded by absurd and irrational pseudoscientific assertions. In this regard respondent seems to us to be overly pessimistic about the capabilities of the jury and of the adversary system generally. Vigorous cross-examination, presentation of contrary evidence, and careful instruction on the burden of proof are the traditional and appropriate means of attacking shaky but admissible evidence. Additionally, in the event the trial court concludes that the scintilla of evidence presented supporting a position is insufficient to allow a reasonable juror to conclude that the position more likely than not is true, the court remains free to direct a judgment and likewise to grant summary judgment. These conventional devices, rather than wholesale exclusion under an uncompromising "general acceptance" test, are the appropriate safeguards where the basis of scientific testimony meets the standards of Rule 702.

Petitioners and, to a greater extent, their *amici* exhibit a different concern. They suggest that recognition of a screening role for the judge that allows for the exclusion of "invalid" evidence will sanction a stifling and repressive scientific orthodoxy and will be inimical to the search for truth. It is true that open debate is an essential part of both legal and scientific analyses. Yet there are important differences between the quest for truth in the courtroom and the quest for truth in the laboratory. Scientific conclusions are subject to perpetual revision. Law, on the other hand, must resolve disputes finally and quickly. The scientific project is advanced by broad and wide-ranging consideration of a multitude of hypotheses, for those that are incorrect will eventually be shown to be so, and that in itself is an advance. Conjectures that are probably wrong are of little use, however, in the project of reaching a quick, final, and binding legal judgment—often of great consequence—about a particular set of events in the past. We recognize that, in practice, a gatekeeping role for the judge, no matter how flexible, inevitably on occasion will prevent the jury from learning of authentic insights and innovations. That, nevertheless, is the balance that is struck by rules of evidence designed not for the exhaustive search for cosmic understanding but for the particularized resolution of legal disputes. * * *

"General acceptance" is not a necessary precondition to the admissibility of scientific evidence under the Federal Rules of Evidence, but the Rules of Evidence—especially Rule 702—do assign to the trial judge the task of ensuring that an expert's testimony both rests on a reliable foundation and is relevant to the task at hand. Pertinent evidence based on scientifically valid principles will satisfy those demands. The inquiries of the district court and the court of appeals focused almost exclusively on "general acceptance," as gauged by publication and the decisions of other courts. Accordingly, the judgment of the court of appeals is vacated, and the case is remanded for further proceedings consistent with this opinion. It is so ordered.

■ REHNQUIST, CHIEF JUSTICE (concurring in part and dissenting in part):

* * * The Court concludes, correctly in my view, that the *Frye* rule did not survive the enactment of the Federal Rules of Evidence, * * * but the Court nonetheless proceeds to construe Rules 702 and 703 very much in the abstract, and then offers some "general observations." * * *

The various briefs filed in this case are markedly different from typical briefs, in that large parts of them do not deal with decided cases or statutory language—the sort of material we customarily interpret. Instead, they deal with definitions of scientific knowledge, scientific method, scientific validity, and peer review—in short, matters far afield from the expertise of judges. This is not to say that such materials are not useful or even necessary in deciding how Rule 703 should be applied; but it is to say that the unusual subject matter should cause us to proceed with great caution in deciding more than we have to, because our reach can so easily exceed our grasp. * * *

I defer to no one in my confidence in federal judges; but I am at a loss to know what is meant when it is said that the scientific status of a theory depends on its "falsifiability," and I suspect some of them will be, too. I do not doubt that Rule 702 confides to the judge some gatekeeping responsibility in deciding questions of the admissibility of proffered expert testimony. But I do not think it imposes on them either the obligation or the authority to become amateur scientists in order to perform that role. I think the Court would be far better advised in this case to decide only the questions presented, and to leave the further development of this important area of the law to future cases.

Daubert v. Merrell Dow Pharmaceuticals, Inc.

43 F.3d 1311 (9th Cir.1995).

■ KOZINSKI, CIRCUIT JUDGE:

* * * For the most part, we don't know how birth defects come about. We do know they occur in 2–3% of births, whether or not the expectant mother has taken Bendectin. Limb defects are even rarer, occurring in fewer than one birth out of every 1000. But scientists simply do not know how teratogens (chemicals known to cause limb reduction defects) do their damage: They cannot reconstruct the biological chain of events that leads from an expectant mother's ingestion of a teratogenic substance to the stunted development of a baby's limbs. Nor do they know what it is about teratogens that causes them to have this effect. No doubt, someday we will have this knowledge, and then we will be able to tell precisely whether and how Bendectin (or any other suspected teratogen) interferes with limb development; in the current state of scientific knowledge, however, we are ignorant.

Not knowing the mechanism whereby a particular agent causes a particular effect is not always fatal to a plaintiff's claim. Causation can be proved even when we don't know precisely *how* the damage occurred, if there is sufficiently compelling proof that the agent must have caused the damage *somehow*. One method of proving causation in these circumstances is to use statistical evidence. If 50 people who eat at a restaurant one evening come down with food poisoning during the night, we can infer that the restaurant's food probably contained something unwholesome, even if none of the dishes is available for analysis. This inference is based on the fact that, in our health-conscious society, it is highly unlikely that 50 people who have nothing in common except that they ate at the same restaurant would get food poisoning from independent sources.

It is by such means that plaintiffs here seek to establish that Bendectin is responsible for their injuries. They rely on the testimony of three groups of scientific experts. One group proposes to testify that there is a statistical link between the ingestion of Bendectin during pregnancy and limb reduction defects. These experts have not themselves conducted epidemiological (human statistical) studies on the effects of Bendectin; rather, they have reanalyzed studies published by other scientists, none of whom reported a statistical association between Bendectin and birth defects. Other experts proffered by plaintiffs propose to testify that Bendectin causes limb reduction defects in humans because it causes such defects in laboratory animals. A third group of experts sees a link between Bendectin and birth defects because Bendectin has a chemical structure that is similar to other drugs suspected of causing birth defects.

The opinions proffered by plaintiffs' experts do not, to understate the point, reflect the consensus within the scientific community. The FDA—an agency not known for its promiscuity in approving drugs—continues to approve Bendectin for use by pregnant women because "available data do not demonstrate an association between birth defects and Bendectin." Every published study here and abroad—and there have been many— concludes that Bendectin is not a teratogen. In fact, apart from the small but determined group of scientists testifying on behalf of the Bendectin plaintiffs in this and many other cases, there doesn't appear to be a single scientist who has concluded that Bendectin causes limb reduction defects. * * *

Federal judges ruling on the admissibility of expert scientific testimony face a far more complex and daunting task in a post-*Daubert* world than before. * * * The first prong of *Daubert* puts federal judges in an uncomfortable position. The question of admissibility only arises if it is first established that the individuals whose testimony is being proffered are experts in a particular scientific field; here, for example, the Supreme Court waxed eloquent on the impressive qualifications of plaintiffs' experts. Yet something doesn't become "scientific knowledge" just because it's uttered by a scientist; nor can an expert's self-serving assertion that his conclusions were "derived by the scientific method" be deemed conclusive * * * * As we read the Supreme Court's teaching in *Daubert*, therefore, though we are largely untrained in science and certainly no match for any of the witnesses whose testimony we are reviewing, it is our responsibility to determine whether those experts' proposed testimony amounts to "scientific knowledge," constitutes "good science," and was "derived by the scientific method."

The task before us is more daunting still when the dispute concerns matters at the very cutting edge of scientific research, where fact meets theory and certainty dissolves into probability. As the record in this case illustrates, scientists often have vigorous and sincere disagreements as to what research methodology is proper, what should be accepted as sufficient proof for the existence of a "fact," and whether information derived by a particular method can tell us anything useful about the subject under study.

Our responsibility, then, unless we badly misread the Supreme Court's opinion, is to resolve disputes among respected, well-credentialed scientists about matters squarely within their expertise, in areas where there is no scientific consensus as to what is and what is not "good science," and occasionally to reject such expert testimony because it was not "derived by the scientific method." Mindful of our position in the hierarchy of the federal judiciary, we take a deep breath and proceed with this heady task. * * *

Our task, then, is to analyze not what the experts say, but what basis they have for saying it. Which raises the question: How do we figure out whether scientists have derived their findings through the scientific method or whether their testimony is based on scientifically valid principles? * * * [T]he Court did list several factors federal judges can consider in determining whether to admit expert scientific testimony under Fed. R. Evid. 702: whether the theory or technique employed by the expert is generally accepted in the scientific community; whether it's been subjected to peer review and publication; whether it can be and has been tested; and whether the known or potential rate of error is acceptable. We read these factors as illustrative rather than exhaustive; similarly, we do not deem each of them to be equally applicable (or applicable at all) in every case. Rather, we read the Supreme Court as instructing us to determine whether the analysis undergirding the experts' testimony falls within the range of accepted standards governing how scientists conduct their research and reach their conclusions.

One very significant fact to be considered is whether the experts are proposing to testify about matters growing naturally and directly out of research they have conducted independent of the litigation, or whether they have developed their opinions expressly for purposes of testifying. That an expert testifies for money does not necessarily cast doubt on the reliability of his testimony, as few experts appear in court merely as an eleemosynary gesture. But in determining whether proposed expert testimony amounts to good science, we may not ignore the fact that a scientist's normal workplace is the lab or the field, not the courtroom or the lawyer's office.

That an expert testifies based on research he has conducted independent of the litigation provides important, objective proof that the research comports with the dictates of good science. For one thing, experts whose findings flow from existing research are less likely to have been biased toward a particular conclusion by the promise of remuneration; when an expert prepares reports and findings before being hired as a witness, that record will limit the degree to which he can tailor his testimony to serve a party's interests. Then, too, independent research carries its own indicia of reliability, as it is conducted, so to speak, in the usual course of business and must normally satisfy a variety of standards to attract funding and institutional support. Finally, there is usually a limited number of scientists actively conducting research on the very subject that is germane to a particular case, which provides a natural constraint on parties' ability to shop for experts who will come to the desired conclusion. That the testimony proffered by an expert is based directly on legitimate, preexisting research unrelated to the litigation provides the most persuasive basis for concluding that the opinions he expresses were "derived by the scientific method."

We have examined carefully the affidavits proffered by plaintiffs' experts, as well as the testimony from prior trials that plaintiffs have introduced in support of that testimony, and find that none of the experts based his testimony on preexisting or independent research. While plaintiffs' scientists are all experts in their respective fields, none claims to have studied the effect of Bendectin on limb reduction defects before being hired to testify in this or related cases.

If the proffered expert testimony is not based on independent research, the party proffering it must come forward with other objective, verifiable evidence that the testimony is based on "scientifically valid principles." One means of showing this is by proof that the research and analysis supporting the proffered conclusions have been subjected to normal scientific scrutiny through peer review and publication.

Peer review and publication do not, of course, guarantee that the conclusions reached are correct; much published scientific research is greeted with intense skepticism and is not borne out by further research. But the test under *Daubert* is not the correctness of the expert's conclusions but the soundness of his methodology. That the research is accepted for publication in a reputable scientific journal after being subjected to the usual rigors of peer review is a significant indication that it is taken seriously by other scientists, i.e., that it meets at least the minimal criteria of good science. If nothing else, peer review and publication "increase the likelihood that substantive flaws in methodology will be detected."

Bendectin litigation has been pending in the courts for over a decade, yet the only review the plaintiffs' experts' work has received has been by judges and juries, and the only place their theories and studies have been published is in the pages of federal and state reporters. None of the plaintiffs' experts has published his work on Bendectin in a scientific journal or solicited formal review by his colleagues. Despite the many years the controversy has been brewing, no one in the scientific community—except defendant's experts—has deemed these studies worthy of verification, refutation or even comment. It's as if there were a tacit understanding within the scientific community that what's going on here is not science at all, but litigation.

Establishing that an expert's proffered testimony grows out of pre-litigation research or that the expert's research has been subjected to peer review are the two principal ways the proponent of expert testimony can show that the evidence satisfies the first prong of Rule 702. Where such evidence is unavailable, the proponent of expert scientific testimony may attempt to satisfy its burden through the testimony of its own experts. For such a showing to be sufficient, the experts must explain precisely how they went about reaching their conclusions and point to some objective source—a learned treatise, the policy statement of a professional association, a published article in a reputable scientific journal or the like—to show that they have followed the scientific method, as it is practiced by (at least) a recognized minority of scientists in their field.

Plaintiffs have made no such showing. As noted above, plaintiffs rely entirely on the experts' unadorned assertions that the methodology they employed comports with standard scientific procedures. In support of these assertions, plaintiffs offer only the trial and deposition testimony of these experts in other cases. While these materials indicate that plaintiffs' experts have relied on animal studies, chemical structure analyses and epidemiological data, they neither explain the methodology the experts followed to reach their conclusions nor point to any external source to validate that methodology. We've been presented with only the experts' qualifications, their conclusions and their assurances of reliability. Under *Daubert*, that's not enough. * * *

In elucidating the second requirement of Rule 702, *Daubert* stressed the importance of the "fit" between the testimony and an issue in the case * * * * Here, the pertinent inquiry is causation. In assessing whether the proffered expert testimony "will assist the trier of fact" in resolving this issue, we must look to the governing substantive standard, which in this case is supplied by California tort law.

Plaintiffs do not attempt to show causation directly; instead, they rely on experts who present circumstantial proof of causation. Plaintiffs' experts testify that Bendectin is a teratogen because it causes birth defects when it is tested on animals, because it is similar in chemical structure to other suspected teratogens, and because statistical studies show that Bendectin use increases the risk of birth defects. Modern tort law permits such proof, but plaintiffs must nevertheless carry their traditional burden; they must prove that their injuries were the result of the accused cause and not some independent factor. In the case of birth defects, carrying this burden is made more difficult because we know that some defects—including limb reduction defects—occur even when expectant mothers do not take Bendectin, and that most birth defects occur for no known reason.

California tort law requires plaintiffs to show not merely that Bendectin increased the likelihood of injury, but that it more likely than not caused their injuries. In terms of statistical proof, this means that plaintiffs must establish not just that their mothers' ingestion of Bendectin increased somewhat the likelihood of birth defects, but that it more than doubled it— only then can it be said that Bendectin is more likely than not the source of their injury. Because the background rate of limb reduction defects is one per thousand births, plaintiffs must show that among children of mothers who took Bendectin the incidence of such defects was more than two per thousand.[13]

None of plaintiffs' epidemiological experts claims that ingestion of Bendectin during pregnancy more than doubles the risk of birth defects. To evaluate the relationship between Bendectin and limb reduction defects, an epidemiologist would take a sample of the population and compare the frequency of birth defects in children whose mothers took Bendectin with the frequency of defects in children whose mothers did not. The ratio

---

13. No doubt, there will be unjust results under this substantive standard. If a drug increases the likelihood of birth defects, but doesn't more than double it, some plaintiffs whose injuries are attributable to the drug will be unable to recover. There is a converse unfairness under a regime that allows recovery to everyone that may have been affected by the drug. Under this regime, all potential plaintiffs are entitled to recover, even though most will not have suffered an injury that can be attributed to the drug. One can conclude from this that unfairness is inevitable when our tools for detecting causation are imperfect and we must rely on probabilities rather than more direct proof. * * *

derived from this comparison would be an estimate of the "relative risk" associated with Bendectin. For an epidemiological study to show causation under a preponderance standard, * * * the study must show that children whose mothers took Bendectin are more than twice as likely to develop limb reduction birth defects as children whose mothers did not.[16] While plaintiffs' epidemiologists make vague assertions that there is a statistically significant relationship between Bendectin and birth defects, none states that the relative risk is greater than two. These studies thus would not be helpful, and indeed would only serve to confuse the jury, if offered to prove rather than refute causation. A relative risk of less than two may suggest teratogenicity, but it actually tends to *dis*prove legal causation, as it shows that Bendectin does not double the likelihood of birth defects. * * *

PROBLEM #9.   *AN EXERCISE IN EPIDEMIOLOGY*

You are the trial judge in a products liability case against the manufacturer of a prescription drug ("Rx") used during pregnancy. The plaintiff's mother ingested the product, and plaintiff was born with serious birth defects. The manufacturer's warning to physicians simply advised that epidemiological studies found an increase in birth defects but that it was not statistically significant ($p < 0.05$). Plaintiff brings strict products liability claims, alleging design defect and failure to warn. The manufacturer moves for summary judgment, arguing (1) that the design of Rx could not be deemed defective because, in risk-utility terms, there was no risk at all; (2) that its warning accurately conveyed all that was known about the supposed risks; and (3) that, even if Rx was "defective" in terms of its design or warnings, plaintiff has failed to prove that Rx actually caused his injuries. Experts for the manufacturer and the plaintiff, respectively, introduced the following studies to address the central question of causation:

- Epidemiological study (association between Rx and birth defects):

	No Rx	Rx
Pregnancies:	10,000	1,000
Birth defects:	100	12
Incidence:	1.0%	1.2%

Relative risk: 1.2

16. A statistical study showing a relative risk of less than two could be combined with other evidence to show it is more likely than not that the accused cause is responsible for a particular plaintiff's injury. For example, a statistical study may show that a particular type of birth defect is associated with some unknown causes, as well as two known potential causes—e.g., smoking and drinking. If a study shows that the relative risk of injury for those who smoke is 1.5 as compared to the general population, while it is 1.8 for those who drink, a plaintiff who does not drink might be able to reanalyze the data to show that the study of smoking did not account for the effect of drinking on the incidence of birth defects in the general population. By making the appropriate comparison—between non-drinkers who smoke and non-drinkers who do not smoke—the teetotaller plaintiff might be able to show that the relative risk of smoking for her is greater than two. * * *

- An unpublished "reanalysis" of the raw data by the plaintiff's expert (she has excluded 1,000 reports from the data set for the non-Rx population and 500 reports from the data set for the Rx population):

	No Rx	Rx
Pregnancies:	9,000	500
Birth defects:	45	6
Incidence:	0.5%	1.2%

Relative risk: 2.4

How do you rule (we have not yet covered the questions raised by (1) and (2), so skip them for now)?

NOTES AND QUESTIONS

1. *It's not over until the fat lady sings*. The body of scientific information relevant to causation issues represents a moving target for courts. In some instances, a litigant will argue on appeal that newly discovered information justifies granting a motion for a new trial, but courts usually decline:

> Although science is a constantly evolving process, the law depends upon a high level of certainty once an outcome has been determined. A trial can be no more than a resolution of an immediate dispute on the basis of present knowledge; its outcome must turn upon the teachings of science as understood at the time of trial as best can be discerned through the presentations of the parties. Where scientific facts are at issue, it is not unexpected, given the nature of the process, that the passage of time will bring forth further scientific data and inquiry relating to the ultimate scientific fact at issue. To reopen the trial's determination of scientific truth, however, runs squarely into the fundamental principle of certainty.

Merrell Dow Pharms., Inc. v. Oxendine, 649 A.2d 825, 831 (D.C.1994). Even so, the court remanded this Bendectin case, and, more than a decade after the original judgment for the plaintiff, the trial court granted extraordinary relief from the judgment based on newly acquired scientific evidence. See Oxendine v. Merrell Dow Pharms., Inc., 1996 WL 680992, *31–35 (D.C.Super.Ct.1996).

2. *A postscript on the Bendectin saga*. As one commentator recently noted, "the wave of Bendectin litigation ultimately cost manufacturers so much that they stopped marketing the product. Although no jury verdict that

Bendectin causes birth defects has ever been upheld on appeal, plaintiffs have received a favorable verdict in approximately 36% of the cases that have gone to trial. The risk of juror error coupled with high litigation costs led manufacturers to withdraw Bendectin from the market notwithstanding the continuing assessment by the FDA and the scientific community that Bendectin provides benefits exceeding its risks." W. Kip Viscusi, Corporate Risk Analysis: A Reckless Act?, 52 Stan. L. Rev. 547, 584 (2000); see also Michael Green, Bendectin and Birth Defects (1996); Joseph Sanders, The Bendectin Litigation: A Case Study in the Life Cycle of Mass Torts, 43 Hastings L.J. 301 (1992). In one verdict reversed on appeal, the jury had awarded the plaintiff almost $34 million. See Merrell Dow Pharms., Inc. v. Havner, 953 S.W.2d 706 (Tex.1997). A generic version of Bendectin may soon be introduced in the United States market in part because the withdrawal of the drug left an unmet therapeutic need for pregnant women with severe nausea resulting in weight loss and dehydration that sometimes necessitated hospitalization. See Gina Kolata, Controversial Drug Makes a Comeback, N.Y. Times, Sept. 26, 2000, at F1.

3. *Extension of* Daubert*'s admissibility formula.* The United States Supreme Court has continued expanding the "gatekeeping" role of trial judges in ruling on the admissibility of expert testimony. See, e.g., Kumho Tire Co. v. Carmichael, 526 U.S. 137, 147–57 (1999) (applying *Daubert* to testimony from an engineer that was based on his experience and observation rather than scientific research); General Elec. Co. v. Joiner, 522 U.S. 136, 142–43 (1997) (holding that an appellate court should review a trial judge's decision to exclude expert scientific testimony with a deferential abuse of discretion standard). A number of states have adopted *Daubert.* See, e.g., Clement v. Griffin, 634 So.2d 412 (La.App.1994); Commonwealth v. Lanigan, 641 N.E.2d 1342 (Mass.1994); E.I. du Pont de Nemours & Co. v. Robinson, 923 S.W.2d 549 (Tex.1995). Several other states have, however, rejected it. See, e.g., People v. Leahy, 882 P.2d 321 (Cal.1994); Dow Chem. Co. v. Mahlum, 970 P.2d 98 (Nev.1998) (affirming plaintiff's verdict in a breast implant case); People v. Wesley, 633 N.E.2d 451 (N.Y.1994); see also Heather G. Hamilton, Note, The Movement from Frye to Daubert: Where Do the States Stand?, 38 Jurimetrics J. 201 (1998).

4. Daubert*'s application in medical products liability litigation.* Not surprisingly, *Daubert* has come to play quite a prominent role in the resolution of products liability lawsuits against pharmaceutical and medical device manufacturers. See Allison v. McGhan Med. Corp., 184 F.3d 1300, 1314 (11th Cir.1999) ("[Plaintiff] does not explain why the results of these animal studies should trump more than twenty controlled epidemiological studies of [silicone gel] breast implants in humans which have found no valid increased risk of autoimmune disease."); Raynor v. Merrell Pharms. Inc., 104 F.3d 1371, 1375–76 (D.C.Cir.1997) (holding that the plaintiff's experts could not testify that Bendectin caused birth defects on the basis of animal and chemical studies in the face of the overwhelming epidemiological evidence finding no effect); Lust v. Merrell Dow Pharms., Inc., 89 F.3d 594, 596–98 (9th Cir.1996) (affirming the exclusion of plaintiff's expert testimony that a fertility drug caused his birth defects); Rosen v. Ciba–

Geigy Corp., 78 F.3d 316, 318 (7th Cir.1996) (affirming the exclusion of plaintiff's expert testimony that short-term use of a nicotine patch caused a heart attack); Porter v. Whitehall Labs., Inc., 9 F.3d 607, 614–15 (7th Cir.1993) (excluding plaintiff's expert testimony, based on nothing more than temporal proximity, that a 30 day prescription of ibuprofen triggered renal failure); Wooley v. Smith & Nephew Richards, Inc., 67 F.Supp.2d 703 (S.D.Tex.1999) (holding a mere temporal association between implant and injury insufficient).

5. *Impaneling court-appointed scientific experts.* Two of the federal judges who were assigned to different class action lawsuits against the manufacturers of silicone-gel breast implants decided to impanel independent experts, as authorized by Federal Rule of Evidence 706, to evaluate the proffered testimony on whether silicone might trigger auto-immune disorders such as scleroderma and lupus. In both instances, the panels reviewed the available data and concluded that no causal association existed. See Hall v. Baxter Healthcare, 947 F.Supp. 1387, 1392–94 (D.Or.1996); Barbara S. Hulka et al., Experience of a Scientific Panel Formed to Advise the Federal Judiciary on Silicone Breast Implants, 342 New Eng. J. Med. 812 (2000) (providing insights by several members of one such panel); Laurens Walker & John Monahan, Scientific Authority: The Breast Implant Litigation and Beyond, 86 Va. L. Rev. 801 (2000); Thomas M. Burton, Implant Makers Get a Boost from Report, Wall St. J., Dec. 2, 1998, at B1 (describing the conclusions of a panel appointed by Judge Sam Pointer of the U.S. District Court for the Northern District of Alabama); see also Troyen A. Brennan, Helping Courts with Toxic Torts: Some Proposals Regarding Alternative Methods for Presenting and Assessing Scientific Evidence in Common Law Courts, 51 U. Pitt. L. Rev. 1, 4–19, 62–71 (1989) (discussing the use of court-appointed experts and scientific panels in litigation); Howard M. Erichson, Mass Tort Litigation and Inquisitorial Justice, 87 Geo. L.J. 1983, 1986–95 (1999) (urging expanded use of court-appointed experts); Lawrence S. Pinsky, Comment, The Use of Scientific Peer Review and Colloquia to Assist Judges in the Admissibility Gatekeeping Mandated by Daubert, 34 Hous. L. Rev. 527, 554–78 (1997) (recommending similar approaches).

6. *Requiring a doubling of the risk.* Although hardly uncontroversial, a number of courts have followed the Ninth Circuit's approach in *Daubert* of requiring epidemiological evidence of a relative risk greater than 2.0. See Bartley v. Euclid, Inc., 158 F.3d 261, 273 (5th Cir.1998); In re Breast Implant Litig., 11 F.Supp.2d 1217, 1225–28 (D.Colo.1998); see also David L. Faigman et al., How Good Is Good Enough? Expert Evidence Under Daubert and Kumho, 50 Case W. Res. L. Rev. 645, 659–67 (2000); Lucinda M. Finley, Guarding the Gate to the Courthouse: How Trial Judges Are Using Their Evidentiary Screening Role to Remake Tort Causation Rules, 49 DePaul L. Rev. 335, 347–76 (1999); Joseph Sanders, From Science to Evidence: The Testimony on Causation in the Bendectin Cases, 46 Stan. L. Rev. 1 (1993). In the absence of epidemiological studies, courts more readily accept other types of evidence. See Kennedy v. Collagen Corp., 161 F.3d 1226, 1229–30 (9th Cir.1998); Ambrosini v. Labarraque, 101 F.3d 129, 135–

41 (D.C.Cir.1996) (reversing the exclusion of plaintiff's expert testimony that Depo–Provera caused birth defects where the epidemiological evidence was unclear); Graham v. Playtex Prods., Inc., 993 F.Supp. 127, 130–34 (N.D.N.Y.1998).

7. *Differential diagnosis.* A plaintiff may attempt to prove specific causation by means other than epidemiological evidence. In one case, the court explained that the plaintiff's "treating physicians based their conclusions on the microscopic appearance of his liver, the Tylenol found in his blood upon his admission to the hospital, the history of several days of Tylenol use after regular alcohol consumption, and the lack of evidence of a viral or any other cause of liver failure. [His experts on liver disease] relied upon a similar methodology; history, examination, lab and pathology data, and study of the peer-reviewed literature." Benedi v. McNeil–P.P.C., Inc., 66 F.3d 1378, 1384 (4th Cir.1995); see also Westberry v. Gislaved Gummi A.B., 178 F.3d 257 (4th Cir.1999) (holding that *Daubert* does not apply to medical diagnosis); Heller v. Shaw Indus., Inc., 167 F.3d 146, 155–58 (3d Cir.1999) (same); Globetti v. Sandoz Pharm. Corp., 111 F.Supp.2d 1174 (N.D.Ala. 2000); Vassallo v. Baxter Healthcare Corp., 696 N.E.2d 909, 917–18 (Mass. 1998) (allowing plaintiff's expert to link atypical autoimmune disease to silicone-gel breast implants notwithstanding the absence of supporting epidemiological data); Jeff L. Lewin, The Genesis and Evolution of Legal Uncertainty About "Reasonable Medical Certainty," 57 Md. L. Rev. 380 (1998). Other courts have applied *Daubert* to diagnoses. See Moore v. Ashland Chem., Inc., 151 F.3d 269, 275 n.7 (5th Cir.1998) (en banc); Siharath v. Sandoz Pharm. Corp., 131 F.Supp.2d 1347 (N.D.Ga.2001); see also In re Breast Implant Litig., 11 F.Supp.2d 1217, 1230 (D.Colo.1998) ("[T]he cause of many diseases remains unknown; therefore, a clinician who suspects that a substance causes a disease in some patients very well might conclude that the substance caused the disease in the plaintiff simply because the clinician has no other explanation."). See generally Jean M. Eggen, Clinical Medical Evidence of Causation in Toxic Tort Cases: Into the Crucible of Daubert, 38 Hous. L. Rev. 369 (2001); Jack E. Karns, Establishing the Standard for a Physician's Patient Diagnosis Using Scientific Evidence: Dealing with the Split of Authority Amongst the Circuit Courts of Appeal, 15 BYU J. Pub. L. 1 (2000); Gary Sloboda, Differential Diagnosis or Distortion?, 35 U.S.F. L. Rev. 301 (2001).

Effective December 1, 2000, an amendment to Rule 702 inserted at the end the following new text: ", if (1) the testimony is based upon sufficient facts or data, (2) the testimony is the product of reliable principles and methods, and (3) the witness has applied the principles and methods reliably to the facts of the case." 192 F.R.D. 340, 418 (2000). The accompanying committee note sent mixed signals about differential diagnosis, see id. at 419–21, but one scholar thought that it "place[d] its imprimatur on opinions in medical cases indicating that another factor is whether the expert has conducted a relatively thorough differential diagnosis." Edward J. Imwinkelried, Expert Witness, Nat'l L.J., Nov. 20, 2000, at A18; see also Federal Judicial Center, Reference Manual on Scientific Evidence 442–46 (2d ed. 2000). Of course, diagnoses of persons other than the plaintiff, which may be published as case reports in the medical literature, only provide anecdotal evidence of causation. See Glastetter v. Novartis Pharms. Corp., 107 F.Supp.2d 1015, 1030–31 (E.D.Mo.2000), aff'd, 252 F.3d 986 (8th Cir.2001); Nelson v. American Home Prods. Corp., 92 F.Supp.2d 954, 969 (W.D.Mo.2000); Willert v. Ortho Pharm. Corp., 995 F.Supp. 979, 981 (D.Minn.1998); Kelley v. American Heyer–Schulte Corp., 957 F.Supp. 873, 881–84 (W.D.Tex.1997); Haggerty v. Upjohn Co., 950 F.Supp. 1160, 1165 (S.D.Fla.1996). Treating physicians may provide expert testimony that helps plaintiffs exclude likely alternative causes of their condition. See Glaser v. Thompson Med. Co., 32 F.3d 969, 978 (6th Cir.1994); see also Baker v. Dalkon Shield Claimants Trust, 156 F.3d 248, 251–53 (1st Cir. 1998) (reversing the exclusion of defendant's expert who suggested alternative causes based on a differential diagnosis); Zuchowicz v. United States, 140 F.3d 381, 385–87 (2d Cir.1998) (allowing physician to relate plaintiff's rare condition to the defendant's drug absent any direct research on the issue); Kuhn v. Sandoz, 14 P.3d 1170 (Kan.2000) (same under *Frye* standard); cf. Wheat v. Pfizer, Inc., 31 F.3d 340, 343 (5th Cir.1994) (agreeing that plaintiff's hepatitis probably resulted from something other than the drug).

8. *Further commentary.* See Kenneth R. Foster & Peter W. Huber, Judging Science: Scientific Knowledge and the Federal Courts (1997); Daniel J. Capra, The Daubert Puzzle, 32 Ga. L. Rev. 699 (1998); Jean Macchiaroli Eggen, Toxic Torts, Causation, and Scientific Evidence After Daubert, 55 U. Pitt. L. Rev. 889, 895–903 (1994); Joseph Sanders, Scientific Validity, Admissibility, and Mass Torts After Daubert, 78 Minn. L. Rev. 1387, 1406–17 (1994); Effie J. Chan, Note, The "Brave New World" of Daubert: True Peer Review, Editorial Peer Review, and Scientific Validity, 70 N.Y.U. L. Rev. 100, 126–34 (1995); Symposium, Scientific Evidence After the Death of Frye, 15 Cardozo L. Rev. 1745 (1994).

Moran v. Pfizer, Inc.

160 F.Supp.2d 508 (S.D.N.Y.2001).

■ PAULEY, DISTRICT JUDGE:

* * * Plaintiff is a 53 year-old resident of New Jersey. While he claims that he does not suffer from erectile dysfunction, in 1998 he sought to enhance his virility. To that end, plaintiff obtained a prescription for Viagra from a doctor in Summit, New Jersey. Viagra is a drug manufactured by Pfizer, a New York corporation with its principal place of business in New York. Plaintiff filled his prescription for Viagra at a pharmacy in New Jersey.

On July 1, 1998, in preparation for a romantic encounter with a woman, plaintiff ingested Viagra. Around 1:00 the next morning, after the tryst, plaintiff left in his car. While stopped at a traffic light, plaintiff saw "blue haze and a blue spot" before his eyes, which looked like a camera flash. Shortly thereafter, plaintiff got into a car accident in Plainfield, New Jersey. Plaintiff, who was alone in his car at the time, struck two parked cars several hundred feet apart and came to rest against a tree on the opposite side of the road. There were no eyewitnesses to the accident and plaintiff does not remember how it occurred. The last thing plaintiff remembers is reaching for a cassette tape in the car radio and seeing "blue lightning streaks" shooting from his fingers to the cassette.

As a result of the crash, plaintiff sustained cuts and bruises on his body and his car was damaged. Plaintiff argues that defendant is liable for the car crash because Viagra caused him to see the blue streaks emanate from his fingers. Defendant argues that there is no evidence that Viagra causes blue lightning streaks, but even if Viagra could cause lightening streaks, plaintiff cannot show that the streaks were the probable cause of the accident. * * *

Laypeople could not be expected to have sufficient knowledge or experience about whether Viagra can cause visual disturbances, and plaintiff has not offered any expert testimony to support his claim that Viagra caused him to see lightning streaks. Plaintiff argues that he does not need expert testimony because it is undisputed Viagra can cause vision to be tinted blue-green in 3% of patients. However, plaintiff does not allege that his vision was tinted blue-green, and evidence that Viagra can cause a patient's vision to be tinted is not sufficient to demonstrate that it can cause a patient to see blue lightning streaks.

Plaintiff also argues, based on an online article, that the Federal Aviation Administration recommends that pilots avoid taking Viagra within six hours of flying because Viagra can cause a patient to have difficulty distinguishing between blue and green, colors that are used extensively in airport lighting and cockpit instrumentation. Even if the online article was admissible, which it is not, plaintiff does not claim that he was unable to distinguish between blue and green. Moreover, contrary to plaintiff's theory of causation, the FDA concluded that "vision abnormalities . . . appear to be nuisances of short duration, sufficient to be dose-limiting, but they are not safety concerns. In particular, the vision disturbance has been fairly well characterized, and it does not appear to pose a risk to men operating motor vehicles or other heavy equipment."

Plaintiff's failure to offer any admissible evidence demonstrating that Viagra can cause the product defect he complains of is fatal to his claims for defective product, failure to warn and negligence. Further, even if plaintiff could demonstrate that Viagra caused him to see blue lightning streaks, he cannot establish that they were the proximate cause of the accident. While plaintiff does not have to establish that Viagra was the sole cause of the accident, he must demonstrate that it was "a substantial factor in causing the harm alleged." Here, plaintiff confesses that he does not remember anything about the accident. Moreover, plaintiff admits that the last thing he remembers is looking at the cassette deck instead of looking at the road. He told the first person who arrived at the accident scene—a police officer—that he was very tired, and there is some dispute as to whether plaintiff told his insurance company that the accident was caused by his arm jamming in the seatbelt. Plaintiff cannot show that seeing the blue lightning streaks more likely caused the accident than any of the other possible causes.

Pure speculation is not a sufficient ground for a jury to find defendant liable. * * * Because plaintiff cannot demonstrate that Viagra causes the defect of which plaintiff complains or that the alleged defect proximately caused plaintiff's car accident, defendant's motion for summary judgment is granted. * * *

NOTES AND QUESTIONS

1. *Causal chains.* One type of recurring fact pattern involving pharmaceuticals may present proximate causation puzzles. A patient taking a drug product may inflict an injury on a third party who then sues the manufacturer. For instance, a drug may cause sedation in the user who then drives an automobile and causes an accident. Cf. Joy v. Eastern Maine Med. Ctr., 529 A.2d 1364 (Me.1987) (addressing the duty of health care providers to warn in such cases). Or, as happened in *Grundberg* (Halcion), a psychoactive drug allegedly causes the patient to kill someone else. See Potter v. Eli Lilly & Co., 926 S.W.2d 449 (Ky.1996) (Prozac); Emily Heller, Drug Maker Hit with $8M Verdict: Jury Finds Maker of Paxil Responsible for Multiple Shooting Deaths, Nat'l L.J., June 25, 2001, at A5. In such cases, it may be difficult to differentiate between therapeutic failures (e.g., a subpotent antidepressant) and side effects as the trigger for the patient's criminal behavior. Chapter 7 will revisit proximate causation issues in connection with claims based on inadequate warnings.

2. MARKET SHARE LIABILITY

Even when questions of defect and actual causation are straightforward, for instance where the manufacture failed to warn of a known risk of illness that is strongly associated with a particular product (also known as a "signature" disease), the plaintiff still must identify who sold the product.

Hymowitz v. Eli Lilly & Co.

539 N.E.2d 1069 (N.Y.1989).

■ WACHTLER, CHIEF JUDGE:

Plaintiffs in these appeals allege that they were injured by the drug diethylstilbestrol (DES) ingested by their mothers during pregnancy. They seek relief against defendant DES manufacturers. While not class actions, these cases are representative of nearly 500 similar actions pending in the courts in this State; the rules articulated by the court here, therefore, must do justice and be administratively feasible in the context of this mass litigation. With this in mind, we now resolve the issue twice expressly left open by this court, and adopt a market share theory, using a national market, for determining liability and apportioning damages in DES cases in which identification of the manufacturer of the drug that injured the plaintiff is impossible. * * *

The history of the development of DES and its marketing in this country has been repeatedly chronicled. Briefly, DES is a synthetic substance that mimics the effect of estrogen, the naturally formed female hormone. It was invented in 1937 by British researchers, but never patented. In 1941, the Food and Drug Administration (FDA) approved the new drug applications (NDAs) of 12 manufacturers to market DES for the treatment of various maladies, not directly involving pregnancy. In 1947, the FDA began approving the NDAs of manufacturers to market DES for the purpose of preventing human miscarriages; by 1951, the FDA had concluded that DES was generally safe for pregnancy use, and stopped requiring the filing of NDAs when new manufacturers sought to produce the drug for this purpose. In 1971, however, the FDA banned the use of DES as a miscarriage preventative, when studies established the harmful latent effects of DES upon the offspring of mothers who took the drug. Specifically, tests indicated that DES caused vaginal adenocarcinoma, a form of cancer, and adenosis, a precancerous vaginal or cervical growth. * * *

All DES was of identical chemical composition. Druggists usually filled prescriptions from whatever was on hand. Approximately 300 manufacturers produced the drug, with companies entering and leaving the market continuously during the 24 years that DES was sold for pregnancy use. The long latency period of a DES injury compounds the identification problem; memories fade, records are lost or destroyed, and witnesses die. Thus the pregnant women who took DES generally never knew who produced the drug they took, and there was no reason to attempt to discover this fact until many years after ingestion, at which time the information is not available. * * *

In a products liability action, identification of the exact defendant whose product injured the plaintiff is, of course, generally required. In DES cases in which such identification is possible, actions may proceed under established principles of products liability. The record now before us, however, presents the question of whether a DES plaintiff may recover against a DES manufacturer when identification of the producer of the specific drug that caused the injury is impossible. * * *

[T]he accepted tort doctrines of alternative liability and concerted action are available in some personal injury cases to permit recovery where the precise identification of a wrongdoer is impossible. * * * [U]se of the alternative liability doctrine generally requires that the defendants have better access to information than does the plaintiff, and that all possible tort-feasors be before the court. See Summers y. Tice, 199 P.2d 1 (Cal. 1948). It is also recognized that alternative liability rests on the notion that where there is a small number of possible wrongdoers, all of whom breached a duty to the plaintiff, the likelihood that any one of them injured the plaintiff is relatively high, so that forcing them to exonerate themselves, or be held liable, is not unfair.

In DES cases, however, there is a great number of possible wrongdoers, who entered and left the market at different times, and some of whom no longer exist. Additionally, in DES cases many years elapse between the ingestion of the drug and injury. Consequently, DES defendants are not in any better position than are plaintiffs to identify the manufacturer of the DES ingested in any given case, nor is there any real prospect of having all the possible producers before the court. Finally, while it may be fair to employ alternative liability in cases involving only a small number of potential wrongdoers, that fairness disappears with the decreasing probability that any one of the defendants actually caused the injury. This is particularly true when applied to DES where the chance that a particular producer caused the injury is often very remote. Alternative liability, therefore, provides DES plaintiffs no relief.

Nor does the theory of concerted action, in its pure form, supply a basis for recovery. This doctrine, seen in drag racing cases, provides for joint and several liability on the part of all defendants having an understanding, express or tacit, to participate in "a common plan or design to commit a tortious act." * * * [D]rug companies were engaged in extensive parallel conduct in developing and marketing DES. There is nothing in the record, however, beyond this similar conduct to show any agreement, tacit or otherwise, to market DES for pregnancy use without taking proper steps to ensure the drug's safety. Parallel activity, without more, is insufficient to establish the agreement element necessary to maintain a concerted action claim. Thus this theory also fails in supporting an action by DES plaintiffs.

In short, extant common-law doctrines, unmodified, provide no relief for the DES plaintiff unable to identify the manufacturer of the drug that injured her. This is not a novel conclusion; in the last decade a number of courts in other jurisdictions also have concluded that present theories do not support a cause of action in DES cases. Some courts, upon reaching this conclusion, have declined to find any judicial remedy for the DES plaintiffs who cannot identify the particular manufacturer of the DES ingested by their mothers. Other courts, however, have found that some modification of existing doctrine is appropriate to allow for relief for those injured by DES of unknown manufacture.

We conclude that the present circumstances call for recognition of a realistic avenue of relief for plaintiffs injured by DES. These appeals present many of the same considerations that have prompted this court in the past to modify the rules of personal injury liability, in order "to achieve the ends of justice in a more modern context," and we perceive that here judicial action is again required to overcome the " 'inordinately difficult problems of proof' " caused by contemporary products and marketing techniques.

Indeed, it would be inconsistent with the reasonable expectations of a modern society to say to these plaintiffs that because of the insidious nature of an injury that long remains dormant, and because so many manufacturers, each behind a curtain, contributed to the devastation, the cost of injury should be borne by the innocent and not the wrongdoers.

This is particularly so where the Legislature consciously created these expectations by reviving hundreds of DES cases [after it modified the statute of limitations to start running only after a victim reasonably would discover an actionable injury]. Consequently, the ever-evolving dictates of justice and fairness, which are the heart of our common-law system, require formation of a remedy for injuries caused by DES.

We stress, however, that the DES situation is a singular case, with manufacturers acting in a parallel manner to produce an identical, generically marketed product, which causes injury many years later, and which has evoked a legislative response reviving previously barred actions. Given this unusual scenario, it is more appropriate that the loss be borne by those that produced the drug for use during pregnancy, rather than by those who were injured by the use, even where the precise manufacturer of the drug cannot be identified in a particular action. We turn then to the question of how to fairly and equitably apportion the loss occasioned by DES, in a case where the exact manufacturer of the drug that caused the injury is unknown.

The past decade of DES litigation has produced a number of alternative approaches to resolve this question. Thus, in a sense, we are now in an enviable position; the efforts of other courts provided examples for contending with this difficult issue, and enough time has passed so that the actual administration and real effects of these solutions now can be observed. With these useful guides in hand, a path may be struck for our own conclusion. * * *

In *Sindell v. Abbott Labs.*, 607 P.2d 924 (Cal.1980), the court synthesized the market share concept by modifying the *Summers v. Tice* alternative liability rationale in two ways. It first loosened the requirement that all possible wrongdoers be before the court, and instead made a "substantial share" sufficient. The court then held that each defendant who could not prove that it did not actually injure plaintiff would be liable according to that manufacturer's market share. The court's central justification for adopting this approach was its belief that limiting a defendant's liability to its market share will result, over the run of cases, in liability on the part of a defendant roughly equal to the injuries the defendant actually caused.

In the recent case of *Brown v. Superior Court*, 751 P.2d 470 (Cal.1988), the California Supreme Court resolved some apparent ambiguity in *Sindell v. Abbott Labs.*, and held that a manufacturer's liability is several only, and, in cases in which all manufacturers in the market are not joined for any reason, liability will still be limited to market share, resulting in a less than 100% recovery for a plaintiff. Finally, it is noteworthy that determining market shares under *Sindell v. Abbott Labs.* proved difficult and engendered years of litigation. After attempts at using smaller geographical units, it was eventually determined that the national market provided the most feasible and fair solution, and this national market information was compiled.

Four years after *Sindell v. Abbott Labs.*, the Wisconsin Supreme Court followed with *Collins v. Lilly & Co.*, 342 N.W.2d 37 (Wis.1984). Deciding the identification issue without the benefit of the extensive California litigation over market shares, the Wisconsin court held that it was prevented from following *Sindell* due to "the practical difficulty of defining and proving market share." Instead of focusing on tying liability closely to the odds of actual causation, as the *Sindell* court attempted, the *Collins* court took a broader perspective, and held that each defendant is liable in proportion to the amount of risk it created that the plaintiff would be injured by DES. Under the *Collins* structure, the "risk" each defendant is liable for is a question of fact in each case, with market shares being relevant to this determination. Defendants are allowed, however, to exculpate themselves by showing that their product could not have caused the injury to the particular plaintiff.

The Washington Supreme Court, writing soon after *Collins v. Lilly & Co.*, took yet another approach. See Martin v. Abbott Labs., 689 P.2d 368 (Wash.1984). * * * Under the Washington scheme, defendants are first allowed to exculpate themselves by proving by the preponderance of the evidence that they were not the manufacturer of the DES that injured plaintiff. Unexculpated defendants are presumed to have equal market shares, totaling 100%. Each defendant then has the opportunity to rebut this presumption by showing that its actual market share was less than presumed. If any defendants succeed in rebutting this presumption, the liability shares of the remaining defendants who could not prove their actual market share are inflated, so that the plaintiff received a 100% recovery. The market shares of defendants is a question of fact in each case, and the relevant market can be a particular pharmacy, or county, or State, or even the country, depending upon the circumstances the case presents. See George v. Parke–Davis, 733 P.2d 507 (Wash.1987).

Turning to the structure to be adopted in New York, we heed both the lessons learned through experience in other jurisdictions and the realities of the mass litigation of DES claims in this State. Balancing these considerations, we are led to the conclusion that a market share theory, based upon a national market, provides the best solution. As California discovered, the reliable determination of any market smaller than the national one likely is not practicable. Moreover, even if it were possible, of the hundreds of cases in the New York courts, without a doubt there are many in which the DES that allegedly caused injury was ingested in another State. Among the thorny issues this could present, perhaps the most daunting is the spectre that the particular case could require the establishment of a separate market share matrix. We feel that this is an unfair, and perhaps impossible burden to routinely place upon the litigants in individual cases.

Nor do we believe that the Wisconsin approach of assessing the "risk" each defendant caused a particular plaintiff, to be litigated anew as a question of fact in each case, is the best solution for this State. Applied on a limited scale this theory may be feasible, and certainly is the most refined approach by allowing a more thorough consideration of how each defendant's actions threatened the plaintiff. We are wary, however, of setting loose, for application in the hundreds of cases pending in this State, a theory which requires the fact finder's individualized and open-ended assessment of the relative liabilities of scores of defendants in every case. Instead, it is our perception that the injustices arising from delayed recoveries and inconsistent results which this theory may produce in this State outweigh arguments calling for its adoption.

Consequently, for essentially practical reasons, we adopt a market share theory using a national market. We are aware that the adoption of a national market will likely result in a disproportion between the liability of individual manufacturers and the actual injuries each manufacturer caused in this State. Thus our market share theory cannot be founded upon the belief that, over the run of cases, liability will approximate causation in this State. Nor does the use of a national market provide a reasonable link between liability and the risk created by a defendant to a particular plaintiff. Instead, we choose to apportion liability so as to correspond to the over-all culpability of each defendant, measured by the amount of risk of injury each defendant created to the public-at-large. Use of a national market is a fair method, we believe, of apportioning defendants' liabilities according to their total culpability in marketing DES for use during pregnancy. Under the circumstances, this is an equitable way to provide plaintiffs with the relief they deserve, while also rationally distributing the responsibility for plaintiffs' injuries among defendants.

To be sure, a defendant cannot be held liable if it did not participate in the marketing of DES for pregnancy use; if a DES producer satisfies its burden of proof of showing that it was not a member of the market of DES sold for pregnancy use, disallowing exculpation would be unfair and unjust. Nevertheless, because liability here is based on the over-all risk produced, and not causation in a single case, there should be no exculpation of a defendant who, although a member of the market producing DES for pregnancy use, appears not to have caused a particular plaintiff's injury. It is merely a windfall for a producer to escape liability solely because it manufactured a more identifiable pill, or sold only to certain drugstores. These fortuities in no way diminish the culpability of a defendant for marketing the product, which is the basis of liability here.

Finally, we hold that the liability of DES producers is several only, and should not be inflated when all participants in the market are not before the court in a particular case. We understand that, as a practical matter, this will prevent some plaintiffs from recovering 100% of their damages. However, we eschewed exculpation to prevent the fortuitous avoidance of liability, and thus, equitably, we decline to unleash the same forces to increase a defendant's liability beyond its fair share of responsibility.[3]

---

3. The dissenter misapprehends the basis for liability here. We have not by the backdoor adopted a theory of concerted action. We avoided extending this theory, because its concomitant requirement of joint and several liability expands the burden on small manufacturers beyond a rational or fair limit. This result is reached by the dissent, not by the majority, so that criticism on this front is misplaced. We are confronted here with an unprecedented identification problem and have provided a solution that rationally apportions liability. We have heeded the practical lessons learned by other jurisdictions,

■ Mollen, Judge (concurring in part and dissenting in part):

* * * I am also in complete agreement with the majority's view that the market share theory of liability, based upon a national market, is an appropriate means by which to accord DES plaintiffs an opportunity to seek recovery for their injuries. However, I respectfully disagree with the majority's conclusion that there should be no exculpation of those defendants who produced and marketed DES for pregnancy purposes, but who can prove, by a preponderance of the evidence, that they did not produce or market the particular pill ingested by the plaintiff's mother. Moreover, in order to ensure that these plaintiffs receive full recovery of their damages, as they are properly entitled to by any fair standard, I would retain the principle of imposing joint and several liability upon those defendants which cannot exculpate themselves.

The emergence of the market share concept of liability in the field of products liability reflects a recognition by several jurisdictions throughout the United States that due to the incidence of mass production and marketing of various drugs and fungible goods, consumers are many times harmed by a product which is not easily traceable to a specific manufacturer, particularly in those situations where the harm occurred many years prior to the discovery of the injuries and the cause thereof. Such is the situation in the DES cases now before us. * * *

Significantly, both the Supreme Courts of Wisconsin and Washington in the *Collins* and *Martin* cases, as did the Supreme Court of California in *Sindell*, provided that the joined or impleaded defendants may exculpate themselves from liability if they can establish, by a preponderance of the evidence, that they did not produce or market the particular DES pill taken by the plaintiff's mother. * * * In fact, *none* of the jurisdictions which have adopted varying theories of collective liability in DES cases has refused to permit exculpation of those defendants which have been able to prove that they could not have produced or marketed the pill which caused the particular plaintiff's injuries, thereby recognizing that to preclude exculpation would directly and unnecessarily contravene the established common-law tort principles of causation.

resulting in our adoption of a national market theory with full knowledge that it concedes the lack of a logical link between liability and causation in a single case. The dissent ignores these lessons and, endeavoring to articulate a theory it perceives to be closer to traditional law, sets out a construct in which liability is based upon chance, not upon the fair assessment of the acts of defendants. Under the dissent's theory, a manufacturer with a large market share may avoid liability in many cases just because it manufactured a memorably shaped pill. Conversely, a small manufacturer can be held jointly liable for the full amount of every DES injury in this State simply because the shape of its product was not remarkable, even though the odds, realistically, are exceedingly long that the small manufacturer caused the injury in any one particular case. Therefore, although the dissent's theory based upon a "shifting the burden of proof" and joint and several liability is facially reminiscent of prior law, in the case of DES it is nothing more than advocating that bare fortuity be the test for liability. When faced with the novel identification problem posed by DES cases, it is preferable to adopt a new theory that apportions fault rationally, rather than to contort extant doctrines beyond the point at which they provide a sound premise for determining liability.

Clearly, the development and underlying purpose of the various concepts of liability in DES cases has been to provide a means whereby the plaintiffs, who cannot identify the actual manufacturer of the pill ingested by their mother, are alleviated of the traditional burden of proof of causation and to shift that burden to the defendants. The various theories of collective liability which have been adopted in the several jurisdictions in an effort to provide plaintiffs with a means to recover for their injuries, were not intended to, and did not, provide DES plaintiffs with an unprecedented strict liability cause of action. However, the majority herein, by precluding exculpation of those defendants in DES cases who produced DES for pregnancy purposes but who can establish, by a preponderance of the evidence, that they did not and could not have produced or marketed the pill which caused the plaintiff's injuries, has created such a radical concept and purports to limit it to DES claims. In the majority's view, the defendant's liability in DES cases is premised upon the over-all risk of injury which they created to the public-at-large in producing and marketing DES for pregnancy purposes and, therefore, exculpation of those defendants who can establish that the plaintiff's mother did not ingest their pill, would be inconsistent with the over-all risk theory of liability. By taking this view, however, the majority, while stating that it is adopting a market share theory of liability, is, in essence, despite its disclaimer of doing so, adopting a concerted action theory of liability, but has eliminated therefrom the requirement that the plaintiffs establish that the defendants tacitly agreed to produce and market DES for pregnancy use without proper testing and without adequate warnings of the potential dangers involved. Such a result represents a radical departure from fundamental tenets of tort law and is unnecessarily unfair and inequitable to the defendants who have proven, or can prove, that they did not produce the pill which caused the injury. * * *

I would adopt a market share theory of liability, based upon a national market, which would provide for the shifting of the burden of proof on the issue of causation to the defendants and would impose liability upon all of the defendants who produced and marketed DES for pregnancy purposes, except those who were able to prove that their product could not have caused the injury. Under this approach, DES plaintiffs, who are unable to identify the actual manufacturer of the pill ingested by their mother, would only be required to establish (1) that the plaintiff's mother ingested DES during pregnancy; (2) that the plaintiff's injuries were caused by DES; and (3) that the defendant or defendants produced and marketed DES for pregnancy purposes. Thereafter, the burden of proof would shift to the defendants to exculpate themselves by establishing, by a preponderance of the evidence, that the plaintiff's mother could not have ingested their particular pill. Of those defendants who are unable to exculpate themselves from liability, their respective share of the plaintiff's damages would be measured by their share of the national market of DES produced and marketed for pregnancy purposes during the period in question.

I would further note that while, on the one hand, the majority would not permit defendants who produced DES for pregnancy purposes to exculpate themselves, the majority at the same time deprives the plaintiffs of the opportunity to recover fully for their injuries by limiting the defendants' liability for the plaintiff's damages to several liability. In my view, the liability for the plaintiff's damages of those defendants who are unable to exculpate themselves should be joint and several thereby ensuring that the plaintiffs will receive full recovery of their damages. In addition to being fair to the DES plaintiffs, the imposition of joint and several liability is consistent with that portion of the revival statute which specifically exempted DES claims from those provisions which provide, with certain exceptions, for several liability of joint tort-feasors. Moreover, in order to ease the financial burden on the specific defendants named in the lawsuit, the defendants would have the option of seeking contribution from their fellow defendants for damages in excess of each defendant's particular market share, and a defendant should be permitted leave to implead those DES manufacturers who the plaintiff has not joined, in order to ensure, where possible, full contribution. Admittedly, adherence to joint and several liability could result in a disproportion between a defendant's potential liability for the damages suffered by the plaintiff and defendant's actual national market share; however, the opportunity to present exculpatory evidence reduces the risk of imposing liability on innocent defendants.

The application of the aforesaid principles, although somewhat innovative and a modification of traditional tort law (i.e., the burden of proof is on the plaintiff to prove proximate causation), would, in view of the exigent circumstances, be in furtherance of a valid public policy of imposing the burden of bearing the cost of severe injuries upon those who are responsible for placing into the stream of commerce the causative instrumentality of such injuries. Adherence to this principle would not be too dissimilar from the accepted doctrine of res ipsa loquitur which provides, in essence, that where an instrumentality which caused the plaintiff's injuries was in the exclusive control of the defendant and the accident which occurred is one which would not ordinarily happen without negligence, these facts are sufficient to justify an inference of negligence and to shift the burden upon the defendant of coming forward with an explanation. Thus, this approach, unlike that taken by the majority, does not represent an unnecessary and radical departure from basic principles of tort law. By characterizing this approach as "nothing more than advocating that bare fortuity be the test for liability" the majority fails to perceive that this is no more and no less than a basic principle of tort law; i.e., a plaintiff may not recover for his or her injuries from a defendant who could not have caused those injuries. When the majority eliminates this fundamental causative factor as a basis for recovery, it effectively indulges in the act of judicial legislating. I would further note that if the Legislature had intended to adopt this radical approach which is at total variance with traditional tort law, it could readily have done so when it enacted the revival statute for, among others, DES plaintiffs. Its refusal to do so can certainly not be deemed to be an invitation to this court to assume the legislative role.

Judged by the aforesaid standard, I conclude that the trial courts' orders in *Tigue & Margolies v. Squibb & Sons* (decided herewith) and *Dolan v. Lilly & Co.* (decided herewith), to the extent that they denied the summary judgment motions of the defendant The Upjohn Company (Upjohn) in both actions and the defendant Rexall Drug Company (Rexall) in the *Tigue* action, were improper. In *Tigue*, Mrs. Tigue, the plaintiff's mother, testified that the DES pill she ingested while she was pregnant with the plaintiff was a white, round tablet. Similarly, Myrna Margolies' mother testified that the DES pill she ingested was a dark red, hard, round pill. Mr. Margolies, the plaintiff's father, also recalled that the pills were a reddish color and Mrs. Margolies' obstetrician stated that the DES pill he prescribed to his patients was not an Upjohn product. Moreover, in the *Dolan* action, Mrs. Dolan, the plaintiff's mother, stated that the DES pill she took was a white, round, hard tablet. This fact was corroborated by Mr. Dolan's testimony. Finally, it was established that Upjohn's DES pill which was produced and marketed for pregnancy purposes, was in the form of a "perle" which is a pharmaceutical term for a dose form consisting of a soft elastic capsule containing a liquid center. Based on the evidence submitted in support of Upjohn's summary judgment motions in these two cases, I would conclude that the plaintiffs have failed to adduce sufficient proof in admissible form to raise a triable issue of fact as to whether their mothers ingested an Upjohn DES pill. Accordingly, Upjohn's motion for summary judgment in those actions should have been granted. * * *

Rexall's motion for summary judgment should have been granted since the plaintiffs failed to raise a triable issue of fact as to whether their mothers could have ingested a Rexall DES product during the pregnancies in question. The evidence submitted in support of Rexall's motion established that until 1978, Rexall sold its products, including its DES pill, exclusively to Rexall Drug Stores. The testimony of the plaintiffs' parents, Mrs. Tigue and Mr. and Mrs. Margolies, established that they had purchased their DES prescriptions from non-Rexall pharmacies during the periods of their respective pregnancies, i.e., 1960 and 1953. Based on this uncontroverted evidence demonstrating Rexall's noninvolvement in these plaintiffs' injuries, Rexall's motion for summary judgment should have been granted. * * *

NOTES AND QUESTIONS

1. *Inculpation and exculpation.* After *Hymowitz*, a lower court refused to dismiss from a lawsuit a California company that had never sold DES in New York or any adjacent states. See In re New York County DES Litig., 615 N.Y.S.2d 882, 885 (App.Div.1994) (rejecting an objection to the exercise of personal jurisdiction); see also In re DES Market Share Litig., 591 N.E.2d 226 (N.Y.1992) (rejecting the argument that the market share theory represented an equitable claim for which the plaintiff would have no right to a jury trial). What if the plaintiff had found her mother's prescription records identifying the particular manufacturer of DES? Would *Hymowitz* require her to use a market share theory, which would mean recovering less than 100% of her damages? Why does the court only allow exculpation by manufacturers of DES marketed solely for non-pregnancy indications? Isn't it possible, given the prevalence of off-label prescribing, that such a manufacturer actually supplied the DES that injured a particular plaintiff? See Miles Labs., Inc. v. Superior Ct., 184 Cal.Rptr. 98 (Ct.App.1982).

2. *Relationship to class actions and choice of law.* The progenitor market share decision, *Sindell v. Abbott Laboratories*, 607 P.2d 924 (Cal.1980), represented a statewide class action lawsuit against manufacturers of DES, and the court defined the relevant market share as limited to the state of California. In that context, perhaps, a theory of proportional liability has far greater appeal. In *Hymowitz*, the court justified using a national market share in part because some of the plaintiffs' mothers may have ingested DES in other states, but then New York tort law may not apply in any event. Cf. Cooney v. Osgood Mach., Inc., 612 N.E.2d 277, 281–83 (N.Y. 1993).

3. *Other formulations.* See Conley v. Boyle Drug Co., 570 So.2d 275, 283 (Fla.1990) (adopting the narrowest possible definition of relevant market); Abel v. Eli Lilly & Co., 343 N.W.2d 164 (Mich.1984) (modified alternative liability theory); see also Rest. (3d) § 15 cmt. c ("The Institute leaves to developing law the question of whether, given the appropriate factors, a rule of proportional liability should be adopted. However, if a court does adopt some form of proportional liability, the liability of each defendant is properly limited to the individual defendant's share of the market."); Richard E. Kaye, Annotation, "Concert of Activity," "Alternate Liability," "Enterprise Liability," or Similar Theory as Basis for Imposing Liability upon One or More Manufacturers of Defective Uniform Product, in Absence of Identification of Manufacturer of Precise Unit or Batch Causing Injury, 63 A.L.R.5th 195 §§ 4, 8 (1998).

4. *Jurisdictions rejecting market share theory even in DES cases.* See, e.g., Wood v. Eli Lilly & Co., 38 F.3d 510 (10th Cir.1994) (applying Oklahoma law); Tidler v. Eli Lilly & Co., 851 F.2d 418 (D.C.Cir.1988) (applying Maryland and D.C. law); Braune v. Abbott Labs., 895 F.Supp. 530 (E.D.N.Y.1995) (applying Georgia law); Mizell v. Eli Lilly & Co., 526 F.Supp. 589 (D.S.C.1981); Smith v. Eli Lilly & Co., 560 N.E.2d 324 (Ill.1990); Mulcahy v. Eli Lilly & Co., 386 N.W.2d 67 (Iowa 1986); Zafft v. Eli Lilly & Co., 676 S.W.2d 241 (Mo.1984); Sutowski v. Eli Lilly & Co., 696 N.E.2d 187 (Ohio 1998); see also Dawson v. Bristol Labs., 658 F.Supp. 1036, 1038–41 (W.D.Ky.1987) (allowing instead the use of a concert of action theory against a manufacturer of tetracycline); Shackil v. Lederle Labs., 561 A.2d 511 (N.J.1989) (DPT vaccine); Senn v. Merrell–Dow Pharms., Inc., 751 P.2d 215 (Or.1988) (same); Gorman v. Abbott Labs., 599 A.2d 1364 (R.I.1991). For additional background on the DES litigation, see Romualdo P. Eclavea, Annotation, Products Liability: Diethylstilbestrol (DES), 2 A.L.R.4th 1091 (1980).

5. *Manufacturing defect claims.* In DES cases, each and every unit sold contained the same defect. Does market share liability make less sense in cases where only some units sold by some manufacturers contain a defect? Contrast Sheffield v. Eli Lilly & Co., 192 Cal.Rptr. 870 (Ct.App.1983) (rejecting market share theory in a case of a defective batch of polio vaccine), with Smith v. Cutter Biological, Inc., 823 P.2d 717 (Haw.1991) (allowing use of market share theory in a case of tainted blood factor concentrates). Along similar lines, courts will refuse to certify class action lawsuits involving medical technologies if there are significant differences among plaintiffs in their use and exposure. See In re Am. Med. Sys., Inc., 75 F.3d 1069, 1081 (6th Cir.1996) (penile prostheses); In re Tetracycline Cases, 107 F.R.D. 719, 730, 733–36 (W.D.Mo.1985) (antibiotics); Baker v. Wyeth–Ayerst Labs., 992 S.W.2d 797, 801 (Ark.1999) (diet drugs).

6. *Medical devices.* A lower court in New York declined to apply *Hymowitz* to litigation against breast implant manufacturers, offering the following explanation:

> This court finds that market share liability should not be applied to breast implants because such products are not fungible and the manufacturers of the implants can often be identified. There are differences in the design and composition of the implants; the warning inserts in each of the products vary; and the products are not generically marketed. Most importantly, the majority of women involved in the breast implant litigation have been able to identify all or some of the manufacturers of their implants. This ability to identify most of the manufacturers is important since both market share and concert of action liability theories came into play so plaintiffs could have recourse to the courts where product identification was impossible. The rationale of the Court of Appeals decision in *Hymowitz* was that market share liability was necessary because the DES was an identical generically marketed product, as a result of which the manufacturers of the product could not be identified. In the present case, silicone breast implant manufacturers make identifiable products, marketed under specific manufacturer names. The reality of a plaintiff's plight when product identification cannot be made is like any other plaintiff who claims injury from a product that has been lost or destroyed. So drastic a departure from traditional tort law is not warranted here.

In re New York State Silicone Breast Implant Litig., 631 N.Y.S.2d 491, 494 (Sup.Ct.1995), aff'd mem., 650 N.Y.S.2d 558 (App.Div.1996); see also Albright v. Upjohn Co., 788 F.2d 1217 (6th Cir.1986) (holding that the plaintiff's lawyer should have been sanctioned under Rule 11 of the Federal Rules of Civil Procedure for naming several manufacturers of tetracycline where the plaintiff's still available medical records had identified only a few of these drug companies as the source of antibiotics that she had received as a child); Thomas C. Willcox, Note, The Application of a Due Diligence Requirement to Market Share Theory in DES Litigation, 19 U. Mich. J.L. Reform 771 (1986).

7. *Further commentary.* See Frederick H. Fern & Leslie S. McHugh, Market Share Liability for Pharmaceuticals: The Distinction Between DES and DPT, 11 J. Legal Med. 391 (1990); David A. Fischer, Products Liability–An Analysis of Market Share Liability, 34 Vand. L. Rev. 1623 (1981); Andrew R. Klein, Beyond DES: Rejecting the Application of Market Share Liability in Blood Products Litigation, 68 Tul. L. Rev. 883 (1994); Aaron D. Twerski, Market Share–A Tale of Two Centuries, 55 Brook. L. Rev. 869 (1989); Note, Market Share Liability: An Answer to the DES Causation Problem, 94 Harv. L. Rev. 668 (1981).

CHAPTER 6

PRODUCTION FAILURES

This chapter addresses products liability claims against sellers of prescription drugs and medical devices that are premised on manufacturing and design defects. A discussion of the more typical failure-to-warn claims is reserved for the next chapter on informational defects.

A. MANUFACTURING DEFECTS

Reiter v. Zimmer Inc.

897 F.Supp. 154 (S.D.N.Y.1995).

■ McKENNA, DISTRICT JUDGE:

Plaintiff Nita Reiter commenced this action against Defendant Zimmer Incorporated alleging that the premature hardening of Zimmer bone cement during hip replacement surgery caused her debilitating personal injuries. * * *

Zimmer bone cement consists of two components: a powder and a liquid. When the two are mixed in the operating room, a chemical reaction begins, and the mixture starts to set or "cure." After a few minutes the mixture becomes a soft putty and can be used to fix the prosthesis. In about 10 minutes, the mixture hardens and the prosthesis cannot be moved. The cement hardens due to the presence of benzoyl peroxide (BPO) in the powder. "The BPO concentration is critical to the reaction rate of the mixed Zimmer Bone Cement and, so, to the length of time available to the surgeon to use the mixed cement."

Reiter contends that the batch of cement used in her operation may have hardened prematurely because it was improperly formulated and blended. It is uncontested that batch #66688200 twice failed a cure test during the blending stages of the formulation * * * *

[Plaintiff's expert George] Stanton contends that the premature hardening of the bone cement used in the operation resulted from Zimmer's failure to comply with the FDA-approved NDA,* that is, with the very procedures proposed by Zimmer. In his final report, Stanton concludes:

---

* The court's repeated reference to an NDA makes little sense because bone cement products qualify as class III medical devices subject to a PMA requirement. See 21 C.F.R. § 888.3027. (Before 1976, however, the FDA would have regulated them as new drugs.)

> [I]t is my professional opinion to a reasonable degree of chemical engineering certainty, [that] the batch of Zimmer bone cement from which the kit used in Mrs. Reiter's surgery was not produced in accordance with FDA approved standards which resulted in the failure (premature hardening) of this critical device, which in turn, resulted in injury to her during the surgery of September, 1989.

While Stanton enumerates several different "failures to comply," the court need not at this time reach highly technical questions relating to Zimmer's alleged non-compliance with procedures described explicitly in the NDA. The court, instead, focuses on Zimmer's alleged failure to comply with industry and FDA standards that it chose to "incorporate by reference" in the NDA.

Stanton complains that Zimmer failed to employ procedures to ensure that the batch of bone cement was sufficiently homogeneous (uniform). The issue of homogeneity was addressed in the NDA both explicitly, by the detailing of certain blending procedures, and implicitly, by the incorporation of industry standards. One such implicit reference appears in Zimmer Engineering Specification (ZES) 2R–01, which states that a quality program in conformity with industry standard ASQC C1 1985 will be maintained. This standard, promulgated by the American Society for Quality Control, requires, inter alia, that "[c]ontrol shall be maintained over production processes to prevent product . . . non-conformity and excessive variability." The standard also requires that "methods and facilities shall be provided to assure conformance with requirements for special process specifications, such as . . . homogenization." Stanton contends that Zimmer's bone cement was formulated in a fashion that resulted in "excessive variability" and did not produce a homogeneous product, which were "substantial contributing factors causing the failure of the Zimmer Bone cement leading directly to Ms. Reiter's injury."

Stanton further observes that ZES 2R–01 references the FDA's Good Manufacturing Practices for Medical Devices, 21 C.F.R. § 820 et seq. Section 820.5 of "Good Manufacturing Practices" requires "a quality assurance program that is appropriate to the specific device manufactured." Section 820.161 requires an investigation when a critical device fails to meet performance specifications.

Reiter's position is that if Zimmer had chosen to omit such references, and FDA approval were received, then Zimmer would only be obligated to follow the manufacturing processes explicitly described in the NDA. Since Zimmer chose to reap the benefits of incorporating industry standards (presumably making FDA approval more likely), Reiter argues, Zimmer must be held to those standards as well, even if they impose requirements not specifically enumerated in the NDA. * * *

The court understands the essence of this argument to be that while it may be possible to pass one particular test, the cure test, by altering the proportion of ingredients, the alteration might result in a defective final product. Furthermore, the alteration was not specifically contemplated by the FDA during its review of the NDA and would not constitute a proper discretionary practice. Good engineering practice—as well as common sense—might suggest discarding a batch that has twice failed a cure test, or inquiring into the basis for the failure (such as improper environmental controls, or substandard ingredients), or conducting additional testing.[3]

The court finds Stanton's argument as to the incorporation of industry and FDA standards to be persuasive, particularly in light of the affidavit submitted by Carl A. Larson, who served as the FDA's Director of the Division of General and Restorative Devices from 1979 to 1992. This Division had primary regulatory responsibility for bone cement, among other medical devices. Larson, who during his tenure was acquainted with both Zimmer personnel and Dr. Frankel (a member of the FDA's Orthopaedic Advisory Panel, which made recommendations to Larson's division), reviewed the affidavit and reports of George Stanton. Larson states: "I agree with Mr. Stanton that bone cement manufacturers, such as Zimmer, are bound to adhere to Good Manufacturing Practices promulgated by the FDA and I agree with the construction that Mr. Stanton places upon these regulations." * * *

Rather than seeing such requirements as additional burdens imposed by state law, which * * * would be preempted by federal law, the court instead views such professional obligations—as the FDA undoubtedly does—as inherent in all medical manufacturing. Since there will undoubtedly be formulation issues that "fall between the cracks" of the NDA, the FDA must assume, particularly in the context of a Class III medical device, that the manufacturer will follow "good engineering practice."

The court's conclusion regarding "incorporation by reference" renders many of Zimmer's arguments irrelevant. For example, Zimmer has argued that the two failed cure tests were not required by the NDA as approved by the FDA in 1982. Even if these tests were not explicitly detailed in the NDA, the two failures may have triggered further obligations, such as an inquiry into their cause, either under the standards incorporated by reference, or under the general professional standard of good engineering practice. * * *

In sum, Reiter has raised substantial factual questions as to Zimmer's compliance with FDA requirements regarding the formulation of batch #66688200 requiring Zimmer's motion for summary judgment [based on federal preemption] be denied.

Rogers v. Johnson & Johnson Products, Inc.

565 A.2d 751 (Pa.1989).

■ Nix, Chief Justice:

* * * Price Rogers entered Lankenau Hospital for the treatment of a broken leg. Dr. John J. Dowling, Lankenau's Chief of Orthopedic Surgery,

---

3. Zimmer has argued that altering the proportion of ingredients was harmless, analogizing it to a man working on a lathe: "What are the odds of a production worker putting a piece of steel on the lathe, grinding it, stopping it and hitting the specifications on that particular one. Everybody knows that it is impossible or it would be entirely coincidental if he did." The analogy between the routine working of a piece of steel and the tinkering with the chemical formulation of a federally regulated critical medical device is a poor one. Altering the proportion of ingredients in Zimmer bone cement might have substantially altered its carefully designed properties.

and Dr. Lawrence Naame, a third year resident on rotation from Thomas Jefferson University Hospital, treated Mr. Rogers. Dr. Dowling recommended surgery which was scheduled for the following day. Dr. Dowling ordered the application of a plaster splint pending the surgery. Unlike a cast, a splint covers only part of an injured limb. Its application immobilizes the injured limb so as to prevent complications from, for example, the broken bone interfering with circulation.

Dr. Naame left the holding room to prepare the splint for application. This required arranging several layers of cotton insulation to be placed under a plaster wrapping product which itself required dipping in tepid or lukewarm water and arranging or "reversing" in several layers. When dipped in water, the product reacted exothermically, as it should have.

After preparing the splint in this fashion, Dr. Naame returned to the holding room. There Dr. Dowling held up the injured leg while both physicians applied the insulation and the plaster wrap so as to form a splint on its underside. Mr. Rogers complained of a sensation of warmth. Dr. Dowling assured him this was to be expected. When the splint began to harden, Dr. Dowling lowered the leg and left the room to arrange for Mr. Rogers' admission into the hospital. Mr. Rogers complained to his wife, who was in the holding room, of a burning sensation. She applied ice to the uppermost part of the splint, at the top of her husband's thigh, and left the room to locate Dr. Dowling. She found him, informed him of her husband's complaints, and accompanied him back to the room. At that point, Mr. Rogers simply requested anesthesia should future painful procedures be required.

Prior to surgery the next morning, Dr. Dowling removed the splint. He discovered second and third degree burns on the back of the leg. Although able to undergo the open reduction surgery, Mr. Rogers experienced a longer, more painful recuperative period, requiring a skin graft, therapy, and home nursing for several months.

Mr. and Mrs. Rogers filed a complaint * * * * At trial, the Rogers' case against Johnson & Johnson consisted of evidence of malfunction, failure to warn, and negligence. They also presented expert testimony eliminating medical malpractice as the cause of burns. Thomas Jefferson University Hospital likewise adduced evidence eliminating medical malpractice as the cause of the plaster's having burned Mr. Rogers. On the other hand, Johnson & Johnson introduced expert testimony indicating that the medical malpractice of the doctors had caused the splint to overheat and to burn Mr. Rogers. * * *

At the close of the evidence the jury was given a verdict form which directed it to decide first whether the Johnson & Johnson plaster was defective as a result of malfunction, second whether it was defective as a result of failure to warn the user, and if the answer to either of these questions was affirmative, to decide thirdly whether the defect was a substantial factor in bringing about the plaintiffs' harm. The jury returned a verdict against Johnson & Johnson on the malfunction theory * * * *

Johnson & Johnson appealed the judgment following the denial of its post-trial motions. The Superior Court reversed and granted a new trial. The Superior Court concluded that because Johnson & Johnson had adduced sufficient evidence of negligence on the part of Dr. Naame to submit that issue to a jury, the plaintiffs had not sustained their burden of proof in eliminating reasonable, secondary causes for the malfunction. * * *

In most instances the plaintiff will produce direct evidence of the product's defective condition. In some instances, however, the plaintiff may not be able to prove the precise nature of the defect in which case reliance may be had on the "malfunction" theory of product liability. This theory encompasses nothing more than circumstantial evidence of product malfunction. It permits a plaintiff to prove a defect in a product with evidence of the occurrence of a malfunction and with evidence eliminating abnormal use or reasonable, secondary causes for the malfunction. It thereby relieves the plaintiff from demonstrating precisely the defect yet it permits the trier-of-fact to infer one existed from evidence of the malfunction, of the absence of abnormal use and of the absence of reasonable, secondary causes. We now accept this evidentiary approach as appropriate in ascertaining the existence of a defect in the manufacturing process.

At the close of the plaintiff's case-in-chief, a defendant manufacturer will have three evidentiary avenues to pursue: the occurrence of the malfunction, the presence of abnormal uses, or the presence of reasonable, secondary causes. In this instance Johnson & Johnson attacked the plaintiffs' evidence eliminating secondary causation by introducing evidence of the doctors' malpractice. This evidence was sufficient to submit the issue of medical malpractice to the jury.

As the Superior Court would have it, however, Johnson & Johnson was entitled to a directed verdict on the malfunction issue once it introduced sufficient evidence of secondary causation, i.e., medical malpractice, to permit this defense to go to the jury. We cannot agree with this circular logic as it essentially mandates the grant of a directed verdict should the defendant manufacturer produce any evidence of reasonable, secondary causation. * * *

The Superior Court erred because it considered incompatible the plaintiffs' evidence of malfunction in light of the defendant, Johnson & Johnson's, evidence of a reasonable secondary cause. It rendered impossible the ability of the plaintiffs to negate secondary causes suggested by Johnson & Johnson's evidence and essentially required a directed verdict in favor of Johnson & Johnson. Contrarily, we believe that so long as the plaintiffs presented a case-in-chief free of secondary causes which justified the inference of a defect in the product, the jury was free to accept their scenario. * * *

■ Flaherty, Justice (dissenting):

The majority, in what could be said to be a res ipsa loquitur approach, holds that so long as the plaintiff presents a case-in-chief free of secondary causes which justif[ies] an inference of defect in the product, the case may be sent to the jury on the "malfunction theory" regardless of whether evidence is admitted negating the very essence of the theory. In my view, sending the malfunction case to the jury without first allowing the defendant to move for a ruling on whether, as a matter of law, the defendant's evidence of secondary causation negates the plaintiff's claim of malfunction is error. Not providing for a legal determination of whether the plaintiff negated defendant's evidence of secondary causes (a legal requirement of stating a malfunction case) before sending the malfunction claim to the jury deprives the defendant of his right to challenge whether the plaintiff has even stated a cause of action.

A malfunction-theory plaintiff argues, in essence, that while he has no direct evidence that the product is defective, he is prepared to establish that the product malfunctioned, from which the jury may infer that the product was defective. Once the plaintiff has established this, he has stated a prima facie case and his evidence will withstand a motion for non-suit.

The defendant, however, may put in evidence that the malfunction was caused by secondary causes separate and apart from any alleged defect in the product. If the defendant produces such evidence, the plaintiff then must negate it, for the survival of his cause of action depends upon his establishing that nothing outside of the product itself caused the malfunction, since if a "secondary cause" created the malfunction, the product itself was not defective and the products liability claim would fail. In other words, a malfunction-theory plaintiff must negate evidence that secondary causes were responsible for the malfunction.

The question which this raises, however, is what a malfunction-theory plaintiff must do in order to negate such secondary cause evidence. It is my view that the problem of determining whether a malfunction-theory plaintiff has negated secondary causes is analogous to deciding whether to grant a motion for a directed verdict; in both cases the proper inquiry for the court is whether the plaintiff put on evidence which, if believed, negates the claim made on the other side, here that there is evidence of secondary causes of the malfunction.

The plaintiff cannot be called upon to negate evidence of secondary causes absolutely, as the Superior Court would have him do, for that would be to place a burden of proof too severe upon the plaintiff, too much in excess of the requirement that the plaintiff must produce a preponderance of evidence in order to prevail. Nor can the trial court be called upon to assess the credibility of plaintiff's witnesses or the weight of the evidence, for those are jury functions. But the trial court is in a position to treat the matter as it would treat a motion for a directed verdict, by simply deciding whether plaintiff's evidence, if believed, negates evidence of secondary causes. * * * It may be that under the standard proposed herein, in which the defendant's motion for directed verdict is defeated if the plaintiff's evidence, if believed, negates evidence of secondary causes, will not change the results in many cases. Nonetheless, a defendant should have the right to move the court to determine whether the plaintiff has met the legal requirements of his case before the case is submitted to the jury.

NOTES AND QUESTIONS

1. *Restatement (Third) formulation.* The new *Restatement* uses the same standard to define prescription drug and medical device manufacturing defects as it does for other consumer goods. See Rest. (3d) § 6(b)(1) (cross-referencing § 2(a), which provides that a product "contains a manufacturing defect when the product departs from its intended design even though all possible care was exercised in the preparation and marketing of the product"). Thus, if a product is "out of specifications" for any reason, it is defective, which is a true strict liability standard. Recall that comment k immunity under *Rest. (2d)* § 402A only applied if the unavoidably unsafe product was "properly prepared."

2. *Manufacturing defect cases.* Recently, plaintiffs' settled class action litigation against Sulzer Orthopedics after it recalled a popular type of hip implant, including nearly 20,000 units already implanted in patients, because of a failure in the manufacturing process that left a residue of lubricating oil on the surface and created a risk of loosening that might require revision surgery. See Elizabeth Olson, Sulzer Offers $1 Billion Settlement for Defective Implants, N.Y. Times, Feb. 4, 2002, at C2; 29 Prod. Safety & Liab. Rep. (BNA) 185 (2001); see also Thomas M. Burton, Baxter Says Its Dialysis Filters Appear to Have Played Role in Patients' Deaths, Wall St. J., Nov. 6, 2001, at A3. For other cases involving manufacturing defects, see Martin v. American Med. Sys., Inc., 116 F.3d 102, 103, 105 (4th Cir.1997) (allowing a patient to pursue a breach of express warranty claim for an implant that was not sterile); Ferren v. Richards Mfg. Co., 733 F.2d 526, 528–30 (8th Cir.1984) (affirming judgment for plaintiff where metal defect in hip implant caused injury, but reversing award of punitive damages); Fender v. Medtronic, Inc., 887 F.Supp. 1326, 1331–33 (S.D.Cal.1995) (holding that manufacturing defect claims for malfunctioning pacemaker leads were not preempted by the FDA's GMP requirements); In re Copley Pharm., Inc., "Albuterol" Prods. Liab. Litig., 158 F.R.D. 485, 487–88 (D.Wyo.1994) (certifying a class action on behalf of patients who were injured by bacterial contamination of four batches of a bronchodilator drug later recalled by the manufacturer); see also Kramer v. Showa Denko K.K., 929 F.Supp. 733 (S.D.N.Y.1996); DiRosa v. Showa Denko K.K., 52 Cal.Rptr.2d 128 (Ct.App.1996) (affirming a judgment for a plaintiff injured by contamination of the amino acid dietary supplement L-tryptophan). In one case, a vaccine manufacturer brought a commercial lawsuit against a medical device manufacturer for supplying defective surgical gloves containing microscopic holes that allowed bacteria to pass from the hand of an employee during processing and ruin several batches of rabies vaccine. See Travenol Labs., Inc. v. Bandy Labs., Inc., 608 S.W.2d 308 (Tex.Civ.App.1980), aff'd, 630 S.W.2d 484 (Tex.App.1982).

3.   *Circumstantial evidence of product defect.* Courts allow plaintiffs to rely on circumstantial evidence of product defectiveness. See Oja v. Howmedica, Inc., 111 F.3d 782, 792–93 (10th Cir.1997) (reversing a directed verdict against a plaintiff's strict liability manufacturing defect claim involving a hip implant). Prescription drugs usually are dispensed in small quantities and rapidly metabolized, and explanted medical devices may not be preserved for testing. In order for a plaintiff to make use of a malfunction theory, however, post-sale explanations for the defect must be rebutted. See Fane v. Zimmer, Inc., 927 F.2d 124, 129–32 (2d Cir.1991) (affirming a directed verdict for manufacturer where a metal brace may have broken because of patient misuse); Readel v. Vital Signs, Inc., 174 F.Supp.2d 754 (N.D.Ill.2001) (denying summary judgment to the seller of a respiratory system valve on a manufacturing defect claim); Mozes v. Medtronic, Inc., 14 F.Supp.2d 1124, 1128–29 (D.Minn.1998) (rejecting res ipsa loquitur where manufacturer of pacemaker leads offered numerous post-sale explanations for failure); Thirsk v. Ethicon, Inc., 687 P.2d 1315, 1317–18 (Colo.Ct.App. 1983) (explaining that surgical bone wax could have been contaminated after sale, but holding that the defendant shoulders the burden of proving it); Fulton v. Pfizer Hosp. Prods. Group, 872 S.W.2d 908, 910–12 (Tenn.Ct. App.1993) (reversing judgment for a plaintiff because no evidence supported the inference that some manufacturing defect caused the pegs in a knee replacement to shear off); see also Rest. (3d) § 3(b) (rule for inference of defectiveness). These decisions all involved medical devices. Why might a circumstantial manufacturing defect case rarely succeed against sellers of pharmaceutical products?

B.   DESIGN DEFECTS

1.   RISK-UTILITY BALANCING

Ezagui v. Dow Chemical Corp.

598 F.2d 727 (2d Cir.1979).

■ LUMBARD, CIRCUIT JUDGE:

* * * Parke–Davis developed Quadrigen during the 1950s as a quadruple antigen product, combining diphtheria toxoids, tetanus toxoids, Salk polio vaccine, and pertussis (whooping cough) vaccine. Vaccines confer protection against diseases by introducing antigens into the body which stimulate the production of immunizing antibodies. This process occurs when lymphocytes, cells contained in the lymph glands, absorb the antigens and produce an antitoxin against the particular disease. With some infectious diseases, such as diphtheria and tetanus, it has been possible to isolate the soluble toxin or poison excreted by these bacteria and to inactivate this toxin with formaldehyde, thereby converting the toxin into what is called a toxoid. This toxoid helps immunize the body against disease by stimulating the production of antibodies, but the toxoid will not cause disease because it has lost its poisonous qualities.

By contrast, the bacterial organism which causes pertussis is so complex as to make impossible the isolation and deactivation of the toxin or poison. Since the ingredient in the pertussis bacteria which stimulates the production of protective antibodies has not been isolated, Parke–Davis and other drug companies have manufactured pertussis vaccine consisting of whole pertussis bacteria, treated to reduce their propensity to cause the disease. Because this treatment cannot completely deactivate the relevant toxin, reactions to pertussis vaccine are more frequent than are reactions to other vaccines.

In the early 1940s, drug manufacturers developed a method for combining pertussis vaccine with diphtheria and tetanus toxoids in a three-way antigen product known as "DTP" and marketed by Parke–Davis under the trade name "Triogen." This combination allowed one shot to do the work of three and was regarded as an important advance. This three-in-one combination produced no apparent increase in toxicity or reactivity.

In 1953 Dr. Jonas Salk developed a polio vaccine. Following commercial development of the Salk Vaccine, Parke–Davis decided to add the new polio vaccine to its "Triogen" product in order to develop a four-way antigen product, whereby one shot would protect against polio as well as diphtheria, tetanus, and pertussis. This new product Parke–Davis marketed under the trade name Quadrigen, beginning in July 1959.

Combining the older Triogen product with the new Salk polio vaccine, however, required a change in preservative which many investigators later believed caused the marked increase in adverse medical reactions experienced with the use of Quadrigen. All vaccines packed in multidose vials require a preservative to maintain their sterility. Prior to the development of the Salk polio vaccine, the universal preservative was merthiolate. Although originally intended to maintain sterility, merthiolate was later shown to act as a stabilizer of the vaccine, decreasing toxicity but maintaining potency. Merthiolate, however, adversely affected the polio vaccine. Accordingly, Parke–Davis selected a different preservative for use in Quadrigen. This preservative was benzethonium chloride, or Phemerol, which was Parke–Davis' trade name for this product. Later research, however, indicated that use of Phemerol caused certain endotoxins in the pertussis vaccine to leak out from the bacterial cell into the fluid which was injected. One of these endotoxins, the lipopolysaccharide, was known to cause a fever which could lead to convulsions and brain damage, as occurred in this case. From the time when they first began to investigate the marked increase in adverse reactions reported by doctors using Quadrigen [prior to the occurrence of this injury], until very recently, Parke–Davis research personnel have been on record as believing that the leakage of these endotoxins was responsible for the measured increase in adverse medical reactions associated with Quadrigen, an increase which finally led to the withdrawal of Quadrigen from the market in November 1962. (The return in 1962 to the older three-in-one product, administered with a separate polio vaccine, reduced the incidence of adverse medical reactions to their pre-Quadrigen levels.) * * *

A jury could reasonably conclude from this evidence that the pertussis vaccine is capable of causing encephalopathy such as that experienced by Mark Ezagui, and that the combination in Quadrigen of the pertussis vaccine with other chemicals materially increased this risk. * * *

PROBLEM #10. *COMBINATION VACCINES*

A researcher in England has suggested that the measles, mumps, and rubella (MMR) vaccine causes autism (a serious neurological disorder), hypothesizing that this represents a synergistic effect when the components are used in combination. See Andrew J. Wakefield et al., Ileal–Lymphoid–Nodular Hyperplasia, Non–Specific Colitis, and Pervasive Developmental Disorder in Children, 351 Lancet 637 (1998). Two years later, the CBS news program "60 Minutes" aired the story. Subsequent research found no link. See Loring Dales et al., Time Trends in Autism and in MMR Immunization Coverage in California, 285 JAMA 1183 (2001); James A Kaye et al., Mumps, Measles, and Rubella Vaccine and the Incidence of Autism Recorded by General Practitioners: A Time Trend Analysis, 322 Brit. Med. J. 460 (2001); see also Sandra Blakeslee, Panel Cautions Against Mercury Preservative, N.Y. Times, Oct. 2, 2001, at A18 (reporting that the Institute of Medicine discounted another theory, which had implicated the preservative thimerosal widely used until recently in childhood vaccines). Assume for the sake of argument that MMR causes autism at a rate of one-in–10,000 children receiving the vaccine (and that using each of the components separately at six month intervals would not reduce their effectiveness). The manufacturers respond that the single combined dose is more convenient (and therefore makes it more likely that kids will get vaccinated). How would a court engage in risk-utility balancing in a case such as this?

NOTES AND QUESTIONS

1. *Childhood vaccines.* The claim in *Ezagui* involved an unusual interaction between the pertussis component and a preservative. More frequently, plaintiffs have assailed the design of the whole-cell pertussis vaccine in isolation. The plaintiffs in these cases have suggested that "fractionated" and "acellular" forms of the pertussis vaccine represented reasonable alternative designs that would not have caused their injuries even though neither form was approved by the FDA during the relevant times. Most courts granted the manufacturer summary judgment on these design defect claims. See Ackley v. Wyeth Labs., Inc., 919 F.2d 397, 398–404 (6th Cir.1990); id. at 401 ("Without an FDA license to produce another design, Wyeth was legally prohibited from distributing either a fractionated cell or an acellular vaccine...."); Pease v. American Cyanamid Co., 795 F.Supp. 755, 757, 760 (D.Md.1992) (explaining that the FDA did not approve an acellular version until 1991, and then only as a booster because of doubts about its effectiveness in infants); White v. Wyeth Labs., Inc., 533 N.E.2d 748, 753 (Ohio 1988) (describing evidence concerning the relative safety and effectiveness of alternative vaccine designs as "speculative at best"); see also Jones v. Lederle Labs., 785 F.Supp. 1123, 1127–28 (E.D.N.Y.1992) (granting a JNOV to the manufacturer), aff'd, 982 F.2d 63, 64 (2d Cir. 1992); cf. Rohrbough v. Wyeth Labs., Inc., 719 F.Supp. 470, 477 & nn.2–3 (N.D.W.Va.1989) (granting summary judgment on lack of causation, but suggesting that the lack of FDA approval would not necessarily defeat a design defect claim), aff'd, 916 F.2d 970, 976 n.11 (4th Cir.1990) (noting "that the alternative pertussis vaccines ... have not yet been adequately shown to be safe and effective for licensure in the United States"). See generally Francis M. Dougherty, Annotation, Products Liability: Pertussis Vaccine Manufacturers, 57 A.L.R.4th 911 (1987 & 2002 Supp.). Nonetheless, a few courts have allowed the design defect issue to go to the jury. See Graham v. Wyeth Labs., 666 F.Supp. 1483, 1496–98 (D.Kan.1987); Toner v. Lederle Labs., 732 P.2d 297, 308 (Idaho 1987). Recall from Chapter 5(A) that Congress displaced much of this tort litigation when it enacted the National Childhood Vaccine Injury Act.

2. *Valuing convenience.* Assume that the elevated risk of injury in *Ezagui* had been less serious; can one justify any increase in risk that does not enhance the therapeutic effect of the product but simply reduces the number of injections required? What if an oral dosage reformulation eliminated the need to provide the vaccine by injection? See Delay Advised in Approving a Flu Therapy, N.Y. Times, July 28, 2001, at A12 (reporting that an FDA advisory committee recommended against the approval of an effective flu vaccine delivered using a nasal spray because of unresolved safety concerns). Note that pharmaceutical companies increasingly try to design time-released or other dosage forms (e.g., transdermal patches) as more convenient for the patient than having to remember to take several pills during the course of a day.

3. *High-dose estrogen contraceptives.* Oral contraceptives contain varying levels of estrogen. In the early 1970s, scientists found that high-dose versions posed a greater risk of cerebral thrombosis. Although the higher-dose versions were no more effective at preventing pregnancy than the available lower-dose versions, doctors sometimes prescribed the higher-dose versions to patients who suffered "break-through bleeding" when using the lower-dose products, a bothersome side effect that may reduce patient compliance with daily dosing directions and, thereby, reduce effectiveness. Courts typically left an analysis of this trade-off to juries. See Brochu v. Ortho Pharm. Corp., 642 F.2d 652, 654–55 & n.4 (1st Cir.1981); Ortho Pharm. Corp. v. Heath, 722 P.2d 410, 414–16 (Colo.1986); Glassman v. Wyeth Labs., 606 N.E.2d 338, 340–41, 343 (Ill.App.Ct.1992).

4. *Contraceptive devices.* Intrauterine devices (IUDs) have triggered significant products liability litigation, including claims that certain devices suffered from design defects. See Jay M. Zitter, Annotation, Liability of Manufacturer or Seller for Injury or Death Allegedly Caused by Use of Contraceptive, 54 A.L.R.5th 1, § 20 (1997 & 2002 Supp.). The most notorious involved the Dalkon Shield, which used a multifilamented tail string that transferred bacteria into the uterus at a far higher rate than other IUDs, causing pelvic inflammatory disease and occasional septic abortions. See In re A.H. Robins Co., 880 F.2d 709 (4th Cir.1989) (summarizing the history of this litigation, and affirming a class certification order and settlement agreement); Palmer v. A.H. Robins Co., 684 P.2d 187 (Colo.1984) (affirming a judgment for one plaintiff). In the end, the Dalkon Shield caused more than 200,000 injuries and almost 20 deaths in the United States. For extended accounts of this mass tort, see Ronald J. Bacigal, The Limits of Litigation: The Dalkon Shield Controversy (1990); Morton Mintz, At Any Cost: Corporate Greed, Women, and the Dalkon Shield (1985); Georgene M. Vairo, The Dalkon Shield Claimants Trust, 61 Fordham L. Rev. 617 (1992).

More recently, lawsuits have alleged design defects against the maker of the CU–7, an IUD that the FDA had regulated as a drug based on the chemical action of the copper used in the device (in the years before it had the power to require premarket approval for medical devices), based on claims that the use of a polypropylene withdrawal string was more likely than a polyethylene string to retract into the uterus where it might cause a perforation or pelvic inflammatory disease. See Adams v. G.D. Searle & Co., 576 So.2d 728, 731–34 (Fla.Ct.App.1991) (reversing a summary judgment for the defendant on a design defect claim); see also Hill v. Searle Labs., 884 F.2d 1064 (8th Cir.1989) (failure-to-warn claim involving the CU–7).

5. *Complexities with risk-utility balancing.* First, how would a jury manage to determine whether any existing (much less theoretical) alternative designs would provide at least the same therapeutic benefit in every case that a physician may encounter? Second, how would a jury assess the risk profile of an alternative treatment? Although they may be able to compare the relative risks of existing products, it is impossible for scientists, let alone courts, to predict with any accuracy the likely safety profile of purely theoretical alternative molecular structures. (In contrast to durable goods where engineers might opine that a particular design modification could improve product safety, it is impossible to anticipate the likely safety and effectiveness of a new molecular entity, which is why the FDA requires extensive clinical trials.) Third, how would a jury decide, for example, which of the following effects of an alternative design would justify a finding that an existing design was defective: (1) reducing by 50% a one-in–100,000 chance of a serious acute side effect such as anaphylactic shock, (2) eliminating an unquantified risk of chronic disease such as cancer (extrapolated from animal studies) that the FDA concluded justified only a precautionary statement in labeling, (3) eliminating a one-in–1,000 risk of blindness, or (4) eliminating a common (one–in–five chance) but nonserious side effect such as nausea or drowsiness?

These are difficult judgments routinely faced by the FDA and medical professionals, and they will depend on the countervailing benefits of the drug or device and the needs of a particular patient. See Grundberg v. Upjohn Co., 813 P.2d 89, 99 (Utah 1991) ("To determine whether a drug's benefit outweighs its risk is inherently complex because of the manufacturer's conscious design choices regarding the numerous chemical properties of the product and their relationship to the vast physiologic idiosyncracies of each consumer for whom the drug is designed."). For one unusual design defect claim premised on a seemingly trivial problem with a life-saving implant, see Bravman v. Baxter Healthcare Corp., 794 F.Supp. 96, 102 (S.D.N.Y.1992) (rejecting claim that an artificial heart valve was defective because it emitted an annoying clicking noise), aff'd, 984 F.2d 71, 76 (2d Cir.1993) ("Despite the alleged noise problems experienced by some patients, the ... heart valve has an impressive record of prolonging the lives of its recipients."), though the appellate court remanded the failure-to-warn claim for trial, see id. at 74–75; see also id. at 74 & n.2 (quoting from Edgar Allan Poe's story "The Tell–Tale Heart").

6. *Causes of patient variability.* The therapeutic requirements of patients vary widely, depending on factors such as the nature of the symptoms, progression of the underlying disease, presence of any concurrent disease conditions or use of other medications, and tolerance of specific side effects. For example, differences in metabolic patterns depending on age, gender, and ethnic background may indicate selection of a drug for some patients even if its risk-utility balance is less favorable for most other persons in the population. Physicians frequently must try different medications at different dosages until they find the one that seems to work best in a particular patient. In some cases, a patient proves to be refractory to the drug of choice but responds well to a second- or third-line therapeutic agent. This may be necessary because of "host reactions" (such as allergies). See John A. Anderson, Allergic Reactions to Drugs and Biological Agents, 268 JAMA 2845 (1992). It is well known, for instance, that certain patients are allergic to penicillin, and approximately 300 persons (representing 0.001% of all treated patients) die each year from anaphylactic reactions. See Goodman and Gilman's The Pharmacological Basis of Therapeutics 1204 (10th ed. 2001). These characteristics make pharmaceutical products fundamentally unlike durable consumer goods (such as toasters or lawn mowers), which presumably anyone equipped with basic information could select and use successfully to achieve the product's intended purpose.

Williams v. Ciba–Geigy Corp.

686 F.Supp. 573 (W.D.La.), aff'd mem., 864 F.2d 789 (5th Cir.1988).

■ VERON, DISTRICT JUDGE:

In this diversity matter under Louisiana law, the plaintiff Carolyn Sue Williams has sued the defendant Ciba–Geigy Corporation in negligence and products liability seeking damages arising out of Stephens–Johnson syndrome, a serious skin condition known to be an adverse reaction to the defendant's product Tegretol (carbamazepine), a prescription drug the plaintiff had taken under a physician's supervision. The defendant moved for summary judgment * * * *

[I]t is presumptively inappropriate for a jury to apply the pure risk-utility test of "unreasonably dangerous per se" to a known and warned-of risk of a prescription drug. Such risks have already been considered in the arduous risk-utility scrutiny of the expert Food and Drug Administration's approval procedures. The plaintiff desirous of having such a risk submitted to a jury must affirmatively show the propriety of the court's so doing. Rather than simply permitting juries to apply, haphazardly and case-by-case, the risk-utility test whenever harm results, the court must require, as a part of the plaintiff's burden of producing evidence, an articulable basis for disregarding the FDA's determination that the drug should be available. For instance, a fact question may arise where the plaintiff produces evidence tending to show that FDA approval was based on erroneous data or on an assumption that the incidence of harmful effects would be significantly lower than the actual incidence the plaintiff can objectively demonstrate. Or, the plaintiff may make out a fact question by producing evidence tending to show that notwithstanding the utility of the drug, the qualitative and quantitative harmful effects, although known and warned of, are such that reasonable minds could conclude that the FDA manifestly erred in its finding that the societal benefits of access to the drug are not outweighed by the risks. * * *

The defendant has submitted a copy of the package insert provided with Tegretol, a copy of the Tegretol entry in the *Physician's Desk Reference* (*PDR*), and the affidavits of five of the plaintiff's treating physicians, all of whom consider the warnings of Stevens–Johnson syndrome adequate and four of whom further consider Tegretol not to be "defective." The plaintiff has submitted as her opposition exhibits bibliographical listings accompanied by abstracts of the contents of each listing * * * * There is no evidence that the FDA's initial or continuing permission to market Tegretol is based on erroneous data or assumptions. Nor does the record reflect what the condition was, in the plaintiff's case, that caused Tegretol to be prescribed.

Tegretol is effective for two basic medical purposes: for the control of epileptic symptoms including psychomotor and grand mal seizures, and for relief of trigeminal neuralgia. * * * [A] layperson might define "trigeminal neuralgia" as suddenly recurring or intensifying severe pain focused roughly in the center of the head below the brain.

No evidence in the record tends to impugn the utility of Tegretol. There is no showing that any drug other than carbamazepine is effective in treating trigeminal neuralgia. Tegretol is indicated only for those sufferers of psychomotor and grand mal seizures who do not respond to, or are endangered by, more conventional anticonvulsants which have serious side effects of their own (one of the most common is phenobarbitol). One of the abstracts submitted by plaintiff outlines dangers of treating liver-damaged patients with carbamazepine, especially in conjunction with other hepatotoxic drugs, however the "[a]uthors stress that physicians should not be discouraged from using carbamazepine as a valuable anticonvulsant." The consequences of the nonavailability of Tegretol for those patients who suffer serious seizures, which can be fatal if not controlled, but who cannot take other anticonvulsants, would be grave indeed.

Proper "risk" evidence for purposes of the risk-utility test is not a mere roster of isolated incidents. Rather, "risk" in a vaccine or pharmaceutical case, as with other cases, concerns not only the qualitative harmful effect, but also the quantitative harm or "incidence" of serious adverse effects, that is, the ratio of instances of harm compared to the total use or consumption of the product. Although the danger may be devastating to those individuals who experience the worst effects, the incidence may be statistically small and the composite risk may not outweigh the value of a high utility drug. There is no question that the qualitative harmful effect of carbamazepine for some individuals can be devastating, indeed fatal, especially where interaction with other prescription drugs is a factor. Many of the possible non-fatal side effects are serious and loathsome conditions, some reversible, some not.

The quantitative risk evidence, however, is very scant. The vast majority of the abstracts submitted by plaintiff simply attribute side effects in particular cases to carbamazepine. Many of the side effects attributed to the drug result from other anticonvulsants as well. * * * [Reported toxic effects] include non-serious effects attributed to Tegretol such as drowsiness, dizziness, unsteadiness, and nausea. A high incidence of *overall* toxic effects in a strong drug such as an anticonvulsant for epilepsy is of little probative value in regard to risk-utility. Cancer chemotherapy may well entail a 100% incidence of relatively serious toxic effects, yet its utility undoubtedly outweighs the *certainty* of the poisoning, nausea, hair loss, and weight loss involved. * * * [A]ssuming the approximately 10–12% risk of severe side effects [in patients given carbamapezine], where doctors have prescribed this drug for patients with the indicated severe and life-threatening conditions and no alternative hope for treatment, reasonable minds could not find this incidence too high.

Finally, * * * [i]n the case of prescription drugs which are unavailable to the consumer except by prescription from the treating physician, warning information listed in the *PDR* should be considered as part and parcel to the product. In this case, the package insert contains substantially or identically the same warnings and information listed in the *PDR*. These warnings are very clear, frank, and comprehensive about the dangers of the drug and ways of reducing the risk. These warnings so greatly diminish the product's danger-in-fact that for this reason alone no reasonable trier of fact could conclude that this highly utile medicine is unreasonably dangerous per se. * * *

———

Restatement (Third) of the Law of Torts: Products Liability § 6
(American Law Inst. 1998):

(c) A prescription drug or medical device is not reasonably safe due to defective design if the foreseeable risks of harm posed by the drug or medical device are sufficiently great in relation to its foreseeable therapeutic benefits that reasonable health-care providers, knowing of such foreseeable risks and therapeutic benefits, would not prescribe the drug or medical device for any class of patients.

Comment f. *Manufacturers' liability for defectively designed prescription drugs and medical devices.* Subsection (c) reflects the judgment that, as long as a given drug or device provides net benefits for a class of patients, it should be available to them, accompanied by appropriate warnings and instructions. Learned intermediaries must generally be relied upon to see that the right drugs and devices reach the right patients. However, when a drug or device provides net benefits to no class of patients—when reasonable, informed health-care providers would not prescribe it to any class of patients—then the design of the product is defective and the manufacturer should be subject to liability for the harm caused.

A prescription drug or device manufacturer defeats a plaintiff's design claim by establishing one or more contexts in which its product would be prescribed by reasonable, informed health-care providers. That some individual providers do, in fact, prescribe defendant's product does not in itself suffice to defeat the plaintiff's claim. Evidence regarding the actual conduct of health-care providers, while relevant and admissible, is not necessarily controlling. The issue is whether, objectively viewed, reasonable providers, knowing of the foreseeable risks and benefits of the drug or medical device, would prescribe it for any class of patients. Given this very demanding objective standard, liability is likely to be imposed only under unusual circumstances. The court has the responsibility to determine when the plaintiff has introduced sufficient evidence so that reasonable persons could conclude that plaintiff has met this demanding standard.

An illustration accompanying comment f was inspired by the following unusual decision.

Tobin v. Astra Pharmaceutical Products, Inc.

993 F.2d 528 (6th Cir.1993).

■ GUY, CIRCUIT JUDGE:

* * * In 1986, Kathy Tobin was 19 years old and pregnant with twins. Her expected date of delivery was in early April 1987. Other than a mitral valve prolapse, or heart murmur, a rather common finding in reproductive-age women, Tobin was a healthy young woman. In mid-October 1986, Tobin was hospitalized for dehydration. She was having difficulty keeping down food and fluids and required hydration. Her condition was diagnosed as viral in origin. She was released after a few days and her pregnancy progressed. In January 1987, Tobin was admitted to the hospital for management of preterm labor. She was given an injection of magnesium sulphate and then was placed on an oral maintenance dose of ritodrine [Yutopar®]. Dosage levels varied, being increased when contractions returned.

Tobin testified that after each dose of ritodrine her pulse would race and her heart felt as if "it was going to jump out of my skin;" her face would also flush and her hands and legs would swell. She was advised that these symptoms were normal side effects of ritodrine. On March 9, 1987, Tobin's obstetricians reduced the dosage because of her rapid heart rate. On March 16, 1987, Tobin informed her doctors that she could not breathe when lying down, and she was told to further reduce the ritodrine dosage. At 1:30 a.m. on March 17, she was admitted to the hospital with symptoms of tachypnea (rapid breathing), dyspnea (shortness of breath), and a gallop rhythm of the heart. At this time, it also was noted that Tobin had a grade I/IV systolic murmur of the heart. X-rays revealed that she had pulmonary edema (fluid in the lungs) and cardiomegaly (enlargement of the heart) caused by congestive heart failure. An electrocardiogram revealed advanced dilated cardiomyopathy. Ritodrine was discontinued, and that afternoon plaintiff delivered healthy twins having a gestational age of 37 weeks.

On March 20, Tobin was discharged from the hospital with instructions to follow up with a cardiologist. The next day she was readmitted for treatment of congestive heart failure, cardiomyopathy, and pulmonary edema. After five days in the hospital, she was again released. She was readmitted on April 10, and on April 15 a mechanical heart, or ventricular assist device, was inserted until a donated heart for a heart transplant could be found. On April 16, Tobin underwent a heart transplant.

Plaintiff filed suit against Duphar B.V., the corporation in the Netherlands that manufactures ritodrine, and against Astra Pharmaceutical, Duphar's United States distributor. After removal to federal court on diversity grounds, the district court granted Duphar's motion to dismiss for lack of personal jurisdiction. Plaintiff proceeded against Astra. After a two-week trial, the jury returned a verdict in favor of the plaintiff. The jury awarded Tobin approximately $4.5 million, finding Astra liable on the basis of defective design and failure to warn for the conditions that led to her heart transplant. The district court denied Astra's motion for j.n.o.v. or in the alternative for a new trial, and Astra timely appealed. * * *

Ritodrine belongs to a class of compounds known as betamimetics. These compounds mimic adrenaline, a natural hormone. A betamimetic, or beta-receptor agonist, exerts its effect by stimulating beta-adrenergic receptors. There are at least two sub-groups of beta receptors, beta–1 and beta–2. The heart contains beta–1 receptors, which, when stimulated, result in an increased heart rate and a rise in systolic pressure concomitant with a decrease in diastolic pressure. The force with which the heart contracts also increases. Stimulation of beta–2 receptors inhibits contractility of smooth muscle, such as that contained in the uterus.

Ritodrine, which at low doses preferentially affects beta–2 receptors, is administered to pregnant women to arrest premature labor. The drug, however, may also exert pronounced beta–1 effects. Ritodrine may unmask occult heart conditions and is specifically contraindicated when a patient suffers from cardiac disease.

Both plaintiff's causation expert, Dr. Waller, and defendant's causation expert, Dr. O'Connell, testified that Tobin's viral infection in October 1986 resulted in myocarditis, an inflammation of the heart muscle. Dr. O'Connell testified that approximately 70 percent of us have been infected by a virus that causes myocarditis and that at least 50 percent of us actually have had the virus infect our heart, and therefore, by definition, have had myocarditis. But Dr. O'Connell testified that most people recover without ever having known it. Dr. Waller's main causation theory was that Tobin would have recovered from the myocarditis, just like the vast majority of people, if it had not been for the added strain of the ritodrine. Dr. O'Connell, on the other hand, testified that plaintiff's cardiomyopathy could be explained by the myocarditis and her twin pregnancy which placed additional strain on her heart. Dr. Waller also felt that there was evidence that ritodrine had a direct effect on plaintiff's heart. * * *

Under Kentucky law, the test for whether a product is in a defective condition and unreasonably dangerous to the user is whether an ordinarily prudent manufacturer, being fully aware of the risks, would have placed the product on the market. Plaintiff argues that the only way to decide whether an ordinarily prudent manufacturer would place a product on the market is to balance the product's risks, its harmful side effects, against its benefits. Defendant argues that Kentucky has never adopted the risk/benefit analysis proffered by plaintiff. * * *

In a nutshell, plaintiff claims that oral ritodrine is bereft of benefits as far as improving neonatal outcome.[8] Weighing no benefits against the serious risks posed by the drug and suffered by the plaintiff, it is clear, plaintiff asserts, that the risks outweigh the benefits and thus no "ordinarily prudent manufacturer" would put the drug on the market. Astra maintains that oral ritodrine is effective in prolonging pregnancy, and therefore in improving neonatal outcome, and that the risks to maternal and fetal health associated with oral ritodrine are outweighed by the benefits of reducing neonatal morbidity and mortality. Astra also maintains that, because of FDA approval, ritodrine's effectiveness is not open to question.

Plaintiff's expert in this area was Dr. Mortensen. Dr. Mortensen, a pediatrician with a master's degree in pharmacology and trained in toxicology, reviewed the test results that were submitted to the FDA with the New Drug Application in 1974. Dr. Mortensen also reviewed several articles discussing betamimetic drugs in general and ritodrine in specific. * * * Dr. Mortensen has experience in clinical studies on the efficacy of drugs. Her testimony centered on the testing procedures used in various studies of the efficacy of ritodrine and the interpretation of the test results. Her testimony on the clinical studies investigating ritodrine was properly allowed.

---

8. Plaintiff does acknowledge that there may be some benefit in improving the overall quality of life for the mother during the remainder of the pregnancy by avoiding repetitive hospitalization.

Before addressing the arguments concerning efficacy, we must first address whether plaintiff should have been allowed to litigate the efficacy issue at all. Defendant argues that "[p]laintiff should not have been permitted to litigate this issue, because it is a mockery of the scientific analysis employed by the FDA and the Advisory Committee which conclusively found that ritodrine was efficacious." We reject the argument that FDA approval preempts state product liability claims based on design defect. * * *

FDA approval is evidence which the jury may consider in reaching its verdict. The jury may weigh FDA approval as it sees fit, especially in a case where the plaintiff has presented evidence to support an articulable basis for disregarding an FDA finding—in this case the finding that ritodrine was effective. Tobin presented an articulable basis for disregarding the FDA's finding that ritodrine was effective in improving neonatal outcome: the individual studies relied on by the FDA were insufficient to support a finding of efficacy as found by the FDA Advisory Committee, and the pooled data requested by the Advisory Committee was statistically invalid.

To understand the arguments of the parties concerning ritodrine's effectiveness, it is necessary to review the New Drug Application that was submitted to the FDA and the results of the required clinical trials, along with subsequent articles that have been published discussing ritodrine. Approval of a new drug by the FDA requires a showing of substantial evidence of efficacy based upon adequate and well-controlled studies. The required clinical studies on ritodrine consisted of Phase I (16 studies in healthy patients to determine safety), Phase II (5 studies in preterm labor patients to determine efficacy), and Phase III (11 studies in preterm labor patients comparing ritodrine patients to non-ritodrine controls to determine safety and efficacy).

The clinical trials were designed to measure a gain in days in the length of pregnancy as a measure of efficacy under the assumption that any increase in the gestational period would reduce neonatal morbidity and mortality. The Phase III studies consisted of tests of oral ritodrine's effectiveness based on three separate testing procedures: a placebo series, in which oral ritodrine was compared to the use of a placebo; an ethanol series comparing ritodrine to the use of ethanol; and a series referred to as the "Creasy studies," in which all patients were treated with injections of intramuscular ritodrine and then half received oral maintenance doses of ritodrine while the other half received placebos. In the Creasy studies, any recurrences of premature labor were treated with injections of intramuscular ritodrine.

After the data from these studies w[ere] submitted to the FDA, the FDA Advisory Committee on Fertility and Maternal Health Drugs found that the required clinical trials failed to demonstrate efficacy. Specifically, "the tenor of the committee was that there was not substantial data to support the efficacy of ritodrine for the treatment of premature labor." The Advisory Committee found that three of the Phase III placebo-controlled studies were flawed because they included women who were not actually in preterm labor. Because the remaining individual studies did not have a sufficient number of patients to establish statistical significance regarding improvement in neonatal outcome, the Advisory Committee requested the data be pooled and resubmitted. The initial data was presented in terms of gain in days; it did not include statistics on neonatal outcome or mortality. The Advisory Committee requested that, when the data was resubmitted, it should include such information. The manufacturer was asked to pool the data from all the studies for an all-patient analysis; stratify all of the patients by gestational age; and analyze neonatal mortality, birth weight, and the incidence of respiratory distress syndrome.

Dr. Peter, who participated in the proceedings before the FDA, testified at trial that this pooled data does not represent statistically valid results. * * * Dr. Little of the committee commented that "obviously, it is not reasonable to pool data." Yet, on the basis of the originally submitted data, which the Advisory Committee had found did not contain substantial evidence to support a finding of efficacy, and the newly reworked data, the committee recommended approval.

The FDA made its own determination regarding efficacy. FDA regulations require that efficacy be established by "at least two 'adequate and well-controlled' studies." Warner–Lambert Co. v. Heckler, 787 F.2d 147, 151 (3d Cir.1986). The FDA determined that four of the Phase III studies met this test, and approved ritodrine in 1980. The four studies are referred to by the names of the project leaders: Fuchs, Barden, Creasy, and Sivasambo. Plaintiff introduced evidence regarding the methodology and conclusions of each study.

In the Fuchs study, the control group of mothers were treated with intravenous ethanol and no follow-up, while ritodrine patients were given initial intravenous doses of ritodrine and follow-up oral doses. The control group was further along in gestation based on each mother's last menstrual period, and the group was found to be in more advanced labor, in that they were more dilated, than the ritodrine group. The Sivasambo study compared ritodrine to librium, which according to recent studies actually increases uterine activity. The Creasy study, described above, did not have an adequate control group, in that all patients were given intramuscular injections of ritodrine at the onset of premature labor and again if contractions returned. In a later publication, Dr. Creasy stated that "further studies have not proved that oral maintenance will decrease the incidence of preterm birth.... [T]hey do show that such an approach will decrease the need for repetitive hospitalization, thus improving the overall quality of life for the remainder of the pregnancy." The final study relied on by the FDA, the Barden study, involved a total of only 25 patients—some given oral ritodrine and others given a placebo.

Astra's evidence focused on the effect of oral ritodrine in prolonging the term of pregnancy, and then separately showed that extending the term of pregnancy improves neonatal outcome. Plaintiff refuted this claim with evidence that, while ritodrine may produce a short-term gain in prolonging pregnancy, there is no evidence of improved neonatal outcome. Plaintiff introduced articles written after the FDA approval. * * *

We do not sit to review the findings of the FDA; our only role in this appeal is to decide if there was sufficient evidence on which the jury could base its verdict. Plaintiff introduced evidence, through the cross-examination of Astra officials, that a reasonably prudent manufacturer would not market ritodrine if the evidence of its efficacy was inconclusive. Plaintiff also introduced sufficient evidence regarding the various clinical studies concerning the efficacy of ritodrine. The jury found that ritodrine, as manufactured and marketed by Astra, was in a defective condition and unreasonably dangerous to plaintiff. We find that there was sufficient evidence before the jury to conclude that a prudent manufacturer knowing all the risks would not market ritodrine. * * *

NOTES AND QUESTIONS

1. *Not ready for prime time?* The court's opinion in *Tobin* is remarkable. First, although it refers to later studies, the court does not base its decision on post-approval data; instead, it allows a jury to conclude (with the assistance, of course, of the parties' experts) that the FDA blew it by using a surrogate end-point (i.e., gestational age) for a clinical end-point (i.e., neonatal health) and by accepting clinical trials that the agency's advisory committee viewed as methodologically flawed. In effect, despite its protestations to the contrary, the court holds that Astra should not have begun marketing even after it received FDA approval. (Does it matter that the FDA had not approved any other tocolytic agents as of 1993, or that neonatal intensive care was more primitive when it approved ritodrine in 1980?) Second, the court marginalizes ritodrine's evident effectiveness in reducing the need for repeated hospitalizations during the pregnancy. Why doesn't this count (and what does this suggest about the emphasis on *"therapeutic* benefits" in *Rest. (3d)* § 6(c))? In effect, the court turns a complex risk-utility judgment (using data from less than ideal clinical trials) into a no-brainer by allowing the jury to conclude that the drug is totally ineffective (meaning that any risk makes the product's design defective). Although this patient suffered a severe injury that may have resulted from use of the drug, the labeling did warn of some cardiac risks, and the court focuses only on utility. Third, the court gives exaggerated significance to the comments of the advisory committee, disregarding the fact that the FDA had undertaken a lengthy internal review and had no obligation to abide by the committee's recommendations. In 1992, based on newly published research, another FDA advisory committee concluded that oral ritodrine lacked effectiveness at current dosages. See F–D–C Rep. ("The Pink Sheet"), Nov. 2, 1992, at 4. The drug remains available in the U.S., though only in an injectable form (oral dosage forms are still marketed in Canada).

2. *Trying to get the inside scoop.* In *Reiter,* the plaintiff introduced an expert affidavit from a former FDA official, but parties to tort litigation generally cannot subpoena agency employees to testify. See 21 C.F.R. § 20.1; David P. Graham & Jacqueline M. Moen, Discovery of Regulatory Information for Use in Private Products Liability Litigation: Getting Past the Road Blocks, 27 Wm. Mitchell L. Rev. 653 (2000); cf. In re Kessler, 100 F.3d 1015 (D.C.Cir.1996) (enforcing a subpoena of FDA's Commissioner in litigation that challenged agency action); United States v. Wood, 57 F.3d 733, 737–38 (9th Cir.1995) (holding that the FDA must disclose relevant internal records to a defendant when it brings a criminal prosecution). Even so, when it approves a product or initiates enforcement action, the FDA leaves a paper trail that parties may wish to use in a products liability case. See, e.g., Sabel v. Mead Johnson & Co., 737 F.Supp. 135, 140–44 (D.Mass.1990) (rejecting hearsay objection to the introduction of a letter from an FDA reviewer to the sponsor recommending revisions in risk labeling). In addition, plaintiffs may try to use the Freedom of Information Act (FOIA), 5 U.S.C. § 552, in order to access relevant records held by the agency. See Edward A. Tomlinson, Use of the Freedom of Information Act for Discovery Purposes, 43 Md. L. Rev. 119 (1984). Manufacturers may try to prevent disclosure by invoking one of FOIA's exemptions, especially the one protecting trade secrets and confidential commercial data. See Webb v. HHS, 696 F.2d 101 (D.C.Cir.1982); see also 21 U.S.C. § 331(j) (directing the FDA to protect trade secrets); 21 C.F.R. § 20.61; Public Citizen Health Research Group v. FDA, 185 F.3d 898 (D.C.Cir.1999); Teich v. FDA, 751 F.Supp. 243 (D.D.C.1990); Lawrence Kaplan, Annotation, What Constitutes "Trade Secrets and Commercial or Financial Information Obtained from Person and Privileged or Confidential," Exempt from Disclosure Under Freedom of Information Act, 139 A.L.R. Fed. 225 (1997).

3. *Rest. (2d) § 402A comment k vs. Rest. (3d) § 6(c).* As discussed in the previous chapter, some courts interpreted comment k as extending blanket immunity from strict products liability claims against sellers of prescription drugs and medical devices, but this did not foreclose design defect claims sounding in negligence (or strict liability design defect claims if the product was not properly prepared or labeled). The new *Restatement* offers a unitary standard for judging design defect claims in such cases. See Rest. (3d) § 6, at 159. If you represented a defendant in a jurisdiction that has not yet sided with either formulation, which would you advocate? (Does the apparent mischief in *Tobin* color your assessment?)

4. *Drugs vs. medical devices.* As explained in the new *Restatement*, § 6(c) "is a significant departure from the general defective design rules ..., in recognition of the unique characteristics of prescription drugs and medical devices." Rest. (3d) § 6, at 158. The black letter formulation of this design defect standard applies equally to prescription drugs and prescription medical devices. This corresponds with the case law applying *Rest. (2d)* § 402A comment k to sellers of certain medical devices, especially implants, but are there any arguments for differentiating between these two broad categories of medical technologies for purposes of engaging in design defect scrutiny?

New drugs are not "designed" in the same sense as durable consumer goods; they are "discovered." At least until recently, the molecular structure of an active drug ingredient could not be redesigned. Instead, if the FDA concludes that the risks of a new drug outweigh its benefits in the intended patient population, the product is not approved and the unsuccessful applicant must restart the process of discovery and testing from scratch. Although it may be appropriate to allow fact-finders to imagine design alternatives in the case of machinery, where some design modifications would require limited added costs (e.g., a hand guard for a power tool), a pharmaceutical manufacturer is not free to redesign an approved new drug. Theoretical molecular redesigns cannot be marketed until the manufacturer discovers this allegedly superior chemical, subjects it to a full battery of preclinical and clinical testing over a period of several years, and the FDA completes its lengthy reviews.

In some cases, a design defect may relate to the proportions of active ingredients used in a combination drug product rather than the design of the chemicals themselves, but relative dosage issues of this sort are better understood as questions about the adequacy of the instructions. Even minor changes in formulation (e.g., different inactive ingredients) would require the submission of an NDA supplement to the FDA (with supporting data to demonstrate bioavailability of the active ingredient). For instance, OxyContin® (an extended-release formulation of oxycodone, a synthetic form of morphine effective in relieving severe or chronic pain such as that experienced by cancer patients) caused deaths among abusers who had managed to defeat the delayed-release mechanism by crushing or dissolving the pills. See Barry Meier, U.S. Asks Painkiller Maker to Help Curb Wide Abuse, N.Y. Times, May 1, 2001, at A12. After the filing of several lawsuits, the manufacturer announced plans to add an ingredient (naltrexone) that could deactivate the oxycodone when crushed, but it explained that the reformulation would have to await FDA approval. See Rita Rubin, Abuse–Resistant OxyContin Planned, USA Today, Aug. 9, 2001, at 2A.

Medical devices differ, however, from prescription drugs in this respect. Medical devices are built rather than discovered, and innovation in this field tends to be incremental. See In re Am. Med. Sys., Inc., 75 F.3d 1069, 1081 n.12 (6th Cir.1996); James S. Benson, Forces Reshaping the Performance and Contribution of the U.S. Medical Device Industry, 51 Food & Drug L.J. 331, 332 (1996) ("[M]edical device product development is inherently iterative, depending heavily on feedback from user experience in real-life clinical settings."); Robert Langreth, Medtronic: Pacing the Field, Forbes, Jan. 8, 2001, at 42 (explaining that one successful device manufacturer's product lines are constantly evolving). Perhaps juries can more easily judge the trade-offs made in the course of designing devices. See Hopkins v. Dow Corning Corp., 33 F.3d 1116, 1119, 1126 (9th Cir.1994) (affirming plaintiff's verdict based in part on an allegation that the manufacturer failed to redesign breast implants to reduce the risk of leakage and rupture). Moreover, the FDA's premarket screening mechanism accommodates the introduction of new and slightly improved models of medical devices (recall from Chapter 3 the phenomenon of "substantial equivalence creep"). Finally, as explained previously, patient variability in drug metabolism makes it difficult to engage in risk-utility balancing for pharmaceuticals, but medical devices generally would not present any such concerns. Nonetheless, focusing on the public policy rationales for reducing the liability of sellers that supply therapeutic products, the new *Restatement* does not differentiate between prescription drugs and medical devices, and courts already have applied § 6(c) to implanted devices. See, e.g., Wheat v. Sofamor, S.N.C., 46 F.Supp.2d 1351 (N.D.Ga.1999); Sita v. Danek Med., Inc., 43 F.Supp.2d 245, 255 (E.D.N.Y.1999); Gebhardt v. Mentor Corp., 191 F.R.D. 180 (D.Ariz.1999). For additional case law involving design defect (and other) claims against medical device firms, see Romualdo P. Eclavea, Annotation, Products Liability in Connection with Prosthesis or Other Product Designed to Be Surgically Implanted in Patient's Body, 1 A.L.R.4th 921 (1980 & 2002 Supp.); Debra T. Landis, Annotation, Products Liability: Medical Machinery Used in Plaintiff's Treatment, 34 A.L.R.4th 532 (1984 & 2002 Supp.).

5. *Time dimension and the state-of-the-art.* As explained at greater length in Chapter 7(A), product manufacturers need only warn of risks "knowable" at the time of sale. Similarly, their obligation to adopt reasonable alternative designs only applies to those redesigns knowable at the time of sale (a.k.a., "the state-of-the-art"). Although a complex issue even in run-of-the-mill products liability cases, this becomes especially tricky with technologically sophisticated products subject to lengthy premarket review by administrative agencies. If risk information comes to light late in the process, sellers generally still can make labeling modifications before sale, but designs become fixed earlier in the R&D process. If the test asks about the availability of a reasonable alternative design, should the question focus on risks and redesigns knowable at the time when the seller (1) discovers the compound, (2) begins clinical trials, (3) files an application with the FDA, (4) receives agency approval, (5) introduces the product into commercial distribution, or (6) sells the unit that injures the plaintiff? Recall that the investigational process unavoidably continues after product approval. Should the test ask instead about the state-of-the-art at the time of the plaintiff's injury, or perhaps even at the time of trial? See generally James A. Henderson, Jr., Coping with the Time Dimension in Products Liability, 69 Cal. L. Rev. 919 (1981); John W. Wade, On the Effect in Product Liability of Knowledge Unavailable Prior to Marketing, 58 N.Y.U. L. Rev. 734 (1983).

6. *Product category liability as the de facto test for design defects in the case of prescription products.* In *Williams v. Ciba–Geigy*, the court held that Tegretol was not "unreasonably dangerous per se" (in effect, defective even without proof of a reasonable alternative design). The *Restatement* rejects the proposition that some types of products may create such a high risk of injury and have so little social utility (e.g., cigarettes) that they should be regarded as defective even without proof of a reasonable alternative design. See Rest. (3d) § 2 cmt. e. This comment concedes, however, that products such as toy guns that shoot hard rubber pellets or prank exploding cigars may have a "manifestly unreasonable" design if courts define the relevant product category (and substitutes) too narrowly. See id. at 22 ("The court would declare the product design to be defective and not reasonably safe because the extremely high degree of danger posed by its use or consumption so substantially outweighs its negligible social utility that no rational, reasonable person, fully aware of the relevant facts, would choose to use, or to allow children to use, the product."); see also James A. Henderson, Jr. & Aaron D. Twerski, Closing the American Products Liability Frontier: The Rejection of Liability Without Defect, 66 N.Y.U. L. Rev. 1263, 1316–31 (1991); David G. Owen, The Graying of Products Liability Law: Paths Taken and Untaken in the New Restatement, 61 Tenn. L. Rev. 1241, 1253–57 (1994). Because particular prescription drugs (and perhaps also medical devices) often represent a class onto themselves without clear therapeutic substitutes, section 6(c) has created a similar standard for judging design defect. Instead of asking whether a reasonable alternative design exists, the test is whether a fully-informed health care provider would ever prescribe the product to any patient. One central objection to the recognition of a broader form of product category liability is that it would allow courts to decide that lawfully marketed products should not be available to consumers. Isn't this objection even more powerful in the case of a medical technology whose sale has been authorized by an expert agency and requires the intervention of a learned intermediary? If a prescription drug manufacturer has provided an adequate warning to the health care providers responsible for selecting a therapeutic intervention for a particular patient, how can a jury properly decide after the fact that the drug should never have been approved for any class of patients and not selected for purposes of treating the plaintiff?

7. *Holdouts.* Courts have not exactly rushed to embrace the *Restatement*'s new test for design defects involving prescription drugs and devices. In evaluating a design defect claim against the manufacturer of Accutane® (isotretinoin), a prescription drug for the treatment of cystic acne, the Nebraska Supreme Court explained its rejection of section 6(c) in the following terms:

> First, it does not accurately restate the law. It has been repeatedly stated that there is no support in the case law for the application of a reasonable physician standard in which strict liability for a design defect will apply only when a product is not useful for any class of persons. Rather, ... the majority of courts apply some form of risk-utility balancing that focuses on a variety of factors, including the existence of a reasonable alternative design. The few cases that the Third Restatement cites to as support for the reasonable physician test also apply a risk-utility test. Thus, § 6(c) does not restate the law and instead seeks to formulate new law with no precedential support.

> Second, the reasonable physician test is criticized as being artificial and difficult to apply. The test requires fact finders to presume that physicians have as much or more of an awareness about a prescription drug product as the manufacturer. The test also ignores concerns of commentators that physicians tend to prescribe drugs they

are familiar with or for which they have received advertising material, even when studies indicate that better alternatives are available.

A third criticism of particular applicability to Freeman's case is that the test lacks flexibility and treats drugs of unequal utility equally. For example, a drug used for cosmetic purposes but which causes serious side effects has less utility than a drug which treats a deadly disease, yet also has serious side effects. In each case, the drugs would likely be useful to a class of patients under the reasonable physician standard for some class of persons. Consequently, each would be exempted from design defect liability. But under a standard that considers reasonable alternative design, the cosmetic drug could be subject to liability if a safer yet equally effective design was available. As a result, the reasonable physician standard of § 6(c) of the Third Restatement has been described as a standard that in effect will never allow liability. However, a standard applying a risk-utility test that focuses on the presence or absence of a reasonable alternative design, although also rarely allowing liability, at least allows the flexibility for liability to attach in an appropriate case.

Fourth, the test allows a consumer's claim to be defeated simply by a statement from the defense's expert witness that the drug at issue had some benefit for any single class of people.... [E]ven though the rule is reformulated, any application of § 6(c) will essentially provide the same blanket immunity from liability for design defects in prescription drugs as did the application of comment k in the few states that interpreted it as such.

Freeman v. Hoffman–La Roche, Inc., 618 N.W.2d 827, 839–40 (Neb.2000).

8. *Prescription vs. OTC products and the debate over the consumer expectations test.* One of the most significant and controversial aspects of the new *Restatement* concerned its rejection of the warranty-inspired consumer expectations test still used by some jurisdictions in design defect cases in favor of a risk-utility test that asks whether a reasonable alternative design exists that would have avoided the plaintiff's injury. See Rest. (3d) § 3 & cmts. d-g; id. at 44–94 (providing an exhaustive survey of the case law and scholarly literature addressing this question); James A. Henderson, Jr. & Aaron D. Twerski, Achieving Consensus on Defective Product Design, 83 Cornell L. Rev. 867 (1998) (same); see also Hansen v. Baxter HealthCare Corp., 764 N.E.2d 35 (Ill.2002) (refusing to abandon the consumer expectations test); Green v. Smith & Nephew AHP, Inc., 629 N.W.2d 727 (Wis. 2001) (rejecting the risk-utility standard on a design defect claim against the seller of latex gloves used by health care workers, and holding that the defendant could be held strictly liable even if it could not have known of the risk of allergic reactions at the time of sale). California uses both tests, depending on the complexity of the product, and a pair of intermediate court decisions involving medical devices reflect this tension. Compare West v. Johnson & Johnson Prods., Inc., 220 Cal.Rptr. 437, 452 (Ct.App.1985) (allowing a plaintiff to use the consumer expectations test in a design defect claim against the manufacturer of a tampon that caused toxic shock syndrome), with Rosburg v. Minnesota Mining & Mfg. Co., 226 Cal.Rptr.

299, 303–05 (Ct.App.1986) (allowing expert testimony about the limited life expectancy of a breast implant to rebut the plaintiff's belief that the device should last a lifetime); see also Brown v. Superior Court, 751 P.2d 470, 477–78 (Cal.1988) (explaining that the consumer expectations test has no place in cases involving prescription drugs); Schindler v. Sofamor, Inc., 774 A.2d 765 (Pa.Super.Ct. 2001) (spinal fixation device could not be expected to last forever in case of nonfusion); cf. Shanks v. Upjohn Co., 835 P.2d 1189, 1193–98 (Alaska 1992) (adopting modified forms of the consumer expectations and risk-utility tests for judging the design of prescription drugs). But cf. Freeman v. Hoffman–La Roche, Inc., 618 N.W.2d 827, 840 (Neb.2000) (using consumer expectations test for Accutane). Other courts have recognized that the consumer expectations test is more apt for nonprescription drugs than for products requiring professional intervention. Even in cases involving OTCs, in jurisdictions that continue to use both tests for design defect, some courts allow plaintiffs to use a risk-utility standard because otherwise an adequate warning might defeat a design claim based on consumer expectations. See Reece v. Good Samaritan Hosp., 953 P.2d 117, 122–23 (Wash.Ct.App.1998). But see Haddix v. Playtex Family Prods. Corp., 138 F.3d 681, 684–86 (7th Cir.1998) (affirming summary judgment for a tampon manufacturer because the plaintiff could not opt to use the risk-utility test for such a simple product and her design defect claim failed under the consumer expectations test where the labeling included a clear warning of the risk of toxic shock syndrome). See generally John P. Ludington, Annotation, Products Liability: Toxic Shock Syndrome, 59 A.L.R.4th 50 (1988 & 2002 Supp.).

9. *Further commentary.* See Richard L. Cupp, Jr., Rethinking Conscious Design Liability for Prescription Drugs: The Restatement (Third) Standard Versus a Negligence Approach, 63 Geo. Wash. L. Rev. 76 (1994); Margaret Gilhooley, When Drugs Are Safe for Some but Not Others: The FDA Experience and Alternatives for Products Liability, 36 Hous. L. Rev. 927 (1999); Michael D. Green, Prescription Drugs, Alternative Designs, and the Restatement (Third): Preliminary Reflections, 30 Seton Hall L. Rev. 207 (1999) (symposium); James A. Henderson, Jr., Prescription Drug Design Liability Under the Proposed Restatement (Third) of Torts: A Reporter's Perspective, 48 Rutgers L. Rev. 471 (1996); David S. Torborg, Comment, Design Defect Liability and Prescription Drugs: Who's in Charge?, 59 Ohio St. L.J. 633 (1998); Dolly M. Trompeter, Comment, Sex, Drugs, and the Restatement (Third) of Torts, Section 6(c): Why Comment E Is the Answer to the Woman Question, 48 Am. U. L. Rev. 1139 (1999); Jeffrey D. Winchester, Note, Section 8(c) of the Proposed Restatement (Third) of Torts: Is It Really What the Doctor Ordered?, 82 Cornell L. Rev. 644 (1997).

2. BIOMATERIALS SUPPLIERS

In re TMJ Implants Products Liability Litigation
97 F.3d 1050 (8th Cir.1996).

■ BOWMAN, CIRCUIT JUDGE:

This appeal arises from a multidistrict litigation proceeding, consolidating approximately 280 products liability actions * * * * Plaintiffs-appellants are the recipients of the Proplast TMJ Interpositional Implant, a prosthetic device used to correct temporomandibular joint (TMJ) disorders. The TMJ connects the upper and lower jaw; it facilitates normal movement of the jawbone. When the articulating surface of the jawbone that fits into the TMJ becomes diseased, normal mobility can be restored by implanting a prosthetic device like the Proplast TMJ Interpositional Implant. The gravamen of the complaint is that the implants failed, abrading the surrounding bone and causing pain to the Recipients.

The implants were invented, designed, tested, manufactured, packaged, and sold by Vitek, Inc., a now bankrupt company founded by Dr. Charles Homsy. Du Pont and Durafilm are the named defendants in this action, however, because they manufactured and supplied some of the raw materials that were used to construct the implants—including polytetrafluoroethylene powder and fiber (PTFE resin) and fluorinated ethylene propylene film (FEP film). Du Pont manufactured both of these materials and sold them under the familiar Teflon trademark. Durafilm distributed FEP film, but did not manufacture it. PTFE resin and FEP film are chemically inert with a wide variety of safe industrial uses. PTFE is used to manufacture everything from bearings in jet aircraft to non-stick surfaces on frying pans. FEP film is used in applications ranging from pipe insulation to solar collectors.

In the late 1960s, Dr. Homsy invented the implant biomaterial Proplast while conducting prosthesis research at Methodist Hospital in Houston, Texas. Proplast is a spongy and highly porous coalesceable gel designed to promote tissue attachment. Dr. Homsy founded Vitek in 1969 to manufacture and distribute his Proplast prosthetic devices while he continued his research at Methodist Hospital. To make Proplast, Vitek combined PTFE resin with carbons and solvents and then subjected this mixture to an eight-step patented process of heating, compressing, and drying. The implant itself is formed by molding the Proplast into the required shape and laminating one side of it with translucent FEP film. The FEP film layer replaced the meniscus or articulating surface of the TMJ and was designed to protect the underlying Proplast from wear in load-bearing joints like the TMJ. Surgeons positioned the implant so that the Proplast side would be anchored eventually by tissue growth while the FEP film side abutted the lower jaw to shield against wear. The chain of distribution for PTFE resin and FEP film thus began with Du Pont or Durafilm as the initial suppliers, then continued on to Vitek as the finished product manufacturer, and finally ended with the Recipients as the ultimate users of the finished product. Each implant, while selling for at least fifty dollars, contained only a few cents' worth of PTFE resin and FEP film.

When Du Pont learned that Dr. Homsy intended to use its Teflon products for medical purposes, Du Pont advised the purchasing agent at Methodist Hospital by a March 13, 1967, letter that its Teflon products were not made for medical applications and that Du Pont had not conducted the necessary long-term studies to determine the suitability of fluorocarbons for medical use. Du Pont's letter also noted several published scientific reports indicating that pure Teflon implants wore badly and had a tendency to disintegrate in load-bearing joints. Consequently, Du Pont required the hospital to sign a disclaimer, acknowledging Du Pont's warnings and agreeing to use its own independent medical and legal judgment as to the safety of Teflon in the implants. * * *

Based on years of clinical studies with Proplast implants in animals and humans and his extensive experience in the manufacturing and marketing of prosthetic devices, Dr. Homsy believed that Proplast was an excellent implant material. Indeed, two FDA advisory committees stated that "the safety and effectiveness of [Proplast] has been established through long-term clinical trials." The FDA authorized the sale of Proplast TMJ implants in 1983. By the late 1980s, however, it had become apparent that the FEP film abraded into particles despite the additional precautions Vitek had taken to ensure that this would not happen. In November 1989, Du Pont informed Vitek and Dr. Homsy that it would no longer fill Vitek's orders for Teflon because of concerns about lawsuits spawned by the disintegrating implants. In January 1991, the FDA ordered Proplast implants removed from the market because of their fragmentation and irritation to human tissue.

The Recipients filed this action against the defendants, asserting strict liability and negligence claims. * * * The Recipients argue that the district court erred in granting summary judgment against them because they have raised factual issues as to whether FEP film was defectively designed. The Recipients insist that, even though FEP film has many safe industrial uses and is not inherently dangerous or defective for all uses, the film was defectively designed for its "reasonably foreseeable" use in the implants. In other words, they claim that FEP film was designed defectively, not because it malfunctioned, but because when incorporated into the implants it caused the implants to function in an unreasonably dangerous manner. We reject this argument because * * * the defect was in the overall design of the implants and not in the FEP film. FEP film is a mere building-block material suitable for many safe uses. The Recipients' argument boils down to nothing more than the fact that Vitek decided to use what proved to be an unsuitable material to manufacture its implants. The erroneous and unfortunate decision to use FEP film in the design of the implant was made by Vitek, however, not by Du Pont or Durafilm. * * * Therefore, as courts in other TMJ implant cases already have held, we hold that the defendants were entitled to summary judgment on the design defect claim.

While the law of design defect clearly extends liability to finished product manufacturers like Vitek, it rarely imposes strict liability on component part suppliers who merely sell their multi-use parts to manufacturers of finished products. The critical inquiry focuses on determining the reason why the component part turned out to be unsuitable for use in the finished product. "If the failure was due to a flaw in the component part, then the component part is itself defective and the cause for the assembled product being defective." In such cases, the component part maker may be held strictly liable. Apperson v. E.I. du Pont de Nemours & Co., 41 F.3d 1103, 1106 (7th Cir.1994) ("Strict liability may extend to manufacturers of component parts for injuries caused by design or manufacturing defects in the component part itself."); Bond v. E.I. du Pont de Nemours & Co., 868 P.2d 1114, 1119 (Colo.Ct.App.1993) ("[A] plaintiff must present evidence from which a jury could find that any 'defect' was in the 'design' of the component part, not the final product.").

If, on the other hand, the finished product was unreasonably dangerous because the component part was unsuited for the particular use that the finished product manufacturer chose to make of it, then the defect is in the design of the finished product rather than in the design of the component part. In these cases, it is the finished product manufacturer and not the component part supplier that may be held strictly liable. In this case, the undisputed facts show as a matter of law that the defect was in the overall design of the implants and not in the design of FEP film. The Recipients simply have failed to show that the disintegration of the implants was due to any design defect in the FEP film itself rather than to Vitek's erroneous decision to incorporate what turned out to be an unsuitable material into its implants.

The Recipients argue that our focus should not be "on the general uses of FEP film but rather on the defective nature of FEP film for its reasonably foreseeable use in TMJ implants." We disagree. "While manufacturers of inherently dangerous raw materials will be held liable for injury caused by their product, courts have treated differently manufacturers of inherently safe components when the final assembly, rather than a manufacturing or design defect in the component itself, renders the component dangerous." Apperson, 41 F.3d at 1107. Indeed, "[t]he alleged foreseeability of the risk of the finished product is irrelevant to determining the liability of the component part manufacturer because imposing such a duty would force the supplier to retain an expert in every finished product manufacturer's line of business and second-guess the finished product manufacturer whenever any of its employees received any information about any potential problems." Kealoha v. E.I. du Pont de Nemours & Co., 844 F.Supp. 590, 594 (D.Haw.1994), aff'd, 82 F.3d 894, 901 (9th Cir.1996).

Making suppliers of inherently safe raw materials and component parts pay for the mistakes of the finished product manufacturer would not only be unfair, but it also would impose an intolerable burden on the business world, especially where, as here, the raw material or component part (the FEP film) accounts for only a few cents' worth of the cost of the entire finished product (the Proplast TMJ implant). See Kealoha, 844 F.Supp. at 595 ("[T]he cost to a manufacturer of an inherently safe raw material to insure against all conceivable misuse of his product would be prohibitively expensive."). As another panel of this court has determined in a previous TMJ case, "[i]t would be unreasonable and impractical to place the burden of testing and developing all devices that incorporate Teflon as a component on Du Pont." Rynders v. E.I. Du Pont de Nemours & Co., 21 F.3d 835,

842 (8th Cir.1994). Suppliers of versatile materials like chains, valves, sand, gravel, etc., cannot be expected to become experts in the infinite number of finished products that might conceivably incorporate their multi-use raw materials or components. *Kealoha*, 844 F.Supp. at 594 ("[T]here would be no end to potential liability if every manufacturer of nuts, bolts and screws could be held liable when their hardware was used in a defective product."). We thus believe that the Recipients' argument must be rejected.
* * *

As the Fifth Circuit recently noted in another TMJ case:

> If Du Pont had designed Teflon otherwise, it would not have been Teflon. Similarly, if a different product would have served more safely in its stead, Dr. Homsy erred by choosing Teflon for use in TMJ implants. The design of Teflon was not, in this context, defective. Any fault lay with Homsy's selection. Teflon therefore is not unreasonably dangerous in design.

Klem v. E.I. du Pont de Nemours Co., 19 F.3d 997, 1003 (5th Cir.1994); accord Hoyt v. Vitek, Inc., 894 P.2d 1225, 1231 (Or.Ct.App.1995) ("In short, if Teflon were designed differently, it would not have the properties that make it useful in so many applications."); Longo v. E.I. du Pont de Nemours & Co., 632 So.2d 1193, 1197 (La.Ct.App.) ("[B]ecause of its unique and peculiar qualities, there appears to be no question but that Teflon could not have been designed with less harmful consequences. If so, it would not have been Teflon."), writ denied, 637 So.2d 464 (La.1994). There is no allegation that FEP film, in and of itself, is inherently dangerous. Indeed, the Recipients concede that FEP film has many safe industrial uses. As the Seventh Circuit noted, "Clearly, Teflon is a raw material with many safe uses; it only became dangerous when Vitek incorporated it into a highly specialized medical device, the Proplast TMJ Implant." *Apperson*, 41 F.3d at 1106; see also Jacobs v. E.I. du Pont de Nemours & Co., 67 F.3d 1219, 1241 (6th Cir.1995). In these circumstances, the responsibility to design a safe medical device is Vitek's alone because, as the finished product manufacturer, it knew the specific end-use it intended to make of the FEP film and was in a far better position to evaluate the film's safety for that particular end-use. Summary judgment thus was properly granted for the defendants on the design defect claim.
* * *

■ Heaney, Circuit Judge (dissenting):

The majority expands the component part supplier doctrine to shield from liability even those suppliers who knew how their product was going to be used and knew that the intended use posed grave danger to the ultimate consumers. I cannot accept such blanket protection for component part manufacturers. In this case, I would permit the Recipients' claims to go to a jury for a determination of what DuPont knew and whether it had a duty to prohibit the sale of Teflon for use in human implants, or at least to provide adequate warnings to Vitek of those known risks.

Underlying the component part supplier doctrine is the premise that the manufacturer of a finished product is generally in a better position to detect its potential dangers than the manufacturer of only a part of the product. Certainly, a finished product manufacturer is responsible for dangers that result from the product design or from the manner in which a component part is integrated into the finished product. As a corollary, manufacturers of a component part generally will not know about such dangers and should not be required to research every possible application of its nondefective, multi-use product.

But the facts of this case place it outside the parameters of the general component part supplier doctrine. The Recipients have presented evidence sufficient for a jury to find that DuPont knew Vitek was going to use the Teflon in the TMJ implants. There is also evidence that DuPont knew that Teflon, used in load-bearing human implants, no matter how the implants were designed, can disintegrate and cause injury to implant recipients. DuPont was aware of several studies demonstrating this precise risk. Moreover, a chemist who worked for DuPont for over thirty years testified that a known characteristic of all Teflon, including FEP film, is that it severely fragments after constant contact with and pressure from sharp edges.

This is not a case, as the majority contends, of an "erroneous decision to incorporate what turned out to be an unsuitable material." Rather, the evidence suggests that DuPont was fully aware of the serious risk of harm Teflon posed when used in human implants. To hold DuPont responsible for these known risks would not require component part suppliers to research every possible application of its product; it recognizes DuPont's actual knowledge, without any further research or speculation. Nor are the Recipients claiming that DuPont should have designed FEP film differently, as the majority suggests, but that if DuPont knew the film was inappropriate for use in human implants, it should not have continued to supply the film.

There is significant "social utility" in making DuPont accountable for what it knew and for its failure to prevent harm to the ultimate consumers. While Vitek may have been in the better position to evaluate the film's safety for the particular use, DuPont's position may well have been sufficient for it to have known of the harm Teflon posed in the human implants. It is my position that where the component part manufacturer knows that its product is going to be used in a particular fashion and knows that, no matter what the design, the product poses a danger to the ultimate consumer, it cannot escape from liability.

NOTES AND QUESTIONS

1. *The high price of success.* DuPont ultimately prevailed in all of the TMJ lawsuits filed against it for supplying raw materials. In addition to the decisions cited above, see, e.g., Anguiano v. E.I. Du Pont De Nemours & Co., 44 F.3d 806 (9th Cir.1995); LaMontagne v. E.I. Du Pont De Nemours

& Co., 41 F.3d 846 (2d Cir.1994). DuPont expended significant resources, however, for its string of victories during the decade that this litigation lasted, paying far more in legal fees than it ever earned on this minor application. See Gary Taylor, A Discovery by DuPont: Hidden Costs of Winning, Nat'l L.J., Mar. 27, 1995, at B1 (reporting one estimate that the company spent more than $40 million defending itself).

2. *Breast implant litigation.* After the largest manufacturer of silicone-gel breast implants filed for bankruptcy protection from the numerous products liability claims, see In re Dow Corning Corp., 211 B.R. 545, 551–54 (Bankr.E.D.Mich.1997), plaintiffs' lawyers began pursuing Dow Chemical as the supplier of the raw silicone. See, e.g., Dow Chem. Co. v. Mahlum, 970 P.2d 98 (Nev.1998) (upholding a compensatory damage award of $4.2 million, but reversing a punitive damage award of $10 million). Dow Chemical usually prevailed, and the lawsuits filed against other companies that had supplied silicone to other manufacturers of breast implants have not succeeded. See In re Silicone Gel Breast Implants Prods. Liab. Litig., 996 F.Supp. 1110 (N.D.Ala.1997); Artiglio v. General Elec. Co., 71 Cal. Rptr.2d 817, 822–23 (Ct.App.1998). Even so, spooked by lawsuits of these sorts, Dow discontinued supplying silicone for other important medical device applications such as hydrocephalus shunts. See RAND Sci. & Tech. Policy Inst., Biomaterials Availability: Potential Effects on Medical Innovation and Health Care, Issue Paper No. 194, Jan. 2000, at 17, 32.

3. *Legislative response.* In the context of such litigation, biomaterials companies refused to supply implant manufacturers with needed components. See Barnaby J. Feder, Implant Industry Is Facing Cutback by Top Suppliers, N.Y. Times, Apr. 25, 1994, at A1. In response to fears of an emerging shortage of raw materials needed to make life-saving medical devices, Congress passed (and, in sharp contrast to other recent tort reform initiatives, the President signed) the Biomaterials Access Assurance Act of 1998, 21 U.S.C. §§ 1601–1606. Under this statute, which displaces applicable state law, a biomaterials supplier that neither manufactured nor sold the allegedly defective implant would face tort liability only if it "failed to meet contractual requirements or specifications" when it furnished raw materials or component parts. See id. § 1604. When named in a lawsuit as a co-defendant, the biomaterials supplier receives certain procedural benefits, including protection from sweeping discovery requests and an opportunity to seek an expedited dismissal with prejudice or summary judgment if the plaintiff cannot establish that the supplier also made or sold the implant or furnished nonconforming biomaterials. See id. § 1605. The biomaterials supplier remains subject to impleader, but only if the claimant or device manufacturer can persuade the trial judge that the negligence or intentionally tortious conduct of the previously dismissed biomaterials supplier caused the harm, and that the manufacturer cannot or should not shoulder the full amount of any tort judgment. See id. § 1606; see also 66 Fed. Reg. 17,562 (2001) (announcing the availability of a draft guidance for implementing a procedure to petition the FDA for a declaration concerning a biomaterials supplier's compliance with establishment registration requirements). See generally Ann Marie Murphy, Note, The Biomaterials

Access Assurance Act of 1998 and Corporate Supplier Liability: Who You Gonna Sue?, 25 Del. J. Corp. L. 715 (2000).

4. *Bulk supplier doctrine.* Even outside of the biomaterials context, companies that sell raw materials or components that are incorporated into finished products will rarely face tort liability. See White v. Weiner, 562 A.2d 378 (Pa.Super.Ct.1989) (upholding summary judgment for a company that had supplied bulk active ingredient to another company that manufactured a prescription drug that caused a patient's death); see also Rest. (3d) § 5 (setting forth the bulk supplier doctrine).

C.   FEAR OF MALFUNCTION

Willett v. Baxter International, Inc.

929 F.2d 1094 (5th Cir.1991).

■ WISDOM, CIRCUIT JUDGE:

The plaintiff, Gene Earl Willett, sued the defendants, Baxter Healthcare Corporation and Carbomedics, Inc., seeking to recover for his fear that his allegedly defective heart valve, manufactured by the defendants, would fail. Mrs. Albert Spriggins, and her husband, intervened in the action, seeking the same recovery. * * * In January of 1988, Dr. White E. Gibson III, a New Orleans cardiovascular surgeon, replaced deteriorating heart valves in both Willett and Mrs. Spriggins with artificial heart valves manufactured by the defendants. In June of 1988, Willett read an article in his local paper that discussed Baxter's voluntary suspension of the marketing of the valves. * * *

Each artificial heart valve has two leaves, made of pyrolitic carbon, that control the flow of blood through the valve. The voluntary recall was prompted by several reports of a phenomenon known as "leaflet escape." Leaflet escape refers to the in vivo escape of one of the two leaflets that controls the flow of blood through the valve.

The plaintiff and the intervenor alleged that their valves were defective in that pyrolitic carbon was not well-suited for use in heart valves because of the possibility of stress fractures in the material. The plaintiff and the intervenor do not deny that their valves are currently functioning properly. Instead, they seek damages for their fear that their valves will fail in the future. * * *

[A]pproximately 19,614 patients received these valves between 1982 and the first quarter of 1990. Since the valves were first implanted, only seventeen cases of leaflet escape have been reported. Of the seventeen reported cases, fifteen involved mitral valves, and two involved aortic valves. All seventeen cases occurred in valves manufactured before April of 1986. The valves of both the plaintiff and the intervenor were manufactured after April of 1986. Of the valves manufactured since April of 1986, no failures have been reported.[4]

From the evidence, a reasonable jury could conclude that leaflet escape is caused by stress fractures in the pyrolitic carbon. From the evidence, it appears that pyrolitic carbon is very resistant to the start of a stress fracture. But once a stress fracture has begun, the fracture will grow at a fairly steady rate, and may eventually lead to leaflet escape.

Baxter published at least three clinical reports documenting the leaflet escape problem in January of 1987, November of 1987, and January of 1988. The articles described the failures that had occurred to date. While the reports stated that the cause (or causes) of the failures was uncertain, the articles suggested that the problem may have been caused by improper surgical technique. Specifically, the reports suggested that, during the surgical procedure, a valve may have been scratched or improperly exposed to certain chemicals. This scratch or improper exposure created a weak spot in the leaflet, where a stress fracture could begin.

In contrast, the plaintiff and the intervenor argue that the manufacturing process inevitably leads to weak spots in the leaflets. They rely on the deposition testimony of one Dr. Harvey Miller Flower, taken from the sealed court records. According to Dr. Flower, soot pockets can form in pyrolitic carbon during manufacture. If not discovered, the soot pocket might weaken the leaflet sufficiently that a stress fracture can begin. Notably, the expert did not testify that another material was more suitable than pyrolitic carbon for use in the valves, or that a different manufacturing or quality control process could have reduced a theoretical soot pocket problem. Dr. Flower also did not testify as to how often undiscovered soot pockets would develop given the manufacturing and quality control process used by the defendants.

The plaintiff and the intervenor provided no evidence that their particular valves actually suffered from a soot pocket problem, and no evidence that their valves were not performing as designed. On the contrary, their surgeon, Dr. Gibson stated, in his affidavit, that the valves implanted in both Willett and Mrs. Spriggins were functioning normally. He also stated that, to a reasonable degree of medical certainty, the valve replacement had saved their lives and greatly improved their quality of life. The district court granted summary judgment in favor of the defendants. The district court held that the valves were functioning normally and were therefore not defective * * * *

First, to establish that a product is unreasonably dangerous per se, a plaintiff must show that the likely harm of the product outweighs its benefit. Based on the summary judgment evidence, a reasonable jury could not find that the pyrolitic carbon heart valves are unreasonably dangerous

---

4. It is unclear whether the defendants changed their manufacturing or quality control process in April of 1986. As a result, it is unclear why the more recently manufactured valves have not failed. The defendants may have solved the problem, or it may simply be that the valves fail over time, and sufficient time has not passed for the more recently manufactured valves to fail.

per se. The undisputed evidence establishes that the valves have extended over nineteen thousand lives. While the valve replacement was not successful in every case, the undisputed evidence established that, even with the risk of leaflet escape, a patient has a much greater chance for life with the valve replacement than without the replacement. From the record, the only reasonable conclusion is that the clear life-saving benefits of the heart valve outweigh its risks.

Second, the plaintiff and the intervenor argue that the existence of soot pockets in some valves is sufficient to create a factual issue as to whether their valves have soot pockets. While we agree that a soot pocket may be a manufacturing defect, the mere possibility of a manufacturing defect is not sufficient to establish the fact of a manufacturing defect in the valves implanted in the plaintiff and the intervenor.

Third, the plaintiff and the intervenor argue that pyrolitic carbon is not suited for use in a heart valve, and that its use establishes a defect in the design of the product. * * * [A] plaintiff would have to present evidence that the defendants knew or should have known of an alternative, either for the heart valve itself or for the pyrolitic carbon in the heart valve, with a failure rate lower than the failure rate established by the summary judgment evidence for the pyrolitic carbon heart valves. The plaintiff and the intervenor presented no evidence of a less risky alternative. * * *

While we recognize that the fear of an unknowable, but potentially fatal, defect in a heart valve is perfectly rational, and almost certainly sincere, we have serious concerns about permitting recovery for such fear absent actual failure of the valve.[20] We do not decide these issues, though, because of our resolution of the defect issue. * * *

PROBLEM #11. *HANDLING Y2K PARANOIA*

In 1989, Walter Stiles, age 49, underwent surgery to implant a pacemaker to assist his failing heart. He received a Cardiotronic Model #75, a

20. The plaintiff and the intervenor argue that there is no difference between allowing recovery for fear and mental anguish as an element of damages if the product in fact fails, and for the fear and mental anguish that the product will fail. We see one critical difference that we illustrate using the facts in this case. Under the current law, if the seventeen persons whose valves actually failed establish a defect, then they can recover mental anguish as a component of their damages. The damages of the seventeen are presumably incorporated into the price of the product and spread among the nineteen thousand who have purchased the valve. In contrast, under the plaintiff's theory, all nineteen thousand would be able to seek recovery for their fear. Again, the probable recovery would be included in the price, but instead of spreading a concentrated loss over a large group, each patient would cover his own probable fear recovery (plus the costs of litigation) by paying a higher price for the heart valve in the first instance. Because no loss-spreading occurs, the money flows in a circle, from each patient (in the form of a higher price) to the company back to the same patient (in the form of a fear recovery), with a substantial portion of the higher price skimmed off for attorneys' fees. In addition, the higher price will place the product beyond the economic reach of at least some of the patients, forcing them to turn to the next best (affordable) alternative. We see little reason to adopt such a system.

medical device first approved by the FDA in 1985. Like many other electronic appliances sold nowadays, the pacemaker was designed with an imbedded computer chip. The chip, which monitored the pacemaker's power source and circuitry, allowed a physician to scan the device periodically without requiring any invasive procedures. During semiannual visits to Mr. Stiles' regular physician, Dr. Laura Manning, the readouts for the pacemaker consistently showed nothing abnormal in its operation.

In 1996, reports began to surface in the media about the so-called "Year 2000 problem" or "millennium bug" in older computer chips. Because dates used only the last two digits of the year, concerns developed that computers would, on Jan. 1, 2000, instead interpret the year as 1900. A great deal of effort and money went into making computers Year 2000 (Y2K) compliant. Upon hearing these reports, Mr. Stiles became alarmed that his pacemaker would malfunction on Jan. 1, 2000. He asked Dr. Manning about this at his Dec. 1998 checkup, but she dismissed his concerns as unfounded. Dr. Manning explained that, at worst, the scanned readouts would provide an incorrect date but there was no reason to fear a malfunction. Mr. Stiles was initially relieved, but he again became worried during the summer of 1999 after having done some additional research on the Internet. Several web sites warned of impending disasters for recipients of pacemakers and other electronic implants. One Internet site directed him to a surgeon in a nearby city, Dr. Ronald Akers, who offered explants of old pacemakers and replacements with Y2K compliant models.

Mr. Stiles was quite agitated when he arrived at Dr. Akers' office and demanded the explant procedure, which Dr. Akers scheduled for Dec. 20, 1999. Realizing that even a short delay could spell disaster, Mr. Stiles became increasingly fearful that he would die at the stroke of midnight on New Year's Eve. In the meantime, the FDA sent an urgent "Dear Doctor" letter warning surgeons against unjustified explant procedures because most pacemakers used computer chips that were not "date aware." On Dec. 15th, the office assistant for Dr. Akers called Mr. Stiles and left a message on his answering machine, saying only that his surgery had been cancelled. Upon arriving at home that evening, Stiles heard the message and became despondent. During a restless night, he suffered a stroke that left him in a permanently vegetative state. Mr. Stiles' pacemaker worked perfectly for another two years until he finally died while in the hospital. His estate plans to sue the manufacturer, Cardiotronic Corp. What claims might Mr. Stiles' estate might bring and what are their probable chances of success?

NOTES AND QUESTIONS

1. *Latent defects and emotional distress.* Other courts have rejected fear of malfunction claims. See Angus v. Shiley Inc., 989 F.2d 142, 147–48 (3d Cir.1993); Walus v. Pfizer, Inc., 812 F.Supp. 41, 44–45 (D.N.J.1993) (collecting cases); Pfizer, Inc. v. Farsian, 682 So.2d 405, 407–08 (Ala.1996), conformed to certified question, 97 F.3d 508 (11th Cir.1996). These issues resemble toxic tort litigation brought by persons exposed to hazardous substances who seek to recover for their enhanced future risk of developing cancer. See Note, Latent Harms and Risk–Based Damages, 111 Harv. L. Rev. 1505 (1998); David Carl Minneman, Annotation, Future Disease or Condition, or Anxiety Relating Thereto, As Element of Recovery, 50 A.L.R.4th 13 (1986 & 2002 Supp.). Recent lawsuits involving the recalled diet drugs fenfluramine and dexfenfluramine (Redux®) have posed these issues as well insofar as plaintiffs allege that they fear developing heart valve abnormalities. See Richard B. Schmitt, Woman Wins $56.6 Million in AHP Case, Wall St. J., Apr. 9, 2001, at B7.

2. *Recalls and prophylactic explant surgery.* If a medical device manufacturer recalls an implant, courts generally have allowed recipients to recover the costs associated explant surgery and accompanying emotional distress. See Larsen v. Pacesetter Sys., Inc., 837 P.2d 1273, 1286–87 (Haw.1992). If, however, explant surgery is not medically-indicated but undertaken at the patient's insistence, courts have rejected such claims. See O'Brien v. Medtronic, Inc., 439 N.W.2d 151 (Wis.Ct.App.1989). Where defects may require explantation in limited circumstances, plaintiffs may request medical monitoring costs. See In re Telectronics Pacing Sys., Inc., 172 F.R.D. 271, 276–78, 284–87 (S.D.Ohio 1997), rev'd on other grds., 221 F.3d 870 (6th Cir.2000); see also 29 Prod. Safety & Liab. Rep. (BNA) 209 (2001) (reporting on a class action lawsuit filed on behalf of recipients of Sulzer hip implants seeking medical monitoring expenses).

Bowling v. Pfizer, Inc.

922 F.Supp. 1261 (S.D.Ohio), aff'd mem., 103 F.3d 128 (6th Cir.1996).

■ NANGLE, DISTRICT JUDGE:

* * * Between 1979 and 1986, Shiley, Inc., a wholly-owned subsidiary of Pfizer, Inc., manufactured a human-implant heart valve known as the Bjork–Shiley convexo/concave heart valve ("c/c heart valve" or "valve"). Somewhere between 50,000 and 100,000 of the valves were implanted in patients world-wide. By 1992, approximately 450 of these valves had fractured resulting in approximately 300 deaths. The valves continue to fracture today and it is anticipated that they will continue to do so in the future.

As early as 1984, consumer groups such as the Washington, D.C.-based Public Citizen, Inc., claimed that the c/c heart valve posed a serious public health threat because it had design and manufacture defects which caused it to have an abnormally high risk of fracture. Defendants have steadfastly denied that the c/c heart valve is any more likely to fracture than any other valve available on the market at that time; however, when Public Citizen petitioned the Food and Drug Administration in 1990 to require defendants to notify implantees of the risks associated with the valves, defendants voluntarily agreed to undertake to find and notify implant patients and their physicians of the alleged risks posed by the valves.

The c/c heart valve has engendered a substantial amount of litigation. Individuals implanted with valves that have fractured, as well as individuals with properly functioning valves, have brought suit against defendants in jurisdictions across the United States. In every suit involving a valve that had actually fractured, defendants were able to settle the case with a confidential agreement. In cases where there had been no fracture, however, defendants were able to get at least 27 courts to dismiss the suits on the ground that there is no right of recovery for emotional distress arising from a valve implantee's fear that a properly functioning valve might fracture in the future.

Although defendants had generally been successful at settling all fracture cases and getting non-fracture cases dismissed, the litigation and attendant poor publicity was nevertheless taking its toll. Defendants were having to devote substantial resources to defending the nation-wide litigation, and a California court denied their motion for summary judgment in a case where a plaintiff had a properly functioning c/c heart valve. Furthermore, criticism of the valve and of the defendants in newspaper articles, television programs and even congressional hearings began to mount. Thus, as Judge Spiegel observed in his order finding the proposed settlement to be fair, defendants had ample reason to settle all claims involving their c/c heart valves.

All of the named plaintiffs in this action had properly functioning c/c heart valves when their complaint was filed on April 19, 1991. The causes of action asserted in their complaint included negligence, strict liability, negligent misrepresentation, fraudulent misrepresentation, intentional infliction of emotional distress, and negligent infliction of emotional distress; and the relief sought included compensatory damages, medical monitoring, and punitive damages. * * *

The settlement applies to all living persons currently implanted with c/c heart valves (approximately 50,000 people) and their current spouses, except those who file valid and timely requests for exclusion. The settlement has three primary components: The Patient Benefit Fund, The Medical and Psychological Consultation Fund, and The Fracture Compensation Mechanism.

A.   The Patient Benefit Fund

The Patient Benefit Fund is a guaranteed fund of $37.5 million, which may increase to as much as $75 million, that is to be used to fund research and development and valve replacement surgery ("explanation") for qualifying class members. The settlement requires defendants to deposit $12.5 million following "Final Approval of the Settlement," and then $6.25 million annually starting on the second anniversary of the Final Approval of the Settlement. Once the defendants have contributed $37.5 million to the Fund, they are entitled to go before the court and argue that further research would be fruitless and that they should not, therefore, be required to make further contributions to the Fund. If they are unsuccessful in their argument, then they are required to continue the annual contribution of $6.25 million until they have deposited a total of $75 million.

In order to administer the benefits available under the Patient Benefit Fund, the settlement creates a seven-member Supervisory Panel to manage the research and to determine whether a class member qualifies for a particular benefit. The Panel is to be comprised of six experts and one layman and all of the fees and expenses of the Panel are to be paid from this Fund. The specific benefits available under the Fund are:

Research and Development. The fund will pay for research and development of diagnostic techniques to identify implantees who have a significant risk of valve fracture, and research to reduce and properly characterize the risks associated with valve replacement surgery.

Payment of Expenses Associated with Explant Surgery. Payment of the usual and customary expenses for valve replacement surgery that are not covered by a third-party payor (i.e. insurance company, government, etc.), where surgery is necessitated by risk of valve fracture.

$38,000.00 for Miscellaneous Expenses. Payment of $38,000.00 to each member who undergoes an explant surgery approved by the Panel and who does not suffer death or permanent bodily injury. This payment is to cover miscellaneous costs of post-hospitalization care, meals, travel, etc.

Temporary Loss of Income. Member's actual lost income, up to $1,500.00 per week for a maximum of 16 total weeks, resulting from a member's inability to work because of hospitalization and recuperation from a qualifying valve replacement surgery. The amount payable is reduced by any payments available from a third-party payor, such as worker's compensation, sick pay, disability insurance, etc. The lost income is only payable from the sixteenth through fifty-second week after surgery.

Permanent Loss of Income. If, after one year, a member is partially disabled from explant surgery and, as a result, suffers a diminished earning capacity and/or extraordinary medical expenses, then he will receive compensation for future income loss that is not covered by workmen's compensation, a disability policy or other third-party source.

Alternative Payment for Death or Permanent Total Disability. If valve replacement surgery results in death or permanent total disability, then a member is entitled to: (1) The same payment available to a member whose valve actually fractures under the Valve Compensation Mechanism; or (2) compensation as set by an arbitration procedure.

Payment for FDA Approved Diagnostic Procedure. If the Food and Drug Administration approves a technique for diagnosing valves with a high risk of fracture, then the Supervisory Panel may use the money from the Fund to pay for the use of the technique on class members where it is reasonably medically necessary.

Additionally, this portion of the settlement permits a class member, who qualifies for valve replacement surgery but chooses not to undergo surgery, to bring an action for damages for alleged emotional distress from fear of fracture of a working valve if the class member has not received any fracture compensation under the settlement. Finally, in the event that class members continue to qualify for explant surgery after the Fund is fully expanded to $75 million, the settlement obligates defendants to continue to pay all of the members' qualifying expenses and benefits listed above even though defendants' total contribution to the Fund would exceed $75 million.

B. The Medical and Psychological Consultation Fund

The Medical and Psychological Consultation Fund is a fund of at least $80 million, which could increase to as much as $130 million, that is intended to provide class members with funds to obtain medical and psychological consultation. The Fund will provide an equal cash payment of between $2,500.00 and $4,000.00 to each member, depending upon how many class members make a claim. Defendants are also required, under this part of the settlement, to pay an additional $10 million into the Fund, which is to be paid to spouses of valve implantees ("Spousal Compensation Fund"). * * *

C. The Valve Fracture Mechanism

The third component of the settlement, the Valve Fracture Mechanism, provides an implantee whose valve has fractured with one of three options for seeking compensation. The first option is a sort of insurance program whereby compensation is determined by a set of formulas that take into account a claimant's family status, age, income and country of residence. The compensation available to a United States resident, for example, ranges from a minimum of $500,000.00 to a maximum of $2,000,000.00, while the payment to members from other countries may be something less but is in no event less than $50,000.00. The settlement creates a Foreign Fracture Panel, which will determine fair compensation for fracture claimants who are residents of countries other than the United States.

The second alternative available to a fracture claimant under the mechanism is binding arbitration. The claimant can bring his or her claim before a three-member panel, whose decision is final and binding. The third option is to bring suit against defendants in an appropriate forum, with all claims and defenses preserved. * * *

An important issue of settlement interpretation that has arisen is whether a class member implanted with a valve that suffers a so-called "single-leg fracture" or "single-strut separation" qualifies for explanation benefits and/or compensation under the Fracture Mechanism. Class and Special Counsel took the position that a member suffering a single-leg separation should receive the same treatment under the settlement that a member suffering a full, dual-leg fracture receives.[12] Defendants disagreed, taking the position that a single-leg separation is qualitatively different from a full, dual-leg fracture and, as a result, a class member suffering such a separation should not be entitled to the same benefits as a member suffering a complete fracture. The parties resolved the issue through an agreement that Class Counsel would negotiate with the defendants each single-leg fracture case on an individual basis. * * *

12. It is the court's understanding that, when only one of the two legs on the c/c valve fractures, the valve continues to function; whereas, when both legs fracture, the valve stops functioning.

CHAPTER 7

INFORMATIONAL DEFECTS

In products liability litigation, failure-to-warn claims have become quite common, supplanting the more traditional and difficult to prove claims such as those alleging defects in manufacture or design. Although prescription drugs by their very nature are most often the subject of lawsuits alleging failures to warn, medical devices and OTC drugs also have been faulted for informational defects. Two difficult questions arise: is there any obligation to warn of a particular risk and, if such a duty exists, was any warning already provided with the product adequate.

A.   TRIGGERING THE DUTY TO WARN

1.   UNKNOWABLE RISKS

Feldman v. Lederle Laboratories

479 A.2d 374 (N.J.1984).

■ SCHREIBER, JUSTICE:

* * * Tetracyclines are a group of antibiotics that was first introduced in 1948. They were produced by different drug manufacturers that marketed the drugs under various trade names.

Defendant first marketed Declomycin in 1959. The *Physicians' Desk Reference (PDR)*, a book used by doctors to determine effects of drugs, contains data furnished by drug manufacturers about drugs, their compositions, usages, and reactions. The 1959 *PDR* entry for Declomycin stated that it had a greater antibiotic potency that made it possible to achieve therapeutic activity with less weight of antibiotic; it had a reduced renal clearance rate that produced a prolongation of the antibacterial levels in the body; and it was therapeutically equally effective as other tetracyclines in infections caused by organisms sensitive to the tetracyclines. The *PDR* is produced annually. Until the 1965 or 1966 edition, the *PDR* did not mention that tooth discoloration was a possible side effect of Declomycin. Since 1965 or 1966 the *PDR* has stated that the drug, when administered to infants and children, could cause tooth discoloration that would be permanent if the drug were given during the developmental stage of the permanent teeth.

Plaintiff, Carol Ann Feldman, was born on February 8, 1960. Her father, Dr. Harold Feldman, asserted that he prescribed Declomycin for her approximately seven or more times from September or October, 1960, when she was eight or nine months old, until the end of 1963. She was given this drug to prevent secondary infections when she had different childhood diseases. In his words, "[i]t was a very effective drug for what I was using it for." He had been introduced to the drug by a medical representative employed by the defendant. The representative gave him a number of samples to be distributed to patients. Plaintiff's baby teeth were discolored gray-brown. Her permanent teeth were more deeply discolored, being primarily gray. The parties agreed that this discoloration had resulted from use of a tetracycline, although they disputed whether Declomycin was the particular tetracycline involved. * * *

The respective experts, Dr. Bonda for the plaintiff and Dr. Guggenheimer for the defendant, agreed that scientific literature existed by 1960 that referred to tooth staining being caused by tetracycline. Dr. Bonda specifically mentioned a 1956 article by Dr. Andre reciting that tetracycline accumulated in mineralized portions of growing bones and teeth of mice; an article by Dr. Milch in the July 1957 *Journal of the National Cancer Institute* reporting that laboratory animals had yellow fluorescents in bones, including teeth, following dosages of tetracycline; a second article by Dr. Milch in the July 1958 issue of the *Journal of Bone and Joint Surgery* again describing fluorescents in the bones and incisor teeth of rodents that had been fed tetracycline; a 1959 article by Dr. Swackman noting that, of 50 children with cystic fibrosis who had received massive doses of tetracycline, 40 had dark tooth staining; a 1960 letter from Dr. Sigrelli, a Columbia University professor, to the *Pediatric Journal* observing that patients with cystic fibrosis of the pancreas who had received tetracyclines as an antibiotic suffered severe discoloration of their teeth, possibly as a result of their tetracycline use; a May 1961 article by Dr. Sigrelli in the *New Jersey/New York State Dental Journal* containing the same information; and an essay by Dr. Bevlander on "The Effect of the Administration of Tetracycline on the Development of Teeth" in the October 1961 issue of the *Journal of Dental Research* reflecting the adverse effect of tetracycline on developing teeth in young laboratory animals. Dr. Bonda concluded the defendant should have begun to investigate the possible effects of all forms of tetracycline on teeth no later than 1956, when the Andre article appeared.

Defendant's expert, Dr. Guggenheimer, on the other hand, noted that before 1962 the literature on tooth discoloration concerned only patients with cystic fibrosis who had been receiving massive doses of tetracyclines. He pointed out that Dr. Milch's papers described only fluorescents, not tooth staining. He testified that Declomycin did not become available until 1959 and that it would take 2½ years for permanent teeth developing in 1959 to erupt. The completion of accurate controlled studies of multiple well-documented cases would have been the only way one could really know whether Declomycin caused tooth discoloration in permanent teeth. Dr. Guggenheimer's testimony is unclear as to whether a correlation between tetracycline and tooth discoloration had been established in 1962. One reading of his testimony indicates that such a correlation was not known to exist and that only by hindsight could that conclusion be drawn. It is also possible to interpret his opinion to be that such correlation had been established in 1962. In any event it is significant that Dr. Guggenheimer gave no opinion as to 1963.

On November 16, 1962, Dr. Swanzey, defendant's Director of Regulatory Agencies Relations, wrote to the Federal Food and Drug Administration (FDA) that the defendant proposed to add to the labels on all its tetracycline products the following warning: "During therapy tetracyclines may form a stable calcium complex in bone-forming tissue with no known harmful effects. Use of any tetracycline during teeth development in the neonatal period or early childhood may cause discoloration of the teeth." Dr. Swanzey explained that it was not necessary to obtain FDA approval before placing a warning on a label, but it was the practice to do so. On cross-examination, however, he indicated that, although no FDA approval was needed to write letters to doctors informing them of this correlation, labeling the product without FDA approval could be considered a misbranding.

The FDA acknowledged receipt of Dr. Swanzey's letter on December 3, 1962, and advised him that the FDA "has been acutely interested by the increasing number of new and/or undesirable effects accompanying or following the use of these products," and would notify the defendant "as soon as any conclusion is reached." Dr. Swanzey telephoned Dr. Barzilai of the FDA, who advised against putting any statement in a circular proposed to be distributed by the defendant and that the FDA had the matter under study. On January 15, 1963, Dr. Swanzey sent to the FDA two articles on bone effects, including a copy of the Bevlander article. Dr. Swanzey also spoke with Dr. Sigrelli, who advised that staining would occur with some tetracyclines, but he had not observed that it occurred with Declomycin.

The FDA, in a letter dated February 4, 1963, proposed that the defendant insert the following warning statement in "all" its tetracycline products:

> Tetracyclines may form a stable calcium complex in any bone forming tissue with no serious harmful effects reported thus far in humans. However, use of any tetracycline drug during tooth development (= last trimester of pregnancy, neonatal period and early childhood) may cause discoloration of the teeth (= yellow-grey-brownish). This effect occurs mostly during long-term use of the drug but it has also been observed in usual short treatment courses.

Dr. Swanzey responded that the suggested statement was satisfactory and would be incorporated in its literature. He added that he assumed that the directive was applicable to Declomycin as well as other tetracycline drugs. The FDA replied that "[t]here is practically no specific clinical evidence to substantiate such a labeling requirement" for Declomycin and the warning would have to appear only on labeling of other tetracycline drugs. On April 12, 1963, the FDA made it clear that the warning statement was to refer not to tetracyclines generally but only to the specific brand names of the implicated products.

In 1963, the defendant received complaints from eight doctors that Declomycin was causing tooth staining. In May, 1963 the defendant referred the FDA again to the side effect of Declomycin. Commencing in mid-December 1963, after receipt of FDA approval, it included the same warning in the Declomycin literature as in other tetracyclines. * * *

This is a strict liability warning case. The product has been made as the manufacturer intended. The plaintiff does not contend that it contained a manufacturing defect. Declomycin's purpose was to act as did other tetracyclines—as an antibiotic. However, it had several advantages over other antimicrobial therapeutics. The plaintiff does not dispute this. Indeed, there is no evidence that plaintiff's usage of Declomycin was not adequate in this respect. Nor was there any proof that it was improperly designed. The crux of the plaintiff's complaint is that her doctor should have been warned of a possible side effect of the drug in infants, discoloration of teeth. * * *

The emphasis of the strict liability doctrine is upon the safety of the product, rather than the reasonableness of the manufacturer's conduct. It is a product-oriented approach to responsibility. Generally speaking, the doctrine of strict liability assumes that enterprises should be responsible for damages to consumers resulting from defective products regardless of fault. The doctrine differs from a negligence theory, which centers on the defendant's conduct and seeks to determine whether the defendant acted as a reasonably prudent person. This difference between strict liability and negligence is commonly expressed by stating that in a strict liability analysis, the defendant is assumed to know of the dangerous propensity of the product, whereas in a negligence case, the plaintiff must prove that the defendant knew or should have known of the danger. This distinction is particularly pertinent in a manufacturing defect context.

When the strict liability defect consists of an improper design or warning, reasonableness of the defendant's conduct is a factor in determining liability. The question in strict liability design defect and warning cases is whether, assuming that the manufacturer knew of the defect in the product, he acted in a reasonably prudent manner in marketing the product or in providing the warnings given. Thus, once the defendant's knowledge of the defect is imputed, strict liability analysis becomes almost identical to negligence analysis in its focus on the reasonableness of the defendant's conduct. * * *

[A]s to warnings, generally conduct should be measured by knowledge at the time the manufacturer distributed the product. Did the defendant know, or should he have known, of the danger, given the scientific, technological, and other information available when the product was distributed; or, in other words, did he have actual or constructive knowledge of the danger? The *Restatement (Second) of Torts* has adopted this test in comment j to section 402A * * * * Under this standard negligence and strict liability in warning cases may be deemed to be functional equivalents. Constructive knowledge embraces knowledge that should have been known based on information that was reasonably available or obtainable and should have alerted a reasonably prudent person to act. Put another way, would a person of reasonable intelligence or of the superior expertise of the defendant charged with such knowledge conclude that defendant should have alerted the consuming public?

Further, a manufacturer is held to the standard of an expert in the field. A manufacturer should keep abreast of scientific advances. * * * Implicit in the requirement that such a manufacturer is held to the standard applicable to experts in the field is the notion that at least in some fields, such as those impacting on public health, a manufacturer may be expected to be informed and affirmatively to seek out information concerning the public's use of its own product.

Furthermore, a reasonably prudent manufacturer will be deemed to know of reliable information generally available or reasonably obtainable in the industry or in the particular field involved. Such information need not be limited to that furnished by experts in the field, but may also include material provided by others. Thus, for example, if a substantial number of doctors or consumers had complained to a drug manufacturer of an untoward effect of a drug, that would have constituted sufficient information requiring an appropriate warning. See Hoffman v. Sterling Drug, Inc., 485 F.2d 132, 146 (3d Cir.1973) (in judgment for plaintiff alleging negligence and strict products liability in failure-to-warn case against prescription drug manufacturer of Aralen, court found jury question whether defendants used foresight appropriate to their enterprise in view of the number of letters from physicians reporting visual injury in patients using Aralen and subsequent medical literature). * * *

In strict liability warning cases, unlike negligence cases, however, the defendant should properly bear the burden of proving that the information was not reasonably available or obtainable and that it therefore lacked actual or constructive knowledge of the defect. The defendant is in a superior position to know the technological material or data in the particular field or specialty. The defendant is the expert, often performing self-testing. It is the defendant that injected the product in the stream of commerce for its economic gain. As a matter of policy the burden of proving the status of knowledge in the field at the time of distribution is properly placed on the defendant.

One other aspect with respect to warnings based on subsequently obtained knowledge should be considered. Communication of the new warning should unquestionably be given to prescribing physicians as soon as reasonably feasible. Although a manufacturer may not have actual or constructive knowledge of a danger so as to impose upon it a duty to warn, subsequently acquired knowledge, both actual and constructive, also may obligate the manufacturer to take reasonable steps to notify purchasers and consumers of the newly-discovered danger.

The timeliness of the warning issue is obliquely present in this case. It is possible that Dr. Feldman already had Declomycin on hand when defendant became aware of Declomycin's side effect. If that state of affairs existed, defendant would have had an obligation to warn doctors and others promptly. This most assuredly would include those to whom defendant had already furnished the product. The extent and nature of post-distribution warnings may vary depending on the circumstances, but in the context of this case, the defendant at a minimum would have had a duty of advising physicians, including plaintiff's father, whom it had directly solicited to use Declomycin. * * *

[The defendant also argued] that it could not lawfully have modified the warnings without FDA approval, an approval that was not obtained until the end of 1963. It raised this defense even though its witness, Dr. Swanzey, testified there was "no prohibition" against inserting the additional warning without FDA approval. * * * We note that the regulation did not prevent a drug manufacturer from adding an additional warning as soon as it was aware of its necessity. Nor has counsel submitted to us any FDA administrative decision to the contrary effect. It would seem anomalous for the FDA to have prevented a drug manufacturer from advising the public immediately of a newly discovered danger while waiting for FDA approval. * * * Furthermore, in 1965 the regulation was amended to require that drug manufacturers inform the public immediately of newly discovered dangers before waiting for the FDA to act. * * *

The trial court erred in fixing the date at which defendant's actual or constructive knowledge was to be measured. It was undisputed that plaintiff had received Declomycin or another tetracycline from approximately September, 1960 until the end of 1963. When the trial court considered the motion, it referred to the conflict in the evidence on whether defendant knew or should have known of the correlation between an infant's ingestion of Declomycin and tooth discoloration in 1960, when the plaintiff first began receiving the drug.

However, the evidence is overwhelming that, at least by mid-November 1962, defendant had sufficient information to warrant that it warn doctors of the possible tooth discoloration effects of Declomycin when administered to infants. According to Dr. Swanzey, then defendant's Director of Regulatory Agency Relations, defendant had "strong suspicions" of the connection between tetracyclines and the discoloration of the teeth by the end of 1962. However, the defendant's actions indicate that its awareness at that time went beyond the stage of suspicion. There was no equivocation in its letter to the FDA on November 16, 1962. The letter proposed that defendant add to the labels on all its tetracycline products, including Declomycin, the following warning: "Use of *any* tetracycline during teeth development in the neonatal period or early childhood may cause discoloration of the teeth." * * *

Apart from plaintiff's evidence to the effect that defendant should have known of the side effect as early as 1960, the record overwhelmingly demonstrates that defendant actually knew of the danger by the end of 1962. Defendant nonetheless continued to market the drug in 1963 and plaintiff continued to ingest the drug that year. * * * In that event defendant would be responsible at least for the enhancement of the condition. We reverse and remand for a new trial.

Carlin v. Superior Court (Upjohn Co.)

920 P.2d 1347 (Cal.1996).

■ MOSK, JUSTICE:

* * * Plaintiff Wilma Peggy Carlin brought an action for damages against Upjohn for injuries she assertedly sustained from ingesting the drug Halcion, which was prescribed for her by a physician between 1987 and 1992. * * * Upjohn demurred, alleging, inter alia, that Carlin failed to state facts sufficient to constitute a cause of action for strict liability * * * * It argues that California courts have "long refused to expand the scope of potential liability of prescription pharmaceutical manufacturers beyond traditional negligence principles." Not so. In prior cases, we have expressly and repeatedly applied a strict liability standard to manufacturers of prescription drugs for failure to warn of known or reasonably scientifically knowable risks. We merely reaffirm those precedents here.

In *Anderson v. Owens–Corning Fiberglas Corp.*, 810 P.2d 549 (Cal. 1991), we summarized prior case law and outlined the general principles of strict liability as they have been applied by California courts for over three decades. * * * Although *Anderson* involved an action against a manufacturer of asbestos, we relied extensively on cases involving a variety of products, *including prescription drugs*. In particular, we were guided by our prior decision in *Brown v. Superior Court,* 751 P.2d 470 (Cal.1988), in which we refused to extend strict liability to the failure to warn of risks that were unknown or *unknowable* at the time of distribution. * * *

We recognized that the knowledge or knowability requirement for failure to warn infuses some negligence concepts into strict liability cases. Indeed, in the failure-to-warn context, strict liability is to some extent a hybrid of traditional strict liability and negligence doctrine. As we explained, however, "the claim that a particular component 'rings of' or 'sounds in' negligence has not precluded its acceptance in the context of strict liability." Indeed, "the strict liability doctrine has incorporated some well-settled rules from the law of negligence and has survived judicial challenges asserting that such incorporation violates the fundamental principles of the doctrine." Thus, although *Anderson*, following *Brown*, incorporated certain negligence concepts into the standard of strict liability for failure to warn, it did not thereby adopt a simple negligence test.

"[F]ailure to warn in strict liability differs markedly from failure to warn in the negligence context. * * * [I]n strict liability, as opposed to negligence, the reasonableness of the defendant's failure to warn is immaterial. Stated another way, a reasonably prudent manufacturer might reasonably decide that the risk of harm was such as not to require a warning as, for example, if the manufacturer's own testing showed a result contrary to that of others in the scientific community. Such a manufacturer might escape liability under negligence principles. In contrast, under strict liability principles the manufacturer has no such leeway; the manufacturer is liable if it failed to give warning of dangers that were known to the scientific community at the time it manufactured or distributed the product." Similarly, a manufacturer could not escape liability under strict liability principles merely because its failure to warn of a known or reasonably scientifically knowable risk conformed to an industry-wide practice of failing to provide warnings that constituted the standard of reasonable care.

We explained the policy behind our strict liability standard for failure to warn as follows: " 'When, in a particular case, the risk qualitatively (e.g., of death or major disability) as well as quantitatively, on balance with the end sought to be achieved, is such as to call for a true choice judgment, medical or personal, the warning must be given. . . .' Thus, the fact that a manufacturer acted as a reasonably prudent manufacturer in deciding not to warn, while perhaps absolving the manufacturer of liability under the negligence theory, will not preclude liability under strict liability principles if the trier of fact concludes that, based on the information scientifically available to the manufacturer, the manufacturer's failure to warn rendered the product unsafe to its users."

Upjohn and amici curiae argue that applying *Anderson* will place manufacturers of prescription drugs in an untenable position because they must comply with regulations set by the Food and Drug Administration, which may preclude them from labeling drugs with warnings of certain side effects. They also contend that *Anderson* would result in overlabeling of pharmaceuticals. Neither claim withstands scrutiny.

We are unpersuaded by Upjohn's argument that a strict liability standard for failure to warn about known or reasonably scientifically knowable risks from prescription drugs is inconsistent with federal regulatory policy. Upjohn concedes that FDA regulations do not expressly preempt common law tort remedies for failure to warn or occupy the entire field of regulation. As numerous courts have concluded, Congress evinced no intention of preempting state tort liability for injuries from prescription drugs.

We disagree with Carlin's argument, however, that FDA regulations are essentially irrelevant in a common law action for failure to warn. We reiterate that strict liability for failure to warn *is not absolute liability*. Under *Anderson*, drug manufacturers are not strictly liable for a risk that was not known or reasonably scientifically knowable. In this context, it is significant that the FDA *precludes* drug manufacturers from warning about every conceivable adverse reaction; they may warn only if there exists significant medical evidence of a possible health hazard. * * *

In appropriate cases, FDA action or inaction, though not dispositive, may be admissible under *Anderson* to show whether a risk was known or reasonably scientifically knowable. Similarly, a drug manufacturer could present evidence to show that there was no "reasonably scientifically knowable risk" because, at the time of distribution, the cause of the alleged adverse effect was too speculative to have been reasonably attributable to the drug by a scientist conducting state-of-the-art research. Thus, when a plaintiff's claim is based on an allegation that a particular risk was "reasonably scientifically knowable," an inquiry may arise as to what a reasonable scientist operating in good faith should have known under the circumstances of the evidence. As we emphasized in *Anderson*, we do not altogether reject strict liability in the failure-to-warn context—for drugs or any other products—simply because some considerations of reasonableness sounding in negligence may be required.

Moreover, in the case of an alleged "known" risk, if state-of-the-art scientific data concerning the alleged risk was fully disclosed to the FDA and it determined, after review, that the pharmaceutical manufacturer *was not permitted to warn*—e.g., because the data was inconclusive or the risk was too speculative to justify a warning—the manufacturer could present such evidence to show that strict liability cannot apply; the FDA's conclusion that there was, in effect, no "known risk" is controlling.

We are also unpersuaded by Upjohn's assertion that applying strict liability to claims of injury for failure to warn will inevitably result in manufacturers inundating consumers with warnings of even speculative risks from prescription drugs. In *Finn v. G.D. Searle & Co.*, 677 P.2d 1147 (Cal.1984), we addressed the potential problems of overlabeling: "[E]xperience suggest[s] that if every report of a possible risk, no matter how speculative, conjectural, or tentative, imposed an affirmative duty to give some warning, a manufacturer would be required to inundate physicians indiscriminately with notice of any and every hint of danger, thereby inevitably diluting the force of any specific warning given." The application of the failure-to-warn theory to pharmaceuticals requires determinations whether available evidence established a causal link between an alleged side effect and a prescription drug, whether any warning should have been given, and, if so, whether the warning was adequate. These are issues of fact involving, inter alia, questions concerning the state of the art, i.e., what was known or reasonably knowable by the application of scientific and medical knowledge available at the time of manufacture and distribution of the prescription drug. They also necessarily involve questions concerning whether the risk, in light of accepted scientific norms, was more than merely speculative or conjectural, or so remote and insignificant as to be negligible.

Moreover, in the case of prescription drugs, the duty to warn runs *to the physician*, not to the patient. Thus, a pharmaceutical manufacturer may not be required to provide warning of a risk known to the medical community.

Nor does Upjohn offer any sound public policy rationale for departing from *Anderson* concerning the liability of manufacturers of prescription drugs for failure to warn of known or reasonably scientifically knowable risks. Thus, we are unpersuaded by the argument, purportedly derived from our reasoning in *Brown*, that manufacturers of prescription drugs should be exempt from the strict liability duty to warn because they might otherwise refrain from developing and marketing drugs, including "cutting-edge vaccines to combat human immunodeficiency virus (HIV)" and other diseases. Our rationale in *Brown*, which involved strict liability for *design defects*, is inapplicable: unlike strict liability for design defects, strict liability for failure to warn does not potentially subject drug manufacturers to liability for flaws in their products that they have not, and could not have, discovered. Drug manufacturers need only warn of risks that are *actually known or reasonably scientifically knowable*.

Upjohn offers no clear or sufficient basis for concluding that research and development will inevitably decrease as a result of imposing strict liability for failure to warn of *known or reasonably scientifically knowable* risks; indeed, requiring manufacturers to internalize the costs of failing to determine such risks may instead *increase* the level of research into safe and effective drugs. In any event, we see no reason to depart from our conclusion in *Anderson* that the manufacturer should bear the costs, in terms of preventable injury or death, of its own failure to provide adequate warnings of known or reasonably scientifically knowable risks. As we observed: "Whatever may be reasonable from the point of view of the manufacturer, the user of the product must be given the option either to refrain from using the product at all or to use it in such a way as to minimize the degree of danger." * * *

■ KENNARD, JUSTICE (concurring in part and dissenting in part):

The manufacture of prescription drugs, a multi billion-dollar industry, has provided many of the 20th century's greatest success stories and some of its worst tragedies. Because they cure disease, alleviate pain, and prolong life, prescription drugs have been a great benefit to society. But prescription drugs sometimes cause severe complications and side effects, inflicting great anguish as well as temporary and even permanent disability on some individuals.

This court's task in the present case is to set rules defining prescription drug manufacturers' tort liability for personal injuries caused by their products' side effects. More particularly, the task is to determine under what circumstances a drug manufacturer should be held liable in tort for personal injury damages proximately caused by a failure to warn about the possibility of a particular drug complication. * * *

At first glance, the majority's holding—that a prescription drug manufacturer need warn only of those risks that are "known or reasonably scientifically knowable"—appears quite reasonable. A close look, however, reveals that the majority imposes on a manufacturer a duty to warn of any risk that arguably may exist. The sheer breadth of that duty threatens two fundamental public interests. First, the majority's holding will result in the problems of overwarning this court has previously recognized, thereby undermining the public interest in consumer protection. Second, by subjecting prescription drug manufacturers to excessive liability, the majority's standard jeopardizes the important public interest of encouraging the development, availability, and affordability of beneficial prescription drugs.

To discern what the majority means by the phrase "known or reasonably scientifically knowable" is no easy task. Throughout its opinion, the majority itself gives different descriptions of the meaning of that phrase. The majority's various characterizations of "knowability" lead me to conclude that the majority considers a risk to be "knowable," even though not actually known to the manufacturer, if the risk at the time of distribution had been or reasonably could have been scientifically identified. The word "risk" simply means the possibility of a loss. Because the majority does not suggest that the degree of probability of loss is of any significance, the majority seemingly equates the identification of a bare possibility of harm with "knowability" and hence a duty to warn. Thus, under the majority's holding, once a prescription drug plaintiff proves that a risk has been or reasonably could have been identified by the scientific community, the manufacturer has a duty to warn regardless of whether warning is otherwise appropriate or reasonable. * * *

In my view, the majority's holding goes too far in imposing liability, because it fails to recognize the complexity involved in scientifically identifying a risk as meaningful and in determining whether a warning is appropriate. As this court has noted, the quality of scientific evidence "may range from extremely vague to highly certain." Scientific studies suggesting associations between products and injuries may themselves be subjected to legitimate question as to the validity of their methods and the soundness of their conclusions. The majority's apparent standard that a prescription drug manufacturer is strictly liable for failure to warn of any "knowable" risk fails to recognize, much less deal with, the complexity of scientific evaluations.

A possible result of such a standard is the destruction of the viability of any warnings. * * * The problems of overwarning are exacerbated if warnings must be given even as to very remote risks, which drug manufacturers may find necessary under the vague standard that the majority adopts today. "Not only would such remote risk warnings crowd out potentially useful warnings but they would also focus consumer attention on the fairy tale bogeyman. One cannot cry wolf without paying the price over the long term."

According to the majority, its standard of liability would not result in inundating consumers with too many warnings, because the manufacturer's duty to warn runs to the physician rather than the patient, and because there is no duty to warn of obvious dangers. It is true, as the majority states, that a prescription drug manufacturer has no duty to ensure that a warning given a physician reaches the patient. But even physicians, the "learned intermediaries," may be overwhelmed by excessive warnings. As this court has recognized, both common sense and experience suggest that to require a manufacturer "to inundate physicians indiscriminately with notice of any and every hint of danger" inevitably dilutes "the force of any specific warning given." And, contrary to the majority's assertion, the absence of a duty to warn of known or obvious dangers has little import in the context of prescription drugs, because few of the sophisticated potential risks of prescription drugs could be considered obvious.

The majority's holding exposes prescription drug manufacturers to such broad liability that they may restrict or cease the development and distribution of life-sustaining and lifesaving drugs, thereby defeating a strong public interest. * * * The concern repeatedly voiced by the courts and legal commentators that the imposition of excessive liability on prescription drug manufacturers may discourage the development and availability of life-sustaining and lifesaving drugs is well founded * * * * To require prescription drug manufacturers to warn of all scientifically knowable risks, as the majority holds, exposes them to excessive liability. Such exposure creates a powerful disincentive on the part of prescription drug manufacturers to develop essential medications, especially when it is joined with the extensive liability exposure for alleged inadequacy of warnings given. * * *

Justice Baxter's dissent [which is not included with this excerpt] expresses the view that a prescription drug manufacturer's liability for failure to warn should be based solely upon negligence principles. Under that approach, a manufacturer is liable for failure to warn only if the plaintiff establishes that a reasonable manufacturer in similar circumstances would have issued warnings. The dissent agrees with the majority that the legal theories of negligent failure to warn and strict liability failure to warn are two different theories of liability: negligence looks to the reasonableness of a manufacturer's conduct while strict liability considers it irrelevant. According to the dissent, the same policy considerations that led this court in *Brown* to adopt a negligence standard for prescription drug design defects apply with equal force when, as here, the alleged defect is a failure to warn of risks associated with the drug.

The dissent cites four reasons for its conclusion. First, it mentions that several commentators have concluded that a product's warning may be characterized as a subset of the product's design. Second, the dissent points out that products liability law has always recognized that prescription drugs may require different legal treatment than other products, and that the tentative draft of the *Restatement Third of Torts* incorporates negligence principles into its new standard for prescription drug manufacturer products liability. Third, it notes that the prescription drug industry is heavily regulated by the federal Food and Drug Administration (FDA), and that one of the FDA's primary functions is to evaluate drug warnings. Fourth, the dissent points out that the imposition of strict liability for failure to warn on prescription drug manufacturers would inhibit and delay the development and marketing of essential drugs.

The negligence standard advocated by the dissent preserves the public interest in the development and availability of life-sustaining and lifesaving drugs because prescription drug manufacturers would be liable only if their decision not to warn was unreasonable. But the dissent's approach would unnecessarily weaken the legal protection afforded injured consumers under products liability law. As mentioned at the outset, a principal objective of products liability law is to relieve injured consumers of the problems of proof inherent in negligence and contractual warranty, common law concepts that were initially applied to consumers injured by defective products. The dissent's approach runs counter to this important goal. * * *

In short, the majority's strict liability standard is too harsh towards the manufacturer of prescription drugs, while the dissent is too harsh towards the injured consumer. I propose an intermediate approach, one that fairly accommodates the competing public policies. Unlike the majority, I would not impose liability on prescription drug manufacturers for their failure to warn of every arguable risk, but only of those risks supported by credible scientific evidence or that upon reasonable inquiry would be supported by credible scientific evidence. * * * In determining the admissibility of new scientific techniques, this court has held that evidence of a technique is admissible only if it has gained acceptance in the particular scientific field to which it belongs. * * * Evidence of a risk would be scientifically credible if the data upon which it is based, the methodology employed, and its conclusions identifying the existence of a risk comply with generally accepted scientific methodology and analysis. Scientific evidence that postulates the possibility of a risk or that is otherwise speculative or conjectural would be inadequate. Also, the relevant inquiry relates to the credibility of the scientific evidence in light of accepted scientific norms, not to the personal professional beliefs or preferences of an otherwise qualified expert.

The plaintiff's identification of such a risk would not by itself subject the manufacturer to liability for failure to warn of the risk associated with the drug prescribed. Against the benefits that may be gained by a warning must be balanced the dangers of overwarning and of less meaningful warnings crowding out necessary warnings, the problems of remote risks, and the seriousness of the possible harm to the consumer. But requiring a plaintiff to prove that these factors supported the giving of a warning would force the plaintiff to independently obtain and evaluate all relevant scientific information bearing on these factors. Because such information is not readily accessible to plaintiffs, who may also lack the resources necessary to analyze and evaluate the information, it would impose too heavy a burden on plaintiffs to require them to prove that a warning should have been given because of factors such as the magnitude of the risk in relation to other risks, the seriousness of the harm, and the probability of the harm. Therefore, I would shift to the manufacturer the burden of proving justification for the failure to warn of the risk established by the consumer's prima facie case.

To satisfy its burden, the manufacturer would have to show that its failure to warn was reasonable in relation to the identified risk. The manufacturer, for instance, could introduce evidence that the risk did not pose a serious threat to health, that it was remote, that the number or relative severity of other risks justified a failure to warn, or that the scientific association between the drug and the risk was weak. The manufacturer's compliance with product safety statutes or regulations such as those of the FDA would also be relevant, but not necessarily controlling.[4]

4. I agree with the majority that a prescription drug manufacturer cannot be held liable for failure to warn if it was pre- cluded from issuing a warning by the FDA. A contrary conclusion would be unreasonable because it would make manufacturer

The same is true of industry standards and practices to the extent they relate to the reasonableness of the manufacturer's decision not to warn.

In my view, this allocation of the burden of proof is appropriate given the manufacturer's superior access to and capability of evaluating the relevant scientific information; it also furthers a goal of products liability law of relieving injured consumers from evidentiary burdens that may be too onerous. Is this solution perfect? Perhaps not. But it does attempt to strike a fair balance between two distinct public interests: compensating consumers injured by defective products, and encouraging the development of prescription drugs, many of which are life sustaining and lifesaving. * * *

The continuing debate over the proper standard of liability for prescription drug warning defects has largely been framed as though the only available alternatives were strict liability and negligence. Both the majority and the dissent in this case address the issue from within that limited framework. For the reasons stated above, however, I am convinced that the framework must be discarded in order to craft a standard of liability that achieves a just resolution of competing public policies. * * *

Restatement (Third) of the Law of Torts: Products Liability § 6 (American Law Inst. 1998):

Comment g. *Foreseeability of risks of harm in prescription drug and medical device cases.* Duties concerning the design and marketing of prescription drugs and medical devices arise only with respect to risks of harm that are reasonably foreseeable at the time of sale. Imposing liability for unforeseeable risks can create inappropriate disincentives for the development of new drugs and therapeutic devices. Moreover, because actuaries cannot accurately assess unknown and unknowable risks, insuring against losses due to unknowable risks would be problematic. Drug and medical device manufacturers have the responsibility to perform reasonable testing prior to marketing a product and to discover risks and risk-avoidance measures that such testing would reveal.

NOTES AND QUESTIONS

1. *When does a risk become knowable?* Courts do not impose a duty to warn of unknowable risks associated with drugs or medical devices. See Moore v. Vanderloo, 386 N.W.2d 108, 116 (Iowa 1986); Castrignano v. E.R. Squibb & Sons, Inc., 546 A.2d 775, 782 (R.I.1988) (refusing to hold the manufacturer of DES liable "for failure to warn of risks inherent in a drug

compliance with both federal and state laws impossible. I also agree with the majority that FDA regulations and action or inaction would be admissible as probative of whether a manufacturer should have warned of a risk.

[because] it neither knew nor could have known by the application of scientific knowledge available at the time of distribution that the drug could produce the undesirable effects suffered by plaintiff"); Kathleen H. Wilson, Note, The Liability of Pharmaceutical Manufacturers for Unforeseen Adverse Drug Reactions, 48 Fordham L. Rev. 735 (1980). In *Feldman*, Lederle did not dispute at trial that Declomycin caused tooth discoloration, whereas, in *Carlin*, Upjohn denied that Halcion had caused any injury. Note that courts generally do not follow *Feldman*'s burden shifting (by imputing knowledge to the manufacturer) approach. See Rest. (3d) § 2 cmt. m & 102–07; see also Grenier v. Medical Eng'g Corp., 243 F.3d 200, 205 (5th Cir.2001) (dismissing the plaintiff's failure-to-warn claim because she "presented no evidence about the cause, frequency, severity, or consequences of 'gel bleed' with regard to the [silicone breast] implants at issue in this case"). Nonetheless, courts recognize a duty to engage in premarket testing, which in practice may come close to imputing time-of-sale knowledge of risks. See Kociemba v. G.D. Searle & Co., 707 F.Supp. 1517, 1528–29 (D.Minn.1989) ("[T]he duty to test is a subpart . . . of the duty to warn."); Rest. (3d) § 2 cmt. m ("The harms that result from unforeseeable risks—for example, in the human body's reaction to a new drug, medical device, or chemical—are not a basis of liability. Of course, a seller bears responsibility to perform reasonable testing prior to marketing a product and to discover risks and risk-avoidance measures that such testing would reveal. A seller is charged with knowledge of what reasonable testing would reveal.").

It is, of course, difficult to identify at what point knowledge about a putative hazard gives rise to a duty to warn. Think back to Problem #9 (Chapter 5(C)(1)) involving published epidemiological studies finding no statistically significant association between Rx and birth defects. Was there any obligation to warn? Some courts have found such a duty on the basis of extremely weak evidence that a substance may have caused an injury. See, e.g., Hermes v. Pfizer, Inc., 848 F.2d 66, 68 (5th Cir.1988) (adverse event reports); Wells v. Ortho Pharm. Corp., 788 F.2d 741, 745–46 (11th Cir. 1986) (manufacturer of spermicide had duty to warn of possible teratogenicity notwithstanding the FDA's conclusion that these drugs did not cause birth defects). For instance, in one case a court held that a reasonable jury could have found a failure to warn of a risk not revealed during clinical trials because of knowledge that a chemically similar product created such a risk. See Wagner v. Roche Labs., 671 N.E.2d 252, 256–58 (Ohio 1996) (Accutane); see also Mulligan v. Lederle Labs., 786 F.2d 859, 864–65 (8th Cir.1986) (sustaining verdict for plaintiff where the manufacturer previously had received reports of similar but not identical adverse reactions); Barson v. E.R. Squibb & Sons, 682 P.2d 832, 836 (Utah 1984) (reports that progesterone caused birth defects should have alerted manufacturer of progesterone-derivative to its teratogenic potential). Other courts demand greater substantiation of a risk allegedly posed by a product before imposing a duty to warn of that risk. See, e.g., Doe v. Miles Labs., Inc., 927 F.2d 187, 194 (4th Cir.1991) (finding no duty to warn where "only one case of AIDS was reported that could possibly have been related to Factor IX treatment ... [and] only a few AIDS cases were related to the use of any blood factor concentrate"); Novak v. United States, 865 F.2d 718, 726 (6th Cir.1989) (warnings accompanying swine flu vaccine not inadequate for failing to alert persons of risk of autoimmune disease because there was "insufficient medical evidence" of causation); Smith v. Ortho Pharm. Corp., 770 F.Supp. 1561, 1582 (N.D.Ga.1991) (rejecting failure-to-warn claim because there was no "reasonably reliable" evidence that spermicide caused birth defects); Finn v. G.D. Searle & Co., 677 P.2d 1147, 1153 (Cal.1984) ("Knowledge of a potential side effect which is based on a single isolated report of a possible link between a prescription drug and an injury may not require a warning.").

2.   *Defensive labeling.* The FDA generally frowns upon "defensive" labeling. See Thomas Scarlett, The Relationship Among Adverse Drug Reaction Reporting, Drug Labeling, Product Liability, and Federal Preemption, 46 Food Drug Cosm. L.J. 31, 40 (1991) ("Although the FDA is not rigidly opposed to adding more precautionary information to labeling, it is conscious of the problem of information overload ... [and it] would not acquiesce in defensive labeling that lacked medical support."). For instance, the agency rejected manufacturers' proposals to contraindicate or otherwise warn against use of their drugs by pregnant women, proposals evidently prompted by the valid fear that birth defects might wrongly be associated with the use of those drugs during pregnancy and therefore expose the manufacturer to potentially meritless but costly products liability litigation. See F–D–C Rep. ("The Pink Sheet"), Dec. 21, 1992, at 3. Similarly, in discussions concerning the labeling of transdermal nicotine patches, manufacturers sought to include a stringent pregnancy warning concerning the teratogenicity of nicotine, but the FDA opted for a milder warning evidently because it did not want to discourage women who would otherwise have smoked during their pregnancy from attempting a cessation program using a patch. See F–D–C Rep. ("The Pink Sheet"), July 20, 1992, at 9. The agency also has directed manufacturers to remove risk information from existing labeling after concluding that there was insufficient data to justify a particular contraindication. See F–D–C Rep. ("The Pink Sheet"), May 24, 1993, at T&G–1.

3.   *Regulatory compliance redux.* Recall from Chapter 5 that most courts treat compliance with FDA requirements as relevant but not dispositive. See Wells v. Ortho Pharm. Corp., 788 F.2d 741, 746 (11th Cir.1986) ("An FDA determination that a warning is not necessary may be sufficient for federal regulatory purposes but still not be sufficient for state tort law purposes."); Brochu v. Ortho Pharm. Corp., 642 F.2d 652, 658 (1st Cir. 1981); Salmon v. Parke, Davis & Co., 520 F.2d 1359, 1362 (4th Cir.1975) ("[C]ompliance with federal laws and regulations concerning a drug, though pertinent, does not in itself absolve a manufacturer of liability."). In support of the general refrain that federal regulations represent only minimum safety requirements open to supplementation by juries, *Feldman* and other courts have emphasized that additional or more forceful warnings may be added to labeling without prior FDA approval. See Motus v. Pfizer Inc., 127 F.Supp.2d 1085, 1096 (C.D.Cal.2000) ("FDA did find that the evidence did not support requiring manufacturers to include additional suicide-related warnings. But FDA never stated that it would be impermissible to include additional warnings."); In re Tetracycline Cases, 747 F.Supp. 543, 549–50 (W.D.Mo.1989) (pointing out that warnings on antibiotics may be added to the label in advance of FDA approval and that there are other means for disseminating warning information which would not conflict with federal requirements).

Even if a manufacturer may add a warning in advance of receiving agency approval, the additional warning may not be used if, after reviewing the supplement, the FDA rejects the modified language. Cf. Lindquist v. Tambrands, Inc., 721 F.Supp. 1058, 1060 (D.Minn.1989). The possibility of agency disapproval means that manufacturers typically await at least informal clearance before changing product labeling. Although *Carlin* suggests otherwise, even a refusal by the FDA to allow the addition of a warning may not protect a manufacturer from tort liability for failing to include precisely that warning. See Wooderson v. Ortho Pharm. Corp., 681 P.2d 1038, 1057 (Kan.1984) (ignoring FDA letter to a manufacturer rejecting addition of requested warning); see also Sterling Drug, Inc. v. Cornish, 370 F.2d 82, 84 (8th Cir.1966) (ignoring manufacturer's argument that the Dear Doctor "letter was not sent sooner because the connection between the drug and the condition was not yet sufficiently established, and because some time was consumed in clearing the letter with the FDA"); May v. Parke, Davis & Co., 370 N.W.2d 371, 380 (Mich.Ct.App.1985) (excluding evidence that the FDA had subsequently rejected another manufacturer's identical proposed warning as unsubstantiated); Charles J. Walsh & Marc S. Klein, The Conflicting Objectives of Federal and State Tort Law Drug Regulation, 41 Food Drug Cosm. L.J. 171, 185–88 (1986).

4. *Are warnings costless?* When resolving failure-to-warn claims against sellers of drugs and devices, many courts appear to regard additional labeling information as essentially costless. See Ross Lab. v. Thies, 725 P.2d 1076, 1079 (Alaska 1986); Cooley v. Carter–Wallace Inc., 478 N.Y.S.2d 375, 376–77 (App.Div.1984) ("Since the cost of providing warnings is often minimal, the balance usually weighs in favor of an obligation to warn."). Other courts pay more attention to the "information costs" in such cases, at least for patient labeling. See Doe v. Miles Lab., Inc., 927 F.2d 187, 194 (4th Cir.1991) ("If pharmaceutical companies were required to warn of every suspected risk that could possibly attend the use of a drug, the consuming public would be so barraged with warnings that it would undermine the effectiveness of these warnings...."); Boruski v. United States, 803 F.2d 1421, 1427 (7th Cir.1986) (rejecting the plaintiff's argument that the warning "ought to be so strong, regardless of medical experience, as to frighten people from receiving the beneficial aspects of the [vaccination] program"); Edmondson v. International Playtex, Inc., 678 F.Supp. 1571, 1574–75 (N.D.Ga.1987); Dunn v. Lederle Lab., 328 N.W.2d 576, 580 (Mich.Ct.App.1982); Vallillo v. Muskin Corp., 514 A.2d 528, 531 n.3 (N.J.Super.Ct.App.Div.1986) ("Warning labels cannot be effective if they take on the characteristics of drug package inserts.").

5. *Hazards of overwarning.* As mentioned in *Carlin*, physicians may not be immune to the consequences of overwarning of prescription drug risks. See Thomas v. Hoffman–LaRoche, 949 F.2d 806, 816 n.40 (5th Cir.1992) (noting that the imposition of liability for failure to warn about reported but unconfirmed adverse experiences with prescription medications could "force drug manufacturers to list, and perhaps contraindicate, every possible risk in order to avoid the possibility of liability"). In the event that labeling included warnings of all possible side effects, the cacophony of risk information could undermine a doctor's ability to appreciate warnings about meaningful hazards. See id. at 816 n.40 ("If manufacturers so respond to the possibility of liability, physicians will begin to ignore or discount the warnings provided by the drug manufacturers. Permitting a jury to find liability on such a basis would undermine the important role of warnings as a device to communicate vital information to physicians."); see also Lars Noah, The Imperative to Warn: Disentangling the "Right to Know" from the "Need to Know" About Consumer Product Hazards, 11 Yale J. on Reg. 293, 381–91 (1994). There is a danger that physicians may alter their prescribing decisions in response to warnings about trivial drug risks, either by taking all warnings less seriously or taking trivial warnings too seriously. Even if physicians are not misled by warnings about trivial risks, they may nonetheless avoid using perfectly safe and effective therapeutic agents for fear of malpractice liability if they disregard a warning. See Chapter 8(A). Patients will be the ultimate losers of excessive and misguided warning efforts undertaken by manufacturers in response to adverse judgments in products liability cases.

Vassallo v. Baxter Healthcare Corp.

696 N.E.2d 909 (Mass.1998).

■ GREANEY, JUSTICE:

* * * In February 1977, at the age of forty-eight, Mrs. Vassallo underwent breast implantation surgery. The silicone gel breast implants that Mrs. Vassallo received were manufactured by Heyer–Schulte Corporation in October 1976. Through a series of corporate transactions, the defendants assumed responsibility for breast implant products manufactured by Heyer–Schulte.

In 1992, Mrs. Vassallo underwent a mammogram after complaining of chest pains that extended up under her left armpit. The mammogram revealed that her breast implants possibly had ruptured. The silicone gel implants were subsequently removed in April 1993, and were replaced with saline implants. During the course of the explant surgery, the surgeon noted severe, permanent scarring of Mrs. Vassallo's pectoral muscles which she attributed to the silicone gel. The implants themselves were encapsulated in scar tissue with multiple nodules of silicone granulomas. Dissection of the scar tissue capsules revealed that the left implant had ruptured, releasing free silicone gel, while the right implant was intact, but had several pinholes through which silicone gel could escape.

The plaintiff's pathology expert, Dr. Douglas Shanklin, indicated that, based on the cellular responses shown in the pathology slides of Mrs. Vassallo's breast tissue taken at the time of explant, the rupture had been longstanding, perhaps for several years. According to Dr. Shanklin, Mrs. Vassallo's pathology slides showed silicone granulomas, giant cells, lymphocytes, and macrophages, all of which indicated a chronic immunological and inflammatory reaction to the silicone implants. Dr. Shanklin also identified deposits of silica and lymphocytic vasculitis, which, he testified, were evidence that Mrs. Vassallo suffered from an autoimmune disease caused by the silicone gel. * * *

There was also extensive testimony as to knowledge, attributable to the defendants, of the risks of silicone gel breast implants up to the time of Mrs. Vassallo's implant surgery in 1977. According to Heyer–Schulte's own internal correspondence, the company was aware of a "Talk Paper," issued by the United States Food and Drug Administration in 1976, that documented migration to the brain, lungs, and heart, and death following injections of liquid silicone into the human body. In 1976, Heyer–Schulte received a report of an animal study, partially funded by Heyer–Schulte and conducted using miniature silicone gel implants supplied by Heyer–Schulte, that documented migration of gel from ruptured implants to the surrounding connective tissues and local inflammatory responses with fibroblastic activity and giant cell formation. The authors of the study stated: "The present tendency by manufacturers of breast implants towards ever thinner envelopes and a filler that is getting further away from gel and closer to silicone liquid must be looked at in the light of these experimental findings, and the question must be asked whether the possible advantages of these changes outweigh the disadvantages."

Heyer–Schulte was also aware that some of their implants were rupturing, having received 129 complaints of ruptured gel implants in 1976. In fact, the president of Heyer–Schulte had written in 1975 that "[p]resently, mammary implants have been designed to be increasingly fragile in response to plastic surgeons' demand for softness, realistic feel and mobility." As a result, Heyer–Schulte knew that its implants were "not consistent as far as durability or destructibility is concerned." The encapsulation of the implant, and the viscous nature of the silicone gel, made it difficult to detect that a rupture had occurred, allowing the silicone to leak into the body for long periods before explantation. By 1975, Heyer–Schulte also knew that, even without a rupture of the implant shell, the silicone gel could leak (known as "gel bleed") through to the exterior surface of the implant and possibly produce "detrimental effect[s]" in the body.

Despite this knowledge of the possible adverse long-term consequences of leaking silicone in the body, Heyer–Schulte conducted few animal, and no clinical, studies to document the safety and efficacy of its silicone gel implants. When Heyer–Schulte began using silicone gel manufactured by Dow Corning in 1976, they relied primarily on the animal testing conducted by Dow Corning, despite the observations of a Heyer–Schulte scientist that "the data . . . [did] not answer questions concerning migration," and "was lacking in quality and left many questions unanswered." Heyer–Schulte did conduct toxicity testing on the Dow Corning gel; the gel passed the seven-day and thirty-day toxicity tests, but failed the ninety-day toxicity test based on the microscopic tissue evaluation that showed considerably greater fibrous tissue reaction and inflammation to the silicone gel than to the control material. There is no indication in the record that Heyer–Schulte ever repeated this ninety-day toxicity test, and the company continued to use the Dow Corning gel in the manufacture of their silicone gel breast implants.

Heyer–Schulte did furnish warnings to physicians concerning their silicone gel implants in a product insert data sheet (PIDS). The 1976 version of the PIDS that accompanied Mrs. Vassallo's implants included warnings that the implant shell could be easily cut or ruptured by excessive stresses, and that Heyer–Schulte could not guarantee gel containment in the case of a rupture. The warnings did not address the issue of gel bleed, the fact that a rupture could result from normal stresses and could persist undetected for a significant time period, or the consequences of gel migration in the body. The PIDS also contained a list of potential complications associated with breast implants, but this list did not address the risks of chronic inflammation, permanent tissue scarring, or possible effects on the immune system. Proposed revisions to the PIDS, which would have included "a warning to the effect that uncontained silicone gel may have untoward consequences," and complications of "migration of the silicone, with mild to severe consequences, including reduction of breast size and absorption of the silicone by the blood and lymph systems, resulting in damage to the liver and kidneys," were rejected by Heyer–Schulte's president in March 1976. The president did issue a letter to doctors dated August 23, 1976, which stated that "[i]f a shell is torn[] with time and normal stresses the gel will migrate," and that "mild inflammation and polynuclear giant cell response characterized as mild foreign body reaction" had been associated with the silicone gel implants. Once again, this letter did not completely address the potential effects of silicone migration on the body's immune system. Mrs. Vassallo stated that, if she had known that the implants could cause permanent scarring, chronic inflammation, and problems with her immune system, she would not have gone ahead with the implantation procedure. * * *

The judge properly allowed the plaintiffs to introduce evidence of complaints made to Heyer–Schulte on a year-by-year basis with an appropriate cautionary instruction to the jury that the complaints were "not admitted for the truth of what the complaints say," but for the jury's "consideration of what Heyer–Schulte was being told and was learning about its product." The complaints of substantially similar defects and consequences were admissible as evidence of notice to Heyer–Schulte of defects in the integrity of its product about which it had failed to warn. * * *

Because the plaintiffs' recoveries can be upheld on the jury's findings of negligence, we need not address the defendants' claims of error concerning the breach of warranty count. We take this opportunity, however, to consider the defendants' argument that we should change our products liability law concerning the implied warranty of merchantability * * * to adopt a "state of the art" standard that conditions a manufacturer's liability on actual or constructive knowledge of the risks.

Our current law, regarding the duty to warn under the implied warranty of merchantability, presumes that a manufacturer was fully informed of all risks associated with the product at issue, regardless of the state of the art at the time of the sale, and amounts to strict liability for failure to warn of these risks. This rule has been justified by the public policy that a defective product, "unreasonably dangerous due to lack of adequate warning[s], [is] not fit for the ordinary purposes for which [it is] used regardless of the absence of fault on [a defendant's] part." * * * [W]e recognize that we are among a distinct minority of States that applies a hindsight analysis to the duty to warn.

The majority of States, either by case law or by statute, follow the principle expressed in *Restatement (Second) of Torts* § 402A comment j (1965), which states that "the seller is required to give warning against [a danger], if he has knowledge, or by the application of reasonable, developed human skill and foresight should have knowledge, of the . . . danger." See Restatement (Third) of Torts: Products Liability, Reporters' Note to comment m, at 104 (1998) ("An overwhelming majority of jurisdictions supports the proposition that a manufacturer has a duty to warn only of risks that were known or should have been known to a reasonable person"). * * * The thin judicial support for a hindsight approach to the duty to warn is easily explained. The goal of the law is to induce conduct that is capable of being performed. This goal is not advanced by imposing liability for failure to warn of risks that were not capable of being known. * * *

We have stated that liability under the implied warranty of merchantability in Massachusetts is "congruent in nearly all respects with the principles expressed in *Restatement (Second) of Torts* § 402A." The main difference has been our application of a hindsight approach to the duty to warn of (and to provide adequate instructions regarding) risks associated with a product. * * * In recognition of the clear judicial trend regarding the duty to warn in products liability cases, and the principles stated in *Restatement (Third) of Torts: Products Liability*, § 2(c) and comment m, we hereby revise our law to state that a defendant will not be held liable under an implied warranty of merchantability for failure to warn or provide instructions about risks that were not reasonably foreseeable at the time of sale or could not have been discovered by way of reasonable testing prior to marketing the product. A manufacturer will be held to the standard of knowledge of an expert in the appropriate field, and will remain subject to a continuing duty to warn (at least purchasers) of risks discovered following the sale of the product at issue. * * *

NOTES AND QUESTIONS

1. *Adverse events and the duty to investigate.* Even if initial reports of adverse reactions do not trigger a duty to warn, companies may be held liable if they have not at least undertaken further inquiries or requested FDA approval of an additional warning as soon as a new hazard is discovered. See Lindsay v. Ortho Pharm. Corp., 637 F.2d 87, 91 (2d Cir.1980) ("The duty is a continuous one, requiring the manufacturer to keep abreast of the current state of knowledge of its products as gained through research, adverse reaction reports, scientific literature, and other available methods."); Sterling Drug, Inc. v. Yarrow, 408 F.2d 978, 991–92 (8th Cir.1969); In re Tetracycline Cases, 747 F.Supp. 543, 550 (W.D.Mo. 1989); Medics Pharm. Corp. v. Newman, 378 S.E.2d 487, 488–89 (Ga.Ct. App.1989); Miller v. Upjohn Co., 465 So.2d 42, 45 (La.Ct.App.1985) (holding that a jury "could reasonably have found that Upjohn was tardy in applying for the warning label"); see also Rest. (3d) § 10 cmt. b (With regard to "prescription drugs and devices, courts traditionally impose a continuing duty of reasonable care to test and monitor after sale to discover product-related risks."); Patricia L. Andel, Inapplicability of the Self–Critical Analysis Privilege to the Drug and Medical Device Industry, 34 San Diego L. Rev. 93 (1997); Bob Van Voris, Plaintiffs Rev Up New Drug Lawsuits, Nat'l L.J., Mar. 26, 2001, at A1 (describing litigation emerging in the wake of the FDA's decision to withdraw phenylpropanolamine (PPA), a popular active ingredient in OTC cold relief and weight loss products linked to hemorrhagic strokes, based in part on allegations that the industry should not have waited several years for the completion of an epidemiological study confirming the suspected risk).

2.   *Post-sale duty to warn.* A product seller may have a duty to warn when after-acquired information reveals a risk of injury unknowable at the time of sale. See Rest. (3d) § 10. In such cases, the courts use a more forgiving negligence-based standard, in recognition of the fact that durable equipment may change hands several times and make it difficult to track down the current owners. See Lovick v. Wil–Rich, 588 N.W.2d 688 (Iowa 1999) (farm machinery). In prescription drug and medical device cases, however, courts have insisted that companies send out letters or use their sales representatives in order to reach health care providers with newly discovered risk information. See Sterling Drug, Inc. v. Yarrow, 408 F.2d 978 (8th Cir.1969). Sellers would find it more difficult, of course, to track down patients who have received a drug or device in order to provide warnings. Courts generally do not impose a tort duty to recall defective products, but a failure to act reasonably in undertaking a government-mandated or voluntary recall may justify imposing liability for any resulting injuries. See Rest. (3d) § 11. A few courts have declined to impose a post-sale duty to convey risk information that has appeared in the medical literature. See May v. Dafoe, 611 P.2d 1275 (Wash.Ct.App.1980) (distinguishing the seller of hospital equipment from drug manufacturers); see also Demmler v. SmithKline Beecham Corp., 671 A.2d 1151, 1154–55 (Pa.Super.Ct.1996) (rejecting an inadequate warning claim for the failure to specify the appropriate therapy in the event that a listed side effect occurred).

3.   *When does a knowable risk become significant?* Another factor relevant to whether a duty to warn exists is the magnitude of the risk posed by the product. In one case, the court held that the manufacturer had a duty to warn of the less than one-in-a-million risk of contracting polio from a vaccine because the risk of contracting polio as a result of not using the vaccine was equally small. See Davis v. Wyeth Labs., Inc., 399 F.2d 121, 130 n.16 (9th Cir.1968); see also McEwen v. Ortho Pharm. Corp., 528 P.2d 522, 530 (Or.1974); Tomer v. American Home Prods. Corp., 368 A.2d 35, 40 (Conn.1976). But see Odom v. G.D. Searle & Co., 979 F.2d 1001, 1003–04 (4th Cir.1992) (rejecting plaintiff's proposed contraindication for an IUD, noting that any additional suggested warning "must bear some reasonable relation to the 1.84% risk" of pelvic inflammatory disease and resulting ectopic pregnancy); Kearl v. Lederle Labs., 218 Cal.Rptr. 453, 468 (Ct.App. 1985) ("[W]hatever duty a manufacturer may have to inform of risks associated with nonuse of a product, such a duty most certainly cannot be imposed when the relationship between use and nonuse is statistically close (and quite possibly immeasurable) and the probability of injury from either course is extremely remote."); Calabrese v. Trenton State College, 392 A.2d 600, 604 (N.J.Super.Ct.App.Div.1978), aff'd, 413 A.2d 315 (N.J.1980).

4. *Allergic reactions*. Manufacturers have an obligation to warn when they knew or should have known that hypersensitive individuals may suffer serious injury. See Basko v. Sterling Drug, Inc., 416 F.2d 417, 430 (2d Cir.1969); see also James A. Henderson, Jr., Process Norms in Products Litigation: Liability for Allergic Reactions, 51 U. Pitt. L. Rev. 761 (1990); Michael K. Barrett, Comment, Latex Gloves: Medical–Legal Issues for Health Care Professionals, 22 J. Legal Med. 263 (2001). Claims against manufacturers of OTC drugs often involve unexpected allergic reactions. See Burlison v. Warner–Lambert Co., 842 F.2d 991 (8th Cir.1988) (cough drop manufacturer had no duty to warn in the absence of evidence that it knew or should have known of possible allergic reactions); Griggs v. Combe, Inc., 456 So.2d 790, 792 (Ala.1984) (OTC drug manufacturer "had no duty to warn of a possible allergic reaction which it had no reason to suspect might occur."); see also Rest. (3d) § 2(c) cmt. k ("[A] warning is required when the harm-causing ingredient is one to which a substantial number of people are allergic."); id. illus. 13 (if product contains aspirin, manufacturer would only need to disclose this ingredient).

2.   Unintended Uses

Proctor v. Davis

682 N.E.2d 1203 (Ill.App.Ct.1997).

■ Hartman, Justice:

Plaintiffs Meyer Proctor and Marjorie Proctor filed this medical malpractice and products liability action against Dr. Michael J. Davis and the Upjohn Company, alleging serious injury resulting from Dr. Davis' injection of the corticosteroid Depo–Medrol, manufactured by Upjohn, directly into Meyer Proctor's left eye on November 7, 1983. A jury exonerated Dr. Davis, but found against Upjohn, awarding Proctor compensatory damages of $3,047,819.76, and punitive damages of $124,573,750, the latter of which the circuit court remitted to $35 million. Proctor and Upjohn appealed from that judgment. * * *

In 1959, the Food and Drug Administration (FDA) approved Upjohn's "New Drug Application" (NDA) for Depo–Medrol, a sterile, aqueous suspension containing methyl prednisone acetate, a corticosteroid, for treatment of various inflammatory bodily disorders. The FDA's approval was limited to intramuscular (in the muscle), intra-articular (in the joint), and intralesional (in a lesion) injections. According to the evidence, Depo–Medrol is an insoluble, toxic material, which is intended to be released in the body over a period of six to eight weeks in human tissue with adequate blood supply; however, the human eye does not possess such a blood supply. Depositing Depo–Medrol into the eye meant that the drug would remain in the eye for a relatively long time. Because of its insolubility, its crystals had an effect on the body's response to it when inserted, including increased intraocular pressure and other trauma. It became a foreign body in the eye, which was very difficult, if not impossible, to remove once injected into the eye.

Shortly after Depo–Medrol's FDA limited approval, two ophthalmologists contacted Upjohn independently, each wishing to use the drug clinically for the treatment of ophthalmic conditions through an unapproved method of administration—periocular (near the eye) injections.[1] This use of Depo–Medrol was neither approved by the FDA nor listed on Depo–Medrol's label (off-label use). Nevertheless, Upjohn immediately provided both with vials of Depo–Medrol without cautioning them that no animal studies had been initiated to test the reaction of the drug upon living tissue before embarking upon human use. Instead, Dr. Porter Crawford, an Upjohn employee responsible for monitoring Depo–Medrol at the time, encouraged this unapproved off-label use * * * * Dr. Crawford sent vials of Depo–Medrol to the inquiring doctor and asked him to let him know when he needed additional supplies. Dr. Crawford also noted that Upjohn would "be anxious to learn how it performs when used this way."

Upjohn dispensed not only vials of Depo–Medrol but, also, financial assistance to doctors who would use Depo–Medrol for the unapproved off-label use of periocular injections, granting one in 1959 $3,000. This doctor later wrote Upjohn that he had given two talks in Chicago in the fall of 1960, extolling the use of Depo–Medrol for subconjunctival injections * * * * Upjohn asked the doctor to prepare a write-up of his cases or publish an article in order to document this off-label use for possible FDA approval. Upjohn noted that "not too many people are actually using this

---

1. At trial, defendant Dr. Davis testified that he believed that by 1983, the technique of periocular injections was widely used in the medical community; he believed physicians were using this technique an estimated one million times each year. Physicians had previously used periocular injections with other steroids to avoid the side effects from other methods of administration, and to provide more direct action on the point of inflammation in the eye. As a new, longer-acting steroid, Depo–Medrol appeared to offer advantages for this type of use. Dr. Davis did not then know of the drug's dangerous propensities, or he would not have used it.

type of therapy and your good results suggest that the work should be scattered about.''

Upjohn itself undertook the task of "scattering about" the unapproved off-label use of Depo–Medrol to the medical community. In 1961, an article on the use of Depo–Medrol was written by the experimenting doctor to whom Upjohn had given $3,000. This doctor informed Dr. Crawford, on August 31, 1961, of the completion of the article, noting separately, however, that he was unable to use any of his animal experiments because the results were "very unsatisfactory." Proctor's expert, Dr. Philip Walson, who reviewed this correspondence, believed the omission of the animal studies created a serious problem because collected data was ignored, and the animal studies, although "unsatisfactory," should have been included in the article touting this use of Depo–Medrol.

Upjohn nevertheless ordered and distributed 2,500 reprints of the article, 500 for "hospital sales" and 2,000 for "sales education," thus becoming part of the "literature" to which the ophthalmic community was exposed. On November 16, 1961, Upjohn requested reprints of another experimenting doctor's article for distribution, which also mentioned the use of subconjunctival injections of Depo–Medrol. More "fodder" priming the sales pump.

On March 8, 1963, Upjohn's Dr. Samuel Stubbs wrote to a different experimenting doctor, requesting case histories on the patients he had treated with Depo–Medrol, which Upjohn would use to supplement its original NDA. Dr. Stubbs informed him that Upjohn would compensate him for his time, and that of his secretary, in preparing the case reports. * * *

Harry P. Davis, Jr., an Upjohn sales representative, wrote to Mr. Crissman at Upjohn on June 12, 1963, informing him that two Ohio physicians were using Depo–Medrol for "severe, chronic or acute, uveitis by retrobulbar injection," but that neither physician was aware that anything had been published on the use of this drug. Dr. Stubbs wrote to these two Ohio doctors on June 26, 1963, informing them of Upjohn's interest and asking for case reports of their experience with the drug. Further, if they were interested in publishing their work, Dr. Stubbs would make the "services of The Upjohn Writing Staff" available to them, would pay for their secretary's time, and would compensate the doctors for work on the case reports, admittedly intending to "plant the seed" in those doctors' minds about publishing an article.

On July 1, 1963, the Ohio doctors responded with eight case reports, which Dr. Stubbs referred to Harold Tucker, one of Upjohn's medical writers, for potential publication. An article written as a result of Upjohn's "expert assistance" proclaimed that positive results from the subconjunctival injection of Depo–Medrol had been confirmed by others. All the while, Upjohn's own expert, Dr. Stubbs, himself questioned the validity of the so-called studies. * * *

The practice of publicizing unapproved uses of drugs, when sponsored by the pharmaceutical company, is not approved by the FDA as proper advertising; it results in continuing, unapproved, potentially dangerous use. Dr. Stubbs was aware that those experimenting physicians would subsequently write publications which appeared in medical journals, for which Upjohn paid secretarial and editorial expenses. These writings, of course, would be addressed to the medical community and become available to ophthalmologists, thereby becoming, incredibly, part of the current medical literature attempting to establish the standard of medical expertise.

In 1965, Dr. Stubbs collected articles in the medical literature and prepared a report for internal use by Upjohn. Based on that report, he and his immediate supervisor recommended that Upjohn consider filing a supplemental NDA to obtain FDA approval for periocular administration of the drug. Without FDA approval, Upjohn could not include that use of Depo–Medrol as an approved method of administration on the drug's labeling. In order to supplement the NDA to provide for periocular administration of Depo–Medrol, Upjohn knew that it was "likely that animal tissue tolerance studies" would have to be performed.

Upjohn elected not to pursue a supplemental NDA for periocular administration. A corporate memorandum recommended that "no further Medical Development work be done with Depo–Medrol administered by [periocular] injection," and that "tissue tolerance studies in animals not be undertaken by Biomedical Research unless a request for [an NDA] supplement is initiated by Marketing, and approved in accordance with the currently effective Pharmaceutical New Product System procedures." * * *

Upjohn knew of potential adverse reactions to the drug, of which it learned over a period of preceding years from drug experience reports (DERs),[9] yet its labeling never referred to unapproved periocular injection of the drug, neither listing it as an appropriate method of administration, including any recommended dosages, nor stating any warnings regarding periocular use. Ophthalmologists, not having been advised of adverse reactions, began making extensive use of periocular injections of Depo–Medrol because the benefits seemingly outweighed the risks. Defendant Dr. Davis, himself, and four others testified to routine periocular administration of the drug.

In October 1980, in response to the FDA's global restructuring of labeling for all corticosteroids, Upjohn proposed a revised Depo–Medrol package insert. The proposed insert included the following statement:

9. When a pharmaceutical company receives a report about an adverse reaction associated with the use of its product, it records it in a DER and forwards it to the FDA. Between the first marketing of Depo–Medrol and the injection of Meyer Proctor that led to this suit, Upjohn received 23 reports indicating adverse experiences associated with its use. The DERs based on these communications were forwarded to the FDA, usually accompanied by a cover letter stating that the use involved was not recommended. Three of these reports (one in 1977 and two in 1983) concerned vision loss following periocular injections with unintentional intraocular injection. Additionally, the medical literature had reported other instances of accidental intraocular injections of corticosteroids like Depo–Medrol, some of which were followed by vision loss.

"ADVERSE REACTIONS REPORTED WITH NONRECOMMENDED ROUTES OF ADMINISTRATION * * * Ophthalmic: (Subconjunctival)—Redness and itching, obtuse, slough at injection site, increased intraocular pressure, decreased vision. (Retrobulbar)—Blindness."

In September 1983, the FDA informed Upjohn that it should not make its proposed changes, but rather should "continue using currently approved labeling" until it received "notification" from the agency. The FDA also told Upjohn that "[i]f important new labeling information becomes available, you should revise your approved product labeling under 21 C.F.R. 314.8." The circuit court excluded this evidence.

In April 1983, Meyer Proctor, a retired public relations worker, consulted Dr. Davis with complaints of blurred vision. Dr. Davis diagnosed Proctor's condition as uveitis, an inflammation of the eye, which can be chronic and can lead to permanent blindness. Dr. Davis began treating this condition with steroid medications applied to both of Proctor's eyes by means of eye drops, which proved to be of only limited value. In May 1983, Proctor developed cystoid macular edema (CME) as a complication of the uveitis, and the vision in his left eye deteriorated to the level of legal blindness. Dr. Davis referred him to a retinal-vitreal specialist for further evaluation and treatment, who concurred in the diagnosis of CME and prescribed Nalfon, a nonsteroidal anti-inflammatory medication. Some improvement in Proctor's vision occurred, but his sight was not restored to normal. After treating Proctor for several months, the specialist referred him back to Dr. Davis, recommending the use of a nonsteroidal anti-inflammatory drug (such as Nalfon), or the systemic or periocular administration of a steroid (such as Depo–Medrol) if continued impairment of vision made further treatment necessary.

On August 1, 1983, Dr. Davis examined Proctor and reinstituted treatment with Nalfon; however, his vision again began to deteriorate. On August 9, 1983, Dr. Davis decided to use periocular injections of Depo–Medrol to treat Proctor's condition, one shot around each eye. Within several weeks, Proctor's vision improved almost to normal, but in November 1983, Proctor experienced renewed problems with the vision in his left eye. In response, on November 7, 1983, Dr. Davis administered another periocular injection of Depo–Medrol near that eye.

All the ophthalmologists who testified at trial regarding the standard of care concluded that Dr. Davis' decision to administer Depo–Medrol via periocular injection both in August and again in November of 1983 was appropriate and within the applicable standard of care. None suggested that anything known at the time, or subsequently discovered, would have made this treatment inappropriate. There were risks associated with this treatment, however. Dr. Davis himself testified that in November 1983 he knew that an inadvertent intraocular injection was a risk of any periocular injection; Depo–Medrol could be "toxic" if inadvertently injected into the eye and cause damage to the eye, including blindness; he had never penetrated the globe of the eye (made an intraocular injection) in more than 1,600 prior periocular injections of Depo–Medrol in his entire career;

and, he believed he would be able to deliver the drug to its intended location without incident in this instance.

During the November 7, 1983 injection, however, Dr. Davis mistakenly inserted the needle and Depo–Medrol into Proctor's left eye. Dr. Davis then referred Proctor to a specialist for evaluation and treatment, who determined that the appropriate treatment was observation, waiting for the drug to clear from the eye, and watching for possible retinal detachment, which eventually occurred. Proctor underwent surgery on November 23, 1983, the Depo–Medrol was removed from Proctor's left eye, and the retina was reattached. The retina again detached, however, and two subsequent operations, on December 13 and 29, 1983, failed to reattach it. In April 1984, Proctor's left eye, having become blind and painful, was surgically removed.
* * *

Upjohn first argues that, after considering all the evidence in the case in the light most favorable to Proctor, it was entitled to either judgment notwithstanding the verdict or a new trial because Proctor failed to prove that a warning was required, because the risk was too remote to require a warning, and because the specialized medical community was already aware of the risks. * * *

From the evidence it is clear that Upjohn knew or should have known that Depo–Medrol is an insoluble, toxic material which, because of its insolubility, when inserted in the eye, became a foreign body, and was very difficult, if not impossible, to remove. * * * If Upjohn did not know what it should have known, it failed in its duty as an expert. It could not fulfill that duty merely by waiting for what it considered sufficient proof of a cause-effect relationship before advising the medical profession with an appropriate alert or warning of the possibility of risk in the use of one of its products. Nor can failure to do so be excused merely by the fact that the potentially endangered users are few in number. The injury here clearly was within the scope of the dangerous propensities of the drug for which Upjohn must be held accountable.

The evidence revealed that Upjohn knew of Depo–Medrol's dangerous propensities before the instant occurrence took place in 1983; yet, there was no reference in the 1983 label or insert that subconjunctival use of Depo–Medrol as practiced upon Proctor in this case was not recommended by Upjohn, nor that FDA approval was never secured for such application.
* * *

The record demonstrates that by 1961, Upjohn had learned that some ophthalmologists were administering Depo–Medrol through periocular injection as an "off-label" use. Upjohn fostered and encouraged this unapproved use as experimentation on human beings with no prior basic scientific studies having been made. This unauthorized use, encouraged by Upjohn, became more widespread in the next two decades, although Upjohn never secured FDA approval for it and never set forth the use, warnings or directions for such periocular injections on its labels or in its literature. None of the dangers attendant to such use, or any reported deleterious side effects which may have developed of which Upjohn was apprised through

DERs, were made known to the prescribing or treating physicians who made this unauthorized off-label use of it. Dr. Davis testified that he did not know of the drug's dangerous propensities, or he would not have used it. Dr. Thomas Deutsch, Upjohn's own expert, asserted that, until he testified in this case, he did not know Depo–Medrol would be difficult or impossible to remove once injected into the eye. * * *

A manufacturer of ethical drugs cannot evade its responsibilities of warning physicians of dangers and risks attendant to the use of its products, by hoping, as in the present case, that the doctors will learn of the dangers themselves. Upjohn's duty to warn was nondelegable; the failure of prescribing and treating physicians to learn of the risks of a drug from other sources does not relieve the manufacturer of liability for harm resulting from its own failure to adequately warn. Here, Upjohn knew of the risks, yet did not share this knowledge with members of the profession acting in decision-making capacities in administering drugs to their patients, and encouraged unapproved use and misleading publicity. * * *

Significantly, Upjohn knew how to warn, and did warn doctors against certain uses of Depo–Medrol by advising them, for example, against intrathecal administration of this drug, which it printed on the insert distributed with the drug in 1983, before the instant insertion of Depo–Medrol into Proctor's eye. Upjohn, in another line or two of print on the insert, easily could have mentioned potential adverse reactions to the drug when injected intraocularly, of which it had learned over a period of preceding years from the DERs. Information regarding questionable reactions or side effects to this Upjohn product contained in DERs in Upjohn's possession was not shared by it with the medical community by any other means. According to Dr. Walson, being on notice of that kind of information from the 1960s up to 1983, there were methodologies and scientific means available to Upjohn to confirm or disaffirm the toxicity of the drug. In his opinion, Upjohn should have included a warning on its label or package insert which said, in effect, do not use the drug in that way, and if so used, this is what may be seen. This was never done. In light of this imbalance of access to information about adverse propensities of Depo–Medrol, it cannot be concluded that physicians had knowledge of the risks equal to Upjohn's. * * *

A drug company cannot absolve itself from the duty to warn by pointing to the unauthorized use of its drug by physicians with whom it has not shared its knowledge of dangerous side effects and injury. Violation of its duty to warn is even more egregious in this case since, as the evidence heard by the jury demonstrated, Upjohn encouraged and participated in disseminating misleading information concerning the use of its drug to the "learned intermediaries," through financial support, technical assistance, and abundant supplies of the drug during the period when Upjohn was receiving adverse information concerning this use of the drug. * * *

The evidence convincingly supports the conclusion that Upjohn promoted, encouraged and advertised the off-label use of Depo–Medrol by providing financial and technical assistance to a limited number of members of the medical community without attempting to communicate to these physicians and the medical community at large the dangers and risks attendant to this use. Although it is assumed that physicians will keep abreast of current medical literature, here, part of the flawed literature was generated by Upjohn. Upjohn even sought to "plant the seed" in doctors' minds about contributing to the literature, and thereby help to mislead the specialized ophthalmic community as to the potential harmful effects attendant to the intraocular injection of a drug which could be impossible to remove. To conclude that the existence of literature in such a case constitutes knowledge on the part of doctors and the medical community equal to that of a drug's manufacturer, would encourage more writings of the type found in this case, fostered by the very defendant upon whom responsibility should be fixed. Such an insidious situation as here existed should be neither countenanced, encouraged nor condoned. The evidence demonstrates that Upjohn knew or should have known of the risks and dangers attendant to the use of Depo–Medrol, thereby requiring warning. Upjohn simply failed to do so. * * *

Upjohn's most persuasive argument is that the punitive damages awarded are excessive and should be reduced. In reviewing punitive damage awards, the question of excessiveness turns on whether the amount is so large that it outruns the justification for exacting punitive damages, namely retribution and deterrence of future outrageous conduct. A reviewing court considers the degree of reprehensibility of defendant's conduct, the relationship between the punitive damage award and the harm caused by the conduct, defendant's gain from the misconduct, and the financial condition of defendant. This court's inquiry is thus one of degree: when arrayed along the spectrum of wrongful acts, was the conduct at issue here so extraordinarily outrageous as to justify extraordinary punitive damages? The circuit court, in its review of the punitive damages awarded, answered that question in the affirmative, although it remitted the jury's award by almost 75%. The original award of more than $124 million amounted to precisely 7% of Upjohn's net worth; the remitted amount is still more than 2% of the company's net worth and more than eleven times the amount of compensatory damages awarded.

When we consider the factors set out by the United States Supreme Court and Illinois courts, we find that the amount of punitive damages awarded in this case far outruns the justification for imposing punitive damages. We agree with the circuit court that Upjohn's conduct was sufficiently reprehensible to support an award of punitive damages, however, there is no reasonable relationship between the amount of the punitive damages and the harm caused by the conduct. Further, although Upjohn is a large corporation with a net worth of approximately $1.7 billion, punishment in the amount of 2% of its net worth is excessive in the extreme. * * * We believe that a punitive damage award twice that of the compensatory damage award will send a strong message to pharmaceutical manufacturers of the necessity to warn of the known potential adverse effects of their drugs. The twin goals of retribution and deterrence would both be met by such an award. Pursuant to Supreme Court Rule 366, we enter a remittitur of the punitive damages to $6,095,639.52. * * *

■ DiVITO, JUSTICE (dissenting):

Meyer Proctor suffered a painful and tragic injury. For that, however, Upjohn bears no responsibility. Succinctly stated, Proctor's injury was the result of an accident involving Dr. Davis' use of a needle, and Upjohn could not have prevented, nor was it responsible for, the doctor's mistake. Judgment notwithstanding the verdict should have been granted because Upjohn had no duty to warn and, even if it did, there was no showing that any alleged failure to warn was a proximate cause of Proctor's injury. Alternatively, reversal and a new trial are warranted because the circuit court improperly excluded critical evidence favorable to Upjohn. * * *

The majority holds that Upjohn is liable for Proctor's injury because it knew that Depo–Medrol was toxic and difficult to remove if injected into the eye, and it failed to warn ophthalmologists of these risks. The record, however, does not justify that conclusion because it contains ample evidence that the medical community, including Dr. Davis, was aware of the risks associated with periocular injection of Depo–Medrol. Drs. Walson, Deutsch, Giles, and Fagman testified that the possibility of intraocular injection was a well-known risk of periocular use of Depo–Medrol. Dr. Walson, plaintiffs' own expert, also testified that he thought that, in 1983, ophthalmologists were aware that inadvertent intraocular injection of Depo–Medrol had caused the loss of an eye for some patients. In addition, there were several reports in the medical literature describing incidents in which vision loss resulted from an inadvertent intraocular injection of Depo–Medrol. Physicians are held to a standard of medical expertise and may be expected to have knowledge of current medical literature. * * *

Not only were the risks associated with periocular use of Depo–Medrol well-known to the medical community, they were also evident to Dr. Davis. Although he testified that he did not know that Depo–Medrol could not be easily removed once injected into the eye, Dr. Davis knew that injecting it into the eye could lead to blindness. From reading medical literature, he knew that accidental intraocular injection was possible and that piercing of the eyeball could cause damage, including blindness. He also testified that he knew Depo–Medrol was toxic to the eye. Even as a medical resident, he and his fellow medical residents were well aware of the drug's toxicity and knew that it should not be used intraocularly. * * *

With respect to the removability of the drug, the relevant question is whether Upjohn had greater knowledge than the medical community about any difficulty in removing Depo–Medrol from the eye. Dr. Stubbs, Upjohn's medical monitor for Depo–Medrol, testified that, based on information in the medical literature available in 1983 and information in drug experience reports sent to Upjohn, he did not believe that Depo–Medrol would be particularly difficult to remove from the eye. Likewise, in the course of testifying about instances reported in the literature concerning the injection of Depo–Medrol into the eye, Dr. Walson made a similar statement concerning the removability of the drug. In addition, two of the three drug experience reports received by Upjohn that described an intraocular injection of Depo–Medrol reported that the Depo–Medrol had been removed by performing a vitrectomy. Thus, the record before us does not support the conclusion that Upjohn had greater knowledge than the medical community of any difficulty in removing the drug in the event of an inadvertent intraocular injection.

Even with the evidence viewed in the light most favorable to plaintiffs, therefore, Upjohn had no duty to warn in this case. The record demonstrates that the medical community and Dr. Davis were well-aware of the potential danger associated with periocular injection of Depo–Medrol and that Upjohn did not have superior knowledge of these risks. * * *

Dr. Davis did testify that he would not have given Proctor a periocular injection of Depo–Medrol had he known it was difficult to remove and might cause blindness. Certainly, it was the role of the jury to evaluate his credibility and to resolve conflicts in the evidence. Nevertheless, judgment notwithstanding the verdict was appropriate because, even viewing the evidence in the light most favorable to plaintiffs, it is clear that, despite his testimony to the contrary, Dr. Davis' treatment decision would have been the same had he received the warnings plaintiffs contend were required.

Dr. Davis' testimony that he would not have treated Proctor with periocular injection of Depo–Medrol if he had received these warnings was completely contradicted by the remainder of his testimony. For example, he testified that he had found this treatment to be safe and effective and had used it without problem on 1,600 occasions prior to the accidental injection of Proctor's eye. In fact, he had used it to restore Proctor's vision when no other treatment had worked. Also contrary to his testimony that he would not have used Depo–Medrol periocularly if he had known the risks, Dr. Davis testified that, at the time he treated Proctor, he was aware that accidental intraocular injection and blindness were possible consequences of periocular injection of Depo–Medrol. Perhaps the best indicator of how knowledge of these risks would have affected his treatment decision was his testimony that, even after he accidentally penetrated Proctor's eye, he continued to treat patients with periocular injections of Depo–Medrol.

Dr. Davis' testimony that periocular injection of Depo–Medrol was the only treatment alternative for Proctor also contradicted his testimony that warnings would have changed his treatment decision. The majority states that there were alternative treatments available, but the record does not support this conclusion. Dr. Davis explained that further use of Nalfon was not a feasible alternative because it had been used without success to treat Proctor's condition. Dr. Davis also explained that intramuscular, that is, systemic, administration of steroids, was contraindicated by certain health conditions Proctor had. As for the majority's suggestion that Dr. Davis could have used a different formulation of Depo–Medrol, the record does not indicate that a different formulation would have been effective. By contrast, Dr. Davis knew that periocular injection was an effective treatment for Proctor because it had restored his vision in the past, and it was not contraindicated by Proctor's other medical conditions.

The testimony of other ophthalmologists also indicated that the warning plaintiffs claim was required would not have changed Dr. Davis' treatment decision. Expert witnesses, Drs. Giles, Fagman, and Deutsch, all testified that Davis' decision to inject Depo–Medrol periocularly was in accordance with the applicable standard of care. Dr. Giles also testified that, even after he accidentally injected Depo–Medrol intraocularly, he continued to treat patients using periocular injection of the drug and found it to be safe and efficacious. It is clear from this evidence that the ophthalmologic community, including Dr. Davis, considered Depo–Medrol to be an appropriate treatment for Proctor's condition and found periocular injection of this drug to be safe and effective despite the possibility of intraocular injection and vision loss.

This uncontradicted evidence compelled the jury to conclude that Upjohn's alleged failure to warn was not a proximate cause of Proctor's injury. The only proximate cause of Proctor's loss of his eye was Dr. Davis' accidental injection of Depo–Medrol into the eye rather than periocularly. Consequently, the circuit court should have granted the motion for judgment notwithstanding the verdict. * * *

The circuit court excluded evidence of post–1983 usage of Depo–Medrol, but Upjohn made offers of proof that, after 1983, Drs. Giles, Deutsch, and Fagman continued to use periocular injection of Depo–Medrol to treat their patients. The evidence that, even after 1983, ophthalmologists continued to view periocular injection of Depo–Medrol as a safe and efficacious treatment severely undermines the argument that Dr. Davis would have treated Proctor differently had he known more about the drug. Moreover, such evidence was highly relevant to the issue of punitive damages. The circuit court erred in excluding this evidence.

The majority holds that this evidentiary ruling was proper because it was consistent with the court's exclusion of post–1983 labeling changes. The majority's "consistency" rationale, however, is not persuasive because, although there are public policy considerations that support the exclusion of the evidence of post–1983 labeling changes, there is no legitimate basis for the exclusion of the evidence of post–1983 usage. Generally, evidence of subsequent remedial measures is inadmissible in negligence and product liability actions for public policy reasons: courts do not want to discourage defendants from making safety improvements, evidence of subsequent remedial measures is not probative, and the jury may view this evidence as proof of negligence. These policy concerns supported the circuit court's exclusion of the post–1983 labeling changes, but they do not justify the exclusion of the post–1983 usage of Depo–Medrol. * * *

Also troubling is the circuit court's exclusion of evidence of Upjohn's attempt to add a warning to its labeling and its exclusion of evidence of FDA labeling controls. * * * Illinois courts have held that evidence of compliance with federal requirements, including FDA requirements, is admissible. The majority distinguishes these cases, however, on the basis that the parties in those cases demonstrated compliance, and Upjohn did not prove that it complied with FDA requirements in this case. The majority, therefore, concludes that Upjohn was not entitled to present evidence of its attempted labeling change or of FDA labeling requirements because these were not relevant either to its duty to warn or to punitive damages. * * *

Even absent proof of compliance, the evidence of Upjohn's attempted labeling change and FDA labeling requirements was highly relevant to the issue of punitive damages because it tended to show that Upjohn's conduct was not willful and wanton. * * * Furthermore, there was no basis for concluding from the record that Upjohn was not complying with an FDA directive when it continued to use labeling that did not contain a warning with respect to ophthalmic use. In response to the FDA's request for format changes to all corticosteroid labels, Upjohn submitted a supplemental application, in which it proposed to revise the Depo–Medrol label to, among other things, include a new warning for ophthalmic uses. In September 1983, the FDA informed Upjohn that it was conducting further review of the labeling format and instructed it to continue to use existing labeling until the FDA notified it of the status of its supplemental application. * * * It was, therefore, logical for Upjohn to wait for the FDA to act on its pending application and to follow the FDA's instruction to use its existing labeling until the FDA notified it of the status of its application. Had the jury been allowed to consider this letter, it may have reached the same conclusion as to Upjohn's actions. * * *

Upjohn also should have been allowed to present evidence of FDA labeling controls. The jury heard Dr. Walson's testimony that the format of the Depo–Medrol labeling was misleading, but Upjohn was not permitted to counter this testimony with evidence that the FDA dictates the format of prescription drug labels. The exclusion of this evidence unfairly prejudiced Upjohn in its ability to justify its failure to warn of the risks associated with ophthalmic use of Depo–Medrol and likely contributed to the jury's punitive damage award.

The majority opinion itself demonstrates the prejudice that resulted from the exclusion of evidence of FDA requirements. According to the majority, Upjohn knew how to warn because it had warned against intrathecal use, and "Upjohn, in another line or two of print on the insert, easily could have mentioned potential adverse reactions to the drug when injected intraocularly." This statement ignores the restrictions that the FDA places on labeling. See Lars Noah, The Imperative to Warn: Disentangling the "Right to Know" from the "Need to Know" About Consumer Product Hazards, 11 Yale J. on Reg. 293, 359 (1994) ("Although in theory drug manufacturers are free to add warnings in advance of FDA approval, they may not enjoy any real flexibility to alter previously approved labeling."). The Depo–Medrol labeling included a warning against intrathecal use because the FDA required this warning. It is not clear what sort of warnings, if any, the FDA would have permitted for periocular use. The FDA must approve all post-marketing labeling changes and, therefore, would not necessarily have permitted Upjohn to "easily" include a warning involving periocular use of the drug. In fact, the record demonstrates that when Upjohn submitted such a warning, it took the FDA several years to respond, and the response instructed Upjohn to continue to use its existing labeling. * * *

Finally, the majority's description of Upjohn's activities with respect to the off-label use of Depo–Medrol must be addressed. * * * Off-label use of drugs is not unusual or illegal, and even the FDA has acknowledged that off-label use of a drug may be appropriate and rational. In addition, contrary to the majority's implication that Upjohn acted improperly by funding research into off-label uses and distributing reprints of articles discussing off-label uses, these practices have been common among drug manufacturers. Dr. Stubbs testified that it was not unusual to supply drugs to physicians who requested them, that fulfilling reprint requests was part of normal sales education, and that, in 1963 and 1964, it was normal for drug manufacturers to compensate doctors for secretarial help in preparing case reports and to supply writing support services. The FDA has recently restricted the manner in which manufacturers may communicate with physicians about off-label uses, but its policy with respect to such communications was not as strict during the period of time relevant to this suit. The majority offers no authority for its suggestion that Upjohn's activities would not have been approved by the FDA and the record does not permit such a conclusion. * * *

NOTES AND QUESTIONS

1. *The relevance of FDA labeling decisions.* In a case similar to *Proctor*, the court credited the testimony from a former FDA Commissioner who had explained that the agency "would not have allowed Upjohn to contact physicians or send a 'Dear Doctor' letter regarding the intrathecal use of Depo–Medrol because it was not an approved use for the drug." Hahn v. Richter, 628 A.2d 860, 863 (Pa.Super.Ct.1993). Why might the FDA resist such labeling? How might Upjohn have described the risk (as revealed by the footnotes excerpted with the majority's opinion, three cases of blindness following accidental intraocular injection had been reported over a 23 year period and associated with an off-label use that occurred approximately one million times in 1983)? How might an ophthalmologist react to such information? Indeed, would Upjohn face heightened exposure to tort liability if it had decided to add such a warning without FDA approval? Recall that the *Feldman* court at least allowed the manufacturer to introduce evidence concerning the FDA's initial resistance to the proposed addition of a warning. Even absent a general duty to warn against off-label uses, if a manufacturer submits a supplemental application seeking approval of a new indication that the agency denies, should the manufacturer have an obligation to disclose that fact in its labeling?

2. *Foreseeable misuse.* Manufacturers must warn of the hazards associated with both the intended use and any foreseeable misuse of a product. It is generally no defense that a plaintiff's injury resulted from misuse if the manufacturer was aware that such misuse might take place and could have warned against it. See Knowlton v. Deseret Med., Inc., 930 F.2d 116, 122–

23 (1st Cir.1991) (device manufacturer knew that its catheter was being used in open-heart surgery); Felice v. Valleylab, Inc., 520 So.2d 920, 926 (La.Ct.App.1987) (manufacturer of electrosurgical device could foresee that it might be used in performing circumcisions and therefore had a duty to warn of the accompanying risk of severe burns). For instance, pharmaceutical manufacturers must warn against the ingestion of excessive doses of a drug product because such failures to abide by instructions are foreseeable. See Docken v. Ciba–Geigy, 739 P.2d 591, 593–95 (Or.Ct.App.1987); see also Richards v. Upjohn Co., 625 P.2d 1192, 1196 (N.M.Ct.App.1980) (because an intramuscular antibiotic solution "had been on the market for over ten years before the recommendation to use it topically was withdrawn," the manufacturer may have had a specific duty to warn against what was now an off-label use); Bristol–Myers Co. v. Gonzales, 548 S.W.2d 416, 423–24 (Tex.Civ.App.1976) (a physician's use of an antibiotic solution as a continuous rather than single-use irrigant for an open wound was reasonably foreseeable by the manufacturer and did not amount to misuse), rev'd on other grds., 561 S.W.2d 801, 804 (Tex.1978); Crocker v. Winthrop Lab., 514 S.W.2d 429, 432–33 (Tex.1974) (holding manufacturer liable for failing to warn of a drug's addictive qualities).

3. *Unforeseeable misuse.* Manufacturers would not, however, have to anticipate "gross misuse" of a drug by a physician. See Rhoto v. Ribando, 504 So.2d 1119, 1124–25 (La.Ct.App.1987); see also Phelps v. Sherwood Med. Indus., 836 F.2d 296, 304 (7th Cir.1987) (jury could find that off-label use of catheter in open-heart surgery amounted to an unforeseeable misuse of the device by the physician); Robak v. Abbott Labs., 797 F.Supp. 475, 476 (D.Md.1992) ("[T]he manufacturer had no duty to warn of any deleterious effects that might be associated with misuse of the product, i.e., its use for treatment of a non-indicated condition."); Peterson v. Parke Davis & Co., 705 P.2d 1001, 1003 (Colo.Ct.App.1985) (because the drug manufacturer warned of toxic effects associated with high dosages, the physician's failure to heed these warnings constituted misuse of the product and justified a verdict in favor of the manufacturer); Pfizer, Inc. v. Jones, 272 S.E.2d 43, 44–45 (Va.1980) (no duty to warn of dangers associated with improper injection method). See generally Lars Noah, Constraints on the Off–Label Uses of Prescription Drug Products, 16 J. Prods. & Toxics Liab. 139 (1994); Kaspar J. Stoffelmayr, Comment, Products Liability and "Off-Label" Uses of Prescription Drugs, 63 U. Chi. L. Rev. 275 (1996).

B.   SCOPE OF THE DUTY TO WARN

Restatement (Third) of the Law of Torts: Products Liability

(American Law Inst. 1998):

> § 6(d) A prescription drug or medical device is not reasonably safe due to inadequate instructions or warnings if reasonable instructions or warnings regarding foreseeable risks of harm are not provided to:

(1) prescribing and other health-care providers who are in a position to reduce the risks of harm in accordance with the instructions or warnings; or

(2) the patient when the manufacturer knows or has reason to know that health-care providers will not be in a position to reduce the risks of harm in accordance with the instructions or warnings.

As explained in the accompanying comment, this subsection "retains the 'learned intermediary' rule. However, in certain limited therapeutic relationships the physician or other health-care provider has a much diminished role as an evaluator or decisionmaker. In these instances it may be appropriate to impose on the manufacturer the duty to warn the patient directly." Id. cmt. b.

1. THE LEARNED INTERMEDIARY RULE

In essentially all jurisdictions, manufacturers of prescription drugs satisfy their common law duty to warn by providing precautionary information to physicians and others who act as learned intermediaries. See, e.g., Thomas v. Hoffman–LaRoche, Inc., 949 F.2d 806, 811 (5th Cir.1992); Stone v. Smith, Kline & French Lab., 731 F.2d 1575, 1579–80 (11th Cir.1984); Niemiera v. Schneider, 555 A.2d 1112, 1117–18 (N.J.1989); Martin v. Hacker, 628 N.E.2d 1308, 1311 (N.Y.1993); Tracy v. Merrell Dow Pharm., Inc., 569 N.E.2d 875, 878 (Ohio 1991); Pittman v. Upjohn Co., 890 S.W.2d 425, 430–31 (Tenn.1994). This rule exists because "the choice involved [in prescribing a particular medication] is essentially a medical one involving an assessment of medical risks in light of the physician's knowledge of this patient's needs and susceptibilities." Davis v. Wyeth Labs., Inc., 399 F.2d 121, 130 (9th Cir.1968); see also Sterling Drug, Inc. v. Cornish, 370 F.2d 82, 85 (8th Cir.1966) ("If the doctor is properly warned of the possibility of a side effect in some patients, and is advised of the symptoms normally accompanying the side effect, there is an excellent chance that injury to the patient can be avoided."). In effect, the physician is regarded as the consumer in the sense of selecting the product for the end-user.

Actually, this duty limitation serves several related purposes. First, courts hesitate to intrude on the doctor-patient relationship. See Swayze v. McNeil Lab., Inc., 807 F.2d 464, 471 (5th Cir.1987) ("In all likelihood, such [direct] warnings would only lead to confusion, and perhaps undermine the physician-patient relationship. When the physician-patient relationship does exist, as here, we hesitate to encourage, much less require, a drug manufacturer to intervene in it."); Dunkin v. Syntex Lab., Inc., 443 F.Supp. 121, 123 (W.D.Tenn.1977) ("[A]ttempts to give detailed warnings to patients could mislead patients and might also tend to interfere with the physician/patient relationship."); Carmichael v. Reitz, 95 Cal.Rptr. 381, 400 (Ct.App.1971) (noting that a patient might decline to take a prescribed drug in response to misunderstood warnings received directly from a manufacturer); In re Certified Questions, 358 N.W.2d 873, 883 (Mich.1984) (Boyle, J., dissenting) (arguing that direct warnings "could potentially cause undue interference with the doctor-patient relationship, cause patient confusion and result in a hampering of the healing process"). In effect, warnings that contradict information supplied by the physician might undermine the patient's trust in the physician's judgment. See Brooks v. Medtronic, Inc., 750 F.2d 1227, 1232 (4th Cir.1984) ("One in a serious medical condition ... faces unwanted, unsettling and potentially harmful risks if advice, almost inevitably involved and longwinded, from non-physicians, contrary to what the doctor of his choice has decided should be done, must be supplied to him during the already stressful period shortly before his trip to the operating room."); McKee v. American Home Prods. Corp., 782 P.2d 1045, 1055 (Wash.1989) (suggesting that package inserts "may confuse and frighten the patient").

Second, physicians can better convey meaningful information to their patients. See *Brooks*, 750 F.2d at 1232 (noting that "the question turns on who is in a better position to disclose risks"); Ferrara v. Berlex Lab., Inc., 732 F.Supp. 552, 555 (E.D.Pa.1990); Martin v. Ortho Pharm. Corp., 661 N.E.2d 352, 357 (Ill.1996) ("[P]rescribing physicians, and not pharmaceutical manufacturers, are in the best position to provide direct warnings to patients concerning the dangers associated with prescription drugs."); MacDonald v. Ortho Pharm. Corp., 475 N.E.2d 65, 74 (Mass.1985) (O'Connor, J., dissenting) ("Doctors, unlike printed warnings, can tailor to the needs and abilities of an individual patient the information that that patient needs in order to make an informed decision whether to use a particular drug."). Manufacturers lack effective means to communicate directly with patients, making it necessary to rely on physicians to convey the relevant information. See *Davis*, 399 F.2d at 130–31 (observing that "it is difficult under such circumstances for the manufacturer, by label or direct communication, to reach the consumer with a warning," and contrasting OTC drugs); Terhune v. A.H. Robins Co., 577 P.2d 975, 978 (Wash.1978) (explaining that "it is ordinarily difficult for the manufacturer to communicate directly with the consumer"). Finally, manufacturers would find it difficult to translate the complex information included in physician labeling for lay patients. See Hill v. Searle Lab., 884 F.2d 1064, 1070 (8th Cir.1989) (noting that "the information regarding risks is often too technical for a patient to make a reasonable choice"); Reaves v. Ortho Pharm. Corp., 765 F.Supp. 1287, 1290 (E.D.Mich.1991) ("As with other prescription drugs, patients are unlikely to understand technical medical information regarding the nature and propensities of oral contraceptives."); Ingram v. Hook's Drugs, Inc., 476 N.E.2d 881, 887 n.4 (Ind.Ct.App.1985) (rejecting the suggestion that patients should have been given precautionary information contained in the package insert for Valium, which included over 20 cautionary instructions and 32 listed side effects, because "[s]uch a voluminous warning would only confuse the normal consumer and be of dubious value").

Warnings can either serve to promote safe use of a product or to disclose unavoidable risks so that the user can make a more informed risk-benefit decision. As explained in the comments accompanying § 6 of the *Restatement (Third)*:

> Failure to instruct or warn is the major basis of liability for manufacturers of prescription drugs and medical devices. When prescribing

health-care providers are adequately informed of the relevant benefits and risks associated with various prescription drugs and medical devices, they can reach appropriate decisions regarding which drug or device is best for specific patients. Sometimes a warning serves to inform health-care providers of unavoidable risks that inhere in the drug or medical device. By definition, such a warning would not aid the health-care provider in reducing the risk of injury to the patient by taking precautions in how the drug is administered or the medical device is used. However, warnings of unavoidable risks allow the health-care provider, and thereby the patient, to make an informed choice whether to utilize the drug or medical device. Beyond informing health-care providers, a drug or device manufacturer may have a duty under the law of negligence to use reasonable measures to supply instructions or warnings to nonprescribing health-care providers who are in positions to act on such information so as to reduce or prevent injury to patients.

Rest. (3d) § 6 cmt. d (1998); see also id. § 2 cmt. i.

The learned intermediary rule has important consequences for litigation. When reduced to the question of whether the warning conveyed to a physician or other health care provider was adequate, plaintiffs will encounter greater difficulties getting a case to a jury. See, e.g., Odom v. G.D. Searle & Co., 979 F.2d 1001, 1003 (4th Cir.1992); Thomas v. Hoffman–LaRoche, 949 F.2d 806, 815–17 (5th Cir.1992); Willett v. Baxter Int'l, Inc., 929 F.2d 1094, 1099 (5th Cir.1991); Anderson v. McNeilab, Inc., 831 F.2d 92, 93 (5th Cir.1987) (per curiam); Finn v. G.D. Searle & Co., 677 P.2d 1147, 1154 (Cal.1984); Felix v. Hoffmann–LaRoche, Inc., 540 So.2d 102, 105 (Fla.1989); Johnson v. American Cyanamid Co., 718 P.2d 1318, 1325–26 (Kan.Ct.App.1986), aff'd on other grds., 758 P.2d 206 (Kan.1988). Although physicians may have an incentive to shift blame to the manufacturer, normally they will testify that they understood the warnings provided by the manufacturer. See Hall v. Merck, Sharp & Dohme, 774 F.Supp. 604, 606–07 (D.Kan.1991); Wooten v. Johnson & Johnson Prods. Inc., 635 F.Supp. 799, 802–04 (N.D.Ill.1986). This stands in contrast to a typical plaintiff's testimony that the warning communicated to them seemed insufficient. Moreover, plaintiffs may have to produce expert testimony to support an inadequacy claim. See Upjohn Co. v. MacMurdo, 562 So.2d 680, 683 (Fla.1990) ("[T]he adequacy or inadequacy of the warning to inform a physician must, except in the more obvious situations, be proved by expert testimony."); Wyeth Lab., Inc. v. Fortenberry, 530 So.2d 688, 692 (Miss. 1988) ("The adequacy of a warning addressed to the medical community may fall into the category of issues requiring expert testimony."). This stands in contrast to a consumer directed warning to which jurors can often apply their own experience.

NOTES AND QUESTIONS

1. *Medical devices.* The learned intermediary rule also applies to implantable medical devices. See Toole v. Baxter Healthcare Corp., 235 F.3d 1307,

1313–14 (11th Cir.2000); Talley v. Danek Med., Inc., 179 F.3d 154 (4th Cir.1999); Jacobs v. E.I. du Pont de Nemours & Co., 67 F.3d 1219, 1239 (6th Cir.1995); Violette v. Smith & Nephew Dyonics, Inc., 62 F.3d 8, 13–14 (1st Cir.1995); Willett v. Baxter Int'l, Inc., 929 F.2d 1094, 1098 (5th Cir.1991); Phelps v. Sherwood Med. Indus., 836 F.2d 296, 303 (7th Cir. 1987); Sita v. Danek Med., Inc., 43 F.Supp.2d 245 (E.D.N.Y.1999); Pumphrey v. C.R. Bard, Inc., 906 F.Supp. 334, 338 (N.D.W.Va.1995); Plenger v. Alza Corp., 13 Cal.Rptr.2d 811, 818 n.6 (Ct.App.1992); Craft v. Peebles, 893 P.2d 138, 155–56 (Haw.1995); see also Lloyd C. Chatfield, II, Medical Implant Litigation and Failure to Warn: A New Extension for the Learned Intermediary Rule?, 82 Ky. L.J. 575 (1993–94).

2. *Further commentary.* See Richard C. Ausness, Learned Intermediaries and Sophisticated Users: Encouraging the Use of Intermediaries to Transmit Product Safety Information, 46 Syracuse L. Rev. 1185 (1996); Margaret Gilhooley, Learned Intermediaries, Prescription Drugs, and Patient Information, 30 St. Louis U. L.J. 633 (1986); Nancy K. Plant, The Learned Intermediary Doctrine: Some New Medicine for an Old Ailment, 81 Iowa L. Rev. 1007 (1996); Charles J. Walsh et al., The Learned Intermediary Doctrine: The Correct Prescription for Drug Labeling, 48 Rutgers L. Rev. 821 (1996); Susan A. Casey, Comment, Laying an Old Doctrine to Rest: Challenging the Wisdom of the Learned Intermediary Doctrine, 19 Wm. Mitchell L. Rev. 931 (1993); see also Pamela R. Ferguson, Liability for Pharmaceutical Products: A Critique of the "Learned Intermediary" Rule, 12 Oxford J. Legal Stud. 59 (1992) (evaluating application of the doctrine by courts in England). See generally Diane Schmauder Kane, Annotation, Construction and Application of Learned–Intermediary Doctrine, 57 A.L.R.5th 1 (1998).

2.   EXCEPTIONS

Only in situations where an individualized prescribing decision is unlikely to be made (for example, when vaccines are being administered to patients in a mass immunization program) would a manufacturer have to provide a warning directly to the patient. See Brazzell v. United States, 788 F.2d 1352 (8th Cir.1986); Plummer v. Lederle Labs., 819 F.2d 349, 356 (2d Cir.1987) ("If the drug is given under clinic-type conditions the manufacturer is obligated to warn consumers directly."); Reyes v. Wyeth Labs., 498 F.2d 1264, 1276–77 (5th Cir.1974); Allison v. Merck & Co., 878 P.2d 948, 958 n.16 (Nev.1994); see also Mazur v. Merck & Co., 964 F.2d 1348, 1365–69 (3d Cir.1992) (holding that a vaccine manufacturer satisfied this duty by delegating to the CDC the responsibility for disseminating patient labeling). A few courts also have suggested that a manufacturer may be unable to rely on the learned intermediary rule in cases where inoculations in a private physician's office resemble a clinic setting. See Givens v. Lederle, 556 F.2d 1341, 1345 (5th Cir.1977); Williams v. Lederle Lab., 591 F.Supp. 381, 389 (S.D.Ohio 1984); Samuels v. American Cyanamid Co., 495 N.Y.S.2d 1006, 1013 (Sup.Ct.1985). But see Stanback v. Parke, Davis & Co., 657 F.2d 642, 647 (4th Cir.1981); Rohrbough v. Wyeth Lab., Inc., 719

F.Supp. 470, 478 (N.D.W.Va.1989), aff'd on other grds., 916 F.2d 970 (4th Cir.1990); Walker v. Merck & Co., 648 F.Supp. 931, 934–35 (M.D.Ga.1986) (treating nurses as learned intermediaries when they administered vaccine), aff'd mem., 831 F.2d 1069 (11th Cir.1987); Dunn v. Lederle Lab., 328 N.W.2d 576, 579 & n.11 (Mich.Ct.App.1982). With regard to childhood vaccines, however, federal legislation has overridden the mass immunization exception. See 42 U.S.C. § 300aa–22(c).

A few courts have extended the mass immunization exception to other products, such as contraceptives, for which a physician may not make an individualized judgment in prescribing a particular medication. See, e.g., Hill v. Searle Labs., 884 F.2d 1064, 1071 (8th Cir.1989) (IUDs); Odgers v. Ortho Pharm. Corp., 609 F.Supp. 867, 878–79 (E.D.Mich.1985) (oral contraceptives); MacDonald v. Ortho Pharm. Corp., 475 N.E.2d 65, 69–70 (Mass. 1985) (same). The overwhelming majority of courts do not, however, recognize any exception for contraceptive drugs or devices. See, e.g., West v. G.D. Searle & Co., 879 S.W.2d 412 (Ark.1994); Lacy v. G.D. Searle & Co., 567 A.2d 398 (Del.1989); Martin v. Ortho Pharm. Corp., 661 N.E.2d 352, 356 (Ill.1996); Humes v. Clinton, 792 P.2d 1032, 1042–43 (Kan.1990); Seley v. G.D. Searle & Co., 423 N.E.2d 831, 840 (Ohio 1981); McKee v. Moore, 648 P.2d 21 (Okla.1982); Wyeth–Ayerst Labs. Co. v. Medrano, 28 S.W.3d 87, 92 (Tex.App.2000).

Restatement (Third) of the Law of Torts: Products Liability § 6 (American Law Inst. 1998):

Comment e. *Direct warnings to patients*. Warnings and instructions with regard to drugs or medical devices that can be sold legally only pursuant to a prescription are, under the "learned intermediary" rule, directed to health-care providers. Subsection (d)(2) recognizes that direct warnings and instructions to patients are warranted for drugs that are dispensed or administered to patients without the personal intervention or evaluation of a health-care provider. An example is the administration of a vaccine in clinics where mass inoculations are performed. In many such programs, health-care providers are not in a position to evaluate the risks attendant upon use of the drug or device or to relate them to patients. When a manufacturer supplies prescription drugs for distribution to patients in this type of unsupervised environment, if a direct warning to patients is feasible and can be effective, the law requires measures to that effect.

Although the learned intermediary rule is generally accepted and a drug manufacturer fulfills its legal obligation to warn by providing adequate warnings to the health-care provider, arguments have been advanced that in two other areas courts should consider imposing tort liability on drug manufacturers that fail to provide direct warnings to consumers. In the first, governmental regulatory agencies have mandated that patients be informed of risks attendant to the use of a drug.

A noted example is the FDA requirement that birth control pills be sold to patients accompanied by a patient package insert. In the second, manufacturers have advertised a prescription drug and its indicated use in the mass media. Governmental regulations require that, when drugs are so advertised, they must be accompanied by appropriate information concerning risk so as to provide balanced advertising. The question in both instances is whether adequate warnings to the appropriate health-care provider should insulate the manufacturer from tort liability.

Those who assert the need for adequate warnings directly to consumers contend that manufacturers that communicate directly with consumers should not escape liability simply because the decision to prescribe the drug was made by the health-care provider. Proponents of the learned intermediary doctrine argue that, notwithstanding direct communications to the consumer, drugs cannot be dispensed unless a health-care provider makes an individualized decision that a drug is appropriate for a particular patient, and that it is for the health-care provider to decide which risks are relevant to the particular patient. The Institute leaves to developing case law whether exceptions to the learned intermediary rule in these or other situations should be recognized.

Even so, the accompanying reporters' note asserts that several courts and commentators seem favorably predisposed to recognizing such exceptions. See id. at 155. Note that, in earlier drafts, the reporters had proposed including these exceptions in the black letter formulation as well as in the comments. For details on this drafting history, and a highly critical response to the reporters' description of the available case law, see Lars Noah, Advertising Prescription Drugs to Consumers: Assessing the Regulatory and Liability Issues, 32 Ga. L. Rev. 141, 161–80 (1997).

Edwards v. Basel Pharmaceuticals

933 P.2d 298 (Okla.1997).

■ SUMMERS, VICE CHIEF JUSTICE:

* * * Alpha Edwards brought a wrongful death action for the death of her husband. He died of a nicotine-induced heart attack as a result of smoking cigarettes while wearing two Habitrol nicotine patches. Habitrol is manufactured by Basel Pharmaceuticals. Plaintiff's theory of liability was that the warnings given in conjunction with the Habitrol patches were inadequate to warn her husband of the fatal risk associated with smoking and overuse of the product. A relatively thorough warning was given to physicians providing the Habitrol patch, but the insert provided for the user did not mention the possibility of a fatal or cardiac related reaction to a nicotine overdose, cautioning that an "overdose might cause you to faint." * * *

When direct warnings to the user of a prescription drug have been mandated by a safety regulation promulgated for the protection of the user, an exception to the learned intermediary doctrine exists, and failure on the part of the manufacturer to warn the consumer can render the drug unreasonably dangerous. According to the material certified by the federal court, the FDA has found a need to require that prescriptions for nicotine patches be accompanied by warnings to the ultimate consumer as well as to the physician, as is required in the distribution of oral contraceptives and intrauterine devices. * * *

The question then becomes whether the manufacturer has fulfilled its legal obligation once the warnings are approved by the FDA and transmitted to the user. Basel contends that because it complied with FDA requirements it had no further duty to warn Mr. Edwards. Jurisdictions split on their answer to this question. * * * It may be that in certain instances compliance with FDA warning procedures will satisfy all state law requirements. But although compliance with FDA standards may prove an effective starting ground, it is not necessarily conclusive. The adequacy of warnings is determined by state law. Our result could improve the safety of prescription drugs by requiring that both standards are met. * * *

In the present case it appears the manufacturer clearly had knowledge of the dangers associated with the Habitrol patch; it furnished detailed warnings to the prescribing physicians. However, as to the warnings the late Mr. Edwards received in his Habitrol insert, state products liability law must be applied to determine their adequacy. * * *

Perez v. Wyeth Laboratories Inc.

734 A.2d 1245 (N.J.1999).

■ O'HERN, JUSTICE:

Our medical-legal jurisprudence is based on images of health care that no longer exist. At an earlier time, medical advice was received in the doctor's office from a physician who most likely made house calls if needed. The patient usually paid a small sum of money to the doctor. Neighborhood pharmacists compounded prescribed medicines. Without being pejorative, it is safe to say that the prevailing attitude of law and medicine was that the "doctor knows best." Pharmaceutical manufacturers never advertised their products to patients, but rather directed all sales efforts at physicians. In this comforting setting, the law created an exception to the traditional duty of manufacturers to warn consumers directly of risks associated with the product as long as they warned health-care providers of those risks.

For good or ill, that has all changed. Medical services are in large measure provided by managed care organizations. Medicines are purchased in the pharmacy department of supermarkets and often paid for by third-party providers. Drug manufacturers now directly advertise products to consumers on the radio, television, the Internet, billboards on public transportation, and in magazines. * * * The question in this case, broadly stated, is whether our law should follow these changes in the marketplace or reflect the images of the past. We believe that when mass marketing of prescription drugs seeks to influence a patient's choice of a drug, a pharmaceutical manufacturer that makes direct claims to consumers for the efficacy of its product should not be unqualifiedly relieved of a duty to provide proper warnings of the dangers or side effects of the product. * * *

This appeal concerns Norplant, a Food and Drug Administration (FDA)-approved, reversible contraceptive that prevents pregnancy for up to five years. The Norplant contraceptive employs six thin, flexible, closed capsules that contain a synthetic hormone, levonorgestrel. The capsules are implanted under the skin of a woman's upper arm during an in-office surgical procedure characterized by the manufacturer as minor. A low, continuous dosage of the hormone diffuses through the capsule walls and into the bloodstream. Although the capsules are not usually visible under the skin, the outline of the fan-like pattern can be felt under the skin. Removal occurs during an in-office procedure, similar to the insertion process.

We have no doubt of the profound public interest in developing new products for reproductive services. We intend no disparagement of the product when we recite plaintiffs' claims concerning the efficacy of Norplant. The procedural posture that brings this case before us requires that we accept as true plaintiffs' version of the facts. The motion to dismiss was in the nature of a motion for judgment on the pleadings.

According to plaintiffs, Wyeth began a massive advertising campaign for Norplant in 1991, which it directed at women rather than at their doctors. Wyeth advertised on television and in women's magazines such as *Glamour*, *Mademoiselle* and *Cosmopolitan*. According to plaintiffs, none of the advertisements warned of any inherent danger posed by Norplant; rather, all praised its simplicity and convenience. None warned of side effects including pain and permanent scarring attendant to removal of the implants. * * *

In 1995, plaintiffs began to file lawsuits in several New Jersey counties claiming injuries that resulted from their use of Norplant. Plaintiffs' principal claim alleged that Wyeth, distributors of Norplant in the United States, failed to warn adequately about side effects associated with the contraceptive. Side effects complained of by plaintiffs included weight gain, headaches, dizziness, nausea, diarrhea, acne, vomiting, fatigue, facial hair growth, numbness in the arms and legs, irregular menstruation, hair loss, leg cramps, anxiety and nervousness, vision problems, anemia, mood swings and depression, high blood pressure, and removal complications that resulted in scarring. * * *

The trial court dismissed plaintiffs' complaints, concluding that even when a manufacturer advertises directly to the public, and a woman is influenced by the advertising campaign, "a physician is not simply relegated to the role of prescribing the drug according to the woman's wishes." Consequently, the court held that the learned intermediary doctrine applied. According to the court, the physician retains the duty to weigh the benefits and risks associated with a drug before deciding whether the drug is appropriate for the patient. * * * The Appellate Division affirmed the trial court's grant of summary judgment in favor of defendants and its determination that the learned intermediary doctrine applied. * * *

[T]he New Jersey Products Liability Act provides:

An adequate product warning or instruction is one that a reasonably prudent person in the same or similar circumstances would have provided with respect to the danger and that communicates adequate information on the dangers and safe use of the product, taking into account the characteristics of, and the ordinary knowledge common to, the persons by whom the product is intended to be used, or in the case of prescription drugs, taking into account the characteristics of, and the ordinary knowledge common to, the prescribing physician. If the warning or instruction given in connection with a drug or device or food or food additive has been approved or prescribed by the federal Food and Drug Administration under the "Federal Food, Drug, and Cosmetic Act," 52 Stat. 1040, 21 U.S.C. § 301 et seq., ... a rebuttable presumption shall arise that the warning or instruction is adequate....

N.J.S.A. 2A:58C–4.

The Senate Judiciary Committee Statement that accompanied L.1987, c.197 recites: "The subsection contains a general definition of an adequate warning and a special definition for warnings that accompany prescription drugs, since, *in the case of prescription drugs, the warning is owed to the physician.*" See N.J.S.A. 2A:58C–1 (providing the Committee Statement) (emphasis added). At oral argument, counsel for Wyeth was candid to acknowledge that he could not "point to a sentence in the statute" that would make the learned intermediary doctrine applicable to the manufacturers' direct marketing of drugs, but rather relied on the Committee Statement. Although the statute provides a physician-based standard for determining the adequacy of the warning due to a physician, the statute does not legislate the boundaries of the doctrine. * * * [I]n 1987, direct-to-consumer marketing of prescription drugs was in its beginning stages. * * *

Our dissenting member suggests that we should await legislative action before deciding that issue. * * * If we decline to resolve the question, we are making the substantive determination that the learned intermediary doctrine applies to the direct marketing of drugs, an issue recently debated but left unanswered by the drafters of the *Restatement.* Either course, then, requires us to adopt a principle of law. The question is which is the better principle. * * *

Judge John Minor Wisdom explained the rationale behind the learned intermediary doctrine. His perspective reflects the then-prevalent attitude about doctor-patient relationships:

This special standard for prescription drugs is an understandable exception to the *Restatement*'s general rule that one who markets goods must warn foreseeable ultimate users of dangers inherent in [the] products.... Prescription drugs are likely to be complex medicines, esoteric in formula and varied in effect. As a medical expert, the prescribing physician can take into account the propensities of the drug, as well as the susceptibilities of [the] patient. [The physician's] task [is to weigh] the benefits of any medication against its potential dangers. The choice [the physician] makes is an informed one, an individualized medical judgment bottomed on a knowledge of both patient and palliative. Pharmaceutical companies then, who must warn ultimate purchasers of dangers inherent in patent drugs sold over the counter, in selling prescription drugs are required to warn only the prescribing physician, who acts as a "learned intermediary" between manufacturer and consumer.

Reyes v. Wyeth Labs., Inc., 498 F.2d 1264, 1276 (5th Cir.1974) (footnote and citation omitted).

A more recent review summarized the theoretical bases for the doctrine as based on four considerations.

First, courts do not wish to intrude upon the doctor-patient relationship. From this perspective, warnings that contradict information supplied by the physician will undermine the patient's trust in the physician's judgment. Second, physicians may be in a superior position to convey meaningful information to their patients, as they must do to satisfy their duty to secure informed consent. Third, drug manufacturers lack effective means to communicate directly with patients, making it necessary to rely on physicians to convey the relevant information. Unlike [over-the-counter products], pharmacists usually dispense prescription drugs from bulk containers rather than as unit-of-use packages in which the manufacturer may have enclosed labeling. Finally, because of the complexity of risk information about prescription drugs, comprehension problems would complicate any effort by manufacturers to translate physician labeling for lay patients. For this reason, even critics of the rule do not suggest that pharmaceutical companies should provide warnings only to patients and have no tort duty to warn physicians.

Lars Noah, Advertising Prescription Drugs to Consumers: Assessing the Regulatory and Liability Issues, 32 Ga. L. Rev. 141, 157–59 (1997) (footnotes omitted).

These premises: (1) reluctance to undermine the doctor-patient relationship; (2) absence in the era of "doctor knows best" of need for the patient's informed consent; (3) inability of drug manufacturer to communicate with patients; and (4) complexity of the subject; are all (with the possible exception of the last) absent in the direct-to-consumer advertising of prescription drugs.

First, with rare and wonderful exceptions, the " 'Norman Rockwell' image of the family doctor no longer exists." Id. at 180 n.78. Informed consent requires a patient-based decision rather than the paternalistic approach of the 1970s. The decision to take a drug is "not exclusively a matter for medical judgment." Second, because managed care has reduced the time allotted per patient, physicians have considerably less time to inform patients of the risks and benefits of a drug. "In a 1997 survey of 1,000 patients, the FDA found that only one-third had received information from their doctors about the dangerous side effects of drugs they were taking." Third, having spent $1.3 billion on advertising in 1998, drug manufacturers can hardly be said to "lack effective means to communicate directly with patients" when their advertising campaigns can pay off in close to billions in dividends. Consumer-directed advertising of pharmaceuticals thus belies each of the premises on which the learned intermediary doctrine rests. * * *

Concerns regarding patients' communication with and access to physicians are magnified in the context of medicines and medical devices furnished to women for reproductive decisions. In *MacDonald v. Ortho Pharmaceutical Corp.*, 475 N.E.2d 65 (Mass.1985), the plaintiff's use of oral contraceptives allegedly resulted in a stroke. The Massachusetts Supreme [Judicial] Court explained several reasons why contraceptives differ from other prescription drugs and thus "warrant the imposition of a common law duty on the manufacturer to warn users directly of associated risks." For example, after the patient receives the prescription, she consults with the physician to receive a prescription annually, leaving her an infrequent opportunity to "explore her questions and concerns about the medication with the prescribing physician." Consequently, the limited participation of the physician leads to a real possibility that their communication during the annual checkup is insufficient. The court also explained that because oral contraceptives are drugs personally selected by the patient, a prescription is often not the result of a physician's skilled balancing of individual benefits and risks but originates, instead, as a product of patient choice. Thus, "the physician is relegated to a ... passive role." Patient choice is an increasingly important part of our medical-legal jurisprudence. New Jersey has long since abandoned the "professional standard" in favor of the objectively-prudent-patient rule, recognizing the informed role of the patient in health-care decisions. * * *

When a patient is the target of direct marketing, one would think, at a minimum, that the law would require that the patient not be misinformed about the product. It is one thing not to inform a patient about the potential side effects of a product; it is another thing to misinform the patient by deliberately withholding potential side effects while marketing the product as an efficacious solution to a serious health problem. Further, when one considers that many of these "life-style" drugs or elective treatments cause significant side effects without any curative effect, increased consumer protection becomes imperative, because these drugs are, by definition, not medically necessary. * * *

FDA regulations are pertinent in determining the nature and extent of any duty of care that should be imposed on pharmaceutical manufacturers with respect to direct-to-consumer advertising. Presently, any duty to warn physicians about prescription drug dangers is presumptively met by compliance with federal labeling. * * * We believe that in the area of direct-to-consumer advertising of pharmaceuticals, the same rebuttable presumption should apply when a manufacturer complies with FDA advertising, labeling and warning requirements. That approach harmonizes the manufacturer's duty to doctors and to the public when it chooses to directly advertise its products, and simultaneously recognizes the public interest in informing patients about new pharmaceutical developments. * * * For all practical purposes, absent deliberate concealment or nondisclosure of after-acquired knowledge of harmful effects, compliance with FDA standards should be virtually dispositive of such claims. By definition, the advertising will have been "fairly balanced." * * *

The more difficult question is whether the role of the physician breaks the chain of causation. Although the physician writes the prescription, the physician's role in deciding which prescription drug is selected has been altered. * * * We have described proximate cause as an expression as much of policy as it is an expression of the effect of sequential events. A proximate cause need not be the sole cause of harm. It suffices if it is a substantial contributing factor to the harm suffered. * * * As a matter of policy then, we could hold that even if deceptive advertising were a substantial contributing factor influencing a patient's choice of a medicine, the intervening role of the physician should insulate the manufacturer who has engaged in deceptive trade practices. * * *

Obviously, the physician is almost always the essential link between the patient and the pharmaceutical. Most ads for drugs caution the patient to consult with a physician. * * * However, we must consider as well a case in which a diabetic patient might have been influenced by advertising to request a drug from a physician without being warned by the manufacturer or the physician of the special dangers posed to a diabetic taking the drug. If an overburdened physician does not inquire whether the patient is a diabetic, the question remains whether the manufacturer should be relieved entirely of responsibility. In the case of direct marketing of drugs, we believe that neither the physician nor the manufacturer should be entirely relieved of their respective duties to warn. Pharmaceutical manufacturers may seek contribution, indemnity or exoneration because of the physician's deficient role in prescribing that drug. * * *

[T]he dramatic shift in pharmaceutical marketing to consumers is based in large part on significant changes in the health-care system from fee-for-service to managed care. Managed care companies negotiate directly with pharmaceutical companies and then inform prescribers which medications are covered by the respective plans. Because managed care has made it more difficult for pharmaceutical companies to communicate with prescribers, the manufacturers have developed a different strategy, marketing to consumers. * * * The direct marketing of drugs to consumers generates a corresponding duty requiring manufacturers to warn of defects in the product. The FDA has established a comprehensive regulatory scheme for direct-to-consumer marketing of pharmaceutical products. Given the presumptive defense that is afforded to pharmaceutical manufacturers that comply with FDA requirements, we believe that it is fair to reinforce the regulatory scheme by allowing, in the case of direct-to-consumer marketing of drugs, patients deprived of reliable medical information to establish that the misinformation was a substantial factor contributing to their use of a defective pharmaceutical product.

Before concluding, we acknowledge that the procedural posture of this case casts defendant's product in an unfair light. Because the case arises on a motion for summary judgment, we are obliged to view the issues in the light most favorable to the claimants. We have no doubt that substantial proofs will be marshaled to show that Norplant is a safe and efficacious product and that Wyeth's advertising, if any, was fairly balanced. An agreed statement of facts submitted to the trial court suggested as much. And Norplant probably does not afford the best context in which to address the general question whether direct-to-consumer marketers of pharmaceutical products are unqualifiedly relieved of a duty to warn consumers of the dangerous propensities of a product. After all, in the case of Norplant, the role of the physician can never be insubstantial because only a physician may implant the device. Just as it is difficult to legislate a rule for every foreseeable circumstance, so too it is difficult to create a special rule of law for a hybrid [drug-device] product such as Norplant.

We are called upon, however, to resolve a question of law that will apply equally as well to an unprincipled marketer of pharmaceutical products as to a principled marketer. To place the issue in context, consider if prescription diet drugs were heavily advertised without warning of a known potential for heart damage. * * * That is the normative situation for which we must decide if a pharmaceutical manufacturer is free to engage in deceptive advertising to consumers. We believe that the answer in such a case should be no. Any question of fairness in imposing on the direct marketer of a product such as Norplant a duty to warn the targeted consumers will be resolved in the proximate cause analysis. * * *

■ Pollock, Justice (dissenting):

With disarming understatement, the majority opinion raises profound questions about the purpose of judicial opinions, the role of courts, and the separation of powers. In raising those questions, the majority rejects the Legislature's endorsement of the learned intermediary doctrine as set forth in N.J.S.A. 2A:58C–4. The majority opinion sustains itself only by ignoring the plain language of an unambiguous statute, the New Jersey Products Liability Act (NJPLA), and by substituting its own policy preference for that of the Legislature. Contrary to the majority opinion, the point of this dissent is not that the court should await legislative action. Rather, the point is that the Legislature has already acted. * * *

New Jersey courts consistently have recognized the vitality of the learned intermediary doctrine. In 1987, the Legislature codified the learned intermediary doctrine in the NJPLA. Thus, although the learned intermediary doctrine remains a common-law rule in most states, it is now a statutory rule in New Jersey. * * * Analysis of the status of the learned intermediary doctrine thus depends on the intent of the Legislature. * * *

The majority has mischaracterized both the statute and the rationale for the learned intermediary doctrine. Contrary to the majority opinion, the statute directs that the warning is owed to the physician not "because drugs were then marketed to the physician," but because the physician is in the best position to make an individualized evaluation of the risks of drugs and warn the patient of those risks. The patient, moreover, cannot obtain the drugs without a prescription written by a physician. Underlying the majority opinion is the assumption that the Legislature in 1987 could not have anticipated the mass-marketing of prescription drugs. That assumption, however, has no basis in the record. * * *

Given the statutory basis for the learned intermediary doctrine in New Jersey, recourse to the *Restatement (Third) of Torts: Products Liability* § 6 (1998) is gratuitous. Furthermore, the *Restatement* generally endorses the traditional rule that a drug manufacturer's duty to warn is owed to the health-care provider, not the consumer. The *Restatement* suggests, however, that it may be appropriate to impose a duty to warn the patient directly "when the manufacturer knows or has reason to know that health-care providers will not be in a position to reduce the risks of harm in accordance with the instructions or warnings." Here, the *Restatement* does not apply for two reasons. First, as prestigious as any *Restatement* may be, it cannot supersede a governing statute. Second, the surgical implantation of Norplant requires the significant involvement of a health-care provider who must make an individualized evaluation of the risk to the patient. Such involvement stands in contrast to the "diminished role as an evaluator or decision maker" that is a predicate for liability under the *Restatement*. That involvement also distinguishes the implantation of Norplant from the administration of mass inoculations, which proceed without an individualized evaluation of the risks to the patient. * * *

Norplant is a poor vehicle to import so momentous a change. Unlike other drugs that concern the majority, the record reveals that Norplant cannot be purchased in a supermarket, is not promoted by health maintenance organizations, approved by compliant physicians to placate overbearing patients, or implanted over the Internet. Through the incorporation of presumed facts, the majority has created a phantom record to support the creation of its exception to the learned intermediary doctrine. That exercise has led the majority to wander from the confines of the present case.

Norplant is not an over-the-counter drug; it can be obtained only with a doctor's prescription. To insert Norplant, a physician or other health-care professional anesthetizes an area in a patient's upper arm, makes a one-eighth-inch incision, and implants six capsules just below the patient's skin. Similar surgery is required to remove the capsules. The use of Norplant thus requires the significant involvement of the prescribing physician. Even Norman Rockwell would recognize the procedure as one performed in accordance with the traditional physician-patient relationship. Presumably, Wyeth's mass-marketing campaign has increased the demand for Norplant and led many women to request it by name. In some contexts, the extent to which pharmaceutical companies seek to influence consumers, like the extent to which they seek to influence physicians, may be disturbing. Here, however, the mass-marketing campaign apparently was ineffectual; none of the bellwether plaintiffs saw any advertising about Norplant. The invasiveness of the Norplant procedure, moreover, would give any patient pause and a physician cause to evaluate the risks. * * *

The majority identifies four premises underlying the learned intermediary doctrine that it asserts are inapplicable when a manufacturer advertises the drug directly to consumers * * * * Contrary to the majority, those four considerations remain relevant to the implantation of Norplant. First, the Norplant System must be implanted surgically. Implicit in the performance of a surgical procedure is respect for the physician-patient relationship. "[T]he physician is in the best position to take into account the propensities of the drug and the susceptibilities of the patient, and to give a highly individualized warning to the ultimate user based on the physician's specialized knowledge." Second, the physician is the only person who can communicate with the patient to obtain the patient's informed consent to the procedure. Third, a pharmaceutical company, such as Wyeth, cannot provide an adequate warning to each individual consumer about the potential side-effects and risks associated with the device. Each patient has individualized risks associated with surgical procedures. Lastly, the Norplant implant, far more than other birth control devices, is a complex contraceptive system that requires detailed instructions and warnings.

To soften the impact of its opinion, the majority creates a rebuttable presumption that a warning is adequate if it complies with FDA regulations. Regrettably, the court has not granted the parties the opportunity to address the creation, nature, or sufficiency of such a presumption. To the extent that such a presumption is essential to the majority's rationale, the parties should have been given that opportunity. * * *

NOTES AND QUESTIONS

1. *An exceptional exception?* No other court has (yet) adopted the exception to the learned intermediary rule announced in *Perez*. See In re Norplant Contraceptive Prods. Liab. Litig., 165 F.3d 374 (5th Cir.1999); Allen v. G.D. Searle & Co., 708 F.Supp. 1142, 1147–48 (D.Or.1989); Vitanza v. Upjohn Co., 778 A.2d 829 (Conn.2001); see also Spychala v. G.D. Searle & Co., 705 F.Supp. 1024, 1032 (D.N.J.1988) (declining to recognize an exception to the learned intermediary rule in an oral contraceptive case even though the plaintiff had argued that the manufacturer's direct advertising to consumers further justified such an exception); cf. Haste v. American Home Prods. Corp., 577 F.2d 1122, 1125 (10th Cir.1978) (holding that direct advertising of a prescription vaccine for livestock did not create an exception to the learned intermediary rule and that the manufacturer had satisfied its duty to warn veterinarians). If plaintiffs in a case like *Perez* had seen and relied on the advertisements, might they assert a misrepresentation claim (see Rest. (3d) § 9), or would the learned intermediary rule present the same duty limitation absent an exception? How about subjects enrolled in clinical trials that sponsors had advertised in print or on television?

2. *The PPI exception.* Contrary to *Edwards*, several courts have rejected the suggestion that the mandatory or voluntary distribution of PPIs would eliminate the learned intermediary rule. See MacPherson v. Searle & Co., 775 F.Supp. 417, 425 (D.D.C.1991); Zanzuri v. G.D. Searle & Co., 748 F.Supp. 1511, 1516 (S.D.Fla.1990); Polley v. Ciba–Geigy Corp., 658 F.Supp. 420, 422 (D.Alaska 1987); Presto v. Sandoz Pharm. Corp., 487 S.E.2d 70, 73–74 (Ga.Ct.App.1997); Martin v. Ortho Pharm. Corp., 661 N.E.2d 352, 356 (Ill.1996); Seley v. G.D. Searle & Co., 423 N.E.2d 831, 840 (Ohio 1981); Taurino v. Ellen, 579 A.2d 925, 930 (Pa.Super.Ct.1990). One court suggested that the learned intermediary rule would not protect a manufacturer against a claim for failure to warn the public of a drug recall. See Nichols v. McNeilab, Inc., 850 F.Supp. 562, 564–65 (E.D.Mich.1993) (distinguishing the notification of a drug withdrawal prompted by safety concerns from the risk information conveyed to patients at the time that a drug is initially prescribed).

3. *Regulatory compliance.* In *Perez*, the court held that compliance with FDA requirements would create a presumption that the risk information communicated to consumers was adequate. An earlier draft of the *Restatement (Third)* had suggested that the scope of judicial review of the content of warnings to consumers under these possible exceptions might be narrower than usual. See Rest. (3d) § 8, cmt. e, at 216 (Tentative Draft No. 2, 1995) ("The Institute leaves to developing case law whether exceptions to the learned intermediary rule in these and other situations are called for and, if so, how broad the scope of judicial review of the content of warnings to consumers should be in the tort context."). Recall, however, from Chapter 5(B)(2) that few states other than New Jersey have codified an FDA compliance defense, and, as suggested in *Edwards*, most courts do not credit compliance with FDA labeling rules. See MacDonald v. Ortho Pharm. Corp., 475 N.E.2d 65, 70–71 (Mass.1985) (explaining that "compliance with FDA requirements, though admissible to demonstrate lack of negligence, is not conclusive").

4. *Keeping doctors in the loop.* In thinking about the desirability of these various exceptions, one should not lose sight of the fact that a medical professional will continue to intervene in the decision to prescribe a drug and make the final judgment about its relative risks and benefits for a particular patient. See Seley v. G.D. Searle & Co., 423 N.E.2d 831, 840 (Ohio 1981) ("The decision to use oral contraception, although involving a higher degree of patient choice than is generally associated with a prescribing decision, remains a joint one made by both doctor and patient."); Gravis v. Parke–Davis & Co., 502 S.W.2d 863, 870 (Tex.Civ.App.1973) (noting that the "entire system of drug distribution in America is set up so as to place the responsibility for distribution and use upon professional people"). As explained in the next chapter, it would constitute professional malpractice to do otherwise.

5. *Further commentary.* See William A. Dreier, Direct-to-Consumer Advertising Liability: An Empty Gift to Plaintiffs, 30 Seton Hall L. Rev. 806 (2000); Jack B. Harrison & Mina J. Jefferson, "Some Accurate Information Is Better Than No Information At All": Arguments Against an Exception to the Learned Intermediary Doctrine Based on Direct-to-Consumer Advertising, 78 Or. L. Rev. 605 (1999); Chester Chuang, Note, Is There a Doctor in the House? Using Failure-to-Warn Liability to Enhance the Safety of Online Prescribing, 75 N.Y.U. L. Rev. 1452 (2000); Bradford B. Lear, Comment, The Learned Intermediary Doctrine in the Age of Direct Consumer Advertising, 65 Mo. L. Rev. 1101 (2000); Catherine A. Paytash, Note, The Learned Intermediary Doctrine and Patient Package Inserts: A Balanced Approach to Preventing Drug–Related Injury, 51 Stan. L. Rev. 1343 (1999).

3.   OTHER SOURCES OF INFORMATION

In re Factor VIII or IX Concentrate Blood Products Litigation

25 F.Supp.2d 837 (N.D.Ill.1998).

■ GRADY, DISTRICT JUDGE:

* * * Plaintiffs in this multidistrict litigation are hemophiliacs and the personal representatives of deceased hemophiliacs who used certain blood products known as "factor concentrates" to treat their hemophilia and, as a result, became infected with the HIV virus. The defendant National Hemophilia Foundation (NHF) is a nonprofit organization that provided information to hemophiliacs about blood products in the 1980s. * * * NHF membership includes chapters (usually on a statewide basis), medical providers and the leading members of the plasma industry. Part of its stated mission is to promote "programs of research; patient, public and professional education; and patient, family and community services." The NHF also develops medical treatment standards or recommendations which are disseminated and relied upon by physicians in their treatment of persons with hemophilia.

The plaintiffs allege that the NHF established itself as the "preeminent authority" and "principal educator" on medical treatment issues impacting persons with hemophilia. The plaintiffs also assert that, early in the AIDS epidemic, the NHF assumed a leadership role in informing, guiding and educating hemophiliacs, their treaters and the media regarding the proper treatment of hemophilia in light of the AIDS risk.

The primary theory of liability is that the NHF was negligent in providing information and advice to its members and for the benefit of the hemophilia community at large. The allegations are that the NHF made false, incorrect and misleading statements regarding the safety of factor concentrates manufactured and distributed by the other defendants in this litigation. Plaintiffs charge that the NHF negligently recommended use of the concentrates when it should have known of the danger of viral contamination, failed to warn its members about that danger, failed to recommend timely recall of the concentrates and failed to disclose certain relationships between NHF board members and the defendant manufacturers. In addition to the negligence allegations, it is claimed that the NHF violated certain fiduciary duties owing to the plaintiffs. Plaintiffs claim that, as a result of the NHF's actions, they and their decedents relied on the NHF, used the concentrates and became infected with the HIV virus. In many cases the infections have resulted in death.

In moving for summary judgment, the NHF argues that its First Amendment rights to free speech and free press would be abridged if courts were to impose liability on it because of its communications. * * * A threshold issue is whether sufficient governmental action exists to implicate the First Amendment. The NHF claims that the imposition of tort liability would be sufficient. This is correct. * * *

The NHF begins by arguing that its publications are noncommercial speech and because of that status can lose protection in only four circumstances—libel, obscenity, incitement and fighting words. * * * It reasons that it is entitled to full First Amendment protection from liability in this litigation unless we find that its speech falls into one of the four unprotected categories. We disagree with the NHF's view of the law. No Supreme Court case has held that the[se] four categories of speech * * * are an exhaustive enumeration of unprotected speech. * * *

The NHF argument is belied by a considerable body of law denying First Amendment protection in situations not involving obscenity, libel, incitement or fighting words. For example: speech that invades privacy, speech that breaches a promise of confidentiality, speech that infringes a copyright, speech that is harassing, speech that infringes a performer's right of publicity, and speech that constitutes fraudulent misrepresentation. Some of these cases are significant for another reason: they illustrate the well-established principle that the protections of the First Amendment do not shield the press from laws of general applicability. * * * It is, of course, true that when the press is confronted with potential liability for the content of its publications, there is a danger of chilling vigorous public discourse. The Supreme Court has recognized this tension in the context of tort liability for defamation. * * *

In regard to plaintiffs' allegations of negligent mistakes in the NHF's publications, the NHF argues that liability cannot be imposed for misstatement alone. * * * The problem with the NHF's argument is that it does not explain why a specific standard articulated in the context of a public figure's ability to recover under libel and invasion of privacy theories applies to this case. The libel and privacy cases did not articulate a broad standard for cases where a defendant is sued for misstatements of fact. Instead, those cases were context-specific, applying only to libel suits brought by public figures. * * *

In this case, the interest of society in providing redress for the grave injuries alleged should be weighed against the danger of chilling the NHF's communications. Here, the chilling effect may be greater because of the large number of claimants. * * * We are not persuaded that this potential chilling effect outweighs the public interest in redressing the kinds of injuries alleged here. For one reason, liability here would not extend to "all the world." The facts of this case involve an organization supplying information to its known membership and, by extension, to the limited community of persons suffering from hemophilia. Moreover, this case involves injuries that are different in nature and gravity from the injuries complained of in [other cases]. * * *

It is essential to recognize the exact nature of the interests being asserted in this litigation. On the one hand, there is the interest of the plaintiffs in redressing serious personal injury and death caused by reliance on erroneous information concerning the safety of medical products. On the other hand, there is the interest of the defendant in being immune from liability for negligent communication of misinformation that has resulted in serious injury or death. The litigation presents no question as to whether there should be liability for erroneous communications which are not negligent or which do not cause serious injury.

Medical and scientific opinions can differ, of course, and there is often a wide range of opinions on a particular medical question. It is traditional in negligence law to distinguish between negligence and errors in judgment, with no liability arising from the latter. But it is also traditional for liability to be imposed upon medical practitioners who fail to use ordinary care in arriving at recommendations that proximately cause injury to patients. The recommendation is a form of expression, since it can be conveyed only orally or in writing, but the First Amendment has never been thought to bar an action for medical malpractice based on such written or spoken expression in a medical context. We see no material difference between such an action and the claims presented here.

The situation would be entirely different if plaintiffs were seeking to impose strict liability upon the NHF for its communications. In that event, the First Amendment would surely be implicated and we would be persuaded by the NHF's argument that there must be open and candid public debate on all medical issues and that the courts should not inhibit nonprofit organizations from contributing to that debate. But the argument is not apposite to negligence liability. In seeking to avoid liability altogether, even for negligent conduct, the NHF simply fails to recognize the interests protected by negligence law (in general or in this particular case) or the need to balance those interests against the values of free speech.

We conclude that negligence law, a law of general applicability, provides a constitutionally acceptable accommodation between the competing interests asserted here, and that the First Amendment does not protect the NHF from liability for the negligent acts and omissions alleged by the plaintiffs in this consolidated litigation.[11] * * *

[I]n response to the plaintiffs' argument that the NHF had a duty to speak concerning several matters,[13] the NHF cites two Supreme Court cases and argues that the First Amendment provides a right not to speak. We reject this argument for several reasons. First, the two cited cases are from areas of law not analogous to this one. Second, there is no case authority for the proposition that the First Amendment provides immunity for defendants in failure to warn cases. Third, adopting the NHF's view of the First Amendment would ignore decades of tort law, dating back to at least 1892, holding that manufacturers can be liable for failing to warn consumers about dangers of their products. We see no principled basis on which the duty to warn could be imposed on manufacturers while organizations such as the NHF would be exempted on First Amendment grounds. * * *

NOTES AND QUESTIONS

1. *First amendment redux.* Does a court's imposition of a duty to warn raise any of the free speech concerns discussed in Chapter 4(C)? Courts generally refuse to impose strict liability against publishers of informational books, including texts that provide therapeutic advice. See Jones v. J.B. Lippincott Co., 694 F.Supp. 1216 (D.Md.1988) (rejecting tort claims brought by a student who suffered an injury from trying a remedy for constipation listed in a nursing textbook); cf. Young v. Mallet, 371 N.Y.S.2d 1, 2 (App.Div.1975) (dismissing, on personal jurisdiction grounds, a tort suit filed against the author and publisher of a child care book that recommended giving children dangerously high doses of vitamin A). The courts view the content of such books as an intangible not covered by products liability doctrines, and they also express concerns about chilling the dissemination of information. See Winter v. G.P. Putnam's Sons, 938 F.2d 1033, 1034–35 (9th Cir.1991); Libertelli v. Hoffman–La Roche, 565 F.Supp. 234 (S.D.N.Y.1983) (dismissing tort claim against the publisher of the PDR for failing to warn of Valium's addictive potential); Rest. (3d) § 19 cmt. d. These objections seem misplaced, especially when one compares the courts' willingness to entertain failure-to-warn claims against pharmaceutical companies. See Lars Noah, Authors, Publishers, and Products Liability: Remedies for Defective Information in Books, 77 Or. L. Rev. 1195, 1212 (1998) ("The conceptual separation between the product itself and information contained within the product, so evident in cases declining to hold

---

11. * * * [T]he determination of whether First Amendment protection exists is different from the determination of whether a duty exists in tort law. The issue before the court is not whether a duty existed in this situation, it is whether and to what extent the NHF is protected by the First Amendment. * * *

13. Plaintiffs argue that the NHF had: (1) a duty to disclose the financial and other relationships of its board with the blood products manufacturers; (2) a duty to disclose all potential risks involved in using the factor concentrates; (3) a duty to warn hemophiliacs about the risk of the sexual transmission of AIDS; and (4) a duty to disclose statements by a certain Dr. Bruce Evatt.

authors and publishers strictly liable, is absent in the prescription drug liability context."). But cf. Smith v. Linn, 563 A.2d 123, 126 (Pa.Super.Ct.1989) (rejecting, in the course of immunizing the author of a diet book from a wrongful death claim brought on behalf of a reader who followed the recommendations, the suggested parallel to failure-to-warn claims against drug manufacturers), aff'd, 587 A.2d 309 (Pa.1991).

2. *Liability for negligence in generating therapeutic information.* The court did not decide whether the NHF owed any tort duties to the plaintiffs. A few courts have allowed tort claims to proceed against the American Association of Blood Banks for failing to recommend to its members certain screening procedures designed to prevent the use of HIV-infected blood. See Snyder v. American Ass'n of Blood Banks, 676 A.2d 1036 (N.J.1996); Weigand v. University Hosp. of NYU Med. Ctr., 659 N.Y.S.2d 395 (Super.Ct.1997). But see N.N.V. v. American Ass'n of Blood Banks, 89 Cal.Rptr.2d 885 (Ct.App.1999) (rejecting such a claim). Some commentators have argued that injured patients may assert similar claims against medical societies responsible for the drafting of practice guidelines. See Matthew R. Giannetti, Note, Circumcision and the American Academy of Pediatrics: Should Scientific Misconduct Result in Trade Association Liability?, 85 Iowa L. Rev. 1507, 1546–66 (2000); Megan L. Sheetz, Note, Toward Controlled Clinical Care Through Clinical Practice Guidelines: The Legal Liability for Developers and Issuers of Clinical Pathways, 63 Brook. L. Rev. 1341 (1997). But cf. Cali v. Danek Med., Inc., 24 F.Supp.2d 941, 949–50 (W.D.Wis.1998) (rejecting fraud claims against medical societies for sponsoring seminars at which allegedly unsafe uses of pedicle screws in spinal fusion were discussed). A similar question arises about the potential tort liability of suppliers of "medical expert systems" that incorporate practice guidelines into computerized decisionmaking products intended for use by physicians. See Brian H. Lamkin, Comment, Medical Expert Systems and Publisher Liability: A Cross–Contextual Analysis, 43 Emory L.J. 731 (1994).

C. MEASURING THE ADEQUACY OF WARNINGS

If a duty to warn does exist in a particular case, the complete failure to provide any warning of the risk would represent an actionable breach. The question becomes more difficult when a manufacturer has conveyed a warning of the risk in question to the appropriate persons but the plaintiff alleges that the warning was inadequate.

1. WARNING HEALTH PROFESSIONALS

Felix v. Hoffmann–LaRoche, Inc.

540 So.2d 102 (Fla.1989).

■ GRIMES, JUSTICE:

* * * This was a suit for the wrongful death of a child attributed to the ingestion of Accutane by his mother during pregnancy. Accutane is a drug

prescribed for serious and disfiguring cases of acne which was approved for marketing in the United States by the Food and Drug Administration in 1982. The mother took the drug late in 1982 while she was pregnant upon the prescription of her physician. The child was born with severe birth defects which led to his early demise.

A critical issue in the case was whether the manufacturer of the drug furnished adequate warnings of the dangers of using the drug during pregnancy. The relevant text of the package insert at that time stated:

CONTRAINDICATIONS: Teratogenicity was observed in rats at a dose of isotretinoin of 150 mg/kg/day. In rabbits a dose of 10 mg/kg/day was teratogenic and embryotoxic, and induced abortion. There are no adequate and well-controlled studies in pregnant women. Because teratogenicity has been observed in animals given isotretinoin, patients who are pregnant or intend to become pregnant while undergoing treatment should not receive Accutane. Women of childbearing potential should not be given Accutane unless an effective form of contraception is used, and they should be fully counseled on the potential risks to the fetus should they become pregnant while undergoing treatment. Should pregnancy occur during treatment, the physician and patient should discuss the desirability of continuing the pregnancy. . . .

WARNINGS: Although no abnormalities of the human fetus have been reported thus far, animal studies with retinoids suggest that teratogenic effects may occur. It is recommended that contraception be continued for one month or until a normal menstrual period has occurred following discontinuation of Accutane therapy. . . .

PRECAUTIONS: *INFORMATION FOR PATIENTS*: . . . . Women of childbearing potential should be instructed to use an effective form of contraception when Accutane therapy is required. (See CONTRAINDICATIONS AND WARNINGS). . . .

PREGNANCY: Category X. See "CONTRAINDICATIONS" section.

Dr. Greenwald prescribed Accutane to the mother for a cystic acne condition of her face and shoulders which had persisted for many years. He characterized Accutane as a miracle drug for people with acne. Dr. Greenwald testified that he understood the warnings which accompanied the drug and said that "category X" meant that the drug should not be used during pregnancy. He also stated that he had prior knowledge of the teratogenic propensities of Accutane from independent research and reading and from seminars he had attended. He defined "teratogenicity" as "the ability of something to turn out a teratogen" and the term "teratogen" as "a mutant, deformed something—a deformed part, a deformed being, a deformed person, a monster, if you will, something very abnormal." Dr. Greenwald testified that he warned the mother against the use of Accutane if she were to become pregnant. The mother denied having received such a warning. * * *

At the outset, it is clear that the manufacturer's duty to warn of Accutane's dangerous side effects was directed to the physician rather than the patient. This is so because the prescribing physician, acting as a "learned intermediary" between the manufacturer and the consumer, weighs the potential benefits against the dangers in deciding whether to recommend the drug to meet the patient's needs. Furthermore, there is no contention that the warning given in this case contained any misstatements. While there have been subsequent incidents of children born with birth defects after their mothers ingested Accutane, there had been no Accutane related teratogenicity in human infants prior to the ingestion of the drug in this case. * * *

[P]etitioner argues that the adequacy of a drug warning can never be decided as a matter of law. Respondents suggest that a pharmaceutical manufacturer would be much less likely to make the capital investment in research, development, obtaining FDA approval, and marketing of a potentially beneficial drug which is accompanied by serious side effects if faced with the knowledge that, no matter how accurate and well-phrased the warning, a jury could decide its adequacy every time the side effect occurred.

While in many instances the adequacy of warnings concerning drugs is a question of fact, we hold that it can become a question of law where the warning is accurate, clear, and unambiguous. The courts of many other jurisdictions have reached the same conclusion. In the instant case, the district court of appeal acknowledged that whether a warning is adequate is usually a jury question. However, in this case the court held that "[i]t is inconceivable that reasonable persons could disagree as to the adequacy of the warnings in conveying to physicians that the prescription drug, Accutane, is dangerous to pregnant women and should not have been prescribed." We agree. While the word "teratogenicity" is not one with which all consumers might be familiar, we are convinced that, as to physicians, the warning concerning the dangerous side effects of Accutane was quite clear.

The district court of appeal also held that even if it could be said that there was a factual dispute concerning the adequacy of the warning, any breach of the duty to warn in this case could not have been the proximate cause of the damage. The court reached this conclusion because the prescribing physician testified that he fully understood the warnings and also had prior knowledge of the teratogenic propensity of Accutane. Therefore, we agree that any inadequacy in the Accutane warning could not have been the proximate cause of the birth defects in this case. Insofar as the liability of the manufacturer is concerned, it makes no difference that the mother testified that Dr. Greenwald did not warn her of the danger of taking Accutane while she was pregnant. While this would present a factual issue in a claim against the doctor, the drug manufacturer could not be penalized for the failure of the doctor to impart knowledge concerning the dangers of the drug of which the doctor had been warned and was aware. * * *

NOTES AND QUESTIONS

1. *Measuring adequacy.* Courts generally require that a warning be communicated with the degree of urgency necessary to cause the user to exercise the level of caution commensurate with the potential danger. See Lindsay v. Ortho Pharm. Corp., 637 F.2d 87, 91 (2d Cir.1980); Werner v. Upjohn Co., 628 F.2d 848, 858 (4th Cir.1980); Williams v. Upjohn Co., 153 F.R.D. 110, 114–15 (S.D.Tex.1994); Seley v. G.D. Searle & Co., 423 N.E.2d 831, 837 (Ohio 1981) ("A reasonable warning not only conveys a fair indication of the nature of the dangers involved, but also warns with the degree of intensity demanded by the nature of the risk."); Richards v. Upjohn Co., 625 P.2d 1192, 1196 (N.M.Ct.App.1980) ("[T]he drug manufacturer must bring the warning home to the doctor."); Janet Fairchild, Annotation, Liability of Manufacturer or Seller for Injury or Death Allegedly Caused by Failure to Warn Regarding Danger in Use of Vaccine or Prescription Drug, 94 A.L.R.3d 748 (1979 & 2002 Supp.). For instance, plaintiffs in drug cases will sometimes complain that a side effect listed in the Adverse Reactions section should instead have appeared in the Warnings or even Contraindications section of the package insert. A warning also may be judged inadequate if its tone, placement, or typeface makes it unlikely to attract the physician's attention. See Sanderson v. Upjohn Co., 578 F.Supp. 338, 339–40 (D.Mass.1984). When a product's labeling warns of the very injury suffered by the plaintiff in clear and precise terms, the manufacturer may succeed on summary judgment. See, e.g., Guevara v. Dorsey Labs., 845 F.2d 364, 366–68 (1st Cir.1988); Anderson v. McNeilab, 831 F.2d 92, 93 (5th Cir.1987); Hunt v. Hoffmann–LaRoche, Inc., 785 F.Supp. 547, 548–50 (D.Md.1992); Bealer v. Hoffman–LaRoche, Inc., 729 F.Supp. 43, 44–45 (E.D.La.1990); Brick v. Barnes–Hines Pharm. Co., 428 F.Supp. 496, 498 (D.D.C.1977); Mikell v. Hoffman–LaRoche, Inc., 649 So.2d 75, 80 (La.Ct.App.1994); Johnson v. American Cyanamid Co., 718 P.2d 1318, 1325–26 (Kan.Ct.App.1986), aff'd, 758 P.2d 206 (Kan.1988); Serna v. Roche Labs., 684 P.2d 1187, 1189–90 (N.M.1984). In at least one case, however, a court held that a warning might be inadequate even if the risk of the very injury suffered by the plaintiff was clearly disclosed, on the grounds that the plaintiff might have been deterred from taking the drug had the risk of some other more serious injury been fully disclosed. See Sanderson v. Upjohn Co., 578 F.Supp. 338, 339–40 (D.Mass.1984); see also McMahon v. Eli Lilly & Co., 774 F.2d 830, 834–35 (7th Cir.1985). But cf. Canesi v. Wilson, 685 A.2d 49, 54 (N.J.App.Div.1996), aff'd in part, 730 A.2d 805 (N.J.1999).

2. *Proximate cause.* If a physician independently understood the risks that the manufacturer failed to warn about adequately, the failure to warn did not cause the patient's injury. See Wheat v. Pfizer, Inc., 31 F.3d 340, 343 (5th Cir.1994); Kirsch v. Picker Int'l, Inc., 753 F.2d 670, 671 (8th Cir.1985); Wooten v. Johnson & Johnson Prods., Inc., 635 F.Supp. 799, 803 (N.D.Ill. 1986); Glucksman v. Halsey Drug Co., 553 N.Y.S.2d 724, 726 (App.Div. 1990); Stewart v. Janssen Pharm., Inc., 780 S.W.2d 910, 912 (Tex.Ct.App. 1989); see also Skotak v. Tenneco Resins, Inc., 953 F.2d 909 (5th Cir.1992) (affirming summary judgment for a manufacturer where the plaintiff was not able to identify his physician); Garside v. Osco Drug, Inc., 976 F.2d 77, 79–83 (1st Cir.1992) (applying a rebuttable presumption that the plaintiff's physician would have heeded a stronger drug interaction warning); cf. Mauldin v. Upjohn Co., 697 F.2d 644, 646–47 (5th Cir.1983) (holding that a jury could find that a stronger warning would have altered the physician's behavior notwithstanding his contrary testimony); Tongate v. Wyeth Labs., 580 N.E.2d 1220, 1228–31 (Ill.App.Ct.1991) (same). Similarly, if a physician fails to diagnose a condition in a patient that would make a warning relevant in the selection of the drug, then any inadequacy in the warning would not have caused the injury. See Dyson v. Winfield, 113 F.Supp.2d 35, 43 (D.D.C.2000). If a physician consciously decides not to relay a warning provided by a manufacturer, any inadequacy in that warning would not qualify as the cause of the patient's injury. See Krasnopolsky v. Warner–Lambert Co., 799 F.Supp. 1342, 1347 (E.D.N.Y.1992).

3. *Dilution.* The use of qualifying language may dilute the impact of an otherwise satisfactory warning. See, e.g., Tinnerholm v. Parke, Davis & Co., 285 F.Supp. 432, 451 (S.D.N.Y.1968) (finding that a warning had been "water[ed] down" by the "shrewd use of descriptive adjectives"), modified, 411 F.2d 48 (2d Cir.1969); McFadden v. Haritatos, 448 N.Y.S.2d 79, 81 (App.Div.1982) (statement that side effects of drug are usually reversible "tends to qualify and dilute the whole of the [adverse reactions] section's admonition"); Ross v. Jacobs, 684 P.2d 1211, 1215–16 (Okla.Ct.App.1984). A manufacturer's overpromotion of a product also may render an otherwise complete warning inadequate. See Salmon v. Parke, Davis & Co., 520 F.2d 1359, 1363–64 (4th Cir.1975); Brown v. Glaxo, Inc., 790 So.2d 35, 40–41 (La.Ct.App.2000); Holley v. Burroughs Wellcome Co., 348 S.E.2d 772, 777 (N.C.1986); Incollingo v. Ewing, 282 A.2d 206, 220 (Pa.1971); see also Globetti v. Sandoz Pharm. Corp., 2001 WL 419160 (N.D.Ala.2001) (allowing fraudulent misrepresentation and concealment claims to proceed against manufacturer of the lactation suppressant Parlodel). But cf. Foster v. American Home Prods. Corp., 29 F.3d 165 (4th Cir.1994) (rejecting a negligent misrepresentation claim against the manufacturer of a brand-name drug where the plaintiff was injured by a generic version). See generally Janet Fairchild, Annotation, Promotional Efforts Directed Toward Prescribing Physician as Affecting Prescription Drug Manufacturer's Liability for Product–Caused Injury, 94 A.L.R.3d 1080 (1979 & 2002 Supp.).

4. *Method of communication.* Even a specific and prominent warning may be found inadequate if it has not been communicated through the most effective channels. For instance, a number of courts have demanded the use of methods other than labeling to convey information to physicians about prescription drug risks, in part because physicians rarely see the actual product they have prescribed for any particular patient. See Sterling Drug, Inc. v. Yarrow, 408 F.2d 978, 992 (8th Cir.1969) ("[I]t was not unreasonable to find that the appellant should have employed all its usual means of communication . . . to warn the prescribing physicians of these dangers."); Baker v. St. Agnes Hosp., 421 N.Y.S.2d 81, 86 (App.Div.1979) ("There are other, well-known methods by which pharmaceutical manufacturers apprise the medical profession of the dangers of a drug."); Finn v. G.D. Searle & Co., 677 P.2d 1147, 1169 n.20 (Cal.1984) (Bird, C.J., dissenting) ("These include advertising and promotional literature, letters to the medical profession and oral communications by sales representatives."). In particular, several courts have focused on the use of pharmaceutical company sales representatives to convey precautionary information about prescription drugs to physicians. See Yarrow v. Sterling Drug, Inc., 263 F.Supp. 159, 163 (D.S.D.1967), aff'd, 408 F.2d 978, 990–94 (8th Cir.1969) (pharmaceutical company held liable for failure to warn of newly discovered side effects, notwithstanding letters it had sent to physicians, because it had not used its sales representatives to convey the information); Stevens v. Parke, Davis & Co., 507 P.2d 653, 663 (Cal.1973); Mahr v. G.D. Searle & Co., 390 N.E.2d 1214, 1232 (Ill.App.Ct.1979); see also Wallace v. Upjohn Co., 535 So.2d 1110, 1117 (La.Ct.App.1988) (sales persons would not be personally liable for failing to warn physicians). When companies do use their sales representatives to disseminate information about possible new side effects, some courts have criticized them for not sending a "Dear Doctor" letter instead. See Sterling Drug, Inc. v. Cornish, 370 F.2d 82, 84 (8th Cir.1966); Hoffman v. Sterling Drug, Inc., 485 F.2d 132, 146–47 (3d Cir.1973) (noting that "some doctors did not take the time to speak to detail men, some did not always accept the product cards or brochures offered, and some did not always listen to what the detail men said about a drug"). Conversely, when "Dear Doctor" letters are circulated, the manufacturer may be held liable for not using sales representatives to convey the information. See id. at 146 ("Nor was mailing drug literature to physicians necessarily an effective way to reach them. . . . [T]he jury could reasonably have found that a considerable amount of such literature winds up in the wastebasket and is not adequate to advise doctors concerning matters of utmost importance."); Yarrow, 408 F.2d at 994 ("The trier of fact could reasonably conclude that the urgency of the circumstances reasonably required more than the relatively slow action and relative lack of emphasis employed in composing and circulating the 'Dear Doctor' letter."). Thus, product labeling alone may sometimes fail to satisfy the duty to warn. Just as in hindsight the content of warning statements may always seem inadequate, a manufacturer's choice of mechanisms for presenting these warnings may always appear to be less than perfect.

Bernhardt v. Pfizer, Inc.

2000 WL 1738645 (S.D.N.Y.2000).

■ McKenna, District Judge:

Lawrence D. Bernhardt and Arnold Liebman have filed product liability actions against Pfizer, Inc. for claims arising out of their use of Cardura, a prescription drug manufactured by defendant. Presently before this court is defendant's motion for judgment on the pleadings pursuant to Fed. R. Civ. P. 12(c) with respect to plaintiffs' claim for mandatory injunctive relief in the form of an emergency notice sent to Cardura users and their physicians. * * *

Pfizer manufactures and markets the antihypertensive drug doxazosin under the brand name "Cardura" for the treatment of hypertension. In 1994, the National Heart, Lung and Blood Institute (NHLBI), a division of the National Institutes of Health (NIH), began an eight-year study called Antihypertensive and Lipid Lowering Treatment to Prevent Heart Attack Trial ("ALLHAT") which included in its scope the comparison of doxazosin to chlorthalidone in the treatment of hypertension. On March 8, 2000, the NHLBI issued a press release announcing that it was discontinuing this part of the ALLHAT study because doxazosin "was found less effective than [chlorthalidone] in reducing some forms of cardiovascular disease." Plaintiffs claim that the ALLHAT findings demonstrate that "Cardura users are twice as likely to be hospitalized for congestive heart failure and have a significantly higher chance of suffering from certain serious cardiac events, including strokes, as compared with patients" who took chlorthalidone to treat hypertension. Plaintiffs seek an order requiring Pfizer to send a notice to Cardura users and their physicians regarding the ALLHAT findings with respect to Cardura. The proposed notice to physicians would state, among other things, that a study by NHLBI "has demonstrated that Cardura (doxazosin) is less effective in preventing heart failure compared to a widely used diuretic drug, chlorthalidone," and the proposed notice to patients, among other things, the same. * * *

Under the doctrine of primary jurisdiction, a district court may refer a matter within its original jurisdiction to the appropriate administrative agency if doing so will "promot[e] proper relationships between the courts and administrative agencies charged with particular regulatory duties." * * * Plaintiffs are not arguing that the ALLHAT findings trigger a statutory or regulatory notification requirement or that Pfizer's inaction violates the FDCA. Rather, plaintiffs ask this court to determine, on the basis of presumably scientific and medical principles to be developed at an adversary preliminary injunction hearing, that the ALLHAT findings warrant a notice to all Cardura users and their physicians. The FDA, not this court, has the relevant expertise.

Congress has granted the FDA the authority to ensure that drugs are safe and effective. The FDA approves the labeling of a drug as part of the new drug approval process. Such labeling is "broadly defined" and has been found to include the "Dear Doctor" and "Dear Patient" notices requested by plaintiffs. See Walls v. Armour Pharm. Co., 832 F. Supp. 1467, 1482–83 (M.D.Fla.1993). The FDA also has the authority to either alert Cardura users and their physicians if it determines that Cardura creates "an imminent danger to health or gross deception of the consumer," or to request Pfizer to revise the labeling for Cardura. Finally, plaintiffs have the ability to request the FDA to take either action pursuant to a "citizen petition" provision.* The above review of the relevant regulatory scheme

---

* The plaintiffs thereupon pursued this option. See Rita Rubin, Taking on a Drug Giant: 2 Patients File Suit Against Pfizer, USA Today, May 23, 2001, at 1D. An FDA advisory committee recommended, however, against issuing the requested notice. See Mel-

convinces this court that whether the notice requested by plaintiffs is warranted is a decision that has been squarely placed within the FDA's informed expert discretion. * * *

2.   WARNING PATIENTS

Questions about the adequacy of warnings directed to patients arise in two contexts. First, a court might decide that the learned intermediary rule does not apply in a particular case. Second, a failure-to-warn claim may relate to a nonprescription drug or medical device.

Hahn v. Sterling Drug, Inc.

805 F.2d 1480 (11th Cir.1986).

■ PER CURIAM:

* * * On December 19, 1982, four year old Valerie Anne Hahn swallowed one and one-half ounces of Campho–Phenique, an over-the-counter topical analgesic. One half hour later, she was convulsing, vomiting, and for a time she stopped breathing. After treatment at the Rockdale County Hospital, she was transferred to the intensive care unit at the Henrietta Eggleston Children's Hospital. After an approximate 24–hour stay in the intensive care unit, Valerie was released and has suffered no permanent disability from the incident.

Earlier in the evening of the 19th, the Hahns allowed their seven year old child to use Campho–Phenique to treat a cold sore. This child evidently misplaced the lid to the container. There was some speculation that the seven year old administered the medicine to Valerie.

Valerie's parents sued Sterling Drug, alleging that Campho–Phenique was a defective product because the warning on the container was inadequate and for the further reason that the product did not have a child-proof cap. The complaint sounds in tort and strict liability. The district court directed a verdict for the defendant, holding that the warning on the package was adequate and that reasonable men could not arrive at a contrary verdict. The warning label on the defendant's product contains the following:

> WARNING: Keep this and all medicines out of children's reach. In case of accidental ingestion, seek professional assistance or contact a poison control center immediately.

> DIRECTIONS: For external use: apply with cotton three or four times daily.

ody Petersen, Panel Suggests Wait in Telling Doctors About Hypertension Drug, N.Y. Times, May 25, 2001, at C11.

Appellants contend that they produced evidence from which a jury could conclude that the danger posed by the product when ingested by small children was great enough to require a more stringent warning. The Hahns rely principally on the testimony of their toxicology expert, Dr. Albert P. Rauber, Professor of Pediatrics at Emory University and also Medical Director of the Georgia Poison Center. Dr. Rauber testified that the warning was very general and that its effect is "watered down" by the fact that the same warning appears on numerous products that are not harmful (i.e., Flintstone Vitamins and Hydrocortisone Cream). Rauber said he was not "satisfied" with the Campho–Phenique label.

The Hahns point to several other facts which could have led a jury to believe that the warning was inadequate. First, the Hahns themselves testified that they had read the label in its entirety and were still unaware that the product could harm their child if ingested. Second, Sterling was aware that many children had been injured after ingesting the product, yet the product continued to use the same warning. Third, the product was known to be quite toxic, and as such it required a more dramatic warning. Fourth, the warning was in a smaller print than other messages on the label. The Hahns say that this was confusing even though the warning was in bold-face type. Fifth, the direction "for external use" was not followed by the word "only." Sixth, the label stated that the product may be used on the gums, possibly indicating to a reasonable person that internal use might be acceptable. Seventh, the label was silent as to the possibility of seizures and respiratory failure if taken internally. Eighth, the warning to contact the poison control center was insufficient since it would have been just as easy to put the word "poison" on the label. Also, the warning is said to be more like a "helpful hint meant merely to please and placate a concerned parent and not a clue that the contents of the bottle are poisonous."

Appellee, of course, argues that no reasonable person could find that the warning on the Campho–Phenique label was inadequate. Sterling relies on Dr. Rauber's admission during cross examination that the warning advised a reasonable person that the product was potentially toxic and that ingestion might create "grave danger." The district court agreed. The court below held that both the references to external use and to the poison control center in combination with the reference to keep this and all medicines out of the reach of children were sufficient to convey the message to an average adult that there is a risk of serious harm if the child swallows the medicine.

At oral argument, Sterling's attorneys conceded that they could not refer to the court any case decided in the Eleventh Circuit or in the Georgia courts which held that the adequacy of a product manufacturer's warning is a proper subject for a directed verdict. * * * As we understand the decided cases in this area of law, the simple question is whether the warning is adequate, given the unsafe nature of the product. It is appropriate for a jury to determine that adequacy. While the jury may or may not consider the intelligence and experience of the consumer-plaintiff, that does not play a part in our rationale in determining whether or not the question should or should not be presented to a jury. * * *

Another issue brought up on appeal that is not a basis for our reversal of the district court but may be important on retrial is whether certain documents should have been admitted at trial. Appellant complained that the district court abused its discretion in refusing to admit into evidence a Food and Drug Administration report that compiled statistics of other ingestions of Campho–Phenique, as well as other documents, on the ground that the reports were irrelevant. Evidence is relevant if it tends to make the existence of any fact that is of consequence to the determination of the action more probable or less probable than it would be without the evidence. It is not clear from the record below whether the plaintiff established that the prior incidents occurred under conditions substantially similar to those of this case, but if upon retrial it develops that the conditions were similar and the evidence of prior accidents might be relevant to either the defendant's notice, the magnitude of danger involved, the defendant's ability to correct known defects, the lack of safety for intended uses, the strength of the product, the standard of care, or the causation, such evidence should not be excluded. * * *

Ramirez v. Plough, Inc.

863 P.2d 167 (Cal.1993).

■ KENNARD, JUSTICE:

* * * Plaintiff Jorge Ramirez, a minor, sued defendant Plough, Inc., alleging that he contracted Reye's syndrome as a result of ingesting a nonprescription drug, St. Joseph Aspirin for Children (SJAC), that was manufactured and distributed by defendant. * * *

In March 1986, when he was less than four months old, plaintiff exhibited symptoms of a cold or similar upper respiratory infection. To relieve these symptoms, plaintiff's mother gave him SJAC. Although the product label stated that the dosage for a child under two years old was "as directed by doctor," plaintiff's mother did not consult a doctor before using SJAC to treat plaintiff's condition. Over a two-day period, plaintiff's mother gave him three SJAC tablets. Then, on March 15, plaintiff's mother took him to a hospital. There, the doctor advised her to administer Dimetapp or Pedialyte (nonprescription medications that do not contain aspirin), but she disregarded the advice and continued to treat plaintiff with SJAC.

Plaintiff thereafter developed Reye's syndrome, resulting in severe neurological damage, including cortical blindness, spastic quadriplegia, and mental retardation. First described by the Australian pathologist Douglas Reye in 1963, Reye's syndrome occurs in children and teenagers during or while recovering from a mild respiratory tract infection, flu, chicken pox, or other viral illness. The disease is characterized by severe vomiting and irritability or lethargy, which may progress to delirium and coma. In 1982, the Centers for Disease Control estimated that Reye's syndrome affected 600 to 1200 children and teenagers in this country each year. The disease is fatal in 20 to 30 percent of cases, with many of the survivors sustaining permanent brain damage. The cause of Reye's syndrome was unknown in 1986 (and apparently remains unknown), but by the early 1980s several studies had shown an association between ingestion of aspirin during a viral illness, such as chicken pox or influenza, and the subsequent development of Reye's syndrome. These studies prompted the United States Food and Drug Administration (FDA) to propose a labeling requirement for aspirin products warning of the dangers of Reye's syndrome. The FDA published a regulation to this effect on March 7, 1986. * * * In 1988, the FDA revised the required warning to state explicitly that Reye's syndrome is reported to be associated with aspirin use, and it made the regulation permanent.

Even before the federal regulation became mandatory, packages of SJAC displayed this warning: "Warning: Reye Syndrome is a rare but serious disease which can follow flu or chicken pox in children and teenagers. While the cause of Reye Syndrome is unknown, some reports claim aspirin may increase the risk of developing this disease. Consult doctor before use in children or teenagers with flu or chicken pox." The package insert contained the same warning, together with this statement: "The symptoms of Reye syndrome can include persistent vomiting, sleepiness and lethargy, violent headaches, unusual behavior, including disorientation, combativeness, and delirium. If any of these symptoms occur, especially following chicken pox or flu, call your doctor immediately, even if your child has not taken any medication. REYE SYNDROME IS SERIOUS, SO EARLY DETECTION AND TREATMENT ARE VITAL."

These warnings were printed in English on the label of the SJAC that plaintiff's mother purchased in March 1986. At that time, plaintiff's mother, who was born in Mexico, was literate only in Spanish. Because she could not read English, she was unable to read the warnings on the SJAC label and package insert. Yet she did not ask anyone to translate the label or package insert into Spanish, even though other members of her household could have done so. Plaintiff's mother had never heard, seen, or relied upon any advertising for SJAC in either English or Spanish. In Mexico, she had taken aspirin for headaches, both as a child and as an adult, and a friend had recommended SJAC.

Plaintiff, by and through his mother as guardian ad litem, filed suit against defendant in August 1989, alleging causes of action for fraud, negligence, and product liability, all premised on the theory of failure to warn about the dangers of Reye's syndrome. * * *

Defendant moved for summary judgment, submitting uncontradicted evidence of the facts as stated above. Defendant argued that it was under no duty to label SJAC with Spanish language warnings, that the English language label warnings were adequate, and that the adequacy of the English warnings was ultimately inconsequential in this case because plaintiff's mother did not read the warnings or have them translated for her. On the motion for summary judgment, the parties agreed that over 148 languages are spoken in the United States. Plaintiff adduced evidence that defendant realized that Hispanics, many of whom have not learned English, constituted an important segment of the market for SJAC, and that defendant had acted on this knowledge by using Spanish language advertisements for SJAC in Los Angeles and New York. The court granted summary judgment. In its order granting the motion, the court stated that there was "no duty to warn in a foreign language" and no causal relationship between plaintiff's injury and defendant's activities. Plaintiff appealed from the judgment for defendant.

The court of appeal reversed. It reasoned that although the question of duty is an issue for the court, the existence of a duty to warn here was undisputed, the actual dispute being as to the adequacy of the warning given. The court noted that the adequacy of a product warning is normally a question of fact, and that a defendant moving for summary judgment has the burden of proving an affirmative defense or the nonexistence of an element of the plaintiff's cause of action. Given the evidence of defendant's knowledge that SJAC was being used by non-English-literate Hispanics, and the lack of evidence as to the costs of Spanish language labeling, the reasonableness of defendant's conduct in not labeling SJAC with a Spanish language warning was, the court concluded, a triable issue of fact.[3] * * *

The FDA has stated that it "encourages the preparation of labeling to meet the needs of non-English speaking or special user populations so long as such labeling fully complies with agency regulations." But the controlling regulation requires only that manufacturers provide full English labeling for all nonprescription drugs except those "distributed solely in the Commonwealth of Puerto Rico or in a Territory where the predominant language is one other than English." The regulation further states that if the label or packaging of any drug distributed in the 50 states contains "any representation in a foreign language," then all required "words, statements, and other information" must appear in the foreign language as well as in English. Finally, the regulation states that "use of label space for any representation in a foreign language" is not a basis to exempt a manufacturer from the general obligation to make required language prominent and conspicuous.

California law parallels and reinforces federal law on the points discussed here. The Health and Safety Code mandates conspicuous English language warnings in section 25900, which provides: "Cautionary statements which are required by law, or regulations adopted pursuant to law, to be printed upon the labels of containers in which dangerous drugs, poisons, and other harmful substances are packaged shall be printed in the

---

3. * * * [A]lthough symbols and pictograms can be used effectively to warn that a substance is flammable or toxic, or to explain its preparation and use, it is doubtful that they are at present able to convey the more complex warning information typically required for nonprescription drugs. In any event, the issue presented for decision in this case is whether manufacturers must warn in foreign languages, not by means of symbols or pictograms.

English language in a conspicuous place in type of conspicuous size in contrast to the typography, layout, or color of the other printed matter on the label." Although warnings in English are expressly required, no California statute requires label or package warnings in any other language. * * *

[Other] statutes demonstrate that the [California] Legislature is able and willing to define the circumstances in which foreign-language communications should be mandated. Given the existence of a statute expressly requiring that package warnings on nonprescription drugs be in English, we think it reasonable to infer that the Legislature has deliberately chosen not to require that manufacturers also include warnings in foreign languages. The same inference is warranted on the federal level. The FDA's regulations abundantly demonstrate its sensitivity to the issue of foreign-language labeling, and yet the FDA regulations do not require it. Presumably, the FDA has concluded that despite the obvious advantages of multilingual package warnings, the associated problems and costs are such that at present warnings should be mandated only in English.

On this point, the FDA's experience with foreign-language patient package inserts for prescription drugs is instructive. Recognizing that "the United States is too heterogeneous to enable manufacturers, at reasonable cost and with reasonable simplicity, to determine exactly where to provide alternative language inserts," the FDA for a time required manufacturers, as an alternative to multilingual or bilingual inserts, to provide Spanish language translations of their patient package inserts on request to doctors and pharmacists. But the FDA later noted that manufacturers were having difficulty obtaining accurate translations, and eventually it abandoned altogether the patient package insert requirement for prescription drugs.

Were we to reject the applicable statutes and regulations as the proper standard of care, there would be two courses of action open to us. The first would be to leave the issue for resolution on a case-by-case basis by different triers of fact under the usual "reasonable person" standard of care. This was the approach that the court of appeal adopted in this case. As a practical matter, such an open-ended rule would likely compel manufacturers to package all their nonprescription drugs with inserts containing warnings in multiple foreign languages because, simply as a matter of foreseeability, it is foreseeable that eventually each nonprescription drug will be purchased by a non-English-speaking resident or foreign tourist proficient only in one of these languages. The burden of including warnings in so many different languages would be onerous, would add to the costs and environmental burdens of the packaging, and at some point might prove ineffective or even counterproductive if the warning inserts became so large and cumbersome that a user could not easily find the warning in his or her own language.

The other alternative would be to use our seldom-exercised power to judicially declare a particularized standard of care, giving precise guidance on this issue. But this determination would involve matters that are peculiarly susceptible to legislative and administrative investigation and determination, based upon empirical data and consideration of the viewpoints of all interested parties. A legislative body considering the utility of foreign-language label warnings for nonprescription medications would no doubt gather pertinent data on a variety of subjects, including the space limitations on nonprescription drug labels and packages, the volume of information that must be conveyed, the relative risks posed by the misuse of particular medications, the cost to the manufacturer of translating and printing warnings in languages other than English, the cost to the consumer of multilingual package warnings in terms of higher prices for, or reduced availability of, products, the feasibility of targeted distribution of products with bilingual or multilingual packaging, the number of persons likely to benefit from warnings in a particular language, and the extent to which nonprescription drug manufacturers as a group have used foreign-language advertisements to promote sales of their products. Legislation and regulations would no doubt reflect findings on these and other pertinent questions.

Lacking the procedure and the resources to conduct the relevant inquiries, we conclude that the prudent course is to adopt for tort purposes the existing legislative and administrative standard of care on this issue. The feasibility and advisability of foreign-language labeling for nonprescription drugs will, no doubt, be reviewed periodically by the FDA and other concerned agencies. Indeed, we are conscious that our decision here may prompt review of this issue by the California Legislature. That is as it should be, for further study might persuade the Legislature, the FDA, or any other concerned agency to revise the controlling statutes or regulations for nonprescription drugs. * * *

We do not, of course, foreclose the possibility of tort liability premised upon the *content* of foreign-language advertising. For example, we do not decide whether a manufacturer would be liable to a consumer who detrimentally relied upon foreign-language advertising that was materially misleading as to product risks and who was unable to read English language package warnings that accurately described the risks. No such issue is presented here. Although plaintiff presented evidence that defendant advertised its product in Spanish, the record contains no evidence of the content of that advertising. And, in any event, plaintiff's mother could not have relied upon defendant's advertising because she admittedly did not see or hear it.

For these reasons, we reject plaintiff's attempt to place on nonprescription drug manufacturers a duty to warn that is broader in scope and more onerous than that currently imposed by applicable statutes and regulations. The FDA has stressed that "it is in the best interest of the consumer, industry, and the marketplace to have uniformity in presentation and clarity of message" in the warnings provided with nonprescription drugs. To preserve that uniformity and clarity, to avoid adverse impacts upon the warning requirements mandated by the federal regulatory scheme, and in deference to the superior technical and procedural lawmaking resources of legislative and administrative bodies, we adopt the legislative/regulatory standard of care that mandates nonprescription drug package warnings in English only.

Plaintiff contends that defendant should be held liable for his injuries even if, as we have concluded, defendant was not required to include Spanish language warnings with SJAC. Plaintiff insists there are other bases of liability that are within the scope of the complaint and that were raised in both the trial court and the court of appeal.

The first alternative ground of liability is an alleged defect in the English language labeling. Plaintiff maintains that the product label represented that SJAC was safe to administer to a child suffering from a common cold. Plaintiff argues that because a cold is a viral illness, and because Reye's syndrome is associated with aspirin use during or while recovering from viral illnesses, defendant should have warned against the use of SJAC for children experiencing or recovering from the symptoms of the common cold. The evidence submitted on the motion for summary judgment precludes liability on this ground. Plaintiff's mother, who administered the SJAC to plaintiff, neither read nor obtained translation of the product labeling. Thus, there is no conceivable causal connection between the representations or omissions that accompanied the product and plaintiff's injury.

The other alternative ground of liability is that defendant should not have marketed SJAC at all because the risks of Reye's syndrome clearly outweighed any benefit to be derived from the product, particularly in light of the availability of non-aspirin pain relievers. We conclude, however, as a matter of law, that defendant may not be held liable for failing to withdraw its product from the market in early 1986, when plaintiff's mother purchased and used it. (Defendant did cease distribution of SJAC effective December 31, 1986.) Although devastating, Reye's syndrome was then and remains now a rare and poorly understood illness. A few scientific studies had shown an association between aspirin and Reye's syndrome, but the methodology of those studies had been questioned and the FDA had determined that further studies were needed to confirm or disprove the association. Pending completion of those studies, the FDA concluded that product warnings were an adequate public safety measure. Although the FDA's conclusion is not binding on us, we think it deserves serious consideration. Plaintiff has submitted nothing that causes us to doubt the FDA's judgment in this matter that in early 1986 aspirin could be considered a reasonably safe product for administration to children, when distributed with appropriate warnings. * * *

■ Mosk, Justice (concurring):

* * * Evidence of the content, timing, duration, and scope of distribution of foreign-language advertising bears substantially on the question whether a non-English-literate consumer has been materially misled about product risks, and a trial court must consider that evidence if properly presented. The majority do not define "materially misleading as to product risks," leaving that issue for another day—a day likely to arrive soon, given

the high probability that foreign-language media will continue to expand in California.

Popular advertisements for over-the-counter drugs generally emphasize their therapeutic effects, not the harmful or fatal consequences of inadvertent misuse. Yet the proper use and inadvertent misuse of drugs occur in very similar ways: swallowing one pill may prove therapeutic, but more may be fatal. Hence, a foreign-language pharmaceutical advertisement will be "materially misleading as to product risks" if a company extols a drug's health benefits in the advertisement yet does not warn a non-English-literate consumer of the risks of misuse in a manner reasonably calculated to reach that consumer before the product is consumed or applied.

If there is such a misrepresentation, then a jury ordinarily should decide the defendant's tort liability. To conclude that notice must be reasonably calculated to reach the non-English-literate consumer is not necessarily to decide that the foreign-language warning must appear in or on the promotional material itself, or on the product's warning label. Notice on a drug's product label, in the foreign languages in which the drug is advertised, not to take or apply the drug before reading a package insert's detailed warning in those languages may, depending on the facts, be sufficient to warn of hazards and yet satisfy federal law. In general, I believe that as long as an over-the-counter drug manufacturer gives reasonable notice, by any legal means, of possible side effects in a foreign language to a non-English-literate consumer whose purchase has been induced in that language, it has met the standard of conduct California tort law demands.

PROBLEM #12. *PULLING IT ALL TOGETHER*

Your client, Jorge Diaz, suffered serious injuries after ingesting Noflux, a recently approved prescription drug indicated for the treatment of gastro-esophageal reflux disease. The package insert included a warning of the adverse event that he had suffered. The manufacturer had aggressively promoted the drug in television advertisements on Univision, a Spanish-language cable television station. These spots complied with the FDA's guidance on broadcast advertising (excerpted in Chapter 4(B)(2)), except that the company had not made a copy of the brief summary available in Spanish as the agency had "strongly encouraged." Mr. Diaz (who is not fluent in English) saw these ads, as had his physician (Gloria Gonzalez), and he specifically requested that Dr. Gonzalez prescribe it for his use. After taking a cursory medical history, Dr. Gonzalez (who is fluent in English) gave her patient several samples of Noflux that one of the manufacturer's detail reps had given her. Assume that the highest court in your jurisdiction has cited both *Perez* and *Ramirez* with approval. What are your prospects?

NOTES AND QUESTIONS

1. *Multilingual labeling.* The FDA regulation addressing foreign language warnings for drug products provides only limited guidance. See 21 C.F.R. § 201.15(c). It does require Spanish labeling for drugs sold in Puerto Rico. Even so, if a prescription drug manufacturer failed to comply with that requirement, but the physician was able to read the English labeling, a plaintiff bringing an inadequate warning claim would fail to establish causation. See Pierluisi v. E.R. Squibb & Sons, Inc., 440 F.Supp. 691 (D.P.R.1977). In issuing its final regulation mandating a Reye syndrome warning, the FDA explained that manufacturers could voluntarily provide the information in a foreign language. See 53 Fed. Reg. 21,633, 21,636 (1988). Notwithstanding the FDA's earlier problems in mandating multilingual PPIs, the Centers for Disease Control (CDC) required that health-care providers supply patients with vaccine information pamphlets in certain foreign languages. See 56 Fed. Reg. 51,798, 51,800 (1991) (promising to provide manufacturers with acceptable translations in Spanish, French, Vietnamese, and Chinese). Under the Clinton administration, HHS issued a requirement that health care providers make interpreters available for Medicaid patients who cannot speak English, a condition of participation that the AMA has assailed as excessively burdensome. See Language Gap, Wash. Post, May 1, 2001, at T6.

Couldn't Plough at least have included the following disclaimer in the labeling of St. Joseph's Aspirin for Children: "Si usted no sabe leer en inglés, por favor no use este producto, hasta que se le haya brindado entrenamiento adecuado." The EPA may require that the labeling of pesticides include just such a disclaimer ("If you cannot read English do not use this product until properly instructed.") in the language(s) spoken by foreseeable users. See 40 Fed. Reg. 28,242, 28,251 (1975); see also Hubbard–Hall Chem. Co. v. Silverman, 340 F.2d 402, 405 (1st Cir.1965) (holding that a jury could find the warning on a pesticide inadequate for users who could not read English "because of its lack of a skull and bones or other comparable symbols"); Stanley Indus., Inc. v. W.M. Barr & Co., 784 F.Supp. 1570, 1576 (S.D.Fla.1992) (same). See generally R. Geoffrey Dillard, Note, Multilingual Warning Labels: Products Liability, "Official English," and Consumer Safety, 29 Ga. L. Rev. 197 (1994); Marjorie A. Caner, Annotation, Products Liability: Failure to Provide Product Warning or Instruction in Foreign Language or to Use Universally Accepted Pictographs or Symbols, 27 A.L.R.5th 697 (1995); Labels in English Pose Risk in Multilingual Nation, N.Y. Times, May 20, 2001, at 30.

2. *Warnings for nonprescription drugs and devices.* Labeling directed to consumers must include clear instructions for avoiding or minimizing the risk. See Cooley v. Carter–Wallace Inc., 478 N.Y.S.2d 375, 379–80 (App.Div. 1984) ("Mere directions for the proper use of a product which fail to warn of specific dangers and risks of harm if the directions are not followed may be inadequate."); see also O'Gilvie v. International Playtex, Inc., 821 F.2d 1438, 1441–43 (10th Cir.1987) (tampons); Torsiello v. Whitehall Labs., 398 A.2d 132, 137–40 (N.J.App.Div.1979) (aspirin products); Michael v. Warner/Chilcott, 579 P.2d 183, 187 (N.M.Ct.App.1978) (sinus medication); Barry v. Don Hall Labs., 642 P.2d 685, 690–91 (Or.Ct.App.1982) (high sugar content of Vitamin C tablets).

3. *Adequacy of PPIs and regulatory compliance.* Again, contrary to *Ramirez*, compliance generally provides no defense to claims of inadequacies in warnings provided to patients. In several cases, for instance, courts have allowed juries to find that the specific warnings provided to patients by manufacturers of oral contraceptives were inadequate even though the labeling fully complied with FDA's PPI regulation. See, e.g., McEwen v. Ortho Pharm. Corp., 528 P.2d 522, 534 (Or.1974). In one case involving labeling for oral contraceptives, warnings emphasizing the risk of "fatal" adverse reactions but failing to use the word "stroke" were found potentially inadequate because a jury might conclude that the resulting permanent disability is a fate worse than death. See MacDonald v. Ortho Pharm. Corp., 475 N.E.2d 65, 72 (Mass.1985); see also Petty v. United States, 740 F.2d 1428, 1437 (8th Cir.1984) ("[T]he risk of death may be conceptually remote, whereas a more specific warning detailing the known risk of serum sickness and its symptoms would alert recipients more concretely to the risks that they actually were assuming."). But see Mampe v. Ayerst Labs., 548 A.2d 798, 801 (D.C.Ct.App.1988) ("We seriously doubt that promotional materials which warn of death as a possible reaction to a drug could be inadequate to warn of a consequence any less severe."); Dunkin v. Syntex Labs., Inc., 443 F.Supp. 121, 124 (W.D.Tenn.1977) (warnings that oral contraceptive created risk of thrombosis, cerebral vascular accident, and fatal blood clotting abnormalities held to be adequate). If the plaintiff discarded the allegedly inadequate PPI without reading it, an inadequate warning claim will fail on causation grounds. See E.R. Squibb & Sons, Inc. v. Cox, 477 So.2d 963, 971 (Ala.1985) (insulin).

4. *Translating complex information for lay persons.* Recall from Chapter 2 that informed consent for participation in clinical trials is geared toward an 8th grade reading level. (The FDA's consumer information brochures are pitched even lower, designed to be understood by those functioning at a 5th grade reading level.) It will be awfully difficult to "dumb down" prescription drug information written for educated medical professionals in a way that will reach most of the population. Many adults in the United States qualify as functionally illiterate, and an even higher percentage experience difficulties in comprehending health information. See Council on Scientific Affairs, Health Literacy, 281 JAMA 552 (1999).

CHAPTER 8

UTILIZATION ERRORS AND MEDICAL MALPRACTICE

Courts face unique difficulties in dealing with medical malpractice claims involving the use of medical technologies. In evaluating the tort liability of health care providers, courts must consider how those providers use drugs and medical devices in order to define the appropriate standard of liability.

In most product defect cases, every entity in the chain of distribution, from the manufacturer down to the retailer, may face strict liability, even if it played no role in causing the defect. However, as discussed in Chapter 6, bulk suppliers generally need not fear liability. In addition, at the other end of the chain, the *Restatement (Third) of the Law of Torts: Products Liability* effectively exempts retailers and users of prescription drugs and medical devices from most forms of strict liability:

(e) A retail seller or other distributor of a prescription drug or medical device is subject to liability for harm caused by the drug or device if:

(1) at the time of sale or other distribution the drug or medical device contains a manufacturing defect as defined in § 2(a) [i.e., when the product departs from its intended design even though all possible care was exercised in the preparation and marketing of the product]; or

(2) at or before the time of sale or other distribution of the drug or medical device the retail seller or other distributor fails to exercise reasonable care and such failure causes harm to persons.

Rest. (3d) § 6(e). In other words, hospitals and pharmacies are not treated as retailers within the chain of distribution except in cases of manufacturing defects. In cases of design or informational defects, hospitals and pharmacies are only liable if they acted negligently. Why is that?

The comment accompanying § 6(e) justified this special rule as follows:

The rule governing most products imposes liability on wholesalers and retailers for selling a defectively designed product, or one without adequate instructions or warnings, even though they have exercised reasonable care in marketing the product. Courts have refused to apply this general rule to nonmanufacturing retail sellers of prescription drugs and medical devices and, instead, have adopted the rule stated in Subsection (e). That rule subjects retailers to liability only if the product contains a manufacturing defect or if the retailer fails to exercise reasonable care in connection with distribution of the drug or medical device. In so limiting the liability of intermediary parties, courts have held that they should be permitted to rely on the special expertise of manufacturers, prescribing and treating health-care providers, and governmental regulatory agencies. They have also emphasized the needs of medical patients to have ready access to prescription drugs at reasonable prices.

Id. cmt. h. Thus, as a general rule, physicians, pharmacists, and hospitals whose patients suffer harm from the use of a prescription drug or device are judged by ordinary negligence standards. Is this any different from the rules applied to manufacturers of such products? Also, given the policy arguments elaborated in the materials that follow, why impose strict liability for manufacturing defects? Aren't these precisely the cases where the need to subject those at the bottom of the chain of distribution to strict liability seems the weakest?

A.   Liability of Users and Prescribers

Physicians "distribute" medical products, in the sense that they utilize these products (or authorize their dispensing) in connection with providing medical services, but courts have concluded that physicians are not in the chain of distribution for products liability purposes. Nevertheless, physicians have legal obligations in connection with the use of medical technologies—they must exercise due care in selecting appropriate products for treating individual patients; they must inform patients fully of the associated risks; and they must, of course, utilize the technology in a non-negligent fashion.

Magrine v. Krasnica

227 A.2d 539 (N.J.Super.Ct.1967), aff'd, 250 A.2d 129 (N.J.1969).

■ Lynch, Judge:

The novelty of this case lies in the attempt by plaintiff, a patient of defendant dentist, to extend the rule of "strict liability" against defendant for personal injuries caused by the breaking of a hypodermic needle in plaintiff's jaw while being used by defendant in an injection procedure. The break was due to a latent defect in the needle. Novelty, of itself, does not foreclose consideration of plaintiff's contentions in this field of developing tort law. Neither does it justify a headlong leap to impose strict liability unless, based on proper policy considerations and reason, such liability should be found. Plaintiff concedes that there is no precedent—anywhere— holding a dentist, or any other "user" of an article, strictly liable for injuries caused by a latent defect therein. * * *

[Defendant] was administering a local anesthetic with a hypodermic needle inserted into the left temporomandibular space, a point at the extreme end of the lower gum beyond the last tooth. The needle extended 1–5/8″ beyond the syringe. It had been assembled by the doctor just before the injection and had been used approximately eight times for about three weeks prior to the accident. It is the custom of the doctor to use about four needles a month and to discard them at the end of the month. As the injection was being made the needle "separated" at the hub, the place where the needle entered the syringe, leaving the entire 1–5/8″ length of the needle in plaintiff's jaw. Defendant does not know what caused the needle to break, but he believes there must have been some sort of defect in it. He does not know from whom he purchased the needle. * * *

We have seen the rapid development of the "strict liability" concept in the products liability field. * * * Plaintiff's argument moves from the major premise that "strict liability" is not confined to "sales," through the minor premise that the basic policy considerations of the doctrine apply to the use of a needle by a dentist, and concludes that he should be held liable though free from negligence. Since the major premise is established, it therefore remains for us to analyze the policy considerations projected by our decisions and other authorities and determine to what extent, if any, they postulate a judgment for plaintiff. * * *

[I]n all of our recent cases strict liability was imposed (except with respect to a retail dealer) upon those who were in "a better position" in the sense that they created the danger (in making the article) * * * or possessed a better capacity or expertise to control, inspect and discover the defect than the party injured. In these respects the dentist here was in no better position than plaintiff. He neither created the defect nor possessed any better capacity or expertise to discover or correct it than she. It is further very clear that strict liability was imposed in our New Jersey cases for the basic reason that those so held liable put the product "in the stream of trade and promote its purchase by the public." * * * Defendant dentist did not put the needle in the stream of commerce or promote its purchase.

It may be logically argued that the foregoing analysis does not effectively distinguish defendant from the retail dealer who, for example, sells food in a sealed container, or otherwise has no opportunity to discover a defect in the article he sells, and who nevertheless is liable for breach of warranty. In this respect such retail dealer is in no better position to discover the defect than the dentist here. Nevertheless, the situations are distinct. In the first place, the Uniform Sales Act and the Uniform Commercial Code, legislative enactments, apply to sales and there can be no judicial construction which could deny a warranty against a retail seller. At common law the implied warranty was originally confined to food. Even so, several courts have refused to impose warranty liability on the "innocent" retailer who has no means of discovering the defect in the goods. Such reasoning is not without a concept of fairness. * * * Of more meaningful significance is a recognition that the essence of the transaction between the retail seller and the consumer relates to the article sold. The seller is in the business of supplying the product to the consumer. It is that, and that alone, for which he is paid. A dentist or a physician offers, and is paid for, his professional services and skill. That is the essence of the relationship between him and his patient. * * *

Plaintiff also invokes the policy consideration of "spreading of the risks"—the concept which suggests that defendant could cover his liability by insurance, or he could be held harmless by impleading his supplier or manufacturer. The "risk distributing theory" is a relevant consideration. But again, we must appreciate the context in which it has been applied in our cases. * * * [A party] who put the goods in the stream of commerce * * * may fairly be assumed to have substantial assets and volume of business, and a large area of contacts over which the risk can be widely spread. It is the "large-scale" enterprise which should bear the loss. The impact of liability upon such a defendant is minuscule in comparison with that of an individual dentist or physician. His means of "spreading the risk" could be by insurance or impleading his supplier or manufacturer. "Malpractice" insurance, however, does not cover implied warranty unless the policy "expressly covers contract claims." In this very case defendant dentist is represented not only by counsel for his insurance carrier but also by his personal counsel because the carrier denies coverage. In any event, there are definite limits as to how far the argument of "risk-spreading" by insurance can go. * * *

So, here, if the dentist or physician were to obtain insurance covering strict liability for equipment failure, the risk would be spread upon his patients by way of increased fees. Can anyone gainsay the fact that medical and dental costs, and insurance therefor, are already bearing hard there? * * * As a matter of principle, the spreading of losses to their patients subverts, rather than supports, the policy consideration that the loss should be imposed on those best able to withstand it, i.e., the manufacturer or other entity which puts the article into the stream of commerce. The "risk distribution" theory has some weight, but not nearly enough when laid beside other more basic considerations. * * *

Something can be said, by way of logical argument, in plaintiff's favor, for the policy consideration that if the dentist be held liable he, as the retail seller of food in a sealed container, can implead the manufacturer and thus be used as a conduit to place the loss where it belongs. This, too, should be regarded as only a "makeweight" argument. While we fully appreciate the appeal of the suggestion that the retail dealer—or the dentist here—is the most convenient conduit to "fight out" liability with the ultimate manufacturer, we are not satisfied that in this case such circuity of action is appropriate. * * * [D]efendant "does not know from whom the needle was purchased; he testified on oral depositions that the needle was manufactured by a certain Precision Bur Co. of New York, New York, but in answers to interrogatories Dr. Krasnica had suggested other possible manufacturers." Thus, plaintiff is not without remedy to reach the supplier by proper use of discovery procedures. If it be shown that identification of the supplier does not eventuate in this particular case, and both plaintiff and defendant are denied recourse to him, then our answer is that this is a "hard case" from which bad law should not flow. It is not the usual situation, for ordinarily the manufacturer can be reached.

In our view it would be bad law to sustain plaintiff's contentions because the relevant policy considerations do not justify imposition of strict liability upon a dentist in the first, or last, instance. Further, the vast body of malpractice law, presumably an expression of the public policy involved in this area of health care, imposes upon a dentist or physician liability only for negligent performance of his services—negligent deviation from the standards of his profession. In the performance of his professional skill he has control of what he does. As to the instrument he uses, he has no control with respect to a latent defect therein. Why, then, should he be held strictly liable for the instruments he uses, as to which he has no control over latent defects, and liable only for negligence in the performance of his professional services, which he does control? * * *

We must consider, also, the consequences if we were to adopt the rule of strict liability here. The same liability, in principle, should then apply to any user of a tool, other equipment or any article which, through no fault of the user, breaks due to a latent defect and injures another. It would apply to any physician, artisan or mechanic and to any user of a defective article—even to a driver of a defective automobile. In our view, no policy consideration positing strict liability justifies application of the doctrine in such cases. No more should it here. * * * Judgment for defendant.

Kelley v. Associated Anesthesiologists, Inc.

589 N.E.2d 1050 (Ill.App.Ct.1992).

■ McCUSKEY, JUSTICE:

* * * Plaintiff, Bryan Kelley, brought an action in medical malpractice against defendants, Associated Anesthesiologists, Inc. and John C. Burdon, M.D. (collectively "Dr. Burdon"), and in products liability against defendant, Burroughs Wellcome Co. Plaintiff's action involved a surgical operation performed during his recovery from an automobile accident. * * *

Dr. Burdon first administered sodium pentothal to put plaintiff to sleep. Dr. Burdon then administered a drip solution of succinylcholine (a muscle relaxant marketed by Burroughs as Anectine) to allow the insertion of a breathing tube into plaintiff's throat. After one unsuccessful attempt at intubation, Dr. Burdon increased the flow of succinylcholine to further relax plaintiff. Plaintiff was then successfully intubated. Plaintiff was removed from the gurney and turned to a prone position on the operating table. Immediately after plaintiff was turned, Dr. Burdon was unable to get a pulse. * * * Plaintiff was revived, but was without a heartbeat for approximately 29 minutes. The drip solution of succinylcholine was inadvertently left on during a portion of this time. Plaintiff is now severely impaired. * * *

The jury returned a verdict in favor of plaintiff and against Dr. Burdon and Burroughs. Based upon counterclaims for contribution filed by defendants, the jury apportioned the verdict 90% against Dr. Burdon and 10% against Burroughs. The trial court entered judgment on the verdicts rendered on plaintiff's claims and on defendants' counterclaims. Burroughs' main contention on appeal is that the trial court erred in denying Burroughs' motion for judgment notwithstanding the verdict. Burroughs argues that plaintiff failed to show causation between his injury and Burroughs' alleged failure to contraindicate administration of Anectine to patients exhibiting symptoms like plaintiff's. * * *

Dr. Burdon testified he was aware of the contents of the package insert. The package insert specifically warned that Anectine may induce hyperkalemia and cardiac arrest in patients recovering from "severe trauma," or in patients with "extensive denervation of skeletal muscle." Evidence presented at trial supported these statements. Dr. Burdon testified the package insert correctly summarized medical literature on the subject, and appropriately listed those persons at risk to experience a hyperkalemic reaction to succinylcholine. Dr. Burdon also testified he was aware of the risk of administering succinylcholine to denervated patients. He stated he had used succinylcholine before on extensively denervated patients without adverse results.

Expert testimony established it was basic knowledge to anesthesiologists that the administration of succinylcholine to an extensively denervated patient entailed the risk of hyperkalemia leading to cardiac arrest. Plaintiff's experts opined the administration of succinylcholine to plaintiff caused hyperkalemia and cardiac arrest, and that Dr. Burdon's failure to stop the flow of succinylcholine delayed efforts to revive plaintiff.

No direct proof was presented which showed Burroughs' product was the proximate cause of plaintiff's injury. No testimony was presented that the package insert was unreasonably dangerous, or that Burroughs' failure to "positively contraindicate" use of Anectine in extensively denervated patients proximately caused plaintiff's injury. Experts for the parties testified it is not necessary to absolutely contraindicate the use of succinylcholine in patients with denervated muscle. The experts further acknowledged the package insert's use of the language with "great caution" was not inappropriate.

Crucial to Dr. Burdon's decision to administer succinylcholine was his determination that plaintiff was not extensively denervated, and therefore not at risk with respect to succinylcholine. Dr. Burdon based his belief on professional literature on the subject and his personal experience in nearly 40 years of practice. Dr. Burdon testified that plaintiff had suffered neither the type nor quantity of "severe" trauma necessary to place plaintiff at risk for cardiac arrest from a hyperkalemic reaction to succinylcholine. Evidence at trial, however, showed that plaintiff was indeed extensively denervated. Since Dr. Burdon failed to identify plaintiff as someone at risk with respect to the administration of succinylcholine, the package insert could not have played a causative role in his injuries. Dr. Burdon never felt plaintiff was in the class of persons in which succinylcholine should be prohibited or used with great caution. * * *

The manner in which Dr. Burdon administered Anectine to plaintiff was not recommended by the package insert. The drip method used by Dr.

Burdon was recommended only for long (rather than short) surgical procedures. The insert also stated the 0.2% solution used by Dr. Burdon was the highest recommended dosage rather than the lowest recommended diluted solution (0.1%). Dr. Burdon testified he felt he was administering Anectine cautiously by using it for a brief period of time. He also testified that a 0.2% solution is the amount he would customarily administer.

The record demonstrates that Dr. Burdon understood the risks involved in administering succinylcholine. Dr. Burdon had used succinylcholine daily for over 30 years. One year prior to the incident, he had read the package insert for Anectine. He had also read the history and content of medical literature regarding succinylcholine. He had used succinylcholine in the past with denervated patients. Even if the insert had absolutely contraindicated the use of succinylcholine in extensively denervated patients, Dr. Burdon would not have heeded the prohibition because he had failed to diagnose plaintiff as being extensively denervated. Under these circumstances, the package insert could not have proximately caused the injury to plaintiff.

We conclude that the trial court should have granted Burroughs' motion for judgment n.o.v. because plaintiff failed to prove the product was unreasonably dangerous or that Burroughs' failure to absolutely contraindicate use of the product in extensively denervated patients was the proximate cause of plaintiff's injury. Accordingly, the judgment of the trial court is vacated as to Burroughs. Based upon our findings, we enter judgment against defendants, Associated Anesthesiologists, Inc. and John C. Burdon, M.D., for the entire amount of the jury verdict.

Tanuz v. Carlberg

921 P.2d 309 (N.M.Ct.App.1996).

■ APODACA, JUDGE:

* * * Plaintiff complained of TMJ pain and was diagnosed as suffering from bilateral derangement of the TMJ. In September 1983, Defendant surgically implanted TMJ implants manufactured by Vitek, Inc. The implants were manufactured using Proplast, a teflon-based substance patented by Vitek. At the time, the Vitek implants were being touted as having a greater success rate than other treatments. Defendant advised Plaintiff to return for routine follow-up care and to return if she experienced pain or discomfort.

On April 27, 1984, Plaintiff returned to Defendant's office, complaining of pain in her TMJs. Defendant's notes from that visit indicate that Plaintiff had failed to make her appointments after the previous visit. He referred her to Dr. Jameson to have her splint replaced. Plaintiff did not see Dr. Jameson after the referral and failed to continue follow-up treatment with Defendant, contrary to his advice. In 1987, Plaintiff began experiencing TMJ pain and self-treated this pain with over-the-counter medication. * * * In October 1993, Plaintiff contacted Defendant's office after watching a television show that discussed problems with Vitek implants. Defendant surgically removed Plaintiff's implants in February 1994.

Plaintiff filed her complaint against Defendant in June 1994. In addition to her strict liability claim, Plaintiff alleged that Defendant was negligent in failing to warn her of the dangers posed by the Vitek implants. Specifically, Plaintiff alleged that Defendant should have contacted her before any official warnings from the manufacturer about the product had arisen, based solely on problems he himself had experienced with his own patients and a growing awareness in the medical community that Vitek implants posed dangers to patients. Plaintiff also alleged that, when Vitek and the Food and Drug Administration alerts appeared in 1990 and 1991, Defendant made inadequate attempts to locate her. * * *

Plaintiff does not contend that Defendant was negligent when he inserted the implants in 1983 or when he assumed care for their removal in 1993 and 1994. * * * [T]he central issue in this case is not whether Defendant owed a duty to exercise reasonable care as information became known later, but whether Defendant breached the duty or applicable standard of care. Breach is an issue for the fact finder unless no reasonable minds could differ. In a medical malpractice action, a plaintiff is required to establish breach through expert medical testimony unless the fact finder can resort to common knowledge. * * *

Defendant testified that Proplast was showing a 93–97% success rate at the time of Plaintiff's initial surgery. Before surgery, Defendant discussed with Plaintiff the nature of the procedure and informed her that her pain may never go away. He told her that the implant could break up, that it was incapable of regeneration, and that anything that is incapable of regeneration can deteriorate. After Plaintiff's surgery, none of the major problems Defendant discussed with Plaintiff at the informed consent meeting occurred. At the time of the last visit, however, he recommended continued follow-up care. Defendant stated that he saw 1400 patients a year, and, as a result, he could not be a "babysitter" for their appointments.

Defendant removed Vitek implants from two of his patients in March (before Plaintiff's last visit) and June 1984. He clinically observed that these patients were getting good results initially but that their erosion problems and pain would return. By the end of 1985, he had removed fifteen implants, constituting a 60% failure rate. At this time, he determined he would no longer use these implants in his patients. The problems he experienced with the implants occurred within the first or second year after surgery, after which time the situation had stabilized. * * *

When asked why he had not attempted to contact Plaintiff after her April 1984 visit, Defendant responded that he advised her during this visit to see Dr. Jameson for a splint, and he assumed that she was treated by Dr. Jameson. When Vitek issued the first safety alert in 1990, Defendant informed his front desk to send it to all of his patients who had implants. Plaintiff was on the mailing list in 1990 and his office assumed that she was reached because the letter was never returned. In October 1991, his office sent an FDA recall notice to Plaintiff and it was returned as undeliverable. Defendant's office assumed that there had been a change of address between 1990 and 1991 because the earlier mailing had not been returned. As a result, his office attempted to contact her at her last known address, listed as the Red River Fish Hatchery on her 1983 intake form and was told she had moved and no one at the fish hatchery knew her new address. He was told by his staff that they went through the records and had used all the abilities that they could have used to contact her. * * *

We believe the testimony noted above shows that the trial court reasonably determined Plaintiff failed to meet her burden that Defendant breached the applicable standard of care. Specifically, Defendant's testimony established that, although there was mounting evidence against the safety of the Vitek implants throughout the 1980s, it was not known until the safety alerts were issued that the Proplast material itself was to blame. This fact is important because, up until that time, it was reasonable for Defendant to conclude that the implants themselves were not inherently defective and that the success or failure with a given patient could be attributed to other causes, such as surgical technique or movement of the implant over time. As such, it was reasonable for Defendant to assume that Plaintiff was not experiencing problems because she did not return to his office, as she was advised to do should she have problems. * * * Although Defendant's 60% failure rate was alarming on its face, the trial court could reasonably rely on Defendant's additional testimony that the problems he experienced with these patients surfaced shortly after their surgery and, as a result, it was reasonable to assume that Plaintiff was asymptomatic.

It was also reasonable for the trial court to disbelieve Plaintiff's assertion that Defendant's efforts in 1990 and 1991 to locate Plaintiff were inadequate. It was reasonable to assume that Plaintiff received the 1990 alert because the letter was not returned. * * * [W]e agree that more steps might have been taken to locate Plaintiff [e.g., certified letters, phone calls, efforts to contact family members], but this factor was most likely considered by the trier-of-fact in the context of Defendant's advice to Plaintiff to return if she began to experience problems. In other words, the trial court could have determined that it would be reasonable to assume that the efforts to locate Plaintiff did not have to exceed those taken because Plaintiff would return to see Defendant or another physician if her implants began to fail. Although the evidence presented by Plaintiff was sufficient to sustain a finding to the contrary, we are compelled under our standard of review to affirm the trial court's determination that Defendant did not breach his duty or the applicable standard of care.

We hold that a physician may not be held strictly liable as a matter of policy for the use of a manufactured implant later shown to be defective. We also hold that a physician has a duty to warn a patient of information obtained following a medical procedure. Under the facts of this case, however, it was reasonable for the trial court, sitting as fact finder, to conclude that Plaintiff had failed to meet her burden of proof that Defendant breached his duty. * * *

NOTES AND QUESTIONS

1. *Exemption from strict products liability.* Thirty years after *Magrine*, and notwithstanding changes in the profession, courts continue to reject strict products liability claims against physicians:

> In analyzing this question, we must consider whether the essence of the transaction is the provision of a service or a product. We hold that health care providers who perform breast implant procedures are, in essence, providing a service. Although the breast implant procedure requires the use of a product, the implant, the health care provider is fundamentally and predominantly offering a service. The provider must have medical knowledge and skill to conduct the procedure. He must advise the patient of the medical consequences and must recommend to the patient the preferable type of procedure. The product may not be purchased independently of the service. One does not "buy" a breast implant procedure in the same way as one would buy a product, such as a lawn-mower. At its heart, the breast implant procedure is a service and not a product.

In re Breast Implant Prod. Liab. Litig., 503 S.E.2d 445, 449 (S.C.1998); see also Silverhart v. Mount Zion Hosp., 98 Cal.Rptr. 187 (Ct.App.1971) (strict liability not applied to dentist whose drill broke during use on patient); Carmichael v. Reitz, 95 Cal.Rptr. 381 (Ct.App.1971) (strict liability inapplicable to physician who prescribed a drug that injured the patient); Barbee v. Rogers, 425 S.W.2d 342 (Tex.1968) (optometrists not liable on strict liability claim for injuries to plaintiff from improper fitting of contact lenses); cf. Magner v. Beth Israel Hosp., 295 A.2d 363 (N.J.Super.Ct.1972) (strict liability inapplicable to dental or medical professionals); Hoven v. Kelble, 256 N.W.2d 379 (Wis.1977) (strict liability inapplicable to medical professionals where plaintiff was injured during lung biopsy procedure). But see Richard L. Cupp, Jr., Sharing Accountability for Breast Implants: Strict Products Liability and Medical Professionals Engaged in Hybrid Sales/Service Cosmetic Product Transactions, 21 Fla. St. U. L. Rev. 873 (1994) (discussing the benefits of applying strict products liability to plastic surgeons who "sell" cosmetic implant devices to patients). The distinction between sales and services extends beyond the medical context. See Rest. (3d) § 19(b) & cmt. f. Thus, just as strict liability does not apply to implant surgeons, persons who install new appliances generally face tort liability only if they acted unreasonably under the circumstances. See Enright v. City of Colorado Springs, 716 P.2d 148 (Colo.Ct.App.1985). For a different approach to holding physicians strictly liable using a state consumer protection statute, see Wright v. Jeckle, 16 P.3d 1268 (Wash.Ct.App.2001) (reinstating plaintiff's claim that the physician's advertising and sale of diet drugs constituted inappropriate entrepreneurial activities in violation of the state's consumer protection act).

2. *Categories of physician negligence.* Physicians have been found negligent in their utilization of medical technologies under a variety of circumstances. See Linda A. Sharp, Annotation, Malpractice: Physician's Liability for Injury or Death Resulting from Side Effects of Drugs Intentionally Administered to or Prescribed for Patients, 47 A.L.R.5th 433 (1997).

a. *Negligent prescribing.* Courts have found physicians negligent for failing to prescribe drugs that are medically appropriate for their patients and that minimize the risk of adverse effects. See, e.g., Haught v. Maceluch, 681 F.2d 291 (5th Cir.1982) (award to mother for mental suffering reinstated based on physician negligence in prescribing drug which resulted in injury to a child during birth); Edwards v. Tardif, 692 A.2d 1266 (Conn. 1997) (wrongful death action based on negligent prescribing without examination of patient); Atlanta Obstet. & Gyn. Group v. Coleman, 398 S.E.2d 16 (Ga.1990) (negligent selection of drug); Bazel v. Mabee, 576 N.W.2d 385 (Iowa Ct.App.1998) (physician negligent for using betadine despite patient's known allergy); Argus v. Scheppegrell, 472 So.2d 573 (La.1985) (physician negligent for continuing to prescribe drugs to addicted patient); Rhoto v. Ribando, 504 So.2d 1119 (La.Ct.App.1987) (physician negligent for inappropriate off-label prescribing); Lynch v. Bay Ridge Obstet. & Gyn. Assoc., 532 N.E.2d 1239 (N.Y.1988) (allowing claim against physician for negligently failing to diagnose a pregnancy and then prescribing a drug that was contraindicated for use in pregnant women); Berkowitz v. Kingsboro, 651 N.Y.S.2d 116 (App.Div.1996) (summary judgment reversed based on claim that physician was negligent in selecting drug to treat infection); Baldino v. Castagna, 478 A.2d 807 (Pa.1984) (physician negligent in prescribing drug); Cooper v. Bowser, 610 S.W.2d 825 (Tex.Civ.App.1980) (negligent prescribing where physician failed to heed warnings regarding preferred length of treatment with certain drugs); Eiss v. Lillis, 357 S.E.2d 539 (Va.1987) (negligent failure to monitor patient's drug therapy).

b. *Failures to warn.* Another category of negligence concerns physician failures to warn the patient of risks associated with the use of the prescribed drug. See, e.g., Songer v. Bowman, 804 P.2d 261 (Colo.Ct.App. 1990) (dermatologist negligent for failing to warn patient of risk of sun exposure during use of topical prescription drug); Summit Bank v. Panos, 570 N.E.2d 960 (Ind.Ct.App.1991) (claim that physician was negligent for failing to warn patient of risk of combining drug with alcohol presents question of fact for a jury); Tenuto v. Lederle Labs., 687 N.E.2d 1300 (N.Y.1997) (physician had a duty to warn plaintiff of risk of contracting polio from child who had received a polio vaccine); Shadrick v. Coker, 963 S.W.2d 726 (Tenn.1998) (informed consent requires physician to inform patient that medical device was not FDA approved); see also James E. Britain, Product Honesty Is the Best Policy: A Comparison of Doctors' and Manufacturers' Duty to Disclose Drug Risks and the Importance of Consumer Expectations in Determining Product Defect, 79 Nw. U. L. Rev. 342 (1984); Gerald F. Tietz, Informed Consent in the Prescription Drug Context: The Special Case, 61 Wash. L. Rev. 367, 395–417 (1986) (urging stricter application of the informed consent duty with respect to drug prescribing).

c. *Undermedicating.* Courts have begun to entertain tort claims against physicians for undertreating pain that would have responded to powerful analgesic products. See Barry R. Furrow, Pain Management and Provider Liability: No More Excuses, 29 J.L. Med. & Ethics 28 (2001); Ben A. Rich, A Prescription for the Pain: The Emerging Standard of Care for Pain Management, 26 Wm. Mitchell L. Rev. 1 (2000). Occasionally, a patient will allege that a physician committed malpractice for failing to switch the patient to a newly approved product that might have worked more effectively. See Reese v. Stroh, 907 P.2d 282, 283–84 (Wash.1995) (noting that the physician had justified his decision based in part on the fact that the FDA had approved the product using surrogate rather than clinical end-points); cf. Bell v. Maricopa Med. Ctr., 755 P.2d 1180, 1182 (Ariz.Ct.App.1988) (alleging malpractice for the failure to use an approved drug for an off-label use); Bridges v. Shelby Women's Clinic, 323 S.E.2d 372, 374–76 (N.C.Ct.App.1984) (same).

d. *Errors in drug administration.* Finally, when health care professionals administer a different drug than the drug prescribed or an improper dosage of the correct drug, courts may find these professionals liable. See, e.g., Baylis v. Wilmington Med. Ctr., Inc., 477 A.2d 1051 (Del.1984) (negligence claim based on improper dose of a drug); Leiker v. Gafford, 778 P.2d 823 (Kan.1989) (negligence for administering excessive dose of a drug); Harrison v. Axelrod, 599 N.Y.S.2d 96 (App.Div.1993) (nurse negligent for administering incorrect dose of prescription drug solution).

3. *New technology and malpractice.* The opportunities for physician negligence increase with advances in medical knowledge and technology. See Mark F. Grady, Why Are People Negligent? Technology, Nondurable Precautions, and the Medical Malpractice Explosion, 82 Nw. U. L. Rev. 293, 298–99, 312 (1988) ("[W]ith the advent of dialysis, there are many compliance opportunities and when someone forgets to test a solution or check a shunt and harm results, there is a negligence claim that could not have existed before dialysis technology was introduced."); Martin J. Hatlie, Editorial, Climbing "The Learning Curve": New Technologies, Emerging Obligations, 270 JAMA 1364, 1365 (1993) ("The difficulty with rapidly emerging treatment modalities is that a 'customary practice' may not yet exist."); Brian Kibble–Smith & Arthur W. Hafner, The Effect of the Information Age on Physicians' Professional Liability, 36 DePaul L. Rev. 69, 86 (1986) ("The physician's duty to keep abreast will be revised as information management technology continues to affect information distribution and access."); Donald E. Kacmar, Note, The Impact of Computerized Medical Literature Databases on Medical Malpractice Litigation: Time for Another Helling v. Carey Wake-up Call?, 58 Ohio St. L.J. 617, 644–48 (1997); Margaret Lent, Note, The Medical and Legal Risks of the Electronic Fetal Monitor, 51 Stan. L. Rev. 807, 828 (1999) (explaining that "several courts have indicated that a physician has a specific duty to 'keep abreast of progress,'" which "obligate[s] physicians to read, interpret, and apply the latest research regarding the drugs, techniques, and procedures employed in their specialities").

4. *Report on errors in medicine.* The Institute of Medicine (IOM) recently issued a report dealing with the frequency and causes of errors in the provision of health care. See Linda T. Kohn et al., To Err Is Human: Building a Safer Health System (2000). One of the largest classes of errors involved the utilization of prescription drugs. See David W. Bates et al., The Costs of Adverse Drug Events in Hospitalized Patients, 277 JAMA 307 (1997) (concluding that 2% of hospital admissions resulted in a preventable adverse drug event, which increased hospital costs by an average of $4,700 per admission for a total of $2.8 million per year for a single 700–bed teaching hospital). Extrapolating from these data, the costs of preventable adverse drug events in hospitals total about $2 billion annually across the country. As the IOM report pointed out, these statistics do not even begin to account for all of the drug-related adverse events that occur outside of hospitals. What is the most significant barrier to reducing such events? In order to track and ultimately prevent patient injuries resulting from improper choice of medication (or inappropriate doses), hospitals and other institutions must be able to identify when such an injury occurs and what error caused the injury. The most obvious source of this information is the treating physician. Consider the competing pressures physicians experience in such circumstances. How might the system alleviate these pressures in order to encourage error reporting and ultimately facilitate error prevention? Commentators have begun to offer some suggestions, see, e.g., Brian A. Liang, Error in Medicine: Legal Impediments to U.S. Reform, 24 J. Health Pol., Pol'y & L. 27 (1999), and the Joint Commission on Accreditation of Healthcare Organizations (JCAHO) recently issued a rule that requires hospitals to inform patients when medical errors occur and that "strongly encourages" internal error reporting. See Revisions to Joint Commission Standards in Support of Patient Safety and Medical/Health Care Error Reduction (2001), available at <www.jcaho.org>.

5. *Handwriting disasters.* Approximately 1,150 pairs of prescription drugs have similar names that may lead to confusion. For example, compare Celebrex® (for arthritis), Cerebyx® (for seizures), and Celexa® (for depression). See FDA, Minimizing Medical Products Errors: A Systems Approach, Jan. 8, 1998 (noting estimates that look-alike and sound-alike drug names cause 20 to 25% of medical errors, and describing strategies to minimize these errors, including the use of short rather than long names, eliminating faxed prescriptions, and storing drugs by category rather than in alphabetical order). Notoriously illegible physician handwriting contributes to the confusion between drug names and also may result in patients receiving inappropriate dosages of the intended drug. In one recent case, a jury ordered a physician, hospital, and pharmacist to pay $450,000 to the family of a man who died of a heart attack after taking an overdose of Plendil® (a blood pressure drug) when he should have received Isordil® (an angina drug) because the prescription was illegible. See Bruce Japsen, Drug Name Confusion a Hazard, Chi. Trib., July 30, 2000, at 1C. Computerized prescribing programs in handheld devices may help to reduce errors once their use becomes widespread. In the meantime, some hospitals have resorted to forcing their staff physicians to attend handwriting classes. See Rene Sanchez, For Doctors' Scrawl, Handwriting's on the Wall, Wash. Post, May 16, 2000, at A1 (describing one such class at the prestigious Cedars-

Sinai Medical Center). The FDA recently ordered several manufacturers to change their labels in order to highlight differences between similar-sounding drug names. See Lauren Neergaard, FDA Pushes to Curb Drug Mix-ups, Boston Globe, Jan. 2, 2002, at E4 (describing label changes using a mixture of upper- and lower-case letters and colors to draw attention to product name differences).

6. *Package inserts and the standard of care.* Courts have struggled in determining the appropriate status of prescription drug labeling in medical malpractice cases. See David Carl Minneman, Annotation, Medical Malpractice: Drug Manufacturer's Package Insert Recommendations as Evidence of Standard of Care, 82 A.L.R.4th 166 (1990 & 2002 Supp.). In some jurisdictions, the package insert may serve as prima facie evidence of the applicable standard of care. See, e.g., Julien v. Barker, 272 P.2d 718, 724 (Idaho 1954); Fournet v. Roule–Graham, 783 So.2d 439, 442–44 (La.Ct.App.2001); Mulder v. Parke Davis & Co., 181 N.W.2d 882, 887 (Minn.1970); Thompson v. Carter, 518 So.2d 609, 612–13 (Miss.1987); Paul v. Boschenstein, 482 N.Y.S.2d 870, 871 (App.Div.1984). In other jurisdictions, it may provide only some relevant evidence on that score. See, e.g., Salgo v. Leland Stanford Jr. Univ., 317 P.2d 170, 180 (Cal.Ct.App.1957); Mozer v. Kerth, 586 N.E.2d 759, 763–64 (Ill.App.Ct.1992); Bissett v. Renna, 710 A.2d 404, 407 (N.H.1998) (holding that "the PDR, by itself, is insufficient to establish the standard of care required of the defendant"); Ramon v. Farr, 770 P.2d 131, 134–35 (Utah 1989). In still other jurisdictions, the package insert amounts to inadmissible hearsay. See, e.g., Rosario v. New York City Health & Hosps. Corp., 450 N.Y.S.2d 805, 807 (App.Div.1982).

It makes little sense for courts to disregard what may be the most evidence-based of all practice guidelines just because doctors habitually ignore them. See Vicki E. Lawrence, Drug Manufacturers' Recommendations and the Common Knowledge Rule to Establish Medical Malpractice, 63 Neb. L. Rev. 859, 875 (1984) ("[I]t is simply unacceptable to allow the manufacturer's recommendation to be ignored on the rationale that it is customarily disregarded by physicians, in light of the fact that the usage and dosage instructions must be supported by sufficient scientific proof in order to receive FDA approval."). In particular, if phrased as a "contraindication," precautionary information would effectively amount to a direction to the physician never to use the drug in those circumstances. See Richardson v. Miller, 44 S.W.3d 1, 8 n.2, 16–17 (Tenn.Ct.App.2000) (holding that the trial judge had erred in excluding label that had specifically warned against the off-label use selected by the physician); see also James R. Bird, Comment, Package Inserts for Prescription Drugs as Evidence in Medical Malpractice Suits, 44 U. Chi. L. Rev. 398, 436–37 (1977) (arguing that courts should differentiate between categories of information in the package insert and give contraindications the greatest weight); cf. Young v. Cerniak, 467 N.E.2d 1045, 1057–58 (Ill.App.Ct.1984) ("[W]e are aware of no case which holds that a drug manufacturer's recommendation regarding dosage, unaccompanied by any warning of adverse consequences if the recommendation is not followed, is proof of the standard of care.").

Morlino v. Medical Center of Ocean County

706 A.2d 721 (N.J.1998).

■ POLLACK, JUSTICE:

* * * On March 5, 1990, four weeks before she was due to deliver her baby, [Angela] Morlino visited the emergency room of the Medical Center. She was diagnosed with "acute pharyngitis," commonly known as a sore throat, and was given a prescription for 500 milligrams of amoxicillin, an antibiotic in the penicillin family. Morlino returned to the emergency room of the Medical Center on March 20. She again sought treatment for a sore throat. Dr. Dugenio took her history, examined her, and diagnosed her condition as acute pharyngitis. He also ordered a variety of tests. * * * Two days later, the results of Morlino's throat culture confirmed the presence of *Hemophilus influenza* bacteria. The culture also revealed that Morlino's infection was resistant to numerous antibiotics such as ampicillin, cephalosporin, erythromycin, clindamycin, nafcillin, and penicillin.

Even before receiving the throat culture results, Dr. Dugenio considered prescribing Cipro. He consulted the PDR, a compilation of information about prescription drugs that is published annually and distributed to the medical professional free of charge. A typical entry includes the trade and chemical names of the drug, a description of the drug, indications and contraindications for its use, warnings, adverse reactions, administrations and dosage, and information on managing and adjusting the dosage of the drug. Generally, the information in a package insert, which accompanies prescription drugs, is the same as that in the PDR.

The PDR contains the following warning for Cipro:

CIPROFLOXACIN SHOULD NOT BE USED IN CHILDREN OR PREGNANT WOMEN. The oral administration of ciprofloxacin caused lameness in immature dogs. Histopathological examination of the weight-bearing joints of these dogs revealed permanent lesions of the cartilage.

Additionally, the PDR characterizes drugs for pregnant women based on the degree to which the drug manufacturer has ruled out a risk to the fetus. Cipro was in "Use–In–Pregnancy Category C," which means:

Risk cannot be ruled out. Human studies are lacking, and animal studies are either positive for fetal risk, or lacking as well. However, potential benefits may justify the potential risk.

From the PDR warnings, Dr. Dugenio understood that he should prescribe Cipro for a pregnant patient only if the potential benefit to the patient outweighed the risk to her and the fetus. In weighing the risks and benefits, Dr. Dugenio was concerned that the *Hemophilus influenzae* bacteria, if untreated, could lead to more serious illnesses, such as infectious mononucleosis, pneumonia, and meningitis. These illnesses could pose serious risks to Morlino and her fetus. The PDR, he noted, did not state that the use of Cipro in pregnant women is contraindicated. * * *

In affirming, the Appellate Division held that the trial court did not err by refusing to read verbatim that part of the two PDR warnings stating that Cipro should not be used by pregnant women and that the "risk cannot be ruled out." The Appellate Division identified three approaches concerning the use of the manufacturer's insert and the parallel PDR warning to establish a medical standard of care. The first approach, adopted by this court in *Sanzari v. Rosenfeld*, 167 A.2d 625 (1961), "is that product packaging inserts do not establish a standard of care but are admissible to show what the physician knew or should have known about the drug." According to the Appellate Division, out-of-state cases support two other approaches. "The second approach is to allow product inserts (and the PDR) into evidence to show the standard of care, provided expert testimony is also presented to explain the standard of care to the jury." The third approach "is that the product insert, standing alone without expert testimony, is evidence of negligence by the physician who fails to adhere to its rules." Rejecting the first and third approaches, the Appellate Division adopted the rule that package inserts and their parallel PDR references may be considered by the jury along with expert testimony to determine the appropriate standard of care. * * *

[T]he jury viewed "blow-ups" of the PDR's relevant sections and heard extensive expert testimony concerning the PDR. Morlino's experts testified about the PDR warnings and their opinion concerning the prescription of Cipro. The experts relied, in part, on the PDR to establish the standard of care and to describe the risk/benefit analysis required for Category C drugs. Also, Dr. Dugenio admitted that he had learned from the PDR not only of the risks of giving Cipro to a pregnant woman, but also of the necessity for a risk/benefit analysis. * * *

[W]e agree with the Appellate Division that the jury was free to consider the PDR warnings on questions of both Dr. Dugenio's knowledge and the standard of care applicable to his conduct. We further hold that the jury may consider package inserts and parallel PDR references, when they are supported by expert testimony, to determine the appropriate standard of care in a medical malpractice case. * * * Physicians frequently rely on the PDR when making decisions concerning the administration and dosage of drugs. Often, the drug manufacturer, which has developed and tested the drug, may be in a better position than the physician to determine the appropriate usage and dosage of drugs.

Nevertheless, drug manufacturers do not design package inserts and PDR entries to establish a standard of medical care. Manufacturers write drug package inserts and PDR warnings for many reasons including compliance with FDA requirements, advertisement, the provision of useful information to physicians, and an attempt to limit the manufacturer's liability. After a drug has been on the market for a sufficient period of time, moreover, physicians may rely more on their own experience and the professional publications of others than on a drug manufacturer's advertisements, inserts, or PDR entries.

Those considerations highlight the reasons expert testimony must accompany the introduction of PDR warnings to establish the applicable standard of care in prescribing a drug. Additionally, expert testimony often is needed to explain the information contained in package inserts or the PDR. Drug manufacturers write explanations and warnings for doctors, not the general public. Comprehension of the terms and their significance may depend on medical expertise. Accordingly, we hold that package inserts and PDR references alone do not establish the standard of care. It follows that a physician's failure to adhere to PDR warnings does not by itself constitute negligence. Reliance on the PDR alone to establish negligence would both obviate expert testimony on an issue where it is needed and could mislead the jury about the appropriate standard of care. * * * Allowing the admission of PDR warnings without accompanying expert testimony could transform drug manufacturers into judges of acceptable medical care. The effect would be to force doctors to follow the PDR's recommendations or run the risk of liability for malpractice.

Whether to prescribe a drug and, if so, what drug to prescribe are issues that demand careful consideration. The decision to prescribe a particular drug ultimately is a matter of judgment for the physician. In addition to considering the individual patient, the physician may consider all available information concerning a drug. The information may include the manufacturer's inserts and PDR warnings, as well as medical journals, advice from colleagues, and the physician's own experience. To confine the treatment choices to those expressly permitted in the PDR would be too restrictive. Such an approach also would be inconsistent with the FDA's position that physicians are not bound by PDR recommendations. * * *

B. LIABILITY OF SUPPLIERS AND DISPENSERS

1. PHARMACISTS

Murphy v. E.R. Squibb & Sons, Inc.

710 P.2d 247 (Cal.1985).

■ MOSK, JUSTICE:

* * * Plaintiff filed an action for personal injuries allegedly resulting from DES taken by her mother in 1951 and 1952 during pregnancy for the purpose of reducing the risk of miscarriage. The complaint sought damages on the theory of strict liability, alleging that the drug was defectively designed, with the result that plaintiff developed clear cell adenocarcinoma at the age of 23. As defendants, plaintiff joined Exclusive Prescription Pharmacy Corporation where plaintiff's mother purchased the DES, and E.R. Squibb & Sons, Inc. * * *

[P]harmacists perform a broad range of tasks, from selling razor blades and dental floss to treating patients in a health care facility by ordering laboratory tests and administering drugs by injection and acting as consultants regarding medication prescribed for patients at such facilities. The discussion which follows relates only to the duties in a community pharmacy of a pharmacist who fills prescriptions for drugs on the order of a physician or other medical care provider, and who has used due care in compounding and labeling the drug.

There are no cases in California deciding whether a retail pharmacy is strictly liable for injuries caused by an inherent defect in a drug. In Florida, North Carolina, and New York a pharmacy is held not to be strictly liable for defects in a prescription drug. These cases rely on section 402A of the *Restatement Second of Torts*, which declares that unavoidably unsafe products such as drugs are not defective if they are accompanied by an appropriate warning, and that a seller is only required to warn of defects of which he knew or should have known. * * *

As might be anticipated, the parties differ sharply as to whether the main function of a pharmacist is to provide a service or to sell a product. Plaintiff asserts that the duties of a pharmacist in filling a prescription do not differ from those of any other retailer: he reads the prescription, fills the container with the proper type and dosage of the medication required, types up a label, attaches it to the container, and exchanges the medication for payment by the customer. In essence, argues plaintiff, a pharmacist is the functional equivalent of "an experienced clerk at a hardware store."

Exclusive paints a dramatically different picture of the role of the pharmacist, characterizing him as a professional who provides an important health service. They point out that with a few exceptions specified by statute, only a physician or a licensed pharmacist may compound or dispense prescription drugs. * * * A pharmacist is required not only to assure that the drug prescribed is properly selected, measured and labeled but * * * he must be alert to errors in prescriptions written by doctors, and contact the doctor in case of doubts or questions regarding the drug prescribed. In addition, the pharmacist may discuss with the patient the proper use of the drug and the potential side effects, and must be aware of the possibility of harmful interaction between various medications which the pharmacist knows the patient is using. * * *

It seems clear to us that the pharmacist is engaged in a hybrid enterprise, combining the performance of services and the sale of prescription drugs. It is pure hyperbole to suggest, as does plaintiff, that the role of the pharmacist is similar to that of a clerk in an ordinary retail store. * * * A pharmacist must not only use skill and care in accurately filling and labeling a prescribed drug, but he must be aware of problems regarding the medication, and on occasion he provides doctors as well as patients with advice regarding such problems. In counseling patients, he imparts the same kind of information as would a medical doctor about the effects of the drugs prescribed. A key factor is that the pharmacist who fills a prescription is in a different position from the ordinary retailer because he cannot offer a prescription for sale except by order of the doctor. In this respect, he is providing a service to the doctor and acting as an extension of the doctor in the same sense as a technician who takes an X-ray or analyzes a blood sample on a doctor's order.

Nevertheless, it cannot be disputed that a sale in fact occurs. There is an obvious distinction between the doctor who provides a patient with a prescription for a defective drug, a dentist who uses a faulty drill, or a hospital that uses a defective needle during surgery, and a pharmacist who fills a prescription. The pharmacist is in the business of selling prescription drugs, and his role begins and ends with the sale. His services are rendered only in connection with the sale, and a patient who goes to a pharmacy to have a prescription filled generally is seeking to purchase the drug rather than to obtain the advice of the pharmacist. By contrast, the doctor, dentist and hospital in the cases cited above are not in the business of selling the drug or device; they use the product in the course of treatment as one element in their efforts to effect a cure, and furnishing the services does not depend on sale of a product.

Ordinarily, in deciding whether the sale or service aspect of an enterprise predominates, we would confine our consideration to the type of factors discussed above. In the case of a pharmacy, however, we must broaden our inquiry. The Legislature has provided that the practice of pharmacy is not only a profession, but also a "dynamic patient-oriented health service that applies a scientific body of knowledge to improve and promote patient health by means of appropriate drug use and drug related therapy." * * *

If pharmacies were held strictly liable for the drugs they dispense, some of them, to avoid liability, might restrict availability by refusing to dispense drugs which pose even a potentially remote risk of harm, although such medications may be essential to the health or even the survival of patients. Furthermore, in order to assure that a pharmacy receives the maximum protection in the event of suit for defects in a drug, the pharmacist may select the more expensive product made by an established manufacturer when he has a choice of several brands of the same drug. As [one] amicus brief warns, "Why choose a new company's inexpensive product, which has received excellent reviews in the literature for its quality, over the more expensive product of an established multinational corporation which will certainly have assets available for purpose of indemnification 10, 20, or 30 years down the line?" * * *

Finally, plaintiff contends that even if the pharmacist is personally exempt from strict liability because he provides a service, the "merchandising organization which employs him ... should not be so exempted." Plaintiff cites no authority in support of this claim, and we perceive no basis in law or rationale for accepting it. The fact that a pharmacy may be owned by an enterprise which also deals in ordinary merchandise does not justify the conclusion that it should be held strictly liable when it performs a service. Moreover, the policy justifying the grant of immunity from strict liability to the practice of pharmacy would only be effectuated if the pharmacy operation itself is exempted. For the reasons stated above, we conclude that the trial court was correct in granting judgment on the pleadings to Exclusive.

■ BIRD, CHIEF JUSTICE (dissenting):

* * * The issue is whether retail druggists and pharmacies, which sell prescription drugs to consumers, are engaged primarily in selling a product or in performing a service. The simple answer is that in the marketing of prescription drugs by retail druggists, as in the marketing of automobiles and other consumer products, the sale aspect predominates over any incidental service provided to the consumer. * * * [S]trict liability applies if the purchase of a product is the "primary objective" or "essence" of the transaction. Strict liability is inapplicable only where the transaction is limited to the provision of a service and does not involve the sale of a product or where the service aspect predominates and any sale included in the transaction is incidental to the provision of the service. * * *

Only 22 percent of patients who purchase prescription drugs are counseled by the retail druggist, who spends an average of only one and one-half hours a day performing this service. Thus, in the vast majority of prescription drug sales transactions, the customer receives only a product and no services from the retail druggist. The predominance of the sale is also reflected by the fixed prices the retail druggist charges for prescription drugs, based on a markup from wholesale cost rather than an hourly fee calculation. The majority dismiss as "pure hyberbole" plaintiff's suggestion that the retail druggist's role is similar to that of a clerk in an "ordinary" retail store. Yet, the average hardware store clerk probably devotes as much or more time to counseling customers on the applications and proper use of the items offered for sale by the store. I doubt that the majority would have any difficulty concluding that the essence of the transaction between the hardware clerk and the customer is a sale rather than a service.

The majority, diverging from the inquiry into the nature of the transaction, contend that the educational and professional standards which must be met to obtain a pharmacist's license somehow dictate the conclusion that the retail druggist and the pharmacy are primarily engaged in the provision of a service. An almost mystical significance is attributed to the retail druggist's admitted expertise and professional status. * * * Nowhere do they explain how the retail druggist's professional status converts the business of selling prescription drugs, in which the provision of services plays a subordinate role, into a business in which the service aspect predominates.

The majority also draw contradictory conclusions from the high standards of knowledge and professional responsibility to which retail druggists are held. On the one hand, they stress the retail druggist's extensive knowledge of the properties, proper dosages, contraindications and side-effects of prescription drugs as support for the view that the retail druggist is primarily a seller of services rather than products. Yet, if anything, the retail druggist's expertise supports the imposition of strict liability. Armed with extensive knowledge of the products he or she sells, the retail druggist may be better equipped than other retailers to identify defective products. This capacity was a prime consideration supporting the application of strict liability to retailers. "[The] retailer himself may play a substantial part in insuring that the product is safe or may be in a position to exert pressure on the manufacturer to that end; the retailer's strict liability thus serves as an added incentive to safety."

On the other hand, the majority stress the statutory and professional restrictions that limit the retail druggist's discretion. Since a retail druggist may not sell a prescription drug except on a doctor's order and is prohibited from substituting a different drug (other than a generic equivalent), they suggest that it would be unfair to treat retail druggists like other retailers who are not subject to such restraints. This reasoning misses the point. The retailer's capacity to select the product sold has never been held to be a prerequisite to the imposition of strict liability. On the contrary, the doctrine has been held to apply to a wholesale-retail tire distributor who supplied whatever tires the manufacturer specified. This rule is consistent with the well-established principle that a retailer is strictly liable even though not equipped to test the product sold. It is also consistent with the focus of the strict liability doctrine on the product rather than on the conduct of the defendant. * * *

Morgan v. Wal–Mart Stores, Inc.

30 S.W.3d 455 (Tex.Ct.App.2000).

■ PATTERSON, JUSTICE:

The issue presented is whether pharmacists have a duty under Texas law to warn of potentially adverse reactions to prescription drugs. Jacquelyn Morgan and Charles Pettus sued Wal–Mart Stores, Inc. individually and as heirs to the estate of their minor child, Cameron Pettus. Plaintiffs alleged that Cameron's death in August 1993 was caused by an adverse reaction to Desipramine, a prescription drug sold to Morgan for Cameron's use by a Wal–Mart pharmacist. A jury found that Wal–Mart's negligent failure to warn of the known dangers of Desipramine was a proximate cause of Cameron's death, and the trial court assessed actual damages of $1,012,000, together with pre-and post-judgment interest. We reverse the judgment of the trial court and render a take-nothing judgment in favor of Wal–Mart. * * *

Cameron began taking Desipramine [for attention deficit hyperactivity disorder] in April 1991 at age twelve * * * * The parties agree that no Wal–Mart pharmacist orally counseled Morgan about Desipramine's possible side effects; they also agree that Wal–Mart did not give Morgan the drug manufacturer's package insert, which contains substantial technical information about Desipramine, including warnings of potential adverse reactions. Pursuant to valid prescriptions from Dr. Schroeder, Morgan purchased Desipramine three more times at Wal–Mart, the last time in February 1993. Morgan testified that at no time did a Wal–Mart pharmacist advise her of anything with respect to the drug.

Irene Franklin, a pharmacist at the Wal–Mart where Morgan purchased Desipramine, testified that during a typical ten-hour shift in 1992 and 1993, she filled about 150 prescriptions. Although Franklin could not recall meeting Morgan, Franklin identified a Wal–Mart business record indicating that on October 24, 1992, she filled a prescription for 25 milligrams of Desipramine for Cameron Pettus. Franklin testified that Wal–Mart computers generate two documents each time a prescription is filled. The first document is a prescription label; the second document contains the patient's receipt and information from a national database about the drug, such as its generic name, common uses, and possible side effects. Franklin testified that it is common practice at Wal–Mart to staple the sheet containing the receipt and drug information to the outside of the bag in which the drug is placed. Morgan specifically denied receiving from Wal–Mart any printed warnings about Desipramine, although she acknowledged that she disposed of all paperwork related to the drug after Cameron's death. * * *

[P]laintiffs alleged Wal–Mart was negligent in the sale of Desipramine "by failing to properly warn intended users of the hazards and harms associated with the use of the product." Plaintiffs contended that Wal–Mart's negligence was the proximate cause of Cameron's health problems and death, as well as their own mental anguish, loss of consortium, and loss of family relationship. * * * On appeal, Wal–Mart argues that as a matter of law its pharmacists had no duty to warn of the potential dangers of Desipramine because that duty rested with the prescribing physician. * * *

While it is apparent then that Wal–Mart owed the plaintiffs a duty to dispense Desipramine in accordance with Dr. Schroeder's prescription, no Texas court has yet considered whether a pharmacist is also obligated to warn customers of potential hazards or side effects of prescribed drugs. A majority of courts considering this question have held that a pharmacist has no such duty when the prescription is proper on its face and neither the physician nor the manufacturer has required that the pharmacist give the customer any warning. The reluctance of courts to hold pharmacists liable for injuries caused by drugs accurately dispensed according to the terms of a valid prescription can be attributed to the application of the "learned intermediary" doctrine, which typically acts as an exception to a manufacturer's duty to warn customers in products liability cases. According to this doctrine, the manufacturer of a prescription drug has a duty to adequately warn the prescribing physician of the drug's dangers. The physician, relying on his medical training, experience, and knowledge of the individual patient, then chooses the type and quantity of drug to be prescribed. The physician assumes the duty to warn the patient of dangers associated with a particular prescribed drug.

A leading case in which the learned intermediary doctrine was applied to a negligence action against a pharmacy is *McKee v. American Home Products Corp.*, 782 P.2d 1045 (Wash.1989). In *McKee*, the plaintiff received prescriptions from her doctor for an appetite suppressant known as Plegine. The Physician's Desk Reference entry for Plegine cautions that it is a potentially addictive amphetamine; therefore, its use should be discontinued within a few weeks to avoid addiction. Notwithstanding, McKee's doctor authorized refills of the drug for ten years, and two pharmacists filled the prescriptions without warning McKee of the possible side effects of extended use. McKee sued the drug manufacturer, the prescribing physician, and the pharmacists for damages sustained as a result of her addiction to Plegine. McKee argued that her pharmacists were negligent in selling her Plegine without warning of its adverse effects and for failing to provide her the drug manufacturer's package insert.

In a 5–4 decision, the Washington Supreme Court concluded that the learned intermediary doctrine, normally applied to the relationship among physician, patient, and manufacturer, applied with equal force to the relationship among physician, patient, and pharmacist. The court reasoned that in both circumstances, the physician was in the best position to "relate the propensities of the drug to the physical idiosyncrasies of the patient." The court therefore held that McKee's pharmacists did not have a duty to warn her of the dangerous propensities of Plegine, nor were they legally obligated to give her the drug manufacturer's package insert containing such warnings. This holding is consistent with the decisions of many other states that have addressed the issue of whether to impose on pharmacists a duty to warn of adverse side effects. * * *

[I]n *Pysz v. Henry's Drug Store*, 457 So.2d 561 (Fla.Ct.App.1984), a pharmacist had filled the plaintiff's prescription for Quaaludes for more than nine years. Pysz alleged that the pharmacist's failure to warn him of the addictive propensities of Quaaludes constituted negligence. The Florida appeals court stated that although a pharmacist might in some instances possess greater knowledge than a physician of the adverse effects of drugs, "it is the physician who has the duty to know the drug that he is prescribing and to properly monitor the patient." The court concluded that the pharmacist, who had properly filled a lawful prescription, had no duty to warn the plaintiff of adverse reactions and affirmed the trial court's dismissal of Pysz's complaint. * * *

In *Stebbins v. Concord Wrigley Drugs, Inc.*, 416 N.W.2d 381 (Mich.Ct. App.1987), Bonnie Stebbins was seriously injured when a car driven by a man taking the antidepressant Tofranil struck her car. Stebbins settled with the other driver and sued his prescribing physician and pharmacist for negligence, alleging that they had failed to warn the patient of Tofranil's side effects, which include drowsiness. The Michigan appeals court began its consideration of the pharmacist's liability by citing the general rule that pharmacists owe patients a high standard of care in filling prescriptions and may be held liable for negligently dispensing a drug other than that prescribed. Relying on *Pysz*, the court concluded that "a pharmacist has no duty to warn the patient of possible side effects of a prescribed medication where the medication is proper on its face and neither the physician nor the manufacturer has required that any warning be given to the patient by the pharmacist." The court emphasized that its decision did not apply to a situation in which a pharmacist knows of a particular patient's unique

medical problems or where a pharmacist fills incompatible prescriptions.
* * *

In *Jones v. Irvin*, 602 F.Supp. 399 (S.D.Ill.1985), the plaintiff alleged she had suffered injuries as a result of her consumption of an excessive amount of Placidyl and other prescribed drugs. The Illinois district court concluded that K–Mart had no duty to notify the customer that she was being overmedicated because the duty to warn of a prescription drug's adverse effects falls squarely on the prescribing physician. Furthermore, the court placed upon the patient the duty to notify the physician of other drugs the patient is taking and upon the drug manufacturer the duty to notify the physician of any adverse effects in administering the drug. The court concluded that "placing these duties to warn on the pharmacist would only serve to compel the pharmacist to second guess every prescription a doctor orders in an attempt to escape liability." As in *Pysz* and *Stebbins*, the district court stressed the narrow application of its holding, stating that it applied only to prescription drugs and that pharmacists still owed customers the highest degree of prudence in filling a prescription.
* * *

While a majority of courts that have considered whether a pharmacist has a duty to warn a patient of the adverse side effects of prescription medication has rejected the imposition of such a duty, unusual factual situations have arisen in which courts have felt compelled to impose a duty beyond mechanically dispensing drugs pursuant to a physician's directions. For example, in *Hand v. Krakowski*, 453 N.Y.S.2d 121 (App.Div.1982), a doctor prescribed certain psychotropic drugs to an alcoholic patient. The drugs were contraindicated with the use of alcohol. Although its records identified the patient as an alcoholic, the pharmacy dispensed the drugs to her over a period of six years without warning her of the danger. The patient died at age fifty-five of pancreatitis associated with a severe degree of cirrhosis. The New York appellate court reversed the summary judgment granted in favor of the defendant pharmacy. The court held that because the dispensing pharmacists knew that the decedent was an alcoholic and knew, or should have known, that the prescribed drugs were contraindicated with alcohol, a fact question existed regarding whether they had a duty to warn the patient of the danger involved. * * *

In sum, courts holding that pharmacists owe their customers a duty beyond accurately filing prescriptions do so based on the presence of additional factors, such as known contraindications, that would alert a reasonably prudent pharmacist to a potential problem. We do not dispute that a pharmacist may be held liable for negligently filling a prescription in such situations, but we cannot discern from the relevant case law a trend towards imposing a more general duty to warn. Nor do we conclude that existing Texas statutory law imposes such a duty. The plaintiffs contend that under the Texas Pharmacy Act and the administrative rules adopted pursuant to the Act, pharmacists have a general duty to warn customers of potential adverse side effects. Plaintiffs argue that the duty arises by implication from the mention of "patient counseling" in the Act's definition of "practice of pharmacy," as well as from several references to pharmacists counseling or communicating with patients in the Administrative Code. Plaintiffs emphasize the Code's repeated references to pharmacists communicating to patients information regarding "common severe side effects or adverse effects or interactions."

While these administrative rules demonstrate that pharmacists in Texas are trusted professionals with varied and important responsibilities, they cannot be reasonably read to impose a legal duty to warn patients of the adverse effects of prescription drugs. The imposition of a generalized duty to warn would unnecessarily interfere with the relationship between physician and patient by compelling pharmacists seeking to escape liability to question the propriety of every prescription they fill. Furthermore, a patient faced with an overwhelming number of warnings from his or her pharmacist may decide not to take a medication prescribed by a physician, who has greater access to and knowledge of the patient's complete medical history and current condition than the pharmacist. Instead of imposing such an onerous and counterproductive duty, the administrative rules reinforce the notion that, although pharmacists act as final auditors of the technical accuracy of a prescription and its appropriateness with respect to a patient's known condition and medication record, they do not possess the extensive knowledge of a physician with respect to a patient's complete medical history and are thus not legally obligated to warn a patient of adverse drug reactions.

Therefore, we hold that any liability of Wal–Mart's for negligently filling Cameron's prescription for Desipramine must be based on neglect in the face of information on which a reasonably prudent pharmacist would have acted. Having reviewed the entire record, we find no basis to conclude that the Wal–Mart pharmacists breached their duty of care when they filled Cameron's prescription for Desipramine. Dr. Schroeder prescribed Desipramine to treat Cameron's ADHD. * * * [A]lthough Cameron experienced severe discomfort while taking Desipramine, at no time did even one of the many doctors that examined him warn Cameron, Morgan, or Pettus of the potential adverse side effects of Desipramine or contact the pharmacists to instruct them to give such a warning. Indeed, the record reveals that the doctors did not attribute Cameron's ailments to Desipramine at all.

Furthermore, it is undisputed that Wal–Mart sold Desipramine to Morgan according to the terms of Dr. Schroeder's prescription. Plaintiffs do not allege that Wal–Mart possessed any special knowledge of Cameron's medical history that would impose upon it an additional duty to warn him, Morgan, or Pettus of the particular dangers of Desipramine. Nor do the plaintiffs contend that Wal–Mart was or should have been aware of any contraindications. * * *

We acknowledge that the pharmacist's role has changed in the last few decades from a mere dispenser of medication to a trusted professional who plays a vital role in patient treatment. We understand that modern pharmacies employ advanced computer systems that can analyze drug interactions in seconds, thus preventing the sale of potentially fatal drugs to consumers, and we encourage the use of such systems. Nonetheless, in light of the learned intermediary doctrine, which we find applicable to the relationship among physician, patient, and pharmacist, we hold that pharmacists have no generalized duty to warn patients of potential adverse reactions to prescription drugs absent some special circumstances not present here. We do not imply that pharmacists may not warn patients of potential adverse reactions or dangerous side effects; we merely hold that pharmacists are not legally obligated to do so. * * *

NOTES AND QUESTIONS

1. *Exemption from strict liability.* Does the fact that many pharmacies today employ "techs" to dispense prescription drugs alter your view of the proper characterization of their role? How about pharmacy chains that now offer 24 hour drive through service? And what if a pharmacist engages in compounding? The majority in *Murphy* refers to the exception for "unavoidably unsafe" products under *Rest. (2d)* § 402A comment k, which we discussed in Chapter 5(A). Does this in fact ever suggest freeing pharmacists of all strict products liability claims? Recall that the new *Restatement* exempts retailers and end users of prescription drugs and medical devices from strict products liability except in cases of manufacturing defects. See Rest. (3d) § 6(e); see also Coyle v. Richardson–Merrell, Inc., 584 A.2d 1383 (Pa.1991) (declining to apply strict liability to a pharmacist for failure to warn a patient of the possible risks of taking Bendectin during pregnancy). See generally David J. Marchitelli, Annotation, Liability of Pharmacist Who Accurately Fills Prescription for Harm Resulting to User, 44 A.L.R.5th 393 (1996 & 2002 Supp.). In *Heredia v. Johnson*, 827 F.Supp. 1522 (D.Nev. 1993), however, the court refused to grant the pharmacy's motion for summary judgment on a strict liability claim:

> This court cannot find that the Nevada Supreme Court would hold that the strict liability doctrine does not apply to defendant simply because the subject transaction was a sale by defendant of a prescription drug. In addition, the summary judgment evidence before the court indicates that the transaction involved a prescription drug that is packaged in a box and includes written information containing an express warning pertinent to this case ("This product should be used with care in cases of perforated eardrum"). The packaging and warning literature are provided by Burroughs Wellcome Company. Questions of fact remain as to whether such a warning actually was distributed with the drug at issue here, whether the warning was ever provided to Payless, or whether Defendant Payless furnished plaintiff with a product different from that which Burroughs Wellcome Company sold to the defendant.

Id. at 1524. In essence the court suggested that a pharmacist's failure to transmit a manufacturer's warning to a consumer about a drug's risks may, under certain circumstances, justify imposing strict products liability.

2. *Categories of pharmacist negligence.* Courts have found pharmacists liable for negligence in a variety of circumstances. These cases tend to fall into one of several categories, especially processing errors, failure to warn the customer of side effects associated with the drug, and failure to monitor drug use. See David B. Brushwood, Pharmacy Malpractice Law and Regulations 104, 233–34, 291–93 (2d ed. 1998).

a. *Processing errors.* When a pharmacist dispenses the wrong drug, or the wrong dosage amount or dosage form, or with the wrong label, he or she may be liable in negligence if the error harms the patient. In these circumstances, no matter how well-trained and careful a pharmacist may be, the existence of the processing error itself is usually sufficient to prove negligence. See, e.g., Lou v. Smith, 685 S.W.2d 809 (Ark.1985) (pharmacist who altered prescription to correct an assumed prescribing error is liable for compensatory and punitive damages after a child suffered a severe reaction to the drug); Forbes v. Walgreen Co., 566 N.E.2d 90, 91 (Ind.Ct. App.1991) (pharmacist liable for dispensing incorrect medication); Attwood v. Albertson's Food Ctrs., Inc., 966 P.2d 351 (Wash.Ct.App.1998) (where pharmacist dispensed incorrect dosage of drug to customer who died, causation is a question of fact for the jury); see also Baas v. Hoye, 766 F.2d 1190 (8th Cir.1985) (holding a pharmacy liable under the Consumer Product Safety Act for failing to dispense prescription drug in a childproof container); Ullman v. Grant, 450 N.Y.S.2d 955 (Sup.Ct.1982). See generally Timothy E. Travers, Annotation, Druggist's Civil Liability for Injuries Sustained as a Result of Negligence in Incorrectly Filling Drug Prescriptions, 3 A.L.R.4th 270 (1981 & 2002 Supp.). Although it resembles strict liability for a manufacturing defect, a presumption of negligence in the case of processing errors differs from *Rest. (3d)* § 6(e)(1) where retailers face strict liability for dispensing a product with a manufacturing defect that they could not have detected.

b. *Failures to warn.* The duty of pharmacists to warn patients about the dangers of prescription drugs continues to evolve and expand. Rather than simply filling prescriptions as written by the physician, the case law suggests that, under some circumstances, the pharmacist has a duty to question the completeness or accuracy of the prescription and to warn the patient of possible harms arising from the use of the prescribed medication. See, e.g., Lasley v. Shrake's Country Club Pharmacy, Inc., 880 P.2d 1129 (Ariz.Ct.App.1994) (mail order pharmacy may have a duty to warn long time customer of danger of addiction from a prescription drug); Ingram v. Hook's Drugs, Inc., 476 N.E.2d 881 (Ind.Ct.App.1985) (pharmacist required to convey to patient warnings included in the prescription); Happel v. Wal–Mart Stores, Inc., 737 N.E.2d 650 (Ill.App.Ct.2000) (pharmacy had duty to warn patient of risks of prescription drug known to be contraindicated for that patient's use); Hand v. Krakowski, 453 N.Y.S.2d 121 (App.Div.1982) (reversing summary judgment for defendant pharmacy on the grounds that the court could find that a pharmacist has a duty to warn a customer of the dangerous interaction between the prescribed drug and alcohol); Riff v. Morgan Pharmacy, 508 A.2d 1247 (Pa.Super.Ct.1986) (pharmacist has a duty to warn patient or physician when incomplete prescription information creates a risk of substantial harm to the patient); Dooley v. Everett, 805 S.W.2d 380 (Tenn.Ct.App.1990) (pharmacy liable for failure to warn customer of drug interaction). See generally Brian L. Porto, Annotation, Civil Liability of Pharmacists or Druggists for Failure to Warn of Potential Drug Interactions in Use of Prescription Drug, 79 A.L.R.5th 409 (2001).

Not all courts have, however, embraced this form of expanded pharmacist liability. See, e.g., Fakhouri v. Taylor, 618 N.E.2d 518 (Ill.App.Ct.1993) (pharmacist has no duty to warn customer where prescribed drug dose exceeds recommended dose in drug package insert); Eldridge v. Eli Lilly & Co., 485 N.E.2d 551 (Ill.App.Ct.1985) (pharmacist has no duty to warn a customer of dangers of drug overdose); Nichols v. Central Merchandise, Inc., 817 P.2d 1131 (Kan.Ct.App.1991) (pharmacy has no duty to warn of possible birth defects associated with a prescription drug); cf. Huggins v. Longs Drug Stores, 862 P.2d 148 (Cal.1993) (rejecting emotional distress claim by parents of child given an excessive dose because of a labeling error by the pharmacist). Should physicians always be the ultimate arbiters of the appropriateness of prescription drug therapy for a particular patient? Under what circumstances, if any, should the pharmacist have an obligation to question the physician's prescribing decision? Should the learned intermediary rule operate to relieve pharmacists from a duty to warn patients in the same way (and for the same reasons) that it insulates manufacturers?

c. *Failures to monitor drug therapy.* Under the right facts, courts have held that pharmacists may owe a duty to monitor a patient's drug therapy in order to detect problems, including addiction, excessive refills, adverse reactions, therapeutic duplication, drug-disease contraindications, or suicide risk. When Congress passed the Omnibus Budget Reconciliation Act of 1990 (OBRA 90), it imposed a requirement that states participating in the federal Medicaid program create prospective drug utilization review standards for pharmacists. See 42 U.S.C. § 1396r–8. Under the utilization review procedures, pharmacists must evaluate whether the drug prescribed by the physician is appropriate for that patient and also offer to provide counseling. See Michael J. Holleran, The Pharmaceutical Access and Prudent Purchasing Act of 1990: Federal Law Shifts the Duty to Warn from Physician to Pharmacist, 26 Akron L. Rev. 77 (1992); Steven W. Huang, The Omnibus Reconciliation Act of 1990: Redefining Pharmacists' Legal Responsibilities, 24 Am. J.L. & Med. 417 (1998). This codification of the pharmacist's duty to monitor prescription drug therapy coincided with the development of a line of cases exploring the contours and limits of a duty in tort. See, e.g., Hooks SuperX, Inc. v. McLaughlin, 642 N.E.2d 514 (Ind. 1994) (holding that, where a pharmacy customer is having a prescription for a drug refilled at an unreasonably faster rate than the rate prescribed, the pharmacist has a duty to suspend refills pending directions from the prescribing physician); Baker v. Arbor Drugs, 544 N.W.2d 727 (Mich.Ct. App.1996) (where pharmacy advertised that its computer monitoring system would warn of therapeutic duplication and drug interactions, pharmacy had duty to monitor prescriptions as advertised); Ferguson v. Williams, 374 S.E.2d 438 (N.C.Ct.App.1988) (although pharmacist has no duty to advise a customer about a drug, if pharmacist has specific knowledge about the customer's special sensitivities and undertakes to advise the customer, pharmacist has duty to provide the customer with accurate advice); cf. Pappas v. Clark, 494 N.W.2d 245 (Iowa Ct.App.1992) (customer's fraudulent acquisition of prescription drugs from pharmacy barred claim that pharmacist negligently failed to monitor the customer's prescription drug use).

3. *Further commentary.* See Jack E. Karns, Pharmacist Liability Relative to Direct Advertising of Services and the Independent Duty to Warn, 9 Widener J. Pub. L. 1 (1999); Edward Cosmere, Comment, Rx for Liability: Advocating the Elimination of the Pharmacist's No Duty to Warn Rule, 33 John Marshall L. Rev. 425 (2000); Lauren Fleisher, Note, From Pill–Counting to Patient Care: Pharmacists' Standard of Care in Negligence Law, 68 Fordham L. Rev. 165 (1999); Symposium, The Evolving Pharmacy Jurisprudence: Changing the Law for a Changing Profession, 44 Drake L. Rev. 377 (1996).

2. HOSPITALS

Cafazzo v. Central Medical Health Services, Inc.

668 A.2d 521 (Pa.1995).

■ MONTEMURO, JUSTICE:

In this case of first impression, we are presented with the question of whether a hospital and a physician can be held subject to strict liability under the *Restatement (Second) of Torts* § 402A for defects in a product incidental to the provision of medical services.

In 1986, appellant Albert Cafazzo underwent surgery for implantation of a mandibular prosthesis. In 1992, some time after it was discovered that this device was defective, a complaint was filed against appellees, the physician who performed the surgery and the hospital where the operation took place, claiming that "all defendants sell, provide or use certain prosthetic devices," and that they should be held strictly liable as having "provided, sold or otherwise placed in the stream of commerce products manufactured by Vitek, Inc., known as Proplast TMJ Implants." The complaint alleged that the prosthesis was defectively designed, unsafe for its intended use, and lacked any warning necessary in order to ensure safety. * * *

In this instance, the manufacturer is in bankruptcy, and unable to sustain liability. Thus, an alternative, and solvent, payor was sought. All other considerations were subordinated to this objective, hence the unequivocal necessity, in appellants' view, for appellees to be designated as sellers irrespective of the actual facts of this matter. However, to ignore the ancillary nature of the association of product with activity is to posit surgery, or indeed any medical service requiring the use of a physical object, as a marketing device for the incorporated object. This is tantamount to deciding that the surgical skills necessary for the implantation of, e.g., mandibular prostheses, are an adjunct to the sale of the implants. Moreover, under such a theory, no product of which a patient in any medical setting is the ultimate consumer, from CT scanners to cotton balls, could escape the assignment of strict liability. Clearly, the relationship of hospital and/or doctor to patients is not dictated by the distribution of such products, even if there is some surcharge on the price of the product. As the New York Court of Appeals has aptly stated:

> Concepts of purchase and sale cannot be separately attached to the healing materials . . . supplied by the hospital for a price as part of the medical services. That the property or title to certain items of medical material may be transferred, so to speak, from the hospital to the patient during the course of medical treatment does not serve to make such a transaction a sale. "Sale" and "transfer" are not synonymous, and not every transfer of personal property constitutes a sale.

Perlmutter v. Beth David Hosp., 123 N.E.2d 792, 794 (N.Y.1954). The thrust of the inquiry is thus not on whether a separate consideration is charged for the physical material used in the exercise of medical skill, but what service is performed to restore or maintain the patient's health. The determinative question becomes not what is being charged, but what is being done. * * *

[W]hile the implant was incidental to the surgical procedure here, it was a necessary adjunct to the treatment administered, as were the scalpel used to make the incision, and any other material objects involved in performing the operation, all of which fulfill a particular role in provision of medical service, the primary activity. Once the illness became evident, treatment of some kind became a matter of necessity to regain health. When one enters the hospital as a patient he goes there, not to buy medicines or pills, not to purchase bandages or iodine or serum or blood, but to obtain a course of treatment in the hope of being cured of what ails him. * * *

[E]ven assuming that providers of medical services could reasonably be termed sellers, in examining the test relied upon by appellants to "prove" their major premise, the policy reasons for strict liability are not present. * * * First, as to the availability of some entity for redress, medical personnel and hospitals are already subject to liability, albeit only where the quality or quantity of the services they provide may be called into question. It is perfectly reasonable to assume, for example, that a physician or hospital possesses the necessary skill and expertise to select a product for use in medical treatment which is fit for its intended purpose. An error of choice might indeed be attributed to negligence or ignorance. However, no allegation has been made that the selection of the Vitek TMJ was made either carelessly or intentionally despite knowledge of its defects. To assign liability for no reason other than the ability to pay damages is inconsistent with our jurisprudence. Where the liability is sought to be imposed on a party which is not a seller under 402A, such liability would indeed be assigned for no reason at all.

Next comes the matter of whether applying strict liability would provide an incentive to safety. As the Superior Court correctly pointed out, the safety of the product depends on the judgment of those connected to the research, development, manufacture, marketing and sale of the product. Moreover, the safety testing and licensing for use of medical devices is a responsibility specifically undertaken by the federal government. Therefore, imposing liability for a poorly designed or manufactured product on the hospitals and doctors who use them on the assurances of the FDA is highly unlikely to effect changes of this sort. Again, selection of the wrong product becomes a matter of professional negligence for which recovery is available. * * *

The net effect of this cost spreading [under a rule of strict liability] would further endanger the already beleaguered health care system. As a practical matter costs would merely be absorbed by the insurers of physicians and hospitals, whose charges would reflect the increase in policy rates without corresponding improvement to any aspect of the health care system. Rather, research and innovation in medical equipment and treatment would be inhibited. The Supreme Court of Wisconsin in *Hoven v. Kelble*, 256 N.W.2d 379 (Wis.1977), has observed, albeit in a slightly different context, that, on balance, the peculiar characteristics of medical services outweigh any of the reasons which might exist to assign strict liability in the medical setting. These include the tendency to be experimental, which would certainly be adversely affected if 402A were applicable; a dependence on factors beyond the control of the professional; and a lack of certainty or assurance of the desired result. In short, medical services are distinguished by factors which make them significantly different in kind from the retail marketing enterprise at which 402A is directed. * * *

■ CAPPY, JUSTICE (dissenting):

* * * [T]his defendant is in a better position than the consumer to prevent the circulation of defective products. The majority commences its analysis of this point by recognizing that the focus of this inquiry is on whether there is "some ongoing relationship with the manufacturer from which some financial advantage inures to the benefit of the latter and which confers some degree of influence on the [putative seller]." The majority, however, rapidly loses sight of its objective. It deduces that since the defendants here have an extensive list of products at their disposal, * * * then the defendants here should also be held immune from strict liability. * * * Such reasoning would lead to the absurd result that a department store, with an inventory of tens of thousands of items, would be less likely to be held strictly liable than the local, family-run convenience store with its modest inventory. Such a "test" does not advance the goals of strict liability, but rather perverts them. * * *

Parker v. St. Vincent Hospital

919 P.2d 1104 (N.M.Ct.App.1996).

■ HARTZ, JUDGE:

[In this case, another TMJ implant recipient sued the hospital under a theory of strict liability. She also sued the hospital on a negligence claim, arguing that the hospital breached a duty to investigate the safety of the implants before supplying and allowing their use in the hospital. The district court granted summary judgment to the defendants.]

According to the weight of authority, a hospital is not a distributor of medical supplies, even though it may bill separately for the item and charge the patient a markup over the hospital's cost. The courts have generally held that the essence of the hospital's role is the provision of services, regardless of whether a product is involved. We are not convinced by this analysis. To be sure, the chief function of hospitals is to provide a service. But when a product is provided as part of the service, and the service provider bills separately for the product, the rule that has emerged outside of the hospital context is that the provision of the product is a distribution for purposes of strict products liability. To depart from this characterization of such a transaction for the special case of hospitals would, in our view, generate unnecessary confusion. If there are sound policy reasons for not imposing strict products liability on hospitals, those policy reasons should be addressed directly, not obscured by artificial semantic distinctions. * * *

[O]ne could expect that the cost of liability arising from defects in a particular product would be shared by those purchasing any product sold by the distributor. For example, the Hospital's liability expenses arising from defective design of an implant would probably be borne by patients using any medical product for which the Hospital is a distributor. The price of pacemakers may go up because of defective jaw implants. To the extent that the cost of injury caused by a defective product is borne by persons who have no occasion to use the product, the first policy [i.e., cost spreading] is not advanced. * * *

[T]he fact that it is easier to prove that a product is defectively designed than to prove that there was negligence in designing the product has a perverse effect in [the hospital] context because ordinarily there is no possibility that a distributor other than the manufacturer created a design defect. That would surely be the case when the hospital does not alter the product and the product is used for its intended purpose. In that event there could be no negligent design by the hospital. * * *

[Although the rationale that strict liability encourages suppliers to select reputable manufacturers when purchasing products] makes sense for other products, it encounters a powerful contrary public policy with regard to medical products. Improving medical care is a national priority. Improvement encompasses both advances in treatment and greater access to care, which is impeded by high costs. In this light, should hospitals be encouraged to deal only with the preeminent suppliers of medical products who have a track record of "well-designed" products and have the financial resources to pay for any injuries caused by defective products? Such encouragement could, for example, impact heavily on the use of generic drugs. * * * Our perception is that public policy strongly favors medical innovation and the use of less expensive alternative products. Protection to the public comes from the expertise of physicians who select the products and, at least to some extent, from regulation by the Food and Drug Administration (FDA). * * *

[T]o the extent that imposition on hospitals of strict products liability for defective design would cause hospitals to devote more resources to reviewing the designs of products it distributes, that additional effort might be contrary to public policy. If, for example, hospitals were to acquire the expert staff and devote the other resources necessary to evaluate the designs of the medical products used in the hospital, hospitals would incur substantial additional costs that would be passed on to its patients. Yet such measures might well provide little benefit in medical care, and could even cause harm. To make each hospital a mini-FDA could duplicate effort while producing a less reliable result because of the much smaller data base. For example, if a hospital must rely on a small sample of uses of a particular product, random fluctuations may cause the hospital to conclude that a product is unsafe (and should not be used at the hospital) when more extensive, better data establish otherwise. * * *

NOTES AND QUESTIONS

1. *Sales vs. service.* Hospitals nowadays generate itemized bills that charge for every item used by a patient (often by scanning a bar code). They also may enter into exclusive purchasing agreements with particular wholesalers and manufacturers (almost the way an automobile dealership does). Moreover, hospitals have the expertise to make selection choices (and patients presumably depend heavily on those choices), and they may have the clout to influence manufacturers' design choices (at least in the medical device industry, innovation may result as much from physician experience and needs as from manufacturer initiative). Nonetheless, most courts refuse to impose strict products liability against hospitals. See Hoff v. Zimmer, 746 F.Supp. 872 (W.D.Wis.1990) (rejecting strict liability against hospital for failure of hip prosthesis); Hector v. Cedars–Sinai Med. Ctr., 225 Cal.Rptr. 595 (Ct.App.1986) (rejecting strict liability against hospital for defective pacemaker); Royer v. Catholic Med. Ctr., 741 A.2d 74 (N.H.1999) (rejecting strict liability against a hospital where the plaintiff received a defective prosthetic knee implant); Easterly v. HSP of Texas, Inc., 772 S.W.2d 211 (Tex.Ct.App.1989) (rejecting strict liability against a hospital supplying an epidural kit containing defective needle). But see Mulligan v. Truman Med. Ctr., 950 S.W.2d 576 (Mo.Ct.App.1997) (allowing a strict liability action for a defective TMJ implant against a hospital). See generally Linda A. Sharp, Annotation, Liability of Hospital or Medical Practitioner Under Doctrine of Strict Liability in Tort, or Breach of Warranty, for Harm Caused by Drug, Medical Instrument, or Similar Device Used in Treating Patient, 65 A.L.R.5th 357 (2001); Jay M. Zitter, Annotation, Liability of Hospital, Physician, or Other Medical Personnel for Death or Injury from Use of Drugs to Stimulate Labor, 1 A.L.R.5th 243 (1992). Under what circumstances, if any, should a hospital be vicariously liable (itself a form of strict tort liability) for an employee's negligent failure to select the most appropriate drug or medical device to treat a patient? See Fleming v. Baptist Gen. Convention, 742 P.2d 1087 (Okla.1987) (allowing a negligence claim against a hospital and physician for improper administration of an injectable drug subcutaneously rather than intravenously).

2. *A duty to investigate the safety of technology used in the hospital?* In *Parker,* the court separately considered the plaintiff's negligence claim alleging that the hospital owed a duty to investigate the safety of the TMJ implants before allowing the devices to be used at the hospital. Although it remanded the case for consideration of this issue, the court observed that, "[i]f a duty to investigate would require considerable effort and expense by hospitals, resulting in higher costs for medical care, but would add little to patient safety, it would be unwise to impose the duty. Safety would not be enhanced, for example, if the hospital were merely duplicating efforts by the FDA, particularly given that the hospital would have a far smaller data base to work from, which could lead it to draw inaccurate inferences. On the other hand, if, as alleged by an expert witness provided by Plaintiffs, hospitals already have a duty under federal law to conduct the sort of investigation Plaintiffs would require, then there may be little reason not to impose liability on a hospital that injures a patient because of failure to perform that duty with due care." 919 P.2d at 1112. How much control does the hospital exert over an individual physician's selection of a drug or medical device to treat a patient within its walls? What other factors might influence this selection? What kinds of medical products might be cheaply and efficiently inspected by a hospital prior to use (and therefore might justify a negligence action if the inspection failed to detect a problem)?

3. *Negligence claims against hospitals.* See Newmann v. United States, 938 F.2d 1258 (11th Cir.1991) (holding a government hospital liable for failure to monitor drug therapy); Kelley v. Wiggins, 724 S.W.2d 443 (Ark.1987) (finding a clinic negligent in administering drug); Fornoff v. Parke Davis & Co., 434 N.E.2d 793 (Ill.App.Ct.1982); Edinburg Hosp. Auth. v. Trevino, 941 S.W.2d 76 (Tex.1997); Harris County Hosp. Dist. v. Estrada, 872 S.W.2d 759 (Tex.Ct.App.1993) (allowing claim against hospital for patient death due to prescribing error that could have been prevented with proper function of hospital charting system).

PROBLEM #13. *THE MALFUNCTIONING PACEMAKER*

Walter Stewart enters Providence Hospital for heart surgery. Because he has been experiencing periodic arrhythmias and tachycardia (racing heartbeat), his cardiologist, Dr. James Grant, plans to implant a pacemaker to alleviate these problems. The pacemaker is manufactured by a small medical device company called Cardiotronica, that specializes in pacemakers and related devices. As is typical with most pacemaker patients, Mr. Stewart does not need the device to make his heart beat; rather he needs the pacemaker to prevent his heart from beating erratically.

The surgery begins well. Dr. Grant successfully attaches the leads of the pacemaker to the correct portions of the heart muscle. After everything is in place, Dr. Grant runs a test on the pacemaker to check that it is functioning properly. Finally, he uses a device to program the pacemaker to respond in specific ways whenever Mr. Stewart's heart begins an abnormal rhythm. The programming device has been supplied by Cardiotronica free of charge to the hospital in exchange for the hospital's agreement to encourage its staff physicians to select Cardiotronica pacemakers for their patients.

Unfortunately, the programming device malfunctions, causing the pacemaker to send rapid electric pulses to Mr. Stewart's heart. Before Dr. Grant and his team can disconnect the pacemaker, Mr. Stewart experiences cardiac arrest and dies. His wife and children want to sue Providence Hospital, Cardiotronica, and Dr. Grant. What claims can they make and what are their chances for success against each defendant?

Chin v. St. Barnabas Medical Center

734 A.2d 778 (N.J.1999).

■ HANDLER, JUSTICE:

* * * Angelina Chin died at the age of forty-five from a massive air embolism during a diagnostic hysteroscopy at St. Barnabas Medical Center. An hysteroscopy is a procedure used to determine abnormalities in a woman's uterus. The doctor uses an hysteroscope, a wand-like instrument with a lens at one end, to view the walls of a woman's uterus on a television monitor. The physician's view of the uterus is enhanced by stretching the uterine walls with a continuous flow of fluid into the uterus. Typically, this type of medical procedure involves minimal risk. In the case of Ms. Chin, however, gas was pumped into her uterus rather than fluid, causing the gas to be introduced into her coronary arteries and resulting in the air embolism that killed her. The record clearly demonstrates that the embolism was the direct result of an incorrect hook-up of the hysteroscope.

Ms. Chin's treating physician, defendant Dr. Herbert Goldfarb, performed the procedure using an hysteroscope manufactured by defendant C.R. Bard, Inc. This type of hysteroscope, called the Hystero–Flo Pump, uses a pump driven by compressed nitrogen to create a vacuum that forces fluid to be drawn into a tube. The fluid passes through the tube, into the hysteroscope unit and finally into the patient's uterus. In order to perform this function, the Bard Hystero–Flo Pump has several tubes. An "irrigation tube" draws fluid into the woman's uterus and a "suction tube" draws waste fluid out of the uterus. Both are connected to the pump. A third tube connects the nitrogen source to the pump. Lastly, an "exhaust hose" carries the by-product of the nitrogen that drives the pump; it is attached to the gas line coming off the pump. When the exhaust hose arrives from the manufacturer, it is attached by three wire clips to indicate that it should remain away from the operating field and remain non-sterile.

In addition to Dr. Goldfarb, three nurses were in the operating room during this procedure. Defendants Nurse Teresa Leib and Nurse Immacula Louis–Charles were assigned to the procedure. Because Leib and Louis–Charles had no experience, familiarity, or training on the Hystero–Flo Pump, they asked defendant Nancy Hofgesang, a nurse who had some experience with the equipment, to assist. She acted as circulating nurse, although she was not officially scheduled by the hospital to be there.

During Ms. Chin's operation, one of the tubes was incorrectly connected to the hysteroscope, causing a closed circuit pathway that permitted the nitrogen gas to enter Ms. Chin's uterus and resulted in the embolism. Defendants presented several theories regarding which tube was wrongly attached. Because Dr. Goldfarb removed the tubes from the pump shortly after Ms. Chin went into cardiac arrest, their exact configuration was ascertainable only by inference. * * *

At trial, defendants presented conflicting testimony regarding which party or parties incorrectly hooked up the apparatus. At the close of evidence, defendant C.R. Bard moved for a directed verdict. The trial court granted the motion and none of the remaining parties argue that C.R. Bard is liable for the death of Ms. Chin. * * * The jury awarded plaintiff two million dollars in damages. It apportioned liability against the several defendants: Dr. Goldfarb, 20% liable; Nurse Leib, 20% liable; Nurse Hofgesang, 25% liable; St. Barnabas Medical Center, 35% liable. Nurse Louis–Charles was found not liable for the death of Ms. Chin. * * *

The primary issue in this case is the application of the principles set forth in our plurality opinion in *Anderson v. Somberg*, 338 A.2d 1 (N.J. 1975). In that case, the court rejected the traditional allocation of the burden of proof; rather than resting with the plaintiff, the burden of proof was shifted to the defendants. Thus, in a case governed by *Anderson*, the jury is instructed that at least one defendant must be found liable and that the defendants bear the burden of exonerating themselves from liability.

The facts in *Anderson v. Somberg* help in understanding the reasoning behind this exception to the usual allocation of burdens of proof. In *Anderson*, a surgical instrument broke during surgery and was lodged in the plaintiff's spinal canal, requiring multiple surgeries and resulting in severe and permanent physical injuries. The plaintiff, who was unconscious at the time, could not be blamed for the mishap. The plaintiff sued his physician, the hospital, the medical supply distributor and the manufacturer of the instrument. No explanation other than the negligence or fault of one of the defendants was available as the cause of the accident. Nevertheless, because the plaintiff could not prove which defendant caused the accident, the jury returned a verdict of no cause of action for each of the defendants. The evidence led to the inference that the break in the medical instrument may have been caused by weak metal, a crack during manufacture, cumulative misuse by other surgeons, or misuse by the operating surgeon. Hence, one, some or all of the defendants indisputably caused the instrument to break; a determination that no defendant was responsible would be an unjust result. * * *

Under the principles of *Anderson v. Somberg*, the plaintiff must show three things in order to shift the burden of proof to the defendants. First, the plaintiff must herself be entirely blameless. The fact pattern to which the principles of *Anderson* most readily apply is where a plaintiff was "clearly helpless or anesthetized" when her injury occurred. Second, the injury must be one that bespeaks negligence on the part of one or more of the defendants. Third, all the potential defendants must be before the court. That is, all those defendants who participated in the chain of events causing plaintiff's injury must be represented. * * *

All three requirements for the application of *Anderson* have been met. Angelina Chin, who was unconscious, helpless, and utterly blameless, suffered a fatal injury that bespeaks negligence on the part of one or more of the defendants. It is not contested that the air embolism could have been caused only by negligent use of the hysteroscope. All the potential defendants, that is, all those who participated in the chain of events leading up to Ms. Chin's injury, were sued in this case. * * * The verdict in this case reflects that the jury reached its determination conscientiously on sufficient evidence. The jurors thoroughly considered the evidence and exonerated Nurse Louis–Charles. Consistent with the jury's verdict, all the testimony indicated that this nurse was not at fault. * * * The jury, weighing the conflicting testimony and contradictory evidence, found various levels of liability among defendants. There is nothing irrational about these findings of fact and they are supported by the evidence. * * *

NOTES AND QUESTIONS

1. *Strict liability in disguise.* Does *Anderson v. Somberg* amount to a rule of strict liability extended to all links in the chain of distribution? See Maciag v. Strato Med. Corp., 644 A.2d 647 (N.J.Super.Ct.1994) (reversing summary judgment in favor of device manufacturer, physicians, and hospital and remanding for trial so that each defendant could explain why it should not be held accountable for the plaintiff's injuries). No other jurisdiction has followed New Jersey's approach.

2. *Durable medical equipment.* Courts have held that hospitals must have adequate equipment to furnish the medical services they offer in a non-negligent manner. In *Washington v. Washington Hospital Center*, 579 A.2d 177 (D.C.1990), the plaintiff suffered a permanent catastrophic brain injury from oxygen deprivation while under general anesthesia. She alleged that the Washington Hospital Center (WHC), a tertiary care hospital, was negligent in failing to provide the anesthesiologists with an end-tidal carbon dioxide monitoring device that allows for the early detection of insufficient oxygen in time to prevent brain injury. After reviewing the expert testimony, statements from professional associations, and articles about anesthesiology practice published in peer-reviewed journals, the court concluded that a reasonable juror could find that the standard of care required WHC to supply such monitors at the time of the plaintiff's injury.

In *Emory University v. Porter*, 120 S.E.2d 668 (Ga.Ct.App.1961), an infant suffered a severe burn to her left foot as a result of remaining in contact with a light bulb in her incubator; her foot was partially amputated as a result. The court rejected her negligence claim against the hospital:

> A hospital owes to its patients only the duty of exercising ordinary care to furnish equipment and facilities reasonably suited to the uses intended and such as are in general use under the same, or similar, circumstances in hospitals in the area. It is not required to furnish the latest or best appliances, or to incorporate in existing equipment the latest inventions or improvements even though such devices may make the equipment safer to use. An appliance is not defective by reason of the failure to have incorporated therein the latest improvement or invention developed for its use. The petition in this case fails to allege that the incubator was defective, or any facts authorizing such a conclusion, and the trial court erred in overruling the motion to dismiss the petition as to the defendant hospital.

Id. at 670.

3. *Reprocessing single-use only devices.* In the early 1980s, device manufacturers began developing and marketing increasingly sophisticated medical devices and surgical instruments. Because of concerns about the difficulty of sterilizing such devices after use (and perhaps to promote sales), manufacturers began to label these devices as "disposable" and "single-use devices" (SUDs). Hospitals, however, continued to re-use certain SUDs to cut costs. This practice has become widespread and can have frightening results. For example, a New Orleans hospital used on eight patients resterilized surgical instruments that had originally been used to operate on a patient with Creutzfeldt–Jakob Disease (CJD). Because ordinary sterilization procedures do not destroy the prions that cause this disease, the other patients may have been exposed. See Possible Exposure Spurs Suit, Orlando Sentinel, Nov. 30, 2000, at A7; see also Valerie Elliott, Stricter Surgery Rules to Counter Fears of CJD, London Times, Aug. 30, 2000 (describing a government plan to create a list of surgical procedures for which instruments may be used only once); Dana Hawkins, News You Can Use: Risky Recycling, U.S. News & World Rep., Sept. 20, 1999, at 62 (describing reports to FDA of contaminated medical devices that caused patient injuries). Such reprocessing and re-use of SUDs makes hospitals vulnerable to negligence claims. As one commentator has explained, the duty of care "includes efforts to establish and maintain appropriate reprocessing protocols and to insure that reuse of the device is safe and presents no increased risk of harm or injury to the patient." Emil P. Wang, Regulatory and Legal Implications of Reprocessing and Reuse of Single–Use Medical Devices, 56 Food & Drug L.J. 77, 93–95 (2001) (explaining that improper re-use of SUDs can support claims against the hospital and physicians based on respondeat superior, direct corporate liability, and breach of the duty to obtain informed consent); see also Janice M. Hogan & Thomas Colonna, Products Liability Implications of Reprocessing and Reuse of Single–Use Medical Devices, 53 Food & Drug L.J. 385 (1998). Why not impose strict products liability in such cases (recall from Chapter 1(C) that the FDA now regulates hospitals engaged in reprocessing in the same manner as original equipment manufacturers)? Would the *Rest. (3d)* already do so by treating these as manufacturing defect claims?

PART III

Economics and Innovation

CHAPTER 9

Pricing and Payment Systems

In 1998, national health care expenditures totaled $1.1 trillion, approximately 13.5 percent of the gross domestic product. A recent survey found that 50 percent of adults took at least one prescription drug in the week preceding the inquiry. See David W. Kaufman et al., Recent Patterns of Medication Use in the Ambulatory Adult Population of the United States, 287 JAMA 337 (2002) (noting that many of those surveyed also took non-prescription drugs and dietary supplements concurrently with prescription medications). Spending on prescription drugs is growing at a far faster rate than spending on other health care products and services. In 2001, spending on prescription drugs reached $175.2 billion, an increase of more than 17 percent over the previous year. See Nat'l Inst. for Health Care Mgmt., Prescription Drug Expenditures in 2001: Another Year of Escalating Costs, available at <www.nihcm.org>; see also Ceci Connolly, Pharmaceutical Spending Continues Steady Increase, Wash. Post, Mar. 29, 2002, at A9; Robert Pear, Spending on Prescription Drugs Increases by Almost 19 Percent, N.Y. Times, May 8, 2001, at A1 (adding that "antidepressants were the best-selling category of prescription medicines"); Bruce Stuart et al., Issues in Prescription Drug Coverage, Pricing, Utilization, and Spending: What We Know and What We Need to Know, App. A (2000), available at <http://aspe.hhs.gov/health/reports/drugstudy/appa-3.htm> (attributing 42 percent of the increase in drug spending to increased rates of prescribing, 36 percent of the increase to a shift in prescribing more costly drugs, and 22 percent to higher drug pricing). Increases in costs for other types of medical technology are more difficult to measure, but all categories of medical expenditures appear to be rising rapidly.

This chapter examines how medical technology is paid for in this country and, more importantly, the consequences for health care of different payment systems. Reimbursement mechanisms have a profound effect on the adoption and use of medical technologies by health care providers. Other factors that influence the demand for technologies—such as the public's unthinking preference for the most sophisticated interventions even when their efficacy is unproven, and physicians' tendency to engage in defensive medicine—clash with the incentives created by public and private reimbursement mechanisms. As third-party payers in both the public and private sectors struggle to maintain control over rising drug prices, several initiatives designed to contain costs have had only limited success.

636

A. PUBLIC INSURANCE

American Medical Association v. Mathews

429 F.Supp. 1179 (N.D.Ill.1977).

■ MARSHALL, DISTRICT JUDGE:

This action challenges the validity of the Maximum Allowable Cost (MAC) regulations of the Department of Health, Education and Welfare (HEW) which establish a mechanism for limiting reimbursement or payment for multiple-source prescription drugs under federally subsidized health care programs (mainly Medicare and Medicaid). The case raises important issues concerning the authority of the defendant, Secretary of HEW, to control spiraling expenditures in federal health programs in the face of claims by the medical profession, selected patients and the drug industry that the Secretary's efforts violate a host of legislative enactments, procedural requirements and the Constitution. We have concluded, for the reasons hereinafter stated, that all of the objections are without merit. Accordingly, judgment will enter dismissing the action.

Plaintiffs are the American Medical Association (AMA), five licensed physicians who are AMA members and who treat patients who receive Medicare and Medicaid benefits, four recipients of Medicare benefits and two Medicaid recipients. The Pharmaceutical Manufacturers Association (PMA) has intervened as a plaintiff. * * *

On November 15, 1974, the Secretary published proposed regulations to establish a procedure for limiting reimbursement or payment for multiple-source drugs under the Medicare and Medicaid programs and certain other federally sponsored health programs. 39 Fed. Reg. 40,302. After reviewing more than 2,600 public comments on the proposal, the Secretary published the final MAC regulations on July 31, 1975. They became effective on August 26, 1976. 40 Fed. Reg. 32,284 (45 C.F.R. § 19.1 et seq.). The regulations undertake to reduce the cost of prescription drugs paid for by the Medicare and Medicaid programs, and they provide a comprehensive scheme for the determination, application and review of cost limitations.

MAC determinations are made by a Pharmaceutical Reimbursement Board, which consists of five full-time HEW employees representing the principal program areas involved in developing and implementing cost determinations. The Board begins the MAC determination process by identifying "multiple-source drugs" for which significant amounts of federal funds are being expended and for which formulators or labelers charge significantly different prices. A "multiple-source drug" is a "drug marketed or sold by two or more formulators or labelers or a drug marketed or sold by the same formulator or labeler under two or more different proprietary names or both under a proprietary name and without such a name." 45 C.F.R. § 19.2(d). For example, the antibiotic ampicillin trihydrate is sold under a variety of trademarked brand names, including Amcill and Totacillin.

After the Board identifies a multiple-source drug, it must seek advice from the Food and Drug Administration (FDA) concerning whether present FDA regulatory control will assure the marketability and bioequivalence of the proposed MAC drug. Unless the FDA advises the Board that the establishment of a MAC should be delayed or withheld, the Board proceeds to determine the "lowest unit price" at which the multiple-source drug is "widely and consistently available" on a national and, when appropriate, a local basis. The Board is required to submit this determination, together with supporting information, to the Pharmaceutical Reimbursement Advisory Committee. The Committee is composed of nine members who are not full-time employees of the federal government and who represent the areas of pharmacy, pharmacology, medicine, pharmaceutical marketing, public health, and consumer affairs. The function of the Committee is to advise the Board on the appropriateness of all proposed MAC determinations, and, upon request, to advise the Board and the Secretary on matters relating to general HEW policies and procedures involving drug reimbursement.

After considering the Committee's advice and recommendations, the Board decides whether to propose the lowest unit price as the maximum allowable cost (MAC) for the drug. If it decides to do so, the proposed MAC is published in the *Federal Register*, thereby triggering provisions in the regulations which afford an opportunity for the public to respond by submitting written comments or by requesting an informal public hearing. The Board may, but need not, grant such a hearing. On the basis of the evidence and submissions, accumulated by these procedures, the Board then makes its final MAC determination and publishes notice of its decision.

Once a MAC is established, reimbursement benefits for that drug under Medicare and Medicaid may not exceed the lowest of three possible computations: (1) the MAC of the drug plus a reasonable dispensing fee; (2) the acquisition cost of the drug plus a reasonable dispensing fee; or (3) the provider's usual and customary charge to the public for the drug. Id. § 19.3(a). However, the MAC limit is not applicable to a brand of the drug "which the prescriber has certified in his own handwriting is medically necessary for that patient." Id. § 19.3(a)(3)(i). Because of this alternative cost limitation scheme, non-multiple-source drugs, which are not covered by MACs, will nonetheless be subject to cost controls (2) or (3) as will specially prescribed "medically necessary" drugs. However, the focus of the plaintiffs' complaint is on the MAC limitations. * * *

[T]he starting point for our statutory analysis is the identification of the different categories of drug services provided under the Medicare and Medicaid programs. Then the different reimbursement standards which apply to each of the various subdivisions of these programs will be analyzed in light of the MAC regulations. It will be apparent that the interplay of these different categories of drug services and different reimbursement standards provides a moderate degree of technical complexity.

Medicare is a nationally uniform federal program of health insurance for the aged and the disabled. It is completely financed and administered by the federal government through the Social Security Administration. Medicare is divided into two parts. Part A, 42 U.S.C. §§ 1395c–1395i, provides federal insurance for inpatient hospital services, post-hospital extended care services (including nursing home services), and post-hospital home health services. This "basic Medicare" program covers the cost of "drugs and biologicals" ordinarily furnished to patients for use in hospitals or extended care facilities, 42 U.S.C. §§ 1395d, 1395x(b)(2), (h)(5), (j)(7), but not those provided to homebound patients, 42 U.S.C. § 1395x(m)(5). Part B of Medicare, 42 U.S.C. §§ 1395j–1395w, establishes a voluntary supplemental insurance program for aged and disabled individuals. It provides protection against the costs of physicians' services and a variety of medical services and equipment which are furnished in and out of medical institutions and which are not covered by the basic plan. This "supplementary Medicare" program covers only the cost of drugs and biologicals which (1) cannot be self-administered, (2) are incidental to a physician's services to patients in his office or to hospital outpatients, (3) are of a kind commonly furnished in physicians' offices, and (4) are commonly rendered without charge or included in the physician's bill. 42 U.S.C. §§ 1395k, 1395x(s)(2). Thus, only a small percentage of drugs, such as injections, are covered under Part B of Medicare. In sum, both Part A and Part B of Medicare generally limit coverage to those drugs which have a close nexus to supervised institutional care.

Medicaid is a federal-state cooperative program that enables participating states to furnish medical assistance to individuals whose economic resources are insufficient to meet the costs of necessary medical care. States electing to participate in the program must submit a plan for approval by the Secretary. Upon approval, the state becomes entitled to federal matching funds to finance the program. Each state has considerable discretion in designing the contours of its program within the guidelines established by 42 U.S.C. § 1396a. The Medicaid program covers physicians' services, extended care services, inpatient and outpatient hospital services, and a wide range of other specified medical services for the needy. Under 42 U.S.C. § 1396d(a)(12), state Medicaid plans may include the costs of all "prescribed drugs," including those furnished in health care institutions and those purchased at pharmacies. Thus, Medicaid potentially provides a more extensive range of coverage for drug costs than Medicare. * * *

Given this maze of reimbursement standards applicable to different categories of drug costs and charges under two different health care programs with different methodologies and philosophies of administration, it is indeed difficult for us to nail down any one reimbursement standard for the purpose of evaluating the consistency of the MAC regulations with the legislative scheme. But we believe that the "reasonable cost" standard of § 1395x(v)(1)(A) is most immediately relevant to the present controversy and most clearly embodies the congressional formula for preventing reimbursement for excessively priced medical items and services. * * * We recognize that all of the sections embody broad terminology of efficiency, economy, necessity and quality of care, and that these terms require administrative interpretation. However, § 1395x(v)(1)(A) contains the most complete methodology of determining unnecessary costs and is the only one to express that determination in formulistic terms. * * * Finally, a reimbursement scheme which disburses different amounts for drug costs to providers who furnish identical services to Medicare and Medicaid patients, or who furnish identical services to the same patients in different circumstances, tends to be illogical, inefficient and uneconomical. The interest in a uniform policy of drug reimbursement is strong. * * * Therefore, we conclude that § 1395x(v)(1)(A) provides the applicable reimbursement standard against which the validity of the MAC regulations must be tested.

Plaintiffs raise numerous arguments alleging that the MAC regulations violate § 1395x(v)(1)(A). To repeat, the crucial language of that section provides that:

> The reasonable cost of any services shall be the cost actually incurred, excluding therefrom any part of incurred cost found to be unnecessary in the efficient delivery of needed health services, and shall be determined in accordance with regulations establishing the method or methods to be used, and the items to be included, in determining such costs for various types or classes of institutions, agencies, and services.

In summary, plaintiffs contend that (1) the MAC regulations inflexibly limit reimbursement to a lower level than "cost actually incurred," (2) the Secretary has not "found," nor do the regulations provide for findings, that drug costs above maximum allowable costs are "unnecessary in the efficient delivery of needed health services," (3) such findings, assuming they were made, were not determined in accordance with preestablished "methods" and procedures, and (4) even assuming such findings were made and such methods were followed, Section 1395x(v)(1)(A) was only intended to curb aberrant extravagance and program abuse by specific health providers, not across-the-board limits on the costs of standard medical supplies purchased on the market.

Plaintiffs' first contention, that the MAC regulations violate this section by inflexibly basing reimbursement on the cost of a MAC drug rather than on the "cost actually incurred" by the provider, relies upon a misconstruction of the statute. Reimbursement under this section was never intended to be based solely on a provider's actual costs. The language of the statute explicitly excludes payments for incurred costs which are unnecessary. Furthermore, in enacting this provision Congress sought to limit costs to "those that would be incurred by a reasonably prudent and cost conscious management," not those that are actually incurred by any health care institution regardless of its operating efficiency. * * *

We also reject plaintiffs' argument that the Secretary has not found, and the regulations fail to make or require a finding, that the difference in price between a MAC drug and a drug actually prescribed represents costs which are "unnecessary in the efficient delivery of needed health services." We note first that the Secretary is empowered to make findings of broad scope and application. The legislative history of the 1972 amendments of

§ 1395x(v)(1)(A) makes clear that the Secretary was not confined to retrospective determinations of reasonable costs on a case-by-case basis. Separate findings as to necessity do not have to be made each time a provider seeks reimbursement for drug costs. Rather, the amendments authorized the Secretary to prospectively establish the reasonable cost for items and services on a class and presumptive basis. * * *

Plaintiffs' next contention is that the Secretary cannot properly find that drug costs above MAC levels are unnecessary without contravening the legislative intent behind § 1395x(v)(1)(A). According to their theory, that section was only intended to authorize cost controls on health care institutions which were inefficient and which charged excessive costs relative to comparable providers operating in similar circumstances, and was not meant to allow across-the-board cost controls on all providers with respect to standard medical supplies purchased on the market.

We believe Congress intended its economizing measure to cover more than merely the problem of the spendthrift. * * * The draftsmen of statutes delegating agency powers do not normally include specific consideration of every evil sought to be corrected, but instead expect the agency to use its expertise to combat new abuses as they arise. Therefore we reject the assertion that the Secretary's findings on unnecessary drug costs represent an attempt to expand his power beyond the scope of the statutory framework. Those findings were clearly directed at eliminating costs which he deemed to be "unnecessary in the efficient delivery of needed health services" within the meaning of § 1395x(v)(1)(A). And given the deference ordinarily accorded to an administrator's statutory interpretations, the MAC regulations are a lawful means of achieving that objective.

Nevertheless, plaintiffs argue, Congress has rejected bills and proposals that would have specifically given the Secretary the authority to establish a MAC-type system of drug reimbursement. However, nearly all of the bills which they cite would impose much stricter federal controls over drug reimbursement than those established by the MAC regulations. The bills generally proposed a formulary system which would limit reimbursement for drug costs and would also restrict types of drugs for which reimbursement could be sought. The MAC regulations only set reimbursement limitations and do not exclude any drug from potential coverage under Medicare or Medicaid. * * *

Plaintiffs also argue that the MAC regulations violate a section of the Social Security Act which is peripherally related to those sections establishing reimbursement standards. The section is 42 U.S.C. § 1395x(t), which defines "drugs" and "biologicals" to:

> ... include only such drugs and biologicals ... as are included ... [in the drug compendia of specified medical and pharmacological organizations], ... or as are approved by the pharmacy and drug therapeutics committee (or equivalent committee) of the medical staff of [participating] (hospitals)....

This section was enacted in 1965 and has never been amended.

Plaintiffs first assert that § 1395x(t) mandates full reimbursement and program coverage for all drugs listed or approved in accordance with that section. They argue that the MAC regulations, by providing full reimbursement for MAC drugs and only partial reimbursement for drugs which cost more than MAC limits and which may be so listed or approved, effectively limit drug coverage to a more restricted category of drugs than those specified in § 1395x(t). We reject this strained interpretation of the statute and of the MAC regulations. The statute was intended to limit payment to only those drugs which were approved by responsible and competent medical organizations. It does not require, but instead permits, reimbursement for all drugs which are approved by the mechanisms specified by the statute. The legislative history supports this reading:

> The intent of the provisions for determining which drugs and biologicals are covered is to *permit* payment for all drugs and biologicals which medical and medically related organizations have evaluated and selected as being proper for use in the course of good patient care.

1965 U.S.C.C.A.N. 1969 (emphasis added). The section was intended to protect patients against poor quality drugs, not to require the government to pay the full cost of all brands of a drug when a portion of that cost has been found unnecessary in the efficient delivery of medical care. Furthermore, the MAC regulations do not affect which drugs are *eligible* for reimbursement; rather, they affect only the *amount* of that reimbursement, and do so only where a physician has not certified that a prescribed drug which costs more than MAC levels is medically necessary for his patient. * * *

Plaintiffs next urge that the MAC regulations constitute unlawful supervision and control over the practice of medicine in violation of 42 U.S.C. § 1395. The section provides, in pertinent part, that:

> Nothing in this subchapter shall be construed to authorize any Federal officer or employee to exercise any supervision or control over the practice of medicine or the manner in which medical services are provided ... or to exercise any supervision or control over the administration or operation of any ... institution, agency, or person [providing health services].

In evaluating the merits of the § 1395 issue, it is helpful to identify at the start those propositions about which the parties agree. First, the MAC regulations will control the level of reimbursement for multiple-source drugs prescribed by physicians for Medicare–Medicaid patients. Second, the MAC limits on reimbursement will not apply where the physician certifies that the particular drug he has prescribed is medically necessary for his patient. Third, the regulations by their terms do not require nor ask the physician to prescribe only those drugs which fall within MAC levels or to alter his medical judgment concerning the proper drugs to prescribe for his patients. Fourth, the regulations will have some effect on the prescribing habits of physicians. The crucial question is whether this effect is sufficient to constitute "supervision or control" within the meaning of § 1395.

Plaintiffs first argue that the test of interference under § 1395 is whether the regulations will have the practical effect of controlling professional judgment in a significant number of instances. Plaintiffs assert that they will, and contend that physicians will be effectively required to prescribe only MAC drugs because neither the hospitals, pharmacists and physicians that furnish the drugs, nor the Medicare–Medicaid patients who procure them, will be able or willing to shoulder the added unreimbursable cost of non-MAC drugs. They argue, therefore, that the regulations will unlawfully restrict the physician's range of practical choice by introducing financial considerations into his decision as to the course of treatment to recommend to his patients. He will be unable to prescribe care solely upon what he analyzes the patient's need to be and must weigh his diagnosis in terms of what the patient (or the hospital or pharmacy) can afford. Plaintiffs envision a situation where the physician will in many instances prescribe drugs which are different from those he would have prescribed in the absence of the MAC regulations.

Analysis of this argument necessitates an inquiry into the impact of cost controls on professional independence. Plaintiffs' prediction of a substantial impact on their medical practice is a claim which is beyond the scope of a motion for judgment on the pleadings and requires evidence for support. But if we assume the validity of their prediction, the resulting effect of the MAC regulations on the aggregate prescription practices of physicians does not fall within the prohibition of § 1395.

Congress made it clear in 1972 that it did not view certain cost limitation mechanisms as within the ambit of § 1395. By enacting a strengthened cost limitation section and authorizing the Secretary to exercise extensive cost control powers, Congress struck a balance between cost controls and professional independence. This balance is not upset by the incidental effects predicted by plaintiffs. The legislative history of § 1395x(v)(1)(A) demonstrates that Congress wanted the judgmental process in the health care delivery system to be influenced and animated by a consciousness of the costs of medical care. * * * In short, Congress did not intend to shield the medical decision-making process from financial consequences. If the MAC regulations have the effect of altering present drug prescription habits in the medical profession to reflect greater cost efficiency, that effect is consistent with congressional intent.

We recognize, however, that Congress did not say that all cost control mechanisms are consistent with § 1395. Congress wanted full reimbursement to be accompanied by an informed medical decision that the incurred costs are necessary in the efficient delivery of health services. Thus, § 19.3(a)(3) of the MAC regulations accommodates professional independence by providing reimbursement of "acquisition cost" or "usual and customary charge" if the physician certifies in his own handwriting that the prescribed drug is medically necessary for his patient. This exception to the MAC limits assures that any changes in physicians' drug prescription practices will result not from a coercive effect of the MAC regulations, but instead from an agreement by physicians that drug products priced within

MAC limits will provide the same level of efficacy as that provided by costlier drug products. It is in precisely those cases where drug prescription judgments are controlled by medically unnecessary factors that the MAC regulations will have their greatest and most clearly intended, if not their only, impact on the medical practice. And Congress intended that impact as a permissible by-product of cost controls, not an intrusion into professional independence.

Plaintiffs contend that the § 19.3(a)(3) certification provision does not save the MAC regulations from a § 1395 violation. They characterize the purpose of the handwritten certification (that a physician reflect for a moment on whether his patient needs a particular drug whose cost exceeds MAC levels) as intended to induce physicians to acquiesce in MAC determinations in close or uncertain cases and as introducing just the sort of bureaucratic interference with medical judgments that § 1395 was designed to prevent. They also perceive a gray area of "medically preferable" drugs between those which are and those which are not medically necessary, and think that physicians may reasonably shrink from making the handwritten certification for these drugs, even though the physicians believe these drugs are safer, more reliable, more effective, or more acceptable to their patients.

We cannot agree that the act of certification is a prohibited intrusion into the physician's medical practice. The handwriting requirement is no more onerous than putting pen to paper, as the physician already does in penning the prescription itself. Furthermore, certification is not intended to affect the physician's judgment but only to document that judgment and to prevent the certification process from becoming a pro forma ritual (if, for instance, the physician need only check off a box on the prescription form). In addition, requiring physicians to certify that particular services are medically necessary is not a novel mechanism. Even before the 1972 amendments, Congress required physicians to certify the medical necessity of tests and treatment for in-hospital, post-hospital and home health care. See 42 U.S.C. § 1395f(a).

Finally, plaintiffs have placed too narrow a construction on the certification provision by arguing that it will cover only medically necessary, but not medically preferable, drugs. The Secretary has given the certification provision a broad scope which minimizes, if not eliminates, plaintiffs' fear of an inhibition on medical judgments. The prescriber need only conclude, "on the basis of a comparative medical judgment," that a particular brand of a multiple-source drug is "better suited" than another brand for the patient's medical needs. 40 Fed. Reg. at 32,295. The MAC regulations contain no provision for governmental review of the physician's certification. We conclude that the MAC regulations do not constitute federal supervision or control over the practice of medicine within the meaning of § 1395. * * *

Our focus now shifts from a resolution of issues of statutory construction, which is a matter assigned primarily to a reviewing court, to a review of the findings and conclusions that form the basis for the regulations, which involve matters essentially within the competence of the administrator. Plaintiff-intervenor PMA raises two arguments in its motion for summary judgment that the Secretary's findings lack an adequate basis in the administrative record and are therefore invalid. * * *

PMA's first contention is that the quality control procedures in the MAC scheme are based on the Secretary's false and unsupported assumption that the Food and Drug Administration's regulatory control activities will assure the quality, therapeutic effectiveness and bioequivalence of MAC-listed drug products. According to the procedures set up by the MAC regulations, the Pharmaceutical Reimbursement Board relies on the FDA to identify drug quality problems prior to the establishment of a MAC and does not make its own independent finding on these issues. Therefore FDA activities play a crucial role in the quality control process. PMA argues that the written comments submitted on the proposed MAC regulations contained persuasive evidence showing the inadequacy of FDA's quality control procedures and that the Secretary's basis and purpose statement and the administrative record failed to adequately respond to this evidence. * * *

The debate on the issue of drug quality centers on the problem of drug bioequivalence. Simply stated, the crucial question in the bioequivalence problem is to what extent can the chemically equivalent drug products of different manufacturers be interchanged without an unacceptable change in the therapeutic effect that will be produced. The issue of interchangeability is important in the context of the MAC regulations, because they provide that a physician who sees no medical necessity for prescribing more expensive drug products for his patient may rely on the fact that less expensive, chemically equivalent drug products will perform with full effectiveness. * * *

The Secretary's actions, however, must be scrutinized by more realistic and modest standards. The Secretary's conclusions on drug quality are legislative judgments on a series of complex, technical issues, based on a wide spectrum of administrative and scientific materials. The Secretary has clearly made a searching and thorough examination of these issues. (His statement of reasons covers some 18 pages in the *Federal Register*.) He was aware of each criticism raised in the comments and responded to them. He recognized that the compendial standards, GMP guidelines and inspection programs have deficiencies and can be improved. He also recognized, as we do, that drug quality is not an objective but a relative criterion, dependent on an analysis of existing technology and balanced by competing considerations concerning the fiscal integrity of the Medicare and Medicaid programs. He has concluded that despite some administrative difficulties, the FDA has been largely successful in assuring that all drug products are of adequate quality and purity to assure safety and effectiveness. And he has provided mechanisms in the MAC regulations to test this general conclusion in the context of each actual MAC proceeding. We find that the Secretary's approach is reasonable and supported by the record. * * *

PMA also challenges the sufficiency of the administrative record to support the Secretary's finding that those portions of the cost of drugs exceeding MAC levels are unnecessary in the efficient delivery of needed health services. Specifically, PMA asserts that the Secretary failed to consider whether the higher prices charged by some drug companies reflect indirect costs that contribute markedly to the efficient delivery of health care. PMA claims that these indirect costs result from the extensive research and development efforts, informational and distribution services, and superior recall capabilities of certain major pharmaceutical manufacturers. * * *

PMA's argument is reducible to the contention that the Secretary failed to consider whether a noncompetitive pricing scheme might more efficiently deliver health services because it assertedly would encourage major drug companies to continue their extensive research and distribution services. * * * The record here documents the Secretary's awareness of the complex of collateral services offered by the major drug manufacturers. Although we have located no explicit finding regarding each factor isolated by the PMA in their briefs, the record contains references supporting the Secretary's implied findings that the costs attributable to these incidental services are on the whole unnecessary. * * *

1.   MEDICAID AND THE BEST PRICE MECHANISM

Medicaid covers more than 41 million individuals, including children, the low-income elderly, the blind and disabled, and it costs the federal and state governments more than $200 billion a year. The federal Medicaid statute and accompanying regulations set out the conditions under which federal funds may be used by state Medicaid programs to pay for benefits such as prescription drugs and medical devices such as dentures, prosthetics, and eyeglasses. See 42 U.S.C. § 1396d(a)(12); 42 C.F.R. § 440.120; see also John K. Inglehart, The American Health Care System: Medicaid, 340 New Eng. J. Med. 403 (1999) (providing an overview of the program).

Health Care Financing Administration, Final Rule, *Medicare and Medicaid Programs; Limits on Payments for Drugs*

52 Fed. Reg. 28,648 (1987).

In 1976, the Department implemented drug reimbursement rules at 45 C.F.R. Part 19 under the authority of statutes pertaining to upper payment limits for Medicaid and other programs. The authority to set an upper payment limit for services available under the Medicaid program is provided under section 1902(a)(30)(A) of the Social Security Act. The Department rules are intended to ensure that the federal government acts as a prudent buyer of drugs under certain federal health programs. The rules set limits on payments for drugs supplied under Medicaid and other programs. Of the federal programs involved, these rules have the greatest impact on the Medicaid program. * * * In addition to limiting the level of payment for multiple source drugs, the MAC program tends to promote substitution of lower cost (generic) drug products for brand-name drugs, since the latter are frequently available only at prices higher than the MAC limits. * * *

[T]he process of approving a MAC for a specific drug is lengthy. This has been of concern particularly since the passage of the Drug Price Competition and Patent Term Extension Act of 1984. This law streamlines the FDA approval process for certain drugs. The result of this law is that therapeutically equivalent (generic) drugs will be coming into the market-place more quickly than in the past. As evidenced by the current MAC program, we are interested in encouraging the use of therapeutically equivalent drugs. We would like to adopt a Medicaid drug policy that would allow us promptly to adjust payment upper limits to reflect the availability of new drug equivalents as they enter the marketplace. * * *

State agencies are encouraged to exercise maximum state flexibility in establishing their own payment methodologies. We do not intend that our adoption of the formula approach to set limits for multiple source drugs be construed as an indicator of the federally preferred payment system. The use of the formula approach is primarily due to the straight-forward application and administrative ease in setting upper limits. We encourage state agencies to establish any program that will substitute lower-priced alternatives for drugs.

We hope that the state agencies will be innovative in these programs and find ways to assure the availability at reasonable prices of multiple-source drugs. One way they could do this would be to encourage retail pharmacy participation in the Medicaid program by permitting them to retain profits from the sale of listed drugs to Medicaid recipients. Other alternative payment systems could include, for example, contracting on a competitive basis for pharmaceutical services with selected pharmacies to which recipients may go for drugs without incurring a copayment or a system which entails charge screens and/or mandatory discounts. Additionally, state agencies may initiate or retain already existing so-called "mini-MAC" programs, which they have established on specific drugs either at levels lower than those established under the current federal MAC limits or on drugs not now covered by MAC limits. This system of aggregate upper limits will allow state agencies to alter payment rates for specific listed drugs without first having to obtain permission from HCFA. The agencies then will be able to respond rapidly to sudden price fluctuations, which may threaten the supply of specific drugs on the HCFA list, without having to pursue a cumbersome approval process. A final advantage of the aggregate limit methodology is the ease of administration at the federal level and the lack of administrative burden on state programs.

The federal upper limit standard that we have adopted for certain multiple source drugs is based on an aggregate payment amount equal to an amount that includes the ingredient cost of the drug calculated according to the formula described below and a reasonable dispensing fee. HCFA will determine to which drugs the formula will be applied. The listing of these drugs and any revisions to the list will be provided to state agencies through Medicaid program issuances on a timely, periodic basis * * * *

[T]he final rule will specify that the drugs to which this formula will be applied must have been evaluated as therapeutically equivalent by the FDA. * * *

The formula to be used in calculating the upper limit of payment for certain multiple source drugs will be 150 percent of the least costly therapeutic equivalent that can be purchased by pharmacists * * * * [W]e chose the markup of 150 percent in order to meet the following two objectives: (1) That the markup be high enough to assure that pharmacists can normally obtain and stock an equivalent product without losing money on acquisition costs of incurring the expense of departure from normal purchasing channels, and (2) that the markup not be so high as to cost the Medicaid program unnecessary money. * * * [I]f a physician certifies that a brand name drug is medically necessary, the upper limit for payment based on the formula will not apply. The upper limit for payment of "other drugs" will apply. * * * [T]he agency payment for certified brand name drugs and drugs other than multiple source drugs for which a specific limit has been established must not exceed, in the aggregate, the level of payment calculated by applying the lower of (1) the EAC [estimated acquisition cost] plus a dispensing fee; or (2) the provider's usual and customary charges to the general public.

Under these rules, the federal requirement for states to use the EAC method of payment will be eliminated. However, because the rule merely establishes an upper limit concept and does not describe the specific methodology for payment, state agencies may continue their practice of establishing EACs for the ingredient costs and adding to it a dispensing fee. Such practices will be acceptable, as will a system of establishing charge/payment screens based on statewide or regional customary and usual prices. The state's findings in regard to whether the statewide aggregate upper limit test is met must demonstrate that aggregate payments do not exceed payment as calculated under the EAC principles. * * *

We expressed the hope that States would recognize the advantage of providing pharmacists with an incentive to participate in the Medicaid program and to stimulate pharmacists to engage in prudent purchasing practices and the substitution of lower cost therapeutically equivalent products. In addition to these effects, we believe that our method of calculating the aggregate upper limit on payment to states may have consequences for other sectors of the industry: in particular on wholesalers and manufacturers. * * *

By using the lowest compendia price for a drug as the benchmark for our listed drug rates, the low price supplier may be encouraged to raise its published price to a point just below the next higher price. Other drug wholesalers and manufacturers may tend to lower their published prices so the range of published prices would begin to narrow and cluster around the low end of the price scale. We would expect to see such pricing patterns develop only for those drugs which had sizable portions of their total sales among Medicaid recipients. However, we suspect that price competition would be carried on in the form of discounts, promotional campaigns and other incentives aimed at the retail pharmacists.

Such tactics would work to the advantage of both retail druggists and wholesalers. Retail pharmacists would gain by being able to purchase drugs at prices below the HCFA list price, while wholesalers could gradually push the benchmark price upwards without losing sales. Although, historically, it has been the large retail outlets that have benefitted the most from wholesale discount practices, if adopted by a substantial number of state agencies, our policy of using published prices as a basis for determining payment levels may cause wholesalers to invent new ways of offering discounts to the smaller independent retail outlets, thereby expanding the practice of discounting to those outlets and enabling them to have access to less expensive sources of pharmaceuticals. The drawback is that neither state programs nor the federal Medicaid program will benefit from such reductions in wholesale prices. * * *

NOTES AND QUESTIONS

1. *Rebate agreements.* In 1990, Congress enacted a law designed to reduce prices on drugs that the federal government purchases or reimburses by demanding that manufacturers give it the benefit, through a rebate or otherwise, of the "best price" that the manufacturer has given any other purchaser. See 42 U.S.C. § 1396r–8(a)(1). Manufacturers must enter into a rebate agreement with the federal government or individual states in order for their drugs to be covered under the Medicaid program. See id. § 1396(b). Under such an agreement, a manufacturer provides a rebate to the states each quarter based on information submitted by the states for the amount of drugs paid for under Medicaid. See Bruce N. Kuhlik, The Medicaid Prescription Drug Rebate and Improved Access to Medicines Requirements of the Omnibus Budget Reconciliation Act of 1990, 46 Food Drug Cosm. L.J. 363 (1991); see also William J. Moore & Robert J. Newman, Drug Formulary Restrictions as Cost–Containment Policy in Medicaid Programs, 36 J.L. & Econ. 71 (1993); Stephen B. Soumerai et al., Determinants of Change in Medicaid Pharmaceutical Cost Sharing, 75 Milbank Q. 11 (1997). Pharmaceutical companies have responded to this "best price" requirement by limiting the substantial discounts that they had previously extended to large institutional purchasers such as HMOs.

2. *Closing a loophole in the best price mechanism.* HCFA (now redesignated as the Center for Medicare and Medicaid Services (CMMS)) recently discovered that several drug companies evaded rules on calculating the best price, costing the agency over $108 million in Medicaid rebates during fiscal years 1998 and 1999. The Office of the Inspector General issued a memorandum explaining how the best price mechanism works and when repackagers of prescription drugs must participate in the best price process:

> The Omnibus Budget Reconciliation Act of 1990 (OBRA 90), which established the Medicaid drug rebate program, defines best price as the lowest price available to any wholesaler, retailer, provider, HMO,

nonprofit, or governmental entity with certain exceptions. The exclusion of sales to repackagers from best price was not addressed in OBRA 90.... In 1997, HCFA issued guidance to drug manufacturers that allowed for the exclusion of sales to certain repackagers from best price. The HCFA issued additional guidance to the manufacturers in July 2000 that reiterated the statutory requirement that sales to HMOs be included in best price regardless of whether the HMO was a repackager.

Medicaid has traditionally represented 11 to 15 percent of the market for prescription drugs. Prior to the passage of OBRA 90, Medicaid took little advantage of its size in the marketplace. However, OBRA 90 allowed Medicaid to take advantage of its purchasing volume by authorizing states to collect rebates from drug manufacturers for drug purchases reimbursed under the Medicaid program. In order for a manufacturer's drugs to be eligible for reimbursement under Medicaid, the manufacturer was required by OBRA 90 to enter into a rebate agreement with HCFA and pay quarterly rebates to the states.

The rebates, for brand name drugs, are based on the difference between an average manufacturer's price (AMP)—the manufacturer's average selling price—and a manufacturer's lowest or best price, thereby affording Medicaid access to a manufacturer's best price. The AMP is defined in the rebate agreement between HCFA and the manufacturers to mean the average price paid by wholesalers for drugs distributed to the retail pharmacy class of trade. The definition also specifically excludes direct sales to hospitals, HMOs, and wholesalers where the drug was relabeled or repackaged under that wholesalers' national drug code. Therefore, AMP is based on sales to the higher paying retail sector and does not include sales to customers that traditionally pay lower prices than the retail sector. Best price is defined by OBRA 90 to mean the lowest price available to any wholesaler, retailer, provider, HMO, nonprofit, or governmental entity with the only exclusions being certain government entities. The definition of best price thus specifically includes certain entities that are excluded from AMP, including HMOs.

Office of the Inspector General, HHS, Memorandum, Medicaid Drug Rebates–Sales to Repackagers Excluded from Best Price Determinations, A–06–00–00056, Mar. 27, 2001, at 2–3; see also David S. Cloud, Schering–Plough Drug Marketing Under Scrutiny, Wall St. J., Mar. 14, 2001, at A3 (describing an investigation of one company for a "repackaging scheme").

3. *Pharmacy dispensing fees.* The provision of prescription drugs to Medicaid beneficiaries involves reimbursement for both the drug itself and the associated costs of dispensing it. New York pharmacists challenged a statute that created a co-payment system to cover pharmacy dispensing costs but that also required pharmacists to dispense drugs to Medicaid recipients who were unable to afford the co-payment. One court held that the statutory scheme was preempted by federal law to the extent that it resulted in the reduction of payments to pharmacists: "To the extent that pharmacies do not receive full compensation, some are likely to drop out of the Medicaid program and reduce the number of providers of health care to poor individuals. And, if they continue as providers, they will simply pass on the costs of the uncollected co-payments to the public at large." Pharmaceutical Soc'y of N.Y. v. Department of Social Serv., 50 F.3d 1168, 1175 (2d Cir.1995); see also Rite Aid v. Houstoun, 171 F.3d 842 (3d Cir.1999) (reviewing a challenge to pharmacy reimbursement rates under state Medicaid program); Florida Pharmacy Ass'n v. Cook, 17 F.Supp.2d 1293 (N.D.Fla.1998) (same).

4. *Limitations on Medicaid reimbursement for drugs and other technology.* Section 1927(d)(2) of the Social Security Act provides that when a state chooses to include outpatient drugs within its Medicaid program it must cover (with a very few exceptions) all FDA-approved prescription drugs for their medically accepted indications. All states currently provide such coverage. States may require that certain drugs be approved by a state agency before physicians may dispense them, and states must conduct drug review prospectively and retrospectively. See 42 U.S.C. § 1396r–8(d), (g). Medicaid programs may not cover drugs which have been deemed less than effective, and therefore not reimbursable, under the Medicare program. See id. § 1396b(i)(5); see also Emile L. Loza, Access to Pharmaceuticals Under Medicaid Managed Care: Federal Law Compiled and State Contracts Compared, 55 Food & Drug L.J. 449 (2000). As for medical devices, states must cover home health services, including medical supplies and equipment. See 42 U.S.C. § 1396a(a)(13)(B)-(C); 42 C.F.R. § 440.70(b)(3). As one commentator has noted, "[i]n many states, to have an item of durable medical equipment (DME) covered by a state's Medicaid program, the item must be listed as a covered item in a state's preapproved list, and a Medicaid recipient's physician must certify that the item is medically necessary for the health of the recipient. The lists are rarely updated." Jennifer K. Squillario, Comment, Medicaid and Durable Medical Equipment: An Ongoing Battle Between Expense and Health, 59 Md. L. Rev. 669, 669–70 (2000); see also DeSario v. Thomas, 139 F.3d 80 (2d Cir.1998), vacated and remanded, 525 U.S. 1098 (1999). There are also specific exceptions to the general drug coverage mandate: States may choose to exclude or restrict access to barbiturates and benzodiazepines, and to drugs for anorexia, weight loss or weight gain, fertility, cosmetic purposes, cough/cold relief, and smoking cessation. States may decline to cover the abortifacient Mifeprex, which the federal government has refused to reimburse in any event. See Amy Goldstein, Medicaid Coverage of RU–486 Limited, Wash. Post, Mar. 31, 2001, at A9. Finally, HCFA recently announced a specific policy on Medicaid coverage of Viagra, concluding that the law requires state Medicaid programs that cover prescription drugs cover Viagra "when medical necessity dictates such coverage for the drug's medically accepted indication" and reassuring states that, because "ninety percent of Medicaid beneficiaries are women and children ... [and] only ten percent of ... beneficiaries are adult males, the number of Medicaid beneficiaries that could be diagnosed with erectile dysfunction is very small." HCFA, Drug Policy, Medicaid Coverage of Viagra, available at

<http://www.hcfa.gov/medicaid/drugs/drpolicy.htm>; see also David F. Chavkin, Medicaid and Viagra: Restoring Potency to an Old Program?, 11 Health Matrix 189 (2001); Erin Lynn Connolly, Note, Constitutional Issues Raised by States' Exclusion of Fertility Drugs from Medicaid Coverage in Light of Mandated Coverage of Viagra, 54 Vand. L. Rev. 451 (2001); Carole L. Stewart, Comment, Mandated Medicaid Coverage of Viagra: Raising the Issues of Questionable Priorities, the Need for a Definition of Medical Necessity, and the Politics of Poverty, 44 Loy. L. Rev. 611 (1998).

5. *Waivers from general federal Medicaid requirements.* Individual states can petition CMMS for permission to implement experimental Medicaid programs or demonstration projects that deviate from federal requirements. See 42 U.S.C. § 1315. Approximately one-third of all states currently operate their Medicaid programs under waivers. See Barry R. Furrow et al., Health Law 608 (2d ed. 2000). Oregon sparked controversy when it proposed a waiver that would allow it to expand its Medicaid coverage to all persons living below the poverty line by specifically ranking covered medical products and services according to their effectiveness and cost, and funding only items that ranked above a particular cut-off point. The framers of the Oregon plan initially intended to engage in a form of explicit health care rationing by evaluating the costs and benefits of various treatments and paying for only those treatments that survived the cost-benefit analysis. See Daniel Callahan, The Oregon Initiative: Ethics and Priority Setting, 1 Health Matrix 157 (1991); Leslie Pickering Francis, Consumer Expectations and Access to Health Care, 140 U. Pa. L. Rev. 1881 (1992); Lawrence Jacobs et al., The Oregon Health Plan and the Political Paradox of Rationing: What Advocates and Critics Have Claimed and What Oregon Did, 24 J. Health Pol. Pol'y & L. 161 (1999); Howard M. Leichter, Oregon's Bold Experiment: Whatever Happened to Rationing?, 24 J. Health Pol. Pol'y & L. 147 (1999). Other states, such as Tennessee, have also enjoyed success with Medicaid demonstration projects. See Symposium, The Law and Policy of Health Care Rationing, 140 U. Pa. L. Rev. 1505 (1992); Philip G. Peters, Jr., Health Care Rationing and Disability Rights, 70 Ind. L.J. 491 (1995). Shortly after George W. Bush took office in 2001, the National Governors' Association proposed a radical restructuring of Medicaid to permit states more flexibility in the administration of benefits. The proposal is designed to offer a full range of medical benefits to the poorest of the states' residents, while broadening access to a more restricted range of benefits for a wider group of low-income people. See Robert Pear, Governors Offer "Radical" Revision of Medicaid Plan, N.Y. Times, Feb. 26, 2001, at A1.

6. *Coverage for experimental therapies.* The public insurance programs severely limit coverage of experimental treatments.

> When public payers are involved, courts interpret "experimentation" in light of the excessively broad definitions offered by the Medicare and Medicaid legislation. The key statutory language for Medicare, the federal health insurance program covering services for the elderly and disabled, states that payment shall not be made for

items or expenses which are "not reasonable and necessary." The Health Care Financing Administration (HCFA), which runs Medicare and Medicaid, equates this with a test of whether the technologies are "safe" and "effective" and not "experimental." However, no regulations have clarified these terms. Indeed, HCFA recognizes that the Medicare law is vague, leaving most coverage questions to the fiscal intermediaries and other Medicare contractors who review payment claims. These Medicare contractors vary widely in their determinations.

In more difficult cases, HCFA issues a "national coverage decision" to indicate to carriers whether a particular technology is covered. Courts may be called upon to review these decisions, yet judicial scrutiny usually focuses on whether proper administrative procedures were followed, and not on the criteria used by HCFA to label a technology experimental. When courts do address these criteria directly, they often mechanically quote from the Medicare pamphlets, which are not much more specific or informative than the statutory language. At best, courts scrutinize whether the determination of a technology's status is reasonable "based on current medical opinion."

The case law surrounding Medicaid, the combined federal-state health insurance program for the poor, is equally vague. The Medicaid statute does not set out specific coverage limitations, but courts have granted states considerable power to determine what services are covered, including the power to exclude experimental services. States are given so much discretion that the Medicaid statute could be read to allow states to exclude even "medically necessary" services, [so] judicial inquiry into whether a technology is experimental is made irrelevant. In any event, Medicaid disputes that end up in court rarely address directly the criteria for labeling a technology as experimental. Courts often defer to the opinion of the prescribing physician, which suggests one approach for determining experimental status. Other courts, however, have recognized that this can result in unfair and inconsistent determinations of benefits. Most of this litigation focuses on the question of who decides what constitutes a "medical necessity." The case law remains relatively silent as to how the term should be construed.

Richard S. Saver, Note, Reimbursing New Technologies: Why Are the Courts Judging Experimental Medicine?, 44 Stan. L. Rev. 1095, 1098–100 (1992).

Weaver v. Reagen

886 F.2d 194 (8th Cir.1989).

■ ROSS, CIRCUIT JUDGE:

* * * On March 20, 1987, the Food and Drug Administration (FDA) announced its approval of AZT under the brand name Retrovir, for the treatment of AIDS. The labeling approved by the FDA for AZT stated:

> Retrovir capsules are indicated for the management of certain adult patients with symptomatic HIV infection (AIDS and advanced [AIDS-related complex (ARC)]) who have a history of cytologically confirmed Pneumocystis carinii pneumonia (PCP) or an absolute CD4 (T4 helper/inducer) lymphocyte count of less than 200/mm in the peripheral blood before therapy is begun.

At the time this action was filed on July 6, 1987, the State of Missouri did not provide any Medicaid coverage for AZT. Three days after the suit was filed, the Missouri Department of Social Services promulgated an emergency rule, providing Medicaid coverage of AZT under certain diagnoses or conditions. Adopted as a permanent rule with minor modifications effective November 12, 1987, Missouri regulations now provide coverage for AZT as follows:

> The availability of the drug Zidovudine, formerly known as Azidothymidine, for Missouri Medicaid coverage shall be limited to only those eligible recipients for whom the prescribing physician has established a medical diagnosis of acquired immunodeficiency syndrome (AIDS) and who have a history of cytologically confirmed Pneumocystis carinii pneumonia (PCP) or an absolute CD4 (T4 helper/inducer) lymphocyte count of less than two hundred (200) per cubic millimeter in the peripheral blood before therapy is begun.

This language is virtually identical to FDA's approval statement for the drug.

At the present time, the drug AZT is the only approved treatment of AIDS or ARC. While there are treatments for particular opportunistic infections which the AIDS patient may develop, AZT is the only approved drug which acts on the HIV virus itself.

Although plaintiff Glenn Weaver, who had suffered from pneumocystis carinii pneumonia (PCP), became eligible for Medicaid coverage of AZT as a result of the change in the Missouri Medicaid rules, the present action was continued when other plaintiffs were granted leave to intervene. The new plaintiffs suffered with AIDS and certain AIDS indicator diseases, but did not meet the restricted medical conditions necessary for coverage of AZT under Missouri's Medicaid rule (history of PCP or an absolute CD4 lymphocyte count below 200). For example, plaintiff Mark Momot was diagnosed as infected with the AIDS virus and suffering from oropharyngeal/esophageal candidiasis, an AIDS indicator disease, as well as significant diarrhea, fever, sweats and lymphadenopathy. In order to prevent or retard the progression of the disease to a more serious illness, his personal physician prescribed AZT. However, because Momot had no history of PCP and his CD4 count had not dropped below 200, Missouri Medicaid denied coverage of his AZT prescription because "he did not meet the diagnosis criteria set forth in the state regulation." * * *

The trial court held that defendants' rule limiting Medicaid coverage of AZT to only those recipients who meet certain diagnostic criteria or conditions violated federal Medicaid law. The district court found that AZT is medically necessary treatment for individuals in the plaintiff class who do not fit within the restrictive criteria of Missouri's Medicaid rule. The court, therefore, enjoined Missouri officials from denying coverage of AZT to "persons eligible for Medicaid and infected with the AIDS virus." * * *

Title XIX of the Social Security Act, commonly known as the Medicaid Act, is a federal-state cooperative program designed to provide medical assistance to persons whose income and resources are insufficient to meet the costs of medical care. Although a state's participation is voluntary, once a state chooses to participate in the program it must comply with federal statutory and regulatory requirements, including the requirement that participating states provide financial assistance for in-patient hospital services, out-patient hospital services, laboratory and x-ray services, skilled nursing facilities and physicians' services.

The participating state may also elect to provide other optional medical services such as prescription drugs. Once a state chooses to offer such optional services it is bound to act in compliance with the Act and the applicable regulations in the implementation of those services, including the requirement that "each service must be sufficient in amount, duration, and scope to reasonably achieve its purpose."

Although a state has considerable discretion in fashioning its Medicaid program, the discretion of the state is not unbridled: "[A state] may not arbitrarily deny or reduce the amount, duration, or scope of a required service . . . to an otherwise eligible recipient solely because of the diagnosis, type of illness or condition." 42 C.F.R. § 440.230(c). "Appropriate limits [may be placed] on a service based on such criteria as medical necessity or utilization control procedures." Id. § 440.230(d). Moreover, the state's plan for determining eligibility for medical assistance must be " 'reasonable' and 'consistent with the objectives' of the Act." This provision has been interpreted to require that a state Medicaid plan provide treatment that is deemed "medically necessary" in order to comport with the objectives of the Act.

In the present case, defendants argue that their reliance on the FDA's approval statement in limiting coverage of AZT to only those patients who meet certain medical criteria is a reasonable exercise of their discretion to place limitations on covered services based on medical necessity and utilization controls. We do not find this argument persuasive.

Contrary to defendants' assertions, FDA approved indications were not intended to limit or interfere with the practice of medicine nor to preclude physicians from using their best judgment in the interest of the patient. Instead, the FDA new drug approval process is intended to ensure that drugs meet certain statutory standards for safety and effectiveness, manufacturing and controls, and labeling, and to ensure that manufacturers market their drugs only for those indications for which the drug sponsor has demonstrated "substantial evidence" of effectiveness. * * * Thus, the fact that FDA has not approved labeling of a drug for a particular use does not necessarily bear on those uses of the drug that are established within the medical and scientific community as medically appropriate. It would be improper for the State of Missouri to interfere with a physician's judgment of medical necessity by limiting coverage of AZT based on criteria that admittedly do not reflect current medical knowledge or practice.

It is also defendants' position on appeal that prescribing AZT outside the FDA approved indications is per se "experimental" in the sense that there is no scientific data derived from clinical trials documenting the efficacy and safety of AZT use outside the FDA guidelines. According to defendants, because such AZT use is experimental, it can never be deemed medically necessary treatment.

In our view, defendants' definition of "experimental" in this context is overly broad. * * * [T]he prescription of AZT beyond its labeled indications is not experimental. The record here establishes that physicians commonly prescribe AZT for patients who have neither a history of PCP nor a CD4 count below 200. Plaintiffs' experts stated that based on their own practice, professional literature, conferences, and contacts with other physicians, AZT is generally accepted by the medical community as an effective and proven treatment for AIDS patients who do not meet the criteria in the FDA indications. * * * Defendants' expert, Dr. John Mills, a professor of medicine at the University of California at San Francisco, does not controvert the affidavits of plaintiffs' experts in which they conclude that AZT may be medically necessary for AIDS patients who do not meet the restrictive diagnostic criteria in Missouri's regulation. Although Dr. Mills stated that the use of AZT beyond labeled indications was experimental in the sense that scientific studies had not conclusively determined its effectiveness, Dr. Mills agreed that "doctors commonly exercise professional medical judgment and prescribe drugs for uses not within the indications articulated by the FDA." Specifically with regard to AZT, Dr. Mills stated that "doctors commonly prescribe AZT for patients not meeting those two criteria" (history of PCP or CD4 count below 200) and in fact, Dr. Mills himself testified that he has prescribed AZT outside the FDA indications. * * *

Missouri's Medicaid rule constitutes an irrebuttable presumption that AZT can never be medically necessary treatment for AIDS patients who have neither a history of PCP nor a CD4 count below 200. The record here establishes that such a presumption is unreasonable in light of the widespread recognition by the medical community and scientific literature that AZT is the only known antiviral treatment for individuals with AIDS.

The Medicaid statute and regulatory scheme create a presumption in favor of the medical judgment of the attending physician in determining the medical necessity of treatment. In denying coverage of AZT to the plaintiff class, the defendants have done nothing to overcome that presumption except to rely on the FDA approval process in a manner expressly rejected by the FDA. In the face of widespread recognition by the medical community and the scientific and medical literature that AZT is the only available treatment for most persons with AIDS, we find that Missouri

Medicaid's approach to its coverage of the drug AZT is unreasonable and inconsistent with the objectives of the Medicaid Act. * * *

NOTES AND QUESTIONS

1. *Medicare and Medicaid coverage of off-label uses.* CMMS provides Medicare reimbursement for approved drugs prescribed for a use approved by the FDA or, in the case of anticancer chemotherapeutic agents, for a use supported by a study appearing in the peer-reviewed medical literature or a citation in one of several identified medical compendia. See 42 U.S.C. § 1395x(t)(2)(B)(ii). In contrast, in a provision added to the statute after the decision in *Weaver*, Congress authorized Medicaid reimbursement of prescription drug expenses only for off-label uses appearing in certain medical compendia, excluding other uses supported by the peer-reviewed medical literature. See id. § 1396r–8(k)(3), (6).

2. *What price for health?* Many people with HIV or AIDS cannot afford the approximately $15,000 annual cost for new "drug cocktails" that dramatically reduce viral load and promise to extend life significantly. Does the fact of their existence make these drug therapies a "right" for those infected with the virus? Put more generally, now that these therapies are standard care for those who can afford them (or whose insurance will cover them), is there some principle that mandates payment for those who cannot pay? Our health care system is not designed this way, and many people in this country remain uninsured. Should government-funded programs such as Medicaid pay for these drugs when patients cannot? Access to minimal health care is not presently recognized as a fundamental right in the United States.

2. MEDICARE REIMBURSEMENT FOR MEDICAL TECHNOLOGIES

Congress established the federal Medicare program, which covers all Social Security recipients and Railroad Retirement beneficiaries who are over age 65, or disabled, or who have permanent kidney failure. As of 1999, the Medicare program insured approximately 40 million people, and by 2030, the program is expected to cover as many as 77 million beneficiaries. Thus, as spending for Medicare continues to balloon to accommodate growing numbers of eligible beneficiaries (and with a possible prescription drug benefit on the horizon threatening an even more drastic spending increase), Congress is going to have to make some difficult choices about Medicare reform. See Marilyn Moon, Medicare, 344 New Eng. J. Med. 928 (2001).

HCFA, Proposed Rule, *Medicare Program: Criteria and Procedures for Making Medical Services Coverage Decisions That Relate to Health Care Technology*
54 Fed. Reg. 4302 (1989).

* * * The Medicare law does not * * * provide an all-inclusive list of specific items, services, treatments, procedures, or technologies covered by

Medicare. Thus, except for the examples of durable medical equipment in section 1861(n) of the Act, and some of the medical and other health services listed in sections 1861(s) and 1862(a) of the Act, the statute does not specify medical devices, surgical procedures, or diagnostic or therapeutic services that should be either covered or excluded from coverage. * * *

Congress understood that questions as to coverage of specific services would invariably arise and would require a specific decision of coverage by those administering the program. Thus, it vested in the Secretary the authority to make those decisions. Section 1862(a)(1)(A) of the Act states: "Notwithstanding any other provisions of this title, no payment may be made under Part A or Part B for any expenses incurred for items or services which * * * are not reasonable and necessary for the diagnosis or treatment of illness or injury or to improve the functioning of a malformed body member." This is a key provision since the words "notwithstanding any other provision of this title" make this an overriding exclusion that may be applicable in a given situation despite the existence of provisions that would otherwise permit coverage. Thus, while Congress provided for the coverage of services such as inpatient hospital care and physicians' services, coverage for those services is prohibited unless they are "reasonable" and "necessary." * * *

Questions regarding coverage of drugs and biologicals are rarely referred to PHS since we have determined as a matter of national policy that drugs or biologicals approved for marketing by FDA are safe and effective when used for indications specified in their labeling. In addition, FDA-approved drugs also may be covered when used for indications other than those specified on their labeling as long as FDA has not specified such use as non-approved. Coverage of non-labeled uses is determined by our contractors taking into consideration the generally accepted medical practice in the community. Treatment Investigational New Drugs (INDs) are approved by FDA but are still considered experimental and not covered by Medicare. Drugs that have not received FDA approval for marketing are considered experimental or investigational and are not covered except for certain cancer drugs distributed by the National Cancer Institute (NCI). * * *

FDA approval for the marketing of a medical device will not necessarily lead to a favorable coverage recommendation, particularly if FDA requirements have been met by means of a notice issued under section 510(k) of the Federal Food, Drug, and Cosmetic Act (FFDCA), rather than by means of a premarket approval application (PMA) made under section 515 of the FFDCA. This is because a section 510(k) notice generally does not involve clinical data showing safety and effectiveness. Only limited safety and effectiveness data are generally required by FDA for purposes of a section 510(k) notice. FDA findings of safety and effectiveness focus on the labeled use of a device only, while our decisions may focus on other uses of a device under average conditions of use (that is, other than in a clinical setting). * * *

Friedrich v. HHS

894 F.2d 829 (6th Cir.1990).

■ Lively, Senior Circuit Judge:

* * * The Medicare Act consists of two parts or programs. Part A provides insurance against the cost of institutional health services. Part B, the portion at issue here, is a voluntary, supplemental medical insurance program that covers 80 percent of the "reasonable charge" for a number of services, including certain physician services, x-rays, lab tests and medical supplies. The purpose of this section is to complement existing insurance coverage for the aged and disabled. Part B is financed through monthly fee charges to the beneficiaries and funding from the government. * * *

Because of the substantial dimensions of the program, Part B is managed for the Secretary by "carriers," insurance companies who administer the payment of qualifying claims. The Secretary pays the carriers' costs resulting from claims administration and the carriers, acting as the Secretary's agents, in turn determine whether a claimed item or service is covered by the program. The carriers make this determination in strict accordance with the Medicare statute and the regulations, instructions and guidelines promulgated by the Secretary. * * *

[U]nder Part B, the Secretary and the insurance carriers are required to deny reimbursement for services that are not "reasonable and necessary for the diagnosis or treatment" of a claimant's illness or injury. 42 U.S.C. § 1395y(a)(1). A finding of what services are "reasonable and necessary" is often made on a case-by-case basis by the carrier. In more difficult cases, however, the Health Care Financing Administration (HCFA), a component of the Department of Health & Human Services (HHS), will make an assessment and then issue a "national coverage determination" clearly indicating to the carriers whether the particular item should be considered covered or not. National coverage determinations issued by HCFA are published in the Part B Carriers Manual (the Manual) and are therefore binding on the carriers and their hearing officers.

In making its assessment of reasonableness and necessity HCFA often relies on the Public Health Service (PHS) for an evaluation of the safety and effectiveness of a particular service and the extent to which it has been accepted by the medical community. Within PHS, every review of this kind is undertaken by the Office of Health Technology Assessment (OHTA) of the National Center for Health Services Research and Health Care Technology Assessment (NCHSRHCTA). OHTA usually places a notice in the *Federal Register* announcing that an assessment is underway and soliciting comments from interested parties. During the assessment process OHTA also seeks information and recommendations from governmental agencies such as the National Institutes of Health (NIH) and the Food and Drug Administration (FDA). OHTA also consults with professional organizations and medical specialty groups to determine whether the procedure is generally accepted by the medical community as being safe and effective, and conducts a review of the medical literature. HCFA then issues a national coverage determination based on its consideration of PHS's recommendations.

The service at issue here, chelation therapy, is a treatment for atherosclerosis (obstructed arteries). The treatment consists of intravenous injections of disodium edetate solution. Proponents of the treatment believe that the disodium edetate, which binds ("chelates") with calcium, removes the calcium-containing plaque that clogs arteries. According to the government, however, this treatment has been widely discredited by the general medical community as being ineffective and unsafe.

An examination of the record indicates that as early as 1970, HCFA had issued instructions restricting Medicare coverage of disodium edetate to treatment for hypercalcemia, ventricular arrhythmias, heart block associated with digitalis toxicity and scleroderma. This position was apparently embraced at the urging of PHS, which had consulted with various medical organizations and the FDA. As early as 1970 the FDA-approved labeling for the drug stated that disodium edetate was indicated for the severe conditions mentioned above, but not "for the treatment of generalized arteriosclerosis associated with advancing age."

The HCFA instructions on disodium edetate remained in effect until 1980, when HCFA replaced most specific drug coverage determinations with general criteria for intermediary and carrier use in determining coverage. The new 1980 criteria permitted payment for any use of an FDA-approved drug determined by the carrier to be reasonable and necessary, except for those uses specifically disapproved by the FDA or for which coverage might be precluded by a national instruction.

Subsequent to the issuance of the 1980 Carriers Manual, HCFA requested that NCHSRHCTA review chelation therapy and make a recommendation as to Medicare coverage. NCHSRHCTA published a notice in the *Federal Register* announcing its planned assessment and requesting interested parties to submit relevant information. NCHSRHCTA additionally sought evaluations of chelation therapy from a number of professional organizations and medical specialty groups. As a result of this notice a large number of opinions by physicians and various medical organizations were obtained. Based on this information, NCHSRHCTA issued a comprehensive report and assessment recommending that the Medicare program not cover chelation therapy. HCFA responded to the assessment by issuing a national coverage determination in February 1982 instructing intermediaries and carriers not to pay for chelation therapy under Medicare. * * *

The plaintiff Michael J. Friedrich, a Medicare Part B beneficiary, requested reimbursement for expenses related to chelation therapy. Friedrich received these treatments in February, March and April of 1983. The total cost of these services was $410.70. The plaintiff's insurance carrier, Nationwide Mutual Insurance, refused to reimburse the claimant for these expenses.

On May 19, 1983, plaintiff filed a claim with Nationwide seeking review of the earlier denial of his claim. The plaintiff's claim was again denied by letter on June 24, 1983. On July 25, 1983, Friedrich requested a carrier hearing review. This hearing was held on March 19, 1984. At the hearing both the plaintiff and his physician, Dr. Frackleton, testified as to the benefits of chelation therapy for the treatment of atherosclerosis. The witnesses also submitted written material. The Secretary offered no contrary evidence. On April 25, 1984, the hearing officer found that "although the evidence and testimony presented at this hearing was impressive and implies the efficacy of chelation therapy as a viable alternative to conventional treatment for coronary artery disease, this does not alter the instructions contained in the carrier's manual that EDTA chelation therapy for the treatment or prevention of atherosclerosis is not covered." Reimbursement was denied on this basis. * * *

The plaintiff argues that the chelation therapy determination represented a departure from Medicare's general policy with respect to coverage. It argues that the general policy is to treat drugs approved for marketing by the FDA as satisfying the statutory "reasonable and necessary" requirement for Medicare reimbursement. He emphasizes the fact that a passage in the Manual states that the disqualification of chelation therapy is an exception to Medicare's general policy on coverage of drugs. The same statement continues, however, by stating that the general rule is to treat FDA-approved drugs prescribed by a physician as covered "if the Medicare contractor determines the use is reasonable and necessary." The Secretary asserts that the purpose of the determination was to restate the Department's consistent policy that, though considered reasonable and necessary for treatment of some illnesses, chelation therapy does not satisfy this statutory requirement when used for the treatment of atherosclerosis.

The record reveals that as early as 1970 the Department of Health, Education and Welfare had advised by notices in the *Federal Register* that disodium edetate was not considered effective for the treatment of generalized arteriosclerosis. (Atherosclerosis is a stage of the chronic disease arteriosclerosis). The Secretary states that this has been the consistent position of the Department and that the 1982 national coverage determination did not represent a change of position.

In 1980 the Secretary began the practice of examining some drugs individually rather than qualifying all FDA-approved drugs if they were found by the Part B carriers to be reasonable and necessary. The 1982 determination implemented this new policy. In effect, it made the determination of reasonableness and necessity with respect to a particular use of chelation therapy rather than leaving that determination to the carriers. The Secretary states that in doing so, he created no new rights or duties; he merely applied the statutory requirements to a particular use of a given drug and method of treatment. The "new policy" referred to in the Manual is the *method* of dealing with FDA-approved drugs, not a new policy with respect to the reasonableness or necessity for use of chelation therapy in the treatment of atherosclerosis. * * * The record as a whole convinces us that the Secretary has been consistent in his determination that chelation therapy is not reasonable and necessary for the diagnosis or treatment of atherosclerosis. Thus the 1982 determination did not represent a departure from a previous evaluation of this medical procedure. * * *

The Medicare program covers the full range of modern medicine and pharmacology. It is comprehensive and operates through a complex structure. National standards are essential if there is to be uniformity and equality in the administration of Medicare. The Secretary has chosen to seek uniformity by requiring Part B carriers to abide by all regulations in the Manual. It is inconceivable to us that the Secretary might be required to comply with the full panoply of APA notice and comment requirements in promulgating national standards for individual drugs and medical procedures. This is a classic case of a rule that fits perfectly the "common theme" of the § 553(b)(A) exception for rules that "accommodate situations where the policies promoted by public participation in rulemaking are outweighed by the countervailing considerations of effectiveness, efficiency, expedition and reduction in expense."

The Medicare Act mandates that only reasonable and necessary medical services are reimbursable. The national coverage determination does not "fill the gaps" in the statute. Thus, it creates no new law. Rather, it interprets the statutory language "reasonable and necessary" as applied to a particular medical service or method of treatment. The district court erred in concluding that the determination is a legislative rule and therefore is invalid for failure of the Secretary to comply with the requirements of 5 U.S.C. § 553(b). * * *

The first step in deciding a procedural due process claim is to identify the interest to which the due process attaches. Here, Friedrich claimed a property interest in Medicare benefits * * * * The only legitimate claim of entitlement under Medicare is to those services that are reasonable and necessary. 42 U.S.C. § 1395y(a)(1). There is no legitimate claim of entitlement to a given medical procedure just because a doctor prescribes it or a patient requests it.

The record in this case reveals that the plaintiff had no more than a unilateral expectation that he would receive reimbursement under the Medicare program for chelation therapy. As we have noted, on advice of the PHS and others, the Secretary has ruled consistently since 1970 that this procedure is not safe and effective for the treatment of atherosclerosis. The various *Federal Register* notices and publications have consistently found that there is little support in the medical community for this course of treatment, and that at best it must be considered experimental. * * *

The record discloses that NCHSRHCTA received and considered large volumes of material, mostly anecdotal, in favor of chelation therapy before HCFA made its final evaluation and issued the national coverage determination in February 1982. We have found the evaluation procedure valid as meeting the requirements for promulgation of an interpretative rule. Friedrich does not have a due process right to have his individual claim considered de novo in the face of the Secretary's determination. Having made a national coverage determination, the Secretary is not required to defend it in response to individual claims by every person who disagrees with the decision to deny coverage. The fact that the hearing officer was bound by the determination did not deny Friedrich process to which he was due. * * *

Goodman v. Sullivan

712 F.Supp. 334 (S.D.N.Y.1989).

■ Walker, District Judge:

* * * Plaintiff was suffering from a progressive speech impediment. In February 1985, plaintiff's physician suggested that plaintiff undergo a diagnostic test known as a magnetic resonance imaging procedure (MRI) to determine the underlying cause of his condition. Plaintiff underwent a MRI and subsequently presented a claim for $675.00 for the cost of the test to the Medicare Part B carrier in his area. The carrier denied plaintiff reimbursement for the MRI on the ground that MRIs were not covered under Medicare Part B as of February 1985. * * *

Plaintiff claims, however, that the regulation denying coverage for any medical procedures unapproved by the Secretary violates 42 U.S.C. § 1395 in that it is contrary to the Act's mandate that the Secretary: (a) pay for all medically necessary treatment and, (b) not interfere with the practice of medicine. Plaintiff maintains that no regulation can establish an irrebuttable presumption of the lack of medical necessity without countermanding the Act. * * * That the Secretary eventually approved MRIs for reimbursement is immaterial. As noted previously, plaintiff does not merely challenge the Secretary's policy regarding MRIs. Rather, plaintiff broadly challenges the validity of the Secretary's regulation denying coverage for any techniques unapproved by the Secretary. * * *

While Congress created specific exclusions from coverage and provided that in no case may payment be made for any expenses incurred for items and services which "are not reasonable and necessary for the diagnosis or treatment of illness or injury," 42 U.S.C. § 1395y(a)(1)(A), it never provided that payment must be made at all times when services are deemed "medically necessary." Neither plaintiff nor the court can locate such language either in the Act or in the legislative history. Rather, Congress delegated to the Secretary the authority to promulgate regulations for administering the Medicare program, and provided the Secretary with great discretion in determining what items or services will be covered under Medicare Part B. The Secretary is specifically provided with discretion in considering whether diagnostic tests shall be covered in 42 U.S.C. § 1395x(s).

Plaintiff mistakenly contends that once a physician has concluded that a service or item is medically necessary, the Secretary cannot deny reimbursement. Congress has not provided that all medically necessary items or services must be covered under Medicare Part B. * * * [T]he rules promulgated by the Secretary do not conflict with the Act but, rather, stay well within the general intent of Congress in enacting Part B of Medicare.

Moreover, the court finds no evidence that either the Secretary's decision to deny plaintiff MRI benefits or the Secretary's regulations themselves interfere with the practice of medicine. * * *

NOTES AND QUESTIONS

1. *Competing proposals for a Medicare drug benefit.* Apart from drugs administered to hospital and skilled nursing facility inpatients, Medicare currently only pays for a very limited group of prescription drugs: immuno-supressants for organ transplant recipients, certain drugs for kidney disease patients, certain oral cancer agents, and hemophilia drugs. Although 73 percent of Medicare beneficiaries have purchased supplemental drug coverage through "Medigap" policies or receive such coverage through employer-sponsored retirement benefits, more than nine million beneficiaries remain without prescription drug coverage. See John K. Inglehart, Medicare and Prescription Drugs, 344 New Eng. J. Med. 1010, 1011 (2001). Proposals for a drug benefit surfaced in the year 2000 as an important issue in the presidential campaign. Republicans and Democrats have floated a variety of plans for prescription drug coverage, but each parties' proposals share certain common elements. The Republican plan generally contemplates a major reform of the Medicare program, providing beneficiaries with a choice between Medicare's traditional fee-for-service plan and private health plans, and providing some prescription drug coverage under both options. Republicans also advocate privatizing drug coverage by providing subsidies to health plans, which would then be free to design drug benefits packages within certain coverage and premium restrictions. Benefits would be phased in over a period of years, beginning with coverage for the lower income Medicare recipients. See Robert Pear, Bush Drug Plan Lacks Support, Senators Assert, N.Y. Times, Jan. 19, 2001, at A1. The Democrats would retain the Medicare program as a purely public insurance program, with management and funding coming exclusively from the federal government, and contemplate a standard, national drug benefit that would provide partial coverage for most Medicare recipients, along with a broader benefit for catastrophic illnesses. Advocates of either strategy must overcome significant hurdles, including questions of how much funding to allocate to the drug benefit program given the possibility that coverage will create greater demand for prescription drugs. The pharmaceutical industry strongly opposes price controls and is expected to oppose the extension to Medicare of the federal supply schedule for pharmaceuticals, which currently enables federal agencies to purchase prescription drugs at prices well below the average wholesale prices for the products. See Dep't of Veterans Affairs, Federal Supply Schedule (2000), available at <http://www.vapbm.org/PBM/menu.asp>. If the government does begin purchasing drugs for Medicare under the terms of the federal supply schedule, experts predict that the prices for drugs charged to private insurers will rise dramatically to compensate for lost revenues. See Inglehart, supra, at 1012–14; see also Joshua P. Cohen, PBMs and a Medicare Prescription Drug Benefit, 55 Food & Drug L.J. 311 (2000).

2. *Renal dialysis benefits.* Not all Medicare beneficiaries are over the age of 65. Medicare Part B covers home dialysis supplies, equipment, and support services, and institutional dialysis services and supplies for patients of any age who suffer from kidney disease. See 42 U.S.C. § 1395x(s)(2)(F), (O); 42 C.F.R. §§ 410.50, 410.52, 405.2101–.2185. Medicare Part A also covers persons with end-stage renal disease after a three-month waiting period. These patients can receive inpatient hospital care for up to ninety days for each "spell of illness." See 42 U.S.C. § 426–1. Well over 90 percent of patients with end-stage renal disease now receive Medicare benefits. See Henry Krakauer et al., The Recent U.S. Experience in the Treatment of End–Stage Renal Disease by Dialysis and Transplantation, 308 New Eng. J. Med. 1558 (1983). As part of covered care for patients with renal disease, the Medicare program pays for erythropoietin (EPO), a biotechnology product approved by the FDA in 1989 to treat anemia problems caused by chronic renal failure. Under HCFA's interim policy for EPO reimbursement for Medicare ESRD and chronic renal failure patients, the total EPO costs were $265 million—an average of $5,300 per patient for EPO alone. HCFA quickly opted to revise the way it calculated payments for EPO (by changing reimbursement rates and dosage units to reflect actual practice), but the newer approach failed to lower the cost to the agency for EPO. See Office of Tech. Assessment, Health Care Technology and Its Assessment in Eight Countries, OTA–BP–H–140, at 317–18 (1995).

3. *Unlawful industry practices seeking reimbursement from government programs.* In 1997, the Department of Justice and the Office of the HHS Inspector General began an investigation of the 20 largest pharmaceutical companies in order to determine whether their pricing practices violated the federal reimbursement system. See Kathleen M. Sanzo & Stephen Paul Mahinka, Expect Big Change in Drug Pricing System, Nat'l L.J., Sept. 4, 2000, at B9 (describing a series of ongoing fraud and abuse investigations of the "pricing, reimbursement and promotional practices of pharmaceutical companies"). TAP Pharmaceuticals recently was charged with bribing physicians to prescribe Lupron and conspiring with a physician to receive inflated Medicare reimbursement for the drug. Although that case settled in September 2001, the government is pursuing similar cases against other pharmaceutical companies for excessive billing to both the Medicare and Medicaid programs. See Melody Petersen, Court Papers Depict Scheme in Drug Billing, N.Y. Times, Feb. 20, 2001, at C1 (describing scheme whereby the companies "publicly reported an average wholesale price for their drugs that was much higher than the price they actually charged doctors and pharmacies"); Robert Pear, Bayer to Pay $14 Million to Settle Charges of Causing Inflated Medicaid Claims, N.Y. Times, Jan. 24, 2001, at A16 (describing an investigation that found that Medicaid sometimes paid two to four times more than commercial customers for certain drugs); see also Thomas N. Bulleit, Jr. & Joan H. Krause, Kickbacks, Courtesies or Cost–Effectiveness?: Application of the Medicare Antikickback Law to the Marketing and Promotional Practices of Drug and Medical Device Manufacturers, 54 Food & Drug L.J. 279 (1999); Alan M. Kirschenbaum & Bruce N. Kuhlik, Federal and State Laws Affecting Discounts, Rebates, and Other

Marketing Practices for Drugs and Devices, 47 Food & Drug L.J. 533 (1992); John B. Reiss, Commentary on Payment and Reimbursement Issues Affecting the Marketing of Drugs, Medical Devices, and Biologics, with Emphasis on the Anti–Kickback Statute and Stark II, 52 Food & Drug L.J. 99 (1997).

TAP Pharmaceuticals v. HHS

163 F.3d 199 (4th Cir.1998).

■ MOTZ, CIRCUIT JUDGE:

TAP Pharmaceuticals, Inc. * * * seeks to challenge a Medicare reimbursement policy. That policy reduces the amount of reimbursement paid for Lupron, a prostate cancer drug manufactured by TAP, to the amount paid for Zoladex, a competing prostate cancer drug made by another drug company. The district court concluded that the interests asserted by TAP in this action do not fall within the "zone of interests" protected by the Medicare Part B program, and that therefore TAP lacked standing to sue. Although we rely on reasons somewhat different than those set forth by the district court, we reach the same conclusion. Accordingly, we affirm.

Lupron and Zoladex treat prostate cancer by means of the same basic chemical mechanism, and they achieve the same level of effectiveness. The two drugs have different rates of action, however, and their particular chemical formulations implicate different adverse reactions. Lupron is administered in liquid form by an intramuscular injection with a 22–gauge needle, while Zoladex is administered as a pellet injected under the skin with a larger, 14– or 16–gauge needle. The larger needle used in administering Zoladex may occasionally cause complications, such as keloid scarring or bleeding hematoma, which are less likely to occur with a Lupron injection. The manufacturer of Zoladex suggests that, at the option of the physician or the patient, a local anesthetic and bandage be used in administering the drug. Such procedures are unnecessary with Lupron. Some doctors prefer Lupron to Zoladex because of its less invasive means of administration.

Many patients who receive Lupron or Zoladex have a portion of their health care costs covered by Medicare Part B, a federal program that provides supplementary medical insurance to the elderly. Generally, Medicare Part B covers "reasonable and necessary" medical services for the "diagnosis or treatment of illness or injury or to improve the functioning of a malformed body member." Though Medicare Part B does not cover most prescription medication, it does cover drugs, like Lupron and Zoladex, which are typically administered by doctors during office or hospital visits. 42 U.S.C. § 1395x(s)(2)(A). Medicare reimburses doctors for a percentage of the cost of such drugs.

In October 1996, Palmetto Government Benefits Administrators, which administers Medicare Part B benefits in South Carolina under the authority of the Health Care Financing Administration and the United States

Department of Health and Human Services (collectively, the Government), adopted the policy that TAP seeks to challenge here. The policy provides that doctors will be reimbursed for the cost of Lupron only at the reimbursement level of the less-expensive Zoladex. Prior to its adoption, Palmetto reimbursed expenditures for each drug on the basis of that drug's own cost.

Palmetto based this change in policy on its conclusion that "there is no therapeutic difference between" the two drugs, although it later acknowledged that TAP's Lupron has a greater duration of action. In the most recent version of the Lupron policy, Palmetto states that "there is no demonstrable difference in clinical efficacy" between Lupron and Zoladex. This latest version of the policy also loosens the restriction on Lupron reimbursement. It allows patients who wish to receive Lupron to make up the difference in cost between Lupron and Zoladex on their own, and it provides that "if there are true medical indications requiring the use of [Lupron] instead of [Zoladex], Medicare will consider reimbursement for the difference in cost if an invoice and documentation of the medical necessity accompanies the claim." * * *

TAP alleges that the new Lupron reimbursement policy violates a Medicare regulation providing that reimbursement for drugs such as Lupron must be "based on the lower of the estimated acquisition cost or the national wholesale average price of the drug." 42 C.F.R. § 405.517(b). TAP asserts that basing reimbursement for Lupron on the cost of Zoladex, rather than on the cost of Lupron itself, violates this regulation. Although the regulation has now been superseded by a 1997 amendment to the Act, which provides that payment for covered drugs is to be made at 95% of the average wholesale price, 42 U.S.C. § 1395u(o)(1), TAP's contention regarding the regulation applies equally well to the statute as amended. Both base reimbursement on the cost of the drug used, while the new Lupron policy bases reimbursement on the cost of another drug. TAP also alleges that * * * Palmetto's conclusion that "there is no therapeutic difference between" Lupron and Zoladex lacked a scientific basis and so its adoption of the new Lupron policy in reliance upon this conclusion was arbitrary and capricious; * * * and finally that Palmetto's reimbursement policy violated 42 U.S.C.A. § 1395y(a)(1)(A), which prohibits payment for any item that is not "reasonable and necessary." * * *

The Government maintains that the only interest arguably protected by the Medicare Part B program is the interest "of the elderly in receiving affordable medical insurance," and that TAP's commercial interests are at odds with this statutory goal. In support of this position, the Government cites the statute's provision of insurance for the cost of "reasonable and necessary" medical care. The Government argues that this statutory language shows Congress's sole intention in enacting this legislation to have been that of protecting the financial integrity of the Medicare program.

TAP contends that the most important interest protected by the Medicare Part B program is the provision of excellent medical care to the elderly. It accordingly denies that the "reasonable and necessary" language in the statute involves a cost limitation, as the Government has argued; instead, TAP maintains that the phrase has long been interpreted by the Government itself to mean merely "safe and effective." TAP also argues that the Government's failed attempts to promulgate a regulation introducing a cost-based limitation show that the existing regulatory scheme has no such limitation. TAP heavily relies on a phrase in the legislative history stating that Medicare Part B seeks "to make the best of modern medicine more readily available to the aged." TAP contends that its commercial interests in selling as much Lupron as possible coincide with this statutory goal.

Both parties provide a distorted picture of the interests "arguably protected" by Medicare Part B. Their conflicting positions suggest what our examination of the statute, the regulations, and the legislative history leads us to conclude: Medicare Part B, like many statutes, embodies a compromise between ideals of achievement and economic feasibility that puts its basic purposes in tension. The Act seeks to "make the best of modern medicine more readily available to the aged," but it tries to do so by covering only "reasonable and necessary" care in a manner that will ensure the financial integrity of the system. Perhaps the clearest indication of the statute's competing goals appears in its provision establishing that health care services will generally be covered at a statutorily-defined percentage of their cost. Through this provision, the Act makes all levels of reasonable and necessary medical care more readily available to the aged, while at the same time discouraging excessive expenditure by requiring beneficiaries to pay for a proportionate share of the cost of the services they use.

To have standing, however, TAP need not assert an interest that coincides precisely with the balance struck by Congress between the Act's conflicting purposes; rather, it need only show that its "interests affected by the agency action" are "among" those that Congress arguably sought to protect. Considering only the statute's interest in providing high-quality medical care does not lead to a resolution favorable to TAP, however. Contrary to TAP's assertions, the interest that it asserts here is not the same as the statute's interest in making the best of medicine more readily available to the aged. TAP seeks to increase distribution of Lupron, but it does not specifically allege that Lupron is the best of medicine, and it has not otherwise definitively contended that Lupron is "better" than Zoladex.

Even if we regard TAP's more general allegations as asserting the superiority of Lupron, the statute's interest in "making the best of modern medicine more readily available to the aged" would not coincide with TAP's interest. Quotation of the entire sentence in which this much-cited fragment of legislative history occurs makes the difference plain: "The provision of insurance against the covered costs would encourage the participating institutions, agencies, and individuals to make the best of modern medicine more readily available to the aged." This statement expresses an expectation that, as a result of the coverage of health care costs under Medicare Part B, hospitals, health care agencies, and doctors will become less reluctant to provide high-quality medical care to elderly patients. Medicare Part B is here envisioned as a means of rectifying a situation in which health care providers denied first-rate services to the aged because they lacked insurance. The main import of the statement, then, is that the statute seeks to make the best of medicine "more readily available" than it would be in the absence of Medicare Part B. The Lupron policy achieves this statutory purpose: Lupron is still covered, reimbursement for a portion of its cost is still provided, and Lupron is thus made more readily available to the aged than it would be in the absence of Medicare Part B. TAP's interest in attacking the Lupron policy must therefore be in something other than making the best of medicine more available in the sense articulated in the legislative history.

TAP actually seeks not to make Lupron "more readily available" than it would be without Medicare Part B, but rather to make it more available than it is now, under the Lupron policy. In this sense, TAP's asserted claim strives for something very different than that which the legislative history identifies as a statutory goal. Moreover, TAP objects to the present reimbursement policy not because it fails to make Lupron more available, but because it fails to make Lupron available on the same basis as Zoladex. The legislative history stating that the statute seeks "to make the best of modern medicine more readily available to the aged," however, cannot be read to express an interest in making different treatments for the same condition available on the same basis. The interest of TAP that is "affected by the agency action in question," therefore, does not coincide with the statute's interest in making the best of medicine more available to Medicare recipients. * * *

HCFA, Notice of Intent to Publish a Proposed Rule, *Medicare Program; Criteria for Making Coverage Decisions*
65 Fed. Reg. 31,124 (1999).

* * * We are issuing this notice to announce our intention to publish a proposed rule and solicit public comments on the criteria we would use to make a national coverage decision (NCD) and our contractors would use to make a local coverage decision (LCD) under section 1862(a)(1) of the Social Security Act (the Act). These coverage decisions are prospective, population-based policies that apply to a clinical subset or class of Medicare beneficiaries and describe the clinical circumstances and setting under which an item or service is available (or not available). We are setting out in this notice the information and approaches we are considering at this time for making coverage decisions. * * *

This notice only deals with the criteria for making national and local coverage decisions under the reasonable and necessary provisions of section 1862(a)(1) of the Act. This notice does not, and we do not anticipate that the proposed rule will, address individual medical necessity determinations and claims adjudication by our contractors and other adjudicators. Finally, this notice does not address Medicare payment policies and we do not anticipate that the proposed rule would include changes to our current rules on Medicare payment.

Given the dynamic nature of the health care system, it is important that the Medicare program be responsive to the rapid advances in health care. Regulations describing our criteria for coverage under the Medicare program would facilitate timely and expanded access for Medicare beneficiaries to appropriate new technologies. Within the scope of the statutory benefit categories, these criteria would expand access for Medicare beneficiaries by covering the following:

1. A breakthrough technology without consideration of cost.

2. A medically beneficial item or service if no other medically beneficial alternative is available.

3. A medically beneficial item or service if it is a different clinical modality compared to an existing covered beneficial alternative, without consideration of cost or magnitude of benefit.

4. A medically beneficial item or service, even if a less expensive alternative, which is not a Medicare benefit, exists. * * *

From the beginning of the Medicare program, one of the goals has been to provide a health insurance system that would make "the best of modern medicine" available to Medicare beneficiaries. Over the last 35 years, there have been significant advances in medical science that have changed the Medicare program and improved the health of beneficiaries and others. * * * While the Congress has demonstrated a strong interest in providing access to necessary medical care for Medicare beneficiaries, the Congress has been equally concerned with ensuring that the Medicare program operates on a sound financial basis. The Congress has established the specific scope of benefits that are included in the program and has defined many of the key terms in section 1861 of the Act. In addition, section 1862(a)(1)(A) of the Act requires that "no payment" may be made under Part A (hospital insurance) or Part B (supplementary medical insurance) for any expenses incurred for items or services that "are not reasonable and necessary for the diagnosis or treatment of illness or injury or to improve the functioning of a malformed body member." If we do not cover the expenses incurred for a particular item or service under this provision, either the Medicare beneficiary or the health care provider or supplier may be financially liable for all of the incurred costs.

The main purpose of our proposed rule will be to explain how the term "reasonable and necessary" applies in making coverage decisions. * * * We have the authority to determine whether an item or service is reasonable and necessary by several distinct approaches. One approach is to make a national coverage decision (NCD). Under 42 C.F.R. 405.732 and 405.860, an NCD either grants, limits, or excludes Medicare coverage for a specific medical service, procedure, or device. An NCD is binding on all carriers, fiscal intermediaries, Peer Review Organizations, and other contractors. * * * While an NCD is subject to judicial review, there are limitations on judicial review. This framework ensures that an NCD is consistently applied throughout the nation and enables a beneficiary to make an informed decision about whether to receive an item or service based on the knowledge that an item or service will be covered (or not covered) by the program.

Due to regional, local, or institutional differences in the practice of medicine, it is not always prudent to issue a prescriptive NCD. Sometimes there is not sufficient information for us to determine whether an item or service is an effective treatment on a national basis. In other circumstances, there are legitimate regional differences in the practice of medicine that would make a preemptive national rule inappropriate.

In the absence of an NCD, a decision concerning Medicare coverage for an individual could be resolved on a case-by-case basis after a claim is submitted. Our regulations separately provide broad appeal rights for certain individuals to administratively challenge our decision to deny payment for a claim before a neutral ALJ and, in some cases, federal court. This case-by-case approach ensures that a beneficiary can present all relevant information concerning a particular need for payment for an item or service. This review only applies to claims that have been denied and is not a mechanism for attaining prior authorization for a specific item or service for an individual.

In order to provide some guidance to beneficiaries and health care providers and suppliers regarding which items and services will (or will not) be covered in a particular area in the absence of an NCD, our contractors may make an LCD. An LCD would provide guidance, in the absence of, or as an adjunct to, an NCD by describing the clinical circumstances and settings under which an item or service is available (or is not available) to a beneficiary under section 1862(a)(1)(A) of the Act. This notice seeks only to define the criteria for how we would make an NCD and our contractors would make an LCD. * * * Before we can make an NCD or LCD, the item or service must fall within a statutory Medicare benefit category and not be otherwise statutorily excluded. Moreover, if regulated by the Food and Drug Administration, the item or service must be lawfully marketed. * * *

We intend that the criteria would make the Medicare coverage process more open, responsive, and understandable to the public. Finally, as mentioned above, we anticipate that the criteria would result in covering more items and services under Medicare. The criteria could also result in us beginning a new NCD to withdraw coverage of a currently covered item or service. In particular, if a new item or service is equivalent in benefit, is in the same clinical modality, is thus substitutable for the existing service, and is lower in costs, we would consider withdrawing coverage for the more expensive currently covered alternative service.

We anticipate applying two criteria when we make an NCD or one of our contractors makes an LCD. First, the item or service must demonstrate medical benefit, and, second, the item or service must demonstrate added value to the Medicare population. * * *

We believe an item or service is medically beneficial if it produces a health outcome better than the natural course of illness or disease with customary medical management of symptoms. We would require the requestor to demonstrate that an item or service is medically beneficial by objective clinical scientific evidence. Given the importance of Medicare coverage decisions for our 39 million current beneficiaries (as well as future beneficiaries), we do not believe we should cover an item or service without adequate information that shows the item or service improves the diagnosis or treatment of an injury or illness, or improves the functioning of a malformed body member. It would be unreasonable and unnecessary to pay for expenses incurred for an item or service that are not proven to be effective for a defined population.

Although mortality and life-expectancy are quantifiable and, thus, "hard" health outcomes, we believe we should move towards "quality of life" as an acceptable health outcome. To help us (and our contractors) make coverage decisions, however, especially assessing comparative benefits, an acceptable health outcome should be quantifiable along a standard scale or metric. * * * We believe a beneficiary's preference, compliance, and well-being are also meaningful outcomes. * * * Another important consideration is how we would measure the magnitude of the improved health outcome. Also, if the treatment includes risks of adverse side-effects, how should we determine that the benefits outweigh the risks?

We believe that an item or service adds value to the existing mix of covered items or services if it substantially improves health outcomes; provides access to a medically beneficial, different clinical modality; or if it can "substitute" for an existing item or service and lower costs for the Medicare population. There are several situations when a new item or service would add value compared to the current mix of services.

One situation is when a new item or service that falls within a Medicare benefit category would be medically beneficial for a beneficiary with a given clinical circumstance and there is no Medicare-covered medically beneficial alternative. We believe this item or service would add value to the program and we should cover it without consideration of costs during the coverage process.

Another situation is when a new item or service would be medically beneficial and it is a different clinical modality than a Medicare-covered medically beneficial alternative(s) (for example, a covered medication versus surgery). Giving Medicare beneficiaries and providers access to competing items or services of different clinical modalities adds value to the program and we believe we should also cover the items or services without consideration of costs during the coverage process. In particular, this adds value to the program because we recognize that there are legitimate differences between beneficiaries, medical practices by region, and delivery systems' capabilities. We believe access to different modalities for a similar medical benefit is warranted.

In making Medicare coverage decisions under these new criteria, we would not compare an item or service that falls within a statutory benefit category to an item or service that is outside the scope of the Medicare program. We do not believe we should compare the effectiveness of an item or service that falls within a statutory benefit category to the effectiveness of a medically beneficial alternative that is not included in a Medicare benefit category. Due to financial circumstances, a beneficiary may not have meaningful access to that alternative. We believe that by only comparing two items or services that are included in a Medicare benefit category, we increase beneficiary access and add value to the program.

Value also would be added when the magnitude of the benefit of an item or service is substantially more than a Medicare-covered alternative of similar clinical modality. We refer to this item or service as a "breakthrough." Even if two services are of the same clinical modality, we believe we should cover the substantially superior service without any consideration of cost during the coverage process.

We believe value would also be added when a new item or service is equivalent in benefit, and is in the same clinical modality (that is, substitutable) for a Medicare-covered alternative, and has equal or lower total costs for the Medicare population. It is possible that a beneficiary would not notice any difference in health outcomes when an item or service is substituted for a Medicare-covered alternative. We would cover a substitutable item or service only if the total costs are equal or lower than the total costs of the Medicare-covered alternative. * * *

NOTES AND QUESTIONS

1. *Added value determinations.* How should HCFA define "same clinical modality" as used in the added value criteria? HCFA requested comments on "how broadly or narrowly we should define 'same clinical modality.' Clearly surgery and prescription medications are not the same. But is an open surgical procedure the same clinical modality as a closed invasive procedure? What if they both require general anesthesia?" 65 Fed. Reg. at 31,128. How would you respond to these definitional questions? On a related note, HCFA requested comments on how it should define "substantially more beneficial" and suggested several options: "One way to define this term is that the benefit is so large that most clinicians would believe that the item or service should be the new standard of care and, thus, completely replace the Medicare-covered alternative. Another is that the benefit is so large that the clinical experts in the relevant clinical discipline believe that the item or service should be the new standard of care and, thus, we should cover the new item or service and withdraw coverage of the Medicare-covered alternative. A third way would be to try to establish a quantifiable statistical 'effect-size' of the new item or service compared with the Medicare-covered alternative." Id. Which option makes the most sense?

2. *Standards of scientific evidence.* HCFA proposes to measure medical benefit and added value using scientific evidence. What difficulties might such an approach raise? Should HCFA use the same standard to evaluate medical technologies and medical procedures (e.g., drugs or devices and surgical procedures)? Does it make sense to generalize clinical trial findings to coverage decisions for "real world" medical care, or does the very controlled (artificial) environment of clinical trials make such generalizations of dubious value?

3. *Coverage of least costly alternatives.* The notice requests comments on the coverage of an item or service that can substitute for an already-covered alternative:

> At a minimum, a substitutable item or service would seem to be one that is the same clinical modality and produces an equivalent health outcome. If the substitutable item or service has greater total costs to the Medicare program, should we deny coverage for the item or service and allow the requestor through the reconsideration process to alter the request to seek a positive coverage decision? Should we simply cover the new item or service but reduce the Medicare payment rate for the incurred expenses to the same rate as the Medicare-covered alternative? This principle has been called the "least costly alternative" adjustment and has been used for many years primarily for coverage of durable medical equipment. Coverage of new items and services under new regulatory requirements may lead to the reexamination of current coverage policies. For example, if the new item or service is "substitutable" for a Medicare-covered alternative and has lower costs for the Medicare program, should we deny coverage for the Medicare-covered alternative or lower the payment for the Medicare-covered alternative so that the total costs for the Medicare program are, at a minimum, equal?

65 Fed. Reg. at 31,128.

B. PRIVATE PAYERS

1. COVERAGE DISPUTES UNDER DRUG BENEFITS PROVISIONS

Sibley-Schreiber v. Oxford Health Plans, Inc.

62 F.Supp.2d 979 (E.D.N.Y.1999).

■ DEARIE, DISTRICT JUDGE:

* * * Plaintiffs bring this class action seeking declaratory judgment, injunctive relief, and to recover damages resulting from defendants' wrongful denial of insurance coverage for the prescription medicine Viagra. * * * Defendants Oxford Health Plans (NY), Inc. and Oxford Health Insurance, Inc. are insurance companies organized and incorporated under the laws of New York State. * * *

Viagra was approved by the FDA as an effective treatment for erectile dysfunction on March 27, 1998. Prior to Viagra, the prescribed course of treatment for erectile dysfunction included painful, complicated, and expensive injections, suppositories, and pumps. These methods were covered, and continue to be covered, under defendants' insurance policies.

On May 1, 1998, defendants stopped paying for Viagra and announced that it would issue a final policy regarding coverage within 45 days (the "no pay" period). On June 15, 1998, Oxford publicly announced that it would pay for only six Viagra pills per month regardless of the number of pills prescribed by the physician (the "six pill" policy). Each plaintiff claims to suffer from "organic impotence." Each plaintiff further alleges that his physician prescribed Viagra soon after the FDA had approved its use for impotence. Plaintiffs challenge defendants' denial of coverage during the 45 day period and the six pill policy.

Defendants argue that plaintiffs failed to exhaust the administrative claims process provided by the insurance plans before filing the instant action. Each plaintiff, however, communicated with defendants on numerous occasions in an effort to get an exception from defendants' publicly announced policies. Each of the named plaintiffs submitted affidavits detailing their efforts at securing coverage for the prescribed medication. * * *

Patient 1's physician recommended that Patient 1 take Viagra every day in order to overcome his erectile dysfunction. The physician sent Oxford a letter of medical necessity. Patient 1's wife called Oxford to inquire whether her husband's prescription for Viagra would be covered and was told that there would be no coverage for at least one month. Patient 1's wife then asked her employer representative to call Oxford on her behalf. The representative was also told that no prescriptions would be covered for at least one month. At no time was Patient 1's wife informed that she could seek further review of the decision during the "no pay" period. After the "six pill" policy was implemented, Patient 1's wife called Oxford again to ask whether an exception was available for her husband since his doctor had prescribed a daily dose of Viagra. She was told there were no exceptions to the policy. Patient 1's wife denies receiving a "Certificate of Coverage & Member Handbook." Patient 1 never presented a prescription for Viagra because he was unable to afford the cost of the full prescription. * * *

Patient 2's physician prescribed 50–milligram tablets of Viagra. This prescription was filled and covered by defendants without question. The 50–milligram dose was ineffective. As a result, Patient 2's doctor instructed him to take two tablets at a time. On April 28, 1998, Patient 2 presented a second prescription for thirty 100–milligram tablets which was rejected by the pharmacy at the direction of the defendants. Patient 2 called the customer service telephone number located on his Oxford membership card. He was informed that defendants would not pay for Viagra for a forty-five day period and that there would be no exceptions. Patient 2 called a second time to speak to an "executive officer" and was again informed that there were no exceptions to the policy. Dr. Sotiropoulos, Patient 2's treating physician, attempted without success to get Oxford to change its decision. After receiving the written notification about the "no pay" period,

Patient 2 made a third telephone call and asked to speak with "a person of higher authority." This "person of higher authority" denied his request for an exception. * * * Patient 2 proceeded to call Oxford for a fourth time and asked to speak with a representative of the "Customer Care" department which he was told was a higher level group than Customer Service. He was told that the "six pill" policy applied to everyone and his request for 15 pills a month was "flatly" denied. Patient 2 was never given any indication that the decision could be "appealed, questioned, or modified." * * *

Section 503(2) of the Employee Retirement Income Security Act (ERISA) requires that "every employee benefit plan shall ... afford a reasonable opportunity to any participant whose claim for benefits has been denied for a full and fair review by the appropriate named fiduciary of the decision denying the claim." 29 U.S.C. § 1133 (1998). There is no statutory requirement that plaintiffs exhaust administrative processes before filing an action in federal court. However, relying on § 1133, "courts have 'developed the requirement that a claimant should ordinarily follow internal plan procedures and exhaust internal plan remedies before seeking judicial relief under ERISA.' " * * *

As set forth in defendants' motion papers, [the Oxford plans] provide a framework for appealing adverse decisions. These review procedures are outlined in a "Certificate of Coverage and Member Handbook." According to the Membership policy for the Freedom Plan, the prescribed "grievance procedure ... should be used when [a member has] a problem with any of [Oxford's] policies, procedures or determinations" other than a determination that a service is not medically necessary. The grievance procedure "may" be initiated by a telephone call to a customer service representative. From there, the policy states that the insured "may" file, either by telephone or in writing, a grievance with the Issues Resolution Department. Subsequently, an unsatisfied insured "may" file a written grievance with the Grievance Review Board. If the insured is still dissatisfied, he "may" appeal in writing to a Committee of the Board of Directors. Finally, an insured "may" appeal a final decision to the New York State Insurance Department or Department of Health. Alternatively, to challenge a determination concerning "medical necessity," an insured "may" appeal within 45 days in writing or by calling the Medical Management Appeals Department. If an insured is not satisfied with the result of that appeal, he "may" appeal to the Board of Directors. Under the Medical Advantage Plan, an insured "may" initiate an appeal process after a denial is issued by submitting a written request. If the insured is still dissatisfied, the insured "may request, verbally or in writing, that the grievance be presented to the Health Plan Grievance Review Board." Neither policy alerts the policyholder that these apparently permissive avenues of redress are preconditions to commencing a legal action.

Exhaustion of the statutorily required administrative process is not always required. Most notably, exhaustion is excused "where claimants make a 'clear and positive showing' that pursuing available administrative remedies would be futile." To fall within the futility doctrine, claimants must "show that it is certain that their claim will be denied on appeal, not merely that they doubt an appeal will result in a different decision." The exhaustion doctrine, however, does not require plaintiffs to "engage in meaningless acts or to needlessly squander resources as a prerequisite to commencing litigation." Courts have been unwilling to conclude that pursuit of the administrative process is futile absent evidence that a plaintiff sincerely attempted to resolve its dispute extrajudicially. Certainly, an allegation of futility is not satisfied by the mere showing that a claim was denied when initially presented to the insurance company. Nor is futility demonstrated by the fact that the members of a review committee consist of the insurance company's management rather than a neutral arbitrator. * * *

According to plaintiffs' affidavits, numerous telephone calls were made to defendants in an effort to get an exception to the "no pay" and six pill policies. Plaintiffs' physicians were required to, and did, submit letters of medical necessity, in some cases on more than one occasion. In one instance, a treating physician interceded on behalf of his needy patient. Regardless of the efforts and opinions of plaintiffs' physicians, defendants consistently denied coverage during the 45 day no-pay period and coverage beyond six pills after that policy was announced. One plaintiff wrote a complaint letter to the New York State Attorney General's office. Despite the fact that plaintiff copied Oxford's Corporate Director of Pharmacy Services, Oxford never responded to the letter. * * *

Exhaustion has been excused when the plaintiff alleged that she was unaware of an appeals process and the defendant insurance company failed to plead or supply proof of the existence of, or plaintiff's knowledge of, the appeal process. Similarly, futility has been demonstrated when an employee made inquires to management on four different occasions about the reinstatement of his pension and was never informed of his right to appeal the denial. Exhaustion has also been satisfied where an insurance company failed to timely respond to a claimant's written request to review its denial of benefits. An insurance company's steadfast refusal to extend benefits in response to a claimant's multiple requests was sufficient to overcome the exhaustion requirement even though the plaintiff filed the complaint two months before the actual denial of benefits. Finally, futility was demonstrated by an insurance company's unexplained refusal to accept a treating physician's opinion that certain services were "medically necessary." * * *

Assuming arguendo that plaintiffs were aware of their need to pursue all administrative appeals and the procedure for pursuing such appeals, there is overwhelming evidence that such efforts would have been futile. While an insured's belief, even in good faith, cannot by itself justify bypassing a contractually binding review process, there are circumstances here, not genuinely in dispute, that make it perfectly clear, as the course of events now confirms, that Oxford would not make any exceptions to the announced policy. Each of the four named plaintiffs called defendants on numerous occasions and received the same "no exceptions" answer to their repeated pleas for consideration. * * *

The named plaintiffs in this case acted entirely reasonably. When faced with Oxford's sudden denial of coverage, they contacted the insurer directly or with the help of the employer's representative for reconsideration and an explanation. They persisted in their request for coverage; they provided medical documentation; they pursued their claims up the hierarchy of Oxford's bureaucracy, and, quite understandably, came eventually to recognize that relief would not come from Oxford at any level. Ultimately, Oxford proved them right. Nevertheless, Oxford now argues that they stopped too soon and despite their entirely reasonable efforts, that misjudgment has cost them the opportunity to press their claims before this court.

Oxford's position seems particularly untenable when seen in the light of the policy language itself. In neither policy handbook is the insured instructed that administrative remedies must be utilized. These materials are strangely silent on the exhaustion requirement that Oxford now embraces with such enthusiasm. Like the named plaintiffs, insureds are left to their own devices, instructed that they should use the grievance procedure and may file a claim or may appeal, as the exhaustion requirement lurks in the background waiting to be deployed should a frustrated policyholder seek to initiate judicial proceedings. The scenario offends notions of fairness and common sense.

Erickson v. Bartell Drug Co.

141 F.Supp.2d 1266 (W.D.Wash.2001).

■ LASNIK, DISTRICT JUDGE:

The parties' cross-motions for summary judgment in this case raise an issue of first impression in the federal courts: whether the selective exclusion of prescription contraceptives from defendant's generally comprehensive prescription plan constitutes discrimination on the basis of sex. In particular, plaintiffs assert that Bartell's decision not to cover prescription contraceptives such as birth control pills, Norplant, Depo–Provera, intra-uterine devices, and diaphragms under its Prescription Benefit Plan for non-union employees violates Title VII, as amended by the Pregnancy Discrimination Act, 42 U.S.C. § 2000e(k).

Title VII makes it unlawful for an employer "to fail or refuse to hire or to discharge any individual, or otherwise to discriminate against any individual with respect to his compensation, terms, conditions, or privileges of employment, because of such individual's race, color, religion, sex, or national origin," 42 U.S.C. § 2000e–2(a)(1). Unfortunately, the legislative history of the Civil Rights Act of 1964, of which Title VII is a part, is not particularly helpful in determining what Congress had in mind when it added protection from discrimination based on sex. * * *

The fact that equality under Title VII is measured by evaluating the relative comprehensiveness of coverage offered to the sexes has been accepted and amplified by the Supreme Court. * * * The other tenet reaffirmed by the PDA (i.e., that discrimination based on any sex-based characteristic is sex discrimination) has also been considered by the courts. The Supreme Court has found that classifying employees on the basis of their childbearing capacity, regardless of whether they are, in fact, pregnant, is sex-based discrimination. * * *

Bartell's exclusion of prescription contraception from its prescription plan is inconsistent with the requirements of federal law. The PDA is not a begrudging recognition of a limited grant of rights to a strictly defined group of women who happen to be pregnant. Read in the context of Title VII as a whole, it is a broad acknowledgment of the intent of Congress to outlaw any and all discrimination against any and all women in the terms and conditions of their employment, including the benefits an employer provides to its employees. Male and female employees have different, sex-based disability and healthcare needs, and the law is no longer blind to the fact that only women can get pregnant, bear children, or use prescription contraception. The special or increased healthcare needs associated with a woman's unique sex-based characteristics must be met to the same extent, and on the same terms, as other healthcare needs. Even if one were to assume that Bartell's prescription plan was not the result of intentional discrimination, the exclusion of women-only benefits from a generally comprehensive prescription plan is sex discrimination under Title VII.

Title VII does not require employers to offer any particular type or category of benefit. However, when an employer decides to offer a prescription plan covering everything except a few specifically excluded drugs and devices, it has a legal obligation to make sure that the resulting plan does not discriminate based on sex-based characteristics and that it provides equally comprehensive coverage for both sexes. In light of the fact that prescription contraceptives are used only by women, Bartell's choice to exclude that particular benefit from its generally applicable benefit plan is discriminatory.

Bartell argues that opting not to provide coverage for prescription contraceptive devices is not a violation of Title VII because: (1) treating contraceptives differently from other prescription drugs is reasonable in that contraceptives are voluntary, preventative, do not treat or prevent an illness or disease, and are not truly a "healthcare" issue; (2) control of one's fertility is not "pregnancy, childbirth, or related medical conditions" as those terms are used in the PDA; (3) employers must be permitted to control the costs of employment benefits by limiting the scope of coverage; (4) the exclusion of all "family planning" drugs and devices is facially neutral; (5) in the thirty-seven years Title VII has been on the books, no court has found that excluding contraceptives constitutes sex discrimination; and (6) this issue should be determined by the legislature, rather than the courts. Each of these arguments is considered in turn.

An underlying theme in Bartell's argument is that a woman's ability to control her fertility differs from the type of illness and disease normally treated with prescription drugs in such significant respects that it is permissible to treat prescription contraceptives differently than all other prescription medicines. The evidence submitted by plaintiffs shows, however, that the availability of affordable and effective contraceptives is of great importance to the health of women and children because it can help to prevent a litany of physical, emotional, economic, and social consequences.

Unintended pregnancies, the condition which prescription contraceptives are designed to prevent, are shockingly common in the United States and carry enormous costs and health consequences for the mother, the child, and society as a whole. Over half of all pregnancies in this country are unintended. A woman with an unintended pregnancy is less likely to seek prenatal care, more likely to engage in unhealthy activities, more likely to have an abortion, and more likely to deliver a low birthweight, ill, or unwanted baby. Unintended pregnancies impose significant financial burdens on the parents in the best of circumstances. If the pregnancy results in a distressed newborn, the costs increase by tens of thousands of dollars. In addition, the adverse economic and social consequences of unintended pregnancies fall most harshly on women and interfere with their choice to participate fully and equally in the "marketplace and the world of ideas."

The availability of a reliable, affordable way to prevent unintended pregnancies would go a long way toward ameliorating the ills described above. Although there are many factors which help explain the unusually high rate of unintended pregnancies in the United States, an important cause is the failure to use effective forms of birth control. Insurance policies and employee benefit plans which exclude coverage for effective forms of contraception contribute to the failure of at-risk women to seek a physician's assistance in avoiding unwanted pregnancies.

The fact that prescription contraceptives are preventative appears to be an irrelevant distinction in this case: Bartell covers a number of preventative drugs under its plan. The fact that pregnancy is a "natural" state and is not considered a disease or illness is also a distinction without a difference. Being pregnant, though natural, is not a state that is desired by all women or at all points in a woman's life. Prescription contraceptives, like all other preventative drugs, help the recipient avoid unwanted physical changes. * * *

Defendant argues that the exclusion of prescription contraceptives from defendant's prescription benefit plan does not run afoul of the PDA and is not, therefore, unlawful. Under the express terms of the PDA, discrimination because of "pregnancy, childbirth, or related medical conditions" is a form of prohibited sex discrimination. * * * Having reviewed the legislative history of the PDA, it is clear that in 1978 Congress had no specific intent regarding coverage for prescription contraceptives. The relevant issue, however, is whether the decision to exclude drugs made for women from a generally comprehensive prescription plan is sex discrimination under Title VII, with or without the clarification provided by the PDA. * * *

Bartell also suggests that it should be permitted to limit the scope of its employee benefit programs in order to control costs. Cost is not, however, a defense to allegations of discrimination under Title VII. While it is undoubtedly true that employers may cut benefits, raise deductibles, or otherwise alter coverage options to comply with budgetary constraints, the method by which the employer seeks to curb costs must not be discriminatory. * * *

Prescription contraceptives are not the only drugs or devices excluded from coverage under Bartell's benefit plan. Bartell argues that it has chosen to exclude from coverage all drugs for "family planning," and that this exclusion is neutral and non-discriminatory. There is no "family planning" exclusion in the benefit plan, however, and the contours of such a theoretical exclusion are not clear. On the list of excluded drugs and devices, contraceptive devices and infertility drugs are the two categories which might be considered "family planning" measures. Contrary to defendant's explanation, there appear to be some drugs which fall under the "family planning" rubric which are covered by the plan. Prenatal vitamins, for example, are frequently prescribed in anticipation of a woman becoming pregnant and are expressly covered under the plan. And although both parties agree that Bartell's plan excludes coverage for Viagra, an impotency drug, it is not clear that it falls into any of the excluded categories. * * *

Employers in general, and Bartell in particular, might justifiably wonder why, when Title VII has been on the books for thirty-seven years, this court is only now holding that it includes a right to prescription contraceptives in certain circumstances. The answer, of course, is that until this case, no court had been asked to evaluate the common practice of excluding contraceptives from a generally comprehensive health plan under Title VII. * * *

Although the court's decision is a matter of first impression for the judiciary, it is not the first tribunal to consider the lawfulness of a contraception exclusion. On December 14, 2000, the EEOC made a finding of reasonable cause on the same issue which is entitled to some deference. * * * As the Commission found, the exclusion of prescription contraceptives from a generally comprehensive insurance policy constitutes sex discrimination under Title VII because the employers "have circumscribed the treatment options available to women, but not to men." * * *

NOTES AND QUESTIONS

1. *Insurance coverage for "lifestyle drugs."* A variety of prescription drugs, such as baldness preparations and wrinkle treatments provide remedies that improve quality of life rather than treating a disease. Health plans rarely cover such prescriptions. See Annotation, What Services, Equipment, or Supplies Are "Medically Necessary" for Purposes of Coverage Under Medical Insurance, 75 A.L.R.4th 763 (1990 & 2002 Supp.). Which categories of drugs would you consider to be "medically necessary" if you were a benefits manager for an insurance company? If you were a consumer suffering with the targeted condition? Consider the following: weight loss drugs, impotence drugs for men, impotence drugs for women, contraceptives, anti-hypertensives, non-sedating antihistamines for seasonal allergies, fertility drugs. And what accounts for the widespread exclusion of OTC drugs (even if "prescribed" by a physician)?

2. *Gender equity in prescription drug coverage.* Would *Bartell* have come out differently if a contraceptive drug existed for men? Many insurance companies quickly included coverage for Viagra under their health plans after its approval for marketing in 1998. Some plans, however, required that the beneficiary have a documented pre-existing condition of "organic" impotence, and limited coverage to six doses per month, while other plans denied coverage because they viewed Viagra as a "quality of life" drug rather than a medical necessity. See Kathryn Kindell, Comment, Prescription for Fairness: Health Insurance Reimbursement for Viagra and Contraceptives, 35 Tulsa L.J. 399, 404–05 (2000); see also Scholl v. QualMed, Inc., 103 F.Supp.2d 850 (E.D.Pa.2000) (dismissing for failure to exhaust administrative remedies a class action suit demanding "full coverage" of Viagra under a health plan's drug benefit clause). Viagra coverage provided useful ammunition for women's advocates who have long argued for insurance coverage of prescription contraceptives. If insurers are willing to pay $10 per pill to enable a man to have intercourse, fundamental fairness dictates that these same plans cover prescription contraceptives to provide women with more control over their sex lives. See Carey Goldberg, Insurance for Viagra Spurs Coverage for Birth Control, N.Y. Times, June 30, 1999, at A1; see also Lisa A. Hayden, Gender Discrimination Within the Reproductive Health Care System: Viagra v. Birth Control, 13 J.L. & Health 171 (1998–99); Kim H. Finley, Comment, Life, Liberty, and the Pursuit of Viagra? Demand for "Lifestyle" Drugs Raises Legal and Public Policy Issues, 28 Cap. U. L. Rev. 837 (2000). As of 1994, only half of the larger indemnity insurance plans offered coverage of prescription contraceptives such as the pill, IUD, or Norplant, and only about 40% of HMOs cover all methods of prescription birth control. See Tamar Lewin, Agency Finds Many Health Plans Should Cover Contraceptive Costs, N.Y. Times, Dec. 15, 2000, at A1; cf. Sylvia A. Law, Sex Discrimination and Insurance for Contraception, 73 Wash. L. Rev. 363, 393–96 (1998) (noting that only 15% of traditional indemnity plans cover prescription contraceptives, while nearly 90% of HMOs provide coverage, and discussing state proposals in California, Connecticut, Georgia, Maryland, and other states, noting that ERISA "still prohibits states from imposing mandatory benefit requirements or anti-discrimination rules that go beyond what is required by federal law"). Prior to the *Bartell* decision, two courts had held that the exclusion of infertility drugs was not discriminatory. See Krauel v. Iowa Methodist Med. Ctr., 95 F.3d 674, 679–80 (8th Cir.1996); Saks v. Franklin Covey Co., 117 F.Supp.2d 318, 328–29 (S.D.N.Y.2000). In the wake of Viagra coverage, several states have passed "contraceptive equity" bills requiring insurers that cover prescription drugs to include prescription birth control coverage. See Sarah E. Bycott, Note, Controversy Aroused: North Carolina Mandates Insurance Coverage of Contraceptives in the Wake of Viagra, 79 N.C. L. Rev. 779 (2001). In 1998, Congress held hearings on the Equity in Prescription Insurance and Contraceptive Coverage Act (EPICC). The bill was designed to equalize the costs of health care between men and women by mandating health plans provided as employee benefits under ERISA provide coverage of prescription contraceptives. See David S. Broder, Thanks, Viagra, Wash. Post, July 26, 1998, at C7. Coverage of the pill, IUDs, Norplant, Depo–Provera, and diaphragm methods was added to the Federal Employees Health Benefits Plan (FEHBP), which covers over 1.2 million female federal employees, in 1998, but the Bush administration has proposed dropping birth control coverage. See Ellen Nakashima, Cut in Birth Control Benefit of Federal Workers Sought, Wash. Post, April 12, 2001, at A29.

3. *Off-label uses.* Private payor coverage varies when physicians prescribe approved drugs or medical devices for off-label uses. See Drusilla S. Raiford et al., Determining Appropriate Reimbursement for Prescription Drugs: Off Label Uses and Investigational Therapies, 49 Food & Drug L.J. 37, 59–61 (1994) (finding that third-party payors relied on certain medical compendia in making coverage determinations); see also Linda Schwab, New York Legislation Mandates Some Off–Label Drug Coverage, 83 J. Nat'l Cancer Inst. 602, 602–03 (1991) (describing laws in New York and Michigan, as well as proposals in California and Texas, to require that private insurers cover some off-label drug uses). Decisions about reimbursement appear to depend, at least in part, on whether the physician is using the drug for a labeled indication or an off-label use. One study found that in oncology, where off-label prescribing is common, oncologists reported an increasing rate of coverage denials or changing reimbursement policies for off-label uses of chemotherapy agents. At times, according to the physicians surveyed, reimbursement policies interfered with delivery of the preferred treatment for some patients. See Thomas Laetz & George Silberman, Reimbursement Policies Constrain the Practice of Oncology, 266 JAMA 2996 (1992). On the other hand, third-party payers usually must add (or explicitly exclude under the contract) newly FDA-approved cancer treatments to their list of reimbursable drugs, even when costs are substantial. See Susan Okie, Cancer Drug Approved Quickly: Gleevec Dramatically Effective Against a Type of Leukemia, Wash. Post, May 11, 2001, at A2 (describing a new treatment costing between $2,000 and $2,400 per month, and noting that the drug's manufacturer plans to subsidize the drug's cost for uninsured patients). If an oncologist wishes to try Gleevec® to treat a patient for a type of cancer other than that which has been formally studied and approved, the patient may have to pay out of pocket, unless the manufacturer is providing the drug gratis as part of a formal clinical trial.

2. INSURANCE COVERAGE FOR EXPERIMENTAL TREATMENTS

Shumake v. Travelers Insurance Co.

383 N.W.2d 259 (Mich.Ct.App.1985).

■ ALLEN, JUDGE:

In this declaratory judgment action, plaintiffs sought reimbursement for Laetrile (amygdalin) and related nutritional therapy prescribed for James Shumake by his physician, Philip E. Binzel, M.D. Dr. Binzel determined that Shumake suffered from a metabolic disorder, a diagnosis he reached based primarily on the fact that Shumake had developed lung cancer. The Laetrile and nutritional supplements were prescribed as a treatment for the metabolic disorder. The trial court held that under the terms of the policy, plaintiffs were entitled to reimbursement in the amount of $17,478.20. Defendant appeals as of right.

Plaintiffs were insured under a group health insurance policy issued by defendant Travelers Insurance Company to James Shumake's former employer, Service Reproduction Company. On May 26, 1978, Shumake underwent surgery for removal of the right upper lobe of his right lung after a cancerous tumor was discovered. His prognosis was guarded, with doctors estimating his chances of survival over the ensuing five years as between 15 and 25 percent. Shumake consulted a general practitioner, Dr. Binzel, who prescribed a course of treatment involving a regimen of Laetrile, enzymes and vitamins, and certain nutritional guidelines. Defendant paid all expenses associated with this treatment from June, 1978, to January 31, 1981. Defendant then notified plaintiffs that expenses for Laetrile and Laetrile-related nutritional supplements were not covered under the subject insurance policy.

The policy at issue provides coverage for 80 percent of "covered medical expenses" which are "necessarily [incurred]." "Covered medical expense" is defined as:

> [The] actual expense to the Employee of the reasonable charges (as defined) not hereinafter excepted incurred by the Employee on account of himself or his Dependent upon the recommendation and approval of the attending physician for the services and supplies listed below and required in connection with the treatment of the Employee or his Dependent for any [accidental bodily injury or sickness].

Included in the list of covered medical expenses are "medical supplies," which are defined to include "[drugs] and medicines covered by written prescription of a physician." The insurance policy does not contain any exclusion which would specifically preclude coverage for Laetrile and Laetrile-related nutritional supplements. Nonetheless, defendant maintains that coverage was properly denied * * * *

Dr. Binzel testified that he did not order laboratory tests because numerous tests would be required to isolate specific nutritional deficiencies and the tests would have been costly. Moreover, he believed that the presence of cancer was indicative of a metabolic disorder and that monitoring the patient's response during the course of therapy was a preferred method for determining whether deficiencies were being adequately treated. It appears from the record before us that Laetrile practitioners generally operated on the central premise that cancer resulted from metabolic imbalances. Proponents believed that if the disorder could be cured, the body's defense mechanisms would then operate to avert a recurrence of cancer.

This issue appears to pose two distinct concerns. First, defendant places substantial weight on the treatment agreement indicating that

Shumake was being treated for a metabolic disorder and not for cancer. Yet, the metabolic disorder and the cancer were intricately related. The purpose of the treatment was to enhance the body's defense mechanisms so that they would take over to ward off cancer. The treatment would never have been prescribed if Shumake had not contracted cancer. By way of affidavit, Binzel stated that he was treating Shumake "for lung cancer and its attendant side effects." Moreover, the crux of defendant's argument on the question of whether Laetrile therapy was "necessarily incurred" is the assertion that the treatment was ineffective in the treatment of cancer—not that it was ineffective in the treatment of a metabolic disorder. Regardless of the efficacy of treatment and the disclaimers in the agreement, we believe that the inescapable result is that Shumake received this treatment because of the cancer. Since we have already determined that he was suffering from a "sickness" as a result of the cancer, coverage cannot be denied on this basis.

In addition, defendant's argument relative to whether Shumake was sick goes to a basic tenet upon which Laetrile practitioners operated, i.e., that cancer was indicative of a metabolic disorder. Although defendant presented substantial evidence which challenges the logic of this reasoning, defendant failed to negate the fact that at the time Shumake's treatment commenced there was a strong and viable minority in the medical community which adhered to these basic tenets and believed that Laetrile was an effective means of controlling cancer. We recognize that the weight of authority held a contrary view. However, we are not prepared to determine as a matter of law that a diagnosis subject to conflicting medical opinions is fallacious merely because a majority of the medical community would arrive at a [different] conclusion. Accordingly, we believe that the evidence presented was sufficient to establish a "sickness."

The next issue presented for our consideration is whether Laetrile and related nutritional treatments were necessarily incurred covered medical expenses and required in connection with Shumake's treatment. Defendant maintains that the treatments have been demonstrated to be ineffective and that, as a result, they cannot be regarded as necessary or required for the treatment of cancer.

The trial court found that "necessarily incurred" was an ambiguous term. It then relied on [a previous decision] to hold that the necessity of a medical treatment or expense should be determined by the attending physician. Defendant points out that such a construction of medical necessity could lead to absurd results. For example, such a construction of the policy would require coverage where a physician prescribed bizarre or archaic treatments, such as bloodletting, simply because the physician deemed it necessary. Defendant therefore urges us to follow the reasoning of *Free v. Travelers Ins. Co.*, 551 F.Supp. 554 (D.Md.1982), which, in construing an identical provision of an insurance policy, found that the language was unambiguous. The *Free* court went on to hold that Laetrile could not be regarded as necessary for the treatment of cancer since the evidence presented at trial overwhelmingly indicated that Laetrile had no value in the treatment of cancer.

We cannot agree with the initial premise of the *Free* opinion, that the terms "necessarily incurred" and "required" for treatment are unambiguous. [The court then reviewed prior decisions equating "necessary" with "appropriate," concluding that necessary means "wise in the light of facts known at the time rendered," and defining necessary to mean "reasonably calculated to shorten and relieve an ordeal of agonizing pain and thereby effectuate the most rapid recovery possible."] * * *

Since the terms "necessary" and "required" are capable of diverse connotations, we find that the provisions in the subject insurance policy are indeed ambiguous. It is a well-established principle that ambiguities in an insurance contract are to be construed against the insurer which drafts the policy and resolved in favor of the insured. A policy should not be construed to defeat coverage unless the language so requires since the purpose of insurance is to insure.

The language "necessarily incurred" or "required" implies that some entity must exercise judgment in determining when a medical expense will be covered. When the insurer does not reserve the right to exercise that judgment itself by way of an exclusion, we believe that the approach of the trial judge * * * is reasonable. A physician is generally better equipped than lawyers and judges to discern what is medically necessary. Cognizant that a rubber stamp approach to a physician's unfettered exercise of discretion could result in coverage for inane treatments, we decline to hold that any treatment or expense is necessary or required merely because it is deemed so by a physician.

However, we do hold that a physician's judgment should be accorded deference. Moreover, since medicine is an evolving science in which treatments are at one time regarded as valid and later discredited, we hold that a decision as to necessity shall be reviewed in light of knowledge which existed at the time the decision was rendered.

Employing such a standard does not dispense with this issue since the gist of defendant's argument is that Laetrile falls within the category of inane cancer treatments and was recognized as ineffective at all times during which Mr. Shumake received treatment. In support of these contentions, defendant relies on the decision of the Commissioner of Food and Drugs on Laetrile, dated July 29, 1977. See 42 Fed. Reg. 39,768 (1977). Further, defendant points to a study on Laetrile which was commissioned by the National Cancer Institute. The results of this study were originally published on January 28, 1982. See Moertel, A Clinical Trial of Amygdalin (Laetrile) in the Treatment of Human Cancer, 306 New Eng. J. Med. 201 (1982). * * *

[T]he FDA concluded that there was "no basis in law or in fact for the use of Laetrile or related substances in the treatment of cancer." A review of the Commissioner's report discloses that, although the FDA acknowledged that Laetrile was generally regarded as ineffective by qualified experts, the FDA did not categorically conclude that Laetrile was ineffective. Rather, the FDA's determination was based on a lack of scientific evidence which might have demonstrated that Laetrile was safe and effective. In other words, Laetrile proponents failed to meet the requisite burden of proof. * * * [The court then reviewed the *Rutherford* litigation, which was excerpted in Chapter 2(D).]

Our review of the Commissioner's report and the *Rutherford* decisions reveals that there was no definitive determination in the scientific community or the courts with respect to Laetrile's effectiveness throughout 1980. Effectiveness had not been proven or disproven. Indeed, these decisions indicate that the debate on Laetrile was still raging in 1980 and that notable institutions were still investigating its use. Moreover, a number of states enacted statutes which permitted intrastate distribution of Laetrile despite the FDA's ban on interstate distribution. Due to the diversity of opinion and Laetrile's questionable status at that time, we believe that a physician could properly exercise discretion so as to determine that Laetrile was necessary and required for the treatment of cancer during this period.

Publication of the Moertel study, however, appears to have terminated the controversy over Laetrile's effectiveness. After administering Laetrile to various control groups while following the regimens recommended by leading Laetrile practitioners, the researchers concluded that:

> [no] substantive benefit was observed in terms of cure, improvement, or stabilization of cancer, improvement of symptoms related to cancer, or extension of life span. The hazards of amygdalin therapy were evidenced in several patients by symptoms of cyanide toxicity or by blood cyanide levels approaching the lethal range. * * * Amygdalin (laetrile) is a toxic drug that is not effective as a cancer treatment.

We have not been provided with any indication that the findings of the Moertel study have been challenged by subsequent studies. At oral argument, plaintiffs' counsel conceded that Laetrile is now recognized as ineffective. In the absence of documentation to refute the Moertel study findings, we would not hold in the future that Laetrile is a necessarily incurred medical expense or required for treatment. However, based on the time frame when these treatments were administered to Shumake and the controversy which was transpiring, we hold that Dr. Binzel's decision as to necessity should be accorded deference.

Finally, defendant argues that the nutritional supplements were not covered under the policy since they could be acquired without a prescription. The policy provides coverage for "drugs and medicines covered by the written prescription of a physician." It is uncontroverted that the nutritional supplements at issue were covered by Binzel's written prescriptions. The policy did not limit its definition of "medical supplies" to drugs which could only be secured with a physician's prescription. Moreover, defendant acknowledged that it provided coverage for nutritional supplements for patients receiving radiation treatments and chemotherapy since malnutrition is often associated with these treatments. Further, Binzel stated that one reason why he prescribed these nutritional supplements was so that he could closely control the dosages that Shumake would receive, a factor which presumably cannot be monitored with medicines that are sold over-the-counter. Since the policy language did not limit coverage to what are generally recognized as "prescription drugs," and the language used must be construed against the insurer, we find that coverage for the nutritional supplements was provided under the terms of the policy. * * *

Richard S. Saver, Note, *Reimbursing New Technologies: Why Are the Courts Judging Experimental Medicine?*
44 STAN. L. REV. 1095 (1992).

That the courts have problems defining "experimentation" in medicine is not surprising. The use of relatively new, untested medical technologies, without the guidance of formal research protocols, generates much confusion. While these technologies may develop new knowledge, their primary purpose is to benefit patients. Such technologies have been appropriately labeled "innovative therapy" as opposed to experimentation. Where innovative therapies and many other treatments fall on the spectrum between experimental and standard care is of more than purely theoretical concern. As most health care payers, both public and private, generally exclude coverage for experimental medical technologies, answering the question of whether a treatment is experimental answers a much more pressing question—who pays?

Simply raising this question implicates a number of basic issues about the American health care system. Health care costs continue to rise at an alarming rate as new technologies strain already limited resources. Natural tensions arise between health care payers who want to limit reimbursement to treatments proven as safe and effective, and individual patients who care more about access to promising treatments. This characterizes the nature of the underlying dispute in experimental exclusion cases. Such cases also often involve multilateral conflicts between patients, medical specialists who use "innovative" technologies, health payers, private sector research advocates, and others. As a result, the experimental exclusion cases severely test the judiciary's ability to resolve competing interests, technical questions, and moral claims about medical technology. * * *

The case law of experimental exclusion is remarkably inconsistent. Decisions involving similarly situated plaintiffs are often resolved inequitably, in part because courts supply their own varied standards for determining when a treatment is "experimental." Because the facts of these cases are distinguishable, no generally accepted legal definition of "experimental" exists. Definitions also vary because of the different contexts in which experimental exclusion cases occur. The public payers (the federal and state governments) run entitlement programs, whereas the private payers (such as insurers) enter into consensual arrangements. In theory, patients and payers have different expectations and obligations, depending on whether the insurance coverage is offered by a self-insured, public, or private payer. Thus, "experimental" may have different meanings depending upon who is spending money on health care. As a result, great uncertainty remains as to what technologies may be excluded as nonreimbursable experimentation. * * *

[P]rivate insurers typically depend upon exclusionary language denying liability for "experimental" technology. Usually insurers include explicit limitations in health plans. Most courts take the approach that such experimental exclusion clauses, without more descriptive language or criteria, are ambiguous. And, because insurance law favors construing ambiguous language against the insurer (in part to discourage unfair contracts of adhesion) courts generally read ambiguous language in health insurance contracts to cover disputed technologies. In some cases, an insurer can overcome the harshness of the ambiguities rule by showing its interpretation of the exclusion clause is reasonable. In most instances, however, courts are reluctant to rely on insurer-supplied definitions of "experimental" if the contract itself did not make them explicit.

Insurers may be unwilling to develop more explicit criteria for experimental status, in part fearing that plans that make noncoverage more visible will drive away customers. Some have relied upon one partially successful strategy for avoiding the ambiguities rule: reserving the right to prescreen for experimental technologies. If patients obtain treatment without first seeking authorization, they may be denied benefits for breach of contract. Insurers can also prevail if their contracts set out clear review and arbitration procedures to resolve whether a particular treatment will be covered.

While courts differ to some extent about when they will apply the ambiguities rule, how they will apply the rule is even less certain. After declaring experimental exclusion clauses ambiguous, courts have supplied their own varying and convoluted definitions for what is "medically necessary" and what is "experimental." A frequently employed variant of the ambiguities rule is the doctrine of "reasonable expectations." Under this doctrine, courts construe insurance policies in light of the reasonable expectations of the insured. This is really the same principle in practical operation as the ambiguities rule. If the insurer intends not to cover something for which the insured could reasonably expect to be reimbursed, then "notice of noncoverage must be conspicuous, plain and clear."

Courts have used the reasonable expectations concept to expand coverage for disputed technologies. Some commentators criticize the reflexive use of the doctrine, arguing that insureds do not reasonably expect coverage for unproven technologies and that from the ex ante position, insureds would rather avoid contracting for costly technology that raises premiums but provides uncertain medical benefit. However, the problem of changing perspectives, which can be quite dramatic where health care is concerned, makes any characterization of the ex ante position somewhat suspect. Moreover, this critique may be incorrect in its assumption that insureds would typically opt for lower premiums as opposed to greater potential protection. This is especially true when the individual costs and benefits of access to promising medical treatments are not counter-balanced by equivalent adjustments to premiums. In any event, courts have difficulty employing the ex ante view when hearing the tragic cases of patients facing life threatening disease. In such "hard cases," there are undeniable sympathies to mandate expanded coverage, regardless of doctrinal justifications.

The imprecise manner in which courts employ either the reasonable expectations doctrine or the ambiguities rule presents efficiency problems. The different approaches to expanding or contracting coverage impair the ability of insurers to rely on legal rules to narrow their insurance risk pools. Insurers compete for the relatively low risk customers in a given pool, luring them away by offering lower premiums that are closer to the customers' expected losses. According to conventional, free market interpretations, the narrowing of pools increases competition, which in turn increases total insurance availability by lowering fees.

In theory, courts could promote efficiency by using the reasonable expectations principle to force insurers to describe more accurately what technologies their policies will cover. But the variation in court decisions makes it difficult for insurers to assess their exposure under this doctrine. Such uncertainty may chill insurers because they are not sure what expenses they will be required to reimburse. Moreover, courts may be indulging in hyperbole when they identify certain expectations as reasonable, given the complexity of typical health insurance policies. Where master health contracts run to 65 pages, perhaps it is time to question how well courts can gauge what insureds "reasonably expect." * * *

Although the judiciary has been criticized for ordering payment for experimental treatment too often, it is difficult to assess patient-plaintiffs' rate of success. For a number of reasons, many patients denied payment for novel technologies never even make it to court. At a time of illness, some patients simply cannot marshal the resources for litigation. Others, facing a limited time horizon in which to begin treatment, will conclude that a lawsuit will take too long. A favorable court decision may provide an empty victory because the plaintiff's condition has changed and the technology can no longer be applied. Furthermore, limitations on damages may make litigation impractical or unappealing. If a plaintiff recovers on a contract theory, the judgment will likely cover only the dollar amount of the disputed claim. The additional expense and burden of litigation itself may be worthwhile only in the rarer situation where a patient can pursue a tort action and possibly recover punitive damages. Further, many cases that could be successfully litigated are settled out of court. By agreeing to settle, the insurer deprives other beneficiaries in the same position of a legal interpretation of the relevant provisions of the policy. Only the most determined or most litigious patients are likely to prevail. * * *

Health care payers may also employ strategies, including delaying the evaluation of technologies, to discourage beneficiaries' appeals. For example, one California HMO, after waiting eight months to evaluate a patient's claim that the cancer drug Interferon should be covered, canceled its coverage for all the members in the patient's workplace. According to a

Gallup poll of oncologists, one patient in eight never receives the physician's preferred treatment because of such reimbursement struggles. * * *

Courts have developed several benchmarks to define experimental status. Different approaches have, of course, been combined by courts. But it is useful to examine each in isolation and consider the problems such standards pose. In the first instance, courts rely on evidence that a physician has prescribed a particular technology. Such a standard is, however, circular. Technologies that get funded are technologies doctors will prescribe; repeated use will standardize the technology's status. Furthermore, this standard is potentially wasteful. To the extent doctors working in the traditional "fee for service" payment system are not under financial constraints with third-party payers, they have little incentive to deny access to even the most speculative of technologies.

Prescribing patterns of physicians working in modern, "managed" care systems, in which cost constraints are more explicit, provide no better guide. In theory, these doctors are driven to prescribe only medically necessary care. In practice, however, many physicians report that administrative policy often interferes with their professional judgment. Furthermore, managed care systems rely upon primary care givers to make most prescription authorizations; these general practitioners may be less aware of technological innovations than medical specialists. * * *

In attempting to determine whether a technology has moved beyond experimental status, courts also rely on evaluations in the medical literature. This approach has the benefit of relying on more rigorously developed and evaluated data than the prescriptive habits of individual physicians. But many new technologies do not generate primary evaluative data. In addition, few medical technologies enjoy an uncritical reception before they are accepted into general practice. Consensus about new treatments may have more to do with whether the treatments follow current fashions in medical theory and less to do with how well they work. Such problems have been evident, for example, in evaluations of colchicine treatments for gout and high-dose aspirin prescriptions for rheumatoid arthritis. Both technologies were ignored or rejected for a time because they did not make sense according to the then-accepted theories of disease mechanism and drug action, even though both had demonstrated effectiveness. Courts must therefore be wary of merely tallying approving and disapproving articles in the mainstream medical literature.

A more troubling aspect of this approach is the inevitable time lag between a technology's acceptance in the medical community and its mainstream publication. Technologies are typically practiced, especially in specialty medical fields, long before they are documented in the conventional medical literature. For example, mainstream publication lagged months behind the development of promising therapies for AIDS and breast cancer. The delay occurred even though less detailed, informal reports on AZT and aerosol pentamidine (as treatments for AIDS) and adjuvant chemotherapy (as a treatment for breast cancer) had been circulating for some time among clinicians. "This elapsed time may seem unacceptable for patients whose mean survival is measured in months or a few years." The significance of mainstream publication must also be questioned when studies indicate that physicians adopt new technologies more because of colleagues' recommendations than because of what appears in the latest medical journals. Finally, for long-term debilitating illnesses such as cancer, where health outcomes are typically measured in 5– and 10–year intervals, evaluations may not be published until many years after the treatment is successfully used by the medical community. Therefore, a literature survey standard provides somewhat useful information where sufficient publications exist, but courts must be careful to avoid simple nose counting. When little has been written about a technology, not much can be inferred. Regardless of the availability of evaluations in the medical literature, fairness demands that other evidence be considered.

In a variation on the literature survey standard, courts may rely upon physician experts who testify about accepted practices in the relevant community of specialists or academic centers. This draws the courts into the awkward but familiar position of having to arbitrate scientific disputes among expert witnesses. The more novel the technology, however, the less likely it is that experts will have sufficient background to adequately inform the trier of fact. As a result, expert testimony may be of little probative value for the ultimate determination by the courts. * * *

When confronted with a seriously ill patient who does not respond to standard treatments, some courts consider evidence that the patient has benefitted or may benefit from a controversial treatment. This standard, though emotionally appealing, may prove difficult to apply. In cases where a plaintiff has already benefitted from a technology, health improvement could be attributable to the well documented "placebo effect," which can cause a patient to improve after use of even ineffective or unsafe technologies. This standard is also unfair to third-party payers. An insurance company or an HMO contracts to provide standard care, not to underwrite any treatment a doctor can convince a patient to try. Shifting the entire cost of developing experimental medicine to third-party payers, who are not in the business of funding research and development, seems unwise.

Several payers have proposed one additional and increasingly controversial standard, suggesting that a technology should be considered experimental unless a government agency such as the FDA approves its use. This standard would normally apply only to cases involving drugs and devices, having little relevance for technologies left untested by government agencies. Where health contracts have ambiguous terms, courts have hesitated to use this standard. But where contracts contain specific language requiring the approval of government agencies, courts have denied reimbursement for treatments based on unapproved technologies.

Payers have undoubtedly advanced the "agency approval" standard as a way of curtailing costs, but it is most unfair, as it cuts against medical custom. Government agencies have limited objectives when evaluating new technologies. For example, when considering new drugs for approval, the FDA analyzes whether a drug is safe and whether it "works" for a specific clinical population. * * * The FDA thus does not even attempt to draw up an exhaustive, definitive list of all the nonexperimental uses of a drug. Indeed, the way in which the drug works, and not the government's evaluation, will determine how physicians use approved drugs in combined treatment regimens or in different but related clinical populations. Therefore, physicians often prescribe drugs for uses that were not tested when the FDA performed its evaluations. Known as "off-label" use, this practice is widespread. An estimated fifty percent of standard cancer therapy, which may involve new combinations of drugs in chemotherapy, is off-label. Insisting on agency approval for all uses of a drug would result not only in lost treatment opportunities, but would also dramatically increase costs, as repeated FDA evaluations would be required. In fact, payers that now routinely deny reimbursement for off-label therapy may unintentionally contribute to the inflation of overall health care costs. To avoid anticipated coverage battles, many clinicians hospitalize patients, where reimbursement for off-label therapy is easier to obtain, rather than administering treatments in the cheaper outpatient setting. Since all approved drugs have been tested for general safety, the FDA has taken the position that physicians may lawfully prescribe drugs for off-label use. Therefore, for payers to require that all uses of a drug go through the lengthy approval process would not only be quite expensive and cumbersome, but would also contravene current practices endorsed by the government.

An FDA approval standard would also, as a practical matter, exclude much of the information generated by physicians practicing in highly specialized fields such as oncology. Modern chemotherapy involves the use of "cocktails," the combination of many different drugs in constantly changing dosage levels and time intervals. There is no convenient way for the FDA to review such combined modality therapy. And for other uses of oncology drugs, it is not feasible to perform the kind of clinical trials necessary to obtain FDA approval.

Currently, a great deal of potentially efficacious treatment is left unscrutinized by government agencies. However, as disputes over access to new technologies widen, the government may become more involved. Because of political pressures, agencies have started to issue advisory opinions on new technologies but such instances are still rare. Therefore, if courts relied exclusively on agency approval as the standard for nonexperimentation, payers would unfairly benefit from government inaction. * * *

NOTES AND QUESTIONS

1. *Coverage disputes.* For other courts' approaches to the problem of experimental treatment coverage, see, e.g., Bechtold v. Physicians Health Plan, 19 F.3d 322 (7th Cir.1994) (upholding health plan's interpretation of contract provision excluding coverage for experimental treatment for breast cancer); Mire v. Blue Cross/Blue Shield of Fla., 43 F.3d 567 (11th Cir.1994); Bushman v. State Mut. Life Assur. Co. of Am., 915 F.Supp. 945 (N.D.Ill. 1996) (dispute over payment for clinical trial of bone marrow transplant);

Westover v. Metropolitan Life Ins. Co., 771 F.Supp. 1172 (M.D.Fla.1991) (upholding plan's denial of plaintiff's claim for chelation therapy benefits to treat artherosclerosis on the grounds that the treatment was experimental and therefore not covered under the plan); Adams v. Blue Cross/Blue Shield, 757 F.Supp. 661 (D.Md.1991); McLaughlin v. Connecticut Gen. Life Ins. Co., 565 F.Supp. 434 (N.D.Cal.1983) (concluding that insurance policy was ambiguous on the issue of coverage of unapproved therapies, and upholding grant of summary judgment to plaintiffs on claim of breach of contract for failure to cover "immuno-augmentative" cancer therapy to treat plaintiff's lung cancer); Free v. Travelers Ins. Co., 551 F.Supp. 554 (D.Md.1982); Miller v. State Farm Mut. Auto. Ins. Co., 424 N.W.2d 31 (Mich.Ct.App.1988); Taulbee v. Travelers Cos., 537 N.E.2d 670 (Ohio Ct.App.1987).

2. *Further commentary.* See Clark C. Havighurst, Health Care Choices: Private Contracts as Instruments of Health Reform (1995); John H. Ferguson et al., Court–Ordered Reimbursement for Unproven Medical Technology, 269 JAMA 2116 (1993); Sharona Hoffman, A Proposal for Federal Legislation to Address Health Insurance Coverage for Experimental and Investigational Treatments, 78 Or. L. Rev. 203 (1999); Dale L. Moore, An IRB Member's Perspective on Access to Innovative Therapy, 57 Alb. L. Rev. 559 (1994); E. Haavi Morreim, From the Clinics to the Courts: The Role Evidence Should Play in Litigating Medical Care, 26 J. Health Pol., Pol'y & L. 409 (2001); Steven R. Salbu, Regulation of Drug Treatments for HIV and AIDS: A Contractarian Model of Access, 11 Yale J. on Reg. 401 (1994); Paul E. Kalb, Note, Controlling Health Care Costs by Controlling Technology: A Private Contractual Approach, 99 Yale L.J. 1109 (1990).

C. TECHNOLOGY ASSESSMENT AND OUTCOMES RESEARCH

Technology assessment, conducted both by federal entities and private institutions, seeks to obtain information about medical technology that is significantly different from the information derived from the FDA's pre-approval processes. Regulatory reviews focus entirely on the safety and effectiveness of a product for a particular clinical use. The FDA generally does not consider data pertaining to the costs and benefits of a new drug or device, or how that new technology compares with currently marketed products or alternative treatments such as surgical interventions. See Maxwell J. Mehlman, Health Care Cost Containment and Medical Technology: A Critique of Waste Theory, 36 Case W. Res. L. Rev. 778, 788 (1986) (explaining that the FDA "has occasionally, albeit rarely, denied approval to market a drug on the basis that it was less safe or less effective than an alternative already on the market").

In the public sector, the Agency for Health Care Policy and Research (AHCPR, now redesignated as the Agency for Healthcare Research and Quality (AHRQ)) conducts technology assessments at the request of other federal agencies. Created in 1989, the AHCPR seeks to promote four important policy goals: enhancing medical practice, reducing costs of care, improving the quality of care, and improving access to services. See J. Jarrett Clinton, Agency for Health Care Policy and Research: Overview of Purpose and Programs, 49 Food & Drug L.J. 449, 458 (1994). The now-defunct Office of Technology Assessment (OTA) also prepared important reports about the relative costs and benefits of a wide variety of medical technologies. See OTA, Identifying Health Technologies that Work: Searching for Evidence (1994).

The Center for Medicare and Medicaid Services has enthusiastically embraced the concept of cost-effectiveness in decisions regarding coverage of services under the Medicare program. The following excerpt depicts the former HCFA's initial approach to technology assessment. As explained later in this chapter, this proposal was withdrawn and replaced with another proposed rule, but the agency's thinking on these issues provides some interesting history.

HCFA, Proposed Rule, *Medicare Program: Criteria and Procedures for Making Medical Services Coverage Decisions that Relate to Health Care Technology*

54 Fed. Reg. 4302 (1989).

In addition to the[] criteria [defining "reasonable and necessary" services], we propose that HCFA and Medicare contractors consider the cost-effectiveness of a service when making coverage decisions. Traditionally, HCFA has interpreted the terms "reasonable and necessary" contained in section 1862(a)(1)(A) of the Act to mean that a service is safe, effective, and widely accepted in the medical community. HCFA is including cost-effectiveness as a proposed criterion because we believe considerations of cost are relevant in deciding whether to expand or continue coverage of technologies, particularly in the context of the current explosion of high-cost medical technologies. We believe the requirement of section 1862(a)(1) that a covered service be "reasonable" encompasses the authority to consider cost as a factor in making Medicare coverage determinations.

The proper role for cost-effectiveness considerations is an important matter. Cost-effectiveness is one of several potential factors to be weighed in a given situation. In many cases, it may have no bearing at all on our conclusion. However, if a service were to be viewed as marginal with respect to safety and effectiveness, but expensive in comparison with available covered alternatives, we think that cost-effectiveness considerations are appropriate. * * * [W]hen there exists a reasonably feasible and medically appropriate alternative pattern of care that is less costly than that furnished, the amount payable is based on the reasonable cost of the least expensive alternative treatment that appropriately meets the patients' needs.

Formal cost-effectiveness analysis is an analytic tool that seeks to compare the incremental cost with the additional effectiveness of the procedure or technology. Beneficial effects are usually quantified in non-monetary terms (for example, increased years of life or reduced infection rates per patient), while costs or savings (both medical and nonmedical) are expressed in dollars. We are aware that cost-effectiveness analysis is a complex field that suffers from data limitations and the inability to quantify some costs. Specifically, for many new technologies, accurate measures of patient benefits or economic impacts (for example, incremental hospital costs) are imprecise because the device or procedure has not been used on many patients. Furthermore, even when data are available, methodological difficulties (for example, selecting a method for projecting future costs) and inherent subjectivity can seriously hamper analysis.

We may not consider cost-effectiveness in every coverage decision. For example, if there is a significant breakthrough or lifesaving technology for which there is no comparable alternative, we could not attempt a comparison to other available technologies since none exist. Another example is consideration of the provisions of section 1861(t)(2) of the Act. That section provides Medicare Part B coverage of outpatient prescription drugs * * * beginning January 1, 1990, and for other covered outpatient prescription drugs beginning January 1, 1991. Specifically, section 1834(c)(5)(C) of the Act prohibits the exclusion from coverage or denial of payment of a covered outpatient drug or class of outpatient drugs, or of any specific use of such a drug for a specific indication, unless the exclusion is based on a finding by the Secretary that the use is not safe and effective. We believe the Act precludes the application of the cost-effectiveness criterion to covered outpatient drugs, and we do not plan to apply the cost-effectiveness criterion to those drugs, although we request comment on the issue.

We believe that a disciplined effort to assess systematically the cost-effectiveness of technologies under coverage review will be useful. We propose to use a flexible definition of cost-effectiveness that encompasses a wide range of impacts: Cost-effectiveness means having improved health outcomes for Medicare patients that justify additional expenditures. In this regard, we would consider a technology cost-effective if, based on analysis, it demonstrated one of the following results:

—It is less costly and at least as effective as an alternative covered technology.

—It is more effective and more costly than a covered alternative, but improved health outcomes justify additional expenditures.

—It is less effective and less costly than an existing alternative, but is a viable alternative for some patients.

To establish the cost-effectiveness of any intervention, we propose to follow a standard set of analytical steps that are well accepted among economists. These steps are:

—Identify the relevant alternative technologies to which the current intervention is to be compared.

—Identify all the relevant outcomes from the alternative technologies and, when possible, quantify them. These may include clinical outcomes such as reduced morbidity and mortality, or qualitative outcomes such as reduced pain, enhanced personal well being, vigor, etc.

—Identify all the relevant costs expected (both Medicare and non-Medicare) from the interventions, including direct medical costs or savings and indirect costs such as enhanced productivity for the disabled, transportation, etc. * * *

—Consider nonquantifiable factors. Since all technology impacts cannot be fit into a conventional cost-effectiveness formula, the range of nonquantifiable factors (for example, ease of use, and access to ambulatory setting) should be described and considered as modifiers of the analysis.

We believe the regular application of these principles by HCFA, as well as by those proposing new technologies for coverage, would vastly improve our knowledge base and be a deterrent to coverage of procedures that may be costly, but have little or no impact on improving health outcomes. * * *

Office of Technology Assessment, *Health Care Technology and Its Assessment in Eight Countries*

OTA–BP–H–140 (1995).

* * * Apart from inflation and its effects on wages and the costs of goods, the increase in resource use is the primary reason for rising health care costs. Nations seeking to control these costs must control the growth and/or use of resources—an effort that inevitably has involved trying to control the processes by which health care technologies are developed, evaluated, adopted, and used.

Yet even without rising costs, controlling technology seems necessary. Choices among technologies have to be made—this occurs at different levels of health care systems. Some choices are made at the national or regional policy level, as when laws and regulations prevent the purchase of equipment or the provision of certain services. Most choices, however, are at the operational level of clinical practice: made by hospital administrators, heads of clinical departments, and health care providers working day to day. The ability to influence these choices, and the means through which that influence is exerted are prominent health policy issues. * * *

As a new technology appears to be of value, clinicians begin to use it and patients begin to ask for it. Diffusion may culminate with the technology's attainment of an appropriate level of use or with the technology's abandonment, either because it was of no value or because a more effective technology has been developed. The technology also may be used too much or too little, as often seems to be the case. In recent years a great deal of attention has been paid to the possibility of assessing the benefits, risks, and costs of technologies before they come into general use and employing the results of these assessments to guide technology adoption and use. * * *

Medical imaging remained relatively unchanged until the computed tomography (CT) scanner was introduced to the market by the EMI Co. in 1972. The CT scanner is a diagnostic device that combines x-ray equipment with a computer and a cathode-ray tube (a television-like device) to produce images of cross-sections of the human body. The principle of CT scanning was developed by the English physicist Hounsfield; he succeeded in producing the first scan of an object in 1967, and in 1971 he was able to scan the head of a live patient. Commercialization of the CT scanner in 1972 initiated a revolution in the field of diagnostic imaging. * * *

CT scanning was rapidly and enthusiastically accepted by the medial community. Despite concerns about its high cost—up to and more than $1 million—it diffused extraordinarily rapidly and came into widespread use throughout the world. * * * Although no randomized studies of the value of CT scanning were done in its early years, clinical experience gradually accumulated that indicated its usefulness in many conditions. It is now a fully accepted diagnostic technology.

Magnetic resonance imaging (MRI) is a more recent innovation in the filed of medical imaging, based on nuclear magnetic resonance (NMR). NMR images are formed without the use of ionizing radiation and reflect the proton density of the tissues being imaged, as well as the velocity with which fluid is flowing through the structures being imaged and the rate at which tissue hydrogen atoms return to their equilibrium states after being excited by radiofrequency energy. The first NMR image was published by Lauterbur of the State University of New York in 1973. Prototype MRI units were developed in the United States, England, and the Netherlands in the late 1970s.

MRI produces images of cross-sections of the human body similar to those produced by CT scanning, with some important differences. A CT scanner depicts the x-ray opacity of body structure. MRI images depict the density or even the chemical environment of hydrogen atoms. These various properties are not necessarily correlated. MRI has several advantages. It gives a high contrast sensitivity in its images, and it can distinguish between various normal and abnormal tissues. Blood flow, circulation of the cerebrospinal fluid, and contraction and relaxation of organs can be assessed. Tissues surrounded by bone can be represented. Also, MRI does not employ potentially dangerous ionizing radiation, as do CT scanning and other imaging methods. It is not necessary to inject toxic contrast agents, as is often done with CT scanning (although contrast agents are being used more and more frequently with MRI scanning). MRI allows for a choice of different imaging planes without moving the patient; CT scanning can produce an image of only one plane at a time, and some planes are not scannable. Finally, images can be obtained from areas of the body where CT scanning fails to produce clear images.

Despite its potential, the initial diffusion of MRI in most countries was less rapid than had been the case with CT scanners. Introduction and diffusion were slowed because of the economic recession in the early 1980s. At the same time health authorities were unwilling to invest heavily in

MRI before any thorough evaluation had taken place. Questions such as these were asked: Is present MRI an advance in imaging technology as compared with CT scanning? Does it produce useful information at a reasonable cost? Does it produce diagnostic information not otherwise available?

MRI has been repeatedly and formally assessed since its introduction. * * * These assessments agree that MRI is a reliable diagnostic device that produces information that can be quite useful. However, evaluation of MRI scanning has been far from optimal. For example, a literature review published in 1988 found that 54 evaluations did poorly when rated by commonly accepted scientific standards, such as use of a "gold standard" comparison of blinded readers of the images (i.e., the expert doing the reading does not know the status of the patient). Only one evaluation had a prospective design. Also, over the period examined there was no improvement in quality of research over time, and this problem continued in later years.

Literature shows that MRI is probably superior to CT, its main competitor, for detection and characterization of posterior fossa (brain) lesions and spinal cord myelopathies, imaging in multiple sclerosis, detecting lesions in patients with refractory partial seizures, and detailed display for guiding complex therapy, as for brain tumors. In other diseases the efficacy of MRI is similar to that of CT. In fact, the best designed study, carried out in a heterogeneous group of patients * * * in a matched pair design, found that sensitivity and specificity of CT scanning were somewhat better than those of MRI. As for the diagnostic or therapeutic impact, little information is available. Investigators in Norway found that 33 percent of patients had their main diagnosis changed by MRI scanning. Plans for surgery changed in 20 percent of the patients, and plans for radiotherapy changed in 8 percent.

Although most MRI scans are of the brain, a specific advantage of MRI lies in diagnosis of spinal cord problems, where MRI may replace myelography, an x-ray procedure involving injection of a potentially dangerous dye. In the spinal cord two studies have examined the relative accuracy of MRI in relation to myelography and CT. The studies found that MRI and CT were roughly equivalent in terms of true positive results but that both were superior to myelography. MRI is gradually replacing both CT scanning and myelography. * * *

The capital cost of an MRI scanner varies greatly, depending particularly on the strength of the magnets. A basic unit costs at least $1,115,000 per year in the mid–1980s. Only about one-third of this operating cost is accounted for by the capital investment in the scanner itself. Other expenses include space, personnel, equipment, and maintenance. The cost per scan in one mid–1980s study was between $370 and $550, and the fee paid for the scan was $500. (The costs apparently do not include payment to the physician.) Other studies have demonstrated that the costs of an MRI scan are considerably more than those of a CT scan. * * *

MRI costs maybe offset by replacement of other diagnostic procedures, particularly myelography. Although myelography requires hospitalization of at least one day, MRI can be done on an outpatient basis. It does not appear to have replaced other modalities, such as CT scanning in the brain, except that it is used preferentially in suspected posterior fossa tumors. In general, however, replacement of other procedures by MRI has not been demonstrated. The result is a considerable increase in costs. The basic issues with CT scanning and MRI scanning is that they provide similar information. It has been difficult to demonstrate much advantage with MRI. * * *

Amy L. Wax, *Technology Assessment and the Doctor–Patient Relationship*

82 VA. L. REV. 1641 (1996).

* * * There are many examples of new medical technologies for which cost is extremely high, and benefit is slight, marginal or unproven. For example, in treating metastatic breast cancer, the use of bone marrow transplantation is extremely expensive, potentially traumatic and risky. Virtually every well-controlled study has failed to show that the treatment has any statistically significant effect on duration of survival. Similarly, a number of drugs recently approved by the FDA show modest, short-lived or ambiguous effects. Demonstrating that these drugs have any benefit whatsoever requires trials of many thousands of patients. Scientists must conduct sophisticated and sometimes problematic statistical analyses in an often unsuccessful attempt to identify subgroups of patients who might be helped by the drug. With respect to diagnostic techniques the situation is not much different. New scanners, screening techniques, and blood tests significantly add to medical expenditures overall, but frequently present only a marginal improvement over existing methods, provide a net health benefit that is very difficult to measure, or have a high error rate that confounds their usefulness.

Careful, accurate, and sophisticated outcomes assessment is the best, and indeed, the only reliable way to identify and measure the magnitude of the costs and benefits of many new therapies. Even under the most rigorous and well-controlled circumstances, it is technically very difficult to quantify with any confidence the effects of innovations that represent only marginal improvements over existing techniques or interventions. Necessarily, measurements are subject to various kinds of error and require assumptions that render them little more than best estimates. These observations apply not just to innovative therapies, but also to established treatments, some of which will also be of questionable or marginal value in some or all patients who have received treatment.

But, even with all of its imperfections and difficulties, technology assessment's irreplaceable role in documenting the cost-benefit ratio makes the technique vitally important to the optimal operation of bedside rationing. Technology assessment allows conscientious physicians to think through the possible approaches to diagnosis and treatment in a systematic and informed manner, rather than relying on intuition, anecdote and limited personal experience. Armed with information about medical benefit, efficacy, side effects and overall expense, physicians who have a scientifically sound understanding of the likely costs and effects of treatment choices can formulate more reasoned treatment plans for individual patients in the least harmful and most cost-effective way. * * *

Although sound information is obviously important in permitting physicians to make more informed judgments, it is even more important in enabling a physician to present the basis for his or her judgment in a way that is likely to gain the assent and cooperation of patients. To the extent that the information provided by technology assessment has the power to foster a reduction in the consumption of medical resources, it will do so mainly by creating the conditions under which patients are more likely to go along with reasonable restraints on the provision of care. All too often, the non-specific demand that health care providers "do everything possible" is a manifestation of ignorance and fear rather than reasoned decision-making based on knowledge and concrete information. Without precise data about costs and benefits, patients will be frightened by the inestimable possibility that a chosen path will sacrifice significant palliation or cure. Patients are more likely to accept tradeoffs and risks when their physician's recommendations are backed by the rigorous, trustworthy, and precise scientific estimates of costs and benefits that outcomes assessment data can provide. And not only does technology assessment enable physicians to provide patients with convincing and precise evidence of the marginality of the benefits offered by many cutting-edge treatments, but it also allows physicians to pinpoint areas of uncertainty and to advise patients about what is known and unknown concerning the effects of new and existing options. If patients can be made to appreciate the (sometimes flimsy) scientific basis for some interventions, they may go along more readily with recommendations that certain particularly expensive therapies or procedures be forgone or put off.

Some examples show how information technology can foster patient-physician joint decision-making that resolves towards less rather than more interventionist care. Mark Hall illustrates the kind of bottom-up rationing that frequently occurs in practice by offering a hypothetical based loosely on a physician's handling of a knee injury his wife received while playing tennis. He states that his wife's physician estimated that there was a ninety percent chance that the injury was a ligament strain (ordinarily treated by resting the affected limb), and a ten percent chance that the injury was a more severe ligament tear, which in turn had a ten percent chance of leading to permanent impairment if left untreated. The most definitive resolution of the diagnostic uncertainty would have been to perform a magnetic resonance imaging scan (costing twelve hundred dollars) immediately. The physician, after consulting with the patient, decided against ordering the scan. A quick recovery proved the gamble harmless.

As Hall points out, this situation does not present the kind of dramatic life-or-death dilemma that dominates the rationing literature. The reality is far less riveting. Through his hypothetical, Hall attempts to provide a more realistic picture of the small, incremental and routine decisions that physicians make every day—decisions like "declining to order a confirming diagnostic test or an extra day in the hospital, prescribing a less expensive drug, or avoiding a referral to a specialist." For each of these decisions, the stakes are comparatively small for individual patients, but the costs of indulging extreme risk aversion at every point add up in the aggregate to significantly greater expense for the system.

Hall's example also illustrates that it is a mistake to think of every medical judgment that can be characterized as not doing everything possible as a sharp departure from norms of acceptable medical practice. First, in most routine cases of medical diagnosis and treatment, it is not readily apparent precisely what doing everything possible would mean. There are often a number of ways to approach a particular medical problem, especially since details of presentation always differ from patient to patient. Flexible conventions, selectively applied through the exercise of individual judgment, are the essence of ordinary medical practice, and can give rise to many alternative strategies for dealing with day-to-day medical scenarios. A measured and gradually escalating sequence of tests and interventions often represents the most acceptable course of action. * * *

Although Hall's story is not primarily about the use of cutting edge technologies, it presents a good example of the kind of decision-making at the margin—decision-making that invites "the prudent trimming of incrementally beneficial services"—that physicians must engage in when determining whether and how to use innovative drugs or treatments. But in order to make decisions at the margins it is necessary to know where the margins are. Hall does not comment on the source or reliability of the probability estimates used in his anecdote. It is easy to devise numbers for use in a hypothetical, but only technology assessment can generate accurate data in a form that can be applied to real-life decision-making. * * *

Paul C. Sorum, *Limiting Cardiopulmonary Resuscitation*
57 ALB. L. REV. 617 (1994).

Researchers at Duke University, studying the outcomes and costs of care of 146 patients who suffered cardiac arrests on the general medical and surgical wards between 1988 and 1991, found that only eighty-four (58%) were revived and only seven (5%) were subsequently able to leave the hospital and lead "meaningful lives" for a period of time. The high cost of caring for the eighty-four initial survivors totaled $1.1 million, or $13,000 per person, due in large part to the expensive care each received in intensive care units after their resuscitations. The researchers pointed out that the cost was about $150,000 for each "meaningful" survivor and, therefore, concluded that "doctors should be reluctant to recommend CPR to people who are gravely ill."

This argument is invalid for four reasons. First, the argument applies equally well to many other treatments routinely given to quite sick or fragile people—e.g., antibiotics that prevent death from pneumonia, chemotherapy that delays the spread of cancer, surgery that relieves a bowel obstruction. In each of these cases, as in the case of a cardiac arrest, if the patients are left to die rather than given treatment, money will be saved (assuming they do die). If monetary savings provide a valid basis to withhold CPR, why not withhold other treatments that have equally high (or higher) monetary consequences?

Second, this amount of money, which initially seems staggering, may not seem so unacceptable upon further examination. It may not be fair to eliminate consideration of the seventy-nine initial survivors who died prior to discharge from the hospital. Their added period of life, as I argued earlier, may very well have been meaningful and valuable to them and their families. Furthermore, $150,000 might not be a high price for preserving a "meaningful" life. To begin with, it would help to know the length and quality of the survivors' lives. This may alter the cost-effectiveness when expressed as cost per year of life gained (rather than as number of survivors) and when adjusted for any decrease in the patients' quality of life (i.e., when expressed as cost per "quality-adjusted life year"). The limited data in other studies on outcomes after discharge suggest that the patients' longevity is limited largely by their age and pre-existing diseases, not by their cardiac arrest, and is quite good; 50% of the survivors live between one and three years or even longer. Furthermore, the patients' mental and physical capacities remain mostly intact. Therefore, the cost per quality-adjusted life year might well be far less than $150,000.

To understand such a cost, it would help to look at the cost-effectiveness of other interventions. [One study has] compared a variety of accepted treatments in terms of the additional dollars spent (as compared with the alternative treatment) for each quality-adjusted life year gained: neonatal intensive care for 1000–1499 gram babies, $5,100; the use of low osmolar contrast media for radiographic studies in patients at high risk for subsequent kidney failure, $22,600; neonatal intensive care for 500–999 gram babies, $30,900; bone marrow transplant for acute nonlymphocytic leukemia, $59,300. The Center for Risk Analysis at the Harvard School of Public Health has compiled the published cost-effectiveness analyses of over 500 interventions intended to prevent premature deaths. The median cost, in 1991 dollars, of interventions in medicine (including measures to prevent, screen for, diagnose, and treat illness) was $17,000 per year of life saved (not adjusted for quality). In consumer product safety the median was $19,000, in transportation safety it was $60,000, in environmental control it was $350,000, and in occupational safety the median cost was $370,000 per year of life saved. The consensus of experts in cost-effectiveness analysis is that in general a medical intervention is cost-effective if the procedure's additional cost, as compared with the costs of the alternatives, is less than $40,000–50,000 for each quality-adjusted life year gained.

Using this guideline to evaluate the allocation of intensive care resources, it is noteworthy, for example, that the charges for intensive care for critically ill patients aged sixty-five and older have been calculated as only $21,768 for each year of life saved (not adjusted for quality of life). On the other hand, the cost per year of life gained by treating critically ill cancer patients in the intensive care unit was found to be $82,845 for patients with solid tumors and $189,399 for those with hematologic malignancies. In the case of CPR, the adjustment of the costs of CPR in the Duke study, in light of the duration and quality of the experiences of the transient and long-term survivors, might well bring the cost per quality-adjusted life year into the range of the guideline of $40,000–50,000 per quality-adjusted life year.

The third criticism of the cost argument is that it unfairly attributes to successful CPR all the costs of subsequent care, implying that once the decision to undertake CPR is made, the option of letting the patient die is lost and the physicians' hands become tied, i.e., they have no choice but to give and continue expensive treatment. In fact, depending on the results of CPR, the patient or patient's surrogate and the physician can decide (either after the CPR or, by advance directives, before) to limit treatment. If they do not, the cost of treatment—which will be far more expensive than CPR itself—must be attributed to that decision, not solely to the decision to undertake CPR. * * *

NOTES AND QUESTIONS

1. *Evidence-based medicine through technology assessment.* While purchasers of medical care seek information about the value of a technological intervention, providers of care seek information that will enable them to choose the most effective medical option for their patients. Evidence about the comparative outcomes of two technologies to diagnose or treat the same condition allows health care providers to select the most useful technology from among the available options. See John M. Eisenberg, Ten Lessons for Evidence–Based Technology Assessment, 282 JAMA 1865 (1999). Sometimes older technologies remain entrenched when newer, better technologies are available; at other times, newer, more expensive technologies replace older therapies without demonstrable added benefit. See David A Grimes, Technology Follies: The Uncritical Acceptance of Medical Innovation, 269 JAMA 3030 (1993); Lars Noah, Medicine's Epistemology: Mapping the Haphazard Diffusion of Knowledge in the Biomedical Community, 44 Ariz. L. Rev. (forthcoming 2002).

2. *Cost-effectiveness of newer prescription drugs.* The increased utilization of prescription drugs accounts for much of the increase in medical spending since the 1980s. According to one recent study, the average price of a prescription drug introduced after 1992 was $71.49, compared with an average of $30.47 for older products. Because newer drugs cost more than older drugs, researchers attempted to determine whether the benefits of the newer drugs justified their greater costs. After controlling for a wide variety of variables, including sex, age, race, income, insurance status, condition for which the drug was prescribed and the length of time that the reporting patient had the condition, other co-existing medical conditions, and other prescription drugs being used, the investigators concluded that replacing older drugs with newer, more costly, drugs reduces morbidity (measured by missed work and school days, and days spent bedridden), mortality, and total medical expenditure. See Frank R. Lichtenberg, The Benefits and Costs of Newer Drugs: Evidence from the 1996 Medical Expenditure Panel Survey (2000), available at <http://www.CESifo.de> ("It is sometimes suggested that, because generic drugs tend to be less expensive than branded drugs, allowing people to use only generic drugs might be an effective means of reducing health expenditure. However generic drugs tend to be much older than branded drugs, and our estimates indicate that denying people access to branded drugs would increase total treatment costs, not reduce them, and would lead to worse outcomes."); see also Peter J. Neumann et al., Are Pharmaceuticals Cost–Effective? A Review of the Evidence, Health Aff., Mar.-Apr. 2000, at 92; P. Saunders & A. Hersheimer, WHO's Model List of Essential Drugs: A Beacon Through Two Decades, 346 Lancet 519 (1995) (discussing the World Health Organization's list of essential drugs); Ron Winslow, Limiting Drugs a Doctor Orders May Cost More, Wall St. J., Mar. 20, 1996, at B1. How would a health insurer that relies on a restricted formulary to limit costs respond to the study findings?

3. *Clot busters.* Two drugs for treating blood clots in heart attack patients appear to be equally effective. The older, off-patent drug, streptokinase, costs between $76 and $300 per dose. The newer agent, a biotechnology product called tissue plasminogen activator (tPA), costs $2,200 per dose. In 1990, two-thirds of the patients treated after heart attack received tPA for a total cost of $210 million, while the streptokinase therapy for the remaining third of the patients cost only $5 million. Many physicians have questioned this prescribing trend in light of studies that found no differences in comparative efficacy. The manufacturer of tPA promoted the drug aggressively by identifying arguable flaws in the data and by warning physicians that they may subject themselves to malpractice liability if they prescribe streptokinase. See Andrew Pollack, The Battle of the Heart Drugs, N.Y. Times, June 30, 1991, at A1; see also Robert McNutt & Arthur Evans, Editorial, Accelerated tPA Versus Streptokinase for Suspected Myocardial Infarction: Waiting for Our Mountain Dew, 15 Med. Decision Making 395 (1995). In contrast, tPA has shown clear benefits when rapidly administered to stroke victims, but health care providers fail to use it. See Laurie Tarkan, Absence of Urgency: A Deadly Problem When Strokes Occur, N.Y. Times, Feb. 13, 2001, at F7 ("Only 2 percent to 3 percent of stroke patients actually receive the new drug, whereas 30 percent to 40 percent of them could benefit from it.").

4. *Cancer screening and cost-effectiveness.* Further advances in scanning technologies raise interesting questions of cost-effectiveness and medical benefit. For example, spiral computed tomography ("spiral CT"), a faster and potentially more accurate type of CT scan, may allow physicians to find smaller lung tumors than traditional x-ray technology. Because spiral CT scans cost at least $300 per scan, some commentators have questioned whether screening at-risk persons for lung cancer will detect lung tumors earlier enough to increase the cure rate for an otherwise frequently fatal disease. Critics suggest that, although patients with lung tumors detected through spiral CT may live longer than patients whose tumors are discovered through conventional scans, the extended life expectancy associated with scanning may be illusory—patients simply live longer after diagnosis because they are being diagnosed earlier with new, expensive technologies. These experts argue that the only way to assess the usefulness of this technology is to conduct a well-designed clinical trial that measures cancer deaths after diagnosis, rather than the length of survival time. See David Brown, A Lung Scan Raises Hopes and Doubts, Wash. Post, Jan. 16, 2001, at A1. Another new type of scanning technology, positron emission tomography (PET), raises similar issues of costs and benefits. The PET scan measures abnormal metabolic activity in cells and therefore can identify cancer cells, which typically operate at a higher metabolic rate than normal cells. Ordinary CT scans may show abnormal tissue as darkened masses within the body, but, without a biopsy, there is no way to determine whether the abnormality is cancerous. PET scans thus can potentially prevent unnecessary biopsy procedures. Medicare now covers the $2,000 scans for a variety of suspected cancerous conditions, but experts suggest that more study is needed to determine whether the costly technology will deliver benefits in the form of reduced treatment costs or extended life-spans. One of the most difficult questions is how to determine the "testing threshold"—that is, the pretest probability that the patient has the disease for which the diagnostic test, if performed, will affect therapeutic choices. "The question then arises: at what probabilities of malignancy is it beneficial or cost-effective to avoid further diagnostic testing or to treat patients empirically? . . . Given the need to balance the risks of diagnostic tissue sampling of lung masses with the risks of failure to diagnose cancer, along with the unknown benefit of early diagnosis of lung cancer, the question of which patients to evaluate is clinically very important." Ethan Balk & Joseph Lau, PET Scans and Technology Assessment: Deja Vu?, 285 JAMA 936 (2001). These same commentators also emphasized the need to evaluate the usefulness of PET in comparison with other relevant technologies, such as CT and MRI, in a well-controlled, scientifically-rigorous clinical trial. See id.; see also David M. Eddy et al., The Value of Mammography Screening in Women Under Age 50 Years, 259 JAMA 1512 (1988) (providing a cost-benefit analysis); Susan Okie, Analysis: Mammograms Don't Cut Cancer Death Risk, Wash. Post, Oct. 19, 2001, at A2.

5. *Tort liability pressures.* Fears of tort liability may drive decisions to use costly new technologies. For example, after years of inadequate treatment for sepsis, a frequently fatal blood infection, hospitals now have access to a costly but effective new treatment. Eli Lilly recently received FDA approval to market Xigris®, which has been demonstrated in clinical trials to reduce sepsis deaths by 20 percent and which the company intends to price at approximately $5000 a dose. One large hospital estimated that the cost of this drug alone would constitute more than 10 percent of the hospital's annual spending for drugs. See Thomas M. Burton, Can Hospitals Afford Not to Prescribe Eli Lilly's Pricey New Sepsis Drug Xigris?, Wall St. J., Sept. 11, 2001, at B1.

6. *Cost consciousness, medical ethics, and patient care.* Does maximum utilization of the newest technologies necessarily promote the highest standards of patient care? Physicians have warned their colleagues that overreliance on technology can depersonalize the physician-patient relationship and, ultimately, hinder patient care. See Chiedozie I. Udeh, New Technologies in Medicine, 283 JAMA 2592 (2000) ("Technology also brings with it the potential for misuse and overuse.... We often forget that for patients and their families, the best physician is rarely the one with all the latest technology. It is usually the one who takes time to carefully examine the patient, discuss the treatment plan, or simply holds a patient's hand to allay his or her fears."); see also Chapter 11(C)(2) (exploring the connection between the ethical concept of medical futility and the pervasiveness of "bedside rationing" of medical technologies). Another commentator has urged physicians and other health care providers to consider the cost of treatments in making choices among medical options, arguing that cost considerations are consistent with medical ethics principles:

> Ironically, at a time when health care policymakers and providers are recognizing that quality health care must be made available to more people and with fewer financial resources, medical science is on the verge of being able to do much more for patients. Advances in molecular biology have been exponential during the last five years, driven to a large extent by the Human Genome Project (HGP). Genetic products are reaching the marketplace, there is a vast pipeline of genetic products in various stages of development, and these visible products are only the predecessors of an entire new generation of therapeutics, diagnostics, and other genetic tests.... Because technology will continue to raise health care costs—perhaps exponentially in the very near future—choices must be made. Technology is becoming an enemy to public health because it has not been made part of a deliberate strategy for managing care. In accordance with the professional dominance and bioethics eras in medical ethics, medical schools have trained physicians not to consider costs, there is no cost-effectiveness requirement for FDA approval, and "only in the past few years have care managers begun convincing technology suppliers regularly to incorporate cost-reduction objectives in their decision-making." The costs of medical technology must be contained, especially in light of the myriad of genetic technologies reaching commerce and the preexisting unmet health care needs of the general public. Ethical norms that recognize and discourage the abuse and waste of health care resources must be fostered.

Michael J. Malinowski, Capitation, Advances in Medical Technology, and the Advent of a New Era in Medical Ethics, 22 Am. J.L. & Med. 331, 332, 346–47 (1996); see also Eric Cassell, The Sorcerer's Book: Medicine's Rampant Technology, 23 Hastings Ctr. Rep. 32 (1993); David Seedhouse, Why Bioethicists Have Nothing Useful to Say About Health Care Rationing, 21 J. Med. Ethics 288 (1995).

7. *Technology assessment in the land down under.* The Australian government was one of the first to use formal, rigorous cost-benefit analyses in deciding whether to provide government subsidies for prescription drugs. Once drugs are approved for marketing, an advisory committee weighs whether the new drug works as well as alternative drugs already available under government subsidy (or provides an advantage compared with a non-drug approach such as surgery) and attempts to determine whether the drug will provide a cost savings to the government by reducing the need for physician visits or hospitalization. If the drug passes muster, the Australian government makes it available for a nominal co-payment to all patients who may benefit. Drugs that fail the cost-benefit analysis remain available in Australia, but consumers must pay the full cost of the product out of their own pockets. See S. Karene Witcher, In the Land Down Under, A Model for National Drug Insurance, Wall St. J., Aug. 31, 2000, at B1.

8. *Further commentary.* See Alexander Morgan Capron, Does Assessment of Medical Practices Have a Future?, 82 Va. L. Rev. 1623 (1996); Allan S. Detsky & Gary Naglie, A Clinician's Guide to Cost–Effectiveness Analysis, 113 Annals Internal Med. 147 (1990); Einer Elhauge, The Limited Regulatory Potential of Medical Technology Assessment, 82 Va. L. Rev. 1525 (1996); Susan Bartlett Foote, Assessing Medical Technology Assessment: Past, Present, and Future, 65 Milbank Q. 59 (1987); Mita K. Giacomini, The Which–Hunt: Assembling Health Technologies for Assessment and Rationing, 24 J. Health Pol. Pol'y & L. 715 (1999); Wendy K. Mariner, Outcomes Assessment in Health Care Reform: Promises and Limitations, 20 Am. J.L. & Med. 37 (1994); Charles Marwick, Pharmacoeconomics: Is a Drug Worth Its Cost?, 272 JAMA 1395 (1994); Louise Russell et al., The Role of Cost–Effectiveness Analysis in Health and Medicine, 276 JAMA 1172 (1996); Sean R. Tunis & Hellen Gelband, Health Care Technology in the United States, 30 Health Pol'y 335 (1994).

PROBLEM #14. *ONLY THE BEST FOR MY BUNDLE OF JOY*

Synagis® is a genetically-engineered antibody that interferes with infection in the lungs by the respiratory syncytial virus (R.S.V.). It doesn't prevent R.S.V. infection, but it reduces the severity of the infection. MedImmune, the manufacturer of Synagis, is pouring substantial resources into the marketing of its product, including television and print advertising, and a brigade of detail representatives. Rhonda Webster, the new mother of baby Stephanie, just saw an advertisement on television promoting Synagis. It showed a doctor giving oxygen to an infant in the hospital with the following voiceover: "If you knew what R.S.V. could do to your precious baby, it would take your breath away. If your baby was born prematurely, call your pediatrician now and ask about Synagis, before it's too late."

Stephanie was born six-weeks prematurely but, after a 10–day stay in the hospital, was discharged and has been a healthy infant ever since. She is now six months old. Rhonda called Stephanie's pediatrician immediately and made an appointment for the next day. Rhonda wasn't sure what

R.S.V. was, but she feared that Stephanie might catch it. With winter just around the corner, Stephanie was already fighting a cold and coughing a bit. The pediatrician checked Stephanie out and found her to be healthy. He told Rhonda that the cough was nothing to worry about and that Stephanie did not need the expensive series of Synagis injections (a total of five shots at a cost of $5,000). Rhonda had done a little research on the Internet, and she insisted that Stephanie was at risk for a serious R.S.V. infection and that she be given Synagis. The Websters' insurance plan covers the drug only for babies born at least six weeks early, who also have other risk factors, such as staying in day care, living with a parent who smokes, or having many siblings in school who could spread the virus at home. (Rhonda has said that they will pay out of pocket if their insurance plan refuses coverage.) Stephanie is the Websters' only child, and Rhonda stays home to care for her. Neither of Stephanie's parents smoke.

Given the following facts about the costs and benefits of Synagis, should the pediatrician give Stephanie the drug? Each year, approximately 100,000 infants are hospitalized with R.S.V. infections leading to bronchitis or pneumonia, and, of this group, somewhere between 500 and 2,000 of the infants die. A clinical trial conducted by MedImmune suggests that Synagis reduces by 55 percent the risk that an infant with R.S.V. infection will be hospitalized. Another independent study estimated that, for every seventeen patients who received Synagis, the treatment would keep one of those patients out of the hospital. That study concluded that the cost of the drug would have to be reduced to $500 in order for it to be cost effective. (At its current price, the cost of one series of Synagis injections would cover the health insurance premiums of a family of four for a year.) Finally, consider that most of the infants afflicted with the worst R.S.V. complications have already spent a substantial amount of time in a hospital NICU to see them through the complications of their prematurity. See Melody Petersen, Doctors Caught in the Middle; Ad Campaign Has Parents Asking for a Costly Drug, N.Y. Times, Jan. 31, 2001, at C1.

Note, *Will Health Care Economic Information Lead to Therapeutic–Class Warfare or Welfare?*
111 Harv. L. Rev. 2384 (1998).

On the frontlines of the annual ninety-three billion dollar prescription drug battleground, pharmaceutical companies are engaged in an increasingly fierce struggle to develop potent drugs, ensure efficient distribution chains, and seize larger market shares. The stakes are enormous: given the size of the market, "even a small share can mean large revenues." In recent years, the terrain has shifted as managed care organizations (MCOs) have emerged as serious market players. MCOs wield enormous influence because they determine which drugs are included on their formularies, which are "lists of drug products approved by the [FDA], arranged by therapeutic category, along with the reimbursement rate for the drug." Formulary inclusion gives a drug manufacturer a tactical advantage over competitors within its therapeutic class.

As prescription drug costs have continued to rise, MCOs have become increasingly concerned with structuring drug utilization schemes that optimize consumer health while minimizing economic expenditures. MCOs hope to reduce overall costs, even at the expense of greater short-term costs, by factoring in the costs and benefits of current health care interventions that prevent later, more expensive illnesses. To do so, MCOs need health care economic information to assess the cost-effectiveness of a given drug to determine whether it should be included on the formulary.

Until recently, however, FDA stifled this information. Rather than adopting an economic standard for evaluating health care economic claims, FDA applied the same clinical-based standard that it used to determine drug effectiveness. * * * Just as pharmaceutical companies had to present "substantial evidence" of safety and effectiveness to gain FDA approval for a new drug, FDA required pharmaceutical companies to demonstrate "substantial evidence" or "substantial clinical evidence" prior to making any cost-effectiveness claims. FDA recodified its policy to consider cost-effectiveness claims within its misbranding provisions in 1976: "Among representations in the labeling of a drug which render such drug misbranded is a false or misleading representation with respect to another drug...." Although a few companies submitted the requisite two adequate and well-controlled studies and ultimately gained approval to make specific pharmacoeconomic claims, many opted to forego this route—because of time and cost concerns—in favor of alternative marketing strategies. Thus, due to FDA's restrictive approach to cost-effectiveness claims, the development and dissemination of health care economic information languished.

Congress recognized the importance of health care economic information to MCOs when it considered the FDA Modernization Act of 1997. Having identified this need, Congress responded by including a health care economic provision in the FDA Modernization Act. This provision defines "health care economic information" to mean "any analysis that identifies, measures, or compares the economic consequences, including the costs of the represented health outcomes, of the use of a drug to the use of another drug, to another health care intervention, or to no intervention." Congress lowered the standard of proof that a manufacturer must meet to substantiate health care economic claims. Under the new framework, Congress now only requires pharmaceutical companies to base health care economic claims on "competent and reliable scientific evidence." Not surprisingly, this new standard is largely context-driven: "the nature of the evidence required to support various components of health care economic analyses depends on which component of the analysis is involved."

Although it relaxed the standard of proof, Congress explicitly limited who can receive health care economic information. This information can be disseminated to formulary committees, MCOs, and other similar entities; however, individual physicians are excluded. Unlike MCOs, which are capable of considering health care economic information through an expert deliberative process, individual physicians typically lack the necessary skills and time to weigh the relevant merits of health care economic claims.

"This limitation is important because it will ensure that the information is presented only to parties who have established procedures and skills to interpret the methods and limitations of economic studies."

Congress also limited potential health care economic claims to already approved drug uses. Specifically, health care economic information provided by pharmaceutical companies will not be considered a false, misleading, or illegal new drug claim as long as it "directly relates to an [approved] indication," as reflected in the approved physician package insert. This section explicitly prohibits drug manufacturers from making any pharmacoeconomic claims relating to unapproved uses of an approved drug. For example, "economic claims based on preventing disease progression would ordinarily not be considered to be directly related to an approved indication for the treatment of symptoms of a disease, for a drug for which the use in prevention of disease progression has not been approved."

Lastly, Congress used this provision to change the default rule for health care economic claims from a requirement of prior approval to one of permissive publication. As noted above, FDA required drug manufacturers to gain premarket approval of any health care economic claim—if it was used in labeling—before publicizing it. Although FDA's current postmarketing reporting regulations still require drug manufacturers to submit health care economic information to FDA at the time such information is initially provided to a formulary committee or other managed care provider, drug manufacturers are now allowed to market their claims immediately. * * *

The trend towards managed care—with its concomitant battle to contain costs while preserving the quality of care—has fueled the demand for accurate health care economic information. Although the FDA Modernization Act explicitly defines the output of CEA, it fails to address methods that will be used to generate that output. The wide disparity in methods currently used to conduct CEA renders the resulting pharmacoeconomic information suspect. A recent survey of MCO decisionmakers found that they considered current health care economic information only "moderately useful" in making drug purchasing decisions, although they ascribed a much higher value to the future usefulness of such information. * * *

One problem that arises from the use of divergent methodologies is the way that researchers identify and calculate the relevant costs that should be included in the numerator of the cost-effectiveness ratio. Although economic theory dictates that a "change in the use of a resource caused by its health intervention should be valued at its opportunity cost," researchers have had a hard time applying this theory in practice. A similar host of problems confronts researchers trying to identify and calculate the relevant benefits that should be included in the denominator of the cost-effectiveness ratio. A comprehensive cost-benefit analysis would weigh all of the benefits accruing to society, even if those benefits do not accrue directly to the MCO. Yet, researchers know that MCOs have an incentive to discount purely societal benefits. Furthermore, researchers have struggled to express these benefits in a meaningful way. One scientific panel suggested incorporating these health benefits variables into a standard unit of measurement called "quality-adjusted life-years" (QALYs). However, "there are a number of methodologic challenges involved in estimating QALYs, including: how to classify health states; whose preferences to use in judging the desirability of the health states; how to measure preferences; and how to adjust for time preferences."

Even if researchers accurately identify and measure the health care costs and benefits associated with a given treatment, three other sources of uncertainty remain. First, researchers must estimate the effectiveness of given treatment interventions. "The quality and validity of a CEA depend crucially on the quality of the underlying data that describe the effectiveness of interventions and the course of illness without intervention." Typically, researchers develop a model based on primary and secondary data sources to estimate effectiveness. On a primary level, researchers might rely on studies conducted specifically to inform the CEA. On a secondary level, researchers might rely on reports of randomized controlled trials, observational studies, uncontrolled experiments, or descriptive series. However, FDA's previous position that "effects need to be demonstrated by adequate and well-controlled studies" rather than simply estimated through "meta-analyses, assumptions[,] or expert opinion" posed a serious obstacle to the development of workable models. It is unclear whether, or how, FDA will alter its treatment of modeling assumptions under the new law. In addition, the new statute only allows consideration of approved drug uses, not off-label uses, even if the latter represent the medical standard of care.

Second, researchers must incorporate consistent discount rates and time preferences. In calculating the cost-effectiveness ratio of a treatment, researchers must calculate the net present value of the costs and benefits. One problem that arises in this calculation is that CEAs frequently incorporate different discount rates that hamper cross-study comparisons. * * * Third, some CEAs fail to address the uncertainty that results from their dependence on a multitude of frequently debatable assumptions. "Cost-effectiveness analyses are subject to uncertainty with regard to estimates of effectiveness, the course of illness, [health-related quality-of-life] consequences and preferences, and health care utilization and costs." Depending on the nature of the assumption and the relative importance of the variable, health care economic outcomes can be significantly affected. However, some studies fail to incorporate appropriate sensitivity analyses that would place the relevant assumptions in an understandable context.

The free market, by itself, is not likely to address completely these methodological shortcomings. * * * The new framework for health care economic information leaves in place the existing incentives for bias and also exacerbates the incentive for researchers to make biased assumptions. First, researchers are still required to make numerous, often subtle assumptions in order to develop workable models. Because most CEAs are done for marketing purposes, "the assumptions made in constructing the models and the data used in the analysis . . . could be biased." * * *

Second, the new framework provides added incentives for bias. The lower standard of proof—competent and reliable scientific evidence—suggests that researchers can afford to make some of the questionable assumptions that they may have been reluctant to make under the stricter standard. Thus, this new standard may actually increase the number of low-quality studies that purport to offer conclusive health care economic information. One expert's observation of CEAs under the former standard is revealing: "There are very few well-done pharmacoeconomic studies in the literature; many are quick and dirty studies done for marketing and promotion. They are beginning to denigrate and give a bad name to the research area." Even if the lower standard will not exacerbate existing incentives for bias, it does nothing to ameliorate these incentives.

Market forces will ameliorate some, but not all, of the incentives to produce low-quality pharmacoeconomic information. Specifically, drug manufacturers, pharmaceutical organizations, and MCOs have incentives to provide or demand high-quality economic information. For instance, a manufacturer of a cost-effective drug can distinguish its product by submitting the CEA for publication in a peer review journal. Journals would effectively screen CEAs for the highest quality studies, and then give those studies their endorsement by publishing them. Although not every CEA would be sufficiently thorough and unbiased, MCOs would have a pool of high-quality, published studies from which to select drugs for their formulary lists. * * *

NOTES AND QUESTIONS

1. *Pharmacoeconomics research.* Drug manufacturers may sponsor studies pitting their product against a competitor's drug (or another form of treatment) in the hope of demonstrating superiority in relative safety, effectiveness, and/or cost. "Pharmacoeconomics," which seeks to document the cost effectiveness of drugs, has attracted sharp methodological criticisms. See Suzanne R. Hill et al., Problems with the Interpretation of Pharmacoeconomic Analyses, 283 JAMA 2116 (2000); Drummond Rennie & Harold S. Luft, Editorial, Pharmacoeconomic Analyses: Making Them Transparent, Making Them Credible, 283 JAMA 2158, 2158–59 (2000). But cf. Peter J. Neumann & Darren E. Zinner, Evaluating and Regulating Pharmacoeconomic Information in the Private Sector, 32 Drug Info. J. 525, 529–30 (1998) (suggesting that editorial peer review can address these methodological concerns adequately).

2. *Conflicts of interest.* Some critics have argued that pharmaceutical manufacturers may stack the deck when they design comparative studies in an effort to ensure a favorable result. See Lisa A. Bero & Drummond Rennie, Influences on the Quality of Published Drug Studies, 12 Int'l J. Tech. Assessment in Health Care 209 (1996); Alan L. Hillman et al., Avoiding Bias in the Conduct and Reporting of Cost–Effectiveness Research Sponsored by Pharmaceutical Companies, 324 New Eng. J. Med. 1362, 1363–64 (1991); Helle Krogh Johansen & Peter C. Gotzsche, Problems in the Design and Reporting of Trials of Antifungal Agents Encountered During Meta–Analysis, 282 JAMA 1752, 1757–58 (1999); Susan Okie, Missing Data on Celebrex: Full Study Altered Picture of Drug, Wash. Post,

Aug. 5, 2001, at A11. These do not always work out as planned. See Thomas M. Burton, Older Treatment for Manic Illness May Be Superior, Wall St. J., Dec. 12, 2000, at B1 (reporting on research sponsored by the manufacturer of Zyprexa which found that another drug works just as well in treating bipolar disorder with fewer side effects and at half the cost). Even so, concerns about conflicts of interest are heightened in this research setting. See Robert G. Evans, Editorial, Manufacturing Consensus, Marketing Truth: Guidelines for Economic Evaluation, 123 Annals Internal Med. 59 (1995); Jerome P. Kassirer & Marcia Angell, Editorial, The Journal's Policy on Cost–Effectiveness Analyses, 331 New Eng. J. Med. 669 (1994) (explaining the decision against even considering cost-effectiveness studies for publication if any author has a personal financial stake in the outcome, and requiring disclosure of industry sponsorship of such studies when conducted by independent researchers).

3.   *Regulating the distribution of pharmacoeconomic information.* Historically, the FDA strictly limited the use of comparative claims. See 21 C.F.R. § 202.1(e)(6)(ii); David A. Kessler et al., Therapeutic–Class Wars: Drug Promotion in a Competitive Marketplace, 331 New Eng. J. Med. 1350, 1352 (1994); Peter J. Neumann et al., The FDA and Regulation of Cost–Effectiveness Claims, Health Aff., Fall 1996, at 54, 59–61 (criticizing the agency's traditional demand for randomized controlled trials to substantiate pharmacoeconomic claims); cf. David Henry & Suzanne Hill, Editorial, Comparing Treatments: Comparison Should Be Against Active Treatments Rather Than Placebos, 310 Brit. Med. J. 1279 (1995) (arguing that governments should sponsor comparative efficacy studies). In 1997, Congress liberalized these restrictions by allowing drug companies to disseminate "health care economic information" so long as it is based on "competent and reliable scientific evidence." Pub. L. No. 105–115, § 114(a), 111 Stat. 2296, 2312 (1997) (codified at 21 U.S.C. § 352(a)). Manufacturers could not, however, provide pharmacoeconomic information to individual health care professionals because of congressional concerns that physicians would not have the time or skill needed to interpret research on the cost effectiveness of drugs. See H.R. Rep. No. 105–310, at 65 (1997). This more paternalistic stance stands in sharp contrast to the provision in the same statute that had liberalized the rules on the distribution of enduring materials that discuss off-label uses. Does it also raise the First Amendment problems discussed in Chapter 4(C)?

D.   DRUG PRICING AND PRICE CONTROLS

HHS, *Report to the President on Prescription Drug Coverage, Utilization, and Prices*
<http://aspe.hhs.gov/health/reports/drugstudy/chap03.htm> (2000).

      * * * Prices and price differentials are important measures for understanding the market for pharmaceuticals in the United States. Analyses of

pharmaceutical pricing, however, are complicated by the intricacies of this market: the process by which drug prices are determined is highly complex, involving numerous interactions and arrangements among manufacturers, wholesalers, retailers, insurers, pharmacy benefit managers (PBMs), and consumers. * * * Cash customers at retail pharmacies include people without coverage and people with indemnity coverage who pay for their own prescriptions and are later reimbursed by their insurer. Prices are set by a series of transactions linking the manufacturer to the cash customer through the wholesaler and the retail pharmacy * * * *

In the first transaction, the manufacturer sells the drug to a wholesaler. The manufacturer establishes a price that varies by the form and strength of the product * * * * When there is only a single manufacturer of a drug, as is often the case with a brand-name drug, there is only one price for a specific product and package size. Once generic versions of the drug become available, the equivalent medication (in form, strength, and package) may be offered at different prices by different manufacturers.

Wholesalers may sometimes receive discounts form manufacturers, based on volume or prompt payment. A manufacturer of a multi-source drug (i.e., one that is produced by more than one manufacturer) may offer a discount to induce wholesalers to promote its particular version of the drug. Thus the manufacturer's price is only a guideline, and may not represent the price that all wholesalers ultimately pay for the drug. The manufacturer's price itself represents both the cost of producing the drug and a share of the manufacturer's research and development costs, taxes, and profits. For any particular drug, the price may reflect the market position of the drug more than the cost of its production; for example, a company may set a higher price for an innovator drug than for one which has several competitors. * * *

In the second transaction, the wholesaler sells the drug to a retail pharmacy at a price reflecting its cost of acquiring the drug plus a markup. This price may be referred to as the wholesale price or acquisition price. A price that is commonly cited in the industry is the "average wholesale price," or AWP. Despite what this name would suggest, the AWP is not the average of the amounts actually paid by retail pharmacies to the wholesalers for a particular drug. Instead it is a published wholesale price or "list price" suggested by the manufacturer of the drug. A wholesaler may sell specific drugs to all pharmacies at prices below the AWP, or may grant a general discount to certain pharmacies. Thus, although the AWP is often used by pharmacies as a cost basis for pricing purposes, it does not represent the actual cost to a retail pharmacy of acquiring the drug. It is merely a wholesale list price that can be used as a benchmark in comparing retail and wholesale prices. Industry sources suggest that the price charged by the manufacturer to the wholesaler typically runs about 20 percent below the list price or AWP. * * *

In the third transaction, the pharmacy sells the drug to a consumer at a price that includes its cost for acquiring the drug from the wholesaler plus a retail markup. Part of this markup is a fixed cost that is not related to the cost of acquiring a specific drug. This is because the cost to the pharmacy of filling a prescription for a low-price drug is likely to be the same as for a high-price drug. As a result, the fixed cost is a higher percentage markup over acquisition cost for a low-price drug than for a high-price one. Different pharmacies have different fixed costs. Because of economies of scale, a large chain pharmacy may have lower costs than a small independent one.

Part of the markup varies by drug. Pharmacies employ a variety of pricing strategies when determining this markup for their sales to cash customers. For example, they may set a lower markup for maintenance medications and a higher markup for acute medications, or may routinely discount certain commonly used medications as "loss leaders," in order to attract cash customers who will then buy other medications or other merchandise. Some industry sources have suggested that retail markups in the range of 20 percent to 25 percent over the pharmacy's acquisition price are typical. This markup includes both the fixed operating costs of the pharmacy as well as taxes and profits. * * *

The simple pricing model just described applies to cash transactions but not to those in which the retail pharmacy is paid by a group insurer, employer, or other third party at the point of sale. * * * [B]ecause management by a PBM is most common, this term will be used as a shorthand for all private entities managing drug benefits. Because a PBM may manage the drug benefit for a large number of individuals, it can negotiate discounts at both ends of the pricing chain: from the manufacturer and from the retail pharmacy. There is little published data about the size of the discounts obtained by PBMs and private insurers, either from manufacturers or from retailers. * * *

The price paid to a retail pharmacy for a given drug is negotiated by the PBM and the pharmacy or pharmacy chain. Typically the PBM will take into account its estimate of the cost to the pharmacy of acquiring the drug (usually assuming that the pharmacy has paid something less than the AWP) and offer a dispensing fee above that amount. This dispensing fee is commonly a fixed dollar add-on (in the range of $2.50) that is not related to the cost of acquiring a specific drug. Because some PBMs cover a large share of the market, a pharmacy will often accept a price that is less than it would charge to cash customers. * * *

Discussions with industry experts conducted during the preparation of this report have provided current information on typical PBM payments to retailers. These experts estimate that payments for brand-name drugs are in the range of AWP minus 13 to 15 percent, plus a $2.50 dispensing fee. * * * For some drugs, however, a pharmacy may be forced to accept reimbursement from the PBM that does not cover the pharmacy's cost of acquiring the drug (let alone its operating costs). The PBM has considerable leverage in this relationship, especially as the proportion of drugs sold through PBM-managed arrangements grows. The pharmacy is left with an option of refusing the large share of business, raising its prices for cash customers, or reducing its operating margin.

For generic drugs, about three-fourths are reimbursed using limits known as maximum allowable cost (MAC). These limits are established by PBMs, based on the lowest estimated acquisition cost for any of the generic equivalents of a given drug. The MAC tends to be 50 to 60 percent below AWP. The remaining one-fourth of generics are reportedly reimbursed, like brand-name drugs, at AWP minus 13 to 15 percent. The dispensing fee for generics tends to be the same as for brand drugs, but sometimes it is 25 or 50 cents higher, to encourage generic substitution by pharmacies.

The second type of discount that the PBM gets is a negotiated rebate paid directly from the manufacturer to the PBM. This rebate does not affect the price paid by a wholesaler to a manufacturer for the drug, the price paid by a retail pharmacy to the wholesaler, or the price paid by the PBM to the pharmacy. It is a separate transaction between the PBM and the manufacturer and thus affects the total amount spent by the PBM. To the extent that a portion of the rebate is passed along, the insurer, employer, or beneficiary may realize a part of these savings.

A key tool in determining whether rebates are available and how large they are is the use of a restrictive formulary, a list of drugs that the PBM has established as preferred for its enrollees. If there are multiple brand-name drugs available for a given condition, the PBM may include some on its formulary and not others. Enrollees who obtain a non-formulary drug may pay higher copayments, or the drug may not be covered at all. Pharmacies dealing with the PBM may be encouraged to contact physicians who have prescribed non-formulary drugs and suggest a formulary alternative. Physicians affiliated with the health plan using the PBM may also face pressure to prescribe formulary drugs. * * *

Manufacturers of brand-name drugs that treat conditions for which an alternative brand-name treatment is available thus have a strong incentive to grant discounts to the PBM in return for the inclusion of their drugs in the formulary. If generic equivalents are available, the manufacturer may also grant a discount to make the price of its brand-name product more competitive. These discounts usually take the form of direct rebates from the manufacturer to the PBM. * * *

Not all drugs dispensed by pharmacies are purchased from wholesalers. Institutions that operate their own outpatient pharmacies, such as hospitals and clinics, may deal directly with manufacturers, either individually or though buying groups. They typically save the wholesaler markup. In addition, they may receive a price lower than that offered by the manufacturer to wholesalers. * * *

Prices paid to manufacturers by the VA, other federal agencies, and certain other entities, such as Indian tribal governments, are set by the Federal Supply Schedule (FSS). Under the Veterans Health Care Act of 1992, manufacturers must make drugs available to covered entities at the FSS price as a condition of eligibility for Medicaid reimbursement. FSS prices are negotiated with manufacturers by the VA. In general, the FSS price may be no higher than the lowest contractual price charged by the manufacturer to any nonfederal purchaser under similar terms and conditions. In order to determine this price, manufacturers supply the VA with information on price discounts and rebates offered to different customers and the terms and conditions involved. * * *

[T]he fact the FSS price is generally lower than other prices may have a variety of explanations. These include the small share of the market that federal purchasers represent (less than 2 percent), the effectiveness of the VA as a price negotiator, and the interest that manufacturers may have in making sure their drugs are available to federal facilities and agencies * * * *

[As explained earlier in this Chapter,] Medicaid programs pay retail pharmacies using fixed cost limits and fixed dispensing fees. For single-source drugs (brand-name drugs without generic equivalents), the cost limit is set at the estimated pharmacy acquisition cost for the drug. For multiple-source drugs (with brand name or generic competitors), the limit is based on a MAC. These are similar in concept to the MACs used by PBMs; some PBMs may simply use the Medicaid MACs, while others develop their own. The Medicaid MACs are published by HCFA every six months and are set at 150 percent of the lowest published price for any equivalent drug, plus a dispensing fee.

Under provisions of the Omnibus Budget Reconciliation Act of 1990, Medicaid programs receive rebates from manufacturers. Participation is generally required for a manufacturer's drugs to be eligible for Medicaid reimbursement. For single source drugs and innovator multiple-source drugs, the rebate must equal the difference between the average manufacturer price (AMP)—the average paid by wholesalers—and the manufacturer's "best price." The best price is the lowest price offered by the manufacturer to any purchaser at any time during the year, excluding the special prices for federal purchasers and certain other covered entities. The minimum rebate must be 15.1 percent of the AMP. For non-innovator multiple source drugs, the rebate is 11 percent of the AMP; the best price concept does not apply. * * *

Patricia M. Danzon & Li–Wei Chao, *Does Regulation Drive out Competition in Pharmaceutical Markets?*

43 J.L. & ECON. 311 (2000).

Most countries regulate manufacturer prices for pharmaceuticals, either directly (France and Italy) or indirectly through controls on insurance reimbursement (Japan) or profits (the United Kingdom). Regulation is often justified by the assumption that price competition is weak for several reasons: patents intentionally limit competition and lead to product differentiation that may be intensified by promotion, insurance makes patients insensitive to prices, and physicians who are primary decision makers may not know product prices and/or may be imperfect agents for patients. Retail pharmacy is also subject to extensive price and entry regulation in countries that regulate manufacturer prices. * * *

Prior studies suggest considerable price competition in some markets. However, theory and casual empirical evidence suggest that regulation may undermine competition, although regulation in principle sets a ceiling, but not a floor, on the manufacturer's price. Generic market shares of off-patent products are significantly higher in countries that permit (relatively) free pricing, such as the United States, the United Kingdom, and Germany, than in countries with strict price or reimbursement regulation, such as France, Italy, and Japan. Whether in practice regulation reinforces or undermines competition is an important empirical question that is of interest to research and policy, as different countries (for example, the United States, Japan, France, and the United Kingdom) evaluate possible changes in their regulatory systems.

Optimal competition policy and the extent of competition in practice differ over the life cycle of a new molecule. Originator products are granted patent protection to provide an opportunity to recoup research and development (R&D) expense. Patents bar competition from generic imitators for the life of the patent, which corresponds to roughly the first 10–12 years of life on the market. However, patent-protected drugs may face competition from "therapeutic substitutes"—drugs with different active ingredients but similar therapeutic effects. After patent expiration, generic imitators can enter the market with minimal R&D expense. * * * [T]here is a strong presumption that price competition between generic substitutes of patent-expired drugs is socially beneficial, assuming that the patent term and structure are designed to yield the socially desired return on R&D.

Generic competition on off-patent drugs offers the potential for significant savings to consumers. Off-patent drugs account for 88 percent of reimbursable packs sold on average for European Union member states, and this off-patent share is expected to grow over the next decade as patents expire on many of the current leading drugs. * * * The design of regulatory systems to promote competition in the off-patent sector is an important issue for all governments concerned with obtaining maximum value from health spending. * * *

In 1992, insurance coverage of drugs through social insurance programs was extensive in all countries in our sample except the United States, where patients paid roughly 50 percent of outpatient drug expense directly out of pocket. Although some countries' social insurance systems nominally require significant patient co-payment, as either a percentage of the price (France, Italy, and Japan) or a fixed payment per script (the United Kingdom and Germany), these nominal co-payments overstate the average marginal co-insurance rate because of exemptions for high-use groups (the elderly and welfare recipients), private supplementary insurance that covers co-payments under the public scheme (France), and stop-loss limits on out-of-pocket payments (Japan). Moreover, all countries except the United States had low or zero co-payments on physician visits, which could be a significant component of the full price of obtaining prescription drugs. * * *

[I]n the United States, many people who were insured for physician and hospital services had no coverage for outpatient drugs and, hence, faced the full price. In addition, many of those with coverage had plans with generic substitution programs, which set a maximum allowable charge (MAC) for generically equivalent drugs and require the patient to pay any excess of the actual price over the MAC * * * *

Given the physician's choice of molecule, pharmacists are authorized in some countries to substitute between generically equivalent products to fill the prescription. In the United States by the 1990s all states had repealed antisubstitution laws and authorized pharmacists to substitute generic equivalents unless the physician explicitly writes "dispense as written." Managed care plans and Medicaid encourage generic substitution for off-patent drugs by paying a maximum allowable charge (MAC, or reference price) for generically equivalent products. * * *

In the United States, manufacturer prices are unregulated. Since the mid–1980s, managed care has changed the nature of competition. Health maintenance organizations (HMOs) and other pharmacy benefit managers (PBMs) create formularies of "preferred" drugs that physicians and patients are encouraged to use. The ability to shift demand toward one or two preferred products within a group of therapeutic substitutes has increased demand elasticity in the managed care sector, which has enabled PBMs to negotiate discounts from list prices for branded products. * * *

NOTES AND QUESTIONS

1. *Formularies.* Health plans may use a variety of formularies to control the prescribing of drugs for their beneficiaries. In an open formulary plan, the insurer agrees to pay for any drug prescribed to the beneficiary, although the insurer may circulate to physicians a list of preferred drugs. At the other extreme, health plans using a closed formulary approach categorically refuse to pay for any nonformulary drug product. Closed formularies typically include the most cost-effective drug in each group of therapeutically-interchangeable drugs. Partially-closed formularies attempt to balance the cost-effectiveness of closed formularies with the prescribing freedom of open formularies. Thus, the partially-closed formulary limits choice with respect to drugs in the most commonly-prescribed therapeutic categories, but otherwise uses an open-formulary approach. Finally, some plans now employ clinical formularies (either closed or partially-closed) for the treatment of specific clinical conditions, such as asthma or stomach ulcers. See Mark A. Buckles, Electronic Formulary Management and Medicaid: Maximizing Economic Efficiency and Quality of Care in the Age of Electronic Prescribing, 11 U. Fla. J.L & Pub. Pol'y 179, 183–85 (2000); see also Connecticut v. Physicians Health Serv. of Conn., Inc., 103 F.Supp.2d 495 (D.Conn.2000) (suit on behalf of state health plan enrollees challenging formulary system); David A. Balto, A Whole New World?: Pharmaceutical Responses to the Managed Care Revolution, 52 Food & Drug L.J. 83 (1997); Arnold J. Rosoff, The Changing Face of Pharmacy Benefits Management:

Information Technology Pursues a Grand Mission, 42 St. Louis U. L.J. 1 (1998); Karen Titlow et al., Drug Coverage Decisions: The Role of Dollars and Values, Health Aff., Mar.-Apr. 2000, at 240. Patients whose physicians prescribe drugs outside of the formulary may be required to pay higher co-payments or may be billed for the full cost of the drug. An increasing number of HMOs allow physicians to override formularies in certain situations, but penalties for deviation from formularies and pre-approval requirements probably limit the number of successful overrides. See AMA Council on Ethical & Judicial Aff., Managed Care Cost Containment Involving Prescription Drugs, 53 Food & Drug L.J. 25, 28 (1998). Do the economic efficiencies of drug formularies justify their potentially negative impact on patient care? What sorts of ethical issues arise with the imposition of strict formulary requirements?

2. *Professional concerns about drug formularies.* The American Medical Association strongly encourages physicians to keep abreast of managed care formularies so that they can prescribe drugs effectively for patients:

> Managed care organizations establish drug formulary systems so that physicians will supplement medical judgment with cost considerations in drug selection. To ensure optimal patient care, various ethical requirements must be established for formulary application.
>
> (1) Physicians who participate in managed care plans should maintain awareness of plan decisions about drug selection by staying informed about pharmacy and therapeutics (P&T) committee actions and by ongoing personal review of formulary composition....
>
> (2) Physicians should be particularly vigilant to ensure that formulary decisions adequately reflect the needs of individual patients and that individual needs are not unfairly sacrificed by decisions based on the needs of the average patient. Physicians are ethically required to advocate for additions to the formulary when they think patients would benefit materially and for exceptions to the formulary on a case-by-case basis when justified by the health care needs of particular patients....
>
> (3) Limits should be placed on the extent to which managed care plans use incentives or pressures to lower prescription drug costs. Financial incentives are permissible when they promote cost-effectiveness, not when they require withholding medically necessary care. Physicians should not be made to feel that they jeopardize their compensation or participation in a managed care plan if they prescribe drugs that are necessary for their patients but that may also be costly....
>
> (4) Managed care plans should develop and implement educational programs on cost-effective prescribing practices. Such initiatives are preferable to financial incentives or pressures by health maintenance organizations or hospitals, which can be ethically problematic.
>
> (5) Patients must be informed of the methods used by their managed care plans to limit prescription drug costs. During enroll-

ment, the plan should disclose the existence of formularies, the provisions for cases in which the physician prescribes a drug that is not included in the formulary and the incentives or other mechanisms used to encourage physicians to consider costs when prescribing drugs. In addition, plans should disclose any relationships with pharmaceutical benefit management companies or pharmaceutical companies that could influence the composition of the formulary. If physicians exhaust all avenues to secure a formulary exception for a significantly advantageous drug, they are still obligated to disclose the option of the more beneficial, more costly drug to the patient, so that the patient can decide whether to pay out-of-pocket.

AMA Council on Ethical & Judicial Aff., *Managed Care Cost Containment Involving Prescription Drugs*, Rep. E–8.135 (1996).

3. *Supply shortages.* For a variety of reasons, drug shortages are becoming increasingly common. Sometimes, a shortage results because of problems with the supply of raw materials, or because of production problems. For example, the FDA temporarily shut down a major manufacturer of the tetanus-diptheria vaccine as a result of GMP violations, and BioPort, the sole manufacturer of an experimental anthrax vaccine, remained shut down for several years because of such problems. Frequently, however, drug shortages arise from deliberate decisions by pharmaceutical companies to cease or drastically reduce production of a product because profits have fallen. Drugs that have lost their patent protection command far lower prices and manufacturers often prefer to produce and market a newer, replacement product that will generate more substantial revenues. Usually, short supplies of drugs do not increase the risks to patients because therapeutic substitutes remain available, but occasionally these shortfalls do endanger patients. See Melody Petersen, Drug Shortages Become a Worry at Hospitals Around the Country, N.Y. Times, Jan. 3, 2001, at A1.

The federal government created a National Pharmaceutical Stockpile (NPS) designed for rapid deployment in the event of public health emergencies. See Reed Abelson & Robert Pear, Concerns About How Quickly the U.S. Can Deliver Drugs, N.Y. Times, Oct. 30, 2001, at B8; see also Rick Weiss, Bioterrorism: An Even More Devastating Threat, Wash. Post, Sept. 17, 2001, at A24. When bioterrorism emerged as a threat to civilians, some feared shortages of antibiotics effective in the treatment of anthrax. See Justin Gillis, Drugmakers Step Forward in Bioterror Fight, Wash. Post, Oct. 31, 2001, at A18; see also Justin Gillis, U.S. Says It Bought Radiation Drug, Wash. Post, Jan. 3, 2002, at A5 (describing the federal government's decision to purchase a large supply of potassium iodide, a drug that provides some protection against thyroid damage from radioactive fallout). In addition, relatively few doses of the vaccine for smallpox, a disease eradicated decades earlier, triggered research into the possibility of diluting the available supplies in order to stretch the doses while waiting for manufacturers to ramp up production under government contracts to purchase 300 million doses. See Rachael Zimmerman, Merck, GlaxoSmithKline Are Front–Runners to Produce Smallpox Vaccine for the U.S.,

Wall St. J., Nov. 2, 2001, at A9. Pricing and payment issues affect the available of other medical technologies as well. For example, declining insurance reimbursements coupled with increasing demand have caused many mammogram centers to become unprofitable and ultimately to close their doors. In many contexts, reimbursements for mammograms no longer cover the cost of performing the diagnostic test. See Barbara Martinez, As More Women Seek Mammograms, Many Have to Wait for Months, Wall St. J., Oct. 30, 2000, at A1.

4. *Direct purchases.* The federal government buys substantial quantities of prescription drugs and devices for use in a variety of programs. By virtue of its sheer size, the government can negotiate for favorable prices, at least if it can coordinate its purchases. See Shankar Vedantam, HHS's Varying Costs for Cipro Criticized, Wash. Post, Oct. 26, 2001, at A16 (reporting that the government negotiated a contract to purchase an antibiotic for the treatment of anthrax for 95¢ per dose, which was far less than the retail price of over $4 and the manufacturer's offer of $1.83, but more than twice the price paid by the government under a preexisting program). Not wanting to be left out, manufacturers of other antibiotics offered free supplies if the FDA would approve labeling revisions to specify use in the treatment of inhalation anthrax. See Charles Ornstein, Drug Firms Rush to Offer Free Anthrax Antibiotics, L.A. Times, Oct. 27, 2001, at A7.

1. PUBLIC EFFORTS AT PRICE CONTROLS

Pharmaceutical Research & Mfrs. of America v. Concannon

249 F.3d 66 (1st Cir.2001).

■ BOWNES, SENIOR CIRCUIT JUDGE:

* * * On May 11, 2000, the Governor of Maine signed into law an Act to Establish Fairer Pricing for Prescription Drugs, 2000 Me. Legis. Ch. 786 (S.P.1026) (L.D.2599), which establishes the "Maine Rx Program." The statute was enacted because of the Maine Legislature's concern that many Maine citizens who were not Medicaid recipients could not afford necessary prescription drugs. It is predicated on the economic reality that volume buying of prescription drugs by Medicaid administrators, insurance companies and health maintenance organizations (HMOs) resulted in substantially lower prices for these entities than for individual purchasers. A minority staff report for the United States House Committee on Government Reform and Oversight [issued in 1998] found that the average retail price for individual elderly purchasers was 86 percent higher than the price charged to the federal government and other favored customers, such as HMOs.

The Program is open to all State residents, and allows enrollees to purchase prescription drugs from participating Maine pharmacies at a discounted price. The discount offered by the pharmacies is reimbursed by the State out of a dedicated fund created with the money raised from "rebate payments" collected from participating drug manufacturers. Me.

Rev. Stat. Ann. tit. 22, § 2681. The obligation to pay the "rebate" is triggered by the retail sale of the manufacturer's drugs to a Program enrollee through a participating pharmacy.

The Act directs the Commissioner of Maine's Department of Health Services to negotiate rebate agreements with manufacturers. These rebate agreements are similar in form to the rebate agreements required of manufacturers participating in the Maine Medicaid outpatient drug program. In negotiating the rebate, the Commissioner is directed to "consider" the rebate amount calculated under the Federal Medicaid Rebate Program, 42 U.S.C. § 1396r–8, and to use his or her "best efforts" to obtain an initial rebate in the same amount. Rebate payments are made quarterly on the basis of retail sales records for that quarter.

In order to create an incentive for manufacturers to enter rebate agreements with the Commissioner, the Act provides that names of manufacturers who do not enter into agreements be released to health care providers and the public. More importantly, the drugs of all noncompliant manufacturers are required to be subject, "as permitted by law," to the "prior authorization requirements" in the State Medicaid program. When subjected to prior authorization, a drug may not be dispensed to a Medicaid beneficiary without the approval of the State Medicaid administrator.

The plaintiff-appellee, Pharmaceutical Research & Manufacturers of America (PhRMA), brought an action in the United States District Court in the District of Maine against defendant-appellants Commissioner of the Maine Department of Human Services and the Maine Attorney General, challenging the constitutionality of the Act. PhRMA claimed that the Act violated the dormant Commerce Clause and was preempted by the federal Medicaid statute under the Supremacy Clause, and moved for a preliminary injunction to prevent the implementation of the Act.

The district court issued the preliminary injunction and found the Act unconstitutional on the two asserted grounds. First, the district court held that the Act had an impermissible extraterritorial reach by regulating the revenues out-of-state pharmaceutical manufacturers receive when selling to out-of-state pharmaceutical distributors, thereby violating the dormant Commerce Clause. As to those distributors located in the State of Maine, the district court held that the Act was preempted under the Supremacy Clause because it conflicted with the federal Medicaid program. * * *

The initial question we face is whether PhRMA has prudential standing to challenge the prior authorization provision of the Act. * * * Maine contends that PhRMA's interest is purely financial and is limited to ensuring that its members' drugs are prescribed instead of competitors' drugs. Nothing in the Medicaid statute, Maine argues, suggests that Congress intended to protect sales of any particular drugs. PhRMA has not asserted an action to enforce rights under the Medicaid statute, however, but rather a preemption-based challenge under the Supremacy Clause. In this type of action, it is the interests protected by the Supremacy Clause, not by the preempting statute, that are at issue. * * * Given that PhRMA has prudential standing grounded in the Supremacy Clause, we think it may fairly assert the rights of Medicaid recipients for purposes of this action. * * *

Under the Supremacy Clause, a federal law may expressly or impliedly preempt state law. As the parties agree, only "implied conflict preemption" is at issue here. Our task, therefore, is to consider if "compliance with both state and federal regulations is impossible" or if "state law interposes an obstacle to the achievement of Congress's discernable objectives." * * *

We perceive no conflict between the Maine Act and Medicaid's structure and purpose. Neither the letter nor the intent of the Medicaid statute prevents states from imposing prior authorization requirements; indeed, they are explicitly permitted. See 42 U.S.C. § 1396r–8(d)(1)(A) (states may "subject to prior authorization any covered outpatient drug"). The statute sets forth only two limitations on a state's use of prior authorization: the state must provide "response by telephone or other telecommunication device within 24 hours of a request for prior authorization;" and, with respect to most drugs, provide for "the dispensing of at least 72–hour supply of a covered outpatient prescription drug in an emergency situation (as defined by the Secretary)." Id. § 1396r–8(d)(5)(A) & (B).

The plain text of the Maine Act appears to incorporate these Medicaid requirements. It provides: "The department shall impose prior authorization requirements in the Medicaid program under this Title, as permitted by law, for the dispensing of prescription drugs...." Me. Rev. Stat. Ann. tit. 22, § 2681(7). We read the language "as permitted by law" to limit the Act's application to only those situations in which prior authorization is permitted by Medicaid. As the Department is charged with administering the Maine Rx Program, we owe deference to its interpretation of the Act.

Moreover, as set forth in the affidavit of Kevin Concannon, Commissioner of the Maine Department of Human Services, Maine has proposed administrative rules governing prior authorization aimed at ensuring that Medicaid recipients will have access to needed medications. Specifically, the decision to place a drug on the prior authorization list may be made only by the State's Medicaid Drug Utilization Review (DUR) Committee, which exclusively comprises physicians and pharmacists licensed to prescribe or dispense medications in Maine. Concannon states: "In making its determination of whether or not a prior authorization requirement is clinically appropriate, the DUR Committee shall be guided by the law of Medicaid, and particularly the principle that Medicaid recipients shall be assured access to all medically necessary prescription drugs."

PhRMA contends that prior authorization, however implemented, necessarily interferes with the delivery of Medicaid services by placing an administrative burden on physicians and patients. This interference is acceptable, it says, when performed in the usual course of the Medicaid regulations concerning prior authorization because there is a countervailing "legitimate" purpose of preventing abuse or overprescription of certain expensive medications. In the case of a prior authorization under the Maine Rx Program, however, PhRMA argues (and the district court agreed) that there is no "Medicaid purpose" or "benefit" to Medicaid that offsets the interference. Hence, it contends, only when a prior authorization is motivated by the refusal to enter into a Maine Rx Program rebate agreement is it preempted.

This argument is unpersuasive. First, we are not convinced that the Medicaid statute is concerned with the motivation behind imposing prior authorization, as long as the 24–hour response and the 72–hour drug-supply requirements are satisfied. Thus, even if the district court's conclusion that "Maine can point to no Medicaid purpose in this new prior authorization requirement" is true, it does not necessarily mean that the prior authorization scheme conflicts with the objectives of the Medicaid program. We see no basis for inflicting the "strong medicine" of preemption on a state statute that, in the absence of an actual conflict, merely fails to directly advance the purpose of the federal program.

Moreover, even assuming that this inquiry into the underlying objectives of the Act is appropriate, we disagree that the Act serves no purpose related to Medicaid. The purposes of the Medicaid statute, read broadly, are consonant with the purposes of the Maine Rx Program. First, the Maine Rx Program furthers Medicaid's aim of providing medical services to those whose "income and resources are insufficient to meet the costs of necessary medical services," 42 U.S.C. § 1396, even if the individuals covered by the Maine Rx Program are not poor enough to qualify for Medicaid. Second, there is some evidence in the record that by making prescription drugs more accessible to the uninsured, Maine may reduce Medicaid expenditures. When people whose incomes fall outside Medicaid eligibility are unable to purchase necessary medication, their conditions may worsen, driving them further into poverty and into the Medicaid program, requiring more expensive treatment that could have been avoided had earlier intervention been possible. See Stephen B. Soumerai & Dennis Ross–Degnan, Inadequate Prescription–Drug Coverage for Medicare Enrollees: A Call to Action, 340 New Eng. J. Med. 722 (1999).

Thus, we disagree with the district court's statement that "If Maine can use its authority over Medicaid authorization to leverage drug manufacturer rebates for the benefit of uninsured citizens, then it can just as easily put the rebates into a state program for highway and bridge construction or school funding." Neither highway construction nor school funding relate in any way to the purposes of providing medical services to the needy or of cost-effective administration of the Medicaid program.

PhRMA further contends that the Maine Rx Program will necessarily harm Medicaid recipients by impeding access to their doctors' first-choice medications. The district court agreed with this argument, concluding that the Maine Act conflicted with the Medicaid provision setting forth a general requirement that a state Medicaid plan contain safeguards to assure that care and services will be provided "in a manner consistent with ... the best interests of the recipients." 42 U.S.C. § 1396a(a)(19). PhRMA vigorously presses the argument that the prior authorization provision is more than a de minimis obstacle to achieving these best interests of the Medicaid recipient because it will effectively require a doctor to shift to her second choice drug where the first choice drug is manufactured by a company that does not participate in the rebate program. The state concedes that it will not authorize payment for the first-choice drug manufactured by a non-participant where there is another drug for the ailment manufactured by a participant, but insists that the Medicaid recipient will always receive medically necessary drugs. At this point in the proceedings, we find insufficient basis for concluding that the Maine Act, on its face, controverts the Medicaid goal of "best interests." * * *

[T]he parties submitted competing affidavits discussing whether the Maine Rx Program will necessarily inflict harm on Medicaid patients. Dr. Scott Howell, Vice President of National Accounts, Managed Care, Smith-Kline Beecham Corporation, states that "when used wrongly," prior authorizations hurt medical professionals and patients by adding administrative burdens, delays, anxiety and confusion. He opines that the Maine Rx Program "will create a high likelihood" of harm by leading to inappropriate prescribing of medications, needlessly burdening doctors, and causing unnecessary inconvenience for Medicaid recipients. "[P]rior authorization of drugs, without regard to safety or efficacy, will lead to drugs being prescribed that are less safe and efficacious."

Dr. Timothy S. Clifford, the Medical Director for the Maine Bureau of Medical Services, which administers the Medicaid program, disagrees with Dr. Howell's affidavit on several points. He contends that the Department will address safety and efficacy concerns in administering the Maine Rx Program's prior authorization requirement; that it will consider the availability of alternative drugs in deciding whether to subject a particular drug to the requirement; and that Medicaid recipients will continue to have access to medically necessary drugs. Dr. Clifford states: "The Department certainly will not subject any single-source drug that fulfills a unique therapeutic function to the prior authorization process, regardless of whether the manufacturer participates in the Maine Rx Program. . . ." Dr. H. Burtt Richardson, Jr., a Maine pediatrician and Maine Medicaid provider, states that he supports the Maine Rx Program "so long as the decision to put a prior authorization on particular drugs is clinically appropriate, feasible for a medical office, and accompanied by the assurance that all Maine Medicaid recipients have access to medically necessary drugs."

These affidavits, along with other materials in the record, fall short of establishing that the Act will inflict inevitable or even probable harm on Medicaid patients or their providers. * * * There is no evidence that the prior authorization procedure is likely to foreclose a patient from receiving a necessary drug. Although prior authorization review is triggered by a manufacturer's refusal to participate in the Maine Rx Program, the record indicates that the final decision to require prior authorization for a particular drug is based primarily on clinical criteria applied by health care professionals.

Since both sides agree that the prior authorization requirement is the "hammer" or "force" that coerces manufacturers to enter into the Program, the possibility that first-choice drugs will not be readily approved where second-choice inferior alternatives exist concerns us. The possibility that the administrative implications of the prior authorization requirement will affect the quality of medical care for Medicaid recipients in more subtle ways, i.e., through inconveniencing prescribing physicians, also concerns us. Dr. Howell's affidavit, however, is controverted by the affidavits of other qualified individuals. We simply cannot say on this record that the Act conflicts with Medicaid's requirement that state Medicaid plans assure that care will be provided in a manner consistent with the recipients' best interests. This decision is without prejudice to PhRMA's right to renew its preemption challenge after implementation of the Act, should there be evidence that Medicaid recipients are harmed by the prior authorization requirement "as applied."

Holding that the Maine Act is not preempted by the Medicaid statute, we next consider whether it violates the dormant Commerce Clause. The Constitution provides that Congress shall have the power "[t]o regulate Commerce with foreign Nations, and among the several States, and with the Indian Tribes." U.S. Const. art. I, § 8, cl. 3. The constitutional provision affirmatively granting Congress the authority to legislate in the area of interstate commerce "has long been understood, as well, to provide 'protection from state legislation inimical to the national commerce [even] where Congress has not acted.'" This negative command, known as the dormant Commerce Clause, prohibits states from acting in a manner that burdens the flow of interstate commerce. The restriction imposed on states by the dormant Commerce Clause is not absolute, and "the States retain authority under their general police powers to regulate matters of legitimate local concern, even though interstate commerce may be affected." * * *

[T]he Maine Act does not regulate the price of any out-of-state transaction, either by its express terms or by its inevitable effect. Maine does not insist that manufacturers sell their drugs to a wholesaler for a certain price. Similarly, Maine is not tying the price of its in-state products to out-of-state prices. There is nothing within the Act that requires the rebate to be a certain amount dependent on the price of prescription drugs in other states. * * *

PhRMA argues strenuously that the effect of the Act will be to regulate the transaction that occurs between the manufacturer and the wholesaler—a transaction that occurs entirely out of state. It argues that as a result of the rebate provision, manufacturers will lose a portion of their profits otherwise obtained from distributors. Admittedly, it is possible that the rebate provisions of the statute may decrease the profits of manufacturers. Simply because the manufacturers' profits might be negatively affected by the Maine Act, however, does not necessarily mean that the Maine Act is regulating those profits. * * *

The rebate program is voluntary and either the manufacturer or the State may withdraw at any time with sixty days' notice. The Act directs the commissioner to "use the commissioner's best efforts" to negotiate the amount of the rebate required from the manufacturer. We note that the commissioner's "best efforts" may become coercive or otherwise inappropriate, but we cannot say so on this facial challenge. This may be an issue that needs to be revisited once the Act takes effect. On a facial challenge, however, the use of the commissioner's "best efforts" indicates that the Act is not "regulating" prices, but merely "negotiating" rebates.

The Act clearly does not interfere with regulatory schemes in other states. Ultimately, the Maine Act simply regulates activity that occurs in state: (1) the purchase of the prescription drugs that triggers the rebate; (2) the negotiation of a rebate amount; and (3) the State's action subjecting a manufacturer's drug to prior authorization and releasing the manufacturer's name to health care providers and the public occurs in state. Because the regulation only applies to in-state activities, there is no extraterritorial reach and the Act is not per se invalid under the Commerce Clause. * * *

The Maine Act is neither an impermissible extraterritorial reach nor is it discriminatory; rather, it regulates evenhandedly and only has incidental effects on interstate commerce. Therefore, we apply [a] lower level of scrutiny * * * * The Maine Rx Program will potentially provide prescription drugs to Maine citizens who could not otherwise afford them. The Maine Legislature has decided that without the Maine Rx Program, needy Maine citizens will continue to be deprived of necessary medical care because of rising prescription drug costs. When measuring manufacturers' possible loss of profits against the increased access to prescription drugs for Maine citizens, the local benefits appear to outweigh the burden on interstate commerce. At the very least, the burden on interstate commerce is not "clearly excessive" as compared to the local benefits. * * *

Having concluded that PhRMA is not likely to succeed on the merits of its constitutional challenges, we need not delve into the three remaining preliminary injunction factors (risk of irreparable harm, the balance of equities and the public interest). This court has recognized that the "sine qua non" of the preliminary injunction analysis is whether the plaintiff is likely to succeed on the merits of the claim. We must conclude that PhRMA has not satisfied its burden to obtain a preliminary injunction preventing the implementation of the Act. * * *

This is a close case but we do not think that, under the applicable law, the State of Maine should be prohibited from putting the Act into play. We heed the dissent of Justice Louis Brandeis in *New State Ice Co. v. Liebmann*, 285 U.S. 262, 310 (1932):

> To stay experimentation in things social and economic is a grave responsibility. Denial of the right to experiment may be fraught with serious consequences to the nation. It is one of the happy incidents of the federal system that a single courageous state may, if its citizens choose, serve as a laboratory; and try novel social and economic experiments without risk to the rest of the country. This Court has the power to prevent an experiment. We may strike down the statute which embodies it * * * * But, in the exercise of this high power, we must be ever on our guard, lest we erect our prejudices into legal

principles. If we would guide by the light of reason, we must let our minds be bold. * * *

NOTES AND QUESTIONS

1. *Bargain hunting across the border.* Many elderly citizens in northern states adjacent to Canada now make regular journeys across the border to purchase prescription drugs at substantially lower prices. For example, the breast cancer drug tamoxifen retails for about $95 for a month's supply in the United States, but costs only $125 for a year's supply in Canada. Pravachol®, a cholesterol-lowering drug, costs $2.71 per pill in the U.S., but only 82 cents per pill in Canada. Recently, some senior citizens have chartered buses for prescription shopping trips to Canada, and some physicians now fax prescriptions to Canadian pharmacies, have the drugs shipped to their U.S. offices, and allow patients to collect them. See Elizabeth Mehren, Bargain Drug Prices Spark Border Crossings, L.A. Times, Dec. 4, 2000, at A1; see also Laura Johannes, Canadian Web Drugstores Offer Deep Discounts and Legal Quandaries, Wall St. J., Jan. 18, 2001, at B1 (describing a process wherein the Canadian web-based pharmacies receive faxed prescriptions from American patients and ship prescriptions across the border); Sarah Lunday, When Purchasing Medicine in Mexico, Buyer Beware, N.Y. Times, Apr. 17, 2001, at F5 (describing concerns about improper manufacturing, labeling, and storage of prescription drugs available in Mexico). In 2000, Congress passed the Medicine Equity and Drug Safety Act, which permits pharmacists and wholesalers to reimport prescription drugs from certain countries, including Canada. See Pub. L. No. 106–387, § 745, 114 Stat. 1549A–35 (codified at 21 U.S.C. § 384). The law has not gone into effect, however, because it requires that the Secretary of HHS demonstrate to Congress that the practice of drug reimportation will "pose no additional risk to the public's health and safety" and will "result in significant reduction in the cost of covered products to the American consumer." Secretary Donna Shalala declined to provide such assurances to Congress. See William Davis, Comment, The Medicine Equity and Drug Safety Act of 2000: Releasing Gray Market Pharmaceuticals, 9 Tul. J. Int'l & Comp. L. 483 (2001); see also Uwe E. Reinhardt, How to Lower the Cost of Drugs, N.Y. Times, Jan. 3, 2001, at A17 (commenting on the Clinton administration's "scuttling" of the drug reimportation bill).

2. *Will other states follow suit?* At least 25 other states now use a variety of approaches, including subsidies, tax credits, and buyers' cooperatives, to assist their elderly citizens with prescription drug purchasing. See Robert Pear, States Creating Plans to Reduce Costs for Drugs, N.Y. Times, Apr. 23, 2001, at A1. Many more states have similar plans under consideration. PhRMA successfully challenged Vermont's plan, which allowed participants to receive drug discounts of up to 30% and required pharmaceutical companies to assume the burden of the price differential. See Pharmaceutical Research & Mfrs. of Am. v. Thompson, 251 F.3d 219 (D.C.Cir.2001) (holding that Vermont could not require pharmaceutical companies to provide the same prescription drug rebates that the federal Medicaid program demands).

3. *Generic substitution laws.* An older approach to concerns about escalating prices allowed or required pharmacists to substitute available generics for prescriptions of brand-name products. One state required pharmacists to dispense bioequivalent generic drugs when available, and allowed physicians to override the generic substitution presumption by choosing a "dispense as written" option. In an unsuccessful challenge to the statute, the plaintiffs argued that the act unconstitutionally burdened interstate commerce and infringed on consumer privacy. See Pharmaceutical Soc'y of the State of N.Y. v. Lefkowitz, 586 F.2d 953 (2d Cir.1978) (holding that the potential savings to consumers justified the minimal burden on interstate commerce and that the physician override provision protected the integrity of the doctor-patient relationship and the prescribing process); see also Henry G. Grabowski & John M. Vernon, Substitution Laws and Innovation in the Pharmaceutical Industry, 43 Law & Contemp. Probs. 43 (1979); Elizabeth Mayo, The Legal Effects of Technical Advances on the Practice of Medicine and Pharmacy, 5 J. Pharmacy & L. 121 (1996); Darrel C. Karl, Note, "Look–Alike" Capsules, Generic Drug Substitution, and the Lanham Act, 32 Cath. U. L. Rev. 345 (1982). A more extreme approach to cost-cutting involves therapeutic substitution—a practice mandating the substitution of cheaper drugs within the same therapeutic class despite lack of evidence of equivalent effectiveness. See J.C. Ballin, Therapeutic Substitution–Usurpation of the Physician's Prerogative, 257 JAMA 528 (1987); American College of Physicians, Therapeutic Substitution and Formulary Systems, 113 Annals Internal Med. 160 (1990); Glenn Ruffenach, When Druggists Second–Guess Doctors, Wall St. J., May 9, 1988, at A25 (describing a law in the state of Washington permitting therapeutic substitution).

4. *Further commentary.* See Andrew S. Krulwich, The Response to Health Care Reform by the Pharmaceutical Industry, 50 Food & Drug L.J. 1 (1995); Douglas Gary Lichtman, Pricing Prozac: Why the Government Should Subsidize the Purchase of Patented Pharmaceuticals, 11 Harv. J.L. & Tech. 123 (1997) (proposing a "mechanism for minimizing the social cost of pharmaceutical patents" by "offering a cash subsidy to any consumer who values a patented drug above its marginal cost but is nonetheless unwilling to pay the monopoly price"); Francis B. Palumbo, The Role of the State as a Drug Purchaser, 56 Food & Drug L.J. 267 (2001); Jerry Stanton, Comment, Lesson for the United States from Foreign Price Controls on Pharmaceuticals, 16 Conn. J. Int'l L. 149 (2000).

2.   Private Efforts at Price Controls

In re Brand Name Prescription Drugs Antitrust Litigation

186 F.3d 781 (7th Cir.1999).

■ Posner, Chief Judge:

Retail pharmacies brought suit under section 1 of the Sherman Act, 15 U.S.C. § 1, against manufacturers and wholesalers of brand-name prescription drugs, charging that the defendants had conspired to deny discounts to the pharmacies. * * * The evidence shows that the manufacturers of brand name (as distinct from generic) prescription drugs engage in price discrimination in the economic sense, selling the identical product to different customers at different prices even though the manufacturers' cost of selling to them is the same. The favored customers are primarily hospitals, health maintenance organizations, and nursing homes; the disfavored are pharmacies. Price discrimination implies market power, that is, the power to charge a price above cost (including in "cost" a profit equal to the cost of equity capital) without losing so much business so fast to competitors that the price is unsustainable. The reason price discrimination implies market power is that assuming the lower of the discriminatory prices covers cost, the higher must exceed cost. There is no general rule against the possession of market power or the use of price discrimination to exploit it, but the plaintiffs argue that the source of the drug manufacturers' market power manifested in their discriminatory pricing is collusion, and if this is right they have a case under section 1.

Manufacturers of brand name prescription drugs generally do not sell directly to the retailers of their drugs, that is, to hospitals, HMO's, nursing homes, and pharmacies, but instead sell to wholesalers for resale to the retailers. A wholesaler is compensated for the warehousing and other functions that he performs in the distribution of his drugs through the difference between the price that he pays his supplier and the price at which he resells to retailers. The danger to a price-discriminating drug manufacturer is that a wholesaler might buy at the discounted price more than he needed to supply his hospital, HMO, and nursing home customers and sell the surplus to pharmacies at a price below the nondiscounted price that the manufacturer wanted them to pay. The industry calls this "diversion" (economists call it "arbitrage") and of course dislikes it. Suppose the manufacturer's profit-maximizing price to an HMO for some drug were $40, his price to a pharmacy for the same drug $65, and the wholesaler tacked on $10 to compensate him for his services in distribution. Suppose that the HMO wanted 10 units of the drug and the pharmacy 2 units. If the wholesaler sold 10 units to the HMO at $50 and 2 units to the pharmacy at $75, as the manufacturer intended, the latter's total revenue would be $530 and the wholesaler's $120 (12 x $10). If instead the wholesaler told the manufacturer that he needed 12 units for the HMO and none for the pharmacy, and the manufacturer therefore sold him 12 units at $40, two of which the wholesaler resold to the pharmacy at some price between $50 and $75 (say, $60), then although the wholesaler's revenue would increase to $140 ($120 plus the added profit from selling 2 units to the pharmacy for $20 above cost rather than $10) and the pharmacy would save $30, the manufacturer would be worse off; his revenue would decline to $480.

Manufacturers could prevent this evasion of their discriminatory pricing scheme by selling directly to the retailers, thus bypassing the wholesalers. The plaintiffs argue that fear that this would happen led the wholesalers to adopt a chargeback system—the focus of this litigation—under which the manufacturer sets a uniform price to the retailers, contracts directly with the favored retailers for discount prices to them, and reimburses the wholesaler for the difference between that and the full, uniform price. In the previous example, the price to the wholesaler would be a flat $65 regardless of whom he was reselling to. But upon proof by him that he had resold to an HMO at, say, $60 ($50, the price agreed upon between the manufacturer and the HMO, plus the wholesaler's service fee, negotiated with the retailer, for performing the wholesale function, and assumed in this example consistent with the previous one to be $10), the manufacturer would reimburse him $15. And so he would net the $10 service fee to compensate him for performing the wholesaling function. The chargeback system eliminates diversion (arbitrage) by requiring the wholesaler, in order to avoid a loss when he resells at a discounted price, to report to the manufacturer his sales to that customer, so that the manufacturer can determine whether the customer is indeed one entitled to a discount. With the chargeback system in place, the manufacturers were content to sell through the wholesalers rather than directly to the retailers. The latter prefer, other things being equal, to deal with a single supplier who stocks the drugs of the different manufacturers (namely a wholesaler) than with each manufacturer separately. And if the manufacturers took over the wholesaling function, they would have to charge a higher price to the retailers to recover the cost of performing that function.

The plaintiffs presented evidence that the wholesalers adopted the chargeback system collectively rather than individually. Even so, the system would be a per se violation of the Sherman Act—and only per se violations are charged in this case—only if it were either a device for eliminating competition among wholesalers, which is not charged, or an instrument of a conspiracy among the manufacturers to eliminate or reduce competition among themselves. If, instead, each manufacturer was engaged in lawful, noncollusive price discrimination, it would no more be illegal per se for the wholesalers to devise collectively a system by which each manufacturer could engage in discriminatory pricing while selling through wholesalers than it would be illegal per se for them to agree on a standard form for inventorying drugs or a common method of inspecting drugs to make sure they are safe. Competitors are permitted by the antitrust laws (and certainly by the per se rule) to engage in cooperative behavior, under trade association auspices or otherwise, provided they don't reduce competition among themselves, or help their suppliers or customers to reduce competition. If the wholesalers in this case were merely helping individual manufacturers maximize their profits by methods permitted by antitrust law, which include noncollusive price discrimination, there was no violation of antitrust law at either the manufacturer or the wholesaler level.

The plaintiffs had therefore to prove that the defendant manufacturers agreed to deny discounts to them. * * * There were two ways in which they might have been able to do this: by presenting direct evidence (admissions or eyewitness accounts) that the manufacturers had agreed to collude; or by presenting circumstantial evidence, economic in character, that their behavior could better be explained on the hypothesis of collusion than on the hypothesis that each was embarked on an individual rather than a concerted course of action—that each, in other words, was merely exploiting the market power it had, rather than seeking to create or amplify such power through an agreement with competitors not to compete.

The direct evidence that the plaintiffs emphasize is testimony about a meeting of wholesalers at which representatives of some drug manufacturers, though none who remain in the case after several settled, were present. The subject was the formation of buying groups by pharmacies that hoped they could obtain discounts by forming leagues which would bargain collectively with manufacturers and wholesalers. The participants in the meeting expressed hostility toward such endeavors and indicated a disinclination to grant these groups any discounts. None of the manufacturer defendants was present, as we have said, and there is no evidence that the manufacturers who were represented at the meeting were acting as agents of the defendants. While the testimony might be evidence that the wholesalers agreed not to discount their own service fees to the buying groups, such an agreement is not among the unlawful acts charged. The complaint is not that the wholesalers were trying to eliminate competition among themselves, by fixing prices or credit terms or other competitive dimensions of the wholesale market, but that they were agents of a manufacturers' conspiracy. The joint adoption of a business method or standard, that is, the chargeback system, independent of any design to reduce competition at either the manufacturer or the wholesaler level, would not raise questions under the per se rule. The only other direct evidence of a manufacturers' conspiracy that merits consideration is a scattering of internal company documents indicating anxiety that competitors might decide to grant such discounts. All firms worry about price cutting by their competitors; these worries are not evidence of price fixing. * * *

The plaintiffs' principal economic evidence was that brand name prescription drugs are indeed priced discriminatorily, to the detriment of the pharmacies; that discrimination requires (and thus demonstrates the existence of) market power; and that the chargeback system facilitates discrimination. * * * The important point is that since the unilateral exercise of a firm's individual market power does not violate the antitrust laws, preventing the frustration of that exercise through arbitrage is not a violation either.

Paradoxical as this may seem, market power is found in many highly competitive markets, for example the markets for scholarly books and journals. (The phenomenon is sometimes referred to as "monopolistic competition.") Publishers of scholarly books commonly publish the same book in hardcover and paperback versions at prices that differ by far more than the difference in costs, and publishers of scholarly journals commonly charge a much higher price to libraries than to individuals even though the cost of making and selling the journal is identical to both classes of purchaser. These price differences are possible because the book, or journal, lacks perfect substitutes (copyright law prevents the sale of identical substitutes without the copyright holder's consent). Brand name prescription drugs ordinarily are patented, and, though the patent may have expired, the physicians who prescribe the drug may continue to prescribe the branded version rather than the generic substitute, whether out of inertia, or because they think the branded version may be produced under better quality control (the rationale for trademarks), or because the patient may feel greater confidence in a familiar brand. The same thing is true if the original brand, whether or not still protected by a patent, now has a therapeutically close substitute sold under a brand name that is less familiar to physicians or patients than the original brand.

It would not be surprising, therefore, if *every* manufacturer of brand name prescription drugs had some market power. If so, every manufacturer would charge different prices depending on the elasticity of demand of different classes of purchaser with respect to price (that is, the responsiveness of quantity demanded to a change in price). The least elastic demanders are the pharmacies, because they must stock a full range of drugs in order to be able to fill prescriptions. They can therefore be expected to be charged the highest prices. In contrast, a hospital, nursing home, or HMO or other managed-care enterprise has a more elastic demand because it can influence (for example through a "formulary," a list of approved or recommended drugs) the physician's choice of which brand (or no brand—a generic) to prescribe. A slight increase in the price of one brand to such a purchaser might cause the manufacturer's sales of that brand to plummet. That manufacturers of brand name prescription drugs grant discounts to the enterprises we have listed but refuse to grant discounts to pharmacies is thus consistent with unilateral profit-maximizing behavior by the manufacturers.

The alternative hypothesis is that the manufacturers refuse to grant discounts to pharmacies because they have agreed among themselves not to. As there is neither an a priori reason nor direct evidence to suppose this hypothesis more likely than the first, and as the plaintiffs bore the burden of persuasion, it was necessary for them to present economic evidence that would show that the hypothesis of collusive action was more plausible than that of individual action. * * * Because price discrimination is as consistent with individual as with collusive behavior, mere proof that discrimination exists does not support, even weakly, an inference of collusion. The plaintiffs have the burden of rebutting, by the normal civil standard of a preponderance of the evidence, the hypothesis of individual maximizing action. They failed to come up with any evidence. * * *

The record does contain a study by a consulting firm which found that many branded drugs have close therapeutic substitutes; this of course is true, but most books also have close substitutes, yet individual books are sufficiently distinctive to enable the publisher to price his books on a discriminatory basis even though he is not colluding with any other publisher. A consumer may rationally pay more for a trademarked product than for its physically identical substitute merely for the greater assurance of quality that a trademark conveys. And all that really matters is that physicians, for whatever reason, in writing prescriptions tend to write a brand name rather than the generic (chemical) name. It is this practice that forces pharmacies to carry a full line of brands and thus prevents them from credibly threatening a manufacturer with refusing to stock his brand unless he offers a discount.

Since the market power conferred by a patent or trademark would vary across brands, evidence of uniform discounts (for example, that all HMOs received a 20 percent discount from the full price on all brands) might be indicative of a conspiracy. The plaintiffs contended in rebuttal at the oral argument of the appeal that this was the case here, but their brief does not make the argument or point to evidence in the record that might support it, so it is forfeited.

All this leaves of the plaintiffs' case is their claim that in the early 1990s the defendant manufacturers agreed among themselves to peg future price increases to the Consumer Price Index. There is enough evidence of such an agreement to create a triable fact. For example, an internal memorandum of defendant Burroughs Wellcome, dated September 1993 and entitled "Price Escalation Proposal," states that "the industry has generally agreed to informally keep its prices in line with CPI or CPI plus 1 to 2 %." The document is subject to interpretation * * * but the interpretation of ambiguous documentary evidence of collusion is for the jury. The district judge threw out the CPI claim not because it was unfounded but because he thought it barred by the *Noerr-Pennington* doctrine, which exempts from antitrust law collusive efforts to obtain governmental protection against the winds of competition. During the period of the alleged CPI conspiracy, the prescription drug industry was under political pressure to limit price increases. Had the industry wanted to obtain a law that would limit annual increases to the rate of inflation as measured by the CPI, plus modest additions, they could without antitrust liability have negotiated the proposal among themselves even though this would have involved their agreeing on how much to seek from government in the way of permitted price increases.

But they didn't want a law; they wanted (they say) to ward off a price-control law by being good boys and keeping their price increases moderate. The distinction is not critical; opposing legislation is a way of participating in the legislative process just as proposing legislation is. It would not make sense to interpret *Noerr-Pennington* in such a way as to encourage industries to channel all their legislative activity into proposing laws (here perhaps a law against passing a price-control law!). But the doctrine does not authorize anticompetitive action in advance of government's adopting the industry's anticompetitive proposal. The doctrine applies when such action is the consequence of legislation or other governmental action, not when it is the means for obtaining such action (or in this case inaction). Otherwise every cartel could immunize itself from antitrust liability by the simple expedient of seeking governmental sanction for the cartel after it was up and going. * * *

To establish damages the plaintiffs would have to prove that the price of brand name prescription drugs would have been higher (and by how much) had the defendants not agreed to peg price increases to the CPI. Since the defendants may have been seeking to moderate their price increases in order to ward off price controls, the price-fixing conspiracy (if there was one) may have resulted in lower rather than higher prices, in which event the defendants' customers were not harmed and cannot obtain damages. * * * We suggest that before proceeding to trial on the CPI issue, the district judge require the plaintiffs to show that they have (in light of the doubts we've expressed) a viable theory of damages; if they do not, there would be no point in a trial on liability, as they do not appear to be seeking injunctive relief against the alleged CPI conspiracy. But these details remain to be sorted out on remand.

NOTES AND QUESTIONS

1. *Pharmaceutical companies and political power.* The United States is the last frontier of unrestricted pharmaceutical pricing, and the pharmaceutical companies regularly rank among the highest profit-makers on the Fortune 500 list of companies (averaging an 18.6 percent return on revenues). Although sales of brand name prescription drugs continue to increase, generic competition has made some inroads into the market. As of 1996, generic drugs accounted for 43 percent of the prescription drug market. See Sheryl Gay Stolberg & Jeff Gerth, In a Drug's Journey to Market, Discovery Is Just the First of Many Steps, N.Y. Times, July 23, 2000, at A15. A recent report detailing the political clout of the pharmaceutical industry found that PhRMA members spent approximately $360 million on political contributions, lobbying efforts, and advertising campaigns during the last five election years, in order to protect its interests. About two-thirds of the political contributions went to Republicans. The spending has paid off in a variety of legislative contexts, by influencing issues such as the possibility of a Medicare drug benefit. See Common Cause, Prescription for Power: How Brand–Name Drug Companies Prevailed Over Consumers in Washington 4–5 (2001), available at <www.commoncause.org>.

2. *Antitrust issues in drug marketing.* Federal prosecutors are investigating whether several drug companies, including Bristol–Myers Squibb, engaged in inappropriate marketing practices in order to persuade physicians to prescribe their products. The company apparently gave oncologists certain drugs free of charge in exchange for agreements to purchase other Bristol–Myers products. The company also "bundles" its oncology drugs in order to increase the marketability of its lesser-selling products. See David S. Cloud, U.S. Scrutinizes Sales Practices of Bristol–Myers, Wall St. J., Feb. 27, 2001, at A3; see also Aimee M. W. Pollak, Note, Should the Exemption from the Robinson–Patman Act Apply to Pharmaceutical Purchases by Nonprofit HMOs?, 73 N.Y.U. L. Rev. 965 (1998).

CHAPTER 10

MANAGING INCENTIVES FOR INNOVATION

A. INTELLECTUAL PROPERTY PROTECTIONS

Fifty years ago, when asked whether he planned to patent his new polio vaccine, Dr. Jonas Salk replied by asking "Can you patent the sun?" How times have changed.

Diamond v. Chakrabarty

447 U.S. 303 (1980).

■ BURGER, CHIEF JUSTICE:

* * * In 1972, respondent Chakrabarty, a microbiologist, filed a patent application, assigned to the General Electric Co. The application asserted 36 claims related to Chakrabarty's invention of "a bacterium from the genus Pseudomonas containing therein at least two stable energy-generating plasmids, each of said plasmids providing a separate hydrocarbon degradative pathway." This human-made, genetically engineered bacterium is capable of breaking down multiple components of crude oil. Because of this property, which is possessed by no naturally occurring bacteria, Chakrabarty's invention is believed to have significant value for the treatment of oil spills.

Chakrabarty's patent claims were of three types: first, process claims for the method of producing the bacteria; second, claims for an inoculum comprised of a carrier material floating on water, such as straw, and the new bacteria; and third, claims to the bacteria themselves. The patent examiner allowed the claims falling into the first two categories, but rejected claims for the bacteria. His decision rested on two grounds: (1) that micro-organisms are "products of nature," and (2) that as living things they are not patentable subject matter under 35 U.S.C. § 101. * * *

The Court of Customs and Patent Appeals, by a divided vote, reversed on the authority of its prior decision in *In re Bergy*, 563 F.2d 1031, 1038 (C.C.P.A.1977), which held that "the fact that microorganisms . . . are alive . . . [is] without legal significance" for purposes of the patent law.[4] * * * The Commissioner of Patents and Trademarks again sought certiorari, and

---

4. *Bergy* involved a patent application for a pure culture of the micro-organism Streptomyces vellosus found to be useful in the production of lincomycin, an antibiotic.

738

we granted the writ as to both *Bergy* and *Chakrabarty*. Since then, *Bergy* has been dismissed as moot, leaving only *Chakrabarty* for decision.

The Constitution grants Congress broad power to legislate to "promote the Progress of Science and useful Arts, by securing for limited Times to Authors and Inventors the exclusive Right to their respective Writings and Discoveries." Art. I, § 8, cl. 8. The patent laws promote this progress by offering inventors exclusive rights for a limited period as an incentive for their inventiveness and research efforts. The authority of Congress is exercised in the hope that "[t]he productive effort thereby fostered will have a positive effect on society through the introduction of new products and processes of manufacture into the economy, and the emanations by way of increased employment and better lives for our citizens."

The question before us in this case is a narrow one of statutory interpretation requiring us to construe 35 U.S.C. § 101, which provides: "Whoever invents or discovers any new and useful process, machine, manufacture, or composition of matter, or any new and useful improvement thereof, may obtain a patent therefor, subject to the conditions and requirements of this title." Specifically, we must determine whether respondent's micro-organism constitutes a "manufacture" or "composition of matter" within the meaning of the statute. * * *

In choosing such expansive terms as "manufacture" and "composition of matter," modified by the comprehensive "any," Congress plainly contemplated that the patent laws would be given wide scope. The relevant legislative history also supports a broad construction. The Patent Act of 1793, authored by Thomas Jefferson, defined statutory subject matter as "any new and useful art, machine, manufacture, or composition of matter, or any new or useful improvement [thereof]." The Act embodied Jefferson's philosophy that "ingenuity should receive a liberal encouragement." Subsequent patent statutes in 1836, 1870, and 1874 employed this same broad language. In 1952, when the patent laws were recodified, Congress replaced the word "art" with "process," but otherwise left Jefferson's language intact. The Committee Reports accompanying the 1952 Act inform us that Congress intended statutory subject matter to "include anything under the sun that is made by man."

This is not to suggest that § 101 has no limits or that it embraces every discovery. The laws of nature, physical phenomena, and abstract ideas have been held not patentable. Thus, a new mineral discovered in the earth or a new plant found in the wild is not patentable subject matter. Likewise, Einstein could not patent his celebrated law that $E = mc^2$; nor could Newton have patented the law of gravity. Such discoveries are "manifestations of . . . nature, free to all men and reserved exclusively to none."

Judged in this light, respondent's micro-organism plainly qualifies as patentable subject matter. His claim is not to a hitherto unknown natural phenomenon, but to a nonnaturally occurring manufacture or composition of matter * * * * [T]he patentee has produced a new bacterium with markedly different characteristics from any found in nature and one having the potential for significant utility. His discovery is not nature's handiwork, but his own; accordingly it is patentable subject matter under § 101. * * *

The petitioner's second argument is that micro-organisms cannot qualify as patentable subject matter until Congress expressly authorizes such protection. His position rests on the fact that genetic technology was unforeseen when Congress enacted § 101. From this it is argued that resolution of the patentability of inventions such as respondent's should be left to Congress. The legislative process, the petitioner argues, is best equipped to weigh the competing economic, social, and scientific considerations involved, and to determine whether living organisms produced by genetic engineering should receive patent protection. * * *

Congress has performed its constitutional role in defining patentable subject matter in § 101; we perform ours in construing the language Congress has employed. In so doing, our obligation is to take statutes as we find them, guided, if ambiguity appears, by the legislative history and statutory purpose. Here, we perceive no ambiguity. The subject-matter provisions of the patent law have been cast in broad terms to fulfill the constitutional and statutory goal of promoting "the Progress of Science and the useful Arts" with all that means for the social and economic benefits envisioned by Jefferson. Broad general language is not necessarily ambiguous when congressional objectives require broad terms. * * *

A rule that unanticipated inventions are without protection would conflict with the core concept of the patent law that anticipation undermines patentability. Mr. Justice Douglas reminded that the inventions most benefiting mankind are those that "push back the frontiers of chemistry, physics, and the like." Congress employed broad general language in drafting § 101 precisely because such inventions are often unforeseeable.

To buttress his argument, the petitioner, with the support of amicus, points to grave risks that may be generated by research endeavors such as respondent's. The briefs present a gruesome parade of horribles. Scientists, among them Nobel laureates, are quoted suggesting that genetic research may pose a serious threat to the human race, or, at the very least, that the dangers are far too substantial to permit such research to proceed apace at this time. We are told that genetic research and related technological developments may spread pollution and disease, that it may result in a loss of genetic diversity, and that its practice may tend to depreciate the value of human life. These arguments are forcefully, even passionately, presented; they remind us that, at times, human ingenuity seems unable to control fully the forces it creates—that with Hamlet, it is sometimes better "to bear those ills we have than fly to others that we know not of."

It is argued that this Court should weigh these potential hazards in considering whether respondent's invention is patentable subject matter under § 101. We disagree. The grant or denial of patents on micro-organisms is not likely to put an end to genetic research or to its attendant risks. The large amount of research that has already occurred when no researcher had sure knowledge that patent protection would be available suggests that legislative or judicial fiat as to patentability will not deter the scientific mind from probing into the unknown any more than Canute could command the tides. Whether respondent's claims are patentable may determine whether research efforts are accelerated by the hope of reward or slowed by want of incentives, but that is all.

What is more important is that we are without competence to entertain these arguments—either to brush them aside as fantasies generated by fear of the unknown, or to act on them. The choice we are urged to make is a matter of high policy for resolution within the legislative process after the kind of investigation, examination, and study that legislative bodies can provide and courts cannot. That process involves the balancing of competing values and interests, which in our democratic system is the business of elected representatives. Whatever their validity, the contentions now pressed on us should be addressed to the political branches of the government, the Congress and the Executive, and not to the courts. * * *

Congress is free to amend § 101 so as to exclude from patent protection organisms produced by genetic engineering. Cf. 42 U.S.C. § 2181(a), exempting from patent protection inventions "useful solely in the utilization of special nuclear material or atomic energy in an atomic weapon." Or it may chose to craft a statute specifically designed for such living things. But, until Congress takes such action, this Court must construe the language of § 101 as it is. The language of that section fairly embraces respondent's invention. * * *

In re Brana

51 F.3d 1560 (Fed.Cir.1995).

■ PLAGER, CIRCUIT JUDGE:

Miguel F. Brana, et al. (applicants), appeal the March 19, 1993 decision of the United States Patent and Trademark Office (PTO) Board of Patent Appeals and Interferences * * * * On June 30, 1988, applicants filed patent application Serial No. 213,690 (the '690 application) directed to 5–nitrobenzo[de]isoquinoline–1,3–dione compounds, for use as antitumor substances * * * * These claimed compounds differ from several prior art benzo[de]isoquinoline–1,3–dione compounds due to the presence of a nitro group (O_2N) at the 5–position and an amino or other amino group (NR^3R^4) at the 8–position of the isoquinoline ring.

The specification states that these non-symmetrical substitutions at the 5– and 8–positions produce compounds with "a better action and a better action spectrum as antitumor substances" than known benzo[de]isoquinolines, namely those in K.D. Paull et al., Computer Assisted Structure–Activity Correlations, Drug Research, 34(II), 1243–46 (1984). Paull describes a computer-assisted evaluation of benzo[de]iso-quinoline–1,3–diones and related compounds which have been screened for antitumor activity by testing their efficacy *in vivo* against two specific implanted murine (i.e., utilizing mice as test subjects) lymphocytic leukemias, P388 and L1210. These two *in vivo* tests are widely used by the National Cancer Institute

(NCI) to measure the antitumor properties of a compound. Paull noted that one compound in particular * * * (hereinafter "NSC 308847"), was found to show excellent activity against these two specific tumor models. Based on their analysis, compound NSC 308847 was selected for further studies by NCI. In addition to comparing the effectiveness of the claimed compounds with structurally similar compounds in Paull, applicants' patent specification illustrates the cytotoxicity of the claimed compounds against human tumor cells, *in vitro*, and concludes that these tests "had a good action."
* * *

At issue in this case is an important question of the legal constraints on patent office examination practice and policy. The question is, with regard to pharmaceutical inventions, what must the applicant prove regarding the practical utility or usefulness of the invention for which patent protection is sought. This is not a new issue; it is one which we would have thought had been settled by case law years ago. We note the Commissioner has recently addressed this question in his Examiner Guidelines for Biotech Applications, see 60 Fed. Reg. 97 (1995).

The requirement that an invention have utility is found in 35 U.S.C. § 101: "Whoever invents ... any new and useful ... composition of matter ... may obtain a patent therefor...." It is also implicit in § 112 ¶ 1, which reads:

> The specification shall contain a written description of the invention, and of the manner and process of making and using it, in such full, clear, concise, and exact terms as to enable any person skilled in the art to which it pertains, or with which it is most nearly connected, to make and use the same, and shall set forth the best mode contemplated by the inventor of carrying out his invention.

Obviously, if a claimed invention does not have utility, the specification cannot enable one to use it. * * *

The first basis for the Board's decision was that the applicants' specification failed to disclose a specific disease against which the claimed compounds are useful, and therefore, absent undue experimentation, one of ordinary skill in the art was precluded from using the invention. In support, the Commissioner argues that the disclosed uses in the '944 application, namely the "treatment of diseases" and "antitumor substances," are similar to the nebulous disclosure found insufficient in [a previous case]. * * * Applicants' specification, however, also states that the claimed compounds have "a better action and a better action spectrum as antitumor substances" than known compounds, specifically those analyzed in Paull. As previously noted, Paull grouped various benzo[de]isoquinoline–1,3–diones, which had previously been tested *in vivo* for antitumor activity against two lymphocytic leukemia tumor models (P388 and L1210), into various structural classifications and analyzed the test results of the groups (i.e., what percent of the compounds in the particular group showed success against the tumor models). Since one of the tested compounds, NSC 308847, was found to be highly effective against these two lymphocytic leukemia tumor models, applicants' favorable comparison implicitly asserts that their claimed compounds are highly effective (i.e., useful) against lymphocytic leukemia. An alleged use against this particular type of cancer is much more specific than the vaguely intimated uses rejected by the courts in [prior cases].

The Commissioner contends, however, that P388 and L1210 are not diseases since the only way an animal can get sick from P388 is by a direct injection of the cell line. The Commissioner therefore concludes that applicants' reference to Paull in their specification does not provide a specific disease against which the claimed compounds can be used. We disagree. As applicants point out, the P388 and L1210 cell lines, though technically labeled tumor models, were originally derived from lymphocytic leukemias in mice. Therefore, the P388 and L1210 cell lines do represent actual specific lymphocytic tumors; these models will produce this particular disease once implanted in mice. If applicants were required to wait until an animal naturally developed this specific tumor before testing the effectiveness of a compound against the tumor *in vivo*, as would be implied from the Commissioner's argument, there would be no effective way to test compounds *in vivo* on a large scale. * * *

The second basis for the Board's rejection was that, even if the specification did allege a specific use, applicants failed to prove that the claimed compounds are useful. Citing various references, the Board found, and the Commissioner now argues, that the tests offered by the applicants to prove utility were inadequate to convince one of ordinary skill in the art that the claimed compounds are useful as antitumor agents. * * *

The references cited by the Board, Pazdur and Martin, do not question the usefulness of any compound as an antitumor agent or provide any other evidence to cause one of skill in the art to question the asserted utility of applicants' compounds. Rather, these references merely discuss the therapeutic predictive value of *in vivo* murine tests—relevant only if applicants must prove the ultimate value in humans of their asserted utility. Likewise, we do not find that the nature of applicants' invention alone would cause one of skill in the art to reasonably doubt the asserted usefulness. The purpose of treating cancer with chemical compounds does not suggest an inherently unbelievable undertaking or involve implausible scientific principles. Modern science has previously identified numerous successful chemotherapeutic agents. * * * Taking these facts—the nature of the invention and the PTO's proffered evidence—into consideration we conclude that one skilled in the art would be without basis to reasonably doubt applicants' asserted utility on its face. The PTO thus has not satisfied its initial burden. Accordingly, applicants should not have been required to substantiate their presumptively correct disclosure to avoid a rejection under the first paragraph of § 112.

We do not rest our decision there, however. Even if one skilled in the art would have reasonably questioned the asserted utility, i.e., even if the PTO met its initial burden thereby shifting the burden to the applicants to offer rebuttal evidence, applicants proffered sufficient evidence to convince one of skill in the art of the asserted utility. In particular, applicants provided through Dr. Kluge's declaration test results showing that several compounds within the scope of the claims exhibited significant antitumor activity against the L1210 standard tumor model *in vivo*. Such evidence alone should have been sufficient to satisfy applicants' burden. The prior art further supports the conclusion that one skilled in the art would be convinced of the applicants' asserted utility. As previously mentioned, prior art * * * disclosed structurally similar compounds which were proven *in vivo* against various tumor models to be effective as chemotherapeutic agents. Although it is true that minor changes in chemical compounds can radically alter their effects on the human body, evidence of success in structurally similar compounds is relevant in determining whether one skilled in the art would believe an asserted utility.

The Commissioner counters that such *in vivo* tests in animals are only preclinical tests to determine whether a compound is suitable for processing in the second stage of testing, by which he apparently means *in vivo* testing in humans, and therefore are not reasonably predictive of the success of the claimed compounds for treating cancer in humans. The Commissioner, as did the Board, confuses the requirements under the law for obtaining a patent with the requirements for obtaining government approval to market a particular drug for human consumption. See Scott v. Finney, 34 F.3d 1058, 1063 (Fed.Cir.1994) ("Testing for the full safety and effectiveness of a prosthetic device is more properly left to the Food and Drug Administration (FDA). Title 35 does not demand that such human testing occur within the confines of Patent and Trademark Office (PTO) proceedings.").

Our court's predecessor has determined that proof of an alleged pharmaceutical property for a compound by statistically significant tests with standard experimental animals is sufficient to establish utility. In re Krimmel, 292 F.2d 948, 953 (C.C.P.A.1961). In concluding that similar *in vivo* tests were adequate proof of utility the court in *In re Krimmel* stated:

> We hold as we do because it is our firm conviction that one who has taught the public that a compound exhibits some desirable pharmaceutical property in a standard experimental animal has made a significant and useful contribution to the art, even though it may eventually appear that the compound is without value in the treatment in humans.

Id. at 953. Moreover, NCI apparently believes these tests are statistically significant because it has explicitly recognized both the P388 and L1210 murine tumor models as standard screening tests for determining whether new compounds may be useful as antitumor agents. * * *

On the basis of animal studies, and controlled testing in a limited number of humans (referred to as Phase I testing), the Food and Drug Administration may authorize Phase II clinical studies. Authorization for a Phase II study means that the drug may be administered to a larger number of humans, but still under strictly supervised conditions. The purpose of the Phase II study is to determine primarily the safety of the drug when administered to a larger human population, as well as its potential efficacy under different dosage regimes. FDA approval, however, is not a prerequisite for finding a compound useful within the meaning of the patent laws. Usefulness in patent law, and in particular in the context of pharmaceutical inventions, necessarily includes the expectation of further research and development. The stage at which an invention in this field becomes useful is well before it is ready to be administered to humans. Were we to require Phase II testing in order to prove utility, the associated costs would prevent many companies from obtaining patent protection on promising new inventions, thereby eliminating an incentive to pursue, through research and development, potential cures in many crucial areas such as the treatment of cancer. In view of all the foregoing, we conclude that applicants' disclosure complies with the requirements of 35 U.S.C. § 112 ¶ 1. * * *

Fujikawa v. Wattanasin

93 F.3d 1559 (Fed.Cir.1996).

■ CLEVENGER, CIRCUIT JUDGE:

Yoshihiro Fujikawa et al. appeal from two decisions of the Board of Patent Appeals and Interferences of the United States Patent & Trademark Office granting priority of invention in two related interferences to Sompong Wattanasin * * * * These interferences pertain to a compound and method for inhibiting cholesterol biosynthesis in humans and other animals. The compound count recites a genus of novel mevalonolactones. The method count recites a method of inhibiting the biosynthesis of cholesterol by administering to a "patient in need of said treatment" an appropriate dosage of a compound falling within the scope of the compound count.

The real parties in interest are Sandoz Pharmaceuticals Corporation, assignee of Wattanasin, and Nissan Chemical Industries, Ltd., assignee of Fujikawa. The inventive activity of Fujikawa, the senior party, occurred overseas. Fujikawa can thus rely only on his effective filing date, August 20, 1987, to establish priority. 35 U.S.C. § 102(g) (1994).* Whether Wattanasin is entitled to priority as against Fujikawa therefore turns on two discrete questions. First, whether Wattanasin has shown conception coupled with diligence from just prior to Fujikawa's effective filing date until reduction to practice. Second, whether Wattanasin suppressed or concealed the invention between reduction to practice and filing. * * *

The Board divided Wattanasin's inventive activity into two phases. The first phase commenced in 1979 when Sandoz began searching for drugs which would inhibit the biosynthesis of cholesterol. Inventor Wattanasin was assigned to this project in 1982, and during 1984–1985 he synthesized three compounds falling within the scope of the compound count. When

---

* As required by an international agreement, Congress subsequently amended this provision to eliminate the differential treatment of foreign entities in claiming priority to an invention. See Pub. L. No. 106–113, § 4806, 113 Stat. 1501 (1999).

tested *in vitro,* each of these compounds exhibited some cholesterol-inhibiting activity, although not all the chemicals were equally effective. Still, according to one Sandoz researcher, Dr. Damon, these test results indicated that, to a high probability, the three compounds "would be active when administered *in vivo* to a patient to inhibit cholesterol biosynthesis, i.e. for the treatment of hypercholesteremia or atherosclerosis." Notwithstanding these seemingly positive results, Sandoz shelved Wattanasin's project for almost two years, apparently because the level of *in vitro* activity in two of the three compounds was disappointingly low.

By January 1987, however, interest in Wattanasin's invention had revived, and the second phase of activity began. Over the next several months, four more compounds falling within the scope of the compound count were synthesized. In October, these compounds were tested for *in vitro* activity, and each of the four compounds yielded positive results. Again, however, there were significant differences in the level of *in vitro* activity of the four compounds. Two of the compounds in particular, numbered 64–935 and 64–936, exhibited *in vitro* activity significantly higher than that of the other two compounds, numbered 64–933 and 64–934.

Soon after, in December 1987, the three most active compounds *in vitro* were subjected to additional *in vivo* testing. For Sandoz, one primary purpose of these tests was to determine the *in vivo* potency of the three compounds relative to that of Compactin, a prior art compound of known cholesterol-inhibiting potency. From the results of the *in vivo* tests, Sandoz calculated an ED_{50} [effective dose for achieving 50% inhibition] for each of the compounds and compared it to the ED_{50} of Compactin. * * *

During this period, Sandoz also began to consider whether, and when, a patent application should be filed for Wattanasin's invention. Several times during the second phase of activity, the Sandoz patent committee considered the question of Wattanasin's invention but decided that it was too early in the invention's development to file a patent application. Each time, however, the patent committee merely deferred decision on the matter and specified that it would be taken up again at subsequent meetings. Finally, in January 1988, with the *in vivo* testing completed, the Committee assigned Wattanasin's invention an "A" rating which meant that the invention was ripe for filing and that a patent application should be prepared. The case was assigned to a Ms. Geisser, a young patent attorney in the Sandoz patent department with little experience in the pharmaceutical field.

Over the next several months the Sandoz patent department collected additional data from the inventor which was needed to prepare the patent application. This data gathering took until approximately the end of May 1988. At that point, work on the case seems to have ceased for several months until Ms. Geisser began preparing a draft sometime in the latter half of 1988. * * * [T]he draft was completed in November and, after several turn-arounds with the inventor, ultimately filed in March of 1989. * * *

We first address Fujikawa's argument that Wattanasin's *in vitro* and *in vivo* tests failed to establish a practical utility for either the compound or method count. The Board held that the *in vitro* tests established a practical utility for the compound and that the *in vivo* tests established a practical utility for both the compound and method counts. For the reasons set out below, we affirm these findings of the Board.

For over 200 years, the concept of utility has occupied a central role in our patent system. Indeed, "[t]he basic *quid pro quo* contemplated by the Constitution and the Congress for granting a patent monopoly is the benefit derived by the public from an invention with substantial utility." Consequently, it is well established that a patent may not be granted to an invention unless substantial or practical utility for the invention has been discovered and disclosed. Similarly, actual reduction to practice, which constitutes in law the final phase of invention, cannot be established absent a showing of practical utility.

In the pharmaceutical arts, our court has long held that practical utility may be shown by adequate evidence of any pharmacological activity. * * * Such activity constitutes a practical utility because "[i]t is inherently faster and easier to combat illnesses and alleviate symptoms when the medical profession is armed with an arsenal of chemicals having known pharmacological activities. Since it is crucial to provide researchers with an incentive to disclose pharmacological activities in as many compounds as possible, we conclude that adequate proof of any such activity constitutes a showing of practical utility."

It may be difficult to predict, however, whether a novel compound will exhibit pharmacological activity, even when the behavior of analogous compounds is known to those skilled in the art. Consequently, testing is often required to establish practical utility. But the test results need not absolutely prove that the compound is pharmacologically active. All that is required is that the tests be "reasonably indicative of the desired [pharmacological] response." In other words, there must be a sufficient correlation between the tests and an asserted pharmacological activity so as to convince those skilled in the art, to a reasonable probability, that the novel compound will exhibit the asserted pharmacological behavior. * * *

Fujikawa contends that Wattanasin has failed to establish an adequate correlation between *in vitro* and *in vivo* results in the field of cholesterol-inhibiting compounds to permit Wattanasin to rely on affirmative *in vitro* results to establish a practical utility for the compound. The Board determined that Wattanasin had reduced the compound count to practice in October 1987 when several compounds falling within the scope of the genus count exhibited activity *in vitro*. In reaching that conclusion, the Board relied on testimony from those skilled in the art that the *in vitro* results convinced them that the claimed compounds would exhibit the desired pharmacological activity when administered *in vivo*. * * *

Having determined that Wattanasin was the de facto first inventor, the remaining question before the Board was whether Wattanasin had suppressed or concealed the invention between the time he reduced to practice and the time he filed his patent application. Suppression or concealment of the invention by Wattanasin would entitle Fujikawa to priority. * * * Admittedly, Sandoz was not overly efficient in preparing a patent application, given the time which elapsed between its reduction to practice in late 1987 and its ultimate filing in March 1989. Intentional suppression, however, requires more than the passage of time. It requires evidence that the inventor intentionally delayed filing in order to prolong the period during which the invention is maintained in secret. Fujikawa presented no evidence that Wattanasin delayed filing for this purpose. On the contrary, all indications are that throughout the period between reduction to practice and filing, Sandoz moved slowly (one might even say fitfully), but inexorably, toward disclosure. We therefore hold that Wattanasin did not intentionally suppress or conceal the invention in this case.

Absent intentional suppression, the only question is whether the 17 month period between the reduction to practice of the compound, or the 15 month period between reduction to practice of the method, and Wattanasin's filing justify an inference of suppression or concealment. The Board held that these facts do not support such an inference. * * *

In our view, the circumstances in this case place it squarely within the class of cases in which an inference of suppression or concealment is not warranted. We acknowledge, of course, that each case of suppression or concealment must be decided on its own facts. Still, the rich and varied case law which this court has developed over many years provides some guidance as to the type of behavior which warrants an inference of suppression or concealment. In this case Wattanasin delayed approximately 17 months between reduction to practice and filing. During much of that period, however, Wattanasin and Sandoz engaged in significant steps towards perfecting the invention and preparing an application. For example, we do not believe any lack of diligence can be ascribed to Wattanasin for the period between October and December 1987 when *in vivo* testing of the invention was taking place. Similarly, at its first opportunity following the *in vivo* testing, the Sandoz patent committee approved Wattanasin's invention for filing. This takes us up to the end of January 1988.

Over the next several months, until May 1988, the Sandoz patent department engaged in the necessary collection of data from the inventor and others in order to prepare Wattanasin's patent application. We are satisfied from the record that this disclosure-related activity was sufficient to avoid any inference of suppression or concealment during this period. Also, as noted above, the record indicates that by August 1988, Ms. Geisser was already at work preparing the application, and that work continued on various drafts until Wattanasin's filing date in March 1989. Thus, the only real period of unexplained delay in this case is the approximately three month period between May and August of 1988.

Given a total delay of 17 months, an unexplained delay of three months, the complexity of the subject matter at issue, and our sense from the record as a whole that throughout the delay Sandoz was moving, albeit slowly, towards filing an application, we conclude that this case does not warrant an inference of suppression or concealment. Consequently, we affirm the Board on this point. * * *

NOTES AND QUESTIONS

1. *Patent prerequisites.* In order to receive patent protection, an invention must satisfy requirements of novelty and usefulness. Novelty requires, among other things, that the invention not have been in public use (as opposed to experimental use) in the United States for more than one year prior to the filing of a patent application. See 35 U.S.C. § 102(b); see also Baxter Int'l, Inc. v. COBE Labs., Inc., 88 F.3d 1054, 1058–61 (Fed.Cir.1996) (finding an absence of novelty because a researcher at NIH who lacked any relationship with the inventor had not restricted access to a modified centrifuge that he used for separating blood components). Pharmaceutical companies generally apply for patents before starting clinical (and sometimes even pre-clinical) trials with a new molecular entity. See Robert Schaffer et al., Clinical Trials May Bar Drug's Patent Protection, Nat'l L.J., May 22, 2000, at B14. See generally F. Scott Kieff, Facilitating Scientific Research: Intellectual Property Rights and the Norms of Science, 95 Nw. U. L. Rev. 691 (2001); Phanesh Koneru, To Promote the Progress of Useful Art[icle]s?: An Analysis of the Current Utility Standards of Pharmaceutical Products and Biotechnological Research Tools, 38 IDEA 625 (1998); William D. Noonan, Patenting Medical Technology, 11 J. Legal Med. 263 (1990); Timothy R. Howe, Comment, Patentability of Pioneering Pharmaceuticals: What's the Use?, 32 San Diego L. Rev. 819 (1995).

2. *Patentable subject matter.* Although most medical technologies are clearly patentable, disputes have arisen with biotechnologies. See Amgen, Inc. v. Chugai Pharm. Co., 927 F.2d 1200, 1206 (Fed.Cir.1991) (holding, in the course of resolving a patent controversy over a DNA sequence encoding erythropoietin (EPO), "that when an inventor is unable to envision the detailed constitution of a gene so as to distinguish it from other materials, as well as a method for obtaining it, conception has not been achieved until reduction to practice has occurred, i.e., until after the gene has been isolated"); see also J.E.M. AG Supply, Inc. v. Pioneer Hi–Bred Int'l, Inc., 534 U.S. 124 (2001) (upholding the patentability of genetically engineered plants on the strength of *Chakrabarty*); David Beier & Robert H. Benson, Biotechnology Patent Protection Act, 68 Denv. U. L. Rev. 173 (1991); Alison E. Cantor, Using the Written Description and Enablement Requirements to Limit Biotechnology Patents, 14 Harv. J.L. & Tech. 267 (2000); John M. Golden, Biotechnology, Technology Policy, and Patentability: Natural Products and Invention in the American System, 50 Emory L.J. 101 (2001); David E. Huizenga, Comment, Protein Variants: A Study on the Differing Standards for Biotechnology Patents in the United States and Europe, 13 Emory Int'l L. Rev. 629 (1999); Kenneth Muhammad, Note, An Analysis of Patent Claim Construction for Newly Invented Monoclonal Antibodies, 18 Temp. Envtl. L. & Tech. J. 95 (1999). The genomics revolution will present numerous difficult patent questions. See Molly A. Holman & Stephen R. Munzer, Intellectual Property Rights in Genes and

Gene Fragments: A Registration Solution for Expressed Sequence Tags, 85 Iowa L. Rev. 735 (2000); Arti K. Rai, Intellectual Property Rights in Biotechnology: Addressing New Technology, 34 Wake Forest L. Rev. 827 (1999); David Manspeizer, Note, The Cheshire Cat, the March Hare, and the Harvard Mouse: Animal Patents Open up a New, Genetically–Engineered Wonderland, 43 Rutgers L. Rev. 417 (1991). The PTO issued new examination guidelines to address some of these questions. See 66 Fed. Reg. 1092 (2001); see also Margaret Graham Tebo, The Big Gene Profit Machine, ABA J., Apr. 2001, at 46; Aaron Zitner, As New Data Shrink Gene Pool, Patent Suits May Be Next Splash, L.A. Times, Feb. 13, 2001, at A1 ("The patent office estimates that it has issued patents on about 1,000 full-length human genes, but it has tens of thousands of applications pending.").

3. *Medical procedure patents.* Controversy once arose over efforts to patent novel surgical techniques. See AMA Council on Ethical & Judicial Affairs, Ethical Issues in the Patenting of Medical Procedures, 53 Food & Drug L.J. 341 (1998). Congress amended the statute to exempt health care providers from any liability for infringing patented medical procedures. See 35 U.S.C. § 287(c); see also Weldon E. Havins, Immunizing the Medical Practitioner "Process" Infringer: Greasing the Squeaky Wheel, Good Public Policy, or What?, 77 U. Det. Mercy L. Rev. 51 (1999); Cynthia M. Ho, Patents, Patients, and Public Policy: An Incomplete Intersection at 35 U.S.C. § 287(c), 33 U.C. Davis L. Rev. 601 (2000); Chris J. Katopis, Patients v. Patents?: Policy Implications of Recent Patent Legislation, 71 St. John's L. Rev. 329 (1997); Joel J. Garris, Note, The Case for Patenting Medical Procedures, 22 Am. J.L. & Med. 85 (1996). How should compounding of drugs (by pharmacists or physicians) be treated? Could a pharmacist secure a process patent to cover novel procedures for compounding a drug using substances no longer protected by composition patents?

1.   COMPOSITION PATENTS

Zenith Laboratories, Inc. v. Bristol–Myers Squibb Co.

19 F.3d 1418 (Fed.Cir.1994).

■ PLAGER, CIRCUIT JUDGE:

The question in this declaratory judgment action is whether a drug compound, which in its manufactured state does not infringe the patent in suit, becomes infringing as a result of transitory chemical changes that occur *in vivo*, that is, as a result of ingestion by the patient. * * *

The chemical compound cefadroxil, an antibiotic of the cephalosporin family effective against bacteria that are resistant to penicillin, was described and claimed in United States Patent No. 3,489,752 (the '752 patent), which issued in 1970; the owner was Bristol. The claims of the '752 patent covered any and all forms of cefadroxil—they described the chemical compound per se. The '752 patent expired in 1987.

In the meantime, Bristol set to work to find a commercially useful crystalline form of the compound that would overcome problems related to manufacture of the product so that it would be usable by humans. The task of developing a commercial production process was assigned to certain of Bristol's chemists. They developed what became known as the Bouzard monohydrate, named after one of the discoverers—a new crystalline form of cefadroxil. Unlike prior forms of cefadroxil, Bouzard monohydrate possesses certain characteristics in its pre-ingested, powdered form, related to bulk density, solubility, and stability (manufacturing-related characteristics), which make it particularly suitable for packaging into capsules.

The Bouzard monohydrate was the subject of the single claim in the '657 patent:

1. Crystalline 7-[D-α-amino-α-(p-hydroxyphenyl-)acetamido]-3-methyl-3-cephem-4-carboxylic acid monohydrate exhibiting essentially the following x-ray diffraction properties: [a 37-line table of relative intensities exhibited by Bouzard monohydrate at various scan angles].

In July 1988, Zenith, the plaintiff in this declaratory judgment action, contracted with a Spanish company, Gema, S.A. of Barcelona, to become the exclusive United States distributor of the form of cefadroxil manufactured by Gema and known as cefadroxil DC. Cefadroxil DC is a hemihydrate form of cefadroxil and thus differs structurally from Bouzard monohydrate. * * * Zenith and Gema sought abbreviated approval on the grounds that cefadroxil DC was bioequivalent to a form of cefadroxil monohydrate (other than Bouzard monohydrate) which had already been approved by the FDA for commercial sale. In October 1990, the FDA granted approval.[3]
* * *

Bristol conceded that cefadroxil DC, being a hemihydrate, did not literally infringe the '657 patent in its pre-ingested form. Bristol nevertheless argued that Zenith was liable under the patent on two grounds: Zenith's product infringed under the doctrine of equivalents; and Zenith's product converted into the patented compound in the patient's stomach, and thus the sale of cefadroxil DC would induce infringement of the '657 patent * * * *

We begin with claim construction: whether the claim of the '657 patent, properly construed, covers Bouzard crystals which might form momentarily in a patient's stomach. Zenith argues that, due to statements made by Bristol during the '657 prosecution, the '657 claim is limited to the pre-ingested, powdered form of Bouzard monohydrate. In those statements Bristol particularly emphasized the superior manufacturing-related benefits of the pre-ingested form of Bouzard monohydrate in relation to prior forms of cefadroxil. Bristol, it is argued, thus relinquished coverage of any forms of cefadroxil DC that do not exhibit these manufacturing-related character-

---

3. The record suggests that the FDA subsequently reconsidered and rescinded this approval after Bristol filed with the FDA a citizens petition seeking to block approval on the grounds cefadroxil DC was a hemihydrate and thus not bioequivalent to cefadroxil monohydrate. * * *

istics—that would obviously include any Bouzard monohydrate formed in a patient's stomach.

Zenith has a point. Prosecution history serves as a limit on the scope of claims by excluding any interpretation of the claim language that would permit the patentee to assert a meaning for the claim that was disclaimed or disavowed during prosecution in order to obtain claim allowance. The prosecution history in this case is replete with arguments by Bristol that the importance of this invention was the discovery of a way to manufacture the known compound so as to make it commercially available for medical treatment.

The difficulty with Zenith's argument, however, is in the nature of the sole claim in the patent. The claim as written and allowed simply describes a compound having specified chemical properties. The question before us is not one of validity: whether the claim would be patentable over the prior art if the suggested restriction were not applicable. The question here is one of infringement: whether there is anything in the claim as issued that limits it to the pre-ingested form * * * *

Zenith's argument suffers from additional infirmities. The '657 claim is a claim for a compound. Its patentability thus derives from the structure of the claimed compound in relation to prior compounds. The relevance to patentability of the properties or characteristics exhibited by the compound is limited to assessing the significance of the structural distinctions of the claimed compound over the prior art. Second, as we later note in more detail, it is not at all clear that the statements concerning these characteristics played a determinative or even significant role in the Patent and Trademark Office's decision to grant the patent. We conclude, therefore, that while the claim as issued is limited to the crystalline form of cefadroxil exhibiting the specified x-ray diffraction pattern, it is not limited to the compound in its pre-ingested form with the manufacturing characteristics which Bristol emphasized during prosecution.

We turn next to the question of whether Bouzard monohydrate is actually found in the stomach of patients who ingest cefadroxil DC. One answer is that no one knows—the scientific fact appears to be that there is no known way to actually sample the contents of patients' stomachs at the precise moment and conduct the x-ray diffraction analyses required to ascertain if all 37 lines described in the patent are present. For its proof Bristol offered instead the testimony of its principal scientific witness, Dr. Harry Brittain, who described various studies and experiments simulating the environment of the human stomach which were conducted under his auspices; Zenith countered with the testimony of its principal scientific witness, Dr. Martha Greenblatt. The trial judge, after hearing all the evidence, concluded that the Bouzard monohydrate in fact does inevitably form in the patient's stomach after ingestion of cefadroxil DC. * * *

In order to establish its case, Bristol had to show that the accused compound infringed the claim contained in the patent. This required Bristol to show that the diffraction pattern of cefadroxil DC following its conversion *in vivo* displayed the same diffraction pattern as that of the claimed compound. The district court, instead of requiring the comparison of the accused compound following conversion to be made with the lines specified in the claim, allowed Bristol to make the comparison with the diffraction pattern exhibited by a sample (the reference pattern) of a material considered by Bristol to be the patented compound.

As we have repeatedly said, it is error for a court to compare in its infringement analysis the accused product or process with the patentee's commercial embodiment or other version of the product or process; the only proper comparison is with the claims of the patent. The difficulty was compounded. The x-ray diffraction pattern exhibited by Bristol's sample (the reference pattern) consisted of a table of only 30 lines of relative intensities. Of this total, the court only compared 22 lines to corresponding lines recited in the claim. Based on its comparison, the court concluded the two were sufficiently similar to permit Bristol to use the reference pattern in its infringement analysis. In fact, the number of lines recited in the claim is 37. Thus, 15 of the lines recited in the claim (representing about 40% of the total) were not considered by the court in its comparison. Although the term "essentially" recited in the claim permits some leeway in the exactness of the comparison with the specified 37 lines of the claim, it does not permit ignoring a substantial number of lines altogether. It is the claim that sets the metes and bounds of the invention entitled to the protection of the patent system.

On the basis of this evidence the trial court concluded that when cefadroxil DC is ingested Bouzard monohydrate is created in a patient's stomach, that that constitutes an infringing use, and that therefore the sale of cefadroxil DC by Zenith would constitute inducement of infringement under 35 U.S.C. § 271(b). Since the finding of infringement was based on testimony which incorporated an improper comparison, and since that comparison was an essential element in the conclusion that infringement occurred, the conclusion that Zenith by selling cefadroxil DC would engage in inducement of infringement is insupportable. Zenith is correct that there was a failure of proof as to whether any crystals, assumed to form in the stomach from ingested cefadroxil DC, literally infringe the '657 claim. In the absence of evidence comparing the '657 claim with the cefadroxil DC after ingestion Bristol has failed to establish any infringing use and therefore we must reverse the district court's conclusion that Zenith's sale of cefadroxil DC induces infringement of the '657 patent. * * *

To prove infringement under the doctrine of equivalents, Bristol bore the burden of showing that cefadroxil DC was the equivalent of Bouzard monohydrate. A necessary part of the function/way/result equivalency analysis is the *function* of the substituted element as seen in the context of the patent, the prosecution history, and the prior art.

In view of Bristol's numerous statements in the prosecution history regarding the superior manufacturing-related benefits of the Bouzard crystal in relation to the prior forms of cefadroxil, it is clear that the primary, if not the only, function of the Bouzard crystal form of the drug as compared to other forms is to facilitate pre-ingestion manufacturing. No other intended function is described or suggested. Since any unanticipated production of the Bouzard crystal in the patient's stomach as a result of ingesting cefadroxil DC does not even remotely perform that function, the "function" part of the function/way/result test of equivalency is not met. As a matter of law, there can be no infringement under the doctrine of equivalents.

Bristol cites a number of cases to demonstrate that the doctrine of equivalents has been applied to find infringement in situations involving *in situ* or *in vivo* conversions. However, these cases do not support Bristol's argument. In [several cases], * * * the substituted compound or ingredient converted *in vivo* or *in situ* to the compound or ingredient called for by the claim, and performed the same function as that of the claim. The infringer was thus using the equivalent element to perform the same function as the claimed compound, a typical case for doctrine of equivalents application.

Even assuming that cefadroxil DC converts *in vivo* to Bouzard monohydrate in measurable amounts, that particular crystalline form does not perform the function of facilitating encapsulation. On the record before us, the trial court was correct in his judgment that Bristol had failed to establish infringement under the doctrine of equivalents. * * *

NOTES AND QUESTIONS

1. *Forms of infringement.* For a similar decision rejecting an infringement claim based on *in vivo* conversion, see Marion Merrell Dow Inc. v. Baker Norton Pharm., Inc., 948 F.Supp. 1050, 1053–57 (S.D.Fla.1996) (terfenadine acid metabolite), dismissed mem., 152 F.3d 941 (Fed.Cir.1998); see also Eitan A. Ogen, Note, Assembling a Theory of Infringement: Third Party Liability Based on In Vivo Production of Patented Pharmaceuticals, 17 Cardozo L. Rev. 117 (1995). A patent holder has a claim against a party that induces another party to infringe. See R2 Med. Sys., Inc. v. Katecho, Inc., 931 F.Supp. 1397, 1442–46 (N.D.Ill.1996) (cardiac monitoring and resuscitation device). For other decisions rejecting infringement claims involving medical technologies, see Young Dental Mfg. Co. v. Q3 Special Prods., Inc., 112 F.3d 1137 (Fed.Cir.1997) (disposable dental prophy angle); California Med. Prods., Inc. v. Tecnol Med. Prods., Inc., 921 F.Supp. 1219 (D.Del.1995) (cervical collar).

2. *Remedies for infringement.* The holder of a patent may seek an injunction and/or damages for lost profits. In a recent pair of jury verdicts, Johnson & Johnson's medical device subsidiary Cordis was awarded almost $600 million in damages from two competitors who allegedly infringed its patent on a stent used to open coronary arteries. See Margaret Cronin Fisk, Patent Victories Reflect 2000 Trend, Nat'l L.J., Feb. 19, 2001, at A1; see also Thomas M. Burton, Jury Says St. Jude Medical Violated Guidant Heart–Defibrillator Patent, Wall St. J., July 5, 2001, at B2 (reporting on a verdict of $140 million). In cases of willful infringement, the plaintiff may recover double damages. See Stryker Corp. v. Intermedics Orthopedics, Inc., 96 F.3d 1409 (Fed.Cir.1996) (affirming the trial judge's finding of willful infringement of a patent for a modular hip implant and an award of double lost profits, and attorneys fees, totaling more than $72 million); Minnesota Mining & Mfg. Co. v. Johnson & Johnson Orthopaedics, Inc., 976 F.2d 1559 (Fed.Cir.1992) (affirming the trial judge's finding of willful infringement of patents for resin-based casting tapes and an award of double lost profits totaling more than $110 million).

2.   Method-of-Use Patents

Eli Lilly & Co. v. Barr Laboratories, Inc.

222 F.3d 973 (Fed.Cir.2000), modified, 251 F.3d 955 (Fed.Cir.2001).

■ Gajarsa, Circuit Judge:

* * * On January 10, 1974, Lilly filed application Serial No. 432,379 ("the '379 application") containing claims for a class of compounds, therapeutic methods of using those compounds, and pharmaceutical compositions comprising those compounds. The '379 application named Bryan B. Molloy and Klaus K. Schmiegel as inventors. After its filing, the '379 application engendered a progeny of divisional applications, continuation applications, and patents that rivals the Hapsburg legacy. When the last patent stemming from the '379 application issued in December 1986, the application had spawned four divisional applications, three continuation applications, and six patents. During that twelve-year period, Lilly obtained six patents relating to fluoxetine hydrochloride [the active ingredient in Prozac®]—the '081 and '549 patents, as well as U.S. Patent Nos. 4,018,895 ("the '895 patent"), 4,194,009 ("the '009 patent"), 4,590,213 ("the '213 patent"), and 4,329,356 ("the '356 patent"). The '213 and '356 patents did not stem from the '379 application, and during the course of this litigation, Lilly disclaimed those patents.

The '009 patent, which expired in April 1994, claimed a class of pharmaceutical compounds, including fluoxetine hydrochloride, for administration in psychotropically effective amounts. The '895, '213, and '356 patents related to methods for treating particular ailments by administering a pharmaceutical compound within a class of compounds that includes fluoxetine hydrochloride. Specifically, the '895 patent, which expired in April 1994, concerned the treatment of humans suffering from depression; the '213 patent concerned the treatment of humans suffering from anxiety; and the '356 patent concerned the treatment of animals suffering from hypertension. * * * On March 31, 1986, Lilly filed continuation application Serial No. 846,448, claiming the benefit of the 1974 filing date of the '379 application under 35 U.S.C. § 120. On December 2, 1986, the application matured into the '549 patent. Claim 7 of the '549 patent, which depends on claim 4, relates to blocking the uptake of the monoamine serotonin in an animal's brain neurons through administration of the compound N-methyl–3-(p-trifluoromethylphenoxy)-3-phenylpropylamine   hydrochloride—commonly referred to as fluoxetine hydrochloride. * * *

Under the patent statutes, a patent enjoys a presumption of validity, which can be overcome only through clear and convincing evidence. See

United States Surgical Corp. v. Ethicon, Inc., 103 F.3d 1554, 1563 (Fed.Cir. 1997). Thus, a moving party seeking to invalidate a patent at summary judgment must submit such clear and convincing evidence of invalidity so that no reasonable jury could find otherwise. Alternatively, a moving party seeking to have a patent held not invalid at summary judgment must show that the nonmoving party, who bears the burden of proof at trial, failed to produce clear and convincing evidence on an essential element of a defense upon which a reasonable jury could invalidate the patent. * * *

Through a statutorily prescribed term, Congress limits the duration of a patentee's right to exclude others from practicing a claimed invention. The judicially-created doctrine of obviousness-type double patenting cements that legislative limitation by prohibiting a party from obtaining an extension of exclusive rights through claims in a later patent that are not patentably distinct from claims in an earlier patent. * * * Obviousness-type double patenting entails a two-step analysis. First, as a matter of law, the court construes the claim in the earlier patent and the claim in the later patent, and it overlays the later claim on the earlier claim to determine whether the later claim encompasses subject matter previously claimed. Second, the court determines whether the differences in subject matter between the two claims is such that the claims are patentably distinct. * * *

We begin by construing claim 1 of the '895 patent and claim 7 of the '549 patent to determine whether the former covers subject matter subsequently claimed in the latter. Claim 1 of the '895 patent pertains to a method of treating depression in humans by administering a compound within the class of compounds * * * * Claim 7 of the '549 patent claims a method for administering the compound fluoxetine hydrochloride to inhibit serotonin uptake. Claim 7 depends on claim 4, which claims a method of blocking the uptake of monoamines by administering a compound found within the same class of compounds that is defined by claim 1 of the '895 patent. Thus, fluoxetine hydrochloride covered in claim 7 of the '549 patent is also one of the compounds encompassed by claim 1 of the '895 patent. It necessarily follows that claim 1 of the '895 patent covered the administration of fluoxetine hydrochloride to treat depression.

Lilly argues that selecting fluoxetine hydrochloride from the class of compounds in claim 1 of the '895 patent to treat depression would not have been obvious to one of ordinary skill in the art because that claim covers thousands of possible compounds. That argument, however, is of no consequence because double patenting is not "concerned with what one skilled in the art would be aware [of] from reading the claims but with what inventions the claims define." Here, claim 1 of the '895 patent, when properly construed, already covered the administration of fluoxetine hydrochloride for treating depression. * * *

Moreover, we find Lilly's argument to be disingenuous because it seeks to use the broad coverage of claim 1 of the '895 patent as both a sword and a shield. Throughout the term of the '895 patent, by virtue of claim 1's broad coverage, Lilly possessed the right to exclude other parties from administering any of the thousands of claimed compounds, including but not limited to fluoxetine hydrochloride, to treat depression. Thus, for example, if another party attempted to use fluoxetine hydrochloride to treat depression, Lilly could have sued for infringement of the '895 patent or asserted its patent as a dominating patent. As a corollary to that expansive right of exclusivity, the '895 patent specification satisfied the written description requirement by allowing persons of ordinary skill in the art "to recognize that the [inventor] invented what is claimed," and the enablement requirement by providing a specification that taught one of ordinary skill in the art "how to make and use the invention as broadly as it is claimed." With the '895 patent now expired, Lilly cannot hide behind its once-advantageous broad coverage, disavow its prior compliance with the written description and best mode requirements, and argue that selecting fluoxetine hydrochloride from the class of compounds defined by claim 1 of the '895 patent would not have been obvious.

Having construed claim 1 of the '895 patent and claim 7 of the '549 patent and concluded that the use of fluoxetine hydrochloride is covered by the earlier claim, we must next determine whether there are any differences between the two claims that are patentably distinct. The only discernible difference between claim 1 of the '895 patent and claim 7 of the '549 patent is that the former addresses the treatment of depression in humans while the latter addresses the treatment of serotonin uptake in animals. Humans are a species of the animal genus, and depression is a species ailment of the genus of ailments caused by defective serotonin uptake. Our case law firmly establishes that a later genus claim is not patentable over an earlier species claim. Accordingly, we hold that the differences between claim 1 of the '895 patent and claim 7 of the '549 patent are not patentably distinct.

Furthermore, the circumstances giving rise to the present case support our conclusion that claim 7 is invalid for obviousness-type double patenting. This case arose when Barr filed an ANDA application seeking FDA approval for marketing fluoxetine hydrochloride as an antidepressant, and Lilly responded by suing for infringement of, inter alia, claim 7 of the '549 patent. Under the '895 patent, which issued in 1977 and expired in 1994, Lilly possessed the right to exclude others from administering any compound, including fluoxetine hydrochloride, within the class of claimed compounds to treat depression. In effect, under the '895 patent, Lilly had the right to exclude others from engaging in the very conduct for which Barr currently seeks FDA approval. Now, by asserting claim 7 of the '549 patent, Lilly attempts to extend the term of exclusivity it enjoyed under the '895 patent for an additional nine years beyond the statutorily prescribed term. * * *

NOTES AND QUESTIONS

1. *Maximizing patent protection.* Lilly's strategy of seeking "second generation" patents (a.k.a. patent stacking) is not uncommon or inevitably unsuccessful. See Melody Petersen, Lilly Set Back in Prozac Patent Case, N.Y. Times, Aug. 10, 2000, at C1 ("Efforts to extend the monopoly on a popular brand-name drug are common in the pharmaceutical industry. . . . [O]ften companies file numerous patent applications on different aspects of the same drug—different uses of the drug, for example, or slightly different formulations—to try to get even more years of exclusive sales."). Method-of-use patents, which identify a previously undisclosed utility, offer one mechanism for doing so. See Fonar Corp. v. General Elec. Co., 107 F.3d 1543, 1550–51 (Fed.Cir.1997) (affirming judgment for holder of patent for the use of MRI scanners in multi-angle oblique imaging); C.R. Bard, Inc. v. Advanced Cardiovascular Sys., Inc., 911 F.2d 670, 673–75 (Fed.Cir.1990) (reviewing a claim by a catheter manufacturer that had patented a method for using catheters in coronary angioplasty alleging that a different manu-facturer of such devices had induced infringement by purchasers).

2. *Conditional sales.* Although the sale and purchase of replacement of parts for a patented medical device generally would not amount to acts of infringement, see Kendall Co. v. Progressive Med. Technology, Inc., 85 F.3d 1570, 1573–76 (Fed.Cir.1996), the reuse of a patented medical device sold for "single use only" may do so, see Mallinckrodt, Inc. v. Medipart, Inc., 976 F.2d 700, 708–09 (Fed.Cir.1992) (allowing the patent holder to bring an infringement claim to enforce such a restriction even if it had an anti-competitive effect); see also B. Braun Med., Inc. v. Abbott Labs., 124 F.3d 1419, 1426–27 (Fed.Cir.1997) (applying the same analysis to a usage restriction imposed by the holder of a patent for an IV tip that reduced the risk of accidental needle sticks when selling it as a component for a kit distributed by another company). One commentator has suggested that the practice of splitting higher-dose pills for sale to patients prescribed lower doses similarly may infringe a seller's method-of-use patent. See Nicolas G. Barzoukas, Pill Splitting Raises Issues of Safety and Patent Coverage, Nat'l L.J., May 22, 2000, at B9.

3.   PROCESS PATENTS

Eli Lilly & Co. v. American Cyanamid Co.
82 F.3d 1568 (Fed.Cir.1996).

■ BRYSON, CIRCUIT JUDGE:

The ongoing struggle between "pioneer" drug manufacturers and generic drug distributors has once more come before our court. Eli Lilly and Company, the "pioneer" drug manufacturer in this case, has filed suit for patent infringement against the appellees, who are involved in various ways in the distribution of a particular generic drug. Lilly sought a preliminary injunction, arguing that the importation and sale of the generic drug in this country infringed Lilly's patent on a process for making a related compound. * * *

The pharmaceutical product at issue in this case is a broad-spectrum antibiotic known as "cefaclor." Cefaclor is a member of the class of cephalosporin antibiotics, all of which are based on the cephem nucleus. Although there are many different cephem compounds, only a few have utility as antibiotic drugs. Each of the known commercial methods for producing cefaclor requires the production of an intermediate cephem compound known as an enol. Once the desired enol cephem intermediate is obtained, it is then subjected to several processing steps in order to produce cefaclor.

Lilly developed cefaclor and patented it in 1975. Until recently, Lilly has been the exclusive manufacturer and distributor of cefaclor in this country. In addition to its product patent on cefaclor, Lilly obtained several patents covering different aspects of the manufacture of cefaclor, including processes for producing enol cephem intermediates. Many of those patents have now expired.

In 1995, Lilly purchased the patent at issue in this case, U.S. Patent No. 4,160,085 (the '085 patent). Claim 5 of that patent defines a method of producing enol cephem compounds, including what is called "compound 6," an enol cephem similar to the one Lilly uses in its process for manufacturing cefaclor. The '085 patent will expire on July 3, 1996.

Compound 6 differs from cefaclor in three respects. Although both compound 6 and cefaclor are based on the cephem nucleus, compound 6 has a hydroxy group at the 3-position on the cephem nucleus, a para-nitrobenzyl carboxylate ester at the 4-position, and a phenylacetyl group at the 7-position. Cefaclor has different groups at each of those positions: it has a chlorine atom at the 3-position, a free carboxyl group at the 4-position, and a phenylglycyl group at the 7-position. Each of those differences between compound 6 and cefaclor contributes to the effectiveness of cefaclor as an orally administered antibiotic drug. The free carboxyl group at the 4-position is believed important for antibacterial activity; the chlorine increases cefaclor's antibiotic potency; and the phenylglycyl group enables cefaclor to be effective when taken orally.

To produce cefaclor from compound 6 requires four distinct steps. First, the hydroxy group is removed from the 3-position and is replaced by a chlorine atom, which results in the creation of "compound 7." Second, compound 7 is subjected to a reaction that removes the phenylacetyl group at the 7-position, which results in the creation of "compound 8." Third, a phenylglycyl group is added at the 7-position, which results in the creation of "compound 9." Fourth, the para-nitrobenzyl carboxylate ester is removed from the 4-position, which results in the creation of cefaclor.

On April 27, 1995, defendants Zenith Laboratories, Inc., and American Cyanamid Company obtained permission from the Food and Drug Administration to distribute cefaclor in this country. Defendant Biocraft Laboratories, Inc., had applied for FDA approval to manufacture and sell cefaclor in the United States but had not yet obtained that approval. All three have obtained large quantities of cefaclor that were manufactured in Italy by defendant Biochimica Opos, S.p.A.

On the same day that Zenith and Cyanamid obtained FDA approval to sell cefaclor in this country, Lilly obtained the rights to the '085 patent and filed suit against Zenith, Cyanamid, Biocraft, and Opos. In its complaint, Lilly sought a declaration that the domestic defendants' importation of cefaclor manufactured by Opos infringed Lilly's rights under several patents, including the '085 patent. Lilly also requested a preliminary injunction, based on the alleged infringement of claim 5 of the '085 patent, to bar the defendants from importing or inducing the importation of cefaclor manufactured by Opos. * * *

The Process Patent Amendments Act of 1988 was enacted to close a perceived loophole in the statutory scheme for protecting owners of United States patents. Prior to the enactment of the 1988 statute, a patentee holding a process patent could sue for infringement if others used the process in this country, but had no cause of action if such persons used the patented process abroad to manufacture products, and then imported, used, or sold the products in this country. * * * Congress changed the law by making it an act of infringement to import into the United States, or to sell or use within the United States "a product which is made by a process patented in the United States ... if the importation, sale, or use of the product occurs during the term of such process patent."

A concern raised during Congress's consideration of the process patent legislation was whether and to what extent the new legislation would affect products other than the direct and unaltered products of patented processes—that is, whether the new statute would apply when a product was produced abroad by a patented process but then modified or incorporated into other products before being imported into this country. Congress addressed that issue by providing that a product that is "made by" a patented process within the meaning of the statute "will ... not be considered to be so made after—(1) it is materially changed by subsequent processes; or (2) it becomes a trivial and nonessential component of another product." 35 U.S.C. § 271(g).

That language, unfortunately, is not very precise. Whether the product of a patented process is a "trivial and nonessential component" of another product is necessarily a question of degree. Even less well defined is the question whether the product of a patented process has been "materially changed" before its importation into this country. While applying that statutory language may be relatively easy in extreme cases, it is not at all easy in a closer case such as this one. * * * [T]he language of the statute refers to changes in the product; the statute permits the importation of an item that is derived from a product made by a patented process as long as that product is "materially changed" in the course of its conversion into the imported item. The reference to a "changed" product is very hard to square with Lilly's proposed test, which turns on the quite different question of whether the use or sale of the imported item impairs the economic value of the process patent. * * *

In the chemical context, a "material" change in a compound is most naturally viewed as a significant change in the compound's structure and properties. Without attempting to define with precision what classes of changes would be material and what would not, we share the district court's view that a change in chemical structure and properties as significant as the change between compound 6 and cefaclor cannot lightly be dismissed as immaterial. Although compound 6 and cefaclor share the basic cephem nucleus, which is the ultimate source of the antibiotic potential of all cephalosporins, the cephem nucleus is common to thousands of compounds, many of which have antibiotic activity, and many of which are dramatically different from others within the cephem family. Beyond the cephem nucleus that they have in common, compound 6 and cefaclor are different in four important structural respects, corresponding to the four discrete chemical steps between the two compounds. While the addition or removal of a protective group, standing alone, might not be sufficient to constitute a "material change" between two compounds (even though it could dramatically affect certain of their properties), the conversion process between compound 6 and cefaclor involves considerably more than the removal of a protective group. * * *

Acknowledging that the task of determining whether a product was "materially changed" prior to its importation would ultimately be left to the courts, the Committee then set out a "two-phased test" to "give the courts congressional guidance in what may be a difficult determination." The first part of the test restated the test set forth in the House report, i.e., that a product "will be considered made by the patented process ... if it would not be possible or commercially viable to make that product but for the use of the patented process." The Senate report provided an analysis of how the first part of the test should be applied in the case of chemical intermediates. The report explained:

> If the only way to have arrived at Y is to have used the patented process at some step, e.g., producing X as an intermediate, Y is infringing. If there is more than one way to have arrived [at] Y, but the patented process is the only commercially viable way to have done so, Y is infringing. If there are commercially viable non-infringing processes to have arrived at X, the connection between the patented process for producing chemical X and the ultimate product, chemical Y, is broken, and Y would be a non-infringing product having satisfied both phases of the test.

As we noted above, the record makes clear that there is at least one commercially viable process for making cefaclor that does not involve the patented method of synthesizing enol cephems (including compound 6). Opos does not use that non-infringing process, but under the test set forth in the Senate report, it is enough to defeat the claim of infringement that there is another way of producing the intermediate, even if the alleged infringer does not use that alternative process.

The Senate Committee described the second portion of the two-part test for identifying a "material change" as follows:

> A product will be considered to have been made by a patented process if the additional processing steps which are not covered by the patent

do not change the physical or chemical properties of the product in a manner which changes the basic utility of the product [produced] by the patented process. However, a change in the physical or chemical properties of a product, even though minor, may be "material" if the change relates to a physical or chemical property which is an important feature of the product produced by the patented process. Usually a change in the physical form of a product (e.g., granules to powder, solid to liquid) or minor chemical conversion (e.g., conversion to a salt, base, acid, hydrate, ester, or addition or removal of a protecti[ve] group) would not be a "material" change.

It seems fairly clear that under this second part of the test, the change from compound 6 to cefaclor would be regarded as a material change. The chemical properties of the two compounds are completely different, the "basic utility" of the products is different, and the chemical structure of the two products is significantly different. The changes between compound 6 and cefaclor go far beyond the minor changes that the report described as not material, such as the conversion to a salt, base, acid, hydrate or ester, or the removal of a protective group. * * *

Lilly also challenges the district court's conclusion that it failed to show that it would suffer irreparable harm if the district court did not grant a preliminary injunction in this case. We conclude that the court did not commit clear error in finding that Lilly failed to prove irreparable harm; the court therefore acted within its discretion in denying Lilly's request for preliminary relief. Because Lilly has not made a strong showing on the issue of infringement, it is not entitled to a presumption of irreparable harm. Nor did the district court commit clear error in rejecting Lilly's arguments that, apart from the presumption, it would suffer irreparable harm in the absence of a preliminary injunction. In particular, the district court found that, under the specific circumstances of this case, "an award of money damages would be an adequate remedy in the event that Lilly ultimately establishes" infringement. In light of the structure of the cefaclor market, the court found that calculating lost profits would be a relatively simple task. The court also found that the two distributors who have been authorized by the FDA to sell cefaclor in this country have adequate assets to satisfy any judgment likely to be awarded if Lilly were to prevail on the merits of its infringement claim.

Lilly contends that the loss of profits on sales of cefaclor because of competition from the appellees will result in irreparable injury to Lilly's overall pharmaceutical research efforts. As the district court pointed out, however, that claim of injury is not materially different from any claim of injury by a business that is deprived of funds that it could usefully reinvest. If a claim of lost opportunity to conduct research were sufficient to compel a finding of irreparable harm, it is hard to imagine any manufacturer with a research and development program that could not make the same claim and thus be equally entitled to preliminary injunctive relief. Such a rule would convert the "extraordinary" relief of a preliminary injunction into a standard remedy, available whenever the plaintiff has shown a likelihood of success on the merits. * * *

■ RADER, CIRCUIT JUDGE (concurring):

* * * The court's majority places great emphasis on the legislative history to resolve the meaning of "material change"—a curious approach given its recognition that the legislative history contains "something . . . for each side." The enactment history is far from dispositive in this case. The record of the enactment of this provision evinces a bitter battle between the pharmaceutical industry and its generic industry competitors. In the first place, neither combatant could convince either house of Congress to enact a statutory standard clearly favorable to their segment of the industry. * * * Without a clear resolution in the statutory language, the battleground shifted to the committee reports. On this front, each combatant could find lobbyists to lace the reports with tutorials to the courts about applying the ambiguous provisions of section 271(g) in future litigation.

With a focus on future litigation, these committee reports became particularly unenlightening as an aid to interpret statutory language. These reports surrendered any pretext of informing members of Congress about the meaning of pending bills before a vote on the floor. Instead, these tutorials, by their own admission, addressed judicial officers, not legislative officers. * * * [T]he directly conflicting and confusing tests set forth in the section analysis leave little doubt that they were inserted by lobbyists for use in future litigation by their clients. In sum, the enactment history maps all the graves on this inconclusive legislative battleground, but shows no route away from the combat zone. * * *

Sadly this decision will create another massive loophole in the protection of patented processes. This decision will, in effect, deny protection to holders of process patents on intermediates as opposed to "final" products. This decision denies protection to a patented process anytime it is not the only way to make an intermediate, even if it is the most economically efficient way to produce the intermediate. In view of the purpose of the statute, compound 6 and cefaclor are essentially the same product. Compound 6 has no commercial use in the U.S. market except to make cefaclor. The patented process is thus in use to make compound 6—a product only four simple, well-known steps from cefaclor. The record shows no other current commercial use of compound 6.

Rather than attempting to distill an elixir from this intoxicating witches brew of enactment history, this court should interpret "material change" consistent with the overriding purpose of the Act—to provide protection to process patent holders. With its eye firmly fixed on the purpose of the Act, this court would avoid eliminating processes for intermediates from the protections of the 1988 Act.

Bio-Technology General Corp. v. Genentech, Inc.

80 F.3d 1553 (Fed.Cir.1996).

■ LOURIE, CIRCUIT JUDGE:

* * * Human growth hormone (hGH) is a 191–amino acid polypeptide hormone secreted by the anterior pituitary gland. It has important meta-

bolic effects, including stimulation of protein synthesis and cellular uptake of amino acids. Genentech is the assignee of two patents relating to hGH that are at issue in this lawsuit. The first patent, U.S. Patent 4,601,980, is directed to a recombinant DNA method for producing a 191– or 192–amino acid human growth hormone product that is identical, or essentially identical, and functionally equivalent to the natural hormone. The product is useful in treating hypopituitary dwarfism in children.

Prior to the '980 invention, hGH could be obtained for therapeutic use only by extracting it from the pituitary glands of human cadavers. Known recombinant DNA methods for producing hGH were deficient; they yielded not only the amino acid sequence of the protein, but also a "leader sequence" of additional amino acids at the beginning of the protein. In the natural synthesis of hGH, the leader sequence enables the protein to emerge from a pituitary cell after expression; the leader is then enzymatically removed. When the product is recombinantly expressed in a bacterial host, however, the leader is not removed and it renders the resulting product biologically inactive.

The invention claimed in the '980 patent solved this problem by providing a method for directly expressing a human growth hormone expression product without a leader sequence. The inventors started with complementary DNA (cDNA) encoding hGH and its leader sequence, and cleaved the cDNA encoding the leader sequence along with a portion of the codons encoding hGH to obtain a cDNA fragment containing hGH codons 24–191. Next, they synthesized a DNA fragment corresponding to the 23 missing codons plus a "start" codon, and fused that DNA fragment to the cDNA fragment. They inserted the resulting semi-synthetic gene into bacterial cells, which directly expressed a 192–amino acid product, met-hGH, consisting of the hGH molecule and one additional amino acid, methionine ("met"), coded for by the start codon. Met-hGH has essentially the same biological activity as the natural hormone, hGH. The '980 patent teaches that the amino acid, methionine, may be cleaved intracellularly in the bacterial host to produce a product that is identical to the natural hormone. Genentech sells met-hGH and hGH under the trademarks Protropin® and Humatrope®, respectively.

The second patent in suit, U.S. Patent 4,342,832, also assigned to Genentech, contains essentially the same disclosure as the '980 patent. The '832 patent claims, however, are directed to a method for constructing a replicable cloning vehicle (e.g., a plasmid) capable, in a microbial organism, of expressing a particular polypeptide (e.g., human growth hormone).

Like Genentech, BTG [Bio–Technology General] manufactures hGH by recombinant DNA techniques using a plasmid that contains a semi-synthetic gene engineered to express hGH without a leader sequence. BTG incorporates the plasmid into bacteria, which then express insoluble met-hGH in the form of biologically-inactive inclusion bodies. In a final step, BTG carries out a purification process that involves recovering soluble met-hGH free of inclusion bodies and cleaving the extra methionine residue to produce the final product, biologically-active hGH. BTG manufactures hGH in Israel, and it plans to import the product for sale in the United States under the trademark Bio–Tropin®.

BTG filed an Investigational New Drug Application (IND) for hGH with the Food and Drug Administration (FDA) in 1985. * * * The FDA approved the NDA in May 1995.

In January 1995, BTG sued Genentech in district court, seeking a declaratory judgment that the '980 and '832 patents are invalid, unenforceable, and not infringed by BTG. Genentech counterclaimed for infringement and moved for a preliminary injunction, arguing that BTG's importation of hGH into the United States would infringe the '980 and '832 patents. After a hearing, the district court found that Genentech had established a reasonable likelihood of success on the merits of its counterclaim * * * *

Claim 2 of the '980 patent reads as follows:

2. A method for producing human growth hormone which method comprises [1] culturing bacterial transformants containing recombinant plasmids which will, in a transformant bacterium, express a gene for human growth hormone unaccompanied by the leader sequence of human growth hormone or other extraneous protein bound thereto, and [2] isolating and purifying said expressed human growth hormone. * * *

Claim 2 uses broad, generic language to define the steps of isolating and purifying the recombinantly produced hGH product. Nothing in the claim language, specification, or prosecution history suggests that the claim is limited to any particular technique for isolating and purifying the product. Further, BTG's process meets these claim limitations. In its NDA, for example, BTG characterized its recovery of soluble, biologically-active hGH from insoluble, biologically-inactive met-hGH in the form of inclusion bodies as a "purification" step. Similarly, at the preliminary injunction hearing there was expert testimony that these processes constitute a "purification" step within the meaning of claim 2. Thus, BTG's process clearly involves "isolating and purifying [the] expressed human growth hormone," as generically defined in claim 2. * * *

The more difficult question is whether hGH is "a product which is made by a process patented in the United States," even though claim 1 of the '832 patent is directed to a method for producing a replicable cloning vehicle (e.g., a plasmid), not hGH. * * * The legislative history precisely anticipated this fact situation and indicated Congress's intent that infringement of a process for making a plasmid is not to be avoided by using it to express its intended protein. Moreover, the '832 patent itself explicitly contemplates that the patented process will be used as part of an overall process for producing hGH; indeed, the patent discloses in detail how to make hGH by carrying out the claimed process and other necessary steps. Thus, it cannot be said as a matter of law that the production of hGH is too remote from the claimed process of making a replicable cloning vehicle. We therefore find no error in the court's conclusion that hGH is a product that is "made by" the '832 patented process. * * *

BTG next argues that the district court's finding of irreparable harm is clearly erroneous. We disagree. The court correctly held that Genentech was entitled to a presumption of irreparable harm because Genentech made a strong showing of infringement and validity, and BTG's asserted defenses lacked substantial merit. BTG did not come forward with persuasive evidence to rebut the presumption of irreparable harm. In addition, the district court determined that Genentech would be harmed if BTG were allowed to enter the market because Genentech would lose revenues and goodwill, and would be required to reduce its research and development activities. BTG has not demonstrated that these findings are clearly erroneous. * * *

NOTES AND QUESTIONS

1. *Compulsory licensing.* Several industrialized countries have limited compulsory licensing rules applicable to medical technologies either where necessary to combat a threat to public health or after a period of non-use by the patent holder. See Reed Boland, RU 486 in France and England: Corporate Ethics and Compulsory Licensing, 20 Law Med. & Health Care 226, 230 (1992); cf. Richard F. Kingham & Grant H. Castle, Data and Marketing Exclusivity for Pharmaceuticals in the European Community, 55 Food & Drug L.J. 209 (2000). Until 1993, Canada used a compulsory licensing system as a mechanism to control the pricing of pharmaceuticals. See Act of June 27, 1969, R.S.C., ch. 49, 7–18 (Can.). Initially, Canadian companies were permitted to market generic copies of drugs still under patent upon payment of minimal royalties to the patent holder. See Novopharm Ltd. v. Janssen Pharm. N.V., 41 C.P.R.3d 194 (Can.1992) (refusing to require more than a 4% royalty). After 1987, Canada limited such compulsory licensing by granting market exclusivity to the foreign patent holder for only the first seven years of the patent term. See Patent Act, R.S.C., ch. P–4, § 39 (1985) (Can.), as amended at S.C. 1987, ch. 41, & S.C. 1993, ch. 2; see also Manitoba Society of Seniors, Inc. v. Canada, 35 C.P.R.3d 66 (Man.Q.B.1991) (rejecting constitutional challenge to the 1987 modification of the compulsory licensing system), aff'd, 45 C.P.R.3d 194 (Man.C.A.1992). In 1993, Canada enacted legislation to eliminate this form of compulsory licensing. See An Act to Amend the Patent Act, 1993 S.C., ch. 2, § 3 (Can.); see also Sheldon Burshtein, Sublicense or Supply Agreement? Supreme Court of Canada Interpretation Benefits Generic Pharmaceutical Industry, 54 Food & Drug L.J. 73 (1999); Philip C. Mendes da Costa, NAFTA–The Canadian Response or Why Does the Canadian Patent Act Keep Changing?, 22 AIPLA Q.J. 65 (1994); Edward Hore, A Comparison of United States and Canadian Laws as They Affect Generic Pharmaceutical Market Entry, 55 Food & Drug L.J. 373 (2000); Christopher Scott Harrison, Comment, Protection of Pharmaceuticals as Foreign Policy: The Canada–U.S. Trade Agreement and Bill C–22 Versus the North American

Free Trade Agreement and Bill C–91, 26 N.C. J. Int'l L. & Com. Reg. 457 (2001). Compulsory licensing remains an option for public health emergencies. See Shankar Vedantam & Terence Chea, Drug Firm Plays Defense in Anthrax Scare: For Now, U.S. Declines to Suspend Bayer's Patent and Authorize Generic Cipro, Wash. Post, Oct. 20, 2001, at A4 (reporting that Canada had invoked its compulsory licensing authority for this antibiotic).

2. *Technology transfer between industrialized and developing countries.* Historically, other countries, especially Third World nations, provided little or no intellectual property protection for pharmaceuticals. See Thomas G. Field, Jr., Pharmaceuticals and Intellectual Property: Meeting Needs Throughout the World, 31 IDEA 3 (1990); Gerald J. Mossinghoff, Research–Based Pharmaceutical Companies: The Need for Improved Patent Protection Worldwide, 2 J.L. & Tech. 307 (1987); F.M. Scherer, The Pharmaceutical Industry and World Intellectual Property Standards, 53 Vand. L. Rev. 2245 (2000); Theresa B. Lewis, Comment, Patent Protection for the Pharmaceutical Industry: A Survey of the Patent Laws of Various Countries, 30 Int'l Law. 835 (1996). Developing countries have sought to justify patent piracy, particularly in connection with medical technologies, as a human rights imperative. See James T. Gathii, Construing Intellectual Property Rights and Competition Policy Consistently with Facilitating Access to Affordable AIDS Drugs to Low–End Consumers, 53 Fla. L. Rev. 727 (2001); Bess–Carolina Dolmo, Note, Examining Global Access to Essential Pharmaceuticals in the Face of Patent Protection Rights: The South African Example, 7 Buff. Hum. Rts. L. Rev. 137 (2001). Conversely, these countries argue that industrialized nations have exploited the rich biological resources of the Third World in the search for new pharmaceuticals. See Michael J. Huft, Comment, Indigenous Peoples and Drug Discovery Research: A Question of Intellectual Property Rights, 89 Nw. U. L. Rev. 1678 (1995); Shayana Kadidal, Note, Plants, Poverty, and Pharmaceutical Patents, 103 Yale L.J. 223 (1993); Gelvina R. Stevenson, Note, Trade Secrets: The Secret to Protecting Indigenous Ethnobiological (Medicinal) Knowledge, 32 N.Y.U. J. Int'l L. & Pols. 1119 (2000).

3. *Free trade agreements.* Under the auspices of the World Trade Organization (WTO), which includes 140 nations as members and accounts for 90% of global trade, the Trade–Related Aspects of Intellectual Property Rights (TRIPS) Agreement seeks to harmonize patent laws around the world and insists that signatories grant at least 20 years of protection to novel and useful pharmaceutical products and processes. See TRIPS arts. 27.1 & 33. The implementation deadline has now passed for most signatories, and the least developed countries must comply by Jan. 1, 2006. For drugs patented after May 15, 1997, the WTO prohibits routine compulsory licensing, but, in case of a national emergency, a signatory may authorize compulsory licensing of patented pharmaceuticals if necessary to protect the public health. See id. art. 27.1 & 31; see also Shanker A. Singham, Competition Policy and the Stimulation of Innovation: TRIPS and the Interface Between Competition and Patent Protection in the Pharmaceutical Industry, 26 Brook. J. Int'l L. 363 (2000); Leslie G. Restaino & Katrine A. Levin, Accord May Provide Means to Stop Copycat Drugs, Nat'l L.J.,

May 14, 2001, at C6. TRIPS and other free trade agreements have spurred revisions in domestic patent laws. See Michelle S. Marks, The Impact of the Patent Term Provisions of the 1994 Uruguay Round Agreements Act on the Drug Price Competition and Patent Term Restoration Act, 51 Food & Drug L.J. 445 (1996); Christopher S. Mayer, Note, The Brazilian Pharmaceutical Industry Goes Walking from Ipanema to Prosperity: Will the New Intellectual Property Law Spur Domestic Investment?, 12 Temp. Int'l & Comp. L.J. 377 (1998); Wendy S. Vicente, Comment, A Questionable Victory for Coerced Argentine Pharmaceutical Patent Legislation, 19 U. Pa. J. Int'l Econ. L. 1101 (1998).

4. *Access to AIDS drugs.* The pharmaceutical industry caught significant flack for a lawsuit that it filed in South Africa to challenge that country's compulsory licensing law. Against the backdrop of the AIDS pandemic on that continent, the timing of the industry's effort to protect its intellectual property rights could not have been worse. See Helene Cooper et al., Patents Pending: AIDS Epidemic Traps Drug Firms in a Vise, Wall St. J., Mar. 2, 2001, at A1. Although a number of manufacturers previously offered to supply their AIDS drugs at deep (appx. 90%) discounts, these treatments remained largely unaffordable throughout Africa. See Paul Blustein & Barton Gellman, HIV Drug Prices Cut for Poorer Countries, Mar. 8, 2001, at A1; Karen DeYoung, AIDS Care for Africa Affordable, Study Says, Wash. Post, Apr. 5, 2001, at A16 (describing a proposal calling on industrialized nations to purchase the drugs for distribution to AIDS patients in poor countries). A generic drug company in India offered to sell versions of the drugs at less than half the deeply discounted prices. See Rachel L. Swarns, AIDS Drug Battle Deepens in Africa, N.Y. Times, Mar. 8, 2001, at A1. Under growing public pressure, the industry dropped its lawsuit. See Karen DeYoung, Makers of AIDS Drugs Drop S. Africa Suit, Wash. Post, Apr. 19, 2001, at A13; Rachel L. Swarns, Drug Makers Drop South Africa Suit over AIDS Medicine, N.Y. Times, Apr. 20, 2001, at A1. Some observers warned that the resolution of this dispute may actually harm the public health: if overseas generic manufacturers experience quality control problems, patients may receive contaminated or subpotent products, or they will have difficulty complying with the complex dosing regimen in countries that lack basic resources, all of which may accelerate drug-resistance problems (much as has happened in the treatment of tuberculosis when patients fail to complete their prescribed courses of antibiotic therapy). See Denise Grady, Generic Medicine for AIDS Raises New Set of Concerns, N.Y. Times, Apr. 24, 2001, at D1.

Responding to demands for access to affordable AIDS drugs throughout Africa, the U.S. government undertook special initiatives to supply such treatments. See Exec. Order No. 13,155, 65 Fed. Reg. 30,521 (2000) (asserting that the AIDS epidemic in Africa poses a threat to national security); Donald G. McNeil, Jr., Bush Keeps Clinton Policy on Poor Lands' Need for AIDS Drugs, N.Y. Times, Feb. 22, 2001, at A9 (reporting that the new office of the U.S. Trade Representative would continue the policy against seeking sanctions when Third World countries apply compulsory licensing laws in such cases). But cf. Barbara Crossette, Brazil's AIDS Chief

Denounces Bush Position on Drug Patents, N.Y. Times, May 3, 2001, at A5 (implying that the policy has changed); Barton Gellman, An Unequal Calculus of Life and Death, Wash. Post, Dec. 27, 2000, at A1 (characterizing these initiatives as empty gestures in practice). For general discussions of these issues, see Matthew Kramer, Comment, The Bolar Amendment Abroad: Preserving the Integrity of American Patents Overseas After the South African Medicines Act, 18 Dick. J. Int'l L. 553 (2000); Mary K. Schug, Note, Promoting Access to AIDS/AIDS Pharmaceuticals in Sub–Saharan Africa Within the Framework of International Intellectual Property Law, 19 Law & Ineq. 229 (2001).

On April 23, 2001, with only a single abstention, the United Nation's Commission on Human Rights adopted a resolution sponsored by Brazil asserting that access to affordable medicines qualifies as a human right. (Do the uninsured poor in the U.S. have any less of a claim to affordable AIDS drugs? What about treatments for other conditions?) The WTO now seems ready to allow for compulsory licensing of patented drugs for the treatment of a broad range of serious diseases. See Celia W. Dugger, A Catch–22 on Drugs for the World's Poor, N.Y. Times, Nov. 16, 2001, at W1; Geoff Winestock & Helene Cooper, Activists Outmaneuver Drug Makers at WTO, Wall St. J., Nov. 14, 2001, at A2.

5. *Patent buyouts.* Some commentators have suggested patent buyouts as a mechanism for controlling price and availability problems with critical pharmaceutical products. See Robert C. Guell & Marvin Fischbaum, Toward Allocative Efficiency in the Prescription Drug Industry, 73 Milbank Q. 213, 221–25 (1995); Michael Kremer, Patent Buyouts: A Mechanism for Encouraging Innovation, 113 Q.J. Econ. 1137, 1163–64 (1998); Evan Ackiron, Note, Patents for Critical Pharmaceuticals: The AZT Case, 17 Am. J.L. & Med. 145, 175–80 (1991). In rare instances, courts have condoned infringement by private parties where the patent holder withholds a license to use the invention in a way that would promote the public health. See Vitamin Technologists v. Wisconsin Alumni Res. Found., 146 F.2d 941 (9th Cir.1944) (process for using irradiation to fortify margarine with vitamin D).

4. Generic Drugs and Patent Extension

Bayer AG v. Elan Pharmaceutical Research Corp.
212 F.3d 1241 (Fed.Cir.2000).

■ Schall, Circuit Judge:

Bayer AG and Bayer Corporation own United States Patent No. 5,264,446. The '446 patent claims a pharmaceutical composition that contains nifedipine crystals of a defined specific surface area (SSA). The patent also claims the composition's method of preparation and a method of treatment using the composition. Bayer sued Elan Pharmaceutical Research Corporation and Elan Corporation, PLC in the United States District Court for the Northern District of Georgia alleging infringement by

Elan of the '446 patent * * * based on Elan's filing of an abbreviated new drug application (ANDA) seeking approval by the Food and Drug Administration (FDA) of a generic version of Bayer's Adalat CC, Bayer's commercial embodiment of the pharmaceutical composition claimed in the '446 patent. * * *

[T]he Hatch–Waxman Act amended the Federal Food, Drug, and Cosmetic Act as well as the patent laws. See Bristol–Myers Squibb Co. v. Royce Lab., Inc., 69 F.3d 1130, 1131–32 (Fed.Cir.1995); Dupont Merck Pharm. Co. v. Bristol–Myers Squibb Co., 62 F.3d 1397, 1399–401 (Fed.Cir. 1995). Under the FDCA, as amended by the Act, a pharmaceutical manufacturer submits an ANDA when seeking expedited FDA approval of a generic version of a drug previously approved by the FDA (a "listed drug"). An ANDA can be filed if the generic drug manufacturer's active ingredient is the "bioequivalent" of the listed drug. When submitting an ANDA, a manufacturer must certify one of four statements concerning the applicable listed drug: (i) the listed drug is not patented (a "Paragraph I certification"); (ii) the listed drug's patent has expired (a "Paragraph II certification"); (iii) the expiration date of the listed drug's patent (a "Paragraph III certification"); or (iv) the listed drug's patent "is invalid or . . . it will not be infringed by the manufacture, use, or sale of the new drug" covered by the ANDA (a "Paragraph IV certification"). 21 U.S.C. § 355(j)(2)(A)(vii)(I)-(IV). If an ANDA is certified under Paragraph IV, the applicant must notify the patent's owner of the certification.

An ANDA certified under Paragraphs I or II is approved immediately after meeting all applicable scientific and regulatory requirements. An ANDA certified under Paragraph III must, even after meeting all applicable scientific and regulatory requirements, wait for approval until the listed drug's patent expires. An ANDA certified under Paragraph IV is approved immediately after meeting all applicable scientific and regulatory requirements unless the listed drug's patent owner brings suit for infringement under 35 U.S.C. § 271(e)(2)(A) within forty-five days of receiving the notice required under 21 U.S.C. § 355(j)(2)(B). If suit is brought, the FDA is required to suspend approval of the ANDA, and the FDA cannot approve the ANDA until the earliest of three dates: (i) the date of the court's decision that the listed drug's patent is either invalid or not infringed; (ii) the date the listed drug's patent expires if the court finds the listed drug's patent infringed; or (iii) subject to modification by the court, the date that is thirty months from the date the owner of the listed drug's patent received notice of the filing of a Paragraph IV certification.

The Act modified the patent laws to provide that "[i]t shall not be an act of infringement to make, use, or sell . . . a patented invention . . . solely for uses reasonably related to the development and submission of information under a Federal law which regulates the manufacture, use, or sale of drugs." 35 U.S.C. § 271(e)(1). A Paragraph IV certification, however, is deemed to be an act of infringement "if the purpose of such a submission is to obtain approval under the [FDCA] to engage in the commercial manufacture, use, or sale of a drug . . . claimed in a patent or the use of which is claimed in a patent before the expiration of such a patent." 35 U.S.C. § 271(e)(2)(A); see also Glaxo, Inc. v. Novopharm, Ltd., 110 F.3d 1562, 1567 (Fed.Cir.1997). "If the court determines that the patent is not invalid and that infringement would occur, and that therefore the ANDA applicant's paragraph IV certification is incorrect, the patent owner is entitled to an order that FDA approval of the ANDA containing the paragraph IV certification not be effective until the patent expires." *Royce Lab.*, 69 F.3d at 1135.

The application that matured into the '446 patent was filed on August 20, 1981; the '446 patent issued on November 23, 1993. The '446 patent relates to solid pharmaceutical compositions, such as tablets, that contain nifedipine crystals of a given SSA, combined with a solid diluent that is adapted for formation into tablets. Nifedipine is a compound that acts on the body's circulation—a coronary vasodilator—and is used to control such medical conditions as high blood pressure. The '446 patent attempts, through its claimed SSA for nifedipine crystals, to address the problem of poor solubility—absorption of nifedipine into the blood—while still maintaining a sustained presence of nifedipine in the blood, i.e., high bioavailability. The patent seeks to achieve its objective without using such disadvantageous means as large-sized tablets, which are hard to swallow, or liquid formulations, which are very expensive and require protection from light.

The '446 patent contains twelve independent claims; the claims cover actual compositions of the nifedipine drug, methods of making the drug, and methods of treatment using the drug. Each claim specifies a SSA range for the nifedipine crystal used. Claim 1, which Bayer asserts against Elan, is representative of the composition claims and recites the broadest SSA range:

> 1. A solid pharmaceutical composition comprising as the active ingredient an effective amount of nifedipine crystals with a specific surface area of 1.0 to 4 m^2/g, in admixture with a solid diluent, to result in a sustained release of nifedipine.

Elan submitted an ANDA to the FDA on April 30, 1997, seeking approval for a product that is bioequivalent to Bayer's Adalat CC product. Elan's ANDA covers a once-daily formulation of nifedipine—an extended release tablet dosage form containing 30 mg of nifedipine. With its ANDA, Elan filed a Certificate of Quality and Analysis (COA). The COA related to an analysis performed by * * * an independent laboratory, on April 17, 1996 with respect to the micronized—finely ground—nifedipine provided to Elan by its nifedipine supplier, Arzneimittelwerk Dresden GmbH (AWD). According to the COA, the measured SSA of the micronized AWD nifedipine crystals was 6.15 m^2/g. The tablets made from these micronized nifedipine crystals and tested for the ANDA process are referred to by the parties as the "biobatch." Elan also filed with its ANDA a Paragraph IV certification, in which it stated that its nifedipine composition did not infringe the '446 patent * * * *

Determination of a claim of infringement involves a two step inquiry. First, the claims are construed, a question of law in which the scope of the asserted claims is defined. Second, the claims, as construed, are compared to the accused device. This is a question of fact. To prevail, the plaintiff must establish by a preponderance of the evidence that the accused device infringes one or more claims of the patent either literally or under the doctrine of equivalents.

Literal infringement requires the patentee to prove that the accused device contains each limitation of the asserted claim(s). If any claim limitation is absent from the accused device, there is no literal infringement as a matter of law. The district court, in deciding the issue of literal infringement, first looked to Elan's ANDA, noting that it "sets a specification for its proposed product of a specific surface area greater than 5 m²/g." The district court also observed that AWD, Elan's nifedipine supplier, cannot sell nifedipine with a SSA under 4.7 m²/g to anyone who will use or sell a product containing AWD's nifedipine in the United States. In addition, the court stated that results in the COA indicated that Elan's biobatch tablets had a SSA of 6.15 m²/g. Faced with this evidence, the court found that Bayer had offered only "unsubstantiated assertions" that there was uncertainty as to whether Elan and AWD would meet Elan's ANDA specification. Thus, Bayer had failed to meet its burden of defeating summary judgment by showing a genuine issue of material fact with respect to the issue of literal infringement of the '446 patent. The district court concluded by noting that Bayer could sue Elan for infringement if Elan begins manufacturing for commercial sale a product with a SSA within 1.0 to 4 m²/g, as claimed by the '446 patent.

Bayer's first argument on appeal is that a genuine issue of material fact exists as to whether Elan's biobatch infringes the '446 patent. Bayer contends that an infringing biobatch is material evidence of infringement under 35 U.S.C. § 271(e)(2). In that regard, Bayer asserts that there is no evidence as to the SSA of Elan's micronized nifedipine crystals just before the crystals were mixed to make biobatch tablets, and it points to certain evidence that nifedipine crystals grow over time before being mixed into tablets, thereby causing the SSA of the crystals to decrease. Bayer also argues that there are genuine issues of material fact as to whether Elan will be able to comply with its SSA specification and thus produce a noninfringing product. Bayer asserts that Elan has not specified a validated test protocol or test equipment to measure the SSA of its nifedipine. It also asserts that Elan has not produced any samples, or test data from samples, under the requirements set forth in Elan's amended ANDA specification.
* * *

The focus, under § 271(e)(2)(A), is on "what the ANDA applicant will likely market if its application is approved, an act that has not yet occurred." *Glaxo*, 110 F.3d at 1569. "[T]his hypothetical inquiry is properly grounded in the ANDA application and the extensive materials typically submitted in its support." Id. Therefore, it is proper for the court to consider the ANDA itself, materials submitted by the ANDA applicant in support of the ANDA, and any other relevant evidence submitted by the applicant or patent holder. However, if the ANDA "is to sell [a] well-defined compound," then the "ultimate question of infringement is usually straightforward."

We believe that the specification in Elan's ANDA mandates a finding of no literal infringement. Elan's specification indicates that "the specific surface area of the micronized nifedipine is to be 5 m^2/g or greater," and that this SSA "will be reflected in certification of analysis provided by Elan's supplier (AWD)." Elan further defines its specification by noting that it is "Elan's intention to measure specific surface area on the micronized nifedipine material prior to use (within 5 working days prior to blend manufacture) to ensure that the ≥ 5 m^2/g specification for specific surface area is met. Material not meeting this specification will not be used for manufacture." Thus, according to Elan's ANDA specification, nifedipine used in its drug cannot have a SSA of less than 5 m^2/g within five working days prior to manufacturing. Significantly, Bayer does not allege that within five working days, the nifedipine's SSA will decrease from 5 m^2/g to a literally infringing size of 4 m^2/g or less. Therefore, under the ANDA specification, Elan cannot literally infringe the '446 patent.

Bayer's focus on the biobatch, whose test data was submitted with Elan's ANDA, is misplaced for two reasons. First, the Act specifically provides an ANDA applicant immunity from allegations of infringement for acts that are necessary in preparing an ANDA. The production of a biobatch, and the submission of a COA regarding this biobatch, are required in the ANDA application process. Thus, even if the biobatch falls within the scope of the claims, the Act specifically indicates that such actions by Elan cannot constitute infringement. In addition, the focus of the infringement inquiry under 35 U.S.C. § 271(e)(2)(A) is on the product that will be sold after the FDA's approval of the ANDA, not on the biobatch that is produced to facilitate FDA approval. The filing of an ANDA is considered an act of infringement under § 271(e)(2)(A), but this "act" is merely a vehicle "to create case or controversy jurisdiction to enable a court to promptly resolve" a dispute concerning an infringement that will happen in the future.

Second, the specification in Elan's ANDA defines its product in a way that directly addresses the question of infringement—the SSA of the nifedipine crystals. Elan is bound by this specification. The dispute between the parties concerns the SSA of the nifedipine that Elan will use in its drug. Elan stated to the FDA that the SSA of its nifedipine composition will not be less than 5 m^2/g, clarifying in an amendment that the SSA will be 5 m^2/g or more five working days before manufacturing. Elan is required, under 21 C.F.R. § 314.94(a)(9), to comply with 21 C.F.R. § 314.50(d)(1)(i) and state the ANDA drug's specification, including its particle size and the process controls used in manufacturing to assure the specification is met. Elan, in its initial ANDA and answers to FDA questions, provided this information and sought approval under 21 U.S.C. § 355(j) based on its specification.

If any of the statements in Elan's specification are false, Elan is subject to civil penalties and the withdrawal of the approval of its drug. Additionally, if Elan introduces a drug into interstate commerce without complying with the approval requirements of 21 U.S.C. § 355, it is subject to various additional penalties, including an injunction, criminal sanctions, seizure of the unapproved drug, and debarment of its corporation and individual officials from submitting or assisting in the submission of an ANDA in the future. Elan also would be subject to criminal prosecution for making false statements to the FDA under 18 U.S.C. § 1001, conspiring to defraud the United States under 18 U.S.C. § 371, and obstructing proceedings before a federal agency under 18 U.S.C. § 1501. If Elan changes its ANDA, it must file the changes with the FDA, and if the changes are to the drug's specification, Elan must obtain approval for the changes before they can be made. In short, the only drug Elan can produce upon approval of the ANDA at issue is a drug that does not literally infringe the '446 patent.

Bayer is correct that in *Glaxo*, we approved of the district court looking to a biobatch for help in deciding the issue of infringement. However, the biobatch in *Glaxo* was properly considered because the ANDA specification in that case did not define the compound in a manner that directly addressed the issue of infringement. The compound in *Glaxo* existed in multiple crystalline forms and mixtures, possibly containing either Form 1 or Form 2 ranitidine hydrochloride (RHCl), and the asserted patent covered mixtures that contained Form 2 RHCl. Thus, the ANDA at issue, which permitted the marketed product to have a Form 1 RHCl purity as low as 90%, did not address the question of infringement—whether a drug produced under the ANDA would contain Form 2 RHCl. Here, however, the ANDA directly addresses the question of infringement; it recites that the SSA of Elan's drug will be 5 m^2/g or above. Thus, we have before us an ANDA specification that, in the words of *Glaxo*, describes a "well-defined compound," and thus "the ultimate question of infringement is ... straightforward." 110 F.3d at 1569. Elan's biobatch does not control the issue of infringement. * * *

If an asserted claim does not literally read on an accused product, infringement may still occur under the doctrine of equivalents if there is not a substantial difference between the limitations of the claim and the accused product. Infringement under the doctrine of equivalents is a question of fact. Prosecution history estoppel is one limitation on the scope of equivalents that a patentee can claim under the doctrine of equivalents and is a question of law. Prosecution history estoppel can occur as a result of (i) amendments made to overcome patentability rejections or (ii) arguments made during prosecution that show "a clear and unmistakable surrender of subject matter."

In addressing whether there was a genuine issue of material fact as to infringement by Elan under the doctrine of equivalents, the district court looked to see whether prosecution history estoppel prevented Bayer from claiming a SSA beyond the upper limit of 4 m^2/g set forth in claim 1 of the '446 patent. In that connection, the court examined the entire prosecution history of the '446 patent to determine what subject matter, if any, a competitor would reasonably conclude was surrendered by Bayer. The court noted that, during prosecution, Bayer argued that the SSA range of 0.5 to 6 m²/g originally claimed in claim 1 provided unexpected results, but the examiner did not agree. The court further noted that, in response to the examiner's rejection * * * , Bayer amended claims 1 through 3 by changing the SSA range to 1.0 to 4 m²/g and canceled claim 4. The district court also considered declarations submitted by Bayer, as well as arguments made by Bayer's attorney, to support Bayer's claim of an unexpected, plateau-like effect for a SSA range of 1.0 to 4 m²/g, with high bioavailability dropping off outside this range. Based on this evidence, the district court determined, as a matter of law, that Bayer had surrendered subject matter outside the claimed range of 1.0 to 4 m²/g * * * *

We need not resolve the question of why Bayer amended its claims and whether its reasons related to patentability because it is clear that, regardless of why it amended its claims, when it did so it unmistakably surrendered coverage to SSAs above 4 m²/g. As a result, it is precluded from asserting that the nifedipine composition that is the subject of Elan's ANDA infringes the '446 patent under the doctrine of equivalents. * * *

In determining whether there has been a clear and unmistakable surrender of subject matter, the prosecution history must be examined as a whole. See Pharmacia & Upjohn Co. v. Mylan Pharm., Inc., 170 F.3d 1373, 1376 (Fed.Cir.1999). * * * Bayer repeatedly argued that its claimed range of 1.0 to 4 m²/g produced unique results and was a superior and inventive range. At the same time, the declarations it submitted praised the benefits of the 1.0 to 4 m²/g SSA range, claiming that this range exhibited a plateau-like effect by producing the maximum dissolution of nifedipine into the blood. * * * This case is very similar to *Pharmacia*. There, we concluded that a patentee had relinquished claim coverage to any type of lactose that was not spray-dried. During prosecution, the patentee argued that the use of spray-dried lactose was "a critical feature" of the claimed invention and that using lactose that was not spray-dried resulted in a pharmaceutical powder that was not readily processed. We held that these statements were "reasonably interpreted as a broad disclaimer of what the invention was not." 170 F.3d at 1378. * * * In this case, during prosecution, Bayer emphasized the inventive nature of its claimed SSA range and the disadvantages of SSAs outside its claimed range. Thus, Bayer's statements, in total, amount to a "clear and unmistakable surrender," so that a competitor would reasonably believe that Bayer had surrendered SSAs outside the claimed range. * * *

NOTES AND QUESTIONS

1. *The Hatch–Waxman compromise.* As explained in *Bayer*, Congress enacted legislation in 1984 to facilitate the introduction of generic drugs without undermining incentives for innovation. See Glaxo, Inc. v. Novopharm, Ltd., 110 F.3d 1562, 1568 (Fed.Cir.1997) ("[The] legislation [was] designed to benefit makers of generic drugs, research-based pharmaceutical companies, and not incidentally the public. The Hatch–Waxman Act, inter alia, allows makers of generic drugs to market generic versions of patented drugs as soon as possible after expiration of the relevant patents, while providing patent holders with limited extensions of patent term in order to recover a portion of the market exclusivity lost during the lengthy process of development and FDA review."). Another court summarized the different ways that the Hatch–Waxman Act simplified clearance of generic drugs:

> Before 1984, a company that wished to make a generic version of an FDA-approved brand-name drug had to file another NDA. Preparation of the second NDA was as time-consuming and costly as the original, because the application had to include new studies showing the drug's safety and effectiveness. In 1984, Congress ... simplified the procedure for obtaining approval of generic drugs.... Subsequent applicants who wished to manufacture generic versions of the original drug were ... allowed to rely on the FDA's previous determination that the drug is safe and effective. As a result of the ANDA innovation under Hatch–Waxman, generic makers can obtain expedited approval to market generic versions of drugs that have undergone the rigors of "pioneer" approval under the NDA process. Moreover, generic makers are permitted to manufacture and use drugs protected by a patent(s) if the otherwise infringing activity is related to the development and submission of an ANDA. Finally, Hatch–Waxman establishes an ANDA certification process, whereby generic makers can obtain expedited approval for their ANDAs before expiration of the pioneer maker's patent.

Mylan Pharm., Inc. v. Henney, 94 F.Supp.2d 36, 39 (D.D.C.2000). Because of implementation problems discussed later in this chapter, Congress has considered revisiting this legislation. See Deirdre Davidson, Reform Eyed for Landmark Drug Law, Legal Times, Sept. 11, 2000, at 1 (describing efforts to sponsor legislation designed to clarify a variety of interpretive problems encountered by the courts); see also Alfred B. Engelberg, Special Patent Provisions for Pharmaceuticals: Have They Outlived Their Usefulness?, 39 IDEA 389 (1999); Joseph P. Reid, A Generic Drug Price Scandal: Too Bitter a Pill for the Drug Price Competition and Patent Term Restoration Act to Swallow?, 75 Notre Dame L. Rev. 309 (1999).

2. *Patent term restoration.* Under Hatch–Waxman, pharmaceutical companies may receive patent extensions for time lost awaiting FDA approval as well as half of the time expended in preapproval clinical trials, but the extension is capped at five years. See 35 U.S.C. § 156; see also Suzan Kucukarslan & Jacqueline Cole, Patent Extension Under the Drug Price Competition and Patent Term Restoration Act of 1984, 49 Food & Drug L.J. 511 (1994). Occasionally, companies succeed in persuading Congress to enact private bills granting them patent extensions on particular products. See Richard M. Cooper, Legislative Patent Extensions, 48 Food & Drug L.J. 59 (1993).

3. *Further commentary.* See Ellen J. Flannery & Peter Barton Hutt, Balancing Competition and Patent Protection in the Drug Industry: The

Drug Price Competition and Patent Term Restoration Act of 1984, 40 Food Drug Cosm. L.J. 269 (1985); John Hudson, Generic Take-up in the Pharmaceutical Market Following Patent Expiry: A Multi–Country Study, 20 Int'l Rev. L. & Econ. 205 (2000); Ralph A. Lewis, Comment, The Emerging Effects of the Drug Price Competition and Patent Term Restoration Act of 1984, 8 J. Contemp. Health L. & Pol'y 361 (1992); James J. Wheaton, Comment, Generic Competition and Pharmaceutical Innovation: The Drug Price Competition and Patent Term Restoration Act of 1984, 35 Cath. U. L. Rev. 433 (1986); Symposium, Striking the Right Balance Between Innovation and Drug Price Competition: Understanding the Hatch–Waxman Act, 54 Food & Drug L.J. 185 (1999).

Fisons plc v. Quigg

876 F.2d 99 (Fed.Cir.1989).

■ NIES, CIRCUIT JUDGE:

* * * Fisons plc had sought extensions of the patent term for each of three patented drugs. The United States Patent and Trademark Office (PTO), which reviews such applications, denied any extension because the PTO found Fisons did not meet the statutory requirements. * * * Fisons owns three patents, United States Patents Nos. 3,419,578; 3,860,618; and 3,975,536, each covering a new human drug product containing the active ingredient cromolyn sodium. Each of these products represents an innovative use or dosage form of cromolyn sodium. In 1973 the Food and Drug Administration (FDA) first approved the chemical compound cromolyn sodium for commercial marketing in inhalation capsule form. Subsequently, the patented products sub judice were also approved.

Patent term extensions are allowed under 35 U.S.C. § 156, if certain requirements set forth therein are met. The issue here is whether Fisons' applications satisfied the following provision in section 156(a)(5)(A): "the permission for the commercial marketing or use of the product after such [FDA] regulatory review period is the first permitted commercial marketing or use of the product under the provision of law under which such regulatory review period occurred." 35 U.S.C. § 156(a)(5)(A). * * *

Applying the definition of "product" provided in section 156(f) to the extension requirement of section 156(a)(5)(A), the PTO and district court interpreted the statute as limiting extensions to the term of the patent on the first permitted marketing or use of a particular active ingredient. Under that interpretation, it follows that because Fisons' patented new products containing cromolyn sodium did not qualify as the first permitted commercial marketing or use of the active ingredient cromolyn sodium, extensions of the patent term for the subject patents were not permissible.

Fisons contends that the term "product" in section 156(a)(5)(A) should not be interpreted to mean an "active ingredient." Rather, per Fisons, the term "product" therein refers to the particular drug product that the FDA approved. Because each application for extension is based on the FDA's first approval of a different use or dose of a product incorporating cromolyn sodium, under Fisons' interpretation, it satisfies the requirement of section 156(a)(5)(A). In support of its interpretation, Fisons points to the last sentence of section 156(a) which states: "The product referred to in paragraphs (4) and (5) is hereinafter in this section referred to as the 'approved product.'" Thus, per Fisons, "product" in paragraph (5) must mean the entire composition of the drug product, not just the active ingredient, inasmuch as FDA approval goes to the former, not merely the latter. One difficulty with this argument is that by its terms the sentence does not apply to paragraph (5), which precedes the sentence. It would do violence to the plain language to make the last sentence into a substantive definition to be read back into paragraph (5). The last sentence is merely a drafting device adopted to simplify the language of subsequent provisions in the section. Accordingly, we cannot agree with Fisons' position. * * *

We have reviewed [the district court's] thoughtful analysis and the extensive legislative history itself. There is strong support for the interpretation adopted by the PTO and the district court inasmuch as some legislators explicitly criticized section 156(a)(5) for not covering new uses and dosages. On the other hand, the statements in the legislative history on which Fisons relies fail to provide the clearly expressed legislative intention, contrary to the statutory language, necessary to avoid the conclusive effect of that language itself.

Fisons makes what can only be characterized as a "policy argument" pointing to statements of lofty goals indicating that Congress broadly sought to encourage pharmaceutical innovation by enacting the 1984 Act. Fisons urges that it makes little sense, in view of such goals, to restrict patent term extensions so as to encourage development only of new chemical entities (NCEs), and not of new uses and doses for such drugs. Per Fisons, developments of new uses and doses for known compounds are as important as NCE developments. It is irrelevant, however, that we might agree with Fisons that, as a matter of policy, Congress might better achieve its goals through a more liberal grant of patent term extension benefits. Matters of policy are for Congress, not the courts, to decide. Accordingly, Fisons' policy arguments are unhelpful in our interpretation of the complex statutory provision at issue. * * *

Eli Lilly & Co. v. Medtronic, Inc.

496 U.S. 661 (1990).

■ SCALIA, JUSTICE:

In 1984, Congress enacted the Drug Price Competition and Patent Term Restoration Act of 1984, which amended the FDCA and the patent laws in several important respects. The issue in this case concerns the proper interpretation of a portion of § 202 of the 1984 Act, codified at 35 U.S.C. § 271(e)(1). That paragraph, as originally enacted, provided:

It shall not be an act of infringement to make, use, or sell a patented invention (other than a new animal drug or veterinary biological product (as those terms are used in the Federal Food, Drug, and Cosmetic Act and the Act of March 4, 1913)) solely for uses reasonably related to the development and submission of information under a Federal law which regulates the manufacture, use, or sale of drugs.

The parties dispute whether this provision exempts from infringement the use of patented inventions to develop and submit information for marketing approval of medical devices under the FDCA. * * * [P]etitioner interprets the statutory phrase, "a Federal law which regulates the manufacture, use, or sale of drugs," to refer only to those individual provisions of federal law that regulate drugs, whereas respondent interprets it to refer to the entirety of any Act (including, of course, the FDCA) at least some of whose provisions regulate drugs. * * *

If § 271(e)(1) referred to "a Federal law which *pertains* to the manufacture, use, or sale of drugs" it might be more reasonable to think that an individual provision was referred to. But the phrase "a Federal law which *regulates* the manufacture, use, or sale of drugs" more naturally summons up the image of an entire statutory scheme of regulation. The portion of § 271(e)(1) that immediately precedes the words "a Federal law" likewise seems more compatible with reference to an entire Act. It refers to "the development and submission of information *under* a Federal law" (emphasis added). It would be more common, if a single section rather than an entire scheme were referred to, to speak of "the development and submission of information *pursuant* to a Federal law," or perhaps "*in compliance with* a Federal law." Taking the action "under a Federal law" suggests taking it in furtherance of or compliance with a comprehensive scheme of regulation. * * *

On the other side of the ledger, however, one must admit that while the provision more naturally means what respondent suggests, it is somewhat difficult to understand why anyone would *want* it to mean that. Why should the touchstone of noninfringement be whether the use is related to the development and submission of information under a provision that happens to be included within an Act that, *in any of its provisions*, not necessarily the one at issue, regulates drugs? * * * As far as the text is concerned, therefore, we conclude that we have before us a provision that somewhat more naturally reads as the court of appeals determined [to cover medical devices], but that is not plainly comprehensible on anyone's view. Both parties seek to enlist legislative history in support of their interpretation, but that sheds no clear light. We think the court of appeals' interpretation is confirmed, however, by the structure of the 1984 Act taken as a whole. * * *

The parties agree that the 1984 Act was designed to respond to two unintended distortions of the 17–year patent term produced by the requirement that certain products must receive premarket regulatory approval. First, the holder of a patent relating to such products would as a practical matter not be able to reap any financial rewards during the early years of the term. When an inventor makes a potentially useful discovery, he ordinarily protects it by applying for a patent at once. Thus, if the discovery relates to a product that cannot be marketed without substantial testing and regulatory approval, the "clock" on his patent term will be running even though he is not yet able to derive any profit from the invention.

The second distortion occurred at the other end of the patent term. In 1984, the Court of Appeals for the Federal Circuit decided that the manufacture, use, or sale of a patented invention during the term of the patent constituted an act of infringement even if it was for the sole purpose of conducting tests and developing information necessary to apply for regulatory approval. Since that activity could not be commenced by those who planned to compete with the patentee until expiration of the entire patent term, the patentee's de facto monopoly would continue for an often substantial period until regulatory approval was obtained. In other words, the combined effect of the patent law and the premarket regulatory approval requirement was to create an effective extension of the patent term.

The 1984 Act sought to eliminate this distortion from both ends of the patent period. Section 201 of the Act established a patent-term extension for patents relating to certain products that were subject to lengthy regulatory delays and could not be marketed prior to regulatory approval. The eligible products were described as [including medical devices.] * * * Section 201 provides that patents relating to these products can be extended up to five years if, inter alia, the product was "subject to a regulatory review period before its commercial marketing or use," and "the permission for the commercial marketing or use of the product after such regulatory review period [was] the first permitted commercial marketing or use of the product under the provision of law under which such regulatory review period occurred." 35 U.S.C. § 156(a).

The distortion at the other end of the patent period was addressed by § 202 of the Act. That added to the provision prohibiting patent infringement, 35 U.S.C. § 271, the paragraph at issue here * * * * This allows competitors, prior to the expiration of a patent, to engage in otherwise infringing activities necessary to obtain regulatory approval. * * *

It seems most implausible to us that Congress, being demonstrably aware of the *dual* distorting effects of regulatory approval requirements in this entire area—dual distorting effects that were roughly offsetting, the disadvantage at the beginning of the term producing a more or less corresponding advantage at the end of the term—should choose to address both those distortions only for drug products; and for other products named in § 201 should enact provisions which not only leave in place an anticompetitive restriction at the end of the monopoly term but simultaneously expand the monopoly term itself, thereby not only failing to eliminate but positively aggravating distortion of the 17–year patent protection. It would take strong evidence to persuade us that this is what Congress wrought, and there is no such evidence here.

Apart from the reason of the matter, there are textual indications that §§ 201 and 202 are meant generally to be complementary. That explains, for example, § 202's exception for "a new animal drug or veterinary biological product (as those terms are used in the Federal Food, Drug, and Cosmetic Act and the Act of March 4, 1913)." Although new animal drugs and veterinary biological products are subject to premarket regulatory licensing and approval under the FDCA, neither product was included in the patent-term extension provision of § 201. They therefore were excepted from § 202 as well. Interpreting § 271(e)(1) as the court of appeals did here appears to create a perfect "product" fit between the two sections. All of the products eligible for a patent term extension under § 201 are subject to § 202 * * * * No interpretation we have been able to imagine can transform § 271(e)(1) into an elegant piece of statutory draftsmanship. To construe it as the court of appeals decided, one must posit a good deal of legislative imprecision; but to construe it as petitioner would, one must posit that and an implausible substantive intent as well. * * *

■ KENNEDY, JUSTICE (dissenting):

* * * Section 271(e)(1), in my view, does not privilege the testing of medical devices such as the cardiac defibrillator. When § 271(e)(1) speaks of a law which regulates drugs, I think that it does not refer to particular enactments or implicate the regulation of anything other than drugs. It addresses the legal regulation of drugs as opposed to other products. Thus, while the section would permit a manufacturer to use a drug for the purpose of obtaining marketing approval under the FDCA, it does not authorize a manufacturer to use or sell other products that, by coincidence, the FDCA also happens to regulate. * * *

The Court asserts that Congress could have specified this result in a clearer manner. That is all too true. But we do not tell Congress how to express its intent. Instead, we discern its intent by assuming that Congress employs words and phrases in accordance with their ordinary usage. In this case, even if Congress could have clarified § 271(e)(1), the Court ascribes a most unusual meaning to the existing language. * * *

Congress did not act in an irrational manner when it drew a distinction between drugs and medical devices. True, like medical devices, some drugs have a very high cost. Testing a patented medical device, however, often will have greater effects on the patent holder's rights than comparable testing of a patented drug. As petitioner has asserted, manufacturers may test generic versions of patented drugs, but not devices, under abbreviated procedures. These procedures, in general, do not affect the market in a substantial manner because manufacturers may test the drugs on a small number of subjects, who may include healthy persons who otherwise would not buy the drug. By contrast, as in this case, manufacturers test and market medical devices in clinical trials on patients who would have purchased the device from the patent holder. * * *

NOTES AND QUESTIONS

1. *Clinical trials exception.* For the most part, lower courts have generously interpreted the exception for clinical trials undertaken to secure FDA

approval. See, e.g., NeoRx Corp. v. Immunomedics, Inc., 877 F.Supp. 202, 206–12 (D.N.J.1994) (holding that scale-up production and shipment overseas to conduct clinical trials in support of FDA approval would be exempt, but shipment to foreign regulatory authorities to secure their approval would not be). But cf. Biogen, Inc. v. Schering AG, 954 F.Supp. 391, 397 (D.Mass.1996) (holding that this safe harbor did not apply where a company "had spent $24 million to stockpile and prepare to market Avonex immediately upon the anticipated, imminent FDA approval in order to access promptly the lucrative market for beta interferon drugs to combat multiple sclerosis"). See generally Courtenay C. Brinckerhoff, Can the Safe Harbor of 35 U.S.C. § 271(e)(1) Shelter Pioneer Drug Manufacturers?, 53 Food & Drug L.J. 643 (1998); Brian D. Coggio & Francis D. Cerrito, The Application of the Patent Laws to the Drug Approval Process, 52 Food & Drug L.J. 345 (1997); Janice M. Mueller, No "Dilettante Affair": Rethinking the Experimental Use Exception to Patent Infringement for Biomedical Research Tools, 76 Wash. L. Rev. 1 (2001); Eyal H. Barash, Comment, Experimental Uses, Patents, and Scientific Progress, 91 Nw. U. L. Rev. 667 (1997); Thomas F. Poche, Note, Clinical Trial Exemption from Patent Infringement: Judicial Interpretation of Section 271(e)(1), 74 B.U. L. Rev. 903 (1994).

2. *Medical devices.* Lower courts have extended the Supreme Court's application of the exception to medical devices. See Abtox, Inc. v. Exitron Corp., 122 F.3d 1019, 1027–29 (Fed.Cir.1997) (applying the exception to research performed on a Class II device prior to marketing); Telectronics Pacing Sys., Inc. v. Ventritex, Inc., 982 F.2d 1520, 1523 (Fed.Cir.1992) (holding that company demonstrations of an implantable defibrillator subject to an IDE at medical conferences "constitute an exempt use reasonably related to FDA approval, because device sponsors are responsible for selecting qualified investigators and providing them with the necessary information to conduct clinical testing"); Intermedics, Inc. v. Ventritex, Inc., 775 F.Supp. 1269 (N.D.Cal.1991), aff'd mem., 991 F.2d 808 (Fed.Cir. 1993); Shashank Upadhye, Understanding Patent Infringement Under 35 U.S.C. Section 271(e): The Collisions Between Patent, Medical Device and Drug Laws, 17 Santa Clara Computer & High Tech. L.J. 1 (2000); Veronica Lanier, Note, Medical Device Eligibility for the Statutory Experimental Use Exception to Patent Infringement, 17 Hastings Comm. & Ent. L.J. 705 (1995). See generally J. Matthew Buchanan, Medical Device Patent Rights in the Age of FDA Modernization: The Potential Effect of Regulatory Streamlining on the Right to Exclude, 30 U. Tol. L. Rev. 305 (1999); Symposium, Intellectual Property and the FDA, 33 Cal. W. L. Rev. 1 (1996).

5.   COPYRIGHT PROTECTION

SmithKline Beecham v. Watson Pharmaceuticals, Inc.

211 F.3d 21 (2d Cir.2000).

■ WINTER, CHIEF JUDGE:

* * * On January 13, 1984, SmithKline obtained FDA approval to sell 2 mg strength Nicorette for prescription-only use. Later, on June 8, 1992,

the FDA approved prescription-only use of 4 mg Nicorette. Finally, on February 9, 1996, the FDA approved both 2 mg and 4 mg Nicorette for OTC sale. Pursuant to 21 U.S.C. § 355(c)(3)(D)(iv), SmithKline obtained a three-year period of exclusivity—essentially an extension of the effective term of SmithKline's Nicorette patent based on additional clinical testing— for OTC sale of Nicorette.

SmithKline's user's guide and audiotape were developed in the course of its research into producing a method of, and product for, quitting smoking. To obtain approval for the OTC sale of Nicorette, SmithKline submitted various versions of the guide and tape to the FDA for review. Between July 1993 and February 1996, SmithKline made approximately 70 changes to the guide and the tape at the FDA's request. Most of the changes related to factual matters, safety, and efficacy. The tape and guide were ultimately included as part of Nicorette's FDA-approved OTC labeling. On April 21, 1998, SmithKline registered a federal copyright for the guide and audiotape script. On February 9, 1999, the day when its exclusivity period for Nicorette expired, SmithKline registered a copyright for the words and music on the tape.

Shortly thereafter, appellees Watson Pharmaceuticals, Inc., Watson Laboratories, Inc., and Circa Pharmaceuticals, Inc. (collectively "Watson") obtained FDA approval for the OTC marketing of a generic version of nicotine gum intended to compete directly with Nicorette. To obtain that approval from the FDA, Watson had to comply with the requirement imposed by the Hatch–Waxman Amendments that "the labeling proposed for [its] new drug [be] the same as the labeling approved for" Nicorette. Thus, Watson's generic nicotine gum was "accompanied by a user guide and audio tape that [we]re virtually identical to SmithKline's."

Before Watson could sell its product to the public, SmithKline initiated the present copyright action, alleging willful infringement of its guide and tape. The district court granted a preliminary injunction that effectively stopped Watson from shipping or selling its product. The district court relied on a March 1999 FDA letter recounting that the agency had explained to Watson that "the 'same labeling' requirement d[oes] not require that the generic's behavioral support materials be identical to the innovator's materials" and indeed that "generic sponsors, like all other sponsors of nicotine-based smoking cessation aids, have discretion to design their own audio support materials." Based on this representation, the district court "concluded that the FDA would have permitted Watson to use a user's guide and audio tape that deviated to some extent from SmithKline's materials . . . [and] that were sufficiently different in wording and otherwise to avoid copyright concerns."

Subsequently, the FDA altered its position. In the face of the preliminary injunction, Watson revised its guide and tape to render them "comparable, but not identical, to SmithKline's." However, on November 23, 1999, the FDA rejected the revised user guide. The FDA "advised Watson that it would approve a revised version of Watson's 'previously approved labeling,' i.e., the virtually identical user's guide previously approved by the FDA." To assist Watson, the FDA "marked up a copy of the previously approved user guide" and bracketed certain portions of text which could be in appropriate cases deleted or "substituted with new text ... similar to the original in tone, content and length." Nevertheless, the bracketed guide gave Watson "very little leeway to deviate from the previously approved user guide." In essence, therefore, the FDA "determined that Watson had to copy verbatim substantially all of the text used in the SmithKline" user's guide.

In December, representatives of the FDA attended a conference with the district court, at which time the court asked the FDA to " 'revisit' the question of whether portions of Watson's proposed user's guide could be rewritten to change the text 'a little bit' to address the copyright concerns." On December 15, the FDA wrote the court and advised that it had "decline[d] to change its approach to Watson's labeling" and that it could not address copyright concerns because it "ha[d] never been directed by Congress to consider potential copyright rights in approving generic drug labeling." In a supplemental decision issued the same day, the FDA "adhered to its decision to require Watson to copy verbatim most of the SmithKline" user guide. In light of the FDA's position, the district court dissolved the preliminary injunction, citing also Watson's efforts to revise its materials, the prejudice caused Watson by delay, and the public interest in a generic nicotine gum product. * * *

We do not doubt that SmithKline has demonstrated the existence of substantial issues under the copyright laws, at least when they are considered in isolation. SmithKline's guide and tape are creative works in which it has a substantial investment, and they are integral to both the marketing and use of Nicorette. Watson's guide and tape are concededly in large part copies of SmithKline's copyrighted materials. Moreover, Watson intends to use the guide and tape in marketing a product in direct competition with SmithKline's gum. Absent more, the propriety of a preliminary injunction would seem clear.

Watson asserts that this copying, having been dictated by the FDA, is a "fair use" protected under 17 U.S.C. § 107. The United States, in its amicus curiae brief, argues instead that in submitting its copyrighted materials for FDA approval, SmithKline gave the FDA an implied, nonexclusive license to permit or require generic drug applicants to copy the user's guide and audiotape in their own nicotine gum packaging. Neither fair use nor implied license is clearly a defense in the present circumstances. Watson's use of SmithKline's copyrighted works in its labeling is rather different from the sorts of copying traditionally deemed to constitute a fair use, e.g., copying for "purposes such as criticism, comment, news reporting, teaching ..., scholarship, or research." Moreover, courts have found implied licenses only in "narrow" circumstances where one party "created a work at [the other's] request and handed it over, intending that [the other] copy and distribute it."

However, we see little need for further examination of these possible defenses. If either were to prevail, some new law, essentially judge-made, would have to be fashioned. In our view, the case can more easily be disposed of on the straightforward ground that the Hatch–Waxman Amendments to the FDCA not only permit but require producers of generic drugs to use the same labeling as was approved for, and is used in, the sale of the pioneer drug, even if that label has been copyrighted. Because those Amendments were designed to facilitate rather than impede the approval and OTC sale of generic drugs, the FDA's requirement that Watson use much of SmithKline's label precludes a copyright infringement action by SmithKline. SmithKline's copyright claim is therefore meritless, and we need not address either the fair use or implied license defenses. * * *

The Hatch–Waxman Amendments reflect the FDA's view that clinical retesting of generic drugs was "unnecessary and wasteful because the drug ha[d] already been determined to be safe and effective," as well as "unethical because it [would] require[] that some sick patients take placebos and be denied treatment known to be effective." H. Rep. No. 98–857, Part I, at 16 (1984), reprinted in 1984 U.S.C.C.A.N. 2647, 2649. Bypassing redundant human testing would also speed up FDA approval for generic entrants and thus introduce price competition more rapidly once the pioneer producer's patent and exclusivity periods expired. See Mead Johnson Pharm. Group v. Bowen, 838 F.2d 1332, 1333 (D.C.Cir.1988) (interpreting congressional purpose of Hatch–Waxman Amendments to be "increas[ing] competition in the drug industry by facilitating the approval of generic copies of drugs").

Except for human clinical tests, the ANDA requires a manufacturer to submit to the FDA the same items as required in the NDA, as well as information to show that the generic drug has the same active ingredients, means of administration, dosage form, strength, pharmacological or therapeutic class, and labeling as the already-approved pioneer drug, and that the generic drug does not infringe any outstanding patents. With specific regard to labeling, the Hatch–Waxman Amendments require that an ANDA "show that the labeling proposed for the [generic] drug is the same as the labeling proposed for the [pioneer] drug ... except for changes required because of [approved] differences [between the pioneer and generic drug] or because the [generic] drug and [pioneer] drug are produced or distributed by different manufacturers." 21 U.S.C. § 355(j)(2)(A)(v). The FDCA defines "label" and "labeling" for these purposes as "a display of written, printed, or graphic matter upon the immediate container of any article" or "accompanying such article," 21 U.S.C. § 321(k) & (m), which the FDA has broadly interpreted to include "[b]rochures, booklets, ... sound recordings, ... and similar pieces of printed, audio, or visual matter descriptive of a drug." 21 C.F.R. § 202.1(*l*)(2).

Applying the Hatch–Waxman Amendments to the present appeal, SmithKline's copyright claim fails. First, its copyrighted user's guide and audiotape constitute "labeling" for purposes of the Hatch–Waxman Amendments. SmithKline has not contended otherwise and understandably so. The guide and tape clearly fall within the statutory and regulatory definitions quoted immediately above. Moreover, they were submitted to the FDA as part of SmithKline's quest for administrative approval of OTC sales of Nicorette. The guide and tape were approved only after more than two years of administrative consideration and after that consideration had led to some 70 changes in the guide and tape at the FDA's request.

Second, the FDA's requirement that Watson use copious amounts of SmithKline's copyrighted material is not a misapplication of the Hatch–Waxman Amendments. As noted, the Amendments require that the labeling for the generic drug be the "same" as the labeling for the pioneer drug. To be sure, as SmithKline noted at oral argument, "same" may be something less than "identical." However, where the language of a document is the "same" as that of a copyrighted work, the former usually infringes the latter. Certainly, a legislative drafter would believe that a sameness requirement would lead to the creation of works that would easily fall within the copyright law's infringement test of "substantial similarity."[2] Indeed, the legislative history of the Hatch–Waxman Amendments suggests that whatever difference may exist between "same" and "identical" is narrow and intended to prevent misstatements rather than infringement:

> [A]n ANDA must contain adequate information to show that the proposed labeling for the generic drug is the same as that of the listed drug. The Committee recognizes that the proposed labeling for the generic drug may not be exactly the same. For example, the name and address of the manufacturers would vary as might the expiration dates for the two products. Another example is that one color is used in the coating of the listed drug and another color is used in that of the generic drug. The FDA might require the listed drug maker to specify the color in its label. The generic manufacturer, which has used a different color, would have to specify a different color in its label.

H. Rep. No. 98–857, Part I, at 22 (1984), reprinted in 1984 U.S.C.C.A.N. 2647, 2655.

Third, if SmithKline's copyright claim has merit, then Watson cannot realistically use the ANDA process to sell its generic nicotine gum because it will either have to change the label and lose FDA approval or be enjoined from using a label that infringes SmithKline's copyright. We are thus faced with a conflict between two statutes. The Hatch–Waxman Amendments require generic drug producers to use labeling that will infringe upon

---

2. Some courts have held that infringement of a copyright in commercial labeling must involve verbatim or near-verbatim copying. However, this heightened standard typically involves a copyrighted label of a "fact-based work," and SmithKline's guide and tape are substantially more creative than the typical commercial labels afforded copyright protection. We need not decide whether the traditional "substantial similarity" infringement test or a heightened "verbatim or near- verbatim" test applies to the instant case. As discussed infra, the plain language of the Hatch–Waxman Amendments, their legislative history, and their interpretation by the FDA all require manufacturers of generic drugs to copy the labeling of pioneer drugs "near-verbatim" to obtain ANDA approval, and this statutory mandate necessarily trumps any copyright interest in the label at issue.

copyrights in labels of pioneer drugs. The Copyright Act seems to prohibit such copying. However, applying the familiar canon that, where two laws are in conflict, courts should adopt the interpretation that preserves the principal purposes of each,[3] the conflict is less stark and more easily resolved than it might seem.

The purposes of the Hatch–Waxman Amendments would be severely undermined if copyright concerns were to shape the FDA's application of the "same" labeling requirement. The Amendments were intended to facilitate the introduction of generic competitors once a pioneer drug's patent term and exclusivity periods had ended by allowing the generic producer to piggy-back upon the pioneer producer's successful FDA application. For example, human testing by the generic producer is not required because it would be time-and resource-consuming even though redundant. For the very same reason, the creation and approval of new labels is avoided by the "same" labeling requirement. If labels that were "substantially similar" to copyrighted labels on pioneer drugs had to be avoided, the administrative process of approving a new label would, in cases like the present one, drain the resources of the FDA and generic producer—not to mention the problem of successive generic producers avoiding infringement of multiple copyrighted labels. Avoiding such infringement would also delay the introduction of the generic product without advancing public health and safety to any perceptible degree. For that reason, Congress left no room for such redundant proceedings and adopted the "same" labeling requirement. The FDA cannot be faithful to that requirement, however, without requiring labels that will often violate copyrights. If copyright law were to prevail, producers of generic drugs will always be delayed in—and quite often prohibited from—marketing the generic product, results at great odds with the purposes of the Hatch–Waxman Amendments.

No such severe undermining of the purpose of the copyright laws would follow from the rejection of SmithKline's claim, however. The creation of labels to be approved by the FDA, such as SmithKline's user's guide and audio tape, is ancillary to the FDA's administrative process. The creativity of the author is focused not only on pleasing and medicating ultimate consumers but also on obtaining the administrative approval of labeling necessary to FDA approval of a drug that will be protected from competition both for the period of the patent term and FDCA exclusivity periods.

Our point here is not only that Congress would have provided explicitly that the Hatch–Waxman Amendments trump the copyright laws had it foreseen the statutory conflict exposed by the present action, although we firmly believe that to be obvious. Our point is also that the profit sought by

---

3. In addition to looking to conflicting statutes' principal purposes, courts have traditionally given weight to statutes' priority of enactment and specificity in reconciling conflicts. Here, of course, both time of enactment and specificity favor our interpretation: the Hatch–Waxman Amendments were enacted subsequent to the Copyright Act of 1976, and the Copyright Act's broad generality contrasts with the Hatch–Waxman Amendments' specific generic drug approval scheme.

the creator of the pioneer drug label flows primarily from the administrative approval of the drug and the patent and exclusivity periods free from competition that follow. The pertinent purpose of the copyright laws—to encourage the production of creative works by according authors a property right in their works so that authors will not have to share profits from their labors with free riders—is not seriously implicated by allowing the "same" labeling requirement to trump a copyright under the Hatch–Waxman Amendments.[5] It is simply not conceivable that, if we reject SmithKline's claim, pioneer drug producers will so fear the copying of labels by future generic drug producers that some pioneer producers—or even one of them—will lack the incentive to create labeling needed for FDA approval.

We emphasize that we do not read the Hatch–Waxman Amendments to repeal other rights under the Copyright Act of copyright owners in Smith-Kline's circumstances. Even though such an owner cannot enforce its copyright against generic drug manufacturers who are required by the Hatch–Waxman Amendments to copy labeling and who do no more than that, it still retains a copyright, if otherwise valid, in the label and might well pursue copyright claims against potential infringers in other circumstances, e.g., use of the copyrighted material in non-labeling advertisements. * * *

6. TRADEMARKS AND LANHAM ACT LITIGATION

Eli Lilly & Co. v. Natural Answers, Inc.

86 F.Supp.2d 834 (S.D.Ind.2000).

■ HAMILTON, DISTRICT JUDGE:

Plaintiff Eli Lilly & Company manufactures and sells fluoxetine hydrochloride under the federally registered trademark Prozac®. Prozac is a prescription drug used to treat clinical depression and some other psychological conditions. Defendant Natural Answers, Inc. manufactures and sells a blend of St. John's Wort and several other herbs under the name Herbrozac. Natural Answers has been advertising Herbrozac over the Internet as "a very potent and synergistic formula, designed to promote Mood Elevation," and as "a powerful, and effective all-natural and herbal

---

5. Although commercial labeling is clearly copyrightable, see 1 Nimmer on Copyright § 2.08[G], at 2–135 ("It is clear that [17 U.S.C. §] 102(a)(5) includes prints and labels used for articles of merchandise under the general protection accorded to pictorial, graphic and sculptural works."), it has been recognized that the "danger lurking in copyright protection for labels is that the tail threatens to wag the dog—proprietors at times seize on copyright protection for the label in order to leverage their thin copyright protection over the text . . . on the label into a monopoly on the typically uncopyrightable product to which it is attached." Id. § 2.08[G][2], at 2–138. "Used in that fashion, the copyright serves 'primarily as a means of harassing competitors,' and thus fails 'nine times out of ten.'" Id. at 2–139. Here, although the labeling at issue is more creative than that in the "familiar" commercial labeling cases, SmithKline's copyright claim is arguably weaker than even the typical commercial labeling case, because the copyrighted text was submitted to obtain FDA approval and consequent market exclusivity.

formula alternative to [the] prescription drug Prozac." Lilly has sued Natural Answers and its founder, Brian Alexander Feinstein, under the Lanham Act for federal trademark infringement and for dilution of Prozac as a famous trademark. On December 16, 1999, Lilly moved for a preliminary injunction to prevent Natural Answers from continuing to market its product using both the Herbrozac name and references to Prozac in its Internet advertising. * * *

Since 1988, using the trademark Prozac, plaintiff Lilly has sold fluoxetine hydrochloride throughout the United States and in many countries around the world. Lilly has marketed the medicine primarily to treat depression. The medicine has also proven useful in treating bulimia nervosa and obsessive-compulsive disorder. Lilly owns United States Trademark Registration No. 1357582 for Prozac as used for pharmaceutical products. The registration was issued September 3, 1985, and has become incontestable as a matter of law.

As a prescription drug, Prozac is not freely available to patients who seek to use it to relieve depression or other conditions. A licensed physician must prescribe the medicine, and a licensed pharmacist must fill the prescription for the patient. Lilly's advertising of Prozac has been aimed at physicians and pharmacists, and not directly to potential consumers. Prozac is the best-selling prescription antidepressant in the United States. Since 1988, doctors have prescribed Prozac more than 240 million times for more than 17 million Americans. Prozac sales in the United States alone have totaled more than $12 billion since 1988.

Over the last eleven years, fluoxetine hydrochloride and the Prozac mark have received an extraordinary amount of attention from the news media. The product has achieved extraordinary fame in American culture. Prozac is the best known brand of a new generation of medications that have been developed and are being developed to treat not only depression but a host of other psychological conditions more effectively than has been possible before.

Lilly has submitted a sampling of newspaper and magazine articles and books about Prozac that evidence this fame. In 1993, for example, Penguin Books USA published Peter D. Kramer's book *Listening to Prozac*, and in 1994, the Berkley Publishing Group published Elizabeth Wurtzel's *Prozac Nation: Young and Depressed in America*. Both books were national bestsellers. * * * Lilly has submitted an article from the *Baltimore Sun* of September 21, 1993, that sums up the fame Prozac achieved within just a few years of its initial launch as a brand. After referring to the use of Prozac in punch lines in a Woody Allen film and a *New Yorker* poem, the author wrote:

> Prozac entered the popular lexicon almost immediately after its introduction six years ago. It's been on the cover of *Newsweek* and shared the stage with Phil and Geraldo; it continues to turn up in the monologues of comedians and the cultural references of the ironic. It's a designer label, a buzzword, a brand name familiar to not only the 4.5 million Americans who have taken it, but also those who wonder if

they, too, might find a cure for whatever ails them in the little green-and-off-white capsule.

As further evidence of Prozac's fame, searches of computerized databases turned up extraordinary numbers of responses. A search of the Internet for "Prozac" using the Altavista search engine on November 29, 1999, found 63,150 web pages. A November 29, 1999, search of the Westlaw database ALLNEWS for the word Prozac and a date after 1997 produced more than 10,000 stories. The Westlaw database Dow Jones Major Newspapers covers only 48 major newspapers. A November 29, 1999, search of that database for "Prozac" over the last ten years turned up more than 12,000 references, or an average of more than 250 stories for each newspaper included in the database.

Defendant Natural Answers' Herbrozac is part of a line of products that Natural Answers calls Herbscriptions. These products are manufactured from a variety of herbs and other natural substances. Natural Answers markets these products over the Internet from a site marked <www.naturalanswers.com/>. Natural Answers has not yet arranged for distribution through "brick-and-mortar" retail stores, but it is actively seeking to do so. * * * As compared to Lilly, which is a worldwide pharmaceutical company established in 1876, with annual sales in the billions of dollars, Natural Answers launched its business in 1999 and has one full-time employee, founder Brian Feinstein. Natural Answers' sales of Herbrozac have amounted to no more than $2000 to date. * * *

Natural Answers tries to walk a fine line in its business. On one hand, Natural Answers attempts to draw a sharp distinction between its herbal formula dietary supplements and the drugs manufactured by pharmaceutical companies like Lilly. Natural Answers takes care to claim that its products are not "intended to diagnose, treat or cure any disease." This distinction is important for both marketing and legal reasons. Natural Answers does not want to subject its products to regulation by the Food and Drug Administration. The FDA treats Natural Answers' dietary supplements as "foods" that are not subject to the FDA's drug approval process. This regulatory treatment of the products as "foods," however, requires Natural Answers to make clear in its labeling that its products are not FDA-approved and are "not intended to diagnose, treat, cure, or prevent any disease." 21 U.S.C. §§ 321(ff), 343(r)(6)(C). Nevertheless, Natural Answers wants to market its products as natural alternatives to manufactured pharmaceuticals. Natural Answers markets its products as "dietary supplements" that are "intended to promote the body's natural functions." Natural Answers markets all the Herbscriptions products as alternatives to drugs. The company's web site makes a direct comparison between "herbs" and "drugs" that portrays herbal formulas in an entirely positive light and as alternatives to drugs.

One way in which Natural Answers tries to suggest the benefits of its products is by giving them names that suggest an association with well-known drug brands or families of drugs. As explained below in the discussion of the similarity of the marks in question, the association between Prozac and Herbrozac is strong and intentional. Natural Answers chose a name similar to Prozac rather than a name similar to other antidepressant drugs because Prozac is the most famous and best-selling antidepressant drug. * * * [T]he other product names in the Herbscriptions line attempt to suggest similar associations. Natural Answers promotes Herbalium as a formula to promote "deep relaxation," and the name is intended to suggest an association with the brand-name drug Valium. Natural Answers promotes Vita–Agra as enhancing men's sexual performance, and the name is intended to suggest an association with the Pfizer brand-name drug Viagra®. Natural Answers promotes Herbocet as a pain reliever, and its name is intended to suggest an association with a family of pain relief drugs using the suffix "cet," such as Lorcet, Darvocet, and Percocet. Natural Answers promotes HerbenolPM as suitable for headaches and a good night's sleep, and the name is intended to suggest an association with TylenolPM®. Natural Answers promotes Herbasprin for pain relief, and the name is intended to suggest an association with aspirin. Similarly, the name of the Natural Answers product Herbadryl is intended to suggest an association with Benadryl®. * * *

The legal line between pharmaceutical drugs and herbal remedies has begun to blur in the market place. Several major pharmaceutical companies have recently begun marketing herbal products based, as Herbrozac is, on St. John's Wort. These companies include Warner–Lambert and Smith-Kline Beecham. This phenomenon lends weight to a possibility that is legally important. It would not be unreasonable for a number of consumers who see or hear the name Herbrozac not only to associate the name with Prozac but also to assume or expect that there is some affiliation between the two. Even though the two products are distributed differently and are subject to very different regulatory regimes, they obviously are marketed to address similar if not identical conditions. The fact that some other major pharmaceutical companies are now marketing herbal products in general, and especially herbal products for mood elevation tends to lend some support to the possibility of confusion with respect to association or affiliation. * * *

To succeed on a trademark infringement claim, a plaintiff must establish that it has a protectable trademark and that the alleged infringer's use of that trademark is likely to cause confusion among consumers. * * * In assessing the likelihood of confusion, the court must consider several factors: (1) the degree of similarity between the parties' marks in appearance and suggestion (or actual copying); (2) the similarity of the products; (3) the area and manner of concurrent use; (4) the degree of care likely to be exercised by consumers; (5) the strength of complainant's mark; (6) actual confusion; and (7) intent to palm off by the infringer. This list of factors is not intended to be a mechanical checklist. No one factor is decisive, and the court must weigh all the facts and circumstances of the particular marks, products, and parties. There are a myriad of variables to be considered, but the most important are the similarity of the marks, the intent of the claimed infringer, and evidence of actual confusion. * * *

There is a strong similarity between the marks Prozac and Herbrozac, in terms of sight, sound, and meaning. Herbrozac includes five of the six letters of Prozac. As for the sixth, the "B" sound in Herbrozac is very similar to the "P" sound at the beginning of Prozac. The net effect is a message that effectively states "herbal Prozac." * * *

There are important differences and similarities between these two products. Herbrozac is not a drug. It is a dietary supplement available directly to consumers who choose to take it. The maker of Herbrozac may not lawfully claim that the product is intended to diagnose, treat, or cure a disease. By contrast, Prozac is a prescription drug that has been proven safe and effective in treating clinical depression and other conditions. There are also physical differences between the products that should not be overlooked. Herbrozac comes in large capsules with a distinctly herbal odor. Prozac comes in small green and off-white pills.

Despite these differences, the difference between a drug and a dietary supplement is primarily an artificial construct of the law, not necessarily a real difference between products. The artificial distinction between drug and dietary supplement is one that Natural Answers seeks to preserve for legal purposes but to obscure for marketing purposes. Natural Answers markets Herbrozac as an alternative to Prozac and other antidepressant drugs. * * * [A] dietary supplement based on herbs lies, for purposes of trademark law, in the natural line of expansion for a manufacturer of pharmaceutical drugs, especially where a drug and dietary supplement are intended and used to affect the same body functions and/or structures. That is, Natural Answers is trying to position its Herbrozac in the closest "competitive proximity" to Prozac that the food and drug laws will possibly allow. * * *

Lilly does not contend that consumers are likely to believe that Herbrozac capsules are really Prozac. Such confusion is not likely because one cannot even purchase Prozac without a prescription from a licensed physician, who is not at all likely to confuse one product for another. Lilly contends, however, that the similarity of the trademarks is likely to confuse some consumers as to whether there is some affiliation or association between the sources of the two products. The Lanham Act applies to use of a product name that "is likely to cause confusion, or to cause mistake, or to deceive as to the affiliation, connection; or association of such person with another person, or as to the origin, sponsorship, or approval of his or her goods, services, or commercial activities by another person." 15 U.S.C. § 1125(a)(1). * * *

The Prozac mark is unusually strong. First, it is a fanciful word that carries no meaning apart from its use to identify a product. It does not describe or suggest the function of the product it names. When the seller of a product coins a word just for the product, as Lilly did with Prozac, trademark protection is at its highest.

Natural Answers asserts that Prozac is now so famous that it has become a "generic" term no longer entitled to trademark protection. A trademark becomes generic when it comes to describe, in common usage in the United States, a class of goods rather than an individual product. * * * Where the plaintiff's trademark has been registered with the United States Patent and Trademark Office, the plaintiff is entitled to a presumption that the mark is not generic, and the burden of proof is on the defendant to come forward with evidence showing that the mark is generic. * * * A trademark can become exceptionally strong and famous without becoming generic, as suggested by the examples of Coca–Cola® and Kodak®.

Natural Answers has not shown that Prozac is likely to be deemed generic. There is no evidence that any other competitors have used the term in a generic way, let alone that Lilly has tolerated such use.[4] There is no evidence that Lilly itself has used the term in a generic way. The parties have not submitted dictionary definitions tending to show the term has seeped into common usage in a generic sense. The media references actually before the court do not use the term "Prozac" in a generic way. They use the term instead to identify plaintiff Lilly's product. They tend to focus on Prozac more than other brands, but they do not use the term "Prozac" to refer to a whole class of different antidepressant drugs. In fact, the references to the new class of antidepressant drugs, of which Prozac is the most widely sold, are much more descriptive: "selective serotonin re-uptake inhibitors." Nor is there any evidence of persons in the trade that the term "Prozac" has taken on a generic meaning, nor has Natural Answers presented any public surveys about the meaning of the term. * * *

Lilly has not presented any evidence of actual confusion here. That is not surprising. Lilly filed suit and sought a preliminary injunction before Herbrozac had reached a level of even $2000 in total sales. In fact, a respectable consumer survey would probably require sampling reactions of more consumers than have actually purchased Herbrozac to date. * * *

Considering all the factors as set forth above, the court concludes that Lilly has shown an unusually strong case on the issue of likelihood of confusion. Most important here are the unusual strength of Lilly's Prozac mark, the strong similarity between Prozac and Herbrozac, and defendant's intentional selection of the Herbrozac name precisely because of its similarity to Prozac for the purpose of suggesting an association or affiliation between the products. Add to this mixture the fairly close "competitive proximity" of the two products, especially as pharmaceutical companies expand into the herbal and dietary supplement business, and Lilly has

---

4. Like many defendants in trademark cases, Natural Answers has tried to portray itself as a tiny David being bullied by a gigantic Goliath. For the holder of a famous trademark on a successful product, however, there is little alternative because the risk of inaction is so great. Delay or failure in enforcing trademark rights will usually give rise to a laches defense. Thus, even when the infringing use is on a new product produced in small volume by a tiny start-up company, the holder of the trademark and the court must assume that the defendant's new product will achieve great commercial success. If the holder of the famous trademark waits, a growing competitor may argue laches. If the holder ignores the first infringer, a later infringer with a more successful product may try to use the holder's failure to contest the small infringing use as evidence of abandonment or of generic meaning.

made a powerful showing of likelihood of success on its claim for trademark infringement.

[In addition, on its separate claim for dilution of a famous trademark,] Lilly has shown that it is likely to prevail in showing that the Herbrozac mark blurs the Prozac mark. Herbrozac is a new product with little national recognition. However, if other manufacturers were to follow Natural Answers' footsteps in naming products, the Prozac mark would become less and less distinctive. * * * [The court issued a preliminary injunction ordering Natural Answers to discontinue using the name Herbrozac.]

NOTES AND QUESTIONS

1. *Trademark infringement.* Recall from Chapter 4(A) that the FDA has begun to pay attention to drug nomenclature in an effort to reduce prescribing errors caused by confusingly similar brand-names. Apart from these types of regulatory concerns, the use of similar brand-names may trigger private litigation. See Erva Pharm., Inc. v. American Cyanamid Co., 755 F.Supp. 36 (D.P.R.1991) (holding that a company selling Supra, a prescription drug for erectile dysfunction, in violation of various FDA requirements could not sue for trademark infringement by a competitor); see also CIBA–GEIGY Corp. v. Bolar Pharm. Co., 719 F.2d 56 (3d Cir.1983) (trade dress infringement); Ortho Pharm. Corp. v. Cosprophar, Inc., 828 F.Supp. 1114, 1125–27 & n.16 (S.D.N.Y.1993) (denying drug manufacturer standing to bring Lanham Act claims against a cosmetic company selling retinol-based anti-wrinkle products, noting that the manufacturer may have violated FDA regulations by promoting the acne drug Retin–A for this off-label use); Jan R. McTavish, What's in a Name? Aspirin and the AMA, 61 Bull. Hist. Med. 343 (1987).

2. *Battling "gray market" imports.* When U.S. companies license the sale of their products overseas, they sometimes find that the foreign licensees attempt to export them back for sale to American consumers. These so-called "gray market" imports are not counterfeits, but they have a similar impact because their lower prices undercut sales by the domestic license holder. Companies have turned to the Lanham Act in an effort to block such imports. See Summit Technology, Inc. v. High–Line Med. Instruments Co., 922 F.Supp. 299, 307–11 (C.D.Cal.1996) (rejecting a Lanham Act claim brought by the manufacturer of an excimer laser system used by ophthalmologists against a company that purchased units in foreign markets for reimportation into the United States); see also Shira R. Yashor, Note, Competing in the Shadowy Gray: Protecting Domestic Trademark Holders from Gray Marketeers Under the Lanham Act, 59 U. Chi. L. Rev. 1363 (1992); cf. Polymer Technology Corp. v. Mimran, 37 F.3d 74, 77–81 (2d Cir.1994) (rejecting trademark infringement claims asserted by the manufacturer of a contact lens solution intended only for sale to health professionals against retailers who sold the product directly to consumers). Recall from the previous chapter that Congress recently enacted legislation authorizing the FDA to allow the re-importation of drugs, but, until the agency chooses to implement that law, most types of gray market imports would run afoul of existing restrictions. See Lars Noah, NAFTA's Impact on the Trade in Pharmaceuticals, 33 Hous. L. Rev. 1293, 1303–09 (1997).

Rhone-Poulenc Rorer Pharmaceuticals, Inc. v. Marion Merrell Dow, Inc.

93 F.3d 511 (8th Cir.1996).

■ Loken, Circuit Judge:

* * * Defendant Marion Merrell Dow (MMD) introduced the first diltiazem drug, Cardizem, in 1982. The FDA approved Cardizem for the treatment of angina; it was also widely prescribed to treat hypertension. In 1989, MMD introduced a sustained release Cardizem product that is taken twice per day. MMD then developed Cardizem CD, a sustained release drug that is taken only once per day. The FDA approved Cardizem CD for hypertension and for angina. Diltiazem was a pioneer new drug, which means that the Cardizem products enjoyed a ten-year period of market exclusivity under the Hatch–Waxman amendments to the Food, Drug, and Cosmetics Act. Cardizem products were immensely successful, generating sales of $1.1 billion in 1992 alone. By the early 1990s, competing drug manufacturers were anxious to penetrate the diltiazem market with less costly alternatives.

[Plaintiff Rhone–Poulenc Rorer (RPR)] launched its diltiazem drug in June 1992. RPR's Dilacor XR, a once-per-day sustained release tablet, initially received FDA new drug approval for the treatment of hypertension but not angina. FDA approval as a new drug, which is more rigorous than approval as a generic substitute, allowed Dilacor XR to compete with Cardizem CD during the latter's period of market exclusivity. FDA classified Dilacor XR as a "BC" drug—one that is not necessarily "bioequivalent"—rather than a bioequivalent "AB" drug. Pharmacists may freely substitute among AB drugs, but only a prescribing physician may substitute one BC drug for another.

Given this FDA classification, to significantly penetrate the diltiazem market RPR had to persuade physicians to prescribe its low-cost product, Dilacor XR, as a substitute for Cardizem CD. MMD of course wanted to persuade the same audience that this is an inappropriate substitution. With this issue as the battleground, the two companies launched advertising campaigns for the allegiance of doctors, pharmacists, and hospitals. Because these are sophisticated consumers, the battle was waged with technical advertisements in professional journals and with marketing presentations by each company's sales representatives. RPR sought to convince prescribing physicians that Dilacor XR is the "same as, only cheaper" than Cardizem CD. MMD's message was, in essence, "not same as," and maybe not cheaper.

The nature of the competing false advertising claims can be briefly summarized. MMD's defensive advertising began with literature telling its sales representatives that Dilacor XR might be only seventy-five percent as bioavailable as Cardizem CD. After agreeing to discontinue that unsubstantiated claim, MMD's next wave of promotional materials advised sales representatives, doctors, and pharmacists that studies showed Dilacor XR only fifty percent as bioavailable as Cardizem CD. In its third wave of advertising, MMD released a four-page brochure in April 1993 reporting the results of a comparative study conducted by an outside laboratory, the "6730 Study." The results, as reported by MMD: "Dilacor XR delivers 81% of a 180–mg dose relative to Cardizem CD" and "74% of a 540–mg dose." RPR sued, contending that these false comparative bioavailability claims violate the Lanham Act.

Throughout this period, RPR's advertising urged doctors and pharmacists to switch their patients from Cardizem products to the low-cost Dilacor XR. In its counterclaims, MMD attacked this advertising as falsely telling medical professionals that Dilacor XR is freely substitutable for Cardizem products when in fact Dilacor XR is not FDA-approved for angina, physicians should monitor patients who switch from Cardizem CD because Dilacor XR does not have "similar bioavailability," and the two drugs are absorbed differently when taken with a meal (the "food effect").

After a bench trial, the district court found that MMD's early literature claiming that Dilacor XR has only seventy-five percent or fifty percent bioavailability violated the Lanham Act. It enjoined MMD from making those claims. However, it found that MMD's advertising based upon the 6730 Study was not false, and it declined to award RPR money damages because RPR failed to prove damage resulting from MMD's earlier false advertising. Turning to MMD's counterclaims, the district court found that RPR's advertising "contain[ed] a hidden message encouraging indiscriminate substitution" that is false in two respects—Dilacor XR is not approved for treatment of angina, and Dilacor XR has a "food effect" that creates a risk of injury if physicians do not monitor patients who are switched to Dilacor XR. Based upon these violations, the court enjoined RPR to "take necessary steps" to advise sales representatives, physicians, pharmacists, and patients (1) of "the food effect associated with Dilacor XR," (2) that physicians should "carefully monitor and titrate" (adjust the dosages) when they switch patients from Cardizem CD to Dilacor XR, and (3) that "Dilacor XR is not approved to treat angina." * * *

MMD advertised Dilacor XR's lower bioavailability in order to persuade medical professionals that Dilacor XR is not a comparable substitute and to undercut Dilacor XR's price advantage. The trial evidence showed that MMD's first claim of seventy-five percent bioavailability was false because it had no substantiation. The second claim of fifty percent bioavailability was false because it was based upon an obvious misinterpretation of data from prior studies. But MMD's third claim of 74% to 81% bioavailability was based upon the specially commissioned 6730 Study. * * *

The Lanham Act prohibits "commercial advertising or promotion [that] misrepresents the nature, characteristics, qualities, or geographic origin of [the advertiser's] or another person's goods, services, or commercial activities." 15 U.S.C. § 1125(a)(1)(B). * * * Thus, the issue before us is whether that advertising was false because the 6730 Study is not a sufficiently reliable basis for comparing the bioavailability of Dilacor XR and Cardizem CD. At trial, RPR presented expert testimony that the 6730 Study was flawed in design and execution, plus evidence that two RPR studies, the "113 Study" and the "115 Study," did not have these flaws and refuted the bioavailability conclusions of the 6730 Study. MMD countered with expert testimony supporting the 6730 Study's methodology and attacking the RPR studies. After weighing this conflicting evidence, the district court concluded that the 6730 Study is a valid study "conducted by standards accepted within the scientific community and consistent with FDA principles." * * *

After carefully reviewing this evidence, we conclude the district court's finding that MMD did not falsely advertise the 6730 Study must be upheld. * * * We note that Lanham Act liability for "tests prove" advertising requires proof that the tests are not "sufficiently reliable" to support the advertised conclusion with "reasonable certainty." To ensure vigorous competition and to protect legitimate commercial speech, courts applying this standard should give advertisers a fair amount of leeway, at least in the absence of a clear intent to deceive or substantial consumer confusion.

RPR also argues that it was entitled to money damages for MMD's earlier false advertising. The Lanham Act provides that a successful plaintiff "shall be entitled" to recover "any damages sustained." 15 U.S.C. § 1117(a). Plaintiff must prove both actual damages and a causal link between defendant's violation and those damages. * * * RPR attempted to prove that MMD's false advertising resulted in $40 to $56 million of lost Dilacor XR sales. However, the district court found that Dilacor XR sales "exceeded [RPR's] initial predictions" and that "Dilacor XR is as well-positioned as should be reasonably expected at this stage in its product history with or without [MMD's] anti-Dilacor campaigns." These findings are not clearly erroneous and are directly responsive to RPR's damage theory. Thus, the district court did not abuse its remedial discretion in declining to award RPR damages. Likewise, because MMD discontinued its earlier false advertising and did not violate the Lanham Act in advertising the 6730 Study results, the court did not abuse its discretion in declining to order MMD to conduct corrective advertising.

The district court found that RPR's advertisements conveyed a false hidden message encouraging indiscriminate substitution of Dilacor XR for Cardizem CD. It ordered RPR to engage in corrective advertising regarding the fact that Dilacor XR is not FDA-approved to treat angina, the need to monitor and titrate patients who switch from Cardizem CD to Dilacor XR, and Dilacor XR's food effect. RPR concedes that its advertisements encouraged physicians to consider the two drugs freely substitutable, and it does not appeal the order that it must effectively disclose the need to monitor and titrate patients who switch drugs. But RPR does contend that the district court erred in ordering corrective advertising disclosing that Dilacor XR is not approved to treat angina and has a "food effect."

Regarding the limited FDA approval issue, RPR notes that it has truthfully advertised Dilacor XR as approved for the treatment of hypertension. The district court erred, RPR argues, because a Lanham Act plaintiff alleging that advertising is false because it conveys a false implicit message must prove actual consumer confusion, and MMD presented no such proof. See Johnson & Johnson–Merck Consumer Pharm. Co. v. Smithkline Beecham Corp., 960 F.2d 294, 297–98 (2d Cir.1992). We note that other Second Circuit cases have said that implicit falsity "should be tested by public reaction," not that a plaintiff such as MMD must prove confusion by consumer research. But we need not resolve that issue because consumer confusion need not be proved if advertising is literally false.[4]

In assessing whether advertising is literally false, "a court must analyze the message conveyed in full context." Here, the record clearly supports the district court's finding that RPR's advertisements were literally false. The court focused on RPR advertisements featuring images such as two similar gasoline pumps or airline tickets with dramatically different prices, accompanied by the slogan, "Which one would you choose." The court found that these ads falsely represented that the two drugs may be indiscriminately substituted, in effect, a representation that Dilacor XR "has certain qualities that it in fact does not actually have." Because the implicit message was literally false, the issue became one of remedy—what corrective advertising would be appropriate. The district court determined that the false message would be remedied if RPR adequately explained the differences in the two products, including the fact that Dilacor XR is not approved to treat angina. There was no abuse of discretion in adopting that remedy. * * *

Sandoz Pharmaceuticals Corp. v. Richardson–Vicks

902 F.2d 222 (3d Cir.1990).

■ BECKER, CIRCUIT JUDGE:

* * * Sandoz manufactures and sells various pharmaceutical products. Its offerings include Triaminic–DM and Triaminicol, leading cough medicines which may be used by children as well as adults. Like Sandoz, Vicks produces and markets a wide array of pharmaceuticals, but, unlike Sandoz, it has not had a market leader in the over-the-counter (OTC) children's cough medicine market. In the fall of 1989, Vicks sought to develop such a leader by introducing a new product, Pediatric 44.

Before its nationwide release of Pediatric 44, Vicks developed a consumer advertising campaign which claimed that Pediatric 44 "starts to work the instant they [the children] swallow" by "shielding irritated cough

---

4. Furthermore, MMD presented evidence of consumer confusion. One physician testified that an RPR representative told him that RPR's formulation of diltiazem "is the same as Cardizem CD." MMD produced affidavits from other physicians stating that they had been told by RPR representatives that the drugs are the same. MMD also produced RPR physician surveys suggesting that consumers viewed the two products as interchangeable.

receptors on contact." Vicks planned to carry this message to consumers via television commercials and print advertisements in consumer magazines, and to pediatricians via "information sheets" mailed to doctors. In addition to claiming that Pediatric 44 "starts working from the very first swallow," the information sheets also state that "Pediatric Formula 44 provides more cough relief in the first thirty minutes [than] those thin, watery cough medicines." To support this statement, the Vicks circular used a bar graph which compared Pediatric 44 with "the leading OTC cough syrup," and showed Pediatric 44 apparently outperforming the competitor.

Vicks's advertising claims with regard to Pediatric 44 are based on the effect of certain locally-acting, inert sugary liquids known as "demulcents," which operate directly on cough receptors in the recipient's throat and respiratory passages. Demulcents are topically acting antitussives, in contrast to centrally acting antitussives, which are the traditional cough antidotes. Because these demulcents work on contact, Vicks claims that Pediatric 44 begins to reduce coughs as soon as it is swallowed.

Vicks performed various tests to support this conclusion. The record contains test results which support, if only marginally, Vicks's arguments that Pediatric 44 starts to work right away, that there is a scientific basis for this claim, and that Pediatrics 44 is superior to its competitors. However, the FDA has never approved any "demulcents" as effective for the relief of coughs, and whether Vicks's level of testing could meet the high standards for drug approval set by the FDA is far from certain.[5] * * *

The first question of law we must address is whether a plaintiff can prevail under the Lanham Act by showing simply that the defendant's advertising claims about its OTC drug's effectiveness are inadequately substantiated under federal guidelines, without also showing that the claims are literally false or are misleading to the consuming public. Sandoz's prime contention on appeal is that it can.

The FTC has the authority under Sections 5 and 12 of the FTC Act, 15 U.S.C. §§ 45 & 52, to find that an inadequately substantiated advertising claim regarding a non-prescription drug is deceptive or misleading, and thus illegal. Sandoz argues that the language in the FTC Act prohibiting "any false advertising" is functionally indistinguishable from the language in the Lanham Act prohibiting "any false description or representation."

---

5. * * * To this point, Vicks has only completed induced cough studies on Pediatric 44. These tests employed healthy subjects whose coughs were artificially induced by the inhalation of citric acid aerosol. Of the five tests performed, each test showed a statistically significant reduction in coughs by the subjects after they received Pediatric 44 as compared to before they received any cough medicine. All but one of the tests, however, were statistically inconclusive regarding whether Pediatric 44 reduced coughs more effectively than Robitussin, a leading OTC children's cough medicine. * * * Vicks undertook, but eventually abandoned, two attempts to measure the effectiveness of Pediatric 44 utilizing "disease state" studies, i.e., studies using individuals actually suffering from upper respiratory infections or other cough-inducing illnesses. Disease state studies are considered more accurate measures of a drug's effectiveness because the drug is tested on subjects actually suffering from the symptoms the drug allegedly combats.

Therefore, according to Sandoz, "it would be absurd" to conclude that an inadequately substantiated claim can violate Sections 5 and 12 of the FTC Act but not Section 43(a) of the Lanham Act.

Vicks, on the other hand, states that Sandoz cannot succeed merely by showing that Vicks's advertising claims are not supported by enough evidence to warrant FDA approval. Rather, Vicks maintains that Sandoz must prove that insufficient substantiation misleads consumers or pediatricians. * * * The key distinctions between the FTC and a Lanham Act plaintiff turns on the burdens of proof and the deference accorded these respective litigants. The FTC, as a plaintiff, can rely on its own determination of deceptiveness. In contrast, a Lanham Act plaintiff must prove deceptiveness in court. * * * [C]onsumer testimony proving actual deception is not necessary when the FTC claims that an advertisement has the capacity to deceive or mislead the public. A Lanham Act plaintiff, on the other hand, is not entitled to the luxury of deference to its judgment. Consequently, where the advertisements are not literally false, plaintiff bears the burden of proving actual deception by a preponderance of the evidence. Hence, it cannot obtain relief by arguing how consumers *could* react; it must show how consumers *actually do* react. * * * We hold that it is not sufficient for a Lanham Act plaintiff to show only that the defendant's advertising claims of its own drug's effectiveness are inadequately substantiated under FDA guidelines; the plaintiff must also show that the claims are literally false or misleading to the public. * * *

Sandoz failed to advance actual evidence of consumer misinterpretation. Furthermore, Sandoz's counsel in oral argument before this court admitted that Sandoz had not proven either that the ingredient in Pediatric 44 designed to shield cough receptors was ineffective or that Vicks's advertising claim was literally false. The district court carefully analyzed the evidence of Vicks's theoretical and empirical justifications for its advertising claims, and we cannot say that its finding that Sandoz did not establish that consumers were misled was clearly erroneous. * * *

[A] target audience's special knowledge of a class of products is highly relevant to any claim that it was misled by an advertisement for such a product. Sandoz never advanced any hard evidence that pediatricians would be misled by Vicks's information sheets or that they would believe that the assertions contained therein were supported by a greater degree of testing data than Vicks actually had compiled. We therefore conclude that the district court's finding that Sandoz had not proven that the pediatrician advertisements were misleading is also not clearly erroneous. * * *

We turn now to the question whether a Lanham Act false labeling claim exists against a manufacturer who lists an ingredient as "inactive" when FDA standards seem to require that such an ingredient be labeled as "active." Sandoz has presented no evidence showing that Pediatric 44's "inactive" label is misleading to the consuming public, and Sandoz did not actively pursue the argument, either here or in the district court, that the "inactive" label in question was deceptive. Instead, it alleges that the label contains a literally false description of the product. * * *

The Lanham Act is primarily intended to protect commercial interests. A competitor in a Lanham Act suit does not act as a " 'vicarious avenger' of the public's right to be protected against false advertising." American Home Prods. Corp. v. Johnson & Johnson, 672 F.Supp. 135, 145 (S.D.N.Y. 1987). Instead, the statute provides a private remedy to a commercial plaintiff who meets the burden of proving that its commercial interests have been harmed by a competitor's false advertising. The FD&C Act, in contrast, is not focused on the truth or falsity of advertising claims. It requires the FDA to protect the public interest by "pass[ing] on the safety and efficacy of all new drugs and . . . promulgat[ing] regulations concerning the conditions under which various categories of OTC drugs . . . are safe, effective and not misbranded." American Home Prod. Corp. v. Johnson & Johnson, 436 F.Supp. 785, 797–98 (S.D.N.Y.1977), aff'd, 577 F.2d 160 (2d Cir.1978).

Sandoz argues that false labeling is actionable under the Lanham Act, and rather conclusively assumes that Vicks's listing of the demulcents in its Pediatric 44 as "inactive" is false. Assuming arguendo that false labeling is actionable under the Lanham Act, Sandoz cannot prevail on its labeling claim because it has not proved that Vicks's labeling is false. Sandoz's counsel argued to the district court that "[i]f [the demulcents] relieve coughs they're active. That's true as a matter of common sense and normal English." Such an interpretation of FDA regulations, absent direct guidance from the promulgating agency, is not as simple as Sandoz proposes.

The FDA has not found conclusively that demulcents must be labelled as active or inactive ingredients within the meaning of 21 C.F.R. § 210.3(b)(7).[10] We decline to find and do not believe that the district court had to find, either "as a matter of common sense" or "normal English," that which the FDA, with all of its scientific expertise, has yet to determine. Because "agency decisions are frequently of a discretionary nature or frequently require expertise, the agency should be given the first chance to exercise that discretion or to apply that expertise." Thus, we are unable to conclude that Vicks's labeling of Pediatric 44's demulcents as inactive is literally false, even if Vicks concurrently claims that these ingredients enable its medicine to work the instant it is swallowed.

Sandoz's position would require us to usurp administrative agencies' responsibility for interpreting and enforcing potentially ambiguous regulations. Jurisdiction for the regulation of OTC drug marketing is vested jointly and exhaustively in the FDA and the FTC, and is divided between them by agreement. Neither of these agencies' constituent statutes creates an express or implied private right of action, and what the FD&C Act and the FTC Act do not create directly, the Lanham Act does not create indirectly, at least not in cases requiring original interpretation of these Acts or their accompanying regulations. * * *

10. Sandoz is free to petition the FDA to investigate these alleged labeling violations. Sandoz represents that it has embarked upon this path already. The fact that it has been unable to get a quick response from the FDA, however, does not create a claim for Sandoz under the Lanham Act.

NOTES AND QUESTIONS

1. *Private remedies for false advertising by competitors.* In addition to providing a private right of action for cases of trademark infringement, the Lanham Act has become an important weapon in the promotional battles between pharmaceutical companies. See Schering Corp. v. Pfizer Inc., 189 F.3d 218 (2d Cir.1999) (reviewing allegations that sales representatives had made misleading claims for prescription antihistamines when detailing physicians); Johnson & Johnson–Merck Consumer Pharm. Co. v. Rhone–Poulenc Rorer Pharm., Inc., 19 F.3d 125 (3d Cir.1994) (OTC antacid); Mylan Labs., Inc. v. Matkari, 7 F.3d 1130, 1137–39 (4th Cir.1993) (labeling for generic drugs allegedly approved by fraud on the FDA); Abbott Labs. v. Mead Johnson & Co., 971 F.2d 6, 13–16 (7th Cir.1992) (holding that the manufacturer of a nonprescription oral electrolyte maintenance solution, which was promoted to health professionals as therapy for infants at risk of dehydration from vomiting or diarrhea, had demonstrated a likelihood of success on the merits of its objections to a competitor's marketing campaign); McNeil–P.C.C., Inc. v. Bristol–Myers Squibb Co., 938 F.2d 1544, 1549–51 (2d Cir.1991) (affirming an injunction issued against the advertising claim that Aspirin Free Excedrin "works better" for headaches than Extra–Strength Tylenol because the scientific studies failed to substantiate analgesic superiority based on nothing other than the use of caffeine in combination with acetaminophen); SmithKline Beecham Consumer Healthcare, L.P. v. Johnson & Johnson–Merck Consumer Pharm. Co., 906 F.Supp. 178 (S.D.N.Y.1995) (OTC heartburn drug), aff'd mem., 100 F.3d 943 (2d Cir.1996); Pfizer, Inc. v. Miles, Inc., 868 F.Supp. 437 (D.Conn.1994) (reviewing objections to various comparative advertising claims by the manufacturers of non-bioequivalent extended-release versions of the antihypertensive drug nifedipine); id. at 460–61 (ordering one company to instruct its sales force to stop disparaging the competitor's drug). See generally Charles J. Walsh & Marc S. Klein, From Dog Food to Prescription Drug Advertising: Litigating False Scientific Establishment Claims Under the Lanham Act, 22 Seton Hall L. Rev. 389 (1992).

2. *False advertising claims by consumers.* Purchasers do not have standing to sue under the Lanham Act. See Serbin v. Ziebart Int'l Corp., 11 F.3d 1163 (3d Cir.1993). If a consumer did not suffer a personal injury that might allow a tortious misrepresentation or similar claim under common law, he or she might have recourse under state statutes that prohibit deceptive acts or practices and provide a private right of action. See Bober v. Glaxo Wellcome PLC, 246 F.3d 934 (7th Cir.2001) (rejecting consumers' objections to nonsubstitutability claims for OTC Zantac 75 and Rx Zantac 150) (excerpted in Chapter 4(B)(2)); Boos v. Abbott Labs., 925 F.Supp. 49, 54–56 (D.Mass.1996).

B.   MARKET EXCLUSIVITY PERIODS

Because inventors usually apply for patents before clinical testing commences, manufacturers of new drugs and medical devices have only a portion of their patent term (which now runs 20 years from filing) left when they receive FDA approval. Recognizing that this may weaken the incentives for innovative activity, Congress established various periods of market exclusivity as a partial substitute. Although weaker than a patent because it only stalls FDA clearance of ANDAs for generic competitors, a period of market exclusivity can provide tremendous financial returns if it runs beyond the date of patent expiration.

1. NEW DRUGS AND MEDICAL DEVICES

Burroughs Wellcome Co. v. Bowen

630 F.Supp. 787 (E.D.N.C.1986).

■ BRITT, DISTRICT JUDGE:

In this action Burroughs Wellcome Company asks the court to overturn a new drug application (NDA) approval issued January 30, 1986, by the Food and Drug Administration (FDA) for an oral leucovorin calcium product manufactured by Lederle Laboratories. Leucovorin calcium is used as an antidote to the adverse effects of chemotherapeutic drugs and other medications. * * *

Lederle is the "pioneer" manufacturer of leucovorin. On June 20, 1952, Lederle obtained new drug approval from the FDA for an injectable dosage form of leucovorin calcium. After the Act was amended in 1962 to require proof of effectiveness, in addition to safety, Lederle submitted additional information on its product. On June 9, 1971, Lederle's NDA for injectable leucovorin was approved as safe and effective. Sometime thereafter Burroughs obtained approval of its own NDA for injectable leucovorin.

In 1979 Burroughs submitted an NDA for an oral dosage form of leucovorin. Burroughs' application was a "paper" NDA; it was based, with the exception of the bioavailability study, on published reports in the medical literature rather than on Burroughs' own clinical investigations or on a prior approved Burroughs product. Burroughs' bioavailability study compared its oral dosage form to Lederle's approved injectable form. On July 8, 1983, Burroughs' application was approved by the FDA's Division of Oncology.

On February 8, 1980, Lederle submitted an NDA to the FDA's Division of Oncology to market an oral dosage form of its leucovorin product. During the course of the Division of Oncology's review Lederle was informed that with respect to the safety and effectiveness of the active ingredient its application was not approvable on the basis of the new clinical reports it had submitted on the oral dosage form. FDA officials encouraged Lederle to submit bioavailability data on its oral form using its own injectable form as the reference drug, and Lederle submitted the requested data. * * *

In its traditional form an NDA contains full reports of testing to show the drug's safety and well-controlled clinical investigations to show the drug's effectiveness, along with manufacturing and chemistry data, proposed labeling, and other studies. A "clinical investigation" is a study of the use of a drug in humans for the purpose of distinguishing the effect of the drug from other influences, such as a placebo effect. The 1984 amendments to the FDC Act codified for the first time the FDA's authority to approve generic copies of drugs on the basis of a showing of bioequivalence to a previously approved drug without requiring resubmission of safety and effectiveness data.

Pursuant to the 1984 amendments there are now two new kinds of drug applications: literature supported NDAs frequently termed "paper" NDAs (section 505(b)(2)), and abbreviated new drug applications (ANDAs) (section 505(j)). A "paper" NDA is one in which the required safety and effectiveness data are not the result of original testing by the NDA applicant, but rather are obtained from literature reports of testing done by others. An ANDA is an application that does not contain any safety or effectiveness testing at all, with the exception of bioavailability testing. The "bioavailability" data show that the ANDA drug, when administered, will provide the same amount of active ingredient to the body as the previously approved drug. Thus, an ANDA is approved on the basis of safety and effectiveness testing done for a previously approved version of the drug.

The 1984 amendments contain five detailed "exclusivity" provisions which prescribe periods of time during which the FDA may not make immediately effective the approval of ANDAs or "paper" NDAs for generic copies of certain previously approved drugs. These exclusivity provisions have no effect on full new drug applications (section 505(b)(1) NDAs), those applications that rely for approval on data sponsored by the applicant or for which the applicant has a right of reference. Furthermore, with the exception of one provision not at issue in this case, the exclusivity provisions do not operate to bar approval as such, but rather to delay the effective date of approval.

"Paper" NDAs and ANDAs are subject to the FDC Act's exclusivity provisions only if they "refer to" a previously approved drug. Thus, Lederle's application, even if properly termed a "paper" NDA or ANDA, is clearly not subject to Burroughs' exclusivity rights. Burroughs has submitted no evidence whatsoever that Lederle's application referred to Burroughs' oral leucovorin product or to any investigations which were conducted by or for Burroughs. * * * Burroughs has failed to establish a strong likelihood of success on the merits of this action. Therefore, Burroughs' motion for a temporary restraining order and a preliminary injunction is hereby denied.

Mead Johnson Pharmaceutical Group v. Bowen

838 F.2d 1332 (D.C.Cir.1988).

■ EDWARDS, CIRCUIT JUDGE:

* * * As a transitional measure, the [Hatch–Waxman] Amendments provided for a ten-year period of exclusivity for drugs "approved" by the FDA between January 1, 1982, and the enactment date of the Amend-

ments, September 24, 1984. See 21 U.S.C. § 355(j)(4)(D)(i). Drugs approved later had shorter periods of exclusivity, while those approved before January 1, 1982, enjoyed no exclusivity at all.

Desyrel is Mead Johnson's trade name for trazodone HCl, an antidepressant drug. Mead submitted a NDA for Desyrel in October 1978. On December 21, 1981, Dr. Marion Finkel of the FDA transmitted a letter to Mead informing it that review of the NDA was complete. This letter stated that approval would be forthcoming upon Mead's submission of revised printed labeling, in accordance with 4½ pages of detailed FDA comments. Following several telephone conversations, Mead submitted revised labeling the next day, incorporating the FDA's requested changes. In its accompanying letter, Mead stated its understanding, based on the telephone discussions, that "final approved labeling can be submitted subsequent to the approval of the NDA." More telephone conversations apparently ensued, and on December 24 the FDA sent Mead a letter which stated in relevant part:

> We have completed our review of [the Desyrel] application as submitted with revised draft labeling on December 22, 1981 and have concluded the drug is safe and effective for use as recommended in the labeling. Accordingly, the application is approved. As agreed to over the phone this approval is granted with the understanding that any remaining issues regarding validation will be promptly and satisfactorily resolved and that final printed labeling will be promptly submitted and revised as follows before the drug is marketed.

There followed five specific requests for minor changes in language under the label's description of adverse reactions (such as changing "memory loss" to "impaired memory").

In the December 1981 supplement to its "Approved Prescription Drug Products" list, the FDA listed Desyrel as approved. In the December 1981 "FDA Drug and Device Product Approvals" list, the FDA also listed Desyrel with an approval date of December 24, 1981. On January 19, 1982, Mead submitted the final printed labeling for Desyrel to the FDA with a cover letter that referenced "Your letter of approval for Desyrel ... dated December 24, 1981." The FDA processed the final labeling as a "supplemental NDA." On February 1, 1982, in a letter to Mead signed by Dr. Paul Leber, a Division Director, the FDA stated: "We have completed our review and the supplement is approved."

After passage of the Hatch–Waxman Amendments, the FDA began to prepare for implementation by requesting drug manufacturers to submit information on their approved drugs. In response to such a request, Mead informed the FDA on October 22, 1984, that the approval date for Desyrel was December 24, 1981, and that it was not entitled to a period of statutory exclusivity. Six months later, however, on April 19, 1985—just days before its patent on the drug was to expire—Mead wrote to the FDA to inform it that it had "reviewed our NDA file for Desyrel," that it had determined that the proper approval date was February 1, 1982, and that it was therefore entitled to an exclusivity period until February 1, 1992. * * *

The FDA rejected the petition in a letter issued August 15, 1985. It found that Desyrel had been approved on December 24, 1981. It stated that the December 24 letter had approved the NDA, with the understanding that final labeling would be submitted before the drug was marketed, but that the letter had "neither stated nor implied" that any further approval was necessary before the drug could be marketed. It added that agreement had been reached by telephone on the changes to be made, and that the ten-year exclusivity period depended only on the date of approval, not the date of marketing. The February 1 letter was clearly only an approval of a "labeling supplement" to a previously approved NDA; its author had had no authority to approve a NDA.[2] * * *

While the term "approved" is not defined in the statute, it had, at the time the Hatch–Waxman Amendments were enacted, a precise and undisputed meaning. By regulation the FDA had specified that "the applicant shall be notified in writing that the application is approved and the application shall be approved on the date of the notification." 21 C.F.R. § 314.105 (1981). As the district court pointed out, the precise date of an "approval" was of great concern to the FDA, the NDA applicant, and competing drug manufacturers, even before the Hatch–Waxman Amendments. The FDA's regulation on this point thus reflected a well-considered, long-standing policy. We have found absolutely no reason to believe that Congress intended the term "approved" in the Hatch–Waxman Amendments to mean anything other than what the FDA understood it to mean. * * *

We note finally that the Sixth Circuit last year decided a case virtually identical to this one. Norwich Eaton Pharm., Inc. v. Bowen, 808 F.2d 486 (6th Cir.1987). There, a drug manufacturer's NDA was approved on December 29, 1981, via a letter similar to the one at issue here, but the final labeling was submitted to the FDA only in June 1985. Nonetheless, the court had no difficulty in holding that the FDA's determination that the drug had been approved on December 29, 1981, was based on a permissible interpretation of the statute. * * *

We hold the FDA's interpretation of the term "approved" in 21 U.S.C. § 355(j)(4)(D)(i) to be consistent with congressional intent; and, even if the term "approved" might be viewed as ambiguous, it is clear that the FDA's construction was a permissible one.

Upjohn Co. v. Kessler

938 F.Supp. 439 (W.D.Mich.1996).

■ BELL, DISTRICT JUDGE:

* * * Upjohn originally developed minoxidil as an antihypertensive agent for the treatment of high blood pressure. When patients using the

---

2. The FDA pointed out that Dr. Leber, the author of the February 1 letter, was a Division Director, and as such was authorized to approve a supplemental NDA, but not a NDA itself. Thus, it stated, if Mead was correct that the Desyrel NDA had not been approved on December 24, then it had never been approved at all. Subsequently, Mead shifted its argument and maintained that "approval" had taken place when it submitted the final labeling on January 19.

drug experienced unwanted hair growth, Upjohn began investigations into the use of the drug for treatment of hair loss. In 1988 the FDA approved Upjohn's new drug application (NDA) for Rogaine, a 2% minoxidil topical solution for the treatment of certain forms of male hair loss. In 1991 Upjohn received FDA approval for the use of Rogaine in the treatment of female hair loss. The FDA approvals limited Rogaine to sale as a prescription drug.

In September 1991, Upjohn initiated communications with the FDA regarding its desire to have Rogaine approved for over-the-counter sales. Such a switch from Rx to OTC status requires approval of a supplemental NDA by the FDA. Upjohn advised that Rogaine had proven to be a safe treatment and that a sufficiently large body of data had been collected that supported the RX-to-OTC switch. On April 9, 1992, Upjohn representatives met with FDA representatives to discuss what information the FDA would require in order to evaluate the proposed Rx-to-OTC switch. Among the concerns raised by FDA representatives at this meeting were the low tolerance for any risk of serious adverse effects due to the cosmetic nature of the drug, the need to address cardiovascular risks and the need to address risks associated with gross over use of the product. Upjohn referenced the ongoing [Phase] IV study in hypertensive patients that it was conducting in connection with its investigation into 5% minoxidil. On April 29, 1993, Upjohn submitted its supplemental NDA to the FDA for OTC Rogaine. Included in the supplemental NDA were the results of the IV study and an application for a 3 year period of exclusivity.

The FDA approved Upjohn's supplemental NDA for the Rx-to-OTC switch on February 9, 1996. Upjohn's patent for minoxidil expired on February 13, 1996. On April 5, 1996, the FDA informed Upjohn by telephone that its claim of exclusivity was denied. On the same date the FDA approved ANDAs for OTC Minoxidil Topical Solution 2% for intervenors Barre National and Lemmon. On April 9, 1996, the FDA approved a similar ANDA for Bausch & Lomb.

On April 12, 1996, Upjohn filed this action for declaratory and injunctive relief. Upjohn contends that the FDA's denial of its request for three years of market exclusivity and approval of the ANDAs prior to February 9, 1999, violates the market exclusivity provisions of the Act, was done arbitrarily and capriciously and not in accordance with law, was in excess of statutory authority, and constituted a taking of property without just compensation in violation of the Fifth Amendment. * * *

Upjohn was informed of the decision by telephone on April 5, 1996. In a subsequent telephone conversation Dr. Lipicky of the FDA explained that the agency's view was that the IV minoxidil study was not essential. Upjohn was also informed that the agency would not be preparing an explanatory letter * * * * [The administrative record that the agency certified to the court consisted primarily of a memorandum from Dr. Robert Temple, Director of the FDA's Office of Drug Evaluation, to Dr.

Janet Woodcock, Director of the FDA's Center for Drug Evaluation and Research (CDER), dated March 20, 1996.]

[T]here are three conditions for approval of a three-year exclusivity period. [See 21 U.S.C. § 355(j)(4)(D)(iv).] In this case there is no dispute that the IV test was a new clinical test or that the test was sponsored by Upjohn. The only issue for the court's consideration is whether there was a rational basis for the FDA's determination that the IV test was not essential to approval. Upjohn contends that the question of whether the test was essential is straight forward and calls for no scientific expertise: the IV test was essential because it was required by the FDA.

Upjohn's argument fails because it is not supported by the evidence presented. There is no question that the FDA expressed its safety concerns at the April 9, 1992, meeting. There is no evidence, however, that the FDA required Upjohn to conduct the IV study as a condition for approval of the Rx-to-OTC switch. The FDA minutes reveal that the FDA representatives expressed several areas of concern: (1) risk of misuse—"What if someone uses more than the labeled dose? What are the blood levels of Rogaine when there is an increase in absorption or gross over use?;" (2) Dr. Botstein noted the need for a focused presentation on cardiovascular risks; and (3) Dr. Temple stated that given the nature of the benefits, a case must be made that there is no discernable risk in terms of serious adverse events. * * * Dr. Temple stated that by now Upjohn should have enough information to determine whether the warnings about cardiovascular events should be removed from the physician's insert. Dr. Lipicky and Dr. Temple commented that they were familiar with the post-marketing surveillance study that had been done in conjunction with the Rx Rogaine, and that the data from the post-marketing study would support the safety of Rogaine.

The 1992 discussion clearly centered on what should be included in the submission, and was not designed to critique the studies or available data. That data was not then before the FDA—the supplemental NDA would not be filed for another year. Nowhere is there any indication that the FDA ever suggested that the available data was insufficient or that the IV test was a necessary prerequisite for approval. In fact there was testimony from Upjohn's Dr. Data that subsequent to the meeting Upjohn seriously considered submitting the supplemental NDA without the IV study.

After submitting the supplemental NDA in 1993 with the completed IV study, Upjohn received numerous questions about the IV study from the FDA. The FDA's interest in the results of the study is not evidence that the FDA requested that the study be done. The FDA is not required to ignore evidence offered by a company in support of its request for approval merely because the evidence is not necessary to approval.

If the FDA did not require Upjohn to conduct the IV study as a condition to approval, was the IV study nevertheless essential to the FDA's ability to make its determination that Rogaine was safe for OTC use? The FDA has defined the term "essential to approval" in its regulations: "Essential to approval means, with regard to an investigation, that there

are no other data available that could support approval of the application."
21 C.F.R. § 314.108(a). There is no question that the FDA had some safety
concerns with respect to the OTC sale of Rogaine. Could that safety
determination be made without reference to the IV test? Was there other
available data which addressed FDA's concern about whether the margin of
safety for topical minoxidil was sufficient to support OTC use? These
questions involve evaluation of the clinical trial and the scientific and
medical significance of that trial to FDA's final determination. They bring
the court into the heart of a chemical and pharmacological debate that is
within the peculiar expertise of the FDA. * * *

The court has reviewed Dr. Temple's 19–page memorandum devoted to
the issue of whether Upjohn's IV study of minoxidil was essential to
approval of OTC Rogaine. In this comprehensive memorandum Dr. Temple
considered the fact that Dr. Lipicky, Director, Division of Cardio–Renal
Drug Products, said that the IV study was essential to his approval
recommendation because it helped answer questions about the safety of
OTC minoxidil raised by the medical reviewer, Dr. Karkowsky. Dr. Temple
also considered Dr. Karkowsky's safety review and the extent to which it
analyzed and relied on the results of the IV study.

Dr. Temple agreed that in order to approve the Rx-to-OTC switch the
FDA should have a high level of confidence that topical minoxidil will
rarely, if ever, have significant hemodynamic effects. Nevertheless, he
concluded that the IV study did not add significantly to the FDA's ability to
reach this conclusion because (1) the IV study did not add much information about concentration-response relationships, at least as analyzed, and
(2) neither the IV or oral studies, as analyzed, shed light on individual
responses—they do not help answer the question of whether the rare
topical patients with concentrations in the 5–10 ng/ml range will have a
response:

> My conclusion is that the original clinical data, including study 84,
> enhanced by 6 benign (so far as we can tell) years of marketing, and
> the cohort study, indicate a very satisfactory record of safety, one
> suitable for an OTC drug. This is not surprising given the documented
> large (order of magnitude) difference between blood levels after topical
> dosing and the blood levels associated with barely detectable effects
> (slight HR increase, no BP effect) after oral dosing with a 2.5 mg b.i.d.
> tablet. The IV study was not essential to this conclusion, although it
> supported it, because concentrations achieved overlapped with those in
> the study of oral minoxidil and gave little new information.

Upjohn contends that the Temple rationale is arbitrary and capricious
because it relied on data available in or before 1988, prior to approval for
Rx Rogaine and because the IV test was the only effective study to address
the margin of safety issue. Upjohn also contends that the 6 benign years of
Rx use are not very helpful to the safety issue because people with
hypertension had been warned away from the drug through the package
insert discussion on risk factors.

Upjohn's dispute with the Temple memorandum is fundamentally a scientific dispute in an area where this court lacks expertise and is required to give the FDA great deference. It appears to this court that although an opposite conclusion, i.e., that the IV test was essential, could have been supported on this record, Dr. Temple's decision did not come out of the blue. Prior to the final decision Upjohn learned that even Dr. Lipicky was leaning against exclusivity. The issue of exclusivity presented the agency with a close question that required more levels of agency attention than was routine. * * *

Dr. Temple's memorandum states in detail the grounds for the decision and the essential facts upon which the decision was based. It appears that he considered the statutory factors governing exclusivity, considered the relevant data, and arrived at a rational decision based upon the evidence. Nothing more is required. See Upjohn Mfg. Co. v. Schweiker, 681 F.2d 480, 483 (6th Cir.1982). The court cannot say that the agency's determination that the IV test was not essential was arbitrary and capricious. * * * In light of the fact that Upjohn has not shown a likelihood of success on the merits, the court does not believe injunctive relief is appropriate. Upjohn's motion for preliminary injunctive will accordingly be denied.

NOTES AND QUESTIONS

1. *Supplemental indications.* The statute provided five years of market exclusivity for the original NDA, coupled with three additional years for supplemental indications based on new research. One company argued that, once it approves such a supplement, the FDA could not approve an ANDA for the original indication(s) because the labeling for the generic would then not be the same as the innovator's product. In the course of rejecting this interpretation of the statute, the court explained the economic motivation for taking this position:

> BMS considers it cold comfort that the FDA would withhold approval of a generic version of captopril for some indications but not others; once the FDA approves the sale of generic captopril for hypertension, the agency can offer BMS no assurance that physicians and pharmacists will not substitute it for Capoten in the treatment of diabetic nephropathy [the supplemental indication for which the additional exclusivity period had not yet expired].

Bristol–Myers Squibb Co. v. Shalala, 91 F.3d 1493, 1496 (D.C.Cir.1996). Although the court held that the innovator company had alleged a sufficient injury to have standing to sue, see id. at 1498–99, it rejected the company's challenge to the FDA's regulation on the merits, see id. at 1499–500:

> [U]nder the Secretary's interpretation of the Act, a pioneer drug manufacturer that obtains approval for a supplemental indication based upon proprietary research will enjoy three years during which the FDA will not approve any ANDA that includes the supplemental indication. BMS claims that economic reality renders the protection

offered by the Secretary largely an illusion. Perhaps so, but why? By BMS's own account, it is because the value of the protection the Congress most clearly conferred upon pioneers would be greater but for some state laws and health insurers that mandate substitution of generic drugs. That is not a sufficient basis upon which to conclude that the Congress intended to confer upon the manufacturers of pioneer drugs the much broader protection that BMS now seeks.

2. *Turnabout is fair play.* When the patent and market exclusivity periods for an innovator drug wind down, manufacturers may respond by seeking approval of a "new and improved" version to combat the threat of generic competition against the original version of the drug. See Mark A. Hurwitz & Richard E. Caves, Persuasion or Information? Promotion and the Shares of Brand Name and Generic Pharmaceuticals, 31 J.L. & Econ. 299, 302–03 (1988). For instance, manufacturers may introduce sustained release formulations that require less frequent dosing or a different form of the active ingredient with greater safety and/or effectiveness. See Marc Borbely, Try This Costly New Drug, Free for One Month!, Wash. Post, May 15, 2001, at T7 (describing Bristol–Myers Squibb's aggressive campaign to persuade diabetics to switch to its new extended release version of Glucophage® in an effort to head off generic competition); Stephen S. Hall, Prescription for Profit, N.Y. Times Mag., Mar. 11, 2001, at 40 (describing Schering–Plough's various strategies to maximize revenues from Claritin® (loratadine), including the planned launch of Clarinex® (desloratadine)); Francesca Kritz, A Side Effect Felt in the Wallet, Wash. Post, Mar. 13, 2001, at T6 (reporting that AstraZeneca will begin marketing Nexium® (esomeprazole magnesium) for gastroesophageal reflux disease just as its blockbuster drug Prilosec® (omeprazole) will lose protection from generics). If the FDA approves such a product, the sponsor of the NDA will receive market exclusivity for either three years (same as a supplemental NDA for an additional indication based on new studies) or five years (same as an entirely new chemical entity). Although the agency will approve ANDAs for generic versions of the original product, the manufacturers of these less expensive copies may find it difficult to take market share from therapeutically superior or more convenient versions of the product.

3. *Active moieties.* The statute provides that, before approving an ANDA, the FDA must wait five years after the approval of an NDA "for a drug, no active ingredient (including any ester or salt of the active ingredient) of which has been approved in any other application." 21 U.S.C. § 355(j)(5)(D)(ii). In trying to interpret identical language used to grant ten years of exclusivity for new chemical entities approved between 1982 and 1984, one court found serious ambiguities in the provision. See Abbott Labs. v. Young, 920 F.2d 984 (D.C.Cir.1990). In 1982, the FDA had approved the anticonvulsant Depakote® (divalproex sodium), but the agency granted the sponsor only two years of market exclusivity under the Hatch–Waxman Act's transitional provisions because, four years earlier, the same company had received an NDA for the anticonvulsant Depakene® (valproic acid). Although their active ingredients differed, the two drugs had the same "active moiety" (and pharmacological action) because divalproex sodium converted into valproic acid once ingested, but Depakote produced fewer gastrointestinal side effects. The question for the court was whether Depakote's "active ingredient (including any ester or salt of the active ingredient)" had previously been approved, in which case the sponsor would receive the shorter period of market exclusivity. Although it was a salt of valproic acid, the FDA had never before approved a drug containing divalproex sodium or any ester or salt of that active ingredient (and, if a company filed an ANDA for divalproex sodium, that is how one would ask the question). Over a sharp dissent, the court held that the language was ambiguous with regard to whether it referred to the active ingredient of the first or the second NDA, but it rejected as unreasonable the government's argument that the word "including" in the parenthetical introduced a nonexhaustive list of examples of similar forms of an active ingredient, which the FDA could interpret as also encompassing an active moiety. Conversely, the court rejected the sponsor's literal reading as implausible because it doubted that Congress had any reason for such an asymmetry (if the FDA had approved the NDA for valproic acid in 1982—after previously approving divalproex sodium—and the question focused on market exclusivity for Depakene, then everyone agrees that the sponsor would receive only two years of protection from generics). The court remanded this interpretive mess to the FDA for further consideration.

4. *Medical devices.* Because of the significant differences in approval systems, the market exclusivity periods provided by the Hatch–Waxman Act have no application to medical devices (though patent term extension and other provisions did apply equally to them). Nonetheless, the Safe Medical Devices Act of 1990 created a somewhat analogous approach for Class III devices subject to PMA requirements. Aside from possible patent constraints, a company wishing to market a device similar to one already approved by the FDA would have to assemble the same data as the innovator, but, six years after approval of a PMA for the same type of Class III device, subsequent manufacturers could file what amounts to an abbreviated PMA by cross-referencing the innovator's safety and effectiveness data. See 21 U.S.C. § 360j(h)(4).

2.   "ORPHAN" PRODUCTS AND INDICATIONS

Genentech, Inc. v. Bowen
676 F.Supp. 301 (D.D.C.1987).

■ HARRIS, DISTRICT JUDGE:

   * * * The pending motions challenge the validity of the FDA's designation, prior to marketing approval, of Lilly's drug as an orphan drug. * * * This case revolves around certain elements of the FDA's implementation of the Orphan Drug Act, Pub. L. No. 97–414, 96 Stat. 2049 (1983) (codified as amended at 21 U.S.C. §§ 360aa–360ee). * * * When the potential market for a drug is small—because the number of persons afflicted with the particular disease or condition which the drug treats is relatively small—it may be impossible for the manufacturer to recover its sizable research and

development investment, much less realize an acceptable return on that investment. The Act is designed to combat the general unwillingness of pharmaceutical manufacturers to invest in the development of commercial drugs for the treatment of diseases which, although devastating to their victims, afflict too small a proportion of the population to make them commercially viable.

The Act seeks to encourage the development of "orphan drugs" by reducing the overall financial cost of development, while enhancing the developer's ability to recover that cost through sale of the drug. Specifically, the Act attempts to reduce development costs by streamlining the FDA's approval process for orphan drugs, by providing tax breaks for expenses related to orphan drug development, by authorizing the FDA to assist in funding the clinical testing necessary for approval of an orphan drug, and by creating an Orphan Products Board to coordinate public and private development efforts. The Act seeks to enhance the orphan drug manufacturer's ability to recover his investment by granting the manufacturer seven years of exclusive marketing rights "for such drug for such [rare] disease or condition." A "rare disease or condition" is one which "affects less than 200,000 persons in the United States," or one which "affects more than 200,000 in the United States and for which there is no reasonable expectation that the cost of developing and making available in the United States a drug for such disease or condition will be recovered from sales in the United States of such drug." 21 U.S.C. § 360bb(a)(2).

Qualification for orphan drug benefits occurs in a two-step process. At any phase of the research and development process, a manufacturer who believes its drug will treat a "rare disease or condition" may apply to the FDA for designation as "a drug for a rare disease or condition" (i.e., an orphan drug). Orphan drug designation enables the manufacturer or sponsor to take advantage of the Act's tax benefits, to request pre-approval clinical testing recommendations, and to request financial assistance from the FDA in conducting the necessary clinical investigations. However, manufacturers receiving orphan drug designation must consent to limited public disclosure of the designation by the FDA and may be asked by the FDA to include in the drug's clinical testing, under an "open protocol" method, persons presently suffering from the rare disease. 21 U.S.C. § 360dd. Although the Act does not limit the number of drugs that may be designated for treatment of a particular rare disease, the FDA's present policy is to not consider requests for orphan drug designation made after that drug has received full FDA marketing approval for that particular disease. See Policy of Eligibility of Drugs for Orphan Designation, 51 Fed. Reg. 4505, 4505 (1986).

While any number of drugs may receive the development-phase benefits of the Act, only one manufacturer may receive exclusive marketing rights. This post-development benefit is reserved for the first manufacturer to receive full FDA approval of its drug as safe and effective for commercial sale. * * * The FDA may authorize another manufacturer to produce "such drug for such disease or condition" only if the exclusive marketer consents in writing or is incapable of providing sufficient quantities of the drug. * * *

The most extensive discussion of the purposes of the Act's exclusivity provision appears in the report prepared by the House Committee on Energy and Commerce to accompany the 1985 amendments to the Act. H.R. Rep. 153, 99th Cong., 1st Sess., reprinted in 1985 U.S.C.C.A.N. 301. * * * The Committee's expectation when it drafted the original provision in 1983 had been that exclusivity "would be used primarily by orphan drugs that [could] not get product patents." However, experience under the Act demonstrated that reliance on the incentives of patent protection for all patentable orphan drugs would be insufficient. First, many patents expire before completion of the clinical testing necessary for FDA marketing approval. Second, in many cases the product patent on a drug is held by an individual or company other than the one that intends to test the drug for use against a rare disease, and prior academic publication in the area precludes issuance of a use patent. Accordingly, the fact that a product patent has been issued does not always ensure that a manufacturer will have a sufficient incentive to apply for permission to market the drug as an orphan drug.

In expanding the exclusivity provision to cover both patented and unpatented orphan drugs, the Committee noted that the provision would only benefit the sponsors of drugs with less than seven years of product patent protection available, and explained the difference between exclusivity under the Act and traditional patent protection. First, traditional patents generally offer much broader protection than orphan drug exclusivity, which is limited to treatment of a particular disease. Second, while the inviolability of a patent is limited only by the holder's ability to enforce his rights in court, orphan drug exclusivity exists only so long as the sponsor adequately supplies the market. * * * In summary, a review of the legislative history reveals bipartisan support for both the purpose of the Orphan Drug Act—the development of safe and effective drugs for persons suffering from diseases so rare that ordinary market forces would not promote development—and the means of achieving the Act's goal—the creation of an economic atmosphere that would lead pharmaceutical manufacturers to invest in developing those drugs.

Human growth hormone (hGH) is a protein naturally produced and secreted by the human pituitary gland. In some children, between 6,000 and 15,000 in the United States, the pituitary gland does not produce enough hGH, resulting in stunted growth. Since 1958, the condition had been treated by supplementing a patient's natural hGH with hGH derived from the pituitary glands of human cadavers. However, in 1985, use of pituitary-derived hGH was effectively eliminated by the discovery that three hGH patients who had been treated with hGH provided by NHPP [the National Institutes of Health's National Hormone and Pituitary Program] had developed Creutzfeldt–Jakob Disease, an extremely rare but fatal condition, apparently due to exposure to a pathogen transmitted by the pituitary-derived hGH. * * *

On October 17, 1985, the FDA granted Genentech, a pharmaceutical developer that specializes in the use of biotechnology (popularly known as "gene splicing"), marketing approval for a human growth product known commercially as Protropin. Genentech's product differs from pituitary-derived hGH in two important respects. First, it is synthesized through a recombinant DNA process utilizing E. coli bacteria, rather than produced in a human gland. Second, Genentech's "r-hGH" product includes an amino acid group not commonly found in pituitary-derived hGH. In terms of chemical structure, Genentech's r-hGH has the same sequence of 191 amino acids found in hGH, with an additional methionine amino acid group attached to one end of the molecule. Because Genentech's drug apparently does not present the risk of Creutzfeldt–Jakob Disease associated with pituitary-derived hGH, its approval in 1985 filled an important health need. On December 12, 1985, the FDA designated Protropin as an orphan drug, thus granting Genentech marketing exclusivity, pursuant to 21 U.S.C. § 360cc, until December 12, 1992. Genentech estimates that it invested approximately $45 million developing its r-hGH product.

On June 12, 1986, the FDA designated an r-hGH drug developed by intervenor-defendant Lilly as an orphan drug for the treatment of human growth hormone deficiency. Unlike Genentech's r-hGH product, the chemical structure of Lilly's product is identical to that of natural, pituitary-derived hGH; that is, Lilly's drug does not contain the additional methionyl group found in Protropin. On October 15, 1986, Lilly submitted to the FDA a New Drug Application (NDA) for its r-hGH product, seeking permission to market the drug commercially.

On November 3, 1986, Genentech submitted a "citizen petition" to the FDA. In it, Genentech took the position that Lilly's drug was, for the purposes of the Orphan Drug Act, the same as Protropin and therefore ineligible for marketing approval until 1992. Genentech asked the FDA to implement procedures under which the manufacturer of an orphan drug with marketing exclusivity would receive notice of, and the opportunity to contest, another manufacturer's claim that its drug was "different" for the purposes of Orphan Drug Act protection. * * *

When Genentech learned that the FDA was preparing to approve the NDA for Lilly's methionyl-free r-hGH product, known commercially as Humatrope, Genentech sought an emergency stay from the FDA. When that request was denied, Genentech filed suit in this court on March 6, 1987, seeking temporary, preliminary, and permanent injunctive relief, in addition to a declaratory judgment that the FDA's application of the Orphan Drug Act violated Genentech's statutory and constitutional rights. * * * On March 8, the FDA approved Lilly's NDA for Humatrope, thereby authorizing Lilly to market the drug commercially and triggering the orphan drug exclusivity provision. Genentech and Nordisk have submitted NDAs for methionyl-free r-hGH products, but the FDA has not yet ruled on either NDA. * * *

Movants contend that Humatrope's orphan drug designation violated both the Orphan Drug Act and the FDA's binding regulations implementing the Act. Their argument is based on the contention that Humatrope and pituitary-derived hGH are the same drug. In light of the peculiar facts of this case, the court cannot accept movants' contention, and therefore must uphold the Humatrope designation.

The dispute presented here involves the proper application of 21 U.S.C. § 360bb(a), the section of the Act governing orphan drug designations, which provides, in relevant part:

> (1) The manufacturer or the sponsor of a drug may request the Secretary to designate the drug as a drug for a rare disease or condition. If the Secretary finds that a drug for which a request is submitted under this subsection is being or will be investigated for a rare disease or condition and—

>> (A) if an application for such drug is approved under section 355 of this title, . . .

> the approval . . . would be for use of such disease or condition, the Secretary shall designate the drug as a drug for such disease or condition.

Movants read this section as requiring that the orphan drug designation of a particular drug occur prior to approval of an NDA for that drug. They then argue that the approval of NDAs for pituitary-derived hGH in the 1970s precluded the orphan drug designation of Humatrope in 1986. Assuming, without deciding, that movants' construction of § 360bb(a) is correct, the court rejects their argument in this case because it is plain that Humatrope and pituitary-derived hGH are not the same drug for the purposes of § 360bb(a).

A review of the Act's legislative history, as all of the parties would agree, sheds no direct light on the question of how broadly or narrowly the word "drug" should be construed in § 360bb(a). The relevant committee reports and floor debates reveal broad, bipartisan support for the noble goal of providing treatment for the presently untreated, but do not evidence any focused consideration of important, but politically tiresome, details like the issue presented here. Instead, Congress directed that the FDA "shall by regulation promulgate procedures for the implementation" of § 360bb(a). Unfortunately, the FDA has not, in the four years since passage of the Act, proposed any regulations defining "drug" for the purposes of § 360bb(a). Thus, the court—lacking either a legislative or administrative pronouncement—is left to apply the Act's broad policy objectives to the unique situation at hand.

Two related aspects of this particular case convince the court that if Congress had been presented with the facts of this case, it would have considered Humatrope and pituitary-derived hGH different drugs for the purposes of § 360bb(a). First, Humatrope, by virtue of its synthetic origin, does not present the danger of contamination with the Creutzfeldt–Jakob prion that is associated with hGH obtained from human cadavers. While movants are correct in noting that none of the reported cases of Creutzfeldt–Jakob Disease has been linked to hGH marketed under the approved

NDAs held by Serono and Kabi, it is also true that so little is known about the contamination process that no manufacturer can warrant that its product is free from contamination. Thus, any pituitary-derived hGH product presents a risk (albeit unquantifiable) of lethal side effects not associated with r-hGH products such as Protropin and Humatrope.

Second, the industry's response to the linking of Creutzfeldt–Jakob Disease to pituitary-derived hGH—withdrawal from the United States market—meant that regardless of the status of the Serono and Kabi NDAs, methionyl-free hGH would not be available to hGH-deficient children in this country. The legislative history is replete with references to the fundamental need to provide treatment for presently untreated patients; the fact that NDAs for pituitary-derived hGH were technically still valid would not have convinced Congress that growth hormone deficiency was not a condition in need of new treatments. One need only imagine a world without methionyl r-hGH (plaintiff's Protropin) to appreciate the unacceptable ramifications of movants' argument when applied to this case. Without Protropin, children in need of supplemental hGH would go without treatment, while movants offered assurances that no additional orphan drug designations were necessary because valid, but unused, NDAs remained in effect. In enacting the Orphan Drug Act, Congress clearly focused on the availability of treatments, not the existence of prior NDAs. The court is satisfied that Congress would have considered Humatrope sufficiently "different" to justify orphan drug designation. * * *

The court expresses no opinion on the still-pending issue of whether Protropin's orphan drug exclusivity barred approval of Humatrope, and, in particular, sets down no universal rule for determining whether two drugs are "different" for the purposes of the Orphan Drug Act. That responsibility is statutorily imposed on the FDA. Until the FDA endeavors to meet that obligation, the courts will be forced to make case-by-case determinations based on the broad policies embodied in the Act. * * *

Baker Norton Pharmaceuticals, Inc. v. FDA

132 F.Supp.2d 30 (D.D.C.2001).

■ HARRIS, DISTRICT JUDGE:

This case involves three groups: plaintiff Baker Norton, defendants Food and Drug Administration and two government officials (collectively "the FDA defendants"), and defendant-intervenor Bristol–Myers Squibb (BMS). Before the court are three motions for summary judgment, submitted by each of the three groups. * * *

When the potential market for a drug is small because the target market is relatively small, it is difficult for a pharmaceutical manufacturer to recover the large research and development costs, and even more difficult to realize a worthwhile return on that investment. The Orphan Drug Act therefore was enacted in 1983 to provide an incentive to develop and test drugs for the treatment of "rare diseases or conditions," which is defined to include diseases or conditions affecting fewer than 200,000 Americans. According to the FDA, in the ten years prior to the passage of the Orphan Drug Act, only ten products for rare diseases were developed and approved for marketing without federal funding. Since the passage of the Orphan Drug Act, the FDA has approved at least 172 orphan drugs and biological products; furthermore, more than 700 orphan-designated products currently are being developed.

Designation and approval of a drug as an orphan drug provides certain benefits to the sponsor of the drug. For example, such a designation permits the FDA to assist the sponsor in studying the drug, and allows the sponsor to claim the benefit of certain tax incentives. 26 U.S.C. § 28. More importantly, orphan drug designation and approval confers seven years of non-patent marketing exclusivity.

In 1992, the FDA promulgated its final orphan drug regulations on how to implement the orphan drug exclusivity right. One of the regulations, 21 C.F.R. § 316.3(b)(13)(i), provided a definition for determining when two drugs are the "same drug" and thus the second drug may not be approved for market exclusivity. In essence, that regulation provides that two drugs will be considered the same drug if they contain the same active moiety, unless the second drug is deemed to be "clinically superior."

To be eligible for orphan drug exclusivity, a drug's sponsor must submit a request to the FDA for designation as an orphan drug. If the FDA determines that the drug targets a rare disease or condition, or that there is no reasonable expectation that the cost of developing and making a drug available will be recovered in the United States, the drug is designated as an orphan drug. Because the drug is designated as an orphan drug before it is approved, more than one applicant may receive orphan designation for what later may be deemed the same "drug" for treatment of the same disease or condition. * * *

Baker Norton developed a drug called Paxene, and BMS developed a drug called Taxol. Although the two drugs are manufactured differently, contain some different inactive ingredients (or "excipients"), and have different profiles of impurities, they both contain paclitaxel as their active component. Paclitaxel is the generic name of a naturally-occurring anti-cancer agent extracted in trace amounts from the Pacific yew tree. Both Taxol and Paxene dissolve paclitaxel in ethanol and polyethoxylated castor oil for delivery by injection into a patient's body. While the castor oil provides adequate solubility of the paclitaxel, it also promotes chemical degradation of the paclitaxel. A principal difference between Taxol and Paxene is how each controls the rate of degradation. One of the ways that BMS controls the degradation rate is by removing certain compounds by passing the castor oil over a solid absorbent. Baker Norton uses citric acid, an inactive ingredient, which changes the physical formation of components so as to reduce the rate of long-term degradation of the paclitaxel.

On March 31, 1997, Baker Norton submitted a new drug application requesting approval for Paxene. Among the potential uses of Paxene is for treating Kaposi's sarcoma, an AIDS-related cancer. Because Kaposi's sarcoma qualifies under the Orphan Drug Act as a "rare disease," Baker Norton also sought designation as an orphan drug. On April 15, 1997, the FDA granted orphan designation. [Previously], BMS requested orphan designation for Taxol for treatment of Kaposi's sarcoma on January 31, 1997, and it filed a supplemental new drug application for Taxol on February 4, 1997.[3] On March 25, 1997, the FDA granted Taxol orphan designation for Kaposi's sarcoma.

What ensued essentially was a race for orphan drug approval since both Taxol and Paxene had been granted orphan drug designation; whichever drug was approved first would receive the seven-year period of market exclusivity. On August 4, 1997, the FDA granted approval to BMS to market Taxol as a second-line treatment for Kaposi's sarcoma. On December 24, 1997, the FDA issued a letter decision to Baker Norton indicating that it had determined Paxene to be safe and effective and, in all other respects, approvable, but that it could not confer final approval until August 4, 2004, due to Taxol's period of exclusivity. Baker Norton could, however, obtain final approval for marketing prior to August 4, 2004, if it could show that Paxene and Taxol should not be considered the "same drug" as defined in 21 C.F.R. part 316. * * *

"There is a presumption in favor of the validity of administrative action, and courts are particularly deferential when an agency is interpreting its own statute and regulations." Pfizer v. Shalala, 1 F.Supp. 2d 38, 44 (D.D.C.1998). Moreover, the "FDA's policies and its interpretation of its own regulations will be paid special deference because of the breadth of Congress' delegation of authority to FDA and because of FDA's scientific expertise." Berlex Labs., Inc. v. FDA, 942 F.Supp. 19, 25 (D.D.C.1996). * * * The court starts with the relevant statutory language of the Orphan Drug Act, which states in pertinent part: "[I]f the Secretary ... approves an application filed pursuant to section 355 ... for a drug designated under section 360bb of this title for a rare disease or condition, the Secretary may not approve another application under section 355 of this title ... for such drug for such disease or condition for a person who is not the holder of such approved application ... until the expiration of seven years from the date of the approval of the approved application." 21 U.S.C. § 360cc(a). * * *

Baker Norton asserts that the FDA's regulation improperly equates the term "drug" in § 360cc(a) with an "active moiety," contrary to legislative intent. * * * Baker Norton asserts that Congress clearly intended for the term "drug" in the context of § 360cc(a) to mean a "finished drug product." Baker Norton reasons that the term "drug" in § 360cc(a) is used in the context of an "application for a drug" under section 355. 21 U.S.C. § 355, which governs applications for approval of new drugs, interprets an "application for a drug" to be an "application for a drug product," not just for an active ingredient or active moiety. When considering an

---

3. BMS filed a supplemental new drug application because the FDA previously had approved Taxol for ovarian cancer usages.

application for a drug product, the inactive ingredients, as well as the manufacturing processes, are important and can distinguish one drug product from another. Because Congress chose to use the phrase "application for a drug" in § 360cc(a) and not another phrase, Baker Norton concludes that Congress clearly intended for the term "drug" to mean a drug product. * * *

Sections 355 and 360cc(a) are different statutory provisions with different purposes. Section 355 aims to protect public health and safety, which it accomplishes by considering the safety of all parts of any new drug proposed for entry in interstate commerce, whereas the Orphan Drug Act seeks to provide a meaningful financial incentive for the development of orphan drugs. What one statutory provision defines as a "drug" may not necessary control another statutory provision's definition of a "drug," even when used in the same phrase. Courts have held that "it is not unusual for the same word to be used with different meanings in the same act, and there is no rule of statutory construction which precludes the courts from giving to the word the meaning which the legislature intended it should have in each instance." * * *

Given the multiple definitions of the term "drug," and the differing purposes that various statutory provisions can serve, the court cannot find that the definition of "drug" in § 360cc(a) is clear and unambiguous. The court finds it more likely that Congress left it to the FDA to determine which definition fits a particular statutory section. Other courts have agreed that the word "drug" in other statutory provisions can be inherently ambiguous, and may cover more than just a finished drug product. * * *

Because the court has determined that the meaning of § 360cc(a) is ambiguous, the court turns to whether the agency's interpretation is based on a permissible construction of the statute. First, Baker Norton asserts that instead of considering whether two drugs have the same "active moiety," the FDA should adopt a "functionality" test: that is, the FDA should consider whether other ingredients in the product may create a functionally different product. Such a test, Baker Norton contends, would prevent companies from claiming that two drugs with the same active moiety are "different" simply by adding ingredients of de minimis import and thereby compromise a prior company's market exclusivity. In Baker Norton's case, Paxene's use of citric acid creates a functionally different drug because the citric acid helps reduce the rate of degradation of paclitaxel. The FDA defendants and BMS assert that a functionality test would vitiate the market exclusivity provision because many drug products could contain the same active moiety yet be functionally different. Whether such a "functionality test" would improve the current regime, however, does not necessarily undermine the permissibility of the FDA's interpretation. Under the *Chevron* test, the court considers only whether the agency's interpretation is permissible, not whether a better interpretation exists.

Baker Norton also maintains that the FDA's regulation is not permissible because it violates the well-established doctrine that grants of monopolies should be narrowly construed. The court finds, however, that the

FDA's interpretation does not produce so sweeping a monopoly as plaintiff would suggest: the market exclusivity rights are limited in time to seven years, and granted only for a particular drug for a particular use. Nothing prevents subsequent applicants from obtaining FDA approval for the same drug for a different use, or a different drug for the same use, or a clinically superior drug with the same active moiety for the same use.

The court finds that the FDA's interpretation is permissible. The interpretation of "same drug" appears to bear out the purpose behind the Orphan Drug Act. The preamble to the 1991 proposed regulations implementing the Orphan Drug Act states:

> With respect to small molecules, it appears sound, for the purposes of consideration of exclusive marketing under the Orphan Drug Act, to adopt a policy that regards two drugs as different if they differ with respect to the chemical structure of their active moieties. First, such differences are highly likely to lead to pharmacologic differences. Second, the development of an agent with a novel active moiety is not a financially or intellectually trivial matter; it represents a considerable effort and a substantial risk, as the results of changes in small molecules are difficult to predict.

56 Fed. Reg. 3338, 3341 (1991). Only one of the 40 comments received during the rulemaking stage suggested an alternate approach for distinguishing among different small-molecule drugs, and that alternate approach was rejected as unworkable.

The regulation's manner of determining "sameness" appears to promote the obvious legislative intent behind the Orphan Drug Act—to promote the development of orphan drugs. The financial incentive for companies to develop such drugs is provided by the period of market exclusivity, which would be undermined if other companies could develop drugs with the same active moiety but minor differences in inactive ingredients. The interests of patients who need such drugs are served by the approval of drugs which have the same active moiety but are clinically superior. See Arent v. Shalala, 70 F.3d 610, 615 (D.C.Cir.1995) ("[A] reviewing court's inquiry . . . is focused on discerning the boundaries of Congress' delegation of authority to the agency; and as long as the agency stays within that delegation, it is free to make policy choices in interpreting the statute, and such interpretations are entitled to deference."). The court therefore finds that the FDA's actions with regard to Baker Norton's application for approval of Paxene are not arbitrary and capricious, or in excess of statutory authority. Accordingly, the court denies plaintiff's motion for summary judgment, and grants the FDA and BMS's motions for summary judgment.

NOTES AND QUESTIONS

1. *Clinical superiority.* The regulations provide that a new drug is "clinically superior" if it offers "[g]reater safety in a substantial portion of the target populations." 21 C.F.R. § 316.3(b)(3)(ii) (listing as an example of "greater safety" the elimination of "an ingredient or contaminant that is associated with relatively frequent adverse effects"); see also 57 Fed. Reg. 62,076, 62,078 (1992) (explaining that even "a small demonstrated ... diminution in adverse reactions may be sufficient to allow a finding of clinical superiority"). In *Berlex Labs., Inc. v. FDA*, 942 F.Supp. 19 (D.D.C. 1996), the court deferred to these regulations in the course of upholding the FDA's decision to approve Biogen's biological drug Avonex®, a beta interferon product used to treat multiple sclerosis. Berlex, which sold the similar orphan drug product Betaseron®, objected because its seven year exclusivity period had not yet expired. The court sustained the FDA's finding that Avonex was not the same drug because it completely avoided one of the side effects (injection site necrosis) associated with Betaseron, disregarding Berlex's response that the overall safety profiles for the two products were comparable. See id. at 23–24. Five years later, Biogen faced the prospect that a competitor would trump its victory over Berlex. See Ronald Rosenberg, Serono Says Drug Better for Skirting Relapses, Boston Globe, May 9, 2001, at 4 (reporting that a comparative efficacy trial demonstrated that a new beta interferon product was clinically superior to Avonex in treating MS patients); see also Naomi Aoki, The Price of Success: Orphan Drug Act Has Spurred Advances–and Disputes, Boston Globe, July 25, 2001, at F1.

2. *Contrasting the different forms of market exclusivity.* A patent generally gives the inventor a 20 year period (measured from the date of filing) of protection against all imitators, and not just in the United States. When the FDA approves a new chemical or molecular entity as a drug, the NDA sponsor receives a five year period of exclusivity, but only against ANDAs. If a sponsor later conducts additional studies in order to secure FDA approval of a supplemental NDA for a new use, it receives a three year period of exclusivity, but only against ANDAs for that particular use. Orphan drug exclusivity provides a seven year period of protection against both ANDAs and NDAs, but only for that use. What, if anything, accounts for these differences?

3. *Orphan medical devices.* In 1988, Congress amended the Orphan Drug Act to provide a few of the same incentives to manufacturers of medical devices used to treat rare diseases or conditions. See Pub. L. No. 100–290, 102 Stat. 90 (1988).

4. *Further commentary.* See Robert A. Bohrer & John T. Prince, A Tale of Two Proteins: The FDA's Uncertain Interpretation of the Orphan Drug Act, 12 Harv. J.L. & Tech. 365 (1999); John J. Flynn, The Orphan Drug Act: An Unconstitutional Exercise of the Patent Power, 1992 Utah L. Rev. 389; David D. Rohde, The Orphan Drug Act: An Engine of Innovation? At What Cost?, 55 Food & Drug L.J. 125 (2000); Janice M. Hogan, Note, Revamping the Orphan Drug Act: Potential Impact on the World Pharmaceutical Market, 26 Law & Pol'y Int'l Bus. 523 (1995); cf. Nina J. Crimm, A Tax Proposal to Promote Pharmacologic Research, to Encourage Conventional Prescription Drug Innovation and Improvement, and to Reduce Product Liability Claims, 29 Wake Forest L. Rev. 1007 (1994).

National Pharmaceutical Alliance v. Henney

47 F.Supp.2d 37 (D.D.C.1999).

■ ROBERTSON, DISTRICT JUDGE:

* * * The pediatric exclusivity provision of FDAMA took effect on November 21, 1997. On March 16, 1998, in compliance with section 355a(b), FDA published a "Draft Pediatric List" of approved drugs for which it suggested that additional pediatric information might produce health benefits in the pediatric population. * * * On May 20, 1998, within the 180–day period prescribed by section 355a(b), FDA published a final "List of Approved Drugs for Which Additional Pediatric Information May Produce Health Benefits in the Pediatric Population." On July 7, 1998, the FDA issued a document entitled "Guidance for Industry: Qualifying for Pediatric Exclusivity Under Section 505A of the Federal Food, Drug, and Cosmetic Act." FDA has neither issued nor proposed regulations for implementing section 355a. It began issuing written requests for pediatric studies on specific drugs soon after publication of the Guidance document. * * *

The complaint alleges that FDA developed the Pediatric List improperly and that FDA's interpretation of the pediatric exclusivity provisions of section 355a is at variance with the statute. * * * The principal issue * * * is whether FDA has authority to grant additional exclusivity periods for drug product *lines* containing a single active moiety in exchange for a pediatric study covering a single drug *product*. * * * The main arguments of both sides focus, correctly, on the FDA's interpretation of the statute. Neither the language of section 355a nor anything in the nature of legislative history speaks directly to the question at issue. * * *

[The] question is whether FDA's interpretation of section 355a is "based on a permissible construction of the statute." Plaintiff asserts that it is not, arguing that FDA has departed from other, consistent interpretations of the term "drug" throughout the [FDCA] to mean "drug product," that Congress wanted extended pediatric exclusivity to be limited to the "drug product" studied in response to a request from FDA, and that FDA's construction conflicts with the statutory purpose of maximizing information about the use of drugs in children by removing the incentive to conduct research. There is little in the way of substantive information in this record, however, that supports these arguments. Congress did not prescribe the exact terms of the bargain it wanted struck with the research-based drug companies, leaving it to FDA to strike the appropriate balance. * * * [Plaintiffs also argue] that FDA acted arbitrarily and capriciously by including in the Pediatric List every drug approved for use in adults for indications that also appear in children. That argument is easily resolved by appropriate deference to the expertise of FDA. * * *

[B]ecause the likelihood of success is slim, plaintiffs would have to make a very substantial showing of severe irreparable injury in order to prevail on their motion [for a preliminary injunction]. * * * [G]eneric drug manufacturers will not realize profits from the sale of their products over the six-month periods of market exclusivity, but that effect was obviously contemplated by Congress when it enacted FDAMA. Plaintiffs have not shown that the loss of six months would allow the creation of impenetrable barriers to market entry or cause business failures among generic manufacturers.

FDAMA has a sunset provision for the year 2002. A report is due to Congress in 2001. The legislative incentive for the conduct of important pharmaceutical testing—which is not otherwise required of drug manufacturers—is thus of limited duration. * * * The public interest would be disserved by an injunction whose operation would be to remove the incentive for testing or actually to stop new testing. As for harm to the parties, it is true that generic drug manufacturers have something to lose and innovator drug manufacturers something to gain from the denial of a preliminary injunction, but that equation was set in place by the enactment of FDAMA. * * *

NOTES AND QUESTIONS

1. *Pediatric indications.* Recall that Eli Lilly & Co. failed in its effort to protect Prozac® with second generation patents. A few months after losing its appeal, the FDA granted the company a six month extension of its market exclusivity period for agreeing to undertake pediatric studies. See Eli Lilly Granted Extension on Prozac, L.A. Times, Nov. 16, 2000, at C2. Other manufacturers of blockbuster drugs nearing the end of their patent lives also have benefitted from this provision. See Chris Adams, Drug–Testing Incentives Are Scrutinized, Wall St. J., Aug. 1, 2001, at B9; Rachel Zimmerman, Pharmaceutical Firms Win Big on Plan to Test Adult Drugs on Kids, Wall St. J., Feb. 5, 2001, at A1 (estimating that the additional six months of market exclusivity on the first 26 drugs to receive this extension will generate an extra $4 billion for the brand-name manufacturers, including nearly $1 billion each on Claritin and Prozac); see also id. (adding that the program has generated valuable information on appropriate dosing for children, but also noting criticisms that some of the studies concern blockbuster drugs used to treat conditions rarely seen in children—such as arthritis, ulcers, hypertension, and adult-onset diabetes—while the law fails to provide any incentive to conduct pediatric studies of older drugs already subject to generic competition). See generally Kurt R. Karst, Comment, Pediatric Testing of Prescription Drugs: The FDA's Carrot and Stick for the Pharmaceutical Industry, 49 Am. U. L. Rev. 739 (2000). Congress recently extended the law, with fairly minor modifications, for another five year period. See Best Pharmaceuticals for Children Act, Pub. L. No. 107–109, 115 Stat. 1408 (2002).

2. *Overlapping exclusivity.* What happens if the pediatric studies lead to a significant alteration in the labeling for the pioneer drug (e.g., adding a specific indication for use in adolescents)? The sponsor of the NDA supplement could get six additional months of protection against any generic competition and/or three years of protection against generic competition on that labeling statement (but not on the drug itself). Should the sponsor receive both exclusivity periods, and would they run sequentially or concurrently? See Juliet Eilperin, Bristol–Myers Presses for Patent, Wash. Post, Nov. 28, 2001, at A33 (reporting that the manufacturer of Glucophage® has argued that it deserves an additional 3½ years of exclusivity, and against any generic competition, after discovering that children could benefit from this diabetes drug). When it extended the sunset date, Congress also closed this apparent loophole. See Alice Dembner, Pediatric Testing Program Extended: Drug Makers Keep Patent Incentive, Boston Globe, Dec. 20, 2001, at A8.

3. GENERIC EXCLUSIVITY

Purepac Pharmaceutical Co. v. Friedman

162 F.3d 1201 (D.C.Cir.1998).

■ RANDOLPH, CIRCUIT JUDGE:

"The active ingredients in most prescription drugs constitute less than 10% of the product; inactive 'excipients' (such as coatings, binders, and capsules) constitute the rest. The term 'generic drug' is used to describe a product that contains the same active ingredients but not necessarily the same excipients as a so-called 'pioneer drug' that is marketed under a brand name." United States v. Generix Drug Corp., 460 U.S. 453, 454–55 (1983). New drugs, including new generic drugs, may not be marketed without the Food and Drug Administration's approval. The Drug Price Competition and Patent Term Restoration Act of 1984, Pub. L. No. 98–417, 98 Stat. 1585, revised the procedures for obtaining the FDA's approval. One of the provisions in the "Hatch–Waxman Amendments," as this Act is known, conferred on the first generic drug applicant a 180–day period during which it would be free of competition from generic applicants who file later. The FDA implemented this provision through a regulation. In *Mova Pharmaceutical Corp. v. Shalala*, 140 F.3d 1060 (D.C.Cir.1998), we sustained a district court injunction against the FDA's enforcement of one of the regulation's requirements, finding it inconsistent with the statute. In response to *Mova*, the FDA revised its system for granting the 180–day exclusivity period. The questions in this case concern the validity of the revision.

In July 1998, the FDA tentatively approved Purepac Pharmaceutical Company's application to market the generic drug ticlopidine hydrochloride, marketed by other companies under the brand-name "Ticlid." Although Purepac's application has become ready for final approval, the FDA is withholding action. Purepac must, the FDA insists, wait until the first ticlopidine applicant—Torpharm, a division of Apotex, Inc.—markets its product for 180 days. At the time of this writing, it is not certain when these 180 days will start running. The FDA has not yet finally approved Torpharm's application.

With matters thus at a standstill, Purepac decided to take legal action. It sued for an injunction and a declaratory judgment, challenging the validity of the FDA's post-*Mova* revision and claiming that Torpharm was not entitled to the 180–day exclusivity period because it had not been sued for patent infringement * * * *

In a paragraph IV certification, the generic applicant must give notice to the owner of the patent and to the holder of the approved application for the drug covered by the patent. FDA approval of the abbreviated application may be made "effective immediately," unless a patent infringement suit is brought against the applicant within forty-five days from the date the patent owner or application holder receives notice of the paragraph IV certification.

No one brought a patent infringement suit against Torpharm (or Purepac) and it is therefore unnecessary to describe the provisions dealing with the various contingencies of such a lawsuit. The section directly in dispute—the section conferring the 180–day period of exclusivity—reads as follows:

> If the application contains a certification described in subclause (IV) of paragraph (2)(A)(vii) and is for a drug for which a previous application has been submitted under this subsection cont[ain]ing such a certification, the application shall be made effective not earlier than one hundred and eighty days after (I) the date the Secretary receives notice from the applicant under the previous application of the first commercial marketing of the drug under the previous application, or (II) the date of a decision of a court in an action described in clause (iii) holding the patent which is the subject of the certification to be invalid or not infringed, whichever is earlier.

21 U.S.C. § 355(j)(5)(B)(iv), as amended by Pub. L. No. 105–115, 111 Stat. 2296 (1997).

The FDA's original regulation implementing this section, promulgated in 1994, provided:

> If an abbreviated new drug application contains a certification that a relevant patent is invalid, unenforceable or will not be infringed and the application is for a generic copy of the same listed drug for which one or more substantially complete abbreviated new drug applications were previously submitted containing a certification that the same patent was invalid, unenforceable or would not be infringed *and the applicant submitting the first application has successfully defended against a suit for patent infringement brought within 45 days of the patent owner's receipt of notice submitted under § 314.95*, approval of the subsequent abbreviated new drug application will be made effective no sooner than 180 days from whichever of the following dates is earlier: (i) The date the applicant submitting the first application first commences commercial marketing of its drug product; or (ii) the date of a decision of the court holding the relevant patent invalid, unenforceable, or not infringed.

59 Fed. Reg. 50,338, 50,367 (1994) (emphasis added). The italicized language embodied what the parties and our *Mova* opinion call the "successful defense" requirement: the first generic applicant was entitled to the 180–day exclusivity period only after it had successfully defended a patent infringement suit.

Mova held that this portion of the regulation was "inconsistent with the statutory text and structure." 140 F.3d at 1076. As the court read the statute, it provided that a later generic applicant could not start marketing its product for 180 days after either commercial marketing by the first applicant, or a court decision declaring the patent invalid or not infringed. Id. at 1069. The FDA's successful defense requirement read the commercial marketing "trigger" out of the statute. As a result, first applicants who were not sued could never receive the benefit of the exclusivity period.

After *Mova*, the FDA issued a "Guidance to Industry" announcing its intention to "formally" remove the successful defense requirement from the regulation and to conduct a rulemaking proceeding to issue new regulations under § 355(j)(5)(B)(iv). In the meantime, the FDA said it would follow the statute as *Mova* interpreted it. That is, the agency would inform "the first applicant to submit a substantially complete" abbreviated application, "with a paragraph IV certification," that the applicant was eligible for 180 days of market exclusivity even though it had not been sued for patent infringement. The FDA added that it expected first applicants to begin marketing their product "promptly upon approval."

In November 1998, while this case was pending, the FDA published an interim rule in the *Federal Register* amending its regulation to eliminate the successful defense requirement. The interim rule accomplished this by deleting from the regulation the following language, italicized above (21 C.F.R. § 314.107(c)(1)): "and the applicant submitting the first application has successfully defended against a suit for patent infringement brought within 45 days of the patent owner's receipt of notice submitted under § 314.95." See 63 Fed. Reg. 59,710, 59,712 (1998). * * *

Purepac maintains that the regulation containing the successful defense requirement did not entitle Torpharm to the 180–day exclusivity period because Torpharm had not been sued for patent infringement. As Purepac sees it, even after *Mova* the FDA still had to require, as a condition for exclusivity, that the first generic applicant be sued for patent infringement, although the FDA could no longer insist that the applicant defend the suit successfully. * * *

We see the FDA's revised system for granting exclusivity as consistent with the statute and with our *Mova* decision. Section 355(j)(5)(B)(iv) does not, on its face, require the first applicant to be sued in order to benefit from market exclusivity. It provides, as we said in *Mova*, that the 180–day exclusivity period for the first applicant begins running upon the occurrence of one of two events, whichever is earlier—commercial marketing by the first applicant, or a court decision in favor of the applicant. The second condition obviously presupposes a lawsuit. The first does not. The words of the statute provide no reason to think, as Purepac must, that the only "commercial marketing" contemplated in § 355(j)(5)(B)(iv) is marketing that takes place while the first applicant is defending a lawsuit or after the lawsuit has concluded. The regulation, as it now stands, is fully consistent with the statute. * * *

There is nothing irrational in the FDA's giving first applicants the 180–day exclusivity period even if they have not been sued. On its face, the statute does the same. Seen in this light, Purepac's real objection is to the words Congress used, not the FDA's revision of its regulation. * * * Purepac also offers a policy reason for reading a lawsuit requirement into § 355(j)(5)(B)(iv). If a first applicant is never sued for patent infringement, it is possible that neither of two "triggers" for the running of the 180 days of market exclusivity—commercial marketing or a judicial decision—would ever occur. Without a lawsuit there would be no judicial decision. If the applicant never begins marketing its product, the 180 days would never run and all later generic applicants would be barred from bringing their products to market. * * * For this reason, *Mova* described a narrower answer to the problem: for first applicants who are not sued, they must bring their products to market within a prescribed period in order to benefit from exclusivity. See 140 F.3d 1071 n.11. There is some indication that the FDA will consider this alternative in the rulemaking promised in its Guidance, or in response to comments on its interim rule. That is the proper time and setting for Purepac to repeat its point and to offer its solution. * * *

Mylan Pharmaceuticals, Inc. v. Henney

94 F.Supp.2d 36 (D.D.C.2000).

■ Urbina, District Judge:

Pharmachemie, B.V. and Mylan Pharmaceuticals, Inc., generic manufacturers of the drug tamoxifen (together, the "Parties"), bring separate actions against Defendant Jane E. Henney, M.D., in her official capacity as Commissioner of the United States Food and Drug Administration, and against Defendant Donna E. Shalala, in her official capacity as Secretary of the United States Department of Health and Human Services (collectively referred to as the "FDA"). The Parties, whose tamoxifen drugs are used in the treatment of breast cancer, bring their actions under the Federal Food, Drug and Cosmetic Act (FDCA) and the Administrative Procedure Act (APA). Barr Laboratories is a manufacturer of the generic drug tamoxifen, currently exclusively licensed by the owner of the patent to market the drug.

Mylan and Pharmachemie both assert that the FDA acted arbitrarily and capriciously in rendering by letter dated March 2, 1999, its decision to grant Barr's request that the FDA stay approval of any version of the drug tamoxifen other than Barr's version. The effect of the March letter is that neither Mylan nor Pharmachemie has the opportunity to market their generic version of tamoxifen until the patent for tamoxifen expires on

August 20, 2002. In essence, both maintain that the March letter violates the FDCA and runs contrary to the agency's own regulations. * * *

[A] generic maker seeking certification of his ANDA under paragraph III must wait for the pioneer maker's patent to expire and, consequently, will not infringe the patent. But a generic maker seeking certification of his ANDA under paragraph IV, on the grounds that the pioneer maker's patent is invalid, triggers a multi-tiered process that potentially enables him to obtain approval of his ANDA and market his generic drug before the pioneer maker's patent expires. * * *

As an incentive to the first generic maker to expose himself to the risk of costly patent litigation, the Hatch–Waxman regime provides that the first to file a paragraph IV certified ANDA is eligible for a 180–day period of marketing protection, commonly known as the 180–day exclusivity period. By its terms, the exclusivity incentive affords the first filer protection from competition from subsequent generic makers for 180 days beginning from the earlier of a commercial marketing or court decision. * * *

The facts material to disposition of this consolidated action date back to August 1985, when a pioneer maker secured the original patent for brand-name tamoxifen, which is a drug used in the treatment of breast cancer. On August 20, 1985, Imperial Chemicals Industries, PLC obtained U.S. Patent 4,536,516, covering tamoxifen. Imperial's subsidiary, Zeneca Inc., is the sole producer of tamoxifen under Imperial's patent. In December 1985, Barr Laboratories, a generic maker of tamoxifen, submitted an ANDA requesting FDA approval to market its own generic version of tamoxifen.

In September 1987, Barr amended its ANDA to include a paragraph IV certification and to challenge the validity of Imperial's tamoxifen patent. After amending its ANDA, Barr sent Imperial notice that it contended Imperial's patent was invalid. The FDA gave effect to Barr's amended paragraph IV certification. In other words, Barr became potentially eligible for the exclusivity incentive. After receiving notice of the challenge, Imperial sued Barr for patent infringement in the United States District Court for the Southern District of New York. On July 21, 1992, the Southern District held that Imperial's tamoxifen patent was invalid because Imperial deliberately, knowingly and fraudulently withheld material information from the Patent and Trademark Office. See Imperial Chem. Ind., PLC v. Barr Lab., Inc., 795 F.Supp. 619, 629 (S.D.N.Y.1992).

Imperial filed a notice of appeal with the United States Court of Appeals for the Federal Circuit, but, before any substantive review by the Federal Circuit, Imperial settled the case with Barr. The settlement was expressly conditioned on Barr's agreement to abandon its challenge to the validity of Imperial's patent. Barr would abandon its challenge by amending its paragraph IV certified ANDA back to a paragraph III certified ANDA. Pursuant to the settlement and as a result of the amendment back, Barr's ANDA was no longer eligible for approval until after August 20, 2002, the date that Imperial's tamoxifen patent was scheduled to expire. In exchange, Imperial paid Barr $21 million and granted Barr a license to market tamoxifen.

After settling the case but during the pendency of the appeal before the Federal Circuit, Imperial and Barr jointly moved to (1) vacate the July 21, 1992, judgment of the Southern District and (2) remand the case with instructions to dismiss without prejudice. The Federal Circuit issued a short order that granted the parties' request, finding that the "parties to the district court proceeding have entered into a settlement agreement resolving the entire dispute." * * *

Within a year of the Federal Circuit's vacatur of the Southern District's decision, in August 1994, Pharmachemie submitted a paragraph III ANDA for its generic version of tamoxifen. In January 1996, Mylan submitted a paragraph IV ANDA for its generic version of tamoxifen. In February 1996, Pharmachemie amended its ANDA to include a paragraph IV certification. After Mylan submitted its paragraph IV ANDA in January 1996, Zeneca sued Mylan for infringement. Because Zeneca brought a patent infringement action against Mylan within 45 days, the 30 month statutory stay of approval was triggered against Mylan and scheduled to expire on July 10, 1998. After Pharmachemie amended its ANDA to reflect a paragraph IV ANDA, Zeneca sued Pharmachemie for patent infringement within 45 days. The 30–month statutory stay was triggered and scheduled to expire in August 1998.

But in June 1998, approximately one month before Mylan's and two months before Pharmachemie's 30 month statutory stays were to expire, Barr filed a petition for stay with the FDA. The petition asked the FDA to continue to credit Barr with the exclusivity incentive to the exclusion of all other generic makers of tamoxifen. Specifically, Barr's petition asked the FDA not to approve any ANDA for a generic version of tamoxifen until 180 days after: (1) Barr's first commercial marketing of generic tamoxifen under its ANDA; or (2) the date of a final decision of a court holding the tamoxifen patent to be invalid or not infringed. Barr's petition came in the midst of the FDA's determination, in light of adverse court decisions, to overhaul its interpretation and application of the exclusivity incentive * * * *

In response to the petition, Janet Woodcock, M.D., Director of the FDA's Center for Drug Evaluation and Research, announced to Barr by letter dated March 2, 1999: "After careful review of your petition and supplement, as well as comments to the petition received by FDA, the Agency grants the petition for the following reasons...." Thus, the FDA granted Barr's petition to preserve its exclusivity incentive and to exclude all other generic makers of tamoxifen. * * *

In its March letter, the FDA gives no effect to the Southern District's decision, rendered in Barr's favor, which held that Imperial's patent for tamoxifen was invalid. Although the district court's decision was vacated during the pendency of appeal and pursuant to a settlement agreement, the FDA, without explanation, sweepingly ignores the existence of the decision altogether. Page four of the March letter states: "Barr has settled its patent litigation without a decision of a court finding the patent invalid, not infringed or unenforceable." While subsequent ANDA applicants have challenged the tamoxifen patent, no court decisions have been rendered in those cases either. Thus, according to the FDA's interpretation, Barr's 180 days of marketing exclusivity has not yet been triggered since there is neither a court decision nor a commercial marketing of tamoxifen under Barr's ANDA. * * * From the plain, comprehensive and inclusive terms of 21 U.S.C. § 355(j)(5)(B)(iii) and (iv), the court discerns clear congressional intent that the draftsmen intended "a decision of a court" to mean all court decisions, whether subsequently vacated, settled, appealed or otherwise mooted. * * *

Moreover, viewed against the sparse legislative history and compromise, the FDA's March letter not only violates the plain language of the statute, but also conflicts with the purposes of Hatch–Waxman. * * * [T]his interpretation is demonstrably at odds with the statute's interest in affording market access and incentives for both generic and non-generic makers. This circuit once cautioned that in cases where the first applicant is never sued, the court-decision trigger will never be satisfied. Later ANDA applicants are thereby at the mercy of the first applicant's decision over when, and if, to market its product. The first applicant could wait indefinitely to begin selling its product, preventing other applicants from entering the market. The court pointed out that this "unfortunate scenario" could happen if the first applicant "colludes with the pioneer drug company to eliminate generic competition." While Imperial and Barr may not have intended to "collude," the chain of events culminating with the FDA's March letter has eliminated generic competition in the tamoxifen market. * * *

Second, the FDA's March letter precludes the possibility of competition in the tamoxifen market until 2002. Courts are advised that statutes should not be interpreted so as to create anticompetitive effects. While this canon may not apply with full force when the FDA is playing in the field of compromise, the FDA's interpretation of the statute as embodied by its March letter excessively favors Barr and Imperial's anticompetitive hold over tamoxifen. The effect of the FDA's interpretation is that from August 20, 1985, the date that Imperial was granted the tamoxifen patent, until August 20, 2002, the date the patent expires, the public will have access only to Imperial's version of tamoxifen, to the exclusion of any generic version of the drug. Barr and Imperial will have benefitted from exclusivity for nearly twenty years. Hatch–Waxman intended to provide an incentive for drug companies to explore new drugs, not a market "windfall" for crafty, albeit industrious, market players. * * *

On or about March 19, 1993, and pursuant to the settlement between Barr and Imperial's subsidiary Zeneca, Barr amended its ANDA from a paragraph IV certification back to a paragraph III certification. To date, Barr has not submitted any further amendments to its ANDA. Mylan and Pharmachemie thus contend that Barr's application can no longer be considered to continue a paragraph IV certification. * * * Regulation

314.94 provides: "An applicant shall submit an amended certification by letter or as an amendment to a pending application [or] an approved application. Once an amendment or letter is submitted, the application will no longer be considered to contain the prior certification." Regulation 314.94, promulgated pursuant to notice-and-comment rulemaking, has the force and effect of law, and must be applied by the agency as written. As written, Regulation 314.94 prohibits the FDA from imposing a 180–day delay period because of Barr's amendment back.

Although Barr changed its certification from a paragraph IV to a paragraph III certification, the agency has not interpreted its regulation to render Barr ineligible for exclusivity after the change. The FDA explains that this regulation regarding changes in patent certification "fulfills a purely administrative function." * * * When first presented, this argument inspired "laughter" and jest from the appeals court. * * * [T]his court continues to be baffled by the internal "housekeeping" argument. * * * In the absence of cogent explanation, the agency's failure to follow its own regulation is fatal. * * *

Because Mylan and Pharmachemie have demonstrated that the FDA's March letter is contrary to its plain meaning and purpose of 21 U.S.C. § 355(j)(5)(B)(iv) and Regulation 314.94, the parties are entitled to declaratory relief. This action will be remanded to the FDA for a permissible construction of the statute. * * *

NOTES AND QUESTIONS

1. *Encouraging generic companies to test the validity of innovator patents.* The prospect of receiving even a relatively short period of market exclusivity against other generics has encouraged companies to challenge patents on brand-name drugs. See Joseph A. Slobodzian, Patent Challenges Are Key to Generics, Nat'l L.J., Feb. 12, 2001, at B1. In some instances, the generic companies have gone too far, and one court awarded attorneys fees and costs to the patent holder when the ANDA applicant filed a baseless paragraph IV certification. See Yamanouchi Pharm. Co. v. Danbury Pharmacal, Inc., 231 F.3d 1339 (Fed.Cir.2000).

2. *Permutations.* In one recent case, a court had to untangle the interaction between market exclusivity periods granted for NDA supplements and for the first filed ANDA. Initially, Glaxo Wellcome filed an NDA for ranitidine hydrochloride in 150 mg and 300 mg tablets, labeled as a prescription drug for the treatment of ulcers (Zantac®). GenPharm was the first company to file a substantially complete ANDA, and, upon the conclusion of patent infringement claims brought by Glaxo, it received a market exclusivity period of 180 days. Subsequently, Glaxo filed an NDA supplement for a lower dose (75 mg) ranitidine hydrochloride tablet with OTC labeling for the treatment of heartburn. Because this required the submission of new clinical trials to secure FDA approval (contrast the *Upjohn* decision excerpted earlier in the Chapter), Glaxo received three years of market exclusivity for OTC Zantac. Novopharm was the first company to file a substantially complete ANDA for the OTC product, so the FDA granted it 180 days of generic exclusivity to commence at the conclusion of Glaxo's period. TorPharm, another company that had filed an ANDA for OTC ranitidine, unsuccessfully challenged the agency's decision to provide this second generic exclusivity period as inconsistent with the statute because the different brand-name products grew out of the same patents previously challenged by GenPharm. See Apotex, Inc. v. Shalala, 53 F.Supp.2d 454, 459–62 (D.D.C.1999).

3. *Struggling to untangle generic exclusivity.* Courts have found it difficult to define exactly when the six month clock starts to run. See Teva Pharm., USA, Inc. v. FDA, 182 F.3d 1003 (D.C.Cir.1999) (holding that the FDA had acted arbitrarily and capriciously when it refused to recognize a dismissal of a declaratory judgment complaint for patent infringement as a "court decision" that would trigger the 180–day period of market exclusivity for the first ANDA applicant); Andrx Pharm., Inc. v. Friedman, 83 F.Supp.2d 179, 185 (D.D.C.2000) ("The statute's second triggering date is the completion of the patent litigation—thus, the statute does provide a time at which subsequent generic competitors may proceed to market, even if the first ANDA applicant never does so. That is, 180 days from the completion of the [patent] litigation, other generics, which have themselves received FDA approval in the form of approved ANDAs, may proceed to market notwithstanding the action or inaction of the first ANDA applicant."); Mylan Pharm., Inc. v. Shalala, 81 F.Supp.2d 30, 36–42, 47 (D.D.C.2000) (invalidating an FDA regulation providing that a court decision in favor of the ANDA sponsor accused of infringing a patent would trigger the 180–day exclusivity period only after opportunities for appeal had been exhausted); Inwood Labs., Inc. v. Young, 723 F.Supp. 1523, 1526–27 (D.D.C.1989) (rejecting the FDA's interpretation of the statute as not entitling the sponsor of the first ANDA to the 180–day exclusivity period if the patent holder declines to pursue an infringement claim in response to a paragraph IV certification, and discounting the agency's concern that the holder of the first ANDA might delay triggering the start of the exclusivity period "in order to harm its competitors"). As hinted at by the court in *Mylan* and elaborated in the next section, this question has implications for resolving antitrust claims against brand-name companies.

4. *Other exclusivity periods for generics.* Some generic drugs come to market through a "paper NDA" rather than an ANDA, and they may receive a three-year market exclusivity period if the applicant had to conduct additional studies in order to secure FDA approval. They also may receive six months of market exclusivity if the sponsor of the generic rather than the brand-name drug conducted pediatric studies.

C. COMPETITION AND ANTITRUST LAW

In re Cardizem CD Antitrust Litigation

105 F.Supp.2d 618 (E.D.Mich.2000).

■ EDMUNDS, DISTRICT JUDGE:

Defendant Hoechst Marion Roussel, Inc. (HMRI), a wholly owned subsidiary of Defendant Hoechst Aktiengesellschaft (Hoechst AG), is the manufacturer of the brand name prescription heart drug Cardizem CD which consists of a once-daily dosage of the chemical compound diltiazem hydrochloride. Cardizem CD is widely prescribed for the treatment of chronic chest pains (angina), high blood pressure (hypertension), and for the prevention of heart attacks and strokes. Until June 23, 1999, when Defendant Andrx Pharmaceuticals, Inc. began to sell Cartia XT, the first generic bioequivalent to Cardizem CD, Defendant HMRI had a monopoly in the $700–million-plus annual United States market for Cardizem CD and its generic bioequivalents.

These cases involve claims that the defendants violated section 1 of the Sherman Antitrust Act, 15 U.S.C. § 1, and various state antitrust and unfair competition statutes. Plaintiffs [various wholesalers, retail pharmacies, and patients] allege the following contract, combination or conspiracy in restraint of trade: Defendant Andrx developed a generic drug which is the bioequivalent to the Hoechst Defendants' prescription drug Cardizem CD. Andrx's generic drug was approved by the FDA for sale and could have entered the U.S. market on or about July 9, 1998. Andrx, however, did not enter the market at that time because it had agreed with its horizontal competitor, HMRI, that it would delay the entry of its generic version of Cardizem CD in exchange for, inter alia, non-refundable payments of $40 million per year from HMRI. Plaintiffs allege that this agreement is embodied in a September 24, 1997, document executed by Defendants HMRI and Andrx.

The HMRI/Andrx Agreement was executed eight days after the FDA preliminarily approved Defendant Andrx's generic drug as the first AB-rated generic bioequivalent for Cardizem CD. It is alleged that, under the terms of the agreement, Defendant Andrx agreed not to market its generic drug when it received FDA approval and not to transfer, assign, or relinquish its right to a 180–day exclusivity period that Andrx would enjoy once it finally did begin to market its generic version of Cardizem CD, and Defendant HMRI paid Andrx $89.83 million, beginning on the date the Andrx product received FDA approval. Thus, it is alleged that the HMRI/Andrx Agreement not only protected HMRI from competition from Andrx, but it also protected HMRI from competition from other generic competitors because Andrx agreed not to give up its FDA first-filer status, thus blocking and delaying other drug manufacturers from introducing generic versions of Cardizem CD in the United States market; i.e., Andrx's delayed entry would postpone the start of its 180–day exclusivity period, and Andrx's agreement not to give up or transfer its right to that 180–day period of exclusivity would preclude other generic competitors from entering the market until that 180–day exclusivity period expired.

After these actions were first filed in August 1998, Defendants' HMRI/Andrx Agreement was widely publicized in the media, was condemned by public officials and health care payors injured by defendants' acts, and was investigated by the FTC. As a result, plaintiffs allege that, in June 1999,

HMRI and Andrx terminated their Agreement, settled their patent infringement action, and Andrx began to market Cartia XT, its generic version of Cardizem CD. * * *

In 1982, Marion Merrell Dow (Dow), HMRI's predecessor, introduced the pioneer drug in the United States containing diltiazem hydrochloride as an active ingredient for treating hypertension and angina. This drug used an immediate release delivery method and was patented and sold under the brand name "Cardizem." The problem with immediate release drugs is that they do not provide for a continuing and slow release of a drug into the patient's bloodstream, so Cardizem patients had to take three or four doses a day. Some patients would forget a dose and this in turn would cause undesirable fluctuations in diltiazem concentrations in the blood. To remedy this problem, Dow introduced an improved, twice-a-day product called "Cardizem SR" in 1989. In 1992, Dow introduced its once-a-day diltiazem hydrochloride formulation under the name Cardizem CD. Cardizem CD's single administration of diltiazem hydrochloride is based on a sustained-release delivery method patented by Elan Corp., P.L.C., an Irish company. Dow and Carderm Capital L.P., a limited partnership, were the licensees of Elan's U.S. patents for sustained-release delivery and absorption of Cardizem CD. Cardizem CD quickly replaced Cardizem SR as the most popular hydrochloride product in the U.S.

The U.S. patent on the compound diltiazem hydrochloride, the active ingredient in Cardizem CD, originally expired in February 1988 but was extended by legislation until November 1992. Thus, it is alleged that after November 1992, Dow for the first time began to face the threat of competition from generic pharmaceutical manufacturers. * * *

Prior to August 1995, Defendant Andrx had been developing its own generic version of Cardizem CD, and provided samples of its proposed generic substitute for Cardizem CD to the Hoechst Defendants so they could perform their own tests to confirm that there was no infringement of the patents claiming Cardizem CD and thus avoid litigation. On September 22, 1995, Andrx filed an ANDA for a generic version of Cardizem CD and made a paragraph IV certification with regard to all unexpired patents listed in the FDA's Orange Book allegedly claiming Cardizem CD.

On November 28, 1995, two months after Andrx's ANDA, the U.S. Patent and Trademark Office issued the " '584 Patent" to Carderm which then licensed it to HMRI. In January 1996, HMRI and Carderm filed a patent infringement suit against Andrx in the District Court for the Southern District of Florida. The filing of the suit triggered the 30–month Hatch–Waxman waiting period, which expired on July 3, 1998. On April 4, 1996, Andrx amended its ANDA to specify a dissolution profile that was even more clearly distinct from that claimed by the '584 patent. Despite notice of this, HMRI continued to prosecute the HMRI/Andrx patent case. Andrx also filed antitrust counterclaims against HMRI in the patent case.

On September 17, 1997, the FDA gave preliminary approval to Andrx's amended ANDA for its generic version of Cardizem CD. Thus, upon expiration of the 30 month waiting period in early July 1998, Andrx would be able to introduce its generic version of Cardizem CD into the U.S. market. Plaintiffs allege that unless the Hoechst Defendants could come up with a way to keep their competitor's generic version off the market, they would lose their monopoly over the market for Cardizem CD and its generic bioequivalents by no later than July 9, 1998. On that date, the 30–month Hatch–Waxman waiting period would expire, and the FDA's approval of Andrx's ANDA would allow Andrx to begin marketing its generic drug notwithstanding the continued pendency of the HMRI/Andrx patent case.

On or before September 24, 1997, HMRI and Andrx entered into the HMRI/Andrx Agreement. Plaintiffs allege that this collusive and anticompetitive agreement had the effect and purpose of allowing the Hoechst Defendants to continue to maintain their monopoly market share while continuing to set artificially high prices for Cardizem CD throughout the U.S. Under the Agreement, HMRI was obligated to start, as of July 9, 1998 (the date the 30–month freeze ended), making quarterly payments to Andrx of ten million dollars. The payments were to end when the HMRI/Andrx patent case, including all appeals, was finally over.

It is alleged that but for the HMRI/Andrx Agreement, Andrx would have begun marketing is generic version of Cardizem CD on or shortly after July 9, 1998, and the FDA could have approved other generic versions of Cardizem CD after the 180–day period of exclusivity granted to Andrx under Hatch–Waxman expired. On August 20, 1998, the first of these state law class actions was filed in California, and on June 9, 1999, HMRI and Andrx announced that they had agreed to settle the HMRI/Andrx patent suit. They claim here that the settlement was possible because Andrx amended its ANDA and reformulated its generic version of Cardizem CD. At the time of settlement, HMRI paid Andrx an additional $50,700,000, bringing its total payments to Andrx to $89,830,000. Since June of 1999, Cartia XT, Andrx's generic version of Cardizem CD, has been sold at a substantial discount to the price of Cardizem CD, and it has captured nearly half of the U.S. market for Cardizem CD and its generic bioequivalents. * * *

To establish antitrust injury, plaintiffs are not required to eliminate the hypothetical possibility that Defendant Andrx might have unilaterally delayed entry into the market even absent the HMRI/Andrx Agreement. * * * Plaintiffs specifically allege that, as a result of the defendants' illegal market allocation agreement and defendants' anticompetitive conduct, plaintiffs and the class paid more than they would have paid for Cardizem CD absent defendants' illegal conduct. They allege that the HMRI/Andrx Agreement eliminated generic competition and thus deprived all U.S. purchasers of the ability to buy Cardizem CD at a competitive price. * * *

Plaintiffs here allege an antitrust injury—having to pay an artificially high price—that flows directly from the alleged antitrust violation, the September 1997 HMRI/Andrx Agreement. The Hatch–Waxman Amendments did not prohibit Andrx from going to market with its generic product on July 9, 1998. Defendant Andrx not only had the unfettered right to do so, plaintiffs allege that it represented to the court presiding over the

HMRI/Andrx patent infringement action that that was what it intended to do. It is further alleged that but for HMRI's promise to pay it tens of millions of dollars to delay, Andrx would have gone to market on July 9, 1998. * * *

Defendants argue that plaintiffs' state law claims are preempted because Congress has so pervasively regulated this particular intersection of patent law, pharmaceutical regulation, and antitrust law that a clear intent to occupy the field can be inferred. Focusing as it must on congressional intent, this court examines defendants' evidence of pervasiveness and its argument that the Hatch–Waxman Amendments preclude enforcement of plaintiffs' state law claims. * * *

The fact that the Hatch–Waxman Amendments set out a statutory scheme designed to encourage drug manufacturers to develop generic forms of brand-name drugs that do not infringe the brand-name drug manufacturer's patents, and the fact that the FDA has adopted regulations to enforce the Hatch–Waxman statutory scheme, does not convince the court that Congress left no room for plaintiffs' state law claims or that plaintiffs' state law claims address the same subject matter addressed in the Hatch–Waxman Amendments or the FDA regulations relating to enforcement of those amendments. Defendants have not convinced the court that the state laws at issue impinge in any way on the federal government's "established scheme" in this area of federal law. The cases defendants rely upon do nothing to advance their position that permitting plaintiffs to bring their state law claims against defendants would frustrate Congress' intent to bring the subject areas of law under a uniform set of federal regulations.

Defendants next argue that plaintiffs' state law claims are preempted because compliance with both the state laws and the Hatch–Waxman Amendments is impossible. Specifically, defendants argue that plaintiffs' state law claims are preempted because the state laws would render illegal the very conduct Congress approved in the Hatch–Waxman Amendments. Defendants' arguments are without merit. As plaintiffs correctly point out, there is nothing in the language of the Hatch–Waxman Amendments or their legislative history that prohibited Defendant Andrx from bringing its generic product to market in July 1998. If it had done so, there would be no violation of the state laws at issue here. Moreover, if Defendant Andrx had unilaterally decided not to market its generic product until resolution of the HMRI/Andrx patent infringement action, there would be no state law violations. However, there is nothing in the language of the Act or its legislative history that impliedly authorizes a patent-holder, like Defendant HMRI, to contract with and pay a generic drug competitor, like Defendant Andrx, to delay its entry into the market beyond the time the statute permits it to go to market so as to artificially inflate the price at which the patented brand-name drug is sold. That is what plaintiffs are alleging here. * * *

The FDA has recently observed that agreements and arrangements between a patent holding drug company and a first-to-apply generic drug company "may contribute to delayed generic competition by forestalling the beginning, or triggering, of the 180–day exclusivity period." 64 Fed. Reg. 42,873, 42,874–75 (1999). Accordingly, such agreements can subvert "Congress's central goal" underlying its passage of the Hatch–Waxman Amendments; i.e., "to bring generic drugs on the market as rapidly as possible." To cure this problem, the FDA has recently announced proposed rule changes to the regulations that place a time limit on when the first-filed ANDA applicant must trigger its rights to obtain the 180–day marketing exclusivity period provided under the Hatch–Waxman Amendments; a "use it or lose it" triggering period is proposed. The FDA explains the problem and proposed remedial regulations as follows:

> The Hatch–Waxman Amendments benefit consumers by bringing lower priced generic versions of previously approved drugs to market, while simultaneously promoting new drug innovation through the restoration of patent life lost during regulatory proceedings. The award of a 180–day period of market exclusivity for certain ANDA applicants with paragraph IV certifications was designed to maintain this balance by rewarding generic firms for their willingness to challenge unenforceable and invalid innovator patents, or design noninfringing drug products. *Recently, however, this balance has been upset and generic competition impeded, in part through the establishment of certain licensing agreements or other commercial arrangements between generic and innovator companies.*

> Under current regulatory provisions, *the first generic applicant* to file a substantially complete ANDA with a paragraph IV certification *can delay generic competition by entering into certain commercial arrangements with an innovator company. The result may be, notwithstanding the intent of the Hatch–Waxman Amendments, rewards are directed to generic companies for hindering rather than speeding generic competition.* A necessary condition for such arrangements is that the economic gains to the innovator from delaying generic competition exceed the potential economic gains to the generic applicant from the 180 days of market exclusivity. *Such instances are becoming more frequent because a successful strategy to extend market exclusivity can mean tens of millions of dollars in increased revenue for an innovator firm.* Under such circumstances, it can be mutually beneficial for the innovator and the generic company that is awarded 180 days of generic exclusivity to enter into agreements that block generic competition for extended periods. This delayed competition harms consumers by slowing the introduction of lower priced products into the market and thwarts the intent of the Hatch–Waxman Amendments.

> *FDA's proposal to establish a 180–day triggering period addresses this problem in several ways.* In most cases, the first generic applicant with a paragraph IV certification would lose its claim to 180–day exclusivity if it withheld its drug product from the market, or failed to obtain a favorable court decision, for more than 180 days after the tentative approval of a subsequent generic applicant for the same drug product. Also, a subsequent generic applicant could not be blocked

from marketing its drug product for longer than, at most, one year from when it received tentative approval (the 180–day triggering period plus the 180–day exclusivity period). *As a result, the potential economic losses to consumers from the increased unavailability of lower priced generic products would be reduced significantly.*

Moreover, *decreasing the length of time that these commercial arrangements could block generic competition lessens the market incentive for entering into such agreements.* Limiting the period during which an agreement between an innovator and the first generic ANDA applicant with a paragraph IV certification could block generic competition provides less incentive, and therefore makes it less likely, that an innovator and a generic company would enter into such an agreement. Consequently, *consumers would benefit because commercial arrangements to block generic competition would be not only less damaging, but would be less likely to occur.*

64 Fed. Reg. at 42,882–83 (emphasis added). The Bureau of Competition and of Policy Planning of the Federal Trade Commission published comments supporting the proposed rule and suggesting that "the FDA consider a requirement that both patent litigation settlement agreements (either full or partial settlements) between branded companies and ANDA applicants and agreements related to the filing of an ANDA by a potential applicant be filed confidentially with the agency in a timely manner and be accessible to federal antitrust authorities on a non-public basis so that the antitrust agencies can be made aware of any anticompetitive issues involved with such settlements." * * *

[N]o court has held that the sixteen year old Hatch–Waxman Amendments provide immunity from the antitrust laws or have repealed the Sherman Act, and defendants have not persuaded this court that it should be the first to do so. Moreover, this court agrees with plaintiffs' argument that both the FDA and the FTC's actions and comments discussed above clarify that neither agency considers that the regulatory scheme of the Hatch–Waxman Amendments conflicts with, or is inconsistent with, existing antitrust laws. Contrary to defendants' arguments, the Hatch–Waxman Amendments are not clearly repugnant to the antitrust laws and thus do not provide an implied exemption from antitrust law. * * *

Defendants argue that: (1) the HRMI/Andrx Agreement is not susceptible to a per se analysis because it is not between actual or potential horizontal competitors and is not the type of agreement that has previously received per se treatment; and (2) it is not actionable under a rule of reason analysis because: a) it is reasonable as a matter of law; and b) plaintiffs have not pled the relevant market and market power. * * * Defendants' arguments lack merit. They ignore plaintiffs' allegations that: (1) the HMRI/Andrx Agreement is also a horizontal market allocation agreement; (2) that its terms affect the price of Cardizem CD; (3) the federal courts have consistently held that the per se rule applies to both horizontal price-fixing and market allocation agreements; and (4) that the agreement is between actual or potential horizontal competitors. * * *

Plaintiffs allege that, due to FDA regulations, once a physician prescribes Cardizem CD, a consumer patient may only purchase Cardizem CD or its FDA-approved AB-rated bioequivalent. Plaintiffs further allege that prior to June 23, 1999, when Andrx's Cartia XT was introduced into the market, HMRI's Cardizem CD comprised a 100% share of the U.S. market for Cardizem CD and its generic bioequivalents. Thus, the physician's prescribing practices and the FDA approval barriers define the relevant market. Accordingly, no heart patient who entered a U.S. pharmacy with a physician's prescription for Cardizem CD could obtain any drug other than Cardizem CD prior to June 23, 1999, when Andrx began shipping Cartia XT. Contrary to Andrx's arguments, a single brand of a product can constitute a relevant market for antitrust purposes. * * *

NOTES AND QUESTIONS

1. *Update.* The trial judge later granted the plaintiffs partial summary judgment. See In re Cardizem CD Antitrust Litig., 105 F.Supp.2d 682 (E.D.Mich.2000) (holding that the agreement was illegal per se). Several states subsequently filed a similar lawsuit. See States Sue Two Drug Makers, Citing Antitrust Concerns, N.Y. Times, May 15, 2001, at C2. The FTC eventually secured a settlement of its charges against Andrx and Aventis (Hoechst's successor). See F.T.C. Accuses Drug Makers of Collusion to Delay Generics, N.Y. Times, Apr. 3, 2001, at C12. In addition to the investigation of the Hoechst agreement with Andrx, the FTC has undertaken inquiries about possible collusion between other companies on the verge of losing patent protection. See Jeff Gerth, Agency Plans to Study Drug Makers' Records to See Whether Deals Delay Generics, N.Y. Times, Oct. 12, 2000, at A16; Sheryl Gay Stolberg & Jeff Gerth, Keeping Down the Competition: How Companies Stall Generics and Keep Themselves Healthy, N.Y. Times, July 23, 2000, at 1 (Abbott Lab's "maneuvering" to delay generic terazosin, which "kept the company's monopoly on Hytrin alive for four years after a patent on the key ingredient ran out," generated $2 billion in revenues before the company signed an FTC consent decree and became the target of several private antitrust suits by purchasers); John R. Wilke, Schering–Plough to Face Antitrust Suit, Wall St. J., Apr. 2, 2001, at A3.

2. *Suits by competitors.* The HMRI/Andrx Agreement, coupled with other allegedly anticompetitive behavior by HMRI's predecessors, triggered an antitrust lawsuit by a potential generic competitor. See Biovail Corp. v. Hoechst AG, 49 F.Supp.2d 750 (D.N.J.1999) (rejecting motions to dismiss); see also Mark Heinzl, Biovail Will Buy Right to Market Aventis Drugs, Wall St. J., Jan. 3, 2001, at B2.

Bristol-Myers Squibb Co. v. IVAX Corp.
77 F.Supp.2d 606 (D.N.J.2000), aff'd in part, 246 F.3d 1368 (Fed.Cir.2001).

■ WALLS, DISTRICT JUDGE:

Bristol–Myers Squibb, a drug manufacturer, has sued Zenith Goldline and IVAX Corporation for infringement of two patents owned by Bristol that claim methods of using the anti-cancer drug Taxol®, a drug based on a natural agent known as paclitaxel. The plaintiff alleges that Zenith Goldline, with the assistance of IVAX, has filed Abbreviated New Drug Application (ANDA) 75–297 with the Food and Drug Administration, to request approval to market paclitaxel. Bristol claims that the filing of the ANDA constitutes infringement of Bristol's rights under U.S. Patent No. 5,641,-803 ("the '803 patent") and No. 5,670,537 ("the '537 patent"), pursuant to the Hatch–Waxman Act, 35 U.S.C. § 271(e)(2)(A). Zenith Goldline and Baker Norton (a subsidiary of IVAX Corporation) assert numerous counterclaims based on federal antitrust provisions and state law. * * *

Paclitaxel is the FDA-designated generic term for an anti-cancer agent derived from the bark of the Pacific Yew tree. Its anti-cancer properties were discovered and developed by researchers at the National Cancer Institute (NCI), an institute of the National Institutes of Health (NIH), beginning in the 1960s. During this period, the federal government developed techniques to extract paclitaxel from yew tree bark and to create a clinically acceptable formulation for treating humans. In the early 1980s, the NCI conducted research and clinical trials concerning the use of paclitaxel to treat ovarian cancer. Eventually, the agency sought a commercial partner to bring a paclitaxel-based drug to market, and in 1991 the NCI and Bristol entered into a cooperative research and development agreement (CRADA) pursuant to the Federal Technology Transfer Act, 15 U.S.C. § 3710a(b).

In 1991 and 1993, Congress held investigatory hearings to determine the extent of Bristol's power to exclude competition pursuant to the CRADA, and to examine Bristol's pricing arrangements. Bristol made various oral and written statements during these hearings. Beginning in 1991, purportedly relying on public assurances by Bristol not to block competition in the development of paclitaxel-related drugs, Baker Norton began to conduct clinical trials involving the use of paclitaxel to treat breast cancer. In 1995, Baker Norton learned that the NCI had obtained U.S. Patent No. 5,496,846 ("the '846 patent"), known as the Wilson patent, which described the use of paclitaxel to treat breast cancer. Accordingly, Baker Norton sought a nonexclusive license to this patent in the spring of 1996 and formally applied to the NIH in September 1996. Soon after, NIH informed Baker Norton that no license was available because the agency had determined that the Wilson patent was a subject invention of the CRADA. Because Bristol had exercised its option under the CRADA for an exclusive license to this patent, Baker Norton's application was rejected.

Baker Norton, seeking to market a paclitaxel-based drug to treat Kaposi's sarcoma, a life-threatening form of cancer that often strikes persons with AIDS, developed and tested Paxene®, a paclitaxel-based drug. The counterclaimants allege that through Baker Norton's application to the NIH for a license to the Wilson patent, Bristol improperly learned that Baker Norton was preparing a New Drug Application to obtain "orphan drug" exclusive marketing privileges regarding the treatment of Kaposi's sarcoma. Orphan drug designation is a form of non-patent marketing exclusivity granted by the FDA pursuant to 21 U.S.C. § 360bb to encourage the development of drugs to treat rare diseases or conditions. The counter-claimants allege that in February 1997, with the assistance of data from NCI researchers, Bristol submitted to the FDA its own application for orphan drug status and a supplemental New Drug Application. These applications were approved, and Bristol was granted a seven-year period of marketing exclusivity. As a result, Baker Norton's New Drug Application, submitted in March 1997, was approved, but Baker Norton was barred from marketing Paxene to treat patients with Kaposi's sarcoma until 2004. * * *

Bristol maintains that because any injury to Baker Norton was the result of Bristol's valid efforts to obtain government action, such efforts are immunized from federal antitrust and state law liability by the *Noerr-Pennington* doctrine. * * * The counterclaimants protest that this doctrine does not immunize an entire course of wrongful acts simply because Bristol requested government approval and licenses as part of its allegedly tortious scheme. * * * Here, there is no question that the counterclaiming plaintiffs' injuries were the "direct result" of decisions made by government agencies. NCI chose to enter a licensing agreement with Bristol; likewise, the FDA made the decision to grant orphan drug exclusivity to the defendant drug company. These decisions cannot fairly be characterized as the result of Bristol's private actions. * * *

The counterclaimants next argue that any antitrust immunity is shed by Bristol's engagement in a course of tortious conduct. They charge that: (1) Bristol improperly received Baker Norton's confidential business infor-mation and obtained an exclusive license to the Wilson patent only after it became aware that Baker Norton had expressed interest in obtaining a nonexclusive license to use paclitaxel to treat breast cancer; (2) Bristol obtained its license to the Wilson patent solely to block competition and has never attempted to bring a breast cancer therapy to market; (3) Bristol misappropriated Baker Norton's confidential business information, learned that Baker Norton was preparing to apply for orphan drug status to market paclitaxel to treat Kaposi's sarcoma and submitted its own request for orphan drug status. Additionally, (4) while the FDA was considering Baker Norton's application for orphan drug status, Bristol met privately with high-level FDA officials in an effort to block the application. * * * Baker Norton and Zenith Goldline assert that the *Noerr-Pennington* doctrine does not protect misconduct in ex parte proceedings before a government agen-cy. * * *

If misconduct were evident, counterclaimants' argument would remain inadequate. In reviewing a publicity campaign that involved the circulation of propaganda which had been disguised as independent commentary, the *Noerr* Court rejected the argument that unethical business conduct could form a basis for antitrust liability. The Court held that even deliberate deception of the public and public officials was of no consequence to liability under the Sherman Act. * * *

In a final effort to save their antitrust claims, Baker Norton and Zenith Goldline proffer that when the government acts in a commercial role, rather than in its political or regulatory capacity, courts should apply a "commercial exception" to the *Noerr-Pennington* doctrine and reject assertions of immunity. They assert that the NCI and its parent NIH began an ongoing commercial relationship with Bristol in 1991, when NCI and Bristol entered the CRADA. They also allege that when NIH granted Bristol an exclusive license to the Wilson patent, the agency had been a commercial partner with Bristol for five years and was in the process of negotiating a royalty agreement under the licensing agreement. * * *

Antitrust immunity is not destroyed by a commercial relationship between the government and a private actor. If that were so, courts would be called upon to frustrate First Amendment rights whenever the government stood to profit from its decisions. There is clear statutory authority to the federal agencies to enter into the CRADA, to grant the patent license, and to designate orphan drug exclusivity to Bristol. Without express declaration of Congress, the counterclaimants' proposed exception cannot swallow the [far]reaching rule of immunity or these statutory grants. The court finds that Bristol was engaged in protected petitioning conduct. The court grants Bristol's motion to dismiss the Sherman Act counterclaims of Baker Norton and Zenith Goldline to the extent that they allege conduct protected by the *Noerr-Pennington* doctrine. * * *

Both counterclaimants assert an estoppel claim, maintaining that Bristol promised during congressional hearings in 1991 and 1993 "that it would not bar all competition in the market for paclitaxel-based drugs and that its monopoly in the paclitaxel-based drug market was limited to ... non-patent exclusivity." The purported promises include statements that: (1) Bristol did not have a monopoly on paclitaxel because the compound [as opposed to methods of administration] is not patentable; (2) Bristol did not have exclusive intellectual property rights to make paclitaxel; (3) any company could file a full [NDA] and market paclitaxel; (4) the NCI did not require a "reasonable pricing clause" in its CRADA with Bristol because paclitaxel is not patentable; (5) " '[c]ompetition' from 'generics' was 'a near certainty in the next several years.... [N]ear-term generic competition for Taxol is a certainty because Taxol is not a patented product;' " and (6) "While Taxol qualified for orphan drug status as a treatment for refractory ovarian cancer, BMS [Bristol] believed that the potential utility of Taxol could place it outside the spirit and intent of the Orphan Drug Act. Therefore, the company voluntarily relinquished Taxol orphan drug status...."

Bristol moves to dismiss on two grounds: that "[s]tatements made to Congress fall—dead center—within the protected zone of petitioning the government," and second, that the counterclaimants have not alleged the elements of promissory estoppel. * * * Here, the statements made by Bristol were offered during congressional hearings headlined, "Exclusive

Agreements Between Federal Agencies and Bristol–Myers Squibb Co. for Drug Development: Is The Public Interest Protected?" and, "Pricing of Drugs Codeveloped by Federal Laboratories and Private Companies." It is apparent that these claims were made in an effort to induce favorable government action, to encourage cooperation between government agencies and drug manufacturers and to defend Bristol's paclitaxel pricing system. It is also likely, as the counterclaimants allege, that these statements were made with anticompetitive intent. Yet, *Noerr* has long protected such a situation from antitrust scrutiny—and, in our circuit, it is likewise protected from state law liability. * * *

[I]t is clear that even misrepresentations made to induce government action are protected by the *Noerr-Pennington* doctrine. The counterclaim for promissory estoppel is barred. Baker Norton and Zenith Goldline have not adequately alleged that Bristol's alleged statements injured them directly. From the well-pled allegations, the court can infer only that their competitor made certain representations in its efforts to obtain government approval. The motion to dismiss the promissory estoppel counterclaim is granted. * * *

NOTES AND QUESTIONS

1. *Inventions financed by the government.* Under the Bayh–Dole Act of 1980, private entities may commercialize breakthroughs supported by government funding, but these products cannot be patented. See Pub. L. No. 96–517, § 6(a), 94 Stat. 3019 (1980) (codified as amended at 35 U.S.C. §§ 200–211); see also Platzer v. Sloan–Kettering Inst., 787 F.Supp. 360, 362 (S.D.N.Y.) ("The Bayh–Dole Act grants non-profit organizations exclusive title to inventions developed through federal funding and allows them to freely license such inventions for profit so long as such profit is used to fund additional scientific research."), aff'd mem., 983 F.2d 1086 (Fed.Cir. 1992). Nonetheless, the sponsor of an NDA may receive a patent for the method of use. For cases involving disputes over the rights to medical technologies developed with federal assistance, see Gen–Probe Inc. v. Center for Neurologic Study, 853 F.Supp. 1215, 1217–18 (S.D.Cal.1993) (holding that no private right of action existed under this statute); Ciba–Geigy Corp. v. Alza Corp., 804 F.Supp. 614, 626–29 (D.N.J.1992) (finding that the statute did not apply to a patent dispute involving transdermal nicotine patches where the inventors had not used federal research grants to first conceive their invention or reduce it to practice). The federal government has made significant investments by sponsoring basic pharmaceutical research, but the financial rewards have gone almost entirely to drug manufacturers. See Alice Dembner, Public Handouts Enrich Drug Makers, Boston Globe, Apr. 5, 1998, at A1 ("NIH spent at least $1 billion on drug and vaccine development in fiscal 1996, but took in only $27 million in royalties from all products."). The government retains "march in" rights that would allow it to call for compulsory licensing of covered inventions.

Under the Federal Technology Transfer Act, Pub. L. No. 99–502, § 2, 100 Stat. 1785 (1986) (codified at 15 U.S.C. § 3710), agencies could enter into cooperative research and developments agreements (CRADAs), assigning to private entities the patents for any inventions developed in collaboration with government researchers. Until 1995, NIH imposed a "reasonable pricing" requirement on products that emerged from a CRADA, which it dropped in the wake of criticism that this amounted to the imposition of price controls. See Peter S. Arno & Michael H. Davis, Why Don't We Enforce Existing Drug Price Controls? The Unrecognized and Unenforced Reasonable Pricing Requirements Imposed upon Patents Deriving in Whole or in Part from Federally–Funded Research, 75 Tul. L. Rev. 631 (2001); Baruch Brody, Public Goods and Fair Prices: Balancing Technological Innovation with Social Well–Being, Hastings Ctr. Rep., Mar.-Apr. 1996. See generally Rebecca S. Eisenberg, Public Research and Private Development: Patents and Technology Transfer in Government–Sponsored Research, 82 Va. L. Rev. 1663 (1996); William M. Sage, Funding Fairness: Public Investment, Proprietary Rights and Access to Health Care Technology, 82 Va. L. Rev. 1737 (1996).

2. *University involvement.* In tandem with the significant role played by the federal government, industry has forged increasingly close ties with academia. See Goldie Blumenstyk & David L. Wheeler, Academic Medical Centers Race to Compete in the $3.2 Billion Drug–Testing Market, Chron. Higher Educ., Mar. 20, 1998, at A39; David Blumenthal et al., Participation of Life–Science Faculty in Research Relationships with Industry, 335 New Eng. J. Med. 1734 (1996); Sheldon Krimsky et al., Academic Corporate Ties in Biotechnology: A Quantitative Study, 16 Sci. Tech. & Hum. Values 275 (1991). Universities have become active participants in patent litigation. See Genentech, Inc. v. Regents of the Univ. of Cal., 143 F.3d 1446 (Fed.Cir.1998); Regents of the Univ. of Minn. v. Glaxo Wellcome Inc., 44 F.Supp.2d 998 (D.Minn.1999); University of Colo. Fdn., Inc. v. American Cyanamid Co., 974 F.Supp. 1339 (D.Colo.1997); Kenneth S. Dueker, Biobusiness on Campus: Commercialization of University–Developed Biomedical Technologies, 52 Food & Drug L.J. 453 (1997); Hamilton Moses, III & Joseph P. Martin, Academic Relationships with Industry, 285 JAMA 933 (2001) (referring to a recent claim asserted by the University of Rochester for a COX–2 inhibitor). As academic researchers and their institutions receive financial stakes in their inventions, serious conflicts of interest may arise. See Marcia Angell, Editorial, Is Academic Medicine for Sale?, 342 New Eng. J. Med. 1516 (2000); Catherine D. DeAngelis, Conflict of Interest and the Public Trust, 284 JAMA 2238 (2000).

Lars Noah, *Sham Petitioning as a Threat to the Integrity of the Regulatory Process*
74 N.C. L. Rev. 1 (1995).

The Federal Trade Commission (FTC) recently announced plans to investigate the petitioning activities of companies in the pharmaceutical and medical device industries. Agency officials expressed concerns that firms were using frivolous patent litigation and petitions to the Food and Drug Administration (FDA) to limit competition and market entry. The financial stakes in these industries are often enormous, and even relatively short delays in FDA approval of competing products could prove extremely valuable to a company with an approved product already on the market. Mark Whitener, Acting Director of the FTC's Bureau of Competition, noted in 1994 that "there is a trend in this market for increasing intervention by pharmaceutical firms in judicial or regulatory proceedings," and he added that some of these efforts may violate the federal antitrust laws.

The FTC's current investigation prompts a number of important questions. Initially, one might ask whether there is any foundation to fears that firms in these or other industries are manipulating regulatory processes. In theory, at least, it seems that pharmaceutical manufacturers could make use of a variety of administrative procedures to delay or perhaps completely prevent market entry by potential competitors. * * *

[T]he next question is how best to minimize the risk of anticompetitive manipulation. By default rather than by design, application of the federal antitrust laws has become the preferred method of response by public and private litigants. Nevertheless, one might wonder whether the confidence expressed by the FTC in using the antitrust laws for these purposes is justified. Because the First Amendment protects persons' right to petition the government for redress of grievances, the Supreme Court has conferred broad immunity from antitrust scrutiny to businesses engaged in legislative lobbying, regulatory proceedings, and litigation. Although "sham petitioning" is excluded from this immunity, serious limitations exist with a remedial approach dependent on the proscriptions of the Sherman Act. * * * The antitrust laws, while perhaps a useful adjunct for combatting the most blatant abuses of regulatory procedure, can never substitute for active policing by agencies to maintain the integrity of their own processes. * * *

The FTC's investigation of petitioning activities in the pharmaceutical industry suggests that the drug approval process may be subject to manipulation by "incumbent firms," namely those companies with approved products already on the market. Although the following hypothetical is only a caricature, it represents a composite derived from a number of actual examples. For the sake of clarity, the illustration proceeds chronologically, first describing the drug approval process, and then identifying how one incumbent firm could try to repel potential competition at different time intervals after it has received all necessary approvals for its own product. * * *

On average, more than a decade elapses between the initial discovery of a new chemical entity and final drug approval. To encourage the development of pharmaceutical products intended for the treatment of rare diseases or conditions, certain investigational drugs may be designated as "orphan" drug products and entitled to special approval rules. Orphan designation for an investigational drug does not ensure ultimate NDA approval, but it does provide special exclusive marketing rights for the first company to receive such approval. There is no limit on how many companies may receive orphan designation for the same investigational drug, and each may conduct clinical trials. Once clinical testing has been completed, however, the [FDA] can approve only one of these products.

Imagine that Alpha Pharmaceutical Company, the incumbent firm, requests orphan drug designation for a combination product ("Rx") for possible use in the treatment of a rare form of cancer. After evaluating the company's evidence that the expected patient population would not exceed 200,000, the FDA grants Alpha's request for orphan designation. Assume also that Rx includes two active ingredients, one of which happens to be regulated as a Schedule II controlled substance. Authority over controlled substances resides with a separate agency, the Drug Enforcement Administration (DEA) of the United States Department of Justice. Before clinical testing of Rx may proceed, Alpha must register as a manufacturer of controlled substances and receive an annual production quota from the DEA for the Schedule II component of the product.

Once it has satisfied both FDA and DEA requirements, Alpha undertakes clinical trials to evaluate the safety and effectiveness of Rx. The statute requires adequate and well-controlled studies, generally defined as independent, double-blind clinical trials. Because the results of its studies are favorable, Alpha prepares and submits an NDA application for the product. After a comprehensive scientific review of the company's chemistry and clinical data, the FDA approves the application. Under the statute, Alpha then is entitled to the seven-year period of market exclusivity reserved as a special incentive for the development of orphan drugs.

One year after Rx is approved, Alpha's competitor "Medica" seeks approval of an apparently similar orphan drug for the same intended use. Both companies had received orphan drug designations for their respective investigational products in the same year. Medica secured a limited DEA registration and procurement quota in order to conduct its own clinical trials in preparation of an NDA application, but Alpha was the first to receive final product approval from the FDA. Although Medica submits evidence that its product would be clinically superior to Rx, Alpha lodges its objection that approval of Medica's product would violate Alpha's statutory right to market exclusivity because the drugs are the same as defined under the FDA's implementing regulations. The agency thereupon rejects Medica's application.

Alpha's own orphan designation is, however, subsequently revoked because of a misrepresentation about the expected size of the patient population, a misrepresentation brought to the Agency's attention by Medica. Alpha therefore loses its seven-year period of market exclusivity for Rx because the product is no longer regarded as an orphan drug. Even so, the NDA for the product is unaffected, leaving Alpha with the more limited form of exclusivity afforded approved new drugs that do not qualify as orphan products—namely, five years of market exclusivity against makers of generic versions of the drug seeking abbreviated approval. Another company could submit a complete NDA application for the same drug during the exclusivity period if it had performed the necessary preclinical and clinical testing. Thus, Medica resubmits its application, and, after another lengthy review, the FDA approves the product. Medica is not initially able to market its product, however, because Alpha temporarily blocks Medica's full manufacturer registration and quota applications by filing objections with DEA.

Finally, when the limited exclusivity period for Rx lapses, Alpha faces the prospect of abbreviated NDA (ANDA) submissions by competitors seeking to market generic versions of this product. * * * Alpha, however, attempts to forestall agency approval of generics by filing a citizen petition asserting general bioequivalence problems that must be resolved before the FDA can evaluate any ANDA applications for this class of products. Even when the agency is prepared to approve generic versions of Rx, perhaps after a significant delay while it has grappled with these bioequivalence issues, Alpha may raise specific objections to the ANDA filings of individual companies.

If these efforts to prevent FDA approval of generic products ultimately prove unsuccessful, even though the company did manage to delay such approvals, Alpha might again attempt to use DEA processes to preserve its market position. Alpha also might file patent infringement lawsuits against the companies marketing generic versions of Rx. Finally, even after these competitors have received the necessary FDA approvals and DEA licenses, Alpha might try to convince state formulary committees not to include the generic products on the list of drugs reimbursable under Medicaid and other health insurance programs, again in hopes of retaining its existing market share.

Thus, an incumbent drug manufacturer may be able to utilize the regulatory processes of the FDA and DEA, as well as the states, in a variety of ways to delay and perhaps completely prevent market entry by competitors. It is precisely this sort of conduct in the pharmaceutical industry that the Federal Trade Commission recently identified as potentially abusive and worthy of closer investigation. This illustration prompts two important questions, namely, whether such conduct should be regarded as objectionable and, if so, whether the antitrust laws provide a meaningful response. To the extent that courts have restricted antitrust scrutiny in such cases, partly in recognition of the First Amendment right to petition, this Article suggests that greater attention should be paid to the procedural mechanisms available to administrative agencies for protecting the integrity of the regulatory process. * * *

Sham petitioning in the regulatory arena is not an unexpected phenomenon. Many commentators have recognized the strategic opportunities available to incumbent firms. As one scholar recently observed: "Entering a market nowadays can require approvals from a myriad of licensing boards, zoning commissions, and environmental regulators. A firm that is repeatedly opposed in such proceedings without regard to the legal merits can have its entry to the market delayed for a long time." In its 1988 enforcement guidelines, the Antitrust Division of the U.S. Department of Justice noted that the "use of governmental processes to disadvantage a competitor and thus to increase market power is in general a more plausible anticompetitive strategy than is pricing below cost because a firm may be able to trigger significant litigation costs and other administrative burdens at little cost to itself." Indeed, such opportunities for deterring market entry may have been part of the political bargain struck between lawmakers and regulated entities * * * *

The fact that a petitioner intentionally causes delay in agency proceedings generally is not, by itself, sufficient to trigger the sham exception. Only in cases where delay appears to be the sole purpose underlying petitions that have no reasonable chance of success on the merits would *Noerr-Pennington* immunity be lost.

Objective baselessness may be difficult to prove in the administrative context, however, because agencies enjoy greater policymaking discretion than do the courts. Indeed, where the standards for approval of licenses and applications make reference to undefined considerations of public interest, it may be impossible to show that a competitor's objections were objectively baseless. Even when agencies must apply more particularized criteria in evaluating applications * * * , incumbent firms generally are free to press objections of this sort even though their only real interest in the matter is the threat of competition. For example, referring back to our drug approval hypothetical, it would be difficult to say that Alpha's objections to Medica's applications to the FDA and DEA, or its array of maneuvers to block generic competition—filing a citizen petition to raise general bioequivalence concerns, objecting to particular ANDAs and DEA registrations, and lobbying state drug formulary committees—are objectively baseless even if the company's ulterior purposes were entirely transparent.

There may be situations when an incumbent firm's claims before an agency clearly are indefensible as a matter of law, and courts have applied the sham exception in the few cases in which this was true. Similarly, a petition may be treated as a sham if its allegations lack any factual support (amounting to fraud), but simple inaccuracies or exaggerations generally would not suffice. Thus, in lobbying state formulary committees, Alpha could reiterate the bioequivalence concerns that it raised unsuccessfully with the FDA, but it could not claim that the generic approvals were procured by bribery of FDA officials if there was no basis for making such an allegation. * * *

One final set of noteworthy questions has arisen from litigation about the sham exception. From the outset, the Supreme Court suggested a sharp distinction between the political arena of the legislature and the adjudicatory setting of judicial and administrative proceedings, with the latter category benefitting from a more expansive sham exception and a correspondingly lesser degree of petitioning immunity. It is not, of course, simple to categorize agency decisionmaking as primarily legislative or adjudicatory. For instance, the various procedural devices available to Alpha Pharmaceuticals arise in settings that may be characterized as primarily legislative (e.g., the citizen petition regarding bioequivalence problems with generics, and the lobbying of state formulary committees) or adjudicative (e.g., objections raised during FDA product approval and DEA licensing proceedings). * * *

Because of the First Amendment interests at stake, courts have given the sham exception a narrow construction. Petitions to the government, therefore, are cloaked in a presumption that they have been brought in good faith. Thus, successful invocation of the sham exception is difficult because "[p]etitioners almost always genuinely desire government action, and [they] seldom have no possibility of getting it." * * *

As previously suggested, the largely unrestricted opportunity to participate brings with it the possibility for strategic manipulation of the regulatory process in pursuit of anticompetitive ends. Although openness and accessibility have long been considered hallmarks of good government, at some point rules favoring public participation may become counterproductive. The central question is whether the potential harms associated with sham petitioning will ever outweigh the values that are served by an open regulatory process. * * *

Although licenses issued by government are regarded as property under the due process clause, only the person whose license or application is at issue would have a sufficiently direct interest in the proceeding to trigger due process rights. For instance, in the hypothetical discussed above, Alpha Pharmaceuticals might have a constitutional right to raise objections if FDA approval of Medica's application would violate Alpha's statutory right to seven years of market exclusivity, but it would not have a similar right to object on some other basis once this period has expired. * * *

Courts have recognized that agencies possess considerable latitude in restricting the scope of an intervenor's participation in order to prevent dilatory tactics. As the Supreme Court once noted, "administrative proceedings should not be a game or a forum to engage in unjustified obstructionism." Moreover, in what appears to be a little-noticed provision, the APA itself directs agencies to take action on license applications with dispatch.

At present, however, many agencies halt proceedings or otherwise delay final decisionmaking when a third party raises objections. These procedures provide obvious invitations for anticompetitive abuse, especially if objections may be filed in a tardy or seriatim fashion. Indeed, intervention procedures may represent political concessions to existing members of a regulated industry as a tool for retarding market entry by potential competitors. They may also reinforce an agency's reluctance to act before all information has been considered; bureaucrats may be more concerned with unimpeachable decisionmaking than with the speedy resolution of matters.

On occasion, agencies do limit the opportunities for intervention in adjudicatory proceedings. When the FDA issued its orphan drug approval regulations, for example, it rejected suggestions that it create a preapproval challenge procedure because it feared that incumbents might try thereby "to delay the marketing of competitors' approvable" orphan drugs. Earlier this year, DEA eliminated the right of incumbents to demand a hearing on a competitor's application to manufacture controlled substances. As the agency explained when it first proposed this modification of its existing procedures:

> [C]urrently registered manufacturers use the regulatory hearing requirement to deter others from applying or to delay entry of competitors into their marketplace. As often as not, a company whose new application is opposed by a current manufacturer retaliates by opposing the annual renewal of the other's registration. This abuse of the regulatory hearing requirement adversely affects competition by delaying new registrations and results in the unnecessary expenditure of DEA resources * * * *

Although agencies permit and even encourage participation by persons with financial interests in licensing and other decisions, neither the constitutional right to petition nor guarantees of due process require that incumbent firms be given opportunities that may be used to block market entry by competitors.

MD Pharmaceutical, Inc. v. DEA

133 F.3d 8 (D.C.Cir.1998).

■ SENTELLE, CIRCUIT JUDGE:

This case arises out of the Drug Enforcement Administration's approval of an application submitted by Mallinckrodt Chemical, Inc. for registration as a bulk manufacturer of methylphenidate, a generic form of the drug commonly known by the brand name of Ritalin. MD Pharmaceutical, Inc., a current producer of methylphenidate, petitions for review * * * *

Methylphenidate is a Schedule II drug, which means that it has a high potential for abuse, that it has a currently accepted medical use, and that abuse of the drug may lead to severe psychological or physical dependence. A company seeking to become a manufacturer of a Schedule II drug must apply for and obtain a certificate of registration from DEA. * * *

On June 20, 1995, DEA issued a final rule altering the certification process in two pertinent respects. Under the amended regulations, which went into effect on July 20 of that year, registered manufacturers retained the right to comment on another firm's application, but no longer had the right to a hearing on an application other than their own. 60 Fed. Reg. 32,099 (1995) (codified at 21 C.F.R. § 1301.43(a) (1996)). The second alteration concerned an applicant's ability to withdraw a pending application. * * *

On July 20, 1995, the date that the new regulations went into effect, Mallinckrodt submitted a letter to DEA requesting withdrawal of its 1994 and 1995 applications. On the same day, Mallinckrodt submitted a new application for registration as a bulk manufacturer of methylphenidate under the newly amended regulations. MD strenuously opposed the withdrawal of the applications, arguing that Mallinckrodt was simply trying to circumvent the hearing requirement under the old rules. * * *

Before reaching the merits, we must address the issue of whether MD has standing to challenge the actions taken by DEA. * * * DEA does not allege that MD has not suffered an injury in fact, nor that the action taken by the government has not caused the alleged injury. * * * MD's competitive injury is fairly traceable to DEA's decision to issue a certificate of registration to Mallinckrodt. * * *

[A] competitor need not be an intended beneficiary to fall within the zone of interests of an entry-restricting statute. * * * MD, as a manufacturer facing potential competition from Mallinckrodt, is a suitable challenger and thus falls within the zone of interests of the statute. When a regulatory system "by its very nature restricts entry into a particular field or transaction," firms that are already operating in the regulated industry have an interest in enforcing the restrictions on potential market entrants. Even though competitors may be motivated by something other than a desire to advance the public interest, they nonetheless fall within the zone of interests of an entry-restricting statute because their interests "are generally congruent with a statutory purpose to restrict entry." The Controlled Substance Act is a quintessential entry-restricting statute. * * * Even more so than traditional licensees, registered manufacturers of controlled substances have an interest in limiting the number of producing firms, because each new market entrant will produce a percentage of the aggregate production quota that would otherwise be produced by existing firms. * * *

MD emphasizes that it submitted detailed comments to DEA regarding Mallinckrodt's proposed registration, which received, in MD's estimation, only short-shrift attention from the agency. 61 Fed. Reg. 37,079 (1996). Petitioner reiterates several of the objections that it unsuccessfully raised before DEA, including Mallinckrodt's alleged history of noncompliance with DEA and FDA regulations, and evidence suggesting that there is adequate competition in the methylphenidate market. MD faults DEA for not dealing with these and other objections in greater detail and with greater specificity. Petitioner also criticizes the agency for failing to identify specific facts to support its conclusion that registration of Mallinckrodt would be consistent with the public interest. * * *

We hold that DEA gave an adequate explanation for its decision to register Mallinckrodt. DEA published an explanation that spans almost eight columns in the *Federal Register* and is largely devoted to answering the many objections raised by MD during the application process. * * * Taken as a whole, DEA's explanation demonstrates that it examined the data, considered the relevant factors, and made a reasonable judgment based on the record. We conclude that the explanation offered by DEA passes muster under the APA. * * *

We decline to reach the merits of MD's objections, however, because there is no longer any live issue with respect to Mallinckrodt's first two applications. * * * Insofar as MD claims that DEA's disposition of the first and second applications somehow tainted the grant of the third, such a claim must rest on the theory that third parties acquire, at the time an application is filed, a vested right in the procedural rules then applicable, which somehow is forever attached to later applications on the same subject. This is altogether untenable. * * *

NOTES AND QUESTIONS

1. *Waging "competition" on multiple fronts.* Although the FTC's original investigation stalled, the agency has become concerned again about anticompetitive strategies used by innovator companies. See Melody Petersen, Two Companies Under Inquiry on Generic Drug Actions, N.Y. Times, Sept. 7, 2000, at C6 (reporting on an FTC inquiry into Bristol–Myers Squibb's efforts to stall IVAX's generic form of Taxol); see also National Ass'n Pharm. Mfrs., Inc. v. Ayerst Labs., 850 F.2d 904, 916–17 (2d Cir.1988) (holding that a letter sent by the manufacturer of brand name products to pharmacists which contained false and disparaging comments about generic products could support an antitrust claim); Michael A. Sanzo, Antitrust Law and Patent Misconduct in the Proprietary Drug Industry, 39 Vill. L. Rev. 1209 (1994); Thomas M. Burton, Bested Interests: Why Generic Drugs Often Can't Compete Against Brand Names, Wall St. J., Nov. 18, 1998, at A1 ("Even when [citizen] petitions fail, they can keep generic drugs off the market for months or years."); John Greenwald, Rx for Nosebleed Prices, Time, May 21, 2001, at 42; Gardiner Harris & Chris Adams, Drug Manufacturers Step up Legal Attacks that Slow Generics, Wall St. J., July 12, 2001, at A1. Frivolous patent litigation also may provide the basis for a private antitrust claim. See Nobelpharma AB v. Implant Innovations, Inc., 141 F.3d 1059, 1068–73 (Fed.Cir.1998); see also David A. Balto, Pharmaceutical Patent Settlements: The Antitrust Risks, 55 Food & Drug L.J. 321 (2000). One strategy involves the listing of marginally-related patents in the FDA's *Orange Book*, which then requires a paragraph IV certification and obligates the agency to delay ANDA approval for 30 months if the patent holder initiates patent infringement litigation. See American Bioscience, Inc. v. Thompson, 269 F.3d 1077 (D.C.Cir.2001); Mylan Pharm, Inc. v. Thompson, 139 F.Supp.2d 1 (D.D.C.2001) (granting a preliminary injunction ordering the manufacturer of BuSpar® to remove a method-of-use patent that it had added to the *Orange Book* one day before the expiration of its composition patent), rev'd, 268 F.3d 1323 (Fed.Cir.2001); Jayne O'Donnell & Julie Appleby, FTC Scrutinizes Validity of Drugmakers' Patent Listings, USA Today, Jan. 8, 2002, at 1A. Manufacturers of OTC drugs engage in similar battles. See Charles C. Mann & Mark Plummer, The Aspirin Wars: Money, Medicine, and 100 Years of Rampant Competition (1991).

2. *Industry consolidation.* As has happened in several other industries, a number of large pharmaceutical manufacturers have merged in recent years. See Steve Sakson, Drugmakers' Prescription: Merge, Wash. Post, Aug. 22, 1995, at D3; Elyse Tanouye, Mergers Will Keep Shuffling Rankings of Drug Makers, Wall St. J., Mar. 15, 1995, at B4. See generally Brian L. Walser, Shared Technical Decisionmaking and the Disaggregation of Sovereignty: International Regulatory Policy, Expert Communities, and the Multinational Pharmaceutical Industry, 72 Tul. L. Rev. 1597 (1998). For instance, the world's largest drug company at the moment, GlaxoSmith-Kline (England), combines Glaxo, Burroughs–Wellcome, and SmithKline Beecham. See Andrew Sorkin, Behind Biggest Drug Merger, Quest for a Research Pipeline, N.Y. Times, Jan. 18, 2000, at C1. Pfizer (U.S.) moved into second place after it acquired Warner–Lambert. See Melody Petersen, Pfizer Gets Its Deal to Buy Warner–Lambert for $90.2 Billion, N.Y. Times, Feb. 8, 2000, at C1. Aventis (France) combines Hoechst AG, Marion Merrell Dow, Roussel–Uclaf, and Rhone–Poulenc Rorer, each of which emerged from earlier combinations. The same holds true of Novartis (Switzerland), which grew out of the merger between Sandoz and Ciba–Geigy, and it soon may add Roche, which in turn controls Genentech. See Elisabeth Olson, In Surprise, Novartis Gets a 20% Stake in Roche, N.Y. Times, May 8, 2001, at W1. In addition, established manufacturers look at successful start up biotechnology companies as attractive targets for acquisition. See, e.g., Johnson & Johnson Gets Approval for Alza Purchase, N.Y. Times, May 11, 2001, at C4; see also Ortho Pharm. Corp. v. Amgen, Inc., 709 F.Supp. 504 (D.Del.1989) (resolving dispute that arose from joint venture); Andrew Sorkin, Bristol Buying Drug Unit of DuPont for $7.8 Billion, N.Y. Times, June 8, 2001, at C5 (describing a major acquisition made by Bristol–Myers Squibb). The medical device industry has remained more decentralized but is not immune to the pressure for mergers. See William M. Brown, Grandfathering Can Seriously Damage Your Wealth: Due Diligence in Mergers and Acquisitions of Medical Device Companies, 36 Gonz. L. Rev. 315 (2000).

3. *Antitrust issues.* This pattern of consolidation has raised a host of antitrust concerns. See David A. Balto & James F. Mongoven, Antitrust Enforcement in Pharmaceutical Industry Mergers, 54 Food & Drug L.J. 255 (1999); Melissa K. Davis, Note, Monopolistic Tendencies of Brand–Name Drug Companies in the Pharmaceutical Industry, 15 J.L. & Com. 357 (1995); Thomas B. Marcotullio, Note, The Battle Against Drugmakers: An Analysis of European Union and United States Merger Enforcement in the Pharmaceutical Industry, 32 Law & Pol'y Int'l Bus. 449 (2001); see also Paul Feldstein, Health Care Economics 442 (3d ed. 1988) (explaining that the four-firm concentration ratio has been relatively low in the pharmaceutical industry, but adding that concentration may be high in sub-markets defined by therapeutic categories). For instance, some drug manufacturers purchased pharmacy benefit management (PBM) companies, which created the potential for preferential treatment of their products in transactions with the PBM's customers. See Stephen Paul Mahinka & Kathleen M. Sanzo, Pharmaceutical Industry Restructuring and New Marketing Approaches: Enforcement Responses, 50 Food & Drug L.J. 313 (1995); Elizabeth L. Mitchell, The Potential for Self–Interested Behavior by Pharmaceutical Manufacturers Through Vertical Integration with Pharmacy Benefit Managers: The Need for a New Regulatory Approach, 54 Food & Drug L.J.

151 (1999); W.E. Afield, Note, The New Drug Buyer: The Changing Definition of the Consumer for Antitrust Enforcement in the Pharmaceutical Industry, 2001 Colum. Bus. L. Rev. 203. Joint marketing agreements may pose similar antitrust questions. Separately, some product approvals have required adjuvant therapies in a way that raised concerns about unlawful tying arrangements. See Mark A. Hurwitz, Note, Bundling Patented Drugs and Medical Services: An Antitrust Analysis, 91 Colum. L. Rev. 1188 (1991); see also Ortho Diagnostic Sys., Inc. v. Abbott Labs., Inc., 920 F.Supp. 455, 463–74 (S.D.N.Y.1996) (rejecting various antitrust claims brought by a competitor against the seller of five blood testing products sold at a discount to blood banks when purchased together). See generally Arti K. Rai, Fostering Cumulative Innovation in the Biopharmaceutical Industry: The Role of Patents and Antitrust, 16 Berkeley Tech. L.J. 813 (2001).

4. *Medical specialty associations.* In some instances, competitors have complained that suppliers of medical technologies have conspired with professional organizations to recommend use of certain therapies. See Scott Hensley, Johnson & Johnson Settles Antitrust Suit over Contact Lenses, Wall St. J., May 23, 2001, at B2; see also Schachar v. American Acad. Ophthalmology, 870 F.2d 397 (7th Cir.1989) (rejecting antitrust claim against medical society for characterizing radial keratotomy as an experimental treatment); Clark C. Havighurst, Applying Antitrust Law to Collaboration in the Production of Information: The Case of Medical Technology Assessment, Law & Contemp. Probs., Spring 1988, at 341, 357–60; Martin Rose & Robert F. Leibenluft, Antitrust Implications of Medical Technology Assessment, 314 New Eng. J. Med. 1490 (1986).

FTC v. Mylan Laboratories, Inc.

62 F.Supp.2d 25 (D.D.C.1999).

■ HOGAN, DISTRICT JUDGE:

* * * The first action is brought by the Federal Trade Commission (FTC) under § 13(a) of the Federal Trade Commission Act, 15 U.S.C. § 53(a), to secure a permanent injunction and other relief against the defendants. Defendants are Mylan Laboratories, Inc., Cambrex Corporation, Profarmaco S.R.L. and Gyma Laboratories of America, Inc. The FTC alleges that the defendants engaged and are engaging in unfair methods of competition in or affecting commerce in violation of § 5(a) of the FTC Act, 15 U.S.C. § 45(a). * * * The second case is an action brought by thirty-two states against defendants for violations of §§ 1 and 2 of the Sherman Act as well as various state antitrust laws. * * *

For purposes of the instant motions to dismiss, the allegations of the complaints are taken as true. The facts below are presented accordingly, and do not constitute factual findings. * * * Typically, the generic manufacturer purchases the active pharmaceutical ingredient (API) from a specialty chemical manufacturer. The generic manufacturer combines the API with inactive filters, binders, colorings and other chemicals to produce a finished product. To sell an API in the United States, the API supplier must file a drug master file (DMF) with the FDA. The DMF explains the processes that the API supplier uses to make the API and to test chemical equivalence and bioequivalence to the brand product. To use an API, the generic manufacturer's ANDA must refer to the API supplier's DMF filed with the FDA. More than one drug manufacturer can reference the DMF of the same API supplier. A generic manufacturer that wants or needs to change its API supplier must obtain FDA approval of an ANDA supplement which includes a reference to the new supplier's DMF and test results regarding the generic manufacturer's product using the new API. This process averages about 18 months, though it can take as long as three years.

Lorazepam and clorazepate are two of the approximately 91 generic drugs that Mylan currently manufactures and sells in tablet form. Lorazepam is used to treat anxiety, tension, agitation, insomnia, and as a preoperative sedative. Doctors issue over 18 million prescriptions a year for lorazepam tablets. Because lorazepam is used to treat chronic conditions and is heavily prescribed for nursing home and hospice patients, lorazepam users tend to stay on the drug for long periods of time. Clorazepate is used to treat anxiety and in adjunct therapy for nicotine and opiate withdrawal. Doctors issue over three million prescriptions a year for clorazepate tablets.

Profarmaco (which is a wholly owned subsidiary of Cambrex) manufactures APIs in Italy. Profarmaco holds DMFs for lorazepam API and clorazepate API, and has supplied such APIs to drug manufacturers in the United States. Foreign firms, like Profarmaco, that supply APIs to the United States typically have distributors in the United States who purchase APIs and resell them to generic drug manufacturers in the United States. Mylan purchases its lorazepam and clorazepate API from Gyma, Profarmaco's U.S. distributor of these products. Several other drug manufacturers have purchased API from SST Corporation, another U.S. distributor of this product.

The plaintiffs in these two cases allege the following anti-competitive conduct on the part of the defendants. Mylan sought from its API suppliers long-term exclusive licenses for the DMFs of certain APIs selected because of limited competition. If Mylan obtained such an exclusive license, no other generic drug manufacturer could use that supplier's API to make the drug in the U.S. Mylan sought exclusive licenses for the DMFs for lorazepam API and clorazepate API as well as one other drug not the subject of these lawsuits.

Mylan entered into contracts with Profarmaco and Gyma such that these companies would license exclusively to Mylan for 10 years. The exclusive licenses would provide Mylan with complete control over Profarmaco's entire supply of lorazepam API and clorazepate API entering the U.S. With complete control of Profarmaco's supply of these products and by refusing to sell to any of its competitors, Mylan would deny its competition access to the most important ingredient for producing lorazepam and clorazepate tablets.

In return for the 10–year exclusive licenses, Mylan offered to pay Cambrex, Profarmaco and Gyma a percentage of gross profits on sales of lorazepam and clorazepate tablets, regardless of who Mylan purchased the API from. Mylan also tried to execute an exclusive licensing arrangement with SST for control of its lorazepam supply. This is significant because Mylan was not authorized by the FDA to sell lorazepam manufactured with SST API (i.e., Mylan's ANDA did not reference SST's DMF). Thus, the States allege that Mylan was entering into a deal for exclusive rights even though it would not have been able to use SST API until after an ANDA supplement had been completed, which usually takes around 18 months. The plaintiffs' argue that Mylan's attempt to obtain control over SST's supply, when Mylan could not even use SST API, demonstrates the anticompetitive nature of Mylan's actions.

On or around January 12, 1998, Mylan raised its price of clorazepate tablets to State Medicaid programs, wholesalers, retail pharmacy chains and other customers by amounts ranging approximately from 1,900 percent to over 3,200 percent, depending on the size of the bottle and the strength. On March 3, 1998, Mylan raised its price of lorazepam tablets by amounts ranging from approximately 1,900 to 2,600 percent. Shortly thereafter, SST raised the price of lorazepam API by approximately 19,000 percent. SST sold the lorazepam API to Geneva, one of Mylan's competitors, which raised its prices to approximately the price of Mylan's tablets. * * *

In addition to an injunction prohibiting defendants' conduct and rescission of defendants' unlawful licensing arrangements, the FTC asks this court to "order other equitable relief, including the disgorgement of $120 million plus interest." Defendants object to the FTC's request on the ground that § 13(b) does not authorize disgorgement or any other form of monetary relief. It is true that the plain language of § 13(b) does not authorize the FTC to seek monetary remedies. The FTC argues, however, that monetary relief is a natural extension of the remedial powers authorized under § 13(b). * * * As defendant cites no relevant case law that prohibits the FTC from seeking disgorgement or any other form of equitable ancillary relief, the court denies defendants' motion on this issue. * * *

The State complaint seeks to recover damages not only for direct purchases from Mylan, but also for purchases from Mylan's competitors. The premise of the States' request is that Mylan's competitors in the generic drug industry, though not parties to the exclusive licenses nor members of the alleged conspiracy, raised their prices as a consequence of Mylan's actions. The States argue that defendants should be liable for the difference between the prices charged by Mylan's competitors and what those prices would have been had Mylan not raised its prices pursuant to an illegal agreement. * * *

The main difficulty with the umbrella theory is that, even in the context of a single level of distribution, ascertaining the appropriate measure of damages is a highly speculative endeavor. There are numerous pricing variables which this court would be bound to consider to approximate the correct measure of damages, including the cost of production, marketing strategy, elasticity of demand, and the price of comparable items (i.e., the brand versions of lorazepam and clorazepate). The interaction of these variables is uncertain. * * * Accordingly, this court will decline the States' invitation to consider umbrella damages and dismiss the States' complaint insofar as it requests such relief. * * *

In light of the court's ruling on the above issues, the States' federal claims against defendant are narrowed to the following cause of action: the States may sue the defendants under § 4 of the Clayton Act for any direct purchases that state entities or state citizens may have made of generic clorazepate and lorazepam from the defendants. Defendants contend that the States' amended complaint fails to allege direct purchases of generic lorazepam or clorazepate tablets from Mylan, and that none of the persons on whose behalf the States purport to sue made such direct purchases from Mylan. Defendants therefore seek dismissal of the States' complaint under Rule 12(b)(6). Although defendants are correct that the States' case is dependent on facts supporting direct purchases by the States, the States have sufficiently alleged direct purchases for the purposes of a motion to dismiss. * * *

To state a Section 2 monopolization claim, a plaintiff must allege facts sufficient to establish both ''(1) the possession of monopoly power in the relevant market and (2) the willful acquisition or maintenance of that power as distinguished from growth or development as a consequence of a superior product, business acumen, or historic accident.'' Mylan alleges that the complaints fail this legal standard in two ways: (1) they fail to sufficiently identify a relevant market; and (2) the complaints fail to allege facts sufficient to show monopoly power.

On the first issue, the complaints specifically identify four relevant markets: (1) generic lorazepam tablets; (2) generic clorazepate tablets; (3) lorazepam API; and (4) clorazepate API. Each of the relevant markets includes only those products approved for sale in the United States. This level of definition is sufficient to survive a motion to dismiss, as it is entirely plausible that plaintiffs will prove a set of facts that supports those market definitions.

Mylan's second claim is that the amended complaint fails to establish the monopoly power element of the monopolization claim. In economic terms, ''[m]onopoly power is the power to raise prices well above competitive levels before customers will turn elsewhere.'' The complaints meet this standard by alleging that Mylan instituted massive and successful price increases for lorazepam and clorazepate. Furthermore, the complaints allege that Mylan constricted the supply of generic lorazepam and clorazepate tablets by denying its competitors the APIs to manufacture these products. Like the ability to control prices, this is evidence of monopoly power. * * *

CHAPTER 11

Evolving Medical Technologies

This chapter reprises elements of many of the problems and concepts encountered in earlier chapters. How well do new medical technologies fit the molds for drugs, devices, or biologics products? Will traditional mechanisms of control, such as FDA regulation, tort liability, or insurance coverage, work effectively to control these new technologies, or is a different approach needed? Finally, this chapter will end with a consideration of how developing medical technologies have shaped the bioethics discourse in the past, and it will explore the potential impact of future technologies on the evolution of ethical norms.

A. Manipulation of Human Tissue Products

The Public Health Service Act defines a "biological product" as "a virus, therapeutic serum, toxin, antitoxin, vaccine, blood, blood component or derivative, allergenic product, or analogous product ... applicable to the prevention, treatment, or cure of a disease or condition of human beings." 42 U.S.C. § 262(i). The newest generation of biotechnology products and processes may not fit neatly into the definition of biological products or, for that matter, into the definitions of "drug" or "device." Other new medical technologies appear to fit within more than one statutory definition.

FDA, *Requirements of Laws and Regulations Enforced by the U.S. Food and Drug Administration: Biological Products*

<www.fda.gov/opacom/morechoices/smallbusiness/blubook.htm> (2001).

Special premarket controls apply to biological products, which have been required to be licensed under Federal law since 1902. They are regulated under the Public Health Service Act. Biological products are legally defined also as "drugs" or "devices" and are therefore subject to all of the adulteration, misbranding, and registration provisions of the federal Food, Drug, and Cosmetic Act. * * *

Since most biological products are derived from living organisms, they are by their nature potentially dangerous if improperly prepared or tested. In fact, the legislation of 1902 bringing biologics under federal license was introduced and enacted following the deaths of 12 children resulting from their having received improperly prepared diphtheria antitoxin.

859

Close surveillance of biologics production, batch testing, and research toward improving the quality of biologics is the responsibility of FDA's Center for Biologics Evaluation and Research (CBER). * * * In addition to the traditional biological products described in the PHS Act, CBER has jurisdiction over selected medical devices, drug products and banked human tissue intended for transplantation. The devices are primarily articles used in blood banks or plasmapheresis centers, such as containers for collecting and processing blood components, blood storage refrigeration units, and blood bank supplies. The drug products and devices are regulated under the provisions of the federal Food, Drug, and Cosmetic Act. Banked human tissue intended for transplantation is regulated under the authority of the PHS Act to prevent the spread of communicable disease. The standards governing banked human tissue are found in 21 C.F.R. § 1270.

Under the Public Health Service Act, a manufacturer wishing to ship a biological product in interstate commerce, or for import or export must obtain a U.S. license. These licenses are granted following a showing that the establishment and product meet specific standards described in [21 C.F.R.] Parts 600 through 680 and Part 211. These regulations are designed to ensure continued safety, purity, potency, and effectiveness. * * * To apply for licensure, the manufacturer must submit information demonstrating that the manufactured product meets the specified standards, and must successfully complete a prelicensing inspection by FDA investigators. Once licensed, most establishments are inspected at least once every two years by FDA * * * *

Prior to the release by the manufacturer of each lot of certain licensed products, specified materials must be submitted to and cleared by CBER. These materials include a sample of the product, of the size specified in the regulations, as well as detailed records (protocols) of the manufacture of each lot of the product, including all results of each test for which results are requested. CBER reviews the protocols and may conduct its own safety, purity, and potency tests on the samples. A product subject to lot release procedures cannot be issued by the manufacturer until notification of official release is received. The CBER supplies standard reference preparations for potency tests of certain licensed products, including antitoxins, bacterial and viral vaccines, and skin tests. Manufacturers are required to obtain and use these preparations in their testing of licensed products. * * *

United States v. Loran Medical Systems, Inc.

25 F.Supp.2d 1082 (C.D.Cal.1997).

■ WILSON, DISTRICT JUDGE:

On June 20, 1996, this court granted a temporary restraining order enjoining Defendants Loran Medical Systems, Inc., Bent Formby and Ernest Thomas, M.D. from importing neonatal rabbit and human fetal cells (the "Cell Product") from Russia for use in the treatment of human diabetes. Defendants claim that injection of the Cell Product into diabetic patients can stimulate the body's production of insulin. * * *

The gravamen of this case is whether the Cell Product falls within the regulatory ambit of the FDA. The government argues that it does, pointing to regulations defining "biological product," which the FDA regulates pursuant to its authority under the Public Health Service Act; and regulations involving "drugs" and "new drugs," which the FDA regulates under its Food and Drug Act authority. * * * A biological product is any "virus, therapeutic serum, toxin, antitoxin or analogous product applicable to the prevention, treatment or cure" of human diseases or injuries. A product is analogous to a toxin or anti-toxin if, irrespective of its source or origin, it can be used in the treatment of disease through a "specific immune process." 21 C.F.R. § 600.3(h)(5)(iii).

The human immune system will naturally react to the injection of any cellular material, whether obtained from a human or non-human source. Defendants inject the Cell Product into an area of the abdomen selected specifically to evade this response and thus reduce the chance that the cells will be rejected. This procedure purportedly allows the rabbit cells to begin producing insulin immediately while the human fetal cells mature.

The government argues that this attempt at evading the body's natural immune system is a "specific immune process" as required by the FDA's regulations. Defendants * * * argue that the PHS Act only authorizes the FDA to regulate products which immunize against a specific disease, such as polio or smallpox. The court disagrees. As described in greater detail below, Congress conferred upon the FDA the broad statutory authority to regulate products analogous to toxins, antitoxins, vaccines, blood, etc. The FDA's assertion of authority over immunological agents such as the Cell Product is a reasonable construction of the PHS Act. * * *

Defendants argue that the Cell Product cannot be a biological product under 42 U.S.C. § 262(a) because it is not biologically or genetically altered in any way. Somatic cell therapy—medical treatment using biologically altered cells—is regulated under the FDA's authority to regulate biological products. See 58 Fed. Reg. 53,250; FDA, Points to Consider in Human Cell Therapy and Gene Therapy (1991). But nothing in the regulation requires alteration before a product is to fall under the FDA's purview. Accordingly, the court finds that the FDA's conclusion that the Cell Product is a biological product that uses a specific immune process is reasonable, and thus the Cell Product is properly under the FDA's authority.

The FD&C Act defines drugs as, inter alia, "articles intended for use in the diagnosis, cure, mitigation, treatment or prevention of disease in [humans]." 21 U.S.C. § 321. The Cell Product was developed for use in the treatment of diabetes. Thus, it meets the statutory definition of a drug. * * * Classifying the Cell Product as a drug is consistent with Congress' intent to give the FDA broad authority in this important area.

All new drugs must undergo premarket review by the FDA. A new drug is any drug that is not already generally recognized among medical experts as safe and effective for its intended use. The exception for "generally recognized" drugs is very narrow. The court's task is to determine whether the drug has a general reputation in the scientific community for safety and effectiveness, not to make an independent determination of these characteristics. * * * While Defendants make sweeping arguments about the worldwide acceptance of the product, they fail to provide specific examples of successful clinical trials or published studies. Moreover, while Defendants provide anecdotal evidence of clinical success, the declarations of Plaintiffs' experts demonstrate that there is a marked lack of consensus in the medical community as to the effectiveness of the Cell Product. Accordingly, the court finds that the FDA has acted reasonably in classifying the Cell Product as a new drug.

The court disposes quickly of defendants' argument that the FDA's exercise of authority over the Cell Product is an attempt to regulate the practice of medicine—an area traditionally left to the states. While the FD&C Act "was not intended to regulate the practice of medicine, it was obviously intended to control the availability of drugs for prescribing by physicians." The court has already determined that the Cell Product is a drug. Accordingly, the FDA has the authority to regulate its use. * * *

NOTES AND QUESTIONS

1. *Vaccines.* The FDA regulates vaccines as both drugs and biologics, which means that, in addition to satisfying new drug approval requirements, manufacturers must test each lot for potency and sterility according to the terms of a biologics license application (BLA) and submit samples of each vaccine lot to CBER for pre-release approval. Once approved for marketing, vaccines also may be required to undergo additional safety and efficacy studies. CBER and the Centers for Disease Control and Prevention (CDC) jointly administer the Vaccine Adverse Event Reporting System (VAERS), a post-market safety surveillance program. See FDA, Vaccines, available at <www.fda.gov/cber/vaccines.htm>.

2. *Blood.* Suppliers of blood and certain blood-derived products must comply with facility registration requirements. See 21 C.F.R. pt. 607; Compliance Policy Guide 7134.01, Registration of Blood Banks and Other Firms Collecting, Manufacturing, Preparing or Processing Human Blood or Blood Products (2000). In an attempt to ensure the safety of the blood supply, all blood banks also must operate in compliance with special GMPs. See 21 CFR pt. 606. As the FDA explained:

> CBER works closely with other parts of the Public Health Service to identify and respond to potential threats to blood safety, to develop safety and technical standards, to monitor blood supplies and to help industry promote an adequate supply of blood and blood products. While a blood supply with zero risk of transmitting infectious disease may not be possible, the blood supply is safer than it has ever been. Over a period of years, FDA has progressively strengthened the overlapping safeguards that protect patients from unsuitable blood and

blood products.... [B]lood donations are now tested for seven different infectious agents. In addition to strengthening these safeguards, FDA has significantly increased its oversight of the blood industry, and "problem" facilities are inspected more often. Blood establishments are now held to quality standards comparable to those expected of pharmaceutical manufacturers.

FDA, Blood Safety, available at <www.fda.gov/cber/blood.htm>. Curiously, the agency previously had announced that it considers human blood and blood products to be drugs. In a preamble to a final rule, the FDA wrote that:

Section 201(g)(1) definition of drug in the [FDCA] reveals that blood and related blood products fall clearly within that definition. That section states "The term 'drug' means ... (B) articles intended for use in the diagnosis, cure, mitigation, treatment, or prevention of disease in man or other animals...." Indications for use of blood products also fall directly within the broad therapeutic scope of the definition. While it is, of course, true that blood is human living tissue, it is incorrect to assume that it must be either a living human tissue or a drug. That human blood and blood products may be characterized as living human tissue for some purposes, and as biologics for purposes of regulation under the Public Health Service Act in no way alters the fact that blood is also a drug subject to regulation under applicable provisions of the Federal Food, Drug, and Cosmetic Act.

38 Fed. Reg. 2965, 2965 (1973). What was the FDA seeking to accomplish by announcing that it can regulate blood as a drug? The agency certainly did not intend to subject blood to the NDA process. Would blood be considered a new drug, or is it GRAS/GRAE?

3. *Overlapping product categories.* As the materials in this section suggest, many products may fit into more than one statutory product category, creating regulatory confusion. See Martha J. Carter, The Ability of Current Biologics Law to Accommodate Emerging Technologies, 51 Food & Drug L.J. 375 (1996); Shane M. Ward, Global Harmonization of Regulatory Requirements for Premarket Approval of Autologous Cell Therapies, 55 Food & Drug L.J. 225 (2000); Martha A. Wells, Overview of FDA Regulation of Human Cellular and Tissue–Based Products, 52 Food & Drug L.J. 401 (1997). Manufacturers seeking a license to market a new biological product that fits the regulatory definition of a drug must obtain an IND to study the product in human clinical trials. If the data from the trials demonstrates the product's safety and effectiveness, then CBER may grant the license. A recent amendment to the FDCA requires the agency "to take measures to minimize differences in the review and approval of products required to have approved biologics license applications under [the PHSA] and products required to have approved new drug applications under [the FDCA]." FDAMA, Pub. L. No. 105–115, § 123(c), 111 Stat. 2324 (1997).

4. *Infectious disease controls in tissue intended for human transplantation.* Even minimally processed tissue can pose significant hazards to the recipient. One patient who received a contaminated bone and cartilage transplant during knee surgery died from a rare bacterial infection. See David Brown, 3 Knee Surgery Deaths Called Unrelated, Wash. Post, Dec. 7, 2001, at A17. In 1997, the FDA issued final rules under the authority of the PHSA governing infectious disease testing, donor screening, and record-keeping for human tissue intended for transplantation. See 62 Fed. Reg. 40,429 (1997) (codified at 21 C.F.R. pt. 1270).

5. *Regulatory oversight of the tissue banking industry.* A recent report by the Office of the Inspector General criticized the FDA's lack of oversight of tissue banks and noted that only two states (Florida and New York) require tissue banks to be licensed and inspected by an accrediting body:

> Some tissue banks have never been inspected by FDA. We found at least 36 tissue banks that have never been inspected, out of 154 tissue establishments that we were able to identify. FDA has indicated that regulation of tissue banks is an unfunded mandate, and that in order to carry out these inspections, the agency has had to borrow resources from other programs, such as blood and plasma. Of the 118 tissue banks that FDA has inspected, 68 have been inspected only once. . . . Information is lacking about the number of tissue banks in operation and the products they produce and distribute. FDA has proposed a regulation to require tissue banks to register and list their products. The regulation would address directly this limitation in knowledge about tissue banking. Because the agency's current regulation focuses on donor screening and testing to prevent transmission of [disease], other important aspects of tissue bank quality are not monitored. Until FDA's good tissue practices rule is finalized, tissue banks have no external requirements for quality and handling of tissue if they are not accredited by [the American Association of Tissue Banks] or licensed by New York or Florida. Of the 154 tissue banks we identified, 67 are neither accredited by AATB nor inspected by Florida or New York.

Office of Inspector Gen., HHS, Oversight of Tissue Banking, OEI–01–00–00441 (2001), at ii-iii, available at <www.hhs.gov/oig/oei/reports/a501.pdf>; see also Barbara Indech, The International Harmonization of Human Tissue Regulation: Regulatory Control over Human Tissue Use and Tissue Banking in Select Countries and the Current State of International Harmonization Efforts, 55 Food & Drug L.J. 343 (2000).

FDA, Proposed Rule, *Establishment Registration and Listing for Manufacturers of Human Cellular and Tissue–Based Products*

63 Fed. Reg. 26,744 (1998).

FDA is putting in place a comprehensive new system of regulation for human cellular and tissue-based products. As a first step toward accomplishing this goal, the agency is proposing regulations that will require establishments that manufacture those products to register and list their products with the agency.

The term "human cellular and tissue-based products" encompasses an array of medical products derived from the human body and used for replacement, reproductive, or therapeutic purposes. Skin, tendons, bone, heart valves, and corneas have long been used as replacements for damaged or diseased tissues. Semen, ova, and embryos are transferred for reproductive purposes. Currently, some human cellular and tissue-based products are being developed for new therapeutic uses. For example, scientists are studying the use of manipulated human cells to treat viral infections, Parkinson's disease, and diabetes, among other diseases.

Human cellular and tissue-based products serve a crucial role in medicine, and they have the potential for providing important new therapies. Yet they also raise public health concerns. With the development of new products, and new uses for existing products, come questions about safety and effectiveness that need to be answered through clinical investigation. Furthermore, all human cellular and tissue-based products, because they contain components of the human body, pose some risk of carrying pathogens that could cause disease in health-care personnel, other handlers of tissue, recipients, and family members or other close contacts of recipients.

FDA has never had a single regulatory program for human cellular and tissue-based products. Instead, it has regulated these products on a case-by-case basis responding as it determined appropriate to the particular characteristics of and concerns raised by each type of product. Some tissues have been regulated as medical devices under section 201 of the Federal Food, Drug, and Cosmetic Act. Corneal lenticules, dura mater, heart valve allografts, and umbilical cord vein grafts fall into this category. Other products have been considered biological products under section 351 of the Public Health Service Act and drugs under the act (hereinafter referred to as biological drugs). Somatic cell therapy products and some gene therapy products fall into this category.

FDA has also relied on section 361 of the PHS Act, which provides the authority to issue regulations to prevent the spread of communicable diseases, to regulate tissues that it has chosen not to regulate as devices or biological drugs. In 1993, in response to concerns about the safety of human tissue intended for transplantation, FDA used this authority to require testing and screening of tissue donors for hepatitis and human immunodeficiency viruses. See 58 Fed. Reg. 65,514 (1993). Until it issued those regulations ("Human Tissues Intended for Transplantation," codified in title 21 of the Code of Federal Regulations (CFR) part 1270), FDA exerted little or no regulatory control over certain types of human cellular and tissue-based products. Instead, human tissue for transplantation was subject to some State regulation and to voluntary accreditation systems. Even today, FDA's human tissue regulations do not address the infectious disease risk of donating, processing, and storing reproductive cells and tissue.

FDA has evaluated its approach to regulating human cellular and tissue-based products and has determined that changes are needed. In light of the development of new products, coupled with a growing awareness of infectious-disease concerns, the agency believes that the current patchwork of regulatory policies is no longer adequate and plans to create a comprehensive regulatory program that will cover a broad range of human cellular and tissue-based products. The agency has considered the relevant provisions of the [FDCA] and the PHS Act and has concluded that these two statutes provide sufficiently broad authority for the proposed regulatory program. The agency announced its plans for reform in two documents released in February 1997: "Reinventing the Regulation of Human Tissue," and "A Proposed Approach to the Regulation of Cellular and Tissue–Based Products" (hereinafter "Proposed Approach document"). * * *

FDA seeks to achieve several goals with its new approach to regulating human cellular and tissue-based products. Primary among them is the improved protection of the public health without the imposition of unnecessary restrictions on research, development, or the availability of new products. Under the new program, the degree of scrutiny afforded different types of products will be commensurate with the risks presented, enabling the agency to use its resources more effectively. Consolidating the regulation of human cellular and tissue-based products into one regulatory program is expected to lead to increased consistency and greater efficiency. Together, these planned improvements should increase the safety of human cellular and tissue-based products, and public confidence in that safety, while encouraging the development of new products.

In developing its proposed approach, FDA examined five issues that it considered fundamental to the proper regulation of the various types of human cellular and tissue-based products. First, the agency asked how the transmission of communicable disease by these products occurs and could be prevented. Second, the agency looked at the types of handling, processing, and manufacturing controls that are necessary to prevent contamination and to preserve the integrity and function of these products. Third, the agency examined concerns about the products' clinical safety and effectiveness. Fourth, FDA considered the type of labeling necessary for proper use of the products and the kind of promotion that would be permissible. Finally, the agency asked how it could best monitor and communicate with the cell and tissue industry.

Through examination of these five public-health and regulatory concerns, FDA was able to develop a proposed comprehensive regulatory scheme tailored to the relevant characteristics of human cellular and tissue-based products. In order to devise an umbrella approach, the agency first focused on the products' common attributes. Then, to ensure appropriate levels of regulation, the agency differentiated between the various types of products based on the public health risks associated with them. For example, the risks posed by cells that are extensively manipulated in a laboratory and then implanted for their systemic effect on a patient are different from those of an unmanipulated tissue that is transplanted into a patient to replace an injured structural tissue.

Taking into account these differences, the agency designed a risk-based tiered approach intended to regulate human cellular and tissue-based products only to the extent necessary to protect public health. Some products will be subject to little or no regulation. For example, no regulatory requirements will be imposed on tissues transplanted into the same patient during the same surgical procedure.

As the potential risk posed by a product increases, so will the level of oversight afforded that product. Thus, minimally processed tissues transplanted from one person to another for their normal structural functions would be subject to infectious disease screening and testing and to requirements for good handling procedures, but would not need FDA premarket review or marketing approval. In contrast, premarket approval would generally be required for cells and tissues that are processed extensively, are combined with noncellular or nontissue components, are labeled or promoted for purposes other than their normal functions, or have a systemic effect. In addition, these products would be subject to requirements for good tissue practices and infectious disease screening and testing, as well as to the good manufacturing practice requirements applicable to drugs and devices.

Although FDA's proposed regulatory approach is far more comprehensive in scope than its present system, some products will not be covered. Among the products not included under the approach are vascularized organs and minimally manipulated bone marrow, both of which fall under the purview of the Health Resources Services Administration. FDA already comprehensively regulates transfusable blood products (e.g., whole blood, red blood cells, platelets, and plasma) under a different regulatory scheme and will not at this time regulate those products as human cellular and tissue-based products. Xenograft transplantation (transplantation using tissues derived from animals) raises different public health issues from transplantation with human tissue, and so will not be subject to the new regulatory program. The new program will also exclude from coverage ancillary products used in cell or tissue propagation, storage, or processing, as well as products that are secreted by or extracted from cells or tissues (e.g., human milk, collagen, urokinase, cytokines, and growth factors), because these products often raise different manufacturing, safety, and effectiveness issues, and generally are covered by other rules, regulations, or standards. * * *

In order to implement its new approach to the regulation of human cellular and tissue-based products, FDA needs to be able to assess the state of the cell and tissue industry. Although some human cellular and tissue-based products are currently regulated by the agency as devices or biological drugs—and thus are covered by registration and listing requirements—others have not been subject to such regulation. As a result, FDA does not know the full size and scope of the cell and tissue industry and its products. Through the current proposal to extend the requirements of registration and product listing to members of the tissue and cell industry not presently under such obligations, FDA seeks to accrue the basic knowledge about the industry that is necessary for its effective regulation. Without reliable data on the tissue and cell industry (e.g., names and addresses of manufacturers and types of products) FDA cannot apply appropriate oversight to a rapidly changing industry. * * * The agency plans to create a single, comprehensive data base with information about human cellular and tissue-based products, maintained by the Center for Biologics Evaluation and Research (CBER). * * *

The main set of regulations being proposed, new part 1271 of title 21 of the CFR, will apply to those human cellular and tissue-based products that the agency will regulate under section 361 of the PHS Act. Proposed part 1271 will cover those products, including products consisting of reproductive cells or tissue, that: (1) are minimally manipulated; (2) are not promoted or labeled for any use other than a homologous use; (3) have not been combined with or modified by the addition of any noncellular or nontissue component that is a drug or device; and (4) do not have a systemic effect, except in cases of autologous use, transplantation into a first-degree blood relative, or reproductive use. For convenience these products will be referred to as "products regulated under section 361" or "361 products." (However, the use of these terms does not indicate that other products will not be regulated under section 361 of the PHS Act. In fact, FDA intends to rely in part on section 361 of the PHS Act when imposing requirements on human cellular and tissue-based products regulated as biological drugs or devices under the act and/or section 351 of the PHS Act.) Examples of products to be regulated under section 361 of the PHS Act include bone, tendons, skin, corneas, and sclera. If all other criteria are met, products with a systemic effect that could come under section 361 of the PHS Act include peripheral and cord blood stem cells used autologously or in first degree blood relatives and sperm, oocytes, and embryos for reproductive use. * * *

Human cellular and tissue-based products subject to regulation as biological drugs or devices are those that do not meet the criteria set out above for regulation under section 361 of the PHS Act. That is, they are: (1) more than minimally manipulated; (2) are promoted or labeled for a nonhomologous use; (3) have been combined with or modified by the addition of a noncellular or nontissue component that is a drug or device; or (4) have a systemic effect (except in cases of autologous use, transplantation into a first degree blood relative, or reproductive use). Examples include: hematopoietic stem cells intended for use in recipients who are not close blood relatives of the cell donor or for uses other than to reconstitute the cellular components of the blood; more than minimally manipulated bone marrow; hematopoietic stem cells that have been expanded or modified as part of gene therapy; cloned and/or activated lymphocyte therapies for cancer or infectious diseases; bone combined with collagen or growth factors; and manipulated cells for autologous structural use (MAS cells), such as expanded chondrocytes to repair damaged knee cartilage.

Under the proposed regulatory system, some products that are currently regulated as medical devices might be regulated as section 361 products instead. One such product under consideration is dura mater, the collagenous connective tissue that covers the human brain and spinal cord. Dura mater is excised from cadavers shortly after death, washed, cut into smaller pieces, sterilized, preserved, and reconstituted before use in neurosurgical, gynecological, oral, otolaryngological, and general surgical procedures. This manner of processing does not change the tissue's original characteristics relating to its ability to carry out reconstruction, repair, or replacement and, therefore, would be considered minimal manipulation as defined in proposed part 1271. Moreover, dura mater does not have a systemic effect. Thus, dura mater that is not combined with or modified by the addition of any nontissue or noncellular component that is a drug or device, and that is not promoted or labeled for any use other than a homologous use, appears to meet the proposed criteria in part 1271 for regulation under section 361 of the PHS Act. * * *

The agency intends to regulate as 361 products human heart valve allografts that meet the criteria of proposed § 1271.10, which are now subject to regulation as medical devices. In the past, these products were considered by FDA to be class III medical devices. * * * The agency now proposes to regulate, as section 361 products, heart valve allografts that are minimally manipulated, do not a have a systemic effect, and are not promoted for a nonhomologous use or combined with a nontissue or noncellular component that is a drug or a device.

FDA is proposing to issue new regulations in part 1271 solely under the authority of section 361 of the PHS Act. Under that section, FDA may make and enforce regulations necessary to prevent the introduction, transmission, or spread of communicable diseases between the States or from foreign countries into the States. Intrastate transactions may also be regulated under section 361 of the PHS Act. See Louisiana v. Mathews, 427 F.Supp. 174, 176 (E.D.La.1977). Because of their nature as derivatives of the human body, all human cellular and tissue-based products pose a potential risk of transmitting diseases. FDA has determined that it may appropriately and effectively regulate certain of these products * * * by controlling the infectious disease risks they present rather than by requiring premarket approval or licensing under the act or the PHS Act. * * * FDA intends to propose regulations to be issued at a later date that would require such measures as the maintenance of "good tissue practices" and various tests for communicable diseases. * * *

Whole blood, blood components, or blood derivative products subject to listing under 21 CFR part 607 are also excluded. Such products include, among others, whole blood, red blood cells, cryoprecipitated AHF, platelets, leukocytes/granulocytes, plasma, blood products for diagnostic use, and blood bank reagents. In contrast, peripheral and cord blood stem cells are not subject to the exception for whole blood, blood components and blood derivative products and therefore are subject to part 1271.

One of the criteria for regulation of a human cellular or tissue-based product under section 361 of the PHS Act and part 1271 is that it be minimally manipulated. Minimal manipulation is defined in § 1271.3(g).

For structural tissue, minimal manipulation is defined as processing that does not alter the original relevant characteristics of the tissue that relate to the tissue's utility for reconstruction, repair, or replacement. For example, separation of structural tissue into components whose relevant characteristics relating to reconstruction or repair are not altered would be considered minimal manipulation, as would extraction or separation of cells from structural tissue in which the remaining structural tissue's relevant characteristics relating to reconstruction and repair remain unchanged. Other examples of procedures that would be considered minimal manipulation include: cutting, grinding, and shaping; soaking in antibiotic solution; sterilization by ethylene oxide treatment or irradiation; cell separation; lyophilization; cryopreservation; and freezing.

For cells (structural and nonstructural) and nonstructural tissues, minimal manipulation is defined as processing that does not alter the relevant biological characteristics and, thus potentially, the function or integrity of the cells or tissues. For example, FDA considers cell selection (e.g., selection of stem cells from amongst lymphocytes and mature cells of other lineages) to be minimal manipulation. * * *

Examples of manipulation not considered minimal, based on current scientific knowledge, include cell expansion, encapsulation, activation, and genetic modification. FDA recognizes that the subsequent accumulation of clinical data and experience about a particular process may demonstrate that it does not alter the original relevant characteristics of the cells or tissue, and the agency will consider this information in determining whether a procedure should be considered minimal as opposed to more-than-minimal manipulation. For example, FDA previously considered demineralized bone products (DMB) to be more than minimally manipulated. * * * After reviewing information provided [by an industry association], the agency believes that the relevant characteristics that relate to DMB's utility for replacement, reconstruction and repair are not altered by processing bone specimens into DMB. Therefore, FDA proposes to regulate DMB under section 361 of the PHS Act provided it is used for homologous function and is not combined with a noncellular or nontissue component that is a drug or device because FDA believes DMB falls within the minimal manipulation definition.

The second criterion for regulation under part 1271 is that a human cellular or tissue-based product not be promoted or labeled for any use other than homologous use. Homologous use is defined in § 1271.3(d) as the use of a cellular or tissue-based product for replacement or supplementation of a recipient's cells or tissues. Homologous use of a structural tissue-based product occurs when the tissue is used for the same basic structural function that it fulfills in its native state, in a location where such structural function normally occurs. Basic function of a structural tissue is what the tissue does from a biological/physiological point of view, or is capable of doing when in its native state. For example, the agency considers structural tissue to be used for a homologous function when it is used to replace an analogous structural tissue that has been damaged or otherwise does not function adequately. Conversely, the agency would consider structural tissue to be performing a nonhomologous function when it is fulfilling a function that is different from the basic function it fulfills in its native state.

Examples of homologous use claims for structural tissues that would fall within the scope of part 1271 include bone allograft obtained from a long bone but labeled for use in a vertebra; skin allograft obtained from the arm but labeled for use as a skin graft on the face; pericardium, a structural membranous covering of the heart, labeled for use as a structural membranous covering for the brain; and heart valves labeled for use as heart valves. An example of a nonhomologous use claim for structural tissue is cartilage labeled for placement under the submucosal layer of the urinary bladder to change the angle of the ureter and thereby prevent backflow of urine from the bladder into the ureter. The cartilage would be performing a structural function (adding volume to change the angle of the ureter) which is different from the function in its native state (to afford flexibility and provide musculoskeletal support).

According to the definition, homologous use of nonstructural cellular or tissue-based products occurs when the cells or tissues are used to perform the function(s) that they performed in the donor. An example of a homologous use claim would be hematopoietic stem cells labeled for use for hematopoietic reconstitution. An example of a nonhomologous use claim for the same cellular product would be a claim for treatment of adrenal leukodystrophies (congenital metabolic deficiencies).

In determining whether a product comes under part 1271 or is instead required to comply with premarketing requirements, FDA has tentatively decided to focus on whether a cellular or tissue-based product is promoted or labeled by its manufacturer for a nonhomologous use, rather than on the intent of the practitioner who uses the product. Accordingly, the actual use of a cellular or tissue-based product for a nonhomologous function would not trigger premarket review requirements if the product was not labeled or promoted for nonhomologous use. This change from the Proposed Approach document comes in response to industry concerns and is expected to lead to the more efficient use of the agency's resources. * * *

Products combined with or modified by the addition of any nontissue or noncellular component that is a drug or device will not be regulated under part 1271. Because "nontissue or noncellular component" is self-explanatory, FDA does not consider it necessary to define the term. However, the agency has modified the phrase "nontissue or noncellular component" with the words "that is a drug or device" in order to clarify that water and buffers would not ordinarily be considered nontissue or noncellular components. In contrast, a product composed of human cells or tissue in combination with a mechanical or synthetic component, such as epithelial cells on a biomatrix to cover burns, would not come under part 1271 and would be regulated under section 351 of the PHS Act and/or the [FDCA].

The final requirement for a product to be regulated under part 1271 is that the product not have a systemic effect. Given that "systemic" is a commonly used medical term, FDA is not proposing a regulatory definition of the word. The agency would consider the insertion of pancreatic islet cells, pituitary cells, or stem cells into an individual to have a mainly systemic effect. In contrast, the insertion of replacement bone would not have a mainly systemic effect; the effect would be limited to the immediate area around the insertion. FDA recognizes that some products may have both systemic and structural effects but intends that a product's primary effect be determinative. * * *

Under § 1271.10(d), there are several exceptions to the requirement that a human cellular or tissue-based product not have a systemic effect to be regulated under part 1271. These exceptions are for cases of autologous or family-related allogeneic systemic use and for reproductive use. * * * Autologous use is defined in § 1271.3(a) as the implantation, transplantation, infusion, or transfer of a cellular or tissue-based product back into the individual from whom the cells or tissue comprising such product were removed. * * * [A]llogeneic use (not defined in this regulation) is the transplantation of cells or tissue obtained from a different individual. FDA is using the phrase "family-related" for situations where the recipient of cells or tissue is a biological parent, child, or sibling of the donor. * * * The third situation in which a product with a systemic effect will be regulated under part 1271 is when the product contains human reproductive cells or tissue and is for reproductive use. In contrast to other tissues with a systemic effect, transfer of reproductive tissues such as semen and ova pose less risk to the health of the recipient from rejection, graft-versus-host disease, and compatibility. In addition, the failure of a reproductive-tissue product will generally cause lesser health risks to the individual than the failure of other systemic products. * * *

Under § 1271.3(f), the term manufacture includes all steps in the recovery, screening, testing, processing, storage, labeling, packaging, or distribution of any human cellular or tissue-based product. The agency interprets certain terms used in the definition of "manufacture" in the following ways. By "recovery" FDA means obtaining cells or tissues from a donor that are intended for use in human transplantation, infusion, implantation, or transfer. "Storage" would include holding human cells or tissue for future distribution or use. "Processing" means any activity, other than recovery, performed on a human cellular or tissue-based product, including preventing contamination and preserving the function and integrity of the product. Processing includes preparation, preservation for storage, removal from storage, and any steps to inactivate and remove adventitious agents. "Distribution" includes any conveyance or shipment of human cellular or tissue-based product (including importation and exportation), whether or not such conveyance or shipment is entirely intrastate and whether or not possession of the human cellular or tissue-based product is taken.

Many entities and individuals that would be considered manufacturers under part 1271 because they recover human cells or tissues expressed concerns that they would be subject to registration requirements. FDA anticipates that individuals engaged solely in the procurement or recovery of cells or tissues and under contract to organizations that coordinate procurement or recovery of human cells or tissues will not have to independently register under part 1271. Registration will be the responsibility of the employer or contracting organization, which will also be required under future rulemaking to ensure that its employees, agents, and contractors that engage in the recovery of cells or tissues comply with applicable regulations or procedures regarding the collection, safe handling, and proper shipment of human cells or tissues. * * *

FDA, Proposed Rule, *Current Good Tissue Practice for Manufacturers of Human Cellular and Tissue–Based Products*
66 Fed. Reg. 1508 (2001).

* * * The regulations now being proposed would require all human cellular and tissue-based products to be manufactured in compliance with current good tissue practice (CGTP). The proposal also contains provisions relating to establishment inspection and enforcement, as well as certain labeling and reporting requirements, which would be applicable to those human cellular and tissue-based products that the agency is proposing to regulate solely under the authority of section 361 of the Public Health Service Act (PHS Act) and not as biological drugs or devices. * * *

On May 14, 1998, the agency proposed regulations that would create a new, unified system for registering establishments that manufacture human cellular and tissue-based products and for listing their products (registration proposed rule at 63 Fed. Reg. 26,744). On September 30, 1999, FDA proposed regulations that would require most cell and tissue donors to be tested and screened for relevant communicable diseases (donor-suitability proposed rule at 64 Fed. Reg. 52,696, 52,719).

With the present rulemaking, the agency is completing the set of proposals that would implement the new regulatory scheme. In the proposed approach document, the agency stated that it would require that cells and tissues be handled according to procedures designed to prevent contamination and to preserve tissue function and integrity. Thus, the agency is now proposing to require that establishments that manufacture human cellular or tissue-based products comply with CGTP, which would include, among other things, proper handling, processing, labeling, and recordkeeping procedures. In addition, the proposed regulations would require each establishment to maintain a "quality program" to ensure compliance with CGTP. * * *

CGTP requirements are intended to prevent the introduction, transmission, and spread of communicable disease through the use of human cellular and tissue-based products by helping to ensure that: (1) The products do not contain relevant communicable disease agents; (2) they are not contaminated during the manufacturing process; and (3) the function and integrity of the products are not impaired through improper manufacturing, all of which could lead to circumstances that increase the risk of communicable disease transmission. * * *

FDA intends to require that a quality program perform certain basic functions, but also intends to provide each establishment with flexibility to devise a program appropriate to its particular activities and characteristics. Thus, FDA expects that quality programs may differ from establishment to establishment, depending on the size of the establishment and the type of manufacturing performed, among other factors. A smaller company that performs limited manufacturing steps might have a less complex quality program than a larger establishment that processes a variety of products. * * *

FDA considers product tracking to be an essential component of its proposed regulatory system for human cellular and tissue-based products. Should the recipient of such a product contract a communicable disease, tracking would permit appropriate follow-up, such as an investigation to determine whether the human cellular or tissue-based product transmitted the disease agent and, if so, would permit steps to be taken to prevent the distribution of other similarly infected products. Similarly, if a donor is discovered, post-donation, to have had a communicable disease, tracking would permit an establishment to locate products from that donor. Thus, a tracking system is closely linked to the agency's regulatory objective of preventing the spread of communicable disease. * * *

In order to stay informed of potential problems with human cellular and tissue-based products related to communicable-disease transmission, and to be able to take appropriate steps in response, FDA needs to receive information from establishments on adverse reactions and certain product deviations that could result in adverse reactions. For this reason, FDA is proposing to require two different kinds of reports from establishments that manufacture human cellular and tissue-based products regulated solely under section 361 of the PHS Act: the reporting of adverse reactions, and the reporting of product deviations. * * *

[O]nly those adverse reactions that involved the transmission of a communicable disease, product contamination, or the failure of a human cellular or tissue-based product's function or integrity would be required to be reported. Moreover, reporting would be limited to those adverse reactions that are fatal or life-threatening, that result in permanent impairment of a body function or permanent damage to body structure, or that necessitate medical or surgical intervention. * * *

FDA, Final Rule, *Human Cells, Tissues, and Cellular and Tissue–Based Products; Establishment Registration and Listing*

66 Fed. Reg. 5447 (2001).

* * * In the three proposed rules, we used the term ''human cellular and tissue-based products.'' In this final rule, we have changed the term to

"human cells, tissues, and cellular and tissue-based products" (abbreviated "HCT/P's"). This change in terminology is a clarification and does not affect the scope of the definition, which continues to encompass an array of articles containing or consisting of human cells or tissues, and intended for implantation, transplantation, infusion, or transfer into human recipients, including investigational products. The definition of "human cells, tissues, or cellular or tissue-based product" is intended to cover HCT/P's at all stages of their manufacture, from recovery through distribution. Some examples of HCT/P's include skin, tendons, bone, heart valves, corneas, hematopoietic stem cells, manipulated autologous chondrocytes, epithelial cells on a synthetic matrix, and semen or other reproductive tissue. * * *

Several comments asserted that we are proposing to regulate the practice of medicine, especially with respect to reproductive tissue and hematopoietic stem cells. We disagree with this comment. This final rule sets out registration and listing requirements for establishments that recover, process, store, label, package, or distribute HCT/P's, or screen or test cell and tissue donors. HCT/P's, including hematopoietic stem cells and reproductive tissues, fall within our jurisdiction. Some HCT/P's will be regulated under the act and/or the PHS Act, while other HCT/P's will be effectively regulated solely by regulations issued under our authority to prevent the spread of communicable disease. We are not attempting to govern practitioners' use of HCT/P's, but rather to ensure that HCT/P's that would be used by practitioners in their treatment of patients are in compliance with applicable regulations, including regulations designed to prevent the transmission or spread of communicable disease.

We received several comments on our proposed regulation of hematopoietic stem cells. One comment supported the proposal that all establishments involved with hematopoietic stem cell therapy register with FDA. Two comments asserted that the proposed regulation would jeopardize patient treatment, impede the development of new therapies, and increase the costs of treatment. One comment asserted that we lack the legal authority to regulate intrastate hematopoietic stem cell transplants. Another comment argued that clinical research involving the use of blood or bone marrow transplantation for treatment of human diseases, but not involving an investigational drug or device, should not require an investigational new drug application or investigational device exemption. * * * We believe that it is necessary to bring the regulation of hematopoietic stem cells in line with the regulation of other HCT/P's, and that we possess the legal authority to take this action. Like other HCT/P's, hematopoietic stem cells may transmit communicable diseases; thus, the basic communicable disease prevention requirements that will be contained in part 1271, including these registration and listing requirements, are as relevant to these cells as to any other HCT/P's. * * *

Several comments questioned the need for the regulation of reproductive cells and tissues, citing current oversight from professional organizations, other Federal agencies, and States. Comments opposed registration for programs involved in egg donation, egg retrieval, semen processing, semen evaluation, or in vitro fertilization (IVF) in assisted reproductive technologies. * * * We stand by our decision to extend regulatory requirements to reproductive cells and tissue. Currently, FDA does not have regulations in place to address the infectious disease risk of donating, processing, and storing reproductive cells and tissue. Because there has been no registration or listing requirement, we have not had accurate information about the industry. * * *

Although we recognize the value of professional efforts to self-regulate, and of regulatory efforts of other agencies and the States, we disagree that these piecemeal, often voluntary, efforts are adequate. Nor will the new regulations in part 1271 be duplicative. State regulation varies from State to State and does not consistently address our concerns about the transmission of communicable disease. The model certification program for embryo laboratories developed by the Centers for Disease Control and Prevention (CDC) is a voluntary program that States may or may not choose to adopt; its primary focus is not on preventing the transmission of communicable disease. No State has yet adopted CDC's model certification program. Membership in professional societies is voluntary. Moreover, many establishments do not report to the Society for Assisted Reproductive Technology. The Clinical Laboratories Improvement Amendment of 1988 (CLIA) covers clinical laboratory testing, including certain procedures performed in embryo laboratories; however, as discussed later in this document, CLIA certification is not equivalent to the requirements we are putting in place. * * *

We proposed to define family-related allogeneic use in proposed § 1271.3(c) as "the implantation, transplantation, infusion, or transfer of a human cellular or tissue-based product into a first-degree blood relative of the individual from whom cells or tissue comprising such product were removed." Under § 1271.10(d), as proposed, HCT/P's with a systemic effect that are for family-related allogeneic use would be regulated under section 361 of the PHS Act (provided that the HCT/P meets all other criteria set out in § 1271.10). This limited exception from the requirement for investigational use exemptions and premarketing submissions was first proposed in the proposed approach. * * * We have decided to change the term from "family-related allogeneic use" to "allogeneic use in a first-degree or second-degree blood relative." Parents, children, and siblings are considered first-degree relatives. Aunts, uncles, nieces, nephews, first cousins, grandparents, and grandchildren are second-degree relatives. Relations by adoption or marriage are not included. * * *

Several comments objected to the word "product" in the term human cellular or tissue-based product, defined in proposed § 1271.3(e). These comments asserted that human cells and tissues are donations, not goods manufactured for sale. Some comments argued that the use of the word "product" might have legal implications; e.g., subjecting eye banks to inappropriate product liability litigation. Comments also noted that the word "product" is inconsistent with terms used in the tissue and eye banking field. We also received an objection to describing embryos and germ cells as "products."

In choosing "human cellular or tissue-based product," we were seeking a term that would describe everything that will be subject to the regulations in part 1271. We needed a term broad enough to cover both cells and tissues, and one that would include within its scope such diverse articles as unprocessed tissue, highly processed cells, and tissues that are combined with certain drugs or devices. Although we have considered removing the word "product" from the definition, we are concerned that another term (e.g., "human cells and tissues") would not be understood to include many of the highly manufactured products to which the regulations apply, or might be misconstrued to apply only to the cell or tissue component of such a product. * * * We recognize, however, that conceptual difficulties may arise in calling certain cells or tissues "products." Thus, as noted earlier in this document, we have expanded the term to "human cells, tissues, and cellular and tissue-based products," abbreviated as "HCT/P's." * * *

In proposed § 1271.10, we set out the criteria for regulating certain HCT/P's solely under section 361 of the PHS Act and the regulations to be contained in part 1271. An HCT/P would be subject to this level of regulation if it: (1) was minimally manipulated; (2) was not promoted or labeled for any use other than a homologous use; (3) was not combined with or modified by the addition of any component that is a drug or a device; and (4) either does not have a systemic effect, or has a systemic effect and is for autologous, family-related allogeneic, or reproductive use. * * *

Our ability to regulate an HCT/P as a drug, device, and/or biological product derives from the act and section 351 of the PHS Act, authorities that are distinct from our authority to issue regulations to prevent the transmission of communicable disease under section 361 of the PHS Act. If an HCT/P does not meet the criteria in § 1271.10 for regulation solely under section 361 of the PHS Act, and the establishment does not qualify for any of the exceptions in final § 1271.15, the HCT/P will be regulated under the act and/or the PHS Act and applicable regulations. * * *

We have * * * rewritten the definition of homologous use in response to the comments' concerns. The new definition reads: "Homologous use means the replacement or supplementation of a recipient's cells or tissues with an HCT/P that performs the same basic function or functions in the recipient as in the donor." The rewording eliminates the distinction between, on the one hand, structural tissues and, on the other, nonstructural tissues and cells. The new wording does not include the statement that, for structural tissues, homologous use occurs "in a location where such structural function normally occurs." This language was understood, contrary to our intention, to limit the use of structural tissue to the same location from which is was derived. However, a use of a structural tissue may be homologous even when it does not occur in the same location as it occurred in the donor. For example, the use of bone for repair, replacement, or reconstruction anywhere in the skeleton of the recipient (including the vertebral column) would be considered homologous use. However, it should be understood that, for the use of a structural tissue to be considered homologous, the HCT/P must perform the same basic function or functions in the recipient as it did in the donor; the use of structural tissue in a location where it does not perform the same basic function as it did in the donor would not be homologous.

We intend to interpret "nonhomologous" narrowly. Examples of uses that would be considered nonhomologous include: The use of dermis as a replacement for dura mater, the use of amniotic membrane in the eye, and the use of cartilage in the bladder. * * * [A]n HCT/P that is intended by the manufacturer for one of these uses would not be regulated solely under section 361 of the PHS Act and these regulations, but as a drug, device, and/or biological product. * * *

After further consideration, we agree that the term "systemic effect" may not cover all of the HCT/P's that we intended to cover. Because the effect of implanted neurons or neural tissue into the brain would likely be restricted to the site where the tissue/cells were placed, this effect might not be included within the meaning of systemic. However, as discussed in the proposed approach, HCT/P's that rely on living cells for their primary function, such as neuronal tissue, raise clinical safety and effectiveness concerns that are not appropriately addressed solely under section 361 of the PHS Act. Such concerns include viability, efficacy, malignant transformation, or rejection after transplantation. Thus, although neuronal cells may not be considered to have a systemic effect, they nonetheless require regulation under the act and/or section 351 of the PHS Act.

Therefore, we have clarified § 1271.10(a)(4) to indicate that an HCT/P that either has systemic effect or depends upon the metabolic activity of living cells for its primary function would not be appropriately regulated solely under section 361 of the PHS Act, and therefore will be regulated as a drug, device, and/or biological product. Cells or tissues such as pancreatic islet cells, which have effects on many different organs throughout the body through the secretion of insulin, are appropriately characterized by the term "systemic effect." Neurons for implantation in the brain would fall into the category of HCT/P's that depend upon the metabolic activity of living cells for their primary function. In contrast, some HCT/P's (such as corneas, skin, or osteochondral allografts) may contain living cells, but do not depend on them for their primary function, which is structural. * * *

NOTES AND QUESTIONS

1. *FDA jurisdiction over tissue products.* The notice of proposed rulemaking provides little legal justification for the FDA's assertion of regulatory authority over the vastly expanding number of tissues and tissue-derived products. As the excerpts above suggest, the agency's current approach to the regulation of cellular and tissue-based products conflates all of the products that fall under the broad heading of "biological products" into two basic categories for purposes of regulatory control. According to the proposal, the degree of tissue manipulation prior to use will dictate the level of regulatory control. How would the following products fit into the FDA's proposed approach to tissue regulation: pulverized and purified human bone mixed with an inactive liquid base and delivered in pre-filled syringes; human bone sculpted into the shape of a screw for use in joint repair surgery; stem cells harvested from human fat tissue to treat anemia in an unrelated donor; a human kidney grown from genetically manipulated stem cells on a biologically-based matrix?

2. *Multiple contributors to the manufacture of a single product.* In assigning responsibility for good tissue practices, the FDA struggled with situations in which several establishments might contribute to the manufacture of a single human tissue or cellular product. In some cases, one establishment might make a donor-suitability determination, a second might recover tissue from a cadaver, a third might process the tissue, and a fourth might finally distribute that tissue. To deal with the problem of divided roles in manufacturing, the FDA's proposal suggested that establishments engaging in limited operations need only comply with regulations that directly apply to their relevant manufacturing activities. See 66 Fed. Reg. 1508, 1511 (2001). The agency considered several mechanisms for allocating regulatory responsibilities among establishments involved in manufacturing cell and tissue products and tried to balance issues of flexibility with concerns about product integrity and function. After considering and rejecting plans to allocate responsibility with the establishment that determines donor suitability, or allowing parties to the manufacturing process to decide among themselves which party bears responsibility for the product, the agency ultimately decided that the best approach is to assign ultimate responsibility to the establishment that distributes the finished product. See id. Is it reasonable for the FDA to expect a final distributor in the chain of manufacturing to assume responsibility for compliance with good tissue practice requirements when multiple establishments may have been involved?

3. *Reproductive tissues.* Until recently, the FDA had not asserted regulatory jurisdiction over in vitro fertilization (IVF) or other fertility treatments. Indeed, agency officials previously testified before Congress that it had no such authority. See Henry T. Greely, Banning "Human Cloning": A Study in the Difficulties of Defining Science, 8 S. Cal. Interdisc. L.J. 131, 151 (1998). In fact, the Fertility Clinic Success Rate and Certification Act of 1992, 42 U.S.C. § 263a–1, suggested no role for the FDA. Instead, Congress directed the CDC to collect information and HHS to develop a model program (for states to implement) to inspect laboratories that work with human embryos. The FDA announced in 1998, and recently reiterated, that its proposed rule governing cellular and tissue-based products would apply to sperm banks and assisted reproduction technology (ART) facilities:

> For purposes of this discussion, references to ART facilities include infertility clinics, and andrology and embryology laboratories. The American Society of Reproductive Medicine (ASRM) has a membership of approximately 330 ART facilities. The ASRM also has a 1996 list of

approximately 110 sperm banks operating in the United States. Based on conversations with consultants, most commercial sperm banking and most ART facilities currently adhere to industry standards similar to those in the proposed rule. The 20 largest sperm banks are estimated to handle 95 percent of the total volume of product for the industry, and these facilities are believed to follow industry standards that are comparable to the CGTP. According to industry consultants, approximately one-third of the 20 largest sperm banks are accredited by the AATB, and the remaining two-thirds are licensed by State health agencies, including the California Department of Health and the New York Department of Health. Sperm banks are also regulated under the Clinical Laboratory Improvement Amendment (CLIA) of 1988. . . .

Most aspects of cellular and tissue product manufacturing in the reproductive tissue industry would become newly regulated under the proposed CGTP rule. The affected establishments within this industry include sperm banks and ART facilities. Reports of the sensitivity of product quality to variations in tissue collection, technician skill, processing methods, environmental conditions, and other factors, indicate that the risk of communicable disease transmission would be reduced by improving the proposed overall product quality, and economic benefits would be seen through improved patient outcomes from facility compliance with the proposed CGTP requirements. The tissue used in commercial sperm banks is washed, processed, and cryopreserved donor sperm used for therapeutic donor insemination. The sperm are obtained generally from paid donors who have been screened and tested for infectious disease and certain genetic disease risks. The tissues used in ART facilities include fresh or cryopreserved oocytes, sperm, zygotes, and embryos. The handling of tissues include but are not limited to: Retrieval of oocytes from a female, collection of sperm from a male, in vitro fertilization (IVF), cryopreservation of fertilized oocytes not transferred in the same treatment cycle, and thawing of frozen fertilized oocytes. The success of in vitro fertilization, measured as the number of deliveries per IVF cycle, has gradually increased over the past decade or so, from 11 percent in 1985 to 18 percent in 1994. More recently, the Centers for Disease Control and Prevention (CDC) have reported average live birth pregnancy rates for ART clinics to be as high as 19.6 percent per cycle in 1995 and 22.6 percent per cycle in 1996.

Despite the increasing effectiveness of infertility treatment through ART, problems can occur in tissue processing. Adverse outcomes owing to problems with product quality can result from contamination that produces infection (e.g., HIV transmission) in the infertility patient. Problems with ART facility processing of sperm or oocytes can also lead to reduced rates of fertilization, and unsuccessful IVF attempts, which would ultimately increase the number of transfer attempts. Each additional transfer attempt increases the risk of communicable disease with each attempt. Where quality problems in tissue processing result in reduced embryo quality and lower probability of pregnancy, the patient, on average, needs to undergo more cycles of IVF to achieve a pregnancy that produces a live birth. The estimated patient cost per cycle ranges from $8,000 to $10,000.

The number of Americans who would potentially benefit from improved reproductive tissue processing is substantial. According to the 1995 National Survey of Family Growth (NSFG), 15.4 percent of American women 15 to 44 years of age, approximately 9.3 million women, have reported receiving infertility services. Approximately 600,000 women report receiving ARTs, defined in NSFG to include artificial insemination and IVF services. The number of ART procedures annually has been increasing in recent years. According to the CDC a total of over 64,000 cycles of ART were performed by U.S. facilities in 1996, compared to approximately 60,000 cycles in 1995. The proposed CGTP rule, therefore, has the potential to benefit thousands of infertile couples.

66 Fed. Reg. 1508, 1525, 1542–43 (2001). After the publication of this proposed rule, the agency sent warning letters to several fertility clinics ordering them to cease the practice of fertility procedures that entail any kind of alteration of human genetic material, including cloning, genetic engineering and "ooplasmic transfer." This last technique involves the transfer of genetic material from one woman's egg into another's, typically to aid an older women in achieving pregnancy. See Antonio Regalado, FDA Warns Reproductive Clinics to Stop Using Fertility Techniques, Wall St. J., July 11, 2001, at B2; Rick Weiss, FDA to Regulate Certain Fertilization Procedures, Wash. Post, July 11, 2001, at A2 (explaining that the FDA now requires physicians performing experimental fertility procedures to file an IND); see also FDA, Letter to Sponsors/Researchers–Human Cells Used in Therapy Involving the Transfer of Genetic Material by Means Other Than the Union of Gamete Nuclei (2001), available at <www.fda.gov/cber/ltr/cytotrans070601.htm>. What problems might arise in the regulation of reproductive tissues as part of the large class of "tissues intended for transplantation"? Why not allow individual states, many of which already regulate assisted reproduction services, to set additional regulatory requirements? See Ronald Chester, Double Trouble: Legal Solutions to the Medical Problems of Unconsented Sperm Harvesting and Drug–Induced Multiple Pregnancies, 44 St. Louis U. L.J. 451 (2000); Weldon E. Havins & James J. Dalessio, The Ever Widening Gap Between the Science of Artificial Reproductive Technology and the Laws Which Govern That Technology, 48 DePaul L. Rev. 825 (1999).

4. *Solid organs.* CBER does not regulate vascularized human organs for transplantation. See 63 Fed. Reg. 26,744, 26,745 (1998) (explicitly disclaiming any intent to regulate solid organs under the agency's proposed approach to the regulation of human cellular and tissue-based products). The federal Health Resources Services Administration (HRSA) provides the primary oversight and funding support for the nation's organ procurement and allocation and coordinates national organ donation activities. Under the National Organ Transplant Act (NOTA), HHS exercises most of the regulatory control over solid organs for transplantation. It has contracted with the United Network for Organ Sharing (UNOS) to run the federal Organ Procurement Transplant Network (OPTN). See 42 U.S.C. § 274, § 1320b–8. Although UNOS is a private nonprofit organization, it creates policies for the OPTN, and, under NOTA, all transplant centers and organ procurement organizations must comply with UNOS policies and rules. See 42 U.S.C. § 1320b–8(a); see also Walter Block et al., Human Organ Transplantation: Economic and Legal Issues, 3 Quinnipiac Health L.J. 87 (2000).

5. *What's a body worth?* Although federal law forbids the sale of tissues or organs, it allows harvesters to recover the "reasonable costs" associated with collecting human tissues. Tissue banks and processing companies currently avoid the statutory prohibition on sale by charging processing fees that ostensibly cover the costs of processing and handling the harvested tissue. Many of these fees appear inflated in light of the actual amount of processing involved. Tendons that are cut from cadavers in minutes are resold to sports medicine surgeons for reconstructive surgery at $2,500 each, and valves recovered from donated hearts currently sell for approximately $7,000. Tissues harvested from a single human body can generate parts with resale values averaging $80,000. See Stephen J. Hedges & William Gaines, Donor Bodies Milled into Growing Profits: Little–Regulated Industry Thrives on Unsuspecting Families, Chi. Trib., May 21, 2000, at C1. In contrast, many of us may recall high school biology textbooks that valued the chemicals and components of the human body at only a few dollars. Regulators and the public are becoming increasingly aware that the harvesting, processing, and transfer of human tissue is a profitable business, and this realization causes reactions ranging from discomfort to outrage. As one commentator has observed:

> [T]he fact that human tissue is rarely advertised and is not traded on exchanges should not lead to the conclusion that commercial activity is absent. On the contrary, money changes hands at numerous points in the chain of distribution from tissue source to ultimate consumer: Transplant patients pay to receive organs, fertility patients purchase ova and sperm, and biotechnology firms sell products derived from human cells. Indeed, it is virtually impossible to imagine how human biological materials would be distributed if commerce in such materials were prohibited. If human tissue and its products could never be exchanged for money or other items of value, then rights to their use and possession would have to be gratuitously transferred at every stage of the chain of distribution. Implementing a system of only uncompensated transfers would—to put it mildly—require a radical overhaul of current medical and scientific practices, but the debate over the acceptability of commerce in human materials is strangely silent on this issue. Instead, the controversies in this area revolve around the issue of who will be entitled to share in the financial returns made possible by the urgent demand for human biological materials, with particular emphasis on whether the human sources of usable tissue (or their surviving relatives) will be permitted to receive compensation. As now conducted, then, the debate over the commercialization of the

human body is not about commercialization at all, but rather about how the financial benefits available will be apportioned.

Julia D. Mahoney, The Market for Human Tissue, 86 Va. L. Rev. 163, 165 (2000).

6. *The tissue banking industry and informed consent.* The Office of the Inspector General recently issued a report dealing with issues surrounding the rapidly expanding tissue banking industry:

> The exact number of tissue donors in this country is unknown. It is clear, though, that the numbers are increasing. In 1999, more than 20,000 donors provided cadaveric tissue, up from perhaps 6,000 donors in 1994. Tissue banks distributed over 750,000 allografts for transplantation in 1999. . . . Tissue banking is subject to more limited regulation than the nation's organ procurement system, even though both organ procurement organizations (OPOs) and tissue banks are involved in approaching families for consent. For example, the National Organ Transplant Act requires OPOs to meet certain organizational and staffing requirements; the Act also requires OPOs to assist hospitals in establishing and implementing protocols for making routine inquiries about organ donation by potential donors. No similar requirements exist for tissue banks.

Office of Inspector Gen., HHS, Informed Consent in Tissue Donation: Expectations and Realities, OEI–01–00–00440 (2001), at 1, available at <www.hhs.gov/oig/oei/reports/a500.pdf>. The report then criticized the growing tension between the donor families' altruistic motives and the now pervasive commercialization of tissue banking:

> Publicly-traded companies have raised capital and brought entrepreneurial energy to tissue processing, leading to development of new processes and products. Yet, it is precisely at this point that tension arises. The concern may be best characterized as unease about a focus on the "bottom line," as portrayed in the following question: If a company's primary interest is financial benefit to its stockholders, is it making choices to put tissue to more lucrative uses over medical needs? A second facet of tension with commercialization relates to the level of salaries and costs incurred by both non-profit and for-profit firms. Although reasonable costs are permitted, there is no definition of, and undoubtedly no consensus about, what constitutes "unreasonable costs." In fact, no guidelines are in place regarding disclosure of costs, and no comparative data are available publicly on the range of costs that would permit such a determination. . . . [I]n an industry that is premised on donation of parts of a loved one's body, it should not be surprising that donor families could feel misled as they question why "everyone is making money off of this altruistic gift except the donor and the donor's family."

Id. at 4–5. Circumstances make the informed consent process for tissue donation particularly challenging. Because families are often in the first stages of shock at the death of a loved one, they may find it difficult to process detailed consent information. Some families may prefer to hear very little detail about the tissue donation process, while others want much more information. Finally, obtaining consent and documenting donor suitability requires detailed questioning about the recently deceased donor's health habits and medical history, in order to reduce the possibility of disease transmission. Such questioning can be particularly intrusive in these circumstances. See id. at 6–7. Because federal laws currently do not address the informed consent process for tissue banks, practices vary widely. Some banks request permission to harvest tissue over the telephone, or employ untrained staff to make the requests. Although all states have enacted some version of the Uniform Anatomical Gift Act, these laws also fail to address the information that tissue banks should provide in obtaining informed consent. Recent Medicare conditions of participation require hospitals receiving Medicare funds to establish donor suitability criteria for tissue donors, as well as organ donors, and require these facilities to train requester to deal with donor families. The conditions of participation do not, however, provide specific guidelines on the informed consent process. The OIG report makes several recommendations to improve the informed consent process:

> The Health Resources and Services Administration should work with groups representing donor families and the tissue banking industry to develop guidelines for conveying information to families about tissue donation.... [HCFA] should address informed consent for tissue donation through conditions of participation for hospitals and for organ procurement organizations.... At the time of obtaining consent, tissue banks should provide families with written materials that provide fuller disclosure about the uses of tissue and the nature of the gift.... Such materials would serve as a way to supplement the information that requester provide to the family during their conversation about donation, while providing requester with the flexibility to adapt that discussion to the unique needs and responses of each donor family.... The tissue banking industry should work with representatives of groups representing donor families to explore a process for periodic public disclosure about tissue banks' financing.

Id. at 13–15.

7. *Live tissue donors and informed consent.* What duty of disclosure do physicians owe to patients from whom they harvest tissues for research or transplant? In *Moore v. Regents of the University of California*, 793 P.2d 479 (Cal.1990), the plaintiff received treatment for hairy-cell leukemia, a rare condition. Afterward, his physicians, employees of UCLA, used the plaintiff's blood, splenic tissue, and other tissue samples for research and eventually developed a cell line on which the university ultimately obtained a patent. The work benefitted the physicians financially and professionally. The court noted that "a physician who treats a patient in whom he also has a research interest has potentially conflicting loyalties" and held that "a physician who is seeking a patient's consent for a medical procedure must, in order to satisfy his fiduciary duty ... disclose personal interests unrelated to the patient's health, whether research or economic, that may affect his medical judgment." Id. at 484–85. For commentary on the *Moore* decision and its implications in the new biotechnology era, see Richard Gold, Owning Our Bodies: An Examination of Property Law and Biotechnology, 32 San Diego L. Rev. 1167 (1995); Jonathan Kahn, Biotechnology and the Legal Constitution of the Self: Managing Identity in Science, the Market, and Society, 51 Hastings L.J. 909 (2000); Anne T. Corrigan, Note, A Paper Tiger: Lawsuits Against Doctors for Non–Disclosure of Economic Interests in Patients' Cells, Tissues and Organs, 42 Case W. Res. L. Rev. 565 (1992); Sharon Nan Perley, Note, From Control over One's Body to Control over One's Body Parts: Extending the Doctrine of Informed Consent, 67 N.Y.U. L. Rev. 335 (1992); Frank J. Wozniak, Annotation, Physician's Use of Patient's Tissues, Cells, or Bodily Substances for Medical Research or Economic Purposes, 16 A.L.R.5th 143 (1993).

1. TISSUE ENGINEERING AND STEM CELLS

Laurel R. Siegel, Comment, *Re-Engineering the Laws of Organ Transplantation*

49 EMORY L.J. 917 (2000).

* * * Researchers have developed new methods of organ production to better combat the supply and rejection problems: tissue engineering. Eventually, these techniques may allow scientists to have access to an unlimited supply of organs. Today, scientists use novel technologies to combine the concepts of biotechnology, molecular and cell biology, materials science, and engineering to better understand the relationship among tissues and to create alternatives for the repair and reconstruction of tissues and organs. The new organs are initially comprised of cells growing and maintaining structure and support on a scaffolding device. To provide scaffolding support, bioartificial organs consist of a biological component: cells or tissues, as well as a biomaterial scaffolding component made of a natural or synthetic material. Allowing the growth of the original tissue without remnants of foreign biomaterials is the primary challenge to this technology. The concept of seeding the patient's own cells onto the scaffolds to control their proliferation forms the basis of tissue engineering. After a period of weeks or months, synthesis of the new tissue replaces the scaffold.

Scientists work with two kinds of cells in tissue engineering: human adult cells and embryonic stem cells ("ES cells"). * * * [W]ith human adult cells, [i]t is theoretically possible to expand, for example, a urothelial strain from a single specimen covering 1 cm squared to a surface area greater than 4000 m squared within eight weeks. One group of physicians has expanded urothelial and muscle cells in vitro (in a petri dish), seeded them onto a matrix, and allowed them to attach to form sheets of cells, before implanting them in vivo (in a living organism). Cell matrices implanted with human bladder muscle cells showed nearly complete replacement of the matrix with sheets of smooth muscle within fifty days, marking the first time composite tissue-engineered structures had been newly created. * * *

Scientists are currently revolutionizing biology with work involving embryonic stem cells. A stem cell is a cell which has not yet differentiated into a specialized cell, such as hair, blood, organ, tissue, or bone. An ES cell, derived from a blastocyst, can be maintained in an undifferentiated state indefinitely and can develop into any of 210 types of cells under certain conditions. When removed from such conditions, the ES cells spontaneously differentiate to form embryoid bodies that contain elements of all germ layers: ectoderm, mesoderm, and endoderm. November 1998 marked the first successful culture of pluripotent [meaning capable of producing multiple different kinds of specialized cells] human stem cells, but it is unknown whether the cells are totipotent [meaning capable of producing every kind of human cell]. Many scientists believe the ability to program the development of cells that could be transplanted into humans will not occur for at least ten years, and even longer before stem cells can be coaxed into creating complex organs such as kidneys or livers.

Each ES cell line contains the genome of a specific individual and can essentially reprogram an adult cell to become an ES cell through at least three principal methods. First, "therapeutic cloning" involves replacing the genetic material of the human egg with the nucleus of the adult cell and cultivating it in vitro until the ES cell-producing blastocyst stage. The ethical objection to this approach lies in the concept of creating a potential human being and then halting its development. A second method entails using any mammalian egg as the recipient of the nucleic material. Scientists first did this in November 1998, using a cow egg as the host for the human genetic material. This approach poses ethical problems of combining human and animal tissue. A third approach entails reprogramming the nuclei of adult cells using ES cell cytoplasm.

Theoretically, embryoid bodies could provide an unlimited supply of specific cell types for transplantation. Researchers must overcome certain obstacles before conducting clinical experiments with human cells. First, donor/recipient compatibility must be researched; possible solutions entail banking cell lines or creating cells genetically identical to the patient's cells by utilizing cloning techniques. Second, scientists need to more clearly understand cell differentiation in culture and whether genetic mutations are introduced during differentiation. Scientists have not yet been able to direct development of embryonic stem cells into specific, differentiated cell types. They are learning, however, to control the differentiation of stem-cell populations into desired cell types, such as cartilage, bone, or liver.

Turning human ES cells into replacement tissues and organs for transplantation without rejection is the ultimate goal. Additionally, researchers hope to manipulate a patient's own cells in culture to replace damaged tissues and avoid the ethical and legal issues of using human embryonic stem cells or creating cells. An alternative involves generating "universal donors" of several cell lines so that everybody could find a match. Existing organs, whether human or otherwise, could potentially be used as scaffolding. * * *

Within the next few years, the growth of the tissue engineering industry will reach the importance of present genetic technology. The ethical issues involved with fetal tissue sources pose a barrier to commercialization. Some scientists think that this can be overcome if adult cells are used or if parents consent for their children's cells to be taken at birth for possible future use. * * *

NOTES AND QUESTIONS

1. *Engineering tissue for autologous use.* The scarcity of human organs and tissues for transplant has encouraged researchers to search for alternatives to improve the supply. "Regenerative medicine" involves using human proteins and cells, rather than foreign substances or objects, to repair injured body parts and cure illnesses. Regenerative medicine combines stem cell research with genetic manipulation technologies. See Terence Chea, Regenerating Approaches in Medicine, Wash. Post, Dec. 4, 2000, at E5. Developing techniques now permit the growth of skin, blood vessels, and bone and other living cells on synthetic "scaffolding" comprised of substances such as coral and porous ceramic. See, e.g., Charles A. Vacanti et al., Replacement of an Avulsed Phalanx with Tissue–Engineered Bone, 344 New Eng. J. Med. 1511 (2001). A recent report published in the *New England Journal of Medicine* documents the creation and transplantation of a tissue-engineered pulmonary artery into a four-year old child with a heart defect. Physicians harvested a piece of the child's peripheral vein, cultured it on a tube-shaped scaffold constructed of biodegradable material, and ultimately used the cultured vessel in reconstructive surgery. See Toshiharu Shin'oka et al., Transplantation of a Tissue–Engineered Pulmonary Artery, 344 New Eng. J. Med. 532, 532–33 (2001). This approach reduces the risk of occlusion that typically occurs with vessels made of prosthetic materials and allows the transplanted graft to grow with the child, reducing the likelihood of future surgeries.

Commentators note that several challenges still exist for tissue engineering in reconstructive surgery. Techniques for isolating and culturing cells still need refining, and researchers continue to experiment with different growth factors. In addition, the cultured cells must proliferate continuously until enough tissue has been generated to accomplish the intended goal. Because cells cultured from a biopsied specimen cease reproducing after a time, scientists have experimented with autologous pluripotent stem cells harvested from bone marrow and, more recently, fat tissue. See Thomas H. Maugh, III, Fat May Be the Answer for Many Illnesses, L.A. Times, Apr. 10, 2001, at A1 (describing new techniques to harvest stem cells from adult fat tissue). Finding appropriate scaffolding poses another scientific challenge. Many materials currently used as scaffolds work well initially but eventually break down, interfering with cell proliferation. These sorts of difficulties are magnified for more complex tissue generation attempts, such as the creation of muscle cells, nerve cells, and multi-tissue solid organs. See Vincent R. Hentz & James Chang, Tissue Engineering for Reconstruction of the Thumb, 344 New Eng. J. Med. 1547, 1547–48 (2001); see also Dan Ferber, Lab–Grown Organs Begin to Take Shape, 284 Science 422 (1999); Will M. Minuth et al., Tissue Engineering: Generation of Differentiated Artificial Tissues for Biomedical Applications, 291 Cell Tissue Res. 1 (1998); Joseph P. Vacanti & Robert Langer, Tissue Engineering: The Design and Fabrication of Living Replacement Devices for Surgical Reconstruction and Transplantation, 354 Lancet 32 (1999).

2.   *Use of stem cells in therapeutic procedures.* In 1994, according to the National Center for Health Statistics National Hospital Discharge Survey, approximately 8,000 stem cell transplant procedures were performed. The FDA estimates that from 200 to 400 peripheral blood stem cell (PBSC) facilities are currently operating in the United States. Only a fraction of these facilities are accredited by the American Association of Blood Banks or the Foundation for the Accreditation of Hematopoietic Cell Therapy. See FDA, Proposed Approach to Regulation of Cellular and Tissue–Based Products (1997), available at <www.fda.gov/cber/cberftp.html>. Stem cells from umbilical cord blood are now used as an alternative to bone marrow transplantation to treat children and adults with blood disorders or blood cancers. When these patients receive chemotherapies that destroy their blood cell producing bone marrow, antigen-matched cord blood transplants can restore blood cell production. See Mary J. Laughlin et al., Hematopoietic Engraftment and Survival in Adult Recipients of Umbilical–Cord Blood from Unrelated Donors, 344 New Eng. J. Med. 1815 (2001) (concluding that cord blood is more effective than bone marrow at regenerating blood cells, with a lower incidence of graft versus host disease, so long as it comes from a donor with identical human leukocyte antigens). Cord blood banks in the U.S. and Europe have now collected over 65,000 units of the stem cell rich blood, and over 1,500 patients have received cord blood infusions. See Eliane Gluckman, Hematopoietic Stem–Cell Transplants Using Umbilical–Cord Blood, 344 New Eng. J. Med. 1860 (2001).

3.   *The FDA's regulatory authority over stem cell research.* The agency's previously discussed proposed approach to the regulation of tissue-based products includes pluripotent stem cells derived from any source. Thus, the FDA would assert that stem cells fall within its regulatory authority under Section 351 or 361 of the Public Health Service Act, and/or as biological drugs or devices, depending on the scientific or medical context in which the cells are used. The agency has issued at least one standards-setting announcement pertaining to stem cells under the umbrella of its proposed approach. See 63 Fed. Reg. 2985 (1998) (requesting suggestions for product standards under the authority of section 361 of the PHSA to ensure the safety and efficacy of stem cell-derived products). How would the FDA defend a decision to regulate stem cell products as drugs? As devices? See Robert P. Brady et al., The Food and Drug Administration's Statutory and Regulatory Authority to Regulate Human Pluripotent Stem Cells (2000), available at <bioethics.gov/stemcell2.pdf> (arguing that the FDA has the "legal discretion to regulate these products in a variety of ways" and that the agency's regulatory approach "is entitled to great deference"); see also

Lori B. Andrews, State Regulation of Embryo Stem Cell Research (2000), available at <bioethics.gov/stemcell2.pdf> (providing an overview of state laws affecting stem cell research and funding); Jennifer Kulynych, Blood as Biological "Drug": Scientific, Legal, and Policy Issues in the Regulation of Placental and Umbilical Cord Stem Cell Transplantation, 32 U. Rich. L. Rev. 407 (1998); Stephen R. Munzer, The Special Case of Property Rights in Umbilical Cord Blood for Transplantation, 51 Rutgers L. Rev. 493 (1999); David A. Suski, Note, Frozen Blood, Neonates, and FDA: The Regulation of Placental–Umbilical Cord Blood, 84 Va. L. Rev. 715 (1998).

4. *Ethical controversies surrounding embryonic stem cells.* As two commentators recently observed, "[t]he promise and potential of human embryonic stem cell research evoke profound clinical enthusiasm; the embryonic human origins of such cells warrants an equally profound ethical concern." Eric Juengst & Michael Fossel, The Ethics of Embryonic Stem Cells–Now and Forever, Cells Without End, 284 JAMA 3180 (2000). Because pluripotent stem cells are derived from human blastocysts which, if implanted in a woman's uterus, could develop into human beings, some religious groups and ethicists have objected vehemently to stem cell research. These stem cells can be obtained from tissue derived from abortions or from embryos created by in vitro fertilization. The debate about the ethical implications of different stem cell sources also becomes relevant when one considers human cloning. Although many of those engaged in the debate emphasize the distinction between "therapeutic cloning" to produce antigen-matched cloned cell lines for transplantation and "reproductive cloning," both types of cloning necessarily commence with the creation of a human embryo. Moreover, some argue that "[c]reating embryos for the sole purpose of obtaining stem cells cannot merit the moral warrants of 'wresting value from tragedy' or 'preserving human cellular life' that have been used to justify collecting stem cells from incidental abortions and unused embryos from in vitro fertilization procedures." On the other hand, the "ethical costs of omission"—of opting against the continuation of stem cell research because of moral or ethical objections—may create its own kind of moral culpability. See id. at 3180–81. The National Bioethics Advisory Commission (NBAC) took the position that the blastocysts from which embryonic stem cells are derived deserve respectful treatment, but that their moral status does not rise to the level of a fully-developed human being. See Robert L. Bartley, Stem Cells: A Wedge Issue?, Wall St. J., June 11, 2001, at A23; see also Robert P. Lanza et al., The Ethical Validity of Using Nuclear Transfer in Human Transplantation, 284 JAMA 3175 (2000); Nicholas Wade, Grappling with the Ethics of Stem Cell Research, N.Y. Times, July 24, 2001, at F3.

5. *Ban on federal funding.* The debate about the appropriateness of federal funding for stem cell research on cells derived from blastocysts continues to rage, and it has resulted in confusing rules about federal funding of research on embryonic stem cells but offered little guidance on the ethical issues. In the case of research using fetal tissue, the previous Bush administration compromised by implementing a moratorium on federal funding for fetal cell implant research rather than banning such research altogether. President Clinton immediately lifted that moratorium upon taking office, but in 1998 Congress banned all federal funding for "the creation of a human embryo or embryos for research purposes." Pub. L. No. 105–277, 112 Stat. 2681 (1998). The law did not appear to prohibit federal funding of research on adult stem cells or stem cells derived from abortions or "salvaged" human embryos, and the NIH issued a policy statement permitting federal funding of research on stem cells that have already been created by privately-funded sources. See Miranda Biven, Administrative Developments: NIH Backs Federal Funding for Stem Cell Research, 27 J.L. Med. & Ethics 95 (1999). On August 25, 2000, the NIH lifted the moratorium on federally-funded research using human pluripotent stem cells derived from human embryos and fetal tissue. See 65 Fed. Reg. 51,976 (2000). The guidelines provided that the NIH would only fund research involving "human pluripotent stem cells derived: (1) from human fetal tissue; or (2) from human embryos that are the result of in vitro fertilization, are in excess of clinical need, and have not reached the stage at which the mesoderm is formed." Id. at 51,979–80. In August 2001, the Bush administration announced that the federal government will fund embryonic stem cell research only on existing stem cell lines. The NIH later counted 72 cell lines that qualified for use in government-funded research, but critics worry that their limited supply and lack of genetic diversity will inhibit scientific progress. See Sheryl Gay Stolberg, Controversy over Cloning Reignites in Congress, N.Y. Times, Dec. 18, 2001, at F1 (noting that several members of Congress plan to revisit the issue early in 2002). Federal funding of embryonic stem cell research remains an important issue because scientists are unsure whether stem cells derived from adult sources have the same pluripotency or medical potential as embryonic stem cells. See Ceci Connolly & Rick Weiss, Stem Cell Research Divides Administration, Wash. Post, June 12, 2001, at A8; see also Nicolas Wade, A New Source for Stem Cells Is Reported, N.Y. Times, Apr. 12, 2001, at A25 (describing research that suggests that stem cells harvested from human placentas are essentially the same as embryonic stem cells); Nicholas Wade, Findings Deepen Debate on Using Embryonic Cells, N.Y. Times, Apr. 3, 2001, at F1 (describing the scientific uncertainty about whether adult stem cells will provide the same degree of therapeutic potency as embryonic stem cells). Meanwhile, corporations continue to pursue embryonic stem cell research with private dollars. One company recently created a public furor when it announced that it had cloned human embryos for the sole purpose of obtaining stem cells for research. See Rick Weiss, First Human Embryos Are Cloned in U.S., Wash. Post, Nov. 26, 2001, at A1.

2. HUMAN CELL CLONING FOR THERAPEUTIC AND REPRODUCTIVE PURPOSES

Gregory J. Rokosz, *Human Cloning: Is the Reach of FDA Authority Too Far a Stretch?*
30 SETON HALL L. REV. 464 (2000).

* * * The term "cloning" has been used differently in various research settings. A strict scientific definition of cloning, however, describes the

process of producing a "precise genetic copy of a molecule, cell, plant, animal, or human being." Cloning technologies are not new and have been used extensively in both horticulture and agriculture to maintain various plant varieties. * * * At the molecular level, cloning of deoxyribonucleic acid (DNA) fragments containing genes has been ongoing for several decades. The process of using bacteria to copy and amplify human DNA fragments and manufacture proteins coded from these fragments has been the foundation for recombinant DNA technology. This technology has led to the production of commercially available quantities of valuable medicines to treat human disease.

Culturing somatic (i.e., body) cells in a laboratory is another form of cloning that results in a cell line genetically identical to the original cell. This cellular cloning technique has been used to test and produce new medicines. In addition, primordial stem-cell therapy, based on cellular cloning techniques, has the potential to revolutionize health care. Clinical trials are already being conducted utilizing nonprimordial stem cells for therapeutic purposes such as cancer treatment.

Attempts to clone genetically identical animals are typically classified as one of two separate methodologies: blastomere separation, or embryo splitting, and nuclear transplantation techniques. Blastomere separation involves the splitting of an early embryo, allowing each split blastomere cell to develop into a separate organism. These cells, considered totipotent, are capable of producing multiple genetically identical organisms when split. This technique exhibits great potential in the area of cattle and livestock breeding. Since 1993, embryo splitting has also been successfully performed with human embryos.

Nuclear transplantation cloning is a more sophisticated cloning method and involves removing the haploid nucleus from an egg cell and replacing it with the diploid nucleus of a donor somatic cell. Early experiments using this technique in frogs, mice, cattle, and rhesus monkeys were successful when embryonic cells served as the donor cell. Dolly's birth, which resulted from the use of an adult cell nucleus donor, was astonishing proof that "cell differentiation and specialization are reversible" and that a fully differentiated adult cell nucleus could be reprogrammed to produce an entire, viable mammal.

It also seems possible to pair somatic cell nuclear transfer techniques with primordial stem-cell research to produce "customized" stem cells reflecting the DNA of a particular patient. A physician might want to generate primordial stem cells containing DNA identical to the recipient patient, thereby ensuring that the "therapy would be compatible with, and not be rejected by, the person for whom the therapy is created." To accomplish this, researchers would use somatic cell nuclear transfer technology to "reprogram somatic cell nuclei to generate more undifferentiated primordial stem cells for that patient."

There are many reasons to permit animal cloning research to continue. Cloning technologies may be used to produce groups of genetically identical animals for research purposes, thus eliminating genetic differences that often lead to experimental variation. Cloning research also has the potential to provide a means of expanding the number of livestock with desirable traits such as enhanced meat or milk production. The use of nuclear transfer technology is also apt to bring about major advances in the production of transgenic livestock, resulting in a wide array of medical benefits for humans. * * * [R]esearch on nuclear transfer cloning techniques used to generate targeted gene alterations in laboratory animals has proven invaluable in studying normal gene function and in developing accurate models of human genetic disease. It is also anticipated that ongoing animal cloning research will further scientific knowledge on cell differentiation. Finally, continued research on nuclear transfer procedures should find significant application in the field of assisted reproduction.

Despite the myriad potential benefits of nuclear transfer cloning research in animals, this technology is not without risks and safety concerns, especially when applied to humans. One concern is for the safety of a surviving clone. Due to the accumulation of genetic mutations throughout life, the older the organism, the greater the predisposition to cancer. Thus, a donor somatic cell used for cloning may contain the accumulated mutations acquired during years of cell division, which may possibly lead to a predisposition for cancer, premature aging, or immunological disease in the resulting clone. In addition, the possibility that some instability in genetic imprinting may exist, particularly in cultured cells, could limit the efficiency of somatic cell nuclear transfer. Researchers have learned "that disturbances in imprinting lead to growth abnormalities in mice and are associated with cancer and rare genetic conditions in children." Other safety concerns would apply to human egg donors, recipients of cloned embryos for gestation, and the nonsurviving cloned embryos. The fact that only 1 live birth resulted from 29 implanted embryos [in the sheep cloning experiment], which in themselves resulted from 277 cellular attempts at cloning, attests to the unresolved safety issues applicable to human cloning.
* * *

The scientific community overwhelmingly believes that any legislative action should be limited to the cloning of human beings, should not include language that impedes important ongoing or potential new research, and should clearly recognize the distinction between the cloning of an entire human being and the healing potential that is derived from biomedical research. Scientific organizations generally do not support the cloning of human beings, but do oppose overly broad legislation that goes beyond this narrow issue and threatens biomedical research that is vital to the discovery of cures for deadly and debilitating diseases. Pro-life groups, on the other hand, * * * believe that human life begins with a fertilized egg, and that any cloning research resulting in a fertilized egg should be banned, regardless of any later intent to implant the egg and to carry a child to term. * * * The current federal legislative stalemate over human cloning prohibitions exemplifies the virtually impossible task of devising statutory language acceptable to both the scientific community and the pro-life constituency. The biotechnology industry, believing that the FDA has clear authority over human cloning attempts, asserts that there is no need to enact legislation in this area. On the other hand, right-to-life organizations would likely prefer the issue to be debated publicly and resolved through the political process, which may allow these organizations to wield more influence.

In February 1998, the FDA, based on safety and efficacy concerns, announced that it had authority to regulate human cloning under its biologics regulations, which deal primarily with human gene therapy and techniques that involve the "material manipulation of human cells that are then reinserted for medical purposes." These regulations and their commentary do not discuss human reproduction, and the FDA had not previously claimed authority over other human reproductive technologies. On October 26, 1998, in a "Dear Colleague" letter issued by Associate Commissioner Stuart L. Nightingale, M.D., the FDA reaffirmed its authority under the PHSA and FFDCA to regulate clinical cloning research for the creation of human beings. According to Nightingale, any such attempts at human cloning would require submission of an IND application and IRB oversight. Support for FDA regulatory authority over human cloning is less certain outside of the scientific community. Serious questions remain regarding whether the FDA does indeed possess the requisite jurisdiction to regulate the practice of human cloning.

The FDA's assertion of jurisdiction over human cloning is sure to elicit various constitutional challenges, such as the violation of the freedom of scientific inquiry under the First Amendment and the violation of a couple's right of privacy or liberty interest in making procreative decisions. A further constitutional challenge to FDA authority over cloning might be based on a lack of authority under the Commerce Clause. * * * Human cloning clinics may well assert that their activities are conducted entirely intrastate and are therefore beyond the reach of FDA jurisdiction. * * *

The FDA includes within its definition of "human cellular and tissue-based products" a variety of "medical products derived from the human body and used for replacement, reproductive, or therapeutic purposes." For example, semen, ova, and embryos used for reproductive purposes fall within this definition. * * * If the proposed regulations are adopted and found to be an appropriate exercise of FDA authority, human cloning products may fall within the category of the rule requiring premarket approval of cellular or tissue-based products that are more than minimally manipulated. Notwithstanding this possibility, the more difficult question is whether such cellular and tissue-based products are sufficiently analogous to other biological products delineated in the statute such that the FDA regulations could survive a judicial challenge. Human embryos produced by cloning technology, however, do not seem to "fit" within the same scientific or medical category as viruses, toxins, antitoxins, vaccines, serums, allergenic products, or blood products.

The statutory background, legislative history, and resulting language of the FFDCA, the PHSA, and the Biologics Act clearly demonstrate that Congress neither contemplated the potential ramifications of human cloning procedures nor drafted the statutory language broadly enough to encompass such a radically new technology. Although embryos produced by cloning techniques and the other biologicals enumerated in the statute are all biologically based, there are significant differences between them. * * * It seems unlikely that a strict interpretation of the plain language of the statute itself would allow the FDA expansive jurisdiction to regulate human cloning, even though the FDA has been inching toward this authority in the administrative arena through its biologicals and gene therapy rules.

In addition, the FDA itself fails to support its claim of cloning jurisdiction with any prior assertion of regulatory authority over either in vitro fertilization or other more aggressive fertility techniques that carry a high-risk profile. Furthermore, the FDA regulations and commentary dealing with human gene therapy do not mention human reproduction despite the fact that, in February 1998, the FDA announced that these same regulations extended to human cloning. The FDA has not generally claimed jurisdiction over human reproductive methods. If human cloning is construed as a new variant of a treatment for infertility, the FDA may have an even weaker argument for regulatory authority because "the FDA is not supposed to regulate the practice of medicine," a power traditionally entrusted to the states.

If the courts do ultimately recognize that human cloning products are sufficiently analogous to viruses, serums, toxins, antitoxins, vaccines, blood products, and allergenic products such that they fall within the statutory envelope of regulatory consideration, the FDA first must demonstrate that these products are "applicable to the prevention, treatment, or cure of a disease or condition of human beings." The resolution of this issue is unclear; however, it is probably more easily addressed than the "analogous product" analysis, and more likely to be resolved in the FDA's favor. The issue then becomes whether human cloning products are utilized to treat or to cure a disease or condition of human beings.

If the statutory interpretation focuses on the use of cloning products to create a pregnancy, then assertion of regulatory jurisdiction would fail because pregnancy is not considered a disease, and although pregnancy arguably could be considered a human condition, such products are not applicable to the prevention, treatment, or cure of the "pregnancy." Human cloning procedures would attempt to create a pregnancy—not to prevent, treat, or cure it.

The FDA could proffer a compelling argument to establish that human cloning products would be used in many instances to treat another disease or human condition—infertility. Under the Americans with Disabilities Act (ADA), courts have already considered infertility to be a physical condition affecting the reproductive system in the context of a disability determination. Although "pregnancy" cannot be classified as a disease, and cloning products cannot be considered applicable to the prevention, treatment, or cure of pregnancy as a human condition, an implanted human embryo created by a cloning procedure could be classified as a biological product that is used to treat the disease or condition of infertility.

Although the issue of whether the FDA has power to regulate human cloning technology as biological products under the PHSA is unclear and has yet to be determined, it seems unlikely that a court would recognize such authority. The FDA's assertion that "analogous biological products" include cloning products would not stand up to judicial scrutiny because such a position would be inconsistent with the express statutory language and legislative history of the PHSA. Even though the FDA's biological regulations seemingly could be construed to include human cloning within their jurisdiction, it is not apparent that the PHSA enables the FDA to promulgate broad regulations that encompass human cloning products. Should Congress decide to confer this power upon the FDA, it could do so by simply amending the PHSA. This approach would undoubtedly have a greater chance of success than would the direct legislative initiatives previously discussed. * * *

NOTES AND QUESTIONS

1. *FDA regulatory authority over human cloning.* The FDA asserted jurisdiction over human cloning by issuing informal correspondence:

> The purpose of this letter is to confirm to institutional review boards (IRBs) that the Food and Drug Administration (FDA) has jurisdiction over clinical research using cloning technology to create a human being, and to inform IRBs of the FDA regulatory process that is required before any investigator can proceed with such a clinical investigation. . . . Clinical research using cloning technology to create a human being is subject to FDA regulation under the Public Health Service Act and the [FDCA]. Under these statutes and FDA's implementing regulations, before such research may begin, the sponsor of the research is required to submit to FDA an IND describing the proposed research plan; to obtain authorization from a properly constituted and functioning IRB; and to obtain a commitment from the investigators to obtain informed consent from all human subjects of the research. Such research may proceed only when an IND is in effect. Since FDA believes that there are major unresolved safety questions pertaining to the use of cloning technology to create a human being, until those questions are appropriately addressed in an IND, the FDA would not permit any such investigation to proceed.

Stuart Nightingale, Dear Colleague Letter, Oct. 26, 1998; see also Kathryn C. Zoon, Letter to Associations–Cloning Technology, Mar. 28, 2001 (reminding recipients of the FDA's assertion of jurisdiction over "clinical research using cloning technology to clone a human being"). In response to announcements by a couple of scientists that they would begin human cloning work, the FDA sent them warning letters. See Rick Weiss, Legal Barriers to Human Cloning May Not Hold Up, Wash. Post, May 23, 2001, at A1; see also Rick Weiss, Scientists Testify on Human Cloning Plans, Wash. Post, Mar. 29, 2001, at A10 (describing statements of an obscure religious group that has announced its intent to begin cloning research at an undisclosed location in the U.S., and noting that the FDA is receiving strident criticism from members of Congress for doing "too little too late to regulate the quickly evolving field of cloning research"). Until recently, the FDA had declined to regulate reproductive technologies.

2. *Cloning products as "drugs."* The FDA letters refer to its authority over "cloning technologies to clone a human being." Presumably, researchers will use previously approved or exempt tools to conduct their work (though perhaps off-label). What then will the agency regard as the focus of regulation? How would you frame an argument that cloning products are drugs under the FDCA? Does your answer depend on whether you are talking about cloned somatic cells for therapeutic purposes or cloned human embryos for reproductive purposes? Can these products be considered "articles" under the drug definition? Rokosz suggests that it "could only refer to the implanted product of a somatic cell nuclear transfer procedure." He notes, however, that "conferring authority upon the FDA to license, preapprove, or otherwise regulate human cloning products as drugs would raise significant constitutional questions as to whether the FDA's regulatory jurisdiction could permissibly include a fundamental procreative liberty.... [T]he FDA would likely argue the existence of a compelling state interest in the safety of the embryo and/or born-alive, cloned person." Rokosz, supra, at 501–07; see also Richard A. Merrill & Bryan J. Rose, FDA Regulation of Human Cloning: Usurpation or Statesmanship?, 15 Harv. J.L. & Tech. 85 (2001). Assuming for the sake of argument that cloning products could be considered "articles" under the statute, can the FDA reasonably argue that these articles are either "intended for use in the diagnosis, cure, mitigation, treatment or prevention of disease" or "intended to affect the structure or function of the body"? If treatment of infertility provided the basis for jurisdiction, that would limit the FDA's authority to situations in which reproductive cloning were used by infertile couples; it would not appear to reach situations in which a fertile woman or man wants to clone herself or himself for some other reason. Suppose a couple with a high risk of genetic disease wanted to maximize their chances of achieving pregnancy with a healthy embryo, and that their embryologist were able to harvest 8 eggs from the woman, fertilize them with the man's sperm, and then screen each embryo for the presence of the unwanted genetic disease. If the embryologist found only one healthy embryo in the lot, the couple might wish to clone that healthy fertilized egg in order to create two or three additional "twins" for implantation in the woman's uterus, in order to maximize the chances of achieving pregnancy in a single IVF cycle. Should the FDA be able to regulate such a procedure (or, more likely, because it involves "cloning a human being," ban it outright)?

3. *Cloning products as "devices."* How would you construct an argument that cloning products are devices under the FDCA? Would cloning products fit the category of "implant . . . or other similar or related article" within the device definition? If so, are these implants "intended for use in the diagnosis of disease or conditions or in the cure, mitigation, treatment, or prevention of disease"? Pregnancy indubitably affects the structure or function of a woman's body, but what about the additional language in the device definition that refers to the mechanism of action: "which does not achieve its primary intended purposes through chemical action ... and which is not dependent upon being metabolized for the achievement of its primary intended purposes"? This language would appear to complicate matters because the implanted cloned embryo's effect upon the body is primarily biochemical rather than mechanical. See Rokosz, supra, at 507–11. How would the arguments about FDA's regulatory authority under the different statutory sections differ if the agency were attempting to assert control over cloning processes for other therapeutic purposes such as primordial stem-cell therapy or customized medical treatments or tissue products designed to match the recipient's DNA?

4. *Other federal limitations on human cloning.* The National Bioethics Advisory Commission published a lengthy report advising the scientific community of its position on legal and ethical issues surrounding human cloning. In a chapter of the report dealing with legal and policy considerations, the NBAC noted various existing constraints:

> At present, the use of [somatic cell nuclear transfer] to create a child would be a premature experiment that exposes the developing child to unacceptable risks. This in itself is sufficient to justify a prohibition on attempts to clone human beings at this time, even if such efforts were to be characterized as the exercise of a fundamental right to attempt to procreate.... Federal law already requires that clinics using assisted reproduction techniques, such as *in vitro* fertilization, be monitored. The requirement would appear to apply, as well, to efforts to use somatic cell nuclear transfer cloning to create a child. This statute, the Fertility Clinic Success Rate and Certification Act of 1992, covers all laboratories and treatments that involve manipulation of human eggs and embryos.... It also directs HHS to develop a model program for inspection and certification of laboratories that use human embryos, to be implemented by the states.

> As this statute is implemented, any clinic or laboratory involved in attempts to initiate pregnancies by somatic cell nuclear transfer cloning should be identifiable to the federal government, and the outcomes of its efforts known to the public. As states move to implement the inspection and certification aspects of the law, a mechanism would exist to prevent attempts to use the technology, if it is shown to be ineffective or dangerous for the tissue donor or resulting child.

> Federal regulations governing the use of human beings also restrict the conduct or funding of any research aimed at cloning human beings. Research that is conducted with federal funds or at institutions that have executed a "multiple assurance agreement" with the federal government is subject to these regulatory provisions, aimed at assuring that human subjects are not exposed to unreasonably risky experiments and are enrolled in research only after giving informed consent.... To the extent that efforts to clone human beings take place at institutions subject to these regulations or in experiments funded by

the federal government, any serious question about the physical harms that might result would make it difficult for such experimentation to be approved.

With regard to federal research funding, President Clinton announced in 1994 that the National Institutes of Health (NIH) should not finance any research that involves creating embryos solely for research that would result in their destruction. Furthermore, Congress has passed prohibitions on the use of ... funds appropriated to the departments of Labor, Education, and HHS for any research that involves exposing embryos to risk of destruction for non-therapeutic research. The net effect of these policies is to eliminate virtually all federal funding for research to perfect methods for cloning human beings, as even research aimed at initiating a pregnancy would probably involve creating and destroying many embryos that fail to develop normally.

NBAC, Cloning Human Beings: Legal and Policy Considerations (1997), at 87–89, available at <http://www.bioethics.gov/pubs.html> (noting also that "a number of state laws regarding the management of embryos arguably could restrict even privately funded research" and that, in states without such legislation, medical malpractice law would serve as the primary means for regulating the clinical application of cloning technology). Do these make FDA control superfluous?

5. *State and federal legislation banning human cloning.* A number of bills in Congress would ban human cloning or various aspects of it. For example, some Republican bills seek to ban human somatic cell nuclear transfer procedures for any purpose. If such a bill were enacted, it would halt all research involving human cloning, including non-reproductive applications such as stem cell therapies. See, e.g., Human Cloning Prohibition Act of 2001, S. 790 (prohibiting "human cloning," which is defined as "human asexual reproduction accomplished by introducing the nuclear material of a human somatic cell into a fertilized or unfertilized oocyte whose nucleus has been removed ... to produce a living organism (at any stage of development) with a human or predominantly human genetic constitution," and providing for civil and criminal penalties including up to ten years in prison). Some of these bills appear to ban somatic cell nuclear transfer processes even if these processes are being used to generate primordial stem cells in order to treat human disease (rather than to create a cloned human embryo to implant in a woman's uterus for gestation). These bills also appear designed to prohibit "customized" stem cell research that uses somatic cell nuclear transfer technology. See Rokosz, supra, at 483–91. In contrast, Democratic bills are more limited in scope and would make it illegal only to "implant the product of somatic cell nuclear transfer into a woman's uterus," punishable by civil fines, exempt certain biomedical research, contain a ten-year sunset provision, and preempt inconsistent state laws. See id. At least two states (California and Michigan) have enacted laws banning cloning. In California, the statute defines cloning as "creating children by the transfer of nuclei from any type of cell to enucleated eggs," though it also has the effect of banning certain infertility treatments unrelated to cloning. See Cal. Health & Safety Code § 24185. For additional discussion of federal and state legislative efforts and the pros and cons of banning human cloning more generally, see Lori B. Andrews, Is There a Right to Clone? Constitutional Challenges to Bans on Human Cloning, 11 Harv. J.L. & Tech. 643 (1998); John A. Robertson, Human Cloning and the Challenge of Regulation, 339 New Eng. J. Med. 119 (1998).

6. *Ethical concerns surrounding cloning.* Health policy experts, ethicists, and scientists have made a variety of ethical arguments against cloning, including concerns about psychological harm to cloned offspring, the commodification of human beings, and the use of cloning technologies to accomplish eugenics goals. See George J. Annas, Why We Should Ban Cloning, 339 New Eng. J. Med. 122 (1998); Dena S. Davis, What's Wrong with Cloning?, 38 Jurimetrics J. 83 (1997); Harold T. Shapiro, Ethical and Policy Issues of Human Cloning, 277 Science 195 (1997); Michael H. Shapiro, I Want a Girl (Boy) Just Like the Girl (Boy) That Married Dear Old Dad (Mom): Cloning Lives, 9 S. Cal. Interdisc. L.J. 1 (1999) (exploring and critiquing the literature on human cloning, and providing several arguments for and against the practice).

7. *Scientific concerns over the safety of cloning human beings.* Apart from questions of ethical propriety or the FDA's regulatory authority over human cloning, many scientists have expressed concern about the safety of human cloning, noting that the safety record in cloned animals is unacceptable. See, e.g., Brian Vastag, At the Cloning Circus Sideshows Abound, While Scientists Seek a Wider Audience, 286 JAMA 1437 (2001) (describing controversy at an NAS scientific workshop on the safety of animal and human cloning); Gina Kolata, Researchers Find Big Risk of Defect in Cloning Animals, N.Y. Times, Mar. 25, 2001, at A1 (noting that fewer than 3% of all animal cloning attempts succeed, and recounting expert's opinions that—ethical objections aside—it would be reckless to clone a human being given the rate of abnormalities that occur in cloned animals); Rick Weiss, Human Cloning Bid Stirs Experts' Anger, Wash. Post, Mar. 7, 2001, at A1 (describing concern in the scientific community about the safety of human cloning based on "cloning's dismal safety record" in animals).

3. XENOTRANSPLANTATION

FDA, Draft Guidance, *Source Animal, Product, Preclinical, and Clinical Issues Concerning the Use of Xenotransplantation Products in Humans*

<http://www.fda.gov/cber/guidelines.htm> (2001).

* * * [X]enotransplantation refers to any procedure that involves the transplantation, implantation, or infusion into a human recipient of either (a) live cells, tissues, or organs from a nonhuman animal source, or (b) human body fluids, cells, tissues or organs that have had ex vivo contact with live nonhuman animal cells, tissues or organs. * * * Recent advances in technology and pharmacology, which have been important for achieving success in allotransplantation, have led to the proposal that xenotransplantation, initially attempted nearly a century ago, may provide a solution to the shortage of human allografts. * * * The use of these different xenotransplantation products has the potential for transmission of infectious disease from nonhuman animals to humans. * * * For these reasons, during product development it is important to consider the safety not only of the recipients and their contacts, but also of the public. * * *

Xenotransplantation products * * * require premarket approval by FDA. If xenotransplantation products are to be used in clinical investigation, they require an appropriate investigational application to FDA. Most xenotransplantation products will be regulated as biological products by CBER. * * * Some products may be combination products consisting of a biologic and a device, such as xenogeneic cells contained in a device used for extracorporeal infusion. Others may be combinations of a biologic and a drug, such as if a novel immunosuppressive agent were to be used only in the context of transplantation of a specific xenotransplantation product. The regulation of combination products is determined by the primary mode of action of the product. * * *

Due to potential infectious disease risks associated with the use of xenotransplantation products, appropriate source animal qualifications should be developed * * * * When xenotransplantation products are transplanted directly after removal from a source animal, it may not be possible to perform all tests on the final product and have the results available prior to use. However, the sponsor should use a biopsy of the organ or a relevant surrogate sample * * * for assay of the xenotransplantation product. * * * For live xenogeneic cells or tissues that are stored, processed, or expanded ex vivo, in addition to safety testing, additional product characterization to measure identity, purity, and potency should be performed. As much as possible, results of these assays should be available prior to xenotransplantation, and used for lot release. * * *

[F]or the preclinical testing of xenotransplantation products, * * * studies to support the safety characterization of therapeutic agents should focus on the intended alteration to the human pathophysiologic state (i.e., activity), as well as unintended effects (i.e., toxicity) to the host system. Such studies serve to assess the potential for clinical risks and constitute an important component of a FDA application. * * * [For clinical trials], [s]ponsors are responsible for ensuring reviews, as appropriate, by local review bodies, including Institutional Review Boards, Institutional Animal Care and Use Committees, and Institutional Biosafety Committees. * * * Because of the potentially serious public health risks of possible zoonotic infections, xenotransplantation should be limited to patients with serious or life-threatening diseases for whom adequately safe and effective alternative therapies are not available. Candidates should be limited to those patients who have potential for a clinically significant improvement with increased quality of life following the procedure. * * *

NOTES AND QUESTIONS

1. *Current state of the technology.* Several types of xenotransplantation procedures have already been attempted in experimental settings. Researchers have implanted neurons from pigs into patients with degenerative neurological disorders. See J. Stephen Fink et al., Porcine Xenografts in Parkinson's Disease and Huntington's Disease Patients: Preliminary Results, 9 Cell Transplant. 273 (2000). Researchers also are attempting to cure diabetes with infusions of pancreatic cells from pigs, see Carl–Gustave Groth et al., Transplantation of Porcine Fetal Pancreas to Diabetic Patients, 344 Lancet 1402 (1994), and they are using cells cultured ex vivo on a murine (mouse) cell line to create skin to aid in wound healing for burn victims. Some recipients of these experimental xenotransplantation technologies have survived for several years after the procedure. As the FDA's draft guidance document suggests, however, problems with recipient immune rejection and concerns about infectious disease transmission pose the biggest obstacles to continued work with xenotransplantation products. Commentators suggest that engineering of these products and cloning of preferred strains of cells may help to reduce such risks. See Louisa E. Chapman & Eda T. Bloom, Clinical Xenotransplantation, 285 JAMA 2304 (2001); see also Fritz H. Bach et al., Uncertainty in Xenotransplantation: Individual Benefit Versus Collective Risk, 4 Nat. Med. 141 (1998); Ravi S. Chari et al., Brief Report: Treatment of Hepatic Failure with Ex Vivo Pig–Liver Perfusion Followed by Liver Transplantation, 331 New Eng. J. Med. 234 (1994); Rick Weiss, Gene Alteration Boosts Pig–Human Transplant Feasibility, Wash. Post, Jan. 4, 2002, at A11.

2. *Characterization of xenotransplantation products.* The agency has issued several other guidance documents dealing with various aspects of xenotransplantation. See, e.g., FDA, Guidance for Industry: Precautionary Measures to Reduce the Possible Risk of Transmission of Zoonoses by Blood and Blood Products from Xenotransplantation Product Recipients and Their Contacts, 64 Fed. Reg. 73,562 (1999); FDA, Guidance for Industry: Public Health Issues Posed by the Use of Nonhuman Primate Xenografts in Humans, 64 Fed. Reg. 16,743 (1999); see also Patrik S. Florencio & Erik D. Ramanathan, Are Xenotransplantation Safeguards Legally Viable?, 16 Berkeley Tech. L.J. 937 (2001). As usual with its assertion of regulatory jurisdiction over new medical technologies, the agency has provided a very limited explanation of the precise statutory basis of its claimed authority. Consider the following products: pig kidneys for direct transplant into human, pig kidneys from genetically-altered (transgenic) pigs that have been modified with human DNA to improve histocompatability, pig pancreatic islet cells that have been cultured and cleansed of pathogens for use in the treatment of diabetes, baboon neuron cells that have been cultured and proliferated in vitro for use in the treatment of spinal cord injuries. Into which statutory category (if any) do these products fit? What sorts of ethical and legal issues does xenotransplantation technology raise? See Fritz H. Bach et al., Ethical and

Legal Issues in Technology: Xenotransplantation, 27 Am. J.L. & Med. 283 (2001) .

3. *This little piggie went to market.* Given the scarcity of human donor organs for transplantation, the market for genetically-modified animal organs with improved human histocompatability could be enormous. PPL Therapeutics PLC, the London-based company that cloned Dolly the sheep, recently announced that it had successfully cloned a litter of DNA-modified pigs. Such genetically-altered animals may one day become a source for organs for human transplantation, especially if scientists can alter the genetic structure of the animals in ways that will reduce the likelihood of adverse immune system responses in the human recipients. See Justin Gillis, DNA–Altered Pigs Are Cloned in Virginia, Wash. Post, Apr. 12, 2001, at E5; see also Jack M. Kress, Xenotransplantation: Ethics and Economics, 53 Food & Drug L.J. 353 (1998); Naomi Aoki, Charlestown Biotech in Pig–Clone Venture, Boston Globe, May 9, 2001, at F5.

B. THE HUMAN GENOME PROJECT AND ITS TECHNOLOGICAL PROGENY

The Human Genome Project (HGP) began in 1990 under the leadership of Dr. James D. Watson. The project's work received federal funding through the NIH and the Department of Energy. Members of an international academic consortium divided the genome into sections for sequencing at different team laboratories. Celera Corporation, then headed by J. Craig Venter, entered the race to sequence the genome in 1998, and its "shotgun" approach to gene sequencing was so efficient that the corporation was able to catch up with the HGP consortium's progress. On June 26, 2000, Francis Collins, the current head of the HGP consortium, and Craig Venter jointly announced that their respective organizations had completed the sequencing of the human genome. See Nicholas Wade, Reading the Book of Life: A Historic Quest, N.Y. Times, June 27, 2000, at F5; see also The Genome International Sequencing Consortium, Initial Sequencing and Analysis of the Human Genome, 409 Nature 860 (2001) (publishing the work of the HGP consortium); Elizabeth Pennisi, The Human Genome, 291 Science 1177 (2001) (describing the work of Celera Corporation). In a show of continued public-private cooperation, the NIH recently agreed to fund Celera Genomics Corporation's new project to map the genome of the laboratory rat. When completed, this map will enable drug researchers to integrate human genomic information with their extensive understanding of rat biology. See Justin Gillis, Government Gives Celera $21 Million to Map Rat Genome, Wash. Post, Mar. 1, 2001, at E5. For a lively history of the early progress of the Human Genome Project, see Robert Cook–Deegan, Gene Wars: Science, Politics, and the Human Genome (1994).

Of course, sequencing the human genome only provides the starting point for the development of new medical technologies. In order to analyze and ultimately apply genomic data for medical purposes, scientists must first "annotate" the genome—that is, provide the "punctuation" for the string of genes that comprise the ribbons of human DNA so that researchers can more readily work with genes and determine their individual functions. Also, most genes code for specific proteins, which in turn may provide structure or serve some other functional purpose in the body by affecting cell metabolism. When the genes that manufacture proteins are defective, disease results. The new discipline of proteomics will enable scientists to analyze simultaneously the many proteins that comprise a cell, rather than studying cell proteins one at a time, so that the role of proteins in the cell can be better understood. Three corporations recently announced that they would collaborate on a project to identify all of the proteins in the human body (the Human Proteome) and demonstrate how these proteins interact with one another. The collaborators project completion of the proteome database by 2004, and they plan to make their results available to drug companies for a fee and to academic researchers for a discounted fee. See Andrew Pollack, Three Companies Will Try to Identify All Human Proteins, N.Y. Times, Apr. 5, 2001, at C4. Scientists currently are working on a variety of promising approaches to disease detection, treatment, and prevention made possible by the HGP.

1. GENETIC TESTING

Consumer Federation of America v. HHS
83 F.3d 1497 (D.C.Cir.1996).

■ WALD, CIRCUIT JUDGE:

In 1992, the United States Department of Health and Human Services issued regulations implementing the 1988 Clinical Laboratory Improvement Amendments ("CLIA" or "Act"), which expands and strengthens federal regulation of laboratories that perform clinical tests on specimens from the human body. * * * In response to growing public concern about the quality of clinical laboratory testing, Congress passed CLIA in 1988 to ensure competence among laboratories testing human specimens for disease diagnosis, prevention, monitoring, and treatment. Prior to CLIA, the federal government regulated only those laboratories which received reimbursement from the federal Medicare program or handled test samples shipped in interstate commerce. All other labs performing clinical tests were free from federal regulation and oversight. Following extensive hearings and investigations, Congress concluded that some of these unregulated facilities "posed a serious threat to the public health." Because they processed tests without sufficient regard for accuracy or reliability, these labs reported incorrect test results at an unacceptably high rate. In particular, significant attention was focused on laboratories reviewing Pap smears, which are used to screen women for indications of cervical cancer. Witnesses presented evidence that many labs were employing inadequately trained cytologists and requiring them to process tests at rates two to three times higher than the recommended maximum workload. As a consequence, the labs reported large numbers of false negative results, contributing to unnecessary suffering and even death in women who did not receive prompt treatment for cervical cancer because the labs failed to identify their Pap smears as abnormal.

Congress identified a number of reasons for these deficiencies, including the absence of uniform standards for personnel performing clinical tests, rates for screening cytology specimens which were so rapid that the risk of improper diagnosis was extremely high, ineffective proficiency testing (or none at all), and the lack of proper quality control measures. To remedy these critical shortcomings, Congress expanded HHS's oversight responsibilities to include all laboratories performing clinical tests on human specimens and revamped the existing regulatory scheme. Two of these reforms are at issue here: a system of personnel qualifications, and proficiency testing requirements for cytologists.

CLIA directs HHS to establish personnel qualifications for all individuals performing clinical tests, and further instructs that the qualifications "shall, as appropriate, be different on the basis of ... the risks and consequences of erroneous results associated with such examinations and procedures." 42 U.S.C. § 263a(f)(1)(C). * * * In its May 1990 Notice of Proposed Rulemaking (NPRM) implementing this provision, HHS proposed a three-tiered scheme of personnel qualifications. Each type of lab test would be placed into one of three categories—"waived" tests (those so simple to perform that the likelihood of an erroneous test result is extremely small, as well as those which pose no reasonable risk of harm to the patient if performed incorrectly), Level I tests, or Level II tests—depending upon the consequences to the patient if the test was performed incorrectly, the complexity of the testing methodology, the degree to which the test requires independent judgment and interpretation, the degree to which interpretation of the test result requires knowledge of external variables, and the training required to perform the test. See 55 Fed. Reg. 20,895, 20,901–02 (1990). Under this scheme, personnel would have to satisfy increasingly rigorous qualifications to perform waived tests, Level I tests, and Level II tests, respectively. * * *

In the final rule, the agency * * * set forth three categories of tests: "waived," "moderate complexity," or "high complexity." As in the NPRM, "waived tests" included those which are so simple to perform that the likelihood of an erroneous test result is extremely small. These tests were exempt from regulation. The remainder of all clinical tests were assigned a score of one to three, for each of seven different criteria: (1) knowledge needed to perform the test; (2) training and experience needed to perform the test; (3) complexity of reagent and materials preparation; (4) characteristics of the steps required to perform the test; (5) availability of materials for calibration, quality control, and proficiency testing; (6) troubleshooting and equipment maintenance required; and (7) degree of interpretation and judgment required. See 42 C.F.R. § 493.17. In contrast to the NPRM, the agency eliminated any express consideration of the risks or consequences to the patient of an erroneous test result. After these values were assigned and totaled, any test with a cumulative score of 12 or less was placed in the "moderate complexity" category, and all other tests (with a score of greater than 12) in the "high complexity" category. HHS then assigned specific personnel qualification requirements to labs in each category. Facilities performing only waived tests must follow accepted laboratory practices and comply with other relevant federal, state, and local requirements, but are not subject to the new CLIA standards. Labs performing moderate and high complexity tests must comply with CLIA regulations regarding proficiency testing, patient test management, quality control and assurance, and personnel standards; the standards for high complexity labs are even stiffer than those imposed on moderate complexity facilities. * * *

Centers for Disease Control, Notice of Intent, *Genetic Testing Under the Clinical Laboratory Improvement Amendments*
65 Fed. Reg. 25,928 (2000).

The Centers for Disease Control and Prevention acts as a scientific advisor to the Health Care Financing Administration in development of requirements for clinical laboratories under the Clinical Laboratory Improvement Amendments (CLIA). The CDC is issuing this notice to advise the public that the Department of Health and Human Services will be preparing a Notice of Proposed Rule Making to revise the CLIA regulations applicable to laboratories performing human genetic testing. Before issuing the NPRM, comments are being solicited on the recommendations of the Clinical Laboratory Improvement Advisory Committee (CLIAC) to change current CLIA requirements to specifically recognize a genetic testing specialty. This new speciality area will address unique testing issues in the pre-analytic, analytic, and post-analytic phases of testing that could affect the accuracy and reliability of test results, and related issues such as informed consent, confidentiality, counseling, and the clinical appropriateness of a genetic test. * * *

Human genetic testing is expected to lead to a whole new era in health care. Some tests may determine not only whether an individual has a particular disease or condition, but also may determine their risk of developing a disease or condition in the future. However, along with the tremendous potential for improving health and preventing disease, genetic testing can also do great harm if errors occur in: (1) the selection of an appropriate test, (2) the performance of the test, (3) the interpretation of the test results, or (4) the clinical application of the test results. False-positive or false-negative results can be especially troublesome when the test is being used to predict future risk of disease in an individual without any current symptoms of disease.

The process of performing a genetic test can be broken into three distinct phases: (1) the pre-analytic phase, which encompasses such events as determining which genetic test, if any, is appropriate to answer the clinical question being asked and collecting an appropriate sample and transporting it to the test site; (2) the analytical phase, which involves steps taken to perform the analysis and analyze the results; and (3) the post-analytic phase, which includes reporting and interpretation of the results. It is important to recognize that the laboratory may need to be involved in carrying out or assisting with all three phases of testing and that errors can occur either within the laboratory or at the interface between the laboratory and the care provider.

In the pre-analytic phase, one recent study found that 20 percent of adenomatous polyposis coli (APC) genetic tests were ordered for inappropriate indications and 19 percent of patients received genetic counseling before testing occurred. See Francis M. Giardiello et al., The Use and Interpretation of Commercial APC Gene Testing for Familial Adenomatous Polyposis, 336 New Eng. J. Med. 823 (1997). Another recent survey of 245 molecular genetic testing laboratories found that 55 percent of the laboratories did not require informed consent prior to testing and 31 percent did not have a written policy on confidentiality. See Margaret M. McGovern et al., Quality Assurance in Molecular Genetic Testing Laboratories, 281 JAMA 835 (1999). This same study found what the authors considered to be substandard laboratory practice, which could lead to adverse clinical outcomes, in 15 percent of the laboratories. In the post-analytic phase of testing, the Giardiello study reported that 31 percent of the cases were misinterpreted by the physician. The McGovern study found that 30 percent of laboratories did not provide access to genetic counseling.

These and other studies point to the need for improvements in laboratory practice and better coordination between the care provider, laboratory, genetic counselor, and the patient to ensure quality in genetic testing. The HHS has sought the advice of experts in laboratory medicine and genetic testing to help identify places in the testing process where testing problems are most likely to occur, and to determine what modifications to current CLIA regulations could provide greater assurance of accurate and reliable testing. Issues for which the laboratory might provide additional assistance to the laboratory user such as informed consent, counseling, and protecting confidentiality were also considered. * * *

In considering whether to create a genetic specialty under CLIA and whether to include the provisions recommended by the CLIAC, it is important to understand the current roles of government and professional organizations in genetic testing, and to note that no single agency or organization is likely to be able to address all of the issues raised by genetic testing. Genetic tests are currently regulated at the federal level through three mechanisms: (1) the Clinical Laboratory Improvement Amendments; (2) the federal Food, Drug, and Cosmetic Act; and (3) during investigational phases of test development, under applicable regulations for the protection of human subjects. In addition, some states regulate and private-sector organizations monitor genetic testing laboratories. * * *

Testing devices and tests that are packaged and sold as kits to multiple laboratories require premarket approval or clearance by the FDA. This premarket review involves an analysis of the device's accuracy as well as its analytical sensitivity and specificity. * * * The majority of new genetic tests are being developed by laboratories for their own use, that is, in-house tests. The FDA established a measure of regulation of in-house tests by instituting controls over the active ingredients (analyte-specific reagents) used by laboratories to perform tests. This regulation subjects reagent manufacturers to certain general controls, such as good manufacturing practices; however, with few exceptions, the current regulatory process does not require a premarket review of these reagents. The regulation requires that the sale of reagents be only to laboratories capable of performing high-complexity tests and requires that certain information accompany both the reagents and the test results. The labels for the reagents must also state that "analytical and performance characteristics are not established." Also, the test results must identify the laboratory that developed the test and its performance characteristics and must include a statement that the test "has not been cleared or approved by the U.S. FDA." In addition, the regulation prohibits direct marketing of in-house developed tests to consumers.

Human subjects participating in the research phase of development of a genetic test are under the protection of human research subjects regulations administered by the National Institutes of Health (NIH) and the FDA. NIH oversees the protection of human research subjects in HHS-funded research, while the FDA oversees the protection of human research subjects in trials of investigational (unapproved) devices, drugs, or biologics being developed for eventual commercial use. Fundamental requirements of these regulations are that experimental protocols involving human subjects be reviewed by an organization's Institutional Review Board (IRB) to assure the safety of the subjects and that risks do not outweigh potential benefits.

Some state agencies may monitor laboratories performing genetic testing, including licensure of personnel and facilities. In some instances, the state Public Health Laboratory and state-operated CLIA program are responsible for quality assurance activities. A few states, such as New York, have promulgated regulations that go beyond the requirements of CLIA. States also administer newborn screening programs and provide other genetic services through maternal and child health programs. Private-sector organizations, in partnership with HCFA and CDC may also develop laboratory and clinical guidelines and standards. A number of organizations are involved in helping to assure the quality of laboratory practices and in developing clinical practice guidelines to ensure the appropriate use of genetic tests. * * *

Michael J. Malinowski & Robin J.R. Blatt, *Commercialization of Genetic Testing Services: The FDA, Market Forces, and Biological Tarot Cards*
71 TUL. L. REV. 1211 (1997).

* * * Concern about the impact of [genetic] testing on society inspired James Watson, codiscoverer of the double-helix structure of DNA and the first head of the HGP, to insist at the outset of the HGP that a respectable

percentage of the annual budget be committed to addressing the project's ethical, legal, and social implications [ELSI]. Nevertheless, most public health officials and other regulators, both federal and state, are only beginning to become aware of the full implications of new genetic technologies. * * * As a result, the regulatory infrastructure necessary for responsible commercialization of genetic technology is being developed in response to, rather than in anticipation of, its commercialization. * * *

Generally, when a gene or biological marker linked to a physical or mental condition is discovered, the basic scientific capability to test for the presence of that marker is a given. Thousands of such linkages have been made subsequent to the commencement of the HGP, and at a rate accelerating with the passage of time, to the point that linkages are being identified almost on a weekly (if not daily) basis. * * * Biotech companies are using such discoveries to develop and commercialize predictive screening tests for an abundance of health conditions in addition to breast and ovarian cancer. Recent discoveries include genetic links to Alzheimer's, bladder cancer, cervical cancer, colon cancer, obesity, prostate cancer, and tumor growth associated with a spectrum of common cancers. Researchers are even developing an "Ides of March" genetic test to serve as a crude indicator of a person's life span. * * *

Unfortunately, the discovery of genetic alterations linked to many health conditions comes well before those discoveries can be turned into therapeutics and reliable predictors of disease in specific individuals. Although the availability of therapeutics to offset genetic predispositions will make genetic testing much less controversial, that time is years away for most conditions. * * * Nevertheless, a deluge of fully commercialized genetic testing services and kits is well within sight. * * * Many developers and manufacturers of genetic tests now are making investigatory, predictive genetic testing available to the public. * * *

In 1994, the Committee on Assessing Genetic Risks assembled by the Institutes of Medicine documented pervasive informal genetic testing by research laboratories, and the ELSI Task Force on Genetic Testing has reached similar conclusions regarding both research and commercial laboratories that report results to patients. The emergence of predictive genetic tests with implications for broad segments of the population, such as the APOE–4 (Alzheimer's) test, is raising concern among public health officials and providers who understand the limitations of this technology and are sensitive to its potential impact on the lives of patients and their families. However, with such understanding comes appreciation for the difficulty of introducing a satisfactory regulatory response to the multitude of genetic technologies approaching and entering commerce.

Predictive genetic testing services, performed in-house by the tests' developers and manufacturers, are square pegs in the rubric of federal regulation. The FDA regulates the production of reagents, probes, or test kits manufactured for use by others in laboratories and, therefore, genetic tests manufactured and sold for others to perform. However, manufacturers and private laboratories may avoid the routine FDA review process for diagnostics and comply with applicable federal regulations by manufacturing and using their own reagents in-house and selling testing services through primary care physicians. Such reagents are called "home brews" because they are manufactured and used within the same facility, and a number of such tests are being developed and made available to the public.

Home brews may be marketed as established products or, to limit product liability where clinical efficacy is not yet established, labeled investigatory. Although the developers of investigatory tests are allowed to charge consumers only enough to recapture costs, commercialization of these tests enables them to generate a revenue stream, gather needed patient data, and build standard-care acceptance of their technologies. Standard-care acceptance means enhanced acceptability among physicians and the public, limits on product liability, and perhaps insurance coverage. Also, the costs of investigatory tests may be considerable, depending upon the stated research objective.

Private laboratories performing genetic testing services also are essentially immune to federal laboratory-quality assurances imposed by the Health Care Finance Administration through the Clinical Laboratory Improvement Amendments. Under CLIA, a laboratory must demonstrate analytical validity of its tests and their components, but there is no clinical validity requirement. In other words, the CLIA validity requirement is satisfied when a genetic test to determine the presence of a specific genetic alteration does so accurately, even though the test may offer no clinical predictability. There is no required express showing that the alteration tested for has any bearing on the subject's health. The only CLIA patient-care safeguard on clinical quality is the requirement that the proposed clinical protocol receive institutional review board approval when an investigatory test enters the human-trial phase. Academic laboratories are required to report to their standing IRBs, but "the situation with respect to IRBs is murkier for biotechnology companies and commercial laboratories. They also may consult an IRB of an academic institution with whom they have ties, or they may form their own IRB—a practice that has the potential for a conflict of interest."

The general lack of regulatory quality control on genetic tests, which raises questions about their fundamental reliability, is exacerbated by the fact that very few specific guidelines for these tests have been formally developed and introduced by the medical profession. "Lack of consensus about what type of screening should be offered means that there is also no clear guidance for state policy makers adopting mandatory screening plans" even on issues such as the testing of fetuses for BRCA1 and BRCA2 variations. Also, reliance on state regulation to monitor (in the ongoing manner necessitated by the research nature of the technology) the quality of genetic testing services is misplaced for, there too, "the field of laboratory licensure and monitoring remains in a state of flux." * * *

[The FDA] has proposed regulations to bring genetic testing services (and home brews in general) more directly within its purview. Specifically, the FDA would like to regulate the active ingredients used in genetic tests.

The FDA's proposal is to classify "active ingredients," chemicals or antibodies that are useful only in testing for one specific disease or condition, as analyte specific reagents (ASRs), which are subject to controls. This labeling would require suppliers of such active ingredients to register with the FDA and provide lists of the ASRs they are supplying to laboratories for use in developing tests. These suppliers then would be held to good manufacturing standards, which require FDA reporting of all adverse events possibly attributable to products. The FDA also has left open the possibility of directly regulating in-house genetic testing services at a later date. * * *

Predictive genetic testing services are, in the aggregate, biological tarot cards subject to misinterpretation by both patients and their physicians. The predictive capability of many genetic tests remains scientifically undefined for the general population. This type of testing must be conclusively distinguished from presymptomatic genetic testing. The latter constitutes a reliable and meaningful predictor only for a small number of conditions—conditions usually caused by a single genetic mutation. Only these few conditions, such as Huntington's and Tay Sachs disease, can be diagnosed conclusively through genetic testing. Even when such conditions can be diagnosed through genetic testing, the rate of expression may vary; with many genetic conditions, severity remains an open question. Most often there is no available treatment, or treatment exists but is price-prohibitive. In addition, in the absence of uniform federal regulatory oversight, the quality of laboratory performance is questionable.

More troubling, due to the absence of adequate clinical data, health care providers cannot interpret the results of predictive genetic tests for most of their patients with any reliability even when they are knowledgeable about genetics. This interpretation problem is exacerbated because the current generation of health care providers does not possess such knowledge. Their lack of genetics education and the novelty of the technology makes providers dependent upon the developers and manufacturers of these tests (both commercial and academic laboratories) for information. This dependency suggests that neither consumers nor their health care providers can reasonably evaluate the technology. * * *

Many consumers and providers are more in awe of the "miracles of modern genetics" than appreciative of its clinical limitations. The demand for predictive genetic testing services may reflect this faith in genetic medicine, a tendency to equate investigational genetic tests with reliable, standard-care diagnostic tests, and the influence of entrepreneurial and academic interests. It also may reflect intolerance for health conditions that deviate from the majority.

The information generated by predictive genetic tests, regardless of its clinical reliability, will deeply impact people's lives. Some of those who have opted to undergo the presymptomatic test for Huntington's, a clinically valid test that conclusively determines future onset, have experienced detrimental psychological reactions to the results even when they are negative. For those whose results are positive, the suicide rate is approximately thirty-five percent higher than among the general population. Further, it appears that genetic information already is disrupting the lives of individuals and their families by subjecting them to discrimination from employers and insurers. * * *

NOTES AND QUESTIONS

1.   *CLIA and FDA jurisdiction over genetic testing.* In 1996, labs performed more than 175,000 genetic tests, and the statistics suggest that testing is growing at the rate of 30 percent each year. Tests for more than 400 genetic diseases are already available, and an additional 330 tests are in the pipeline. See Rick Weiss, Ignorance Undercuts Gene Tests' Potential, Wash. Post, Dec. 2, 2000, at A1. As explained above, CLIA regulations set out criteria under which HHS assigns an in vitro diagnostic test to a "complexity category." That category, in turn, determines the level of regulation. Laboratories that perform only "waived tests" are subject to minimal regulation, whereas those labs that perform moderate or high complexity tests must meet regulatory standards dealing with personnel, proficiency testing, quality assurance, and inspections. See 42 C.F.R. pt. 493. Responsibility for the categorization determination shifted recently from the CDC to the FDA in order to "allow[] manufacturers to submit premarket applications for [IVD] products and requests for complexity categorization of these products under CLIA to one agency." FDA, Draft Guidance for Administrative Procedures for CLIA Categorization (2000), available at <www.fda.gov/cdrh>; see also 64 Fed. Reg. 73,561 (1999) (transferring to FDA various functions under CLIA).

2.   *FDA regulation of "home brews."* The FDA regulates "diagnostic kits" as medical devices. See 21 U.S.C. § 360k(a). Recall that the agency places new devices into three classes. See id. § 360c(a)(1). The complexity of genetic diagnostic products (and lack of pre–1976 predicate devices) frequently leads to Class III designation, requiring the submission of a PMA. However, as explained above, many laboratories were circumventing the premarket approval process by manufacturing and using their own diagnostic analyte specific reagents (ASRs) in house (so-called "home brews") and then marketing the test process as a service. In 1996, the FDA declared that "at a future date, the agency may reevaluate whether additional controls over the in house tests developed by such laboratories may be needed to provide an appropriate level of consumer protection. Such controls may be especially relevant as testing for the presence of genes associated with cancer or dementing diseases becomes more widely available." 61 Fed. Reg. 10,484 (1996) (declaring the agency's intent to regulate the reagents used in in-house genetic testing as Class III devices and a subgroup of these as "restricted" devices). The FDA finalized the proposed rule a year later, regulating all ASRs as restricted (but not Class III) medical devices:

> Under the authority of section 520(e) of the act, the final rule restricts the sale, distribution or use of all ASR's subject to the rule.

FDA has determined that these restrictions are necessary to provide a reasonable assurance of the safety and effectiveness of ASRs, commensurate with their potentiality for harmful effect or the collateral measures necessary to their use. The final rule restricts ordering the use of in-house developed tests using ASRs to physicians or other health care practitioners authorized by applicable state law to access such tests. The final rule also restricts the sale of ASRs to those clinical laboratories regulated under Clinical Laboratory Improvement Amendments of 1988 (CLIA) as qualified to perform high complexity testing. . . .

FDA does not intend, at this time, to regulate ASRs used in genetic testing differently from other restricted class I medical devices that are exempt from premarket notification requirements. The ASR regulations are drafted to classify most ASRs used to develop in-house tests as class I devices because FDA believes this degree of regulatory control is commensurate with the need to bring consistency to the manufacture of these devices and to assure their safety and effectiveness when used by health and scientific personnel trained in laboratory practices. FDA considered identifying a subset of ASRs that are used to develop tests intended for predictive genetic diagnosis as ASRs that pose unique risks to the public health because of the substantial clinical impact of the information generated using these devices. For the genetic tests currently in use, FDA is aware that both the genetic test and the ASR used in the genetic test are developed by the laboratory in-house. Because these ASRs are not being commercially marketed independently of the tests, they do not currently fall within the scope of this regulation. Nonetheless, FDA considered designating as class III devices those ASRs that would be marketed independently for use in tests intended for use in overtly healthy people to identify a genetic predisposition to a dementing disease, or to fatal or potentially fatal medical disorders (e.g., cancers or Alzheimer's disease), in situations where penetrance is poorly defined or variable and latency is 5 years or longer. However, after reviewing the comments and currently available information, FDA has not yet identified criteria that would logically distinguish among genetic tests in order to determine which have the requisite impact to trigger more stringent controls. FDA has determined that the special issues related to genetic testing or predictive genetic testing do not warrant establishing a more stringent degree of regulatory control over ASRs used in these tests at this time. FDA believes that regulating most ASRs as restricted class I devices exempt from premarket notification establishes appropriate initial controls in the event more stringent requirements are later determined to be necessary for ASRs used in genetic tests.

62 Fed. Reg. 62,243, 62,244–46 (1997). Why are ASRs, which are complex chemicals, regulated as any sort of "devices" under the FDCA? How can the FDA argue that it's appropriate to regulate any class of ASRs as restricted medical devices? Finally, how can the agency assert regulatory jurisdiction over home-brews, which never leave the laboratory where they

are manufactured? See Richard A. Merrill, Genetic Testing: A Role for FDA?, 41 Jurimetrics J. 63 (2000).

3. *Limitations of genetic testing.* With the completion of the human genome map, the identification of genes that contribute to the development of a wide variety of diseases, traits, and conditions continues to accelerate. Once identified, it is usually possible to test an individual's genome for the presence of a mutation on a gene or genes associated with a disease or trait. Although the current state of technology permits identification of such mutations, it offers little in the way of gene therapy or prophylaxis. With mutations on the BRCA–1 or BRCA–2 genes that increase the risk of breast and ovarian cancer, for example, affected women can increase surveillance in order to detect developing cancer early, but there is no way at present to "engineer" a cure for the mutation so that the disease can be prevented. The only available prophylaxis is oophrectomy or mastectomy while the tissue is still healthy, an option that many women understandably prefer to avoid. See Gail Geller et al., "Decoding" Informed Consent: Insights from Women Regarding Breast Cancer Susceptibility Testing, 27 Hastings Ctr. Rep. 28 (1997). In the case of another type of familial cancer—hereditary diffuse gastric cancer—recent reports recommend predictive genetic testing to identify affected family members with germ-line mutations in the CDH1 gene and suggest "consideration of prophylactic gastrectomy in young, asymptomatic carriers" of the mutation. See David G. Huntsman et al., Early Gastric Cancer in Young, Asymptomatic Carriers of Germ–Line E–Cadherin Mutations, 344 New Eng. J. Med. 1904, 1904 (2001); see also Jeffrey N. Weitzel & Laurence E. McCahill, The Power of Genetics to Target Surgical Prevention, 344 New Eng. J. Med. 1942, 1943 (2001) (suggesting that "[t]he risks and benefits of prophylactic surgery must be balanced against the efficacy of screening, the risk of cancer, and the lethality of the particular form of cancer"). Many physicians cannot accurately calculate and convey a genetic test's "positive predictive value"—the likelihood that a person who tests positive for a mutation will actually get the disease. Thus, many patients tested receive false reassurance, or become inappropriately worried about their future risk of disease. A test's predictive value depends in part on the degree of penetrance of the genetic condition; in other words, the presence of some mutations indicates a high likelihood that the disease will develop, while for other mutations, the likelihood of disease is far lower, or more subject to influence by other genes and non-genetic factors such as environment.

4. *Discrimination and disclosure.* Health care professionals who test patients for the presence of genetic mutations often fail to provide appropriate counseling to the individuals tested about the implications of the test results. Moreover, healthy people whose genetic test results indicate that they are at increased risk for future disease may be subject to discrimination by employers or health insurers, though state and federal legislation has begun to make inroads against discriminatory practices. See Henry T. Greely, Health Insurance, Employment Discrimination, and the Genetics Revolution, in The Code of Codes: Scientific and Social Issues in the Human Genome Project 264 (Daniel J. Kevles & Leroy Hood eds., 1992); Mark A. Rothstein, Discrimination Based on Genetic Information, 33

Jurimetrics J. 13 (1992); Rick Weiss, Ignorance Undercuts Gene Tests' Potential, Wash. Post, Dec. 2, 2000, at A1. There are other privacy concerns as well. The American Society of Human Genetics (ASHG) has issued a statement dealing with the problems of disclosing genetic information to the tested individual and his or her family members. The ASHG statement deals with such thorny issues as whether it is appropriate for a physician to disclose the results of a genetic test to the tested individual's estranged family members if the results indicate the presence of a preventable genetic disease. See ASHG Statement: Professional Disclosure of Familial Genetic Information, 62 Am. J. Human Genetics 474 (1998); see also National Society of Genetic Counselors Code of Ethics, in Prescribing Our Future: Ethical Challenges in Genetic Counseling 169–71 (1993); Alice Wexler, Mapping Fate: A Memoir of Family, Risk, and Genetic Research (1995) (chronicling the author's family history of Huntington's disease, the development of a genetic test for the Huntington's marker, and the author's struggle with the decision to be tested); Jeffrey N. Weitzel, Genetic Cancer Risk Assessment: Putting It All Together, 86 Cancer 2483 (1999).

5. *Gene chips.* Another new technology—gene expression chips—enables scientists to assess in thousands of genes simultaneously which genes are active within a cell at any given time, which will facilitate understanding of how gene activity switches on and off within cells and how cell function changes over time. See Hadley C. King & Animesh A. Sinha, Gene Expression Profile Analysis by DNA Microarrays: Promise and Pitfalls, 286 JAMA 2280 (2001); Nicholas Wade, Now, the Hard Part: Putting the Genome to Work, N.Y. Times, June 27, 2000, at F1. Gene chips are actually glass slides with microscopic pieces of genetic material attached to them. When biological samples come into contact with the chips, the genetic material from the gene chips binds with complementary material in the sample. The resulting patterns of binding allow researchers to understand the precise mechanism of disease and protein production at the genetic level. See Justin Gillis, Corning's Latest Reinvention: Glass Firm Enters the Uncertain Gene–Chip Market, Wash. Post, May 9, 2001, at E1. Gene chips may also prove useful in testing with more speed and accuracy the toxic effects of chemicals and drugs on the body—a new technique called toxicogenomics. Once perfected, toxicogenomics could allow physicians to select optimal medications for individuals based on their particular genetic sensitivities. See Andrew Pollack, DNA Chip May Help Usher in a New Era of Product Testing, N.Y. Times, Nov. 28, 2000, at F2 (also discussing the "mixed blessing" that such technology might represent for pharmaceutical companies).

2.   THERAPEUTIC APPLICATIONS

Edward A. Marshall, Note, *Medical Malpractice in the New Eugenics: Relying on Innovative Tort Doctrine to Provide Relief When Gene Therapy Fails*
35 GA. L. REV. 1277 (2001).

Mapping the human genome, the 3.12 billion nucleotide "letter" sequence that makes up human DNA, has taken place years ahead of even the most optimistic estimates of the scientific community. Isolating a protein that corresponds with one of the 30,000 human genes, which years ago could have taken up to a decade, now can be done in a matter of seconds simply by searching a computer database. Even more remarkable than the present advances in genetic biotechnology, however, is the inevitable transformation that genetic research will effectuate on the practice of medicine in the future. * * *

The basic premise behind gene therapy is deceptively simple: after determining what gene or genes are "defective" within a given individual's genome, a "normal" copy of the imperfect gene is inserted in an individual to alter the production of proteins within the cell. This alteration, if successful, would prevent the manifestation of a "genetic" disorder by repairing the malfunctioning sequence of nucleotides on the strands of DNA. This section explores the basic procedural model of how gene therapy "works," describes different categories of human gene therapy, and explores obstacles to successful gene therapy that must be overcome before it is available for widespread application in humans.

1. *Inserting a More Perfect Gene.* For gene therapy to be effective as a treatment for a "genetic" disorder, a physician must not only identify the defective gene or genes within a patient, but must also devise a method for inserting a "normal" copy of the gene (the transgene) into a patient's cells. No microscopic tweezers have yet been developed that can accomplish this task. Instead, geneticists have developed, and continue to develop, transgenic "vectors" that act as vehicles, carrying the transgenic materials into the patient and penetrating the patient's cells.

The "vectors" studied and employed thus far in human genetic alteration are genetically altered viruses—with the viral component replaced with the transgene sought to be introduced into the patient's cells. In fact, the genetically manipulated cold virus, also known as the adenovirus, is the most common transgenic vector currently being used. When vectors penetrate the cell, the transgene is then integrated with the patient's genome, and the process of transcription then produces the mRNA that, through transcription, should produce the same proteins that would have been synthesized from a "normal" gene.

2. *Types of Human Gene Therapy.* The process of gene therapy could theoretically be employed to manipulate two types of human cells. The first, somatic cells, are cells that are "component[s] of the body," such as white blood cells or bone marrow stem cells, that are incapable of being fertilized and, thus, not involved in the process of reproduction. Due to the non-reproductive nature of somatic cells, somatic cell gene therapy is analogous to conventional enzyme therapy or organ transplants in that the effects extend only to the patient herself. This is significant as, even after a successful somatic cell gene therapy procedure, any preexisting defect in the patient's genes could still be passed on to her children. More importantly, after a negligently performed somatic gene therapy, there is essentially no direct effect on subsequent generations.

The opposite is true when the manipulated cells are germ-line cells, which produce eggs and sperm. These cells, unlike somatic cells, are involved in the process of reproduction, and genes contained in these cells are thus capable of being passed on to the offspring of an individual. Since a negligent germ-line gene therapy procedure could detrimentally affect a patient's offspring, the ramifications of the procedure present a multigenerational problem as well as ethical considerations not involved in somatic cell gene therapy.

Somatic gene therapy has been available for treatment in humans affected by ADA–SCID (an immune disorder resulting in the death of white blood cells) since 1990, and geneticists expect human somatic gene therapy treatments for various other diseases to become available in the near future. Germ-line therapy, however, has not yet been performed in humans. Looking to the future, the widespread use of germ-line therapy in humans is questionable as, despite the efficacy of being able to "cure" multiple generations of a given defect with a single treatment, the moral and ethical controversy surrounding germ-line therapy may prove an insurmountable barrier.

3. *Biological Obstacles to Widespread Use of Gene Therapy in Humans.* Despite the success gene therapy has achieved in limited contexts, it remains to a large extent a "hellishly difficult" procedure. The first challenge is to identify an adequate vector in which to transport the transgene. The most common vector currently being employed by geneticists to transport transgenes into human cells is the adenovirus. While capable of carrying the therapeutic gene into the human body, the adenovirus often triggers an immune response that can destroy the needed gene, and may endanger the patient. In fact, complications resulting from the use of an adenovirus vector can be fatal. Researchers continue to experiment with other vectors that may prove superior in effectuating the gene replacement while creating fewer risks.

The second barrier facing the practice of eugenics that may stall widespread use of gene therapy involves establishing more site-specific gene insertion procedures. Integration of a transgene into the human genome ideally would involve target gene-replacement, with the transgene actually taking the place of the defective gene on the patient's chromosome. At present, however, gene therapy technology only allows for gene-addition procedures, which "simply add functional copies of the gene that is defective in the patient to the genomes of the recipient cells ... [with] the introduced genes ... inserted at random or nearly random sites in the chromosomes of the host cells." The problem with this type of gene therapy is twofold. First, the distance between the inserted transgene and the location along the chromosome where the "normal" gene is ordinarily present may disrupt the interaction with the surrounding genes that send signals initiating and halting protein synthesis. Second, placing the transgene at random along the chromosome increases the probability that it will alter the structure of another, "normal" gene, thereby disrupting an essential genetic process. Fortunately, these problems of gene addition may soon be resolved through recently developed targeting and selection strategies, which have already produced limited success in inserting a transgene at the appropriate place along the genetic sequence. In fact, geneticists predict that "[i]n the future, targeted gene replacements will probably become the method of choice for ... gene therapy treatment of human diseases." * * *

NOTES AND QUESTIONS

1. *Prospects for gene therapy.* A number of commentators have suggested that the promise of gene therapy may remain unfulfilled, but others disagree. Although the science has not progressed as rapidly as initial reports predicted, physicians and researchers have achieved some success in developing gene therapy techniques. Researchers have already achieved some success in using gene therapy to treat diseases such as severe combined immunodeficiency (SCID). Progress in the treatment of other diseases such as hemophilia, Parkinson's disease, cystic fibrosis, and certain chronic infectious diseases also continues. See W. French Anderson, The Best of Times, the Worst of Times, 288 Science 627 (2000). One recent experimental protocol involved transferring a gene encoding for human blood factor VIII into autologous cells (fibroblasts) and then cloning the cells and reintroducing them into the patients' bodies to treat severe hemophilia. See David A. Roth et al., Nonviral Transfer of the Gene Encoding Coagulation Factor VIII in Patients with Severe Hemophilia A, 344 New Eng. J. Med. 1735 (2001) (describing successful transfer of genetically-modified and cloned factor VIII-producing cells in four out of six studied subjects with effects lasting ten months and no serious side effects); see also Louis J. Elsas, II, Medical Genetics: Present and Future Benefits, 49 Emory L.J. 801 (2000) (providing an overview of the different categories of genetic medicine, and discussing the current and projected development of these technologies); Randal J. Kaufman, Advances Toward Gene Therapy for Hemophilia at the Millennium, 10 Human Gene Ther. 2091 (1999); Daniel G. Miller & George Stamatoyannopoulos, Gene Therapy for Hemophilia, 344 New Eng. J. Med. 1782 (2001) (providing an optimistic discussion of the future of gene therapy for this condition, and reviewing several scientific concerns surrounding the current technology).

2. *Federal jurisdiction over gene therapy.* Federal guidelines governing research with rDNA were first issued in 1976. See 41 Fed. Reg. 27,902 (1976); see also 62 Fed. Reg. 4782 (1997) (describing restructuring and function of the RAC). For those protocols that receive public funding, the researcher must comply with both FDA requirements and NIH regulations and oversight. See 59 Fed. Reg. 34,496 (1994) (superceding all previous NIH guidelines); see also 63 Fed. Reg. 26,018 (1998). More recently, the FDA issued a guidance document that stated that "all gene therapy products and most somatic cell therapy products are regulated by the FDA" under its proposed approach to the regulation of cellular and tissue-based products. See FDA, Guidance for Human Somatic Cell Therapy and Gene Therapy (1998), at 4, available at <www.fda.gov/cber>. The FDA regulates experimental gene therapy protocols like other experimental drug and biological product therapies; the agency expects researchers to obtain an IND for the gene therapy product. See id. According to the FDA, existing statutory and regulatory authority easily encompasses the regulation of human gene therapy products and processes:

> As a consequence of scientific and biotechnological progress during the past decade, new therapies involving somatic cells and genetic material are being investigated, and commercial development of products for use in somatic cell therapies and gene therapies is occurring. Existing FDA statutory authorities, although enacted prior to the advent of somatic cell and gene therapies, are sufficiently broad in scope to encompass these new products and require that areas such as quality control, safety, potency, and efficacy be thoroughly addressed prior to marketing.... This statement is intended to present the agency's current approach to regulating somatic cell and gene therapy products. For the purpose of this statement, somatic cell therapy products are defined as autologous (i.e., self), allogeneic (i.e., intra-species), or xenogeneic (i.e., inter-species) cells that have been propagated, expanded, selected, pharmacologically treated, or otherwise altered in biological characteristics ex vivo to be administered to humans and applicable to the prevention, treatment, cure, diagnosis, or mitigation of disease or injuries. Cellular products intended for use as somatic cell therapy are biological products subject to regulation pursuant to the PHS Act and also fall within the definition of drugs in the FDCA.

58 Fed. Reg. 53,248 (1993); see also Judith A. Cregan, Light, Fast, and Flexible: A New Approach to Regulation of Human Gene Therapy, 32 McGeorge L. Rev. 261 (2000); David A. Kessler et al., Regulation of Somatic–Cell Therapy and Gene Therapy by the Food and Drug Administration, 329 New Eng. J. Med. 1169 (1993); Michael J. Malinowski & Maureen A. O'Rourke, A False Start? The Impact of Federal Policy on the Genotechnology Industry, 13 Yale J. on Reg. 163 (1996); Joseph M. Rainsbury, Biotechnology on the RAC–FDA/NIH Regulation of Human Gene Therapy, 55 Food & Drug L.J. 575 (2000); Christine Wilgoos, Note, FDA Regulation: An Answer to the Questions of Human Cloning and Germline Therapy, 27 Am. J.L. & Med. 101 (2001). What problems exist with the FDA's assertion of jurisdiction over gene therapy "products"? Is the fact that most of these "products" are actually complex scientific *processes*, frequently customized for the individual patient, fatal to the claimed categorization of gene therapy as a biologic or drug?

3. *Flaws in oversight.* In 1999, Jesse Gelsinger, an 18–year-old patient with a rare metabolic disorder, died from a reaction to an experimental gene therapy treatment at the University of Pennsylvania. Gelsinger had a mild form of the disorder and was doing well on a combination of a restricted diet and medications, but he volunteered to test the gene therapy for safety so that it could later be used in infants with a more severe and deadly form of the disease. After receiving a large dose of corrective genes via a weakened cold virus vector, he suffered an "overwhelming inflammatory reaction." The FDA temporarily suspended all human research at Penn's Institute for Human Gene Therapy. The RAC later began an inquiry into his death and the protocol that caused it. See Eliot Marshall, Gene Therapy on Trial, 288 Science 951 (2000); Sheryl Gay Stolberg, The Biotech Death of Jesse Gelsinger, N.Y. Times Mag., Nov. 28, 1999, at 137. The FDA investigated the protocol and discovered a number of violations of the human subjects protection regulations. See Wilder J. Leavitt, Note, Regulating Human Gene Therapy: Legislative Overreaction to Human Subject Protection Failures, 53 Admin. L. Rev. 315 (2001). In addition, revelations of flaws in the informed consent process and inappropriate financial connections between the PI and a sponsoring biotechnology company led Paul Gelsinger, Jesse's father, to file a lawsuit against the University of Pennsylvania, which decided to settle. See Sheryl Gay Stolberg, Gene Therapy Ordered Halted at University, N.Y. Times, Jan. 22, 2000, at A1; Rick Weiss & Deborah Nelson, Penn Settles Gene Therapy Suit: University Pays Undisclosed Sum to Family of Teen Who Died, Wash. Post, Nov. 4, 2000, at A4.

4. *Ethical concerns.* Most gene therapy protocols at this point affect only the patient's somatic cells; these therapies do not modify reproductive cells, and therefore cannot affect the genome of the patients' children. Germ-line therapies—therapies that alter reproductive cells—could theoretically eradicate genetic disease in future generations, though some ethicists and scientists have expressed concern about unforeseen effects on the genome and the resurgence of eugenics. See George J. Annas, The Man on the Moon, Immortality, and Other Millennial Myths: The Prospects and Perils of Human Genetic Engineering, 49 Emory L.J. 753 (2000); Paul R. Billings et al., Human Germline Gene Modification: A Dissent, 353 Lancet 1873 (1999); Maxwell J. Mehlman, The Human Genome Project and the Courts: Gene Therapy and Beyond, 83 Judicature 124 (1999); Maxwell J. Mehlman, The Law of Above Averages: Leveling the New Genetic Enhancement Playing Field, 85 Iowa L. Rev. 517 (2000); Michael H. Shapiro, The Technology of Perfection: Performance Enhancement and the Control of Attributes, 65 S. Cal. L. Rev. 11 (1991). For an excellent overview of the practical, ethical, and scientific arguments for and against somatic and germline gene therapy, see Bernard Gert et al., Morality and the New Genetics: A Guide for Students and Health Care Providers (1996).

5. *Pharmacogenomics—the latest designer drug technology.* The improved understanding of the human genome now promises new developments in customized medicine. Pharmacogenomics refers to the science of utilizing genetic variations to facilitate drug development and to create optimal patient treatments. Moreover, because human beings exhibit a great deal of genetic variation, better understanding of individual differences presents an opportunity for physicians to tailor "designer drugs" to suit their patients' individual genetic quirks. See Amalia M. Issa, Ethical Considerations in Pharmacogenomics Research, 21 Trends in Pharmacol. Sci. 247 (2000); Allen D. Roses, Pharmacogenetics and the Practice of Medicine, 405 Nature 857 (2000); Janice Hopkins Tanne, The New Word in Designer Drugs, 316 Brit. Med. J. 1930 (1998) (explaining that an improved ability to predict an individual patient's response to certain therapies can avoid expensive but inefficacious treatments in certain patients); see also Human Genome Project Information, Pharmacogenomics (2001), available at <www.ornl.gov/hgmis/medicine/pharma.html>.

The possibility of genetic testing to predict an individual patient's response to a particular drug therapy has met with mixed responses from pharmaceutical companies. One major drug manufacturer has filed for patents on genetic tests to assess the efficacy of its asthma medication, but apparently it intends to obtain the patent in order to prevent others from testing patient responses to its blockbuster drug. Other companies have shown some interest in genetic tests as a possible vehicle to keep drugs that are dangerous to a small percentage of patients on the market by pre-testing patients to weed out those who will have an adverse reaction. But some critics suggest that pharmaceutical companies are wary of genetic testing and "personalized" medicine because they fear that such testing will expose the limitations of their drugs and, ultimately, decrease sales. See Geeta Anand, Big Drug Makers Try to Postpone Custom Regimens, Wall St. J., June 18, 2001, at B1. Conversely, where multiple drugs exist to treat a condition, and patients respond to some better than others, pharma-cogenomics could replace today's trial-and-error approach in a way that would benefit the industry: patients would begin therapy more quickly, they would better comply with dosing schedules, and they might suffer fewer side effects. See Todd R. Golub, Genome–Wide Views of Cancer, 344 New Eng. J. Med. 601 (2001) (explaining that the developing science of molecular medicine will enable physicians to prescribe drugs that target diseases more efficiently with fewer harmful side effects, and speculating that such technologies will prove particularly important in oncology); Kathryn A. Phillips et al., Potential Role of Pharmacogenomics in Reducing Adverse Drug Reactions, 286 JAMA 2270 (2001). A number of pharmaceuti-cal companies are developing new drugs using information from gene databases to design proteins that target enzymes associated with particular diseases. See, e.g., Barry Werth, The Billion Dollar Molecule: One Compa-ny's Quest for the Perfect Drug (1994); Andrew Pollack, Drug Developed from Gene Study Tested on People, N.Y. Times, Feb. 26, 2001, at C14 (describing early trials of a small-molecule drug discovered through gene database hunting and designed to treat cardiovascular disease).

How might pharmacogenomics pose a challenge to existing regulatory mechanisms? Taken to an improbable extreme of complete customization, drug manufacturing would come to resemble pharmacy compounding and, in products liability terms, represent the provision of a service rather than sale of a product. Even the more probable tendency toward fragmenting patient populations into smaller subsets will pose challenges. Will clinical trials become even larger? Will more drugs qualify for orphan status? Should they in order to counteract the financial disincentives resulting from smaller market shares? Might some patient populations lose out? Will labeling suffice to educate physicians about pharmacogenomic data? Will diagnostic tests have to be bundled with these drug products? See Lars

Noah, The Coming Pharmacogenomics Revolution: Tailoring Drugs to Fit Patients' Genetic Profiles (forthcoming 2002).

PROBLEM #15. *THE REGULATORY PITFALLS OF CUSTOMIZED MEDICINES*

You are the in-house attorney for a biotechnology company called Bio–Orb. You've just had a meeting with the scientific director, who informs you excitedly that they are ready to begin Phase III clinical trials of their new drug product, Lodropol, which is intended to treat hypertension. There are several classes of hypertension drugs currently on the market, including calcium channel blockers (CCBs), ACE inhibitors, and diuretics. Some patients respond well to one type of blood pressure drug, some to another, but individual response is unpredictable. Until now, physicians have had to prescribe by trial and error until they find a drug that will reduce their patient's blood pressure without causing unwanted side effects. For some patients, none of the available drugs are both safe and effective. Trial and error prescribing suggests that approximately one-third of hypertension patients ("the BP subpopulation") experience adverse reactions to CCBs and ACE inhibitors, and at the same time find that diuretics do not control their condition adequately.

Bio–Orb used molecular medicine techniques and an improved understanding of genetics to target the precise biochemical mechanism responsible for elevating blood pressure. Its molecular biologists and geneticists isolated the gene responsible for the adverse reactions in the BP subpopulation, and they used this information to develop Lodropol—a drug that is closely related in chemical structure to CCBs but theoretically should not cause the same adverse reactions. The company's scientists also developed a genetic test to predict which patients fall into the BP subpopulation. Bio–Orb believes that Lodropol will control hypertension with virtually no side effects in this patient subpopulation. (It is less certain how effective the drug will be for other high blood pressure patients.)

Bio–Orb plans to seek FDA permission to conduct large-scale Phase III clinical trials on Lodropol. The scientific director wants your advice about how to design a protocol that will produce the best evidence of Lodropol's efficacy within the bounds of legal constraints on human subjects research. She asks you to look at the patient selection issues (for example, should they test the product on all hypertension patients, or just the BP subpopulation?), placebo controls, and the risk-benefit assessment, among other things.

Assuming that the clinical trials go well, the scientific director wants to know what sorts of problems to expect during the drug licensing process. How will the agency assess risk and benefit for this unusual product? What other problems might arise? The company is also exploring the possibility of separately commercializing the genetic test to predict which patients can most benefit from Lodropol. The director wonders whether there is any legal or practical downside to marketing such a test?

C.   BIOETHICAL CHALLENGES POSED BY MEDICAL TECHNOLOGY

The preface to this casebook refers to broad and narrow definitions of "technology." The broad sense of the word encompasses all scientific and medical knowledge, whereas the narrower sense refers to the products and processes developed through the application of scientific knowledge and used, directly or indirectly, in medical care. The advent of new medical technologies, in both the broad and narrow meaning of the term, has shaped bioethical norms in a variety of interesting ways. The discipline of bioethics began in the 1960s in response to ethical dilemmas associated with medical research and new medical technologies such as hemodialysis. Bioethics seeks to apply several fundamental principles, including beneficence, patient autonomy, nonmaleficence, and justice, in making medical decisions for individual patients in the clinical setting and for society as a whole. Beneficence refers to the obligation to further the patient's best interests, and nonmaleficence requires the caregiver to avoid harming the patient, or to minimize the harm when it is unavoidable. See John C. Fletcher et al., Introduction to Clinical Ethics 4–12 (2d ed. 1997). The following section introduces some scenarios in which the intersection of technology and medicine has created new ethical problems in medicine, and it examines some challenges for the future.

Michael H. Shapiro, *Is Bioethics Broke?: On the Idea of Ethics and Law "Catching Up" with Technology*
33 IND. L. REV. 17 (1999).

* * * Debates about technology and how we manage it often seem to shift without notice between critiques of ethical and legal evaluation, on the one hand, and critiques of the technological uses that draw our attention and dismay, on the other. Those who object to acquiring or using certain kinds of knowledge may criticize those who secured or applied it. * * * If the critical reactions derive from a failure within bioethics to deal with material problems, or from infirm perception or reasoning, then the criticisms are at least partly well taken. However, if the disagreement stems from deep differences in values, it is misleading and question-begging to say that the discipline, or some segment of it, is at fault for anything other than taking a different position from that of its critics. Of course, those in deep moral disagreement are very likely to find their opponents guilty of material omissions and failures of insight. Although it is sometimes hard to separate critiques of applied technology from critiques of technology assessment, complaints about a technological use and complaints about how we morally and legally assess it are not the same. * * *

The complaint that current ethical analysis is a turtle chasing a hare often rests on a simple matter: such analysis may not provide answers, at least definitive this-is-the-way-it-is-and-must-be answers, to difficult moral issues. If a medical laboratory can determine cell counts within a narrow range of uncertainty, or that the fibula is fragmented, or that your zorch is inflamed, why is ethics unable to yield definitive answers? If it cannot, what good is it? Here is a brief illustration of the sorts of expectations some have when appealing to the discipline of bioethics for answers.

Scientists trying to map genes think they are on the verge of figuring out how to build an artificial life form. J. Craig Venter hopes to salvage DNA from dead bacteria to construct an artificial organism. His interest centers on a tiny bacterium called *Mycoplasma genitalium*. It lives in the human genital tract and lungs, causing no known disease, but has the distinction of having fewer genes than any other organism mapped so far, making it a good model for figuring out precisely which genes are essential for life. "We are attempting to understand what the definition of life is," said Dr. Venter of Celera Genomics Corp. in Rockville, Md. "We are trying to understand what the minimum set of genes is." Before he goes any further, Dr. Venter said he wants advice from experts on ethics and religion. "We are asking whether it is ethical to synthetically make life," he said. * * *

Although some may think that ethics experts have special knowledge about rightness and goodness, that view is doubted by many, including most ethical theorists and "ethicists." Indeed, some modern democratic movements seem to reject the very possibility of special moral insight or expertise. Perhaps it would be too strong to call it a mass delusion, but many within democratic systems think that one person's views on most matters are as good as another's. In particular, bottom-line moral conclusions are thought to be as fit for one citizen as for another if one assumes that the relevant situational facts are available to all. It may well be true, for example, as Professor Robert Holmes urges, that neither meta-, normative, nor applied ethicists can "make better moral judgments in particular situations than anyone else." * * *

There is at least one sense in which the claim that "technology has outrun ethics and law" is not that puzzling. People often complain of having too much information or too much choice and perhaps even too many ethical theories on the philosophy supermarket shelves. The "too much" label is a somewhat tendentious description; we may well be better off overall with more information and opportunities. Nevertheless, increased choice and knowledge bear certain costs, at least for some decision makers—e.g., a sense of oppression from a felt responsibility to assure the best outcome by canvassing all options and considering all information. * * *

The problem with biomedical technology, however, is not simply that we have more options and information of the same sort that we had before * * * * We have new kinds of choices: choices over the traits of offspring (prenatal and preconception testing; cloning); choices concerning control of mind and behavior (antipsychotic drugs; intellect-enhancing drugs); choices about lifesaving efforts (organ transplantation); and so on. Furthermore, we have new, possibly exaggerated visions of ourselves, our powers, and our progression. We may see our thought and behavior as less "free" and more "determined," and worry over the blurring of the boundaries between ourselves and other forms of life, or even machines. We encounter new difficulties of description and evaluation that may seem deeper and reflect far greater dangers than do those arising from choice in other contexts. The fact that we cannot get a precise fix on what these dangers might be makes matters worse because of the very namelessness of the risks. The range and difficulty of choice over matters we have never or only marginally dealt with before may seem to exceed our capacities for rational choice. What is that wretched state in which one permanently loses all faculties of thought and feeling, but one's bodily functions continue? Should we choose to say it is death because the person we knew seems irretrievably gone, despite his body's endurance? Who is the natural parent of a cloned offspring, or is there even any such thing?

This expanded range of choice reflects moral/conceptual difficulties, not just an increase in things to choose from. However, this is not what prevents moral and legal analysis from gaining on technology. Such analysis does not progress or advance in the same way as technology. They are not even on the same race track. Determining how Sarah Jr. shall be constructed when we have her germ line in hand in an early embryo cannot be answered just by gathering more information, or running brilliant experiments, or even by getting smarter. * * *

Consider the debate about objectification, an important idea concerning a central premise of bioethical analysis. We are rightly concerned with the risk of transforming our view of ourselves as persons into a view of ourselves as manipulable objects. It is said that bioethics undervalues risks of objectification—our descent from persons to objects. Objectification, however, is one of the most heavily discussed issues in bioethics. Indeed, in bioethics more people credit the risk of objectification than discount it. If something is wrong with bioethics here, it is that it overestimates that risk. In any case, search the literature for articles that do more than throw the term around. You will find some—but they do not characterize the field.

Instead, you will find material suggesting that simply using the term "products" to refer to children born of artificial technology indicates that we have already plunged into the abyss and are treating, say, babies born of in vitro fertilization (IVF) as things to be used as we wish. There is zero evidence to back this up; there is not even evidence to support the colorable view that investing heavy monetary, physical, and psychic resources in creating the child will result in intrusive parental control designed to assure a proper return on the investment. Even the term "objectification," used to describe a legitimate concern of bioethics, has itself been reduced to an analytically used slogan. * * *

The indictment of applied biology is often accompanied by claims that bioethics is infirm because it has failed to stop or even slow the onslaught of personhood-impairing technological advances. It has failed because its intellectual structure is impoverished or beholden to the wrong groups or values and so hastens our decline. This is so whether bioethics is viewed as a scholarly discipline, a body of law and legal practices, a set of customs and clinical practices, a set of attitudes and perspectives held by various groups, or any or all of these. Whatever it is, it is said to lack relevant perspectives, embrace the wrong values and value priorities, use the wrong paradigms and models and other modes of thought, and to be patriarchal and too oriented toward establishment culture.

The task here is to expose the vulnerabilities of these attacks. In this "critique of the critique" of biological technology and bioethics, I will complain, among other things, about how debates on the uses of life science technologies are framed and pursued in confused, confusing, and often misleading terms. * * * The explanation lies largely in a showing of how practices which radically rearrange life processes to suit specific wants generate conceptual and normative monsters: persons, entities, relationships, situations, and behaviors that escape the major abstractions we use to describe, explain, and evaluate human actions and circumstances. Of course, we encounter daily anomalies that do not fit nicely into our conceptual bins, but the failures recited here are special not only because they fit so poorly, but because they deal with foundational matters: whether we will come into or continue our existence, in what form, and under what constraints and circumstances. * * *

Our conceptual system is not assaulted because we cannot identify a clear boundary between negligence and due care, or between due and undue process. Nor is everyday language fatally flawed because there is no clear border between being tall and not being tall. Few would claim that we should abandon all concepts and distinctions because some of their applications are unclear, indeterminate, or change with time. Even simple conceptual vagueness, however, can lead to serious normative/conceptual problems as the world changes. Six-footers used to be giants and still are among some groups, but among other groups—think of the N.B.A.—six feet is pretty short. Do persons projected to be no more than six feet tall need growth hormone? Do early embryos from short people require genetic enhancement?

Similarly, * * * it is no garden-variety puzzle to be unable to identify a single natural mother when a fertilized ovum from one woman is gestated by another woman, who of course has no genetic connection to it. Here, the very structure of elemental notions like "mother" is in question. The concept itself has been fragmented as a result of our reconfiguration of the reproductive process.

This divide-conquer-and-confuse aspect of some biological technologies leads us to other characteristics of bioethical problems. Among the more notable are the reinforcement of the idea of the determinate, predictable, controllable, algorithmic person; the introduction of new purposes for our old life processes, as in producing fetuses to provide transplantable tissue rather than to reproduce; providing opportunities to further existing purposes with greater precision, as in controlling behavior with psychotropic drugs; and, more generally, substantially increasing our control over life processes, enabling greater predictability of traits and behavior. The very existence of such choice over matters not previously under our control is itself something of a conceptual anomaly.

Think, for example, of being able to determine the entire genome of a person-to-be through cloning, or of being able to heavily influence particular traits. If we can "construct" a person through technological alteration of her physiological system or her germ line, what sort of being should we construct? What new or strengthened purposes ought to be installed for life functions? What purposes for reproduction should be added or extended? The possibility of bone marrow transplantation suggests having babies—not just fetuses—to provide compatible tissue for transplantation. The prospect of cloning may inspire reproductive acts resting on the (mistaken) view that clones are locked into some common fate shared by all who have their defining genome. A given act of cloning may thus reflect the novel purpose, not simply of having children, but of perpetuating a line of identical persons raised to pursue some sharply bounded set of tasks requiring that their talents be matched to their assigned roles in life. Here, then, biological technology restructures reproductive processes in a way that generates anomalous lineage relationships, reinforces the images of persons as determinate entities, and provides us with additional reasons, possibly mistaken or objectionable, for using procreational mechanisms.

So, the arguably distinctive features of classic bioethical problems are that they involve, at the most abstract level, the directed revision of life processes and what this entails: the idea of the determinate person; the substitution of new purposes in using human capacities; and the general expansion of choice in constructing, controlling, and predicting life processes, in partial displacement of the natural randomness of life. These distinctive features of bioethics are not fully independent. The core idea is still the reordering of life processes into unclassified forms, giving us relationships (e.g., gestational mothers and "their" children and the children's "genetic parents"); entities (such as cryopreserved embryos); and powers (over our own fundamental structures, individually and collectively) that we often do not know how to deal with. Some believe that this transforms our vision of persons as free into an anti-vision of persons as machine-like or lower-animal-like—predictable, explainable, and controllable. * * *

One can plausibly criticize a discipline as conceptually and normatively impoverished because it fails to consider all material matters; that it proceeds illogically, incoherently, or otherwise carelessly or irrationally; that it is beset by conflicts of interest and imbalances of power; that it is biased, rigidly constrained by ideology, afflicted with false consciousness; and so on. It is less plausible, however, to complain because one simply disagrees with an outcome, without express regard to the approach used; or because (unthinkingly) the critic and the criticized assign different meanings to the same terms or concepts used in the decision making process. For example, rights-talk by one party may be at a different level of generality from that used by another; or a claim about prima facie rights might be taken as an absolute claim by another; or a claim about non-interference rights might be conflated with a claim about rights to affirmative assistance. * * *

Consider, for example, the idea of a commercial transaction as applied to human reproduction. A surrogacy arrangement can be as much a commercial exchange as the purchase of a clothes dryer. But saying this and abruptly ending the analysis is an immense descriptive and normative/conceptual error. Some indeed use the comparison to attack surrogacy as causing or constituting human commodification (the commercial version of objectification) by stressing the similarities between the two transactions—and then stopping without considering their differences. It is hard to see how the analysis could possibly be complete without doing both; there is no other rational way to deal with a purported parallelism. Moreover, the analogy is mishandled if one does not see that what even counts as "similarity" or "difference" may be contested. If a commentator or a discipline characteristically fail to confront both similarities and differences and the difficulties in recognizing them as such, then its decision making processes are indeed infirm. Making comparisons with blinders on may reflect lack of time for reflection, or lack of acuity. Disagreement about the results of the comparison, of course, does not nullify its worth; one's final judgment, however, is far better informed.

Moreover, an analogy may be useful in some contexts and not in others. For example, some nontrivial constitutional value probably applies to most forms of assisted sexual reproduction—artificial insemination (AI), IVF, etc.: with respect to sexual union in the general biological sense, they are identical. The social relationships involved may vary, but few doubt the status of these processes as human reproduction entitled to some constitutional protection. Some commentators, however, think that human asexual reproduction is so radically different that all constitutional bets are off: it is outside the Fourteenth Amendment's procreational autonomy ballpark. Its distance from paradigmatic sexual reproduction cannot be measured because the notion of "distance" does not readily apply. What is contested here is the very status of sexual recombination as a defining characteristic of human reproduction; the birth of a child is, for some, not enough to trigger constitutional protections of procreation.

For such observers then, comparison to a paradigm may work pretty well for AI, IVF, and even posthumous reproduction, but not for human cloning. The paradigm does not help establish anything one way or the other, or so one might argue. The asexual nature of cloning drives some critics to say, in effect, that it makes no sense to talk of the linear distance between sexual and asexual reproduction: they are utterly distinct and rival processes that should not bear the same designation—"procreation."

The upshot is that use of analogy or comparison to a paradigm need not be universally serviceable; the processes are not completely worthless merely because they sometimes fail. Much the same applies to entire disciplines: if the discipline reaches a decision different from yours, it will take a lot more beyond this bare fact to establish a failure of process and an impeachment of its practitioners. * * *

In general, the talk about law and ethics being behind science and technology has to be reconstructed to make sense. Law and ethics are categorically different from science and technology and from each other, despite isomorphisms in argument structure and the "fuzziness" of the fact/value distinction. They concern science and technology, they are about science and technology (and everything else), but they are a different order of existence, and it is thus impossible to apply the same sense of progress to both domains. Their canons of verification differ strongly, despite the structural similarities. There is no race between law and ethics on the one hand, and science and technology on the other. In many instances, indecision, paradox, and indeterminacy are not usefully considered flaws in law or in ethics because they are inherent in them. One is not deficient for failing to come up with a certainly correct answer when it is impossible to find one. * * *

I am not even remotely suggesting that progress is simply a function of process. The temptation to forego substance because of its uncertainties in favor of choosing fair procedures is understandable, and in various situations resort to procedural solutions may be the only available pragmatic strategy for securing an acceptable bottom-line decision. However, there can be no assurance that the process will culminate in a morally convincing answer or a situation that all would say is the best of the alternatives. Indeed, conscientious decisionmakers who find themselves planted within some procedural scheme, say, a committee to distribute scarce medical resources, will experience precisely the same difficulties encountered by those who, not knowing how to generate a right answer, established the procedure in the first place. What would be clearly amiss, then, is to assert that because we cannot resolve a matter definitively, something is wrong with moral and legal theory generally and bioethics in particular. There are many who cannot abide such uncertainty and the shortage of answers it entails. The only sensible response is: get used to it, because there is no honest alternative.

NOTES AND QUESTIONS

1. *"Normal" height and above-average aspirations.* Shapiro points out that, in some contexts, conceptual vagueness creates serious difficulties for medical decisionmaking. Take his example of the contextual variations in defining "normal" height. Controversy has emerged over the use of human growth hormone in normal children of short stature. See Committee on Drugs and Committee on Bioethics, American Academy of Pediatrics, Considerations Related to the Use of Recombinant Human Growth Hormone in Children, 99 Pediatrics 122 (1997); Patricia McLaughlin, If Shortness Isn't a Disease, Why Are We Testing a Cure?, Hous. Chron., Nov. 1, 1993, at 3; see also Alice Dreger, When Medicine Goes Too Far in the Pursuit of Normality, N.Y. Times, July 28, 1998, at F4 ("Instead of constantly enhancing the norm—forever upping the ante of the 'normal' with new technologies—we should work on enhancing the concept of normal by broadening appreciation of anatomical variation."). In the relatively near future, parents may be able to use preimplantation genetic selection or genetic manipulation to choose or create taller children. Apart from the medical side-effects of such interventions, what other consequences would result if they became routine?

2. *Further commentary.* See Roger B. Dworkin, Limits: The Role of the Law in Bioethical Decision Making 18 (1996) (criticizing the law's role in bioethics, and opining that "our [legal institutional] tools for dealing with social problems posed by rapid change in biology and medicine are limited at best"); Owen D. Jones, Sex Selection: Regulating Technology Enabling the Predetermination of a Child's Gender, 6 Harv. J.L. & Tech. 1 (1992); Michael H. Shapiro, Constitutional Adjudication and Standards of Review Under Pressure from Biological Technologies, 11 Health Matrix 351 (2001); Michael H. Shapiro, Illicit Reasons and Means for Reproduction: On Excessive Choice and Categorical and Technological Imperatives, 47 Hastings L.J. 1081 (1996) (providing a critique of objectification arguments against the use of reproductive technologies).

1. HIGH-TECH DEFINITIONS OF DEATH

In re Bowman

617 P.2d 731 (Wash.1980).

■ UTTER, JUDGE:

* * * Death is both a legal and medical question. * * * Until recently, the definition of death was both medically and legally a relatively simple matter. When the heart stopped beating and the lungs stopped breathing, the individual was dead according to physicians and according to the law. The traditional definition did not include the criterion of lack of brain activity because no method existed for diagnosing brain death. Moreover, until recently, no mechanical means have been available to maintain heart and lung action; and respiration, heart action, and brain function are so closely related that without artificial support, the cessation of any one of them will bring the other two to a halt within a very few minutes. Thus, *Black's Law Dictionary* 488 (4th ed. 1951), based upon older medical technology, defines death as:

> The cessation of life; the ceasing to exist; defined by physicians as a total stoppage of the circulation of the blood, and a cessation of the animal and vital functions consequent thereon, such as respiration, pulsation, etc.

With the recent advancement of medical science, the traditional common law "heart and lungs" definition is no longer adequate. Some of the specific factors compelling a more refined definition are: (1) modern medicine's technological ability to sustain life in the absence of spontaneous heartbeat or respiration, (2) the advent of successful organ transplantation capabilities which creates a demand for viable organs from recently deceased donors, (3) the enormous expenditure of resources potentially wasted if persons in fact dead are being treated medically as though they were alive, and (4) the need for a precise time of death so that persons who have died may be treated appropriately.

The numerous legal issues which look to the time and presence of death as determining factors require a legal response to these new developments. Inheritance, liability for death claims under an insurance contract, proximate cause and time of death in homicide cases, and termination of life support efforts are but a few of the areas in which legal consequences follow from a determination of whether death has occurred. * * *

While 20 years ago a victim of cardiac arrest had little chance of survival, now, however, up to one in five victims returns to productive life. This advance in technology has produced a tragic problem not known before, of those whose cardiorespiratory systems may be kept functioning but whose brains have suffered massive and irreversible damage resulting in brain death. * * *

The determination by a physician that the symptoms of brain death are present, in accordance with acceptable medical standards, emphasizes that cessation of brain function is a symptom of the loss that makes a person dead, rather than the loss itself. It is the law's determination that brain death is the legal equivalent of death because—under current medical science—the capacity for life is irretrievably lost when the entire brain, including the brain stem, has ceased functioning. * * *

The medical profession has established criteria by which to measure whether brain death has occurred. * * * In 1968, a Harvard Medical School committee developed criteria which now constitute the basis of accepted medical standards for the determination of brain death. Ad Hoc Committee of the Harvard Medical School to Examine the Definition of Brain Death, A Definition of Irreversible Coma, 205 JAMA 337 (1968). These "Harvard criteria" require (1) unreceptivity and unresponsivity to even the most intensely painful stimuli; (2) no spontaneous movements or spontaneous breathing for at least 1 hour; (3) no reflexes, as shown by no ocular movement, no blinking, no swallowing, and fixed and dilated pupils. The report further recommended flat electroencephalograms (EEGs) as a confirmatory test, and that hypothermia and use of central nervous system depressants as causes be eliminated. * * * More recently, refinements in the criteria have been proposed. See Refinements in Criteria for the Determination of Death: An Appraisal, 221 JAMA 48 (1972); An Appraisal of the Criteria of Cerebral Death: A Summary Statement, 237 JAMA 982 (1977). * * *

Both courts and legislatures have responded to these medical advances and adopted brain death as a standard of death. * * * [We] adopt the provisions of the Uniform Determination of Death Act which state:

> An individual who has sustained either (1) irreversible cessation of circulatory and respiratory functions, or (2) irreversible cessation of all functions of the entire brain, including the brain stem, is dead. A determination of death must be made in accordance with accepted medical standards.

This standard reflects both the former common law standard and the evolutionary change in medical technology. * * *

Steven Goldberg, *The Changing Face of Death: Computers, Consciousness, and Nancy Cruzan*

43 STAN. L. REV. 659 (1991).

The law of death and dying is exquisitely sensitive to our notion of what it means to be human. When the crucial aspects of "personhood" are irretrievably lost, we feel that an individual has died. But what are those crucial aspects? Changes in the legal definition of death over time suggest that our sense of what is unique to the human experience alters as science progresses. * * *

[T]he next few decades may bring a dramatic change in our sense of human uniqueness and a corresponding change in the definition of death. The engine of change will be developments in artificial intelligence, the field of study devoted to building thinking computers. It is not the rational power of those computers that will shake us but rather the prospect that they might become self-aware. * * * [T]he current heated debate over whether such a thing is possible demonstrates the centrality of self-awareness to our sense of human uniqueness. * * *

In terms of legal doctrine, the centrality of human self-consciousness is best demonstrated by the modern approach to the definition of death. As Robert Veatch notes, any concept of human death depends directly on those qualities thought to make humans unique. By that standard, the modern trend is clear. In the space of a few decades, technology has pushed us from a world in which a beating heart symbolizes life to a world in which circulation, breathing, eating, and even responding to external stimuli are less important than human consciousness.

The interdependence of respiration, circulation, and brain function, coupled with the inability of technology to replace essential bodily functions, made the determination of death relatively uncontroversial in the first half of this century. The absence of respiration and heart function signified death. Beginning in the 1950s, however, artificial respirators and other life-support systems began to change the situation. It became possible to keep the body alive even though the brain had ceased functioning. It eventually became possible to replace virtually every part of the body except the brain with an artificial substitute.

These revolutionary technological developments caused a tremor in mankind's sense of self. A government commission, the Artificial Heart Assessment Panel at the National Heart and Lung Institute, responded by discussing "the problem of the 'man-machine symbiosis'—that is, the extent to which technological processes should be imposed upon, or substituted for, the natural processes of human beings." The panel focused its discussion on the artificial heart. As the panel put it, "[t]he heart has held pre-eminence in poetry and in common speech as the seat of bravery, love, joy, and generosity. Will its replacement by a mechanical pump and motor not merely place technology deep in man's bosom but place man more deeply in the bosom of technology?"

The development of the artificial heart and other mechanical life-support devices hardly forced mankind to admit equivalence with machines. The human thirst for uniqueness was easily satisfied by transferring all important characteristics to what was now the one remaining irreplaceable organ, the brain. A focus on the heart was dismissed as "symbolism" and "irrational." * * *

But the transfer of focus to the brain left difficult problems for medicine and law. Confronted for the first time with comatose individuals who had essential bodily functions sustained by machines, members of neither profession were certain of how to proceed. On the one hand, no one wanted to end the existence of someone who was likely to regain brain function, but on the other hand, the sense of respect for human dignity, the cost of medical treatment, and the need for transplant organs counseled for ending life support in certain cases. The result was a growing interest in "brain death," a concept that permitted death to be declared while the heart was still beating.

In this country, an influential step toward defining death in terms of the brain was the report of an ad hoc committee at the Harvard Medical School (the Committee) in 1968. The Committee emphasized that with modern technology, respiration and a heartbeat could be maintained "even when there is not the remotest possibility of an individual recovering consciousness following massive brain damage." Accordingly, the Committee believed that it was essential to try to redefine the point at which death occurs. The Committee proposed standards for determining when a patient should be declared dead because his or her brain was permanently nonfunctioning.

It became apparent, however, that the word "brain" itself was too broad for the purpose of defining death. The Committee recognized that a distinction must be made between "higher" brain and "lower" brain functions. Generally speaking, consciousness and cognition are carried on in the higher brain, that is, in the cerebrum, particularly the neocortex. By contrast, vegetative functions such as breathing and blood pressure are carried out by the brain stem, a portion of the lower brain. The distinction is critical because in many heart attacks and accidents the disturbance of circulatory or respiratory functions is too brief to destroy the brain stem, but it is sufficient to destroy the neocortex. The result of such a disturbance is an individual who is alive under a "whole brain" definition of death, because the lower part of the brain still works, but who would not be alive if a "higher brain" definition were used. Such individuals are in what is often termed a "persistent vegetative state." They can be kept alive with intravenous feeding and antibiotics, but they are unlikely to ever recover further. These individuals often need no mechanical aid to breathe; they maintain a heartbeat, react to light, and respond with other merely physical reflexes, but they lack all awareness and cognition. * * *

It is important to keep in mind the rapidity of these developments in order to understand the legal regime that grew out of them. In the space of a few decades, the centuries-old identification of death with the cessation of heartbeat and respiration was giving way to a brain-centered definition. Fundamental moral issues were being addressed at the same time that new diagnostic techniques were being developed. * * * [T]he net result was that the legal definition of death moved to a recognition that death of the whole brain meant death of the human being, even if the heart and lungs were still being artificially maintained. But the formal definition of death does not tell the whole story. For while death was defined in terms of the whole brain, legal decisions on the cessation of treatment, including that of mechanical feeding, recognized that treatment could end not only when the whole brain was dead, but also when the higher brain alone was destroyed.

The legal definition of death moved quickly to reflect the considerations set forth in the report of the Committee. An influential step in this direction was the 1972 article by Alexander Capron and Leon Kass proposing a model brain-death statute. Drawing in part on the Committee's report, the authors proposed that if artificial means were needed to keep respiration and circulation going, a person would be considered dead if "he has experienced an irreversible cessation of spontaneous brain functions." The authors emphasized that by "brain functions" they meant the whole brain, so that someone who had lost only higher brain functions would not be defined as dead. But the authors did not defend the proposition that lower brain functioning alone—a condition marked by spontaneous reflexes but no consciousness—constituted human life. On the contrary, they stipulated that "the exclusion of patients without neocortical function from the category of death may appear somewhat arbitrary." They defended the exclusion on the ground that they were taking a "modest" step to bring the definition of death in line with modern medicine and emphasized that modern medicine was not yet able to routinely diagnose irreversible higher brain death as clearly as whole brain death. Significantly, they left the door open to the notion that individuals with higher brain death should be allowed to die by stressing in a footnote to the article that they were distinguishing the question "is he dead?," from the question "should he be allowed to die?"

Two influential reports by the Presidents' Commission for the Study of Ethical Problems in Medicine and Biomedical and Behavioral Research took the same tack. The first, a 1981 report entitled *Defining Death*, opted for a whole-brain rather than a higher-brain definition of death. The second, a 1983 report entitled *Deciding to Forego Life–Sustaining Treatment*, stated that families could justifiably remove artificial feeding tubes from patients with no higher brain functions thus causing the death of those patients.

The law has generally paralleled these approaches. In most jurisdictions, statute or common law provides that an individual is dead if her whole brain has ceased functioning, even if breathing and circulation are artificially maintained. At the same time, prior to the *Cruzan* decision, "an unbroken stream of cases ha[d] authorized procedures for the cessation of treatment of patients in persistent vegetative states," that is, patients who suffered higher-brain death. Many of these cases involve the removal of feeding tubes from these patients. The courts' opinions have employed various theories, ranging from an assessment of the patient's previously expressed wishes to an analysis of the benefits of continued treatment, but the results have been the same. * * * So in the space of just a few decades, a remarkable consensus has developed in the medical and legal communities that those who have been permanently deprived of self-awareness by cessation of higher brain functioning can be allowed to die. Clearly, the emphasis on the higher brain has been driven by a concern for those qualities that make humans special. * * *

NOTES AND QUESTIONS

1. *Withdrawal of life-sustaining treatment.* In *Cruzan v. Director, Missouri Department of Health*, 497 U.S. 261 (1990), the plaintiff sustained permanent brain damage that left her in a persistent vegetative state. Her family sought court permission to withdraw life-sustaining nutrition and hydration that was delivered through a tube. The Supreme Court framed the constitutional question very narrowly, asking only whether the state of Missouri could constitutionally require a health care surrogate decision-maker to present "clear and convincing evidence" of Ms. Cruzan's wishes in order to permit the withdrawal of treatment. The Court concluded, by a bare majority, that the clear and convincing evidence requirement did not impermissibly infringe on Ms. Cruzan's 14th Amendment liberty interests. Although the *Cruzan* decision explicitly recognizes a constitutional right to refuse unwanted medical treatment by competent patients, it does not stand for the more general proposition that there is a constitutional "right to die." See Yale Kamisar, When Is There a Constitutional "Right to Die"? When Is There No Constitutional "Right to Live"?, 25 Ga. L. Rev. 1203 (1991); Thomas W. Mayo, Constitutionalizing the "Right to Die," 49 Md. L. Rev. 103 (1990).

2. *Further commentary.* See Alexander Morgan Capron & Leon R. Kass, A Statutory Definition of the Standards for Determining Human Death: An Appraisal and a Proposal, 121 U. Pa. L. Rev. 87 (1972); William C. Charron, Death: A Philosophical Perspective on the Legal Definitions, 1975 Wash. U. L.Q. 979; David Randolph Smith, Legal Recognition of Neocortical Death, 71 Cornell L. Rev. 850 (1986) (noting that advances in medical technology make it essential to examine the legal issues raised by cardiopulmonary, whole brain, and neocortical definitions of death); Stuart J. Younger & Edward T. Bartlett, Human Death and High Technology: The Failure of the Whole–Brain Formulation, 99 Annals Internal Med. 252 (1983); Eelco F.M. Wijdicks, The Diagnosis of Brain Death, 344 New Eng. J. Med. 1215 (2001) (reviewing the criteria for establishing brain death, including techniques for excluding conditions that mimic brain death).

3. *Technology's impact on changing conceptions of viability.* Advances in medical technology also impact medical decisionmaking at the beginning of life. As the Supreme Court explained in *Planned Parenthood v. Casey*, 505 U.S. 833, 871 (1992), "[t]he woman's right to terminate her pregnancy before viability is the most central principle" of *Roe v. Wade*, 410 U.S. 113 (1973). The Court rejected *Roe*'s trimester framework, however, in part because advances in neonatology had undercut the "rigid" trimester framework and made babies born before the end of the second trimester viable. See Webster v. Reproductive Health Serv., 492 U.S. 490 (1989).

2. TECHNOLOGY, RATIONING, AND THE CONCEPT OF FUTILITY

With the continuing advance of medical technology, patients and physicians have more treatment options than ever. Yet, at the same time, many available interventions appear to be of questionable therapeutic value. The proliferation of medical technology requires that physicians and ethicists think seriously about what constitutes medically appropriate care. Previous chapters in this casebook presented the question of medical benefit at a different level of generality. For example, Chapter 3 described how the FDA makes risk-benefit evaluations when it decides whether to approve a medical technology for marketing, and Chapter 9 considered the process by which payers make cost-benefit determinations when deciding whether to reimburse providers and patients for the use of particular technologies. But the FDA does not evaluate the appropriateness of new technology as part of the available array of medical interventions for a particular condition. It may approve a new type of neonatal incubator for very premature infants because the product works safely and effectively without ever pausing to consider whether providing the incubator for such infants is medically appropriate. Insurers may decide to reimburse patients for an extremely expensive oncology drug because it permits the average patient to live a month or two longer without pausing to evaluate whether the treatment provides a net benefit to the dying patient. Considerations of medical futility ask whether a technological intervention is medically appropriate for a particular patient apart from its safety or cost.

Mark A. Hall, *Rationing Health Care at the Bedside*
69 N.Y.U. L. REV. 693 (1994).

When we are ill, we desperately want our doctors to do everything within their power to heal us, regardless of the costs involved. Medical technology has advanced so far, however, that literal adherence to this credo for everyone would consume the entire gross domestic product. Therefore, the fundamental problem of how best to ration limited medical resources among competing beneficial uses must be resolved in order for this country to construct a workable system for financing and delivering health care.

This axiomatic statement of the problem assumes the necessity of rationing, which some policy analysts and most politicians continue to dispute. President Clinton adamantly asserted that his 1993 health care reform proposal would not cause rationing, a claim disputed by this critics.

Both sides of the political debate assume, then, that it is desirable and feasible to avoid rationing. As a few politicians and most policy analysts recognize, however, it is a fundamental law of the psychology of human wants that rationing in some form is inevitable. Every spending decision is necessarily a rationing decision simply because resources devoted to one person or one use are not available for someone or something else. Therefore, the question cannot be put whether rationing is avoidable, since we have always rationed health care resources on a massive scale, only according to irrational and unethical principles. * * * [F]or those who are fully insured, we devote vast resources to save lives and restore health once an illness or accident occurs, but we spend relatively little on safety, health education, and health prevention measure. Even within traditional medicine, care is rationed by limiting benefits for mental health, dental, and nursing home services. * * *

In searching for an acceptable form of rationing, we are plagued by two basic questions: (1) Who should decide what care is not worth the costs, and (2) What criteria of benefit should be used to make this determination? The substantive criteria problem is the one that has received more attention to date in the health care rationing literature. Numerous volumes have been written on questions such as whether the short supply of transplantable organs should be distributed based on simple queue or lottery systems or on elaborate concepts of medical need or medical benefit, and whether social worth factors can be prevented from tainting these concepts. Extensive literature has also developed around routine medical technologies asking whether medical resources generally should be rationed according to age or instead according to some more quantitative formula for cost-benefit or cost effectiveness. In the latter case, the literature discusses whether medical benefit should be defined in terms of lengths of life, quality of life, or some more intermediate end point such as diagnostic certainty.

These are tremendously important questions deserving of continuing inquiry, but they avoid what I see as the more fundamental question: Who should be the rationing decision maker? This question is more basic for three reasons. First, some decisionmaking mechanisms would obviate the need for an explicit consensus on criteria. For instance, the competitive market mechanism leaves the substantive criteria to individual choice as in other sectors of the economy where rationing is largely hidden. Second, even if we adopt more collective forms of rationing, it is highly unlikely that we will agree on a single, substantive criterion, or a lexical ordering of several rationing criteria. Therefore, the criteria question inevitably will be influenced by whatever decisionmaking framework we choose, whether political, medical professional, or market oriented. Third, even if agreement on general criteria were reached, their precise definition and application would depend on the broad range of discretion exercised by whomever implemented the criteria.

Fundamentally, three different rationing mechanisms are conceivable. Cost-sensitive treatment decisions can be made by patients, by physicians, or by third parties, primarily private and governmental insurers, but also various regulatory or review organizations. Although patient and third-party rationing are each systematically flawed, legal doctrine and ethical theory have leveled their strongest attack against physician rationing. * * *

Elsewhere in our economy, cost-benefit trade-offs are usually made through the purchasing decisions of individual consumers. For example, nutrition resources are allocated at both the macro and micro levels through the aggregation of countless, individual decisions of how much food to buy, of what quality, and from what source. This simple market mechanism, however, is not generally available or desirable for health care because of the unpredictability of illness and the complexities of medical judgment. We purchase insurance rather than pay out of pocket because we want to protect ourselves from the uncertain costs of health care and the anxiety of making spending decisions under the strain of serious illness. Moreover, even without insurance, we make few of our medical decisions ourselves because the complexity of treatment compels us to delegate extensive authority to our doctors.

These two structural elements—insurance and physician agency— make consumer rationing untenable for many health care purchasing decisions. Some role for consumer rationing may be preserved to the extent that insurance is incomplete, requiring, for instance, patients to pay deductibles and co-insurance. Consumer rationing may also occur to the extent that informed consent requirements place the ultimate authority in the hands of patients. But because consumers will always rely on insurance to insulate themselves from some health care costs, and because patients will always rely to a significant degree on their physicians' recommendations, medical spending decisions are necessarily made through the agency of insurance and the agency of physicians.

Insurers can ration through cost-sensitive rules about what treatment they will pay for, although to date this has seldom happened, either by private or governmental insurers. Oregon became the first state to attempt explicit rule-based rationing when it ranked over 600 condition-treatment pairings—e.g., surgery for appendicitis—according to medical effectiveness for purposes of allocating limited Medicaid funding. Other efforts are under way to develop a host of much more detailed and nuanced clinical practice guidelines, which could also serve as rule-based rationing tools.

As important as these efforts are, they will never produce a wholly satisfactory rationing scheme. The complexities of human mental and biological functioning and the state of medical science are such that no set of rules could possibly be detailed enough to capture all of the judgmental and value-laden aspects of medical decision making. A complete and scientifically valid set of rationing rules would entail the impossible task of developing rigorous empirical information for each of the almost 10,000 diagnostic entries in the World Health Organization's *International Classification of Diseases* and the almost 10,000 medical interventions listed in the AMA's *Current Procedural Terminology*. Moreover, even if such rules were completed and continuously updated, they would fail to reflect varying consumer preferences for different medical risks and health outcomes. Since these preferences cannot be fully captured in either patient-generated decisions or in third-party rules, we necessarily must resort to some degree of physician rationing * * * *

Despite the imperfections of rule-based third-party rationing, no one disputes that those who foot the bill for health care have a right to set some external limits on the particular items of service they will fund. Thus, for third-party rationing, the debate is only over establishing appropriate limits for its role and scope. In contrast, physician-based rationing remains controversial at a level of fundamental principle that questions whether it may occur at all. * * *

Victor Fuchs, an economist who champions health care rationing, expresses the common attitude of concern about the physician's role in rationing decisions: "The commitment of the individual physician to the individual patient is one of the most valuable features of American medical care. It would therefore be a great mistake to turn each physician into an explicit maximizer of the social-benefit/social-cost ratio in his or her daily practice." Embracing this concern, the dominant position among medical ethicists and the medical profession in general is a nearly absolute moral prohibition against physicians every considering the costs of treatment to any degree. This Article refers to this cost-is-no-object position as the physician's ethic of absolute quality. This ethic advocates that from the physician's perspective literally any marginal medical benefit, no matter how small, is worth absolutely any price because doctors in their role as healers should behave as if each of our lives is priceless. Adherents believe that rationing either is not necessary or that it must be imposed from external, societal sources. * * *

A divergent wing of less absolutist physicians and ethicists are more accommodating to bedside rationing. They recognize the necessity of rationing, are willing to contemplate that physicians will incorporate economic costs into their clinical judgments to some extent, and see this as preferable in some instances to rationing by market forces or by insurer or governmental fiat. Still, most adherents to this minority view impose the constraint that physicians be strictly insulated from any personal financial gain from their economizing decisions. These adherents believe that physicians should be allowed to mediate among the health care needs within a group of patients, but that they should not be financially rewarded for rationing. * * *

[M]uch of the opposition to bedside rationing can be explained by the fear that doctors will play God by overtly sacrificing life or health for some social agenda. Thus, many of the critics of physician rationing cited above focus on dramatic, life-or-death decisions such as terminating all treatment for the elderly or for severely injured children. But it is possible to support some measure of incremental bedside rationing and also to agree with the notion that it would be too corrosive of the treatment relationship for physicians to make high stakes, high drama rationing decisions without consulting their patients or relying on explicit regulatory or contractual authority. A more useful picture of bedside rationing involves physicians declining to order a confirming diagnostic test or an extra day in the hospital, prescribing a less expensive drug, or avoiding a referral to a specialist when the stakes are low or when their confidence in diagnosis and prognosis is fairly high already. * * *

[B]edside rationing would not require explicit cost-benefit calculations, although such calculations would not be prohibited. Instead, various mechanisms—education, peer influence, and financial incentives—would cause physicians to internalize cost consideration within their intuitive clinical judgment, encouraging then to adopt a more conservative, less interventionist practice style. Cost-benefit trade-offs would be largely subliminal in physicians' thought process, just as medical risk-benefit calculations at present are more often made through heuristic judgment rather than with rigorous calculation. * * *

Finally, it is important to realize that the argument over the choice of rationing mechanisms too often falsely pits unchannelled incentives against inflexible standards. This is not a winner-take-all contest; the ideal is likely to lie within a range of different mixtures between the two. As Richard Epstein has observed, the fact that the stakes are so high does not dictate one answer or the other but only underscores the importance of arriving at the correct result. We will never know which mixes are acceptable until the merits and flaws of each approach and their proper domains receive rigorous empirical inquiry and analytical debate. The problem is that in order to even broach this subject in a constructive manner, we must overcome the ethical and legal taboo against physicians ever considering the costs of their treatment decisions. * * *

Paul C. Sorum, *Limiting Cardiopulmonary Resuscitation*
57 Alb. L. Rev. 617 (1994).

Cardiopulmonary resuscitation (CPR) is the treatment for cardiac arrest. Cardiac arrest is the loss of an effective pumping action of the heart, so that blood flow ceases to the vital organs (including the brain, the kidneys, and the heart itself). * * * The aim of CPR is twofold: first, to maintain a sufficient flow of oxygenated blood to the vital organs to prevent damage or, more accurately, to delay its onset; second, to restore effective cardiac function. The patient will usually receive the following interventions: manual compressions of the chest ("closed-chest cardiac massage"); one or more jolts of electricity to the chest ("defibrillation") designed to interrupt the disorganized activity so that an orderly heartbeat can re-emerge; artificial ventilation of the lungs through a mask over the patient's mouth or through a tube inserted through the mouth down into the windpipe; and intravenous medications and fluids. These procedures usually last from a few minutes to a half an hour, until the patient's cardiac function has been restored or until he or she has been declared dead.

CPR has a history similar to that of many other medical technologies. It was invented at the end of the 1950s primarily for patients who, because of shocks from electrical lines, the effects of anesthesia, or heart attacks, developed ventricular fibrillation—the sudden onset of chaotic electrical activity in the muscle wall of the ventricle, leading to disorganized quivering of the heart with no forward movement of blood. But quickly it was used, even by its inventors, on patients without ventricular fibrillation as well, that is, on types of patients for whom it was not originally intended. Soon everyone in the hospital was, unless declared otherwise, a candidate for CPR, even when the cause of the arrest was chronic, not acute. CPR became a right for all patients, although a rite of passage to death for most. As a result, the hospital house staff who trained in the 1970s and 1980s, who were called on to perform most of the attempted resuscitations, were— as I have personally experienced—frequently disturbed, even revolted, by what seemed cruel and fruitless assaults on severely ill and demented patients. By the end of the 1980s, many physicians and ethicists were proposing in the medical journals that physicians should limit the use of CPR. They have advanced three types of arguments to justify restricting CPR: 1) its lack of effectiveness (in particular, its "futility" for certain categories of patients); 2) the high cost of its consequences; and 3) the wish of many patients to forgo it. * * *

The results of CPR in adults are not encouraging. Most patients die either immediately or within a few days. Only about a tenth of recipients live long enough to leave the hospital. It seems, therefore, that CPR is a highly atypical medical procedure in that most patients are worse off after it than before it. Yet the patients' condition just before CPR is cardiac arrest, and the results of no CPR are, most people believe, even worse than those of CPR: every patient who suffers a true cardiac arrest and does not receive CPR dies. The issue seems to be how many patients will hang on to meaningful life.

Yet some groups of patients have worse results than others. Patients who are gravely ill at the time of their cardiac arrests almost never survive to be discharged from the hospital. Numerous physicians and ethicists * * * have, therefore, argued that CPR is, for these groups of patients, a "futile" treatment (in the sense that it offers them no benefit). Under such circumstances, because a physician is not obligated to undertake or even offer a treatment that is clearly futile, the physician can and should decide to exclude these patients from receiving CPR, i.e., declare them DNR ("do not resuscitate"). The physician needs to inform them or their surrogates of this decision but does not need to consult with them about it.

The result has been, as would be expected, a heated debate over the validity of the futility argument. To find a path through this thicket, it is necessary to consider the moral grounds on which a physician might refuse a patient's request for CPR. Here it is particularly useful to examine the three rationales for withholding CPR: * * * 1) that the patient's current quality of life is, from the patient's point of view, unacceptable, i.e., worse than death; 2) that the patient's quality of life, while currently acceptable, would become unacceptable to the patient (again as judged, in advance, by the patient or his or her surrogates) after he or she has suffered the insults of the arrest and the resuscitation; and 3) that CPR would offer "no medical benefit" because it would "almost certainly not be successful." The first two rationales are based on the choice of the patient (or of his or her surrogate) * * * * Only the third rationale might authorize the physician to make the decision. We need, therefore, to examine more closely those cases in which resuscitation is said to offer "no medical benefit."

The American Heart Association in its official 1992 guidelines for CPR distinguishes three categories of patients for whom CPR might be deemed of no medical benefit: 1) the patient who, for practical purposes, is already dead—for example, a patient who has already undergone full resuscitation without success or one who suffered a cardiac arrest more than ten minutes ago; 2) the patient whose cardiac arrest is the culmination of a relentlessly deteriorating and terminal condition—for example, a patient in an intensive care unit who is receiving maximal therapy but whose blood pressure or oxygen level is nonetheless progressively falling; and 3) the patient whose serious underlying disease puts him or her in a category in which survival after an arrest and resuscitation until discharge from the hospital would be unprecedented, or, as others would insist, a category in which survival is rare if not actually unprecedented—for example, a patient with widely metastatic cancer, multiple organ failure, or sepsis. The first two categories, in which the futility of CPR is obvious, need not concern us much: CPR would be unsuccessful immediately in the first and quickly in the second, for these patients are either dead or about to die, regardless of our attempts to resuscitate. The real debate about futility thus narrows down to whether CPR can be deemed futile in the third scenario where survival to hospital discharge would be unprecedented or at least rare, as in fact the American Heart Association and the other major proponents of the futility argument have claimed. This is indeed an important issue, for with this third category of patients, unlike with the first two, we are facing potentially enormous psychological and economic costs.

Two objections can be offered to declaring that CPR is futile for patients with little or no hope of subsequently leaving the hospital. First, when a variety of studies of the outcomes of CPR are examined, no category of patients is without some survivors to discharge. It would be very difficult, if not impossible, therefore, to draw the line between those for whom CPR is futile and those for whom it is not. Second, and more importantly, it is, in my opinion, illegitimate for a physician to deny the option of CPR to his or her patient on the grounds that the patient is going to die soon anyway. In doing this, the physician either is declaring, without consulting the patient or his or her surrogate, that the patient's life is no longer worth living or, at least, would no longer be worth living after the arrest and resuscitation, or is deciding that the meager benefit to the patient and others of keeping the patient alive for a short time is not worth the expected enormous monetary and psychological costs.

In the first case, the physician is substituting his or her own values or estimation of the worth of a particular form of living for the patient's. Yet patients frequently adjust to and find some benefit in even painful and restricted modes of existence. Physicians tend, therefore, to underestimate how the patient rates his or her quality of life. In the second case, the physician is placing the interests of society, the institution, or another group (such as personnel in the intensive care unit) above the patient's interests. In both cases the physician would, in my judgment, be acting contrary to the current dictates of medical ethics and the law, which obligate the physician to act primarily in accordance with the patient's values, not his or her own, and in accordance with the interests of the patient, not of others.

The second argument used to justify restricting the use of CPR focuses on cost. The increasingly high cost of health care in the United States alarms the public and politicians alike. Theoretically, no particular percentage of the Gross National Product (GNP) spent on health care is intrinsically too high. * * * Although restraining the costs, development, and use of new and more expensive medical technologies will be difficult, if not impossible, a number of medical economists, ethicists, and policymakers have concluded that some system of rationing of health services is necessary. * * * [Chapter 9(C) excerpts this discussion.]

[E]ven if we still believe that CPR should be restricted for economic reasons, we need to realize that this rationing should be done by society (or its representatives), not by individual physicians. The patient-physician relationship in America is based on the premise that the physician will act primarily in the individual patient's best interests, not in the interests of society. Society may decide to establish rules for rationing or to appoint agents to impose rationing (such as directors or triage officers of intensive care units), but it cannot, in the current American climate, expect individual physicians to withhold CPR from their patients in order to save money. This seems to be the position of most physicians and would likely be upheld by most judges and juries. Many commentators thus argue that, to resolve the dilemmas of futility and cost, society—in the form, for example, of proposals by presidential commissions, statements by religious authorities, state laws, and judicial rulings—needs to take a clearer stand. The conclusion of my consideration of the rationales of ineffectiveness and cost for restricting the use of CPR is that patient (or surrogate) choice provides the only legitimate ground for physicians to withhold CPR from their patients. * * *

NOTES AND QUESTIONS

1. *The debate about the definition of medical futility.* For more on the debate about how to define the medically appropriate use of CPR and other expensive medical technologies, see Leslie J. Blackhall, Must We Always Use CPR?, 317 New Eng. J. Med. 1281 (1987); Kathleen M. Boozang, Death Wish: Resuscitating Self–Determination for the Critically Ill, 35 Ariz. L. Rev. 23 (1993); Nancy M.P. King & Gail Henderson, Treatments of Last Resort: Informed Consent and the Diffusion of New Technology, 42 Mercer L. Rev. 1007 (1991); Steven Miles, Futility and Medical Professionalism, 25

Seton Hall L. Rev. 873 (1995); Lawrence J. Schneiderman et al., Medical Futility: Its Meaning and Ethical Implications, 112 Annals Internal Med. 949 (1990); Symposium, Legal and Ethical Implications of Innovative Medical Technology, 57 Alb. L. Rev. 551 (1994); Symposium, Medical Futility, 20 Law Med. & Health Care 307 (1992). For criticisms of futility arguments, see Council on Ethical & Judicial Affairs, AMA, Guidelines for the Appropriate Use of Do–Not–Resuscitate Orders, 265 JAMA 1868 (1991); John D. Lantos et al., The Illusion of Futility in Clinical Practice, 87 Am. J. Med. 81 (1989); Robert D. Truog et al., The Problem with Futility, 326 New Eng. J. Med. 1560 (1992); Stuart J. Youngner, Who Defines Futility?, 260 JAMA 2094 (1988). As the excerpts above suggest, concepts of medical futility are closely linked with the process of technology assessment. See George J. Annas & Frances H. Miller, The Empire of Death: How Culture and Economics Affect Informed Consent in the U.S., the U.K., and Japan, 20 Am. J.L. & Med. 357 (1994); Alexander M. Capron, Medical Futility: Strike Two, Hastings Ctr. Rep., Sept.-Oct. 1994, at 42 (reporting a study of care offering a less than 1% chance of two-month survival); Ian L. Cohen et al., Mechanical Ventilation for the Elderly Patient in Intensive Care: Incremental Charges and Benefits, 269 JAMA 1025 (1993); Ezekiel J. Emanuel & Linda L. Emanuel, The Economics of Dying: The Illusion of Cost Savings at the End of Life, 330 New Eng. J. Med. 540 (1994); Donald J. Murphy & Thomas E. Finucane, New Do–Not–Resuscitate Policies: A First Step in Cost Control, 153 Archives Internal Med. 1641 (1993); A.A. Scitovsky, "The High Cost of Dying" Revisited, 72 Milbank Q. 561 (1994); Peter A. Singer & Frederick H. Lowy, Rationing, Patient Preferences, and Cost of Care at the End of Life, 152 Archives Internal Med. 478 (1992).

2. *Medical futility and the care of premature infants.* Questions of medical futility also arise at the beginning of life, with decisions about the care of premature or severely handicapped infants. Physicians and families often find it difficult to make decisions about appropriate levels of medical intervention because the ethical principle of autonomy does not apply. Instead, decisionmakers must attempt to determine what is in the infant's best interest—a difficult task because the outcome of any treatment remains uncertain. See, e.g., In re Baby K, 16 F.3d 590 (4th Cir.1994); In re K.I., 735 A.2d 448 (D.C.1999); Iafelice v. Zarafu, 534 A.2d 417 (N.J.App. Div.1987); see also Thomas A. Warnock, Comment, Scientific Advancements: Will Technology Make the Unpopular Wrongful Birth/Life Causes of Action Extinct?, 19 Temp. Envtl. L. & Tech. J. 173 (2001).

3. Defining Categories of Disease

Lars Noah, *Pigeonholing Illness: Medical Diagnosis as a Legal Construct*

50 Hastings L.J. 241 (1999).

    * * * The concept of disease, which is so fundamental to medical practice, has numerous important applications in the law. It helps to inform or delineate reimbursable illnesses covered by health insurance,

risk-benefit calculations performed by regulatory agencies charged with
licensing therapeutic products, the scope of compensable injuries in tort
actions, the potential relevance of psychiatric evidence in criminal trials,
and impairments subject to antidiscrimination laws and disability benefit
programs. Diagnostic judgments have become so pervasive and readily
accepted in these varied contexts that we may lose sight of their overall
significance. Novel diseases occasionally attract critical scrutiny, as has
happened recently with the perceived proliferation of psychiatric syndrome
evidence in criminal trials, but commentators invariably advocate doctrinal
responses designed to assist decisionmakers in properly assimilating such
information. Little or no attention is paid to the ways in which medical
professionals react to the external pressures emanating from, or mediated
by, legal institutions with regard to defining and diagnosing disease conditions. * * *

Traditionally, medical professionals defined categories of diseases (nosology) and identified such conditions in particular patients (diagnosis) for
purposes of selecting appropriate treatments and predicting the likely
course of the patient's illness (prognosis). Increasingly, however, diagnostic
judgments have come to serve other purposes. Perhaps such a development
is neither surprising nor worrisome, at least so long as these diagnoses do
not interfere with therapeutic purposes. But once the definition and identification of illness begin primarily to serve the needs of non-medical decisionmakers such as insurers, regulatory agencies, and litigants, closer
scrutiny of the diagnostic process is warranted. In at least some situations,
researchers apparently cater to patient demands for useful new disease
categories, and physicians authenticate complaints, certifying to bureaucrats that particular patients suffer from a qualifying illness. * * *

"Diseases" are not things awaiting discovery by researchers and physicians. Instead, they are convenient short-hand descriptions of illnesses
experienced by patients that facilitate investigating and selecting possible
courses of treatment. But conceptions of illness do not serve only medical
purposes; scholars and physicians alike have recognized that diseases are
socially constructed and mutable. Nosology and diagnosis can describe a
patient's health or illness experience only imperfectly. * * *

Patients seek out medical care in hopes of finding a treatment for some
bothersome condition. They usually care little about the name of their
affliction. Similarly, physicians diagnose patients as a means to the end of
identifying the most appropriate therapy. It may be that, if there are
several plausible diagnoses for a condition but further specification would
serve no purpose given the nature of available treatments, the health care
professional will not pursue additional diagnostic inquiries for their own
sake. Similarly, physicians may have to revisit their initial diagnosis in the
event that the patient's condition does not improve with the prescribed
therapy. * * *

[T]he FDA's decision to approve a new drug or other medical product
will entail a risk-benefit calculation, so the perceived importance of the
therapeutic benefit naturally will influence the agency's licensing judg-

ments. In this manner, the FDA takes into account the significance of a targeted health condition, or the status of that condition as a treatable disease, when making product approval decisions. * * *

Asymptomatic conditions may pose difficult questions for the FDA when it reviews new drugs intended to manage these conditions. An asymptomatic condition does not really qualify as an "illness" because the patient cannot perceive any complaints, though it may still represent a disease condition detected by a physician. For example, hypertension, hypercholesterolemia, and hyperlipidemia generally do not manifest symptoms, but they are viewed as risk-factors in coronary heart disease and stroke. * * * [T]he agency usually demands that an applicant demonstrate a drug's effectiveness in achieving clinical endpoints rather than surrogate markers associated with those clinical endpoints. By reconceptualizing hypertension as a freestanding disease entity, however, a pharmaceutical manufacturer would only have to demonstrate that its new drug product effectively reduced blood pressure without also having to show that this resulted in reduced morbidity or mortality. Classifying asymptomatic conditions as diseases may, however, also undermine the prospects for approval of a drug whose side effects include one of these conditions—for instance, a drug intended to treat some other condition may fare less well in the agency's risk-benefit calculus if it causes the "disease" of hypertension than if it merely causes elevated blood pressure.

The status of obesity as a condition or a disease has been a recurrent issue for the FDA. In approving the fat-substitute olestra, the agency noted that it had received several comments supporting this novel food additive as a useful response to the adverse health effects of obesity. The FDA also has approved prescription weight loss drugs in recent years based in part on the assumption that obesity represents a disease. Indeed, historically, the FDA did not regard obesity as a disease, leading Congress to expand the drug definition so that the agency could assert its regulatory authority over weight loss products. Although obese individuals face a variety of health problems, some scientists regard most types of obesity as a symptom of one among several possible underlying disorders rather than a disease process itself. If only regarded as a symptom, proposed new obesity treatments will fare less well in the agency's risk-benefit calculus and product approval decisions in the future. * * *

Along with administrative agencies and courts, legislatures have expressed a distinct preference for basing eligibility for certain statutory benefits on presumably objective diagnostic judgments made by medical professionals. * * * [S]uch programs ask medical professionals to certify the legitimacy of asserted disabilities—in effect, dispensing diagnoses that may serve no particular therapeutic purpose. * * * Some have criticized the development of a cottage industry of medical or educational professionals available to certify that a student suffers from a learning disability as well as the growing tendency to define new types of such disabilities. Attention deficit disorder (ADD) has attracted particular notice in recent years. ADD, sometimes also referred to as attention deficit hyperactivity disorder (ADHD), has become a common diagnosis for what in the past would have been characterized as behavioral or socialization problems. Generally identified in disruptive elementary school students, and frequently treated with the psychoactive drug methylphenidate hydrochloride (Ritalin), ADD has been implicated in all manner of educational difficulties. * * *

If diseases are created rather than discovered, as the social constructivists argue, what forces influence that process? Much of the pressure is internal to the patient and the medical profession, but some of it comes from outside, including from the legal profession. Just as social forces have shaped medical practice, legal institutions influence both nosology and diagnosis. * * * Legal institutions have, of course, altered medical practice quite directly, most notably through malpractice decisions. At the federal level, however, Congress generally has disclaimed any intent to interfere with the practice of medicine. * * * This Article has described one very important aspect of medical practice, diagnosis, that legal institutions have influenced indirectly and unintentionally, though pervasively. In a sense, regulators and courts function as something of a feedback mechanism for the medical profession as it defines and identifies diseases.

The recent emergence of novel diseases, such as multiple chemical sensitivity and chronic fatigue syndrome, may reflect a confluence of two factors. First, patients with previously undiagnosed complaints obviously may become frustrated and demand some medical—but preferably not a psychiatric—label for their symptoms. They may do so for entirely personal reasons, but many patients also understand the potential legal utility of a medical diagnosis, which is only partially counterbalanced by concerns about their future insurability and even social stigma. Second, some researchers and practitioners have been willing to respond to such opportunities by defining and identifying new syndromes in these patients. As [one commentator] has written, there is a "widespread belief that those who are stressed and mentally ill are an immense market for somatic diagnoses, making the diagnosis of these syndromes vulnerable to abuse." Researchers may try to capitalize on what they hope will prove to be a major biomedical breakthrough, and some clinicians may become opportunistic popularizers of novel diseases.

To the extent that legal and related external pressures influence the labeling of diseases and their diagnosis in particular patients, is there anything troublesome about that? Do these external constraints corrupt an essentially scientific, taxonomic process? Should medical professionals be forced to undertake a patient advocacy role that competes and may even conflict with their more traditional role of treating ill patients? The phrase *primum non nocere* expressed one of the central maxims of the Hippocratic tradition—above all, physicians should do no harm in dealing with their patients. If the medical community defines or identifies diseases for reasons other than their use in helping to select a course of treatment, however, diagnostic judgments may run afoul of this bioethical principle of nonmaleficence. Indeed, there may be significant costs to patients, the medical profession, and society. * * *

[D]efining a condition as a disease may help secure insurance coverage for treatments, improve the odds that the FDA will approve new therapeutic products for marketing, allow tort plaintiffs to side-step tricky causation questions, assist criminal defendants in avoiding conviction, and expand eligibility for disability programs and workers' compensation benefits. For instance, pharmaceutical companies seeking FDA approval of new drugs (or hoping to guarantee the availability of insurance reimbursement for prescriptions) care whether the scientific community categorizes hypertension, obesity, or premenstrual syndrome as diseases. Lawyers who represent parties in the ongoing breast implant litigation have an obvious stake in the direction of research on [atypical] connective-tissue disorders. Also, as noted in connection with the discussion of both tort and criminal litigation, nosological innovations may help promote and perhaps also disguise significant doctrinal modifications.

Patient and social advocacy groups sometimes influence nosology. Traditionally, at a time when disability programs reflected a medical or rehabilitative rather than a civil rights model, condition-specific associations formed to promote clinical research into their members' particular disease. More recently, most notably in the case of AIDS, patients have formed advocacy groups to lobby legislators and regulators to support research and accelerate the availability of potential treatments. But some experts warn that such "lobbying could undermine scientific objectivity in decisions such as which diseases are researched and how much funding those projects receive." In some situations, as in the case of chronic fatigue syndrome, patient support groups have formed primarily to demand that medical professionals and the public take their ailments seriously.

The selection of diagnostic criteria also may have important legal consequences. For instance, the CDC's surveillance activities draw the attention of patient advocacy groups because of the inevitable use of these diagnostic criteria for other purposes: "Although the CDC's various case definitions were developed primarily for surveillance activities, these definitions have become the diagnostic standard used by other federal, state, and local agencies to determine eligibility for entitlements and benefits." In addition to the availability of disability benefits, CDC definitions may affect reimbursement to health care providers, FDA review of therapeutic agents, and federal funding of biomedical research. Over time, clinical researchers may narrow the definition of novel diseases, potentially leading to conflicts between patient advocacy groups and clinicians—patients may feel "disenfranchised" if their illness falls outside of increasingly refined diagnostic criteria.

The debate about the existence of "Gulf War syndrome" provides a recent illustration of an advocacy group aggressively lobbying for the formal recognition of a new ailment. Gulf War syndrome (GWS) has aspects of both MCS [multiple chemical sensitivity] (premised on possible exposure to biological agents and other toxins during combat) and post-traumatic stress disorder. PTSD itself emerged as a diagnosis for Vietnam veterans suffering from psychiatric problems that had been identified in previous generations of soldiers as shell shock or combat fatigue. Recognition of GWS would entitle many veterans of the Persian Gulf War to medical and disability benefits. To date, however, biomedical researchers have failed to find much scientific support for these nosological claims.

Both the AMA and the APA [American Psychiatric Association] have published important diagnostic guides, in some cases consciously geared toward forensic or reimbursement uses. These professional societies engage in more than a taxonomic endeavor when they compile and promote these manuals. As the significance of their diagnostic manuals grows, groups with a stake in the outcome attempt to exert some influence, and the drafting process inevitably becomes more politicized and less driven by scientific expertise.

Although the APA explicitly cautioned that DSM–IV was intended primarily for therapeutic rather than forensic or reimbursement purposes, that caveat has a decidedly hollow ring to it. Recognition in the DSM has become essential for securing health insurance coverage, so much so that patient groups and pharmaceutical companies may lobby the APA to include new disorders. Paradoxically, the DSM's diagnostic criteria for mental disorders may end up serving primarily non-therapeutic purposes, whether tied to reimbursement, forensic testimony, or basic research. * * *

Some commentators have applauded the tendency of litigation to promote scientific research on important subjects, but, if definitions of disease serve primarily forensic rather than therapeutic purposes, the odds of objective and rigorous scientific testing may decrease. Instead, legal institutions may embrace and unwittingly promote unorthodox medicine. Also, to the extent that legal institutions contribute to rapid nosological revisions, they may harm both the scientific enterprise and patient care. If nosologies become moving targets, biomedical researchers cannot adequately investigate their clinical utility before revised definitions render their work moot. Revisions also increase the risk of diagnostic errors as clinicians cannot keep up with changes in nomenclature, which in turn complicates communication among colleagues about their patients. None of this is meant to discount scientific and other non-legal motivations for pursuing basic disease research, but one should not dismiss the peculiar incentives created or mediated by different legal institutions and their possible adverse consequences for biomedical work. * * *

What does it mean to be ill? It depends in part on whom you ask. Physicians, historians, philosophers, and sociologists have struggled to answer this important question. It also depends on why you want to know. The traditional response would emphasize therapeutic purposes, in which case the medical model of disease made perfect sense. If, however, non-therapeutic motives underlie the question, then the range of possible answers might proliferate and depart substantially from the medical model. Legal institutions, by looking to medical professionals for answers to non-therapeutic questions about disease, have failed to appreciate these distinctions.

Why should we care that legal institutions misunderstand the answers that they receive to their non-therapeutic questions about the meaning of disease? At one level, it may distort decisions having important personal, financial, and societal consequences, and legal decisionmakers may wish to reorient their understandings of illness for that reason alone. At another level, * * * the misunderstanding and distortion may rebound in various ways that influence the behavior of medical professionals. In this respect, legal institutions do more than make a mistake in relying on diagnostic judgments for their own non-therapeutic purposes; by becoming dependent on these medical judgments, they also distort nosology and diagnosis in ways that may threaten clinical research and patient care. * * *

Courts and agencies can try to delink themselves from an overreliance on the gatekeeping role traditionally placed on treating physicians, and the medical profession should insist on a clearer demarcation between diagnostic judgments for therapeutic purposes and forensic diagnoses. Organized medicine should not unnecessarily multiply nosologies in response to reimbursement pressures or perceived forensic opportunities, and physicians should not feel pressured into becoming zealous advocates for their patients outside of the therapeutic relationship. Otherwise, health care professionals risk losing sight of the primary purpose for making a diagnosis, namely, caring for a patient with an illness.

NOTES AND QUESTIONS

1. *Psychoactive medications and behavior modification.* Exploding rates of Ritalin® prescribing for ADHD have generated intense controversy in the medical and educational communities. Recent studies demonstrate that the United States manufactures and uses 85% of the world's supply of the drug and that prescribing rates for very young children are increasing substantially. See Lawrence H. Diller, The Run on Ritalin: Attention Deficit Disorder and Stimulant Treatment in the 1990s, 26 Hastings Ctr. Rep. 12 (1996); Gina Kolata, Boom in Ritalin Sales Raises Ethical Issues, N.Y. Times, May 15, 1996, at C8. But see Larry S. Goldman et al., Diagnosis and Treatment of Attention–Deficit/Hyperactivity Disorder in Children and Adolescents, 279 JAMA 1100 (1998) (finding little evidence of substantial rates of ADHD misdiagnosis or overprescribing of Ritalin for the disorder). Brain imaging studies suggest that Ritalin produces chemical changes in the brain that closely resemble the effects of cocaine. See Brian Vastag, Pay Attention: Ritalin Acts Much Like Cocaine, 286 JAMA 905 (2001). Moreover, one survey indicated a high level of abuse, finding that one in five college students take Ritalin for recreational purposes. See House Panel Hears Tales of Ritalin Excesses in Schools, Chi. Trib., May 17, 2000, at 12.

Prescription drug treatment for other behavioral problems in children is also on the rise. One study found that 1% to 1.5% of children aged 2 to 4 who were enrolled in two Medicaid programs and a managed care plan were prescribed stimulants, antidepressants, or antipsychotic drugs. Prescribing of selective seratonin reuptake inhibitors for children aged 5 or younger increased 10–fold between 1993 and 1997. Physicians have expressed concern that the safety and efficacy of such drugs has not been established in very young children and that the long-term use of such drugs could inhibit normal brain development. See Joseph T. Coyle, Psychotrophic Drug Use in Very Young Children, 283 JAMA 1059 (2000). Some research on older children suggests that drugs are quite effective for treating certain psychiatric conditions. For example, a recent study of the psychotrophic drug Luvox® (fluvoxamine) in children aged 6 to 17 found that it effectively alleviated symptoms of social phobia and anxiety. See John T. Walkup et al., Fluvoxamine for the Treatment of Anxiety Disorders in Children and Adolescents, 344 New Eng. J. Med. 1279 (2001). An editorial accompanying the study noted that the International Narcotics Control Board of the United Nations has "expressed concern about the inappropriate medicalization of social problems in developed countries and the widespread use of drugs to treat behavioral symptoms instead of treating the underlying causes," and it urged readers to consider "whether conditions in children and adolescents are sufficiently serious and disabling to necessitate pharmacologic intervention." Joseph T. Coyle, Drug Treatment of Anxiety Disorders in Children, 344 New Eng. J. Med. 1326 (2001). The editorial also suggested that, because other well-designed studies had found that behavioral therapy was at least as effective as drugs in treating anxiety disorders in adolescents and children, behavioral therapy "might be preferred to pharmacotherapy as an initial treatment" because of the low risk or side effects and to avoid the risk of long-term effects of psychoactive drugs on the developing brain. See id. at 1327; see also Carol Marbin Miller, Use of Drugs to Control Kids Worries Specialists, Miami Herald, July 2, 2001 (reporting that significant numbers of children in state foster care were receiving the schizophrenia drug Risperdal® as a "chemical restraint"). The marketing of psychoactive drugs to treat arguably normal personality variations in adults is also on the rise. Pharmaceutical companies employ promotional strategies intended to medicalize common personality traits, such as "social anxiety disorder" (shyness) in order to create a demand for a pharmacological intervention. See Shankar Vedantam, Drug Ads Hyping Anxiety Make Some Uneasy, Wash. Post, July 16, 2001, at A1 (describing the very successful marketing of Paxil®, and noting that "pharmaceutical companies, traditionally in the business of finding new drugs for existing disorders, are increasingly in the business of seeking new disorders for existing drugs"). For further commentary on the use of drugs to modify arguably normal behavior, see Michael H. Shapiro, Law, Culpability, and the Neural Sciences, in The Neurotransmitter Revolution: Serotonin, Social Behavior and the Law 179 (R. Masters & M. McGuire eds., 1994); Leticia M. Diaz, Regulating the Administration of Mood–Altering Drugs to Juveniles: Are We Legally Drugging Our Children?, 25 Seton Hall Legis. J. 83 (2001).

2. *PMS, PMDD, and Prozac.* In another recent development, Eli Lilly, the makers of Prozac®, obtained FDA approval to market the drug under the brand name Sarafem® for treatment of "premenstrual dysmorphic disorder" (PMDD), an allegedly more severe and distinct form of premenstrual syndrome (PMS). See Peter D. Kramer, The Way We Live Now: Female Troubles, N.Y. Times Mag., Oct. 1, 2000, at 17 (commenting that "the pill is a pretty pink-and-lavender capsule, available in a light blue box ... sold under the liltingly soft name Sarafem, which sounds like the angels known for the quality of their spiritual love," and pointing out that it "isn't a new drug at all, only Prozac in drag"). Repackaging and marketing the drug for this new indication will provide Lilly with market exclusivity through 2007—an attractive proposition for the company because it lost patent protection on Prozac in August 2001. Other manufacturers of antidepressants, including Pfizer (Zoloft®) and GlaxoSmithKline (Paxil®) also are pursuing approval to market their products for the treatment of PMDD. Many members of the medical community have expressed skepticism, however, about whether PMDD is in fact a real disease, or "simply a way for drug companies to cast a wider net in search of new customers." Tara Parker–Pope, Drug Companies Push Use of Antidepressants to Treat Severe PMS, Wall St. J., Feb. 23, 2001, at B1; Joe Sharkey, It's a Mad, Mad, Mad, Mad World, N.Y. Times, Sept. 28, 1997, at D1. Another commentator has expressed concern that PMDD "stigmatizes women by characterizing them as having a mental illness once a month" when many psychiatrists do not believe that the condition is a valid medical disorder. Others counter that PMDD is a serious problem that prevents afflicted women from functioning personally and professionally, and applaud the male-dominated medical profession's interest in the problem. PMDD is currently categorized as a disorder under consideration in the latest edition of the APA's *Diagnostic and Statistical Manual*. See Shankar Vedantam, Renamed Prozac Fuels Women's Health Debate, Wash. Post, Apr. 29, 2001, at A1 (also noting that Eli Lilly spent $17 million in direct-to-consumer advertising for Sarafem during a four-month period and $16 million in medical journal ads over a seven-month period); see also Shankar Vedantam, Drug Use, and Concern, Is on the Rise, Phil. Inquirer, Mar. 19, 2001, at C1 (describing burgeoning prescribing of antidepressants, antipsychotic medications, and antianxiety medications and the concern of some critics that these drugs are being overprescribed, in part to compensate for managed care limits on therapy sessions).

*

STATUTORY APPENDIX*

Federal Food, Drug, and Cosmetic Act
Public Health Service Act (§§ 351, 361)

FEDERAL FOOD, DRUG, AND COSMETIC ACT

Table of Contents

* Current through Feb. 2002. Note that some of the headings and subheadings have been modified in minor ways to promote clarity. Only the most relevant statutory sections are excerpted here; ellipses are used only to identify material deleted within sections.

SEC. 201 [21 U.S.C. § 321]. DEFINITIONS. For the purposes of this chapter—

(a) (1) The term "State", except as used in the last sentence of section 372(a) of this title, means any State or Territory of the United States, the District of Columbia, and the Commonwealth of Puerto Rico.

(2) The term "Territory" means any Territory or possession of the United States, including the District of Columbia, and excluding the Commonwealth of Puerto Rico and the Canal Zone.

(b) The term "interstate commerce" means (1) commerce between any State or Territory and any place outside thereof, and (2) commerce within the District of Columbia or within any other Territory not organized with a legislative body.

(c) The term "Department" means Department of Health and Human Services.

(d) The term "Secretary" means the Secretary of Health and Human Services.

(e) The term "person" includes individual, partnership, corporation, and association.

(f) The term "food" means (1) articles used for food or drink for man or other animals, (2) chewing gum, and (3) articles used for components of any such article.

(g) (1) The term "drug" means

(A) articles recognized in the official United States Pharmacopoeia, official Homeopathic Pharmacopoeia of the United States, or official National Formulary, or any supplement to any of them; and

(B) articles intended for use in the diagnosis, cure, mitigation, treatment, or prevention of disease in man or other animals; and

(C) articles (other than food) intended to affect the structure or any function of the body of man or other animals; and

(D) articles intended for use as a component of any article specified in clause (A), (B), or (C). A food or dietary supplement for which a claim, subject to sections 403(r)(1)(B) and 403(r)(3) of this title or sections 403(r)(1)(B) and 403(r)(5)(D) of this title, is made in accordance with the requirements of section 403(r) of this title is not a drug solely because the label or the labeling contains such a claim. A food, dietary ingredient, or dietary supplement for which a truthful and not misleading statement is made in accordance with section 403(r)(6) of this title is not a drug under clause (C) solely because the label or the labeling contains such a statement.

(2) The term "counterfeit drug" means a drug which, or the container or labeling of which, without authorization, bears the trademark, trade name, or other identifying mark, imprint, or device, or any likeness thereof, of a drug manufacturer, processor, packer, or distributor other than the

person or persons who in fact manufactured, processed, packed, or distributed such drug and which thereby falsely purports or is represented to be the product of, or to have been packed or distributed by, such other drug manufacturer, processor, packer, or distributor.

(h) The term "device" (except when used in paragraph (n) of this section and in sections 301(i), 403(f), 502(c), and 602(c)) means an instrument, apparatus, implement, machine, contrivance, implant, in vitro reagent, or other similar or related article, including any component, part, or accessory, which is—

(1) recognized in the official National Formulary, or the United States Pharmacopoeia, or any supplement to them,

(2) intended for use in the diagnosis of disease or other conditions, or in the cure, mitigation, treatment, or prevention of disease, in man or other animals, or

(3) intended to affect the structure or any function of the body of man or other animals,

and which does not achieve its primary intended purposes through chemical action within or on the body of man or other animals and which is not dependent upon being metabolized for the achievement of its primary intended purposes.

(i) The term "cosmetic" means (1) articles intended to be rubbed, poured, sprinkled, or sprayed on, introduced into, or otherwise applied to the human body or any part thereof for cleansing, beautifying, promoting attractiveness, or altering the appearance, and (2) articles intended for use as a component of any such articles; except that such term shall not include soap.

(j) The term "official compendium" means the official United States Pharmacopoeia, official Homeopathic Pharmacopoeia of the United States, official National Formulary, or any supplement to any of them.

(k) The term "label" means a display of written, printed, or graphic matter upon the immediate container of any article; and a requirement made by or under authority of this Act that any word, statement, or other information appear on the label shall not be considered to be complied with unless such word, statement, or other information also appears on the outside container or wrapper, if any there be, of the retail package of such article, or is easily legible through the outside container or wrapper.

(*l*) The term "immediate container" does not include package liners.

(m) The term "labeling" means all labels and other written, printed, or graphic matter (1) upon any article or any of its containers or wrappers, or (2) accompanying such article.

(n) If an article is alleged to be misbranded because the labeling or advertising is misleading, then in determining whether the labeling or advertising is misleading there shall be taken into account (among other things) not only representations made or suggested by statement, word, design, device, or any combination thereof, but also the extent to which the labeling or advertising fails to reveal facts material in the light of such representations or material with respect to consequences which may result from the use of the article to which the labeling or advertising relates under the conditions of use prescribed in the labeling or advertising thereof or under such conditions of use as are customary or usual.

(o) The representation of a drug, in its labeling, as an antiseptic shall be considered to be a representation that it is a germicide, except in the case of a drug purporting to be, or represented as, an antiseptic for inhibitory use as a wet dressing, ointment, dusting powder, or such other use as involves prolonged contact with the body.

(p) The term "new drug" means—

(1) Any drug (except a new animal drug or an animal feed bearing or containing a new animal drug) the composition of which is such that such drug is not generally recognized, among experts qualified by scientific training and experience to evaluate the safety and effectiveness of drugs, as safe and effective for use under the conditions prescribed, recommended, or suggested in the labeling thereof, except that such a drug not so recognized shall not be deemed to be a "new drug" if at any time prior to the enactment of this Act it was subject to the Food and Drugs Act of June 30, 1906, as amended, and if at such time its labeling contained the same representations concerning the conditions of its use; or

(2) Any drug (except a new animal drug or an animal feed bearing or containing a new animal drug) the composition of which is such that such drug, as a result of investigations to determine its safety and effectiveness for use under such conditions, has become so recognized, but which has not, otherwise than in such investigations, been used to a material extent or for a material time under such conditions.

* * *

(aa) The term "abbreviated drug application" means an application submitted under section 505(j) for the approval of a drug that relies on the approved application of another drug with the same active ingredient to establish safety and efficacy, and—(1) in the case of section 306, includes a supplement to such an application for a different or additional use of the drug but does not include a supplement to such an application for other than a different or additional use of the drug, and (2) in the case of sections 307 and 308, includes any supplement to such an application.

(bb) The term "knowingly" or "knew" means that a person, with respect to information—(1) has actual knowledge of the information, or (2) acts in deliberate ignorance or reckless disregard of the truth or falsity of the information.

(cc) For purposes of section 306, the term "high managerial agent"—

(1) means—(A) an officer or director of a corporation or an association, (B) a partner of a partnership, or (C) any employee or other agent of a corporation, association, or partnership, having duties such that the conduct of such officer, director, partner, employee, or agent may fairly be

assumed to represent the policy of the corporation, association, or partnership, and

(2) includes persons having management responsibility for—(A) submissions to the Food and Drug Administration regarding the development or approval of any drug product, (B) production, quality assurance, or quality control of any drug product, or (C) research and development of any drug product.

(dd) For purposes of sections 306 and 307, the term "drug product" means a drug subject to regulation under section 505, 512, or 802 of this Act or under section 351 of the Public Health Service Act.

(ee) The term "Commissioner" means the Commissioner of Food and Drugs.

(ff) The term "dietary supplement"—

(1) means a product (other than tobacco) intended to supplement the diet that bears or contains one or more of the following dietary ingredients: (A) a vitamin; (B) a mineral; (C) an herb or other botanical; (D) an amino acid; (E) a dietary substance for use by man to supplement the diet by increasing the total dietary intake; or (F) a concentrate, metabolite, constituent, extract, or combination of any ingredient described in clause (A), (B), (C), (D), or (E);

(2) means a product that—(A)(i) is intended for ingestion in a form described in section 411(c)(1)(B)(i) of this title; or (ii) complies with section 411(c)(1)(B)(ii) of this title; (B) is not represented for use as a conventional food or as a sole item of a meal or the diet; and (C) is labeled as a dietary supplement; and

(3)(A) include[s] an article that is approved as a new drug under section 505 or licensed as a biologic under section 351 of the Public Health Service Act (42 U.S.C. § 262) and was, prior to such approval, certification, or license, marketed as a dietary supplement or as a food unless the Secretary has issued a regulation, after notice and comment, finding that the article, when used as or in a dietary supplement under the conditions of use and dosages set forth in the labeling for such dietary supplement, is unlawful under section 402(f) of this title; and

(B) [does] not include—(i) an article that is approved as a new drug under section 505 of this title, certified as an antibiotic under section 507, or licensed as a biologic under section 351 of the Public Health Service Act (42 U.S.C. § 262), or (ii) an article authorized for investigation as a new drug, antibiotic, or biological for which substantial clinical investigations have been instituted and for which the existence of such investigations has been made public, which was not before such approval, certification, licensing, or authorization marketed as a dietary supplement or as a food unless the Secretary, in the Secretary's discretion, has issued a regulation, after notice and comment, finding that the article would be lawful under this chapter.

* * *

(ii) The term "compounded positron emission tomography drug"—

(1) means a drug that (A) exhibits spontaneous disintegration of unstable nuclei by the emission of positrons and is used for the purpose of providing dual photon positron emission tomographic diagnostic images; and (B) has been compounded by or on the order of a practitioner who is licensed by a State to compound or order compounding for a drug described in subparagraph (A), and is compounded in accordance with that State's law, for a patient or for research, teaching, or quality control; and

(2) includes any nonradioactive reagent, reagent kit, ingredient, nuclide generator, accelerator, target material, electronic synthesizer, or other apparatus or computer program to be used in the preparation of such a drug.

(jj) The term "antibiotic drug" means any drug (except drugs for use in animals other than humans) composed wholly or partly of any kind of penicillin, streptomycin, chlortetracycline, chloramphenicol, bacitracin, or any other drug intended for human use containing any quantity of any chemical substance which is produced by a micro-organism and which has the capacity to inhibit or destroy micro-organisms in dilute solution (including a chemically synthesized equivalent of any such substance) or any derivative thereof.

(kk) PRIORITY SUPPLEMENT.—The term "priority supplement" means a drug application referred to in section 101(4) of the Food and Drug Administration Modernization Act of 1997 (111 Stat. 2298).

SEC. 301 [21 U.S.C. § 331]. PROHIBITED ACTS. The following acts and the causing thereof are hereby prohibited:

(a) The introduction or delivery for introduction into interstate commerce of any food, drug, device, or cosmetic that is adulterated or misbranded.

(b) The adulteration or misbranding of any food, drug, device, or cosmetic in interstate commerce.

(c) The receipt in interstate commerce of any food, drug, device, or cosmetic that is adulterated or misbranded, and the delivery or proffered delivery thereof for pay or otherwise.

(d) The introduction or delivery for introduction into interstate commerce of any article in violation of section 404 or 505.

(e) The refusal to permit access to or copying of any record as required by section 412 or 703; or the failure to establish or maintain any record, or make any report, required under section 412, 505(i) or (k), 512(a)(4)(C), 512(j), (l), or (m), 515(f), or 519, or the refusal to permit access to or verification or copying of any such required record.

(f) The refusal to permit entry or inspection as authorized by section 704.

(g) The manufacture within any Territory of any food, drug, device, or cosmetic that is adulterated or misbranded.

(h) The giving of a guaranty or undertaking referred to in section 333(c)(2) of this title, which guaranty or undertaking is false, except by a person who relied upon a guaranty or undertaking to the same effect signed by, and containing the name and address of, the person residing in the United States from whom he received in good faith the food, drug, device, or cosmetic; or the giving of a guaranty or undertaking referred to in section 333(c)(3) of this title, which guaranty or undertaking is false.

(i) (1) Forging, counterfeiting, simulating, or falsely representing, or without proper authority using any mark, stamp, tag, label, or other identification device authorized or required by regulations promulgated under the provisions of section 404, or 721.

(2) Making, selling, disposing of, or keeping in possession, control, or custody, or concealing any punch, die, plate, stone, or other thing designed to print, imprint, or reproduce the trademark, trade name, or other identifying mark, imprint, or device of another or any likeness of any of the foregoing upon any drug or container or labeling thereof so as to render such drug a counterfeit drug.

(3) The doing of any act which causes a drug to be a counterfeit drug, or the sale or dispensing, or the holding for sale or dispensing, of a counterfeit drug.

(j) The using by any person to his own advantage, or revealing, other than to the Secretary or officers or employees of the Department, or to the courts when relevant in any judicial proceeding under this Act, any information acquired under authority of section 404, 409, 412, 505, 510, 512, 513, 514, 515, 516, 518, 519, 520, 704, 708, or 721 concerning any method or process which as a trade secret is entitled to protection, or the violating of section 408(i)(2) or any regulation issued under that section. This paragraph does not authorize the withholding of information from either House of Congress or from, to the extent of matter within its jurisdiction, any committee or subcommittee of such committee or any joint committee of Congress or any subcommittee of such joint committee.

(k) The alteration, mutilation, destruction, obliteration, or removal of the whole or any part of the labeling of, or the doing of any other act with respect to, a food, drug, device, or cosmetic, if such act is done while such article is held for sale (whether or not the first sale) after shipment in interstate commerce and results in such article being adulterated or misbranded.

* * *

(n) The using, in labeling, advertising or other sales promotion of any reference to any report or analysis furnished in compliance with section 704.

(o) In the case of a prescription drug distributed or offered for sale in interstate commerce, the failure of the manufacturer, packer, or distributor thereof to maintain for transmittal, or to transmit, to any practitioner licensed by applicable State law to administer such drug who makes written request for information as to such drug, true and correct copies of all printed matter which is required to be included in any package in which that drug is distributed or sold, or such other printed matter as is approved by the Secretary. Nothing in this paragraph shall be construed to exempt any person from any labeling requirement imposed by or under other provisions of this Act.

(p) The failure to register in accordance with section 510, the failure to provide any information required by section 510(j) or 510(k), or the failure to provide a notice required by section 510(j)(2).

(q) (1) The failure or refusal to (A) comply with any requirement prescribed under section 518 or 520(g), (B) furnish any notification or other material or information required by or under section 519 or 520(g), or (C) comply with a requirement under section 522.

(2) With respect to any device, the submission of any report that is required by or under this Act that is false or misleading in any material respect.

(r) The movement of a device in violation of an order under section 304(g) or the removal or alteration of any mark or label required by the order to identify the device as detained.

* * *

(t) The importation of a drug in violation of section 801(d)(1), the sale, purchase, or trade of a drug or drug sample or the offer to sell, purchase, or trade a drug or drug sample in violation of section 503(c), the sale, purchase, or trade of a coupon, the offer to sell, purchase, or trade such a coupon, or the counterfeiting of such a coupon in violation of section 503(c)(2), the distribution of a drug sample in violation of section 503(d) or the failure to otherwise comply with the requirements of section 503(d), or the distribution of drugs in violation of section 503(e) or the failure to otherwise comply with the requirements of section 503(e).

(u) The failure to comply with any requirements of the provisions of, or any regulations or orders of the Secretary, under section 512(a)(4)(A), 512(a)(4)(D), or 512(a)(5).

(v) The introduction or delivery for introduction into interstate commerce of a dietary supplement that is unsafe under section 413.

(w) The making of a knowingly false statement in any record or report required or requested under subparagraph (A) or (B) of section 801(d)(3), the failure to submit or maintain records as required by sections 801(d)(3)(A) and 801(d)(3)(B), the release into interstate commerce of any article imported into the United States under section 801(d)(3) or any finished product made from such article (except for export in accordance with section 801(e) or 802 or section 351(h) of the Public Health Service Act), or the failure to export or destroy any component, part or accessory not incorporated into a drug, biological product or device that will be exported in accordance with section 801(e) or 802 or section 351(h) of the Public Health Service Act.

(x) The falsification of a declaration of conformity submitted under section 514(c) or the failure or refusal to provide data or information requested by the Secretary under paragraph (3) of such section.

(y) In the case of a drug, device, or food—(1) the submission of a report or recommendation by a person accredited under section 523 that is false or misleading in any material respect; (2) the disclosure by a person accredited under section 523 of confidential commercial information or any trade secret without the express written consent of the person who submitted such information or secret to such person; or (3) the receipt by a person accredited under section 523 of a bribe in any form or the doing of any corrupt act by such person associated with a responsibility delegated to such person under this Act.

(z) The dissemination of information in violation of section 551.

(aa) The importation of a covered product in violation of section 804, the falsification of any record required to be maintained or provided to the Secretary under such section, or any other violation of regulations under such section.

SEC. 302 [21 U.S.C. § 332]. INJUNCTION PROCEEDINGS.

(a) The district courts of the United States and the United States courts of the Territories shall have jurisdiction, for cause shown to restrain violations of section 301, except paragraphs (h), (i), and (j).

(b) In case of violation of an injunction or restraining order issued under this section, which also constitutes a violation of this Act, trial shall be by the court, or, upon demand of the accused, by a jury.

SEC. 303 [21 U.S.C. § 333]. PENALTIES.

(a) (1) Any person who violates a provision of section 301 shall be imprisoned for not more than one year or fined not more than $1,000, or both.

(2) Notwithstanding the provisions of paragraph (1) of this section, if any person commits such a violation after a conviction of him under this section has become final, or commits such a violation with the intent to defraud or mislead, such person shall be imprisoned for not more than three years or fined not more than $10,000, or both.

(b) (1) Notwithstanding subsection (a), any person who violates section 301(t) by—

(A) knowingly importing a drug in violation of section 801(d)(1),

(B) knowingly selling, purchasing, or trading a drug or drug sample or knowingly offering to sell, purchase, or trade a drug or drug sample, in violation of section 503(c)(1),

(C) knowingly selling, purchasing, or trading a coupon, knowingly offering to sell, purchase, or trade such a coupon, or knowingly counterfeiting such a coupon, in violation of section 503(c)(2), or

(D) knowingly distributing drugs in violation of section 503(e)(2)(A), shall be imprisoned for not more than 10 years or fined not more than $250,000, or both.

(2) Any manufacturer or distributor who distributes drug samples by means other than the mail or common carrier whose representative, during the course of the representative's employment or association with that manufacturer or distributor, violated section 301(t) because of a violation of section 503(c)(1) or violated any State law prohibiting the sale, purchase, or trade of a drug sample subject to section 503(b) or the offer to sell, purchase, or trade such a drug sample shall, upon conviction of the representative for such violation, be subject to the following civil penalties:

(A) A civil penalty of not more than $50,000 for each of the first two such violations resulting in a conviction of any representative of the manufacturer or distributor in any 10–year period.

(B) A civil penalty of not more than $1,000,000 for each violation resulting in a conviction of any representative after the second conviction in any 10–year period. For the purposes of this paragraph, multiple convictions of one or more persons arising out of the same event or transaction, or a related series of events or transactions, shall be considered as one violation.

(3) Any manufacturer or distributor who violates section 301(t) because of a failure to make a report required by section 503(d)(3)(E) shall be subject to a civil penalty of not more than $100,000.

(4)(A) If a manufacturer or distributor or any representative of such manufacturer or distributor provides information leading to the institution of a criminal proceeding against, and conviction of, any representative of that manufacturer or distributor for a violation of section 301(t) because of a sale, purchase, or trade or offer to purchase, sell, or trade a drug sample in violation of section 503(c)(1) or for a violation of State law prohibiting the sale, purchase, or trade or offer to sell, purchase, or trade a drug sample, the conviction of such representative shall not be considered as a violation for purposes of paragraph (2).

(B) If, in an action brought under paragraph (2) against a manufacturer or distributor relating to the conviction of a representative of such manufacturer or distributor for the sale, purchase, or trade of a drug or the offer to sell, purchase, or trade a drug, it is shown, by clear and convincing evidence—

(i) that the manufacturer or distributor conducted, before the institution of a criminal proceeding against such representative for the violation which resulted in such conviction, an investigation of events or transactions which would have led to the reporting of information leading to the institution of a criminal proceeding against, and conviction of, such representative for such purchase, sale, or trade or offer to purchase, sell, or trade, or

(ii) that, except in the case of the conviction of a representative employed in a supervisory function, despite diligent implementation by the manufacturer or distributor of an independent audit and security system designed to detect such a violation, the manufacturer or distributor could not reasonably have been expected to have detected such violation, the conviction of such representative shall not be considered as a conviction for purposes of paragraph (2).

(5) If a person provides information leading to the institution of a criminal proceeding against, and conviction of, a person for a violation of section 301(t) because of the sale, purchase, or trade of a drug sample or the offer to sell, purchase, or trade a drug sample in violation of section 503(c)(1), such person shall be entitled to one-half of the criminal fine imposed and collected for such violation but not more than $125,000.

(6) Notwithstanding subsection (a), any person who is a manufacturer or importer of a covered product pursuant to section 804(a) and knowingly fails to comply with a requirement of section 804(e) that is applicable to such manufacturer or importer, respectively, shall be imprisoned for not more than 10 years or fined not more than $250,000, or both.

(c) No person shall be subject to the penalties of subsection (a)(1) of this section, (1) for having received in interstate commerce any article and delivered it or proffered delivery of it, if such delivery or proffer was made in good faith, unless he refuses to furnish on request of an officer or employee duly designated by the Secretary the name and address of the person from whom he purchased or received such article and copies of all documents, if any there be, pertaining to the delivery of the article to him; or (2) for having violated section 301(a) or (d), if he establishes a guaranty or undertaking signed by, and containing the name and address of, the person residing in the United States from whom he received in good faith the article, to the effect, in case of an alleged violation of section 301(a), that such article is not adulterated or misbranded, within the meaning of this chapter designating this Act or to the effect, in case of an alleged violation of section 301(d), that such article is not an article which may not, under the provisions of section 404 or 505, be introduced into interstate commerce; or (3) for having violated section 301(a), where the violation exists because the article is adulterated by reason of containing a color additive not from a batch certified in accordance with regulations promulgated by the Secretary under this Act, if such person establishes a guaranty or undertaking signed by, and containing the name and address of, the manufacturer of the color additive, to the effect that such color additive was from a batch certified in accordance with the applicable regulations promulgated by the Secretary under this Act; or (4) for having violated section 301(b), (c) or (k) by failure to comply with section 502(f) in respect to an article received in interstate commerce to which neither section 503(a) nor 503(b)(1) is applicable, if the delivery or proffered delivery was made in good faith and the labeling at the time thereof contained the same directions for use and warning statements as were contained in the labeling at the time of such receipt of such article; or (5) for having violated section 301(i)(2) if such person acted in good faith and had no reason to believe that use of the punch, die, plate, stone, or other thing involved would result in a drug being a counterfeit drug, or for having violated section 301(i)(3) if the person doing the act or causing it to be done acted in good faith and had no reason to believe that the drug was a counterfeit drug.

* * *

(e) (1) Except as provided in paragraph (2), any person who distributes or possesses with the intent to distribute any anabolic steroid for any use in humans other than the treatment of disease pursuant to the order of a physician shall be imprisoned for not more than three years or fined under title 18, United States Code, or both.

(2) Any person who distributes or possesses with the intent to distribute to an individual under 18 years of age, any anabolic steroid for any use in humans other than the treatment of disease pursuant to the order of a physician shall be imprisoned for not more than six years or fined under title 18, United States Code, or both.

(f) (1) Except as provided in paragraph (2), whoever knowingly distributes, or possesses with intent to distribute, human growth hormone for any use in humans other than the treatment of a disease or other recognized medical condition, where such use has been authorized by the Secretary of Health and Human Services under section 505 and pursuant to the order of a physician, is guilty of an offense punishable by not more than 5 years in prison, such fines as are authorized by title 18, or both.

(2) Whoever commits any offense set forth in paragraph (1) and such offense involves an individual under 18 years of age is punishable by not more than 10 years imprisonment, such fines as are authorized by title 18, or both.

(3) Any conviction for a violation of paragraphs (1) and (2) of this subsection shall be considered a felony violation of the Controlled Substances Act for the purposes of forfeiture under section 413 of such Act.

(4) As used in this subsection the term "human growth hormone" means somatrem, somatropin, or an analogue of either of them.

(5) The Drug Enforcement Administration is authorized to investigate offenses punishable by this subsection.

(g) (1)(A) Except as provided in subparagraph (B), any person who violates a requirement of this Act which relates to devices shall be liable to the United States for a civil penalty in an amount not to exceed $15,000 for each such violation, and not to exceed $1,000,000 for all such violations adjudicated in a single proceeding.

(B) Subparagraph (A) shall not apply—

(i) to any person who violates the requirements of section 519(a) or 520(f) unless such violation constitutes (I) a significant or knowing departure from such requirements, or (II) a risk to public health,

(ii) to any person who commits minor violations of section 519(e) or 519(f) (only with respect to correction reports) if such person demonstrates substantial compliance with such section, or

(iii) to violations of section 501(a)(2)(A) which involve one or more devices which are not defective. * * *

(3)(A) A civil penalty under paragraph (1) or (2) shall be assessed by the Secretary by an order made on the record after opportunity for a hearing provided in accordance with this subparagraph and section 554 of title 5, United States Code. Before issuing such an order, the Secretary shall give written notice to the person to be assessed a civil penalty under such order of the Secretary's proposal to issue such order and provide such person an opportunity for a hearing on the order. In the course of any investigation, the Secretary may issue subpoenas requiring the attendance and testimony of witnesses and the production of evidence that relates to the matter under investigation.

(B) In determining the amount of a civil penalty, the Secretary shall take into account the nature, circumstances, extent, and gravity of the violation or violations and, with respect to the violator, ability to pay, effect on ability to continue to do business, any history of prior such violations, the degree of culpability, and such other matters as justice may require. * * *

SEC. 304 [21 U.S.C. § 334]. SEIZURE.

(a) (1) Any article of food, drug, or cosmetic that is adulterated or misbranded when introduced into or while in interstate commerce or while held for sale (whether or not the first sale) after shipment in interstate commerce, or which may not, under the provisions of section 404 or 505, be introduced into interstate commerce, shall be liable to be proceeded against while in interstate commerce, or at any time thereafter, on libel of information and condemned in any district court of the United States or United States court of a Territory within the jurisdiction of which the article is found. No libel for condemnation shall be instituted under this Act, for any alleged misbranding if there is pending in any court a libel for condemnation proceeding under this Act based upon the same alleged misbranding, and not more than one such proceeding shall be instituted if no such proceeding is so pending, except that such limitations shall not apply (A) when such misbranding has been the basis of a prior judgment in favor of the United States, in a criminal, injunction, or libel for condemnation proceeding under this Act, or (B) when the Secretary has probable cause to believe from facts found, without hearing, by him or any officer or employee of the Department that the misbranded article is dangerous to health, or that the labeling of the misbranded article is fraudulent, or would be in a material respect misleading to the injury or damage of the purchaser or consumer. In any case where the number of libel for condemnation proceedings is limited as above provided the proceeding pending or instituted shall, on application of the claimant, seasonably made, be removed for trial to any district agreed upon by stipulation between the parties, or, in case of failure to so stipulate within a reasonable time, the claimant may apply to the court of the district in which the seizure has been made, and such court (after giving the United States attorney for such district reasonable notice and opportunity to be heard) shall by order, unless good cause to the contrary is shown, specify a district of reasonable proximity to the claimant's principal place of business, to which the case shall be removed for trial.

(2) The following shall be liable to be proceeded against at any time on libel of information and condemned in any district court of the United States or United States court of a Territory within the jurisdiction of which they are found: (A) any drug that is a counterfeit drug, (B) any container of a counterfeit drug, (C) any punch, die, plate, stone, labeling, container, or other thing used or designed for use in making a counterfeit drug or drugs, and (D) any adulterated or misbranded device. * * *

(b) The article, equipment, or other thing proceeded against shall be liable to seizure by process pursuant to the libel, and the procedure in cases under this section shall conform, as nearly as may be, to the procedure in admiralty; except that on demand of either party any issue of fact joined in any such case shall be tried by jury. When libel for condemnation proceedings under this section, involving the same claimant and the same issues of adulteration or misbranding, are pending in two or more jurisdictions, such pending proceedings, upon application of the claimant seasonably made to the court of one such jurisdiction, shall be consolidated for trial by order of such court, and tried in (1) any district selected by the claimant where one of such proceedings is pending; or (2) a district agreed upon by stipulation between the parties. If no order for consolidation is so made within a reasonable time, the claimant may apply to the court of one such jurisdiction and such court (after giving the United States attorney for such district reasonable notice and opportunity to be heard) shall by order, unless good cause to the contrary is shown, specify a district of reasonable proximity to the claimant's principal place of business, in which all such pending proceedings shall be consolidated for trial and tried. Such order of consolidation shall not apply so as to require the removal of any case the date for trial of which has been fixed. The court granting such order shall give prompt notification thereof to the other courts having jurisdiction of the cases covered thereby.

(c) The court at any time after seizure up to a reasonable time before trial shall by order allow any party to a condemnation proceeding, his attorney or agent, to obtain a representative sample of the article seized and a true copy of the analysis, if any, on which the proceeding is based and the identifying marks or numbers, if any, of the packages from which the samples analyzed were obtained.

(d) (1) Any food, drug, device, or cosmetic condemned under this section shall, after entry of the decree, be disposed of by destruction or sale as the court may, in accordance with the provisions of this section, direct and the proceeds thereof, if sold, less the legal costs and charges, shall be paid into the Treasury of the United States; but such article shall not be sold under such decree contrary to the provisions of this Act or the laws of the jurisdiction in which sold. After entry of the decree and upon the payment of the costs of such proceedings and the execution of a good and sufficient bond conditioned that such article shall not be sold or disposed of contrary to the provisions of this Act or the laws of any State or Territory in which sold, the court may by order direct that such article be delivered to the owner thereof to be destroyed or brought into compliance with the provisions of this Act, under the supervision of an officer or employee duly designated by the Secretary, and the expenses of such supervision shall be paid by the person obtaining release of the article under bond. If the article was imported into the United States and the person seeking its release establishes (A) that the adulteration, misbranding, or violation did not occur after the article was imported, and (B) that he had no cause for believing that it was adulterated, misbranded, or in violation before it was released from customs custody, the court may permit the article to be delivered to the owner for exportation in lieu of destruction upon a showing by the owner that all of the conditions of section 801(e) can and will be met. The provisions of this sentence shall not apply where condemnation is based upon violation of section 402(a)(1), (2), or (6), section 501(a)(3), section 502(j), or section 601(a) or (d). Where such exportation is made to the original foreign supplier, then paragraphs (1) and (2) of section 801(e) and the preceding sentence shall not be applicable; and in all cases of exportation the bond shall be conditioned that the article shall not be sold or disposed of until the applicable conditions of section 801(e) have been met. Any article condemned by reason of its being an article which may not, under section 404 or 505, be introduced into interstate commerce, shall be disposed of by destruction.

(2) The provisions of paragraph (1) of this subsection shall, to the extent deemed appropriate by the court, apply to any equipment or other thing which is not otherwise within the scope of such paragraph and which is referred to in paragraph (2) of subsection (a).

(3) Whenever in any proceeding under this section, involving paragraph (2) of subsection (a), the condemnation of any equipment or thing (other than a drug) is decreed, the court shall allow the claim of any claimant, to the extent of such claimant's interest, for remission or mitigation of such forfeiture if such claimant proves to the satisfaction of the court (i) that he has not committed or caused to be committed any prohibited act referred to in such paragraph (2) and has no interest in any drug referred to therein, (ii) that he has an interest in such equipment or other thing as owner or lienor or otherwise, acquired by him in good faith, and (iii) that he at no time had any knowledge or reason to believe that such equipment or other thing was being or would be used in, or to facilitate, the violation of laws of the United States relating to counterfeit drugs.

(e) When a decree of condemnation is entered against the article, court costs and fees, and storage and other proper expenses, shall be awarded against the person, if any, intervening as claimant of the article.

* * *

(g) (1) If during an inspection conducted under section 704 of a facility or a vehicle, a device which the officer or employee making the inspection has reason to believe is adulterated or misbranded is found in such facility or vehicle, such officer or employee may order the device detained (in accordance with regulations prescribed by the Secretary) for a reasonable period which may not exceed twenty days unless the Secretary determines that a period of detention greater than twenty days is required to institute an action under subsection (a) or section 302, in which case he may authorize a detention period of not to exceed thirty days. Regulations of the Secretary prescribed under this paragraph shall require that before a device may be ordered detained under this paragraph the Secretary or an officer or employee designated by the Secretary approve such order. A detention order under this paragraph may require the labeling or marking of a device during the period of its detention for the purpose of identifying the device as detained. Any person who would be entitled to claim a device if it were seized under subsection (a) may appeal to the Secretary a detention of such device under this paragraph. Within five days of the date an appeal of a detention is filed with the Secretary, the Secretary shall after affording opportunity for an informal hearing by order confirm the detention or revoke it.

(2)(A) Except as authorized by subparagraph (B), a device subject to a detention order issued under paragraph (1) shall not be moved by any person from the place at which it is ordered detained until—(i) released by the Secretary, or (ii) the expiration of the detention period applicable to such order, whichever occurs first.

(B) A device subject to a detention order under paragraph (1) may be moved—(i) in accordance with regulations prescribed by the Secretary, and (ii) if not in final form for shipment, at the discretion of the manufacturer of the device for the purpose of completing the work required to put it in such form.

SEC. 305 [21 U.S.C. § 335]. HEARING BEFORE REPORT OF CRIMINAL VIOLATION.

Before any violation of this Act is reported by the Secretary to any United States attorney for institution of a criminal proceeding, the person against whom such proceeding is contemplated shall be given appropriate notice and an opportunity to present his views, either orally or in writing, with regard to such contemplated proceeding.

SEC. 306 [21 U.S.C. § 335a]. DEBARMENT, TEMPORARY DENIAL OF APPROVAL, AND SUSPENSION.

(a) MANDATORY DEBARMENT.

(1) CORPORATIONS, PARTNERSHIPS, AND ASSOCIATIONS.—If the Secretary finds that a person other than an individual has been convicted, after the date of enactment of this section, of a felony under Federal law for conduct relating to the development or approval, including the process for development or approval, of any abbreviated drug applica-

tion, the Secretary shall debar such person from submitting, or assisting in the submission of, any such application.

(2) INDIVIDUALS.—If the Secretary finds that an individual has been convicted of a felony under Federal law for conduct—(A) relating to the development or approval, including the process for development or approval, of any drug product, or (B) otherwise relating to the regulation of any drug product under this Act, the Secretary shall debar such individual from providing services in any capacity to a person that has an approved or pending drug product application.

(b) PERMISSIVE DEBARMENT.

(1) IN GENERAL.—The Secretary, on the Secretary's own initiative or in response to a petition, may, in accordance with paragraph (2), debar— (A) a person other than an individual from submitting or assisting in the submission of any abbreviated drug application, or (B) an individual from providing services in any capacity to a person that has an approved or pending drug product application.

(2) PERSONS SUBJECT TO PERMISSIVE DEBARMENT.—The following persons are subject to debarment under paragraph (1):

(A) CORPORATIONS, PARTNERSHIPS, AND ASSOCIATIONS.— Any person other than an individual that the Secretary finds has been convicted—

(i) for conduct that—

(I) relates to the development or approval, including the process for the development or approval, of any abbreviated drug application; and

(II) is a felony under Federal law (if the person was convicted before the date of enactment of this section), a misdemeanor under Federal law, or a felony under State law, or

(ii) of a conspiracy to commit, or aiding or abetting, a criminal offense described in clause (i) or a felony described in subsection (a)(1),

if the Secretary finds that the type of conduct which served as the basis for such conviction undermines the process for the regulation of drugs.
* * *

(c) DEBARMENT PERIODS AND CONSIDERATIONS.

(1) EFFECT OF DEBARMENT.—The Secretary—

(A) shall not accept or review (other than in connection with an audit under this section) any abbreviated drug application submitted by or with the assistance of a person debarred under subsection (a)(1) or (b)(2)(A) during the period such person is debarred,

(B) shall, during the period of a debarment under subsection (a)(2) or (b)(2)(B), debar an individual from providing services in any capacity to a person that has an approved or pending drug product application and shall not accept or review (other than in connection with an audit under this section) an abbreviated drug application from such individual, and

(C) shall, if the Secretary makes the finding described in paragraph (6) or (7) of section 307(a), assess a civil penalty in accordance with section 307.

(2) DEBARMENT PERIODS.

(A) IN GENERAL.—The Secretary shall debar a person under subsection (a) or (b) for the following periods:

(i) The period of debarment of a person (other than an individual) under subsection (a)(1) shall not be less than 1 year or more than 10 years, but if an act leading to a subsequent debarment under subsection (a) occurs within 10 years after such person has been debarred under subsection (a)(1), the period of debarment shall be permanent.

(ii) The debarment of an individual under subsection (a)(2) shall be permanent.

(iii) The period of debarment of any person under subsection (b)(2) shall not be more than 5 years. The Secretary may determine whether debarment periods shall run concurrently or consecutively in the case of a person debarred for multiple offenses.

(B) NOTIFICATION.—Upon a conviction for an offense described in subsection (a) or (b) or upon execution of an agreement with the United States to plead guilty to such an offense, the person involved may notify the Secretary that the person acquiesces to debarment and such person's debarment shall commence upon such notification.

(3) CONSIDERATIONS.—In determining the appropriateness and the period of a debarment of a person under subsection (b) and any period of debarment beyond the minimum specified in subparagraph (A)(i) of paragraph (2), the Secretary shall consider where applicable—

(A) the nature and seriousness of any offense involved,

(B) the nature and extent of management participation in any offense involved, whether corporate policies and practices encouraged the offense, including whether inadequate institutional controls contributed to the offense,

(C) the nature and extent of voluntary steps to mitigate the impact on the public of any offense involved, including the recall or the discontinuation of the distribution of suspect drugs, full cooperation with any investigations (including the extent of disclosure to appropriate authorities of all wrongdoing), the relinquishing of profits on drug approvals fraudulently obtained, and any other actions taken to substantially limit potential or actual adverse effects on the public health,

(D) whether the extent to which changes in ownership, management, or operations have corrected the causes of any offense involved and provide reasonable assurances that the offense will not occur in the future,

(E) whether the person to be debarred is able to present adequate evidence that current production of drugs subject to abbreviated drug applications and all pending abbreviated drug applications are free of fraud or material false statements, and

(F) prior convictions under this Act or under other Acts involving matters within the jurisdiction of the Food and Drug Administration.

(d) TERMINATION OF DEBARMENT.

(1) APPLICATION.—Any person that is debarred under subsection (a) (other than a person permanently debarred) or any person that is debarred under subsection (b) of this section may apply to the Secretary for termination of the debarment under this subsection. * * *

(e) PUBLICATION AND LIST OF DEBARRED PERSONS.—The Secretary shall publish in the Federal Register the name of any person debarred under subsection (a) or (b), the effective date of the debarment, and the period of the debarment. The Secretary shall also maintain and make available to the public a list, updated no less often than quarterly, of such persons, of the effective dates and minimum periods of such debarments, and of the termination of debarments.

(f) TEMPORARY DENIAL OF APPROVAL.

(1) IN GENERAL.—The Secretary, on the Secretary's own initiative or in response to a petition, may, in accordance with paragraph (3), refuse by order, for the period prescribed by paragraph (2), to approve any abbreviated drug application submitted by any person—

(A) if such person is under an active Federal criminal investigation in connection with an action described in subparagraph (B),

(B) if the Secretary finds that such person—

(i) has bribed or attempted to bribe, has paid or attempted to pay an illegal gratuity, or has induced or attempted to induce another person to bribe or pay an illegal gratuity to any officer, employee, or agent of the Department of Health and Human Services or to any other Federal, State, or local official in connection with any abbreviated drug application, or has conspired to commit, or aided or abetted, such actions, or

(ii) has knowingly made or caused to be made a pattern or practice of false statements or misrepresentations with respect to material facts relating to any abbreviated drug application, or the production of any drug subject to an abbreviated drug application, to any officer, employee, or agent of the Department of Health and Human Services, or has conspired to commit, or aided or abetted, such actions, and

(C) if a significant question has been raised regarding—(i) the integrity of the approval process with respect to such abbreviated drug application, or (ii) the reliability of data in or concerning such person's abbreviated drug application. * * *

(3) INFORMAL HEARING.—Within 10 days of the date an order is issued under paragraph (1), the Secretary shall provide such person with an opportunity for an informal hearing, to be held within such 10 days, on the decision of the Secretary to refuse approval of an abbreviated drug application. Within 60 days of the date on which such hearing is held, the Secretary shall notify the person given such hearing whether the Secretary's refusal of approval will be continued, terminated, or otherwise modified. Such notification shall be final agency action.

(g) SUSPENSION AUTHORITY.

(1) IN GENERAL.—If—

(A) the Secretary finds—

(i) that a person has engaged in conduct described in subparagraph (B) of subsection (f)(1) in connection with 2 or more drugs under abbreviated drug applications, or

(ii) that a person has engaged in flagrant and repeated, material violations of good manufacturing practice or good laboratory practice in connection with the development, manufacturing, or distribution of one or more drugs approved under an abbreviated drug application during a 2–year period, and—(I) such violations may undermine the safety and efficacy of such drugs, and (II) the causes of such violations have not been corrected within a reasonable period of time following notice of such violations by the Secretary, and

(B) such person is under an active investigation by a Federal authority in connection with a civil or criminal action involving conduct described in subparagraph (A),

the Secretary shall issue an order suspending the distribution of all drugs the development or approval of which was related to such conduct described in subparagraph (A) or suspending the distribution of all drugs approved under abbreviated drug applications of such person if the Secretary finds that such conduct may have affected the development or approval of a significant number of drugs which the Secretary is unable to identify. The Secretary shall exclude a drug from such order if the Secretary determines that such conduct was not likely to have influenced the safety or efficacy of such drug.

(2) PUBLIC HEALTH WAIVER.—The Secretary shall, on the Secretary's own initiative or in response to a petition, waive the suspension under paragraph (1) (involving an action described in paragraph (1)(A)(i)) with respect to any drug if the Secretary finds that such waiver is necessary to protect the public health because sufficient quantities of the drug would not otherwise be available. The Secretary shall act on any petition seeking action under this paragraph within 180 days of the date the petition is submitted to the Secretary.

(h) TERMINATION OF SUSPENSION.—The Secretary shall withdraw an order of suspension of the distribution of a drug under subsection (g) if the person with respect to whom the order was issued demonstrates in a petition to the Secretary—

(1)(A) on the basis of an audit by the Food and Drug Administration or by experts acceptable to the Food and Drug Administration, or on the basis of other information, that the development, approval, manufacturing, and distribution of such drug is in substantial compliance with the applicable requirements of this Act, and

(B) changes in ownership, management, or operations—

(i) fully remedy the patterns or practices with respect to which the order was issued, and

(ii) provide reasonable assurances that such actions will not occur in the future, or

(2) the initial determination was in error.

The Secretary shall act on a submission of a petition under this subsection within 180 days of the date of its submission and the Secretary may consider the petition concurrently with the suspension proceeding. Any information submitted to the Secretary under this subsection does not constitute an amendment or supplement to a pending or approved abbreviated drug application.

(i) PROCEDURE.—The Secretary may not take any action under subsection (a), (b), (c), (d)(3), (g), or (h) with respect to any person unless the Secretary has issued an order for such action made on the record after opportunity for an agency hearing on disputed issues of material fact. In the course of any investigation or hearing under this subsection, the Secretary may administer oaths and affirmations, examine witnesses, receive evidence, and issue subpoenas requiring the attendance and testimony of witnesses and the production of evidence that relates to the matter under investigation.

(j) JUDICIAL REVIEW.

(1) IN GENERAL.—Except as provided in paragraph (2), any person that is the subject of an adverse decision under subsection (a), (b), (c), (d), (f), (g), or (h) may obtain a review of such decision by the United States Court of Appeals for the District of Columbia or for the circuit in which the person resides, by filing in such court (within 60 days following the date the person is notified of the Secretary's decision) a petition requesting that the decision be modified or set aside.

(2) EXCEPTION.—Any person that is the subject of an adverse decision under clause (iii) or (iv) of subsection (b)(2)(B) may obtain a review of such decision by the United States District Court for the District of Columbia or a district court of the United States for the district in which the person resides, by filing in such court (within 30 days following the date the person is notified of the Secretary's decision) a complaint requesting that the decision be modified or set aside. In such an action, the court shall determine the matter de novo.

(k) CERTIFICATION.—Any application for approval of a drug product shall include—

(1) a certification that the applicant did not and will not use in any capacity the services of any person debarred under subsection (a) or (b), in connection with such application, and

(2) if such application is an abbreviated drug application, a list of all convictions, described in subsections (a) and (b) which occurred within the previous 5 years, of the applicant and affiliated persons responsible for the development or submission of such application.

* * *

SEC. 307 [21 U.S.C. § 335b]. CIVIL PENALTIES.

(a) IN GENERAL.—Any person that the Secretary finds—

(1) knowingly made or caused to be made, to any officer, employee, or agent of the Department of Health and Human Services, a false statement or misrepresentation of a material fact in connection with an abbreviated drug application,

(2) bribed or attempted to bribe or paid or attempted to pay an illegal gratuity to any officer, employee, or agent of the Department of Health and Human Services in connection with an abbreviated drug application,

(3) destroyed, altered, removed, or secreted, or procured the destruction, alteration, removal, or secretion of, any material document or other material evidence which was the property of or in the possession of the Department of Health and Human Services for the purpose of interfering with that Department's discharge of its responsibilities in connection with an abbreviated drug application,

(4) knowingly failed to disclose, to an officer or employee of the Department of Health and Human Services, a material fact which such person had an obligation to disclose relating to any drug subject to an abbreviated drug application,

(5) knowingly obstructed an investigation of the Department of Health and Human Services into any drug subject to an abbreviated drug application,

(6) is a person that has an approved or pending drug product application and has knowingly—(A) employed or retained as a consultant or contractor, or (B) otherwise used in any capacity the services of, a person who was debarred under section 306, or

(7) is an individual debarred under section 306 and, during the period of debarment, provided services in any capacity to a person that had an approved or pending drug product application,

shall be liable to the United States for a civil penalty for each such violation in an amount not to exceed $250,000 in the case of an individual and $1,000,000 in the case of any other person.

(b) PROCEDURE.

(1) IN GENERAL.

(A) ACTION BY THE SECRETARY.—A civil penalty under subsection (a) shall be assessed by the Secretary on a person by an order made on the record after an opportunity for an agency hearing on disputed issues of material fact and the amount of the penalty. In the course of any investigation or hearing under this subparagraph, the Secretary may administer oaths and affirmations, examine witnesses, receive evidence, and issue subpoenas requiring the attendance and testimony of witnesses and the production of evidence that relates to the matter under investigation.

(B) ACTION BY THE ATTORNEY GENERAL.—In lieu of a proceeding under subparagraph (A), the Attorney General may, upon request of the Secretary, institute a civil action to recover a civil money penalty in the amount and for any of the acts set forth in subsection (a). Such an action may be instituted separately from or in connection with any other claim, civil or criminal, initiated by the Attorney General under this Act.

(2) AMOUNT.—In determining the amount of a civil penalty under paragraph (1), the Secretary or the court shall take into account the nature, circumstances, extent, and gravity of the act subject to penalty, the person's ability to pay, the effect on the person's ability to continue to do business, any history of prior, similar acts, and such other matters as justice may require.

(3) LIMITATION ON ACTIONS.—No action may be initiated under this section—(A) with respect to any act described in subsection (a) of this section that occurred before the date of enactment of this section, or (B) more than 6 years after the date when facts material to the act are known or reasonably should have been known by the Secretary but in no event more than 10 years after the date the act took place.

(c) JUDICIAL REVIEW.—Any person that is the subject of an adverse decision under subsection (b)(1)(A) may obtain a review of such decision by the United States Court of Appeals for the District of Columbia or for the circuit in which the person resides, by filing in such court (within 60 days following the date the person is notified of the Secretary's decision) a petition requesting that the decision be modified or set aside.

(d) RECOVERY OF PENALTIES.—The Attorney General may recover any civil penalty (plus interest at the currently prevailing rates from the date the penalty became final) assessed under subsection (b)(1)(A) in an action brought in the name of the United States. The amount of such penalty may be deducted, when the penalty has become final, from any sums then or later owing by the United States to the person against whom the penalty has been assessed. In an action brought under this subsection, the validity, amount, and appropriateness of the penalty shall not be subject to judicial review.

(e) INFORMANTS.—The Secretary may award to any individual (other than an officer or employee of the Federal Government or a person who materially participated in any conduct described in subsection (a)) who provides information leading to the imposition of a civil penalty under this section an amount not to exceed—(1) $250,000, or (2) one-half of the penalty so imposed and collected, whichever is less. The decision of the Secretary on such award shall not be reviewable.

SEC. 308 [21 U.S.C. § 335c]. AUTHORITY TO WITHDRAW APPROVAL OF ANDAs.

(a) IN GENERAL.—The Secretary—

(1) shall withdraw approval of an abbreviated drug application if the Secretary finds that the approval was obtained, expedited, or otherwise facilitated through bribery, payment of an illegal gratuity, or fraud or material false statement, and

(2) may withdraw approval of an abbreviated drug application if the Secretary finds that the applicant has repeatedly demonstrated a lack of ability to produce the drug for which the application was submitted in accordance with the formulations or manufacturing practice set forth in the abbreviated drug application and has introduced, or attempted to introduce, such adulterated or misbranded drug into commerce.

(b) PROCEDURE.—The Secretary may not take any action under subsection (a) with respect to any person unless the Secretary has issued an order for such action made on the record after opportunity for an agency hearing on disputed issues of material fact. In the course of any investigation or hearing under this subsection, the Secretary may administer oaths and affirmations, examine witnesses, receive evidence, and issue subpoenas requiring the attendance and testimony of witnesses and the production of evidence that relates to the matter under investigation.

(c) APPLICABILITY.—Subsection (a) shall apply with respect to offenses or acts regardless of when such offenses or acts occurred.

(d) JUDICIAL REVIEW.—Any person that is the subject of an adverse decision under subsection (a) may obtain a review of such decision by the United States Court of Appeals for the District of Columbia or for the circuit in which the person resides, by filing in such court (within 60 days following the date the person is notified of the Secretary's decision) a petition requesting that the decision be modified or set aside.

SEC. 309 [21 U.S.C. § 336]. REPORT OF MINOR VIOLATIONS.

Nothing in this Act shall be construed as requiring the Secretary to report for prosecution, or for the institution of libel or injunction proceedings, minor violations of this Act whenever he believes that the public interest will be adequately served by a suitable written notice or warning.

SEC. 310 [21 U.S.C. § 337]. PROCEEDINGS IN NAME OF UNITED STATES.

(a) Except as provided in subsection (b), all such proceedings for the enforcement, or to restrain violations, of this Act shall be by and in the name of the United States. Subpoenas for witnesses who are required to attend a court of the United States, in any district, may run into any other district in any proceeding under this section.

     * * *

PROVISIONS GOVERNING DRUGS AND MEDICAL DEVICES

SEC. 501 [21 U.S.C. § 351]. ADULTERATED DRUGS AND DEVICES.

A drug or device shall be deemed to be adulterated—

(a) (1) If it consists in whole or in part of any filthy, putrid, or decomposed substance; or

(2)(A) if it has been prepared, packed, or held under insanitary conditions whereby it may have been contaminated with filth, or whereby it may have been rendered injurious to health; or (B) if it is a drug and the methods used in, or the facilities or controls used for, its manufacture, processing, packing, or holding do not conform to or are not operated or administered in conformity with current good manufacturing practice to assure that such drug meets the requirements of this chapter as to safety and has the identity and strength, and meets the quality and purity characteristics, which it purports or is represented to possess; or (C) if it is a compounded positron emission tomography drug and the methods used in, or the facilities and controls used for, its compounding, processing, packing, or holding do not conform to or are not operated or administered in conformity with the positron emission tomography compounding standards and the official monographs of the United States Pharmacopoeia to assure that such drug meets the requirements of this Act as to safety and has the identity and strength, and meets the quality and purity characteristics, that it purports or is represented to possess; or

(3) if its container is composed, in whole or in part, of any poisonous or deleterious substance which may render the contents injurious to health; or

(4) if (A) it bears or contains, for purposes of coloring only, a color additive which is unsafe within the meaning of section 721(a), or (B) it is a color additive the intended use of which in or on drugs or devices is for purposes of coloring only and is unsafe within the meaning of section 721(a); or

(5) if it is a new animal drug which is unsafe within the meaning of section 512; or

(6) if it is an animal feed bearing or containing a new animal drug, and such animal feed is unsafe within the meaning of section 512.

(b) If it purports to be or is represented as a drug the name of which is recognized in an official compendium, and its strength differs from, or its quality or purity falls below, the standard set forth in such compendium. Such determination as to strength, quality, or purity shall be made in accordance with the tests or methods of assay set forth in such compendium, except that whenever tests or methods of assay have not been prescribed in such compendium, or such tests or methods of assay as are prescribed are, in the judgment of the Secretary, insufficient for the making of such determination, the Secretary shall bring such fact to the attention of the appropriate body charged with the revision of such compendium, and if such body fails within a reasonable time to prescribe tests or methods of assay which, in the judgment of the Secretary, are sufficient for purposes of this paragraph, then the Secretary shall promulgate regulations prescribing appropriate tests or methods of assay in accordance with which such determination as to strength, quality, or purity shall be made. No drug defined in an official compendium shall be deemed to be adulterated under this paragraph because it differs from the standard of strength, quality, or purity therefor set forth in such compendium, if its difference in strength, quality, or purity from such standard is plainly stated on its label. Whenever a drug is recognized in both the United States Pharmacopoeia and the Homeopathic Pharmacopoeia of the United States it shall be subject to the requirements of the United States Pharmacopoeia unless it is labeled and offered for sale as a homeopathic drug, in which case it shall be subject to the provisions of the Homeopathic Pharmacopoeia of the United States and not to those of the United States Pharmacopoeia.

(c) If it is not subject to the provisions of paragraph (b) of this section and its strength differs from, or its purity or quality falls below, that which it purports or is represented to possess.

(d) If it is a drug and any substance has been (1) mixed or packed therewith so as to reduce its quality or strength or (2) substituted wholly or in part therefor.

(e) (1) If it is, or purports to be or is represented as, a device which is subject to a performance standard established under section 514 unless such device is in all respects in conformity with such standard.

(2) If it is declared to be, purports to be, or is represented as, a device that is in conformity with any standard recognized under section 514(c) unless such device is in all respects in conformity with such standard.

(f) (1) If it is a class III device—

(A)(i) which is required by a regulation promulgated under subsection (b) of section 515 to have an approval under such section of an application for premarket approval and which is not exempt from section 515 under section 520(g), and (ii)(I) for which an application for premarket approval or a notice of completion of a product development protocol was not filed with the Secretary within the ninety-day period beginning on the date of the promulgation of such regulation, or (II) for which such an application was filed and approval of the application has been denied, suspended, or withdrawn, or such a notice was filed and has been declared not completed or the approval of the device under the protocol has been withdrawn;

(B)(i) which was classified under section 513(f) into class III, which under section 515(a) is required to have in effect an approved application for premarket approval, and which is not exempt from section 515 under section 520(g), and (ii) which has an application which has been suspended or is otherwise not in effect; or

(C) which was classified under section 520(*l*) into class III, which under such section is required to have in effect an approved application under section 515, and which has an application which has been suspended or is otherwise not in effect.

(2)(A) In the case of a device classified under section 513(f) into class III and intended solely for investigational use, paragraph (1)(B) shall not apply with respect to such device during the period ending on the ninetieth day after the date of the promulgation of the regulations prescribing the procedures and conditions required by section 520(g)(2).

(B) In the case of a device subject to a regulation promulgated under subsection (b) of section 515, paragraph (1) shall not apply with respect to such device during the period ending—(i) on the last day of the thirtieth calendar month beginning after the month in which the classification of the device in class III became effective under section 513, or (ii) on the ninetieth day after the date of the promulgation of such regulation, whichever occurs later.

(g) If it is a banned device.

(h) If it is a device and the methods used in, or the facilities or controls used for, its manufacture, packing, storage, or installation are not in conformity with applicable requirements under section 520(f)(1) or an applicable condition prescribed by an order under section 520(f)(2).

(i) If it is a device for which an exemption has been granted under section 520(g) for investigational use and the person who was granted such exemption or any investigator who uses such device under such exemption fails to comply with a requirement prescribed by or under such section.

SEC. 502 [21 U.S.C. § 352]. MISBRANDED DRUGS AND DEVICES.

A drug or device shall be deemed to be misbranded—

(a) If its labeling is false or misleading in any particular. Health care economic information provided to a formulary committee, or other similar entity, in the course of the committee or the entity carrying out its responsibilities for the selection of drugs for managed care or other similar organizations, shall not be considered to be false or misleading under this paragraph if the health care economic information directly relates to an indication approved under section 505 or under section 351(a) of the Public Health Service Act for such drug and is based on competent and reliable scientific evidence. The requirements set forth in section 505(a) or in section 351(a) of the Public Health Service Act shall not apply to health care economic information provided to such a committee or entity in accordance with this paragraph. Information that is relevant to the substantiation of the health care economic information presented pursuant to this paragraph shall be made available to the Secretary upon request. In this paragraph, the term ''health care economic information'' means any analysis that identifies, measures, or compares the economic consequences, including the costs of the represented health outcomes, of the use of a drug to the use of another drug, to another health care intervention, or to no intervention.

(b) If in package form unless it bears a label containing (1) the name and place of business of the manufacturer, packer, or distributor; and (2) an accurate statement of the quantity of the contents in terms of weight, measure, or numerical count: *Provided*, That under clause (2) of this paragraph reasonable variations shall be permitted, and exemptions as to small packages shall be established, by regulations prescribed by the Secretary.

(c) If any word, statement, or other information required by or under authority of this Act to appear on the label or labeling is not prominently placed thereon with such conspicuousness (as compared with other words, statements, designs, or devices, in the labeling) and in such terms as to render it likely to be read and understood by the ordinary individual under customary conditions of purchase and use.

(e) (1)(A) If it is a drug, unless its label bears, to the exclusion of any other nonproprietary name (except the applicable systematic chemical name or the chemical formula),

(i) the established name (as defined in subparagraph (3)) of the drug, if such there is such a name;

(ii) the established name and quantity or, if determined to be appropriate by the Secretary, the proportion of each active ingredient, including the quantity, kind, and proportion of any alcohol, and also including whether active or not the established name and quantity or if determined to be appropriate by the Secretary, the proportion of any bromides, ether, chloroform, acetanilide, acetophenetidin, amidopyrine, antipyrine, atropine, hyoscine, hyoscyamine, arsenic, digitalis, digitalis glucosides, mercury, ouabain, strophanthin, strychnine, thyroid, or any derivative or preparation of any such substances, contained therein, except that the requirement for stating the quantity of the active ingredients, other than the quantity of those specifically named in this subclause, shall not apply to nonprescription drugs not intended for human use; and

(iii) the established name of each inactive ingredient listed in alphabetical order on the outside container of the retail package and, if determined to be appropriate by the Secretary, on the immediate container, as prescribed in regulation promulgated by the Secretary, except that nothing in this subclause shall be deemed to require that any trade secret be divulged, and except that the requirements of this subclause with respect to alphabetical order shall apply only to nonprescription drugs that are not also cosmetics and that this subclause shall not apply to nonprescription drugs not intended for human use.

(B) for any prescription drug the established name of such drug or ingredient, as the case may be, on such label (and on any labeling on which a name for such drug or ingredient is used) shall be printed prominently and in type at least half as large as that used thereon for any proprietary name or designation for such drug or ingredient; except, that to the extent that compliance with the requirements of subclause (ii) or (iii) of clause (A) or this clause is impracticable, exemptions shall be established by regulations promulgated by the Secretary.

(2) If it is a device and it has an established name, unless its label bears, to the exclusion of any other nonproprietary name, its established name (as defined in subparagraph (4)) prominently printed in type at least half as large as that used thereon for any proprietary name or designation for such device, except that to the extent compliance with the requirements of this subparagraph is impracticable, exemptions shall be established by regulations promulgated by the Secretary.

(3) As used in subparagraph (1), the term "established name", with respect to a drug or ingredient thereof, means (A) the applicable official name designated pursuant to section 508, or (B), if there is no such name and such drug, or such ingredient, is an article recognized in an official compendium, then the official title thereof in such compendium, or (C) if neither clause (A) nor clause (B) of this subparagraph applies, then the common or usual name, if any, of such drug or of such ingredient, except that where clause (B) of this subparagraph applies to an article recognized in the United States Pharmacopeia and in the Homeopathic Pharmacopoeia under different official titles, the official title used in the United States Pharmacopeia shall apply unless it is labeled and offered for sale as a homeopathic drug, in which case the official title used in the Homeopathic Pharmacopoeia shall apply.

(4) As used in subparagraph (2), the term "established name" with respect to a device means (A) the applicable official name of the device designated pursuant to section, 508, (B) if there is no such name and such device is an article recognized in an official compendium, then the official title thereof in such compendium, or (C) if neither clause (A) nor clause (B) of this subparagraph applies, then any common or usual name of such device.

(f) Unless its labeling bears (1) adequate directions for use; and (2) such adequate warnings against use in those pathological conditions or by children where its use may be dangerous to health, or against unsafe dosage or methods or duration of administration or application, in such manner and form, as are necessary for the protection of users, except that where any requirement of clause (1) of this paragraph, as applied to any drug or device, is not necessary for the protection of the public health, the Secretary shall promulgate regulations exempting such drug or device from such requirement.

(g) If it purports to be a drug the name of which is recognized in an official compendium, unless it is packaged and labeled as prescribed therein. The method of packing may be modified with the consent of the Secretary. Whenever a drug is recognized in both the United States Pharmacopoeia and the Homeopathic Pharmacopoeia of the United States, it shall be subject to the requirements of the United States Pharmacopoeia with respect to packaging and labeling unless it is labeled and offered for sale as a homeopathic drug, in which case it shall be subject to the provisions of the Homeopathic Pharmacopoeia of the United States, and not those of the United States Pharmacopoeia, except that in the event of inconsistency between the requirements of this paragraph and those of paragraph (e) as to the name by which the drug or its ingredients shall be designated, the requirements of paragraph (e) shall prevail.

(h) If it has been found by the Secretary to be a drug liable to deterioration, unless it is packaged in such form and manner, and its label bears a statement of such precautions, as the Secretary shall by regulations require as necessary for the protection of the public health. No such regulation shall be established for any drug recognized in an official compendium until the Secretary shall have informed the appropriate body charged with the revision of such compendium of the need for such packaging or labeling requirements and such body shall have failed within a reasonable time to prescribe such requirements.

(i) (1) If it is a drug and its container is so made, formed, or filled as to be misleading; or (2) if it is an imitation of another drug; or (3) if it is offered for sale under the name of another drug.

(j) If it is dangerous to health when used in the dosage or manner, or with the frequency or duration prescribed, recommended, or suggested in the labeling thereof.

    * * *

(n) In the case of any prescription drug distributed or offered for sale in any State, unless the manufacturer, packer, or distributor thereof includes in all advertisements and other descriptive printed matter issued or caused to be issued by the manufacturer, packer, or distributor with respect to that drug a true statement of (1) the established name as defined in section 502(e), printed prominently and in type at least half as large as that used for any trade or brand name thereof, (2) the formula showing quantitatively each ingredient of such drug to the extent required for labels under section 502(e), and (3) such other information in brief summary relating to side effects, contraindications, and effectiveness as shall be required in regulations which shall be issued by the Secretary in accordance with the procedure specified in section 701(e) of this Act, except that (A) except in extraordinary circumstances, no regulation issued under this paragraph shall require prior approval by the Secretary of the content of any advertisement, and (B) no advertisement of a prescription drug, published after the effective date of regulations issued under this paragraph applicable to advertisements of prescription drugs, shall with respect to the matters specified in this paragraph or covered by such regulations, be subject to the provisions of sections 12 to 17 of the Federal Trade Commission Act, as amended (15 U.S.C. §§ 52–57). This paragraph (n) shall not be applicable to any printed matter which the Secretary determines to be labeling as defined in section 201(m) of this Act. Nothing in the Convention on

Psychotropic Substances, signed at Vienna, Austria, on February 21, 1971, shall be construed to prevent drug price communications to consumers.

(o) If it was manufactured, prepared, propagated, compounded, or processed in an establishment in any State not duly registered under section 510, if it was not included in a list required by section 510(j), if a notice or other information respecting it was not provided as required by such section or section 510(k), or if it does not bear such symbols from the uniform system for identification of devices prescribed under section 510(e) as the Secretary by regulation requires.

(p) If it is a drug and its packaging or labeling is in violation of an applicable regulation issued pursuant to section 3 or 4 of the Poison Prevention Packaging Act of 1970.

(q) In the case of any restricted device distributed or offered for sale in any State, if (1) its advertising is false or misleading in any particular, or (2) it is sold, distributed, or used in violation of regulations prescribed under section 520(e).

(r) In the case of any restricted device distributed or offered for sale in any State, unless the manufacturer, packer, or distributor thereof includes in all advertisements and other descriptive printed matter issued or caused to be issued by the manufacturer, packer, or distributor with respect to that device (1) a true statement of the device's established name as defined in section 502(e), printed prominently and in type at least half as large as that used for any trade or brand name thereof, and (2) a brief statement of the intended uses of the device and relevant warnings, precautions, side effects, and contraindications and, in the case of specific devices made subject to a finding by the Secretary after notice and opportunity for comment that such action is necessary to protect the public health, a full description of the components of such device or the formula showing quantitatively each ingredient of such device to the extent required in regulations which shall be issued by the Secretary after an opportunity for a hearing. Except in extraordinary circumstances, no regulation issued under this paragraph shall require prior approval by the Secretary of the content of any advertisement and no advertisement of a restricted device, published after the effective date of this paragraph shall, with respect to the matters specified in this paragraph or covered by regulations issued hereunder, be subject to the provisions of sections 12 through 15 of the Federal Trade Commission Act (15 U.S.C. §§ 52–55). This paragraph shall not be applicable to any printed matter which the Secretary determines to be labeling as defined in section 201(m).

(s) If it is a device subject to a performance standard established under section 514, unless it bears such labeling as may be prescribed in such performance standard.

(t) If it is a device and there was a failure or refusal (1) to comply with any requirement prescribed under section 518 respecting the device, (2) to furnish any material or information required by or under section 519 respecting the device, or (3) to comply with a requirement under section 522.

SEC. 503 [21 U.S.C. § 353]. EXEMPTIONS AND CONSIDERATIONS FOR CERTAIN PRODUCTS.

(a) The Secretary is directed to promulgate regulations exempting from any labeling or packaging requirement of this Act drugs and devices which are, in accordance with the practice of the trade, to be processed, labeled, or repacked in substantial quantities at establishments other than those where originally processed or packed, on condition that such drugs and devices are not adulterated or misbranded under the provisions of this Act upon removal from such processing, labeling, or repacking establishment.

(b) (1) A drug intended for use by man which—

(A) because of its toxicity or other potentiality for harmful effect, or the method of its use, or the collateral measures necessary to its use, is not safe for use except under the supervision of a practitioner licensed by law to administer such drug; or

(B) is limited by an approved application under section 505 to use under the professional supervision of a practitioner licensed by law to administer such drug; shall be dispensed only (i) upon a written prescription of a practitioner licensed by law to administer such drug, or (ii) upon an oral prescription of such practitioner which is reduced promptly to writing and filed by the pharmacist, or (iii) by refilling any such written or oral prescription if such refilling is authorized by the prescriber either in the original prescription or by oral order which is reduced promptly to writing and filed by the pharmacist. The act of dispensing a drug contrary to the provisions of this paragraph shall be deemed to be an act which results in the drug being misbranded while held for sale.

(2) Any drug dispensed by filling or refilling a written or oral prescription of a practitioner licensed by law to administer such drug shall be exempt from the requirements of section 502, except paragraphs (a), (i)(2) and (3), (k), and (l), and the packaging requirements of paragraphs (g), (h), and (p), if the drug bears a label containing the name and address of the dispenser, the serial number and date of the prescription or of its filling, the name of the prescriber, and, if stated in the prescription, the name of the patient, and the directions for use and cautionary statements, if any, contained in such prescription. This exemption shall not apply to any drug dispensed in the course of the conduct of a business of dispensing drugs pursuant to diagnosis by mail, or to a drug dispensed in violation of paragraph (1) of this subsection.

(3) The Secretary may by regulation remove drugs subject to sections 502(d) and 505 from the requirements of paragraph (1) of this subsection when such requirements are not necessary for the protection of the public health.

(4)(A) A drug which is subject to paragraph (1) shall be deemed to be misbranded if at any time prior to dispensing its label fails to bear at a minimum, the symbol "Rx only." (B) A drug to which paragraph (1) does not apply shall be deemed to be misbranded if at any time prior to dispensing the label of the drug bears the symbol described in subparagraph (A).

(5) Nothing in this subsection shall be construed to relieve any person from any requirement prescribed by or under authority of law with respect to drugs now included or which may hereafter be included within the classifications stated in section 3220 of the Internal Revenue Code (26 U.S.C. § 3220) or to marihuana as defined in section 3238(b) of the Internal Revenue Code (26 U.S.C. § 3238(b)).

(c) (1) No person may sell, purchase, or trade or offer to sell, purchase, or trade any drug sample. For purposes of this paragraph and subsection (d), the term "drug sample" means a unit of a drug, subject to subsection (b), which is not intended to be sold and is intended to promote the sale of the drug. Nothing in this paragraph shall subject an officer or executive of a drug manufacturer or distributor to criminal liability solely because of a sale, purchase, trade, or offer to sell, purchase, or trade in violation of this paragraph by other employees of the manufacturer or distributor.

(2) No person may sell, purchase, or trade, offer to sell, purchase, or trade, or counterfeit any coupon. For purposes of this paragraph, the term "coupon" means a form which may be redeemed, at no cost or at a reduced cost, for a drug which is prescribed in accordance with subsection (b).

(3)(A) No person may sell, purchase, or trade, or offer to sell, purchase, or trade, any drug—

(i) which is subject to subsection (b), and

(ii)(I) which was purchased by a public or private hospital or other health care entity, or (II) which was donated or supplied at a reduced price to a charitable organization described in section 501(c)(3) of the Internal Revenue Code of 1954.

(B) Subparagraph (A) does not apply to—

(i) the purchase or other acquisition by a hospital or other health care entity which is a member of a group purchasing organization of a drug for its own use from the group purchasing organization or from other hospitals or health care entities which are members of such organization,

(ii) the sale, purchase, or trade of a drug or an offer to sell, purchase, or trade a drug by an organization described in subparagraph (A)(ii)(II) to a nonprofit affiliate of the organization to the extent otherwise permitted by law,

(iii) a sale, purchase, or trade of a drug or an offer to sell, purchase, or trade a drug among hospitals or other health care entities which are under common control,

(iv) a sale, purchase, or trade of a drug or an offer to sell, purchase, or trade a drug for emergency medical reasons, or

(v) a sale, purchase, or trade of a drug, an offer to sell, purchase, or trade a drug, or the dispensing of a drug pursuant to a prescription executed in accordance with subsection (b).

For purposes of this paragraph, the term "entity" does not include a wholesale distributor of drugs or a retail pharmacy licensed under State law and the term "emergency medical reasons" includes transfers of a drug between health care entities or from a health care entity to a retail pharmacy undertaken to alleviate temporary shortages of the drug arising from delays in or interruptions of regular distribution schedules.

(d) (1) Except as provided in paragraphs (2) and (3), no person may distribute any drug sample. For purposes of this subsection, the term "distribute" does not include the providing of a drug sample to a patient by a—(A) practitioner licensed to prescribe such drug, (B) health care professional acting at the direction and under the supervision of such a practitioner, or (C) pharmacy of a hospital or of another health care entity that is acting at the direction of such a practitioner and that received such sample pursuant to paragraph (2) or (3).

(2)(A) The manufacturer or authorized distributor of record of a drug subject to subsection (b) may, in accordance with this paragraph, distribute drug samples by mail or common carrier to practitioners licensed to prescribe such drugs or, at the request of a licensed practitioner, to pharmacies of hospitals or other health care entities. Such a distribution of drug samples may only be made—(i) in response to a written request for drug samples made on a form which meets the requirements of subparagraph (B), and (ii) under a system which requires the recipient of the drug sample to execute a written receipt for the drug sample upon its delivery and the return of the receipt to the manufacturer or authorized distributor of record.

(B) A written request for a drug sample required by subparagraph (A)(i) shall contain—(i) the name, address, professional designation, and signature of the practitioner making the request,

(ii) the identity of the drug sample requested and the quantity requested, (iii) the name of the manufacturer of the drug sample requested, and (iv) the date of the request.

(C) Each drug manufacturer or authorized distributor of record which makes distributions by mail or common carrier under this paragraph shall maintain, for a period of 3 years, the request forms submitted for such distributions and the receipts submitted for such distributions and shall maintain a record of distributions of drug samples which identifies the drugs distributed and the recipients of the distributions. Forms, receipts, and records required to be maintained under this subparagraph shall be made available by the drug manufacturer or authorized distributor of record to Federal and State officials engaged in the regulation of drugs and in the enforcement of laws applicable to drugs.

(3) The manufacturer or authorized distributor of record of a drug subject to subsection (b) may, by means other than mail or common carrier, distribute drug samples only if the manufacturer or authorized distributor of record makes the distributions in accordance with subparagraph (A) and carries out the activities described in subparagraphs (B) through (F) as follows:

(A) Drug samples may only be distributed—(i) to practitioners licensed to prescribe such drugs if they make a written request for the drug samples, or (ii) at the written request of such a licensed practitioner, to pharmacies of hospitals or other health care entities. A written request for drug samples shall be made on a form which contains the practitioner's name, address, and professional designation, the identity of the drug sample requested, the quantity of drug samples requested, the name of the manufacturer or authorized distributor of record of the drug sample, the date of the request and signature of the practitioner making the request.

(B) Drug manufacturers or authorized distributors of record shall store drug samples under conditions that will maintain their stability, integrity, and effectiveness and will assure that the drug samples will be free of contamination, deterioration, and adulteration.

(C) Drug manufacturers or authorized distributors of record shall conduct, at least annually, a complete and accurate inventory of all drug samples in the possession of representatives of the manufacturer or authorized distributor of record. Drug manufacturers or authorized distributors of record shall maintain lists of the names and address of each of their representatives who distribute drug samples and of the sites where drug samples are stored. Drug manufacturers or authorized distributors of record shall maintain records for at least 3 years of all drug samples distributed, destroyed, or returned to the manufacturer or authorized distributor of record, of all inventories maintained under this subparagraph, of all thefts or significant losses of drug samples, and of all requests made under subparagraph (A) for drug samples. Records and lists maintained under this subparagraph shall be made available by the drug manufacturer or authorized distributor of record to the Secretary upon request.

(D) Drug manufacturers or authorized distributors of record shall notify the Secretary of any significant loss of drug samples and any known theft of drug samples.

(E) Drug manufacturers or authorized distributors of record shall report to the Secretary any conviction of their representatives for violations of subsection (c)(1) or a State law because of the sale, purchase, or trade of a drug sample or the offer to sell, purchase, or trade a drug sample.

(F) Drug manufacturers or authorized distributors of record shall provide to the Secretary the name and telephone number of the individual responsible for responding to a request for information respecting drug samples.

(e) (1)(A) Each person who is engaged in the wholesale distribution of a drug subject to subsection (b) and who is not the manufacturer or an authorized distributor of record of such drug shall, before each wholesale distribution of such drug (including each distribution to an authorized distributor of record or to a retail pharmacy), provide to the person who receives the drug a statement (in such form and containing such information as the Secretary may require) identifying each prior sale, purchase, or trade of such drug (including the date of the transaction and the names and addresses of all parties to the transaction).

(B) Each manufacturer of a drug subject to subsection (b) shall maintain at its corporate offices a current list of the authorized distributors of record of such drug.

(2)(A) No person may engage in the wholesale distribution in interstate commerce of drugs subject to subsection (b) in a State unless such person is licensed by the State in accordance with the guidelines issued under subparagraph (B), or has registered with the Secretary in accordance with paragraph (3).

(B) The Secretary shall by regulation issue guidelines establishing minimum standards, terms, and conditions for the licensing of persons to make wholesale distributions in interstate commerce of drugs subject to subsection (b). Such guidelines shall prescribe requirements for the storage and handling of such drugs and for the establishment and maintenance of records of the distributions of such drugs.

(3) Any person who engages in the wholesale distribution in interstate commerce of drugs that are subject to subsection (b) in a State that does not have a program that meets the guidelines established under paragraph (2)(B) shall register with the Secretary the following:

(A) The person's name and place of business.

(B) The name of each establishment the person owns or operates that is engaged in the wholesale distribution of drugs in a State that does not have a program to license persons engaged in such distribution.

(4) For the purposes of this subsection and subsection (d)—

(A) the term "authorized distributors of record" means those distributors with whom a manufacturer has established an ongoing relationship to distribute such manufacturer's products, and

(B) the term "wholesale distribution" means distribution of drugs subject to subsection (b) to other than the consumer or patient but does not include intracompany sales and does not include distributions of drugs described in subsection (c)(3)(B).

(f) (1)(A) A drug intended for use by animals other than man, other than a veterinary feed directive drug intended for use in animal feed or an animal feed bearing or containing a veterinary feed directive drug, which—

(i) because of its toxicity or other potentiality for harmful effect, or the method of its use, or the collateral measures necessary for its use, is not safe for animal use except under the professional supervision of a licensed veterinarian, or

(ii) is limited by an approved application under subsection (b) of section 512 to use under the professional supervision of a licensed veterinarian, shall be dispensed only by or upon the lawful written or oral order of a licensed veterinarian in the course of the veterinarian's professional practice.

(B) For purposes of subparagraph (A), an order is lawful if the order—

(i) is a prescription or other order authorized by law,

(ii) is, if an oral order, promptly reduced to writing by the person lawfully filling the order, and filed by that person, and

(iii) is refilled only if authorized in the original order or in a subsequent oral order promptly reduced to writing by the person lawfully filling the order, and filed by that person.

(C) The act of dispensing a drug contrary to the provisions of this paragraph shall be deemed to be an act which results in the drug being misbranded while held for sale.

(2) Any drug when dispensed in accordance with paragraph (1) of this subsection—

(A) shall be exempt from the requirements of section 502, except subsections (a), (g), (h), (i)(2), (i)(3), and (p) of such section, and

(B) shall be exempt from the packaging requirements of subsections (g), (h), and (p) of such section, if—

(i) when dispensed by a licensed veterinarian, the drug bears a label containing the name and address of the practitioner and any directions for use and cautionary statements specified by the practitioner, or

(ii) when dispensed by filling the lawful order of a licensed veterinarian, the drug bears a label containing the name and address of the dispenser, the serial number and date of the order or of its filling, the name of the licensed veterinarian, and the directions for use and cautionary statements, if any, contained in such order. The preceding sentence shall not apply to any drug dispensed in the course of the conduct of a business of dispensing drugs pursuant to diagnosis by mail.

(3) The Secretary may by regulation exempt drugs for animals other than man subject to section 512 from the requirements of paragraph (1) when such requirements are not necessary for the protection of the public health.

(4) A drug which is subject to paragraph (1) shall be deemed to be misbranded if at any time prior to dispensing its label fails to bear the statement "Caution: Federal law restricts this drug to use by or on the order of a licensed veterinarian." A drug to which paragraph (1) does not apply shall be deemed to be misbranded if at any time prior to dispensing its label bears the statement specified in the preceding sentence.

(g) (1) The Secretary shall designate a component of the Food and Drug Administration to regulate products that constitute a combination of a drug, device, or biological product. The Secretary shall determine the primary mode of action of the combination product. If the Secretary determines that the primary mode of action is that of—

(A) a drug (other than a biological product), the persons charged with premarket review of drugs shall have primary jurisdiction,

(B) a device, the persons charged with premarket review of devices shall have primary jurisdiction, or

(C) a biological product, the persons charged with premarket review of biological products shall have primary jurisdiction.

(2) Nothing in this subsection shall prevent the Secretary from using any agency resources of the Food and Drug Administration necessary to ensure adequate review of the safety, effectiveness, or substantial equivalence of an article.

(3) The Secretary shall promulgate regulations to implement market clearance procedures in accordance with paragraphs (1) and (2) not later than 1 year after the date of enactment of this subsection.

(4) As used in this subsection:

(A) The term "biological product" has the meaning given the term in section 351(i) of the Public Health Service Act (42 U.S.C. § 262(i)).

(B) The term "market clearance" includes—(i) approval of an application under section 505, 507, 515, or 520(g), (ii) a finding of substantial equivalence under this part, and (iii) approval of a biologics license application under subsection (a) of section 351 of the Public Health Service Act (42 U.S.C. § 262).

SEC. 503A [21 U.S.C. § 353a]. PHARMACY COMPOUNDING.

(a) IN GENERAL.—Sections 501(a)(2)(B), 502(f)(1), and 505 shall not apply to a drug product if the drug product is compounded for an identified individual patient based on the unsolicited receipt of a valid prescription order or a notation, approved by the prescribing practitioner, on the prescription order that a compounded product is necessary for the identified patient, if the drug product meets the requirements of this section, and if the compounding—

(1) is by—(A) a licensed pharmacist in a State licensed pharmacy or a Federal facility, or (B) a licensed physician,

on the prescription order for such individual patient made by a licensed physician or other licensed practitioner authorized by State law to prescribe drugs; or

(2)(A) is by a licensed pharmacist or licensed physician in limited quantities before the receipt of a valid prescription order for such individual patient; and

(B) is based on a history of the licensed pharmacist or licensed physician receiving valid prescription orders for the compounding of the drug product, which orders have been generated solely within an established relationship between—

(i) the licensed pharmacist or licensed physician; and

(ii)(I) such individual patient for whom the prescription order will be provided; or (II) the physician or other licensed practitioner who will write such prescription order.

(b) COMPOUNDED DRUG.

(1) LICENSED PHARMACIST AND LICENSED PHYSICIAN. A drug product may be compounded under subsection (a) if the licensed pharmacist or licensed physician—

(A) compounds the drug product using bulk drug substances, as defined in regulations of the Secretary published at section 207.3(a)(4) of title 21 of the Code of Federal Regulations—

(i) that (I) comply with the standards of an applicable United States Pharmacopoeia or National Formulary monograph, if a monograph exists, and the United States Pharmacopoeia chapter on pharmacy compounding; (II) if such a monograph does not exist, are drug substances that are components of drugs approved by the Secretary; or (III) if such a monograph does not exist and the drug substance is not a component of a drug approved by the Secretary, that appear on a list developed by the Secretary through regulations issued by the Secretary under subsection (d);

(ii) that are manufactured by an establishment that is registered under section 510 (including a foreign establishment that is registered under section 510(i)); and

(iii) that are accompanied by valid certificates of analysis for each bulk drug substance;

(B) compounds the drug product using ingredients (other than bulk drug substances) that comply with the standards of an applicable United States Pharmacopoeia or National Formulary monograph, if a monograph exists, and the United States Pharmacopoeia chapter on pharmacy compounding;

(C) does not compound a drug product that appears on a list published by the Secretary in the Federal Register of drug products that have been withdrawn or removed from the market because such drug products or components of such drug products have been found to be unsafe or not effective; and

(D) does not compound regularly or in inordinate amounts (as defined by the Secretary) any drug products that are essentially copies of a commercially available drug product.

(2) DEFINITION.—For purposes of paragraph (1)(D), the term "essentially a copy of a commercially available drug product" does not include a drug product in which there is a change, made for an identified individual patient, which produces for that patient a significant difference, as determined by the prescribing practitioner, between the compounded drug and the comparable commercially available drug product.

(3) DRUG PRODUCT.—A drug product may be compounded under subsection (a) only if—

(A) such drug product is not a drug product identified by the Secretary by regulation as a drug product that presents demonstrable difficulties for compounding that reasonably demonstrate an adverse effect on the safety or effectiveness of that drug product; and

(B) such drug product is compounded in a State—

(i) that has entered into a memorandum of understanding with the Secretary which addresses the distribution of inordinate amounts of compounded drug products interstate and provides for appropriate investigation by a State agency of complaints relating to compounded drug products distributed outside such State; or

(ii) that has not entered into the memorandum of understanding described in clause (i) and the licensed pharmacist, licensed pharmacy, or licensed physician distributes (or causes to be distributed) compounded drug products out of the State in which they are compounded in quantities that do not exceed 5 percent of the total prescription orders dispensed or distributed by such pharmacy or physician.

The Secretary shall, in consultation with the National Association of Boards of Pharmacy, develop a standard memorandum of understanding for use by the States in complying with subparagraph (B)(i).

(c) ADVERTISING AND PROMOTION.—A drug may be compounded under subsection (a) only if the pharmacy, licensed pharmacist, or licensed physician does not advertise or promote the compounding of any particular drug, class of drug, or type of drug. The pharmacy, licensed pharmacist, or licensed physician may advertise and promote the compounding service provided by the licensed pharmacist or licensed physician.

(d) REGULATIONS.

(1) IN GENERAL.—The Secretary shall issue regulations to implement this section. Before issuing regulations to implement subsections (b)(1)(A)(i)(III), (b)(1)(C), or (b)(3)(A), the Secretary shall convene and consult an advisory committee on compounding unless the Secretary determines that the issuance of such regulations before consultation is necessary to protect the public health. The advisory committee shall include represen-

tatives from the National Association of Boards of Pharmacy, the United States Pharmacopoeia, pharmacy, physician, and consumer organizations, and other experts selected by the Secretary.

(2) LIMITING COMPOUNDING.—The Secretary, in consultation with the United States Pharmacopoeia Convention, Incorporated, shall promulgate regulations identifying drug substances that may be used in compounding under subsection (b)(1)(A)(i)(III) for which a monograph does not exist or which are not components of drug products approved by the Secretary. The Secretary shall include in the regulation the criteria for such substances, which shall include historical use, reports in peer reviewed medical literature, or other criteria the Secretary may identify.

(e) APPLICATION.—This section shall not apply to—(1) compounded positron emission tomography drugs as defined in section 201(ii); or (2) radiopharmaceuticals.

(f) DEFINITION.—As used in this section, the term "compounding" does not include mixing, reconstituting, or other such acts that are performed in accordance with directions contained in approved labeling provided by the product's manufacturer and other manufacturer directions consistent with that labeling.

* * *

SEC. 505 [21 U.S.C. § 355]. NEW DRUGS.

(a) No person shall introduce or deliver for introduction into interstate commerce any new drug, unless an approval of an application filed pursuant to subsection (b) or (j) is effective with respect to such drug.

(b) (1) Any person may file with the Secretary an application with respect to any drug subject to the provisions of subsection (a). Such person shall submit to the Secretary as a part of the application (A) full reports of investigations which have been made to show whether or not such drug is safe for use and whether such drug is effective in use; (B) a full list of the articles used as components of such drug; (C) a full statement of the composition of such drug; (D) a full description of the methods used in, and the facilities and controls used for, the manufacture, processing, and packing of such drug; (E) such samples of such drug and of the articles used as components thereof as the Secretary may require; and (F) specimens of the labeling proposed to be used for such drug. The applicant shall file with the application the patent number and the expiration date of any patent which claims the drug for which the applicant submitted the application or which claims a method of using such drug and with respect to which a claim of patent infringement could reasonably be asserted if a person not licensed by the owner engaged in the manufacture, use, or sale of the drug. If an application is filed under this subsection for a drug and a patent which claims such drug or a method of using such drug is issued after the filing date but before approval of the application, the applicant shall amend the application to include the information required by the preceding sentence. Upon approval of the application, the Secretary shall publish information submitted under the two preceding sentences. The Secretary shall, in consultation with the Director of the National Institutes of Health and with representatives of the drug manufacturing industry, review and develop guidance, as appropriate, on the inclusion of women and minorities in clinical trials required by clause (A).

(2) An application submitted under paragraph (1) for a drug for which the investigations described in clause (A) of such paragraph and relied upon by the applicant for approval of the application were not conducted by or for the applicant and for which the applicant has not obtained a right of reference or use from the person by or for whom the investigations were conducted shall also include—

(A) a certification, in the opinion of the applicant and to the best of his knowledge, with respect to each patent which claims the drug for which such investigations were conducted or which claims a use for such drug for which the applicant is seeking approval under this subsection and for which information is required to be filed under paragraph (1) or subsection (c)—

(i) that such patent information has not been filed,

(ii) that such patent has expired,

(iii) of the date on which such patent will expire, or

(iv) that such patent is invalid or will not be infringed by the manufacture, use, or sale of the new drug for which the application is submitted; and

(B) if with respect to the drug for which investigations described in paragraph (1)(A) were conducted information was filed under paragraph (1) or subsection (c) for a method of use patent which does not claim a use for which the applicant is seeking approval under this subsection, a statement that the method of use patent does not claim such a use.

(3)(A) An applicant who makes a certification described in paragraph (2)(A)(iv) shall include in the application a statement that the applicant will give the notice required by subparagraph (B) to—

(i) each owner of the patent which is the subject of the certification or the representative of such owner designated to receive such notice, and

(ii) the holder of the approved application under subsection (b) for the drug which is claimed by the patent or a use of which is claimed by the patent or the representative of such holder designated to receive such notice.

(B) The notice referred to in subparagraph (A) shall state that an application has been submitted under this subsection for the drug with respect to which the certification is made to obtain approval to engage in the commercial manufacture, use, or sale of the drug before the expiration of the patent referred to in the certification. Such notice shall include a detailed statement of the factual and legal basis of the applicant's opinion that the patent is not valid or will not be infringed.

(C) If an application is amended to include a certification described in paragraph (2)(A)(iv), the notice required by subparagraph (B) shall be given when the amended application is submitted.

(4)(A) The Secretary shall issue guidance for the individuals who review applications submitted under paragraph (1) or under section 351 of the Public Health Service Act, which shall relate to promptness in conducting the review, technical excellence, lack of bias and conflict of interest, and knowledge of regulatory and scientific standards, and which shall apply equally to all individuals who review such applications.

(B) The Secretary shall meet with a sponsor of an investigation or an applicant for approval for a drug under this subsection or section 351 of the Public Health Service Act if the sponsor or applicant makes a reasonable written request for a meeting for the purpose of reaching agreement on the design and size of clinical trials intended to form the primary basis of an effectiveness claim. The sponsor or applicant shall provide information necessary for discussion and agreement on the design and size of the clinical trials. Minutes of any such meeting shall be prepared by the Secretary and made available to the sponsor or applicant upon request.

(C) Any agreement regarding the parameters of the design and size of clinical trials of a new drug under this paragraph that is reached between the Secretary and a sponsor or applicant shall be reduced to writing and made part of the administrative record by the Secretary. Such agreement shall not be changed after the testing begins, except—

(i) with the written agreement of the sponsor or applicant;

(ii) pursuant to a decision, made in accordance with subparagraph (D) by the director of the reviewing division, that a substantial scientific issue essential to determining the safety or effectiveness of the drug has been identified after the testing has begun.

(D) A decision under subparagraph (C)(ii) by the director shall be in writing and the Secretary shall provide to the sponsor or applicant an opportunity for a meeting at which the director and the sponsor or applicant will be present and at which the director will document the scientific issue involved.

(E) The written decisions of the reviewing division shall be binding upon, and may not directly or indirectly be changed by, the field or compliance division personnel unless such field or compliance division personnel demonstrate to the reviewing division why such decision should be modified.

(F) No action by the reviewing division may be delayed because of the unavailability of information from or action by field personnel unless the reviewing division determines that a delay is necessary to assure the marketing of a safe and effective drug.

(G) For purposes of this paragraph, the reviewing division is the division responsible for the review of an application for approval of a drug under this subsection or section 351 of the Public Health Service Act (including all scientific and medical matters, chemistry, manufacturing, and controls).

(c) (1) Within one hundred and eighty days after the filing of an application under subsection (b), or such additional period as may be agreed upon by the Secretary and the applicant, the Secretary shall either—

(A) approve the application if he then finds that none of the grounds for denying approval specified in subsection (d) applies, or

(B) give the applicant notice of an opportunity for a hearing before the Secretary under subsection (d) on the question whether such application is approvable. If the applicant elects to accept the opportunity for hearing by written request within thirty days after such notice, such hearing shall commence not more than ninety days after the expiration of such thirty days unless the Secretary and the applicant otherwise agree. Any such hearing shall thereafter be conducted on an expedited basis and the Secretary's order thereon shall be issued within ninety days after the date fixed by the Secretary for filing final briefs.

(2) If the patent information described in subsection (b) could not be filed with the submission of an application under subsection (b) because the application was filed before the patent information was required under subsection (b) or a patent was issued after the application was approved under such subsection, the holder of an approved application shall file with the Secretary the patent number and the expiration date of any patent which claims the drug for which the application was submitted or which claims a method of using such drug and with respect to which a claim of patent infringement could reasonably be asserted if a person not licensed by the owner engaged in the manufacture, use, or sale of the drug. If the holder of an approved application could not file patent information under subsection (b) because it was not required at the time the application was approved, the holder shall file such information under this subsection not later than thirty days after the enactment of this sentence; and if the holder of an approved application could not file patent information under subsection (b) because no patent had been issued when an application was filed or approved, the holder shall file such information under this subsection not later than thirty days after the date the patent involved is issued. Upon the submission of patent information under this subsection, the Secretary shall publish it.

(3) The approval of an application filed under subsection (b) which contains a certification required by paragraph (2) of such subsection shall be made effective on the last applicable date determined under the following:

(A) If the applicant only made a certification described in clause (i) or (ii) of subsection (b)(2)(A) or in both such clauses, the approval may be made effective immediately.

(B) If the applicant made a certification described in clause (iii) of subsection (b)(2)(A), the approval may be made effective on the date certified under clause (iii).

(C) If the applicant made a certification described in clause (iv) of subsection (b)(2)(A), the approval shall be made effective immediately unless an action is brought for infringement of a patent which is the subject of the certification before the expiration of forty-five days from the date the notice provided under paragraph (3)(B) is received. If such an action is brought before the expiration of such days, the approval may be made effective upon the expiration of the thirty-month period beginning on the date of the receipt of the notice provided under paragraph (3)(B) or such shorter or longer period as the court may order because either party to the action failed to reasonably cooperate in expediting the action, except that—

(i) if before the expiration of such period the court decides that such patent is invalid or not infringed, the approval may be made effective on the date of the court decision,

(ii) if before the expiration of such period the court decides that such patent has been infringed, the approval may be made effective on such date as the court orders under section 271(e)(4)(A) of title 35, United States Code or

(iii) if before the expiration of such period the court grants a preliminary injunction prohibiting the applicant from engaging in the commercial manufacture or sale of the drug until the court decides the issues of patent validity and infringement and if the court decides that such patent is invalid or not infringed, the approval shall be made effective on the date of such court decision.

In such an action, each of the parties shall reasonably cooperate in expediting the action. Until the expiration of forty-five days from the date the notice made under paragraph (3)(B) is received, no action may be brought under section 2201 of title 28 United States Code for a declaratory judgment with respect to the patent. Any action brought under such section 2201 shall be brought in the judicial district where the defendant has its principal place of business or a regular and established place of business.

(D)(i) If an application (other than an abbreviated new drug application) submitted under subsection (b) for a drug, no active ingredient (including any ester or salt of the active ingredient) of which has been approved in any other application under subsection (b), was approved during the period beginning January 1, 1982, and ending on the date of enactment of this subsection, the Secretary may not make the approval of another application for a drug for which the investigations described in clause (A) of subsection (b)(1) and relied upon by the applicant for approval of the application were not conducted by or for the applicant and for which the applicant has not obtained a right of reference or use from the person by or for whom the investigations were conducted effective before the expiration of ten years from the date of the approval of the application previously approved under subsection (b).

(ii) If an application submitted under subsection (b) for a drug, no active ingredient (including any ester or salt of the active ingredient) of which has been approved in any other application under subsection (b), is approved after the date of the enactment of this clause, no application which refers to the drug for which the subsection (b) application was submitted and for which the investigations described in clause (A) of subsection (b)(1) and relied upon by the applicant for approval of the application were not conducted by or for the applicant and for which the applicant has not obtained a right of reference or use from the person by or for whom the investigations were conducted may be submitted under subsection (b) before the expiration of five years from the date of the approval of the application under subsection (b), except that such an application may be submitted under subsection (b) after the expiration of four years from the date of the approval of the subsection (b) application if it contains a certification of patent invalidity or noninfringement described in clause (iv) of subsection (b)(2)(A). The approval of such an application shall be made effective in accordance with this paragraph except that, if an action for patent infringement is commenced during the one-year period beginning forty-eight months after the date of the approval of the subsection (b) application, the thirty-month period referred to in subparagraph (C) shall be extended by such amount of time (if any) which is required for seven and one-half years to have elapsed from the date of approval of the subsection (b) application.

(iii) If an application submitted under subsection (b) for a drug, which includes an active ingredient (including any ester or salt of the active ingredient) that has been approved in another application approved under subsection (b), is approved after the date of enactment of this clause, and if such application contains reports of new clinical investigations (other than bioavailability studies) essential to the approval of the application and conducted or sponsored by the applicant, the Secretary may not make the approval of an application submitted under subsection (b) for the conditions of approval of such drug in the approved subsection (b) application effective before the expiration of three years from the date of the approval of the application under subsection (b) if the investigations described in clause (A) of subsection (b)(1) and relied upon by the applicant for approval of the application were not conducted by or for the applicant and if the applicant has not obtained a right of reference or use from the person by or for whom the investigations were conducted.

(iv) If a supplement to an application approved under subsection (b) is approved after the date of enactment of this clause, and the supplement contains reports of new clinical investigations (other than bioavailability studies) essential to the approval of the supplement and conducted or sponsored by the person submitting the supplement, the Secretary may not make the approval of an application submitted under subsection (b) for a change approved in the supplement effective before the expiration of three years from the date of the approval of the supplement under subsection (b) if the investigations described in clause (A) of subsection (b)(1) and relied upon by the applicant for approval of the application were not conducted by or for the applicant and if the applicant has not obtained a right of reference or use from the person by or for whom the investigations were conducted.

(v) If an application (or supplement to an application) submitted under subsection (b) for a drug, which includes an active ingredient (including any ester or salt of the active ingredient) that has been approved in another application under subsection (b), was approved during the period beginning January 1, 1982, and ending on the date if enactment of this clause, the Secretary may not make the approval of an application submitted under this subsection and for which the investigations described in clause (A) of subsection (b)(1) and relied upon by the applicant for approval of the application were not conducted by or for the applicant and for which the applicant has not obtained a right of reference or use from the person by or for whom the investigations were conducted and which refers to the drug for which the subsection (b) application was submitted effective before the expiration of two years from the date of enactment of this clause.

(4) A drug manufactured in a pilot or other small facility may be used to demonstrate the safety and effectiveness of the drug and to obtain approval for the drug prior to manufacture of the drug in a larger facility, unless the Secretary makes a determination that a full scale production facility is necessary to ensure the safety or effectiveness of the drug.

(d) If the Secretary finds, after due notice to the applicant in accordance with subsection (c) and giving him an opportunity for a hearing, in accordance with said subsection, that (1) the investigations, reports of which are required to be submitted to the Secretary pursuant to subsection (b), do not include adequate tests by all methods reasonably applicable to show whether or not such drug is safe for use under the conditions prescribed, recommended, or suggested in the proposed labeling thereof; (2) the results of such tests show that such drug is unsafe for use under such conditions or do not show that such drug is safe for use under such conditions; (3) the methods used in, and the facilities and controls used for, the manufacture, processing, and packing of such drug are inadequate to preserve its identity, strength, quality, and purity; (4) upon the basis of the information submitted to him as part of the application, or upon the basis of any other information before him with respect to such drug, he has insufficient information to determine whether such drug is safe for use under such conditions; or (5) evaluated on the basis of the information submitted to him as part of the application and any other information before him with respect to such drug, there is a lack of substantial evidence that the drug will have the effect it purports or is represented to have under the conditions of use prescribed, recommended, or suggested in the proposed labeling thereof; or (6) the application failed to contain the patent information prescribed by subsection (b); or (7) based on a fair evaluation of all material facts, such labeling is false or misleading in any particular; he shall issue an order refusing to approve the application. If, after such notice and opportunity for hearing, the Secretary finds that clauses (1) through (6) do not apply, he shall issue an order approving the application. As used in this subsection and subsection (e), the term "substantial evidence" means evidence consisting of adequate and well-controlled investigations, including clinical investigations, by experts qualified by scientific training and experience to evaluate the effectiveness of the drug involved, on the basis of which it could fairly and responsibly be concluded by such experts that the drug will have the effect it purports or is represented to have under the conditions of use prescribed, recommended, or suggested in the labeling or proposed labeling thereof. If the Secretary determines, based on relevant science, that data from one adequate and well-controlled clinical investigation and confirmatory evidence (obtained prior to or after such investigation) are sufficient to establish effectiveness, the Secretary may consider such data and evidence to constitute substantial evidence for purposes of the proceeding sentence.

(e) The Secretary shall, after due notice and opportunity for hearing to the applicant, withdraw approval of an application with respect to any drug under this section if the Secretary finds (1) that clinical or other experience, tests, or other scientific data show that such drug is unsafe for use under the conditions of use upon the basis of which the application was approved; (2) that new evidence of clinical experience, not contained in such application or not available to the Secretary until after such application was approved, or tests by new methods, or tests by methods not deemed reasonably applicable when such application was approved, evaluated together with the evidence available to the Secretary when the application was approved, shows that such drug is not shown to be safe for use under the conditions of use upon the basis of which the application was approved; or (3) on the basis of new information before him with respect to such drug, evaluated together with the evidence available to him when the application was approved, that there is a lack of substantial evidence that the drug will have the effect it purports or is represented to have under the conditions of use prescribed, recommended, or suggested in the labeling thereof; or (4) the patent information prescribed by subsection (c) was not filed within thirty days after the receipt of written notice from the Secretary specifying the failure to file such information; or (5) that the application contains any untrue statement of a material fact: *Provided,* That if the Secretary (or in his absence the officer acting as Secretary) finds that there is an imminent hazard to the public health, he may suspend the approval of such application immediately, and give the applicant prompt notice of his action and afford the applicant the opportunity for an expedited hearing under this subsection; but the authority conferred by this proviso to suspend the approval of an application shall not be delegated. The Secretary may also, after due notice and opportunity for hearing to the applicant, withdraw the approval of an application submitted under subsection (b) or (j) with respect to any drug under this section if the Secretary finds (1) that the applicant has failed to establish a system for maintaining required records, or has repeatedly or deliberately failed to maintain such records or to make required reports, in accordance with a regulation or order under subsection (k) or to comply with the notice requirements of section 510(k)(2), or the applicant has refused to permit access to, or copying or verification of, such records as required by paragraph (2) of such subsection; or (2) that on the basis of new information before him, evaluated together with the evidence before him when the application was approved, the methods used in, or the facilities and controls used for, the manufacture, processing, and packing of such drug are inadequate to assure and preserve its identity, strength, quality, and purity and were not made adequate within a reasonable time after receipt of written notice from the Secretary specifying the matter complained of; or (3) that on the basis of new information before him, evaluated together with the evidence before him when the application was approved, the labeling of such drug, based on a fair evaluation of all material facts, is false or misleading in any particular and was not corrected within a reasonable time after receipt of written notice from the Secretary specifying the matter complained of. Any order under this subsection shall state the findings upon which it is based.

(f) Whenever the Secretary finds that the facts so require, he shall revoke any previous order under subsection (d) or (e) refusing, withdrawing, or suspending approval of an application and shall approve such application or reinstate such approval, as may be appropriate.

(g) Orders of the Secretary issued under this section shall be served (1) in person by any officer or employee of the department designated by the Secretary or (2) by mailing the order by registered mail or by certified mail addressed to the applicant or respondent at his last-known address in the records of the Secretary.

(h) An appeal may be taken by the applicant from an order of the Secretary refusing or withdrawing approval of an application under this section. Such appeal shall be taken by filing in the United States court of appeals for the circuit wherein such applicant resides or has his principal place of business, or in the United States Court of Appeals for the District of Columbia Circuit, within sixty days after the entry of such order, a written petition praying that the order of the Secretary be set aside. A copy of such petition shall be forthwith transmitted by the clerk of the court to the Secretary, or any officer designated by him for that purpose, and thereupon the Secretary shall certify and file in the court the record upon which the order complained of was entered, as provided in section 2112 of title 28, United States Code. Upon the filing of such petition such court shall have exclusive jurisdiction to affirm or set aside such order, except that until the filing of the record the Secretary may modify or set aside his order. No objection to the order of the Secretary shall be considered by the court unless such objection shall have been urged before the Secretary or unless there were reasonable grounds for failure so to do. The finding of the Secretary as to the facts, if supported by substantial evidence, shall be conclusive. If any person shall apply to the court for leave to adduce additional evidence, and shall show to the satisfaction of the court that such additional evidence is material and that there were reasonable grounds for failure to adduce such evidence in the proceeding before the Secretary, the court may order such additional evidence to be taken before the Secretary and to be adduced upon the hearing in such manner and upon such terms and conditions as to the court may seem proper. The Secretary may modify his findings as to the facts by reason of the additional evidence so taken, and he shall file with the court such modified findings which, if supported by substantial evidence, shall be conclusive, and his recommendation, if any, for the setting aside of the original order. The judgment of the court affirming or setting aside any such order of the Secretary shall be final, subject to review by the Supreme Court of the United States upon certiorari or certification as provided in section 1254 of title 28 of the United States Code. The commencement of proceedings under this subsection shall not, unless specifically ordered by the court to the contrary, operate as a stay of the Secretary's order.

(i) (1) The Secretary shall promulgate regulations for exempting from the operation of the foregoing subsections of this section drugs intended solely for investigational use by experts qualified by scientific training and experience to investigate the safety and effectiveness of drugs. Such regulations may, within the discretion of the Secretary, among other conditions relating to the protection of the public health, provide for conditioning such exemption upon—

(A) the submission to the Secretary, before any clinical testing of a new drug is undertaken, of reports, by the manufacturer or the sponsor of the investigation of such drug, or preclinical tests (including tests on animals) of such drug adequate to justify the proposed clinical testing;

(B) the manufacturer or the sponsor of the investigation of a new drug proposed to be distributed to investigators for clinical testing obtaining a signed agreement from each of such investigators that patients to whom the drug is administered will be under his personal supervision, or under the supervision of investigators responsible to him, and that he will not supply such drug to any other investigator, or to clinics, for administration to human beings;

(C) the establishment and maintenance of such records, and the making of such reports to the Secretary, by the manufacturer or the sponsor of the investigation of such drug, of data (including but not limited to analytical reports by investigators) obtained as the result of such investigational use of such drug, as the Secretary finds will enable him to evaluate the safety and effectiveness of such drug in the event of the filing of an application pursuant to subsection (b); and

(D) the submission to the Secretary by the manufacturer or the sponsor of the investigation of a new drug of a statement of intent regarding whether the manufacturer or sponsor has plans for assessing pediatric safety and efficacy.

(2) Subject to paragraph (3), a clinical investigation of a new drug may begin 30 days after the Secretary has received from the manufacturer or sponsor of the investigation a submission containing such information about the drug and the clinical investigation, including—

(A) information on design of the investigation and adequate reports of basic information, certified by the applicant to be accurate reports, necessary to assess the safety of the drug for use in clinical investigation; and

(B) adequate information on the chemistry and manufacturing of the drug, controls available for the drug, and primary data tabulations from animal or human studies.

(3)(A) At any time, the Secretary may prohibit the sponsor of an investigation from conducting the investigation (referred to in this paragraph as a "clinical hold") if the Secretary makes a determination described in subparagraph (B). The Secretary shall specify the basis for the clinical hold, including the specific information available to the Secretary which served as the basis for such clinical hold, and confirm such determination in writing.

(B) For purposes of subparagraph (A), a determination described in this subparagraph with respect to a clinical hold is that—

(i) the drug involved represents an unreasonable risk to the safety of the persons who are the subjects of the clinical investigation, taking into account the qualifications of the clinical investigators, information about the drug, the design of the clinical investigation, the condition for which the drug is to be investigated, and the health status of the subjects involved; or

(ii) the clinical hold should be issued for such other reasons as the Secretary may by regulation establish (including reasons established by regulation before the date of the enactment of the Food and Drug Administration Modernization Act of 1997).

(C) Any written request to the Secretary from the sponsor of an investigation that a clinical hold be removed shall receive a decision, in writing and specifying the reasons therefor, within 30 days after receipt of such request. Any such request shall include sufficient information to support the removal of such clinical hold.

(4) Regulations under paragraph (1) shall provide that such exemption shall be conditioned upon the manufacturer, or the sponsor of the investigation, requiring that experts using such drugs for investigational purposes certify to such manufacturer or sponsor that they will inform any human beings to whom such drugs, or any controls used in connection therewith, are being administered, or their representatives, that such drugs are being

used for investigational purposes and will obtain the consent of such human beings or their representatives, except where it is not feasible or it is contrary to the best interests of such human beings. Nothing in this subsection shall be construed to require any clinical investigator to submit directly to the Secretary reports on the investigational use of drugs.

(j) (1) Any person may file with the Secretary an abbreviated application for the approval of a new drug.

(2)(A) An abbreviated application for a new drug shall contain—

(i) information to show that the conditions of use prescribed, recommended, or suggested in the labeling proposed for the new drug have been previously approved for a drug listed under paragraph (7) (hereinafter in this subsection referred to as a "listed drug");

(ii)(I) if the listed drug referred to in clause (i) has only one active ingredient, information to show that the active ingredient of the new drug is the same as that of the listed drug;

(II) if the listed drug referred to in clause (i) has more than one active ingredient, information to show that the active ingredients of the new drug are the same as those of the listed drug, or

(III) if the listed drug referred to in clause (i) has more than one active ingredient and if one of the active ingredients of the new drug is different and the application is filed pursuant to the approval of a petition filed under subparagraph (C), information to show that the other active ingredients of the new drug are the same as the active ingredients of the listed drug, information to show that the different active ingredient is an active ingredient of a listed drug or of a drug which does not meet the requirements of section 201(p), and such other information respecting the different active ingredient with respect to which the petition was filed as the Secretary may require;

(iii) information to show that the route of administration, the dosage form, and the strength of the new drug are the same as those of the listed drug referred to in clause (i) or, if the route of administration, the dosage form, or the strength of the new drug is different and the application is filed pursuant to the approval of a petition filed under subparagraph (C), such information respecting the route of administration, dosage form, or strength with respect to which the petition was filed as the Secretary may require;

(iv) information to show that the new drug is bioequivalent to the listed drug referred to in clause (i), except that if the application is filed pursuant to the approval of a petition filed under subparagraph (C), information to show that the active ingredients of the new drug are of the same pharmacological or therapeutic class as those of the listed drug referred to in clause (i) and the new drug can be expected to have the same therapeutic effect as the listed drug when administered to patients for a condition of use referred to in clause (i);

(v) information to show that the labeling proposed for the new drug is the same as the labeling approved for the listed drug referred to in clause (i) except for changes required because of differences approved under a petition filed under subparagraph (C) or because the new drug and the listed drug are produced or distributed by different manufacturers;

(vi) the items specified in clauses (B) through (F) of subsection (b)(1);

(vii) a certification, in the opinion of the applicant and to the best of his knowledge, with respect to each patent which claims the listed drug referred to in clause (i) or which claims a use for such listed drug for which the applicant is seeking approval under this subsection and for which information is required to be filed under subsection (b) or (c)—(I) that such patent information has not been filed, (II) that such patent has expired, (III) of the date on which such patent will expire, or (IV) that such patent is invalid or will not be infringed by the manufacture, use, or sale of the new drug for which the application is submitted; and

(viii) if with respect to the listed drug referred to in clause (i) information was filed under subsection (b) or (c) for a method of use patent which does not claim a use for which the applicant is seeking approval under this subsection, a statement that the method of use patent does not claim such a use.

The Secretary may not require that an abbreviated application contain information in addition to that required by clauses (i) through (viii).

(B) (i) An applicant who makes a certification described in subparagraph (A)(vii)(IV) shall include in the application a statement that the applicant will give the notice required by clause (ii) to—

(I) each owner of the patent which is the subject of the certification or the representative of such owner designated to receive such notice, and

(II) the holder of the approved application under subsection (b) for the drug which is claimed by the patent or a use of which is claimed by the patent or the representative of such holder designated to receive such notice.

(ii) The notice referred to in clause (i) shall state that an application, which contains data from bioavailability or bioequivalence studies, has been submitted under this subsection for the drug with respect to which the certification is made to obtain approval to engage in the commercial manufacture, use, or sale of such drug before the expiration of the patent referred to in the certification. Such notice shall include a detailed statement of the factual and legal basis of the applicant's opinion that the patent is not valid or will not be infringed.

(iii) If an application is amended to include a certification described in subparagraph (A)(vii)(IV), the notice required by clause (ii) shall be given when the amended application is submitted.

(C) If a person wants to submit an abbreviated application for a new drug which has a different active ingredient or whose route of administration, dosage form, or strength differ from that of a listed drug, such person shall submit a petition to the Secretary seeking permission to file such an application. The Secretary shall approve or disapprove a petition submitted under this subparagraph within ninety days of the date the petition is submitted. The Secretary shall approve such a petition unless the Secretary finds—

(i) that investigations must be conducted to show the safety and effectiveness of the drug or of any of its active ingredients, the route of administration, the dosage form, or strength which differ from the listed drug; or

(ii) that any drug with a different active ingredient may not be adequately evaluated for approval as safe and effective on the basis of the information required to be submitted in an abbreviated application.

(3)(A) The Secretary shall issue guidance for the individuals who review applications submitted under paragraph (1), which shall relate to promptness in conducting the review, technical excellence, lack of bias and conflict of interest, and knowledge of regulatory and scientific standards, and which shall apply equally to all individuals who review such applications.

(B) The Secretary shall meet with a sponsor of an investigation or an applicant for approval for a drug under this subsection if the sponsor or applicant makes a reasonable written request for a meeting for the purpose of reaching agreement on the design and size of bioavailability and bioequivalence studies needed for approval of such application. The sponsor or applicant shall provide information necessary for discussion and agreement on the design and size of such studies. Minutes of any such meeting shall be prepared by the Secretary and made available to the sponsor or applicant.

(C) Any agreement regarding the parameters of design and size of bioavailability and bioequivalence studies of a drug under this paragraph that is reached between the Secretary and a sponsor or applicant shall be reduced to writing and made part of the administrative record by the Secretary. Such agreement shall not be changed after the testing begins, except—

(i) with the written agreement of the sponsor or applicant;

(ii) pursuant to a decision, made in accordance with subparagraph (D) by the director of the reviewing division, that a substantial scientific issue essential to determining the safety or effectiveness of the drug has been identified after the testing has begun.

(D) A decision under subparagraph (C)(ii) by the director shall be in writing and the Secretary shall provide to the sponsor or applicant an opportunity for a meeting at which the director and the sponsor or applicant will be present and at which the director will document the scientific issue involved.

(E) The written decisions of the reviewing division shall be binding upon, and may not directly or indirectly be changed by, the field or compliance office personnel unless such field or compliance office personnel demonstrate to the reviewing division why such decision should be modified.

(F) No action by the reviewing division may be delayed because of the unavailability of information from or action by field personnel unless the reviewing division determines that a delay is necessary to assure the marketing of a safe and effective drug.

(G) For purposes of this paragraph, the reviewing division is the division responsible for the review of an application for approval of a drug under this subsection (including scientific matters, chemistry, manufacturing, and controls).

(4) Subject to paragraph (5), the Secretary shall approve an application for a drug unless the Secretary finds—

(A) the methods used in, or the facilities and controls used for, the manufacture, processing, and packing of the drug are inadequate to assure and preserve its identity, strength, quality, and purity;

(B) information submitted with the application is insufficient to show that each of the proposed conditions of use have been previously approved for the listed drug referred to in the application;

(C) (i) if the listed drug has only one active ingredient, information submitted with the application is insufficient to show that the active ingredient is the same as that of the listed drug;

(ii) if the listed drug has more than one active ingredient, information submitted with the application is insufficient to show that the active ingredients are the same as the active ingredients of the listed drug, or

(iii) if the listed drug has more than one active ingredient and if the application is for a drug which has an active ingredient different from the listed drug, information submitted with the application is insufficient to show—

(I) that the other active ingredients are the same as the active ingredients of the listed drug, or

(II) that the different active ingredient is an active ingredient of a listed drug or a drug which does not meet the requirements of section 201(p), or no petition to file an application for the drug with the different ingredient was approved under paragraph (2)(C);

(D) (i) if the application is for a drug whose route of administration, dosage form, or strength of the drug is the same as the route of administration, dosage form, or strength of the listed drug referred to in the application, information submitted in the application is insufficient to show that the route of administration, dosage form, or strength is the same as that of the listed drug, or

(ii) if the application is for a drug whose route of administration, dosage form, or strength of the drug is different from that of the listed drug referred to in the application, no petition to file an application for the drug with the different route of administration, dosage form, or strength was approved under paragraph (2)(C);

(E) if the application was filed pursuant to the approval of a petition under paragraph (2)(C), the application did not contain the information required by the Secretary respecting the active ingredient, route of administration, dosage form, or strength which is not the same;

(F) information submitted in the application is insufficient to show that the drug is bioequivalent to the listed drug referred to in the application or, if the application was filed pursuant to a petition approved under paragraph (2)(C), information submitted in the application is insufficient to show that the active ingredients of the new drug are of the same pharmacological or therapeutic class as those of the listed drug referred to in paragraph (2)(Λ)(i) and that the new drug can be expected to have the same therapeutic effect as the listed drug when administered to patients for a condition of use referred to in such paragraph;

(G) information submitted in the application is insufficient to show that the labeling proposed for the drug is the same as the labeling approved for the listed drug referred to in the application except for changes required because of differences approved under a petition filed under paragraph (2)(C) or because the drug and the listed drug are produced or distributed by different manufacturers;

(H) information submitted in the application or any other information available to the Secretary shows that (i) the inactive ingredients of the drug are unsafe for use under the conditions prescribed, recommended, or suggested in the labeling proposed for the drug, or (ii) the composition of the drug is unsafe under such conditions because of the type or quantity of inactive ingredients included or the manner in which the inactive ingredients are included;

(I) the approval under subsection (c) of the listed drug referred to in the application under this subsection has been withdrawn or suspended for grounds described in the first sentence of subsection (e), the Secretary has published a notice of opportunity for hearing to withdraw approval of the listed drug under subsection (c) for grounds described in the first sentence of subsection (e), the approval under this subsection of the listed drug referred to in the application under this subsection has been withdrawn or suspended under paragraph (6), or the Secretary has determined that the listed drug has been withdrawn from sale for safety or effectiveness reasons;

(J) the application does not meet any other requirement of paragraph (2)(A); or

(K) the application contains an untrue statement of material fact.

(5)(A) Within one hundred and eighty days of the initial receipt of an application under paragraph (2) or within such additional period as may be agreed upon by the Secretary and the applicant, the Secretary shall approve or disapprove the application.

(B) The approval of an application submitted under paragraph (2) shall be made effective on the last applicable date determined under the following:

(i) If the applicant only made a certification described in subclause (I) or (II) of paragraph (2)(A)(vii) or in both such subclauses, the approval may be made effective immediately.

(ii) If the applicant made a certification described in subclause (III) of paragraph (2)(A)(vii), the approval may be made effective on the date certified under subclause (III).

(iii) If the applicant made a certification described in subclause (IV) of paragraph (2)(A)(vii), the approval shall be made effective immediately unless an action is brought for infringement of a patent which is the subject of the certification before the expiration of forty-five days from the date the notice provided under paragraph (2)(B)(i) is received. If such an action is brought before the expiration of such days, the approval shall be made effective upon the expiration of the thirty-month period beginning on the date of the receipt of the notice provided under paragraph (2)(B)(i) or such shorter or longer period as the court may order because either party to the action failed to reasonably cooperate in expediting the action, except that—

(I) if before the expiration of such period the court decides that such patent is invalid or not infringed, the approval shall be made effective on the date of the court decision,

(II) if before the expiration of such period the court decides that such patent has been infringed, the approval shall be made effective on such date as the court orders under section 271(e)(4)(A) of title 35, United States Code or

(III) if before the expiration of such period the court grants a preliminary injunction prohibiting the applicant from engaging in the commercial manufacture or sale of the drug until the court decides the issues of patent validity and infringement and if the court decides that such patent is invalid or not infringed, the approval shall be made effective on the date of such court decision.

In such an action, each of the parties shall reasonably cooperate in expediting the action. Until the expiration of forty-five days from the date the notice made under paragraph (2)(B)(i) is received, no action may be brought under section 2201 of title 28, United States Code, for a declaratory judgment with respect to the patent. Any action brought under section 2201 shall be brought in the judicial district where the defendant has its principal place of business or a regular and established place of business.

(iv) If the application contains a certification described in subclause (IV) of paragraph (2)(A)(vii) and is for a drug for which a previous application has been submitted under this subsection continuing such a certification, the application shall be made effective not earlier than one hundred and eighty days after—

(I) the date the Secretary receives notice from the applicant under the previous application of the first commercial marketing of the drug under the previous application, or

(II) the date of a decision of a court in an action described in clause (iii) holding the patent which is the subject of the certification to be invalid or not infringed, whichever is earlier.

(C) If the Secretary decides to disapprove an application, the Secretary shall give the applicant notice of an opportunity for a hearing before the Secretary on the question of whether such application is approvable. If the applicant elects to accept the opportunity for hearing by written request within thirty days after such notice, such hearing shall commence not more than ninety days after the expiration of such thirty days unless the Secretary and the applicant otherwise agree. Any such hearing shall thereafter be conducted on an expedited basis and the Secretary's order thereon shall be issued within ninety days after the date fixed by the Secretary for filing final briefs.

(D) (i) If an application (other than an abbreviated new drug application) submitted under subsection (b) for a drug, no active ingredient (including any ester or salt of the active ingredient) of which has been approved in any other application under subsection (b), was approved during the period beginning January 1, 1982, and ending on the date of enactment of this subsection, the Secretary may not make the approval of an application submitted under this subsection which refers to the drug for which the subsection (b) application was submitted effective before the expiration of ten years from the date of the approval of the application under subsection (b).

(ii) If an application submitted under subsection (b) for a drug, no active ingredient (including any ester or salt of the active ingredient) of which has been approved in any other application under subsection (b), is approved after the date of enactment of this subsection, no application may be submitted under this subsection which refers to the drug for which the subsection (b) application was submitted before the expiration of five years from the date of the approval of the application under subsection (b), except that such an application may be submitted under this subsection after the expiration of four years from the date of the approval of the subsection (b) application if it contains a certification of patent invalidity or noninfringement described in subclause (IV) of paragraph (2)(A)(vii). The approval of such an application shall be made effective in accordance with subparagraph (B) except that, if an action for patent infringement is commenced during the one-year period beginning forty-eight months after the date of the approval of the subsection (b) application, the thirty-month period referred to in subparagraph (B)(iii) shall be extended by such amount of time (if any) which is required for seven and one-half years to have elapsed from the date of approval of the subsection (b) application.

(iii) If an application submitted under subsection (b) for a drug, which includes an active ingredient (including any ester or salt of the active ingredient) that has been approved in another application approved under subsection (b), is approved after the date of enactment of this subsection, and if such application contains reports of new clinical investigations (other than bioavailability studies) essential to the approval of the application and conducted or sponsored by the applicant, the Secretary may not make the approval of an application submitted under this subsection for the conditions of approval of such drug in the subsection (b) application effective before the expiration of three years from the date of the approval of the application under subsection (b) for such drug.

(iv) If a supplement to an application approved under subsection (b) is approved after the date of enactment of this subsection, and the supplement contains reports of new clinical investigations (other than bioavailability studies) essential to the approval of the supplement and conducted or sponsored by the person submitting the supplement, the Secretary may not make the approval of an application submitted under this subsection for a change approved in the supplement effective before the expiration of three years from the date of the approval of the supplement under subsection (b).

(v) If an application (or supplement to an application) submitted under subsection (b) for a drug, which includes an active ingredient (including any ester or salt of the active ingredient) that has been approved in another application under subsection (b), was approved during the period beginning January 1, 1982, and ending on the date of enactment of this subsection, the Secretary may not make the approval of an application submitted under this subsection which refers to the drug for which the subsection (b) application was submitted or which refers to a change approved in a supplement to the subsection (b) application effective before the expiration of two years from the date of enactment of this subsection.

(6) If a drug approved under this subsection refers in its approved application to a drug the approval of which was withdrawn or suspended for grounds described in the first sentence of subsection (e) or was withdrawn or suspended under this paragraph or which, as determined by the Secretary, has been withdrawn from sale for safety or effectiveness

reasons, the approval of the drug under this subsection shall be withdrawn or suspended—

(A) for the same period as the withdrawal or suspension under subsection (e) or this paragraph, or

(B) if the listed drug has been withdrawn from sale, for the period of withdrawal from sale or, if earlier, the period ending on the date the Secretary determines that the withdrawal from sale is not for safety or effectiveness reasons.

(7)(A)(i) Within sixty days of the date of enactment of this subsection, the Secretary shall publish and make available to the public—

(I) a list in alphabetical order of the official and proprietary name of each drug which has been approved for safety and effectiveness under subsection (c) before the date of enactment of this subsection;

(II) the date of approval if the drug is approved after 1981 and the number of the application which was approved; and

(III) whether in vitro or in vivo bioequivalence studies, or both such studies, are required for applications filed under this subsection which will refer to the drug published.

(ii) Every thirty days after the publication of the first list under clause (i) the Secretary shall revise the list to include each drug which has been approved for safety and effectiveness under subsection (c) or approved under this subsection during the thirty-day period.

(iii) When patent information submitted under subsection (b) or (c) respecting a drug included on the list is to be published by the Secretary, the Secretary shall, in revisions made under clause (ii), include such information for such drug.

(B) A drug approved for safety and effectiveness under subsection (c) or approved under this subsection shall, for purposes of this subsection, be considered to have been published under subparagraph (A) on the date of its approval or the date of enactment, whichever is later.

(C) If the approval of a drug was withdrawn or suspended for grounds described in the first sentence of subsection (e) or was withdrawn or suspended under paragraph (6) or if the Secretary determines that a drug has been withdrawn from sale for safety or effectiveness reasons, it may not be published in the list under subparagraph (A) or, if the withdrawal or suspension occurred after its publication in such list, it shall be immediately removed from such list—

(i) for the same period as the withdrawal or suspension under subsection (e) or paragraph (6), or

(ii) if the listed drug has been withdrawn from sale, for the period of withdrawal from sale or, if earlier, the period ending on the date the Secretary determines that the withdrawal from sale is not for safety or effectiveness reasons. A notice of the removal shall be published in the Federal Register.

(8) For purposes of this subsection:

(A) The term "bioavailability" means the rate and extent to which the active ingredient or therapeutic ingredient is absorbed from a drug and becomes available at the site of drug action.

(B) A drug shall be considered to be bioequivalent to a listed drug if—

(i) the rate and extent of absorption of the drug do not show a significant difference from the rate and extent of absorption of the listed drug when administered at the same molar dose of the therapeutic ingredient under similar experimental conditions in either a single dose or multiple doses; or

(ii) the extent of absorption of the drug does not show a significant difference from the extent of absorption of the listed drug when administered at the same molar dose of the therapeutic ingredient under similar experimental conditions in either a single dose or multiple doses and the difference from the listed drug in the rate of absorption of the drug is intentional, is reflected in its proposed labeling, is not essential to the attainment of effective body drug concentrations on chronic use, and is considered medically insignificant for the drug.

(9) The Secretary shall, with respect to each application submitted under this subsection, maintain a record of—(A) the name of the applicant, (B) the name of the drug covered by the application, (C) the name of each person to whom the review of the chemistry of the application was assigned and the date of such assignment, and (D) the name of each person to whom the bioequivalence review for such application was assigned and the date of such assignment.

The information the Secretary is required to maintain under this paragraph with respect to an application submitted under this subsection shall be made available to the public after the approval of such application.

(k) (1) In the case of any drug for which an approval of an application filed under subsection (b) or (j) is in effect, the applicant shall establish and maintain such records, and make such reports to the Secretary, of data relating to clinical experience and other data or information, received or otherwise obtained by such applicant with respect to such drug, as the Secretary may by general regulation, or by order with respect to such application, prescribe on the basis of a finding that such records and reports are necessary in order to enable the Secretary to determine, or facilitate a determination, whether there is or may be ground for invoking subsection (e) of this section. Regulations and orders issued under this subsection and under subsection (i) shall have due regard for the professional ethics of the medical profession and the interests of patients and shall provide, where the Secretary deems it to be appropriate, for the examination, upon request, by the persons to whom such regulations or orders are applicable, of similar information received or otherwise obtained by the Secretary.

(2) Every person required under this section to maintain records, and every person in charge or custody thereof, shall, upon request of an officer or employee designated by the Secretary, permit such officer or employee at all reasonable times to have access to and copy and verify such records.

(*l*) Safety and effectiveness data and information which has been submitted in an application under subsection (b) for a drug and which has not previously been disclosed to the public shall be made available to the public, upon request, unless extraordinary circumstances are shown—

(1) if no work is being or will be undertaken to have the application approved,

(2) if the Secretary has determined that the application is not approvable and all legal appeals have been exhausted,

(3) if approval of the application under subsection (c) is withdrawn and all legal appeals have been exhausted,

(4) if the Secretary has determined that such drug is not a new drug, or

(5) upon the effective date of the approval of the first application under subsection (j) which refers to such drug or upon the date upon which the approval of an application under subsection (j) which refers to such drug could be made effective if such an application had been submitted.

(m) For purposes of this section, the term "patent" means a patent issued by the Patent and Trademark Office of the Department of Commerce.

(n) (1) For the purpose of providing expert scientific advice and recommendations to the Secretary regarding a clinical investigation of a drug or the approval for marketing of a drug under section 505 or section 351 of the Public Health Service Act, the Secretary shall establish panels of experts or use panels of experts established before the date of enactment of the Food and Drug Administration Modernization Act of 1997, or both.

(2) The Secretary may delegate the appointment and oversight authority granted under section 904 to a director of a center or successor entity within the Food and Drug Administration.

(3) The Secretary shall make appointments to each panel established under paragraph (1) so that each panel shall consist of—

(A) members who are qualified by training and experience to evaluate the safety and effectiveness of the drugs to be referred to the panel and who, to the extent feasible, possess skill and experience in the development, manufacture, or utilization of such drugs;

(B) members with diverse expertise in such fields as clinical and administrative medicine, pharmacy, pharmacology, pharmacoeconomics, biological and physical sciences, and other related professions;

(C) a representative of consumer interests, and a representative of interests of the drug manufacturing industry not directly affected by the matter to be brought before the panel; and

(D) two or more members who are specialists or have other expertise in the particular disease or condition for which the drug under review is proposed to be indicated.

Scientific, trade, and consumer organizations shall be afforded an opportunity to nominate individuals for appointment to the panels. No individual who is in the regular full-time employ of the United States and engaged in the administration of this Act may be a voting member of any panel. The Secretary shall designate one of the members of each panel to serve as chairman thereof.

(4) Each member of a panel shall publicly disclose all conflicts of interest that member may have with the work to be undertaken by the panel. No member of a panel may vote on any matter where the member or the immediate family of such member could gain financially from the advice given to the Secretary. The Secretary may grant a waiver of any conflict of interest requirement upon public disclosure of such conflict of interest if such waiver is necessary to afford the panel essential expertise, except that the Secretary may not grant a waiver for a member of a panel when the member's own scientific work is involved.

(5) The Secretary shall, as appropriate, provide education and training to each new panel member before such member participates in a panel's activities, including education regarding requirements under this Act and related regulations of the Secretary, and the administrative processes and procedures related to panel meetings.

(6) Panel members (other than officers or employees of the United States), while attending meetings or conferences of a panel or otherwise engaged in its business, shall be entitled to receive compensation for each day so engaged, including travel time, at rates to be fixed by the Secretary, but not to exceed the daily equivalent of the rate in effect for positions classified above grade GS–15 of the General Schedule. While serving away from their homes or regular places of business, panel members may be allowed travel expenses (including per diem in lieu of subsistence) as authorized by section 5703 of title 5, United States Code, for persons in the Government service employed intermittently.

(7) The Secretary shall ensure that scientific advisory panels meet regularly and at appropriate intervals so that any matter to be reviewed by such a panel can be presented to the panel not more than 60 days after the matter is ready for such review. Meetings of the panel may be held using electronic communication to convene the meetings.

(8) Within 90 days after a scientific advisory panel makes recommendations on any matter under its review, the Food and Drug Administration official responsible for the matter shall review the conclusions and recommendations of the panel, and notify the affected persons of the final decision on the matter, or of the reasons that no such decision has been

reached. Each such final decision shall be documented including the rationale for the decision.

SEC. 505A [21 U.S.C. § 355a]. PEDIATRIC STUDIES OF DRUGS.

(a) DEFINITIONS.—As used in this section, the term "pediatric studies" or "studies" means at least one clinical investigation (that, at the Secretary's discretion, may include pharmacokinetic studies) in pediatric age groups (including neonates in appropriate cases) in which a drug is anticipated to be used.

(b) MARKET EXCLUSIVITY FOR NEW DRUGS.—If, prior to approval of an application that is submitted under section 505(b)(1), the Secretary determines that information relating to the use of a new drug in the pediatric population may produce health benefits in that population, the Secretary makes a written request for pediatric studies (which shall include a timeframe for completing such studies), and such studies are completed within any such timeframe and the reports thereof submitted in accordance with subsection (d)(2) or accepted in accordance with subsection (d)(3)—

(1)(A)(i) the period referred to in subsection (c)(3)(D)(ii) of section 505, and in subsection (j)(5)(D)(ii) of such section, is deemed to be five years and six months rather than five years, and the references in subsections (c)(3)(D)(ii) and (j)(5)(D)(ii) of such section to four years, to forty-eight months, and to seven and one-half years are deemed to be four and one-half years, fifty-four months, and eight years, respectively; or

(ii) the period referred to in clauses (iii) and (iv) of subsection (c)(3)(D) of such section, and in clauses (iii) and (iv) of subsection (j)(5)(D) of such section, is deemed to be three years and six months rather than three years; and

(B) if the drug is designated under section 526 for a rare disease or condition, the period referred to in section 527(a) is deemed to be seven years and six months rather than seven years; and

(2)(A) if the drug is the subject of—

(i) a listed patent for which a certification has been submitted under subsection (b)(2)(A)(ii) or (j)(2)(A)(vii)(II) of section 505 and for which pediatric studies were submitted prior to the expiration of the patent (including any patent extensions); or

(ii) a listed patent for which a certification has been submitted under subsections (b)(2)(A)(iii) or (j)(2)(A)(vii)(IV) of section 505,

the period during which an application may not be approved under section 505(c)(3) or section 505(j)(4)(B) shall be extended a period of six months after the date the patent expires (including any patent extensions); or

(B) if the drug is the subject of a listed patent for which certification has been submitted under subsection (b)(2)(A)(iv) or (j)(2)(A)(vii)(IV) of section 505, and in the patent infringement litigation resulting from the certification the court determines that the patent is valid and would be infringed, the period during which an application may not be approved under section 505(c)(3) or section 505(j)(4)(B) shall be extended by a period of six months after the date the patent expires (including any patent extensions).

(c) MARKET EXCLUSIVITY FOR ALREADY–MARKETED DRUGS.—If the Secretary determines that information relating to the use of an approved drug in the pediatric population may produce health benefits in that population and makes a written request to the holder of an approved application under section 505(b)(1) for pediatric studies (which shall include a timeframe for completing such studies), the holder agrees to the request, the studies are completed within any such timeframe, and the reports thereof are submitted in accordance with subsection (d)(2) or accepted in accordance with subsection (d)(3)—

(1)(A)(i) the period referred to in subsection (c)(3)(D)(ii) of section 505, and in subsection (j)(5)(D)(ii) of such section, is deemed to be five years and six months rather than five years, and the references in subsections (c)(3)(D)(ii) and (j)(5)(D)(ii) of such section to four years, to forty-eight months, and to seven and one-half years are deemed to be four and one-half years, fifty-four months, and eight years, respectively; or

(ii) the period referred to in clauses (iii) and (iv) of subsection (c)(3)(D) of such section, and in clauses (iii) and (iv) of subsection (j)(5)(D) of such section, is deemed to be three years and six months rather than three years; and

(B) if the drug is designated under section 526 for a rare disease or condition, the period referred to in section 527(a) is deemed to be seven years and six months rather than seven years; and

(2)(A) if the drug is the subject of—

(i) a listed patent for which a certification has been submitted under subsection (b)(2)(A)(ii) or (j)(2)(A)(vii)(II) of section 505 and for which pediatric studies were submitted prior to the expiration of the patent (including any patent extensions); or

(ii) a listed patent for which a certification has been submitted under subsection (b)(2)(A)(iii) or (j)(2)(A)(vii)(III) of section 505,

the period during which an application may not be approved under section 505(c)(3) or section 505(j)(4)(B) shall be extended by a period of six months after the date the patent expires (including any patent extensions); or

(B) if the drug is the subject of a listed patent for which certification has been submitted under subsection (b)(2)(A)(iv) or (j)(2)(A)(vii)(IV) of section 505, and in the patent infringement litigation resulting from the certification the court determines that the patent is valid and would be infringed, the period during which an application may not be approved under section 505(c)(3) or section 505(j)(4)(B) shall be extended by a period of six months after the date the patent expires (including any patent extensions).

(d) CONDUCT OF PEDIATRIC STUDIES.

(1) AGREEMENT FOR STUDIES.—The Secretary may, pursuant to a written request from the Secretary under subsection (b) or (c), after consultation with—(A) the sponsor of an application for an investigational new drug under section 505(i); (B) the sponsor of an application for a new drug under section 505(b)(1); or (C) the holder of an approved application for a drug under section 505(b)(1)—agree with the sponsor or holder for the conduct of pediatric studies for such drug. Such agreement shall be in writing and shall include a timeframe for such studies.

(2) WRITTEN PROTOCOLS TO MEET THE STUDIES REQUIRE-MENT.—If the sponsor or holder and the Secretary agree upon written protocols for the studies, the studies requirement of subsection (b) or (c) is satisfied upon the completion of the studies and submission of the reports thereof in accordance with the original written request and the written agreement referred to in paragraph (1). In reaching an agreement regarding written protocols, the Secretary shall take into account adequate representation of children of ethnic and racial minorities. Not later than 60 days after the submission of the report of the studies, the Secretary shall determine if such studies were or were not conducted in accordance with the original written request and the written agreement and reported in accordance with the requirements of the Secretary for filing and so notify the sponsor or holder.

(3) OTHER METHODS TO MEET THE STUDIES REQUIRE-MENT.—If the sponsor or holder and the Secretary have not agreed in writing on the protocols for the studies, the studies requirement of subsection (b) or (c) is satisfied when such studies have been completed and the reports accepted by the Secretary. Not later than 90 days after the submission of the reports of the studies, the Secretary shall accept or reject such reports and so notify the sponsor or holder. The Secretary's only responsibility in accepting or rejecting the reports shall be to determine, within the 90 days, whether the studies fairly respond to the written request, have been conducted in accordance with commonly accepted scientific principles and protocols, and have been reported in accordance with the requirements of the Secretary for filing.

(4) WRITTEN REQUEST TO HOLDERS OF APPROVED APPLICA-TIONS FOR DRUGS THAT HAVE MARKET EXCLUSIVITY.—

(A) REQUEST AND RESPONSE.—If the Secretary makes a written request for pediatric studies (including neonates, as appropriate) under subsection (c) to the holder of an application approved under section 505(b)(1), the holder, not later than 180 days after receiving the written request, shall respond to the Secretary as to the intention of the holder to act on the request by—(i) indicating when the pediatric studies will be initiated, if the holder agrees to the request; or (ii) indicating that the holder does not agree to the request.

(B) NO AGREEMENT TO REQUEST.–(i) REFERRAL.—If the holder does not agree to a written request within the time period specified in subparagraph (A), and if the Secretary determines that there is a continuing need for information relating to the use of the drug in the pediatric population (including neonates, as appropriate), the Secretary shall refer the drug to the Foundation for the National Institutes of Health established under section 499 of the Public Health Service Act (42 U.S.C. § 290b) (referred to in this paragraph as the "Foundation") for the conduct of the pediatric studies described in the written request. (ii) PUBLIC NOTICE.—The Secretary shall give public notice of the name of the drug, the name of the manufacturer, and the indications to be studied made in a referral under clause (i).

(C) LACK OF FUNDS.—On referral of a drug under subparagraph (B)(i), the Foundation shall issue a proposal to award a grant to conduct the requested studies unless the Foundation certifies to the Secretary, within a timeframe that the Secretary determines is appropriate through guidance, that the Foundation does not have funds available under section 499(j)(9)(B)(i) to conduct the requested studies. If the Foundation so certifies, the Secretary shall refer the drug for inclusion on the list established under section 409I of the Public Health Service Act for the conduct of the studies.

(D) EFFECT OF SUBSECTION.—Nothing in this subsection (including with respect to referrals from the Secretary to the Foundation) alters or amends section 301(j) of this Act or section 552 of title 5 or section 1905 of title 18, United States Code.

(E) NO REQUIREMENT TO REFER.—Nothing in this subsection shall be construed to require that every declined written request shall be referred to the Foundation.

(F) WRITTEN REQUESTS UNDER SUBSECTION (b).—For drugs under subsection (b) for which written requests have not been accepted, if the Secretary determines that there is a continuing need for information relating to the use of the drug in the pediatric population (including neonates, as appropriate), the Secretary shall issue a written request under subsection (c) after the date of approval of the drug.

(e) DELAY OF EFFECTIVE DATE FOR CERTAIN APPLICATION.—If the Secretary determines that the acceptance or approval of an application under section 505(b)(2) or 505(j) for a new drug may occur after submission of reports of pediatric studies under this section, which were submitted prior to the expiration of the patent (including any patent extension) or the applicable period under clauses (ii) through (iv) of section 505(c)(3)(D) or clauses (ii) through (iv) of section 505(j)(5)(D), but before the Secretary has determined whether the requirements of subsection (d) have been satisfied, the Secretary shall delay the acceptance or approval under section 505(b)(2) or 505(j) until the determination under subsection (d) is made, but any such delay shall not exceed 90 days. In the event that requirements of this section are satisfied, the applicable six-month period under subsection (b) or (c) shall be deemed to have been running during the period of delay.

(f) NOTICE OF DETERMINATIONS ON STUDIES REQUIREMENT.—
The Secretary shall publish a notice of any determination that the requirements of subsection (d) have been met and that submissions and approvals under subsection (b)(2) or (j) of section 505 for a drug will be subject to the provisions of this section.

(g) LIMITATIONS.—A drug to which the six-month period under subsection (b) or (c) has already been applied—

(1) may receive an additional six-month period under subsection (c)(1)(A)(ii) for a supplemental application if all other requirements under this section are satisfied, except that such a drug may not receive any additional such period under subsection (c)(2); and

(2) may not receive any additional such period under subsection (c)(1)(B).

(h) RELATIONSHIP TO REGULATIONS.—Notwithstanding any other provision of law, if any pediatric study is required pursuant to regulations promulgated by the Secretary and such study meets the completeness, timeliness, and other requirements of this section, such study shall be deemed to satisfy the requirement for market exclusivity pursuant to this section.

(i) LABELING SUPPLEMENTS.—

(1) PRIORITY STATUS FOR PEDIATRIC SUPPLEMENTS.—Any supplement to an application under section 505 proposing a labeling change pursuant to a report on a pediatric study under this section—(A) shall be considered to be a priority supplement; and (B) shall be subject to the performance goals established by the Commissioner for priority drugs.

(2) DISPUTE RESOLUTION.—

(A) REQUEST FOR LABELING CHANGE AND FAILURE TO AGREE.—If the Commissioner determines that an application with respect to which a pediatric study is conducted under this section is approvable and that the only open issue for final action on the application is the reaching of an agreement between the sponsor of the application and the Commissioner on appropriate changes to the labeling for the drug that is the subject of the application, not later than 180 days after the date of submission of the application—(i) the Commissioner shall request that the sponsor of the application make any labeling change that the Commissioner determines to be appropriate; and (ii) if the sponsor of the application does not agree to make a labeling change requested by the Commissioner, the Commissioner shall refer the matter to the Pediatric Advisory Subcommittee of the Anti–Infective Drugs Advisory Committee.

(B) ACTION BY THE PEDIATRIC ADVISORY SUBCOMMITTEE OF THE ANTI–INFECTIVE DRUGS ADVISORY COMMITTEE.—Not later than 90 days after receiving a referral under subparagraph (A)(ii), the Pediatric Advisory Subcommittee of the Anti–Infective Drugs Advisory Committee shall—(i) review the pediatric study reports; and (ii) make a recommendation to the Commissioner concerning appropriate labeling changes, if any.

(C) CONSIDERATION OF RECOMMENDATIONS.—The Commissioner shall consider the recommendations of the Pediatric Advisory Subcommittee of the Anti–Infective Drugs Advisory Committee and, if appropriate, not later than 30 days after receiving the recommendation, make a request to the sponsor of the application to make any labeling change that the Commissioner determines to be appropriate.

(D) MISBRANDING.—If the sponsor of the application, within 30 days after receiving a request under subparagraph (C), does not agree to make a labeling change requested by the Commissioner, the Commissioner may deem the drug that is the subject of the application to be misbranded.

(E) NO EFFECT ON AUTHORITY.—Nothing in this subsection limits the authority of the United States to bring an enforcement action under this Act when a drug lacks appropriate pediatric labeling. Neither course of action (the Pediatric Advisory Subcommittee of the Anti–Infective Drugs Advisory Committee process or an enforcement action referred to in the preceding sentence) shall preclude, delay, or serve as the basis to stay the other course of action.

(j) DISSEMINATION OF PEDIATRIC INFORMATION.—

(1) IN GENERAL.—Not later than 180 days after the date of submission of a report on a pediatric study under this section, the Commissioner shall make available to the public a summary of the medical and clinical pharmacology reviews of pediatric studies conducted for the supplement, including by publication in the Federal Register.

(2) EFFECT OF SUBSECTION.—Nothing in this subsection alters or amends section 301(j) of this Act or section 552 of title 5 or section 1905 of title 18, United States Code.

(k) CLARIFICATION OF INTERACTION OF MARKET EXCLUSIVITY UNDER THIS SECTION AND MARKET EXCLUSIVITY AWARDED TO AN APPLICANT FOR APPROVAL OF A DRUG UNDER SECTION 505(j).—If a 180–day period under section 505(j)(5)(B)(iv) overlaps with a 6–month exclusivity period under this section, so that the applicant for approval of a drug under section 505(j) entitled to the 180–day period under that section loses a portion of the 180–day period to which the applicant is entitled for the drug, the 180–day period shall be extended from—(1) the date on which the 180–day period would have expired by the number of days of the overlap, if the 180–day period would, but for the application of this subsection, expire after the 6–month exclusivity period; or (2) the date on which the 6–month exclusivity period expires, by the number of days of the overlap if the 180–day period would, but for the application of this subsection, expire during the six-month exclusivity period.

(*l*) PROMPT APPROVAL OF DRUGS UNDER SECTION 505(j) WHEN PEDIATRIC INFORMATION IS ADDED TO LABELING.—

(1) GENERAL RULE.—A drug for which an application has been submitted or approved under section 505(j) shall not be considered ineligi-

ble for approval under that section or misbranded under section 502 on the basis that the labeling of the drug omits a pediatric indication or any other aspect of labeling pertaining to pediatric use when the omitted indication or other aspect is protected by patent or by exclusivity under clause (iii) or (iv) of section 505(j)(5)(D).

(2) LABELING.—Notwithstanding clauses (iii) and (iv) of section 505(j)(5)(D), the Secretary may require that the labeling of a drug approved under section 505(j) that omits a pediatric indication or other aspect of labeling as described in paragraph (1) include—(A) a statement that, because of marketing exclusivity for a manufacturer—(i) the drug is not labeled for pediatric use; or (ii) in the case of a drug for which there is an additional pediatric use not referred to in paragraph (1), the drug is not labeled for the pediatric use under paragraph (1); and (B) a statement of any appropriate pediatric contraindications, warnings, or precautions that the Secretary considers necessary.

(3) PRESERVATION OF PEDIATRIC EXCLUSIVITY AND OTHER PROVISIONS.—This subsection does not affect—(A) the availability or scope of exclusivity under this section; (B) the availability or scope of exclusivity under section 505 for pediatric formulations; (C) the question of the eligibility for approval of any application under section 505(j) that omits any other conditions of approval entitled to exclusivity under clause (iii) or (iv) of section 505(j)(5)(D); or (D) except as expressly provided in paragraphs (1) and (2), the operation of section 505.

(m) REPORT.—The Secretary shall conduct a study and report to Congress not later than January 1, 2001, based on the experience under the program established under this section. The study and report shall examine all relevant issues, including—

(1) the effectiveness of the program in improving information about important pediatric uses for approved drugs;

(2) the adequacy of the incentive provided under this section;

(3) the economic impact of the program on taxpayers and consumers, including the impact of the lack of lower cost generic drugs on patients, including on lower income patients; and

(4) any suggestions for modification that the Secretary determines to be appropriate.

(n) SUNSET.—A drug may not receive any 6–month period under subsection (b) or (c) unless—(1) on or before October 1, 2007, the Secretary makes a written request for pediatric studies of the drug; (2) on or before October 1, 2007, an application for the drug is accepted for filing under section 505(b); and (3) all requirements of this section are met.

SEC. 506 [21 U.S.C. § 356]. FAST TRACK PRODUCTS.

(a) DESIGNATION OF DRUG AS A FAST TRACK PRODUCT.

(1) IN GENERAL.—The Secretary shall, at the request of the sponsor of a new drug, facilitate the development and expedite the review of such

drug if it is intended for the treatment of a serious or life-threatening condition and it demonstrates the potential to address unmet medical needs for such a condition. (In this section, such a drug is referred to as a "fast track product.")

(2) REQUEST FOR DESIGNATION.—The sponsor of a new drug may request the Secretary to designate the drug as a fast track product. A request for the designation may be made concurrently with, or at any time after, submission of an application for the investigation of the drug under section 505(i) or section 351(a)(3) of the Public Health Service Act.

(3) DESIGNATION.—Within 60 calendar days after the receipt of a request under paragraph (2), the Secretary shall determine whether the drug that is the subject of the request meets the criteria described in paragraph (1). If the Secretary finds that the drug meets the criteria, the Secretary shall designate the drug as a fast track product and shall take such actions as are appropriate to expedite the development and review of the application for approval of such product.

(b) APPROVAL OF APPLICATION FOR A FAST TRACK PRODUCT.

(1) IN GENERAL.—The Secretary may approve an application for approval of a fast track product under section 505(c) or section 351 of the Public Health Service Act upon a determination that the product has an effect on a clinical endpoint or on a surrogate endpoint that is reasonably likely to predict clinical benefit.

(2) LIMITATION.—Approval of a fast track product under this subsection may be subject to the requirements—

(A) that the sponsor conduct appropriate post-approval studies to validate the surrogate endpoint or otherwise confirm the effect on the clinical endpoint; and

(B) that the sponsor submit copies of all promotional materials related to the fast track product during the preapproval review period and, following approval and for such period thereafter as the Secretary determines to be appropriate, at least 30 days prior to dissemination of the materials.

(3) EXPEDITED WITHDRAWAL OF APPROVAL.—The Secretary may withdraw approval of a fast track product using expedited procedures (as prescribed by the Secretary in regulations which shall include an opportunity for an informal hearing) if—

(A) the sponsor fails to conduct any required post-approval study of the fast track drug with due diligence;

(B) a post-approval study of the fast track product fails to verify clinical benefit of the product;

(C) other evidence demonstrates that the fast track product is not safe or effective under the conditions of use;

(D) the sponsor disseminates false or misleading promotional materials with respect to the product.

(c) REVIEW OF INCOMPLETE APPLICATIONS FOR APPROVAL OF A FAST TRACK PRODUCT.

(1) IN GENERAL.—If the Secretary determines, after preliminary evaluation of clinical data submitted by the sponsor, that a fast track product may be effective, the Secretary shall evaluate for filing, and may commence review of portions of, an application for the approval of the product before the sponsor submits a complete application. The Secretary shall commence such review only if the applicant—

(A) provides a schedule for submission of information necessary to make the application complete; and

(B) pays any fee that may be required under section 736.

(2) EXCEPTION.—Any time period for review of human drug applications that has been agreed to by the Secretary and that has been set forth in goals identified in letters of the Secretary (relating to the use of fees collected under section 736 to expedite the drug development process and the review of human drug applications) shall not apply to an application submitted under paragraph (1) until the date on which the application is complete.

(d) AWARENESS EFFORTS.—The Secretary shall—

(1) develop and disseminate to physicians, patient organizations, pharmaceutical and biotechnology companies, and other appropriate persons a description of the provisions of this section applicable to fast track products; and

(2) establish a program to encourage the development of surrogate endpoints that are reasonably likely to predict clinical benefit for serious or life-threatening conditions for which there exist significant unmet medical needs.

SEC. 506A [21 U.S.C. § 356a]. MANUFACTURING CHANGES.

(a) IN GENERAL.—With respect to a drug for which there is in effect an approved application under section 505 or 512 or a license under section 351 of the Public Health Service Act, a change from the manufacturing process approved pursuant to such application or license may be made, and the drug as made with the change may be distributed, if—

(1) the holder of the approved application or license (referred to in this section as a "holder") has validated the effects of the change in accordance with subsection (b); and

(2)(A) in the case of a major manufacturing change, the holder has complied with the requirements of subsection (c); or

(B) in the case of a change that is not a major manufacturing change, the holder complies with the applicable requirements of subsection (d).

(b) VALIDATION OF EFFECTS OF CHANGES.—For purposes of subsection (a)(1), a drug made with a manufacturing change (whether a major manufacturing change or otherwise) may be distributed only if, before distribution of the drug as so made, the holder involved validates the effects of the change on the identity, strength, quality, purity, and potency of the drug as the identity, strength, quality, purity, and potency may relate to the safety or effectiveness of the drug.

(c) MAJOR MANUFACTURING CHANGES.

(1) REQUIREMENT OF SUPPLEMENTAL APPLICATION.—For purposes of subsection (a)(2)(A), a drug made with a major manufacturing change may be distributed only if, before the distribution of the drug as so made, the holder involved submits to the Secretary a supplemental application for such change and the Secretary approves the application. The application shall contain such information as the Secretary determines to be appropriate, and shall include the information developed under subsection (b) by the holder in validating the effects of the change.

(2) CHANGES QUALIFYING AS MAJOR CHANGES.—For purposes of subsection (a)(2)(A), a major manufacturing change is a manufacturing change that is determined by the Secretary to have substantial potential to adversely affect the identity, strength, quality, purity, or potency of the drug as they may relate to the safety or effectiveness of a drug. Such a change includes a change that—

(A) is made in the qualitative or quantitative formulation of the drug involved or in the specifications in the approved application or license referred to in subsection (a) for the drug (unless exempted by the Secretary by regulation or guidance from the requirements of this subsection);

(B) is determined by the Secretary by regulation or guidance to require completion of an appropriate clinical study demonstrating equivalence of the drug to the drug as manufactured without the change; or

(C) is another type of change determined by the Secretary by regulation or guidance to have a substantial potential to adversely affect the safety or effectiveness of the drug.

(d) OTHER MANUFACTURING CHANGES.

(1) IN GENERAL.—For purposes of subsection (a)(2)(B), the Secretary may regulate drugs made with manufacturing changes that are not major manufacturing changes as follows:

(A) The Secretary may in accordance with paragraph (2) authorize holders to distribute such drugs without submitting a supplemental application for such changes.

(B) The Secretary may in accordance with paragraph (3) require that, prior to the distribution of such drugs, holders submit to the Secretary supplemental applications for such changes.

(C) The Secretary may establish categories of such changes and designate categories to which subparagraph (A) applies and categories to which subparagraph (B) applies.

(2) CHANGES NOT REQUIRING SUPPLEMENTAL APPLICATION.

(A) SUBMISSION OF REPORT.—A holder making a manufacturing change to which paragraph (1)(A) applies shall submit to the Secretary a report on the change, which shall contain such information as the Secretary determines to be appropriate, and which shall include the information developed under subsection (b) by the holder in validating the effects of the change. The report shall be submitted by such date as the Secretary may specify.

(B) AUTHORITY REGARDING ANNUAL REPORTS.—In the case of a holder that during a single year makes more than one manufacturing change to which paragraph (1)(A) applies, the Secretary may in carrying out subparagraph (A) authorize the holder to comply with such subparagraph by submitting a single report for the year that provides the information required in such subparagraph for all the changes made by the holder during the year.

(3) CHANGES REQUIRING SUPPLEMENTAL APPLICATION.

(A) SUBMISSION OF SUPPLEMENTAL APPLICATION.—The supplemental application required under paragraph (1)(B) for a manufacturing change shall contain such information as the Secretary determines to be appropriate, which shall include the information developed under subsection (b) by the holder in validating the effects of the change.

(B) AUTHORITY FOR DISTRIBUTION.—In the case of a manufacturing change to which paragraph (1)(B) applies:

(i) The holder involved may commence distribution of the drug involved 30 days after the Secretary receives the supplemental application under such paragraph, unless the Secretary notifies the holder within such 30-day period that prior approval of the application is required before distribution may be commenced.

(ii) The Secretary may designate a category of such changes for the purpose of providing that, in the case of a change that is in such category, the holder involved may commence distribution of the drug involved upon the receipt by the Secretary of a supplemental application for the change.

(iii) If the Secretary disapproves the supplemental application, the Secretary may order the manufacturer to cease the distribution of the drugs that have been made with the manufacturing change.

SEC. 506B [21 U.S.C. § 356b]. REPORTS OF POSTMARKETING STUDIES.

(a) SUBMISSION.

(1) IN GENERAL.—A sponsor of a drug that has entered into an agreement with the Secretary to conduct a postmarketing study of a drug

shall, submit to the Secretary, within 1 year after the approval of such drug and annually thereafter until the study is completed or terminated, a report of the progress of the study or the reasons for the failure of the sponsor to conduct the study. The report shall be submitted in such form as is prescribed by the Secretary in regulations issued by the Secretary.

(2) AGREEMENTS PRIOR TO EFFECTIVE DATE.—Any agreement entered into between the Secretary and a sponsor of a drug, prior to the date of enactment of the Food and Drug Administration Modernization Act of 1997, to conduct postmarketing study of a drug shall be subject to the requirements of paragraph (1). An initial report for such an agreement shall be submitted within 6 months after the date of the issuance of the regulations under paragraph (1).

(b) CONSIDERATION OF INFORMATION AS PUBLIC INFORMA-TION.—Any information pertaining to a report described in subsection (a) shall be considered to be public information to the extent that the informa-tion is necessary—(1) to identify the sponsor; and (2) to establish the status of a study described in subsection (a) and the reasons, if any, for any failure to carry out the study.

(c) STATUS OF STUDIES AND REPORTS.—The Secretary shall annually develop and publish in the Federal Register a report that provides informa-tion on the status of the postmarketing studies—(1) that sponsors have entered into agreements to conduct; and (2) for which reports have been submitted under subsection (a)(1).

SEC. 506C [21 U.S.C. § 356c]. DISCONTINUANCE OF A LIFE SAVING PRODUCT.

(a) IN GENERAL.—A manufacturer that is the sole manufacturer of a drug—

(1) that is—(A) life-supporting; (B) life-sustaining; or (C) intended for use in the prevention of a debilitating disease or condition;

(2) for which an application has been approved under section 505(b) or 505(j); and

(3) that is not a product that was originally derived from human tissue and was replaced by a recombinant product,

shall notify the Secretary of a discontinuance of the manufacture of the drug at least 6 months prior to the date of the discontinuance.

(b) REDUCTION IN NOTIFICATION PERIOD.—The notification period required under subsection (a) for a manufacturer may be reduced if the manufacturer certifies to the Secretary that good cause exists for the reduction, such as a situation in which—(1) a public health problem may result from continuation of the manufacturing for the 6–month period; (2) a biomaterials shortage prevents the continuation of the manufacturing for the 6–month period; (3) a liability problem may exist for the manufacturer if the manufacturing is continued for the 6–month period; (4) continuation of the manufacturing for the 6–month period may cause substantial economic hardship for the manufacturer; (5) the manufacturer has filed for bankruptcy under chapter 7 or 11 of title 11, United States Code; or (6) the manufacturer can continue the distribution of the drug involved for 6 months.

(c) DISTRIBUTION.—To the maximum extent practicable, the Secretary shall distribute information on the discontinuation of the drugs described in subsection (a) to appropriate physician and patient organizations.

SEC. 508 [21 U.S.C. § 358]. AUTHORITY TO DESIGNATE OFFICIAL NAMES.

(a) The Secretary may designate an official name for any drug or device if he determines that such action is necessary or desirable in the interest of usefulness and simplicity. Any official name designated under this section for any drug or device shall be the only official name of that drug or device used in any official compendium published after such name has been prescribed or for any other purpose of this Act. In no event, however, shall the Secretary establish an official name so as to infringe a valid trademark.

(b) Within a reasonable time after the effective date of this section, and at such other times as he may deem necessary, the Secretary shall cause a review to be made of the official names by which drugs are identified in the official United States Pharmacopoeia, the official Homeopathic Pharmacopoeia of the United States, and the official National Formulary, and all supplements thereto, and at such times as he may deem necessary shall cause a review to be made of the official names by which devices are identified in any official compendium (and all supplements thereto) to determine whether revision of any of those names is necessary or desirable in the interest of usefulness and simplicity.

(c) Whenever he determines after any such review that (1) any such official name is unduly complex or is not useful for any other reason, (2) two or more official names have been applied to a single drug or device, or to two or more drugs which are identical in chemical structure and pharmacological action and which are substantially identical in strength, quality, and purity, or to two or more devices which are substantially equivalent in design and purpose or (3) no official name has been applied to a medically useful drug or device, he shall transmit in writing to the compiler of each official compendium in which that drug or drugs or device are identified and recognized his request for the recommendation of a single official name for such drug or drugs or device which will have usefulness and simplicity. Whenever such a single official name has not been recommended within one hundred and eighty days after such request, or the Secretary determines that any name so recommended is not useful for any reason, he shall designate a single official name for such drug or drugs or device. Whenever he determines that the name so recommended is useful, he shall designate that name as the official name of such drug or drugs or device. Such designation shall be made as a regulation upon public notice and in accordance with the procedure set forth in section 553 of title 5, United States Code.

(d) After each such review, and at such other times as the Secretary may determine to be necessary or desirable, the Secretary shall cause to be compiled, published, and publicly distributed a list which shall list all revised official names of drugs or devices designated under this section and shall contain such descriptive and explanatory matter as the Secretary may determine to be required for the effective use of those names.

(e) Upon a request in writing by any compiler of an official compendium that the Secretary exercise the authority granted to him under subsection 508(a), he shall upon public notice and in accordance with the procedure set forth in section 553 of title 5, United States Code designate the official name of the drug or device for which the request is made.

SEC. 509 [21 U.S.C. § 359]. NONAPPLICABILITY TO COSMETICS.

This chapter, as amended by the Drug Amendments of 1962, shall not apply to any cosmetic unless such cosmetic is also a drug or device or component thereof.

SEC. 510 [21 U.S.C. § 360]. REGISTRATION OF PRODUCERS OF DRUGS AND DEVICES.

(a) As used in this section—

(1) the term "manufacture, preparation, propagation, compounding, or processing" shall include repackaging or otherwise changing the container, wrapper, or labeling of any drug package or device package in furtherance of the distribution of the drug or device from the original place of manufacture to the person who makes final delivery or sale to the ultimate consumer or user; and

(2) the term "name" shall include in the case of a partnership the name of each partner and, in the case of a corporation, the name of each corporate officer and director, and the State of incorporation

(b) On or before December 31 of each year every person who owns or operates any establishment in any State engaged in the manufacture, preparation, propagation, compounding, or processing of a drug or drugs or a device or devices shall register with the Secretary his name, places of business, and all such establishments.

(c) Every person upon first engaging in the manufacture, preparation, propagation, compounding, or processing of a drug or drugs or a device or devices in any establishment which he owns or operates in any State shall immediately register with the Secretary his name, place of business, and such establishment

(d) Every person duly registered in accordance with the foregoing subsections of this section shall immediately register with the Secretary any additional establishment which he owns or operates in any State and in which he begins the manufacture, preparation, propagation, compounding, or processing of a drug or drugs or a device or devices.

(e) The Secretary may assign a registration number to any person or any establishment registered in accordance with this section. The Secretary may also assign a listing number to each drug or class of drugs listed under subsection (j). Any number assigned pursuant to the preceding sentence shall be the same as that assigned pursuant to the National Drug Code. The Secretary may by regulation prescribe a uniform system for the identification of devices intended for human use and may require that persons who are required to list such devices pursuant to subsection (j) shall list such devices in accordance with such system.

(f) The Secretary shall make available for inspection, to any person so requesting, any registration filed pursuant to this section; except that any list submitted pursuant to paragraph (3) of subsection (j) and the information accompanying any list or notice filed under paragraph (1) or (2) of that subsection shall be exempt from such inspection unless the Secretary finds that such an exemption would be inconsistent with protection of the public health.

(g) The foregoing subsections of this section shall not apply to—

(1) pharmacies which maintain establishments in conformance with any applicable local laws regulating the practice of pharmacy and medicine and which are regularly engaged in dispensing prescription drugs or devices, upon prescriptions of practitioners licensed to administer such drugs or devices to patients under the care of such practitioners in the course of their professional practice, and which do not manufacture, prepare, propagate, compound, or process drugs or devices for sale other than in the regular course of their business of dispensing or selling drugs or devices at retail;

(2) practitioners licensed by law to prescribe or administer drugs or devices and who manufacture, prepare, propagate, compound, or process drugs or devices solely for use in the course of their professional practice;

(3) persons who manufacture, prepare, propagate, compound, or process drugs or devices solely for use in research, teaching, or chemical analysis and not for sale;

(4) any distributor who acts as a wholesale distributor of devices, and who does not manufacture, repackage, process, or relabel a device; or

(5) such other classes of persons as the Secretary may by regulation exempt from the application of this section upon a finding that registration by such classes of persons in accordance with this section is not necessary for the protection of the public health.

In this subsection, the term "wholesale distributor" means any person (other than the manufacturer or the initial importer) who distributes a device from the original place of manufacture to the person who makes the final delivery or sale of the device to the ultimate consumer or user.

(h) Every establishment in any State registered with the Secretary pursuant to this section shall be subject to inspection pursuant to section 704 and every such establishment engaged in the manufacture, propagation, compounding, or processing of a drug or drugs or of a device or devices classified in class II or III shall be so inspected by one or more officers or employees duly designated by the Secretary at least once in the two-year period beginning with the date of registration of such establishment pursuant to this section and at least once in every successive two-year period thereafter.

(i) (1) Any establishment within any foreign country engaged in the manufacture, preparation, propagation, compounding, or processing of a drug or a device that is imported or offered for import into the United States shall register with the Secretary the name and place of business of the establishment and the name of the United States agent for the establishment.

(2) The establishment shall also provide the information required by subsection (j).

(3) The Secretary is authorized to enter into cooperative arrangements with officials of foreign countries to ensure that adequate and effective means are available for purposes of determining, from time to time, whether drugs or devices manufactured, prepared, propagated, compounded, or processed by an establishment described in paragraph (1), if imported or offered for import into the United States, shall be refused admission on any of the grounds set forth in section 801(a).

(j) (1) Every person who registers with the Secretary under subsection (b), (c), or (d) shall, at the time of registration under any such subsection, file with the Secretary a list of all drugs and a list of all devices and a brief statement of the basis for believing that each device included in the list is a device rather than a drug (with each drug and device in each list listed by its established name (as defined in section 502(e)) and by any proprietary name) which are being manufactured, prepared, propagated, compounded, or processed by him for commercial distribution and which he has not included in any list of drugs or devices filed by him with the Secretary under this paragraph or paragraph (2) before such time of registration. Such list shall be prepared in such form and manner as the Secretary may prescribe and shall be accompanied by—

(A) in the case of a drug contained in the applicable list and subject to section 505 or 512, or a device intended for human use contained in the applicable list with respect to which a performance standard has been established under section 514 or which is subject to section 515, a reference to the authority for the marketing of such drug or device and a copy of all labeling for such drug or device;

(B) in the case of any other drug or device contained in an applicable list—

(i) which drug is subject to section 503(b)(1), or which device is a restricted device, a copy of all labeling for such drug or device, a representative sampling of advertisements for such drug or device, and, upon request made by the Secretary for good cause, a copy of all advertisements for a particular drug product or device, or

(ii) which drug is not subject to section 503(b)(1) or which device is not a restricted device, the label and package insert for such drug or device and a representative sampling of any other labeling for such drug or device;

(C) in the case of any drug contained in an applicable list which is described in subparagraph (B), a quantitative listing of its active ingredient or ingredients, except that with respect to a particular drug product the Secretary may require the submission of a quantitative listing of all ingredients if he finds that such submission is necessary to carry out the purposes of this Act; and

(D) if the registrant filing a list has determined that a particular drug product or device contained in such list is not subject to section 505 or 512, or the particular device contained in such list is not subject to a performance standard established under section 514 or to section 515 or is not a restricted device a brief statement of the basis upon which the registrant made such determination if the Secretary requests such a statement with respect to that particular drug product or device.

(2) Each person who registers with the Secretary under this section shall report to the Secretary once during the month of June of each year and once during the month of December of each year the following information:

(A) A list of each drug or device introduced by the registrant for commercial distribution which has not been included in any list previously filed by him with the Secretary under this subparagraph or paragraph (1) of this subsection. A list under this subparagraph shall list a drug or device by its established name (as defined in section 502(e)), and by any proprietary name it may have and shall be accompanied by the other information required by paragraph (1).

(B) If since the date the registrant last made a report under this paragraph (or if he has not made a report under this paragraph, since the effective date of this subsection) he has discontinued the manufacture, preparation, propagation, compounding, or processing for commercial distribution of a drug or device included in a list filed by him under subparagraph (A) or paragraph (1); notice of such discontinuance, the date of such discontinuance, and the identity (by established name (as defined in section 502(e)) and by any proprietary name) of such drug or device.

(C) If since the date the registrant reported pursuant to subparagraph (B) a notice of discontinuance he has resumed the manufacture, preparation, propagation, compounding, or processing for commercial distribution of the drug or device with respect to which such notice of discontinuance was reported; notice of such resumption, the date of such resumption, the identity of such drug or device (each by established name (as defined in section 502(e)) and by any proprietary name), and the other information required by paragraph (1), unless the registrant has previously reported such resumption to the Secretary pursuant to this subparagraph.

(D) Any material change in any information previously submitted pursuant to this paragraph or paragraph (1).

(3) The Secretary may also require each registrant under this section to submit a list of each drug product which (A) the registrant is manufacturing, preparing, propagating, compounding, or processing for commercial distribution, and (B) contains a particular ingredient. The Secretary may not require the submission of such a list unless he has made a finding that the submission of such a list is necessary to carry out the purposes of this Act.

(k) Each person who is required to register under this section and who proposes to begin the introduction or delivery for introduction into interstate commerce for commercial distribution of a device intended for human use shall, at least ninety days before making such introduction or delivery, report to the Secretary (in such form and manner as the Secretary shall by regulation prescribe)—

(1) the class in which the device is classified under section 513 or if such person determines that the device is not classified under such section, a statement of that determination and the basis for such person's determination that the device is or is not so classified, and

(2) action taken by such person to comply with requirements under section 514 or 515 which are applicable to the device.

(l) A report under subsection (k) is not required for a device intended for human use that is exempted from the requirements of this subsection under subsection (m) or is within a type that has been classified into class I under section 513. The exception established in the preceding sentence does not apply to any class I device that is intended for a use which is of substantial importance in preventing impairment of human health, or to any class I device that presents a potential unreasonable risk of illness or injury.

(m) (1) Not later than 60 days after the date of enactment of the Food and Drug Administration Modernization Act of 1997, the Secretary shall publish in the Federal Register a list of each type of class II device that does not require a report under subsection (k) to provide reasonable assurance of safety and effectiveness. Each type of class II device identified by the Secretary as not requiring the report shall be exempt from the requirement to provide a report under subsection (k) as of the date of the publication of the list in the Federal Register.

(2) Beginning on the date that is 1 day after the date of the publication of a list under this subsection, the Secretary may exempt a class II device from the requirement to submit a report subsection (k), upon the Secretary's own initiative or a petition of an interested person, if the Secretary determines that such report is not necessary to assure the safety and effectiveness of the device. The Secretary shall publish in the Federal Register notice of the intent of the Secretary to exempt the device, or of the

petition, and provide a 30–day period for public comment. Within 120 days after the issuance of the notice in the Federal Register, the Secretary shall publish an order in the Federal Register that sets forth the final determination of the Secretary regarding the exemption of the device that was the subject of the notice. If the Secretary fails to respond to a petition within 180 days of receiving it, the petition shall be deemed to be granted.

(n) The Secretary shall review the report required in subsection (k) and make a determination under section 513(f)(1) not later than 90 days after receiving the report.

* * *

SEC. 513 [21 U.S.C. § 360c]. DEVICE CLASSES.

(a) (1) There are established the following classes of devices intended for human use:

(A) CLASS I, GENERAL CONTROLS.

(i) A device for which the controls authorized by or under section 501, 502, 510, 516, 518, 519, or 520 or any combination of such sections are sufficient to provide reasonable assurance of the safety and effectiveness of the device.

(ii) A device for which insufficient information exists to determine that the controls referred to in clause (i) are sufficient to provide reasonable assurance of the safety and effectiveness of the device or to establish special controls to provide such assurance, but because it—

(I) is not purported or represented to be for a use in supporting or sustaining human life or for a use which is of substantial importance in preventing impairment of human health, and

(II) does not present a potential unreasonable risk of illness or injury, is to be regulated by the controls referred to in clause (i).

(B) CLASS II, SPECIAL CONTROLS.—A device which cannot be classified as a class I device because the general controls by themselves are insufficient to provide reasonable assurance of the safety and effectiveness of the device, and for which there is sufficient information to establish special controls to provide such assurance, including the promulgation of performance standards, postmarket surveillance, patient registries, development and dissemination of guidelines (including guidelines for the submission of clinical data in premarket notification submissions in accordance with section 510(k)), recommendations, and other appropriate actions as the Secretary deems necessary to provide such assurance. For a device that is purported or represented to be for a use in supporting or sustaining human life, the Secretary shall examine and identify the special controls, if any, that are necessary to provide adequate assurance of safety and effectiveness and describe how such controls provide such assurance.

(C) CLASS III, PREMARKET APPROVAL.—A device which because—

(i) it (I) cannot be classified as a class I device because insufficient information exists to determine that the application of general controls are sufficient to provide reasonable assurance of the safety and effectiveness of the device, and (II) cannot be classified as a class II device because insufficient information exists to determine that the special controls described in subparagraph (B) would provide reasonable assurance of its safety and effectiveness, and

(ii)(I) is purported or represented to be for a use in supporting or sustaining human life or for a use which is of substantial importance in preventing impairment of human health, or (II) presents a potential unreasonable risk of illness or injury, is to be subject, in accordance with section 515, to premarket approval to provide reasonable assurance of its safety and effectiveness.

If there is not sufficient information to establish a performance standard for a device to provide reasonable assurance of its safety and effectiveness, the Secretary may conduct such activities as may be necessary to develop or obtain such information.

(2) For purposes of this section and sections 514 and 515, the safety and effectiveness of a device are to be determined—(A) with respect to the persons for whose use the device is represented or intended, (B) with respect to the conditions of use prescribed, recommended, or suggested in the labeling of the device, and (C) weighing any probable benefit to health from the use of the device against any probable risk of injury or illness from such use.

(3)(A) Except as authorized by subparagraph (B), the effectiveness of a device is, for purposes of this section and sections 514 and 515, to be determined, in accordance with regulations promulgated by the Secretary, on the basis of well-controlled investigations, including 1 or more clinical investigations where appropriate, by experts qualified by training and experience to evaluate the effectiveness of the device, from which investigations it can fairly and responsibly be concluded by qualified experts that the device will have the effect it purports or is represented to have under the conditions of use prescribed, recommended, or suggested in the labeling of the device.

(B) If the Secretary determines that there exists valid scientific evidence (other than evidence derived from investigations described in subparagraph (A))—

(i) which is sufficient to determine the effectiveness of a device, and

(ii) from which it can fairly and responsibly be concluded by qualified experts that the device will have the effect it purports or is represented to have under the conditions of use prescribed, recommended, or suggested in the labeling of the device, then, for purposes of this section and sections 514 and 515, the Secretary may authorize the effectiveness of the device to be determined on the basis of such evidence.

(C) In making a determination of a reasonable assurance of the effectiveness of a device for which an application under section 515 has been submitted, the Secretary shall consider whether the extent of data that otherwise would be required for approval of the application with respect to effectiveness can be reduced through reliance on postmarket controls.

(D) (i) The Secretary, upon the written request of any person intending to submit an application under section 515, shall meet with such person to determine the type of valid scientific evidence (within the meaning of subparagraphs (A) and (B)) that will be necessary to demonstrate for purposes of approval of an application the effectiveness of a device for the conditions of use proposed by such person. The written request shall include a detailed description of the device, a detailed description of the proposed conditions of use of the device, a proposed plan for determining whether there is a reasonable assurance of effectiveness, and, if available, information regarding the expected performance from the device. Within 30 days after such meeting, the Secretary shall specify in writing the type of valid scientific evidence that will provide a reasonable assurance that a device is effective under the conditions of use proposed by such person.

(ii) Any clinical data, including one or more well-controlled investigations, specified in writing by the Secretary for demonstrating a reasonable assurance of device effectiveness shall be specified as result of a determination by the Secretary that such data are necessary to establish device effectiveness. The Secretary shall consider, in consultation with the applicant, the least burdensome appropriate means of evaluating device effectiveness that would have a reasonable likelihood of resulting in approval.

(iii) The determination of the Secretary with respect to the specification of valid scientific evidence under clauses (i) and (ii) shall be binding upon the Secretary, unless such determination by the Secretary could be contrary to the public health.

(b) (1) CLASSIFICATION PANELS.—For purposes of—

(A) determining which devices intended for human use should be subject to the requirements of general controls, performance standards, or premarket approval, and

(B) providing notice to the manufacturers and importers of such devices to enable them to prepare for the application of such requirements to devices manufactured or imported by them,

the Secretary shall classify all such devices (other than devices classified by subsection (f)) into the classes established by subsection (a). For the purpose of securing recommendations with respect to the classification of devices, the Secretary shall establish panels of experts or use panels of experts established before the date of the enactment of this section, or both. Section 14 of the Federal Advisory Committee Act shall not apply to the duration of a panel established under this paragraph.

(2) The Secretary shall appoint to each panel established under paragraph (1) persons who are qualified by training and experience to evaluate the safety and effectiveness of the devices to be referred to the panel and who, to the extent feasible, possess skill in the use of, or experience in the development, manufacture, or utilization of, such devices. The Secretary shall make appointments to each panel so that each panel shall consist of members with adequately diversified expertise in such fields as clinical and administrative medicine, engineering, biological and physical sciences, and other related professions. In addition, each panel shall include as nonvoting members a representative of consumer interests and a representative of interests of the device manufacturing industry. Scientific, trade, and consumer organizations shall be afforded an opportunity to nominate individuals for appointment to the panels. No individual who is in the regular full-time employ of the United States and engaged in the administration of this Act may be a member of any panel. The Secretary shall designate one of the members of each panel to serve as chairman thereof.

(3) Panel members (other than officers or employees of the United States), while attending meetings or conferences of a panel or otherwise engaged in its business, shall be entitled to receive compensation at rates to be fixed by the Secretary, but not at rates exceeding the daily equivalent of the rate in effect for grade GS–18 of the General Schedule, for each day so engaged, including travel time; and while so serving away from their homes or regular places of business each member may be allowed travel expenses (including per diem in lieu of subsistence) as authorized by section 5703 of title 5, United States Code for persons in the Government service employed intermittently.

(4) The Secretary shall furnish each panel with adequate clerical and other necessary assistance.

(5) Classification panels covering each type of device shall be scheduled to meet at such times as may be appropriate for the Secretary to meet applicable statutory deadlines.

(6)(A) Any person whose device is specifically the subject of review by a classification panel shall have—

   (i) the same access to data and information submitted to a classification panel (except for data and information that are not available for public disclosure under section 552 of title 5, United States Code) as the Secretary;

   (ii) the opportunity to submit, for review by a classification panel, information that is based on the data or information provided in the application submitted under section 515 by the person, which information shall be submitted to the Secretary for prompt transmittal to the classification panel; and

   (iii) the same opportunity as the Secretary to participate in meetings of the panel.

(B) Any meetings of a classification panel shall provide adequate time for initial presentations and for response to any differing views by persons whose devices are specifically the subject of a classification panel review, and shall encourage free and open participation by all interested persons.

(7) After receiving from a classification panel the conclusions and recommendations of the panel on a matter that the panel has reviewed, the Secretary shall review the conclusions and recommendations, shall make a final decision on the matter in accordance with section 515(d)(2), and shall notify the affected persons of the decision in writing and, if the decision differs from the conclusions and recommendations of the panel, shall include the reasons for the difference.

(8) A classification panel under this subsection shall not be subject to the annual chartering and annual report requirements of the Federal Advisory Committee Act.

(c) (1) CLASSIFICATION PANEL ORGANIZATION AND OPERA-TION.—The Secretary shall organize the panels according to the various fields of clinical medicine and fundamental sciences in which devices intended for human use are used. The Secretary shall refer a device to be classified under this section to an appropriate panel established or authorized to be used under subsection (b) for its review and for its recommendation respecting the classification of the device. The Secretary shall by regulation prescribe the procedure to be followed by the panels in making their reviews and recommendations. In making their reviews of devices, the panels, to the maximum extent practicable, shall provide an opportunity for interested persons to submit data and views on the classification of the devices.

(2)(A) Upon completion of a panel's review of a device referred to it under paragraph (1), the panel shall, subject to subparagraphs (B) and (C), submit to the Secretary its recommendation for the classification of the device. Any such recommendation shall (i) contain (I) a summary of the reasons for the recommendation, (II) a summary of the data upon which the recommendation is based, and (III) an identification of the risks to health (if any) presented by the device with respect to which the recommendation is made, and (ii) to the extent practicable, include a recommendation for the assignment of a priority for the application of the requirements of section 514 or 515 to a device recommended to be classified in class II or class III.

(B) A recommendation of a panel for the classification of a device in class I shall include a recommendation as to whether the device should be exempt from the requirements of section 510, 519, or 520(f).

(C) In the case of a device which has been referred under paragraph (1) to a panel, and which—

(i) is intended to be implanted in the human body or is purported or represented to be for a use in supporting or sustaining human life, and

(ii)(I) has been introduced or delivered for introduction into interstate commerce for commercial distribution before the date of enactment of this section, or (II) is within a type of device which was so introduced or delivered before such date and is substantially equivalent to another device within that type,

such panel shall recommend to the Secretary that the device be classified in class III unless the panel determines that classification of the device in such class is not necessary to provide reasonable assurance of its safety and effectiveness. If a panel does not recommend that such a device be classified in class III, it shall in its recommendation to the Secretary for the classification of the device set forth the reasons for not recommending classification of the device in such class.

(3) The panels shall submit to the Secretary within one year of the date funds are first appropriated for the implementation of this section their recommendations respecting all devices of a type introduced or delivered for introduction into interstate commerce for commercial distribution before the date of enactment of this section.

(d) CLASSIFICATION.

(1) Upon receipt of a recommendation from a panel respecting a device, the Secretary shall publish in the Federal Register the panel's recommendation and a proposed regulation classifying such device and shall provide interested persons an opportunity to submit comments on such recommendation and the proposed regulation. After reviewing such comments, the Secretary shall, subject to paragraph (2), by regulation classify such device.

(2)(A) A regulation under paragraph (1) classifying a device in class I shall prescribe which, if any, of the requirements of section 510, 519, or 520(f) shall not apply to the device. A regulation which makes a requirement of section 510, 519, or 520(f) inapplicable to a device shall be accompanied by a statement of the reasons of the Secretary for making such requirement inapplicable.

(B) A device described in subsection (c)(2)(C) shall be classified in class III unless the Secretary determines that classification of the device in such class is not necessary to provide reasonable assurance of its safety and effectiveness. A proposed regulation under paragraph (1) classifying such a device in a class other than class III shall be accompanied by a full statement of the reasons of the Secretary (and supporting documentation and data) for not classifying such device in such class and an identification of the risks to health (if any) presented by such device.

(3) In the case of devices classified in class II and devices classified under this subsection in class III and described in section 515(b)(1) the Secretary may establish priorities which, in his discretion, shall be used in applying sections 514 and 515, as appropriate, to such devices.

(e) CLASSIFICATION CHANGES.

(1) Based on new information respecting a device, the Secretary may, upon his own initiative or upon petition of an interested person, by

regulation (A) change such device's classification, and (B) revoke, because of the change in classification, any regulation or requirement in effect under section 514 or 515 with respect to such device. In the promulgation of such a regulation respecting a device's classification, the Secretary may secure from the panel to which the device was last referred pursuant to subsection (c) a recommendation respecting the proposed change in the device's classification and shall publish in the Federal Register any recommendation submitted to the Secretary by the panel respecting such change. A regulation under this subsection changing the classification of a device from class III to class II may provide that such classification shall not take effect until the effective date of a performance standard established under section 514 for such device.

(2) By regulation promulgated under paragraph (1), the Secretary may change the classification of a device from class III—(A) to class II if the Secretary determines that special controls would provide reasonable assurance of the safety and effectiveness of the device and that general controls would not provide reasonable assurance of the safety and effectiveness of the device, or (B) to class I if the Secretary determines that general controls would provide reasonable assurance of the safety and effectiveness of the device.

(f) INITIAL CLASSIFICATION AND RECLASSIFICATION OF CERTAIN DEVICES.—

(1) Any device intended for human use which was not introduced or delivered for introduction into interstate commerce for commercial distribution before the date of enactment of this section, is classified in class III unless—(A) the device—(i) is within a type of device (I) which was introduced or delivered for introduction into interstate commerce for commercial distribution before such date and which is to be classified pursuant to subsection (b), or (II) which was not so introduced or delivered before such date and has been classified in class I or II, and (ii) is substantially equivalent to another device within such type, or (B) the Secretary in response to a petition submitted under paragraph (2) has classified such device in class I or II. A device classified in class III under this paragraph shall be classified in that class until the effective date of an order of the Secretary under paragraph (2) or (3) classifying the device in class I or II.

(2)(A) Any person who submits a report under section 510(k) for a type of device that has not been previously classified under this Act, and that is classified into class III under paragraph (1), may request, within 30 days after receiving written notice of such a classification, the Secretary to classify the device under the criteria set forth in subparagraphs (A) through (C) of subsection (a)(1). The person may, in the request, recommend to the Secretary a classification for the device. Any such request shall describe the device and provide detailed information and reasons for the recommended classification.

(B) (i) Not later than 60 days after the date of the submission of the request under subparagraph (A), the Secretary shall by written order classify the device involved. Such classification shall be the initial classification of the device for purposes of paragraph (1) and any device classified under this paragraph shall be a predicate device for determining substantial equivalence under paragraph (1).

(ii) A device that remains in class III under this subparagraph shall be deemed to be adulterated within the meaning of section 501(f)(1)(B) until approved under section 515 or exempted from such approval under section 520(g).

(C) Within 30 days after the issuance of an order classifying a device under this paragraph, the Secretary shall publish a notice in the Federal Register announcing such classification.

(3)(A) The Secretary may initiate the reclassification of a device classified into class III under paragraph (1) of this subsection or the manufacturer or importer of a device classified under paragraph (1) may petition the Secretary (in such form and manner as he shall prescribe) for the issuance of an order classifying the device in class I or class II. Within thirty days of the filing of such a petition, the Secretary shall notify the petitioner of any deficiencies in the petition which prevent the Secretary from making a decision on the petition.

(B) (i) Upon determining that a petition does not contain any deficiency which prevents the Secretary from making a decision on the petition, the Secretary may for good cause shown refer the petition to an appropriate panel established or authorized to be used under subsection (b). A panel to which such a petition has been referred shall not later than ninety days after the referral of the petition make a recommendation to the Secretary respecting approval or denial of the petition. Any such recommendation shall contain (I) a summary of the reasons for the recommendation, (II) a summary of the data upon which the recommendation is based, and (III) an identification of the risks to health (if any) presented by the device with respect to which the petition was filed. In the case of a petition for a device which is intended to be implanted in the human body or which is purported or represented to be for a use in supporting or sustaining human life, the panel shall recommend that the petition be denied unless the panel determines that the classification in class III of the device is not necessary to provide reasonable assurance of its safety and effectiveness. If the panel recommends that such petition be approved, it shall in its recommendation to the Secretary set forth its reasons for such recommendation.

(ii) The requirements of paragraphs (1) and (2) of subsection (c) (relating to opportunities for submission of data and views and recommendations respecting priorities and exemptions from sections 510, 519, and 520(f)) shall apply with respect to consideration by panels of petitions submitted under subparagraph (A).

(C) (i) Within ninety days from the date the Secretary receives the recommendation of a panel respecting a petition (but not later than 210 days after the filing of such petition) the Secretary shall by order deny or approve the petition. If the Secretary approves the petition, the Secretary shall order the classification of the device into class I or class II in accordance with the criteria prescribed by subsection (a)(1)(A) or (a)(1)(B). In the case of a petition for a device which is intended to be implanted in the human body or which is purported or represented to be for a use in supporting or sustaining human life, the Secretary shall deny the petition unless the Secretary determines that the classification in class III of the device is not necessary to provide reasonable assurance of its safety and effectiveness. An order approving such petition shall be accompanied by a full statement of the reasons of the Secretary (and supporting documentation and data) for approving the petition and an identification of the risks to health (if any) presented by the device to which such order applies.

(ii) The requirements of paragraphs (1) and (2)(A) of subsection (d) (relating to publication of recommendations, opportunity for submission of comments, and exemption from sections 510, 519, and 520(f)) shall apply with respect to action by the Secretary on petitions submitted under subparagraph (A).

(4) If a manufacturer reports to the Secretary under section 510(k) that a device is substantially equivalent to another device—(A) which the Secretary has classified as a class III device under subsection (b), (B) which was introduced or delivered for introduction into interstate commerce for commercial distribution before December 1, 1990, and (C) for which no final regulation requiring premarket approval has been promulgated under section 515(b), the manufacturer shall certify to the Secretary that the manufacturer has conducted a reasonable search of all information known or otherwise available to the manufacturer respecting such other device and has included in the report under section 510(k) a summary of and a citation to all adverse safety and effectiveness data respecting such other device and respecting the device for which the section 510(k) report is being made and which has not been submitted to the Secretary under section 519. The Secretary may require the manufacturer to submit the adverse safety and effectiveness data described in the report.

(5) The Secretary may not withhold a determination of the initial classification of a device under paragraph (1) because of a failure to comply with any provision of this Act unrelated to a substantial equivalence decision, including a finding that the facility in which the device is manufactured is not in compliance with good manufacturing requirements as set forth in regulations of the Secretary under section 520(f) (other than a finding that there is a substantial likelihood that the failure to comply with such regulations will potentially present a serious risk to human health).

(g) INFORMATION.—Within sixty days of the receipt of a written request of any person for information respecting the class in which a device has been classified or the requirements applicable to a device under this chapter, the Secretary shall provide such person a written statement of the classification (if any) of such device and the requirements of this chapter applicable to the device.

(h) DEFINITIONS.—For purposes of this section and sections 501, 510, 514, 515, 516, 519 and 520—

(1) a reference to "general controls" is a reference to the controls authorized by or under sections 501, 502, 510, 516, 518, 519, and 520,

(2) a reference to "class I", "class II", or "class III" is a reference to a class of medical devices described in subparagraph (A), (B), or (C) of subsection (a)(1), and

(3) a reference to a "panel under section 513" is a reference to a panel established or authorized to be used under this section.

(i) (1)(A) For purposes of determinations of substantial equivalence under subsection (f) and section 520(l), the term "substantially equivalent" or "substantial equivalence" means, with respect to a device being compared to a predicate device, that the device has the same intended use as the predicate device and that the Secretary by order has found that the device—

(i) has the same technological characteristics as the predicate device, or

(ii)(I) has different technological characteristics and the information submitted that the device is substantially equivalent to the predicate device contains information, including appropriate clinical or scientific data if deemed necessary by the Secretary or a person accredited under section 523, that demonstrates that the device is as safe and effective as a legally marketed device, and (II) does not raise different questions of safety and effectiveness than the predicate device.

(B) For purposes of subparagraph (A), the term "different technological characteristics" means, with respect to a device being compared to a predicate device, that there is a significant change in the materials, design, energy source, or other features of the device from those of the predicate device.

(C) To facilitate reviews of reports submitted to the Secretary under section 510(k), the Secretary shall consider the extent to which reliance on postmarket controls may expedite the classification of devices under subsection (f)(1) of this section.

(D) Whenever the Secretary requests information to demonstrate that devices with differing technological characteristics are substantially equivalent, the Secretary shall only request information that is necessary to making substantial equivalence determinations. In making such request, the Secretary shall consider the least burdensome means of demonstrating substantial equivalence and request information accordingly.

(E) (i) Any determination by the Secretary of the intended use of a device shall be based upon the proposed labeling submitted in a report for the device under section 510(k). However, when determining that a device can be found substantially equivalent to a legally marketed device, the director of the organizational unit responsible for regulating devices (in this subparagraph referred to as the "Director") may require a statement in labeling that provides appropriate information regarding a use of the device not identified in the proposed labeling if, after providing an opportunity for consultation with the person who submitted such report, the Director determines and states in writing— (I) that there is a reasonable likelihood that the device will be used for an intended use not identified in the proposed labeling for the device; and (II) that such use could cause harm.

(ii) Such determination shall—(I) be provided to the person who submitted the report within 10 days from the date of the notification of the Director's concerns regarding the proposed labeling; (II) specify the limitations on the use of the device not included in the proposed labeling; and (III) find the device substantially equivalent if the requirements of subparagraph (A) are met and if the labeling for such device conforms to the limitations specified in subclause (II).

(iii) The responsibilities of the Director under this subparagraph may not be delegated.

(iv) This subparagraph has no legal effect after the expiration of the five-year period beginning on the date of the enactment of the Food and Drug Administration Modernization Act of 1997.

(F) Not later than 270 days after the date of the enactment of the Food and Drug Administration Modernization Act of 1997, the Secretary shall issue guidance specifying the general principles that the Secretary will consider in determining when a specific intended use of a device is not reasonably included within a general use of such device for purposes of a determination of substantial equivalence under subsection (f) or section 520(*l*).

(2) A device may not be found to be substantially equivalent to a predicate device that has been removed from the market at the initiative of the Secretary or that has been determined to be misbranded or adulterated by a judicial order.

(3)(A) As part of a submission under section 510(k) respecting a device, the person required to file a premarket notification under such section shall provide an adequate summary of any information respecting safety and effectiveness or state that such information will be made available upon request by any person.

(B) Any summary under subparagraph (A) respecting a device shall contain detailed information regarding data concerning adverse health effects and shall be made available to the public by the Secretary within 30 days of the issuance of a determination that such device is substantially equivalent to another device.

SEC. 514 [21 U.S.C. § 360d]. PERFORMANCE STANDARDS.

(a) PROVISION OF STANDARDS.

(1) The special controls required by section 513c(a)(1)(B) shall include performance standards for a class II device if the Secretary determines that a performance standard is necessary to provide reasonable assurance of the safety and effectiveness of the device. A class III device may also be considered a class II device for purposes of establishing a standard for the device under subsection (b) if the device has been reclassified as a class II device under a regulation under section 513(e) but such regulation provides that the reclassification is not to take effect until the effective date of such a standard for the device.

(2) A performance standard established under this section for a device—

(A) shall include provisions to provide reasonable assurance of its safe and effective performance;

(B) shall, where necessary to provide reasonable assurance of its safe and effective performance, include—

(i) provisions respecting the construction, components, ingredients, and properties of the device and its compatibility with power systems and connections to such systems,

(ii) provisions for the testing (on a sample basis or, if necessary, on an individual basis) of the device or, if it is determined that no other more practicable means are available to the Secretary to assure the conformity of the device to the standard, provisions for the testing (on a sample basis or, if necessary, on an individual basis) by the Secretary or by another person at the direction of the Secretary,

(iii) provisions for the measurement of the performance characteristics of the device,

(iv) provisions requiring that the results of each or of certain of the tests of the device required to be made under clause (ii) show that the device is in conformity with the portions of the standard for which the test or tests were required, and

(v) a provision requiring that the sale and distribution of the device be restricted but only to the extent that the sale and distribution of a device may be restricted under a regulation under section 520(e); and

(C) shall, where appropriate, require the use and prescribe the form and content of labeling for the proper installation, maintenance, operation, and use of the device.

(3) The Secretary shall provide for periodic evaluation of performance standards established under subsection (b) to determine if such standards should be changed to reflect new medical, scientific, or other technological data.

(4) In carrying out his duties under this section and subsection (b), the Secretary shall, to the maximum extent practicable—(A) use personnel, facilities, and other technical support available in other Federal agencies, (B) consult with other Federal agencies concerned with standard-setting and other nationally or internationally recognized standard-setting entities, and (C) invite appropriate participation, through joint or other conferences, workshops, or other means, by informed persons representative of scientific, professional, industry, or consumer organizations who in his judgment can make a significant contribution.

(b) ESTABLISHMENT OF A STANDARD.

(1)(A) The Secretary shall publish in the Federal Register a notice of proposed rulemaking for the establishment, amendment, or revocation of any performance standard for a device.

(B) A notice of proposed rulemaking for the establishment or amendment of a performance standard for a device shall—

(i) set forth a finding with supporting justification that the performance standard is appropriate and necessary to provide reasonable assurance of the safety and effectiveness of the device,

(ii) set forth proposed findings with respect to the risk of illness or injury that the performance standard is intended to reduce or eliminate,

(iii) invite interested persons to submit to the Secretary, within 30 days of the publication of the notice, requests for changes in the classification of the device pursuant to section 513(e) based on new information relevant to the classification, and

(iv) invite interested persons to submit an existing performance standard for the device, including a draft or proposed performance standard, for consideration by the Secretary.

(C) A notice of proposed rulemaking for the revocation of a performance standard shall set forth a finding with supporting justification that the performance standard is no longer necessary to provide reasonable assurance of the safety and effectiveness of a device.

(D) The Secretary shall provide for a comment period of not less than 60 days.

(2) If, after publication of a notice in accordance with paragraph (1), the Secretary receives a request for a change in the classification of the device, the Secretary shall, within 60 days of the publication of the notice, after consultation with the appropriate panel under section 513, either deny the request or give notice of an intent to initiate such change under section 513(e).

(3)(A) After the expiration of the period for comment on a notice of proposed rulemaking published under paragraph (1) respecting a performance standard and after consideration of such comments and any report from an advisory committee under paragraph (5), the Secretary shall (i) promulgate a regulation establishing a performance standard and publish in the Federal Register findings on the matters referred to in paragraph (1), or (ii) publish a notice terminating the proceeding for the development of the standard together with the reasons for such termination. If a notice of termination is published, the Secretary shall (unless such notice is issued because the device is a banned device under section 516 of this title) initiate a proceeding under section 513(e) to reclassify the device subject to the proceeding terminated by such notice.

(B) A regulation establishing a performance standard shall set forth the date or dates upon which the standard shall take effect, but no such regulation may take effect before one year after the date of its publication unless (i) the Secretary determines that an earlier effective date is necessary for the protection of the public health and safety, or (ii) such standard has been established for a device which, effective upon the effective date of the standard, has been reclassified from class III to class II. Such date or dates shall be established so as to minimize, consistent with the public health and safety, economic loss to, and disruption or dislocation of, domestic and international trade.

(4)(A) The Secretary, upon his own initiative or upon petition of an interested person may by regulation, promulgated in accordance with the requirements of paragraphs (1), (2), and (3)(B) of this subsection, amend or revoke a performance standard.

(B) The Secretary may declare a proposed amendment of a performance standard to be effective on and after its publication in the Federal Register and until the effective date of any final action taken on such amendment if he determines that making it so effective is in the public interest. A proposed amendment of a performance standard made so effective under the preceding sentence may not prohibit, during the period in which it is so effective, the introduction or delivery for introduction into interstate commerce of a device which conforms to such standard without the change or changes provided by such proposed amendment.

(5)(A) The Secretary—

(i) may on his own initiative refer a proposed regulation for the establishment, amendment, or revocation of a performance standard, or

(ii) shall, upon the request of an interested person which demonstrates good cause for referral and which is made before the expiration of the period for submission of comments on such proposed regulation refer such proposed regulation, to an advisory committee of experts, established pursuant to subparagraph (B), for a report and recommendation with respect to any matter involved in the proposed regulation which requires the exercise of scientific judgment.

If a proposed regulation is referred under this subparagraph to an advisory committee, the Secretary shall provide the advisory committee with the data and information on which such proposed regulation is based. The advisory committee shall, within sixty days of the referral of a proposed regulation and after independent study of the data and information furnished to it by the Secretary and other data and information before it, submit to the Secretary a report and recommendation respecting such regulation, together with all underlying data and information and a statement of the reason or basis for the recommendation. A copy of such report and recommendation shall be made public by the Secretary.

(B) The Secretary shall establish advisory committees (which may not be panels under section 513) to receive referrals under subparagraph (A). The Secretary shall appoint as members of any such advisory committee persons qualified in the subject matter to be referred to the committee and of appropriately diversified professional background, except that the Secretary may not appoint to such a committee any individual who is in the regular full-time employ of the United States and engaged in the administration of this Act. Each such committee shall include as nonvoting members a representative of consumer interests and a representative of interests of the device manufacturing industry. Members of an advisory committee who are not officers or employees of the United States, while attending conferences or meetings of their committee or otherwise serving at the request of the Secretary, shall be entitled to receive compensation at rates to be fixed by the Secretary, which rates may not exceed the daily equivalent of the rate in effect for grade GS–18 of the General Schedule, for each day (including travel time) they are so engaged; and while so serving away from their homes or regular places of business each member may be allowed travel expenses, including per diem in lieu of subsistence, as authorized by section 5703 of title 5 of the United States Code for persons in the Government service employed intermittently. The Secretary shall designate one of the members of each advisory committee to serve as chairman thereof. The Secretary shall furnish each advisory committee with clerical and other assistance, and shall by regulation prescribe the procedures to be followed by each such committee in acting on referrals made under subparagraph (A).

(c) RECOGNITION OF A STANDARD.

(1)(A) In addition to establishing a performance standard under this section, the Secretary shall, by publication in the Federal Register, recognize all or part of an appropriate standard established by a nationally or internationally recognized standard development organization for which a person may submit a declaration of conformity in order to meet a premarket submission requirement or other requirement under this Act to which such standard is applicable.

(B) If a person elects to use a standard recognized by the Secretary under subparagraph (A) to meet the requirements described in such subparagraph, the person shall provide a declaration of conformity to the Secretary that certifies that the device is in conformity with such standard. A person may elect to use data, or information, other than data required by a standard recognized under subparagraph (A) to meet any requirement regarding devices under this Act.

(2) The Secretary may withdraw such recognition of a standard through publication of a notice in the Federal Register if the Secretary determines that the standard is no longer appropriate for meeting a requirement regarding devices under this Act.

(3)(A) Subject to subparagraph (B), the Secretary shall accept a declaration of conformity that a device is in conformity with a standard recognized under paragraph (1) unless the Secretary finds—

(i) that the data or information submitted to support such declaration does not demonstrate that the device is in conformity with the standard identified in the declaration of conformity; or

(ii) that the standard identified in the declaration of conformity is not applicable to the particular device under review.

(B) The Secretary may request, at any time the data or information relied on by the person to make a declaration of conformity with respect to a standard recognized under paragraph (1).

(C) A person making a declaration of conformity with respect to a standard recognized under paragraph (1) shall maintain the data and information demonstrating conformity of the device to the standard for a period of two years after the date of the classification or approval of the device by the Secretary or a period equal to the expected design life of the device, whichever is longer.

SEC. 515 [21 U.S.C. § 360e]. PREMARKET APPROVAL.

(a) GENERAL REQUIREMENT.—A class III device—

(1) which is subject to a regulation promulgated under subsection (b); or

(2) which is a class III device because of section 513(f), is required to have, unless exempt under section 520(g), an approval under this section of an application for premarket approval.

(b) REGULATION TO REQUIRE PREMARKET APPROVAL.

(1) In the case of a class III device which—

(A) was introduced or delivered for introduction into interstate commerce for commercial distribution before the date of enactment of this section; or

(B) is (i) of a type so introduced or delivered, and (ii) is substantially equivalent to another device within that type,

the Secretary shall by regulation, promulgated in accordance with this subsection, require that such device have an approval under this section of an application for premarket approval.

(2)(A) A proceeding for the promulgation of a regulation under paragraph (1) respecting a device shall be initiated by the publication in the

Federal Register of a notice of proposed rulemaking. Such notice shall contain—(i) the proposed regulation; (ii) proposed findings with respect to the degree of risk of illness or injury designed to be eliminated or reduced by requiring the device to have an approved application for premarket approval and the benefit to the public from use of the device; (iii) opportunity for the submission of comments on the proposed regulation and the proposed findings; and (iv) opportunity to request a change in the classification of the device based on new information relevant to the classification of the device.

(B) If, within fifteen days after publication of a notice under subparagraph (A), the Secretary receives a request for a change in the classification of a device, he shall, within sixty days of the publication of such notice and after consultation with the appropriate panel under section 513, by order published in the Federal Register, either deny the request for change in classification or give notice of his intent to initiate such a change under section 513(e).

(3) After the expiration of the period for comment on a proposed regulation and proposed findings published under paragraph (2) and after consideration of comments submitted on such proposed regulation and findings, the Secretary shall (A) promulgate such regulation and publish in the Federal Register findings on the matters referred to in paragraph (2)(A)(ii), or (B) publish a notice terminating the proceeding for the promulgation of the regulation together with the reasons for such termination. If a notice of termination is published, the Secretary shall (unless such notice is issued because the device is a banned device under section 516) initiate a proceeding under section 513(e) to reclassify the device subject to the proceeding terminated by such notice.

(4) The Secretary, upon his own initiative or upon petition of an interested person, may by regulation amend or revoke any regulation promulgated under this subsection. A regulation to amend or revoke a regulation under this subsection shall be promulgated in accordance with the requirements prescribed by this subsection for the promulgation of the regulation to be amended or revoked.

(c) APPLICATION FOR PREMARKET APPROVAL.

(1) Any person may file with the Secretary an application for premarket approval for a class III device. Such an application for a device shall contain—

(A) full reports of all information, published or known to or which should reasonably be known to the applicant, concerning investigations which have been made to show whether or not such device is safe and effective;

(B) a full statement of the components, ingredients, and properties and of the principle or principles of operation, of such device;

(C) a full description of the methods used in, and the facilities and controls used for, the manufacture, processing, and, when relevant, packing and installation of, such device;

(D) an identifying reference to any performance standard under section 514 which would be applicable to any aspect of such device if it were a class II device, and either adequate information to show that such aspect of such device fully meets such performance standard or adequate information to justify any deviation from such standard;

(E) such samples of such device and of components thereof as the Secretary may reasonably require, except that where the submission of such samples is impracticable or unduly burdensome, the requirement of this subparagraph may be met by the submission of complete information concerning the location of one or more such devices readily available for examination and testing;

(F) specimens of the labeling proposed to be used for such device; and

(G) such other information relevant to the subject matter of the application as the Secretary, with the concurrence of the appropriate panel under section 513, may require.

(2) Upon receipt of an application meeting the requirements set forth in paragraph (1), the Secretary—

(A) may on the Secretary's own initiative, or

(B) shall, upon the request of an applicant unless the Secretary finds that the information in the application which would be reviewed by a panel substantially duplicates information which has previously been reviewed by a panel appointed under section 513,

refer such application to the appropriate panel under section 513 for study and for submission (within such period as he may establish) of a report and recommendation respecting approval of the application, together with all underlying data and the reasons or basis for the recommendation.

(d) ACTION ON APPLICATION FOR PREMARKET APPROVAL.

(1)(A) As promptly as possible, but in no event later than one hundred and eighty days after the receipt of an application under subsection (c) (except as provided in section 520(l)(3)(D)(ii) or unless, in accordance with subparagraph (B)(i), an additional period as agreed upon by the Secretary and the applicant), the Secretary, after considering the report and recommendation submitted under paragraph (2) of such subsection, shall—

(i) issue an order approving the application if he finds that none of the grounds for denying approval specified in paragraph (2) of this subsection applies; or

(ii) deny approval of the application if he finds (and sets forth the basis for such finding as part of or accompanying such denial) that one or more grounds for denial specified in paragraph (2) of this subsection apply.

In making the determination whether to approve or deny the application, the Secretary shall rely on the conditions of use included in the proposed labeling as the basis for determining whether or not there is a reasonable assurance of safety and effectiveness, if the proposed labeling is neither false nor misleading. In determining whether or not such labeling is false or misleading, the Secretary shall fairly evaluate all material facts pertinent to the proposed labeling.

(B) (i) The Secretary may not enter into an agreement to extend the period in which to take action with respect to an application submitted for a device subject to a regulation promulgated under subsection (b) unless he finds that the continued availability of the device is necessary for the public health.

(ii) An order approving an application for a device may require as a condition to such approval that the sale and distribution of the device be restricted but only to the extent that the sale and distribution of a device may be restricted under a regulation under section 520(e).

(iii) The Secretary shall accept and review statistically valid and reliable data and any other information from investigations conducted under the authority of regulations required by section 520(g) to make a determination of whether there is a reasonable assurance of safety and effectiveness of a device subject to a pending application under this section if—

(I) the data or information is derived from investigations of an earlier version of the device, the device has been modified during or after the investigations (but prior to submission of an application under subsection (c)) and such a modification of the device does not constitute a significant change in the design or in the basic principles of operation of the device that would invalidate the data or information; or

(II) the data or information relates to a device approved under this section, is available for use under this Act, and is relevant to the design and intended use of the device for which the application is pending.

(2) The Secretary shall deny approval of an application for a device if, upon the basis of the information submitted to the Secretary as part of the application and any other information before him with respect to such device, the Secretary finds that—

(A) there is a lack of a showing of reasonable assurance that such device is safe under the conditions of use prescribed, recommended, or suggested in the proposed labeling thereof;

(B) there is a lack of a showing of reasonable assurance that the device is effective under the conditions of use prescribed, recommended, or suggested in the proposed labeling thereof;

(C) the methods used in, or the facilities or controls used for, the manufacture, processing, packing, or installation of such device do not conform to the requirements of section 520(f);

(D) based on a fair evaluation of all material facts, the proposed labeling is false or misleading in any particular; or

(E) such device is not shown to conform in all respects to a performance standard in effect under section 514 of this title compliance with which is a condition to approval of the application and there is a lack of adequate information to justify the deviation from such standard.

Any denial of an application shall, insofar as the Secretary determines to be practicable, be accompanied by a statement informing the applicant of the measures required to place such application in approvable form (which measures may include further research by the applicant in accordance with one or more protocols prescribed by the Secretary).

(3)(A) (i) The Secretary shall, upon the written request of an applicant, meet with the applicant, not later than 100 days after the receipt of an application that has been filed as complete under subsection (c), to discuss the review status of the application.

(ii) The Secretary shall, in writing and prior to the meeting, provide to the applicant a description of any deficiencies in the application that, at that point, have been identified by the Secretary based on an interim review of the entire application and identify the information that is required to correct those deficiencies.

(iii) The Secretary shall notify the applicant promptly of—

(I) any additional deficiency identified in the application,

(II) any additional information required to achieve completion of the review and final action on the application, that was not described as a deficiency in the written description provided by the Secretary under clause (ii).

(B) The Secretary and the applicant may, by mutual consent, establish a different schedule for a meeting required under this paragraph.

(4) An applicant whose application has been denied approval may, by petition filed on or before the thirtieth day after the date upon which he receives notice of such denial, obtain review thereof in accordance with either paragraph (1) or (2) of subsection (g), and any interested person may obtain review, in accordance with paragraph (1) or (2) of subsection (g), of an order of the Secretary approving an application.

(5) In order to provide for more effective treatment or diagnosis of life-threatening or irreversibly debilitating human diseases or conditions, the Secretary shall provide review priority for devices—

(A) representing breakthrough technologies,

(B) for which no approved alternatives exist,

(C) which offer significant advantages over existing approved alternatives, or

(D) the availability of which is in the best interest of the patients.

(6)(A) (i) A supplemental application shall be required for any change to a device subject to an approved application under this subsection that affects safety or effectiveness, unless such change is a modification in a manufacturing procedure or method of manufacturing and the holder of the approved application submits a written notice to the Secretary that describes in detail the change, summarizes the data or information supporting the change, and informs the Secretary that the change has been made under the requirements of section 520(f).

(ii) The holder of an approved application who submits a notice under clause (i) with respect to a manufacturing change of a device may distribute the device 30 days after the date on which the Secretary receives the notice, unless the Secretary within such 30–day period notifies the holder that the notice is not adequate and describes such further information or action that is required for acceptance of such change. If the Secretary notifies the holder that a supplemental application is required, the Secretary shall review the supplement within 135 days after the receipt of the supplement. The time used by the Secretary to review the notice of the manufacturing change shall be deducted from the 135–day review period if the notice meets appropriate content requirements for premarket approval supplements.

(B) (i) Subject to clause (ii), in reviewing a supplement to an approved application, for an incremental change to the design of a device that affects safety or effectiveness, the Secretary shall approve such supplement if—

(I) nonclinical data demonstrate that the design modification creates the intended additional capacity, function, or performance of the device; and

(II) clinical data from the approved application and any supplement to the approved application provide a reasonable assurance of safety and effectiveness for the changed device.

(ii) The Secretary may require, when necessary, additional clinical data to evaluate the design modification of the device to provide a reasonable assurance of safety and effectiveness.

(e) WITHDRAWAL AND TEMPORARY SUSPENSION OF APPROVAL APPLICATION.

(1) The Secretary shall, upon obtaining, where appropriate, advice on scientific matters from a panel or panels under section 513, and after due notice and opportunity for informal hearing to the holder of an approved application for a device, issue an order withdrawing approval of the application if the Secretary finds—

(A) that such device is unsafe or ineffective under the conditions of use prescribed, recommended, or suggested in the labeling thereof;

(B) on the basis of new information before him with respect to such device, evaluated together with the evidence available to him when the application was approved, that there is a lack of a showing of reasonable assurance that the device is safe or effective under the conditions of use prescribed, recommended, or suggested in the labeling thereof;

(C) that the application contained or was accompanied by an untrue statement of a material fact;

(D) that the applicant (i) has failed to establish a system for maintaining records, or has repeatedly or deliberately failed to maintain records or to make reports, required by an applicable regulation under section 519(a), (ii) has refused to permit access to, or copying or verification of, such records as required by section 704, or (iii) has not complied with the requirements of section 510;

(E) on the basis of new information before him with respect to such device, evaluated together with the evidence before him when the application was approved, that the methods used in, or the facilities and controls used for, the manufacture, processing, packing, or installation of such device do not conform with the requirements of section 520(f) and were not brought into conformity with such requirements within a reasonable time after receipt of written notice from the Secretary of nonconformity;

(F) on the basis of new information before him, evaluated together with the evidence before him when the application was approved, that the labeling of such device, based on a fair evaluation of all material facts, is false or misleading in any particular and was not corrected within a reasonable time after receipt of written notice from the Secretary of such fact; or

(G) on the basis of new information before him, evaluated together with the evidence before him when the application was approved, that such device is not shown to conform in all respects to a performance standard which is in effect under section 514 compliance with which was a condition to approval of the application and that there is a lack of adequate information to justify the deviation from such standard.

(2) The holder of an application subject to an order issued under paragraph (1) withdrawing approval of the application may, by petition filed on or before the thirtieth day after the date upon which he receives notice of such withdrawal, obtain review thereof in accordance with either paragraph (1) or (2) of subsection (g).

(3) If, after providing an opportunity for an informal hearing, the Secretary determines there is reasonable probability that the continuation of distribution of a device under an approved application would cause serious, adverse health consequences or death, the Secretary shall by order temporarily suspend the approval of the application approved under this section. If the Secretary issues such an order, the Secretary shall proceed expeditiously under paragraph (1) to withdraw such application.

(f) PRODUCT DEVELOPMENT PROTOCOL.

(1) In the case of a class III device which is required to have an approval of an application submitted under subsection (c) of this section, such device shall be considered as having such an approval if a notice of completion of testing conducted in accordance with a product development

protocol approved under paragraph (4) has been declared completed under paragraph (6).

(2) Any person may submit to the Secretary a proposed product development protocol with respect to a device. Such a protocol shall be accompanied by data supporting it. If, within thirty days of the receipt of such a protocol, the Secretary determines that it appears to be appropriate to apply the requirements of this subsection to the device with respect to which the protocol is submitted, the Secretary—

(A) may, at the initiative of the Secretary, refer the proposed protocol to the appropriate panel under section 513 for its recommendation respecting approval of the protocol; or

(B) shall so refer such protocol upon the request of the submitter, unless the Secretary finds that the proposed protocol and accompanying data which would be reviewed by such panel substantially duplicate a product development protocol and accompanying data which have previously been reviewed by such a panel.

(3) A proposed product development protocol for a device may be approved only if—

(A) the Secretary determines that it is appropriate to apply the requirements of this subsection to the device in lieu of the requirement of approval of an application submitted under subsection (c); and

(B) the Secretary determines that the proposed protocol provides—

(i) a description of the device and the changes which may be made in the device,

(ii) a description of the preclinical trials (if any) of the device and a specification of (I) the results from such trials to be required before the commencement of clinical trials of the device, and (II) any permissible variations in preclinical trials and the results therefrom,

(iii) a description of the clinical trials (if any) of the device and a specification of (I) the results from such trials to be required before the filing of a notice of completion of the requirements of the protocol, and (II) any permissible variations in such trials and the results therefrom,

(iv) a description of the methods to be used in, and the facilities and controls to be used for, the manufacture, processing, and, when relevant, packing and installation of the device,

(v) an identifying reference to any performance standard under section 514 to be applicable to any aspect of such device,

(vi) if appropriate, specimens of the labeling proposed to be used for such device,

(vii) such other information relevant to the subject matter of the protocol as the Secretary, with the concurrence of the appropriate panel or panels under section 513, may require, and

(viii) a requirement for submission of progress reports and, when completed, records of the trials conducted under the protocol which records are adequate to show compliance with the protocol.

(4) The Secretary shall approve or disapprove a proposed product development protocol submitted under paragraph (2) within one hundred and twenty days of its receipt unless an additional period is agreed upon by the Secretary and the person who submitted the protocol. Approval of a protocol or denial of approval of a protocol is final agency action subject to judicial review under chapter 7 of title 5, United States Code.

(5) At any time after a product development protocol for a device has been approved pursuant to paragraph (4), the person for whom the protocol was approved may submit a notice of completion—

(A) stating (i) his determination that the requirements of the protocol have been fulfilled and that, to the best of his knowledge, there is no reason bearing on safety or effectiveness why the notice of completion should not become effective, and (ii) the data and other information upon which such determination was made, and

(B) setting forth the results of the trials required by the protocol and all the information required by subsection (c)(1).

(6)(A) The Secretary may, after providing the person who has an approved protocol and opportunity for an informal hearing and at any time prior to receipt of notice of completion of such protocol, issue a final order to revoke such protocol if he finds that—

(i) such person has failed substantially to comply with the requirements of the protocol,

(ii) the results of the trials obtained under the protocol differ so substantially from the results required by the protocol that further trials cannot be justified, or

(iii) the results of the trials conducted under the protocol or available new information do not demonstrate that the device tested under the protocol does not present an unreasonable risk to health and safety.

(B) After the receipt of a notice of completion of an approved protocol the Secretary shall, within the ninety-day period beginning on the date such notice is received, by order either declare the protocol completed or declare it not completed. An order declaring a protocol not completed may take effect only after the Secretary has provided the person who has the protocol opportunity for an informal hearing on the order. Such an order may be issued only if the Secretary finds—

(i) such person has failed substantially to comply with the requirements of the protocol,

(ii) the results of the trials obtained under the protocol differ substantially from the results required by the protocol, or

(iii) there is a lack of a showing of reasonable assurance of the safety and effectiveness of the device under the conditions of use prescribed, recommended, or suggested in the proposed labeling thereof.

(C) A final order issued under subparagraph (A) or (B) shall be in writing and shall contain the reasons to support the conclusions thereof.

(7) At any time after a notice of completion has become effective, the Secretary may issue an order (after due notice and opportunity for an informal hearing to the person for whom the notice is effective) revoking the approval of a device provided by a notice of completion which has become effective as provided in subparagraph (B) if he finds that any of the grounds listed in subparagraphs (A) through (G) of subsection (e)(1) of this section apply. Each reference in such subparagraphs to an application shall be considered for purposes of this paragraph as a reference to a protocol and the notice of completion of such protocol, and each reference to the time when an application was approved shall be considered for purposes of this paragraph as a reference to the time when a notice of completion took effect.

(8) A person who has an approved protocol subject to an order issued under paragraph (6)(A) revoking such protocol, a person who has an approved protocol with respect to which an order under paragraph (6)(B) was issued declaring that the protocol had not been completed, or a person subject to an order issued under paragraph (7) revoking the approval of a device may, by petition filed on or before the thirtieth day after the date upon which he receives notice of such order, obtain review thereof in accordance with either paragraph (1) or (2) of subsection (g).

(g) REVIEW.

(1) Upon petition for review of—

(A) an order under subsection (d) approving or denying approval of an application or an order under subsection (e) withdrawing approval of an application, or

(B) an order under subsection (f)(6)(A) revoking an approved protocol, under subsection (f)(6)(B) declaring that an approved protocol has not been completed, or under subsection (f)(7) revoking the approval of a device,

the Secretary shall, unless he finds the petition to be without good cause or unless a petition for review of such order has been submitted under paragraph (2), hold a hearing, in accordance with section 554 of title 5, United States Code, on the order. The panel or panels which considered the application, protocol, or device subject to such order shall designate a member to appear and testify at any such hearing upon request of the Secretary, the petitioner, or the officer conducting the hearing, but this requirement does not preclude any other member of the panel or panels from appearing and testifying at any such hearing. Upon completion of such hearing and after considering the record established in such hearing, the Secretary shall issue an order either affirming the order subject to the hearing or reversing such order and, as appropriate, approving or denying approval of the application, reinstating the application's approval, approving the protocol, or placing in effect a notice of completion.

(2)(A) Upon petition for review of—

(i) an order under subsection (d) approving or denying approval of an application or an order under subsection (e) withdrawing approval of an application, or

(ii) an order under subsection (f)(6)(A) revoking an approved protocol, under subsection (f)(6)(B) declaring that an approved protocol has not been completed, or under subsection (f)(7) revoking the approval of a device,

the Secretary shall refer the application or protocol subject to the order and the basis for the order to an advisory committee of experts established pursuant to subparagraph (B) for a report and recommendation with respect to the order. The advisory committee shall, after independent study of the data and information furnished to it by the Secretary and other data and information before it, submit to the Secretary a report and recommendation, together with all underlying data and information and a statement of the reasons or basis for the recommendation. A copy of such report shall be promptly supplied by the Secretary to any person who petitioned for such referral to the advisory committee.

(B) The Secretary shall establish advisory committees (which may not be panels under section 513) to receive referrals under subparagraph (A). The Secretary shall appoint as members of any such advisory committee persons qualified in the subject matter to be referred to the committee and of appropriately diversified professional backgrounds, except that the Secretary may not appoint to such a committee any individual who is in the regular full-time employ of the United States and engaged in the administration of this Act. Members of an advisory committee (other than officers or employees of the United States), while attending conferences or meetings of their committee or otherwise serving at the request of the Secretary, shall be entitled to receive compensation at rates to be fixed by the Secretary, which rates may not exceed the daily equivalent for grade GS–18 of the General Schedule for each day (including travel time) they are so engaged; and while so serving away from their homes or regular places of business each member may be allowed travel expenses, including per diem in lieu of subsistence, as authorized by section 5703 of title 5 of the United States Code for persons in the Government service employed intermittently. The Secretary shall designate the chairman of an advisory committee from its members. The Secretary shall furnish each advisory committee with clerical and other assistance, and shall by regulation prescribe the procedures to be followed by each such committee in acting on referrals made under subparagraph (A).

(C) The Secretary shall make public the report and recommendation made by an advisory committee with respect to an application and shall by order, stating the reasons therefor, either affirm the order referred to the advisory committee or reverse such order and, if appropriate, approve or deny approval of the application, reinstate the application's approval, approve the protocol, or place in effect a notice of completion.

(h) SERVICE OF ORDERS.—Orders of the Secretary under this section shall be served (1) in person by any officer or employee of the department designated by the Secretary, or (2) by mailing the order by registered mail or certified mail addressed to the applicant at his last known address in the records of the Secretary.

(i) REVISION.

(1) Before December 1, 1995, the Secretary shall by order require manufacturers of devices, which were introduced or delivered for introduction into interstate commerce for commercial distribution before May 28, 1976, and which are subject to revision of classification under paragraph (2), to submit to the Secretary a summary of and citation to any information known or otherwise available to the manufacturer respecting such devices, including adverse safety or effectiveness information which has not been submitted under section 519. The Secretary may require the manufacturer to submit the adverse safety or effectiveness data for which a summary and citation were submitted, if such data are available to the manufacturer.

(2) After the issuance of an order under paragraph (1) but before December 1, 1995, the Secretary shall publish a regulation in the Federal Register for each device—

(A) which the Secretary has classified as a class III device, and

(B) for which no final regulation has been promulgated under section 515,

revising the classification of the device so that the device is classified into class I or class II, unless the regulation requires the device to remain in class III. In determining whether to revise the classification of a device or to require a device to remain in class III, the Secretary shall apply the criteria set forth in section 513(a). Before the publication of a regulation requiring a device to remain in class III or revising its classification, the Secretary shall publish a proposed regulation respecting the classification of a device under this paragraph and provide reasonable opportunity for the submission of comments on any such regulation. No regulation requiring a device to remain in class III or revising its classification may take effect before the expiration of 90 days from the date of its publication in the Federal Register as a proposed regulation.

(3) The Secretary shall, as promptly as is reasonably achievable, but not later than 12 months after the effective date of the regulation requiring a device to remain in class III, establish a schedule for the promulgation of

a section 515 regulation for each device which is subject to the regulation requiring the device to remain in class III.

SEC. 516 [21 U.S.C. § 360f]. BANNED DEVICES.

(a) GENERAL RULE.—Whenever the Secretary finds, on the basis of all available data and information, that—

(1) a device intended for human use presents substantial deception or an unreasonable and substantial risk of illness or injury; and

(2) in the case of substantial deception or an unreasonable and substantial risk of illness or injury which the Secretary determined could be corrected or eliminated by labeling or change in labeling and with respect to which the Secretary provided written notice to the manufacturer specifying the deception or risk of illness or injury, the labeling or change in labeling to correct the deception or eliminate or reduce such risk, and the period within which such labeling or change in labeling was to be done, such labeling or change in labeling was not done within such period;

he may initiate a proceeding to promulgate a regulation to make such device a banned device.

(b) SPECIAL EFFECTIVE DATE.—The Secretary may declare a proposed regulation under subsection (a) to be effective upon its publication in the Federal Register and until the effective date of any final action taken respecting such regulation if (1) he determines, on the basis of all available data and information, that the deception or risk of illness or injury associated with the use of the device which is subject to the regulation presents an unreasonable, direct, and substantial danger to the health of individuals, and (2) before the date of the publication of such regulation, the Secretary notifies the manufacturer of such device that such regulation is to be made so effective. If the Secretary makes a proposed regulation so effective, he shall, as expeditiously as possible, give interested persons prompt notice of his action under this subsection, provide reasonable opportunity for an informal hearing on the proposed regulation, and either affirm, modify, or revoke such proposed regulation.

SEC. 517 [21 U.S.C. § 360g]. JUDICIAL REVIEW.

(a) APPLICATION OF SECTION.—Not later than thirty days after—

(1) the promulgation of a regulation under section 513 classifying a device in class I or changing the classification of a device to class I or an order under subsection (f)(2) of such section reclassifying a device or denying a petition for reclassification of a device,

(2) the promulgation of a regulation under section 514 establishing, amending, or revoking a performance standard for a device,

(3) the issuance of an order under section 514(b)(2) or 515(b)(2)(B) denying a request for reclassification of a device,

(4) the promulgation of a regulation under paragraph (3) of section 515(b) requiring a device to have an approval of a premarket application, a

regulation under paragraph (4) of that section amending or revoking a regulation under paragraph (3), or an order pursuant to section 515(g)(1) or 515(g)(2)(C),

(5) the promulgation of a regulation under section 516 (other than a proposed regulation made effective under subsection (b) of such section upon the regulation's publication) making a device a banned device,

(6) the issuance of an order under section 520(f)(2),

(7) an order under section 520(g)(4) disapproving an application for an exemption of a device for investigational use or an order under section 520(g)(5) withdrawing such an exemption for a device,

(8) an order pursuant to section 513(i),

(9) a regulation under section 515(i)(2) or 520(*l*)(5)(B), or

(10) an order under section 520(h)(4)(B),

any person adversely affected by such regulation or order may file a petition with the United States Court of Appeals for the District of Columbia or for the circuit wherein such person resides or has his principal place of business for judicial review of such regulation or order. A copy of the petition shall be transmitted by the clerk of the court to the Secretary or other officer designated by him for that purpose. The Secretary shall file in the court the record of the proceedings on which the Secretary based his regulation or order as provided in section 2112 of title 28, United States Code. For purposes of this section, the term "record" means all notices and other matter published in the Federal Register with respect to the regulation or order reviewed, all information submitted to the Secretary with respect to such regulation or order, proceedings of any panel or advisory committee with respect to such regulation or order, any hearing held with respect to such regulation or order, and any other information identified by the Secretary, in the administrative proceeding held with respect to such regulation or order, as being relevant to such regulation or order.

(b) ADDITIONAL DATA, VIEWS, AND ARGUMENTS.—If the petitioner applies to the court for leave to adduce additional data, views, or arguments respecting the regulation or order being reviewed and shows to the satisfaction of the court that such additional data, views, or arguments are material and that there were reasonable grounds for the petitioner's failure to adduce such data, views, or arguments in the proceedings before the Secretary, the court may order the Secretary to provide additional opportunity for the oral presentation of data, views, or arguments and for written submissions. The Secretary may modify his findings, or make new findings by reason of the additional data, views, or arguments so taken and shall file with the court such modified or new findings, and his recommendation, if any, for the modification or setting aside of the regulation or order being reviewed, with the return of such additional data, views, or arguments.

(c) STANDARD FOR REVIEW.—Upon the filing of the petition under subsection (a) of this section for judicial review of a regulation or order, the court shall have jurisdiction to review the regulation or order in accordance with chapter 7 of title 5, United States Code and to grant appropriate relief, including interim relief, as provided in such chapter. A regulation described in paragraph (2) or (5) of subsection (a) and an order issued after the review provided by section 515(g) shall not be affirmed if it is found to be unsupported by substantial evidence on the record taken as a whole.

(d) FINALITY OF JUDGMENT.—The judgment of the court affirming or setting aside, in whole or in part, any regulation or order shall be final, subject to review by the Supreme Court of the United States upon certiorari or certification, as provided in section 1254 of title 28.

(e) REMEDIES.—The remedies provided for in this section shall be in addition to and not in lieu of any other remedies provided by law.

(f) STATEMENT OF REASONS.—To facilitate judicial review under this section or under any other provision of law of a regulation or order issued under section 513, 514, 515, 516, 518, 519, 520, or 521 each such regulation or order shall contain a statement of the reasons for its issuance and the basis, in the record of the proceedings held in connection with its issuance, for its issuance.

SEC. 518 [21 U.S.C. § 360h]. NOTIFICATION AND OTHER REMEDIES.

(a) NOTIFICATION.—If the Secretary determines that—

(1) a device intended for human use which is introduced or delivered for introduction into interstate commerce for commercial distribution presents an unreasonable risk of substantial harm to the public health, and

(2) notification under this subsection is necessary to eliminate the unreasonable risk of such harm and no more practicable means is available under the provisions of this Act (other than this section) to eliminate such risk,

the Secretary may issue such order as may be necessary to assure that adequate notification is provided in an appropriate form, by the persons and means best suited under the circumstances involved, to all health professionals who prescribe or use the device and to any other person (including manufacturers, importers, distributors, retailers, and device users) who should properly receive such notification in order to eliminate such risk. An order under this subsection shall require that the individuals subject to the risk with respect to which the order is to be issued be included in the persons to be notified of the risk unless the Secretary determines that notice to such individuals would present a greater danger to the health of such individuals than no such notification. If the Secretary makes such a determination with respect to such individuals, the order shall require that the health professionals who prescribe or use the device provide for the notification of the individuals whom the health professionals treated with the device of the risk presented by the device and of any action which may be taken by or on behalf of such individuals to eliminate or reduce such risk. Before issuing an order under this subsection, the Secretary shall consult with the persons who are to give notice under the order.

(b) REPAIR, REPLACEMENT, OR REFUND.

(1)(A) If, after affording opportunity for an informal hearing, the Secretary determines that—

(i) a device intended for human use which is introduced or delivered for introduction into interstate commerce for commercial distribution presents an unreasonable risk of substantial harm to the public health,

(ii) there are reasonable grounds to believe that the device was not properly designed or manufactured with reference to the state of the art as it existed at the time of its design or manufacture,

(iii) there are reasonable grounds to believe that the unreasonable risk was not caused by failure of a person other than a manufacturer, importer, distributor, or retailer of the device to exercise due care in the installation, maintenance, repair, or use of the device, and

(iv) the notification authorized by subsection (a) would not by itself be sufficient to eliminate the unreasonable risk and action described in paragraph (2) of this subsection is necessary to eliminate such risk,

the Secretary may order the manufacturer, importer, or any distributor of such device, or any combination of such persons, to submit to him within a reasonable time a plan for taking one or more of the actions described in paragraph (2). An order issued under the preceding sentence which is directed to more than one person shall specify which person may decide which action shall be taken under such plan and the person specified shall be the person who the Secretary determines bears the principal, ultimate financial responsibility for action taken under the plan unless the Secretary cannot determine who bears such responsibility or the Secretary determines that the protection of the public health requires that such decision be made by a person (including a device user or health professional) other than the person he determines bears such responsibility.

(B) The Secretary shall approve a plan submitted pursuant to an order issued under subparagraph (A) unless he determines (after affording opportunity for an informal hearing) that the action or actions to be taken under the plan or the manner in which such action or actions are to be taken under the plan will not assure that the unreasonable risk with respect to which such order was issued will be eliminated. If the Secretary disapproves a plan, he shall order a revised plan to be submitted to him within a reasonable time. If the Secretary determines (after affording opportunity for an informal hearing) that the revised plan is unsatisfactory or if no revised plan or no initial plan has been submitted to the Secretary within the prescribed time, the Secretary shall (i) prescribe a plan to be carried out by the person or persons to whom the order issued under subparagraph (A) was directed, or (ii) after affording an opportunity for an informal hearing, by order prescribe a plan to be carried out by a person who is a manufacturer, importer, distributor, or retailer of the device with respect to which the order was issued but to whom the order under subparagraph (A) was not directed.

(2) The actions which may be taken under a plan submitted under an order issued under paragraph (1) are as follows:

(A) To repair the device so that it does not present the unreasonable risk of substantial harm with respect to which the order under paragraph (1) was issued.

(B) To replace the device with a like or equivalent device which is in conformity with all applicable requirements of this Act.

(C) To refund the purchase price of the device (less a reasonable allowance for use if such device has been in the possession of the device user for one year or more—(i) at the time of notification ordered under subsection (a), or (ii) at the time the device user receives actual notice of the unreasonable risk with respect to which the order was issued under paragraph (1), whichever first occurs).

(3) No charge shall be made to any person (other than a manufacturer, importer, distributor or retailer) for availing himself of any remedy, described in paragraph (2) and provided under an order issued under paragraph (1), and the person subject to the order shall reimburse each person (other than a manufacturer, importer, distributor, or retailer) who is entitled to such a remedy for any reasonable and foreseeable expenses actually incurred by such person in availing himself of such remedy.

(c) REIMBURSEMENT.—An order issued under subsection (b) of this section with respect to a device may require any person who is a manufacturer, importer, distributor, or retailer of the device to reimburse any other person who is a manufacturer, importer, distributor, or retailer of such device for such other person's expenses actually incurred in connection with carrying out the order if the Secretary determines such reimbursement is required for the protection of the public health. Any such requirement shall not affect any rights or obligations under any contract to which the person receiving reimbursement or the person making such reimbursement is a party.

(d) EFFECT ON OTHER LIABILITY.—Compliance with an order issued under this section shall not relieve any person from liability under Federal or State law. In awarding damages for economic loss in an action brought for the enforcement of any such liability, the value to the plaintiff in such action of any remedy provided him under such order shall be taken into account.

(e) RECALL AUTHORITY.

(1) If the Secretary finds that there is a reasonable probability that a device intended for human use would cause serious, adverse health consequences or death, the Secretary shall issue an order requiring the appropriate person (including the manufacturers, importers, distributors, or retailers of the device)—

(A) to immediately cease distribution of such device, and

(B) to immediately notify health professionals and device user facilities of the order and to instruct such professionals and facilities to cease use of such device.

The order shall provide the person subject to the order with an opportunity for an informal hearing, to be held not later than 10 days after the date of the issuance of the order, on the actions required by the order and on whether the order should be amended to require a recall of such device. If, after providing an opportunity for such a hearing, the Secretary determines that inadequate grounds exist to support the actions required by the order, the Secretary shall vacate the order.

(2)(A) If, after providing an opportunity for an informal hearing under paragraph (1), the Secretary determines that the order should be amended to include a recall of the device with respect to which the order was issued, the Secretary shall, except as provided in subparagraphs (B) and (C), amend the order to require a recall. The Secretary shall specify a timetable in which the device recall will occur and shall require periodic reports to the Secretary describing the progress of the recall.

(B) An amended order under subparagraph (A)—

(i) shall—(I) not include recall of a device from individuals, and (II) not include recall of a device from device user facilities if the Secretary determines that the risk of recalling such device from the facilities presents a greater health risk than the health risk of not recalling the device from use, and

(ii) shall provide for notice to individuals subject to the risks associated with the use of such device. In providing the notice required by clause (ii), the Secretary may use the assistance of health professionals who prescribed or used such a device for individuals. If a significant number of such individuals cannot be identified, the Secretary shall notify such individuals pursuant to section 705(b).

(3) The remedy provided by this subsection shall be in addition to remedies provided by subsections (a), (b), and (c).

SEC. 519 [21 U.S.C. § 360i]. RECORDS AND REPORTS ON DEVICES.

(a) GENERAL RULE.—Every person who is a manufacturer or importer of a device intended for human use shall establish and maintain such records, make such reports, and provide such information, as the Secretary may by regulation reasonably require to assure that such device is not adulterated or misbranded and to otherwise assure its safety and effectiveness. Regulations prescribed under the preceding sentence—

(1) shall require a device manufacturer or importer to report to the Secretary whenever the manufacturer or importer receives or otherwise becomes aware of information that reasonably suggests that one of its marketed devices—(A) may have caused or contributed to a death or

serious injury, or (B) has malfunctioned and that such device or a similar device marketed by the manufacturer or importer would be likely to cause or contribute to a death or serious injury if the malfunction were to recur;

(2) shall define the term "serious injury" to mean an injury that—(A) is life threatening, (B) results in permanent impairment of a body function or permanent damage to a body structure, or (C) necessitates medical or surgical intervention to preclude permanent impairment of a body function or permanent damage to a body structure;

(3) shall require reporting of other significant adverse device experiences as determined by the Secretary to be necessary to be reported;

(4) shall not impose requirements unduly burdensome to a device manufacturer or importer taking into account his cost of complying with such requirements and the need for the protection of the public health and the implementation of this Act;

(5) which prescribe the procedure for making requests for reports or information shall require that each request made under such regulations for submission of a report or information to the Secretary state the reason or purpose for such request and identify to the fullest extent practicable such report or information;

(6) which require submission of a report or information to the Secretary shall state the reason or purpose for the submission of such report or information and identify to the fullest extent practicable such report or information;

(7) may not require that the identity of any patient be disclosed in records, reports, or information required under this subsection unless required for the medical welfare of an individual, to determine the safety or effectiveness of a device, or to verify a record, report, or information submitted under this Act; and

(8) may not require a manufacturer or importer of a class I device to—

(A) maintain for such a device records respecting information not in the possession of the manufacturer or importer, or

(B) to submit for such a device to the Secretary any report or information—(i) not in the possession of the manufacturer or importer, or (ii) on a periodic basis, unless such report or information is necessary to determine if the device should be reclassified or if the device is adulterated or misbranded. In prescribing such regulations, the Secretary shall have due regard for the professional ethics of the medical profession and the interests of patients. The prohibitions of paragraph (7) of this subsection continue to apply to records, reports, and information concerning any individual who has been a patient, irrespective of whether or when he ceases to be a patient. The Secretary shall by regulation require distributors to keep records and make such records available to the Secretary upon request. Paragraphs (4) and (8) apply to distributors to the same extent and in the same manner as such paragraphs apply to manufacturers and importers.

(b) USER REPORTS.

(1)(A) Whenever a device user facility receives or otherwise becomes aware of information that reasonably suggests that a device has or may have caused or contributed to the death of a patient of the facility, the facility shall, as soon as practicable but not later than 10 working days after becoming aware of the information, report the information to the Secretary and, if the identity of the manufacturer is known, to the manufacturer of the device. In the case of deaths, the Secretary may by regulation prescribe a shorter period for the reporting of such information.

(B) Whenever a device user facility receives or otherwise becomes aware of—

(i) information that reasonably suggests that a device has or may have caused or contributed to the serious illness of, or serious injury to, a patient of the facility, or

(ii) other significant adverse device experiences as determined by the Secretary by regulation to be necessary to be reported,

the facility shall, as soon as practicable but not later than 10 working days after becoming aware of the information, report the information to the manufacturer of the device or to the Secretary if the identity of the manufacturer is not known.

(C) Each device user facility shall submit to the Secretary on an annual basis a summary of the reports made under subparagraphs (A) and (B). Such summary shall be submitted on January 1 of each year. The summary shall be in such form and contain such information from such reports as the Secretary may require and shall include—

(i) sufficient information to identify the facility which made the reports for which the summary is submitted,

(ii) in the case of any product which was the subject of a report, the product name, serial number, and model number,

(iii) the name and the address of the manufacturer of such device, and

(iv) a brief description of the event reported to the manufacturer.

(D) For purposes of subparagraphs (A), (B), and (C), a device user facility shall be treated as having received or otherwise become aware of information with respect to a device of that facility when medical personnel who are employed by or otherwise formally affiliated with the facility receive or otherwise become aware of information with respect to that device in the course of their duties.

(2) The Secretary may not disclose the identity of a device user facility which makes a report under paragraph (1) except in connection with—(A) an action brought to enforce section 301(q), (B) a communication to a manufacturer of a device which is the subject of a report under paragraph (1). This paragraph does not prohibit the Secretary from disclosing the

identity of a device user facility making a report under paragraph (1) or any information in such a report to employees of the Department of Health and Human Services, to the Department of Justice, or to the duly authorized committees and subcommittees of the Congress.

(3) No report made under paragraph (1) by—

(A) a device user facility,

(B) an individual who is employed by or otherwise formally affiliated with such a facility, or

(C) a physician who is not required to make such a report,

shall be admissible into evidence or otherwise used in any civil action involving private parties unless the facility, individual, or physician who made the report had knowledge of the falsity of the information contained in the report.

(4) A report made under paragraph (1) does not affect any obligation of a manufacturer who receives the report to file a report as required under subsection (a).

(5) With respect to device user facilities:

(A) The Secretary shall by regulation plan and implement a program under which the Secretary limits user reporting under paragraphs (1) through (4) to a subset of user facilities that constitutes a representative profile of user reports for device deaths and serious illnesses or serious injuries.

(B) During the period of planning the program under subparagraph (A), paragraphs (1) through (4) continue to apply.

(C) During the period in which the Secretary is providing for a transition to the full implementation of the program, paragraphs (1) through (4) apply except to the extent that the Secretary determines otherwise.

(D) On and after the date on which the program is fully implemented, paragraphs (1) through (4) do not apply to a user facility unless the facility is included in the subset referred to in subparagraph (A).

(E) Not later than 2 years after the date of the enactment of the Food and Drug Administration Modernization Act of 1997, the Secretary shall submit to the Committee on Commerce of the House of Representatives, and to the Committee on Labor and Human Resources of the Senate, a report describing the plan developed by the Secretary under subparagraph (A) and the progress that has been made toward the implementation of the plan.

(6) For purposes of this subsection:

(A) The term "device user facility" means a hospital, ambulatory surgical facility, nursing home, or outpatient treatment facility which is not a physician's office. The Secretary may by regulation include an outpatient diagnostic facility which is not a physician's office in such term.

(B) The terms "serious illness" and "serious injury" mean illness or injury, respectively, that—

(i) is life threatening,

(ii) results in permanent impairment of a body function or permanent damage to a body structure, or

(iii) necessitates medical or surgical intervention to preclude permanent impairment of a body function or permanent damage to a body structure.

(c) PERSONS EXEMPT.—Subsection (a) shall not apply to—

(1) any practitioner who is licensed by law to prescribe or administer devices intended for use in humans and who manufactures or imports devices solely for use in the course of his professional practice;

(2) any person who manufactures or imports devices intended for use in humans solely for such person's use in research or teaching and not for sale (including any person who uses a device under an exemption granted under section 520(g)); and

(3) any other class of persons as the Secretary may by regulation exempt from subsection (a) of this section upon a finding that compliance with the requirements of such subsection by such class with respect to a device is not necessary to (A) assure that a device is not adulterated or misbranded or (B) otherwise to assure its safety and effectiveness.

(e) DEVICE TRACKING.

(1) The Secretary may by order require a manufacturer to adopt a method of tracking a class II or class III device—(A) the failure of which would be reasonably likely to have serious adverse health consequences; or (B) which is—(i) intended to be implanted in the human body for more than one year, or (ii) a life sustaining or life supporting device used outside a device user facility.

(2) Any patient receiving a device subject to tracking under paragraph (1) may refuse to release, or refuse permission to release, the patient's name, address, social security number, or other identifying information for the purpose of tracking.

(f) REPORTS OF REMOVALS AND CORRECTIONS.

(1) Except as provided in paragraph (2), the Secretary shall by regulation require a manufacturer or importer of a device to report promptly to the Secretary any correction or removal of a device undertaken by such manufacturer or importer if the removal or correction was undertaken—(A) to reduce a risk to health posed by the device, or (B) to remedy a violation of this Act caused by the device which may present a risk to health. A manufacturer or importer of a device who undertakes a correction or removal of a device which is not required to be reported under this paragraph shall keep a record of such correction or removal.

(2) No report of the corrective action or removal of a device may be required under paragraph (1) if a report of the corrective action or removal is required and has been submitted under subsection (a).

(3) For purposes of paragraphs (1) and (2), the terms "correction" and "removal" do not include routine servicing.

SEC. 520 [21 U.S.C. § 360j]. GENERAL PROVISIONS RESPECTING CONTROL OF DEVICES.

(a) GENERAL RULE.—Any requirement authorized by or under section 501, 502, 510, or 519 applicable to a device intended for human use shall apply to such device until the applicability of the requirement to the device has been changed by action taken under section 513, 514, or 515 or under subsection (g) of this section, and any requirement established by or under section 501, 502, 510, or 519 which is inconsistent with a requirement imposed on such device under section 514 or 515 or under subsection (g) of this section shall not apply to such device.

(b) CUSTOM DEVICES.—Sections 514 and 515 do not apply to any device which, in order to comply with the order of an individual physician or dentist (or any other specially qualified person designated under regulations promulgated by the Secretary after an opportunity for an oral hearing) necessarily deviates from an otherwise applicable performance standard or requirement prescribed by or under section 515 if

(1) the device is not generally available in finished form for purchase or for dispensing upon prescription and is not offered through labeling or advertising by the manufacturer, importer, or distributor thereof for commercial distribution, and

(2) such device—

(A)(i) is intended for use by an individual patient named in such order of such physician or dentist (or other specially qualified person so designated) and is to be made in a specific form for such patient, or (ii) is intended to meet the special needs of such physician or dentist (or other specially qualified person so designated) in the course of the professional practice of such physician or dentist (or other specially qualified person so designated), and

(B) is not generally available to or generally used by other physicians or dentists (or other specially qualified persons so designated).

(c) TRADE SECRETS.—Any information reported to or otherwise obtained by the Secretary or his representative under section 513, 514, 515, 516, 518, 519, or 704 or under subsection (f) or (g) of this section which is exempt from disclosure pursuant to subsection (a) of section 552 of title 5, United States Code by reason of subsection (b)(4) of such section shall be considered confidential and shall not be disclosed and may not be used by the Secretary as the basis for the reclassification of a device from class III to class II or class I or as the basis for the establishment or amendment of a performance standard under section 514 for a device reclassified from class III to class II, except (1) in accordance with subsection (h), and (2) that such information may be disclosed to other officers or employees concerned with carrying out this Act or when relevant in any proceeding under this Act (other than section 513 or 514).

(d) NOTICE AND FINDINGS.—Each notice of proposed rulemaking under section 513, 514, 515, 516, 518, or 519, or under this section, any other notice which is published in the Federal Register with respect to any other action taken under any such section and which states the reasons for such action, and each publication of findings required to be made in connection with rulemaking under any such section shall set forth—(1) the manner in which interested persons may examine data and other information on which the notice or findings is based, and (2) the period within which interested persons may present their comments on the notice or findings (including the need therefor) orally or in writing, which period shall be at least sixty days but may not exceed ninety days unless the time is extended by the Secretary by a notice published in the Federal Register stating good cause therefor.

(e) RESTRICTED DEVICES.

(1) The Secretary may by regulation require that a device be restricted to sale, distribution, or use—

(A) only upon the written or oral authorization of a practitioner licensed by law to administer or use such device, or

(B) upon such other conditions as the Secretary may prescribe in such regulation,

if, because of its potentiality for harmful effect or the collateral measures necessary to its use, the Secretary determines that there cannot otherwise be reasonable assurance of its safety and effectiveness. No condition prescribed under subparagraph (B) may restrict the use of a device to persons with specific training or experience in its use or to persons for use in certain facilities unless the Secretary determines that such a restriction is required for the safe and effective use of the device. No such condition may exclude a person from using a device solely because the person does not have the training or experience to make him eligible for certification by a certifying board recognized by the American Board of Medical Specialties or has not been certified by such a Board. A device subject to a regulation under this subsection is a restricted device.

(2) The label of a restricted device shall bear such appropriate statements of the restrictions required by a regulation under paragraph (1) as the Secretary may in such regulation prescribe.

(f) GOOD MANUFACTURING PRACTICE REQUIREMENTS.

(1)(A) The Secretary may, in accordance with subparagraph (B), prescribe regulations requiring that the methods used in, and the facilities and controls used for, the manufacture, pre-production design validation (including a process to assess the performance of a device but not including an evaluation of the safety or effectiveness of a device), packing, storage, and installation of a device conform to current good manufacturing practice, as prescribed in such regulations, to assure that the device will be safe and effective and otherwise in compliance with this Act.

(B) Before the Secretary may promulgate any regulation under subparagraph (A) he shall—(i) afford the advisory committee established under paragraph (3) an opportunity to submit recommendations to him with respect to the regulation proposed to be promulgated, (ii) afford opportunity for an oral hearing; and (iii) ensure that such regulation conforms, to the extent practicable, with internationally recognized standards defining quality systems, or parts of the standards, for medical devices. The Secretary shall provide the advisory committee a reasonable time to make its recommendation with respect to proposed regulations under subparagraph (A).

(2)(A) Any person subject to any requirement prescribed by regulations under paragraph (1) may petition the Secretary for an exemption or variance from such requirement. Such a petition shall be submitted to the Secretary in such form and manner as he shall prescribe and shall—

(i) in the case of a petition for an exemption from a requirement, set forth the basis for the petitioner's determination that compliance with the requirement is not required to assure that the device will be safe and effective and otherwise in compliance with this Act,

(ii) in the case of a petition for a variance from a requirement, set forth the methods proposed to be used in, and the facilities and controls proposed to be used for, the manufacture, packing, storage, and installation of the device in lieu of the methods, facilities, and controls prescribed by the requirement, and

(iii) contain such other information as the Secretary shall prescribe.

(B) The Secretary may refer to the advisory committee established under paragraph (3) any petition submitted under subparagraph (A). The advisory committee shall report its recommendations to the Secretary with respect to a petition referred to it within sixty days of the date of the petition's referral. Within sixty days after—

(i) the date the petition was submitted to the Secretary under subparagraph (A), or

(ii) if the petition was referred to an advisory committee, the expiration of the sixty-day period beginning on the date the petition was referred to the advisory committee,

whichever occurs later, the Secretary shall by order either deny the petition or approve it.

(C) The Secretary may approve—

(i) a petition for an exemption for a device from a requirement if he determines that compliance with such requirement is not required to assure that the device will be safe and effective and otherwise in compliance with this Act, and

(ii) a petition for a variance for a device from a requirement if he determines that the methods to be used in, and the facilities and controls to be used for, the manufacture, packing, storage, and installation of the device in lieu of the methods, controls, and facilities prescribed by the requirement are sufficient to assure that the device will be safe and effective and otherwise in compliance with this Act.

An order of the Secretary approving a petition for a variance shall prescribe such conditions respecting the methods used in, and the facilities and controls used for, the manufacture, packing, storage, and installation of the device to be granted the variance under the petition as may be necessary to assure that the device will be safe and effective and otherwise in compliance with this Act.

(D) After the issuance of an order under subparagraph (B) respecting a petition, the petitioner shall have an opportunity for an informal hearing on such order.

(3) The Secretary shall establish an advisory committee for the purpose of advising and making recommendations to him with respect to regulations proposed to be promulgated under paragraph (1)(A) and the approval or disapproval of petitions submitted under paragraph (2). The advisory committee shall be composed of nine members as follows:

(A) Three of the members shall be appointed from persons who are officers or employees of any State or local government or of the Federal Government.

(B) Two of the members shall be appointed from persons who are representative of interests of the device manufacturing industry; two of the members shall be appointed from persons who are representative of the interests of physicians and other health professionals; and two of the members shall be representative of the interests of the general public.

Members of the advisory committee who are not officers or employees of the United States, while attending conferences or meetings of the committee or otherwise engaged in its business, shall be entitled to receive compensation at rates to be fixed by the Secretary, which rates may not exceed the daily equivalent of the rate in effect for grade GS–18 of the General Schedule, for each day (including travel time) they are so engaged; and while so serving away from their homes or regular places of business each member may be allowed travel expenses, including per diem in lieu of subsistence, as authorized by section 5703 of title 5 of the United States Code for persons in the Government service employed intermittently. The Secretary shall designate one of the members of the advisory committee to serve as its chairman. The Secretary shall furnish the advisory committee with clerical and other assistance. Section 14 of the Federal Advisory Committee Act shall not apply with respect to the duration of the advisory committee established under this paragraph.

(g) EXEMPTION FOR DEVICES FOR INVESTIGATIONAL USE.

(1) It is the purpose of this subsection to encourage, to the extent consistent with the protection of the public health and safety and with ethical standards, the discovery and development of useful devices intended for human use and to that end to maintain optimum freedom for scientific investigators in their pursuit of that purpose.

(2)(A) The Secretary shall, within the one hundred and twenty-day period beginning on the date of enactment of this section, by regulation prescribe procedures and conditions under which devices intended for human use may upon application be granted an exemption from the requirements of section 502, 510, 514, 515, 516, 519, or 721 or subsection (e) or (f) of this section or from any combination of such requirements to permit the investigational use of such devices by experts qualified by scientific training and experience to investigate the safety and effectiveness of such devices.

(B) The conditions prescribed pursuant to subparagraph (A) shall include the following:

(i) A requirement that an application be submitted to the Secretary before an exemption may be granted and that the application be submitted in such form and manner as the Secretary shall specify.

(ii) A requirement that the person applying for an exemption for a device assure the establishment and maintenance of such records, and the making of such reports to the Secretary of data obtained as a result of the investigational use of the device during the exemption, as the Secretary determines will enable him to assure compliance with such conditions, review the progress of the investigation, and evaluate the safety and effectiveness of the device.

(iii) Such other requirements as the Secretary may determine to be necessary for the protection of the public health and safety.

(C) Procedures and conditions prescribed pursuant to subparagraph (A) for an exemption may appropriately vary depending on (i) the scope and duration of clinical testing to be conducted under such exemption, (ii) the number of human subjects that are to be involved in such testing, (iii) the need to permit changes to be made in the device subject to the exemption during testing conducted in accordance with a clinical testing plan required under paragraph (3)(A), and (iv) whether the clinical testing of such device is for the purpose of developing data to obtain approval for the commercial distribution of such device.

(3) Procedures and conditions prescribed pursuant to paragraph (2)(A) shall require, as a condition to the exemption of any device to be the subject of testing involving human subjects, that the person applying for the exemption—

(A) submit a plan for any proposed clinical testing of the device and a report of prior investigations of the device (including, where appropriate, tests on animals) adequate to justify the proposed clinical testing—

(i) to the local institutional review committee which has been established in accordance with regulations of the Secretary to supervise clinical testing of devices in the facilities where the proposed clinical testing is to be conducted, or

(ii) to the Secretary, if—

(I) no such committee exists, or

(II) the Secretary finds that the process of review by such committee is inadequate (whether or not the plan for such testing has been approved by such committee),

for review for adequacy to justify the commencement of such testing; and, unless the plan and report are submitted to the Secretary, submit to the Secretary a summary of the plan and a report of prior investigations of the device (including, where appropriate, tests on animals);

(B) promptly notify the Secretary (under such circumstances and in such manner as the Secretary prescribes) of approval by a local institutional review committee of any clinical testing plan submitted to it in accordance with subparagraph (A);

(C) in the case of a device to be distributed to investigators for testing, obtain signed agreements from each of such investigators that any testing of the device involving human subjects will be under such investigator's supervision and in accordance with subparagraph (D) and submit such agreements to the Secretary; and

(D) assure that informed consent will be obtained from each human subject (or his representative) of proposed clinical testing involving such device, except where subject to such conditions as the Secretary may prescribe, the investigator conducting or supervising the proposed clinical testing of the device determines in writing that there exists a life threatening situation involving the human subject of such testing which necessitates the use of such device and it is not feasible to obtain informed consent from the subject and there is not sufficient time to obtain such consent from his representative.

The determination required by subparagraph (D) shall be concurred in by a licensed physician who is not involved in the testing of the human subject with respect to which such determination is made unless immediate use of the device is required to save the life of the human subject of such testing and there is not sufficient time to obtain such concurrence.

(4)(A) An application, submitted in accordance with the procedures prescribed by regulations under paragraph (2), for an exemption for a device (other than an exemption from section 516) shall be deemed approved on the thirtieth day after the submission of the application to the Secretary unless on or before such day the Secretary by order disapproves the application and notifies the applicant of the disapproval of the application.

(B) The Secretary may disapprove an application only if he finds that the investigation with respect to which the application is submitted does not conform to procedures and conditions prescribed under regulations under paragraph (2). Such a notification shall contain the order of disapproval and a complete statement of the reasons for the Secretary's disapproval of the application and afford the applicant opportunity for an informal hearing on the disapproval order.

(5) The Secretary may by order withdraw an exemption granted under this subsection for a device if the Secretary determines that the conditions applicable to the device under this subsection for such exemption are not met. Such an order may be issued only after opportunity for an informal hearing, except that such an order may be issued before the provision of an opportunity for an informal hearing if the Secretary determines that the continuation of testing under the exemption with respect to which the order is to be issued will result in an unreasonable risk to the public health.

(6)(A) Not later than 1 year after the date of the enactment of the Food and Drug Administration Modernization Act of 1997, the Secretary shall by regulation establish, with respect to a device for which an exemption under this subsection is in effect, procedures and conditions that, without requiring an additional approval of an application for an exemption or the approval of a supplement to such an application, permit—

(i) developmental changes in the device (including manufacturing changes) that do not constitute a significant change in design or in basic principles of operation and that are made in response to information gathered during the course of an investigation; and

(ii) changes or modifications to clinical protocols that do not affect—

(I) the validity of data or information resulting from the completion of an approved protocol, or the relationship of likely patient risk to benefit relied upon to approve a protocol;

(II) the scientific soundness of an investigational plan submitted under paragraph (3)(A); or

(III) the rights, safety, or welfare of the human subjects involved in the investigation.

(B) Regulations under subparagraph (A) shall provide that a change or modification described in such subparagraph may be made if—

(i) the sponsor of the investigation determines, on the basis of credible information (as defined by the Secretary) that the applicable conditions under subparagraph (A) are met; and

(ii) the sponsor submits to the Secretary, not later than 5 days after making the change or modification, a notice of the change or modification.

(7)(A) In the case of a person intending to investigate the safety or effectiveness of a class III device or any implantable device, the Secretary shall ensure that the person has an opportunity, prior to submitting an application to the Secretary or to an institutional review committee, to submit to the Secretary, for review, an investigational plan (including a clinical protocol). If the applicant submits a written request for a meeting with the Secretary regarding such review, the Secretary shall, not later than 30 days after receiving the request, meet with the applicant for the purpose of reaching agreement regarding the investigational plan (including a clinical protocol). The written request shall include a detailed description of the device, a detailed description of the proposed conditions of use of the device, a proposed plan (including a clinical protocol) for determining whether there is a reasonable assurance of effectiveness, and, if available information regarding the expected performance from the device.

(B) Any agreement regarding the parameters of an investigational plan (including a clinical protocol) that is reached between the Secretary and a sponsor or applicant shall be reduced to writing and made part of the administrative record by the Secretary. Any such agreement shall not be changed, except—(i) with the written agreement of the sponsor or applicant; or (ii) pursuant to a decision, made in accordance with subparagraph (C) by the director of the office in which the device involved is reviewed, that a substantial scientific issue essential to determining the safety or effectiveness of the device involved has been identified.

(C) A decision under subparagraph (B)(ii) by the director shall be in writing, and may be made only after the Secretary has provided to the sponsor or applicant an opportunity for a meeting at which the director and the sponsor or applicant are present and at which the director documents the scientific issue involved.

(h) RELEASE OF INFORMATION RESPECTING SAFETY AND EFFECTIVENESS.

(1) The Secretary shall promulgate regulations under which a detailed summary of information respecting the safety and effectiveness of a device which information was submitted to the Secretary and which was the basis for—

(A) an order under section 515(d)(1)(A) approving an application for premarket approval for the device or denying approval of such an application or an order under section 515(e) withdrawing approval of such an application for the device,

(B) an order under section 515(f)(6)(A) revoking an approved protocol for the device, an order under section 515(f)(6)(B) declaring a protocol for the device completed or not completed, or an order under section 515(f)(7) revoking the approval of the device, or

(C) an order approving an application under subsection (g) for an exemption for the device from section 516 or an order disapproving, or withdrawing approval of, an application for an exemption under such subsection for the device,

shall be made available to the public upon issuance of the order. Summaries of information made available pursuant to this paragraph respecting a device shall include information respecting any adverse effects on health of the device.

(2) The Secretary shall promulgate regulations under which each advisory committee established under section 515(g)(2)(B) shall make available to the public a detailed summary of information respecting the safety and effectiveness of a device which information was submitted to the advisory committee and which was the basis for its recommendation to the Secretary made pursuant to section 515(g)(2)(A). A summary of information upon which such a recommendation is based shall be made available pursuant to this paragraph only after the issuance of the order with respect to which the recommendation was made and each summary shall include information respecting any adverse effect on health of the device subject to such order.

(3) Except as provided in paragraph (4), any information respecting a device which is made available pursuant to paragraph (1) or (2) of this subsection (A) may not be used to establish the safety or effectiveness of another device for purposes of this Act by any person other than the person who submitted the information so made available, and (B) shall be made available subject to subsection (c) of this section.

(4)(A) Any information contained in an application for premarket approval filed with the Secretary pursuant to section 515(c) (including information from clinical and preclinical tests or studies that demonstrate the safety and effectiveness of a device, but excluding descriptions of methods of manufacture and product composition and other trade secrets) shall be available, 6 years after the application has been approved by the Secretary, for use by the Secretary in—

(i) approving another device;

(ii) determining whether a product development protocol has been completed, under section 515 for another device;

(iii) establishing a performance standard or special control under this Act; or

(iv) classifying or reclassifying another device under section 513 and subsection (1)(2).

(B) The publicly available detailed summaries of information respecting the safety and effectiveness of devices required by paragraph (1)(A) shall be available for use by the Secretary as the evidentiary basis for the agency actions described in subparagraph (A).

(i) PROCEEDINGS OF ADVISORY PANELS AND COMMITTEES.—Each panel under section 513 and each advisory committee established under section 514(b)(5)(B) or 515(g) or under subsection (f) of this section shall make and maintain a transcript of any proceeding of the panel or committee. Each such panel and committee shall delete from any transcript made pursuant to this subsection information which under subsection (c) of this section is to be considered confidential.

(j) TRACEABILITY.—Except as provided in section 519(e), no regulation under this Act may impose on a type or class of device requirements for the traceability of such type or class of device unless such requirements are necessary to assure the protection of the public health.

(k) RESEARCH AND DEVELOPMENT.—The Secretary may enter into contracts for research, testing, and demonstrations respecting devices and may obtain devices for research, testing, and demonstration purposes without regard to section 3648 and 3709 of the Revised Statutes (31 U.S.C. 529, 41 U.S.C. 5).

(*l*) TRANSITIONAL PROVISIONS FOR DEVICES CONSIDERED AS NEW DRUGS.

(1) Any device intended for human use—

(A) for which on the date of enactment of the Medical Device Amendments of 1976 (hereinafter in this subsection referred to as the "enactment date") an approval of an application submitted under section 505(b) was in effect;

(B) for which such an application was filed on or before the enactment date and with respect to which application no order of approval or refusing to approve had been issued on such date under subsection (c) or (d) of such section;

(C) for which on the enactment date an exemption under subsection (i) of such section was in effect;

(D) which is within a type of device described in subparagraph (A), (B), or (C) and is substantially equivalent to another device within that type;

(E) which the Secretary in a notice published in the Federal Register before the enactment date has declared to be a new drug subject to section 505; or

(F) with respect to which on the enactment date an action is pending in a United States court under section 302, 303, or 304 for an alleged violation of a provision of section 301 which enforces a requirement of section 505 or for an alleged violation of section 505(a),

is classified in class III unless the Secretary in response to a petition submitted under paragraph (2) has classified such device in class I or II.

(2) The Secretary may initiate the reclassification of a device classified into class III under paragraph (1) of this subsection or the manufacturer or importer of a device classified under paragraph (1) may petition the Secretary (in such form and manner as he shall prescribe) for the issuance of an order classifying the device in class I or class II. Within thirty days of the filing of such a petition, the Secretary shall notify the petitioner of any deficiencies in the petition which prevent the Secretary from making a decision on the petition. Except as provided in paragraph (3)(D)(ii), within one hundred and eighty days after the filing of a petition under this paragraph, the Secretary shall, after consultation with the appropriate panel under section 513, by order either deny the petition or order the

classification, in accordance with the criteria prescribed by section 513(a)(1)(A) or 513(a)(1)(B), of the device in class I or class II.

(3)(A) In the case of a device which is described in paragraph (1)(A) and which is in class III—

(i) such device shall on the enactment date be considered a device with an approved application under section 515, and

(ii) the requirements applicable to such device before the enactment date under section 505 shall continue to apply to such device until changed by the Secretary as authorized by this Act.

(B) In the case of a device which is described in paragraph (1)(B) and which is in class III, an application for such device shall be considered as having been filed under section 515 on the enactment date. The period in which the Secretary shall act on such application in accordance with section 515(d)(1) shall be one hundred and eighty days from the enactment date (or such greater period as the Secretary and the applicant may agree upon after the Secretary has made the finding required by section 515(d)(1)(B)(i)) less the number of days in the period beginning on the date an application for such device was filed under section 505 and ending on the enactment date. After the expiration of such period such device is required, unless exempt under subsection (g) of this section, to have in effect an approved application under section 515.

(C) A device which is described in paragraph (1)(C) and which is in class III shall be considered a new drug until the expiration of the ninety-day period beginning on the date of the promulgation of regulations under subsection (g) of this section. After the expiration of such period such device is required, unless exempt under subsection (g), to have in effect an approved application under section 515.

(D) (i) Except as provided in clauses (ii) and (iii), a device which is described in subparagraph (D), (E), or (F) of paragraph (1) and which is in class III is required, unless exempt under subsection (g) of this section, to have on and after sixty days after the enactment date in effect an approved application under section 515.

(ii) If—

(I) a petition is filed under paragraph (2) for a device described in subparagraph (D), (E), or (F) of paragraph (1), or

(II) an application for premarket approval is filed under section 360e of this title for such a device,

within the sixty-day period beginning on the enactment date (or within such greater period as the Secretary, after making the finding required under section 515(d)(1)(B), and the petitioner or applicant may agree upon), the Secretary shall act on such petition or application in accordance with paragraph (2) or section 515 except that the period within which the Secretary must act on the petition or application shall be within the one hundred and twenty-day period beginning on the date the petition or application is filed. If such a petition or application is filed within such sixty-day (or greater) period, clause (i) of this subparagraph shall not apply to such device before the expiration of such one hundred and twenty-day period, or if such petition is denied or such application is denied approval, before the date of such denial, whichever occurs first.

(iii) In the case of a device which is described in subparagraph (E) of paragraph (1), which the Secretary in a notice published in the Federal Register after March 31, 1976, declared to be a new drug subject to section 505, and which is in class III—

(I) the device shall, after eighteen months after the enactment date, have in effect an approved application under section 515 unless exempt under subsection (g) of this section, and

(II) the Secretary may, during the period beginning one hundred and eighty days after the enactment date and ending eighteen months after such date, restrict the use of the device to investigational use by experts qualified by scientific training and experience to investigate the safety and effectiveness of such device, and to investigational use in accordance with the requirements applicable under regulations under subsection (g) of this section to investigational use of devices granted an exemption under such subsection.

If the requirements under subsection (g) of this section are made applicable to the investigational use of such a device, they shall be made applicable in such a manner that the device shall be made reasonably available to physicians meeting appropriate qualifications prescribed by the Secretary.

(5)(A) Before December 1, 1991, the Secretary shall by order require manufacturers of devices described in paragraph (1), which are subject to revision of classification under subparagraph (B), to submit to the Secretary a summary of and citation to any information known or otherwise available to the manufacturers respecting the devices, including adverse safety or effectiveness information which has not been submitted under section 519. The Secretary may require a manufacturer to submit the adverse safety or effectiveness data for which a summary and citation were submitted, if such data are available to the manufacturer.

(B) Except as provided in subparagraph (C), after the issuance of an order under subparagraph (A) but before December 1, 1992, the Secretary shall publish a regulation in the Federal Register for each device which is classified in class III under paragraph (1) revising the classification of the device so that the device is classified into class I or class II, unless the regulation requires the device to remain in class III. In determining whether to revise the classification of a device or to require a device to remain in class III, the Secretary shall apply the criteria set forth in section 513(a). Before the publication of a regulation requiring a device to remain in class III or revising its classification, the Secretary shall publish a proposed regulation respecting the classification of a device under this subparagraph and provide an opportunity for the submission of comments on any such regulation. No regulation under this subparagraph requiring a device to remain in class III or revising its classification may take effect before the expiration of 90 days from the date of the publication in the Federal Register of the proposed regulation.

(C) The Secretary may by notice published in the Federal Register extend the period prescribed by subparagraph (B) for a device for an additional period not to exceed 1 year.

(m) HUMANITARIAN DEVICE EXEMPTION.

(1) To the extent consistent with the protection of the public health and safety and with ethical standards, it is the purpose of this subsection to encourage the discovery and use of devices intended to benefit patients in the treatment and diagnosis of diseases or conditions that affect fewer than 4,000 individuals in the United States.

(2) The Secretary may grant a request for an exemption from the effectiveness requirements of sections 514 and 515 for a device for which the Secretary finds that—

(A) the device is designed to treat or diagnose a disease or condition that affects fewer than 4,000 individuals in the United States,

(B) the device would not be available to a person with a disease or condition referred to in subparagraph (A) unless the Secretary grants such an exemption and there is no comparable device, other than under this exemption, available to treat or diagnose such disease or condition, and

(C) the device will not expose patients to an unreasonable or significant risk of illness or injury and the probable benefit to health from the use of the device outweighs the risk of injury or illness from its use, taking into account the probable risks and benefits of currently available devices or alternative forms of treatment.

The request shall be in the form of an application submitted to the Secretary. Not later than 75 days after the date of the receipt of the application, the Secretary shall issue an order approving or denying the application.

(3) No person granted an exemption under paragraph (2) with respect to a device may sell the device for an amount that exceeds the costs of research and development, fabrication, and distribution of the device.

(4) Devices granted an exemption under paragraph (2) may only be used—

(A) in facilities that have established, in accordance with regulations of the Secretary, a local institutional review committee to supervise clinical testing of devices in the facilities, and

(B) if, before the use of a device, an institutional review committee approves the use in the treatment or diagnosis of a disease or condition referred to in paragraph (2)(A), unless a physician determines in an emergency situation that approval from a local institutional review committee can not be obtained in time to prevent serious harm or death to a patient.

In a case described in subparagraph (B) in which a physician uses a device without an approval from an institutional review committee, the physician shall, after the use of the device, notify the chairperson of the local institutional review committee of such use. Such notification shall include the identification of the patient involved, the date on which the device was used, and the reason for the use.

(5) The Secretary may require a person granted an exemption under paragraph (2) to demonstrate continued compliance with the requirements of this subsection if the Secretary believes such demonstration to be necessary to protect the public health or if the Secretary has reason to believe that the criteria for the exemption are no longer met.

(6) The Secretary may suspend or withdraw an exemption from the effectiveness requirements of sections 514 and 515 for a humanitarian device only after providing notice and an opportunity for an informal hearing.

SEC. 521 [21 U.S.C. § 360k]. STATE AND LOCAL REQUIREMENTS RESPECTING DEVICES.

(a) GENERAL RULE.—Except as provided in subsection (b), no State or political subdivision of a State may establish or continue in effect with respect to a device intended for human use any requirement—

(1) which is different from, or in addition to, any requirement applicable under this Act to the device, and

(2) which relates to the safety or effectiveness of the device or to any other matter included in a requirement applicable to the device under this Act.

(b) EXEMPT REQUIREMENTS.—Upon application of a State or a political subdivision thereof, the Secretary may, by regulation promulgated after notice and opportunity for an oral hearing, exempt from subsection (a), under such conditions as may be prescribed in such regulation, a requirement of such State or political subdivision applicable to a device intended for human use if—

(1) the requirement is more stringent than a requirement under this Act which would be applicable to the device if an exemption were not in effect under this subsection; or

(2) the requirement—(A) is required by compelling local conditions, and (B) compliance with the requirement would not cause the device to be in violation of any applicable requirement under this Act.

SEC. 522 [21 U.S.C. § 360*l*]. POSTMARKET SURVEILLANCE.

(a) IN GENERAL.—The Secretary may by order require a manufacturer to conduct postmarket surveillance for any device of the manufacturer which is a class II or class III device the failure of which would be reasonably likely to have serious adverse health consequences or which is intended to be—(1) implanted in the human body for more than one year, or (2) a life sustaining or life supporting device used outside a device user facility.

(b) SURVEILLANCE APPROVAL.—Each manufacturer required to conduct a surveillance of a device shall, within 30 days of receiving an order from the Secretary prescribing that the manufacturer is required under this section to conduct such surveillance, submit, for the approval of the Secretary, a plan for the required surveillance. The Secretary, within 60 days of the receipt of such plan, shall determine if the person designated to conduct the surveillance has appropriate qualifications and experience to undertake such surveillance and if the plan will result in the collection of useful data that can reveal unforeseen adverse events or other information necessary to protect the public health. The Secretary, in consultation with the manufacturer, may by order require a prospective surveillance period of up to 36 months. Any determination by the Secretary that a longer period is necessary shall be made by mutual agreement between the Secretary and the manufacturer or, if no agreement can be reached, after the completion of a dispute resolution process as described in section 562.

SEC. 523 [21 U.S.C. § 360m]. ACCREDITED PERSONS.

(a) IN GENERAL.

(1) REVIEW AND CLASSIFICATION OF DEVICES.—Not later than 1 year after the date of the enactment of the Food and Drug Administration Modernization Act of 1997, the Secretary shall, subject to paragraph (3), accredit persons for the purpose of reviewing reports submitted under section 510(k) and making recommendations to the Secretary regarding the initial classification of devices under section 513(f)(1).

(2) REQUIREMENTS REGARDING REVIEW.

(A) IN GENERAL.—In making a recommendation to the Secretary under paragraph (1), an accredited person shall notify the Secretary in writing of the reasons for the recommendation.

(B) TIME PERIOD FOR REVIEW.—Not later than 30 days after the date on which the Secretary is notified under subparagraph (A) by an accredited person with respect to a recommendation of an initial classification of a device, the Secretary shall make a determination with respect to the initial classification.

(C) SPECIAL RULE.—The Secretary may change the initial classification under section 513(f)(1) that is recommended under paragraph (1) by an accredited person, and in such case shall provide to such person, and the person who submitted the report under section 510(k) for the device, a statement explaining in detail the reasons for the change.

(3) CERTAIN DEVICES.

(A) IN GENERAL.—An accredited person may not be used to perform a review of—(i) a class III device; (ii) a class II device which is intended to be permanently implantable or life sustaining or life supporting; or (iii) a class II device which requires clinical data in the report submitted under section 510(k) for the device, except that the number of class II devices to which the Secretary applies this clause for a year, less the number of such reports to which clauses (i) and (ii) apply, may not exceed 6 percent of the number that is equal to the total number of reports submitted to the Secretary under such section for such year less the number of such reports to which such clauses apply for such year.

(B) ADJUSTMENT.—In determining for a year the ratio described in subparagraph (A)(iii), the Secretary shall not include in the numerator class III devices that the Secretary reclassified into class II, and the Secretary shall include in the denominator class II devices for which reports under section 510(k) were not required to be submitted by reason of the operation of section 510(m).

(b) ACCREDITATION.

(1) PROGRAMS.—The Secretary shall provide for such accreditation through programs administered by the Food and Drug Administration, other government agencies, or by other qualified nongovernment organizations.

(2) ACCREDITATION.

(A) IN GENERAL.—Not later than 180 days after the date of the enactment of the Food and Drug Administration Modernization Act of 1997, the Secretary shall establish and publish in the Federal Register criteria to accredit or deny accreditation to persons who request to perform the duties specified in subsection (a). The Secretary shall respond to a request for accreditation within 60 days of the receipt of the request. The accreditation of such person shall specify the particular activities under subsection (a) for which such person is accredited.

(B) WITHDRAWAL OF ACCREDITATION.—The Secretary may suspend or withdraw accreditation of any person accredited under this paragraph, after providing notice and an opportunity for an informal hearing, when such person is substantially not in compliance with the requirements of this section or poses a threat to public health or fails to act in a manner that is consistent with the purposes of this section.

(C) PERFORMANCE AUDITING.—To ensure that persons accredited under this section will continue to meet the standards of accreditation, the Secretary shall—(i) make onsite visits on a periodic basis to each accredited person to audit the performance of such person; and (ii) take such additional measures as the Secretary determines to be appropriate.

(D) ANNUAL REPORT.—The Secretary shall include in the annual report required under section 903(g) the names of all accredited persons and the particular activities under subsection (a) for which each such person is accredited and the name of each accredited person whose accreditation has been withdrawn during the year.

(3) QUALIFICATIONS.—An accredited person shall, at a minimum, meet the following requirements:

(A) Such person may not be an employee of the Federal Government.

(B) Such person shall be an independent organization which is not owned or controlled by a manufacturer, supplier, or vendor of devices and which has no organizational, material, or financial affiliation with such a manufacturer, supplier, or vendor.

(C) Such person shall be a legally constituted entity permitted to conduct the activities for which it seeks accreditation.

(D) Such person shall not engage in the design, manufacture, promotion, or sale of devices.

(E) The operations of such person shall be in accordance with generally accepted professional and ethical business practices and shall agree in writing that as a minimum it will—(i) certify that reported information accurately reflects data reviewed; (ii) limit work to that for which competence and capacity are available; (iii) treat information received, records, reports, and recommendations as proprietary information; (iv) promptly respond and attempt to resolve complaints regarding its activities for which it is accredited; and (v) protect against the use, in carrying out subsection (a) with respect to a device, of any officer or employee of the person who has a financial conflict of interest regarding the device, and annually make available to the public disclosures of the extent to which the person, and the officers and employees of the person, have maintained compliance with requirements under this clause relating to financial conflicts of interest.

(4) SELECTION OF ACCREDITED PERSONS.—The Secretary shall provide each person who chooses to use an accredited person to receive a section 510(k) report a panel of at least two or more accredited persons from which the regulated person may select one for a specific regulatory function.

(5) COMPENSATION OF ACCREDITED PERSONS.—Compensation for an accredited person shall be determined by agreement between the accredited person and the person who engages the services of the accredited person, and shall be paid by the person who engages such services.

(c) DURATION.—The authority provided by this section terminates—

(1) 5 years after the date on which the Secretary notifies Congress that at least 2 persons accredited under subsection (b) are available to review at least 60 percent of the submissions under section 510(k), or

(2) 4 years after the date on which the Secretary notifies Congress that the Secretary has made a determination described in paragraph (2)(B) of

subsection (a) for at least 35 percent of the devices that are subject to review under paragraph (1) of such subsection,

whichever occurs first.

ORPHAN DRUG PROVISIONS

SEC. 525 [21 U.S.C. § 360aa]. DRUGS FOR RARE DISEASES OR CONDITIONS.

(a) The sponsor of a drug for a disease or condition which is rare in the States may request the Secretary to provide written recommendations for the non-clinical and clinical investigations which must be conducted with the drug before—(1) it may be approved for such disease or condition under section 505, or (2) if the drug is a biological product, it may be licensed for such disease or condition under section 351 of the Public Health Service Act. If the Secretary has reason to believe that a drug for which a request is made under this section is a drug for a disease or condition which is rare in the States, the Secretary shall provide the person making the request written recommendations for the nonclinical and clinical investigations which the Secretary believes, on the basis of information available to the Secretary at the time of the request under this section, would be necessary for approval of such drug for such disease or condition under section 505 or licensing of such drug for such disease or condition under section 351 of the Public Health Service Act.

(b) The Secretary shall by regulation promulgate procedures for the implementation of subsection (a).

SEC. 526 [21 U.S.C. § 360bb]. DESIGNATION OF DRUGS FOR RARE DISEASES.

(a) (1) The manufacturer or the sponsor of a drug may request the Secretary to designate the drug as a drug for a rare disease or condition. A request for designation of a drug shall be made before the submission of an application under section 505(b) for the drug, the submission of an application for certification of the drug under section 357 of this title, or the submission of an application for licensing of the drug under section 351 of the Public Health Service Act. If the Secretary finds that a drug for which a request is submitted under this subsection is being or will be investigated for a rare disease or condition and—

(A) if an application for such drug is approved under section 505, or

(B) if a license for such drug is issued under section 351 of the Public Health Service Act,

the approval, certification, or license would be for use for such disease or condition, the Secretary shall designate the drug as a drug for such disease or condition. A request for a designation of a drug under this subsection shall contain the consent of the applicant to notice being given by the Secretary under subsection (b) respecting the designation of the drug.

(2) For purposes of paragraph (1), the term "rare disease or condition" means any disease or condition which (A) affects less than 200,000 persons

in the United States, or (B) affects more than 200,000 in the United States and for which there is no reasonable expectation that the cost of developing and making available in the United States a drug for such disease or condition will be recovered from sales in the United States of such drug. Determinations under the preceding sentence with respect to any drug shall be made on the basis of the facts and circumstances as of the date the request for designation of the drug under this subsection is made.

(b) A designation of a drug under subsection (a) shall be subject to the condition that—(1) if an application was approved for the drug under section 505(b) or a license was issued for the drug under section 351 of the Public Health Service Act, the manufacturer of the drug will notify the Secretary of any discontinuance of the production of the drug at least one year before discontinuance, and (2) if an application has not been approved for the drug under section 505(b) or a license has not been issued for the drug under section 351 of the Public Health Service Act and if preclinical investigations or investigations under section 505(i) are being conducted with the drug, the manufacturer or sponsor of the drug will notify the Secretary of any decision to discontinue active pursuit of approval of an application under section 505(b) or approval of a license under section 351 of the Public Health Service Act.

(c) Notice respecting the designation of a drug under subsection (a) shall be made available to the public.

(d) The Secretary shall by regulation promulgate procedures for the implementation of subsection (a).

SEC. 527 [21 U.S.C. § 360cc]. PROTECTION FOR DRUGS FOR RARE DISEASES.

(a) Except as provided in subsection (b), if the Secretary—

    (1) approves an application filed pursuant to section 505, or

    (2) issues a license under section 351 of the Public Health Service Act

for a drug designated under section 526 for a rare disease or condition, the Secretary may not approve another application under section 505 or issue another license under section 351 of the Public Health Service Act for such drug for such disease or condition for a person who is not the holder of such approved application, of such certification, or of such license until the expiration of seven years from the date of the approval of the approved application, the issuance of the certification, or the issuance of the license. Section 505(c)(2) does not apply to the refusal to approve an application under the preceding sentence.

(b) If an application filed pursuant to section 505 is approved for a drug designated under section 526 for a rare disease or condition, or if a license is issued under section 351 of the Public Health Service Act for such a drug, the Secretary may, during the seven-year period beginning on the date of the application approval, or of the issuance of the license, approve another application under section 355 of this title, or issue a license under section 351 of the Public Health Service Act, for such drug for such disease or condition for a person who is not the holder of such approved application, of such certification, or of such license if—

(1) the Secretary finds, after providing the holder notice and opportunity for the submission of views, that in such period the holder of the approved application, or of the license cannot assure the availability of sufficient quantities of the drug to meet the needs of persons with the disease or condition for which the drug was designated; or

(2) such holder provides the Secretary in writing the consent of such holder for the approval of other applications, or the issuance of other licenses before the expiration of such seven-year period.

SEC. 528 [21 U.S.C. § 360dd]. OPEN PROTOCOLS FOR INVESTIGATIONS.

If a drug is designated under section 526 as a drug for a rare disease or condition and if notice of a claimed exemption under section 505(i) or regulations issued thereunder is filed for such drug, the Secretary shall encourage the sponsor of such drug to design protocols for clinical investigations of the drug which may be conducted under the exemption to permit the addition to the investigations of persons with the disease or condition who need the drug to treat the disease or condition and who cannot be satisfactorily treated by available alternative drugs.

ELECTRONIC PRODUCT RADIATION CONTROL

SEC. 531 [21 U.S.C. § 360hh]. DEFINITIONS.—As used in this subchapter—

(1) the term "electronic product radiation" means—(A) any ionizing or non-ionizing electromagnetic or particulate radiation, or (B) any sonic, infrasonic, or ultrasonic wave, which is emitted from an electronic product as the result of the operation of an electronic circuit in such product;

(2) the term "electronic product" means—(A) any manufactured or assembled product which, when in operation, (i) contains or acts as part of an electronic circuit and (ii) emits (or in the absence of effective shielding or other controls would emit) electronic product radiation, or (B) any manufactured or assembled article which is intended for use as a component, part, or accessory of a product described in clause (A) and which when in operation emits (or in the absence of effective shielding or other controls would emit) such radiation * * *

SEC. 532 [21 U.S.C. § 360ii]. ELECTRONIC PRODUCT RADIATION CONTROL PROGRAM.

(a) The Secretary shall establish and carry out an electronic product radiation control program designed to protect the public health and safety from electronic product radiation. As a part of such program, he shall—

(1) pursuant to section 534, develop and administer performance standards for electronic products;

(2) plan, conduct, coordinate, and support research, development, training, and operational activities to minimize the emissions of and the exposure of people to, unnecessary electronic product radiation;

(3) maintain liaison with and receive information from other Federal and State departments and agencies with related interests, professional organizations, industry, industry and labor associations, and other organizations on present and future potential electronic product radiation;

(4) study and evaluate emissions of, and conditions of exposure to, electronic product radiation and intense magnetic fields;

(5) develop, test, and evaluate the effectiveness of procedures and techniques for minimizing exposure to electronic product radiation; and

(6) consult and maintain liaison with the Secretary of Commerce, the Secretary of Defense, the Secretary of Labor, the Atomic Energy Commission, and other appropriate Federal departments and agencies on (A) techniques, equipment, and programs for testing and evaluating electronic product radiation, and (B) the development of performance standards pursuant to section 534 to control such radiation emissions.

(b) In carrying out the purposes of subsection (a), the Secretary is authorized to—

(1)(A) collect and make available, through publications and other appropriate means, the results of, and other information concerning, research and studies relating to the nature and extent of the hazards and control of electronic product radiation; and (B) make such recommendations relating to such hazards and control as he considers appropriate;

(2) make grants to public and private agencies, organizations, and institutions, and to individuals for the purposes stated in paragraphs (2), (4), and (5) of subsection (a);

(3) contract with public or private agencies, institutions, and organizations, and with individuals, without regard to section 3324 of title 31 United States Code and section 3709 of the Revised Statutes of the United States Code (41 U.S.C. § 5); and

(4) procure (by negotiation or otherwise) electronic products for research and testing purposes, and sell or otherwise dispose of such products.

(c) (1) Each recipient of assistance under this subchapter pursuant to grants or contracts entered into under other than competitive bidding procedures shall keep such records as the Secretary shall prescribe, including records which fully disclose the amount and disposition by such recipient of the proceeds of such assistance, the total cost of the project or undertaking in connection with which such assistance is given or used, and the amount of that portion of the cost of the project or undertaking supplied by other sources, and such other records as will facilitate an effective audit.

(2) The Secretary and the Comptroller General of the United States, or any of their duly authorized representatives, shall have access for the purpose of audit and examination to any books, documents, papers, and

records of the recipients that are pertinent to the grants or contracts entered into under this subchapter under other than competitive bidding procedures.

SEC. 533 [21 U.S.C. § 360jj]. STUDIES BY THE SECRETARY.

(a) The Secretary shall conduct the following studies, and shall make a report or reports of the results of such studies to the Congress on or before January 1, 1970, and from time to time thereafter as he may find necessary, together with such recommendations for legislation as he may deem appropriate:

(1) A study of present State and Federal control of health hazards from electronic product radiation and other types of ionizing radiation, which study shall include, but not be limited to—

(A) control of health hazards from radioactive materials other than materials regulated under the Atomic Energy Act of 1954;

(B) any gaps and inconsistencies in present controls;

(C) the need for controlling the sale of certain used electronic products, particularly antiquated X-ray equipment, without upgrading such products to meet the standards for new products or separate standards for used products;

(D) measures to assure consistent and effective control of the aforementioned health hazards;

(E) measures to strengthen radiological health programs of State governments; and

(F) the feasibility of authorizing the Secretary to enter into arrangements with individual States or groups of States to define their respective functions and responsibilities for the control of electronic product radiation and other ionizing radiation;

(2) A study to determine the necessity for the development of standards for the use of nonmedical electronic products for commercial and industrial purposes; and

(3) A study of the development of practicable procedures for the detection and measurement of electronic product radiation which may be emitted from electronic products manufactured or imported prior to the effective date of any applicable standard established pursuant to this subchapter.

(b) In carrying out these studies, the Secretary shall invite the participation of other Federal departments and agencies having related responsibilities and interests, State governments—particularly those of States which regulate radioactive materials under section 274 of the Atomic Energy Act of 1954, as amended, and interested professional, labor, and industrial organizations. Upon request from congressional committees interested in these studies, the Secretary shall keep these committees currently informed as to the progress of the studies and shall permit the committees to send observers to meetings of the study groups.

(c) The Secretary or his designee shall organize the studies and the participation of the invited participants as he deems best. Any dissent from the findings and recommendations of the Secretary shall be included in the report if so requested by the dissenter.

SEC. 534 [21 U.S.C. § 360kk]. PERFORMANCE STANDARDS FOR ELECTRONIC PRODUCTS.

(a) (1) The Secretary shall by regulation prescribe performance standards for electronic products to control the emission of electronic product radiation from such products if he determines that such standards are necessary for the protection of the public health and safety. Such standards may include provisions for the testing of such products and the measurement of their electronic product radiation emissions, may require the attachment of warning signs and labels, and may require the provision of instructions for the installation, operation, and use of such products. Such standards may be prescribed from time to time whenever such determinations are made, but the first of such standards shall be prescribed prior to January 1, 1970. In the development of such standards, the Secretary shall consult with Federal and State departments and agencies having related responsibilities or interests and with appropriate professional organizations and interested persons, including representatives of industries and labor organizations which would be affected by such standards, and shall give consideration to—

(A) the latest available scientific and medical data in the field of electronic product radiation;

(B) the standards currently recommended by (i) other Federal agencies having responsibilities relating to the control and measurement of electronic product radiation, and (ii) public or private groups having an expertise in the field of electronic product radiation;

(C) the reasonableness and technical feasibility of such standards as applied to a particular electronic product;

(D) the adaptability of such standards to the need for uniformity and reliability of testing and measuring procedures and equipment; and

(E) in the case of a component, or accessory described in paragraph (2)(B) of section 531, the performance of such article in the manufactured or assembled product for which it is designed.

(2) The Secretary may prescribe different and individual performance standards, to the extent appropriate and feasible, for different electronic products so as to recognize their different operating characteristics and uses.

(3) The performance standards prescribed under this section shall not apply to any electronic product which is intended solely for export if (A) such product and the outside of any shipping container used in the export of such product are labeled or tagged to show that such product is intended for export, and (B) such product meets all the applicable requirements of the country to which such product is intended for export.

(4) The Secretary may by regulation amend or revoke any performance standard prescribed under this section.

(5) The Secretary may exempt from the provisions of this section any electronic product intended for use by departments or agencies of the United States provided such department or agency has prescribed procurement specifications governing emissions of electronic product radiation and provided further that such product is of a type used solely or predominantly by departments or agencies of the United States.

(b) The provisions of subchapter II of chapter 5 of title 5 of the United States Code (relating to the administrative procedure for rulemaking), and of chapter 7 of such title (relating to judicial review), shall apply with respect to any regulation prescribing, amending, or revoking any standard prescribed under this section.

(c) Each regulation prescribing, amending, or revoking a standard shall specify the date on which it shall take effect which, in the case of any regulation prescribing, or amending any standard, may not be sooner than one year or not later than two years after the date on which such regulation is issued, unless the Secretary finds, for good cause shown, that an earlier or later effective date is in the public interest and publishes in the Federal Register his reason for such finding, in which case such earlier or later date shall apply.

(d) (1) In a case of actual controversy as to the validity of any regulation issued under this section prescribing, amending, or revoking a performance standard, any person who will be adversely affected by such regulation when it is effective may at any time prior to the sixtieth day after such regulation is issued file a petition with the United States court of appeals for the circuit wherein such person resides or has his principal place of business, for a judicial review of such regulation. A copy of the petition shall be forthwith transmitted by the clerk of the court to the Secretary or other officer designated by him for that purpose. The Secretary thereupon shall file in the court the record of the proceedings on which the Secretary based the regulation, as provided in section 2112 of title 28 of the United States Code.

(2) If the petitioner applies to the court for leave to adduce additional evidence, and shows to the satisfaction of the court that such additional evidence is material and that there were reasonable grounds for the failure to adduce such evidence in the proceeding before the Secretary, the court may order such additional evidence (and evidence in rebuttal thereof) to be taken before the Secretary, and to be adduced upon the hearing, in such manner and upon such terms and conditions as to the court may seem proper. The Secretary may modify his findings, or make new findings, by reason of the additional evidence so taken, and he shall file such modified or new findings, and his recommendations, if any, for the modification or setting aside of his original regulation, with the return of such additional evidence.

(3) Upon the filing of the petition referred to in paragraph (1) of this subsection, the court shall have jurisdiction to review the regulation in accordance with chapter 7 of title 5 of the United States Code and to grant appropriate relief as provided in such chapter.

(4) The judgment of the court affirming or setting aside, in whole or in part, any such regulation of the Secretary shall be final, subject to review by the Supreme Court of the United States upon certiorari or certification as provided in section 1254 of title 28 of the United States Code.

(5) Any action instituted under this subsection shall survive, notwithstanding any change in the person occupying the office of Secretary or any vacancy in such office.

(6) The remedies provided for in this subsection shall be in addition to and not substitution for any other remedies provided by law.

(e) A certified copy of the transcript of the record and administrative proceedings under this section shall be furnished by the Secretary to any interested party at his request, and payment of the costs thereof, and shall be admissible in any criminal, exclusion of imports, or other proceeding arising under or in respect of this subchapter irrespective of whether proceedings with respect to the regulation have previously been initiated or become final under this section.

(f) (1)(A) The Secretary shall establish a Technical Electronic Product Radiation Safety Standards Committee (hereafter in this part referred to as the "Committee") which he shall consult before prescribing any standard under this section. The Committee shall be appointed by the Secretary, after consultation with public and private agencies concerned with the technical aspect of electronic product radiation safety, and shall be composed of fifteen members each of whom shall be technically qualified by training and experience in one or more fields of science or engineering applicable to electronic product radiation safety, as follows:

(i) Five members shall be selected from governmental agencies, including State and Federal Governments;

(ii) Five members shall be selected from the affected industries after consultation with industry representatives; and

(iii) Five members shall be selected from the general public, of which at least one shall be a representative of organized labor.

(B) The Committee may propose electronic product radiation safety standards to the Secretary for his consideration. All proceedings of the Committee shall be recorded and the record of each such proceeding shall be available for public inspection.

(2) Payments to members of the Committee who are not officers or employees of the United States pursuant to subsection (c) of section 208 of the Public Health Service Act shall not render members of the Committee officers or employees of the United States for any purpose.

(g) The Secretary shall review and evaluate on a continuing basis testing programs carried out by industry to assure the adequacy of safeguards against hazardous electronic product radiation and to assure that electronic products comply with standards prescribed under this section.

(h) Every manufacturer of an electronic product to which is applicable a standard in effect under this section shall furnish to the distributor or dealer at the time of delivery of such product, in the form of a label or tag permanently affixed to such product or in such manner as approved by the Secretary, the certification that such product conforms to all applicable standards under this section. Such certification shall be based upon a test, in accordance with such standard, of the individual article to which it is attached or upon a testing program which is in accord with good manufacturing practice and which has not been disapproved by the Secretary (in such manner as he shall prescribe by regulation) on the grounds that it does not assure the adequacy of safeguards against hazardous electronic product radiation or that it does not assure that electronic products comply with the standards prescribed under this section.

SEC. 535 [21 U.S.C. § 360*ll*]. NOTIFICATION OF DEFECTS IN AND REPAIR OR REPLACEMENT OF ELECTRONIC PRODUCTS.

(a) (1) Every manufacturer of electronic products who discovers that an electronic product produced, assembled, or imported by him has a defect which relates to the safety of use of such product by reason of the emission of electronic product radiation, or that an electronic product produced, assembled, or imported by him on or after the effective date of an applicable standard prescribed pursuant to section 534 fails to comply with such standard, shall immediately notify the Secretary of such defect or failure to comply if such product has left the place of manufacture and shall (except as authorized by paragraph (2)) with reasonable promptness furnish notification of such defect or failure to the persons (where known to the manufacturer) specified in subsection (b) of this section.

(2) If, in the opinion of such manufacturer, the defect or failure to comply is not such as to create a significant risk of injury, including genetic injury, to any person, he may, at the time of giving notice to the Secretary of such defect or failure to comply, apply to the Secretary for an exemption from the requirement of notice to the persons specified in subsection (b). If such application states reasonable grounds for such exemption, the Secretary shall afford such manufacturer an opportunity to present his views and evidence in support of the application, the burden of proof being on the manufacturer. If, after such presentation, the Secretary is satisfied that such defect or failure to comply is not such as to create a significant risk of injury, including genetic injury, to any person, he shall exempt such manufacturer from the requirement of notice to the persons specified in subsection (b) of this section and from the requirements of repair or replacement imposed by subsection (f) of this section.

(b) The notification (other than to the Secretary) required by paragraph (1) of subsection (a) of this section shall be accomplished—

(1) by certified mail to the first purchaser of such product for purposes other than resale, and to any subsequent transferee of such product; and

(2) by certified mail or other more expeditious means to the dealers or distributors of such manufacturer to whom such product was delivered.

(c) The notifications required by paragraph (1) of subsection (a) of this section shall contain a clear description of such defect or failure to comply with an applicable standard, an evaluation of the hazard reasonably related to such defect or failure to comply, and a statement of the measures to be taken to repair such defect. In the case of a notification to a person referred to in subsection (b) of this section, the notification shall also advise the person of his rights under subsection (f) of this section.

(d) Every manufacturer of electronic products shall furnish to the Secretary a true or representative copy of all notices, bulletins, and other communications to the dealers or distributors of such manufacturer or to purchasers (or subsequent transferees) of electronic products of such manufacturer regarding any such defect in such product or any such failure to comply with a standard applicable to such product. The Secretary shall disclose to the public so much of the information contained in such notice or other information obtained under section 537 as he deems will assist in carrying out the purposes of this subchapter, but he shall not disclose any information which contains or relates to a trade secret or other matter referred to in section 1905 of title 18 United States Code unless he determines that it is necessary to carry out the purposes of this subchapter.

(e) If through testing, inspection, investigation, or research carried out pursuant to this subchapter, or examination of reports submitted pursuant to section 537, or otherwise, the Secretary determines that any electronic product—

(1) does not comply with an applicable standard prescribed pursuant to section 534; or

(2) contains a defect which relates to the safety of use of such product by reason of the emission of electronic product radiation;

he shall immediately notify the manufacturer of such product of such defect or failure to comply. The notice shall contain the findings of the Secretary and shall include all information upon which the findings are based. The Secretary shall afford such manufacturer an opportunity to present his views and evidence in support thereof, to establish that there is no failure of compliance or that the alleged defect does not exist or does not relate to safety of use of the product by reason of the emission of such radiation hazard. If after such presentation by the manufacturer the Secretary determines that such product does not comply with an applicable standard prescribed pursuant to section 534, or that it contains a defect which relates to the safety of use of such product by reason of the emission of electronic product radiation, the Secretary shall direct the manufacturer to furnish the notification specified in subsection (c) to the persons specified in paragraphs (1) and (2) of subsection (b) (where known to the manufacturer), unless the manufacturer has applied for an exemption from the requirement of such notification on the ground specified in paragraph (2) of subsection (a) and the Secretary is satisfied that such noncompliance or defect is not such as to create a significant risk of injury, including genetic injury, to any person.

(f) If any electronic product is found under subsection (a) or (e) to fail to comply with an applicable standard prescribed under this subchapter or to have a defect which relates to the safety of use of such product, and the notification specified in subsection (c) is required to be furnished on account of such failure or defect, the manufacturer of such product shall (1) without charge, bring such product into conformity with such standard or remedy such defect and provide reimbursement for any expenses for transportation of such product incurred in connection with having such product brought into conformity or having such defect remedied, (2) replace such product with a like or equivalent product which complies with each applicable standard prescribed under this subchapter and which has no defect relating to the safety of its use, or (3) make a refund of the cost of such product. The manufacturer shall take the action required by this subsection in such manner, and with respect to such persons, as the Secretary by regulations shall prescribe.

(g) This section shall not apply to any electronic product that was manufactured before the date of the enactment of this subchapter.

SEC. 536 [21 U.S.C. § 360mm]. IMPORTS.

(a) Any electronic product offered for importation into the United States which fails to comply with an applicable standard prescribed under this subchapter, or to which is not affixed a certification in the form of a label or tag in conformity with section 534(h) shall be refused admission into the United States. The Secretary of the Treasury shall deliver to the Secretary of Health and Human Services, upon the latter's request, samples of electronic products which are being imported or offered for import into the United States, giving notice thereof to the owner or consignee, who may have a hearing before the Secretary of Health and Human Services. If it appears from an examination of such samples or otherwise that any electronic product fails to comply with applicable standards prescribed pursuant to section 534, then, unless subsection (b) applies and is complied with, (1) such electronic product shall be refused admission, and (2) the Secretary of the Treasury shall cause the destruction of such electronic product unless such article is exported, under regulations prescribed by the Secretary of the Treasury, within 90 days after the date of notice of refusal of admission or within such additional time as may be permitted by such regulations.

(b) If it appears to the Secretary of Health and Human Services that any electronic product refused admission pursuant to subsection (a) can be brought into compliance with applicable standards prescribed pursuant to section 534, final determination as to admission of such electronic product may be deferred upon filing of timely written application by the owner or consignee and the execution by him of a good and sufficient bond providing for the payment of such liquidated damages in the event of default as the Secretary of Health and Human Services may by regulation prescribe. If such application is filed and such bond is executed the Secretary of Health and Human Services may, in accordance with rules prescribed by him, permit the applicant to perform such operations with respect to such electronic product as may be specified in the notice of permission.

(c) All expenses (including travel, per diem or subsistence, and salaries of officers or employees of the United States) in connection with the destruction provided for in subsection (a) and the supervision of operations provided for in subsection (b) of this section, and all expenses in connection with the storage, cartage, or labor with respect to any electronic product refused admission pursuant to subsection (a), shall be paid by the owner or consignee, and, in event of default, shall constitute a lien against any future importations made by such owner or consignee.

(d) It shall be the duty of every manufacturer offering an electronic product for importation into the United States to designate in writing an agent upon whom service of all administrative and judicial processes, notices, orders, decisions, and requirements may be made for and on behalf of said manufacturer, and to file such designation with the Secretary, which designation may from time to time be changed by like writing, similarly filed. Service of all administrative and judicial processes, notices, orders, decisions, and requirements may be made upon said manufacturer by service upon such designated agent at his office or usual place of residence with like effect as if made personally upon said manufacturer, and in default of such designation of such agent, service of process, notice, order, requirement, or decision in any proceeding before the Secretary or in any judicial proceeding for enforcement of this subchapter or any standards prescribed pursuant to this subchapter may be made by posting such process, notice, order, requirement, or decision in the Office of the Secretary or in a place designated by him by regulation.

SEC. 537 [21 U.S.C. § 360nn]. INSPECTION AND REPORTS.

(a) If the Secretary finds for good cause that the methods, tests, or programs related to electronic product radiation safety in a particular factory, warehouse, or establishment in which electronic products are manufactured or held, may not be adequate or reliable, officers or employees duly designated by the Secretary, upon presenting appropriate credentials and a written notice to the owner, operator, or agent in charge, are thereafter authorized (1) to enter, at reasonable times, any area in such factory, warehouse, or establishment in which the manufacturer's tests (or testing programs) required by section 534(h) are carried out, and (2) to inspect, at reasonable times and within reasonable limits and in a reasonable manner, the facilities and procedures within such area which are related to electronic product radiation safety. Each such inspection shall be commenced and completed with reasonable promptness. In addition to other grounds upon which good cause may be found for purposes of this subsection, good cause will be considered to exist in any case where the manufacturer has introduced into commerce any electronic product which does not comply with an applicable standard prescribed under this part and with respect to which no exemption from the notification requirements has been granted by the Secretary under section 535(a)(2) or 535(e).

(b) Every manufacturer of electronic products shall establish and maintain such records (including testing records), make such reports, and provide such information, as the Secretary may reasonably require to enable him to determine whether such manufacturer has acted or is acting in compliance with this subchapter and standards prescribed pursuant to this subchapter and shall, upon request of an officer or employee duly designated by the Secretary, permit such officer or employee to inspect appropriate books, papers, records, and documents relevant to determining whether such manufacturer has acted or is acting in compliance with standards prescribed pursuant to this subchapter.

(c) Every manufacturer of electronic products shall provide to the Secretary such performance data and other technical data related to safety as may be required to carry out the purposes of this subchapter. The Secretary is authorized to require the manufacturer to give such notification of such performance and technical data at the time of original purchase to the ultimate purchaser of the electronic product, as he determines necessary to carry out the purposes of this subchapter after consulting with the affected industry.

(d) Accident and investigation reports made under this subchapter by any officer, employee, or agent of the Secretary shall be available for use in any civil, criminal, or other judicial proceeding arising out of such accident. Any such officer, employee, or agent may be required to testify in such proceedings as to the facts developed in such investigations. Any such report shall be made available to the public in a manner which need not identify individuals. All reports on research projects, demonstration projects, and other related activities shall be public information.

(e) The Secretary or his representative shall not disclose any information reported to or otherwise obtained by him, pursuant to subsection (a) or (b), which concerns any information which contains or relates to a trade secret or other matter referred to in section 1905 of title 18 of the United States Code, except that such information may be disclosed to other officers or employees of the Department and of other agencies concerned with carrying out this subchapter or when relevant in any proceeding under this subchapter. Nothing in this section shall authorize the withholding of information by the Secretary, or by any officers or employees under his control, from the duly authorized committees of the Congress.

(f) The Secretary may by regulation (1) require dealers and distributors of electronic products, to which there are applicable standards prescribed under this subchapter and the retail prices of which is not less than $50, to furnish manufacturers of such products such information as may be necessary to identify and locate, for purposes of section 535, the first purchasers of such products for purposes other than resale, and (2) require manufacturers to preserve such information. Any regulation establishing a requirement pursuant to clause (1) of the preceding sentence shall (A) authorize such dealers and distributors to elect, in lieu of immediately furnishing such information to the manufacturer, to hold and preserve such information until advised by the manufacturer or Secretary that such information is needed by the manufacturer for purposes of section 535, and (B) provide that the dealer or distributor shall, upon making such election, give prompt notice of such election (together with information identifying the notifier and the product) to the manufacturer and shall, when advised by the manufacturer or Secretary, of the need therefor for the purposes of section 535, immediately furnish the manufacturer with the required information. If a dealer or distributor discontinues the dealing in or distribution of electronic products, he shall turn the information over to the manufacturer. Any manufacturer receiving information pursuant to this subsection concerning first purchasers of products for purposes other than resale shall treat it as confidential and may use it only if necessary for the purpose of notifying persons pursuant to section 535(a).

SEC. 538 [21 U.S.C. § 360oo]. PROHIBITED ACTS.

(a) It shall be unlawful—

(1) for any manufacturer to introduce, or to deliver for introduction, into commerce, or to import into the United States, any electronic product which does not comply with an applicable standard prescribed pursuant to section 534;

(2) for any person to fail to furnish any notification or other material or information required by section 535 or 537; or to fail to comply with the requirements of section 535;

(3) for any person to fail or to refuse to establish or maintain records required by this subchapter or to permit access by the Secretary or any of his duly authorized representatives to, or the copying of, such records, or to permit entry or inspection, as required by or pursuant to section 537;

(4) for any person to fail or to refuse to make any report required pursuant to section 537(b) or to furnish or preserve any information required pursuant to section 537(f); or

(5) for any person (A) to fail to issue a certification as required by section 534(h), or (B) to issue such a certification when such certification is not based upon a test or testing program meeting the requirements of section 534(h) or when the issuer, in the exercise of due care, would have reason to know that such certification is false or misleading in a material respect.

(b) The Secretary may exempt any electronic product, or class thereof, from all or part of subsection (a), upon such conditions as he may find necessary to protect the public health or welfare, for the purpose of research, investigations, studies, demonstrations, or training, or for reasons of national security.

SEC. 539 [21 U.S.C. § 360pp]. ENFORCEMENT.

(a) The district courts of the United States shall have jurisdiction, for cause shown, to restrain violations of section 538 and to restrain dealers and distributors of electronic products from selling or otherwise disposing of electronic products which do not conform to an applicable standard prescribed pursuant to section 534 except when such products are disposed of by returning them to the distributor or manufacturer from whom they were obtained. The district courts of the United States shall also have jurisdiction in accordance with section 1355 of title 28 of the United States Code to enforce the provisions of subsection (b) of this section.

(b) (1) Any person who violates section 538 shall be subject to a civil penalty of not more than $1,000. For purposes of this subsection, any such violation shall with respect to each electronic product involved, or with respect to each act or omission made unlawful by section 538, constitute a separate violation, except that the maximum civil penalty imposed on any person under this subsection for any related series of violations shall not exceed $300,000.

(2) Any such civil penalty may on application be remitted or mitigated by the Secretary. In determining the amount of such penalty, or whether it should be remitted or mitigated and in what amount, the appropriateness of such penalty to the size of the business of the person charged and the gravity of the violation shall be considered. The amount of such penalty, when finally determined, may be deducted from any sums owing by the United States to the person charged.

(c) Actions under subsections (a) and (b) may be brought in the district court of the United States for the district wherein any act or omission or transaction constituting the violation occurred, or in such court for the district where the defendant is found or transacts business, and process in such cases may be served in any other district of which the defendant is an inhabitant or wherever the defendant may be found.

(d) Nothing in this subchapter shall be construed as requiring the Secretary to report for the institution of proceedings minor violations of this subchapter whenever he believes that the public interest will be adequately served by a suitable written notice or warning.

(e) Except as provided in the first sentence of section 542, compliance with this subchapter or any regulations issued thereunder shall not relieve any person from liability at common law or under statutory law.

(f) The remedies provided for in this subchapter shall be in addition to and not in substitution for any other remedies provided by law.

SEC. 540 [21 U.S.C. § 360qq]. ANNUAL REPORT.

(a) The Secretary shall prepare and submit to the President for transmittal to the Congress on or before April 1 of each year a comprehensive report on the administration of this part for the preceding calendar year. Such report shall include—

(1) a thorough appraisal (including statistical analyses, estimates, and long-term projections) of the incidence of biological injury and effects, including genetic effects, to the population resulting from exposure to

electronic product radiation, with a breakdown, insofar as practicable, among the various sources of such radiation;

(2) a list of Federal electronic product radiation control standards prescribed or in effect in such year, with identification of standards newly prescribed during such year;

(3) an evaluation of the degree of observance of applicable standards, including a list of enforcement actions, court decisions, and compromises of alleged violations by location and company name;

(4) a summary of outstanding problems confronting the administration of this part in order of priority;

(5) an analysis and evaluation of research activities completed as a result of Government and private sponsorship, and technological progress for safety achieved during such year;

(6) a list, with a brief statement of the issues, of completed or pending judicial actions under this subchapter;

(7) the extent to which technical information was disseminated to the scientific, commercial, and labor community and consumer-oriented information was made available to the public; and

(8) the extent of cooperation between Government officials and representatives of industry and other interested parties in the implementation of this subchapter including a log or summary of meetings held between Government officials and representatives of industry and other interested parties.

(b) The report required by subsection (a) shall contain such recommendations for additional legislation as the Secretary deems necessary to promote cooperation among the several States in the improvement of electronic product radiation control and to strengthen the national electronic product radiation control program.

SEC. 541 [21 U.S.C. § 360rr]. FEDERAL–STATE COOPERATION.

The Secretary is authorized (1) to accept from State and local authorities engaged in activities related to health or safety or consumer protection, on a reimbursable basis or otherwise, any assistance in the administration and enforcement of this subchapter which he may request and which they may be able and willing to provide and, if so agreed, may pay in advance or otherwise for the reasonable cost of such assistance, and (2) he may, for the purpose of conducting examinations, investigations, and inspections, commission any officer or employee of any such authority as an officer of the Department.

SEC. 542 [21 U.S.C. § 360ss]. STATE STANDARDS.

Whenever any standard prescribed pursuant to section 534 with respect to an aspect of performance of an electronic product is in effect, no State or political subdivision of a State shall have any authority either to establish, or to continue in effect, any standard which is applicable to the same aspect of performance of such product and which is not identical to the Federal standard. Nothing in this subchapter shall be construed to prevent the Federal Government or the government of any State or political subdivision thereof from establishing a requirement with respect to emission of radiation from electronic products procured for its own use if such requirement imposes a more restrictive standard than that required to comply with the otherwise applicable Federal standard.

DISSEMINATION OF TREATMENT INFORMATION

SEC. 551 [21 U.S.C. § 360aaa]. REQUIREMENTS FOR DISSEMINATION OF TREATMENT INFORMATION ON DRUGS OR DEVICES.

(a) IN GENERAL.—Notwithstanding sections 301(d), 502(f), and 505, and section 351 of the Public Health Service Act (42 U.S.C. § 262), a manufacturer may disseminate to—(1) a health care practitioner; (2) a pharmacy benefit manager; (3) a health insurance issuer; (4) a group health plan; or (5) a Federal or State governmental agency; written information concerning the safety, effectiveness, or benefit of a use not described in the approved labeling of a drug or device if the manufacturer meets the requirements of subsection (b).

(b) SPECIFIC REQUIREMENTS.—A manufacturer may disseminate information under subsection (a) on a new use only if—

(1) (A) in the case of a drug, there is in effect for the drug an application filed under subsection (b) or (j) of section 505 or a biologics license issued under section 351 of the Public Health Service Act; or

(B) in the case of a device, the device is being commercially distributed in accordance with a regulation under subsection (d) or (e) of section 513, an order under subsection (f) of such section, or the approval of an application under section 515;

(2) the information meets the requirements of section 552;

(3) the information to be disseminated is not derived from clinical research conducted by another manufacturer or if it was derived from research conducted by another manufacturer, the manufacturer disseminating the information has the permission of such other manufacturer to make the dissemination;

(4) the manufacturer has, 60 days before such dissemination, submitted to the Secretary—(A) a copy of the information to be disseminated; and (B) any clinical trial information the manufacturer has relating to the safety or effectiveness of the new use, any reports of clinical experience pertinent to the safety of the new use, and a summary of such information;

(5) the manufacturer has complied with the requirements of section 554 (relating to a supplemental application for such use);

(6) the manufacturer includes along with the information to be disseminated under this subsection—

(A) a prominently displayed statement that discloses—

(i) that the information concerns a use of a drug or device that has not been approved or cleared by the Food and Drug Administration;

(ii) if applicable, that the information is being disseminated at the expense of the manufacturer;

(iii) if applicable, the name of any authors of the information who are employees of, consultants to, or have received compensation from, the manufacturer, or who have a significant financial interest in the manufacturer;

(iv) the official labeling for the drug or device and all updates with respect to the labeling;

(v) if applicable, a statement that there are products or treatments that have been approved or cleared for the use that is the subject of the information being disseminated pursuant to subsection (a)(1); and

(vi) the identification of any person that has provided funding for the conduct of a study relating to the new use of a drug or device for which such information is being disseminated; and

(B) a bibliography of other articles from a scientific reference publication or scientific or medical journal that have been previously published about the use of the drug or device covered by the information disseminated (unless the information already includes such bibliography).

(c) ADDITIONAL INFORMATION.—If the Secretary determines, after providing notice of such determination and an opportunity for a meeting with respect to such determination, that the information submitted by a manufacturer under subsection (b)(3)(B), with respect to the use of a drug or device for which the manufacturer intends to disseminate information, fails to provide data, analyses, or other written matter that is objective and balanced, the Secretary may require the manufacturer to disseminate—

(1) additional objective and scientifically sound information that pertains to the safety or effectiveness of the use and is necessary to provide objectivity and balance, including any information that the manufacturer has submitted to the Secretary or, where appropriate, a summary of such information or any other information that the Secretary has authority to make available to the public; and

(2) an objective statement of the Secretary, based on data or other scientifically sound information available to the Secretary, that bears on the safety or effectiveness of the new use of the drug or device.

SEC. 552 [21 U.S.C. § 360aaa–1]. INFORMATION AUTHORIZED TO BE DISSEMINATED.

(a) AUTHORIZED INFORMATION.—A manufacturer may disseminate information under section 551 on a new use only if the information—

(1) is in the form of an unabridged—

(A) reprint or copy of an article, peer-reviewed by experts qualified by scientific training or experience to evaluate the safety or effectiveness of the drug or device involved, which was published in a scientific or medical journal (as defined in section 556(5)), which is about a clinical investigation with respect to the drug or device, and which would be considered to be scientifically sound by such experts; or

(B) reference publication, described in subsection (b), that includes information about a clinical investigation with respect to the drug or device that would be considered to be scientifically sound by experts qualified by scientific training or experience to evaluate the safety or effectiveness of the drug or device that is the subject of such a clinical investigation; and

(2) is not false or misleading and would not pose a significant risk to the public health.

(b) REFERENCE PUBLICATION.—A reference publication referred to in subsection (a)(1)(B) is a publication that—

(1) has not been written, edited, excerpted, or published specifically for, or at the request of, a manufacturer of a drug or device;

(2) has not been edited or significantly influenced by such a manufacturer;

(3) is not solely distributed through such a manufacturer but is generally available in bookstores or other distribution channels where medical textbooks are sold;

(4) does not focus on any particular drug or device of a manufacturer that disseminates information under section 551 and does not have a primary focus on new uses of drugs or devices that are marketed or under investigation by a manufacturer supporting the dissemination of information; and

(5) presents materials that are not false or misleading.

SEC. 553 [21 U.S.C. § 360aaa–2]. ESTABLISHMENT OF LISTS.

(a) IN GENERAL.—A manufacturer may disseminate information under section 551 on a new use only if the manufacturer prepares and submits to the Secretary biannually—

(1) a list containing the titles of the articles and reference publications relating to the new use of drugs or devices that were disseminated by the manufacturer to a person described in section 551(a) for the 6–month period preceding the date on which the manufacturer submits the list to the Secretary; and

(2) a list that identifies the categories of providers (as described in section 551(a)) that received the articles and reference publications for the 6–month period described in paragraph (1).

(b) RECORDS.—A manufacturer that disseminates information under section 551 shall keep records that may be used by the manufacturer when, pursuant to section 555, such manufacturer is required to take corrective action and shall be made available to the Secretary, upon request, for purposes of ensuring or taking corrective action pursuant to such section. Such records, at the Secretary's discretion, may identify the recipient of information provided pursuant to section 551 or the categories of such recipients.

SEC. 554 [21 U.S.C. § 360aaa–3]. REQUIREMENT REGARDING SUB-MISSION OF SUPPLEMENTAL APPLICATION FOR NEW USE; EXEMPTION FROM REQUIREMENT.

(a) IN GENERAL.—A manufacturer may disseminate information under section 551 on a new use only if—

(1)(A) the manufacturer has submitted to the Secretary a supplemental application for such use; or

(B) the manufacturer meets the condition described in subsection (b) or (c) (relating to a certification that the manufacturer will submit such an application); or

(2) there is in effect for the manufacturer an exemption under subsection (d) from the requirement of paragraph (1).

(b) CERTIFICATION ON SUPPLEMENTAL APPLICATION; CONDITION IN CASE OF COMPLETED STUDIES.—For purposes of subsection (a)(1)(B), a manufacturer may disseminate information on a new use if the manufacturer has submitted to the Secretary an application containing a certification that—

(1) the studies needed for the submission of a supplemental application for the new use have been completed; and

(2) the supplemental application will be submitted to the Secretary not later than 6 months after the date of the initial dissemination of information under section 551.

(c) CERTIFICATION ON SUPPLEMENTAL APPLICATION; CONDITION IN CASE OF PLANNED STUDIES.

(1) IN GENERAL.—For purposes of subsection (a)(1)(B), a manufacturer may disseminate information on a new use if—

(A) the manufacturer has submitted to the Secretary an application containing—

(i) a proposed protocol and schedule for conducting the studies needed for the submission of a supplemental application for the new use; and

(ii) a certification that the supplemental application will be submitted to the Secretary not later than 36 months after the date of the initial dissemination of information under section 551 (or, as applicable, not later than such date as the Secretary may specify pursuant to an extension under paragraph (3)); and

(B) the Secretary has determined that the proposed protocol is adequate and that the schedule for completing such studies is reasonable.

(2) PROGRESS REPORTS ON STUDIES.—A manufacturer that submits to the Secretary an application under paragraph (1) shall submit to the Secretary periodic reports describing the status of the studies involved.

(3) EXTENSION OF TIME REGARDING PLANNED STUDIES.— The period of 36 months authorized in paragraph (1)(A)(ii) for the completion of studies may be extended by the Secretary if—

(A) the Secretary determines that the studies needed to submit such an application cannot be completed and submitted within 36 months; or

(B) the manufacturer involved submits to the Secretary a written request for the extension and the Secretary determines that the manufacturer has acted with due diligence to conduct the studies in a timely manner, except that an extension under this subparagraph may not be provided for more than 24 additional months.

(d) EXEMPTION FROM REQUIREMENT OF SUPPLEMENTAL APPLICATION.

(1) IN GENERAL.—For purposes of subsection (a)(2), a manufacturer may disseminate information on a new use if—

(A) the manufacturer has submitted to the Secretary an application for an exemption from meeting the requirement of subsection (a)(1); and

(B) (i) the Secretary has approved the application in accordance with paragraph (2); or

(ii) the application is deemed under paragraph (3)(A) to have been approved (unless such approval is terminated pursuant to paragraph (3)(B)).

(2) CONDITIONS FOR APPROVAL.—The Secretary may approve an application under paragraph (1) for an exemption if the Secretary makes a determination described in subparagraph (A) or (B), as follows:

(A) The Secretary makes a determination that, for reasons defined by the Secretary, it would be economically prohibitive with respect to such drug or device for the manufacturer to incur the costs necessary for the submission of a supplemental application. In making such determination, the Secretary shall consider (in addition to any other considerations the Secretary finds appropriate)—

(i) the lack of the availability under law of any period during which the manufacturer would have exclusive marketing rights with respect to the new use involved; and

(ii) the size of the population expected to benefit from approval of the supplemental application.

(B) The Secretary makes a determination that, for reasons defined by the Secretary, it would be unethical to conduct the studies necessary for the supplemental application. In making such determination, the

Secretary shall consider (in addition to any other considerations the Secretary finds appropriate) whether the new use involved is the standard of medical care for a health condition.

(3) TIME FOR CONSIDERATION OF APPLICATION; DEEMED APPROVAL.

(A) IN GENERAL.—The Secretary shall approve or deny an application under paragraph (1) for an exemption not later than 60 days after the receipt of the application. If the Secretary does not comply with the preceding sentence, the application is deemed to be approved.

(B) TERMINATION OF DEEMED APPROVAL.—If pursuant to a deemed approval under subparagraph (A) a manufacturer disseminates written information under section 551 on a new use, the Secretary may at any time terminate such approval and under section 555(b)(3) order the manufacturer to cease disseminating the information.

(e) REQUIREMENTS REGARDING APPLICATIONS.—Applications under this section shall be submitted in the form and manner prescribed by the Secretary.

SEC. 555 [21 U.S.C. § 360aaa–4]. CORRECTIVE ACTIONS; CESSATION OF DISSEMINATION.

(a) POSTDISSEMINATION DATA REGARDING SAFETY AND EFFECTIVENESS.

(1) CORRECTIVE ACTIONS.—With respect to data received by the Secretary after the dissemination of information under section 551 by a manufacturer has begun (whether received pursuant to paragraph (2) or otherwise), if the Secretary determines that the data indicate that the new use involved may not be effective or may present a significant risk to public health, the Secretary shall, after consultation with the manufacturer, take such action regarding the dissemination of the information as the Secretary determines to be appropriate for the protection of the public health, which may include ordering that the manufacturer cease the dissemination of the information.

(2) RESPONSIBILITIES OF MANUFACTURERS TO SUBMIT DATA.—After a manufacturer disseminates information under section 551, the manufacturer shall submit to the Secretary a notification of any additional knowledge of the manufacturer on clinical research or other data that relate to the safety or effectiveness of the new use involved. If the manufacturer is in possession of the data, the notification shall include the data. The Secretary shall by regulation establish the scope of the responsibilities of manufacturers under this paragraph, including such limits on the responsibilities as the Secretary determines to be appropriate.

(b) CESSATION OF DISSEMINATION.

(1) FAILURE OF MANUFACTURER TO COMPLY WITH REQUIREMENTS.—The Secretary may order a manufacturer to cease the dissemination of information pursuant to section 551 if the Secretary determines that

the information being disseminated does not comply with the requirements established in this subchapter. Such an order may be issued only after the Secretary has provided notice to the manufacturer of the intent of the Secretary to issue the order and (unless paragraph (2)(B) applies) has provided an opportunity for a meeting with respect to such intent. If the failure of the manufacturer constitutes a minor violation of this subchapter, the Secretary shall delay issuing the order and provide to the manufacturer an opportunity to correct the violation.

(2) SUPPLEMENTAL APPLICATIONS.—The Secretary may order a manufacturer to cease the dissemination of information pursuant to section 551 if—

(A) in the case of a manufacturer that has submitted a supplemental application for a new use pursuant to section 554(a)(1), the Secretary determines that the supplemental application does not contain adequate information for approval of the new use for which the application was submitted;

(B) in the case of a manufacturer that has submitted a certification under section 554(b), the manufacturer has not, within the 6–month period involved, submitted the supplemental application referred to in the certification; or

(C) in the case of a manufacturer that has submitted a certification under section 554(c) but has not yet submitted the supplemental application referred to in the certification, the Secretary determines, after an informal hearing, that the manufacturer is not acting with due diligence to complete the studies involved.

(3) TERMINATION OF DEEMED APPROVAL OF EXEMPTION RE-GARDING SUPPLEMENTAL APPLICATIONS.—If under section 554(d)(3) the Secretary terminates a deemed approval of an exemption, the Secretary may order the manufacturer involved to cease, disseminating the information. A manufacturer shall comply with an order under the preceding sentence not later than 60 days after the receipt of the order.

(c) CORRECTIVE ACTIONS BY MANUFACTURERS.

(1) IN GENERAL.—In any case in which under this section the Secretary orders a manufacturer to cease disseminating information, the Secretary may order the manufacturer to take action to correct the information that has been disseminated, except as provided in paragraph (2).

(2) TERMINATION OF DEEMED APPROVAL OF EXEMPTION RE-GARDING SUPPLEMENTAL APPLICATIONS.—In the case of an order under subsection (b)(3) to cease disseminating information, the Secretary may not order the manufacturer involved to take action to correct the information that has been disseminated unless the Secretary determines that the new use described in the information would pose a significant risk to the public health.

SEC. 556 [21 U.S.C. § 360aaa–5]. DEFINITIONS.

For purposes of this subchapter:

(1) The term "health care practitioner" means a physician, or other individual who is a provider of health care, who is licensed under the law of a State to prescribe drugs or devices.

(2) The terms "health insurance issuer" and "group health plan" have the meaning given such terms under section 2791 of the Public Health Service Act.

(3) The term "manufacturer" means a person who manufactures a drug or device, or who is licensed by such person to distribute or market the drug or device.

(4) The term "new use"—(A) with respect to a drug, means a use that is not included in the labeling of the approved drug; and (B) with respect to a device, means a use that is not included in the labeling for the approved or cleared device.

(5) The term "scientific or medical journal" means a scientific or medical publication—

(A) that is published by an organization—

(i) that has an editorial board;

(ii) that utilizes experts, who have demonstrated expertise in the subject of an article under review by the organization and who are independent of the organization, to review and objectively select, reject, or provide comments about proposed articles; and

(iii) that has a publicly stated policy, to which the organization adheres, of full disclosure of any conflict of interest or biases for all authors or contributors involved with the journal or organization;

(B) whose articles are peer-reviewed and published in accordance with the regular peer-review procedures of the organization;

(C) that is generally recognized to be of national scope and reputation;

(D) that is indexed in the Index Medicus of the National Library of Medicine of the National Institutes of Health; and

(E) that is not in the form of a special supplement that has been funded in whole or in part by one or more manufacturers.

SEC. 557 [21 U.S.C. § 360aaa–6]. RULES OF CONSTRUCTION.

(a) UNSOLICITED REQUEST.—Nothing in section 551 shall be construed as prohibiting a manufacturer from disseminating information in response to an unsolicited request from a health care practitioner.

(b) DISSEMINATION OF INFORMATION ON DRUGS OR DEVICES NOT EVIDENCE OF INTENDED USE.—Notwithstanding subsection (a), (f), or (o) of section 502, or any other provision of law, the dissemination of information relating to a new use of a drug or device, in accordance with section 551, shall not be construed by the Secretary as evidence of a new intended use of the drug or device that is different from the intended use of the drug or device set forth in the official labeling of the drug or device. Such dissemination shall not be considered by the Secretary as labeling, adulteration, or misbranding of the drug or device.

(c) PATENT PROTECTION.—Nothing in section 551 shall affect patent rights in any manner.

(d) AUTHORIZATION FOR DISSEMINATION OF ARTICLES AND FEES FOR REPRINTS OF ARTICLES.—Nothing in section 551 shall be construed as prohibiting an entity that publishes a scientific journal (as defined in section 556(5)) from requiring authorization from the entity to disseminate an article published by such entity or charging fees for the purchase of reprints of published articles from such entity.

GENERAL PROVISIONS RELATING TO DRUGS AND DEVICES

SEC. 561 [21 U.S.C. § 360bbb]. EXPANDED ACCESS TO UNAPPROVED THERAPIES.

(a) EMERGENCY SITUATIONS.—The Secretary may, under appropriate conditions determined by the Secretary, authorize the shipment of investigational drugs or investigational devices for the diagnosis, monitoring, or treatment of a serious disease or condition in emergency situations.

(b) INDIVIDUAL PATIENT ACCESS TO INVESTIGATIONAL PRODUCTS INTENDED FOR SERIOUS DISEASES.—Any person, acting through a physician licensed in accordance with State law, may request from a manufacturer or distributor, and any manufacturer or distributor may, after complying with the provisions of this subsection, provide to such physician an investigational drug or investigational device for the diagnosis, monitoring, or treatment of a serious disease or condition if—

(1) the licensed physician determines that the person has no comparable or satisfactory alternative therapy available to diagnose, monitor, or treat the disease or condition involved, and that the probable risk to the person from the investigational drug or investigational device is not greater than the probable risk from the disease or condition;

(2) the Secretary determines that there is sufficient evidence of safety and effectiveness to support the use of the investigational drug or investigational device in the case described in paragraph (1);

(3) the Secretary determines that provision of the investigational drug or investigational device will not interfere with the initiation, conduct, or completion of clinical investigations to support marketing approval; and

(4) the sponsor, or clinical investigator, of the investigational drug or investigational device submits to the Secretary a clinical protocol consistent with the provisions of section 505(i) or 520(g), including any regulations promulgated under section 505(i) or 520(g), describing the use of the investigational drug or investigational device in a single patient or a small group of patients.

(c) TREATMENT INVESTIGATIONAL NEW DRUG APPLICATIONS AND TREATMENT INVESTIGATIONAL DEVICE EXEMPTIONS.— Upon submission by a sponsor or a physician of a protocol intended to provide widespread access to an investigational drug or investigational device for eligible patients (referred to in this subsection as an "expanded access protocol"), the Secretary shall permit such investigational drug or investigational device to be made available for expanded access under a treatment investigational new drug application or treatment investigational device exemption if the Secretary determines that—

(1) under the treatment investigational new drug application or treatment investigational device exemption, the investigational drug or investigational device is intended for use in the diagnosis, monitoring, or treatment of a serious or immediately life-threatening disease or condition;

(2) there is no comparable or satisfactory alternative therapy available to diagnose, monitor, or treat that stage of disease or condition in the population of patients to which the investigational drug or investigational device is intended to be administered;

(3)(A) the investigational drug or investigational device is under investigation in a controlled clinical trial for the use described in paragraph (1) under an investigational drug application in effect under section 505(i) or investigational device exemption in effect under section 520(g); or (B) all clinical trials necessary for approval of that use of the investigational drug or investigational device have been completed;

(4) the sponsor of the controlled clinical trials is actively pursuing marketing approval of the investigational drug or investigational device for the use described in paragraph (1) with due diligence;

(5) in the case of an investigational drug or investigational device described in paragraph (3)(A), the provision of the investigational drug or investigational device will not interfere with the enrollment of patients in ongoing clinical investigations under section 505(i) or 520(g);

(6) in the case of serious diseases, there is sufficient evidence of safety and effectiveness to support the use described in paragraph (1); and

(7) in the case of immediately life-threatening diseases, the available scientific evidence, taken as a whole, provides a reasonable basis to conclude that the investigational drug or investigational device may be effective for its intended use and would not expose patients to an unreasonable and significant risk of illness or injury.

A protocol submitted under this subsection shall be subject to the provisions of section 505(i) or 520(g), including regulations promulgated under section 505(i) or 520(g). The Secretary may inform national, State, and local medical associations and societies, voluntary health associations, and other appropriate persons about the availability of an investigational drug or investigational device under expanded access protocols submitted under this subsection. The information provided by the Secretary, in accordance with the preceding sentence, shall be the same type of information that is required by section 402(j)(3) of the Public Health Service Act.

(d) TERMINATION.—The Secretary may, at any time, with respect to a sponsor, physician, manufacturer, or distributor described in this section, terminate expanded access provided under this section for an investigational drug or investigational device if the requirements under this section are no longer met.

(e) DEFINITIONS.—In this section, the terms "investigational drug", "investigational device", "treatment investigational new drug application", and "treatment investigational device exemption" shall have the meanings given the terms in regulations prescribed by the Secretary.

SEC. 562 [21 U.S.C. § 360bbb–1]. DISPUTE RESOLUTION.

If, regarding an obligation concerning drugs or devices under this Act or section 351 of the Public Health Service Act, there is a scientific controversy between the Secretary and a person who is a sponsor, applicant, or manufacturer and no specific provision of the Act involved, including a regulation promulgated under such Act, provides a right of review of the matter in controversy, the Secretary shall, by regulation, establish a procedure under which such sponsor, applicant, or manufacturer may request a review of such controversy, including a review by an appropriate scientific advisory panel described in section 505(n) or an advisory committee described in section 515(g)(2)(B). Any such review shall take place in a timely manner. The Secretary shall promulgate such regulations within 1 year after the date of the enactment of the Food and Drug Administration Modernization Act of 1997.

SEC. 563 [21 U.S.C. § 360bbb–2]. CLASSIFICATION OF PRODUCTS.

(a) REQUEST.—A person who submits an application or submission (including a petition, notification, and any other similar form of request) under this Act for a product, may submit a request to the Secretary respecting the classification of the product as a drug, biological product, device, or a combination product subject to section 503(g) or respecting the component of the Food and Drug Administration that will regulate the product. In submitting the request, the person shall recommend a classification for the product, or a component to regulate the product.

(b) STATEMENT.—Not later than 60 days after the receipt of the request described in subsection (a), the Secretary shall determine the classification of the product under subsection (a), or the component of the Food and Drug Administration that will regulate the product, and shall provide to the person a written statement that identifies such classification or such component, and the reasons for such determination. The Secretary may not modify such statement except with the written consent of the person, or for public health reasons based on scientific evidence.

(c) INACTION OF SECRETARY.—If the Secretary does not provide the statement within the 60–day period described in subsection (b), the recommendation made by the person under subsection (a) shall be considered to be a final determination by the Secretary of such classification of the product, or the component of the Food and Drug Administration that will regulate the product, as applicable, and may not be modified by the Secretary except with the written consent of the person, or for public health reasons based on scientific evidence.

GENERAL ADMINISTRATIVE PROVISIONS, etc.

SEC. 701 [21 U.S.C. § 371]. REGULATIONS AND HEARINGS.

(a) The authority to promulgate regulations for the efficient enforcement of this Act, except as otherwise provided in this section, is vested in the Secretary.

(b) The Secretary of the Treasury and the Secretary of Health and Human Services shall jointly prescribe regulations for the efficient enforcement of the provisions of section 801, except as otherwise provided therein. Such regulations shall be promulgated in such manner and take effect at such time, after due notice, as the Secretary of Health and Human Services shall determine.

(c) Hearings authorized or required by this Act shall be conducted by the Secretary or such officer or employee as he may designate for the purpose.

(d) The definitions and standards of identity promulgated in accordance with the provisions of this Act shall be effective for the purposes of the enforcement of this Act, notwithstanding such definitions and standards as may be contained in other laws of the United States and regulations promulgated thereunder.

(e) (1) Any action for the issuance, amendment, or repeal of any regulation under section 403(j), 404(a), 406, 501(b), or 502(d) or (h) of this Act * * * shall be begun by a proposal made (A) by the Secretary on his own initiative, or (B) by petition of any interested person, showing reasonable grounds therefor, filed with the Secretary. The Secretary shall publish such proposal and shall afford all interested persons an opportunity to present their views thereon, orally or in writing. As soon as practicable thereafter, the Secretary shall by order act upon such proposal and shall make such order public. Except as provided in paragraph (2), the order shall become effective at such time as may be specified therein, but not prior to the day following the last day on which objections may be filed under such paragraph.

(2) On or before the thirtieth day after the date on which an order entered under paragraph (1) is made public, any person who will be adversely affected by such order if placed in effect may file objections thereto with the Secretary, specifying with particularity the provisions of the order deemed objectionable, stating the grounds therefor, and requesting a public hearing upon such objections. Until final action upon such objections is taken by the Secretary under paragraph (3), the filing of such objections shall operate to stay the effectiveness of those provisions of the order to which the objections are made. As soon as practicable after the time for filing objections has expired the Secretary shall publish a notice in the Federal Register specifying those parts of the order which have been

stayed by the filing of objections and, if no objections have been filed, stating that fact.

(3) As soon as practicable after such request for a public hearing, the Secretary, after due notice, shall hold such a public hearing for the purpose of receiving evidence relevant and material to the issues raised by such objections. At the hearing, any interested person may be heard in person or by representative. As soon as practicable after completion of the hearing, the Secretary shall by order act upon such objections and make such order public. Such order shall be based only on substantial evidence of record at such hearing and shall set forth, as part of the order, detailed findings of fact on which the order is based. The Secretary shall specify in the order the date on which it shall take effect, except that it shall not be made to take effect prior to the ninetieth day after its publication unless the Secretary finds that emergency conditions exist necessitating an earlier effective date, in which event the Secretary shall specify in the order his findings as to such conditions.

(f) (1) In a case of actual controversy as to the validity of any order under subsection (e), any person who will be adversely affected by such order if placed in effect may at any time prior to the ninetieth day after such order is issued file a petition with the Circuit Court of Appeals of the United States for the circuit wherein such person resides or has his principal place of business, for a judicial review of such order. A copy of the petition shall be forthwith transmitted by the clerk of the court to the Secretary or other officer designated by him for that purpose. The Secretary thereupon shall file in the court the record of the proceedings on which the Secretary based his order, as provided in section 2112 of title 28, U.S. Code.

(2) If the petitioner applies to the court for leave to adduce additional evidence, and shows to the satisfaction of the court that such additional evidence is material and that there were reasonable grounds for the failure to adduce such evidence in the proceeding before the Secretary, the court may order such additional evidence (and evidence in rebuttal thereof) to be taken before the Secretary, and to be adduced upon the hearing, in such manner and upon such terms and conditions as to the court may seem proper. The Secretary may modify his findings as to the facts, or make new findings, by reason of the additional evidence so taken, and he shall file such modified or new findings, and his recommendation, if any, for the modification or setting aside of his original order, with the return of such additional evidence.

(3) Upon the filing of the petition referred to in paragraph (1) of this subsection, the court shall have jurisdiction to affirm the order, or to set it aside in whole or in part, temporarily or permanently. If the order of the Secretary refuses to issue, amend, or repeal a regulation and such order is not in accordance with law the court shall by its judgment order the Secretary to take action, with respect to such regulation, in accordance with law. The findings of the Secretary as to the facts, if supported by substantial evidence, shall be conclusive.

(4) The judgment of the court affirming or setting aside, in whole or in part, any such order of the Secretary shall be final, subject to review by the Supreme Court of the United States upon certiorari or certification as provided in section 1254 of title 28, United States Code.

(5) Any action instituted under this subsection shall survive notwithstanding any change in the person occupying the office of Secretary or any vacancy in such office.

(6) The remedies provided for in this subsection shall be in addition to and not in substitution for any other remedies provided by law.

(g) A certified copy of the transcript of the record and proceedings under subsection (e) shall be furnished by the Secretary to any interested party at his request, and payment of the costs thereof, and shall be admissible in any criminal libel for condemnation, exclusion of imports, or other proceeding arising under or in respect to this Act, irrespective of whether proceedings with respect to the order have previously been instituted or become final under subsection (f).

(h) (1)(A) The Secretary shall develop guidance documents with public participation and ensure that information identifying the existence of such documents and the documents themselves are made available to the public both in written form and, as feasible, through electronic means. Such documents shall not create or confer any rights for or on any person, although they present the views of the Secretary on matters under the jurisdiction of the Food and Drug Administration.

(B) Although guidance documents shall not be binding on the Secretary, the Secretary shall ensure that employees of the Food and Drug Administration do not deviate from such guidances without appropriate justification and supervisory concurrence. The Secretary shall provide training to employees in how to develop and use guidance documents and shall monitor the development and issuance of such documents.

(C) For guidance documents that set forth initial interpretations of a statute or regulation, changes in interpretation or policy that are of more than a minor nature, complex scientific issues, or highly controversial issues, the Secretary shall ensure public participation prior to implementation of guidance documents, unless the Secretary determines that such prior public participation is not feasible or appropriate. In such cases, the Secretary shall provide for public comment upon implementation and take such comment into account.

(D) For guidance documents that set forth existing practices or minor changes in policy, the Secretary shall provide for public comment upon implementation.

(2) In developing guidance documents, the Secretary shall ensure uniform nomenclature for such documents and uniform internal procedures for approval of such documents. The Secretary shall ensure that guidance documents and revisions of such documents are properly dated and indicate the nonbinding nature of the documents. The Secretary shall periodically

review all guidance documents and, where appropriate revise such documents.

(3) The Secretary, acting through the Commissioner, shall maintain electronically and update and publish periodically in the Federal Register a list of guidance documents. All such documents shall be made available to the public.

(4) The Secretary shall ensure that an effective appeals mechanism is in place to address complaints that the Food and Drug Administration is not developing and using guidance documents in accordance with this subsection.

(5) Not later than July 1, 2000, the Secretary after evaluating the effectiveness of the Good Guidance Practices document, published in the Federal Register at 62 Fed. Reg. 8961, shall promulgate a regulation consistent with this subsection specifying the policies and procedures of the Food and Drug Administration for the development, issuance, and use of guidance documents.

SEC. 702 [21 U.S.C. § 372]. EXAMINATIONS AND INVESTIGATIONS.

(a) The Secretary is authorized to conduct examinations and investigations for the purposes of this Act through officers and employees of the Department or through any health, food, or drug officer or employee of any State, Territory, or political subdivision thereof, duly commissioned by the Secretary as an officer of the Department. In the case of food packed in the Commonwealth of Puerto Rico or a Territory the Secretary shall attempt to make inspection of such food at the first point of entry within the United States when, in his opinion and with due regard to the enforcement of all the provisions of this Act, the facilities at his disposal will permit of such inspection. For the purposes of this subsection the term "United States" means the States and the District of Columbia.

(b) Where a sample of a food, drug, or cosmetic is collected for analysis under this Act the Secretary shall, upon request, provide a part of such official sample for examination or analysis by any person named on the label of the article, or the owner thereof, or his attorney or agent; except that the Secretary is authorized, by regulations, to make such reasonable exceptions from, and impose such reasonable terms and conditions relating to, the operation of this subsection as he finds necessary for the proper administration of the provisions of this Act.

(c) For purposes of enforcement of this Act, records of any department or independent establishment in the executive branch of the Government shall be open to inspection by any official of the Department duly authorized by the Secretary to make such inspection.

(d) The Secretary is authorized and directed, upon request from the Under Secretary of Commerce for Intellectual Property and Director of the United States Patent and Trademark Office, to furnish full and complete information with respect to such questions relating to drugs as the Director may submit concerning any patent application. The Secretary is further authorized, upon receipt of any such request, to conduct or cause to be conducted, such research as may be required.

(e) Any officer or employee of the Department designated by the Secretary to conduct examinations, investigations, or inspections under this Act relating to counterfeit drugs may, when so authorized by the Secretary—

(1) carry firearms;

(2) execute and serve search warrants and arrest warrants;

(3) execute seizure by process issued pursuant to libel under section 304;

(4) make arrests without warrant for offenses under this Act with respect to such drugs if the offense is committed in his presence or, in the case of a felony, if he has probable cause to believe that the person so arrested has committed, or is committing, such offense; and

(5) make, prior to the institution of libel proceedings under section 304(a)(2), seizures of drugs or containers or of equipment, punches, dies, plates, stones, labeling, or other things, if they are, or he has reasonable grounds to believe that they are, subject to seizure and condemnation under such section 304(a)(2). In the event of seizure pursuant to this paragraph (5), libel proceedings under section 304(a)(2) shall be instituted promptly and the property seized be placed under the jurisdiction of the court.

SEC. 703 [21 U.S.C. § 373]. RECORDS OF INTERSTATE SHIPMENT.

For the purpose of enforcing the provisions of this Act, carriers engaged in interstate commerce, and persons receiving food, drugs, devices, or cosmetics in interstate commerce or holding such articles so received, shall, upon the request of an officer or employee duly designated by the Secretary, permit such officer or employee, at reasonable times, to have access to and to copy all records showing the movement in interstate commerce of any food, drug, device, or cosmetic, or the holding thereof during or after such movement, and the quantity, shipper, and consignee thereof; and it shall be unlawful for any such carrier or person to fail to permit such access to and copying of any such record so requested when such request is accompanied by a statement in writing specifying the nature or kind of food, drug, device, or cosmetic to which such request relates, except that evidence obtained under this section, or any evidence which is directly or indirectly derived from such evidence, shall not be used in a criminal prosecution of the person from whom obtained, and except that carriers shall not be subject to the other provisions of this Act by reason of their receipt, carriage, holding, or delivery of food, drugs, devices, or cosmetics in the usual course of business as carriers.

SEC. 704 [21 U.S.C. § 374]. FACTORY INSPECTION.

(a) (1) For purposes of enforcement of this Act, officers or employees duly designated by the Secretary, upon presenting appropriate credentials and a written notice to the owner, operator, or agent in charge, are authorized

(A) to enter, at reasonable times, any factory, warehouse, or establishment in which food, drugs, devices, or cosmetics are manufactured, processed, packed, or held, for introduction into interstate commerce or after such introduction, or to enter any vehicle being used to transport or hold such food, drugs, devices, or cosmetics in interstate commerce; and (B) to inspect, at reasonable times and within reasonable limits and in a reasonable manner, such factory, warehouse, establishment, or vehicle and all pertinent equipment, finished and unfinished materials, containers, and labeling therein. In the case of any factory, warehouse, establishment, or consulting laboratory in which prescription drugs, non-prescription drugs intended for human use, or restricted devices are manufactured, processed, packed, or held, the inspection shall extend to all things therein (including records, files, papers, processes, controls, and facilities) bearing on whether prescription drugs, non-prescription drugs intended for human use, or restricted devices which are adulterated or misbranded within the meaning of this Act, or which may not be manufactured, introduced into interstate commerce, or sold, or offered for sale by reason of any provision of this Act, have been or are being manufactured, processed, packed, transported, or held in any such place, or otherwise bearing on violation of this Act. No inspection authorized by the preceding sentence or by paragraph (3) shall extend to financial data, sales data other than shipment data, pricing data, personnel data (other than data as to qualification of technical and professional personnel performing functions subject to this Act), and research data (other than data relating to new drugs, antibiotic drugs, and devices and subject to reporting and inspection under regulations lawfully issued pursuant to section 505(i) or (k), section 519 or 520(g), and data relating to other drugs or devices which in the case of a new drug would be subject to reporting or inspection under lawful regulations issued pursuant to section 505(j)). A separate notice shall be given for each such inspection, but a notice shall not be required for each entry made during the period covered by the inspection. Each such inspection shall be commenced and completed with reasonable promptness.

(2) The provisions of the second sentence of paragraph (1) shall not apply to—

(A) pharmacies which maintain establishments in conformance with any applicable local laws regulating the practice of pharmacy and medicine and which are regularly engaged in dispensing prescription drugs or devices, upon prescriptions of practitioners licensed to administer such drugs or devices to patients under the care of such practitioners in the course of their professional practice, and which do not, either through a subsidiary or otherwise, manufacture, prepare, propagate, compound, or process drugs or devices for sale other than in the regular course of their business of dispensing or selling drugs or devices at retail;

(B) practitioners licensed by law to prescribe or administer drugs, or prescribe or use devices, as the case may be, and who manufacture, prepare, propagate, compound, or process drugs, or manufacture or process devices, solely for use in the course of their professional practice;

(C) persons who manufacture, prepare, propagate, compound, or process drugs or manufacture or process devices, solely for use in research, teaching, or chemical analysis and not for sale;

(D) such other classes of persons as the Secretary may by regulation exempt from the application of this section upon a finding that inspection as applied to such classes of persons in accordance with this section is not necessary for the protection of the public health. * * *

(b) Upon completion of any such inspection of a factory, warehouse, consulting laboratory, or other establishment, and prior to leaving the premises, the officer or employee making the inspection shall give to the owner, operator, or agent in charge a report in writing setting forth any conditions or practices observed by him which, in his judgment, indicate that any food, drug, device, or cosmetic in such establishment (1) consists in whole or in part of any filthy, putrid, or decomposed substance, or (2) has been prepared, packed, or held under insanitary conditions whereby it may have become contaminated with filth, or whereby it may have been rendered injurious to health. A copy of such report shall be sent promptly to the Secretary.

(c) If the officer or employee making any such inspection of a factory, warehouse, or other establishment has obtained any sample in the course of the inspection, upon completion of the inspection and prior to leaving the premises he shall give to the owner, operator, or agent in charge a receipt describing the samples obtained.

(d) Whenever in the course of any such inspection of a factory or other establishment where food is manufactured, processed, or packed, the officer or employee making the inspection obtains a sample of any such food, and an analysis is made of such sample for the purpose of ascertaining whether such food consists in whole or in part of any filthy, putrid, or decomposed substance, or is otherwise unfit for food, a copy of the results of such analysis shall be furnished promptly to the owner, operator, or agent in charge.

(e) Every person required under section 519 or 520(g) to maintain records and every person who is in charge or custody of such records shall, upon request of an officer or employee designated by the Secretary, permit such officer or employee at all reasonable times to have access to, and to copy and verify, such records.

(f) (1) A person accredited under section 523 to review reports made under section 510(k) and make recommendations of initial classifications of devices to the Secretary shall maintain records documenting the training qualifications of the person and the employees of the person, the procedures used by the person for handling confidential information, the compensation arrangements made by the person, and the procedures used by the person to identify and avoid conflicts of interest. Upon the request of an officer or employee designated by the Secretary, the person shall permit the officer or employee, at all reasonable times, to have access to, to copy, and to verify, the records.

(2) Within 15 days after the receipt of a written request from the Secretary to a person accredited under section 523 for copies of records described in paragraph (1), the person shall produce the copies of the records at the place designated by the Secretary.

SEC. 705 [21 U.S.C. § 375]. PUBLICITY.

(a) The Secretary shall cause to be published from time to time reports summarizing all judgments, decrees, and court orders which have been rendered under this Act, including the nature of the charge and the disposition thereof.

(b) The Secretary may also cause to be disseminated information regarding food, drugs, devices, or cosmetics in situations involving, in the opinion of the Secretary, imminent danger to health, or gross deception of the consumer. Nothing in this section shall be construed to prohibit the Secretary from collecting, reporting, and illustrating the results of the investigations of the Department.

SEC. 708 [21 U.S.C. § 379]. CONFIDENTIAL INFORMATION.

The Secretary may provide any information which is exempt from disclosure pursuant to subsection (a) of section 552 of title 5, United States Code by reason of subsection (b)(4) of such section to a person other than an officer or employee of the Department if the Secretary determines such other person requires the information in connection with an activity which is undertaken under contract with the Secretary, which relates to the administration of this Act, and with respect to which the Secretary (or an officer or employee of the Department) is not prohibited from using such information. The Secretary shall require as a condition to the provision of information under this section that the person receiving it take such security precautions respecting the information as the Secretary may by regulation prescribe.

SEC. 709 [21 U.S.C. § 379a]. PRESUMPTION.

In any action to enforce the requirements of this Act respecting a device, food, drug, or cosmetic the connection with interstate commerce required for jurisdiction in such action shall be presumed to exist.

SEC. 736 [21 U.S.C. § 379h]. AUTHORITY TO ASSESS AND USE DRUG FEES.

(a) TYPES OF FEES.—Beginning in fiscal year 1998, the Secretary shall assess and collect fees in accordance with this section as follows:

(1) HUMAN DRUG APPLICATION AND SUPPLEMENT FEE.

(A) IN GENERAL.—Each person that submits, on or after September 1, 1992, a human drug application or a supplement shall be subject to a fee as follows:

(i) A fee established in subsection (b) for a human drug application for which clinical data (other than bioavailability or bioequivalence studies) with respect to safety or effectiveness are required for approval.

(ii) A fee established in subsection (b) for a human drug application for which clinical data with respect to safety or effectiveness are not required or a supplement for which clinical data (other than bioavailability or bioequivalence studies) with respect to safety or effectiveness are required.

(B) PAYMENT.—The fee required by subparagraph (A) shall be due upon submission of the application or supplement.

(C) EXCEPTION FOR PREVIOUSLY FILED APPLICATION OR SUPPLEMENT.—If a human drug application or supplement was submitted by a person that paid the fee for such application or supplement, was accepted for filing, and was not approved or was withdrawn (without a waiver), the submission of a human drug application or a supplement for the same product by the same person (or the person's licensee, assignee, or successor) shall not be subject to a fee under subparagraph (A).

(D) REFUND OF FEE IF APPLICATION REFUSED FOR FILING.—The Secretary shall refund 75 percent of the fee paid under subparagraph (B) for any application or supplement which is refused for filing.

(E) EXCEPTION FOR DESIGNATED ORPHAN DRUG OR INDICATION.—A human drug application for a prescription drug product that has been designated as a drug for a rare disease or condition pursuant to section 526 shall not be subject to a fee under subparagraph (A), unless the human drug application includes an indication for other than a rare disease or condition. A supplement proposing to include a new indication for a rare disease or condition in a human drug application shall not be subject to a fee under subparagraph (A), if the drug has been designated pursuant to section 526 as a drug for a rare disease or condition with regard to the indication proposed in such supplement.

(F) REFUND OF FEE IF APPLICATION WITHDRAWN.—If an application or supplement is withdrawn after the application or supplement was filed, the Secretary may refund the fee or a portion of the fee if no substantial work was performed on the application or supplement after the application or supplement was filed. The Secretary shall have the sole discretion to refund a fee or a portion of the fee under this subparagraph. A determination by the Secretary concerning a refund under this paragraph shall not be reviewable.

(2) PRESCRIPTION DRUG ESTABLISHMENT FEE.

(A) IN GENERAL.—Except as provided in subparagraph (B) each person that—

(i) is named as the applicant in a human drug application; and

(ii) after September 1, 1992, had pending before the Secretary a human drug application or supplement,

shall be assessed an annual fee in subsection (b) for each prescription drug establishment listed in its approved human drug application as an establishment that manufactures the prescription drug product named in the application. The annual establishment fee shall be assessed in each fiscal year in which the prescription drug product named in the application is assessed a fee under paragraph (3) unless the prescription drug establishment listed in the application does not engage in the manufacture of the prescription drug product during the fiscal year. The establishment fee shall be payable on or before January 31 of each year. Each such establishment shall be assessed only one fee per establishment, notwithstanding the number of prescription drug products manufactured at the establishment.
* * *

(3) PRESCRIPTION DRUG PRODUCT FEE.

(A) IN GENERAL.—Except as provided in subparagraph (B), each person—

(i) who is named as the applicant in a human drug application for a prescription drug product which is listed under section 510, and

(ii) who, after September 1, 1992, had pending before the Secretary a human drug application or supplement,

shall pay for each such prescription drug product the annual fee established in subsection (b) of this section. Such fee shall be payable for the fiscal year in which the product is first submitted for listing under section 510, or is submitted for relisting under section 510 if the product has been withdrawn from listing and relisted. After such fee is paid for that fiscal year, such fee shall be payable on or before January 31 of each year. Such fee shall be paid only once for each product for a fiscal year in which the fee is payable.

(B) EXCEPTION.—The listing of a prescription drug product under section 510 shall not require the person who listed such product to pay the fee prescribed by subparagraph (A) if such product is the same product as a product approved under an application filed under section 505(b)(2) or 505(j), under an abbreviated application filed under section 507 (as in effect on the day before the date of enactment of the Food and Drug Administration Modernization Act of 1997), or under an abbreviated new drug application pursuant to regulations in effect prior to the implementation of the Drug Price Competition and Patent Term Restoration Act of 1984.

(b) FEE AMOUNTS.—Except as provided in subsections (c), (d), (f), and (g), the fees required under subsection (a) shall be determined and assessed as follows:

(1) APPLICATION AND SUPPLEMENT FEES.

(A) FULL FEES.—The application fee under subsection (a)(1)(A)(i) shall be $250,704 in fiscal year 1998, $256,338 in each of fiscal years

1999 and 2000, $267,606 in fiscal year 2001, and $258,451 in fiscal year 2002.

(B) OTHER FEES.—The fee under subsection (a)(1)(A)(ii) shall be $125,352 in fiscal year 1998, $128,169 in each of fiscal years 1999 and 2000, $133,803 in fiscal year 2001, and $129,226 in fiscal year 2002.

(2) TOTAL FEE REVENUES FOR ESTABLISHMENT FEES.—The total fee revenues to be collected in establishment fees under subsection (a)(2) shall be $35,600,000 in fiscal year 1998, $36,400,000 in each of fiscal years 1999 and 2000, $38,000,000 in fiscal year 2001, and $36,700,000 in fiscal year 2002.

(3) TOTAL FEE REVENUES FOR PRODUCT FEES.—The total fee revenues to be collected in product fees under subsection (a)(3) in a fiscal year shall be equal to the total fee revenues collected in establishment fees under subsection (a)(2) in that fiscal year.

* * *

(d) FEE WAIVER OR REDUCTION.

(1) IN GENERAL.—The Secretary shall grant a waiver from or a reduction of one or more fees assessed under subsection (a) where the Secretary finds that—(A) such waiver or reduction is necessary to protect the public health, (B) the assessment of the fee would present a significant barrier to innovation because of limited resources available to such person or other circumstances, (C) the fees to be paid by such person will exceed the anticipated present and future costs incurred by the Secretary in conducting the process for the review of human drug applications for such person, (D) assessment of the fee for an application or a supplement filed under section 505(b)(1) pertaining to a drug containing an active ingredient would be inequitable because an application for a product containing the same active ingredient filed by another person under section 505(b)(2) could not be assessed fees under subsection (a)(1), or (E) the applicant involved is a small business [meaning an entity that has fewer than 500 employees] submitting its first human drug application to the Secretary for review. * * *

(e) EFFECT OF FAILURE TO PAY FEES.—A human drug application or supplement submitted by a person subject to fees under subsection (a) shall be considered incomplete and shall not be accepted for filing by the Secretary until all fees owed by such person have been paid.

(f) ASSESSMENT OF FEES.

(1) LIMITATION.—Fees may not be assessed under subsection (a) for a fiscal year beginning after fiscal year 1997 unless appropriations for salaries and expenses of the Food and Drug Administration for such fiscal year (excluding the amount of fees appropriated for such fiscal year) are equal to or greater than the amount of appropriations for the salaries and expenses of the Food and Drug Administration for the fiscal year 1997 (excluding the amount of fees appropriated for such fiscal year) multiplied by the adjustment factor applicable to the fiscal year involved. * * *

(g) CREDITING AND AVAILABILITY OF FEES.

(1) IN GENERAL.—Fees collected for a fiscal year pursuant to subsection (a) shall be credited to the appropriation account for salaries and expenses of the Food and Drug Administration and shall be available in accordance with appropriation Acts until expended without fiscal year limitation. Such sums as may be necessary may be transferred from the Food and Drug Administration salaries and expenses appropriation account without fiscal year limitation to such appropriation account for salaries and expenses with such fiscal year limitation. The sums transferred shall be available solely for the process for the review of human drug applications.
* * *

(j) CONSTRUCTION.—This section may not be construed to require that the number of full-time equivalent positions in the Department of Health and Human Services, for officers, employers, and advisory committees not engaged in the process of the review of human drug applications, be reduced to offset the number of officers, employees, and advisory committees so engaged.

SEC. 751 [21 U.S.C. § 379r]. NATIONAL UNIFORMITY FOR NONPRESCRIPTION DRUGS.

(a) IN GENERAL.—Except as provided in subsection (b), (c)(1), (d), (e), or (f), no State or political subdivision of a State may establish or continue in effect any requirement—(1) that relates to the regulation of a drug that is not subject to the requirements of section 503(b)(1) or 503(f)(1)(A); and (2) that is different from or in addition to, or that is otherwise not identical with, a requirement under this Act, the Poison Prevention Packaging Act of 1970 (15 U.S.C. 1471 et seq.), or the Fair Packaging and Labeling Act (15 U.S.C. 1451 et seq.).

(b) EXEMPTION.—

(1) IN GENERAL.—Upon application of a State or political subdivision thereof, the Secretary may by regulation, after notice and opportunity for written and oral presentation of views, exempt from subsection (a), under such conditions as may be prescribed in such regulation, a State or political subdivision requirement that—(A) protects an important public interest that would otherwise be unprotected, including the health and safety of children; (B) would not cause any drug to be in violation of any applicable requirement or prohibition under Federal law; and (C) would not unduly burden interstate commerce.

(2) TIMELY ACTION.—The Secretary shall make a decision on the exemption of a State or, political subdivision requirement under paragraph (1) not later than 120 days after receiving the application of the State or political subdivision under paragraph (1).

(c) SCOPE.

(1) IN GENERAL.—This section shall not apply to—(A) any State or political subdivision requirement that relates to the practice of pharmacy; or (B) any State or political subdivision requirement that a drug be

dispensed only upon the prescription of a practitioner licensed by law to administer such drug.

(2) SAFETY OR EFFECTIVENESS.—For purposes of subsection (a), a requirement that relates to the regulation of a drug shall be deemed to include any requirement relating to public information or any other form of public communication relating to a warning of any kind for a drug.

(d) EXCEPTIONS.—

(1) IN GENERAL.—In the case of a drug described in subsection (a)(1) that is not the subject of an application approved under section 505 or section 507 (as in effect on the day before the date of enactment of the Food and Drug Administration Modernization Act of 1997) or a final regulation promulgated by the Secretary establishing conditions under which the drug is generally recognized as safe and effective and not misbranded, subsection (a) shall apply only with respect to a requirement of a State or political subdivision of a State that relates to the same subject as, but is different from or in addition to, or that is otherwise not identical with—(A) a regulation in effect with respect to the drug pursuant to a statute described in subsection (a)(2); or (B) any other requirement in effect with respect to the drug pursuant to an amendment to such a statute made on or after the date of enactment of the Food and Drug Administration Modernization Act of 1997.

(2) STATE INITIATIVES.—This section shall not apply to a State requirement adopted by a State public initiative or referendum enacted prior to September 1, 1997.

(e) NO EFFECT ON PRODUCT LIABILITY LAW.—Nothing in this section shall be construed to modify or otherwise affect any action or the liability of any person under the product liability law of any State.

(f) STATE ENFORCEMENT AUTHORITY.—Nothing in this section shall prevent a State or political subdivision thereof from enforcing, under any relevant civil or other enforcement authority, a requirement that is identical to a requirement of this Act.

SEC. 756 [21 U.S.C. § 379v]. SAFETY REPORT DISCLAIMERS.

With respect to any entity that submits or is required to submit a safety report or other information in connection with the safety of a product (including a product that is a food, drug, device, dietary supplement, or cosmetic) under this Act (and any release by the Secretary of that report or information), such report or information shall not be construed to reflect necessarily a conclusion by the entity or the Secretary that the report or information constitutes an admission that the product involved malfunctioned, caused or contributed to an adverse experience, or otherwise caused or contributed to a death, serious injury, or serious illness. Such an entity need not admit, and may deny, that the report or information submitted by the entity constitutes an admission that the product involved malfunctioned, caused or contributed to an adverse experience, or caused or contributed to a death, serious injury, or serious illness.

SEC. 801 [21 U.S.C. § 381]. IMPORTS AND EXPORTS.

(a) The Secretary of the Treasury shall deliver to the Secretary of Health and Human Services, upon his request, samples of food, drugs, devices, and cosmetics which are being imported or offered for import into the United States, giving notice thereof to the owner or consignee, who may appear before the Secretary of Health and Human Services and have the right to introduce testimony. The Secretary of Health and Human Services shall furnish to the Secretary of the Treasury a list of establishments registered pursuant to subsection (i) of section 510 and shall request that if any drugs or devices manufactured, prepared, propagated, compounded, or processed in an establishment not so registered are imported or offered for import into the United States, samples of such drugs or devices be delivered to the Secretary of Health and Human Services, with notice of such delivery to the owner or consignee, who may appear before the Secretary of Health and Human Services and have the right to introduce testimony. If it appears from the examination of such samples or otherwise that (1) such article has been manufactured, processed, or packed under insanitary conditions or, in the case of a device, the methods used in, or the facilities or controls used for, the manufacture, packing, storage, or installation of the device do not conform to the requirements of section 520(f) or (2) such article is forbidden or restricted in sale in the country in which it was produced or from which it was exported, or (3) such article is adulterated, misbranded, or in violation of section 505, then such article shall be refused admission, except as provided in subsection (b) of this section. The Secretary of the Treasury shall cause the destruction of any such article refused admission unless such article is exported, under regulations prescribed by the Secretary of the Treasury, within ninety days of the date of notice of such refusal or within such additional time as may be permitted pursuant to such regulations. Clause (2) of the third sentence of this paragraph shall not be construed to prohibit the admission of narcotic drugs the importation of which is permitted under the Controlled Substances Import and Export Act.

(b) Pending decision as to the admission of an article being imported or offered for import, the Secretary of the Treasury may authorize delivery of such article to the owner or consignee upon the execution by him of a good and sufficient bond providing for the payment of such liquidated damages in the event of default as may be required pursuant to regulations of the Secretary of the Treasury. If it appears to the Secretary of Health and Human Services that an article included within the provisions of clause (3) of subsection (a) of this section can, by relabeling or other action, be brought into compliance with the Act or rendered other than a food, drug, device, or cosmetic, final determination as to admission of such article may be deferred and, upon filing of timely written application by the owner or consignee and the execution by him of a bond as provided in the preceding provisions of this subsection, the Secretary may, in accordance with regulations, authorize the applicant to perform such relabeling or other action specified in such authorization (including destruction or export of rejected articles or portions thereof, as may be specified in the Secretary's authorization). All such relabeling or other action pursuant to such authorization shall in accordance with regulations be under the supervision of an officer or employee of the Department of Health and Human Services designated by the Secretary, or an officer or employee of the Department of the Treasury designated by the Secretary of the Treasury.

(c) All expenses (including travel, per diem or subsistence, and salaries of officers or employees of the United States) in connection with the destruction provided for in subsection (a) of this section and the supervision of the relabeling or other action authorized under the provisions of subsection (b) of this section, the amount of such expenses to be determined in accordance with regulations, and all expenses in connection with the storage, cartage, or labor with respect to any article refused admission under subsection (a) of this section, shall be paid by the owner or consignee and, in default of such payment, shall constitute a lien against any future importations made by such owner or consignee.

(d) (1) Except as provided in paragraph (2) and section 804, no drug subject to section 503(b) or composed wholly or partially of insulin which is manufactured in a State and exported may be imported into the United States unless the drug is imported by the manufacturer of the drug.

(2) The Secretary may authorize the importation of a drug the importation of which is prohibited by paragraph (1) if the drug is required for emergency medical care.

(3) No component of a drug, no component part or accessory of a device, or other article of device requiring further processing, which is ready or suitable for use for health-related purposes, and no food additive, color additive, or dietary supplement, including a product in bulk form, shall be excluded from importation into the United States under subsection (a) if—

(A) the importer of such article of a drug or device or importer of the food additive, color additive, or dietary supplement submits a statement to the Secretary, at the time of initial importation, that such article of a drug or device, food additive, color additive, or dietary supplement is intended to be further processed by the initial owner or consignee, or incorporated by the initial owner or consignee into a drug, biological product, device, food, food additive, color additive, or dietary supplement that will be exported by such owner or consignee from the United States in accordance with section 801(e) or 802 or section 351(h) of the Public Health Service Act;

(B) the initial owner or consignee responsible for such imported article maintains records that identify the use of such imported article and upon request of the Secretary submits a report that provides an accounting of the exportation or the disposition of the imported article, including portions that have been destroyed, and the manner in which such person complied with the requirements of this paragraph; and

(C) any imported component, part, article, or accessory of a drug or device and any food additive, color additive, or dietary supplement not incorporated or further processed as described in subparagraph (A) is destroyed or exported by the owner or consignee.

(4) The importation into the United States of blood, blood components, source plasma, or source leukocytes or of a component, accessory, or part thereof is not permitted pursuant to paragraph (3) unless the importation complies with section 351(a) of the Public Health Service Act or the Secretary permits the importation under appropriate circumstances and conditions, as determined by the Secretary. The importation of tissue or a component or part of tissue is not permitted pursuant to paragraph (3) unless the importation complies with section 361 of the Public Health Service Act.

(e) (1) A food, drug, device, or cosmetic intended for export shall not be deemed to be adulterated or misbranded under this chapter if it—

(A) accords to the specifications of the foreign purchaser,

(B) is not in conflict with the laws of the country to which it is intended for export,

(C) is labeled on the outside of the shipping package that it is intended for export, and

(D) is not sold or offered for sale in domestic commerce.

(2) Paragraph (1) does not apply to any device—

(A) which does not comply with an applicable requirement of section 514 or 515,

(B) which under section 520(g) is exempt from either such section, or

(C) which is a banned device under section 516,

unless, in addition to the requirements of paragraph (1), either (i) the Secretary has determined that the exportation of the device is not contrary to public health and safety and has the approval of the country to which it is intended for export or (ii) the device is eligible for export under section 802.

(3) A new animal drug that requires approval under section 512 shall not be exported pursuant to paragraph (1) if such drug has been banned in the United States.

(4)(A) Any person who exports a drug, animal drug, or device may request that the Secretary—(i) certify in writing that the exported drug, animal drug, or device meets the requirements of paragraph (1) or section 802; or (ii) certify in writing that the drug, animal drug, or device being exported meets the applicable requirements of this Act upon a showing that the drug or device meets the applicable requirements of this Act. The Secretary shall issue such a certification within 20 days of the receipt of a request for such certification.

(B) If the Secretary issues a written export certification within the 20 days prescribed by subparagraph (A), a fee for such certification may be charged but shall not exceed $175 for each certification. Fees collected for a fiscal year pursuant to this subparagraph shall be credited to the appropriation account for salaries and expenses of the Food and Drug Administration and shall be available in accordance with appropriations Acts until expended without fiscal year limitation. Such fees shall be collected in each fiscal year in an amount equal to the amount specified in appropriations Acts for such fiscal year and shall only be collected End available for the costs of the Food and Drug Administration.

(f) (1) If a drug (other than insulin, an antibiotic drug, an animal drug, or a drug exported under section 802) being exported in accordance with subsection (e) is being exported to a country that has different or additional labeling requirements or conditions for use and such country requires the drug to be labeled in accordance with those requirements or uses, such drug may be labeled in accordance with such requirements and conditions for use in the country to which such drug is being exported if it also is labeled in accordance with the requirements of this Act.

(2) If, pursuant to paragraph (1), the labeling of an exported drug includes conditions for use that have not been approved under this Act, the labeling must state that such conditions for use have not been approved under this Act. A drug exported under section 802 is exempt from this section.

(g) (1) With respect to a prescription drug being imported or offered for import into the United States, the Secretary, in the case of an individual who is not in the business of such importations, may not send a warning notice to the individual unless the following conditions are met:

(A) The notice specifies, as applicable to the importation of the drug, that the Secretary has made a determination that—

(i) importation is in violation of section 801(a) because the drug is or appears to be adulterated, misbranded, or in violation of section 505;

(ii) importation is in violation of section 801(a) because the drug is or appears to be forbidden or restricted in sale in the country in which it was produced or from which it was exported;

(iii) importation is or appears to be in violation of section 801(d)(1); or

(iv) importation otherwise is or appears to be in violation of Federal law.

(B) The notice does not specify any provision described in subparagraph (A) that is not applicable to the importation of the drug.

(C) The notice states the reasons underlying such determination by the Secretary, including a brief application to the principal facts involved of the provision of law described in subparagraph (A) that is the basis of the determination by the Secretary.

(2) For purposes of this section, the term "warning notice," with respect to the importation of a drug, means a communication from the Secretary (written or otherwise) notifying a person, or clearly suggesting to

the person, that importing the drug for personal use is, or appears to be, a violation of this Act.

SEC. 802 [21 U.S.C. § 382]. EXPORTS OF CERTAIN UNAPPROVED PRODUCTS.

(a) A drug or device—

(1) which, in the case of a drug—(A)(i) requires approval by the Secretary under section 505 before such drug may be introduced or delivered for introduction into interstate commerce; or (ii) requires licensing by the Secretary under section 351 of the Public Health Service Act or by the Secretary of Agriculture under the Act of March 4, 1913 (known as the Virus–Serum Toxin Act) before it may be introduced or delivered for introduction into interstate commerce; (B) does not have such approval or license; and (C) is not exempt from such sections or Act; and

(2) which, in the case of a device—(A) does not comply with an applicable requirement under section 514 or 515; (B) under section 520(g) is exempt from either such section; or (C) is a banned device under section 516,

is adulterated, misbranded, and in violation of such sections or Act unless the export of the drug or device is, except as provided in subsection (f), authorized under subsection (b), (c), (d), or (e) or section 801(e)(2). If a drug or device described in paragraphs (1) and (2) may be exported under subsection (b) and if an application for such drug or device under section 505 or 515 or section 351 of the Public Health Service Act was disapproved, the Secretary shall notify the appropriate public health official of the country to which such drug will be exported of such disapproval.

(b) (1)(A) A drug or device described in subsection (a) may be exported to any country, if the drug or device complies with the laws of that country and has valid marketing authorization by the appropriate authority—

(i) in Australia, Canada, Israel, Japan, New Zealand, Switzerland, or South Africa; or

(ii) in the European Union or a country in the European Economic Area (the countries in the European Union and the European Free Trade Association) if the drug or device is marketed in that country or the drug or device is authorized for general marketing in the European Economic Area.

(B) The Secretary may designate an additional country to be included in the list of countries described in clauses (i) and (ii) of subparagraph (A) if all of the following requirements are met in such country:

(i) Statutory or regulatory requirements which require the review of drugs and devices for safety and effectiveness by an entity of the government of such country and which authorize the approval of only those drugs and devices which have been determined to be safe and effective by experts employed by or acting on behalf of such entity and qualified by scientific training and experience to evaluate the safety and effectiveness of drugs and devices on the basis of adequate and well-controlled investigations, including clinical investigations, conducted by experts qualified by scientific training and experience to evaluate the safety and effectiveness of drugs and devices.

(ii) Statutory or regulatory requirements that the methods used in, and the facilities and controls used for—

(I) the manufacture, processing, and packing of drugs in the country are adequate to preserve their identity, quality, purity, and strength; and

(II) the manufacture, preproduction design validation, packing, storage, and installation of a device are adequate to assure that the device will be safe and effective.

(iii) Statutory or regulatory requirements for the reporting of adverse reactions to drugs and devices and procedures to withdraw approval and remove drugs and devices found not to be safe or effective.

(iv) Statutory or regulatory requirements that the labeling and promotion of drugs and devices must be in accordance with the approval of the drug or device.

(v) The valid marketing authorization system in such country or countries is equivalent to the systems in the countries described in clauses (i) and (ii) of subparagraph (A).

The Secretary shall not delegate the authority granted under this subparagraph.

(C) An appropriate country official, manufacturer, or exporter may request the Secretary to take action under subparagraph (B) to designate an additional country or countries to be added to the list of countries described in clauses (i) and (ii) of subparagraph (A) by submitting documentation to the Secretary in support of such designation. Any person other than a country, requesting such designation shall include, along with the request, a letter from the country indicating the desire of such country to be designated.

(2) A drug described in subsection (a) may be directly exported to a country which is not listed in clause (i) or (ii) of paragraph (1)(A) if—

(A) the drug complies with the laws of that country and has valid marketing authorization by the responsible authority in that country; and

(B) the Secretary determines that all of the following requirements are met in that country:

(i) Statutory or regulatory requirements which require the review of drugs for safety and effectiveness by an entity of the government of such country and which authorize the approval of only those drugs which have been determined to be safe and effective by experts employed by or acting on behalf of such entity and qualified by scientific training and experience to evaluate the safety and effectiveness of drugs on the basis of adequate and well-controlled investigations, including clinical investigations, conducted by experts qualified by scientific training and experience to evaluate the safety and effectiveness of drugs.

(ii) Statutory or regulatory requirements that the methods used in, and the facilities and controls used for the manufacture, processing, and packing of drugs in the country are adequate to preserve their identity, quality, purity, and strength.

(iii) Statutory or regulatory requirements for the reporting of adverse reactions to drugs and procedures to withdraw approval and remove drugs found not to be safe or effective.

(iv) Statutory or regulatory requirements that the labeling and promotion of drugs must be in accordance with the approval of the drug.

(3) The exporter of a drug described in subsection (a) which would not meet the conditions for approval under this Act or conditions for approval of a country described in clause (i) or (ii) of paragraph (1)(A) may petition the Secretary for authorization to export such drug to a country which is not described in clause (i) or (ii) of paragraph (1)(A) or which is not described in paragraph (2). The Secretary shall permit such export if—

(A) the person exporting the drug—

(i) certifies that the drug would not meet the conditions for approval under this Act or the conditions for approval of a country described in clause (i) or (ii) of paragraph (1)(A); and

(ii) provides the Secretary with credible scientific evidence, acceptable to the Secretary, that the drug would be safe and effective under the conditions of use in the country to which it is being exported; and

(B) the appropriate health authority in the country to which the drug is being exported—

(i) requests approval of the export of the drug to such country;

(ii) certifies that the health authority understands that the drug is not approved under this Act or in a country described in clause (i) or (ii) of paragraph (1)(A); and

(iii) concurs that the scientific evidence provided pursuant to subparagraph (A) is credible scientific evidence that the drug would be reasonably safe and effective in such country.

The Secretary shall take action on a request for export of a drug under this paragraph within 60 days of receiving such request.

(c) A drug or device intended for investigational use in any country described in clause (i) or (ii) of subsection (b)(1)(A) may be exported in accordance with the laws of that country and shall be exempt from regulation under section 505(i) or 520(g).

(d) A drug or device intended for formulation, filling, packaging, labeling, or further processing in anticipation of market authorization in any country described in clause (i) or (ii) of subsection (b)(1)(A) may be exported for use in accordance with the laws of that country.

(e) (1) A drug or device which is used in the diagnosis, prevention, or treatment of a tropical disease or another disease not of significant prevalence in the United States and which does not otherwise qualify for export under this section shall, upon approval of an application, be permitted to be exported if the Secretary finds that the drug or device will not expose patients in such country to an unreasonable risk of illness or injury and the probable benefit to health from the use of the drug or device (under conditions of use prescribed, recommended, or suggested in the labeling or proposed labeling of the drug or device) outweighs the risk of injury or illness from its use, taking into account the probable risks and benefits of currently available drug or device treatment.

(2) The holder of an approved application for the export of a drug or device under this subsection shall report to the Secretary—

(A) the receipt of any credible information indicating that the drug or device is being or may have been exported from a country for which the Secretary made a finding under paragraph (1)(A) to a country for which the Secretary cannot make such a finding; and

(B) the receipt of any information indicating adverse reactions to such drug.

(3)(A) If the Secretary determines that—

(i) a drug or device for which an application is approved under paragraph (1) does not continue to meet the requirements of such paragraph; or

(ii) the holder of an approved application under paragraph (1) has not made the report required by paragraph (2),

the Secretary may, after providing the holder of the application an opportunity for an informal hearing, withdraw the approved application.

(B) If the Secretary determines that the holder of an approved application under paragraph (1) or an importer is exporting a drug or device from the United States to an importer and such importer is exporting the drug or device to a country for which the Secretary cannot make a finding under paragraph (1) and such export presents an imminent hazard, the Secretary shall immediately prohibit the export of the drug or device to such importer, provide the person exporting the drug or device from the United States prompt notice of the prohibition, and afford such person an opportunity for an expedited hearing.

(f) A drug or device may not be exported under this section—

(1) if the drug or device is not manufactured, processed, packaged, and held in substantial conformity with current good manufacturing practice

requirements or does not meet international standards as certified by an international standards organization recognized by the Secretary;

(2) if the drug or device is adulterated under clause (1), (2)(A), or (3) of section 501(a) or subsection (c) or (d) of section 501;

(3) if the requirements of subparagraphs (A) through (D) of section 801(e)(1) have not been met;

(4)(A) if the drug or device is the subject of a notice by the Secretary or the Secretary of Agriculture of a determination that the probability of reimportation of the exported drug or device would present an imminent hazard to the public health and safety of the United States and the only means of limiting the hazard is to prohibit the export of the drug or device; or

(B) if the drug or device presents an imminent hazard to the public health of the country to which the drug or device would be exported;

(5) if the labeling of the drug or device is not—

(A) in accordance with the requirements and conditions for use in—

(i) the country in which the drug or device received valid marketing authorization under subsection (b); and

(ii) the country to which the drug or device would be exported; and

(B) in the language and units of measurement of the country to which the drug or device would be exported or in the language designated by such country; or

(6) if the drug or device is not promoted in accordance with the labeling requirements set forth in paragraph (5).

In making a finding under paragraph (4)(B), (5), or (6) the Secretary shall consult with the appropriate public health official in the affected country.

(g) The exporter of a drug or device exported under subsection (b)(1) shall provide a simple notification to the Secretary identifying the drug or device when the exporter first begins to export such drug or device to any country listed in clause (i) or (ii) of subsection (b)(1)(A). When an exporter of a drug or device first begins to export a drug or device to a country which is not listed in clause (i) or (ii) of subsection (b)(1)(A), the exporter shall provide a simple notification to the Secretary identifying the drug or device and the country to which such drug or device is being exported. Any exporter of a drug or device shall maintain records of all drugs or devices exported and the countries to which they were exported.

(h) For purposes of this section—(1) a reference to the Secretary shall in, the case of a biological product which is required to be licensed under the Act of March 4,1913 (37 Stat. 832–833) (commonly known as the Virus–Serum Toxin Act) be considered to be a reference to the Secretary of Agriculture, and (2) the term "drug" includes drugs for human use as well as biologicals under section 351 of the Public Health Service Act or the Act of March 4, 1913 (37 Stat. 832–833) (commonly known as the Virus–Serum Toxin Act).

(i) Insulin and antibiotic drugs may be exported without regard to the requirements in this section if the insulin and antibiotic drugs meet the requirements of section 801(e)(1).

SEC. 803 [21 U.S.C. § 383]. OFFICE OF INTERNATIONAL RELATIONS.

(a) There is established in the Department of Health and Human Services an Office of International Relations.

(b) In carrying out the functions of the office under subsection (a), the Secretary may enter into agreements with foreign countries to facilitate commerce in devices between the United States and such countries consistent with the requirements of this Act. In such agreements, the Secretary shall encourage the mutual recognition of—(1) good manufacturing practice regulations promulgated under section 520(f), and (2) other regulations and testing protocols as the Secretary determines to be appropriate.

(c) (1) The Secretary shall support the Office of the United States Trade Representative, in consultation with the Secretary of Commerce, in meetings with representatives of other countries to discuss methods and approaches to reduce the burden of regulation and harmonize regulatory requirements if the Secretary determines that such harmonization continues consumer protections consistent with the purposes of this Act.

(2) The Secretary shall support the Office of the United States Trade Representative, in consultation with the Secretary of Commerce, in efforts to move toward the acceptance of mutual recognition agreements relating to the regulation of drugs, biological products, devices, foods, food additives, and color additives, and the regulation of good manufacturing practices, between the European Union and the United States.

(3) The Secretary shall regularly participate in meetings with representatives of other foreign governments to discuss and reach agreement on methods and approaches to harmonize regulatory requirements.

(4) The Secretary shall, not later than 180 days after the date of enactment of the Food and Drug Administration Modernization Act of 1997, make public a plan that establishes a framework for achieving mutual recognition of good manufacturing practices inspections.

(5) Paragraphs (1) through (4) shall not apply with respect to products defined in section 201(ff).

SEC. 804 [21 U.S.C. 384]. IMPORTATION OF COVERED PRODUCTS.

(a) REGULATIONS—The Secretary, after consultation with the United States Trade Representative and the Commissioner of Customs, shall promulgate regulations permitting pharmacists and wholesalers to import into the United States covered products.

(b) LIMITATION—Regulations under subsection (a) shall—

(1) require that safeguards be in place to ensure that each covered product imported pursuant to such subsection complies with section 505 (including with respect to being safe and effective for its intended use), with sections 501 and 502, and with other applicable requirements of this Act;

(2) require that an importer of a covered product pursuant to subsection (a) comply with the applicable provisions of this section, including subsection (d); and

(3) contain any additional provisions determined by the Secretary to be appropriate as a safeguard to protect the public health or as a means to facilitate the importation of such products.

(c) RECORDS—Regulations under subsection (a) shall require that records regarding the importation of covered products pursuant to such subsection be provided to and maintained by the Secretary for a period of time determined to be necessary by the Secretary.

(d) IMPORTATION—Regulations under subsection (a) shall require an importer of a covered product pursuant to such subsection to provide to the Secretary the following information and records:

(1) The name and amount of the active ingredient of such product and description of the dosage form.

(2) The date that the product is shipped and the quantity of the product that is shipped, points of origin and destination for the product, the price paid for the product by the importer, and (once the product is distributed) the price for which such product is sold by the importer.

(3) Documentation from the foreign seller specifying the original source of the product and the amount of each lot of the product originally received.

(4) The manufacturer's lot or control number of the product imported.

(5) The name, address, and telephone number of the importer, including the professional license number of the importer, if any.

(6) For a product that is coming directly from the first foreign recipient of the product from the manufacturer:

(A) Documentation demonstrating that such product came from such recipient and was received by the recipient from such manufacturer.

(B) Documentation of the amount of each lot of the product received by such recipient to demonstrate that the amount being imported into the United States is not more than the amount that was received by the recipient.

(C) In the case of the initial imported shipment, documentation demonstrating that each batch of such shipment was statistically sampled and tested for authenticity and degradation.

(D) In the case of all subsequent shipments from such recipient, documentation demonstrating that a statistically valid sample of such shipments was tested for authenticity and degradation.

(E) Certification from the importer or manufacturer of such product that the product is approved for marketing in the United States and meets all labeling requirements under this Act.

(7) For a product that is not coming directly from the first foreign recipient of the product from the manufacturer:

(A) Documentation demonstrating that each batch in all shipments offered for importation into the United States was statistically sampled and tested for authenticity and degradation.

(B) Certification from the importer or manufacturer of such product that the product is approved for marketing in the United States and meets all labeling requirements under this Act.

(8) Laboratory records, including complete data derived from all tests necessary to assure that the product is in compliance with established specifications and standards.

(9) Documentation demonstrating that the testing required by paragraphs (6) through (8) was performed at a qualifying laboratory (as defined in subsection (k)).

(10) Any other information that the Secretary determines is necessary to ensure the protection of the public health.

(e) TESTING—Regulations under subsection (a)—

(1) shall require that testing referred to in paragraphs (6) through (8) of subsection (d) be conducted by the importer of the covered product pursuant to subsection (a), or the manufacturer of the product;

(2) shall require that if such tests are conducted by the importer, information needed to authenticate the product being tested, and to confirm that the labeling of such product complies with labeling requirements under this Act, be supplied by the manufacturer of such product to the pharmacist or wholesaler, and shall require that such information be kept in strict confidence and used only for purposes of testing under this Act; and

(3) may include such additional provisions as the Secretary determines to be appropriate to provide for the protection of trade secrets and commercial or financial information that is privileged or confidential.

(f) COUNTRY LIMITATION—Regulations under subsection (a) shall provide that covered products may be imported pursuant to such subsection only from a country, union, or economic area that is listed in subparagraph (A) of section 802(b)(1) or designated by the Secretary, subject to such limitations as the Secretary determines to be appropriate to protect the public health.

(g) SUSPENSION OF IMPORTATIONS—The Secretary shall require that importations of specific covered products or importations by specific importers pursuant to subsection (a) be immediately suspended upon discovery of a pattern of importation of such products or by such importers that is counterfeit or in violation of any requirement pursuant to this section, until an investigation is completed and the Secretary determines that the public is adequately protected from counterfeit and violative covered products being imported pursuant to subsection (a).

(h) PROHIBITED AGREEMENTS—No manufacturer of a covered product may enter into a contract or agreement that includes a provision to prevent the sale or distribution of covered products imported pursuant to subsection (a).

(i) STUDIES; REPORTS—

(1) STUDY BY SECRETARY—

(A) IN GENERAL—The Secretary shall conduct, or contract with an entity to conduct, a study on the imports permitted pursuant to subsection (a), including consideration of the information received under subsection (d). In conducting such study, the Secretary or entity shall—

(i) evaluate the compliance of importers with regulations under subsection (a), and the number of shipments pursuant to such subsection, if any, that have been determined to be counterfeit, misbranded, or adulterated, and determine how such compliance contrasts with the number of shipments of prescription drugs transported within the United States that have been determined to be counterfeit, misbranded, or adulterated; and

(ii) consult with the United States Trade Representative and the Commissioner of Patents and Trademarks to evaluate the effect of importations pursuant to subsection (a) on trade and patent rights under Federal law.

(B) REPORT—Not later than two years after the effective date of final regulations under subsection (a), the Secretary shall prepare and submit to the Congress a report describing the findings of the study under subparagraph (A).

(2) STUDY BY GENERAL ACCOUNTING OFFICE—The Comptroller General of the United States shall conduct a study to determine the effect of this section on the price of covered products sold to consumers at retail. Not later than 18 months after the effective date of final regulations under subsection (a), the Comptroller General shall prepare and submit to the Congress a report describing the findings of such study.

(j) CONSTRUCTION—Nothing in this section shall be construed to limit the statutory, regulatory, or enforcement authority of the Secretary relating to the importation of covered products, other than with respect to section 801(d)(1) as provided in this section.

(k) DEFINITIONS—

(1) COVERED PRODUCT—

(A) IN GENERAL—For purposes of this section, the term "covered product" means a prescription drug, except that such term does not include a controlled substance in schedule I, II, or III under section

202(c) of the Controlled Substances Act or a biological product as defined in section 351 of the Public Health Service Act.

(B) CHARITABLE CONTRIBUTIONS; PARENTERAL DRUGS—Notwithstanding any other provision of this section, section 801(d)(1)—

(i) continues to apply to a covered product donated or otherwise supplied for free by the manufacturer of the drug to a charitable or humanitarian organization, including the United Nations and affiliates, or to a government of a foreign country; and

(ii) continues to apply to a covered product that is a parenteral drug the importation of which pursuant to subsection (a) is determined by the Secretary to pose a threat to the public health.

(2) OTHER TERMS—For purposes of this section:

(A) The term "importer" means a pharmacist or wholesaler.

(B) The term "pharmacist" means a person licensed by a State to practice pharmacy, including the dispensing and selling of prescription drugs.

(C) The term "prescription drug" means a drug subject to section 503(b).

(D) The term "qualifying laboratory" means a laboratory in the United States that has been approved by the Secretary for purposes of this section.

(E) The term "wholesaler" means a person licensed as a wholesaler or distributor of prescription drugs in the United States pursuant to section 503(e)(2)(A). Such term does not include a person authorized to import drugs under section 801(d)(1).

(l) CONDITIONS—This section shall become effective only if the Secretary demonstrates to the Congress that the implementation of this section will—

(1) pose no additional risk to the public's health and safety; and

(2) result in a significant reduction in the cost of covered products to the American consumer.

(m) SUNSET—Effective upon the expiration of the five-year period beginning on the effective date of final regulations under subsection (a), this section ceases to have any legal effect.

SEC. 903 [21 U.S.C. § 393]. FOOD AND DRUG ADMINISTRATION.

(a) IN GENERAL.—There is established in the Department of Health and Human Services the Food and Drug Administration (hereinafter in this section referred to as the "Administration").

(b) MISSION.—The Administration shall—

(1) promote the public health by promptly and efficiently reviewing clinical research and taking appropriate action on the marketing of regulated products in a timely manner;

(2) with respect to such products, protect the public health by ensuring that—

(A) foods are safe, wholesome, sanitary, and properly labeled;

(B) human and veterinary drugs are safe and effective;

(C) there is reasonable assurance of the safety and effectiveness of devices intended for human use;

(D) cosmetics are safe and properly labeled; and

(E) public health and safety are protected from electronic product radiation;

(3) participate through appropriate processes with representatives of other countries to reduce the burden of regulation, harmonize regulatory requirements, and achieve appropriate reciprocal arrangements; and

(4) as determined to be appropriate by the Secretary, carry out paragraphs (1) through (3) in consultation with experts in science, medicine, and public health, and in cooperation with consumers, users, manufacturers, importers, packers, distributors, and retailers of regulated products.

(c) INTERAGENCY COLLABORATION.—The Secretary shall implement programs and policies that will foster collaboration between the Administration, the National Institutes of Health, and other science-based Federal agencies, to enhance the scientific and technical expertise available to the Secretary in the conduct of the duties of the Secretary with respect to the development, clinical investigation, evaluation, and postmarket monitoring of emerging medical therapies, including complementary therapies, and advances in nutrition and food science.

(d) COMMISSIONER.

(1) APPOINTMENT.—There shall be in the Administration a Commissioner of Food and Drugs (hereinafter in this section referred to as the "Commissioner") who shall be appointed by the President by and with the advice and consent of the Senate.

(2) GENERAL POWERS.—The Secretary, through the Commissioner, shall be responsible for executing this chapter and for—

(A) providing overall direction to the Food and Drug Administration and establishing and implementing general policies respecting the management and operation of programs and activities of the Food and Drug Administration;

(B) coordinating and overseeing the operation of all administrative entities within the Administration;

(C) research relating to foods, drugs, cosmetics, and devices in carrying out this Act;

(D) conducting educational and public information programs relating to the responsibilities of the Food and Drug Administration; and

(E) performing such other functions as the Secretary may prescribe.

(e) TECHNICAL AND SCIENTIFIC REVIEW GROUPS.—The Secretary through the Commissioner of Food and Drugs may, without regard to the provisions of title 5 governing appointments in the competitive service and without regard to the provisions of chapter 51 and subchapter III of chapter 53 of such title relating to classification and General Schedule pay rates, establish such technical and scientific review groups as are needed to carry out the functions of the Administration, including functions under the Federal Food, Drug, and Cosmetic Act, and appoint and pay the members of such groups, except that officers and employees of the United States shall not receive additional compensation for service as members of such groups.

(f) AGENCY PLAN FOR STATUTORY COMPLIANCE.—

(1) IN GENERAL.—Not later than 1 year after the date of enactment of the Food and Drug Administration Modernization Act of 1997, the Secretary, after consultation with appropriate scientific and academic experts, health care professionals, representatives of patient and consumer advocacy groups, and the regulated industry, shall develop and publish in the Federal Register a plan bringing the Secretary into compliance with each of the obligations of the Secretary under this Act. The Secretary shall review the plan biannually and shall revise the plan as necessary, in consultation with such persons.

(2) OBJECTIVES OF AGENCY PLAN.—The plan required by paragraph (1) shall establish objectives and mechanisms to achieve such objectives, including objectives related to—

(A) maximizing the availability and clarity of information about the process for review of applications and submissions (including petitions, notifications, and any other similar forms of request) made under this Act;

(B) maximizing the availability and clarity of information for consumers and patients concerning new products;

(C) implementing inspection and postmarket monitoring provisions of this Act;

(D) ensuring access to the scientific and technical expertise needed by the Secretary to meet obligations described in paragraph (1);

(E) establishing mechanisms, by July 1, 1999, for meeting the time periods specified in this Act for the review of all applications and submissions described in sub-paragraph (A) and submitted after the date of enactment of the Food and Drug Administration Modernization Act of 1997; and

(F) eliminating backlogs in the review of applications and submissions described in subparagraph (A), by January 1, 2000.

(g) ANNUAL REPORT.—The Secretary shall annually prepare and publish in the Federal Register and solicit public comment on a report that— (1) provides detailed statistical information on the performance of the Secretary under the plan described in subsection (f); (2) compares such performance of the Secretary with the objectives of the plan and with the statutory obligations of the Secretary; and (3) identifies any regulatory policy that has a significant negative impact on compliance with any objective of the plan or any statutory obligation and sets forth any proposed revision to any such regulatory policy.

SEC. 904 [21 U.S.C. § 394]. SCIENTIFIC REVIEW GROUPS.

Without regard to the provisions of title 5, United States Code, governing appointments in the competitive service and without regard to the provisions of chapter 51 and subchapter III of chapter 53 of such title relating to classification and General Schedule pay rates, the Commissioner of Food and Drugs may—(1) establish such technical and scientific review groups as are needed to carry out the functions of the Food and Drug Administration (including functions prescribed under this Act); and (2) appoint and pay the members of such groups, except that officers and employees of the United States shall not receive additional compensation for service as members of such groups.

SEC. 906 [21 U.S.C. § 396]. PRACTICE OF MEDICINE.

Nothing in this Act shall be construed to limit or interfere with the authority of a health care practitioner to prescribe or administer any legally marketed device to a patient for any condition or disease within a legitimate health care practitioner-patient relationship. This section shall not limit any existing authority of the Secretary to establish and enforce restrictions on the sale or distribution, or in the labeling, of a device that are part of a determination of substantial equivalence, established as a condition of approval, or promulgated through regulations. Further, this section shall not change any existing prohibition on the promotion of unapproved uses of legally marketed devices.

SEC. 907 [21 U.S.C. § 397]. CONTRACTS FOR EXPERT REVIEW.

(a) IN GENERAL.

(1) AUTHORITY.—The Secretary may enter into a contract with any organization or any individual (who is not an employee of the Department) with relevant expertise, to review and evaluate, for the purpose of making recommendations to the Secretary on, part or all of any application or submission (including a petition, notification, and any other similar form of request) made under this Act for the approval or classification of an article or made under section 351(a) of the Public Health Service Act (42 U.S.C. § 262(a)) with respect to a biological product. Any such contract shall be subject to the requirements of section 708 relating to the confidentiality of information.

(2) INCREASED EFFICIENCY AND EXPERTISE THROUGH CONTRACTS.—The Secretary may use the authority granted in paragraph (1) whenever the Secretary determines that use of a contract described in paragraph (1) will improve the timeliness of the review of an application or submission described in paragraph (1), unless using such authority would

reduce the quality, or unduly increase the cost, of such review. The Secretary may use such authority whenever the Secretary determines that use of such a contract will improve the quality of the review of an application or submission described in paragraph (1), unless using such authority would unduly increase the cost of such review. Such improvement in timeliness or quality may include providing the Secretary increased scientific or technical expertise that is necessary to review or evaluate new therapies and technologies.

(b) REVIEW OF EXPERT REVIEW.

(1) IN GENERAL.—Subject to paragraph (2), the official of the Food and Drug Administration responsible for any matter for which expert review is used pursuant to subsection (a) shall review the recommendations of the organization or individual who conducted the expert review and shall make a final decision regarding the matter in a timely manner.

(2) LIMITATION.—A final decision by the Secretary on any such application or submission shall be made within the applicable prescribed time period for review of the matter as set forth in this Act or in the Public Health Service Act (42 U.S.C. § 201 et seq.).

PUBLIC HEALTH SERVICE ACT

SEC. 351 [42 U.S.C. § 262]. REGULATION OF BIOLOGICAL PRODUCTS.

(a) BIOLOGICS LICENSE.

(1) No person shall introduce or deliver for introduction into interstate commerce any biological product unless—

(A) a biologics license is in effect for the biological product; and

(B) each package of the biological product is plainly marked with—

(i) the proper name of the biological product contained in the package;

(ii) the name, address, and applicable license number of the manufacturer of the biological product; and

(iii) the expiration date of the biological product.

(2)(A) The Secretary shall establish, by regulation, requirements for the approval, suspension, and revocation of biologics licenses.

(B) The Secretary shall approve a biologics license application—

(i) on the basis of a demonstration that—

(I) the biological product that is the subject of the application is safe, pure, and potent; and

(II) the facility in which the biological product is manufactured, processed, packed, or held meets standards designed to assure that the biological product continues to be Safe, pure, and potent; and

(ii) if the applicant (or other appropriate person) consents to the inspection of the facility that is the subject of the application, in accordance with subsection (c) of this section.

(3) The Secretary shall prescribe requirements under which a biological product undergoing investigation shall be exempt from the requirements of paragraph (1).

(b) FALSELY LABELING OR MARKING PACKAGE OR CONTAINER; ALTERING LABEL OR MARK.—No person shall falsely label or mark any package or container of any biological product or alter any label or mark on the package or container of the biological product so as to falsify the label or mark.

(c) INSPECTION OF ESTABLISHMENT FOR PROPAGATION AND PREPARATION.—Any officer, agent, or employee of the Department of Health and Human Services, authorized by the Secretary for the purpose, may during all reasonable hours enter and inspect any establishment for the propagation or manufacture and preparation of any biological product.

(d) RECALL OF PRODUCT PRESENTING IMMINENT HAZARD; VIOLATIONS.

(1) Upon a determination that a batch, lot, or other quantity of a product licensed under this section presents an imminent or substantial

hazard to the public health, the Secretary shall issue an order immediately ordering the recall of such batch, lot, or other quantity of such product. An order under this paragraph shall be issued in accordance with section 554 of title 5.

(2) Any violation of paragraph (1) shall subject the violator to a civil penalty of up to $100,000 per day of violation. The amount of a civil penalty under this paragraph shall, effective December 1 of each year beginning 1 year after the effective date of this paragraph, be increased by the percent change in the Consumer Price Index for the base quarter of such year over the Consumer Price Index for the base quarter of the preceding year, adjusted to the nearest 1/10 of 1 percent. For purposes of this paragraph, the term "base quarter," as used with respect to a year, means the calendar quarter ending on September 30 of such year and the price index for a base quarter is the arithmetical mean of such index for the 3 months comprising such quarter.

(e) INTERFERENCE WITH OFFICERS.—No person shall interfere with any officer, agent, or employee of the Service in the performance of any duty imposed upon him by this section or by regulations made by authority thereof.

(f) PENALTIES FOR OFFENSES.—Any person who shall violate, or aid or abet in violating, any of the provisions of this section shall be punished upon conviction by a fine not exceeding $500 or by imprisonment not exceeding one year, or by both such fine and imprisonment, in the discretion of the court.

(g) CONSTRUCTION WITH OTHER LAWS.—Nothing contained in this chapter shall be construed as in any way affecting, modifying, repealing, or superseding the provisions of the Federal Food, Drug, and Cosmetic Act [21 U.S.C. 301 et seq.].

(h) EXPORTATION OF PARTIALLY PROCESSED BIOLOGICAL PRODUCTS.—A partially processed biological product which—

(1) is not in a form applicable to the prevention, treatment, or cure of diseases or injuries of man;

(2) is not intended for sale in the United States; and

(3) is intended for further manufacture into final dosage form outside the United States,

shall be subject to no restriction on the export of the product under this chapter or the Federal Food, Drug, and Cosmetic Act [21 U.S.C. § 301 et. seq.] if the product is manufactured, processed, packaged, and held in conformity with current good manufacturing practice requirements or meets international manufacturing standards as certified by an international standards organization recognized by the Secretary and meets the requirements of section 801(e)(1) of the Federal Food, Drug, and Cosmetic Act [21 U.S.C. § 381(e)].

(i) "BIOLOGICAL PRODUCT" DEFINED.—In this section, the term "biological product" means a virus, therapeutic serum, toxin, antitoxin, vaccine, blood, blood component or derivative, allergenic product, or analogous product, or arsphenamine or derivative of arsphenamine (or any other trivalent organic arsenic compound), applicable to the prevention, treatment, or cure of a disease or condition of human beings.

(j) APPLICATION OF FEDERAL FOOD, DRUG, AND COSMETIC ACT.—The Federal Food, Drug, and Cosmetic Act [21 U.S.C. § 301 et seq.] applies to a biological product subject to regulation under this section, except that a product for which a license has been approved under subsection (a) shall not be required to have an approved application under section 505 of such Act [21 U.S.C. § 355].

SEC. 361 [42 U.S.C. § 264]. REGULATIONS TO CONTROL COMMUNICABLE DISEASES.

(a) PROMULGATION AND ENFORCEMENT BY SURGEON GENERAL.—The Surgeon General, with the approval of the Secretary, is authorized to make and enforce such regulations as in his judgment are necessary to prevent the introduction, transmission, or spread of communicable diseases from foreign countries into the States or possessions, or from one State or possession into any other State or possession. For purposes of carrying out and enforcing such regulations, the Surgeon General may provide for such inspection, fumigation, disinfection, sanitation, pest extermination, destruction of animals or articles found to be so infected or contaminated as to be sources of dangerous infection to human beings, and other measures, as in his judgment may be necessary.

(b) APPREHENSION, DETENTION, OR CONDITIONAL RELEASE OF INDIVIDUALS.—Regulations prescribed under this section shall not provide for the apprehension, detention, or conditional release of individuals except for the purpose of preventing the introduction, transmission, or spread of such communicable diseases as may be specified from time to time in Executive orders of the President upon the recommendation of the National Advisory Health Council and the Surgeon General.

(c) APPLICATION OF REGULATIONS TO PERSONS ENTERING FROM FOREIGN COUNTRIES.—Except as provided in subsection (d) of this section, regulations prescribed under this section, insofar as they provide for the apprehension, detention, examination, or conditional release of individuals, shall be applicable only to individuals coming into a State or possession from a foreign country or a possession.

(d) APPREHENSION AND EXAMINATION OF PERSONS REASONABLY BELIEVED TO BE INFECTED.—On recommendation of the National Advisory Health Council, regulations prescribed under this section may provide for the apprehension and examination of any individual reasonably believed to be infected with a communicable disease in a communicable stage and (1) to be moving or about to move from a State to another State; or (2) to be a probable source of infection to individuals who, while infected with such disease in a communicable stage, will be moving from a State to another State. Such regulations may provide that if upon examination any such individual is found to be infected, he may be detained for such time and in such manner as may be reasonably necessary. For purposes of this subsection, the term "State" includes, in addition to the several States, only the District of Columbia.

*

INDEX

References are to pages.

†

1–58778–169–7

90000